What are the social and emotional effects of social networking? *pp. 94–95, 258–259*

Why can we remember so little from our first four years of life? *pp. 196, 208, 209*

How do women and men differ at reading others' nonverbal emotions? *p. 268*

Can the brain repair itself after damage? *pp. 2, 50, 51, 60*

Can self-control really make us healthier, more successful, and better able to cope with stress? How can we strengthen our self-control? *pp. 92–93, 166, 174–175, 258–259, 261, 265, 283–285, 292, 297*

How can we get a better night's sleep? *pp. 62–64*

Are memories of childhood sexual abuse often repressed? If so, can they be recovered? *pp. 208–209*

How many college students have experienced depression in the last year? *p. 380*

What are the effects of nature and nurture on our intelligence? *pp. 235–238*

How, by adopting a healthier lifestyle, might people find some relief from depression? *p. 418*

What are the effects of a *growth mindset* on our success and well-being? *pp. 26, 238*

How do sleep, friends, and genetics affect weight? *pp. 253–254*

How does the stress of significant life changes—even happy ones—affect our health? *p. 277*

(SEE INSIDE THE BACK COVER FOR MORE OF THIS TEXT'S TOP-RATED APPLICATION QUESTIONS.)

Psychology

IN EVERYDAY LIFE

FIFTH EDITION

(left to right) LWA/Getty Images; Huy Lam/Getty Images; Thomas Barwick/Getty Images; Rawpixel.com/Shutterstock; Sollina Images/Getty Images; Peathegee Inc/Getty Images

David G. Myers
Hope College
Holland, Michigan

C. Nathan DeWall
University of Kentucky
Lexington, Kentucky

worth publishers
Macmillan Learning
New York

Senior Vice President, Content Strategy: Charles Linsmeier
Program Director, Social Sciences: Shani Fisher
Executive Program Manager: Carlise Stembridge
Development Manager, Social Sciences: Christine Brune
Development Editors: Nancy Fleming, Trish Morgan, Danielle Slevens
Assistant Editor: Anna Munroe
Executive Marketing Manager: Katherine Nurre
Marketing Assistant: Steven Huang
Director of Media Editorial & Assessment, Social Sciences: Noel Hohnstine
Executive Media Editor, Psychology: Laura Burden
Media Editorial Assistant: Conner White
Supplements Editor: Betty Probert
Director, Content Management Enhancement: Tracey Kuehn
Senior Managing Editor: Lisa Kinne
Senior Content Project Manager: Won McIntosh
Director of Digital Production: Keri deManigold
Senior Media Project Manager: Chris Efstratiou
Media Project Manager: Eve Conte
Senior Workflow Supervisor: Susan Wein
Executive Permissions Editor: Robin Fadool
Photo Researcher and Lumina Project Manager: Donna Ranieri
Director of Design, Content Management: Diana Blume
Design Services Manager: Natasha Wolfe
Design Manager, Cover: John Callahan
Interior Design: Maureen McCutcheon
Layout Design: Lee Ann McKevitt
Cover Design: Evelyn Pence
Interior Illustrations: Shawn Barber, Keith Kasnot, Matthew McAdams, Evelyn Pence, and Don Stewart
Art Manager: Matthew McAdams
Composition: Lumina Datamatics, Inc.
Printing and Binding: LSC Communications

Cover Photos: (left to right) LWA/Getty Images; Huy Lam/Getty Images; Thomas Barwick/Getty Images; GlebSStock/Shutterstock; Disability Images/Huntstock, Inc.; Rawpixel.com/Shutterstock; Sollina Images/Getty Images; Peathegee Inc/Getty Images

Library of Congress Control Number: 2019947272

ISBN-13: 978-1-319-13372-6
ISBN-10: 1-319-13372-X

Printed in the United States of America
6 24 23 22

David Myers' royalties from the sale of this book are assigned to the David and Carol Myers Foundation, which exists to receive and distribute funds to other charitable organizations.

Worth Publishers
One New York Plaza
Suite 4600
New York, NY 10004-1562
www.macmillanlearning.com

[DM] **For Charles Linsmeier, with gratitude for two decades of faithful support, and for your leadership of our teaching mission.**

[ND] **For Ken Burns, with thanks for your friendship, encouragement, and inspiration.**

ABOUT THE AUTHORS

Photographer Steven Herppich, courtesy of Hope College Public Affairs and Marketing

Carol Myers

David, in South Africa with daughter Laura, a "sociobehavioural scientist" at the University of Cape Town's Desmond Tutu HIV Foundation.

David Myers received his B.A. in chemistry from Whitworth University, and his psychology Ph.D. from the University of Iowa. He has spent his career at Hope College in Michigan, where he has taught dozens of introductory psychology sections. Hope College students have invited him to be their commencement speaker and voted him "outstanding professor." His research and writings have been recognized by the Gordon Allport Intergroup Relations Prize, an Honored Scientist award from the Federation of Associations in Behavioral & Brain Sciences, an Award for Service on Behalf of Personality and Social Psychology, a Presidential Citation from APA Division 2, election as an American Association for the Advancement of Science Fellow, and three honorary doctorates.

With support from National Science Foundation grants, Myers' scientific articles have appeared in three dozen scientific periodicals, including *Science, American Scientist, Psychological Science,* and *American Psychologist.* In addition to his scholarly and textbook writing, he digests psychological science for the general public. His writings have appeared in four dozen magazines, from *Today's Education* to *Scientific American.* He also has authored five general audience books, including *The Pursuit of Happiness* and *Intuition: Its Powers and Perils.*

David Myers has chaired his city's Human Relations Commission, helped found a thriving assistance center for families in poverty, and spoken to hundreds of college, community, and professional groups worldwide.

Drawing on his experience, he also has written articles and a book *(A Quiet World)* about hearing loss, and he is advocating a transformation in American assistive listening technology (see HearingLoop.org). For his leadership, he has received awards from the American Academy of Audiology, the hearing industry, and the Hearing Loss Association of America.

David and Carol Myers met and married while undergraduates, and have raised sons Peter and Andrew, and a daughter, Laura. They have one grandchild, Allie (seen on page 82).

J.A Laub Photography, LLC

Nathan DeWall is professor of psychology at the University of Kentucky. He received his bachelor's degree from St. Olaf College, a master's degree in social science from the University of Chicago, and a master's degree and Ph.D. in social psychology from Florida State University. DeWall received the College of Arts and Sciences Outstanding Teaching Award, which recognizes excellence in undergraduate and graduate teaching. The Association for Psychological Science identified DeWall as a "Rising Star" early in his career for "making significant contributions to the field of psychological science." He is in the top 1 percent of all cited scientists in psychology and psychiatry on the Institute for Scientific Information list, according to the Web of Science.

DeWall conducts research on close relationships, self-control, and aggression. With funding from the National Institutes of Health, the National Science Foundation, and the John Templeton Foundation, he has published over 200 scientific articles and chapters. DeWall's research awards include the SAGE Young Scholars Award from the Foundation for Personality and Social Psychology, the Young Investigator Award from the International Society for Research on Aggression, and the Early Career Award from the International Society for Self and Identity. His research has been covered by numerous media outlets, including Good Morning America, *The Wall Street Journal, Newsweek, The Atlantic Monthly, The New York Times, The Los Angeles Times, Harvard Business Review, USA Today,* National Public Radio, the BBC, and *The Guardian.* He has lectured nationally and internationally, including in Hong Kong, China, the Netherlands, England, Greece, Hungary, Sweden, Australia, and France.

Nathan is happily married to Alice DeWall and is the proud father of Beverly "Bevy" and Ellis. He enjoys playing with his two golden retrievers, Finnegan and Atticus. As an ultramarathon runner, he completed numerous races, including the Badwater 135 in 2017

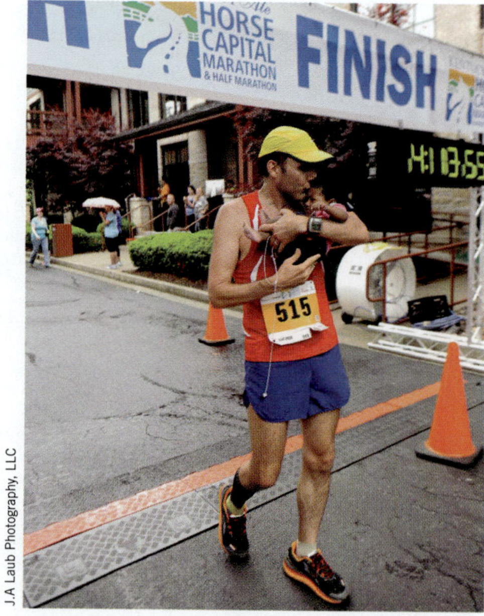

J.A Laub Photography, LLC

(dubbed "the World's toughest foot race"). In his spare time now, he writes novels, watches sports, tends his chickens, and plays guitar and sings in a rock band called *Roar Shock.*

BRIEF CONTENTS

CONTENTS

PSYCHOLOGY IS FASCINATING, and so relevant to our everyday lives. Psychology's insights enable people to be better students, more tuned-in friends and partners, more effective co-workers, and wiser parents. With this new edition, we hope to captivate students with what psychologists are learning about our human nature, to help them think more like psychological scientists, and, as the title implies, to help them relate psychology to their own lives—their thoughts, feelings, and behaviors. And we hope to make the *teaching* of psychology easier and more enjoyable for you, the instructor. Our integrated resources aim to support your class preparation, and to bring your students to class better prepared.

We have created this very brief, uniquely student-friendly book with supportive input from hundreds of instructors and students (by way of surveys, focus groups, content and design reviews, and class testing). Compacting our introduction of psychology's key topics keeps both the length and the price manageable, with loose-leaf and digital-only options being especially affordable for students. And we write with the goal of making psychology accessible to all students, regardless of their personal or academic backgrounds. It has been gratifying to hear from instructors who have been delighted to find that this affordable, accessible text offers a complete, college-level survey of the field that they can proudly offer to their students.

What's New in the Fifth Edition?

In addition to our thorough, line-by-line updating of every chapter, and our ongoing efforts to *make no assumptions* about student readers' gender identity, sexual orientation, culture, relationship or family status, age, economic or educational background, or physical ability, we offer much that is new in this fifth edition:

1. **Over 900 new research citations.** Our ongoing scrutiny of dozens of scientific periodicals and science news sources, enhanced by commissioned reviews and countless emails from instructors and students, enables integrating our field's most important, thought-provoking, and student-relevant new discoveries. Part of the pleasure that sustains this work is learning something new every day! ***See MacmillanLearning.com for a chapter-by-chapter list of significant Content Changes.***
2. **Think, Consider, Improve.** This new theme highlights how throughout the text, students are encouraged to
   - *think critically,* by examining sources and evidence;
   - *consider other voices and ideas,* by being open to diverse perspectives; and
   - *improve their everyday life,* by using evidence-based principles to boost their relationships, academic success, stress-management, and so much more. Students may start by taking advantage of the NEW Student Preface—***Student Success: How to Apply Psychology to Live Your Best Life*** on p. xxix.
3. **Chapter 4, Sex, Gender, and Sexuality.** A lot has changed in the field of psychology since the last edition was written, especially in this fast-moving subfield. We sought extra reviews from experts and instructors and made extensive updates to this coverage. We've worked to be appropriately inclusive and fully up-to-date in our presentation—representing the abundance of current research in this area, but also encompassing the lived experiences of many people, which may not yet be well represented in the literature.
4. **Post-Truth World.** Chapter 1 has a new section, "Psychological Science in a Post-Truth World," which is accompanied by my [DM's] new tutorial animation, "Thinking Critically in Our Post-Truth World" in LaunchPad, and also at tinyurl.com/PostTruthMyers.
5. **Everyday Life Questions.** The revised "In Your Everyday Life" questions now appear periodically in the margins (rather than at the end of the chapter), with new "*Improve* Your Everyday Life" questions added to the mix.
6. **Fully mobile-compatible, accessible e-book.** The e-book can now go with any student, anywhere, and it meets accessibility standards.
7. **"Thinking Critically About . . ." infographics.** All of these infographics have been revised and updated for the new edition, with two entirely new pieces on "Sexual Aggression" (Chapter 4) and "How to Be Persuasive" (Chapter 11; See **FIGURE 1**). They are also now accompanied by *new corresponding activities in LaunchPad.*
8. **Concept Practice activities.** LaunchPad offers 120 of these dynamic, new, interactive mini-tutorials that teach and reinforce the course's foundational ideas. We've included callouts from the text pages to especially pertinent, helpful online resources. (See **FIGURE 2** for a sample.)

Thinking Critically About:
How to Be Persuasive

LOQ 11-5 How can we share our views more effectively?

Would you like to be persuasive with those whose views differ from yours?

Do not:

Loudly argue your position before listening. Yelling backfires.

Humiliate people, or imply that they are ignorant. Insults breed defensiveness.

Bore people with complex and forgettable information.

Therefore, with that said, direct your attention to this very dull and wonky and boring statistic that you will never remember. Now, however, on the other hand, here are yet more data points that are even more dry and overly complicated than the last... Let us continue...

Do:

Identify your shared values or goals, such as, "We all want to graduate, yes? Find a better job? Let's study for the test before we take time off to hang out."

Appeal to others' admirable motives. Relate your aims to their yearnings.[1] For example:

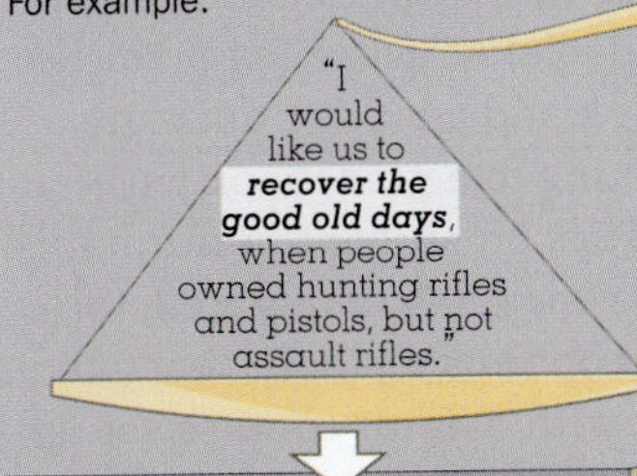

"I would like us to ***recover the good old days***, when people owned hunting rifles and pistols, but not assault rifles."
"I would prefer to ***make a change***, so that in the future people may own hunting rifles and pistols, but no one will have assault rifles."

Political conservatives tend to respond to nostalgia. Those promoting gun safety legislation to this group should frame their message as an affirmation of yesteryear.

Political liberals respond better to future-focused messages.

Make your message vivid. People remember dramatic visual examples well. Pictures of unvaccinated children suffering from preventable diseases, or hungry children starving speak to the heart as well as the head.

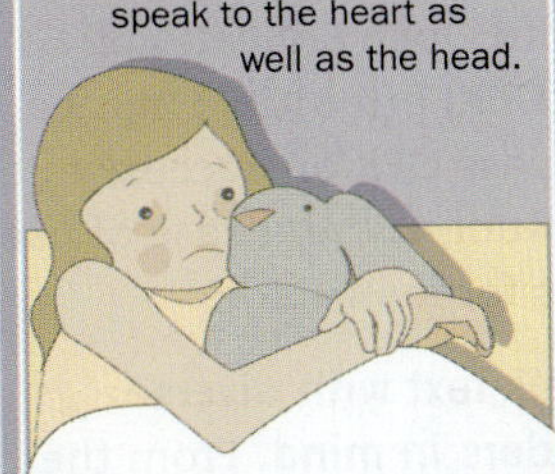

Repeat your message. People often come to believe repeated falsehoods, but they also tend to believe oft-repeated truths.

Science Science Evidence-based Science Evidence-based Science Evidence-based Evidence-based Consider alternatives Consider alternatives Science

Engage your audience in restating your message or, better yet, acting on it. Engage them in actively owning it—not just passively listening.

1. Lammers & Baldwin, 2018.

FIGURE 1 Sample "Thinking Critically About" infographic from Chapter 11, Social Psychology

LaunchPad For an animated tutorial on correlations, engage online with *Concept Practice: Positive and Negative Correlations.* See also the *Video: Correlational Studies* for another helpful tutorial animation.

FIGURE 2 Sample LaunchPad callout from Chapter 1

9. **Active Learning.** Our Instructor's Resources have long been considered the "gold standard" in the field, and they nicely support students' active learning in class. There are additional NEW Classroom Exercises, Student Projects, Demonstrations, and Lecture/Discussion Topics that work well for think-pair-share, small group, and large group activities.

Why Should I Use *Psychology in Everyday Life,* Fifth Edition, and Its Resources?

There are several reasons we think you should consider using this text and its resources for your classes:

1. **These resources are top quality.** Our resources offer *up-to-date, carefully checked content and assessment you can rely on,* with a study system that follows best practices from learning and memory research. This new fifth edition includes *hundreds of new citations* representing the field's most important, thought-provoking, and student-relevant new discoveries. We have worked with dozens of helpful reviewers, and with our editors run the text manuscript through *eight* drafts. Our dedicated Media and Test Bank authors and editors have focused similar intensity on their work. (For example, our Test Bank questions go through four stages of checking to ensure there is appropriate coverage for each new edition.)

2. **This text and its resources make life easier for instructors like you.** We've imagined the worst-case scenario of being asked to teach a course on a Friday and walking into the classroom ready to go on a Monday. Step 1: Assign a book students tell us they love! Step 2: You have what you need with *LaunchPad's full course solution* (e-book, adaptive quizzing and other assessments, clicker questions, classroom activities and other Instructor Resources, abundant videos, and numerous engaging student tutorials and activities for each chapter—all reporting to an easy-to-use gradebook). Or you may opt for the simplified (and extra-affordable) *Achieve Read & Practice* (e-book and adaptive quizzing, reporting to a gradebook with analytics on student performance). These engaging, integrated, top-notch options are both ready to use as is, with default courses set up, or you can readily tweak them to suit your needs. Our popular adaptive quizzing system has been shown to bring students to class better prepared, and help them do better in class.

3. ***Psychology in Everyday Life* is among the most affordable options available.** The digital-only or looseleaf options compete with Open Educational Resources (OER) printouts on price, and far surpass OER on success in the course for students, and ease of use and success for instructors.

4. **We wrote this text with diverse student readers in mind.** From the first edition, we have endeavored to make no assumptions in terms of students' gender identity, sexual orientation, culture, relationship or family status, age, economic or educational background, or physical ability. The text includes abundant, integrated coverage of psychology's diversity, and plenty of everyday life applications to draw all students into the content. Since this text's first edition, one of its Eight Guiding Principles has been "To convey respect for human unity and diversity." (See p. xxiii. See also **TABLE 1** The Psychology of Gender, Gender Identity, and Sexuality, and **TABLE 2**, The Psychology of Culture, Ethnicity, and Race.)

5. **These resources teach critical thinking.** "To teach critical thinking" has been the first of the "Eight Guiding Principles" that have guided our work on this text since the first edition. (See p. xxii.) Chapter 1 takes a critical-thinking approach to introducing students to psychology's research methods and the idea that *psychology is a science.* Critical thinking is a key term on p. 2 and is encouraged throughout the text and its resources. For example, we offer "Thinking Critically About . . ." infographics in each chapter, with accompanying activities in LaunchPad. See **TABLE 3**, Critical Thinking, for a deeper list of coverage.

6. **This text is perfect for nursing and premed students.** *Psychology in Everyday Life* maps well onto the new MCAT's psychology section. Since 2015, the MCAT has devoted 25 percent of its questions to the "Psychological, Social, and Biological Foundations of Behavior." The new section's topics match up almost exactly with the topics in this text. See **TABLE 4** for a sample. For a complete pairing of the new MCAT psychology topics with this book's contents, see MacmillanLearning.com. In addition, the Test Bank questions for *Psychology in Everyday Life,* Fifth Edition, are keyed to the new MCAT.

TABLE 1 The Psychology of Gender, Gender Identity, and Sexuality

Coverage of the *psychology of gender, gender identity,* and *sexuality* can be found on the following pages:

(*Continued*)

TABLE 1 The Psychology of Gender, Gender Identity, and Sexuality (*continued*)

Coverage of the *psychology of gender, gender identity,* and *sexuality* can be found on the following pages:			
heterosexual, pp. 100, 117, 121–123 pansexual, pp. 121, 122, 125 same-sex, pp. 80, 100, 101, 107, 115, 121–125, 317, 331, 416 Sexual response cycle, p. 118 Sexuality, pp. 117–121 male-female differences in, p. 126 natural selection and, pp. 126–127 Sexualization of girls, p. 121 Sexually transmitted infections, p. 119	Sexually violent media effects, pp. 186 Smell, sense of, p. 158 Social clock, p. 101 Social connectedness, pp. 109, 111 the brain and, p. 109 Social media use/texting, p. 109 Social power, pp. 108, 110 Social scripts pornography and, p. 322 sexual behavior and, p. 121, 127, 322 Spermarche, p. 112 Stereotype threat, p. 243	Stress and the immune system, p. 279 Stress responses, p. 278 tend-and-befriend, p. 278 Suicide, p. 395 Teen pregnancy, pp. 120–121 Testosterone, pp. 97, 111, 117, 125, 320–321 replacement therapy, p. 117 #Time's Up, p. 314 Touch, p. 153 Transgender depression rates and community acceptance, pp. 277, 362 gender dysphoria, p. 116	identity, p. 116 prevalence, p. 116 self-reporting rates increasing, p. 122 social acceptance rates, p. 116 social identity, p. 93 therapy, expectations, p. 416 Trauma and earlier death for women, p. 87 Trial marriage, p. 100 Violent crime, p. 108 Vulnerability to psychological disorders, p. 108 Women in psychology, pp. 3–4, pp. F-1–F-5

7. You won't find better service and support anywhere. The Macmillan representatives who market and sell these resources, help set up instructors' courses, and in many other ways service instructor and student course needs, are the best in the business. Many of these folks have become personal friends. We've been grateful to be working with a family-owned publisher that has been so supportive of our teaching mission and has encouraged us to create the best teaching and learning materials.

Tell Me More About *Psychology in Everyday Life*

THE WRITING

We've written this book to be optimally accessible. The vocabulary is sensitive to students' widely varying reading levels and backgrounds. A ***Spanish-language Glosario*** at the back of the book offers additional assistance for ESL Spanish speakers. And *Psychology in Everyday Life* is concise—making it easier to fit into one-term courses. It offers a complete survey of the field, but it is a more manageable survey, with an emphasis on the most humanly significant concepts. We continually asked ourselves while working, "Would an educated person need to know this? Would this help students live better lives?"

NO ASSUMPTIONS

Even more than in other Myers/DeWall texts, we have written *Psychology in Everyday Life* with the diversity of student readers in mind:

- *Gender:* Extensive coverage of gender development, changing gender roles, and gender identity.
- *Culture:* No assumptions about readers' cultural backgrounds or experiences.
- *Economic Background:* No references to backyards, summer camp, vacations.
- *Education:* No assumptions about past or current learning environments; the writing is accessible to all.
- *Physical Abilities:* No assumptions about full vision, hearing, movement, or other abilities.
- *Life Experiences:* Examples are included from urban, suburban, and rural/outdoor settings.
- *Relationship or Family Status:* Examples and ideas are made relevant for all students, whether they have children or are still living at home, are married or cohabiting or single; and with no assumptions about sexual orientation or gender identity.

EVERYDAY LIFE APPLICATIONS

Throughout this text, as its title suggests, we relate the findings of psychology's research to the real world. This edition includes:

- "In Your Everyday Life" and "*Improve* Your Everyday Life" questions throughout each chapter, helping students make the concepts more meaningful (and memorable), and apply psychology to improve their own lives. These questions can also be used as group discussion topics.
- "Assess Your Strengths" personal self-assessments in LaunchPad, allowing students to actively apply key principles to their own experiences and develop their strengths.
- fun notes and quotes in small boxes throughout the text, applying psychology's findings to sports, literature, world religions, music, business, and more.
- an emphasis throughout the text on critical thinking in everyday life,

TABLE 2 The Psychology of Culture, Ethnicity, and Race

Coverage of *culture, ethnicity,* and *race* can be found on the following pages:

- Academic achievement, pp. 95, 241–242, 286
- Achievement motivation, p. 259
- Adolescence,
  - onset and end of, p. 90
  - positive parent-teen relationships in, p. 94
- Aggression, pp. 321–323
- Animal cultures and learning, p. 223
- Animal research, views on, p. 24
- Beauty ideals, p. 325
- Behavioral effects of culture, pp. 8–9
- Biopsychosocial approach, pp. 8–9
  - to aggression, pp. 320–323
  - to drug use, pp. 378–380
  - to learning, pp. 180–182
  - to pain, pp. 153–155
  - to personality, pp. 351–352
  - to psychological disorders, pp. 364–365
- Body image, p. 391
- Categorizing mixed-race people, p. 319
- Child raising, pp. 88, 90
- Collectivism, pp. 356–357
  - conformity, p. 308
  - moral reasoning and, p. 92
  - self-esteem and, p. 297
  - therapy and, pp. 415–416
  - within-culture differences, p. 357
- Conflict, pp. 330–332
  - enemy perceptions, p. 330
  - mirror-image perceptions, p. 330
- Conformity, p. 308
- Cooperative learning, pp. 331–332
- Corporal punishment practices, p. 177
- Creativity and intercultural experience, p. 221
- Cultural values
  - child raising and, pp. 88, 90
  - moral reasoning and, p. 92
  - psychotherapy and, pp. 415–416
- Culture
  - child raising and, pp. 88, 90
  - context effects and, p. 137
  - defined, p. 9
  - emotional expression and, pp. 269–271
  - intelligence test bias and, pp. 242–243
  - the self and, pp. 356–357
  - similarity, pp. 9, 326
  - smiling and, p. 271
  - violence and, p. 322
- Culture-specific disorders, p. 364
  - *amok,* p. 364
  - eating disorders, pp. 364, 390–392
  - *susto,* p. 364
  - *taijin kyofusho,* p. 364
- Deaf culture, pp. 50, 53, 225, 241
- Deindividuation, p. 312
- Depression
  - Google search data, p. 17
  - risk of, p. 383
  - suicide and, p. 395
- Developmental similarities across cultures, p. 70
- Discrimination
  - against obese people, pp. 254, 315
  - defined, p. 315
  - ingroup networking and, p. 318
  - unconscious prejudices and, p. 316
- Dissociative identity disorder, p. 392
- Diversity,
  - increased acceptance of, p. 316
  - in psychology, pp. 3, F-1–F-5
  - psychotherapy and, pp. 415–416
- Divorce, pp. 100, 256
- Dysfunctional behavior diagnoses, p. 362
- Eating disorders, p. 391
- Emerging adulthood, p. 96
- Emotional expression, p. 268
- Enemy perceptions, p. 330
- Family self, p. 90
- Father presence
  - pregnancy and, p. 121
  - violence and, p. 322
- Flow, p. B-2
- Foot-in-the-door phenomenon, pp. 303–304
- Framing and organ donation, p. 219
- Fundamental attribution error, p. 302
- Gender
  - aggression and, p. 108
  - discrimination, p. 317
  - prejudice, p. 317
- Gender roles, pp. 110, 113–114
  - division of labor and, pp. 113–114
- General adaptation syndrome, p. 278
- Grief, expressions of, p. 102
- Group polarization, pp. 313–314
- Groupthink, p. 315
- Happiness, pp. 293, 295–296, 297
- Hate crimes, p. 318
- Hate speech, p. 312
- HIV/AIDS, p. 119
- Identity formation, p. 94
- Immigration, pp. 13, 184, 225, 256, 284, 318, 330, 331
- Implicit bias, p. 316
- Individualism, pp. 302, 308, 312, 356–357
  - moral reasoning and, p. 92
  - psychotherapy and, pp. 415–416
  - self-esteem and, p. 297
- Ingroup bias, p. 318
- Intelligence, p. 229
  - racial and ethnic differences, pp. 241–242
- Intelligence testing,
  - bias, pp. 242–243
  - stereotype threat, p. 243
- Intergroup contact, p. 316
- Internet as social amplifier, p. 314
- Interracial marriage, views on, p. 316
- Job satisfaction, p. B-5
- Just-world phenomenon, p. 318
- Language development,
  - classifying objects, p. 116
  - persistence of childhood language, p. 79
  - second languages and, pp. 225–226
  - sign language, p. 225
  - universal grammar, p. 223
  - verbal interaction encouraged in, p. 90
- Leadership style, cultural influences on, pp. B-7–B-8
- Life cycle, p. 70
- Marriage, p. 327
- Mating preferences, p. 126
- Media violence, effects of, p. 186
- Memory, p. 195
- Mental disorders
  - rates of, pp. 361–362
  - stress and, p. 364
- Mere exposure effect, p. 324
- Microaggressions, p. 315
- Mirror-image perceptions, p. 330
- Moral reasoning, p. 92
- Motivation, p. 250
- Motor development, massage and, p. 79
- Naturalistic observation, pp. 16–17
- Need to belong, social identity and, p. 256
- Obedience during Holocaust, p. 310
- Obesity,
  - sleep loss and, p. 254
  - worldwide rates of, p. 254
- Observational learning, p. 185
- Optimism, p. 286
- Ostracism, racial, p. 257
- Other-race effect, pp. 318–319
- Pain
  - physical and social, p. 257
  - social-cultural influences on, p. 154
- Parent-teen relations, p. 95
- Partner selection, p. 325
- Peace, promoting, pp. 330–332
  - contact, p. 331
  - cooperation, pp. 331–332
  - superordinate goals, p. 331
- Personal control
  - loss of, p. 284
  - tyranny of choice and, p. 284
- Personality traits and Big Five dimensions, p. 348
- Phobias, p. 368
- Physical attractiveness, p. 326
- Poverty, explanations of, p. 303
- Power differences between men and women, p. 108
- Prejudice, pp. 315–320
  - against immigrants, p. 318
  - against Jews, pp. 303, 310
  - against Muslims, pp. 317, 318, 319
  - belief systems, p. 317
  - contact, cooperation, and, pp. 331–332
  - explicit, p. 316
  - forming categories, p. 319
  - gender, p. 317
  - gender nonconforming, p. 362
  - group polarization and, pp. 313–314
  - implicit, p. 316
  - Kenneth Clark and Mamie Phipps Clark and, p. 25
  - LGBTQ, p. 317
  - major depressive disorder and, p. 380
  - own-age bias, p. 319
  - racial and ethnic, pp. 316–318
  - representativeness heuristic and, p. 216
  - risk of disorder and, p. 362
  - roots of, pp. 317–320
  - stress and, p. 277
- Prosocial behavior, p. 184
- Psychological disorders, definitions of "normal," p. 362

(*Continued*)

TABLE 2 The Psychology of Culture, Ethnicity, and Race (*continued*)

Coverage of *culture, ethnicity,* and *race* can be found on the following pages:

- dissociative identity disorder, p. 392
- eating disorders, 391
- schizophrenia, pp. 388–389
- treatment of, pp. 415–416
- Race-influenced perceptions, pp. 316–317
- Racial similarities, pp. 241–242
- Racism
  - Google search data, p. 17
  - Oprah Winfrey and, p. 165
  - ostracism and, p. 257
  - representativeness heuristic and, p. 216
  - scapegoat theory and, p. 318
  - social inequalities and divisions and, p. 318
- Religious involvement and longevity, p. 291
- Representativeness heuristic, p. 216
- Resilience, p. 524
- Risk assessment, p. 216
- Same-sex attraction, cultural attitudes toward, p. 122
- Scapegoat theory, p. 318
- Schizophrenia, pp. 388–389
- Self-esteem, p. 297
- Self-serving bias, pp. 355, 357
- Separation anxiety, p. 86
- Sexual aggression, cultural differences in, p. 115
- Sexual risk taking among teens, p. 120
- Social clock, p. 101
- Social identity, p. 93
- Social inequalities and divisions, p. 318
- Social influence, p. 308
- Social loafing, p. 312
- Social networking, pp. 257–258
- Social support, p. 287
- Social trust, p. 88
- Social-cultural psychology, p. 7
- Stereotype threat, p. 243
- Stereotypes, pp. 216, 315, 318, 319, 342
- Stress
  - gender-nonconforming people and, p. 277
  - racism and, p. 277
  - same-sex orientation and, p. 277
  - transgender people and, p. 277
- Substance use,
  - cultural expectations, p. 372
  - rates of, pp. 361, 380
- Suicide, p. 395
- Taste preference, p. 253
- Terrorism,
  - fear/aggression and, p. 318
  - group polarization and, p. 313
  - vivid cases and, p. 319
- Therapy, p. 416
- Trait stability, p. 350
  - in Japanese people, p. 348
- Trauma, pp. 342, 368
- Universal emotions, p. 270
- Universal expressions, pp. 9, 270
- Video-game playing, compulsive, p. 373
- Violence, p. 322
- Weight, p. 254
- WEIRD cultures, p. 9
- Well-being, p. 297

including the "Statistical Reasoning in Everyday Life" appendix, helping students to become more informed consumers and everyday thinkers.

- added emphasis on *clinical* applications. *Psychology in Everyday Life* offers a great sensitivity to clinical issues throughout the text. For example, Chapter 13, Psychological Disorders, includes lengthy coverage of substance-related disorders, with guidelines for determining *substance use disorder* and new coverage of *substance/medication-induced disorders*. See **TABLE 5** for a listing of coverage of clinical psychology concepts and issues throughout the text.

See inside the front and back covers for a listing of students' top-rated applications to everyday life from this text.

Scattered throughout this book, students will find interesting and informative review notes and quotes from researchers and others that will encourage them to be active learners and to apply their new knowledge to everyday life.

STUDY SYSTEM FOLLOWS BEST PRACTICES FROM LEARNING AND MEMORY RESEARCH

This text's learning system harnesses the *testing effect,* which documents the benefits of actively retrieving information through regular testing (**FIGURE 3**). Thus, our LearningCurve system, which has been very popular with students, offers an adaptive quizzing program that provides a personalized study plan. In the text, each chapter offers **Retrieve & Remember** questions interspersed throughout (**FIGURE 4**). Creating these *desirable difficulties* for students along the way optimizes the testing effect, as does *immediate feedback* via answers that are available for checking.

FIGURE 3 How to learn and remember
For my [DM's] 5-minute animated guide to more effective studying, visit tinyurl.com/HowToRemember.

RETRIEVE & REMEMBER

ANSWERS IN APPENDIX E

9. What does a good theory do?
10. Why is replication important?

FIGURE 4 Sample Retrieve & Remember feature

In addition, each main section of text begins with a numbered question that establishes a **learning objective** and directs student reading. The Chapter Review section repeats these questions as a further self-testing opportunity (with answers available to check). The Chapter Review section also offers a self-test on the **Terms and Concepts to Remember,** and **Chapter Test** questions in multiple formats to promote optimal retention.

TABLE 3 Critical Thinking

***Critical thinking* coverage can be found on the following pages:**

Are intelligence tests biased?, pp. 242–243
Are personality tests able to predict behavior?, pp. 347–349
Attachment style, development of, pp. 85–88
Attention-deficit/hyperactivity disorder (ADHD), p. 363
Can memories of childhood sexual abuse be repressed and then recovered?, p. 209
Causation and the violence-viewing effect, pp. 185–186
Choosing a research design, pp. 22–23
Classifying psychological disorders, pp. 365–366
Confirmation bias, p. 215
Continuity vs. stage theories of development, pp. 70–71
Correlation and causation, pp. 18–22, 89, 94, 102, 186, 291
Critical thinking defined, pp. 2–3
Critical thinking and the scientific attitude, 2–3
Critiquing the evolutionary perspective on sexuality, p. 127
Discovery of hypothalamus reward centers, p. 44
The divided brain, pp. 51–53
Do lie detectors lie?, p. 267
Do other species have language?, pp. 227–228
Do other species share our cognitive abilities?, pp. 222–223
Do video games teach, or release, violence?, pp. 322–323
Does meditation enhance health?, pp. 290–291
Does stress cause illness?, p. 283
Effectiveness of alternative psychotherapies, p. 414
Emotion and the brain, pp. 39, 43–45
Emotional intelligence, p. 231
Evolutionary science and human origins, pp. 128–129
Extrasensory perception, pp. 160–162
Fear of flying vs. probabilities, p. 217
Framing, p. 219
Freud's contributions, pp. 341–343
Gender bias in the workplace, p. 110
Genetic and environmental influences on schizophrenia, pp. 388–390
Group differences in intelligence, pp. 240–242
Hindsight bias, p. 12
How can we avoid belief perseverance?, p. 218
How do nature and nurture shape prenatal development?, pp. 73–74
How do twin and adoption studies help us understand the effects of nature and nurture?, pp. 76–77
How does the brain process language?, p. 226
How much is gender socially constructed vs. biologically influenced?, pp. 111–116
How to be persuasive, p. 306
How valid is the Rorschach inkblot test?, p. 341
Humanistic perspective, evaluating, p. 345
Hypnosis: dissociation or social influence?, pp. 155–156
Importance of checking fears against facts, p. 217
Interaction of nature and nurture in overall development, p. 70
The internet as social amplifier, p. 314
Is breast milk better than formula? p. 20
Is dissociative identity disorder a real disorder?, pp. 392–393
Is psychotherapy effective?, pp. 412–413
Is repression a myth?, p. 342
Limits of case studies, naturalistic observation, and surveys, pp. 16–18
Limits of common sense, pp. 12–13
Making good (and bad) decisions and judgments, pp. 215–220
Natural endorphins discovery, pp. 35–36
Nature, nurture, and perceptual ability, pp. 149–150
Near-death experiences, pp. 377–388
Obesity and weight-control challenges, p. 254
Overconfidence, pp. 13, 218
Parenting styles, p. 89
Perceiving order in random events, p. 13
Posttraumatic stress disorder (PTSD), p. 369
Powers and limits of parental involvement on development, pp. 95–96
Powers and perils of intuition, pp. 219–220
Problem-solving strategies, pp. 214–215
Psychic phenomena, pp. 4, 160–162
Psychological science in a post-truth world, pp. 13–14
Psychology: a discipline for critical thought, pp. 2, 4, 12, 13–14
Religious involvement and longevity, pp. 291–292
Scientific attitude, p. 4
Scientific method, pp. 14–18
A scientific model for studying psychology, p. 171
Sexual aggression, p. 115
Sexual desire and ovulation, p. 117
Similarities and differences in social power between men and women, pp. 108, 110
The stigma of introversion, p. 347
Stress and cancer, pp. 280–281
Subliminal sensation and persuasion, p. 134
Superforecasters avoid overconfidence, p. 13
Technology and "big data" observations, pp. 16–17
Therapeutic lifestyle change, p. 418
Tolerance and addiction, p. 373
Using only 10 percent of our brain, p. 49
Using psychology to debunk popular beliefs, pp. 2–3
Values and psychology, pp. 24–25
What does selective attention teach us about consciousness?, pp. 54–56
What factors influence sexual orientation?, pp. 123–125
What is the connection between the brain and the mind?, p. 40
What is the scientific attitude?, pp. 2–4
Which therapies work best?, pp. 413–414
Why do we sleep? pp. 59–60
Wording effects, p. 17

A DESIGN STUDENTS LOVE

In response to unanimous support from students across previous editions, the new fifth edition printed text retains the easy-to-read three-column design, rich with visual support. In written reviews, students have compared our three-column design with a traditional one-column design (without knowing which was ours). They have overwhelmingly preferred the three-column design. It was, they said, "less intimidating" and "less overwhelming," and it "motivated" them to read on.

This design responds to students' expectations, based on what they have told us about their reading, both online and in print. The narrow column width eliminates the strain of reading across a wide page, and is more similar to phone and other online reading. Illustrations appear near the pertinent text narrative, which helps students see them in the appropriate context. Key terms are defined near where they are introduced. The e-book design has similarly easy-to-read narrative columns, with illustrations and definitions presented in context.

key terms Look for complete definitions of each important term near the term's introduction in the narrative.

TABLE 4 Sample MCAT Correlation with *Psychology in Everyday Life*, Fifth Edition

MCAT 2015	*Psychology in Everyday Life*, Fifth Edition, Correlations	
Content Category 6C: Responding to the world		**Page Number**
Emotion	Emotion: Arousal, Behavior, and Cognition; Embodied Emotion; Expressed and Experienced Emotion	261–272
Three components of emotion (i.e., cognitive, physiological, behavioral)	Emotion: Arousal, Behavior, and Cognition	261–265
Universal emotions (e.g., fear, anger, happiness, surprise, joy, disgust, and sadness)	The Basic Emotions	265
	Culture and Emotion—including the universal emotions	269–271
Adaptive role of emotion	*Emotion as the body's adaptive response*	262, 265–266, 270, 278
	Emotions and the Autonomic Nervous System	265–266
Theories of emotion		
James-Lange theory	*James-Lange Theory: Arousal Comes Before Emotion*	262
Cannon-Bard theory	*Cannon-Bard Theory: Arousal and Emotion Happen at the Same Time*	262–263
Schachter-Singer theory	*Schachter and Singer Two-Factor Theory: Arousal + Label = Emotion*	263
Zajonc; LeDoux; Lazarus	*Zajonc, LeDoux, and Lazarus: Emotion and the Two-Track Brain*	263–265
The role of biological processes in perceiving emotion	*Emotions and the Autonomic Nervous System*	265–266
Brain regions involved in the generation and experience of emotions	*The Physiology of Emotions*	266–267
	Zajonc, LeDoux, and Lazarus: Emotion and the Two-Track Brain	263–265
The role of the limbic system in emotion	*Emotions and the Autonomic Nervous System* *The Limbic System*	265–266 43–45
	Physiological differences among specific emotions	266–267
Emotion and the autonomic nervous system	*Emotions and the Autonomic Nervous System*	265–266
Physiological markers of emotion (signatures of emotion)	*The Physiology of Emotions*	266–267
Stress	Stress, Health, and Human Flourishing	275–300
The nature of stress	Stress: Some Basic Concepts	276–279
Appraisal	*Stress appraisal*	276
Different types of stressors (i.e., cataclysmic events, personal)	*Stressors—Things That Push Our Buttons*	277
Effects of stress on psychological functions	*Stress Reactions—From Alarm to Exhaustion*	277–279
Stress outcomes/response to stressors	*Stress Reactions—From Alarm to Exhaustion*	277–279
Physiological	*Stress Reactions—From Alarm to Exhaustion*	277–279
	Stress Effects and Health	279–282
	Thinking Critically About: Stress and Health	283
Emotional	*Stress and Heart Disease: The Effects of Personality; The Effects of Pessimism and Depression*	281–282
	Coping With Stress	282
	Posttraumatic Stress Disorder	368–369
Behavioral	*Stress Reactions—From Alarm to Exhaustion*	277–279
	Coping With Stress	282–288
Managing stress (e.g., exercise, relaxation techniques, spirituality)	Managing Stress Effects: aerobic exercise; relaxation and meditation; faith communities	288–292

TABLE 5 Clinical Psychology

Coverage of *clinical psychology* can be found on the following pages:

(*Continued*)

TABLE 5 Clinical Psychology (*Continued*)

Coverage of *clinical psychology* can be found on the following pages:

Lifestyle change, therapeutic effects of, p. 418
Loss of a child, psychiatric hospitalization and, p. 102
Major depressive disorder, pp. 380–386
Medical model of mental disorders, p. 364
Mental health professional, finding, p. 416
Neurotransmitter imbalances and related disorders, p. 35
Nonsuicidal self-injury, pp. 395–396
  eating disorders and, p. 391
Obsessive-compulsive disorder, p. 368
  prevalence, p. 362
Operant conditioning techniques, p. 408
Ostracism, negative effects of, pp. 256–257
Pain, controlling psychologically, pp. 154–156
Panic disorder, p. 367
Paraprofessional therapists, p. 415
Personality disorders, pp. 393–395
Person-centered therapy, p. 404
Phobias, p. 368
  prevalence, p. 362
Placebo effect, pp. 21, 412, 417, 419–420, 421
Posttraumatic growth, pp. 369, 424
Posttraumatic stress disorder, pp. 368–369
  prevalence, p. 362
Preventive mental health, p. 423
Psychoactive drugs, types of, pp. 372, 374–379, 380
Psychoanalysis, pp. 336–337, 341–342, 402–403
Psychodynamic theory, pp. 336–340
Psychodynamic therapy, pp. 403–404
Psychological disorders, pp. 361–399
  classification of, pp. 365–366
  risk of harm in, pp. 396–397
  gender differences in, pp. 9, 108, 374, 382
  preventing, and building resilience, pp. 422–424
Psychosurgery, p. 422
Psychotherapies, pp. 402–411
  evaluating, pp. 412–414
Rorschach inkblot test, p. 341
Savant syndrome, pp. 229–230
Schizophrenia, pp. 386–390
  Big Five personality inventory for, p. 348
  brain scans and, p. 41
  dopamine and, p. 35
  genetics and risk for, pp. 389–390
  hallucinations, auditory, and, p. 48
  parent-blaming and, p. 95
  placebo effect and, p. 21
  prenatal environment and risk of, pp. 388–389
  prevalence, p. 362
Self-actualization, p. 250
Sleep disorders, p. 63
Stigma and psychological disorders, p. 366
Substance use disorders, pp. 371–380
Suicide, p. 395
  gender differences in, p. 108
  bipolar disorder and, p. 382
  by firearms, pp. 217, 320
  eating disorders and risk of, p. 391
  faith factor and, p. 291
  increase with spread of social media, p. 94
  increased risk for people with same-sex attraction, p. 122
  major depressive disorder and, p. 381
  ostracism and, p. 256
  social networking and teen, p. 258
  survivor grief and, p. 288
Testosterone replacement therapy, p. 117
Therapeutic alliance, p. 415
Transgender/gender-nonconforming and rate of disorder, p. 362
Violence,
  brain damage and, p. 396
  mental illness and, p. 396

EIGHT GUIDING PRINCIPLES

We have retained the goals—the guiding principles—that have animated all of my [DM's] texts since their first editions:

Facilitating the Learning Experience

1. To teach critical thinking By presenting research as intellectual detective work, we model a scientific mindset. Students will discover how critical thinking can help them evaluate competing ideas and popular claims—from ESP and memory construction to group differences in intelligence and alternative therapies. Our "Thinking Critically About" infographic features help engage students in this learning. (See p. xii, and Table 3 on p. xix, for more about critical thinking in this text.)

2. To provide applications of principles Throughout the narrative, illustrations, and online resources we relate psychology's findings to real-world applications. We make psychology meaningful to students by showing how it relates to their lives—their life span development, their search for relationships and happiness, their understanding of negative forces, such as prejudice, and so much more. The "Everyday Life" questions throughout each chapter, and our "Assess Your Strengths" activities in LaunchPad invite students to apply important concepts to their own lives, and to learn ways to develop key personal strengths. (See **TABLE 6**, Positive Psychology, for more about how we encourage understanding of happiness and human strengths, and see the new Student Preface—Student Success: How To Apply Psychology to Live Your Best Life on p. xxix.)

3. To reinforce learning at every step Everyday examples and thought-provoking questions encourage students to process the material actively. Self-testing opportunities throughout the text and online resources help students learn and retain important concepts and terminology.

Demonstrating the Science of Psychology

4. To show the process of inquiry We try to show students not just the outcome of research, but how the research process works, often by putting them in the role of experimenter or participant in classic studies. We introduce research stories as mysteries that unravel as one clue

TABLE 6 Positive Psychology

Coverage of *positive psychology* topics can be found in the following chapters:

Topic	Chapter
Altruism/compassion	1, 6, 3, 10, 11, 14
Coping	3, 9, 10, 13, 14
Courage	1, 11, 12, 13, App. B, App. F
Creativity	1, 2, 7, 8, 10, 12, 13, App. B
Emotional intelligence	8
Empathy	1, 3, 4, 5, 6, 9, 11, 12, 13, 14
Flow	10, App. B
Gratitude	10
Happiness/life satisfaction	1, 3, 4, 7, 8, 9, 10, 11, 12, App. B
Humility	1, 12, App. B
Humor	3, 10, 13
Integrity	1, 3
Justice	3
Leadership	1, 4, 10, 12, App. B
Love	1, 3, 4, 9, 10, 11, 12
Morality	3, 6, 8, 11, 12, 13
Optimism	1, 10, 12, 14
Personal control	10, 11
Resilience	3, 4, 10, 14
Self-awareness	8, 12, 14
Self-control	1, 3, 9, 10
Self-discipline	3, 8, 9, 10, 12
Self-efficacy	12
Self-esteem	3, 9, 10, 12, 13, App. B
Spirituality	1, 3, 4, 9, 10, 11
Toughness (grit)	3, 8, 9, 10
Wisdom	1, 8, App. B

after another falls into place. Our "How Would You Know?" activities in LaunchPad allow students to play the role of researcher in thinking about research questions and how they may be studied effectively.

5. **To be as up-to-date as possible** While retaining psychology's classic studies and concepts, we also present the most important recent developments. In this edition, 896 references are dated 2016–2019. Likewise, new photos and new everyday examples are drawn from today's world.

6. **To put facts in the service of concepts** Our intention is not to overwhelm students with facts, but to reveal psychology's major concepts—to teach students how to think, and to offer psychological ideas worth thinking about. Learning Objective Questions and Retrieve & Remember questions throughout each chapter help students focus on the most important concepts. Concept Practice and Topic Tutorial activities in LaunchPad help ensure student understanding of key points.

Promoting Big Ideas and Broadened Horizons

7. **To enhance comprehension by providing continuity** Many chapters have a significant issue or theme that links subtopics and ties the chapter together. The Learning chapter conveys the idea that bold thinkers can serve as intellectual pioneers. The Thinking, Language, and Intelligence chapter raises the issue of human rationality and irrationality. The Psychological Disorders chapter conveys empathy for, and understanding of, troubled lives. Other threads, such as cognitive neuroscience, dual processing, and individual and group diversity, weave throughout the whole book, and students hear a consistent voice.

8. **To convey respect for human unity and diversity** Throughout the book, readers will see evidence of human kinship in our shared biology—our common mechanisms of seeing and learning, hungering and feeling, loving and hating. They will also better understand our diversity—our individual diversity in development and aptitudes, temperament and personality, and disorder and health; and our cultural diversity in attitudes and expressive styles, child-raising and care for the elderly, and life priorities and experiences.

Tell Me More About LaunchPad and Achieve Read & Practice

LAUNCHPAD

It has been a joy for me [ND] to teach the course with **LaunchPad** (LaunchPadWorks.com), which my students love. LaunchPad makes it easy to engage students effectively starting on Day 1 of the class when I make a LaunchPad assignment. With immediate engagement, and active learning throughout the course, most students have fun with the material and stay in my class.

LaunchPad facilitates active learning as it solves key challenges in the course (**FIGURE 5**). In combination with the meticulously created text, these online resources give students everything they need to prepare for class and exams, while giving you, the instructor, everything *you* need to quickly set up a course, shape the content to your syllabus, craft presentations and lectures, assign and assess homework, and guide the progress of individual students and the class as a whole:

- Our **NEW e-book** can now go with any student, anywhere. It is fully mobile-compatible and meets accessibility standards.
- **LearningCurve game-like quizzing** motivates students and adapts to their needs based on their performance. It is the perfect tool to get students to engage before class, and review after. Additional reporting tools and metrics will help you assess the progress of individual students and the class as a whole.
- **iClicker offers active learning simplified, and now includes the REEF mobile app (iClicker.com).** iClicker's simple, flexible tools in LaunchPad help you give students a voice and facilitate active learning

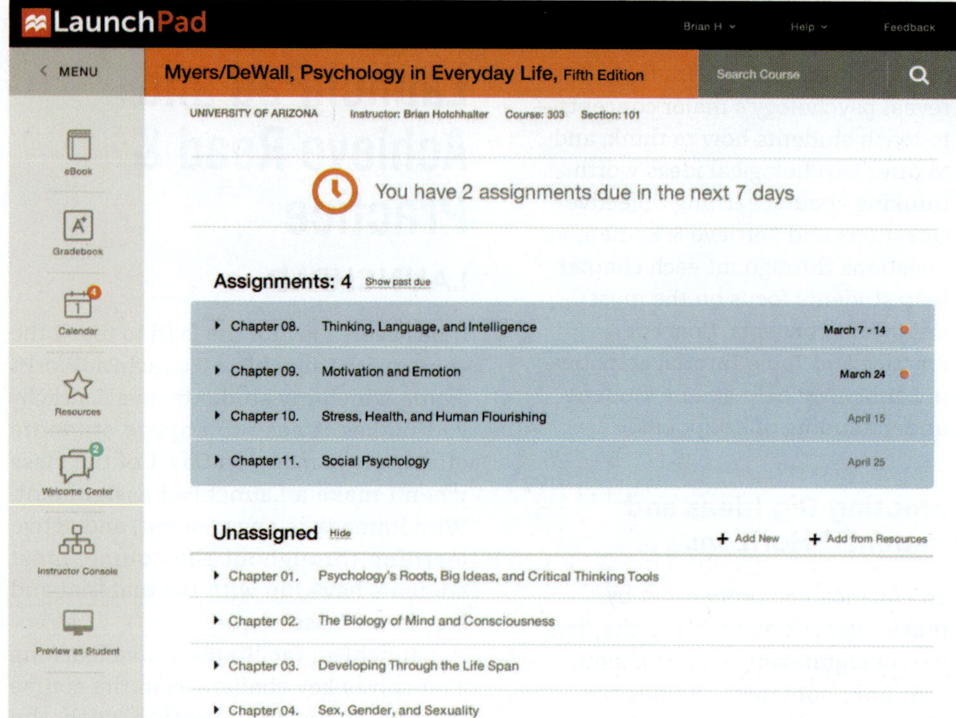

FIGURE 5 Sample from LaunchPad

in the classroom. Students can use iClicker remotes, or the REEF mobile app on their phone, tablet, or laptop to participate more meaningfully. LaunchPad includes a robust collection of iClicker questions for each chapter—readily available for use in your class.

- **The NEW Concept Practice collection** offers 120 dynamic, interactive mini-tutorials that teach and reinforce the course's foundational ideas. Each brief activity (only 5 minutes to complete) addresses one or two concepts, in a consistent format—review, practice, quiz, and conclusion.
- The **Topic Tutorials: PsychSim6,** Thomas Ludwig's (Hope College) award-winning interactive psychology simulations, were designed for the mobile web. PsychSim immerses students in the world of psychological research, placing them in the role of scientist or participant in activities that highlight important concepts, processes, and experimental approaches.
- In the **Assess Your Strengths** activities, students apply what they are learning from the text to their own lives and experiences by considering key "strengths." Each activity starts with a personalized video introduction from us [DM and ND], explaining how that strength ties in to the content of the chapter. Next, students assess themselves on the strength (critical thinking, quality of sleep, self-control, relationship strength, belonging, hope, and more) using scales developed by researchers across psychological science. After showing students their results, we offer tips for nurturing that strength in their own lives. Finally, students take a quiz to help solidify their learning.
- **NEW "Thinking Critically About . . ." infographic activities** for each chapter teach and reinforce critical-thinking skills.
- **LMS integration** into your school's system is readily available. Check with your local sales representative for details.
- **The Video Assignment Tool** makes it easy to assign and assess video-based activities and projects, and provides a convenient way for students to submit video coursework.
- **The Gradebook** gives a clear window on performance for the whole class, for individual students, and for individual assignments.
- A **streamlined interface** helps students manage their schedule of assignments, while ***social commenting tools*** let them connect with classmates and learn from one another. 24/7 help is a click away, accessible from a link in the upper right-hand corner.
- LaunchPad offers curated **optional pre-built chapter units,** which can be used as is or customized. Or choose not to use them and build your course from scratch.
- Our **Instructor Resources** include suggestions for lectures, classroom exercises and demonstrations, and student projects (with an indication in the *Lecture Guide* of which ones work best for think-pair-share, small group, and large group activities); ***Lecture Guides*** (summarizing key text discussions and connecting instructor resources with text learning objectives); the best ***Test Banks*** in the industry (carefully authored, professionally edited, and tightly coordinated with the text by the same fabulous editor since the first edition); and nice starter image slides with textbook graphics.
- In addition, we offer access to the **Macmillan Community** (Community .Macmillan.com). Created by instructors *for* instructors, this is an ideal forum for interacting with fellow educators—including Macmillan authors—in your discipline. Join ongoing conversations

about everything from course prep and presentations to assignments and assessments to teaching with media, keeping pace with—and influencing—new directions in your field. It includes exclusive access to classroom resources, blogs (including my [DM's] TalkPsych.com), webinars, professional development opportunities, and more.

ACHIEVE READ & PRACTICE

Achieve Read & Practice is the marriage of our LearningCurve adaptive quizzing and our mobile, accessible e-book in one, easy-to-use and affordable product (**FIGURE 6**). New, built-in analytics make it easier than ever for instructors to track student progress and intervene to help students succeed. Instructors who class-tested Achieve Read & Practice were surprised by its truly easy interface, and pleased with their course results. In a study of 227 students at 6 institutions, instructors found a significant improvement in the proportion of students who stayed on track with the assigned reading, and they found that students who retook quizzes (a helpful feature of Achieve Read & Practice) earned higher grades in the course. (Access the full report at MacmillanLearning.com/Catalog/Page/LearningScience.)

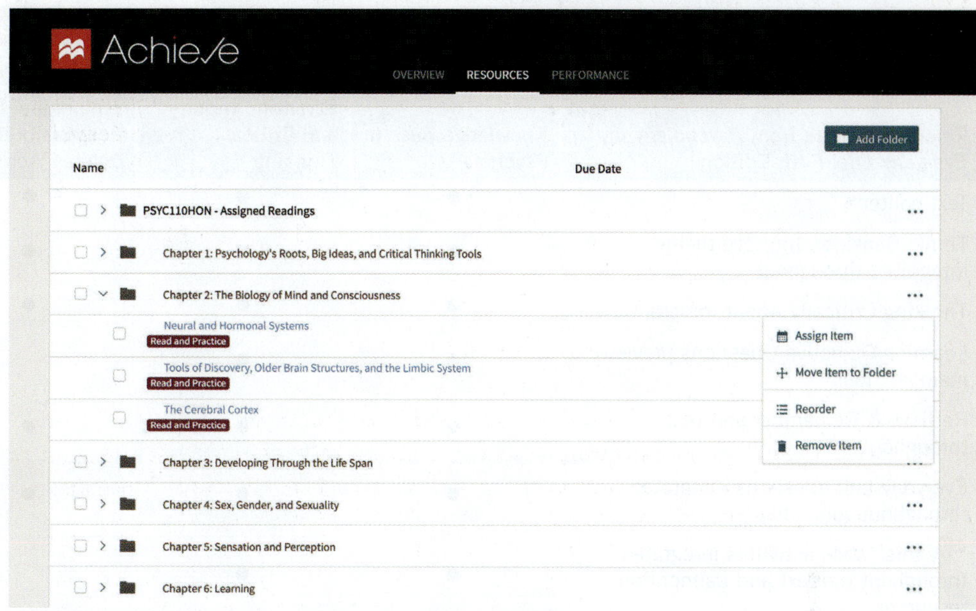

FIGURE 6 Sample from Achieve Read & Practice

What About APA Assessment Tools?

In 2011, the American Psychological Association (APA) approved the new **Principles for Quality Undergraduate Education in Psychology.** These broad-based principles and their associated recommendations were designed to "produce psychologically literate citizens who apply the principles of psychological science at work and at home." (See apa.org/education/undergrad/principles.aspx.)

APA's more specific **2013 Learning Goals and Outcomes,** from their *Guidelines for the Undergraduate Psychology Major,* Version 2.0, were designed to gauge progress in students graduating with psychology majors. (See apa.org/ed/precollege/about/psymajor-guidelines.pdf.) Many psychology departments use these goals and outcomes to help establish their own benchmarks for departmental assessment purposes.

Table 7 outlines the way *Psychology in Everyday Life,* Fifth Edition, can help you and your department to address the APA's Learning Goals and Outcomes. In addition, all of the Test Bank items for this text are coded for the APA Outcomes.

In Appreciation

Aided by input from thousands of instructors and students over the years, this has become a better, more effective, more accurate book than two authors alone (these authors at least) could write. Our indebtedness continues to the innumerable researchers who have been so willing to share their time and talent to help us accurately report their research, and to the hundreds of instructors who have taken the time to offer feedback.

Our gratitude extends to the colleagues who contributed criticism, corrections, and creative ideas related to the content, pedagogy, and format of this new edition and its resources. For their expertise and encouragement, and the gift of their time to the teaching of psychology, we thank the reviewers and consultants listed here:

Andrea Brown
College of Southern Nevada

Douglas Dinero
Onondaga Community College

Angela B. Dortch
Ivy Tech Community College

Jessica Fede
Johnson and Wales University

Jerry Green
Tarrant County College

Dann Hazel
Polk State College

Regina M. Hughes
Collin College

Lee Kooler
Modesto Junior College

Martin Lance
Forsyth Technical Community College

Jon Mandracchia
Missouri Western State University

TABLE 7 ***Psychology in Everyday Life*, Fifth Edition, Corresponds to APA Learning Goals**

Relevant Feature from *Psychology in Everyday Life*, Fifth Edition	APA Learning Goals				
	Knowledge Base in Psychology	Scientific Inquiry and Critical Thinking	Ethical and Social Responsibility in a Diverse World	Communication	Professional Development
Text content	●	●	●	●	●
Think, Consider, Improve theme integrated throughout	●	●	●		●
Thinking Critically About infographics	●	●	●		●
Learning Objective Questions previewing main sections	●	●		●	
Retrieve & Remember self-tests throughout	●	●	●	●	●
Everyday Life questions integrated throughout each chapter	●	●	●	●	●
"Try this" style activities integrated throughout the text and LaunchPad resources	●	●		●	●
Chapter Tests	●	●		●	
Statistical Reasoning in Everyday Life appendix		●		●	●
Psychology at Work appendix	●	●	●	●	●
"The Story of Psychology" timeline (Appendix F)	●		●		●
Career Fields in Psychology appendix, with Pursuing a Psychology Career online appendix	●		●		●
LaunchPad with LearningCurve formative quizzing	●	●		●	●
Assess Your Strengths feature in LaunchPad	●	●	●	●	●
"How Would You Know?" activities in LaunchPad	●	●	●	●	●

Kellie McCants-Price
Anne Arundel Community College

Michelle Merwin
The University of Tennessee at Martin

Hayley Kleitz Nelson
Delaware County Community College

Thelisa E. Nutt
Tarrant County College District—Southeast Campus

David L. Roby
Texas Southmost College

Edie Sample
Metropolitan Community College

Todd J. Smith
Morehead State University

Anita P. Tam
Greenville Technical College

Rachelle Tannenbaum
Anne Arundel Community College

Melissa S. Terlecki
Cabrini University

Carol Wilkinson
Whatcom Community College

Christine J. Ziemer
Missouri Western State University

We'd like to offer special thanks to the reviewers and consultants who helped us update and improve the content of Chapter 4, Sex, Gender, and Sexuality, and who helped us shape the new Thinking Critically About: Sexual Aggression infographic feature in Chapter 4:

Michael Bailey
Northwestern University

Andrea Brown
College of Southern Nevada

Christia Brown
University of Kentucky

Ann Coker
University of Kentucky

Jane Dickie
Hope College

Sara Dorer
Hope College

Angela B. Dortch
Ivy Tech Community College

Heather V. Ganginis Del Pino
Montgomery College

Jerry Green
Tarrant County College

Ruth Hallongren
Triton College

Regina M. Hughes
Collin College

Kellie McCants-Price
Anne Arundel Community College

Michelle Merwin
The University of Tennessee at Martin

Hayley Kleitz Nelson
Delaware County Community College

Thelisa E. Nutt
Tarrant County College District—Southeast Campus

Claire Renzetti
University of Kentucky

David L. Roby
Texas Southmost College

We'd also like to offer our thanks to the instructors who shared their input and expertise to help us shape the content of our new Student Preface—Student Success: How to Apply Psychology to Live Your Best Life:

Andrea Brown
College of Southern Nevada

Douglas Dinero
Onondaga Community College

Angela B. Dortch
Ivy Tech Community College

Timothy Flemming
Georgia State University

Dann Hazel
Polk State College

David L. Roby
Texas Southmost College

Edie Sample
Metropolitan Community College

Melissa S. Terlecki
Cabrini University

Carol Wilkinson
Whatcom Community College

We especially appreciate the consultation of Vernon Padgett (Rio Hondo College), who engaged his students to offer feedback on the format and organization for the new edition, and for the following instructors who gathered student feedback on cover options:

Douglas Dinero
Onondaga Community College

Timothy Flemming
Georgia State University

Dann Hazel
Polk State College

Carol Wilkinson
Whatcom Community College

And we appreciate the instructors who engaged their students to help us select the best of the application questions from the text, to appear inside the front and back covers of this new edition:

Jiliene G. Seiver
Bellevue College

Melissa S. Terlecki
Cabrini University

We also appreciate Salena Brody's (University of Texas, Dallas) careful review of our Psychology Timeline (Appendix F), including her added entries relating to the contributions of women and members of minority groups, and the new classroom exercises, lecture/discussion topics, and think-pair-share activities she created for the Instructor's Resources on diversity in psychology.

At Worth Publishers a host of people played key roles in creating this fifth edition.

Executive Program Manager Carlise Stembridge has been a valued team leader, thanks to her dedication, creativity, and sensitivity. Carlise oversees, encourages, and guides our author-editor team, and she serves as an important liaison with our colleagues in the field.

Noel Hohnstine and Laura Burden expertly coordinated creation of the media resources. Betty Probert efficiently edited and produced the Test Bank questions (working with Chrysalis Wright, University of Central Florida), Instructor's Resources, and Lecture Guides and, in the process, also helped fine-tune the whole book. Anna Munroe provided invaluable support in commissioning and organizing the multitude of reviews, coordinating our development and production schedules, and providing editorial guidance. Lee McKevitt did a splendid job of laying out each page. Robin Fadool and Donna Ranieri worked together to create the lovely photo program.

Won McIntosh and Susan Wein masterfully kept the book to its tight schedule, and Natasha Wolfe skillfully coordinated creation of the beautiful new design.

As you can see, although this book has two authors it is a *team* effort. A special salute is due to our book development editors, who have invested so much in creating *Psychology in Everyday Life*. My [DM] longtime editor Christine Brune saw the need for a short, accessible, student-friendly introductory psychology text, and she energized and guided the rest of us in bringing her vision to reality. Development editor Nancy Fleming is one of those rare editors who is gifted at "thinking big" about a chapter—and with a kindred spirit to our own—while also applying her sensitive, graceful, line-by-line touches. Her painstaking, deft editing was a key part of achieving the hoped-for brevity and accessibility. Development Editors Trish Morgan and Danielle Slevens also amazed us with their meticulous focus, impressive knowledge, and helpful editing. And Deborah Heimann did an excellent job with the copyediting.

To achieve our goal of supporting the teaching of psychology, these resources not only must be authored, reviewed, edited, and produced, but also made available to teachers of psychology, with effective guidance and professional and friendly servicing close at hand. For their exceptional success in doing all this, our author team is grateful to Macmillan Learning's professional sales and marketing team. We are especially grateful to Executive Marketing Manager

Kate Nurre, and Learning Solutions Specialists Robyn Burnett and Elizabeth Chaffin Woosley for tirelessly working to inform our teaching colleagues of our efforts to assist their teaching, and for the joy of working with them.

At Hope College, the supporting team members for this edition included Kathryn Brownson, who researched countless bits of information and edited and proofed hundreds of pages. Kathryn is a knowledgeable and sensitive adviser on many matters. At the University of Kentucky, Lorie Hailey has showcased a variety of indispensable qualities, including a sharp eye and a strong work ethic.

Again, I [DM] gratefully acknowledge the editing assistance and mentoring of my writing coach, poet Jack Ridl, whose influence resides in the voice you will be hearing in the pages that follow. He, more than anyone, cultivated my delight in dancing with the language, and taught me to approach writing as a craft that shades into art. Likewise, I [ND] am grateful to my intellectual hero and mentor, Roy Baumeister, who taught me how to hone my writing and embrace the writing life. I'm also indebted to John Tierney, who has offered unending support and served as a role model of how to communicate to a general audience.

And we have enjoyed our ongoing work with each other on this our seventh co-authored book. Nathan's fresh insights and contributions continue to enrich this book as we work together on each chapter. With support from our wonderful editors, this is a team project. In addition to our work together on the textbook, Nathan and I contribute to the monthly "Teaching Current Directions in Psychological Science" column in the *APS Observer* (tinyurl.com/MyersDeWall). I [DM] also blog at TalkPsych.com, where I share exciting new findings, everyday applications, and observations on all things psychology.

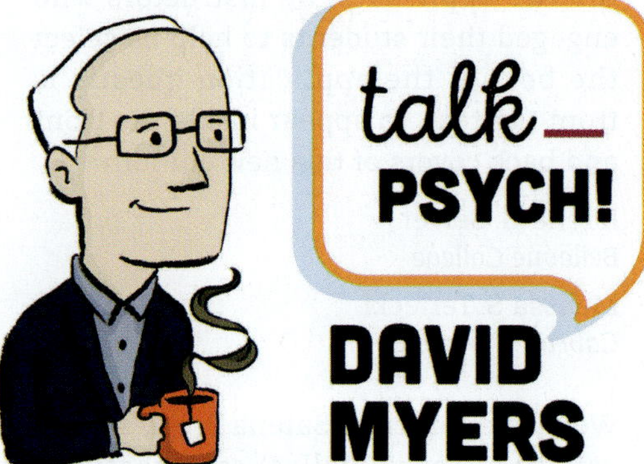

Finally, our gratitude extends to the many students and instructors who have written to offer suggestions, or just an encouraging word. It is for them, and those about to begin their study of psychology, that we have done our best to introduce the field we love.

* * *

The day this book went to press was the day we started gathering information and ideas for the next edition. Your input will influence how this book continues to evolve. So, please, do share your thoughts.

David G. Myers

Hope College
Holland, Michigan 49422-9000 USA
DavidMyers.org
@DavidGMyers

Nathan DeWall

University of Kentucky
Lexington, Kentucky 40506-0044 USA
NathanDeWall.com
@cndewall

Student Success

HOW TO APPLY PSYCHOLOGY TO LIVE YOUR BEST LIFE

You will see in the chapters to come that some things—including our temperament, body type, sexual orientation, and basic personality traits—can be checked with willpower, yet are largely beyond our power to change. In such ways it's better to accept than to fight who we are.

In other ways, we *can* change and become the person we aspire to be. Consider four life areas where we can use psychology to live our best life: self-care and self-improvement, time management and study tips, social life, and finding meaning and pursuing goals.

Self-Care and Self-Improvement

In order to care for others, we first need to care for ourselves. With family, work, and school commitments, it can be difficult to make time to achieve our goals, sustain our health, and have fun. Although you will experience occasional disappointment, failure is part of growth. No one gets everything right all of the time.

SELF-CONTROL

To care for ourselves and work on self-improvement takes **self-control**—the ability to monitor impulses and delay short-term gratification for greater long-term rewards. What's your level of self-control? On a scale from **1 *(not at all like me)* to 5 *(very much like me)*,** indicate how much each of the following statements reflects how you typically are (Tangney et al., 2004):

1. ___ I am good at resisting temptation.
2. ___I have a hard time breaking bad habits.
3. ___I am lazy.
4. ___I say inappropriate things.
5. ___I do certain things that are bad for me, if they are fun.
6. ___I refuse things that are bad for me.
7. ___I wish I had more self-discipline.
8. ___People would say that I have iron self-discipline.
9. ___Pleasure and fun sometimes keep me from getting work done.
10. ___I have trouble concentrating.
11. ___I am able to work effectively toward long-term goals.
12. ___Sometimes I can't stop myself from doing something, even if I know it is wrong.
13. ___I often act without thinking through all the alternatives.

Here's how to tally your total score:

- ***Reverse*** your rating for items 2, 3, 4, 5, 7, 9, 10, 12, and 13 (1=5, 2=4, 3=3, 4=2, 5=1).
- Now ***add*** your ratings for all items to establish your ***total score.***
- Total scores range from 13 to 65, with an average score of 39 in two studies of college students (Tangney et al., 2004). Higher scores indicate a greater degree of self-control.

> **LaunchPad** Alternatively, you can engage online (and have your score automatically calculated) with this self-assessment in the activity *Assess Your Strengths: How Much Self-Control Do You Have, and Why Is This Worth Working to Increase?*

Consider research-based strategies for improving your self-control by watching my [ND's] Video: Self-Control—Our Greatest Inner Strength, available in LaunchPad or at tinyurl.com/DeWallSelf-Control.

SELF-IMPROVEMENT

Here are some tips for improving your self-care:

- **Set and announce your goals.** Specific and realistic goals—such as "draft that paper by next Friday"—direct attention, promote effort, and motivate persistence (see Appendix B, Psychology at Work). Moreover, after letting friends or family know our goal, we're more likely to follow through.
- **Develop an action plan.** Create a strategy that specifies how you will progress toward your goals (more about this in Appendix B). People who flesh out goals with detailed plans become more focused, and are more likely to finish on time. Fantasizing your ultimate success (a great paper in on time, a good course grade, a sports victory) helps. But imagining the step-by-step details of actually getting there helps more.
- **Form beneficial habits.** Is there some behavior, such as exercising, that you would like to make automatic? Make yourself do it every day for two months and you will have transformed a hard-to-do behavior into a must-do habit. (More on this in Chapter 6, Learning.) If you struggle, try not to get discouraged. It's better to begin again after failure than to fail to set any goal.
- **Plan for a full night's sleep.** Want to be gloomy, fatigued, unfocused, and at risk for sickness? Sleep deprivation can take you there. Sometimes it is difficult—or even impossible—to get adequate sleep. Work commitments, family stresses, and other challenges can interfere. As the father of two small children, I [ND] sometimes struggle to get enough sleep. Screen

time and social time can also get in the way. The first step in changing your sleep routine starts with a question, "Do I want to increase my happiness, energy, focus, and health?" If so, try to find a way to give your body more of the sleep it craves. (More on this in Chapter 2, The Biology of Behavior and Consciousness.)

- **Create a supportive environment.** It's easier to eat healthy when you don't have junk food around. At meals, control portion size by using smaller plates and bowls. To focus on a project, remove distractions. At night, stash your phone so you can sleep undisturbed. Spend time with friends who bring out the best rather than the worst in you.
- **Control substance use.** Many psychoactive drugs, such as nicotine, are highly addictive and can readily hijack our daily lives, long-term goals, and good health. Although some drugs, such as caffeine, may be safely consumed in moderation, many others will seriously disrupt our best life unless avoided entirely. (More on this in Chapter 13, Psychological Disorders.)
- **Make time for exercise.** Daily or every-other-day aerobic exercise is a great time investment. Even in small amounts, aerobic exercise boosts health, increases energy, lifts mood, improves memory, and calms anxiety. (More on this in Chapter 10, Stress, Health, and Human Flourishing, and Chapter 14, Therapy.)
- **Incorporate mindfulness meditation.** Practicing mindfulness can help you achieve a better life balance by managing your stress and regulating your emotions more healthfully. (More on this in Chapter 10.)
- **Build resilience, coping skills, and a better lifestyle.** If we become more resilient and learn to manage our emotions, we will be better able to get through stressful times. There are also a number of lifestyle changes we can make to improve our mental health. (For more information, see Chapter 10, and "Thinking Critically About: Therapeutic Lifestyle Change" in Chapter 14.)

LaunchPad Consider ways to build your resilience by engaging online with *Assess Your Strengths: How Resilient Are You, and Why Should You Build More Resilience?*

Time Management and Study Tips

Some students fail. Some survive. And some thrive. So, what choices can you make to thrive?

Success begins with a plan for how you will manage your time and maximize your studying efforts. As legendary basketball coach John Wooden (1977) said, "When you fail to prepare, you're preparing to fail."

The first step in improving your time management and study skills is recognizing how you're currently operating.

It may seem as if there are not enough hours in the week to get everything done. That may be true, or it may be that you are not using your time as efficiently as you could. To assess your need for study skills and time management techniques, complete the survey below by answering YES or NO:[1]

1. _____Have you estimated how many hours you will need to study each week?
2. _____Do you tend to complete your assignments on time?
3. _____Have you estimated how long it takes to read one chapter in each of your textbooks?
4. _____Do you begin to work on long-term assignments at the beginning of the term?
5. _____Do you make lists of things to do in your head rather than on paper or a digital scheduling program?
6. _____Do you participate in social activities even when you know you should be studying?
7. _____Do you schedule time to study for exams?
8. _____Do you have a job that requires more than 20 hours a week?
9. _____Do you know exactly what tasks you are going to do when you sit down to study?
10. _____Do you attempt the assignments from your most difficult class first?

Give yourself one point for each *NO* answer to questions 5, 6, and 8, and one point for each *YES* answer to all the other questions. How many total points did you earn? People who score higher than 7 tend already to have good time management and study skills; people who score below 5 benefit most from learning how to improve. We can all use a reminder of best practices. Here are a few tips:

Manage your time. Your time is your most precious resource. Managing your time requires intentionally planning *when* you will progress toward your goals. Start by creating a "time budget" that mirrors your goals so that you can enjoy life, be energized, and complete your study, work, and family tasks. You need to plan time for recreation and friends; social media; sleep, eating, and personal care; class time and study; and any employment or home obligations. And precisely when will you do each? *Create weekly and daily schedules that make guilt-free space for each activity*. To become the person you wish to be, live intentionally, day by day.

Manage your mental energy. Some tasks are more mentally demanding than others. Plan your day to make space for such tasks when you have the most energy. Allow time to rest and recover before engaging the next demanding task. By becoming a better mental energy accountant, you will know when to spend your limited energy and when to save it.

Play offense. Car troubles, family problems, and work challenges happen. Sometimes we have to play "defense" against

[1] Source: Van Blerkom, D. L. (2012). *Orientation to learning* (7th ed.). Boston: Wadsworth.

stock_colors/Getty Images

Time for success Making a realistic, day-to-day schedule will allow you time for what you *need* to do as well as time for what you *want* to do.

life's demands and problems, leaving us stressed and short of our goals. The solution: When possible, play "offense" against your environment. Rather than just letting the day happen to you, start each day with a plan. Control how you spend your time. Establishing routines and making decisions in advance conserves energy by reducing daily decision making. If you know you are going to study two hours in the morning before class, you won't waste time weighing what to do.

Study smart. To remember what you read, use the SQ3R (Survey, Question, Read, Retrieve, Review) system: Survey the chapter organization; identify Questions your reading should answer; Read actively, seeking answers; Retrieve and rehearse key ideas; and finally, Review the chapter's organization and concepts. Those last two "R's" are especially important: You will retain information best through repeated self-testing and rehearsal of previously studied material. Getting *immediate feedback* makes this *testing effect* even stronger. This was the idea behind our effective online adaptive quizzing system, LearningCurve, and the frequent self-testing opportunities throughout the text. *Distributing* your study time, rather than cramming, will also help. Establishing a schedule, and sticking to it, will spread the load out across the term. For more information, see "Use Psychology to Improve Your Life and Become a Better Student" at the end of Chapter 1 and "Improving Memory" in Chapter 7, and view my [DM's] 5-minute animation at tinyurl .com/HowToRemember.

Social Life

Living your best life requires social support—not trying to manage everything on your own, and not just relying on social media for contact with friends and family. Here are some tips for forming and maintaining healthy, supportive relationships:

- **Prioritize people.** We humans are social animals. We need to belong. (See Chapter 9, Motivation and Emotion.) We are happier and healthier when supported by, and giving support to, our friends. So, make the effort to make friends, such as by joining a club, sports team, or fellowship group. Get to know your instructors by visiting during their office hours. And do not take your friends and loved ones for granted. Attend to them. Affirm them. Share your daily experiences and feelings with them.
- **Enjoy social media and your phone without letting them control you.** Use social media and your phone to stay connected with friends and family, but without displacing the face-to-face relationships for which we are made, or hijacking your time and other priorities. (More on this in Chapter 9.) And when posting on social media, remember that someday a potential employer may be Googling your name. (For tips on thinking smarter about your social media newsfeed, see my [DM's] new tutorial animation, "Thinking Critically in Our Post-Truth World" in LaunchPad, and also at tinyurl.com/PostTruthMyers.)
- **Embrace a speak-up culture rather than a call-out culture.** To disagree is to be human. You will disagree with others, and others will disagree with you. Indeed, we often learn by exploring these other perspectives. (This is why it is so important for psychological scientists to practice humility. See Chapter 1.) When you disagree, avoid *calling out* others (publicly shaming those with whom you disagree). Instead, try to *speak up:* Approach the person and express your disagreement calmly. We have a natural tendency to explain others' behaviors based on their personality traits ("He's a selfish jerk") rather than their situation ("He's sleep-deprived and stressed"). Resist this tendency by taking the other person's perspective. (See Chapter 11 for more on persuasive strategies.)
- **It's time to be the adult in the room.** As we age, we pass through different stages of development. (See Chapter 3, Developing Through the Life Span.) Most adolescents seek social acceptance while still depending on family. The transition from adolescence to adulthood requires becoming more independent. As adults, we need to own our goals, attitudes, values, and beliefs, and to make our own decisions and solve our own problems. We need to move on to having healthy adult relationships with family and friends.

LaunchPad To assess and nurture your feelings of belonging and your relationship strength, engage online with these two activities (1) *Assess Your Strengths: How Strong Is Your Need to Belong, and How Can you Strengthen Your Feelings of Belonging?* and (2) *Assess Your Strengths: How Strong Is Your Relationship, and How Might You Increase Its Strength?*

Finding Meaning and Pursuing Goals

To have meaning is to have a life filled with purpose, coherence, and significance. Most people want a meaningful life, but they report feeling unfulfilled in some area of their lives. They may not be fully engaged in their work (see Appendix B). Or they may feel stuck in a daily routine that brings money without meaning. To live your best life, take the following steps to promote meaning and pursue goals:

- **Imagine your possible self.** Who is the person you wish to be? Who is the "possible self" (see Chapter 12, Personality) you dream of becoming? "The first step to better times is to imagine them," a fortune cookie once reminded me [DM]. Thus, your first step is to *define who you hope to be and what you aim to achieve.* With that vision in mind, you can then lay out specific goals and strategies that will take you where you want to go.
- **Live your dream daily.** Here's a good rule for success: Whatever you hope to achieve, do *something toward that every day.* Do you want to be kinder, more educated, more assertive? Then, every day, do a kind act, learn something new, or practice asserting yourself. Although many days you may accomplish less than you'd hoped, even small daily steps toward a goal can, over time, take you to your destination—transforming your possible self into your actual self.
- **Adopt a "growth mindset."** It's surprisingly powerful to believe that our abilities are changeable through energy and effort. Some things we should accept, but many things we have the power to change. If you see your math or writing ability as like a muscle—something that gets stronger with training and practice—you will, in fact, develop more skill. (More on this in Chapter 8, Thinking, Language, and Intelligence.) Your mindset matters.
- **Find your calling.** No need to rush it. Most students change their vocational plans along the way, and you likely will, too. But notice what sorts of activities absorb you and make time fly. Is it being with people? Working with your hands? Solving problems with your mind? Watch for work and activities that will enable you to do what you love and to love what you do, and pursue those paths.

Mariusz Szczawinski/Alamy

Social success Nurturing relationships is an important part of a successful life. Make time and energy for important others, and you will have better physical and psychological health.

LaunchPad To further develop your goal-setting ability, engage online with the activity *Assess Your Strengths: How Might Your Willingness to Think of the Future Affect Your Ability to Achieve Long-Term Goals?*

* * * * *

Throughout this book you will encounter additional pointers to a flourishing life—counting your blessings, expressing gratitude, finding *flow,* acting happy, training your willpower, becoming mindful, opting for optimism, and more. In such ways, you can not only survive, you can thrive. Don't be too hard on yourself if you experience setbacks. If you try to do a little better each day, you can, over time, accomplish goals that might seem impossible at the outset. As Reinhold Niebuhr suggested, seek the serenity to accept things you cannot change, but also feel empowered to change the things you can.

asiseeit/Getty Images

CHAPTER 1

SURVEY THE CHAPTER

Psychology's Roots, Critical Thinking, and Self-Improvement Tools

Hoping to understand themselves and others, millions turn to psychology, as you now do. What do psychologists really know? You might think that psychologists analyze personality, examine crime scenes, testify in court, and offer advice about parenting, love, happiness, and overcoming personal problems. Do psychologists do all these things? *Yes,* and much more. Consider some of the questions psychologists study that you may also wonder about:

- Have you ever found yourself reacting to something as one of your biological parents would — perhaps in a way you vowed you *never* would — and then wondered how much of your personality you inherited? *How much are we shaped by our genes, and how much by our home and community environments?*
- Have you ever worried about how to act among people of a different culture, race, gender identity, or sexual orientation, or among people with differing abilities? *How are we alike as members of the human family? How do we differ?*
- Have you ever awakened from a nightmare and wondered why you had such a crazy dream? *Why do we dream?*

- Have you ever played peekaboo with a 6-month-old and wondered why the baby finds your disappearing/reappearing act so delightful? *What do babies actually perceive and think?*
- Have you ever wondered what leads to success in life? *Does the intelligence we are born with explain why some people get richer, think more creatively, or relate more sensitively? Or does gritty effort, and a belief that we can grow smarter, matter more?*
- Have you ever become depressed or anxious and wondered whether you'll ever feel "normal"? *What triggers our bad moods—and our good ones? What's the line between a routine mood swing and a psychological disorder?*

As you will see, psychological science has produced some fascinating and sometimes surprising answers to these questions. Psychology's roots are broad, reaching back into philosophy and biology, and its branches now spread out across the world.

Psychology Is a Science

Learning Objective Question LOQ 1-1

How is psychology a science? How does critical thinking feed a scientific attitude, and smarter thinking for everyday life?[1]

Once upon a time, on a planet in our neighborhood of the universe, there came to be people. These creatures became intensely interested in themselves and one another. They wondered, "Who are we? Why do we think and feel and act as we do? And how are we to understand—and to manage—those around us?"

To be human is to be curious about ourselves and the world around us. The ancient Greek naturalist and philosopher Aristotle (384–322 B.C.E.) wondered about learning and memory, motivation and emotion, perception and personality. We may chuckle at some of his guesses, like his suggestion that a meal makes us sleepy by causing gas and heat to collect around what he thought was the source of our personality, the heart. But credit Aristotle with asking the right questions.

CRITICAL THINKING AND THE SCIENTIFIC ATTITUDE

Psychology asks similar questions. But today's psychologists search for answers differently, by scientifically studying how we act, think, and feel. They do so with critical thinking and the scientific attitude.

Critical thinking[2] is smart thinking. Whether reading a research report or an online opinion, critical thinkers ask questions. *How do they know that? Who benefits? Is the conclusion based on a personal story and gut feelings or on scientific evidence? How do we know one event caused the other? How else could we explain things?*

Critical thinkers wince when people say something is true based on gut feelings: "I *feel like* climate change is [or isn't] happening." "I *feel like* self-driving cars are more [or less] dangerous." "I *feel like* my candidate is more honest." Such beliefs (commonly mislabeled as feelings) may or may not be true. Critical thinkers are open to the possibility that they (or you) might be wrong. Sometimes the best evidence confirms what we believe to be true. Sometimes it challenges these claims and leads us to a different way of thinking. To believe everything—or to reject everything—is to be a fool.

Some deeply religious people may view critical thinking and scientific inquiry, including psychology's, as a threat. Yet many of the leaders of the scientific revolution, including Copernicus and Newton, were deeply religious people acting on the idea that "in order to love and honor God, it is necessary to fully appreciate the wonders of his handiwork" (Stark, 2003a,b).[3]

> From a humorous Twitter feed:
> "The problem with quotes on the internet is that you never know if they're true."
> —Abraham Lincoln

In psychology, critical thinking has led to some surprising findings. Believe it or not . . .

- massive losses of brain tissue early in life may have few long-term effects (see Chapter 2).
- within days, newborns can recognize their mother's odor (Chapter 3).
- after brain damage, some people can learn new skills, yet at the mind's conscious level be unaware that they have these skills (Chapter 7).
- most of us—male and female, old and young, wealthy and not wealthy, with and without disabilities—report roughly the same levels of personal happiness (Chapter 10).
- an electric shock delivered to the brain (*electroconvulsive therapy*) may relieve severe depression when all else has failed (Chapter 14).

The more people use critical thinking, the better they separate fiction from fact (Bensley et al., 2014). In psychology, this same critical inquiry has also overturned some popular beliefs. When we let the evidence speak for itself, we learn that . . .

- sleepwalkers are *not* acting out their dreams (Chapter 2).
- our past experiences are *not* recorded word for word in our brain. Neither brain stimulation nor hypnosis will let us replay and relive long-buried memories (Chapter 7).
- most of us do *not* suffer from low self-esteem, and high self-esteem is not all good (Chapter 12).
- opposites do *not* generally attract (Chapter 11).

---

[1] To assist your learning of psychology, numbered Learning Objective Questions appear at the beginning of major sections. You can test your understanding by trying to answer the question before, and then again after, you read the section.

[2] Throughout the text, the most important concepts are **boldfaced.** As you study, you can find these terms defined nearby, and all together in the Glossary and Glosario.

[3] This book's information sources are cited in parentheses, with name and date. Every citation can be found in the end-of-book References, with complete documentation.

In later chapters, you'll see many more examples in which psychology's critical thinking has challenged old beliefs and led us onto new paths. All of science, including psychology, lets the facts speak for themselves.

Science-aided thinking is smart thinking. No matter how sensible-seeming or wild an idea, the smart thinker asks: *Does it work?* A scientific attitude prepares us to think smarter. (See Thinking Critically About: The Scientific Attitude.)

IN YOUR EVERYDAY LIFE

Were you surprised to learn that psychology is a science? How would you explain that now if someone asked you about it?[4]

RETRIEVE & REMEMBER

ANSWERS IN APPENDIX E

1. Describe what's involved in critical thinking.
2. Describe the three parts of the scientific attitude.

(a)

(b)

Yesterday's lack of diversity At this 1964 meeting of the Society of Experimental Psychologists (a), Eleanor Gibson was easy to spot among the many male members, all in a sea of White faces. By contrast, women now are 55 percent of Association for Psychological Science members and 75 percent of psychology graduate students, as is clear in this photo of graduate students from Lehigh University (b). People of color have made enormous contributions to the field (see, for example, coverage of Kenneth Clark and Mamie Phipps Clark later in this chapter), and psychology's diversity continues to grow. For more on the history of these changes, see the Historical Timeline at the end of this text and in LaunchPad (LaunchPadWorks.com).

PSYCHOLOGICAL SCIENCE'S BIRTH AND DEVELOPMENT

LOQ 1-3 How has psychology's focus changed over time?

Psychology as we know it was born on a December day in 1879, in a small, third-floor room at a German university. There, Wilhelm Wundt and his assistants created a machine to measure how long it took people to press a telegraph key after hearing a ball hit a platform (Hunt, 1993). (Most hit the key in about one-tenth of a second.) Wundt's attempt to measure "atoms of the mind"—the fastest and simplest mental processes—was psychology's first experiment. And that modest third-floor room took its place in history as the first psychological laboratory.

Psychology's earliest explorers—"Magellans of the mind," Morton Hunt (1993) called them—came from many disciplines and countries. Wundt was both a philosopher and a physiologist. Charles Darwin, whose thinking on species variation in the natural world led to *evolutionary psychology*, was an English naturalist. Ivan Pavlov, who taught us much about learning, was a Russian physiologist. Sigmund Freud, a famous personality theorist and therapist, was an Austrian physician. Jean Piaget, who explored children's developing minds, was a Swiss biologist. William James, who shared his love of psychology in his 1890 textbook, was an American philosopher.

Few of psychology's early pioneers were women. In the late 1800s, psychology, like most fields, was a man's world. William James helped break that mold when he chose to mentor Mary Whiton Calkins, by accepting her into his graduate seminar. Although Calkins went on to outscore all the male students on the Ph.D. exams, Harvard University denied her the degree she had earned. In its place, she was told, she could have a degree from Radcliffe College, Harvard's undergraduate "sister" school for women. Calkins resisted the unequal treatment and turned down the offer. But she continued her research on memory, which her colleagues honored in 1905

[4] Thinking about these *In* Your Everyday Life questions and *Improve* Your Everyday Life questions—and how they relate to your own life—will help you make psychology's concepts more personally meaningful, and therefore more memorable.

critical thinking thinking that does not blindly accept arguments and conclusions. Rather, it examines assumptions, assesses the source, uncovers hidden values, weighs evidence, and assesses conclusions.

Thinking Critically About:

The Scientific Attitude

LOQ 1-2 What are the three key elements of the scientific attitude, and how do they support scientific inquiry?

Three basic attitudes helped make modern science possible.

1 CURIOSITY:

Does it work?

When put to the test, can its **predictions be confirmed?**

Can some people read minds? ●

Are stress levels related to health and well-being? ○

● *No one has yet been able to demonstrate extrasensory mind-reading.*

○ *Many studies have found that higher stress relates to poorer health.*

2 SKEPTICISM:

What do you mean?

How do you know?

Sifting reality from fantasy requires a healthy skepticism—an attitude that is not cynical (doubting everything), but also not gullible (believing everything).

Do our facial expressions and body postures affect how we actually feel? ●

Do parental behaviors determine their children's sexual orientation? ○

● *Our facial expressions and body postures can affect how we feel.*

○ *Chapter 4 explains that there is not a relationship between parental behaviors and their children's sexual orientation.*

3 HUMILITY:

That was unexpected! Let's explore further.

Researchers must be willing to be surprised and follow new ideas. People and other animals don't always behave as our ideas and beliefs would predict.

One of psychology's mottos: The rat is always right.

Wilhelm Wundt (1832–1920) Wundt established the first psychology laboratory at the University of Leipzig, Germany.

William James (1842–1910) and Mary Whiton Calkins (1863–1930) James was a legendary teacher-writer who authored an important 1890 psychology text. He mentored Calkins, who became famous for her memory research and for being the first woman to be president of the American Psychological Association.

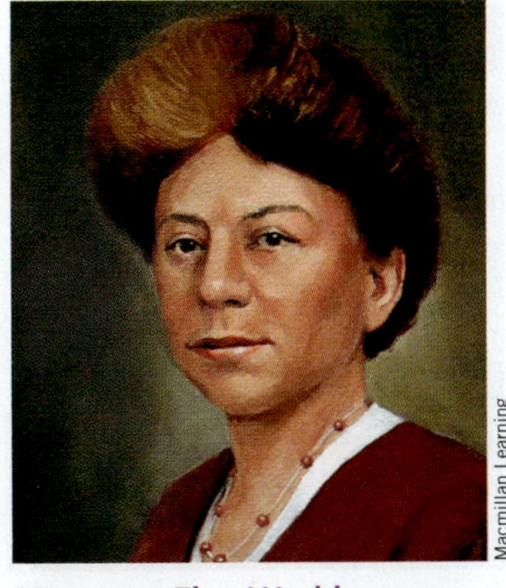

Margaret Floy Washburn (1871–1939) After Harvard refused to grant Calkins the degree she had earned, Washburn became the first woman to receive a psychology Ph.D. She focused on animal behavior research in *The Animal Mind.*

by electing her the first female president of the American Psychological Association (APA). Animal behavior researcher Margaret Floy Washburn became the first woman to officially receive a psychology Ph.D. and the second, in 1921, to become an APA president. (Between 1997 and 2019, more than half of the elected presidents of the science-focused Association for Psychological Science were women.)

The rest of the story of psychology—the story this book tells—develops at many levels, in the hands of many people, with interests ranging from therapy to the study of nerve cell activity. As you might expect, agreeing on a definition of psychology has not been easy.

For the early pioneers, *psychology* was defined as "the science of mental life"—inner sensations, images, thoughts, and emotions. As it developed, psychology became organized into different branches. **Structuralism** (promoted by Wundt) focused on the structure of the mind, and **functionalism** (promoted by James) focused on how the mind functions.

And so it continued until the 1920s, when the first of two larger-than-life American psychologists challenged the idea of studying internal, mental processes. John B. Watson, and later B. F. Skinner, insisted that *psychology* must be "the scientific study of observable *behavior*." After all, they said, science is rooted in observation. What you cannot observe and measure, you cannot scientifically study. You cannot observe a sensation, a feeling, or a thought, but you *can* observe and record people's *behavior* as they are *conditioned*—as they respond to and learn in different situations. Many agreed, and **behaviorism** was one of psychology's two major forces well into the 1960s.

The other major force was Sigmund Freud's *psychoanalytic psychology,* which emphasized the ways our unconscious mind and childhood experiences affect our behavior. Some students wonder: Is psychology mainly about Freud's teachings on unconscious sexual conflicts and the mind's defenses against its own wishes and impulses? *No.* Today's psychological science does not support Freud's theory of sexuality. It does, however, agree that much of the human mind operates outside our conscious awareness. (In chapters to come, we'll look more closely at Freud and others mentioned here.)

As the behaviorists had rejected the early 1900s definition of *psychology,* other groups in the 1960s rejected the behaviorists' definition. In the 1960s, **humanistic psychologists,** led by Carl Rogers and Abraham Maslow, found both behaviorism and Freudian psychology too limiting. Rather than focusing on conditioned responses or childhood memories, Rogers and Maslow drew attention to our growth potential, to our needs for love and acceptance, and to environments that nurture or limit personal growth.

Another group searching for a new path in the 1960s pioneered a *cognitive revolution,* which led the field back to its early interest in how our mind processes and retains information. **Cognitive psychology** today continues its scientific exploration of how we perceive, process, and remember information, and of how thinking and emotion

structuralism an early school of thought promoted by Wundt that focused on the structure of the human mind.

functionalism an early school of thought promoted by James and influenced by Darwin that focused on how the mind functions.

behaviorism the view that psychology (1) should be an objective science that (2) studies behavior without reference to mental processes. Most psychologists today agree with (1) but not with (2).

humanistic psychology a historically important perspective that emphasized human growth potential.

cognitive psychology the study of mental processes, such as occur when we perceive, learn, remember, think, communicate, and solve problems.

John B. Watson (1878–1958) and Rosalie Rayner (1898–1935) Working with Rayner, Watson championed psychology as the scientific study of behavior. In a controversial study on a baby who became famous as "Little Albert," he and Rayner showed that fear could be learned. (More about this in Chapter 6.)

B. F. Skinner (1904–1990) This leading behaviorist rejected the idea of studying inner thoughts and feelings. He believed psychology should study how consequences shape behavior.

Sigmund Freud (1856–1939) The controversial ideas of this famous personality theorist and therapist have influenced humanity's self-understanding.

interact in anxiety, depression, and other disorders. The marriage of cognitive psychology (the science of the mind) and neuroscience (the science of the brain) gave birth to **cognitive neuroscience.** This specialty, with researchers in many disciplines, studies the brain activity underlying mental activity.

Today's psychology builds upon the work of many earlier scientists and schools of thought. To include psychology's concern with observable behavior *and* with inner thoughts and feelings, we now define **psychology** as the *science of behavior and mental processes.*

Let's unpack this definition. *Behavior* is anything a human or nonhuman animal *does*—any action we can observe and record. Yelling, smiling, blinking, sweating, talking, and questionnaire marking are all observable behaviors. *Mental processes* are our internal, subjective experiences—sensations, perceptions, dreams, thoughts, beliefs, and feelings.

By now you've learned that the key word in today's psychology is *science.* Psychology is less a set of findings than a way of asking and answering questions. Our aim, then, is not merely to report results but also to show you how psychologists play their game. You will see how researchers evaluate conflicting opinions and ideas. And you will learn more about how you, whether as a beginner scientist or simply a curious person, can think harder and smarter when explaining events and making choices in your own life.

IN YOUR EVERYDAY LIFE

How would you have defined psychology before taking this class? How do you think psychology might change in the future as more women, and others from historically excluded groups, contribute their ideas to the field?

RETRIEVE & REMEMBER

ANSWERS IN APPENDIX E

3. What event defined the start of scientific psychology?
4. From the 1920s through the 1960s, the two major forces in psychology were ________ and ________ psychology.
5. How did the cognitive revolution affect the field of psychology?

LaunchPad Our online learning tools will help you excel in this course. Take advantage of the LearningCurve adaptive quizzing that adjusts to your individual needs, "Assess Your Strengths" personal self-assessments, interactive simulations, and "How Would You Know?" research activities. For more information, see LaunchPadWorks.com. And for an excellent tour of psychology's roots, view the 9.5-minute *Video: The History of Psychology.*

TODAY'S PSYCHOLOGY

LOQ 1-4 What are psychology's current perspectives, and what are some of its subfields?

Today there are more than 1 million psychologists around the world (Zoma & Gielen, 2015). The International Union of Psychological Science has 82 member nations, from Albania to Zimbabwe. Psychology is *growing* and it is *globalizing.* The story of psychology is being written in many places, with studies ranging from the exploration of nerve cell activity to international conflicts. Modern psychology is shaped by many forces.

Psychologists' wide-ranging interests make it hard to picture a psychologist at work. You might start by imagining a neuroscientist probing an animal's brain, an intelligence researcher studying how quickly infants become bored with a familiar scene, or a therapist listening closely to a client's anxieties. Psychologists examine behavior and mental processes from many viewpoints, which are described in **TABLE 1.1.** These perspectives range from the biological to the social-cultural, and their settings range from the laboratory to the clinic. But all share a common goal: *describing and explaining behavior and the mind underlying it.*

Psychology also relates to many other fields. You'll find psychologists teaching

TABLE 1.1 Psychology's Current Perspectives

Perspective	Focus	Sample Questions	Examples of Subfields Using This Perspective
Neuroscience	How the body and brain enable emotions, memories, and sensory experiences	How do pain messages travel from the hand to the brain? How is blood chemistry linked with moods and motives?	Biological; cognitive; clinical
Evolutionary	How the natural selection of traits passed down from one generation to the next has promoted the survival of genes	How has our evolutionary past influenced our modern-day mating preferences? Why do humans learn some fears so much more easily than others?	Biological; developmental; social
Behavior genetics	How our genes and our environment influence our individual differences	To what extent are psychological traits such as intelligence, personality, sexual orientation, and vulnerability to depression products of our genes? Of our environment?	Personality; developmental; legal/ forensic
Psychodynamic	How behavior springs from unconscious drives and conflicts	How can someone's personality traits and disorders be explained in terms of their childhood relationships?	Clinical; counseling; personality
Behavioral	How we learn observable responses	How do we learn to fear particular objects or situations? What is the most effective way to alter our behavior, say, to lose weight or stop smoking?	Clinical; counseling; industrial-organizational
Cognitive	How we encode, process, store, and retrieve information	How do we use information in remembering? Reasoning? Solving problems?	Cognitive neuroscience; clinical; counseling; industrial-organizational
Social-cultural	How behavior and thinking vary across situations and cultures	How are we affected by the people around us, and by our surrounding culture?	Developmental; social; clinical; counseling

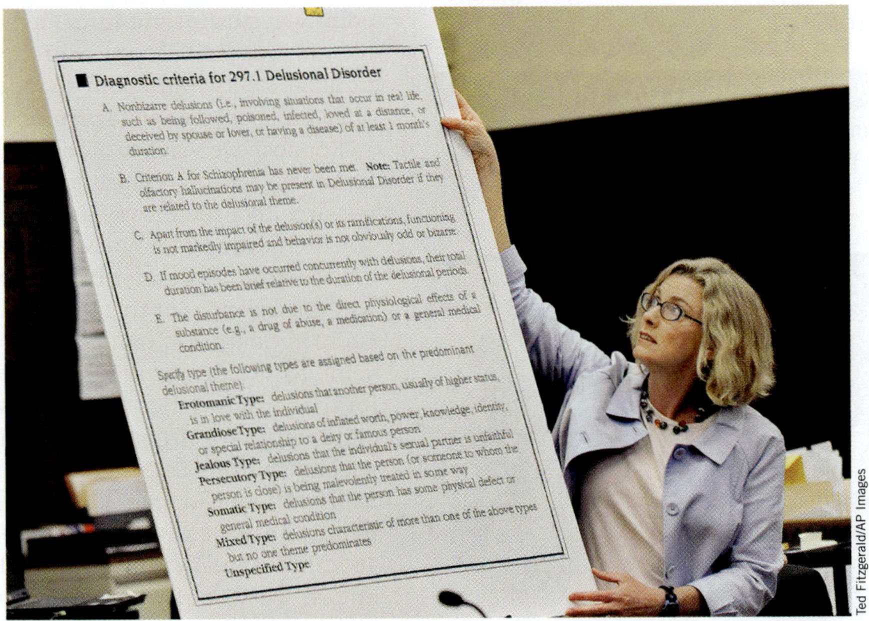

Psychology in court *Forensic psychologists* apply psychology's principles and methods in the criminal justice system. They may assess witnesses or testify in court about a defendant's state of mind and future risk.

in psychology departments, medical schools, law schools, business schools, and theological seminaries. You'll see them working in hospitals, factories, and corporate offices.

In this course, you will hear about

- ***biological psychologists*** exploring the links between brain and mind.
- ***developmental psychologists*** studying our changing abilities from womb to tomb.
- ***cognitive psychologists*** experimenting with how we perceive, think, and solve problems.

cognitive neuroscience the interdisciplinary study of the brain activity linked with mental activity (including perception, thinking, memory, and language).

psychology the science of behavior and mental processes.

- *personality psychologists* investigating our persistent traits.
- *social psychologists* exploring how we view and affect one another.
- *health psychologists* investigating the psychological, biological, and behavioral factors that promote or impair our health.
- *industrial-organizational psychologists* studying and advising on workplace-related behaviors and system and product designs.

Psychology is both a science and a profession. Some psychologists conduct *basic research,* to build the field's knowledge base. Others conduct *applied research,* tackling practical problems. Many do both.

Psychology also influences modern cultures. Knowledge transforms us. After learning about psychology's findings, people less often judge psychological disorders as moral failures. They less often regard women as men's inferiors. They less often view children as ignorant, willful beasts in need of taming. And as thinking changes, so do actions. "In each case," noted Hunt (1990, p. 206), "knowledge has modified attitudes, and, through them, behavior." Once aware of psychology's well-researched ideas—about how body and mind connect, how we construct our perceptions, how we learn and remember, how people across the world are alike and different—your own mind may never be quite the same.

"I'm a social scientist, Michael. That means I can't explain electricity or anything like that, but if you ever want to know about people I'm your man."

The New Yorker Collection, 1986, J.B. Handelsman from cartoonbank.com

Now let's consider some of modern psychology's big ideas, which you will find woven throughout this book: the *biopsychosocial approach* to understanding our behavior and mental processes, the surprising *dual processing* in our two-track mind, and the way psychology explores human challenges *(clinical psychology)* as well as strengths *(positive psychology)*.

IN YOUR EVERYDAY LIFE

Which of psychology's theoretical perspectives is most interesting to you? Why?

Paul Sakuma/AP Images

Photo 12/Alamy

Life after studying psychology The study of psychology, and its critical thinking strategies, have helped prepare people for varied occupations. Facebook founder Mark Zuckerberg studied psychology and computer science while in college. Actor and film producer Natalie Portman majored in psychology and co-authored a scientific article in college—and on one of her summer breaks filmed *Star Wars: Episode I.*

RETRIEVE & REMEMBER

ANSWERS IN APPENDIX E

6. The ________-________ perspective in psychology focuses on how behavior and thought differ from situation to situation and from culture to culture, while the ________ perspective emphasizes observation of how we respond to and learn in different situations.

The Biopsychosocial Approach

LOQ 1-5 How do psychologists use the biopsychosocial approach, and how can it help us understand our diverse world?

Each of us is part of a larger social system—a family, ethnic group, culture, and *socioeconomic* class (level of income). But we also define ourselves individually by gender, physical ability, and sexual orientation. We share a biologically rooted human nature. Yet many biological, psychological, and social-cultural influences fine-tune our assumptions, values, and behaviors. The **biopsychosocial approach** integrates these three *levels of analysis*—the biological, psychological, and social-cultural. Each level's viewpoint gives us insight into a behavior or mental process. Each asks different questions and has limits, but together they offer the most complete picture.

Suppose we want to study gender differences. Although early psychological research focused mostly on men, federal research agencies now expect researchers to examine gender differences. You will see throughout this book (and especially in Chapter 4) that *gender* is not the same as *sex. Gender* refers to the behavioral characteristics that people associate with *boy, girl, man,* or *woman* in a specific culture. *Sex* refers to the biologically influenced characteristics, which people inherit thanks to their genes. To study gender similarities and differences, we would want to know about biological influences. But we would also want to understand how the group's **culture**—the shared ideas and behaviors that one generation passes on to the

Roy Toft/Getty Images

Antonia Brune

A smile is a smile the world around Throughout this book, you will see examples not only of our incredible diversity but also of the similarities that define our shared human nature. People vary in when and how often they smile, but a naturally happy smile *means* the same thing to all of us everywhere.

next—views gender. Critical thinking has taught psychologists to be careful about making statements about people in general if the evidence comes from studies done in only one time and place. Participants in many studies have come from the WEIRD cultures—Western, Educated, Industrial, Rich, and Democratic (Henrich et al., 2010). We are also increasingly aware that the categories we use to divide people are socially constructed. In terms of gender and sex, we will see that many individuals' *gender identity* differs from their sex.

If we knew about a group's culturally influenced gender expectations, our view would still be incomplete. We would also need some understanding of how the group's *individuals* differ from one another because of their personal abilities and learning.

Studying all these influences in various people around the world, researchers have found some gender differences—in what we dream, in how we express and detect emotion, and in our risk for alcohol use disorder, eating disorders, and depression. Psychologically as well as biologically, we differ. But research shows we are also alike. Whether female or male, we learn to walk at about the same age. We experience the same sensations of light and sound. We remember vivid emotional events and forget everyday details. We feel the same pangs of hunger, desire, and fear. We exhibit similar overall intelligence and well-being.

We are each in certain respects like all others, like some others, and like no other. Studying all kinds of people helps us see our similarities and our differences, our human kinship and our diversity.

Psychologists have used the biopsychosocial approach to study many of the field's big questions. One of the biggest and most persistent is the **nature–nurture issue:** How do we judge the contributions of *nature* (biology) and *nurture* (experience)? Today's psychologists explore this age-old question by asking, for example:

- How are intelligence and personality differences influenced by heredity and by environment?
- Is our *sexual orientation* written in our genes?
- Can life experiences affect the expression of the genes we inherit?
- Should we treat depression as a disorder of the brain or a disorder of thought—or both?

In most cases, *nurture works on what nature provides.* However, in Chapter 3, you'll also learn about *epigenetics*—how experience in turn influences genetic expression. And in Chapter 2 you will see that our species has been graced with the great biological gift of brain *plasticity:* an enormous ability to learn and adapt. Every psychological event—every thought,

Jane Barlow/Getty Images

Hemis/Alamy

Culture and kissing Kissing crosses cultures. Yet how we do it varies. Imagine yourself kissing someone on the lips. Do you tilt your head right or left? In Western cultures, in which people read from left to right, about two-thirds of couples kiss right, as in Prince Harry and Meghan's wedding kiss, and in Auguste Rodin's sculpture, *The Kiss.* People reading Hebrew and Arabic read from right to left, and in one study 77 percent of those readers kissed tilting left (Shaki, 2013).

biopsychosocial approach an approach that integrates different but complementary views from biological, psychological, and social-cultural viewpoints.

culture the enduring behaviors, ideas, attitudes, values, and traditions shared by a group of people and handed down from one generation to the next.

nature–nurture issue the age-old controversy over the relative influence of genes and experience in the development of psychological traits and behaviors. Today's psychological science sees traits and behaviors arising from the interaction of nature and nurture.

A nature-made nature–nurture experiment Identical twins have the same genes. This makes them ideal participants in studies designed to shed light on hereditary and environmental influences on personality, intelligence, and other traits. Fraternal twins have different genes but often share a similar environment. Twin studies provide a wealth of findings—described in later chapters—showing the importance of both nature and nurture.

every emotion—is also a biological event. Thus, depression can be both a brain disorder *and* a thought disorder. (You'll learn more about this in Chapter 13.)

IN YOUR EVERYDAY LIFE

Think of one of your own unique traits. (This can be anything from whether you usually complete assignments on time or late to whether you become energized by social interactions or recharge by spending time alone.) How do you think that trait was influenced by nature and nurture?

Dual Processing With Our Two-Track Mind

LOQ 1-6 What are we learning about *dual processing* from psychological science?

Today's psychological science explores how our perception, thinking, memory, and attitudes all operate on two independent levels: a conscious, aware track, and an unconscious, automatic, unaware track (Wang, 2017). It has been a surprise to learn how much information processing happens without our awareness.

Our conscious mind *feels* like the boss of our body, and we do process much information on our brain's conscious track, with full awareness. But at the same time, a large unconscious, automatic track is also processing information outside of our awareness. Today's researchers call it **dual processing.** We know more than we know we know.

Vision is a great example of our dual processing. As science often reveals, truth can be stranger than fiction.

During a stay at Scotland's University of St. Andrews, I [DM] came to know research psychologists Melvyn Goodale and David Milner (2004, 2006). They studied a local woman, D. F., who was overcome by carbon monoxide one day. The resulting brain damage left her unable to consciously perceive objects. Yet she *acted* as if she *could* see them. Slip a postcard into a mail slot? *Yes,* she could do so without error. Report the width of a block in front of her? *No,* but she could grasp it with just the right finger-thumb distance. How could a woman who is perceptually blind grasp and guide objects accurately? A scan of D. F.'s brain revealed the answer.

The eye sends information to different brain areas, and each of these areas has a different task. A scan of D. F.'s brain revealed normal activity in an area concerned with reaching for and grasping objects, but not in another area concerned with consciously recognizing objects. A few other patients have a reverse pattern of damage. As you might expect, their symptoms are the reverse of D. F.'s. They can see and recognize objects, but they have difficulty pointing toward or grasping them.

We think of our vision as one system: We look. We see. We respond to what we see. Actually, vision is a two-track system (Foley et al., 2015). Our *visual perception track* enables us to think about the world—to recognize things and to plan future actions. Our *visual action track* guides our moment-to-moment actions.

Our thinking, memory, and attitudes also operate on two levels—conscious and unconscious. More than we realize, much of our mental life happens automatically, off screen. Like jumbo jets, we fly mostly on autopilot. This may be a strange new idea for some of you. It was for me [DM]. I long believed that my own intentions and deliberate choices ruled my life. In many ways they do. But as you will see in later chapters, there is much, much more to being human.

Clinical Psychology

LOQ 1-7 How is psychology also a helping profession?

Psychology is a science, but it is also a profession that helps people have healthier relationships, overcome feelings of anxiety or depression, and raise thriving children. *Counseling psychology* and *clinical psychology* grew out of different historical traditions. Early counseling psychologists offered job skills guidance, whereas clinical psychologists worked alongside psychiatrists to assess and provide psychotherapy to people in the first psychology clinics. Today's counseling psychologists and clinical psychologists have a lot in common. **Counseling psychologists** help people to cope with challenges and crises (including school, work, and relationship issues) and to improve their personal and social functioning. **Clinical psychologists** often assess and treat people with mental, emotional, and behavior disorders. Both counseling and clinical psychologists give and interpret tests, provide counseling and therapy to people with all levels of psychological difficulties, and undergo the same licensing exams. They sometimes also conduct basic and applied research. By contrast, **psychiatrists,** who also may provide psychotherapy, are medical doctors. They are licensed to prescribe drugs and otherwise

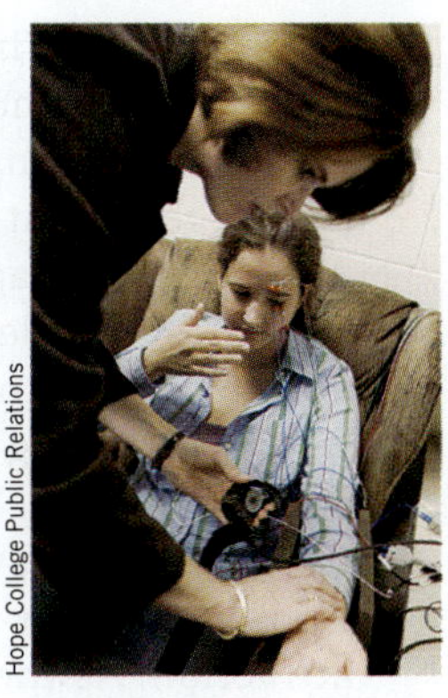

Psychology: A science and a profession Psychologists experiment with, observe, test, and help change behavior. Here we see psychologists testing a child, measuring emotion-related physiology, and doing face-to-face therapy.

treat physical causes of psychological disorders.

Rather than seeking to change people to fit their environment, **community psychologists** work to create social and physical environments that are healthy for all (Bradshaw et al., 2009; Trickett, 2009). To prevent bullying, for example, they might consider ways to improve the culture of the school and neighborhood, and how to increase bystander intervention (Polanin et al., 2012).

Positive Psychology

LOQ 1-8 What is *positive psychology?*

Psychology's first hundred years focused on understanding and treating troubles, such as abuse and anxiety, depression and disease, prejudice and poverty. Much of today's psychology continues the exploration of such challenges. Without slighting the need to repair damage and cure disease, Martin Seligman and others (2002, 2005, 2011) have called for more research on *human flourishing,* on understanding and developing the emotions and traits that help us to thrive. These psychologists call their approach **positive psychology.** They believe that happiness is a by-product of a pleasant, engaged, and meaningful life. Thus, positive psychology focuses on building a "good life" that engages our skills, and a "meaningful life" that points beyond ourselves. Positive psychology uses scientific methods to explore

- ***positive emotions,*** such as satisfaction with the past, happiness with the present, and optimism about the future.
- ***positive character traits,*** such as creativity, courage, compassion, integrity, self-control, leadership, wisdom, and spirituality. Current research examines the roots and fruits of such qualities, sometimes by studying the lives of individuals who offer striking examples.
- ***positive institutions,*** such as healthy families, supportive neighborhoods, effective schools, and socially responsible media.

Will psychology have a more positive mission in this century? Can it help us all to flourish? An increasing number of scientists worldwide believe it can.

IN YOUR EVERYDAY LIFE

When you signed up for this course, what did you know about different psychology specialties?

LaunchPad Want to learn more? See Appendix C, Career Fields in Psychology, at the end of this book, and go to our online *Pursuing a Psychology Career* resource to learn about the many interesting options available to those with bachelor's, master's, and doctoral degrees in psychology. To review and test your understanding of psychology's perspectives and subfields, engage online with *Concept Practice: Psychology's Current Perspectives* and *Concept Practice: Psychology's Subfields.*

RETRIEVE & REMEMBER

ANSWERS IN APPENDIX E

7. Match the specialty (i through iii) with the description (a through c).

i. Clinical psychology	a. works to create social and physical environments that are healthy for all
ii. Psychiatry	b. studies, assesses, and treats people with psychological disorders but usually does not provide medical therapy
iii. Community psychology	c. is a branch of medicine dealing with psychological disorders

dual processing the principle that our mind processes information at the same time on separate conscious and unconscious tracks.

counseling psychology a branch of psychology that assists people with problems in living (often related to school, work, or relationships) and in achieving greater well-being.

clinical psychology a branch of psychology that studies, assesses, and treats people with psychological disorders.

psychiatry a branch of medicine dealing with psychological disorders; practiced by physicians who sometimes provide medical (for example, drug) treatments as well as psychological therapy.

community psychology a branch of psychology that studies how people interact with their social environments and how social institutions (such as schools and neighborhoods) affect individuals and groups.

positive psychology the scientific study of human flourishing, with the goals of discovering and promoting strengths and virtues that help individuals and communities to thrive.

The Need for Psychological Science

Some people think psychology merely proves what we already know and then dresses it in jargon: "You get paid for using fancy methods to tell me what my grandmother knew?" Indeed, although sometimes mistaken, Grandma's common sense is often right. As the baseball great Yogi Berra (1925–2015) once said, "You can observe a lot by watching." (We also have Berra to thank for other gems, such as "Nobody ever goes there any more—it's too crowded," and "If the people don't want to come out to the ballpark, nobody's gonna stop 'em.") We're all behavior watchers, and sometimes we get it right. For example, many people believe that love breeds happiness, and it does. (We have what Chapter 9 calls a deep "need to belong.")

THE LIMITS OF COMMON SENSE

LOQ 1-9 How does our everyday thinking sometimes lead us to a wrong conclusion?

Common sense is indeed important. But it can also lead us astray. Our gut feelings may tell us that lie detectors work and that eyewitnesses recall events accurately. But as you will see in chapters to come, hundreds of scientific findings challenge these beliefs.

Hunches are a good starting point, even for smart thinkers. But thinking critically means checking assumptions, weighing evidence, inviting criticism, and testing conclusions. Does the death penalty prevent murders? Whether your gut tells you Yes or No, you need evidence. You might ask, *Do U.S. states with a death penalty have lower homicide rates? After states pass death-penalty laws, do their homicide rates drop? Do homicide rates rise in states that abandon the death penalty?* If we ignore the answers to such questions (which the evidence suggests are *No, No,* and *No*), our gut feelings may steer us down the wrong path.

With its standards for gathering and sifting evidence, psychological science helps us avoid errors and think smarter. Before moving on to our study of how psychologists use psychology's methods in their research, let's look more closely at three common flaws in commonsense thinking—*hindsight bias, overconfidence,* and *perceiving patterns in random events.*

Did We Know It All Along? Hindsight Bias

Consider how easy it is to draw the bull's-eye *after* the arrow strikes. After the game, we credit the coach if a "gutsy play" wins the game and fault her for the same "stupid play" if it doesn't. After a war or an election, its outcome usually seems obvious. Although history may therefore seem like a series of predictable events, the actual future is seldom foreseen. No one's diary recorded, "Today the Hundred Years War began."

This **hindsight bias** is easy to demonstrate by giving half the members of a group a true psychological finding, and giving the other half the opposite, false result. Tell the first group, for example: "Psychologists have found that separation weakens romantic attraction. As the saying goes, 'Out of sight, out of mind.'" Ask them to imagine why this might be true. Most people can, and after hearing an explanation, nearly all will then view this true finding as unsurprising—just common sense. Tell the second group the opposite: "Psychologists have found that separation strengthens romantic attraction. As the saying goes, 'Absence makes the heart grow fonder.'" People given this *false* statement can also easily imagine it, and most will also see it as unsurprising. When opposite findings both seem like common sense, we have a problem!

More than 800 scholarly papers have shown hindsight bias in people young and old from around the world (Roese & Vohs, 2012). Hindsight errors in people's recollections and explanations show why we need psychological research. Just asking people how and why they felt or acted as they did can be misleading. Why? It's not that common sense is usually wrong. Rather, common sense describes, after the fact, what *has* happened better than it predicts what *will* happen.

Everett Collection/Newscom

Hindsight bias When drilling its Deepwater Horizon oil well in 2010, BP employees took shortcuts and ignored warning signs, without intending to harm people, the environment, or their company's reputation. *After* an explosion killed 11 employees and caused the largest ever marine oil spill, with the benefit of hindsight, the foolishness of those judgments became obvious.

Overconfidence

We humans also tend to be *overconfident*—we think we know more than we do. Consider the solutions beside these three word puzzles (called anagrams), which people like you were asked to unscramble in one study (Goranson, 1978).

WREAT → WATER
ETRYN → ENTRY
GRABE → BARGE

About how many seconds do you think it would have taken you to unscramble each anagram? Knowing the answer makes us overconfident. Surely the solution would take only 10 seconds or so? In reality, the average problem solver spends 3 minutes, as you also might, given a similar puzzle without the solution: OCHSA. (When you're ready, check your answer against the footnote below.[5])

Fun anagram solutions from Wordsmith (wordsmith.org):
Snooze alarms = Alas! No more z's
Dormitory = dirty room
Slot machines = cash lost in 'em

Are we any better at predicting our social behavior? At the beginning of the school year, one study had students predict their own behavior (Vallone et al., 1990). Would they drop a course, vote in an upcoming election, call their parents regularly (and so forth)? On average, the students felt 84 percent sure of their self-predictions. But later quizzes about their actual behavior showed their predictions were correct only 71 percent of the time. It turns out that only about 2 percent of people do an excellent job predicting social behavior. Psychologist Philip Tetlock (1998, 2005) and science writer Dan Gardner (2016) call them "superforecasters." What is a superforecaster's defining feature? A lack of overconfidence. Faced with a difficult prediction, a superforecaster "gathers facts, balances clashing arguments, and settles on an answer."

[5] The solution to the OCHSA anagram is CHAOS.

IMPROVE YOUR EVERYDAY LIFE

Do you have a hard time believing you may be overconfident? Could overconfidence be at work in that self-assessment? How can reading this section about overconfidence help reduce your tendency to be overconfident?

Perceiving Order in Random Events

We have a built-in eagerness to make sense of our world. People see a face on the Moon, hear Satanic messages in music, or perceive the Virgin Mary's image on a grilled cheese sandwich. Even in random, unrelated data we often find patterns, because *random sequences often don't look random* (Falk et al., 2009; Nickerson, 2002, 2005). Flip a coin 50 times and you may be surprised at the streaks of heads or tails—much like supposed "hot" and "cold" streaks in sports. In actual random sequences, patterns and streaks (such as repeating numbers) occur more often than people expect (Oskarsson et al., 2009). When embezzlers try to generate random-like sequences when specifying how much to steal, their nonrandom patterns can alert fraud experts (Poundstone, 2014).

Why are people prone to patterned behaviors? For most people, a random, unpredictable world is uncomfortable (Tullett et al., 2015). Making sense of our world is a stress-buster (Ma et al., 2017). It helps us stay calm and get on with daily living.

Some happenings, such as winning the lottery twice, seem so amazing that we struggle to believe they are due to chance. But as statisticians have noted, "with a large enough sample, any outrageous thing is likely to happen" (Diaconis & Mosteller, 1989). An event that happens to but 1 in 1 billion people every day occurs about 7 times a day, more than 2500 times a year.

The point to remember: We trust our gut feelings more than we should. Our commonsense thinking is flawed by three powerful tendencies—hindsight bias, overconfidence, and perceiving patterns in random events. But scientific thinking can help us sift reality from illusion.

RETRIEVE & REMEMBER

ANSWERS IN APPENDIX E

8. Why, after friends start dating, do we often feel that we *knew* they were meant to be together?

LaunchPad Play the role of a researcher using scientific inquiry to think smarter about random hot streaks in sports. Engage online with the activity *How Would You Know If There Is a "Hot Hand" in Basketball?*

PSYCHOLOGICAL SCIENCE IN A POST-TRUTH WORLD

LOQ 1-10 Why is it so easy to believe untruths?

In 2017, when the Oxford English Dictionary's word of the year was *post-truth*, it seemed like many people's emotions and personal beliefs tended to override their acceptance of objective facts. "Never," said psychology and law professor Dan Kahan (2015), "have human societies *known so much* . . . but *agreed so little* about what they collectively know."

Consider two examples of widely shared misinformation in the United States:

Belief: *The U.S. crime rate is rising.* Every recent year, 7 in 10 Americans have told Gallup that there is more crime "than there was a year ago" (Swift, 2016).

Fact: For several decades, both violent and property crime rates have been *falling*. In 2015, the violent crime rate was less than half the 1990 rate (BJS, 2017; Statista, 2017).

Belief: *Many immigrants are criminals.* Memorable incidents feed this narrative. Stories of an immigrant murdering, burglarizing, or lying spread through social networks and news outlets.

Fact: Most immigrants are *not* criminals. Compared with native-born Americans, immigrants are 44 percent less likely to be imprisoned (CATO, 2017).

hindsight bias the tendency to believe, after learning an outcome, that we could have predicted it. (Also known as the *I-knew-it-all-along phenomenon.*)

Joe Dator The New Yorker Collection/The Cartoon Bank

"I'm sorry, Jeannie, your answer was correct, but Kevin shouted his incorrect answer over yours, so he gets the points."

Political party bias has also distorted Americans' thinking. Indeed, psychologist Peter Ditto and his colleagues (2015) reported that researchers have found "partisan bias in both liberals and conservatives, and at virtually identical levels." One study found that American Democrats discriminated against Republican candidates for college scholarships as much as Republicans discriminated against identically qualified Democratic candidates (Iyengar & Westwood, 2015). So, no American can smugly think, "Yes but that doesn't apply to *me*."

U.S. Democrats and Republicans share concern about failures to separate fact from fiction. In his farewell address, President Barack Obama (2017) warned that without a "common baseline of facts," democracy is threatened. Then "we start accepting only information, whether it's true or not, that fits our opinions, instead of basing our opinions on the evidence that is out there." Republican Senator John McCain (2017) similarly expressed alarm about "the growing inability, and even unwillingness, to separate truth from lies."

So why do post-truth era people so often, in the words of psychologist Tom Gilovich (1991), "know what isn't so?"

False news Some false news gets fed to us intentionally. It's "lies in the guise of news" (Kristof, 2017). And false news persists. In one analysis of 126,000 stories tweeted by 3 million people, falsehoods—especially false political news—spread "significantly farther, faster, deeper, and more broadly than the truth" (Vosoughi et al., 2018).

Repetition In experiments, statements become more believable when they are repeated (Dechêne et al., 2010). What we hear over and over—perhaps a made-up smear of a political opponent—gets remembered and comes to seem true (Fazio et al., 2015).

Availability of powerful examples In the media, "if it bleeds it leads." Gruesome violence—a horrific murder, a mass killing, a plane crash—gets reported, with vivid images that implant in our memory and color our judgments. No wonder Americans grossly overestimate their risk of being victimized by crime, terror, and plane crashes.

Group identity and the echo chamber of the like-minded Our social identities matter. Feeling good about our groups helps us feel good about ourselves. On social media we tend to friend people who think as we do. We often read news sources that support our views and criticize news sources that do not.

The good news is that we can build a real-truth world by embracing critical thinking and a scientific mindset. By actively seeking information with *curiosity, skepticism,* and *humility,* we can usually know what really is so.

"We have . . . become sloppier than ever: Tweet first, research later. Post first, rescind later. Guess first, confirm later." —Luvvie Ajayi, *I'm Judging You: The Do-Better Manual,* 2016

LaunchPad To experience my [DM's] animated walk through some important, scientific thinking strategies, view the 4-minute *Video: Thinking Critically in a "Post-Truth" World.*

How Do Psychologists Ask and Answer Questions?

As we've noted, the basis of all science, including psychology, is the scientific attitude, which has three essential ingredients: curiosity, skepticism, and humility. Psychologists arm their scientific attitude with the *scientific method.* They observe events, form theories, and then refine their theories in the light of new observations.

THE SCIENTIFIC METHOD

LOQ 1-11 How do theories advance psychological science?

Chatting with friends and family, we often use *theory* to mean "mere hunch." In science, a **theory** *explains* behaviors or events by offering ideas that *organize* what we have observed. By using deeper principles to organize isolated facts, a theory summarizes and simplifies. It connects the observed dots so that a clear picture emerges.

A theory of how sleep affects memory, for example, helps us organize countless sleep-related observations into a short list of principles. Imagine that we observe over and over that people with good sleep habits tend to answer questions correctly in class, and they do well at test time. We might therefore theorize that sleep improves memory. So far so good: Our principle neatly summarizes a list of observations about the effects of a good night's sleep.

Yet no matter how reasonable a theory may sound—and it does seem reasonable to suggest that sleep boosts memory—we must put it to the test. A good theory produces testable *predictions,* called **hypotheses.** Such predictions specify what results would support the theory and what results would not.

To test our theory about the sleep effects on memory, we might hypothesize that when sleep deprived, people will remember less from the day before. To test that hypothesis, we might measure how well people remember course materials they studied either before a good night's sleep or before a shortened night's sleep (**FIGURE 1.1**). The results will either support our theory or lead us to revise or reject it.

Our theories can bias our observations. The urge to see what we expect to see is strong, both inside and outside the laboratory. Having theorized that better memory springs from more sleep, we may see what we expect: We may perceive sleepy people's comments as less accurate.

As a check on their own biases, psychologists, when reporting their studies, use precise, measurable **operational definitions** of research procedures and concepts. *Sleep deprived,* for example, may be defined as "2 or more hours less" than the person's natural sleep. These exact descriptions will allow anyone to **replicate** (repeat) the research. Other people can then re-create the study with different participants and in different situations. If they get similar results, we can be more confident that the findings are reliable. Replication is confirmation.

Replication is an essential part of good science. In psychology, replication efforts have produced mixed results. One cluster of replications brought encouraging news: All but 2 of 13 experiments replicated (Klein et al., 2014). But when 270 psychologists recently worked together to redo 100 psychological studies, the results made news: Only 36 percent of the results were replicated (Open Science Collaboration, 2015). But then another team of scientists found most of the failed replications flawed (inaccurate re-creations of the original studies). This team argued that "the reproducibility of psychological science" is "quite high" (Gilbert et al., 2016). A subsequent replication effort yielded slightly more promising results, with 62 percent of the results replicating (Camerer et al., 2018). (None of the nonreproducible findings in these replication efforts appear in this text.) Despite the differing findings, it's clear that psychological science benefits from more replications and from more sharing of research methods and data (Gilmore & Adolph, 2017; Nosek et al., 2015; Open Science Collaboration, 2017). More and more psychologists use **preregistration** to publicly communicate their planned study design, hypotheses, data collection, and analyses (Nosek et al., 2018). Preregistration benefits psychological science by encouraging openness and transparency (Nelson et al., 2018).

Psychology is not alone in its quest for reproducible research. Other fields, including genetics, behavioral neuroscience, and brain imaging, also have nonreplicated findings (Baxter & Burwell, 2017; Carter et al., 2017; Eklund et al., 2016). Especially when based on a small sample, a single failure to replicate can itself need replication (Maxwell et al., 2015). In all scientific fields, replications either confirm findings, or enable us to revise our understanding.

"Failure to replicate is not a bug; it is a feature. It is what leads us along the path—the wonderfully twisty path—of scientific discovery." —Lisa Feldman Barrett, "Psychology Is Not in Crisis," 2015

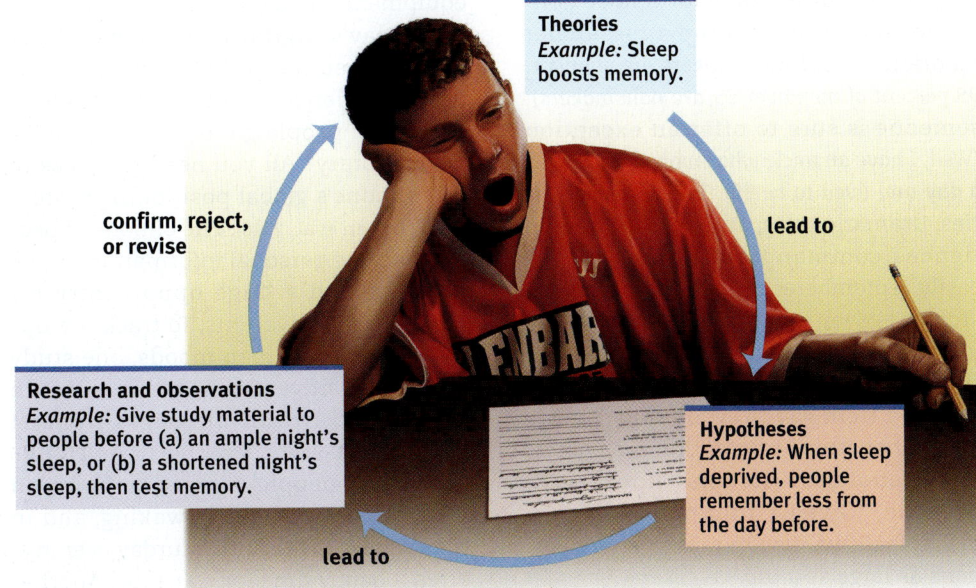
Theories
Example: Sleep boosts memory.
lead to
Hypotheses
Example: When sleep deprived, people remember less from the day before.
lead to
Research and observations
Example: Give study material to people before (a) an ample night's sleep, or (b) a shortened night's sleep, then test memory.
confirm, reject, or revise

FIGURE 1.1 The scientific method A self-correcting process for asking questions and observing nature's answers.

theory an explanation using principles that organize observations and predict behaviors or events.

hypothesis a testable prediction, often implied by a theory.

operational definition a carefully worded statement of the exact procedures (operations) used in a research study. For example, *human intelligence* may be operationally defined as what an intelligence test measures.

replication repeating the essence of a research study, usually with different participants in different situations, to see whether the basic finding can be reproduced.

preregistration publicly communicating planned study design, hypotheses, data collection, and analyses.

Let's summarize. A good theory

- effectively ***organizes*** observations.
- leads to clear ***predictions*** that anyone can use to check the theory or to create practical applications of it.
- often stimulates ***replications*** and more research that supports the theory (as happened with sleep and memory studies, as you'll see in Chapter 2), or leads to a revised theory that better organizes and predicts what we observe.

We can test our hypotheses and refine our theories in several ways.

- ***Descriptive*** methods describe behaviors, often by using (as we will see) case studies, naturalistic observations, or surveys.
- ***Correlational*** methods associate different factors. (You'll see the word *factor* often in descriptions of research. It refers to anything that contributes to a result.)
- ***Experimental*** methods manipulate, or vary, factors to discover their effects.

To think critically about popular psychology claims, we need to understand the strengths and weaknesses of these methods. (For more information about some of the statistical methods that psychological scientists use in their work, see Appendix A, Statistical Reasoning in Everyday Life.)

RETRIEVE & REMEMBER

ANSWERS IN APPENDIX E

9. What does a good theory do?
10. Why is replication important?

DESCRIPTION

LOQ 1-12 How do psychologists use case studies, naturalistic observations, and surveys to observe and describe behavior, and why is random sampling important?

In daily life, we all observe and describe other people, trying to understand why they think, feel, and act as they do. Psychologists do much the same, though objectively and systematically, using

- ***case studies*** (in-depth analyses of individuals or groups).
- ***naturalistic observations*** (recording the natural behavior of many individuals).
- ***surveys*** and interviews (asking people questions).

The Case Study

A **case study** examines one individual or group in depth, in the hope of revealing things true of us all. Some examples: Medical case studies of people who lost specific abilities after damage to certain brain regions gave us much of our early knowledge about the brain. Jean Piaget taught us about children's thinking after he carefully watched and questioned just a few children. Studies of various animals, including only a few chimpanzees, have revealed their capacity for understanding and communicating.

Intensive case studies are sometimes very revealing. They often suggest directions for further study, and they show us what *can* happen. But individual cases may also mislead us. The individual being studied may be *atypical* (unlike the larger population). Viewing such cases as general truths can lead to false conclusions. Indeed, anytime a researcher mentions a finding (*Smokers die younger: 95 percent of men over 85 are nonsmokers*), someone is sure to offer an exception (*Well, I have an uncle who smoked two packs a day and lived to be 89*). These vivid stories, dramatic tales, and personal experiences command attention and are easily remembered. Stories move us, but stories—even when they are psychological case examples—can mislead. A single story of someone who supposedly changed from gay to straight is *not* evidence that sexual orientation is a choice. As psychologist Gordon Allport (1954, p. 9) said, "Given a thimbleful of [dramatic] facts we rush to make generalizations as large as a tub."

The point to remember: Individual cases can suggest fruitful ideas. What is true of all of us can be seen in any one of us. But just because something is true of one of us (the atypical uncle), we should not assume it is true of all of us (most long-term smokers *do* suffer ill health and early death). To find those general truths, we must look to methods beyond the case study.

RETRIEVE & REMEMBER

ANSWERS IN APPENDIX E

11. We cannot assume that case studies always reveal general principles that apply to all of us. Why not?

LaunchPad See the *Video: Case Studies* for an animated tutorial.

Naturalistic Observation

A second descriptive method records responses in natural environments. These **naturalistic observations** may be used to describe cultural differences in parenting, student lunchroom self-seating patterns, or chimpanzee family structures.

Until recently, naturalistic observation was mostly "small science"—possible with pen and paper rather than fancy equipment and a big budget (Provine, 2012). But today's digital technologies have transformed naturalistic observations into big science. Want to keep track of how often people go to the gym, a café, or the library? All you need is access to their phone's global positioning system (GPS) (Harari et al., 2016). The billions of people entering personal information online have created a huge opportunity for "big data" observations. To track the ups and downs of human moods, one study counted positive and negative words in 504 million Twitter messages from 84 countries (Golder & Macy, 2011). As **FIGURE 1.2** shows, people seemed happier on weekends, shortly after waking, and in the evenings. (Are late Saturday evenings often a happy time for you, too?) Another study found that negative emotion words (especially anger-related words) in 148 million tweets from 1347 U.S. counties predicted the counties' heart

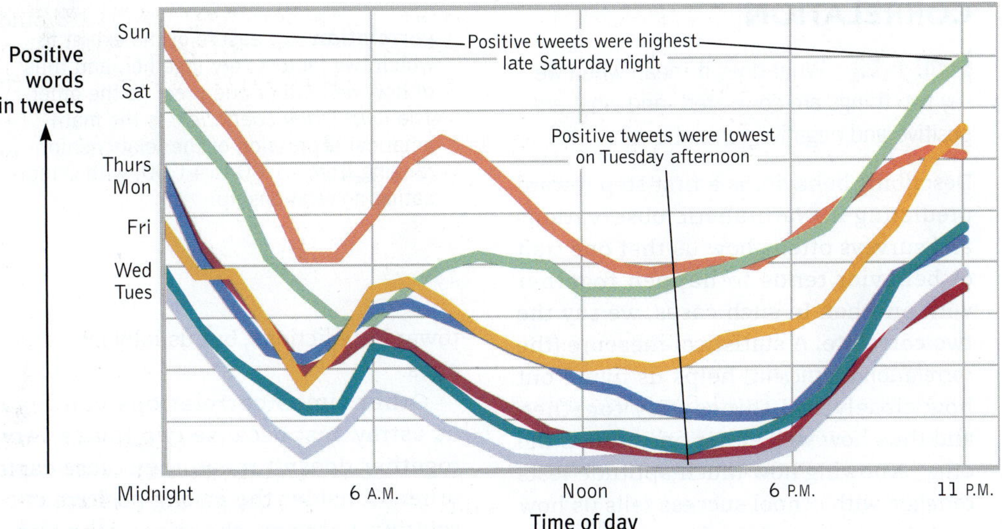

FIGURE 1.2 Twitter message moods, by time and by day This graph illustrates how, without knowing anyone's identity, researchers can use big data to study human behavior on a massive scale. It now is also possible to associate people's moods with, for example, their locations or with the weather, and to study the spread of ideas through social networks. (Data from Golder & Macy, 2011.)

disease rates *better* than smoking and obesity rates (Eichstaedt et al., 2015). Google data—on the words people search and the questions they ask—can pinpoint a geographical area's level of racism and depression (Stephens-Davidowitz, 2017).

Like the case study method, naturalistic observation does not *explain* behavior. It *describes* it. Nevertheless, descriptions can be revealing: The starting point of any science is description.

RETRIEVE & REMEMBER

ANSWERS IN APPENDIX E

12. Using tools such as smart-phone apps and body-worn sensors, researchers are able to sample naturally occurring slices of daily life. What are the advantages and disadvantages of this kind of naturalistic observation?

LaunchPad See the *Video: Naturalistic Observation* for a helpful tutorial animation.

The Survey

A **survey** looks at many cases, asking people to report their own behavior or opinions. Questions about everything from sexual practices to political opinions are put to the public. Here are some recent survey findings:

- Compared with those born in the 1960s and 1970s, twice as many millennials born in the 1990s reported having no sexual partners since age 18 (Twenge et al., 2017).
- 1 in 2 people across 24 countries reported believing in the "existence of intelligent alien civilizations in the universe" (Glocalities, 2017).
- 68 percent of all humans—some 4.6 billion people—say that religion is important in their daily lives (from Gallup World Poll data analyzed by Diener et al., 2011).

But asking questions is tricky, and the answers often depend on the way you word your questions and on who answers them.

Wording Effects Even subtle changes in the wording of questions can have major effects. Should violence be allowed to appear in children's television programs? People are much more likely to approve "not allowing" such things than "forbidding" or "censoring" them. In one national survey, only 27 percent of Americans approved of "government censorship" of media sex and violence, though 66 percent approved of "more restrictions on what is shown on television" (Lacayo, 1995). People are much more approving of "gun safety" laws than of "gun control" laws, and of "revenue enhancers" than of "taxes." Wording is a delicate matter, and some words can trigger positive or negative reactions. Critical thinkers will reflect on how a question's phrasing might affect the opinions people express.

Random Sampling For an accurate picture of a group's experiences and attitudes, there's only one game in town. In a *representative sample,* a smaller group can accurately reflect the larger **population** you want to study and describe.

So how do you obtain a representative sample? Say you want to survey the total student population to get your peers' reaction to an upcoming tuition increase. To be sure your sample represents the whole student population, you would want to choose a **random sample,** in which every person in the entire population has an equal chance of being picked. You would not want to ask for volunteers, because the students

case study a descriptive technique in which one individual or group is studied in depth in the hope of revealing universal principles.

naturalistic observation a descriptive technique of observing and recording behavior in naturally occurring situations without trying to change or control the situation.

survey a descriptive technique for obtaining the self-reported attitudes or behaviors of a group, usually by questioning a representative, *random sample* of that group.

population all those in a group being studied, from which random samples may be drawn. (*Note:* Except for national studies, this does *not* refer to a country's whole population.)

random sample a sample that fairly represents a population because each member has an equal chance of inclusion.

who step forward to help would not be a random sample of all the students. But you could assign each student a number, and then use a random-number generator to select a sample.

With very large samples, estimates become quite reliable. *E* is estimated to represent 12.7 percent of the letters in written English. *E*, in fact, is 12.3 percent of the 925,141 letters in Melville's *Moby-Dick*, 12.4 percent of the 586,747 letters in Dickens' *A Tale of Two Cities*, and 12.1 percent of the 3,901,021 letters in 12 of Mark Twain's works (*Chance News*, 1997).

Time and money will affect the size of your sample, but you would try to involve as many people as possible. Why? Because large representative samples are better than small ones. (But a smaller representative sample of 100 is better than a larger *unrepresentative* sample of 500.)

Political pollsters sample voters in national election surveys just this way. Using only 1500 randomly sampled people, drawn from all areas of a country, they can provide a remarkably accurate snapshot of the nation's opinions. Without random sampling, large samples—including call-in phone samples and TV or website polls—often give misleading results. And it's worth remembering that even with the best-designed poll there can still sometimes be surprising results, as we saw in the result of the 2016 U.S. presidential election.

The point to remember: Before accepting survey findings, think critically. Consider the wording of the questions and the sample. The best basis for generalizing is from a representative, random sample of a population.

RETRIEVE & REMEMBER

ANSWERS IN APPENDIX E

13. What is an unrepresentative sample, and how do researchers avoid it?

CORRELATION

LOQ 1-13 What does it mean when we say two things are correlated, and what are positive and negative correlations?

Describing behavior is a first step toward predicting it. Naturalistic observations and surveys often show us that one trait or behavior tends to happen together with another. In such cases, we say the two **correlate.** A statistical measure (the *correlation coefficient*) helps us figure out how closely two things vary together, and thus how well either one *predicts* the other. Knowing how much aptitude tests *correlate* with school success tells us how well the scores *predict* school success.

- ***A positive correlation*** (above 0 to +1.00) indicates a *direct* relationship, meaning that two things increase together or decrease together. Across people, height correlates positively with weight.
- ***A negative correlation*** (below 0 to −1.00) indicates an *inverse* relationship: As one thing increases, the other decreases. The number of hours spent watching videos each week correlates negatively with grades. Negative correlations can go as low as −1.00. This means that, like children on opposite ends of a seesaw, one set of scores goes down precisely as the other goes up.
- A coefficient near zero is a weak correlation, indicating little or no relationship.

Though informative, psychology's correlations usually explain only part of the variation among individuals. As we will see, there is a positive correlation between parents' abusiveness and their children's later abusiveness when they become parents. But this does not mean that most abused children become abusive. The correlation simply indicates a statistical relationship: Most abused children do *not* grow into abusers. But nonabused children are even less likely to become abusive. Correlations point us toward predictions, but usually imperfect ones.

correlation a measure of the extent to which two factors vary together, and thus of how well either one predicts the other. The *correlation coefficient* is the mathematical expression of the relationship, ranging from −1.00 to +1.00, with 0 indicating no relationship.

Other times correlations can lead us astray. Just because two things vary together doesn't mean they *cause* each other. Consider the strong positive correlation between chocolate consumption in 23 countries and their number of Nobel laureates (Messerli, 2012). Eating more chocolate will not cause a country to have more Nobel laureates! But for whatever reason, chocolate-loving countries have knowledge-loving Nobel laureates.

The point to remember: A correlation coefficient helps us see the world more clearly by revealing the extent to which two things relate. Just remember that revealing relationships does not mean *explaining* them. (See Thinking Critically About: Correlation and Causation.)

RETRIEVE & REMEMBER

ANSWERS IN APPENDIX E

14. Indicate whether each of the following statements describes a positive correlation or a negative correlation.

a. The more husbands viewed internet pornography, the worse their marital relationships (Muusses et al., 2015). ________

b. The less sexual content teens saw on TV, the less likely they were to have sex (Collins et al., 2004). ________

c. The longer children were breast-fed, the greater their later academic achievement (Horwood & Fergusson, 1998). ________

d. The more income rose among a sample of poor families, the fewer symptoms of mental illness their children experienced (Costello et al., 2003). ________

LOQ 1-14 Why do correlations enable prediction but not cause-effect explanation?

Mental illness *correlates* with smoking—meaning that those who experience mental illness are also more likely to be smokers.[1] Does this tell us anything about what *causes* mental illness or smoking? **NO.**

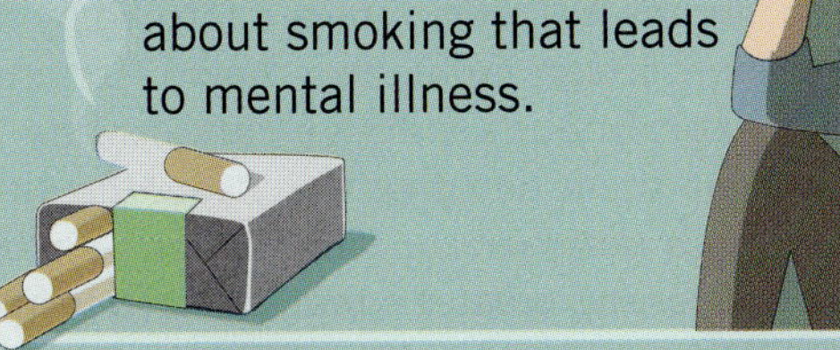

There may be something about smoking that leads to mental illness.

Those with mental illness may be more likely to smoke.

OR

There may be some *third variable*, such as a stressful home life, for example, that triggers *both* smoking and mental illness.

So, then, how would you interpret these recent findings:
a) sexual hook-ups correlate with college women's experiencing depression, and
b) *delaying* sexual intimacy correlates with positive outcomes such as greater relationship satisfaction and stability?[2]

Possible explanations:

1. Sexual restraint	→	Better mental health and stronger relationships
2. Depression	→	People being more likely to hook up
3. Some third factor, such as lower impulsivity	→	Sexual restraint, psychological well-being, and better relationships

Correlations do help us predict. Consider: Self-esteem correlates negatively with (and therefore predicts) depression. The lower people's self-esteem, the greater their risk for depression.

Possible interpretations:

1. Low self-esteem	→	Depression
2. Depression	→	Low self-esteem
3. Some third factor, such as distressing events or biological predisposition	→	Both low self-esteem and depression

You try it!
A survey of over 12,000 adolescents found that the more teens feel loved by their parents, the less likely they are to behave in unhealthy ways—having early sex, smoking, abusing alcohol and drugs, exhibiting violence.[3] What are three possible ways we could interpret that finding?[4]

***The point to remember:* Correlation does not prove causation.**
Correlation suggests a possible cause-effect relationship but does not prove it. Remember this principle and you will be wiser as you read and hear news of scientific studies.

1. Belluck, 2013. 2. Fielder et al., 2013; Willoughby et al., 2014. 3. Resnick et al., 1997. 4. *ANSWERS*: A. Parental love may produce healthy teens. B. Well-behaved teens may feel more parental love and approval. C. Some third factor, such as income or neighborhood, may influence both parental love AND teen behaviors.

RETRIEVE & REMEMBER

ANSWERS IN APPENDIX E

15. Length of marriage positively correlates with hair loss in men. Does this mean that marriage causes men to lose their hair (or that balding men make better husbands)?

Nancy Brown/Getty Images

LaunchPad For an animated tutorial on correlations, engage online with *Concept Practice: Positive and Negative Correlations.* See also the *Video: Correlational Studies* for another helpful tutorial animation.

EXPERIMENTATION

LOQ 1-15 How do experiments clarify or reveal cause-effect relationships?

Descriptions, even with big data, don't prove causation. Correlations don't prove causation. To isolate cause and effect, psychologists have to simplify. In our everyday lives, many things affect our actions and influence our thoughts. Psychologists sort out this complexity by using **experiments.** With experiments, researchers can focus on the possible effects of one or more factors by

- manipulating the factors of interest.
- holding constant ("controlling") other factors.

Let's consider a few experiments to see how this works.

Random Assignment: Minimizing Differences

Researchers have compared infants who are breast-fed with those who are bottle-fed with formula. The results are mixed. Some studies, but not others, show that children's intelligence test scores are a tad higher if they were breast-fed (Horta et al., 2015; von Stumm & Plomin, 2015; Walfisch et al., 2014; Yang et al., 2018). Others have found that the longer they were breast-fed, the higher their later intelligence test scores (Jedrychowski et al., 2012; Victora et al., 2015). So should we say that mother's milk may *correlate* modestly but positively with later intelligence? If so, do smarter mothers have smarter children? Or do the nutrients in mother's milk contribute to brain development? Even big data from a million or a billion mothers and their offspring wouldn't tell us.

To find the answer, we would have to isolate the effects of mother's milk from the effects of other factors, such as mother's age, education, and intelligence. How might we do that? By experimenting. With parental permission, one British research team directly experimented with breast milk. They **randomly assigned** 424 hospitalized premature infants either to formula feedings or to breast-milk feedings (Lucas et al., 1992). By doing this, they created two otherwise similar groups:

- an **experimental group,** in which babies received the treatment (breast milk).
- a contrasting **control group** without the treatment.

Random assignment (whether by means of a random-number generator or by the flip of a coin) minimizes any preexisting differences between the two groups. If one-third of the volunteers for an experiment can wiggle their ears, then about one-third of the people in each group will be ear wigglers. So, too, with age, intelligence, attitudes, and other characteristics, which will be similar in the experimental and control groups. When groups are formed by random assignment, and they differ at the experiment's end, we can assume the treatment had an effect. (Note the difference between *random sampling*—which in *surveys* creates a representative survey sample—and *random assignment,* which in *experiments* equalizes the experimental and control groups.)

Lane Oatey/Getty Images

Is breast best? The British experiment found that, at least for premature infants, breast milk is indeed best for developing intelligence. On intelligence tests taken at age 8, those nourished with breast milk scored significantly higher than those who had been formula-fed.

The point to remember: Unlike correlational studies, which uncover *naturally occurring* relationships, an experiment *manipulates* (varies) a factor to determine its effect.

LaunchPad See the *Video: Random Assignment* for a tutorial animation.

The Double-Blind Procedure: Eliminating Bias

In the breast-milk experiment, babies didn't have expectations that could affect the experiment's outcome. Adults, however, do have expectations.

Consider: Three days into a cold, many of us start taking zinc tablets. If we find our cold symptoms lessening, we may credit the pills. But after a few days, most colds are naturally on their way out. Was the zinc cure truly effective? To find out, we could experiment.

And that is precisely how new drugs and new methods of psychotherapy are evaluated (Chapter 14). Researchers use random assignment to form the groups. An experimental group receives the treatment, such as an antidepressant medication. A control group receives a **placebo** (an inactive substance — perhaps a look-alike pill with no drug in it). Often, the people who take part in these studies are *blind* (uninformed) about which treatment, if any, they are receiving.

Many studies use a **double-blind procedure** — neither those taking part in the study nor those collecting the data know which group is receiving the treatment. In such studies, researchers can check a treatment's actual effects apart from the participants' belief in its healing powers and the staff's enthusiasm for its potential. Just *thinking* you are getting a treatment can boost your spirits, relax your body, and relieve your symptoms. This **placebo effect** is well documented in reducing pain, depression, anxiety, and, in schizophrenia, sound-based hallucinations (Dollfus et al., 2016; Kirsch, 2010). Athletes have run faster when given a fake performance-enhancing drug (McClung & Collins, 2007). Decaf-coffee drinkers have reported increased vigor and alertness — when they thought their brew had caffeine in it (Dawkins et al., 2011). People have felt better after receiving a phony mood-enhancing drug (Michael et al., 2012). And the more expensive the placebo, the more "real" it seems — a fake pill that cost $2.50 worked better than one costing 10 cents (Waber et al., 2008). To know how effective a therapy really is, researchers must control for a possible placebo effect.

"If I don't think it's going to work, will it still work?"

RETRIEVE & REMEMBER

ANSWERS IN APPENDIX E

16. What measures do researchers use to prevent the *placebo effect* from confusing their results?

Variables

Here is an even more potent experiment example: The drug Viagra was approved for use after 21 clinical trials. One trial was an experiment in which researchers randomly assigned 329 men with erectile disorder to either an experimental group (Viagra takers) or a control group (placebo takers). The pills looked identical, and the procedure was double-blind — neither the men taking the pills nor the people giving them knew who received the placebo. The result: At peak doses, 69 percent of Viagra-assisted attempts at intercourse were successful, compared with 22 percent for men receiving the placebo (Goldstein et al., 1998). Viagra performed.

A similar experiment on a drug approved to increase women's sexual arousal produced a result described as, um, anticlimactic — an additional "half of one satisfying sexual encounter a month" (Ness, 2016; Tavernise, 2016).

This simple experiment manipulated just one factor — the drug (Viagra versus no Viagra). We call the manipulated factor an **independent variable:** We can vary it *independently* of other factors, such as the men's age, weight, and personality. These other factors, which could influence a study's results, are called **confounding variables.** Thanks to random assignment, the confounding variables should be roughly equal in both groups.

Experiments examine the effect of one or more independent variables on some behavior or mental process that can be measured. We call this kind of affected behavior the **dependent variable** because it can vary *depending* on what takes place during the experiment. Experimenters give both variables precise *operational definitions*. They specify exactly how the

- independent variable (in this study, the precise drug dosage and timing) is manipulated.
- dependent variable (in this study, the men's responses to questions about their sexual performance) is measured.

experiment a method in which researchers vary one or more factors (independent variables) to observe the effect on some behavior or mental process (the dependent variable). By *random assignment* of participants, researchers aim to control other factors.

random assignment assigning participants to experimental and control groups by chance, thus minimizing any preexisting differences between the groups.

experimental group in an experiment, the group exposed to the treatment, that is, to one version of the independent variable.

control group in an experiment, the group *not* exposed to the treatment; the control group serves as a comparison with the experimental group for judging the effect of the treatment.

placebo [pluh-SEE-bo; Latin for "I shall please"] an inactive substance or condition that is sometimes given to those in a control group in place of the treatment given to the experimental group.

double-blind procedure in an experiment, a procedure in which both the participants and the research staff are ignorant (blind) about who has received the treatment or a placebo.

placebo effect results caused by expectations alone.

independent variable in an experiment, the factor that is manipulated; the variable whose effect is being studied.

confounding variable in an experiment, a factor other than the factor being studied that might influence a study's results.

dependent variable in an experiment, the factor that is measured; the variable that may change when the independent variable is manipulated.

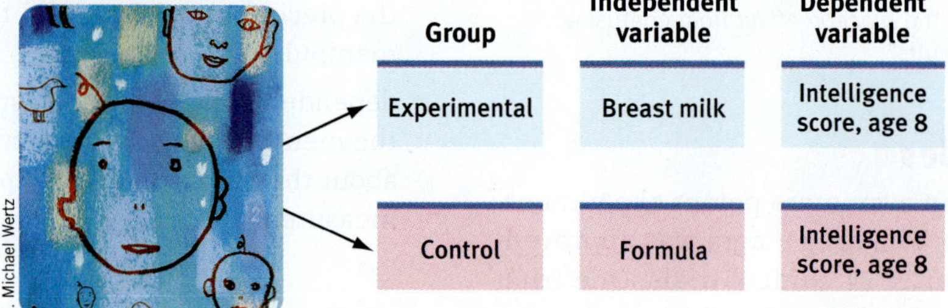

FIGURE 1.3 Experimentation To study cause and effect, psychologists control for confounding variables by randomly assigning some participants to an experimental group, others to a control group. Measuring the dependent variable (intelligence test score in later childhood) will determine the effect of the independent variable (type of milk fed as babies).

Operational definitions answer the "What do you mean?" question with a level of precision that enables others to replicate (repeat) the study.

Let's review these terms using the British breast-milk experiment (**FIGURE 1.3**). A *variable* is anything that can vary (infant nutrition, intelligence). Experiments aim to *manipulate* an *independent* variable (type of milk), *measure* a *dependent* variable (later intelligence test score), and control *confounding* variables. An experiment has at least two different groups: an *experimental group* (infants who received breast milk) and a *comparison* or *control group* (infants who did not receive breast milk). *Random assignment* works to control all other (confounding) variables by equating the groups before any manipulation begins. In this way, an experiment tests the effect of at least one independent variable (what we manipulate) on at least one dependent variable (the outcome we measure).

In another experiment, psychologists tested whether landlords' perceptions of an applicant's ethnicity would influence the availability of rental housing. The researchers sent identically worded emails to 1115 Los Angeles–area landlords (Carpusor & Loges, 2006). They varied the sender's name to imply different ethnic groups: "Patrick McDougall," "Said Al-Rahman," and "Tyrell Jackson." Then they tracked the percentage of landlords' positive replies. How many emails triggered invitations to view the apartment? For McDougall, 89 percent; for Al-Rahman, 66 percent; and for Jackson, 56 percent. In this experiment, what was the independent variable? What was the dependent variable?[6]

"[We must guard] against not just racial slurs, but . . . against the subtle impulse to call Johnny back for a job interview, but not Jamal." —U.S. President Barack Obama, eulogy for state senator and church-shooting victim Clementa Pinckney, June 26, 2015

RETRIEVE & REMEMBER

ANSWERS IN APPENDIX E

17. By using *random assignment*, researchers are able to control for ____________, which are other factors besides the independent variable(s) that may influence research results.

LaunchPad **See the *Videos: Experiments* and *Confounding Variables* for helpful tutorial animations.**

[6] The independent variable, which the researchers manipulated, was the implied ethnicity of the applicants' names. The dependent variable, which the researchers measured, was the rate of positive responses from the landlords.

CHOOSING A RESEARCH DESIGN

LOQ 1-16 How would you know which research design to use?

Throughout this book, you will read about amazing psychological science discoveries. But how do psychological scientists choose research methods and design their studies in ways that provide meaningful results? Understanding how research is done—how testable questions are developed and studied—is key to appreciating all of psychology. **TABLE 1.2** compares the features of psychology's main research methods. In later chapters, you will read about other research designs, including *twin studies* and *cross-sectional* and *longitudinal research* (Chapter 3).

In psychological research, no questions are off limits, except untestable (or unethical) ones. Does free will exist? Are people born evil? Is there an afterlife? Psychologists can't test those questions, but they *can* test whether free will beliefs, aggressive personalities, and a belief in life after death influence how people think, feel, and act (Dechesne et al., 2003; Shariff et al., 2014; Webster et al., 2014).

Having chosen their question, psychologists then select the most appropriate research design—*experimental, correlational, case study, naturalistic observation, twin study, longitudinal,* or *cross-sectional*—and determine how to set it up most effectively. They consider how much money and time are available, ethical issues, and other limitations. For example, it wouldn't be ethical for a researcher studying child development to use the experimental method and randomly assign children to loving versus punishing homes.

Next, psychological scientists decide how to measure the behavior or mental process being studied. For example, researchers studying aggressive behavior could measure participants' willingness to blast a stranger with supposed intense noise.

TABLE 1.2 Comparing Research Methods

Research Method	Basic Purpose	How Conducted	What Is Manipulated	Weaknesses
Descriptive	To observe and record behavior	Do case studies, naturalistic observations, or surveys	Nothing	No control of variables; single cases may be misleading
Correlational	To detect naturally occurring relationships; to assess how well one variable predicts another	Collect data on two or more variables; no manipulation	Nothing	Cannot establish cause and effect
Experimental	To explore cause and effect	Manipulate one or more factors; use random assignment	The independent variable(s)	Sometimes not possible for practical or ethical reasons

To help you build your understanding, your critical thinking, and your *scientific literacy skills,* we created research activities in LaunchPad. In these "How Would You Know?" activities, you get to play the role of the researcher, making choices about the best ways to test interesting questions. Some examples: How Would You Know If Having Children Relates to Being Happier?, How Would You Know If a Cup of Coffee Can Warm Up Relationships?, and How Would You Know If People Can Learn to Reduce Anxiety?

RETRIEVE & REMEMBER

ANSWERS IN APPENDIX E

18. Match the term on the left (i through iii) with the description on the right (a through c).

i. Double-blind procedure	a. helps researchers generalize from a small set of survey responses to a larger population
ii. Random sampling	b. helps minimize preexisting differences between experimental and control groups
iii. Random assignment	c. controls for the placebo effect; neither researchers nor participants know who receives the real treatment

19. Why, when testing a new drug to control blood pressure, would we learn more about its effectiveness from giving it to half the participants in a group of 1000 than to all 1000 participants?

Researchers want to have confidence in their findings, so they carefully consider confounding variables—factors other than those being studied that may affect their interpretation of results.

Psychological research is a fun and creative adventure. Researchers *design* each study, *measure* target behaviors, *interpret* results, and learn more about the fascinating world of behavior and mental processes along the way.

IN YOUR EVERYDAY LIFE

If you could conduct a study on any psychological question, which question would you choose? How would you design the study?

PREDICTING EVERYDAY BEHAVIOR

LOQ 1-17 How can simplified laboratory experiments help us understand general principles of behavior?

When you see or hear about psychology research, do you ever wonder whether people's behavior in a research laboratory will predict their behavior in real life? Does detecting the blink of a faint red light in a dark room say anything useful about flying an airplane at night? Or, suppose an experiment shows that a man aroused by viewing a violent, sexually explicit film will then be more willing to push buttons that he thinks will deliver a noise blast to a woman. Does that really say anything about whether viewing violent pornography makes men more likely to abuse women?

Before you answer, consider this. The experimenter *intends* to simplify reality—to create a mini-environment that imitates and controls important features of everyday life. Just as a wind tunnel lets airplane designers re-create airflow forces under controlled conditions, a laboratory experiment lets psychologists re-create psychological forces under controlled conditions.

An experiment's purpose is not to re-create the exact behaviors of everyday life, but to test *theoretical principles* (Mook, 1983). In aggression studies, deciding whether to push a button that delivers a shock may not be the same as slapping someone in the face, but the principle is the same. *It is the resulting principles—not the specific findings—that help explain everyday behaviors.* Many investigations show that principles derived in the laboratory do typically generalize to the everyday world (Mitchell, 2012).

The point to remember: Psychological science focuses less on specific behaviors than on revealing general principles that help explain many behaviors.

LaunchPad To review and test your understanding of research methods, engage online with *Concept Practice: Psychology's Research Methods and The Language of Experiments,* and the interactive *Topic Tutorial: PsychSim6, Understanding Psychological Research.* For a 9.5-minute video synopsis of psychology's scientific research strategies, see the *Video: Research Methods.*

Psychology's Research Ethics

LOQ 1-18 Why do psychologists study animals, and what ethical guidelines safeguard human and animal research participants? How do psychologists' values influence what they study and how they apply their results?

We have reflected on how a scientific approach can restrain biases. We have seen how case studies, naturalistic observations, and surveys help us describe behavior. We have also noted that correlational studies assess the association between two factors, showing how well one predicts another. We have examined the logic underlying experiments, which use controls and random assignment to isolate the causal effects of independent variables on dependent variables.

Hopefully, you are now prepared to understand what lies ahead and to think critically about psychological matters. But before we plunge in, let's address some common questions about psychology's ethics and values.

LaunchPad See the *Video: Research Ethics* for a helpful tutorial animation.

STUDYING AND PROTECTING ANIMALS

Many psychologists study nonhuman animals because they find them fascinating. They want to understand how different species learn, think, and behave. Psychologists also study animals to learn about people. We humans are not *like* animals; we *are* animals, sharing a common biology. Animal experiments have therefore led to treatments for human diseases—insulin for diabetes, vaccines to prevent polio and rabies, transplants to replace defective organs.

Humans are more complex. But some of the same processes by which we learn are present in other animals, even sea slugs and honeybees. The simplicity of the sea slug's nervous system is precisely what makes it so revealing of the neural mechanisms of learning. Ditto for the honeybee, which resembles humans in how it learns to cope with stress (Dinges et al., 2017).

"Rats are very similar to humans except that they are not stupid enough to purchase lottery tickets."—Dave Barry, July 2, 2002

Sharing such similarities, should we not respect our animal relatives? The animal protection movement protests the use of animals in psychological, biological, and medical research. Out of this heated debate, two issues emerge.

The basic question: Is it right to place the well-being of humans above that of other animals? In experiments on stress and cancer, is it right that mice get tumors in the hope that people might not? Humans raise and slaughter 56 billion animals a year (Worldwatch Institute, 2017). Is this use and consumption of other animals as natural as the behavior of carnivorous hawks, cats, and whales?

For those who give human life top priority, a second question emerges: What safeguards should protect the well-being of animals in research? One survey of animal researchers gave an answer. Some 98 percent supported government regulations protecting primates, dogs, and cats. And 74 percent also backed regulations providing for the humane care of rats and mice (Plous & Herzog, 2000). Many professional associations and funding agencies already have such guidelines. British Psychological Society (BPS) guidelines call for housing animals under reasonably natural living conditions, with companions for social animals (Lea, 2000). American Psychological Association (APA) guidelines state that researchers must provide "humane care and healthful conditions" and that testing should "minimize discomfort" (APA, 2012). The European Parliament also mandates standards for animal care and housing (Vogel, 2010). Most universities screen research proposals, often through an animal care ethics committee, and laboratories are regulated and inspected.

MARY ALTAFFER/AP Images

Animal research benefiting animals Psychologists have helped zoos enrich animal environments, for example by giving animals more choices to reduce the "learned helplessness" of captivity (Kurtcyz, 2015; Weir, 2013). Thanks partly to research on the benefits of novelty, control, and stimulation, these gorillas are enjoying an improved quality of life in New York's Bronx Zoo.

Animals have themselves benefited from animal research. After measuring stress hormone levels in samples of millions of dogs brought each year to animal shelters, research psychologists devised handling and stroking methods to reduce stress and ease the dogs' move to adoptive homes (Tuber et al., 1999). Other studies have helped improve care and management in animals' natural habitats. By revealing our behavioral kinship with animals and the remarkable intelligence of chimpanzees, gorillas, and other animals, experiments have led to increased empathy and protection for other species. At its best, a psychology concerned for humans and sensitive to animals serves the welfare of both.

STUDYING AND PROTECTING HUMANS

What about human participants? Does the image of white-coated scientists seeming to deliver electric shocks trouble you? Actually, most psychological studies are free of such stress. Blinking lights, flashing words, and pleasant social interactions are more common. Moreover, psychology's experiments are mild compared with the stress and humiliation often inflicted in reality TV "experiments." In two episodes of *The Bachelor,* a man dumped his new fiancée — on camera — for a woman who earlier had been runner-up (Bonos, 2018; Collins, 2009).

Occasionally, researchers do temporarily stress or deceive people. This happens only when they believe it is unavoidable. Some experiments won't work if participants know everything beforehand. (Wanting to be helpful, the participants might try to confirm the researcher's predictions.)

The APA and Britain's BPS ethics codes urge researchers to

- obtain the potential participants' **informed consent** to take part.
- protect participants from out-of-the-ordinary harm and discomfort.
- keep information about individual participants confidential.
- fully **debrief** participants (explain the research afterward, including any temporary deception).

As with nonhuman animals, most university ethics committees have guidelines that screen research proposals and safeguard participants' well-being.

VALUES IN PSYCHOLOGY

Values affect what we study, how we study it, and how we interpret results. Consider our choice of research topics. Should we study worker productivity or worker morale? Sex discrimination or gender differences? Conformity or independence? Values can also color "the facts"—our observations and interpretations. Sometimes we see what we want or expect to see (**FIGURE 1.4**).

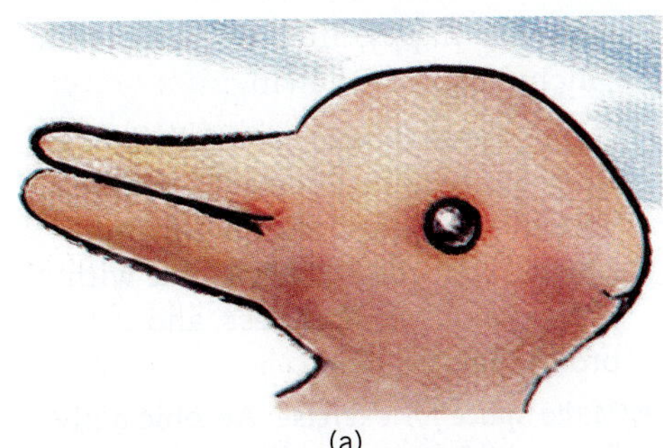

(a)

Rubberball/Mike Kemp/Getty Images

(b)

FIGURE 1.4 What do you see? Our expectations influence what we perceive in (a). Did you see a duck or a rabbit? Show some friends this image with the rabbit photo (b) covered up and see if they are more likely to perceive a duck. (Inspired by Shepard, 1990.)

Even the words we use to describe traits and tendencies can reflect our values. Labels describe and labels evaluate. One person's *rigidity* is another's *consistency*. One person's *undocumented worker* is another's *illegal alien*. One person's *faith* is another's *fanaticism*. One country's *enhanced interrogation techniques* is an enemy country's use of *torture*. Our words—*firm* or *stubborn, careful* or *picky, discreet* or *secretive*—reveal our attitudes.

Applied psychology also contains hidden values. If you defer to "professional" guidance — on raising children, achieving self-fulfillment, coping with sexual feelings, getting ahead at work — you are accepting value-laden advice. A science of behavior and mental processes can help us reach our goals, but it cannot decide what those goals should be.

Others have a different worry about psychology: that it is becoming dangerously powerful. Might psychology, they ask, be used to manipulate people? Knowledge, like all power, can be used for good or evil. Nuclear power has been used to light up cities — and to demolish them. Persuasive power has been used to educate people — and to deceive them. Although psychology does indeed have the power to deceive, its purpose is to enlighten. Every day, psychologists explore ways to enhance learning, creativity, and compassion. Psychology speaks to many of our world's great problems — war, inequality, climate change, prejudice, family crises, crime — all of which involve attitudes and behaviors. Psychology also speaks to our deepest longings — for nourishment, for love, for happiness. And, as you have seen, one of the new developments in this field — positive psychology — has as its goal exploring and promoting human strengths. Many of life's questions are beyond psychology, but even a first psychology course can shine a bright light on some very important ones.

Macmillan Learning

Macmillan Learning

Psychology speaks In making its historic 1954 school desegregation decision, the U.S. Supreme Court cited the expert testimony and research of psychologists Kenneth Clark and Mamie Phipps Clark (1947). The Clarks reported that, when given a choice between Black and White dolls, most African-American children chose the White doll. This choice indicated that the children had likely absorbed and accepted anti-Black prejudice.

informed consent giving people enough information about a study to enable them to decide whether they wish to participate.

debriefing after an experiment ends, explaining to participants the study's purpose and any deceptions researchers used.

IN YOUR EVERYDAY LIFE

What other questions or concerns do you have about psychology?

RETRIEVE & REMEMBER

ANSWERS IN APPENDIX E

20. How are animal and human research participants protected?

Use Psychology to Improve Your Life and Become a Better Student

LOQ 1-19 How can psychological principles help you to learn, remember, and thrive?

Psychology is not just about understanding others, but also about understanding ourselves. It is only through such learning that we can be—and show to the world—our very best selves. This book is all about how you can *use* psychology. You may do so in these three ways:

Think: Think critically, by examining sources and evidence before accepting arguments and conclusions.

Consider: Consider other voices and ideas by being open to diverse perspectives. By engaging with people who differ from you, your world will be enriched. As actor Angelina Jolie (2017) remarked, "What a dull and pointless life it would be if everyone was the same."

Improve: Use psychology's evidence-based principles—on relationships, achieving success, handling stress, finding meaning, and much more—to improve your everyday life.

Think, Consider, and Improve: These principles run through the entire book. In chapters to come, we will offer evidence-based suggestions that you can use to live a happy, effective, flourishing life, including the following:

- ***Manage your time to get a full night's sleep.*** Unlike sleep-deprived people, who live with fatigue and gloomy moods, well-rested people live with greater energy, happiness, and productivity.
- ***Make space for exercise.*** Aerobic activity not only increases health and energy, it also is an effective remedy for mild to moderate depression and anxiety.
- ***Set long-term goals, with daily aims.*** Flourishing, successful people take time each day to work toward their goals, such as exercising or sleeping more, or eating more healthfully. Over time, they often find that their daily practice becomes a habit.
- ***Have a growth mindset.*** Rather than seeing their abilities as fixed, successful people view their mental abilities as like a muscle—something that grows stronger with effortful use.
- ***Prioritize relationships.*** We humans are social animals. We flourish when connected in close relationships. We are both happier and healthier when supported by (and when supporting) caring friends.

Psychology's research also shows how we can learn and retain information. Many students assume that the way to cement new learning is to reread. What helps more—and what this book therefore encourages—is *repeated self-testing and rehearsal* of previously studied material. Memory researchers call this the **testing effect** (Roediger & Karpicke, 2006). (This is also known as the *retrieval practice effect* or as *test-enhanced learning*.) In one study, English-speaking students who had been tested repeatedly recalled the meaning of 20 previously learned Lithuanian words better than those who had spent the same time restudying the 20 words (Ariel & Karpicke, 2018). Repetitive testing's rewards also make it reinforcing: Students who used repetitive testing once found it helped, and more often used it later when learning new material. Many other studies, including in college classrooms, confirm that *frequent quizzing and self-testing boosts students' retention* (Cho et al., 2017; Foss & Pirozzolo, 2017; Trumbo et al., 2016).

We have designed this book to help you benefit from the testing effect and other memory research findings. As you will see in Chapter 7, to master information you must *actively process it*. In one digest of 225 studies, students who were learning actively scored highest in science, technology, engineering, and mathematics (the STEM fields) (Freeman et al., 2014). Likewise, when learning a new language, those who practice *speaking* it learn better than those who passively listen to it (Hopman & MacDonald, 2018). So don't treat your mind like your stomach, something to be filled passively. Treat it more like a muscle that grows stronger with exercise. Countless experiments reveal that people learn and remember best when they put material into their own words, rehearse it, and then retrieve and review it again.

The **SQ3R** study method converts these principles into practice (McDaniel et al., 2009; Robinson, 1970). SQ3R is an acronym—an abbreviation formed from the first letter of each of its five steps: Survey, Question, Read, Retrieve,[7] Review.

To study a chapter, first *survey*, taking a bird's-eye view. Scan the table of contents at the chapter's opening to visually survey the upcoming content. Scan the headings, and notice how the chapter is organized.

Before you read each main section, try to answer its numbered Learning Objective *Question* (for this section: "How can psychological principles help you to learn, remember, and thrive?"). By testing your understanding *before* you read the section, you will discover what you don't yet know.

Then *read*, actively searching for the answer to each question. At each sitting, read only as much of the chapter (usually a single main section) as you can absorb

[7] Also sometimes called "Recite."

without tiring. Read actively and think critically. Ask your own questions. Take notes. Relate the ideas to your personal experiences and to your own life. *Does the idea support or challenge my assumptions? How convincing is the evidence?* Write out what you know. "Writing is often a tool for learning," say researchers (Arnold et al., 2017).

Having read a section, *retrieve* its main ideas—"Active retrieval promotes meaningful learning" (Karpicke, 2012). So test yourself—even better, test yourself repeatedly. To get you started, we offer periodic Retrieve & Remember questions throughout each chapter (see, for example, the questions at the end of this section). After trying to answer these questions, check the answers in Appendix E, and reread the material as needed. Researchers have found that "trying and failing to retrieve the answer is actually helpful to learning" (Roediger & Finn, 2010). Testing yourself after you read will help you learn and retain the information more effectively.

Finally, *review:* Read over any notes you have taken, again with an eye on the chapter's organization, and quickly review the whole chapter. Write or say what a concept is before rereading the material to check your understanding.

Survey, question, read, retrieve, review. We have organized this book's chapters to help you use the SQ3R study system. Each chapter begins with a *survey* of the content to come. Headings and Learning Objective *Questions* suggest issues and concepts you should consider as you move through the section. The length of the sections is controlled so you can easily *read* them. The Retrieve & Remember questions will challenge you to *retrieve* what you have learned, and thus *retain* it better. The *In* Your Everyday Life and *Improve* Your Everyday Life questions appearing throughout the chapter will help make the chapter's concepts more personally meaningful, and therefore more memorable. The end-of-chapter Review is set up as a self-test, with the collected Learning Objective Questions and key terms listed, along with Chapter Test questions in a variety of formats. In the e-book, answer-checking is a click away. In the printed text, answers may be found in Appendix D and Appendix E.

Four additional study tips may further boost your learning:

Distribute your study time. One of psychology's oldest findings is that *if you want to retain information, spaced practice is better than massed practice.* So space your time over several study periods—perhaps one hour a day, six days a week—rather than cramming it into one week-long or all-night study blitz. You'll remember material better if you read just one main section (not the whole chapter) in a single sitting. Then turn to something else.

Spacing your study sessions requires discipline and knowing how to manage your time. Richard O. Straub explains time management in a helpful preface at the beginning of this text.

Learn to think critically. We again mention critical thinking because it is so important. Whether you are reading or listening to class discussions, think smartly. Try to spot people's assumptions and values. Can you detect a bias underlying an argument? Weigh the evidence. Is it a personal story that might not represent the whole group? Or is it scientific evidence based on sound experiments? Assess conclusions. Are other explanations possible?

Process class information actively. Listen for a lecture's main ideas and sub-ideas. *Write them down.* Ask questions during and after class. In class, as in your own study, process the information actively and you will understand and retain it better. Make the information your own by making connections between what you read and what you already know. Engage with the "Your Everyday Life" questions found throughout each chapter to relate what you read to your own life. Tell someone else about it. (As any teacher will confirm, to teach is to remember.)

Also, take notes *by hand.* Handwritten notes, in your own words, typically engage more active processing, with better retention, than does word-for-word note taking on laptops (Mueller & Oppenheimer, 2014).

Overlearn. Psychology tells us that we tend to be overconfident—we overestimate how much we know. You may understand a chapter as you read it, but that feeling of familiarity can trick you. By using the Retrieve & Remember and Chapter Test questions as well as our other online learning opportunities, you can test your knowledge and *overlearn* in the process.

Memory experts offer simple, scientifically supported advice for how to improve your retention and your grades (Bjork & Bjork, 2011, p. 63):

> Spend less time on the input side and more time on the output side, such as summarizing what you have read from memory or getting together with friends and asking each other questions. Any activities that involve testing yourself—that is, activities that require you to retrieve or generate information, rather than just representing information to yourself—will make your learning both more durable and flexible.

So go ahead and jump right in. Learn psychology. Learn it well. And discover how it can help you be the happiest, most effective, and most successful you.

IMPROVE YOUR EVERYDAY LIFE

Of all of these helpful principles, which ones seem most relevant and important for improving your own life and studies? How will you add them to your usual routines?

RETRIEVE & REMEMBER

ANSWERS IN APPENDIX E

21. The ________ ________ describes the enhanced memory that results from repeated retrieval (as in self-testing) rather than from simple rereading of new information.
22. What does SQ3R stand for?

testing effect enhanced memory after retrieving, rather than simply rereading, information. Also sometimes called the *retrieval practice effect* or *test-enhanced learning*.

SQ3R a study method incorporating five steps: *S*urvey, *Q*uestion, *R*ead, *R*etrieve, *R*eview.

Psychology's Roots, Critical Thinking, and Self-Improvement Tools

LEARNING OBJECTIVES

TEST YOURSELF Answer these repeated Learning Objective Questions on your own (before checking the answers in Appendix D) to improve your retention of the concepts (McDaniel et al., 2009, 2015).

Psychology Is a Science

1-1: How is psychology a science? How does critical thinking feed a scientific attitude, and smarter thinking for everyday life?

1-2: What are the three key elements of the scientific attitude, and how do they support scientific inquiry?

1-3: How has psychology's focus changed over time?

1-4: What are psychology's current perspectives, and what are some of its subfields?

1-5: How do psychologists use the biopsychosocial approach, and how can it help us understand our diverse world?

1-6: What are we learning about *dual processing* from psychological science?

1-7: How is psychology also a helping profession?

1-8: What is *positive psychology?*

The Need for Psychological Science

1-9: How does our everyday thinking sometimes lead us to a wrong conclusion?

1-10: Why is it so easy to believe untruths?

How Do Psychologists Ask and Answer Questions?

1-11: How do theories advance psychological science?

1-12: How do psychologists use case studies, naturalistic observations, and surveys to observe and describe behavior, and why is random sampling important?

1-13: What does it mean when we say two things are correlated, and what are positive and negative correlations?

1-14: Why do correlations enable prediction but not cause-effect explanation?

1-15: How do experiments clarify or reveal cause-effect relationships?

1-16: How would you know which research design to use?

1-17: How can simplified laboratory experiments help us understand general principles of behavior?

Psychology's Research Ethics

1-18: Why do psychologists study animals, and what ethical guidelines safeguard human and animal research participants? How do psychologists' values influence what they study and how they apply their results?

Use Psychology to Improve Your Life and Become a Better Student

1-19: How can psychological principles help you to learn, remember, and thrive?

TERMS AND CONCEPTS TO REMEMBER

TEST YOURSELF Write down the definition in your own words, then check your answer.

critical thinking, *p. 3*
structuralism, *p. 5*
functionalism, *p. 5*
behaviorism, *p. 5*
humanistic psychology, *p. 5*
cognitive psychology, *p. 5*
cognitive neuroscience, *p. 7*
psychology, *p. 7*
biopsychosocial approach, *p. 9*
culture, *p. 9*
nature–nurture issue, *p. 9*
dual processing, *p. 11*
counseling psychology, *p. 11*
clinical psychology, *p. 11*
psychiatry, *p. 11*
community psychology, *p. 11*
positive psychology, *p. 11*
hindsight bias, *p. 13*
theory, *p. 15*
hypothesis, *p. 15*
operational definition, *p. 15*
replication, *p. 15*
preregistration, *p. 15*
case study, *p. 17*
naturalistic observation, *p. 17*
survey, *p. 17*
population, *p. 17*
random sample, *p. 17*
correlation, *p. 18*
experiment, *p. 21*
random assignment, *p. 21*
experimental group, *p. 21*
control group, *p. 21*
placebo [pluh-SEE-bo], *p. 21*
double-blind procedure, *p. 21*
placebo effect, *p. 21*
independent variable, *p. 21*
confounding variable, *p. 21*
dependent variable, *p. 21*
informed consent, *p. 25*
debriefing, *p. 25*
testing effect, *p. 27*
SQ3R, *p. 27*

CHAPTER TEST

TEST YOURSELF Answer the following questions on your own first, then check your answers in Appendix E.

1. How can critical thinking help you evaluate claims in the media, even if you're not a scientific expert on the issue?

2. As scientists, psychologists

- **a.** keep their methods private so others will not repeat their research.
- **b.** assume the truth of articles published in leading scientific journals.
- **c.** reject evidence that competes with traditional findings.
- **d.** are willing to ask questions and to reject claims that cannot be verified by research.

3. In 1879, in psychology's first experiment, ___________ and his students measured the time lag between hearing a ball hit a platform and pressing a key.

4. William James would be considered a(n) ___________. Wilhelm Wundt would be considered a(n) ___________.

- **a.** functionalist; structuralist
- **b.** structuralist; functionalist
- **c.** evolutionary theorist; structuralist
- **d.** functionalist; evolutionary theorist

5. In the early twentieth century, ___________ redefined psychology as "the scientific study of observable behavior."

- **a.** John B. Watson
- **b.** Abraham Maslow
- **c.** William James
- **d.** Sigmund Freud

6. Nature is to nurture as

- **a.** personality is to intelligence.
- **b.** biology is to experience.
- **c.** intelligence is to biology.
- **d.** psychological traits are to behaviors.

7. "Nurture works on what nature provides." Describe what this means, using your own words.

8. Which of the following is true regarding gender differences and similarities?

- **a.** Differences between the genders outweigh any similarities.
- **b.** Despite some gender differences, the underlying processes of human behavior are the same.
- **c.** Both similarities and differences between the genders depend more on biology than on environment.
- **d.** Gender differences are so numerous that it is difficult to make meaningful comparisons.

9. ___________ ___________ is the principle that our mind processes information on two tracks at the same time—one with our full awareness and the other outside of our awareness.

10. A psychologist treating emotionally troubled adolescents at a local mental health agency is most likely to be a(n)

- **a.** research psychologist.
- **b.** psychiatrist.
- **c.** industrial-organizational psychologist.
- **d.** clinical psychologist.

11. A mental health professional with a medical degree who can prescribe medication is a ___________.

12. Martin Seligman and other researchers who explore various aspects of human flourishing refer to their field of study as ___________ ___________.

13. ___________ ___________ refers to our tendency to perceive events as predictable and obvious after the fact.

14. A theory-based prediction is called a(n) ___________.

15. Which of the following is NOT one of the *descriptive* methods psychologists use to observe and describe behavior?

- **a.** A case study
- **b.** Naturalistic observation
- **c.** Correlational research
- **d.** A phone survey

16. For your survey, you need to establish a group of people who represent the country's entire adult population. To do this, you will need to question a ___________ sample of the population.

17. A study finds that the more childbirth training classes women attend, the less pain medication they require during childbirth. This finding can be stated as a ___________ (positive/negative) correlation.

18. Knowing that two events are correlated provides

- **a.** a basis for prediction.
- **b.** an explanation of why the events are related.
- **c.** proof that as one increases, the other also increases.
- **d.** an indication that an underlying third factor is at work.

19. Here are some recently reported correlations, with interpretations drawn by journalists. Knowing just these correlations, can you come up with other possible explanations for each of these?

a. Alcohol use is associated with violence. (One interpretation: Drinking triggers, or unleashes, aggressive behavior.)

b. Educated people live longer, on average, than less-educated people. (One interpretation: Education lengthens life and improves health.)

c. Teens engaged in team sports are less likely to use drugs, smoke, have sex, carry weapons, and eat junk food than are teens who do not engage in team sports. (One interpretation: Team sports encourage healthy living.)

d. Adolescents who frequently see smoking in movies are more likely to smoke. (One interpretation: Movie stars' behavior influences impressionable teens.)

20. To explain behaviors and clarify cause and effect, psychologists use ___________.

21. To test the effect of a new drug on depression, we randomly assign people to control and experimental groups. Those in the control group take a pill that contains no medication. This pill is a ___________.

22. In a double-blind procedure,

a. only the participants know whether they are in the control group or the experimental group.

b. experimental and control group members will be carefully matched for age, sex, income, and education level.

c. neither the participants nor the researchers know who is in the experimental group or control group.

d. someone separate from the researcher will ask people to volunteer for the experimental group or the control group.

23. A researcher wants to know whether noise level affects workers' blood pressure. In one group, she varies the level of noise in the environment and records participants' blood pressure. In this experiment, the level of noise is the ___________ ___________.

24. The laboratory environment is designed to

a. exactly re-create the events of everyday life.

b. re-create psychological forces under *controlled* conditions.

c. re-create psychological forces under *random* conditions.

d. reduce the use of animals and humans in psychological research.

25. In defending their experimental research with animals, psychologists have noted that

a. animals' biology and behavior can tell us much about our own.

b. animal experimentation sometimes helps animals as well as humans.

c. animals are fascinating creatures and worthy of study.

d. all of these statements are correct.

Continue testing yourself with **LearningCurve** or **Achieve Read & Practice** to learn and remember most effectively.

GlebSStock/Shutterstock

CHAPTER 2

The Biology of Behavior and Consciousness

SURVEY THE CHAPTER

Xiaoping Ren, a Chinese transplant surgeon, is building an international team that hopes to undertake an extremely daring medical venture—a full-body transplant (Kean, 2016; Tatlow, 2016). Wang Huanming, who is paralyzed from the neck down, is one of ten volunteers for this mind-boggling experiment. What would Wang have done? His fully-functioning head would be transferred to a brain-dead person's still-functioning body.

Ignore, for now, the experiment's serious ethical and technical issues. Just imagine that it could work. With the same brain and a new body, would Wang still be Wang? After recovering, to whose home should he return? If the old Wang was a skilled musician, would the new Wang retain that skill—or would that depend on the muscle memories stored in the new body? And if he (assuming the new body was male) later had a child, whom should the birth certificate list as the father?

Most of us twenty-first-century people (you, too?) presume that, even with a new body, Wang would still be Wang. We presume that our brain, designed by our genes and sculpted by our experience, provides our identity and enables our mind. No brain, no mind.

No principle is more central to today's psychology, or to this book, than this: *Everything psychological is also biological.* Your every idea, every mood, every urge is a biological happening. You love, laugh, and cry with your body. To think, feel, or act without a body would be like running without legs. Without your body—your brain, your heart, your appearance—you truly would be nobody. Moreover, your body and your brain influence and are influenced by your experience.

We may talk separately of biological and psychological influences, but they are two sides of the same coin. In combination with social-cultural influences, they form the *biopsychosocial approach.* In later chapters, we'll look at how those influences interact in our development (Chapter 3), our sensory perceptions (Chapter 5), our learning and memory (Chapters 6 and 7), and our well-being (Chapters 10, 13, and 14). In this chapter, we explore these interactions in our two-track mind. Our exploration starts small and builds—from nerve cells to brain functions to brain states, including sleeping and dreaming.

"You're certainly a lot less fun since the operation."

The Power of Plasticity

Learning Objective Question LOQ 2-1 How do biology and experience enable neural plasticity?

Your brain is sculpted not only by your genes but also by your life. Under the surface of your awareness, your brain is constantly changing, building new pathways as it adjusts to new experiences. This neural change is called **plasticity**.

The mind's eye Daniel Kish, who is completely blind, enjoys going for walks in the woods. To stay safe, he uses echolocation—the same navigation method used by bats and dolphins. Blind echolocation experts such as Kish engage the brain's visual centers to navigate their surroundings (Thaler et al., 2011, 2014). Although Kish is blind, his flexible brain helps him to "see."

Although neural plasticity is strongest in childhood, it continues throughout life (Gutchess, 2014).

To see plasticity at work, consider London's taxi driver trainees. They spend years learning and remembering the city's 25,000 street locations and connections. Only half of these trainees pass the difficult final test. But passing produces big rewards: a better income and an enlarged hippocampus, a brain center that processes spatial memories. London's bus drivers, who navigate a smaller set of roads, gain no similar neural rewards (Maguire et al., 2000, 2006).

We also see plasticity in well-practiced pianists, who have a larger-than-usual auditory cortex area, a sound-processing region (Bavelier et al., 2000; Pantev et al., 1998). After years of practice, the brains of ballerinas and jugglers reflect other changes related to improved performance (Draganski et al., 2004; Hänggi et al., 2010; Herholz & Zatorre, 2012). Your brain, too, is a work in progress. It changes with the focus and practice you're devoting to the ideas, skills, and people you care about the most. The brain you're born with is not the brain you will die with.

Plasticity is part of what makes the human brain unique (Gómez-Robles et al., 2015). More than for any other species, our brain is designed to change, and thus to adapt to our changing world.

RETRIEVE & REMEMBER

ANSWERS IN APPENDIX E

1. How does learning a new skill affect the structure of our brain?

Neural Communication

LOQ 2-2 What are the parts of a neuron, and what is an *action potential?*

The human body is complexity built from simplicity. Our amazing internal communication system is formed by basic building blocks: **neurons**, or nerve cells. Throughout life, new neurons are born and unused ones wither away (O'Leary et al., 2014; Shors, 2014).

A NEURON'S STRUCTURE

Neurons differ, but each consists of a **cell body** and its branching fibers (**FIGURE 2.1**). The neuron's often bushy **dendrite** fibers receive and integrate information, conducting it toward the cell body (Stuart & Spruston, 2015). From there, the cell's single **axon** fiber sends out messages to other neurons or to muscles or glands (**FIGURE 2.2**). Dendrites listen. Axons speak.

The messages neurons carry are electrical signals, or nerve impulses, called **action potentials**. These impulses travel down axons at different speeds. Supporting our nerve cells are spidery **glial cells** ("glue cells"). Neurons are like queen bees—on their own, they cannot feed or sheathe themselves. Glial cells are worker bees. They provide nutrients and *myelin*—the layer of fatty tissue that insulates some neurons. They also guide neural connections and clean up after neurons send messages to one another. Glia play a role in information

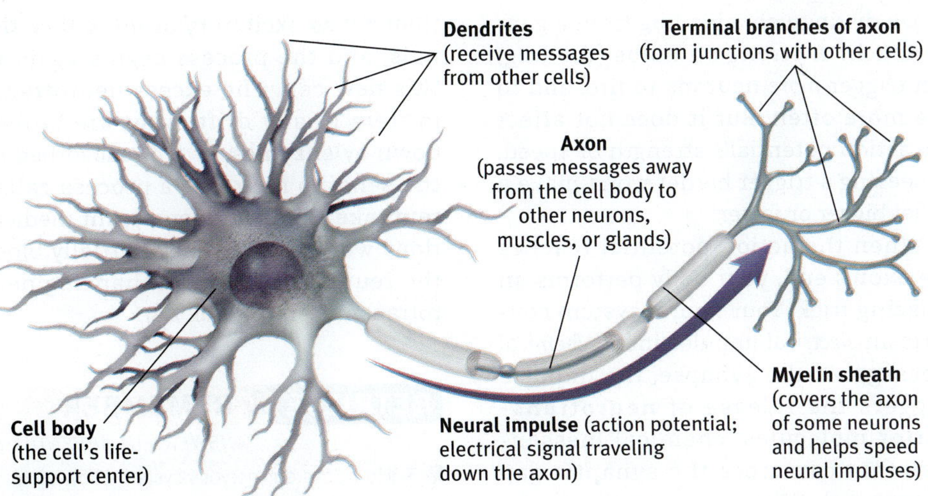

FIGURE 2.1 A motor neuron

processing—learning, thinking, and memory (Fields, 2011; Martín et al., 2015).

Some action potentials trudge along at a sluggish 2 miles (3 kilometers) per hour, and others race along at 200 or more miles (320 kilometers) per hour. Can you guess which reacts faster, a human brain or a high-speed computer? The computer wins every time. Even our brain's top speed is 3 million times slower than electricity zipping through a wire. Thus, unlike the nearly instant reactions of a computer, your "quick" reaction to a sudden event, such as a child darting in front of your car, may take a quarter-second or more. Your brain is vastly more complex than a computer, but slower at executing simple responses.

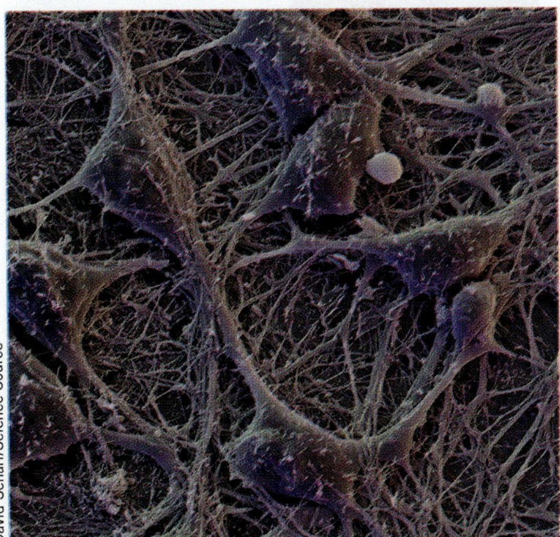

FIGURE 2.2 Neurons communicating
When we learn about neurons, we often see them one at a time to learn their parts. But our billions of neurons exist in a vast and densely interconnected web. One neuron's terminal branches send messages to neighboring dendrites. Read on to learn more about this complex and fascinating electrochemical communication process.

Neurons interweave so tightly that even with a microscope, you would struggle to see where one ends and another begins. But end they do, at meeting places called **synapses**. At these points, two neurons are separated by a tiny *synaptic gap* less than a millionth of an inch wide. "Like elegant ladies air-kissing so as not to muss their makeup, dendrites and axons don't quite touch," noted poet Diane Ackerman (2004). How, then, does a neuron send information across the gap? The answer is one of the important scientific discoveries of our age.

> "All information processing in the brain involves neurons 'talking to' each other at synapses." —Neuroscientist Solomon H. Snyder, 1984

IN YOUR EVERYDAY LIFE

Does it surprise you to learn that despite your brain's complexity, your reaction time is slower than a computer's? What does this tell you about which tasks might be more readily performed by humans versus computers?

RETRIEVE & REMEMBER

ANSWERS IN APPENDIX E

2. When a neuron fires an action potential, the information travels through the axon, the dendrites, and the cell body, but not in that order. Place these three structures in the correct order.

LaunchPad For an interactive, animated explanation of this process, engage online with *Concept Practice: Action Potentials.*

HOW NEURONS COMMUNICATE

LOQ 2-3 How do neurons communicate?

Each neuron is itself a miniature decision-making device, reacting to signals it receives from hundreds, even thousands, of other neurons. Most of these signals are *excitatory,* somewhat like pushing a

plasticity the brain's ability to change, especially during childhood, by reorganizing after damage or by building new pathways based on experience.

neuron a nerve cell; the basic building block of the nervous system.

cell body the part of a neuron that contains the nucleus; the cell's life-support center.

dendrites neuron extensions that receive and integrate messages and conduct them toward the cell body.

axon the neuron extension that sends messages to other neurons or to muscles and glands.

action potential a nerve impulse; a brief electrical charge that travels down an axon.

glial cells (glia) cells in the nervous system that support, nourish, and protect neurons; they also play a role in learning, thinking, and memory.

synapse [SIN-aps] the junction between the axon tip of a sending neuron and the dendrite or cell body of a receiving neuron. The tiny gap at this junction is called the *synaptic gap* or *synaptic cleft.*

neuron's gas pedal. Others are *inhibitory*, more like pushing its brake.

If the excitatory signals exceed the inhibitory signals by a minimum intensity, or **threshold**, the combined signals trigger an action potential. (Think of it this way: If the excitatory party animals outvote the inhibitory party poopers, the party's on.) The neuron fires, sending an impulse down its axon, carrying information to another cell. Neurons then need a short break before they can fire again. This resting pause, called a **refractory period**, lasts a tiny fraction of an eyeblink.

A neuron's firing doesn't vary in intensity. The neuron's reaction is an **all-or-none response**. Like guns, neurons either fire or they don't. How, then, do we distinguish a big hug from a gentle touch? A strong stimulus (the hug) can trigger *more* neurons to fire, and to fire more often. But it does not affect the action potential's strength or speed. Squeezing a trigger harder won't make a bullet bigger or faster.

When the action potential reaches the axon's end, your body performs an amazing trick. Your neural system converts an *electrical* impulse into a *chemical* message. At the synapse, the impulse triggers the release of **neurotransmitter** molecules, chemical messengers that can cross the synaptic gap (**FIGURE 2.3**). Within one 10,000th of a second, these molecules bind to receptor sites on the receiving neuron, as neatly as keys fitting into locks. They then act as excitatory or inhibitory signals, and the process begins again in this new cell. The excess neurotransmitters finally drift away, are broken down by enzymes, or are reabsorbed by the sending neuron—a process called **reuptake**. Some antidepressant medications work because they partially block the reuptake of mood-enhancing neurotransmitters (**FIGURE 2.4**).

RETRIEVE & REMEMBER

ANSWERS IN APPENDIX E

- 3. How does our nervous system allow us to experience the difference between a slap and a tap on the back?
- 4. What happens in the *synaptic gap?*

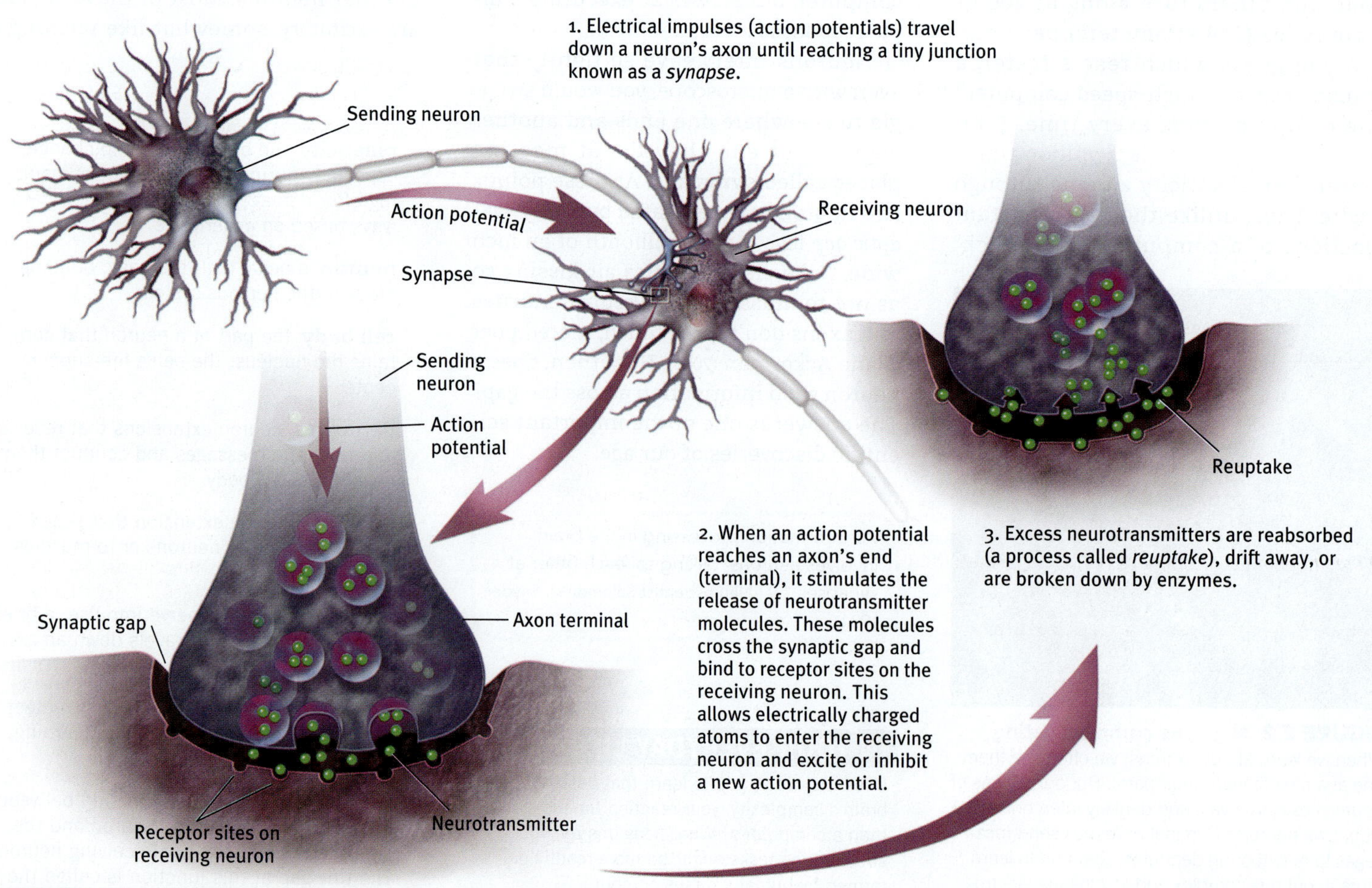
1. Electrical impulses (action potentials) travel down a neuron's axon until reaching a tiny junction known as a *synapse*.
Sending neuron
Action potential
Receiving neuron
Synapse
Sending neuron
Action potential
Axon terminal
Synaptic gap
Receptor sites on receiving neuron
Neurotransmitter
2. When an action potential reaches an axon's end (terminal), it stimulates the release of neurotransmitter molecules. These molecules cross the synaptic gap and bind to receptor sites on the receiving neuron. This allows electrically charged atoms to enter the receiving neuron and excite or inhibit a new action potential.
Reuptake
3. Excess neurotransmitters are reabsorbed (a process called *reuptake*), drift away, or are broken down by enzymes.

FIGURE 2.3 How neurons communicate

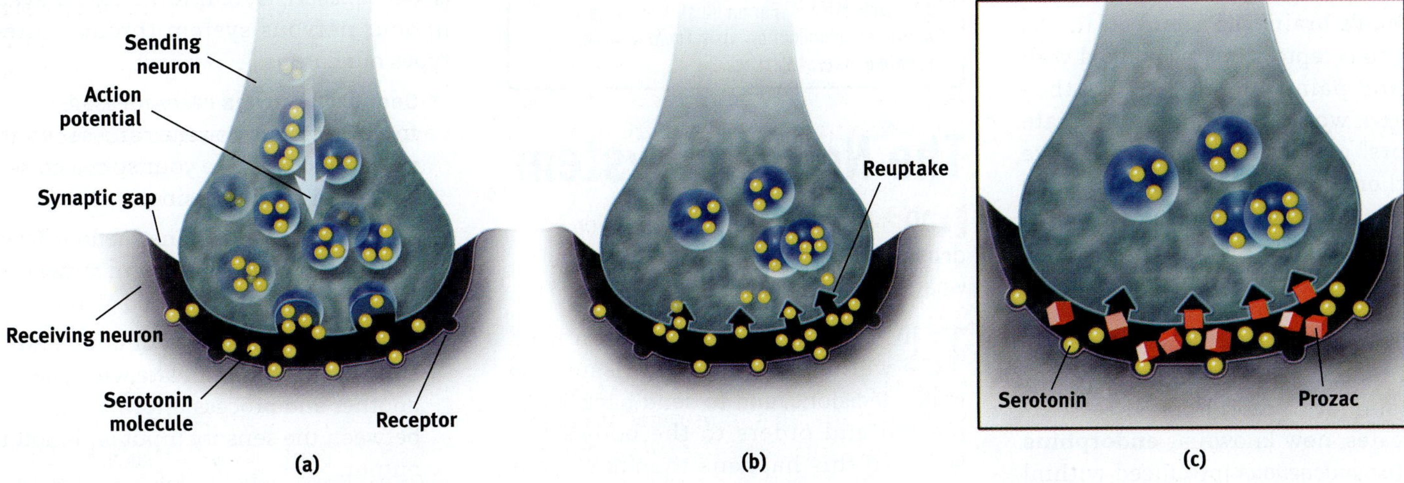
Message is sent across synaptic gap.
Message is received; excess serotonin molecules are reabsorbed by sending neuron.
Prozac partially blocks normal reuptake of the neurotransmitter serotonin; excess serotonin in synapse enhances its mood-lifting effect.
Sending neuron
Action potential
Synaptic gap
Receiving neuron
Serotonin molecule
Receptor
Reuptake
Serotonin
Prozac
(a)
(b)
(c)

FIGURE 2.4 Biology of antidepressants Selective serotonin reuptake inhibitors (SSRIs) are popularly prescribed antidepressants. They relieve depression by partially blocking the reuptake of the neurotransmitter serotonin. Shown here is the action of the SSRI Prozac.

HOW NEUROTRANSMITTERS INFLUENCE US

LOQ 2-4 How do neurotransmitters affect our mood and behavior?

Dozens of different neurotransmitters have their own pathways in the brain. As they travel along these paths, they carry specific but different messages that influence our motions and emotions. *Dopamine* levels, for example, influence our movement, learning, attention, and feelings of pleasure and reward. *Serotonin* levels can make us more or less moody, hungry, sleepy, or aroused. **TABLE 2.1** outlines the effects of these and other neurotransmitters.

TABLE 2.1 Some Neurotransmitters and Their Functions

Neurotransmitter	Function	Examples of Malfunctions
Acetylcholine (ACh)	Enables muscle action, learning, and memory	With Alzheimer's disease, ACh-producing neurons deteriorate.
Dopamine	Influences movement, learning, attention, and emotion	Oversupply linked to schizophrenia. Undersupply linked to tremors and decreased mobility in Parkinson's disease.
Serotonin	Affects mood, hunger, sleep, and arousal	Undersupply linked to depression. Some drugs that raise serotonin levels are used to treat depression.
Norepinephrine	Helps control alertness and arousal	Undersupply can depress mood.
GABA (gamma-aminobutyric acid)	A major inhibitory neurotransmitter	Undersupply linked to seizures, tremors, and insomnia.
Glutamate	A major excitatory neurotransmitter; involved in memory	Oversupply can overstimulate the brain, producing migraines or seizures (which is why some people avoid MSG, monosodium glutamate, in food).
Endorphins	Neurotransmitters that influence the perception of pain or pleasure	Oversupply with opiate drugs can suppress the body's natural endorphin supply.

"When it comes to the brain, if you want to see the action, follow the neurotransmitters." —Neuroscientist Floyd Bloom, 1993

In Chapter 1, we promised to show you how psychologists play their game. Here's an example. An exciting neurotransmitter discovery emerged when researchers attached a harmless radioactive tracer to morphine, an **opiate** drug that elevates mood and eases pain (Pert & Snyder, 1973).

threshold the level of stimulation required to trigger a neural impulse.

refractory period in neural processing, a brief resting pause that occurs after a neuron has fired; subsequent action potentials cannot occur until the axon returns to its resting state.

all-or-none response a neuron's reaction of either firing (with a full-strength response) or not firing.

neurotransmitters neuron-produced chemicals that cross the synaptic gap to carry messages to other neurons or to muscles and glands.

reuptake a neurotransmitter's reabsorption by the sending neuron.

opiate a chemical, such as opium, morphine, or heroin, that depresses neural activity, temporarily lessening pain and anxiety.

As researchers tracked the morphine in an animal's brain, they noticed it was binding to receptors in areas linked with mood and pain sensations. Why, they wondered, would these natural "opiate receptors" exist? Might the brain have these chemical locks because our body produces a natural key—some built-in painkiller—to open them?

Further work revealed the answer. When we are in pain or exercising vigorously, the brain does, indeed, produce several types of neurotransmitter molecules similar to morphine. These natural opiates, now known as **endorphins** (short for *endogenous* [produced within] *morphine*), help explain why we can be unaware of pain after an extreme injury. They also explain the painkilling effects of acupuncture, and the good feeling known as "runner's high" (Boecker et al., 2008; Fuss et al., 2015).

If our natural endorphins lessen pain and boost mood, why not increase this effect by flooding the brain with artificial opiates, such as heroin and morphine? Because it would disrupt the brain's chemical balancing act. When flooded with artificial opiates, it may shut down its own "feel-good" chemistry. If the artificial opiates are then withdrawn, the brain will be deprived of any form of relief. Nature charges a price for suppressing the body's own neurotransmitter production.

Throughout this book, you'll hear more about the many roles neurotransmitters play in our daily lives. But let's first continue our journey into the brain.

IN YOUR EVERYDAY LIFE

Can you recall a time, perhaps after a workout, when you felt the effects of endorphins? How would you describe those feelings?

RETRIEVE & REMEMBER

ANSWERS IN APPENDIX E

5. Serotonin, dopamine, and endorphins are all chemical messengers called ________.

LaunchPad For an illustrated review of neural communication, visit *Topic Tutorial: PsychSim6, Neural Messages.*

The Nervous System

LOQ 2-5 What are the two major divisions of the nervous system, and what are their basic functions?

To live is to take in information from the world and the body's tissues, to make decisions, and to send back information and orders to the body's tissues. All this happens thanks to your body's **nervous system** (FIGURE 2.5). Your brain and spinal cord form the **central nervous system (CNS)**, your body's decision maker. Your **peripheral nervous system (PNS)** gathers information from other body parts and transmits CNS decisions to the rest of your body.

Nerves are electrical cables formed from bundles of axons. They link your central nervous system with your body's sensory receptors, muscles, and glands. Your optic nerve, for example, bundles a million axons into a single cable carrying messages from each eye to your brain (Mason & Kandel, 1991). Information travels in your nervous system through three types of neurons.

- **Sensory neurons** carry messages from your body's tissues and sensory receptors inward to your spinal cord and brain for processing.
- **Motor neurons** carry instructions from your central nervous system outward to your body's muscles and glands.
- **Interneurons** within your brain and spinal cord communicate with one another and process information between the sensory input and motor output.

Your complexity resides mostly in your interneuron systems. Your nervous system has a few million sensory neurons, a few million motor neurons, and billions and billions of interneurons.

THE PERIPHERAL NERVOUS SYSTEM

The peripheral nervous system has two parts—somatic and autonomic. Your **somatic nervous system** monitors sensory input and triggers motor output, controlling your skeletal muscles (which

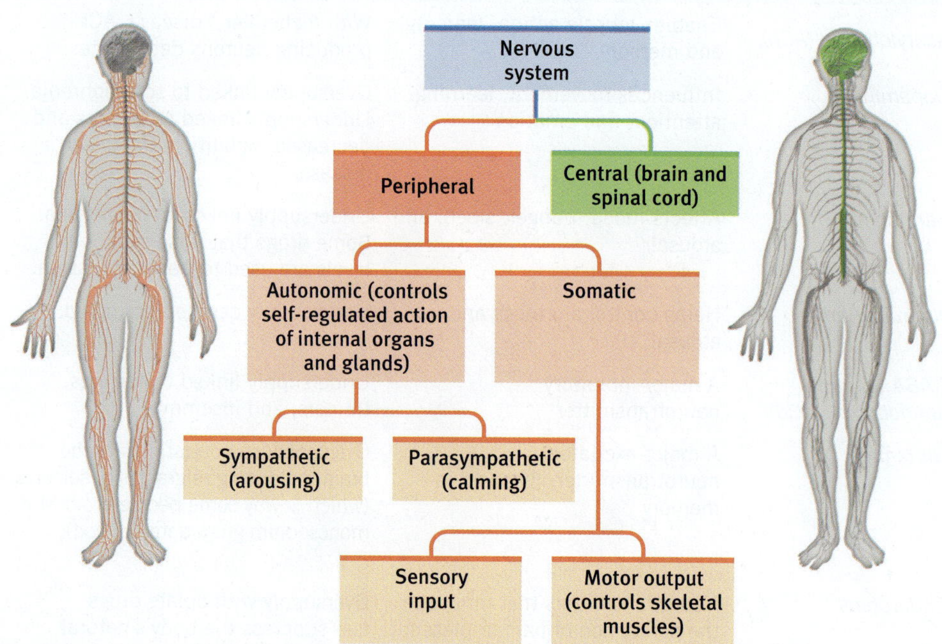

FIGURE 2.5 The functional divisions of the human nervous system

is why it is also called the *skeletal nervous system*). As your friend taps your shoulder, your somatic nervous system reports the information to your brain and carries back instructions that trigger your head to turn. Your **autonomic nervous system (ANS)** controls your glands and the muscles of your internal organs, including those of your heart and digestive system. Like an automatic pilot, this system may be consciously overridden, but usually it operates on its own (autonomously).

Within your autonomic nervous system, two subdivisions help you cope with challenges (**FIGURE 2.6**). If something alarms or challenges you (perhaps giving a speech), your **sympathetic nervous system** will arouse you, making you more alert, energetic, and ready for action. It will increase your heartbeat, blood pressure, and blood-sugar level. It will also slow your digestion and cool you with perspiration. When the stress dies down (the speech is over), your **parasympathetic nervous system** will calm you, conserving your energy as it decreases your heartbeat, lowers your blood sugar, and so on. In everyday situations, the sympathetic and parasympathetic divisions work together to steady our internal state.

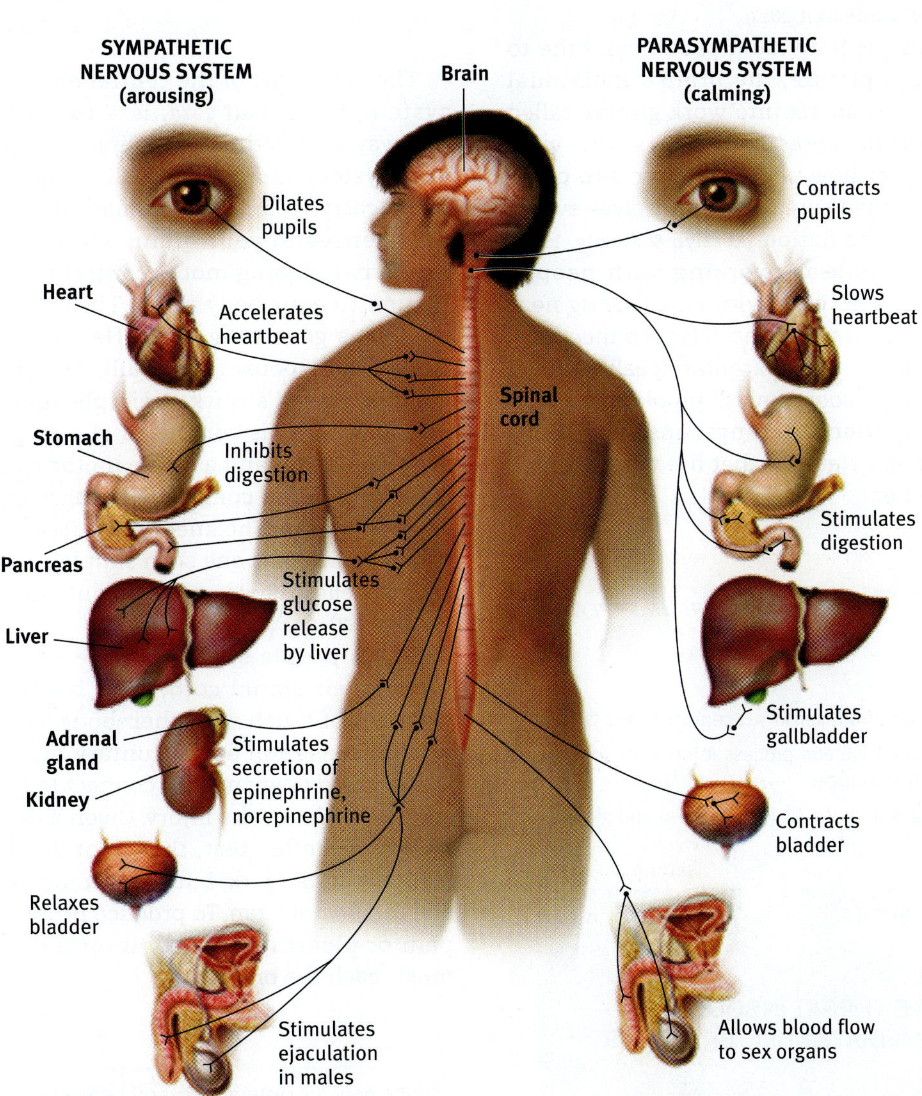

FIGURE 2.6 The dual functions of the autonomic nervous system The autonomic nervous system controls the more autonomous (or self-regulating) internal functions. Its sympathetic division arouses the body and expends energy. Its parasympathetic division calms the body and conserves energy, allowing routine maintenance activity. For example, sympathetic stimulation accelerates heartbeat, whereas parasympathetic stimulation slows it.

endorphins [en-DOR-fins] "morphine within"—natural, opiate-like neurotransmitters linked to pain control and to pleasure.

nervous system the body's speedy, electrochemical communication network, consisting of all the nerve cells of the central and peripheral nervous systems.

central nervous system (CNS) the brain and spinal cord.

peripheral nervous system (PNS) the sensory and motor neurons connecting the central nervous system to the rest of the body.

nerves bundled axons that form neural cables connecting the central nervous system with muscles, glands, and sense organs.

sensory neurons neurons that carry incoming information from the body's tissues and sensory receptors to the brain and spinal cord.

motor neurons neurons that carry outgoing information from the brain and spinal cord to the muscles and glands.

interneurons neurons within the brain and spinal cord; they communicate internally and process information between sensory inputs and motor outputs.

somatic nervous system peripheral nervous system division that controls the body's skeletal muscles. Also called the *skeletal nervous system*.

autonomic [aw-tuh-NAHM-ik] **nervous system (ANS)** peripheral nervous system division that controls the glands and the muscles of the internal organs (such as the heart). Its *sympathetic* subdivision arouses; its *parasympathetic* subdivision calms.

sympathetic nervous system autonomic nervous system subdivision that arouses the body, mobilizing its energy.

parasympathetic nervous system autonomic nervous system subdivision that calms the body, conserving its energy.

I [DM] recently experienced my ANS in action. Before sending me into an MRI (magnetic resonance imaging) machine for a shoulder scan, the technician asked if I had ever had claustrophobia (panic feelings when confined). "No, I'm fine," I assured her, with perhaps a hint of macho swagger. Moments later, my sympathetic nervous system had a different idea. I found myself on my back, stuck deep inside a coffin-sized box and unable to move. Claustrophobia overtook me. My heart began pounding and I felt a desperate urge to escape. Just as I was about to cry out for release, I felt my calming parasympathetic nervous system kick in. My heart rate slowed and my body relaxed, though my arousal surged again before the 20-minute confinement ended. "You did well!" the technician said, unaware of my ANS roller-coaster ride.

IN YOUR EVERYDAY LIFE

Think back to a stressful moment when you felt your sympathetic nervous system kick in. What was your body preparing you for? Were you able to sense your parasympathetic nervous system's response when the challenge had passed?

THE CENTRAL NERVOUS SYSTEM

From neurons "talking" to other neurons arises the complexity of the central nervous system's brain and spinal cord.

It is the *brain* that enables our humanity—our thinking, feeling, and acting. Tens of billions of neurons, each communicating with thousands of other neurons, yield an ever-changing wiring diagram. By one estimate, based on small tissue samples, our brain has some 86 billion neurons (Azevedo et al., 2009; Herculano-Houzel, 2012).

Just as individual pixels combine to form a picture, the brain's individual neurons cluster into work groups called *neural networks*. To understand why, consider how people cluster into cities rather than spreading themselves evenly across the nation (Kosslyn & Koenig, 1992). Like people networking with people, neurons network with neighboring neurons by means of short, fast connections. Learning—to play a guitar, speak a foreign language, solve a math problem—occurs as experience strengthens those connections. Neurons that fire together wire together.

"The body is made up of millions and millions of crumbs."

The other part of the central nervous system, the *spinal cord*, is a two-way highway connecting the peripheral nervous system and the brain. Some nerve fibers carry incoming information from your senses to your brain, while others carry outgoing motor-control information to your body parts. The neural pathways governing our **reflexes**, our automatic responses to stimuli, illustrate the spinal cord's work. A simple spinal reflex pathway is composed of a single sensory neuron and a single motor neuron. These often communicate through an interneuron. The knee-jerk reflex, for example, involves one such simple pathway. A headless warm body could do it (**FIGURE 2.7**).

When people suffer damage to the top of their spinal cord, their brain is truly out of touch with their body. They lose all sensation and voluntary movement in body regions that connect to the spinal cord below its injury. Given a doctor's knee-reflex test, their foot would respond with a jerk, but they would not feel the doctor's tap. To produce physical pain or pleasure, sensory information must reach the brain.

> "If the nervous system be cut off between the brain and other parts, the experiences of those other parts are nonexistent for the mind. The eye is blind, the ear deaf, the hand insensible and motionless." —William James, *Principles of Psychology*, 1890

RETRIEVE & REMEMBER

ANSWERS IN APPENDIX E

6. Match the type of neuron (i–iii) to its description (a–c).

Type:	Description:
i. Motor neurons	a. Carry incoming messages from sensory receptors to the CNS.
ii. Sensory neurons	b. Communicate within the CNS and process information between incoming and outgoing messages.
iii. Interneurons	c. Carry outgoing messages from the CNS to muscles and glands.

Ballistic stress In 2018, Hawaiians received this terrifying alert, amid concerns about North Korean nuclear warheads. "We fully felt we were about to die," reported one panicked mother (Nagourney et al., 2018). Thirty-eight minutes later, the alert was declared a false alarm.

EMERGENCY ALERTS now

Emergency Alert
BALLISTIC MISSILE THREAT INBOUND TO HAWAII. SEEK IMMEDIATE SHELTER. THIS IS NOT A DRILL.
Slide for more

7. How was the ANS involved in Hawaiians' terrified responses, and in calming their bodies once they realized it was a false alarm?

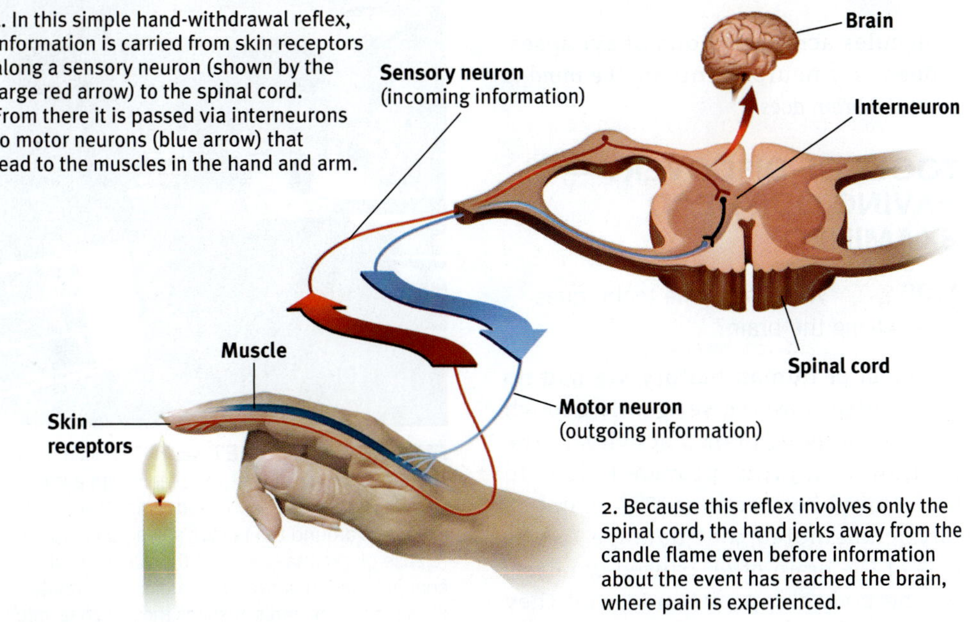
1. In this simple hand-withdrawal reflex, information is carried from skin receptors along a sensory neuron (shown by the large red arrow) to the spinal cord. From there it is passed via interneurons to motor neurons (blue arrow) that lead to the muscles in the hand and arm.
Sensory neuron
(incoming information)
Brain
Interneuron
Muscle
Spinal cord
Skin receptors
Motor neuron
(outgoing information)
2. Because this reflex involves only the spinal cord, the hand jerks away from the candle flame even before information about the event has reached the brain, where pain is experienced.

FIGURE 2.7 A simple reflex

The Endocrine System

LOQ 2-6 How does the endocrine system transmit information and interact with the nervous system?

So far, we have focused on the body's speedy electrochemical information system. But your body has a second communication system, the **endocrine system** (**FIGURE 2.8**). Glands in this system secrete **hormones**, another form of chemical messenger. Hormones travel through our bloodstream and influence many aspects of our life—growth, reproduction, metabolism, and mood.

Some hormones are chemically identical to neurotransmitters. The endocrine system and nervous system are therefore close relatives. Both produce molecules that act on receptors elsewhere. Like many relatives, they also differ. The speedier nervous system zips messages from eyes to brain to hand in a fraction of a second. Endocrine messages trudge along in the bloodstream, taking several seconds or more to travel from the gland to the target tissue. The nervous system transmits information to specific receptor sites with text-message speed. The endocrine system is more like delivering an old-fashioned letter.

But slow and steady sometimes wins the race. The effects of endocrine messages tend to outlast those of neural messages. Have you ever felt angry long after the cause of your angry feelings was resolved (say, your friend apologized for her rudeness)? You may have experienced an "endocrine hangover" from lingering emotion-related hormones. Consider what happens behind the scenes when you hear burglar-like noises outside your window. Your ANS may order your **adrenal glands** to release *epinephrine* and *norepinephrine* (also called *adrenaline* and *noradrenaline*). In response, your heart rate, blood pressure, and blood sugar will rise, giving you a surge of energy known as the *fight-or-flight response*. When the "burglar" turns out to be a playful friend, the hormones—and your alert, aroused feelings—will linger a while.

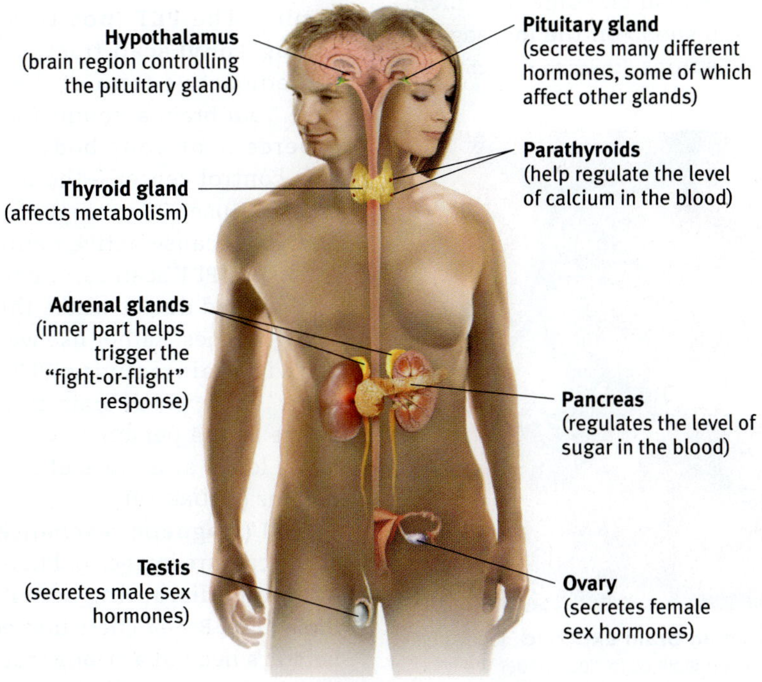

Hypothalamus
(brain region controlling the pituitary gland)

Pituitary gland
(secretes many different hormones, some of which affect other glands)

Parathyroids
(help regulate the level of calcium in the blood)

Thyroid gland
(affects metabolism)

Adrenal glands
(inner part helps trigger the "fight-or-flight" response)

Pancreas
(regulates the level of sugar in the blood)

Testis
(secretes male sex hormones)

Ovary
(secretes female sex hormones)

FIGURE 2.8 The endocrine system

reflex a simple, automatic response to a sensory stimulus, such as the knee-jerk response.

endocrine [EN-duh-krin] **system** the body's "slow" chemical communication system; a set of glands that secrete hormones into the bloodstream.

hormones chemical messengers that are manufactured by the endocrine glands, travel through the bloodstream, and affect other tissues.

adrenal [ah-DREEN-el] **glands** a pair of endocrine glands that sit just above the kidneys and secrete hormones (epinephrine and norepinephrine) that help arouse the body in times of stress.

The endocrine glands' control center is the **pituitary gland**. This pea-sized structure, located in the brain's core, is controlled by a nearby brain area, the *hypothalamus* (more on that shortly). The pituitary releases a number of hormones. One is a growth hormone that stimulates physical development. Another is *oxytocin,* which enables contractions during birthing, milk flow in nursing, and orgasm. Oxytocin also promotes social bonding (De Dreu et al., 2010; Marsh et al., 2017; Pfundmair et al., 2017).

Pituitary secretions also direct other endocrine glands to release their hormones. The pituitary, then, is a *master gland* (whose own master is the hypothalamus). For example, under the brain's influence, the pituitary triggers your sex glands to release sex hormones. These in turn influence your brain and behavior.

This feedback system (brain → pituitary → other glands → hormones → body and brain) reveals the interplay between the nervous and endocrine systems. The nervous system directs endocrine secretions, which then affect the nervous system. In charge of this whole electrochemical orchestra is that flexible master conductor we call the brain.

IN YOUR EVERYDAY LIFE

Do you remember feeling the lingering effects of a hormonal response, such as anger, after some particularly aggravating event? How did it feel? How long did it last?

RETRIEVE & REMEMBER

ANSWERS IN APPENDIX E

8. Why is the pituitary gland called the "master gland"?
9. How are the nervous and endocrine systems alike, and how do they differ?

The Brain

When you think *about* your brain, you're thinking *with* your brain—by releasing billions of neurotransmitter molecules across trillions of synapses. Indeed, say neuroscientists, *the mind is what the brain does.*

TOOLS OF DISCOVERY—HAVING OUR HEAD EXAMINED

LOQ 2-7 What are some techniques for studying the brain?

For most of human history, we had no device high-powered yet gentle enough to reveal a living brain's activity. In the past, brain injuries provided clues to brain-mind connections. For example, physicians noted that damage to one side of the brain often caused paralysis on the body's opposite side, and they correctly guessed that the body's right side is wired to the brain's left side, and vice versa. Other early observers linked vision problems with damage to the back of the brain, and speech problems with damage to the left-front brain. Gradually, a map of the brain began to emerge.

Now the human brain has invented new ways to study itself. A new generation of mapmakers is at work charting formerly unknown territory, stimulating various brain parts and watching the results. Some use microelectrodes to snoop on the messages of individual neurons (Ishiyama & Brecht, 2017).

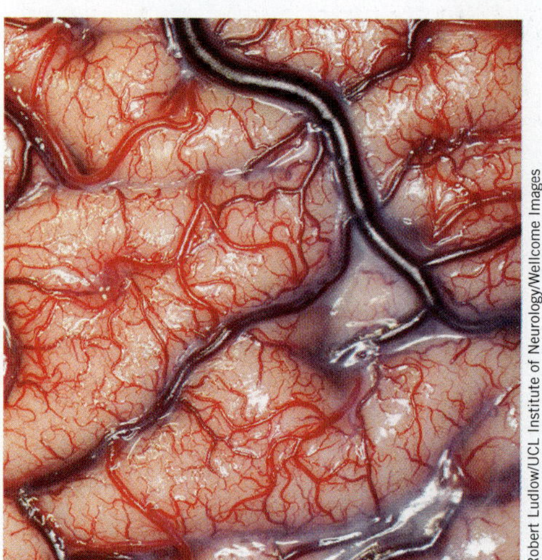

Robert Ludlow/UCL Institute of Neurology/Wellcome Images

A living human brain exposed Today's neuroscience tools enable us to "look under the hood" and glimpse the brain at work, enabling the mind.

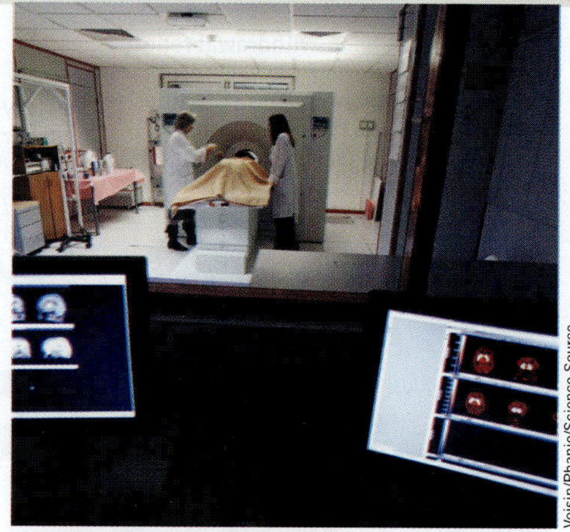

Voisin/Phanie/Science Source

FIGURE 2.9 The PET scan To obtain a PET scan, researchers inject volunteers with a low and harmless dose of a short-lived radioactive sugar. Detectors around the person's head pick up the release of gamma rays from the sugar, which has concentrated in active brain areas. A computer then processes and translates these signals into a map of the brain at work.

Some attach larger electrodes to the scalp to eavesdrop with an **EEG (electroencephalograph)** on the chatter of billions of neurons. Some use **MEG (magnetoencephalography)** to observe how certain tasks influence brain activity (Uhlhaas et al., 2018).

Others use scans that peer into the thinking, feeling brain and give us a Superman-like ability to see what's happening. The **PET (positron emission tomography) scan** tracks a temporarily radioactive form of the sugar glucose. Your brain accounts for only about 2 percent of your body weight. But this control center—the heart of your smarts—uses 20 percent of your body's energy. Because active neurons gobble glucose, a PET scan can track the radioactivity and detect where this "food for thought" goes. Rather like weather radar showing rain activity, PET-scan "hot spots" show which brain areas are most active as the person solves math problems, looks at images of faces, or daydreams (**FIGURE 2.9**).

MRI (magnetic resonance imaging) scans capture images of brain structures by briefly disrupting activity in brain molecules. Researchers first position the person's head in a strong magnetic field, which aligns the spinning atoms of brain

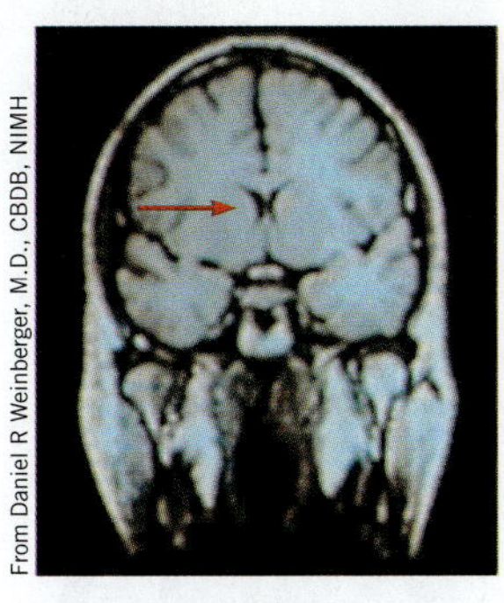
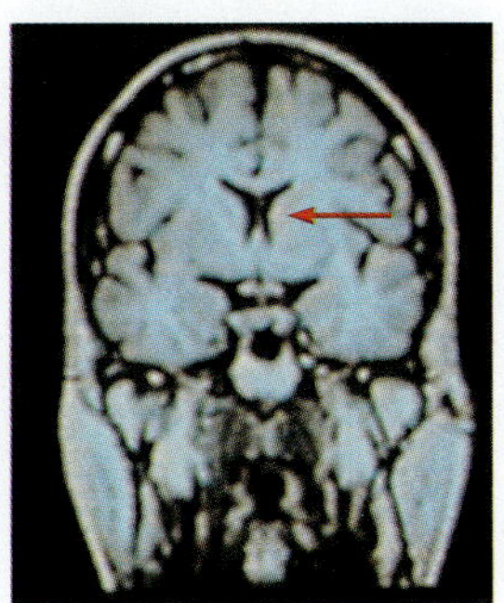

From Daniel R Weinberger, M.D., CBDB, NIMH

(a) (b)

FIGURE 2.10 MRI scan of a healthy individual (a) and a person with schizophrenia (b) Note the enlarged ventricle—the fluid-filled brain region at the tip of the arrow—in the brain of the person with schizophrenia (b).

molecules. Then, with a brief pulse of radio waves, they disrupt the spinning. When the atoms return to their normal spin, they give off signals that provide a detailed picture of soft tissues, including the brain. MRI scans have revealed, for example, that some people with schizophrenia, a disabling psychological disorder, have enlarged fluid-filled brain areas (**FIGURE 2.10**).

A special application of MRI, **fMRI (functional MRI)**, also reveals the brain's *functions* (see **TABLE 2.2** to compare these imaging techniques). Where the brain is especially active, blood goes. By comparing MRI scans taken less than a second apart, researchers can watch parts of the brain activate as a person thinks or acts in certain ways. As the person looks at a photo, for example, the fMRI shows blood rushing to the back of the brain, which processes visual information. This technology enables a very crude sort of mind reading. Neuroscientists scanned 129 people's brains as they did eight different mental tasks (such as reading, gambling, and rhyming). Later, viewing another person's brain images, they were able, with 80 percent accuracy, to identify which of these mental tasks the person was doing (Poldrack et al., 2009).

What the telescope did for astronomy, these brain-snooping tools are doing for psychology. By revealing how the living, working brain divides its labor, these tools have taught us more about the brain in the past 30 years than we had learned in the prior 30,000 years. Around the world, researchers are unlocking the mysteries of how our brain uses electrical and chemical processes to take in, organize, interpret, store, and use information. One giant study, the $40 million Human Connectome Project, is mapping long-distance brain fiber connections in search of "what makes us uniquely human and what makes every person different from all others" (2013; Gorman, 2014; Smith et al., 2015). Such efforts have led to the creation of a new brain map with 100 neural centers not previously described (Glasser et al., 2016). To be learning

pituitary gland the most influential endocrine gland. Under the influence of the hypothalamus, the pituitary regulates growth and controls other endocrine glands.

EEG (electroencephalograph) a device that uses electrodes placed on the scalp to record waves of electrical activity sweeping across the brain's surface. (The record of those brain waves is an *electroencephalogram.*)

MEG (magnetoencephalography) a brain-imaging technique that measures magnetic fields from the brain's natural electrical activity.

PET (positron emission tomography) scan a view of brain activity showing where a radioactive form of glucose goes while the brain performs a given task.

MRI (magnetic resonance imaging) a technique that uses magnetic fields and radio waves to produce computer-generated images of soft tissue. MRI scans show brain anatomy.

fMRI (functional MRI) a technique for revealing blood flow and, therefore, brain activity by comparing successive MRI scans. fMRI scans show brain function.

TABLE 2.2 Types of Neural Measures

Name	How Does It Work?	Sample finding
EEG (Electroencephalogram)	Electrodes placed on the scalp measure electrical activity in neurons.	Symptoms of depression and anxiety correlate with increased activity in the right frontal lobe, a brain area associated with behavioral withdrawal and negative emotion (Thibodeau et al., 2006).
MEG (Magnetoencephalography)	A head coil records magnetic fields from the brain's natural electrical currents.	Soldiers with posttraumatic stress disorder (PTSD), compared with those who do not have PTSD, show stronger magnetic fields in the visual cortex when they view trauma-related images (Todd et al., 2015).
PET (Positron emission tomography)	Tracks where a temporarily radioactive form of glucose goes while the brain of the person given it performs a task.	Monkeys with an anxious temperament have brains that use more glucose in regions related to fear, memory, and expectations of reward and punishment (Fox et al., 2015).
MRI (Magnetic resonance imaging)	People sit or lie down in a chamber that uses magnetic fields and radio waves to provide a map of brain structure.	People with a history of violence tend to have smaller frontal lobes, especially in regions that aid moral judgment and self-control (Glenn & Raine, 2014).
fMRI (Functional magnetic resonance imaging)	Measures blood flow to brain regions by comparing continuous MRI scans.	Years after surviving a near plane crash, passengers who viewed material related to their trauma showed greater activation in the brain's fear, memory, and visual centers than when they watched footage related to the 9/11 terrorist attacks (Palombo et al., 2015).

RETRIEVE & REMEMBER

ANSWERS IN APPENDIX E

10. Match the scanning technique (i–iii) with the correct description (a–c).

Technique:	Description:
i. fMRI scan	a. tracks radioactive glucose to reveal brain *activity*.
ii. PET scan	b. tracks successive images of brain tissue to show brain *function*.
iii. MRI scan	c. uses magnetic fields and radio waves to show brain *anatomy*.

about the brain now is like studying geography while the early explorers were mapping the world.

OLDER BRAIN STRUCTURES

Brain structures determine our abilities. In sharks and other primitive vertebrates (animals with backbones), a not-so-complex brain mainly handles basic survival functions: breathing, resting, and feeding. In lower mammals, such as rodents, a more complex brain enables emotion and greater memory. In advanced mammals, such as humans, a brain that processes more information also enables the ability to plan ahead.

The brain's increasing complexity arises from new systems built on top of the old, much as new layers cover old ones in Earth's landscape. Digging down, one discovers the fossil remnants of the past—brainstem components performing for us much as they did for our distant ancestors. Let's start with the brain's base and work up.

The Brainstem

LOQ 2-8 What structures make up the brainstem, and what are the functions of the brainstem, thalamus, reticular formation, and cerebellum?

The **brainstem** is the brain's oldest and innermost region. Its base is the **medulla**, the slight swelling in the spinal cord just after it enters the skull (**FIGURE 2.11**). Here lie the controls for your heartbeat and breathing. Just above the medulla sits the *pons*, which helps coordinate movements and control sleep.

imageBROKER/Alamy

As some severely brain-damaged patients illustrate, we need no higher brain or conscious mind to orchestrate our heart's pumping and our lungs' breathing. The brainstem handles those tasks. If a cat's brainstem is severed from the rest of the brain above it, the animal will still live and breathe. It will even run, climb, and groom (Klemm, 1990). But cut off from the brain's higher regions, it won't *purposefully* run or climb to get food.

The brainstem is a crossover point. Here, you'll find a peculiar sort of cross-wiring, with most nerves to and from each side of the brain connecting to the body's opposite side. Thus, the right brain controls the left side of the body, and vice versa (**FIGURE 2.12**). This cross-wiring is one of the brain's many surprises.

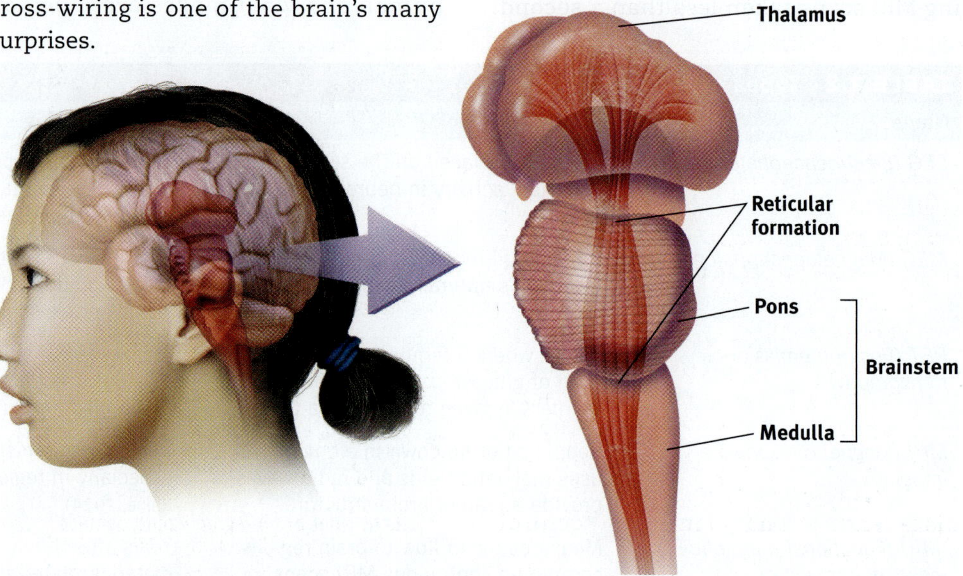

FIGURE 2.11 The brainstem and thalamus The brainstem, including the pons and medulla, is an extension of the spinal cord. The thalamus is attached to the top of the brainstem. The reticular formation passes through both structures.

RETRIEVE & REMEMBER

ANSWERS IN APPENDIX E

11. The ________ is a crossover point where nerves from the left side of the brain are mostly linked to the right side of the body, and vice versa.

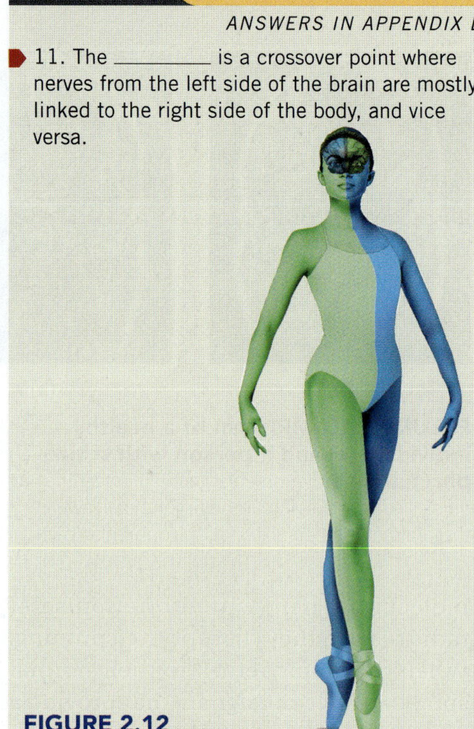

FIGURE 2.12 The body's wiring

Andrew Swift

The Thalamus

Sitting at the top of the brainstem is the **thalamus**, which acts as the brain's sensory control center. This joined pair of egg-shaped structures receives information from all your senses except smell. It then forwards those messages to their final destination in other brain regions that deal with seeing, hearing, tasting, and touching. Your thalamus also receives some higher brain regions' replies, which it forwards to your medulla and cerebellum for processing. Think of the thalamus as being to sensory information what London is to England's trains: a hub through which traffic passes on its way to various destinations.

The Reticular Formation

Inside the brainstem, between your ears, lies your **reticular** ("netlike") **formation**. This nerve network extends upward from your spinal cord, through your brainstem, and into your thalamus (see Figure 2.11). As sensory messages travel from your spinal cord to your thalamus, this long structure acts as a filter, relaying important information to other brain areas. Have you multitasked today? You can thank your reticular formation (Wimmer et al., 2015).

The reticular formation also controls arousal, as researchers discovered in 1949. Electrically stimulating the reticular formation of a sleeping cat almost instantly produced an awake, alert animal (Moruzzi & Magoun, 1949). When a cat's reticular formation was cut off from higher brain regions, without damaging nearby sensory pathways, the effect was equally dramatic. The cat lapsed into a coma and never woke up.

The Cerebellum

At the rear of the brainstem is the **cerebellum**, meaning "little brain," which is what its two wrinkled halves resemble **(FIGURE 2.13)**. This baseball-sized structure plays an important role in a lot that happens just outside your awareness. Quickly answer these questions. How long have you been reading this text? Does your clothing feel soft or rough against your skin? How's your mood today? If you answered easily, thank your cerebellum. It helps you judge time, discriminate textures and sounds, and control your emotions (Bower & Parsons, 2003). It aids your vocabulary, reading, and ability to store information (Moore et al., 2017). Your cerebellum also coordinates voluntary movement. When a soccer player masterfully controls the ball, give the cerebellum some credit. If you injured your cerebellum or drugged it with alcohol, you would have trouble walking, keeping your balance, or shaking hands. The cerebellum also helps process and store memories for things you cannot consciously recall, such as how to ride a bicycle. (Stay tuned for more about memory storage in Chapter 7.)

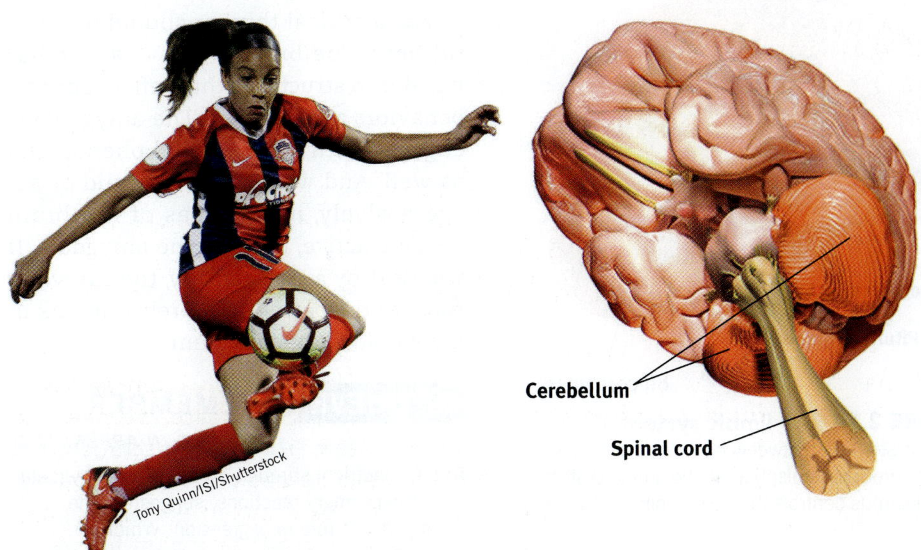

FIGURE 2.13 The brain's organ of agility Hanging at the back of the brain, the cerebellum coordinates our voluntary movements, as when USA women's soccer player Mallory Pugh controls the ball.

* * *

Note: These older brain functions all occur without any conscious effort. This illustrates one of our recurring themes: *Our two-track brain processes most information outside of our awareness.* We are aware of the *results* of our brain's labor (say, our current visual experience) but not of *how* we construct the visual image. Likewise, whether we are asleep or awake, our brainstem manages its life-sustaining functions, freeing our newer brain regions to think, talk, dream, or savor a memory.

RETRIEVE & REMEMBER

ANSWERS IN APPENDIX E

12. In what brain region would damage be most likely to (a) disrupt your ability to jump rope? (b) disrupt your ability to hear? (c) leave you in a coma? (d) cut off the very breath and heartbeat of life?

THE LIMBIC SYSTEM

LOQ 2-9 What are the structures and functions of the limbic system?

We've traveled through the brain's oldest parts, but we've not yet reached its newest and highest regions, the *cerebral hemispheres* (the two halves of the brain).

brainstem the oldest part and central core of the brain, beginning where the spinal cord swells as it enters the skull; responsible for automatic survival functions.

medulla [muh-DUL-uh] the base of the brainstem; controls heartbeat and breathing.

thalamus [THAL-uh-muss] the brain's sensory control center, located on top of the brainstem; directs sensory messages to the cortex and transmits replies to the cerebellum and medulla.

reticular formation nerve network running through the brainstem and into the thalamus; plays an important role in controlling arousal.

cerebellum [sehr-uh-BELL-um] the "little brain" at the rear of the brainstem; functions include processing sensory input, coordinating movement output and balance, and enabling nonverbal learning and memory.

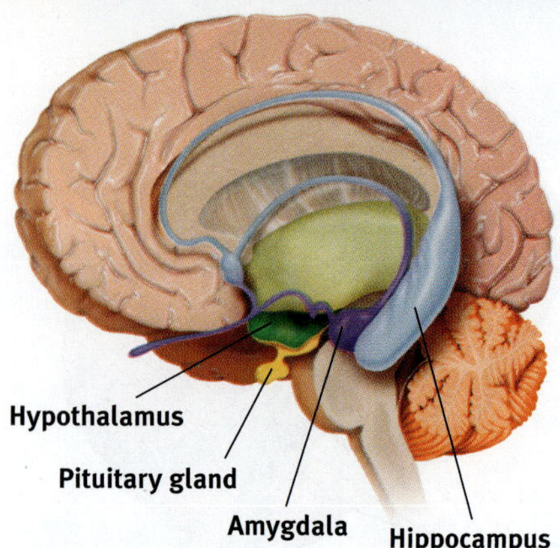

FIGURE 2.14 The limbic system This neural system sits between the brain's older parts and its cerebral hemispheres. The limbic system's hypothalamus controls the nearby pituitary gland.

Before we do, we must pass the **limbic system**, which lies between the oldest and newest brain areas (*limbus* means "border"). The limbic system contains the *amygdala*, the *hypothalamus*, and the *hippocampus* (**FIGURE 2.14**).

The Amygdala

The **amygdala**—two lima-bean-sized neural clusters—enables aggression and fear. In 1939, researchers surgically removed a rhesus monkey's amygdala, turning the normally ill-tempered animal into the most mellow of creatures (Klüver & Bucy, 1939).

What, then, might happen if we electrically stimulated the amygdala of a normally mellow domestic animal, such as a cat? Do so in one spot and the cat prepares to attack, hissing with its back arched, its pupils wide, its hair on end. Move the electrode only slightly within the amygdala, cage the cat with a small mouse, and now it cowers in terror.

Many experiments have confirmed the amygdala's role in processing emotions and perceiving rage and fear. Monkeys and humans with amygdala damage become less fearful of strangers (Harrison et al., 2015). After her amygdala was destroyed by a rare genetic disease, one woman no longer experienced fear. Facing a snake, speaking in public, even being threatened with a gun—she's not afraid (Feinstein et al., 2013).

But a critical thinker should be careful here. The brain is not neatly organized into structures that reflect specific behaviors and feelings. The amygdala is engaged with other mental phenomena as well. And when we feel afraid or act aggressively, many areas of our brain become active, not just the amygdala. If you destroy a car's battery, the car won't run. Yet the battery is merely one link in the whole working system.

RETRIEVE & REMEMBER

ANSWERS IN APPENDIX E

13. Electrical stimulation of a cat's amygdala provokes angry reactions, suggesting the amygdala's role in aggression. Which *autonomic nervous system* division is activated by such stimulation?

The Hypothalamus

Just below *(hypo)* your thalamus is your **hypothalamus**, an important link in the command chain that helps your body maintain a steady internal state. Some neural clusters in the hypothalamus influence hunger. Others regulate thirst, body temperature, and sexual behavior.

To monitor your body state, the hypothalamus tunes in to your blood chemistry and any incoming orders from other brain parts. For example, picking up signals from your brain's information-processing center, the *cerebral cortex*, that you are thinking about sex, your hypothalamus will secrete hormones. These hormones will in turn trigger the nearby "master" gland of the endocrine system, your pituitary (see Figure 2.14), to influence your sex glands to release *their* hormones. These hormones will intensify the thoughts of sex in your cerebral cortex. (Note the interplay between the nervous and endocrine systems: The brain influences the endocrine system, which in turn influences the brain.)

A remarkable discovery about the hypothalamus illustrates how progress in science often occurs—when curious, smart-thinking investigators keep an open mind. Two young psychologists, James Olds and Peter Milner (1954), were trying to implant an electrode in a rat's reticular formation when they made a magnificent mistake. They placed the electrode incorrectly (Olds, 1975). Curiously, the rat, as though seeking more stimulation, kept returning to the location where it had been stimulated by this misplaced electrode. When Olds and Milner discovered that they had actually placed the device in a region of the hypothalamus, they realized they had stumbled upon a brain center that provides pleasurable rewards. In later studies, rats allowed to control their own stimulation in this and other *reward centers* in the brain did so at a feverish pace—pressing a pedal up to 1000 times an hour, until they dropped from exhaustion.

Animal researchers have discovered similar reward centers in or near the hypothalamus in goldfish, dolphins, monkeys, and other species (Hamid et al., 2016). One general reward system triggers the release of the neurotransmitter dopamine. Specific centers help us enjoy the pleasures of eating, drinking, and sex. Animals, it seems, come equipped with built-in systems that reward activities essential to survival.

Do we humans also have limbic centers for pleasure? Some evidence indicates we do. When we meet likeable people, our brain bursts with reward center activity (Zerubavel et al., 2018). Stimulating reward centers can also calm the cruelest individuals. But as one neurosurgeon found when implanting electrodes in violent patients' limbic system areas, the patients reported only mild pleasure. Unlike Olds and Milner's rats, the human patients were not driven to a frenzy (Deutsch, 1972; Hooper & Teresi, 1986). And some studies reveal that stimulating the human brain's reward circuits may trigger more *desire* than pure enjoyment (Kringelbach & Berridge, 2012).

The Hippocampus

The **hippocampus**—a seahorse-shaped brain structure—processes conscious, *explicit* memories of facts and events. Healthy hippocampal development

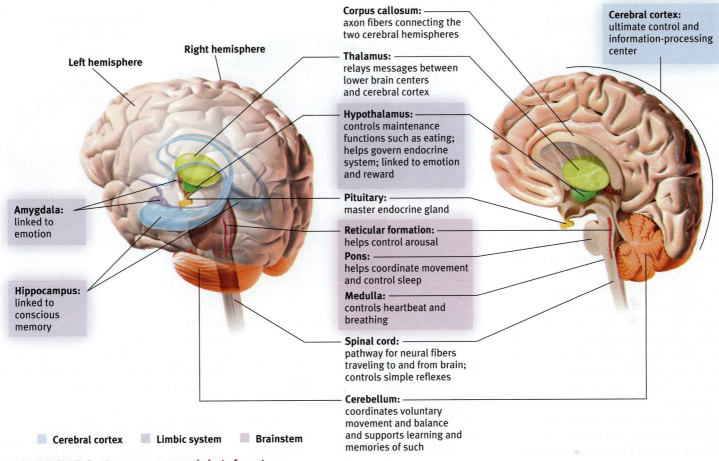

Left hemisphere

Right hemisphere

Corpus callosum: axon fibers connecting the two cerebral hemispheres

Cerebral cortex: ultimate control and information-processing center

Thalamus: relays messages between lower brain centers and cerebral cortex

Hypothalamus: controls maintenance functions such as eating; helps govern endocrine system; linked to emotion and reward

Amygdala: linked to emotion

Pituitary: master endocrine gland

Reticular formation: helps control arousal

Pons: helps coordinate movement and control sleep

Medulla: controls heartbeat and breathing

Hippocampus: linked to conscious memory

Spinal cord: pathway for neural fibers traveling to and from brain; controls simple reflexes

Cerebellum: coordinates voluntary movement and balance and supports learning and memories of such

Cerebral cortex   Limbic system   Brainstem

FIGURE 2.15 Brain structures and their functions

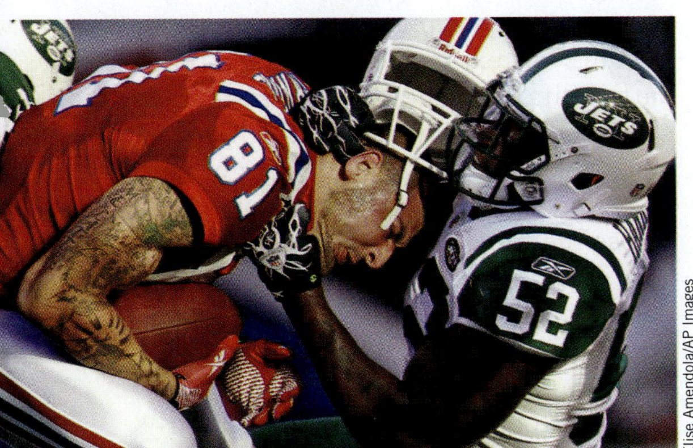

Elise Amendola/AP Images

Has professional football damaged players' brains? When researchers analyzed the brains of 111 deceased National Football League players, 99 percent showed signs of degeneration related to frequent head trauma (Mez et al., 2017). In 2017, NFL player Aaron Hernandez (#81) died by suicide while imprisoned for murder. An autopsy demonstrated that his brain, at age 27, was already showing advanced degeneration (Kilgore, 2017). Will today's more protective gear and rules protect players' brains?

predicts better academic achievement (Wilkey et al., 2018). Humans who lose their hippocampus to surgery or injury lose their ability to form new memories of facts and events (Clark & Maguire, 2016). Children who survive a hippocampal brain tumor will later struggle to remember new information (Jayakar et al., 2015). Birds with a damaged hippocampus will be unable to recall where they buried seeds (Kamil & Cheng, 2001; Sherry & Vaccarino, 1989). National Football League players who experience one or more loss-of-consciousness concussions may later have a shrunken hippocampus and poor memory (Strain et al., 2015).

Later in this chapter, we'll see how the hippocampus helps store the day's experiences while we sleep. In Chapter 7, we'll explore how the hippocampus interacts with our frontal lobes to create our conscious memory.

* * *

FIGURE 2.15 locates the brain areas we've discussed—as well as the cerebral cortex, our final stop on our journey through the brain.

limbic system neural system (including the *amygdala, hypothalamus,* and *hippocampus*) located below the cerebral hemispheres; associated with emotions and drives.

amygdala [uh-MIG-duh-la] two lima-bean-sized neural clusters in the limbic system; linked to emotion.

hypothalamus [hi-po-THAL-uh-muss] a neural structure lying below (*hypo*) the thalamus; directs several maintenance activities (eating, drinking, body temperature), helps govern the endocrine system via the pituitary gland, and is linked to emotion and reward.

hippocampus a neural center located in the limbic system; helps process for storage explicit (conscious) memories of facts and events.

RETRIEVE & REMEMBER

ANSWERS IN APPENDIX E

14. What are the three key structures of the limbic system, and what functions do they serve?

LaunchPad To review and assess your understanding, engage online with *Concept Practice: The Limbic System.*

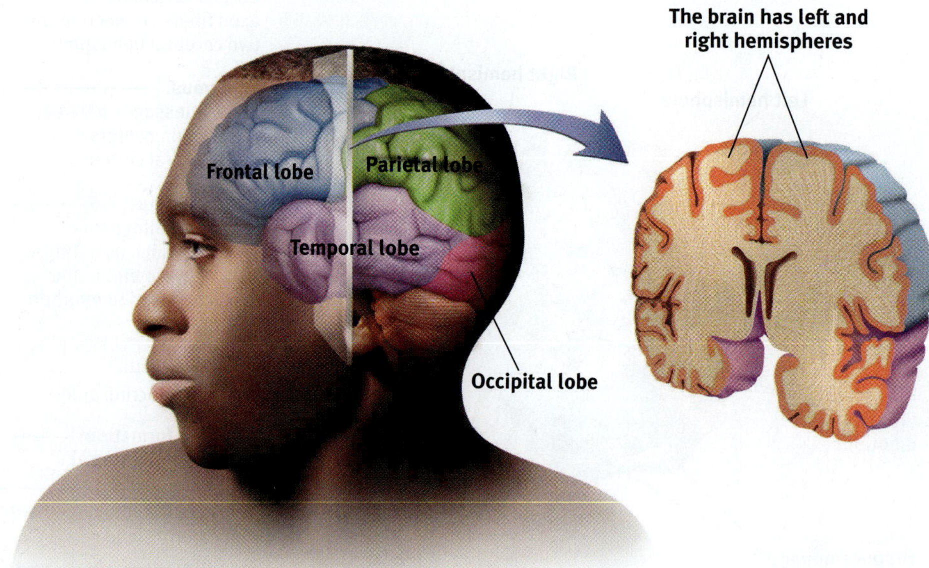

FIGURE 2.16 The cortex and its basic subdivisions

THE CEREBRAL CORTEX

Older brain networks sustain basic life functions and enable memory, emotions, and basic drives. High above these older structures is the *cerebrum*—two large hemispheres that contribute 85 percent of the brain's weight. Covering those hemispheres, like bark on a tree, is the **cerebral cortex**, a thin surface layer of interconnected neurons. In our brain's evolutionary history, the cerebral cortex is a relative newcomer. Its newer neural networks form specialized work teams that enable your thinking, sensing, and speaking. The cerebral cortex is your brain's thinking crown, your body's ultimate control and information-processing center.

Structure of the Cortex

LOQ 2-10 What are the four lobes of the cerebral cortex, and where are they located?

If you opened a human skull, exposing the brain, you would see a wrinkled organ, shaped somewhat like an oversized walnut. Without these wrinkles, a flattened cerebral cortex would require triple the area—roughly that of a large pizza. The brain's left and right hemispheres are filled mainly with axons connecting the cortex to the brain's other regions. The cerebral cortex—that thin surface layer—contains some 20 to 23 billion nerve cells and 300 trillion synaptic connections (de Courten-Myers, 2005). Being human takes a lot of nerve.

Each hemisphere's cortex is subdivided into four *lobes*, separated by deep folds (**FIGURE 2.16**). You can roughly trace the four lobes, starting with both hands on your forehead. The **frontal lobes** lie directly behind your forehead. As you move your hands over the top of your head, toward the rear, you're sliding over your **parietal lobes**. Continuing to move down, toward the back of your head, you'll slide over your **occipital lobes**. Now move each hand forward, to the sides of your head, and just above each ear you'll find your **temporal lobes.** Each hemisphere has these four lobes. Each lobe carries out many functions. And many functions require the cooperation of several lobes.

Functions of the Cortex

LOQ 2-11 What are the functions of the motor cortex, somatosensory cortex, and association areas?

More than a century ago, surgeons found damaged areas of the cerebral cortex during autopsies of people who had been partially paralyzed or speechless. This rather crude evidence was interesting, but it did not prove that *specific* parts of the cortex control complex functions like movement or speech. A laptop with a broken power cord might go dead, but we would be fooling ourselves if we thought we had "localized" the internet in the cord.

Motor Functions Early scientists had better luck showing simple brain-behavior links. In 1870, for example, German physicians Gustav Fritsch and Eduard Hitzig made an important discovery. By electrically stimulating parts of an animal's cortex, they could make other parts of its body move. The movement happened only when they stimulated an arch-shaped region at the back of the frontal lobe, running roughly ear to ear across the top of the brain. Moreover, if they stimulated this region in the left hemisphere, the right leg would move. And if they stimulated part of the right hemisphere, the opposite leg—on the left—reacted. Fritsch and Hitzig had discovered what is now called the **motor cortex**.

Lucky for brain surgeons and their patients, the brain has no sensory receptors. Knowing this, in the 1930s, Otfrid Foerster and Wilder Penfield were able to map the motor cortex in hundreds of wide-awake patients by stimulating different cortical areas and observing the body's responses. They discovered that

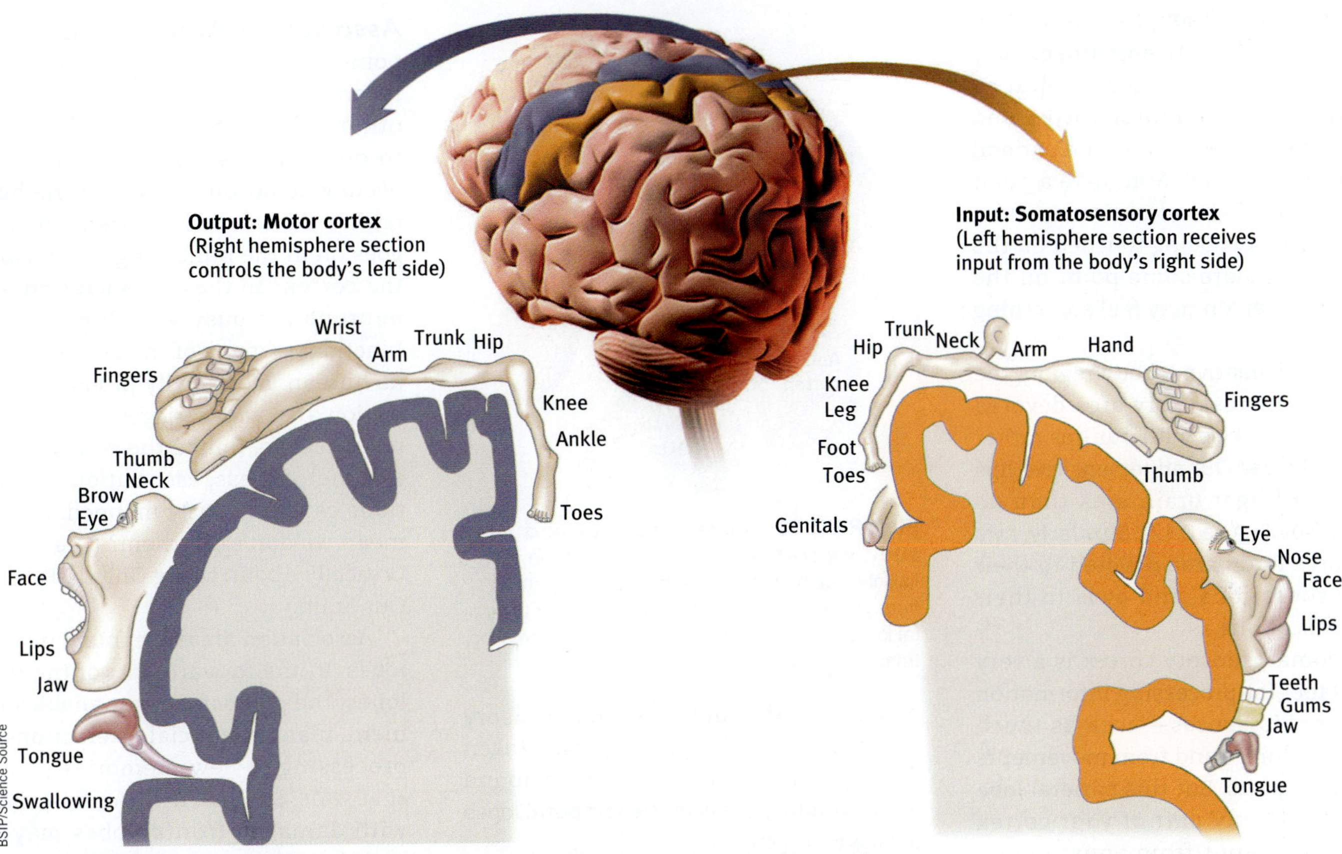

FIGURE 2.17 Motor cortex and somatosensory cortex tissue devoted to each body part As you can see from this classic though inexact representation, the amount of cortex devoted to a body part in the motor cortex (in the frontal lobes) or in the somatosensory cortex (in the parietal lobes) is not proportional to that body part's size. Rather, the brain devotes more tissue to sensitive areas and to areas requiring precise control. So, your fingers have a greater representation in the cortex than does your upper arm.

body areas requiring precise control, such as the fingers and mouth, occupied the greatest amount of cortical space (**FIGURE 2.17**).

As is so often the case in science, new answers have triggered new questions. Might electrodes implanted in the motor cortex identify what neurons control specific activities? If so, could people learn to mentally control these implanted devices, perhaps to direct a robotic limb? Clinical trials are now under way with people who have severe paralysis or have lost a limb (Andersen et al., 2010; Nurmikko et al., 2010). Some who received implants have indeed learned to control robotic limbs (Clausen et al., 2017).

RETRIEVE & REMEMBER

ANSWERS IN APPENDIX E

15. Try moving your right hand in a circular motion, as if cleaning a table. Then start your right foot doing the same motion as your hand. Now reverse the right foot's motion, but not the hand's. Finally, try moving the *left* foot opposite to the right hand.

1. Why is reversing the right foot's motion so hard?

2. Why is it easier to move the left foot opposite to the right hand?

Sensory Functions The motor cortex sends messages out to the body. What parts of the cortex receive incoming messages from our senses of touch and

cerebral [seh-REE-bruhl] **cortex** a thin layer of interconnected neurons covering the cerebral hemispheres; the body's ultimate control and information-processing center.

frontal lobes the portion of the cerebral cortex lying just behind the forehead; involved in speaking and muscle movements and in making plans and judgments.

parietal [puh-RYE-uh-tuhl] **lobes** the portion of the cerebral cortex lying at the top of the head and toward the rear; receives sensory input for touch and body position.

occipital [ahk-SIP-uh-tuhl] **lobes** the portion of the cerebral cortex lying at the back of the head; includes areas that receive information from the visual fields.

temporal lobes the portion of the cerebral cortex lying roughly above the ears; includes areas that receive information from the ears.

motor cortex the cerebral cortex area at the rear of the frontal lobes; controls voluntary movements.

movement? Penfield supplied the answer. An area now called the **somatosensory cortex** receives this sensory input. It runs parallel to the motor cortex and just behind it, at the front of the parietal lobes (see Figure 2.17). Stimulate a point on the top of this band of tissue, and a person may report being touched on the shoulder. Stimulate some point on the side, and the person may feel something on the face.

The more sensitive a body region, the larger the somatosensory area devoted to it. Why do we kiss with our lips rather than rub elbows? Our supersensitive lips project to a larger brain area than do our arms (see Figure 2.17). Similarly, rats have a large brain area devoted to their whisker sensations, and owls to their hearing sensations.

Your somatosensory cortex is a very powerful tool for processing information from your skin senses—such as touch and temperature—and from movements of your body parts. But this parietal lobe area isn't the only part of your cortex that receives input from your senses. After surgeons removed a large tumor from his right *occipital lobe,* in the back of his brain, a friend of mine [DM's] became blind to the left half of his field of vision. Why? Because in an intact brain, visual information travels from the eyes to the *visual cortex,* in the occipital lobes (**FIGURE 2.18**). From your occipital lobes, visual information travels to other areas that specialize in tasks such as identifying words, detecting emotions, and recognizing faces (**FIGURE 2.19**).

If you have normal vision, you might see flashes of light or dashes of color if stimulated in your occipital lobes. (In a sense, we *do* have eyes in the back of our head!)

Any sound you now hear is processed by your *auditory cortex* in your *temporal lobes* (just above your ears; see Figure 2.18). Most of this auditory information travels a roundabout route from one ear to the auditory receiving area above your opposite ear. If stimulated in your auditory cortex, you alone might hear a sound. People with schizophrenia sometimes have auditory **hallucinations** (false sensory experiences). Brain-imaging scans taken during these hallucinations have found active auditory areas in the temporal lobes (Lennox et al., 1999).

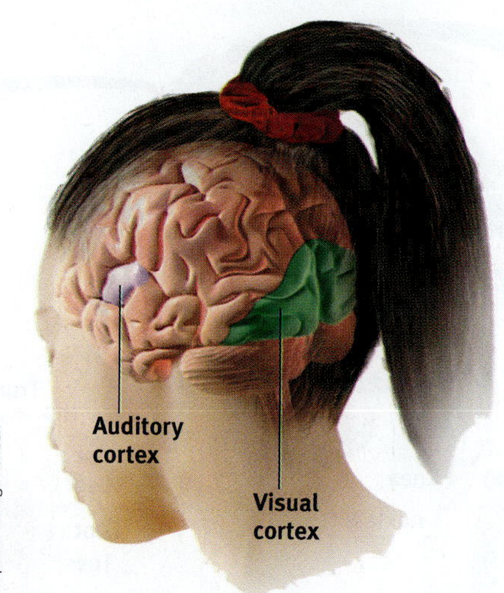

FIGURE 2.18 The visual cortex and auditory cortex The visual cortex in the occipital lobes at the rear of your brain receives input from your eyes. The auditory cortex in your temporal lobes—above your ears—receives information from your ears.

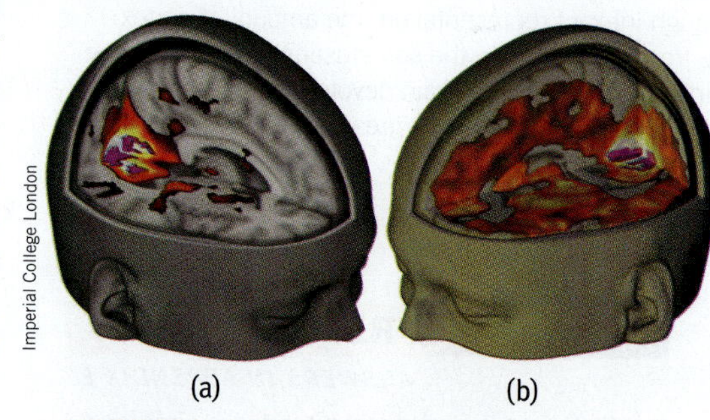

FIGURE 2.19 Seeing without eyes The psychoactive drug LSD often produces vivid *hallucinations.* Why? It dramatically increases communication between the visual cortex (in the occipital lobe) and other brain regions. (a) This fMRI (functional MRI) scan shows a research participant with closed eyes who has been given a placebo. (b) In this fMRI, the same person is under the influence of LSD (color represents increased blood flow) (Carhart-Harris et al., 2016; Cormier, 2016).

RETRIEVE & REMEMBER

ANSWERS IN APPENDIX E

16. Our brain's ________ cortex registers and processes body touch and movement sensations. The ________ cortex controls our voluntary movements.

Association Areas So far, we have pointed out small areas of the cortex that receive messages from our senses, and other small areas that send messages to our muscles. Together, these areas occupy about one-fourth of the human brain's thin, wrinkled cover. What, then, goes on in the remaining vast regions of the cortex? In these **association areas**, neurons are busy with higher mental functions—many of the tasks that make us human. Electrically probing an association area won't trigger any observable response. So, unlike the somatosensory and motor areas, association area functions can't be neatly mapped. Does this mean we don't use them? (See Thinking Critically About: Using Only 10 Percent of Our Brain.)

Association areas are found in all four lobes. In the forward part of the frontal lobes, the *prefrontal cortex* enables judgment, planning, social interactions, and processing of new memories (de la Vega et al., 2016; Silwa & Frehwald, 2017). People with damaged frontal lobes may have high intelligence test scores and great cake-baking skills. Yet they would not be able to plan ahead to *begin* baking a cake for a birthday party (Huey et al., 2006). And if they did begin to bake, they might forget the recipe (MacPherson et al., 2016).

Frontal lobe damage can alter personality, as it did in the famous case of railroad worker Phineas Gage. One afternoon in 1848, Gage, then 25 years old, was using an iron rod to pack gunpowder into a rock. A spark ignited the gunpowder, shooting the rod up through his left cheek and out the top of his skull, causing massive damage to his frontal lobes (**FIGURE 2.20a**). To everyone's amazement, he was immediately able to sit up and speak. After the wound healed, he returned to work. But friendly, soft-spoken Gage was now irritable, profane, and dishonest. The accident had destroyed frontal lobe areas that enable control over emotions (Van Horn et al., 2012). This person, said his friends, was "no longer Gage." His mental abilities and memories were unharmed, but for the next few years, his personality was not.

Thinking Critically About:

Using Only 10 Percent of Our Brain

LOQ 2-12 Do we really use only 10 percent of our brain?

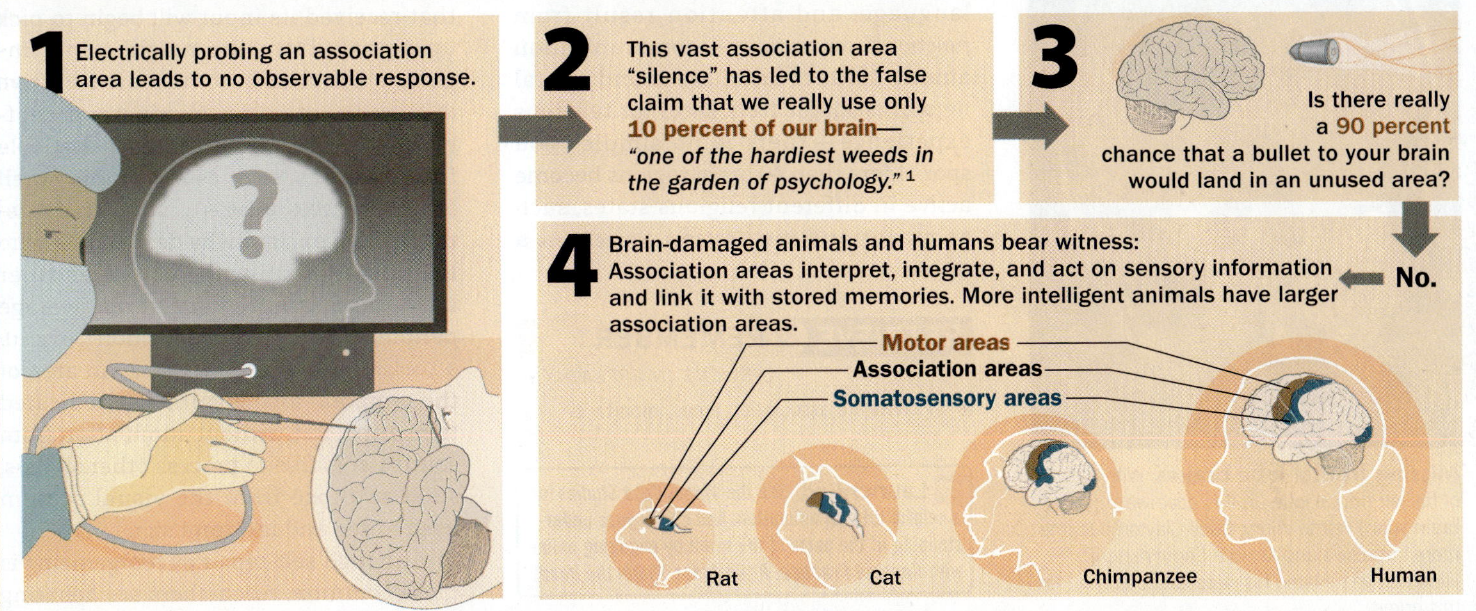

1 Electrically probing an association area leads to no observable response.
2 This vast association area "silence" has led to the false claim that we really use only 10 percent of our brain—"one of the hardiest weeds in the garden of psychology."[1]
3 Is there really a 90 percent chance that a bullet to your brain would land in an unused area?
No.
4 Brain-damaged animals and humans bear witness: Association areas interpret, integrate, and act on sensory information and link it with stored memories. More intelligent animals have larger association areas.
Motor areas
Association areas
Somatosensory areas
Rat
Cat
Chimpanzee
Human

1. McBurney, 1996, p. 44

(Gage later lost his railroad job, but over time he adapted to his injury and found work as a stagecoach driver [Macmillan & Lena, 2010].)

Without the frontal lobe brakes on his impulses, Gage became less inhibited. When his frontal lobes ruptured, his moral compass seemed to disconnect from his behavior. Studies of others with damaged frontal lobes reveal similar losses — their moral judgments seem untouched by normal emotions. Would you agree with the idea of pushing someone in front of a runaway train to save five others? Most people would not, but those with damage to the frontal lobe often do (Koenigs et al., 2007). The frontal lobes help steer us away from violent actions (Molenberghs et al., 2015; Yang & Raine, 2009). In 1972, Cecil Clayton

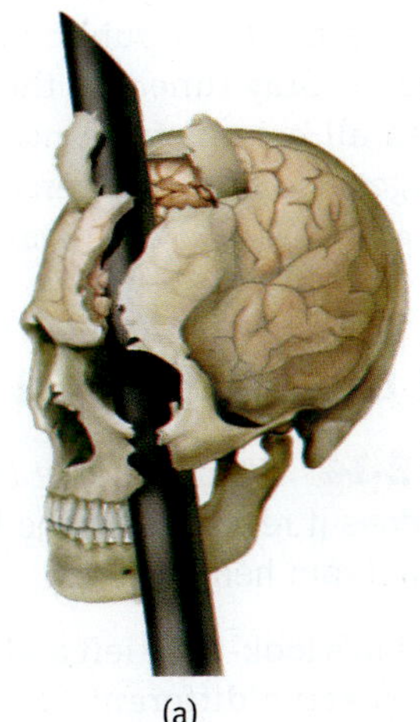

(a)

Warren Anatomical Museum in the Francis A. Countway Library of Medicine. Gift of Jack and Beverly Wilgus

(b)

FIGURE 2.20 A blast from the past (a) Phineas Gage's skull was kept as a medical record. Using measurements and modern neuroimaging techniques, researchers have reconstructed the probable path of the rod through Gage's brain (Van Horn et al., 2012). (b) This photo shows Gage after his accident. (The image has been reversed to show the features correctly. Early photos, including this one, were actually mirror images.)

somatosensory cortex the cerebral cortex area at the front of the parietal lobes; registers and processes body touch and movement sensations.

hallucination a false sensory experience, such as hearing something in the absence of an external auditory stimulus.

association areas cerebral cortex areas involved primarily in higher mental functions, such as learning, remembering, thinking, and speaking.

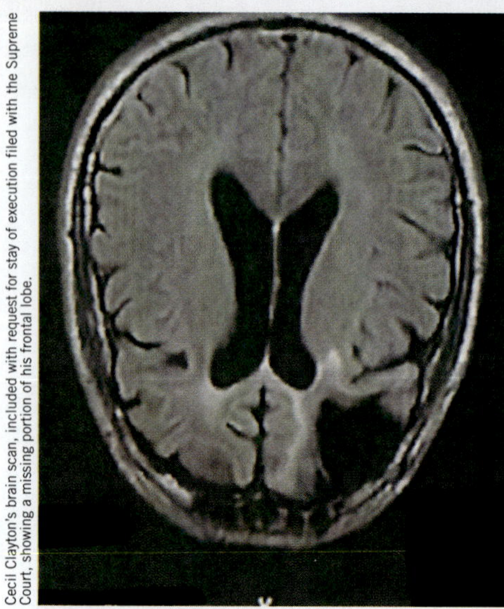

Missing frontal lobe brakes With part of his left frontal lobe (in this downward-facing brain scan) lost to injury, Cecil Clayton became more impulsive and killed a deputy sheriff. Nineteen years later, his state executed him for this crime.

lost 20 percent of his left frontal lobe in a sawmill accident. His intelligence test score dropped to an elementary school level. He became increasingly impulsive. In 1996, he shot and killed a deputy sheriff. In 2015, when he was 74, the State of Missouri executed him (Williams, 2015).

Damage to association areas in other lobes would result in different losses. If a stroke or head injury destroyed part of your parietal lobes, you might lose mathematical and spatial reasoning (Ibos & Freedman, 2014). If the damaged area was on the underside of the right temporal lobe, which lets you recognize faces, you would still be able to describe facial features and to recognize someone's sex and approximate age. Yet you would be strangely unable to identify the person as, say, Ariana Grande, or even your grandmother.

Nevertheless, complex mental functions don't reside in any one spot in your brain. Performing simple tasks may activate tiny patches of your brain, far less than 10 percent. During a complex task, a scan would show many islands of brain activity working together—some running automatically in the background, and others under conscious control (Chein & Schneider, 2012). Memory, language, and attention result from *functional connectivity*—communication among distinct brain areas and neural networks (Knight, 2007). Ditto for religious experience—there is no simple "God spot." More than 40 brain regions become active in different religious states, such as prayer and meditation (Fingelkurts & Fingelkurts, 2009).

RETRIEVE & REMEMBER

ANSWERS IN APPENDIX E

17. Why are association areas important?

LaunchPad See the *Video: Case Studies* for a helpful tutorial animation. And check your understanding of the parts of the brain by engaging online with *Concept Practice: Brain Areas Within the Head.*

RESPONSES TO DAMAGE

LOQ 2-13 How does the brain modify itself after some kinds of damage?

Earlier, we learned about the brain's *plasticity*—how our brain adapts to new situations. What happens when we experience mishaps, big and little? Let's explore the brain's ability to modify itself after damage.

Brain-damage effects were discussed in several places in this chapter. Most can be traced to two hard facts. (1) Severed brain and spinal cord neurons, unlike cut skin, usually do not repair themselves. If a spinal cord is severed, the person will probably be paralyzed permanently. (2) Some brain functions seem forever linked to specific areas. A newborn with damage to facial recognition areas on both temporal lobes was never able to recognize faces (Farah et al., 2000).

But there is good news: The brain often attempts self-repair by *reorganizing* existing tissue. Some brain tissue—especially in a young child's brain—can reorganize even after serious damage (Kolb, 1989) (**FIGURE 2.21**). If a slow-growing left-hemisphere tumor disrupts language, the right hemisphere may take over the task (Thiel et al., 2006). If a finger is lost, the somatosensory cortex that received its input will begin to pick up signals from the neighboring fingers, which then become more sensitive (Oelschläger et al., 2014). Blindness or deafness makes unused brain areas available for other uses, such as sound and smell (Amedi et al., 2005; Bauer et al., 2017). This plasticity helps explain why deaf people who learned sign language before another language may have better-than-average peripheral and motion detection (Bosworth & Dobkins, 1999; Shiell et al., 2014). An area of the temporal lobe is normally dedicated to hearing. But without stimulation from sounds, it is free to process other signals, such as those from the visual system used to see and interpret signs.

Although self-repair by reorganizing is more common, researchers are debating whether the brain can also mend itself through **neurogenesis**—producing new neurons (Boldrini et al., 2018; Sorrells et al., 2018). Researchers have found baby neurons deep in the brains of adult mice, birds, monkeys, and humans (He & Jin, 2016; Jessberger et al., 2008). These neurons may then migrate elsewhere and form connections with neighboring neurons (Aimone et al., 2010; Egeland et al., 2015; Gould, 2007).

Might surgeons someday be able to rebuild damaged brains, much as damaged fields in public parks can be reseeded? Stay tuned. In the meantime, we can all benefit from natural aids to neurogenesis, such as exercise and sleep (Iso et al., 2007; Pereira et al., 2007; Sexton et al., 2016).

THE DIVIDED BRAIN

LOQ 2-14 What is a *split brain*, and what does it reveal about the functions of our two brain hemispheres?

Our brain's look-alike left and right hemispheres serve different functions. This *lateralization* is clear after some types of brain damage. Language processing, for example, seems to reside mostly in your left hemisphere. A left-hemisphere

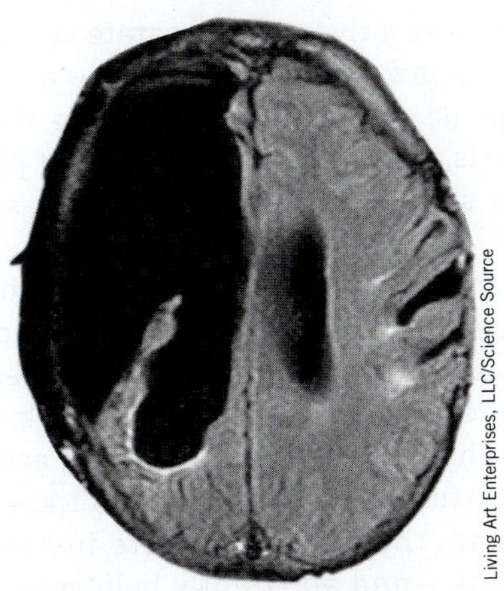
Living Art Enterprises, LLC/Science Source

Joe McNally/Hulton Archive/Getty Images

FIGURE 2.21 Brain work is child's play This 6-year-old had surgery to end her life-threatening seizures. Although most of an entire hemisphere was removed (see MRI of hemispherectomy), her remaining hemisphere compensated by putting other areas to work. One Johns Hopkins medical team reflected on the child hemispherectomies they had performed. Although use of the opposite arm was compromised, the team reported being "awed" by how well the children had retained their memory, personality, and humor (Vining et al., 1997). The younger the child, the greater the chance that the remaining hemisphere can take over the functions of the one that was surgically removed (Choi, 2008; Danelli et al., 2013).

accident, stroke, or tumor could leave you unable to read, write, or speak. You might be unable to reason, do arithmetic, or understand others. Similar right hemisphere damage seldom has such dramatic effects.

Does this mean that the right hemisphere is just along for the ride—a silent junior partner or "minor" hemisphere? Many believed this was the case until 1960, when researchers found that the "minor" right hemisphere was not so limited after all. The unfolding of this discovery is a fascinating chapter in psychology's history.

Splitting the Brain: One Skull, Two Minds

In 1961, two neurosurgeons believed that the uncontrollable seizures of some patients with severe epilepsy was caused by abnormal brain activity bouncing back and forth between the two cerebral hemispheres. If so, they wondered, could they end this biological tennis game by cutting through the **corpus callosum**, the wide band of axon fibers connecting the two hemispheres and carrying messages between them (**FIGURE 2.22**)? The neurosurgeons knew that psychologists Roger Sperry, Ronald Myers, and Michael Gazzaniga had divided cats' and monkeys' brains in this manner, with no serious ill effects.

So the surgeons operated. The result? The seizures all but disappeared. The patients with these **split brains** were surprisingly normal, their personality and intellect hardly affected. Waking from surgery, one even joked that he had a "splitting headache" (Gazzaniga, 1967). By sharing their experiences, these patients have greatly expanded our understanding of interactions between the intact brain's two hemispheres.

To appreciate these studies, we need to focus for a minute on the peculiar nature of our visual wiring, illustrated in **FIGURE 2.23**. Note that each eye receives sensory information from the entire visual field. But information from the left half of your field of vision goes to your right hemisphere, and information from the right half of your visual field goes to your left hemisphere. In an intact brain, data received by either hemisphere are quickly transmitted to the other side, across the corpus callosum.

In a person with a severed corpus callosum, this information sharing does not take place. Because the surgery had cut the communication lines between the patient's two hemispheres, Sperry and Gazzaniga were able to quiz each hemisphere separately. They could send information to the patient's left hemisphere by having the person stare at a dot and

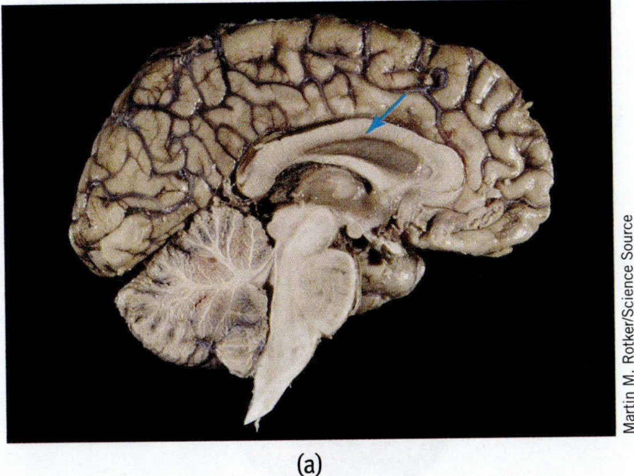
Martin M. Rotker/Science Source

(a)

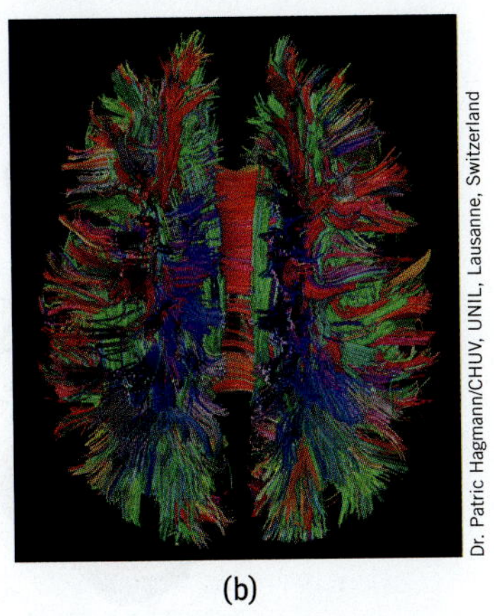
Dr. Patric Hagmann/CHUV, UNIL, Lausanne, Switzerland

(b)

FIGURE 2.22 The corpus callosum This large band of neural fibers connects the two brain hemispheres. (a) To photograph this half brain, a surgeon separated the hemispheres by cutting through the corpus callosum (see blue arrow) and lower brain regions. (b) This high-resolution diffusion spectrum image, showing a top-facing brain from above, reveals brain neural networks within the two hemispheres, and the corpus callosum neural bridge between them.

neurogenesis the formation of new neurons.

corpus callosum [KOR-pus kah-LOW-sum] a large band of neural fibers connecting the two brain hemispheres and carrying messages between them.

split brain a condition resulting from surgery that separates the brain's two hemispheres by cutting the fibers (mainly those of the corpus callosum) connecting them.

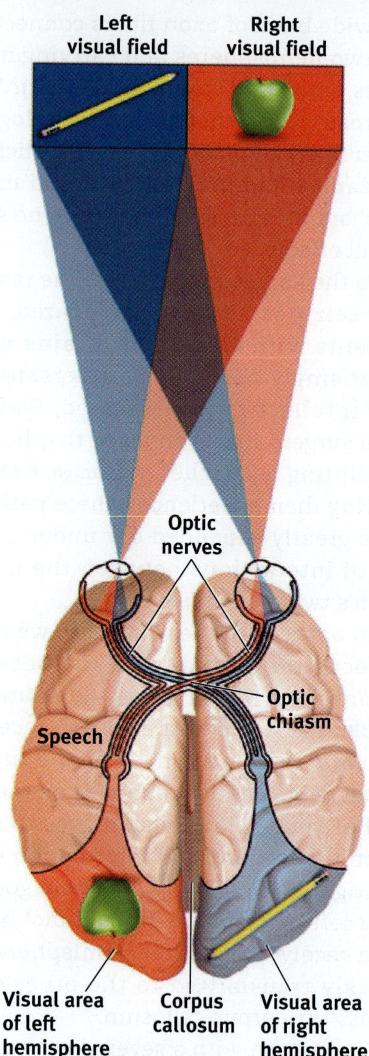

FIGURE 2.23 The information highway from eye to brain

by then flashing a stimulus (a word or photo) to the right of the dot. To send a message to the right hemisphere, they would flash the item to the left of the dot. (If they tried to do this with you, the hemisphere receiving the information would instantly pass the news to the other side of your intact brain.)

In an early experiment, Gazzaniga (1967, 2016) flashed the word *HEART* across the screen in such a way that *HE* appeared to the left of the dot, and *ART* appeared to the right (**FIGURE 2.24b**). Asked to *say* what they had seen, the patients reported the letters sent to the left hemisphere, which usually controls speech—"*ART*." Asked to point *with their left hand* to what they had seen, they were startled when that hand (controlled by the right hemisphere) pointed to "*HE*" (Figure 2.24c). One skull was housing two minds.

A few people who have had split-brain surgery have for a time been bothered by the unruly independence of their left hand. It seems the left hand truly didn't know what the right hand was doing. One hand might unbutton a shirt while the other buttoned it, or put grocery store items back on the shelf after the other hand put them in the cart. It was as if each hemisphere was thinking, "I've half a mind to wear my green (blue) shirt today." Indeed, said Sperry (1964), split-brain surgery leaves people "with two separate minds." Today's researchers believe that a split-brain patient's mind resembles a river with separate streams, each unaware of its influence on the other (Pinto et al., 2017). (Reading these reports, can you imagine a patient playing a solitary game of "rock, paper, scissors"—left hand versus right?)

What happens when the "two minds" disagree? If a split-brain patient follows an order ("Walk") sent to the right hemisphere, the left hemisphere won't know why the legs start walking. But if asked, the patient doesn't say "I don't know." Instead, the left hemisphere instantly invents—and apparently believes—an explanation ("I'm going into the house to get a Coke"). Thus, Gazzaniga (1988), who has called split-brain patients "the most fascinating people on Earth," concluded that the conscious left hemisphere resembles an interpreter that instantly

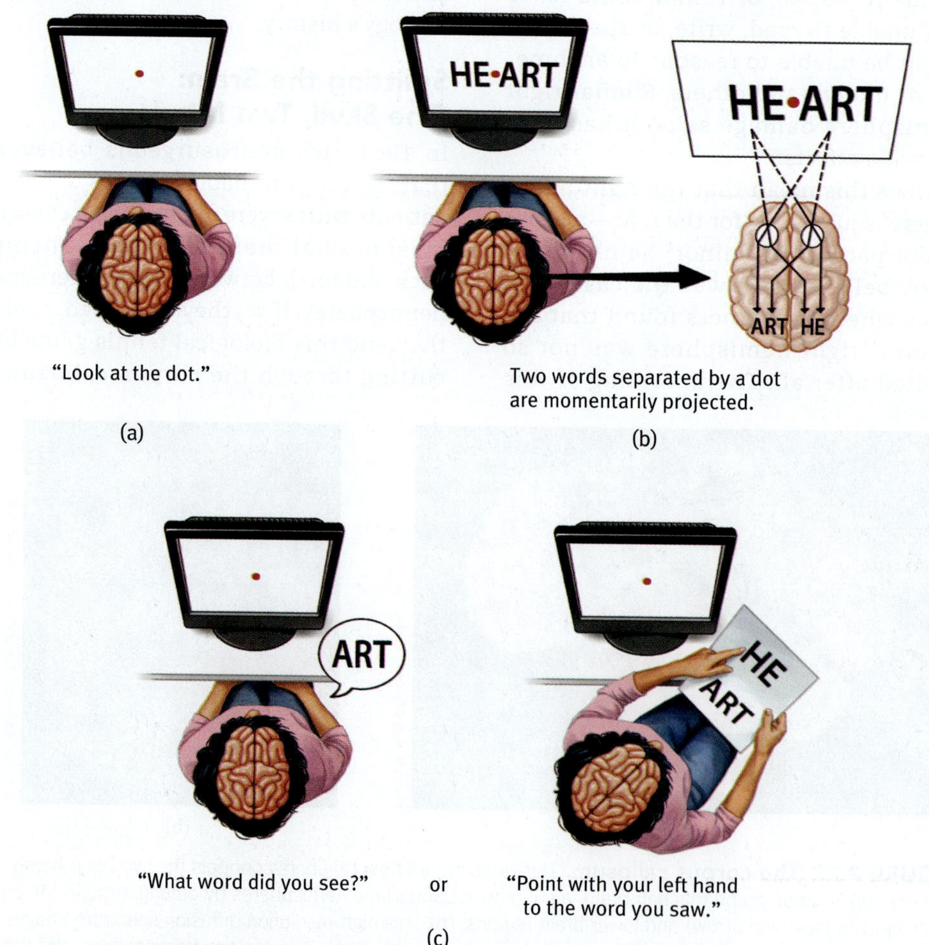

FIGURE 2.24 Testing the divided brain (Gazzaniga, 1983.)

constructs theories to explain our behavior. There goes our brain, running on autopilot as usual. It feels and acts and later explains itself (Kahneman, 2011).

RETRIEVE & REMEMBER

ANSWERS IN APPENDIX E

18. (a) If we flash a red light to the right hemisphere of a person with a split brain, and flash a green light to the left hemisphere, will each observe its own color? (b) Will the person be aware that the colors differ? (c) What will the person verbally report seeing?

LaunchPad Have you ever been asked if you are "left-brained" or "right-brained"? Consider this popular misconception by engaging online with the activity *How Would You Know If People Can Be "Left-Brained" or "Right-Brained"?*

Right-Left Differences in Intact Brains

So, what about the 99.99+ percent of us with undivided brains? Does each of *our* hemispheres also perform distinct functions? The short answer is Yes. If you were performing a *perceptual* task, a brain scan would show increased activity (brain waves, blood flow, and glucose consumption) in your *right* hemisphere. If you were speaking or doing math calculations, the scan would show increased activity in your *left* hemisphere.

A dramatic demonstration of lateralization happens before some types of brain surgery. To locate the patient's language centers, the surgeon injects a sedative into the neck artery feeding blood to the left hemisphere, which usually controls speech. Before the injection, the patient is lying down, arms in the air, chatting with the doctor. Can you predict what happens when the drug puts the left hemisphere to sleep? Within seconds, the patient's right arm falls limp. If the left hemisphere is controlling language, the patient will be speechless until the drug wears off.

To the brain, language is language, whether spoken or signed. Just as hearing people usually use the left hemisphere to process spoken language, deaf people usually use the left hemisphere to process sign language (Corina et al., 1992; Hickok et al., 2001). Thus, a left-hemisphere stroke disrupts a deaf person's signing, much as it disrupts a hearing person's speaking (Corina, 1998). The same brain area is involved in both. (For more on how the brain enables language, see Chapter 8.)

Let's not forget that our left and right brain hemispheres work together. The left hemisphere is good at making quick, exact interpretations of language. But the right hemisphere excels in *making inferences* (reasoned conclusions) (Beeman & Chiarello, 1998; Bowden & Beeman, 1998; Mason & Just, 2004). It also *helps fine-tune our speech* to make meaning clear—as when we say "Let's eat, Grandpa!" instead of "Let's eat Grandpa!" (Heller, 1990). And it *helps orchestrate our self-awareness*. People with partial paralysis sometimes stubbornly deny their condition. They may claim they can move a paralyzed limb—if the damage causing the paralysis is in the right hemisphere (Berti et al., 2005).

Simply looking at the two hemispheres, so alike to the naked eye, who would suppose they each contribute uniquely to the harmony of the whole? Yet a variety of observations—of people with split brains and those with intact brains, and even of other species' brains—leaves little doubt. We have unified brains with specialized parts (Hopkins & Cantalupo, 2008; MacNeilage et al., 2009). And one product of all that brain activity is consciousness, our next topic.

Roz Chast The New Yorker Collection/The Cartoon Bank

IN YOUR EVERYDAY LIFE

Why do you think our brain evolved into so many interconnected structures with varying functions?

LaunchPad For a helpful animated review of this research, see *Topic Tutorial: PsychSim6, Hemispheric Specialization.*

Brain States and Consciousness

LOQ 2-15 What do we mean by *consciousness*, and how does selective attention direct our perceptions?

How does our brain create our mind? Such questions fascinate **biological psychologists**, who study the links between biological (genetic, neural, hormonal) processes and psychological processes. In **cognitive neuroscience**, people from many fields join forces to study the connections between brain activity and mental processes. One of the great mysteries these scientists are trying to solve is **consciousness**: our subjective awareness of ourselves and our environment (Feinberg & Mallatt, 2016). Because consciousness is subjective, it gives us a unique lens for viewing our sensory experiences, feelings, thoughts, and sense of identity.

biological psychology the scientific study of the links between biological and psychological processes.

cognitive neuroscience the interdisciplinary study of the brain activity linked with cognition (including perception, thinking, memory, and language).

consciousness our subjective awareness of ourselves and our environment.

Consciousness enables us to exert voluntary control and to communicate our mental states to others. When we learn a complex concept or behavior, it is consciousness that focuses our attention. It lets us assemble information from many sources as we reflect on the past, adapt to the present, and plan for the future.

Can consciousness persist in a permanently motionless, noncommunicative body? Possibly, depending on the underlying condition. By measuring brain responses to magnetic stimulation, researchers can assess whether a motionless person is experiencing consciousness (Koch, 2017, 2018). A hospitalized 23-year-old woman showed no outward signs of conscious awareness (Owen, 2017; Owen et al., 2006). But when researchers asked her to *imagine* playing tennis, fMRI scans revealed activity in a brain area that normally controls arm and leg movements. Even in a motionless body, the researchers concluded, the brain—and the mind—may still be active (**FIGURE 2.25**).

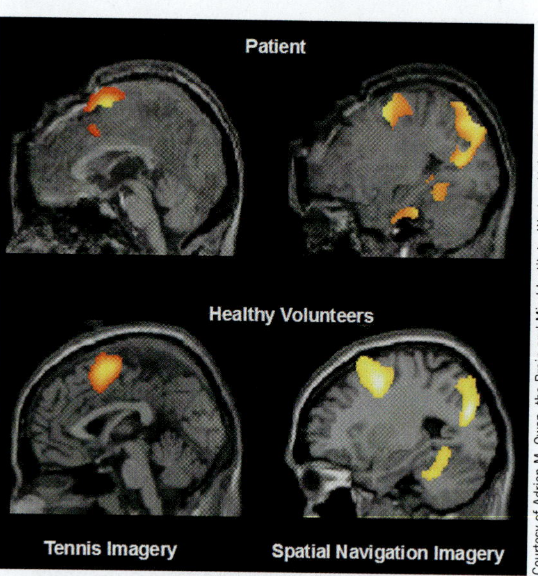

FIGURE 2.25 Evidence of awareness? When a noncommunicative patient was asked to imagine playing tennis or navigating her home, her brain (top) exhibited activity similar to a healthy person's brain (bottom). Researchers wonder if such fMRI scans might enable a "conversation" with some unresponsive patients, by instructing them, for example, to answer *yes* to a question by imagining playing tennis (top and bottom left), and *no* by imagining walking around their home (top and bottom right).

"I am a brain, Watson. The rest of me is a mere appendix." —Sherlock Holmes, in Arthur Conan Doyle's "The Adventure of the Mazarin Stone," 1921

Consciousness is not located in any one small brain area. Conscious awareness is a product of coordinated, cortex-wide activity (Chennu et al., 2014; Mashour, 2018). If a stimulus activates enough brain-wide coordinated neural activity, it crosses a threshold for consciousness. In a brain scan, your conscious awareness of a loved one's presence would appear as a pattern of strong signals bouncing back and forth among many brain areas (Blanke, 2012; Boly et al., 2011; Olivé et al., 2015). Less important stimuli—perhaps a word flashed too briefly for you to consciously perceive—may trigger only visual cortex activity that quickly fades (Silverstein et al., 2015). Our brain is a whole system, and our mental experiences arise from coordinated brain activity.

When we consciously focus on a new or complex task, our brain uses **sequential processing**, giving full attention to one thing at a time. But sequential processing is only one track in the two-track mind. Even while your conscious awareness is intensely focused elsewhere, your mind's other track is taking care of routine business (breathing and heart function, body balance, and hundreds of other tasks) by means of **parallel processing**. Some "80 to 90 percent of what we do is unconscious," says Nobel laureate and memory expert Eric Kandel (2008). Unconscious parallel processing is faster than conscious sequential processing, but both are essential.

In addition to normal waking awareness, consciousness comes to us in altered states, aspects of which are discussed in other chapters. These include meditating, daydreaming, sleeping, hypnosis (Chapter 5), and drug-induced hallucinating (Chapter 13). Here we take a close look at the role of attention, and two altered states we all experience—sleep and dreams.

SELECTIVE ATTENTION

Your conscious awareness focuses, like a flashlight beam, on a *very* small part of all that you experience. Psychologists call this **selective attention**. Until reading this sentence, you were unaware that your nose is jutting into your line of vision. Now, suddenly, the spotlight shifts, and your nose stubbornly intrudes on the words before you. While focusing on these words, you've also been blocking other parts of your environment from awareness, though your normal side vision would let you see them easily. You can change that. As you stare at the X below, notice what surrounds these sentences (the edges of the page or screen, the desktop, the floor).

X

Have you, like 60 percent of American drivers, read or sent a text message or viewed a phone map while driving in the last month (Gliklich et al., 2016)? Such digital distraction can have tragic consequences, as our selective attention shifts more than we realize (Stavrinos et al., 2017). One study left people in a room for 28 minutes with full internet and television access. How many times did their attention shift between the two? Participants guessed it was about 15 times. Not even close! The actual number (verified by eye-tracking equipment) averaged 120 (Brasel & Gips, 2011).

"Has a generation of texters, surfers, and twitterers evolved the enviable ability to process multiple streams of novel information in parallel? Most cognitive psychologists doubt it." —Steven Pinker, "Not at All," 2010

Rapid toggling between activities is today's great enemy of sustained, focused attention. When we switch attentional gears, and especially when shifting from mobile phone use to noticing and avoiding cars around us, we pay a toll—a slight and sometimes fatal delay in coping (Rubenstein et al., 2001). When a driver attends to a conversation, activity in brain areas vital to driving decreases an average of 37 percent (Just et al., 2008). To stay safe, drivers should limit external distractions (Mackenzie & Harris, 2017).

Each day, about 9 Americans are killed in traffic accidents due to distracted driving (CDC, 2018b). One video cam study of teen drivers found that driver distraction from passengers or phones occurred just before 58 percent of their crashes (AAA, 2015). Talking with passengers makes the risk of an accident 1.6 times higher than normal. Using a cell phone (even a hands-free set) makes the risk 4 times higher than normal—equal to the risk of drunk driving (McEvoy et al., 2005, 2007).

Talking is distracting, but texting wins the danger game. In an 18-month video cam study that tracked the driving habits of long-haul truckers, their risk of a collision increased 23 times when they were texting (Olson et al., 2009)! Mindful of such findings, 48 of 50 U.S. states now ban texting while driving. So the next time you're behind the wheel, put the brakes on your texts. Your passengers and fellow drivers will thank you.

Driven to distraction In driving-simulation experiments, people whose attention is diverted by texting and cell-phone conversation make more driving errors.

Our conscious attention is so powerfully selective that we become "blind" to all but a tiny sliver of the immense ocean of visual stimuli constantly before us. In one famous study (**FIGURE 2.26**), people watched a 1-minute video of basketball players, three in black shirts and three in white shirts, tossing a ball (Becklen & Cervone, 1983; Neisser, 1979). Researchers told viewers to press a key each time they saw a black-shirted player pass the ball. Most viewers were so intent on their task that they failed to notice a young woman carrying an umbrella stroll across the screen midway through the video. Watching a replay of the video, they were amazed to see her! With their attention focused elsewhere, the viewers experienced **inattentional blindness**. In another study, two smart-aleck researchers had a gorilla-suited assistant thump his chest and move through the swirl of players. Did he steal the show? No—half the pass-counting viewers failed to see him, too (Simons & Chabris, 1999).

The invisible gorilla struck again in a study of 24 radiologists who were asked to search for signs of cancer in lung scans. All but 4 of them missed the little image of a gorilla embedded in the scan (Drew et al., 2013). They did, however, spot the much tinier groups of cancer cells, which were the focus of their attention.

Given that most of us miss people strolling by in gorilla suits while our attention is focused elsewhere, imagine the fun that magicians can have by distracting us. Misdirect our attention and we will miss the hand slipping into the pocket. "Every time you perform a magic trick, you're engaging in experimental psychology," says magician Teller, a master of mind-messing methods (2009). Clever thieves know this, too. One psychologist was surprised by a woman exposing herself. Only later did he realize her crime partner had picked his pocket (Gallace, 2012).

In other experiments, people exhibited a form of inattentional blindness

FIGURE 2.26 Inattentional blindness Viewers who were attending to basketball tosses among the black-shirted players usually failed to notice the umbrella-toting woman sauntering across the screen (Neisser, 1979).

sequential processing processing one aspect of a stimulus or problem at a time; generally used to process new information or to solve difficult problems.

parallel processing processing many aspects of a stimulus or problem at the same time.

selective attention focusing conscious awareness on a particular stimulus.

inattentional blindness failing to see visible objects when our attention is directed elsewhere.

(a)

(b)

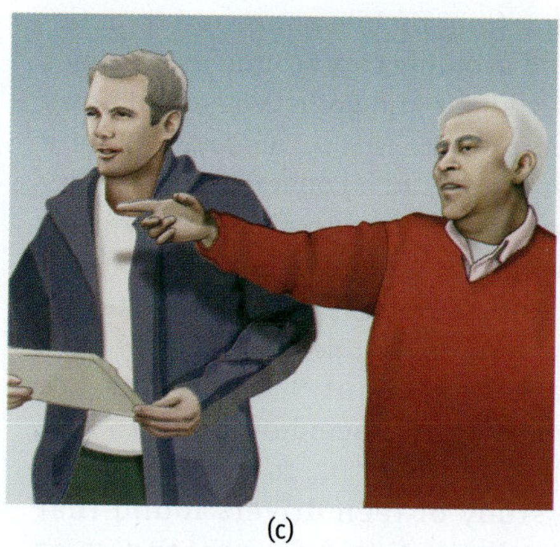
(c)

FIGURE 2.27 Change blindness While a man (in red) provides directions to another (a), two experimenters rudely pass between them carrying a door (b). During this interruption, the original worker switches places with another person wearing different-colored clothing (c). Most people, focused on their direction giving, do not notice the switch (Simons & Levin, 1998).

called **change blindness**. In laboratory experiments, viewers didn't notice that, after a brief visual interruption, a big Coke bottle had disappeared, a railing had risen, clothing had changed color—and a direction seeker had changed places with a new person (**FIGURE 2.27**) (Chabris & Simons, 2010; Resnick et al., 1997). Out of sight, out of mind.

The point to remember: Our conscious mind is in one place at a time. But outside our conscious awareness, the other track of our two-track mind remains active—even during sleep, as we see next.

IN YOUR EVERYDAY LIFE

Can you recall a recent time when, as your attention focused on one thing, you were oblivious to something else (perhaps to pain, to someone's approach, or to background music)?

RETRIEVE & REMEMBER

ANSWERS IN APPENDIX E

19. Explain two attentional principles that magicians may use to fool us.

LaunchPad Watch the thought-provoking *Video: Automatic Skills—Disrupting a Pilot's Performance.* And for more on the limits of our attention, engage online with *Concept Practice: Selective Attention and Multitasking.*

SLEEP AND DREAMS

We humans have about a 16-hour battery life before, each night, we lay down on our comfy wireless charging pad and slip into sleep. We may feel "dead to the world," but we are not. Our perceptual window remains open a crack, and our two-track mind continues to process information outside our conscious awareness. We move around on the bed but manage not to fall out. If someone speaks our name, our unconscious body will perk up. Although the roar of my [ND's] neighborhood garbage truck leaves me undisturbed, my baby's cry will shatter my sleep. Our auditory cortex responds to sound stimuli during sleep (Kutas, 1990).

Sleep's mysteries puzzled scientists for centuries. Now, in laboratories around the world, some of these mysteries are being solved as people sleep, attached to recording devices, while others observe. By recording brain waves and muscle movements, and by watching and sometimes waking sleepers, researchers are glimpsing things that a thousand years of common sense never told us.

Biological Rhythms and Sleep

LOQ 2-16 What is the *circadian rhythm*, and what are the stages of our nightly sleep cycle?

Like the ocean, life has its rhythmic tides. Let's look more closely at two of these biological rhythms—our 24-hour biological clock and our 90-minute sleep cycle.

Circadian Rhythm Have you ever pulled an all-nighter? You might remember feeling groggiest in the middle of the night, but you gain a new sense of alertness with the arrival of your normal wake-up time. This happens thanks to your body's internal biological clock, its **circadian rhythm** (from the Latin *circa*, "about," and *diem*, "day"). Your wake-up call is a sign that your internal clock is doing its job—keeping you roughly in tune with the 24-hour cycle of day and night. As morning nears, body temperature rises. Then it peaks during the day, dips for a time in early afternoon (when many people take naps), and begins to drop again in the evening. Thinking is sharpest and memory most accurate as we approach our daily peak in circadian arousal.

Age and experience can alter our circadian rhythm. Most 20-year-olds are evening-energized "owls," with performance improving across the day (May & Hasher, 1998). After age 20, our clocks begin to shift. The older you get, the more you look forward to bedtime. Most older adults are morning-loving "larks," with

performance declining as the day wears on (Roenneberg et al., 2004). For our ancestors (and for today's hunter-gatherers), a grandparent who awakened easily and early helped protect the family from predators (Samson et al., 2017). Most retirement homes are quiet by mid-evening, when the night has hardly begun for many young adults.

IN YOUR EVERYDAY LIFE

Would you consider yourself a night owl or a morning lark? When do you usually feel most energetic? What time of day works best for you to study?

Sleep Stages Seeking sleep, we crawl into bed and fake it until we make it. Eventually, sleep overtakes us, and consciousness fades as different parts of our brain's cortex stop communicating (Massimini et al., 2005). Yet the sleeping brain is active and has its own biological rhythm. About every 90 minutes, we cycle through distinct sleep stages. This basic fact came to light when 8-year-old Armond Aserinsky went to bed one night in 1952. His father, Eugene, needed to test an electroencephalograph he had repaired that day (Aserinsky, 1988; Seligman & Yellen, 1987). Placing electrodes near Armond's eyes to record the rolling eye movements then believed to occur during sleep, Aserinsky watched the machine go wild, tracing deep zigzags on the graph paper. Could the machine still be broken? As the night proceeded and the activity recurred, Aserinsky realized that the periods of fast, jerky eye movements were accompanied by energetic brain activity. Awakened during one such episode, Armond reported having a dream. Aserinsky had discovered what we now know as **REM sleep** (*r*apid *e*ye *m*ovement sleep; sometimes called *R sleep*).

Similar procedures used with thousands of volunteers showed the cycles were a normal part of sleep (Kleitman, 1960) (**FIGURE 2.28**). To appreciate these studies, imagine yourself as a participant. As the hour grows late, you feel sleepy and get ready for bed. A researcher comes in and tapes electrodes to your scalp (to detect your brain waves), on your chin (to detect muscle tension), and just outside the corners of your eyes (to detect eye movements). Other devices may record your heart rate, breathing rate, and genital arousal.

When you are in bed with your eyes closed, the researcher in the next room sees on the EEG the relatively slow **alpha waves** of your awake but relaxed state (**FIGURE 2.29**). As you adapt to all this equipment, you grow tired. Then, in a moment you won't remember, your breathing slows and you slip into **sleep**. The EEG now shows the irregular brain waves of the non-REM sleep stage called *NREM-1* (or *N1*) sleep (Silber et al., 2007).

During this brief N1 sleep you may experience fantastic images resembling hallucinations. You may have a sensation of falling (when your body may suddenly jerk) or of floating weightlessly. These are *hypnagogic* (also called *hypnic*) sensations (from the Greek root words meaning "leading to sleep"). Your brain may later treat them as real memories. People who claim they were abducted by aliens—often shortly after getting into bed—commonly recall being floated off from (or pinned down on) their beds (Clancy, 2005).

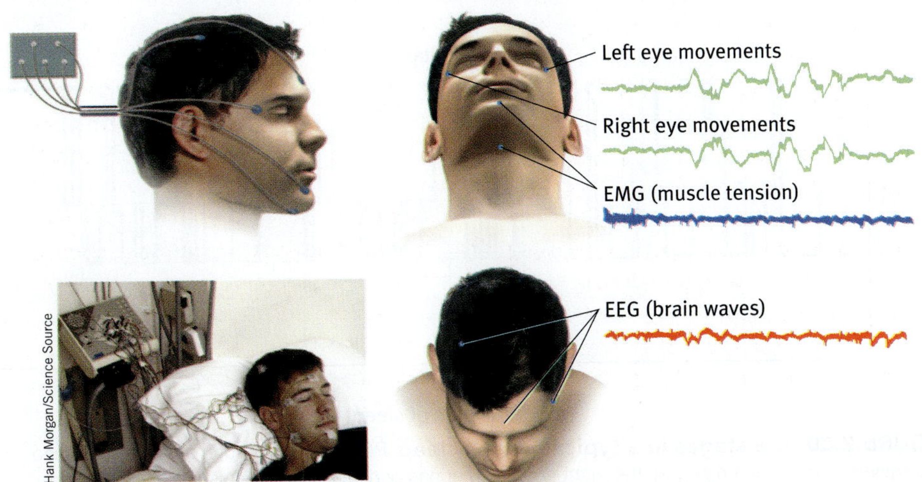

FIGURE 2.28 Measuring sleep activity Sleep researchers measure brain-wave activity, eye movements, and muscle tension with electrodes that pick up weak electrical signals from the brain, eyes, and facial muscles (Dement, 1978).

change blindness failing to notice changes in the environment; a form of *inattentional blindness.*

circadian [ser-KAY-dee-an] **rhythm** our internal biological clock; regular bodily rhythms (for example, of temperature and wakefulness) that occur on a 24-hour cycle.

REM (R) sleep rapid eye movement sleep; a recurring sleep stage during which vivid dreams commonly occur. Also known as *paradoxical sleep,* because the muscles are relaxed (except for minor twitches) but other body systems are active.

alpha waves relatively slow brain waves of a relaxed, awake state.

sleep a periodic, natural loss of consciousness—as distinct from unconsciousness resulting from a coma, general anesthesia, or hibernation. (Adapted from Dement, 1999.)

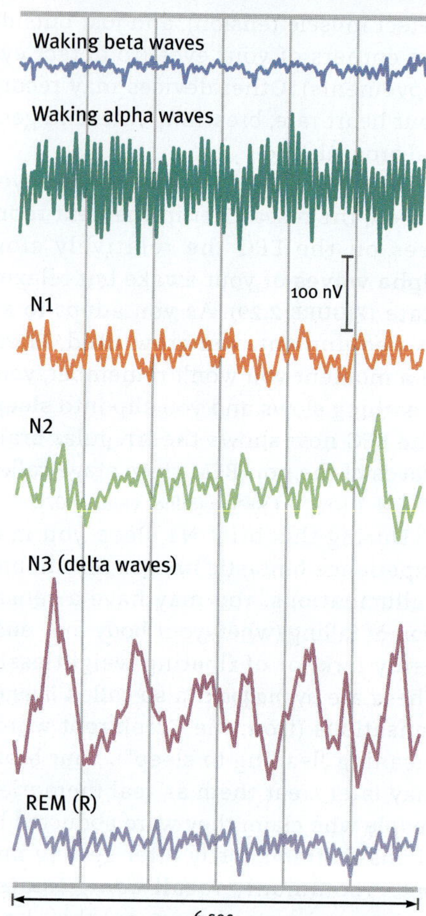

FIGURE 2.29 Brain waves and sleep stages The beta waves of an alert, waking state and the regular alpha waves of an awake, relaxed state differ from the slower, larger delta waves of deep N3 sleep. Although the rapid REM (R) sleep waves resemble the near-waking N1 sleep waves, the body is more internally aroused during REM sleep than during NREM sleep (the N1, N2, and N3 stages).

You then relax more deeply and begin about 20 minutes of *NREM-2 (N2)* sleep. The EEG will show bursts of rapid, rhythmic brain-wave activity. Although you could still be awakened without too much difficulty, you are now clearly asleep.

Then you enter the deep sleep of *NREM-3 (N3)*. During this slow-wave sleep, which lasts for about 30 minutes, your brain emits large, slow **delta waves**. You would be hard to awaken. Have you ever said, "That thunder was so loud last night!" only to have a friend respond, "What thunder?" Those who missed the storm may have been in delta sleep. (It is at the end of this stage that children may wet the bed.)

LaunchPad To better understand EEG readings and their relationship to consciousness, sleep, and dreams, experience the tutorial and simulation of *Topic Tutorial: PsychSim6, EEG and Sleep Stages.*

REM (R) Sleep About an hour after you first dive into sleep, a strange thing happens. You reverse course. From N3, you head back through N2 (where you'll ultimately spend about half your night). You then enter the most puzzling sleep phase—REM (R) sleep (**FIGURE 2.30**). And the show begins. For about 10 minutes, your brain waves become rapid and saw-toothed, more like those of the nearly awake N1 sleep. But unlike N1, during REM sleep your heart rate rises and your breathing becomes rapid and irregular. Every half-minute or so, your eyes dart around in a brief burst of activity behind your closed lids. These eye movements announce the beginning of a dream—often emotional, usually story-like, and richly hallucinatory. Dreams aren't real, but REM sleep tricks your brain into responding as if they were (Andrillon et al., 2015).

Except during very scary dreams, your genitals become aroused during REM sleep. You may have an erection or increased vaginal lubrication and clitoral engorgement, regardless of whether the dream's content is sexual (Karacan et al., 1966). Men's common "morning erection" stems from the night's last REM

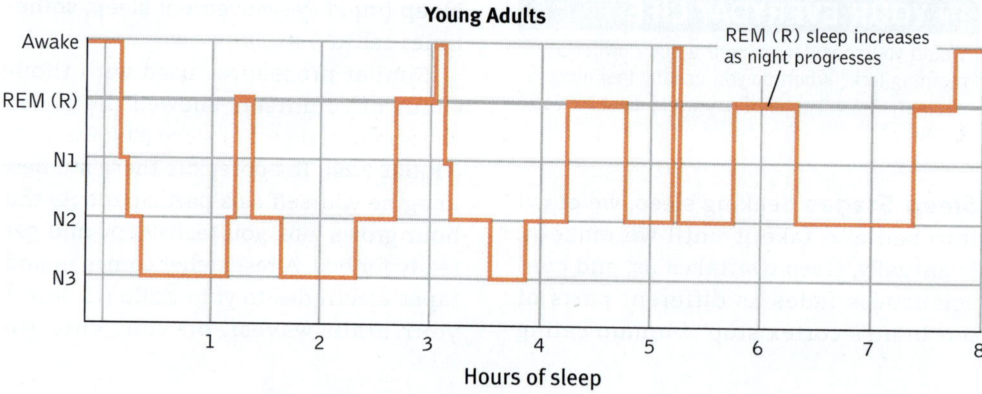

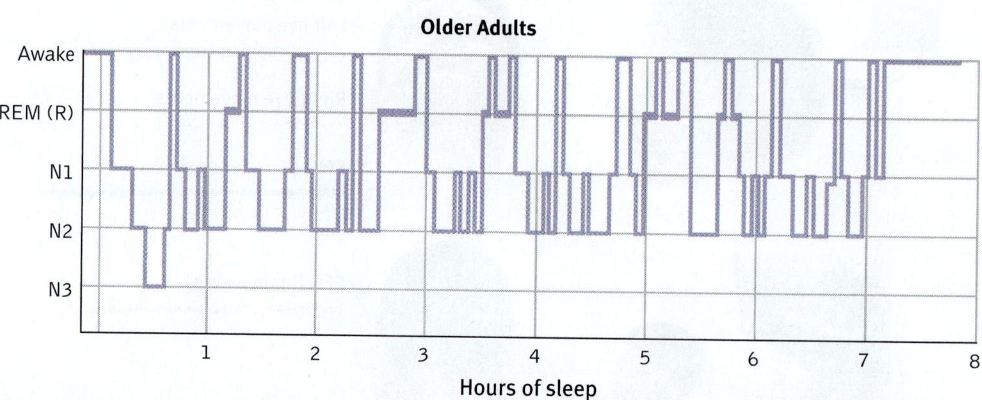

FIGURE 2.30 The stages in a typical night's sleep People pass through a multistage sleep cycle several times each night. As the night goes on, periods of deep sleep diminish and, for younger adults, REM (R) sleep increases. As people age, sleep becomes more fragile, with awakenings common among older adults (Kamel & Gammack, 2006; Neubauer, 1999).

period, often just before waking. (Many men who have occasional erectile problems get sleep-related erections, suggesting the problem is not between their legs.)

During REM sleep, your brain's motor cortex is active but your brainstem blocks its messages. This leaves your muscles relaxed, so much so that, except for an occasional finger, toe, or facial twitch, you are essentially paralyzed. Moreover, you cannot easily be awakened. REM sleep is thus sometimes called *paradoxical* sleep. The body is internally aroused, with waking-like brain activity, but externally calm—except for those darting eyes.

Horses, which spend 92 percent of each day standing and can sleep standing, must lie down for muscle-paralyzing REM sleep (Morrison, 2003).

The sleep cycle repeats itself about every 90 minutes for younger adults (with shorter, more frequent cycles for older adults). As the night goes on, deep N3 sleep grows shorter and disappears, and REM and N2 sleep periods get longer (see Figure 2.30). By morning, we have spent 20 to 25 percent of an average night's sleep—some 100 minutes—in REM sleep. In sleep lab studies, 37 percent of participants have reported rarely or never having dreams that they "can remember the next morning" (Moore, 2004). Yet even they, more than 80 percent of the time, could recall a dream if awakened during REM sleep. Each year, we spend about 600 hours experiencing some 1500 dreams. Over a typical lifetime, this adds up to more than 100,000 dreams—all swallowed by the night but not acted out, thanks to REM's protective paralysis.

RETRIEVE & REMEMBER

ANSWERS IN APPENDIX E

Tatan Syuflana/AP Photo

20. Why would communal sleeping provide added protection for those whose safety depends upon vigilance, such as these refugees in Paris?
21. What are the four sleep stages, and in what order do we normally travel through those stages?
22. Match the cognitive experience (a–c) with the sleep stage (i–iii).

Sleep stage:	Cognitive experience:
i. N1	a. story-like dream
ii. N3	b. fleeting images
iii. REM	c. minimal awareness

Why Do We Sleep?

LOQ 2-17 How do our sleep patterns differ? What five theories describe our need to sleep?

True or false? "Everyone needs 8 hours of sleep." *False.* The first clue to how much sleep a person needs is their age. Newborns often sleep two-thirds of their day, most adults no more than one-third. But there is more to our sleep differences than age.

Some adults thrive on fewer than 6 hours a night. Others regularly rack up 9 hours or more. Some of us are awake between nightly sleep periods, breaking the night into a "first sleep" and a "second sleep" (Randall, 2012). And for those who can nap, a 15-minute midday snooze can be as effective as an additional hour at night (Horne, 2011). Heredity influences sleep patterns, and researchers are tracking the sleep-regulating genes in humans and other animals (Hayashi et al., 2015; Mackenzie et al., 2015).

Sleep patterns are also culturally influenced. Canadian, American, British, German, and Japanese adults average 7 hours of sleep on workdays and 7 to 8 hours on other days (NSF, 2013). Earlier school start times, more extracurricular activities, and fewer parent-set bedtimes lead American adolescents to get less sleep than their Australian counterparts (Short et al., 2013). Thanks to modern lighting, shift work, and social media diversions, many who would have gone to bed at 9:00 P.M. in days past are now up until 11:00 P.M. or later. With sleep, as with waking behavior, biology and environment interact.

Whether for work or play, bright light can disrupt our biological clock, tricking the brain into thinking night is morning. The process begins in our eyes' retinas, which contain light-sensitive proteins.

delta waves large, slow brain waves associated with deep sleep.

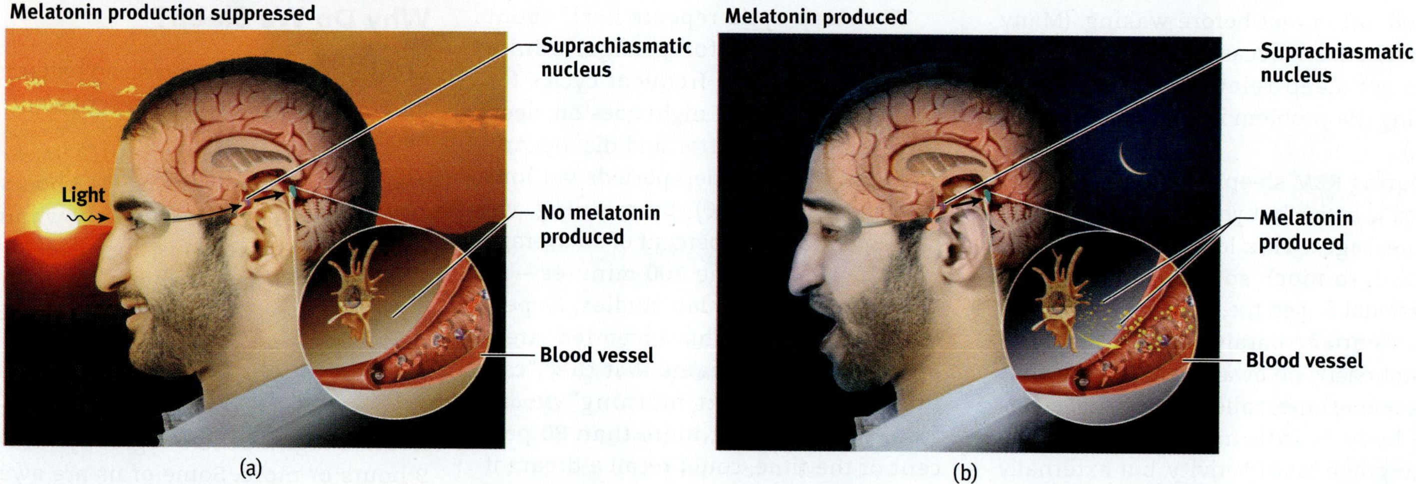

FIGURE 2.31 The biological clock (a) Light striking the eye's retina signals the suprachiasmatic nucleus (SCN) to suppress production of the sleep hormone melatonin. (b) At night, the SCN quiets down, allowing the release of melatonin into the bloodstream.

Bright light sets off an internal alarm by activating these proteins, which then signal a brain structure called the **suprachiasmatic nucleus** (**FIGURE 2.31**). This brain structure in turn decreases production of the sleep-supporting hormone *melatonin* (Chang et al., 2015; Gandhi et al., 2015).

Sleep Theories So, our sleep patterns differ from person to person and from culture to culture. But why do we *need* to sleep? Psychologists offer five possible reasons:

1. ***Sleep protects***. When darkness shut down the day's hunting, gathering, and social activities, our distant ancestors were better off asleep in a cave, out of harm's way. Those who didn't wander around dark cliffs were more likely to leave descendants. This fits a broader principle: Sleep patterns tend to suit a species' place in nature. Animals with the greatest need to graze and the least ability to hide tend to sleep less (see **FIGURE 2.32**). Animals also sleep less, with no ill effects, during times of mating and migration (Siegel, 2012).
2. ***Sleep helps us recover***. Sleep gives your body and brain the chance to repair, rewire, and reorganize. It helps restore the immune system and repair brain tissue. Sleep gives resting neurons time to repair themselves, while pruning or weakening unused connections (Ascády & Harris, 2017; Ding et al., 2016; Li et al., 2017). Bats and many other small animals burn a lot of calories, producing *free radicals*, molecules that are toxic to neurons. Sleep sweeps away this toxic waste (Xie et al., 2013). Think of it this way: When consciousness leaves your house, workers come in to clean, saying "Good night. Sleep tidy."
3. ***Sleep helps us restore and rebuild fading memories of the day's experiences***. To sleep is to strengthen. Sleep strengthens neural connections and replays recent learning (Pace-Schott et al., 2015; Yang et al., 2014). It reactivates recent experiences stored in the hippocampus and shifts them for permanent storage elsewhere in the cortex (Racsmány et al., 2010; Urbain et al., 2016). Adults, children, and infants trained to perform tasks recall them better after a night's sleep, or even after a short nap, than after several hours awake (Friedrich et al., 2015; Horváth et al., 2017; Sandoval et al., 2017; Seehagen et al., 2015). Sleep, it seems, strengthens memories in a way that being awake does not.
4. ***Sleep feeds creative thinking***. A full night's sleep boosts our thinking and learning. After working on a task, then sleeping on it, people solve problems more insightfully than do those who stay awake (Barrett, 2011; Sio et al., 2013). They also are better at spotting connections among novel pieces of information (Ellenbogen et al., 2007; Whitehurst et al., 2016). To think smart and see connections, it often pays to sleep on it.
5. ***Sleep supports growth***. During slow-wave sleep, the pituitary gland releases a hormone we need for muscle development. A regular full night's sleep can "*dramatically* improve your athletic ability" (Maas & Robbins, 2010). Well-rested athletes have faster reaction times, more energy, and greater endurance. Teams that build 8 to 10 hours of daily sleep into their training show improved performance.

"Maybe 'Bring Your Pillow To Work Day' wasn't such a good idea."

Kruglov_Orda/Shutterstock

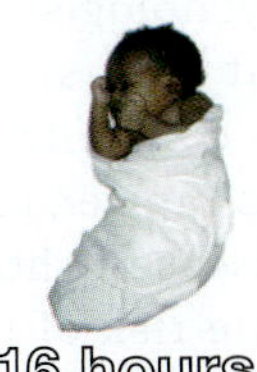

Andrew D. Myers

Utekhina Anna/Shutterstock

Steffen Foerster/Shutterstock

RubberBall Productions/Getty Images

Eric Isselée/Shutterstock

pandapaw/Shutterstock

FIGURE 2.32 Animal sleep time Would you rather be a brown bat and sleep 20 hours a day or a giraffe and sleep 2 hours a day? (Data from NIH, 2010.)

Given all the benefits of sleep, it's no wonder that sleep loss—our next topic of discussion—hits us so hard.

"Sleep faster, we need the pillows." —Yiddish proverb

RETRIEVE & REMEMBER

ANSWERS IN APPENDIX E

23. What are five proposed reasons for our need for sleep?

Sleep Deprivation and Sleep Disorders

LOQ 2-18 How does sleep loss affect us, and what are the major sleep disorders?

Sleep commands roughly one-third of our lives—some 25 years, on average. With enough sleep, we awaken refreshed and in a better mood. We work more efficiently and accurately. But when our body yearns for sleep and does not get it, we feel terrible. Trying to stay awake, we will eventually lose. In the tiredness battle, sleep always wins.

The Effects of Sleep Loss Today, more than ever, our sleep patterns leave us not only sleepy but drained of energy and our sense of well-being. Some researchers see today's tiredness as a "Great Sleep Recession" (Keyes et al., 2015). After several 5-hour nights, we run up a sleep debt that won't be wiped out by one long snooze. "The brain keeps an accurate count of sleep debt for at least two weeks," reported sleep researcher William Dement (1999, p. 64).

College students are especially sleep deprived. In one national survey, 69 percent reported "feeling tired" or "having little energy" on at least several days in the two previous weeks (AP, 2009). Small wonder so many fall asleep in class. The going needn't get boring before students start snoring.

Sleep loss also affects our mood. Tiredness triggers testiness—less sleep predicts more conflicts in students' friendships and romantic relationships (Gordon & Chen, 2014; Tavernier & Willoughby, 2014). Sleep loss can also predict depression (Baglioni et al., 2016). Researchers who studied 15,500 12- to 18-year-olds found that those who slept 5 or fewer hours a night had a 71 percent higher risk of depression than those who slept 8 hours or more (Gangwisch et al., 2010). The link does not reflect an effect of depression on sleep. In long-term studies, sleep loss predicts depression, not vice versa (Gregory et al., 2009). REM sleep's processing of emotional experiences helps protect against depression (Walker & van der Helm, 2009). After a good night's sleep, we often do feel better the next day.

Chronic sleep loss can suppress the immune system, lowering our resistance to illness. With fewer immune cells, we are less able to battle viral infections and cancer (Möller-Levet et al., 2013; Motivala & Irwin, 2007; Opp & Krueger, 2015). One experiment exposed volunteers to a cold virus. Those who had averaged less than 5 hours of sleep a night were 4.5 times more likely to develop a cold than those who slept more than 7 hours a night (Prather et al., 2015). Sleep's protective effect may help explain why people who sleep 7 to 8 hours a night tend to outlive their sleep-deprived agemates (Dew et al., 2003; Parthasarathy et al., 2015; Scullin & Bliwise, 2015).

When sleepy frontal lobes confront visual attention tasks, reactions slow and errors increase (Caldwell, 2012; Lim & Dinges, 2010). For drivers in an unexpected situation, slow responses can spell disaster. Drowsy driving has contributed to an estimated 1 in 6 deadly American traffic accidents (AAA, 2010). Consider the engineer of a New Jersey Transit commuter train, whose fatigue from *sleep apnea* caused him to crash the train, killing one bystander (McGeehan, 2018). One 2-year study examined the driving accident rates of more than 20,000 Virginia 16- to 18-year-olds in two major cities. Students whose high schools started later (compared with those starting at least 60 minutes earlier) experienced fewer vehicle crashes (Morgenthaler et al., 2016; Vorona et al., 2011).

Deliberate, experimental manipulation of driver fatigue on the road would be illegal and unethical. But twice each year, most North Americans participate in a revealing sleep-manipulation experiment: We "spring forward" to daylight savings time and "fall back" to standard time. A search of millions of Canadian and American records showed that accidents increased immediately after the spring-forward change, which shortens sleep (Coren, 1996) (**FIGURE 2.33**).

suprachiasmatic nucleus (SCN) a pair of cell clusters in the hypothalamus that controls circadian rhythm. In response to light, the SCN adjusts melatonin production, thus modifying our feelings of sleepiness.

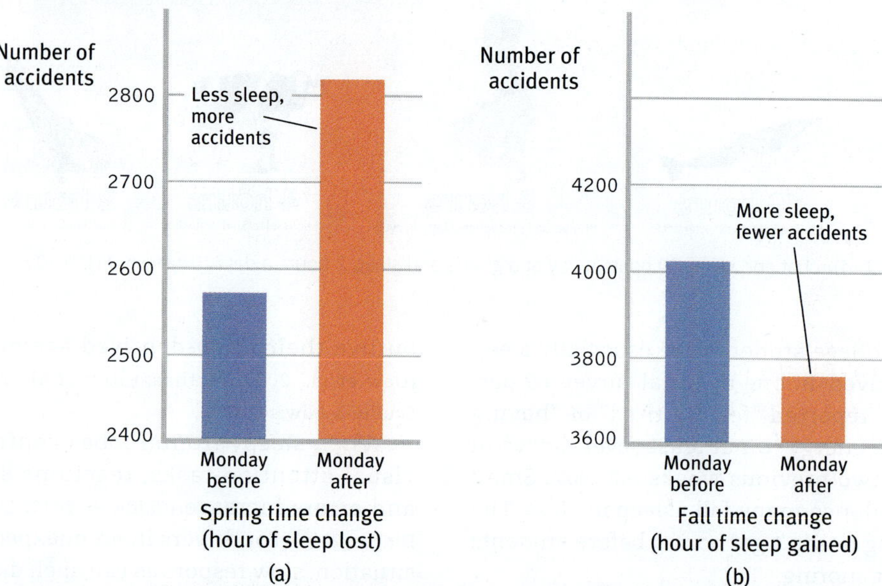

FIGURE 2.33 Less sleep = more accidents (a) On the Monday after the spring time change, when people lose one hour of sleep, accidents increased, as compared with the Monday before. (b) In the fall, traffic accidents normally increase because of greater snow, ice, and darkness, but they diminished after the time change. (Data from Coren, 1996.)

Sleep also affects academic outcomes. When Seattle high schools started an hour later, students got more sleep, attended more classes, and earned better grades (Dunster et al., 2018).

So, sleep loss can destroy our mood, lower our resistance to infection, decrease driver safety, and reduce school performance. It can also make us gain weight. Children and adults who sleep less than normal are heavier than average. And in recent decades, people have been sleeping less and weighing more (Shiromani et al., 2012; Suglia et al., 2014). Here's how it happens. Sleep deprivation

- increases *ghrelin*, a hunger-arousing hormone, and decreases its hunger-suppressing partner, *leptin* (Shilsky et al., 2012).
- decreases metabolic (energy use) rate (Buxton et al., 2012).
- increases production of *cortisol*, a stress hormone that triggers fat production.
- enhances limbic brain responses to the mere sight of food and decreases cortical responses that help us resist temptation (Benedict et al., 2012; Greer et al., 2013; St-Onge et al., 2012).

These effects may help explain the weight gain common among sleep-deprived college students.

FIGURE 2.34 summarizes the effects of sleep deprivation. But there is good news! Psychologists have discovered a treatment that strengthens memory, increases concentration, boosts mood, moderates hunger, reduces obesity, fortifies the disease-fighting immune system, lessens the risk of fatal accidents, and boosts school performance. Even better news: The treatment feels good, it can be self-administered, and it's free! If you are a typical college student, often going to bed late, you might feel trapped in a cycle of sleeplessness. Your stressful living situation might make sleep seem more of a luxury than a necessity. One night this week, try to add 15 minutes to your sleep. If you feel more rested and less like a zombie, try adding more sleep as often as you can. For some additional tips on getting better quality sleep, see **TABLE 2.3**.

LaunchPad To see whether you are one of the many sleep-deprived students, engage online with the self-assessment activity *Assess Your Strengths: Are You Sleep Deprived? How Can You Improve Your Sleep?* And consider how researchers have addressed these issues by engaging online with *How Would You Know If Sleep Deprivation Affects Academic Performance?*

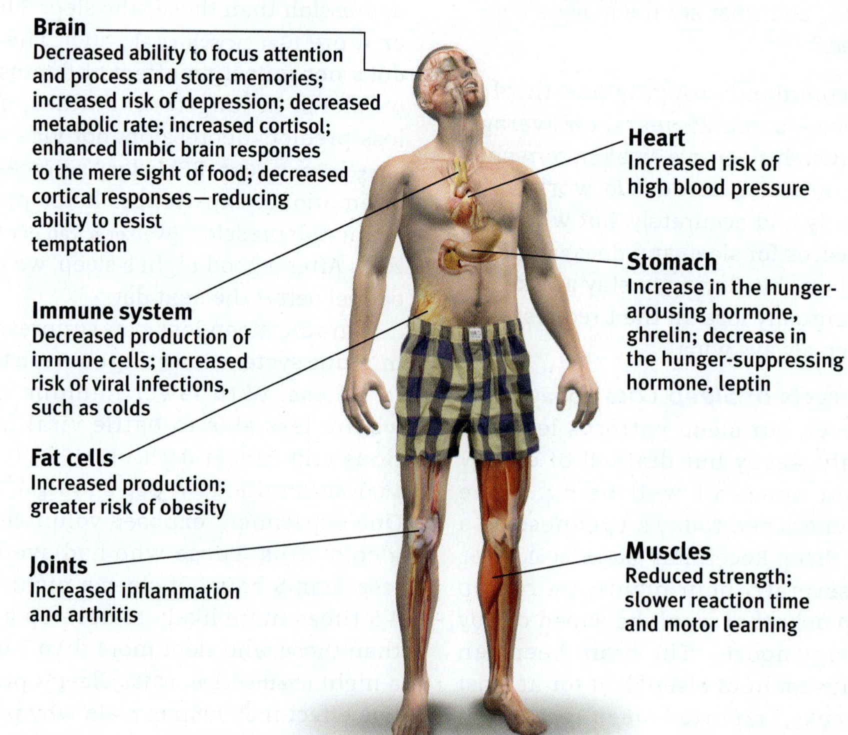

FIGURE 2.34 How sleep deprivation affects us

TABLE 2.3 Get a Better Night's Sleep: Natural Sleep Aids
• Exercise regularly but not in the late evening. (Late afternoon is best.)
• Avoid caffeine after early afternoon, and avoid food and drink near bedtime. The exception would be a glass of milk, which provides raw materials for the manufacture of serotonin, a neurotransmitter that facilitates sleep.
• Relax before bedtime, using dimmer light.
• Sleep on a regular schedule (rise at the same time even after a restless night) and avoid long naps.
• Hide time displays so you aren't tempted to check repeatedly.
• Reassure yourself that temporary sleep loss causes no great harm.
• Focus your mind on nonarousing, engaging thoughts, such as song lyrics or vacation travel (Gellis et al., 2013). (Thinking about falling asleep may keep you awake.)
• Manage stress. Realize that for any stressed organism, being vigilant is natural and adaptive. Less stress = better sleep.

insomnia recurring problems in falling or staying asleep.

narcolepsy a sleep disorder in which a person has uncontrollable sleep attacks, sometimes lapsing directly into REM sleep.

sleep apnea a sleep disorder in which a sleeping person repeatedly stops breathing until blood oxygen is so low the person awakens just long enough to draw a breath.

night terrors a sleep disorder characterized by high arousal and an appearance of being terrified; unlike nightmares, night terrors occur during N3 sleep and are infrequently remembered.

dream a sequence of images, emotions, and thoughts passing through a sleeping person's mind.

Major Sleep Disorders Do you have trouble sleeping when anxious or excited? Most of us do. (*Warning:* A smart phone tucked under your pillow as an alarm clock increases the likelihood that you'll have a bad night's sleep.) An occasional loss of sleep is nothing to worry about. But for those who have a major sleep disorder—**insomnia, narcolepsy, sleep apnea**, sleepwalking (*somnambulism*), sleeptalking, or **night terrors**—trying to sleep can be a nightmare. (See **TABLE 2.4** for a summary of these disorders.)

IMPROVE YOUR EVERYDAY LIFE

What have you learned about sleep that you could apply to yourself?

RETRIEVE & REMEMBER

ANSWERS IN APPENDIX E

24. A well-rested person would be more likely to have ________ (trouble concentrating/quick reaction times) and a sleep-deprived person would be more likely to ________ (gain weight/fight off a cold).

Dreams

LOQ 2-19 What do we dream about, and what are five explanations of *why* we dream?

Now playing at an inner theater near you: the premiere showing of a sleeping person's dream. This never-before-seen mental movie features engaging characters wrapped in a plot that is original and unlikely, yet seemingly real.

REM **dreams** are vivid, emotional, and often bizarre (Loftus & Ketcham, 1994).

TABLE 2.4 Sleep Disorders

Disorder	Rate	Description	Effects
Insomnia	1 in 10 adults; 1 in 4 older adults	Ongoing difficulty falling or staying asleep.	Chronic tiredness. Reliance on sleeping pills and alcohol, which reduce REM sleep and lead to tolerance—a state in which increasing doses are needed to produce an effect.
Narcolepsy	1 in 2000 adults	Sudden attacks of overwhelming sleepiness.	Risk of falling asleep at a dangerous moment. Narcolepsy attacks usually last less than 5 minutes, but they can happen at the worst and most emotional times. Everyday activities, such as driving, require extra caution.
Sleep apnea	1 in 20 adults	Stopping breathing repeatedly while sleeping.	Fatigue and depression (as a result of slow-wave sleep deprivation). Associated with obesity (especially among men).
Sleepwalking and sleeptalking	1–15 in 100 in the general population for sleepwalking (NSF, 2016); about half of young children for sleeptalking (Reimão & Lefévre, 1980)	Doing normal waking activities (sitting up, walking, speaking) while asleep. Sleeptalking can occur during any sleep stage. Sleepwalking happens in N3 sleep.	Few serious concerns. Sleepwalkers return to their beds on their own or with the help of a family member, rarely remembering their trip the next morning.
Night terrors	1 in 100 adults; 1 in 30 children	Appearing terrified, talking nonsense, sitting up, or walking around during N3 sleep; different from nightmares.	Doubling of a child's heart and breathing rates during the attack. Luckily, children remember little or nothing of the fearful event the next day. As people age, night terrors become more and more rare.

Waking from one, we may wonder how our brain can so creatively, colorfully, and completely construct this inner world. Caught for a moment between our dreaming and waking consciousness, we may even be unsure which world is real. A 4-year-old may awaken and scream for his parents, terrified of the bear in the house.

"I love to sleep. Do you? Isn't it great? It really is the best of both worlds. You get to be alive and unconscious." —Comedian Rita Rudner, 1993

Each of us spends about 6 years of our life in dreams—brain videos that remain locked behind our moving eyelids and usually vanish with the new day. The discovery of the link between REM sleep and dreaming gave us a key to that lock. Now, instead of relying on a dreamer's hazy recall hours later, researchers can catch dreams as they happen. They can awaken people during or within 3 minutes of a REM sleep period to hear a vivid account.

What We Dream Few REM dreams are sweet. For both women and men, 8 in 10 are bad dreams (Domhoff, 2007). Common themes are failing in an attempt to do something; being attacked, pursued, or rejected; or experiencing misfortune (Hall et al., 1982). Dreams with sexual imagery occur less often than you might think (though more often after consuming sexual media [Van den Buick et al., 2016]). In one study, only 1 in 10 dreams among young men and 1 in 30 among young women had sexual overtones (Domhoff, 1996). More commonly, our dreams feature people and places from the day's nonsexual experiences (Nikles et al., 2017).

A popular sleep myth: If you dream you are falling and hit the ground (or if you dream of dying), you die. Unfortunately, those who could confirm these ideas are not around to do so. Many people, however, have had such dreams and are alive to report them.

Our two-track mind continues to monitor our environment while we sleep. Sensory stimuli—a particular odor or a phone's ringing—may be instantly woven into the dream story. In a classic experiment, researchers lightly sprayed cold water on dreamers' faces (Dement & Wolpert, 1958). Compared with sleepers who did not get the cold-water treatment, these people were more likely to dream about a waterfall, a leaky roof, or even about being sprayed by someone.

Why We Dream Dream theorists have proposed several explanations of why we dream, including these five:

1. ***To satisfy our own wishes***. In 1900, Sigmund Freud offered what he thought was "the most valuable of all the discoveries it has been my good fortune to make." He proposed that dreams act as a safety valve, discharging feelings that the dreamer could not express in public. He called the dream's remembered story line its **manifest content**. For Freud, this apparent content was a censored, symbolic version of the dream's underlying meaning—the **latent content**, or unconscious drives and wishes (often erotic) that would be threatening if expressed directly. Thus, a gun appearing in a dream could be a penis in disguise.

   Freud's critics say it is time to wake up from Freud's dream theory, which they regard as a scientific nightmare. Scientific studies offer "no reason to believe any of Freud's specific claims about dreams and their purposes," said dream researcher William Domhoff (2003). Do we dream of phallic-shaped foods any more than would be expected? *No* (Stephens-Davidowitz, 2017). Cucumbers, for example, are the seventh most dreamed-of vegetable and the seventh most common vegetable. Legend has it that even Freud, who loved to smoke cigars, agreed that "sometimes, a cigar is just a cigar." Other critics have noted that dreams could be interpreted in many different ways. Freud's wish-fulfillment theory of dreams has in large part given way to other theories.

2. ***To file away memories***. The *information-processing* perspective proposes that dreams may help sift, sort, and secure the day's events in our memory. Some studies support this view. When tested the day after learning a task, those who had slept undisturbed did better than those who had been deprived of both slow-wave and REM sleep (Stickgold, 2012).

   Brain scans confirm the link between REM sleep and memory. Brain regions that were active as rats learned to navigate a maze (or as people learned to identify the difference between objects) became active again later during REM sleep (Louie & Wilson, 2001; Maquet, 2001). So precise were these activity patterns that scientists could tell where in the maze the rat would be if awake.

   Students, take note. Sleep researcher Robert Stickgold (2000) believes many students suffer from a kind of sleep bulimia, sleep deprived on weekdays and binge sleeping on the weekend. He warned, "If you don't get good sleep and enough sleep after you learn new stuff, you won't integrate it effectively into your memories." That helps explain why high school students with top grades slept about 25 minutes longer each night than their lower-achieving classmates (Wolfson & Carskadon, 1998). Sacrificing sleep time to study actually *worsens* academic performance by making it harder the next day to understand class material or do well on a test (Gillen-O'Neel et al., 2013).

3. ***To develop and preserve neural pathways***. Dreams—the brain activity linked to REM sleep—may give the sleeping brain a workout that helps it develop. As we'll see in Chapter 3, stimulating experiences preserve and expand the brain's neural pathways.

Infants, whose neural networks are fast developing, spend much of their abundant sleep time in REM sleep.

4. ***To make sense of neural static.*** Other theories propose that dreams are born when random neural activity spreads upward from the brainstem (Antrobus, 1991; Hobson, 2003, 2004, 2009). Our ever-alert brain attempts to make sense of the activity, pasting the random bits of information into a meaningful image. Brain scans taken while people were dreaming have revealed increased activity in the emotion-related limbic system and in areas that process visual images (Schwarz, 2012). Damage either of these areas and dreaming itself may be impaired (Domhoff, 2003).
5. ***To reflect cognitive development.*** Some dream researchers prefer to see dreams as a reflection of brain maturation and cognitive development (Domhoff, 2010, 2011; Foulkes, 1999). For example, before age 9, children's dreams seem more like a slide show and less like an active story in which the child is an actor. Dreams at all ages tend to feature the kind of thinking and talking we demonstrate when awake. They seem to draw on our current knowledge and concepts we understand.

Despite their differences, today's dream researchers agree on one thing: We need REM sleep. Deprived of it in sleep labs or in real life, people return more and more quickly to the REM stage when finally allowed to sleep undisturbed. They literally sleep like babies—with increased REM sleep, known as **REM rebound**.

IN YOUR EVERYDAY LIFE

Which explanation for why we dream makes the most sense to you? How well does it explain your own dreams?

RETRIEVE & REMEMBER

ANSWERS IN APPENDIX E

25. What five theories propose explanations for why we dream?

* * *

We have glimpsed the truth of this chapter's overriding principle: *Biological and psychological explanations of behavior are partners, not competitors.* We are privileged to live in a time of breathtaking discovery about the interplay of our biology and our behavior and mental processes. Yet what is unknown still dwarfs what is known. We can describe the brain. We can learn the functions of its parts. We can study how the parts communicate. We can observe sleeping and waking brains. But how do we get mind out of meat? How does the electrochemical whir in a hunk of tissue the size of a head of lettuce give rise to a feeling of joy, a creative idea, or a crazy dream?

The mind seeking to understand the brain—that is indeed among the ultimate scientific challenges. And so it will always be. To paraphrase scientist John Barrow, a brain simple enough to be understood is too simple to produce a mind able to understand it.

manifest content according to Freud, the remembered story line of a dream.

latent content according to Freud, the underlying meaning of a dream.

REM rebound the tendency for REM sleep to increase following REM sleep deprivation.

CHAPTER 2 REVIEW The Biology of Behavior and Consciousness

LEARNING OBJECTIVES

TEST YOURSELF Answer these repeated Learning Objective Questions on your own (before checking the answers in Appendix D) to improve your retention of the concepts (McDaniel et al., 2009, 2015).

The Power of Plasticity

2-1: How do biology and experience enable neural plasticity?

Neural Communication

2-2: What are the parts of a neuron, and what is an *action potential?*

2-3: How do neurons communicate?

2-4: How do neurotransmitters affect our mood and behavior?

The Nervous System

2-5: What are the two major divisions of the nervous system, and what are their basic functions?

The Endocrine System

2-6: How does the endocrine system transmit information and interact with the nervous system?

The Brain

2-7: What are some techniques for studying the brain?

2-8: What structures make up the brainstem, and what are the functions of the brainstem, thalamus, reticular formation, and cerebellum?

2-9: What are the structures and functions of the limbic system?

2-10: What are the four lobes of the cerebral cortex, and where are they located?

2-11: What are the functions of the motor cortex, somatosensory cortex, and association areas?

2-12: Do we really use only 10 percent of our brain?

2-13: How does the brain modify itself after some kinds of damage?

2-14: What is a *split brain*, and what does it reveal about the functions of our two brain hemispheres?

Brain States and Consciousness

2-15: What do we mean by *consciousness,* and how does selective attention direct our perceptions?

2-16: What is the *circadian rhythm,* and what are the stages of our nightly sleep cycle?

2-17: How do our sleep patterns differ? What five theories describe our need to sleep?

2-18: How does sleep loss affect us, and what are the major sleep disorders?

2-19: What do we dream about, and what are five explanations of *why* we dream?

TERMS AND CONCEPTS TO REMEMBER

TEST YOURSELF Write down the definition in your own words, then check your answer.

plasticity, *p.* 33
neuron, *p.* 33
cell body, *p.* 33
dendrites, *p.* 33
axon, *p.* 33
action potential, *p.* 33
glial cells (glia), *p.* 33
synapse [SIN-aps], *p.* 33
threshold, *p.* 35
refractory period, *p.* 35
all-or-none response, *p.* 35
neurotransmitters, *p.* 35
reuptake, *p.* 35
opiate, *p.* 35
endorphins [en-DOR-fins], *p.* 37
nervous system, *p.* 37
central nervous system (CNS), *p.* 37
peripheral nervous system (PNS), *p.* 37
nerves, *p.* 37
sensory neurons, *p.* 37
motor neurons, *p.* 37
interneurons, *p.* 37
somatic nervous system, *p.* 37
autonomic [aw-tuh-NAHM-ik] **nervous system (ANS),** *p.* 37
sympathetic nervous system, *p.* 37
parasympathetic nervous system, *p.* 37
reflex, *p.* 39
endocrine [EN-duh-krin] **system,** *p.* 39
hormones, *p.* 39
adrenal [ah-DREEN-el] **glands,** *p.* 39
pituitary gland, *p.* 41
EEG (electroencephalograph), *p.* 41
MEG (magnetoencephalography), *p.* 41
PET (positron emission tomography) scan, *p.* 41
MRI (magnetic resonance imaging), *p.* 41
fMRI (functional MRI), *p.* 41
brainstem, *p.* 43
medulla [muh-DUL-uh], *p.* 43
thalamus [THAL-uh-muss], *p.* 43
reticular formation, *p.* 43
cerebellum [sehr-uh-BELL-um], *p.* 43
limbic system, *p.* 45
amygdala [uh-MIG-duh-la], *p.* 45
hypothalamus [hi-po-THAL-uh-muss], *p.* 45
hippocampus, *p.* 45
cerebral [seh-REE-bruhl] **cortex,** *p.* 47
frontal lobes, *p.* 47
parietal [puh-RYE-uh-tuhl] **lobes,** *p.* 47
occipital [ahk-SIP-uh-tuhl] **lobes,** *p.* 47
temporal lobes, *p.* 47
motor cortex, *p.* 47
somatosensory cortex, *p.* 49
hallucination, *p.* 49
association areas, *p.* 49
neurogenesis, *p.* 51
corpus callosum [KOR-pus kah-LOW-sum], *p.* 51
split brain, *p.* 51
biological psychology, *p.* 53
cognitive neuroscience, *p.* 53
consciousness, *p.* 53
sequential processing, *p.* 55
parallel processing, *p.* 55
selective attention, *p.* 55
inattentional blindness, *p.* 55
change blindness, *p.* 57
circadian [ser-KAY-dee-an] **rhythm,** *p.* 57
REM (R) sleep, *p.* 57
alpha waves, *p.* 57
sleep, *p.* 57
delta waves, *p.* 59
suprachiasmatic nucleus (SCN), *p.* 61
insomnia, *p.* 63
narcolepsy, *p.* 63
sleep apnea, *p.* 63
night terrors, *p.* 63
dream, *p.* 63
manifest content, *p.* 65
latent content, *p.* 65
REM rebound, *p.* 65

CHAPTER TEST

TEST YOURSELF Answer the following questions on your own first, then check your answers in Appendix E.

1. What do psychologists mean when they say the brain is "plastic"?
2. The neuron fiber that passes messages through its branches to other neurons or to muscles and glands is the ________.
3. The tiny space between the axon of one neuron and the dendrite or cell body of another is called the
   a. axon terminal.
   b. branching fiber.
   c. synaptic gap.
   d. threshold.
4. Regarding a neuron's response to stimulation, the intensity of the stimulus determines
   a. whether or not an impulse is generated.
   b. how fast an impulse is transmitted.
   c. how intense an impulse will be.
   d. whether reuptake will occur.
5. In a sending neuron, when an action potential reaches an axon terminal, the impulse triggers the release of chemical messengers called ________.
6. Endorphins are released in the brain in response to
   a. morphine or heroin.
   b. pain or vigorous exercise.
   c. the all-or-none response.
   d. all of the above.
7. The autonomic nervous system
   a. is also referred to as the skeletal nervous system.
   b. controls the glands and the muscles of our internal organs.
   c. is a voluntary system under our conscious control.
   d. monitors sensory input and triggers motor output.
8. The sympathetic nervous system arouses us for action and the parasympathetic nervous system calms us down. Together, the two systems make up the ________ nervous system.
9. The neurons of the spinal cord are part of the ________ nervous system.
10. The most influential endocrine gland, known as the "master gland," is the
    a. pituitary.
    b. hypothalamus.
    c. thyroid.
    d. pancreas.
11. The ________ ________ secrete(s) epinephrine and norepinephrine, helping to arouse the body during times of stress.
12. The part of the brainstem that controls heartbeat and breathing is the
    a. cerebellum.
    b. medulla.
    c. cortex.
    d. thalamus.
13. The thalamus functions as a
    a. memory bank.
    b. balance center.
    c. breathing regulator.
    d. sensory control center.
14. The lower brain structure that governs arousal is the
    a. spinal cord.
    b. cerebellum.
    c. reticular formation.
    d. medulla.
15. The part of the brain that coordinates voluntary movement and enables nonverbal learning and memory is the ________.
16. Two parts of the limbic system are the amygdala and the
    a. cerebral hemispheres.
    b. hippocampus.
    c. thalamus.
    d. pituitary.
17. A cat's ferocious response to electrical brain stimulation would lead you to suppose the electrode had touched the ________.
18. The neural structure that most directly regulates eating, drinking, and body temperature is the
    a. endocrine system.
    b. hypothalamus.
    c. hippocampus.
    d. amygdala.
19. The initial reward center discovered by Olds and Milner was located in the ________.
20. If a neurosurgeon stimulated your right motor cortex, you would most likely
    a. see light.
    b. hear a sound.
    c. feel a touch on the right arm.
    d. move your left leg.

21. How do different neural networks communicate with one another to let you respond when a friend greets you at a party?

22. Which of the following body regions has the greatest representation in the somatosensory cortex?

a. Upper arm

b. Toes

c. Lips

d. All regions are equally represented.

23. The "uncommitted" areas that make up about three-fourths of the cerebral cortex are called ________ ________.

24. Judging and planning are enabled by the ________ lobes.

25. The flexible brain's ability to respond to damage is especially evident in the brains of

a. split-brain patients.

b. young adults.

c. young children.

d. right-handed people.

26. An experimenter flashes the word HERON across the visual field of a man whose corpus callosum has been severed. HER is transmitted to his right hemisphere and ON to his left hemisphere. When asked to indicate what he saw, the man says he saw ________ but his left hand points to ________.

27. Studies of people with split brains and brain scans of those with undivided brains indicate that the left hemisphere excels in

a. processing language.

b. visual perceptions.

c. making inferences.

d. neurogenesis.

28. Damage to the brain's right hemisphere is most likely to reduce a person's ability to

a. recite the alphabet rapidly.

b. make inferences.

c. understand verbal instructions.

d. solve arithmetic problems.

29. Failure to see visible objects because our attention is occupied elsewhere is called ________ ________.

30. Inattentional blindness is a product of our ________ attention.

31. Our body temperature tends to rise and fall in sync with a biological clock, which is referred to as ________ ________.

32. During the NREM-1 (N1) sleep stage, a person is most likely to experience

a. deep sleep.

b. hallucinations.

c. night terrors or nightmares.

d. rapid eye movements.

33. The brain emits large, slow delta waves during ________ sleep.

34. As the night progresses, what happens to the REM (R) stage of sleep?

35. Which of the following is NOT one of the reasons that have been proposed to explain why we need sleep?

a. Sleep has survival value.

b. Sleep helps us recuperate.

c. Sleep rests the eyes.

d. Sleep plays a role in the growth process.

36. What is the difference between narcolepsy and sleep apnea?

37. In interpreting dreams, Freud was most interested in their

a. information-processing function.

b. physiological function.

c. manifest content, or story line.

d. latent content, or hidden meaning.

38. Which dream theory best explains why we often dream of daily things we've seen or done?

39. The tendency for REM sleep to increase following REM sleep deprivation is referred to as ________ ________.

Continue testing yourself with **LearningCurve** or **Achieve Read & Practice** to learn and remember most effectively.

Sollina Images/Getty Images

Developing Through the Life Span

CHAPTER 3

SURVEY THE CHAPTER

Life is a journey, from womb to tomb. So it is for me [DM], and so it will be for you. My story, and yours, began when a man and a woman together contributed 20,000+ genes to an egg that became a unique person. Those genes contained the codes for the building blocks that, with astonishing precision, form our body and predispose our traits. My grandmother gave to my mother a rare hearing-loss pattern, which she, in turn, passed on to me (the least of her gifts). My father was a good-natured extravert, and sometimes I forget to stop talking. (As a child, though, my talking was slowed by embarrassing stuttering, for which Seattle Public Schools provided speech therapy.)

Along with my parents' nature, I also received their nurture. Like you, I was born into a particular culture, with its own way of viewing the world. My values have been shaped by a family culture filled with talking and laughter, by a religious culture that speaks of love and justice, and by an academic culture that encourages critical thinking (asking, *What do you mean? How do you know?*).

We are formed by our genes, and by our contexts, so our stories all differ. But in many ways we are each like nearly everyone else on Earth. Being human, you and I have a need to belong. My mental video library, which began after age 4, is filled with scenes of social attachment. Over time, my attachments to parents loosened as peer friendships grew. After lacking confidence to date in high school, I fell in love with a college classmate and married at age 20. Natural selection disposes us to survive and pass on our genes. Sure enough, two years later a child entered our lives, and I experienced a new form of love that surprised me with its intensity.

But life is marked by change. That child now lives 2000 miles away, and one of his two siblings calls South Africa her home. The tight rubber bands linking parent and child have loosened, as yours likely have as well.

Change also marks most vocational lives. I spent my teen years working in the family insurance agency, then became a premed chemistry major and a hospital aide. After discarding my half-completed medical school applications, I found my calling as a psychology professor and author. I predict that in 10 years you, too, will be doing things not in your current plan.

Stability also marks our development. Our life situations change, but we experience a continuous self. When I look in the mirror I do not see the person I once was, but I feel like the person I have always been. I am the same person who, as a late teen, played basketball and discovered love. A half-century later, I still play basketball. And I still love—with less passion but more security—the life partner with whom I have shared life's griefs and joys.

We experience a continuous self, but that self morphs through stages—for me, growing up, raising children, enjoying a career, and, eventually, life's final stage, which will demand my presence. As I make my way through this cycle of life to death, I am mindful that life's journey is a continuing process of development. That process is seeded by nature and shaped by nurture, animated by love and focused by work, begun with wide-eyed curiosity and completed, for those blessed to live to a good old age, with peace and never-ending hope.

Across the life span, we grow from newborn to toddler, from toddler to teenager, and from teenager to mature adult. At each stage of life there are physical, cognitive, and social milestones. Let's begin by exploring three key themes in developmental psychology.

Developmental Psychology's Major Issues

Learning Objective Question LOQ 3-1

What are the three major issues studied by developmental psychologists?

Why do researchers find human development interesting? Like most of us, they want to understand more about how we've become our current selves, and how we may change in the years ahead. **Developmental psychology** examines our physical, cognitive, and social development across the life span. Developmental psychologists often do **cross-sectional studies** (comparing people of different ages) and **longitudinal studies** (following people across time) to explore three major issues:

1. ***Nature and nurture:*** How does our genetic inheritance (our *nature*) interact with our experiences (our *nurture*) to influence our development?
2. ***Continuity and stages:*** What parts of development are gradual and continuous, like riding an escalator? What parts change abruptly in separate stages, like climbing rungs on a ladder?
3. ***Stability and change:*** Which of our traits persist through life? How do we change as we age?

LaunchPad See the *Video: Longitudinal and Cross-Sectional Studies* for a helpful tutorial animation.

NATURE AND NURTURE

The unique gene combination created when our mother's egg absorbed our father's sperm helped form us as individuals. Genes predispose both our shared humanity and our individual differences.

But it also is true that our experiences form us. Our family and peer relationships teach us how to think and act. Even differences initiated by our nature may be amplified by our nurture. We are not formed by either nature or nurture, but by the interaction between them. Biological, psychological, and social-cultural forces interact.

Mindful of how others differ from us, however, we often fail to notice the similarities stemming from our shared biology. Regardless of our culture, we humans share the same life cycle. We speak to our infants in similar ways and respond similarly to their coos and cries (Bornstein et al., 1992a,b). Although ethnic groups have differed in some ways, including average school achievement, the differences are "no more than skin deep" (Rowe et al., 1994). To the extent that family structure, peer influences, and parental education predict behavior in one of these ethnic groups, they do so for the others as well. Compared with the person-to-person differences within groups, the differences between groups are small. We share a human nature.

CONTINUITY AND STAGES

Do adults differ from infants as a giant redwood differs from its seedling—differences mostly created by constant, gradual growth? Or do we change in some ways as a caterpillar differs from a butterfly—in distinct stages?

Researchers who focus on experience and learning typically view development as a slow, ongoing process. Those who emphasize the influence of our biology tend to see development as a process of maturation, as we pass through a series of stages or steps, guided by instructions programmed into our genes. Progress through the various stages may be quick or slow, but we all pass through the stages in the same order.

Are there clear-cut stages of psychological development, as there are physical stages such as walking before running? The *stage theories* we will consider—of Jean Piaget on cognitive development, Lawrence Kohlberg on moral development, and Erik Erikson on psychosocial development—propose

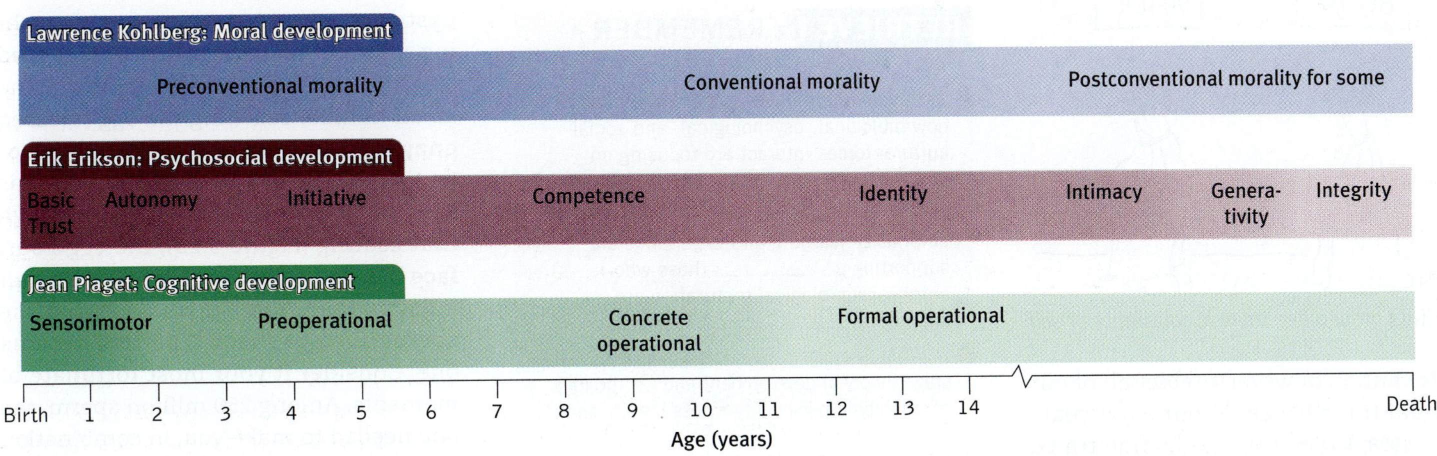

FIGURE 3.1 Comparing the stage theories With thanks to Dr. Sandra Gibbs, Muskegon Community College, for inspiring this illustration.

developmental phases (summarized in **FIGURE 3.1**). But we will also see research that casts doubt on the idea that life passes through neatly defined age-linked stages.

Although many modern developmental psychologists do not identify as stage theorists, the stage concept remains useful. The human brain does experience growth spurts during childhood and puberty that correspond roughly to Piaget's stages (Thatcher et al., 1987). And stage theories help us focus our attention on the forces and interests that affect us at different points in the life span. This close attention can help us understand how people of one age think and act differently when they arrive at a later age.

Stages of the life cycle

STABILITY AND CHANGE

As we follow lives through time, do we find more evidence for stability or change? If reunited with a long-lost childhood friend, do we instantly realize that "it's the same old Andy"? Or do long-ago friends now seem like strangers? (At least one man I [DM] know would choose the second option. At his 40-year college reunion, he failed to recognize a former classmate. That understandably upset classmate was his first wife!)

> "When I look at myself in the first grade and I look at myself now, I'm basically the same. The temperament is not that different." —Donald Trump to his biographer in *Never Enough*, 2015

We experience both stability and change. People predict that they will not change much in the future (Quoidbach et al., 2013). In some ways, they are correct. Some of our characteristics, such as *temperament* (emotional excitability), are very stable. When a research team studied 1000 people from age 3 to 32, they were struck by the consistency of temperament and emotionality across time (Slutske et al., 2012). Out-of-control 3-year-olds were later the most likely to engage in teen smoking, adult criminal behavior, or out-of-control gambling. Researchers also confirmed stability of moods when they followed 174 Scots

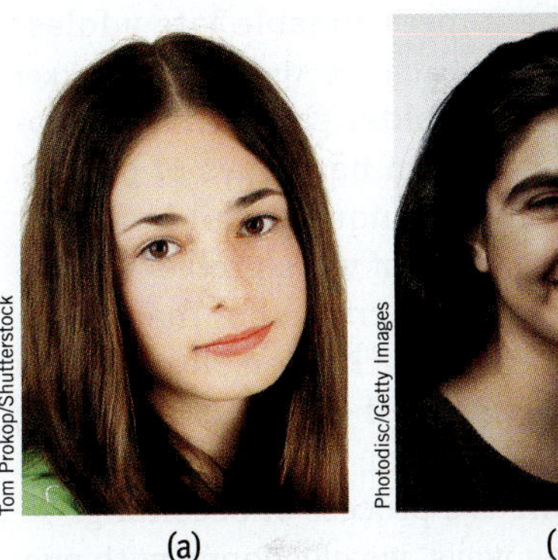
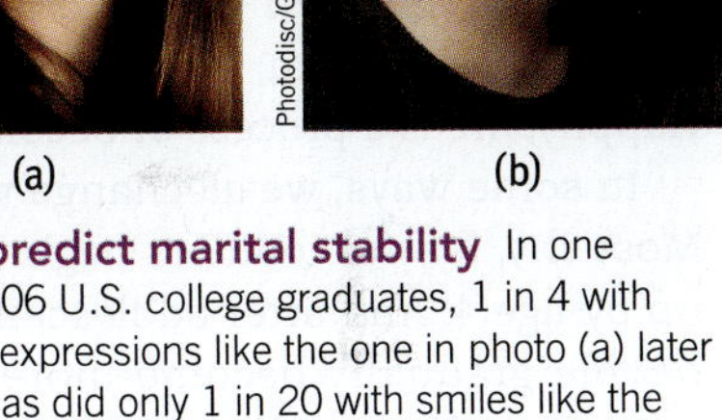

(a) (b)

Smiles predict marital stability In one study of 306 U.S. college graduates, 1 in 4 with yearbook expressions like the one in photo (a) later divorced, as did only 1 in 20 with smiles like the one in photo (b) (Hertenstein et al., 2009).

across 63 years—from age 14 to 77 (Harris et al., 2016). Moreover, children observed being repeatedly cruel to animals often became violent adults (Hensley et al., 2018). But on a happier note, other research showed that the widest smilers in childhood and college photos were, years later, the adults most likely to enjoy enduring marriages (Hertenstein et al., 2009).

developmental psychology a branch of psychology that studies physical, cognitive, and social development throughout the life span.

cross-sectional study research that compares people of different ages at the same point in time.

longitudinal study research that follows and retests the same people over time.

As adults grow older, there is continuity of self.

We cannot, however, predict all of our eventual traits based on our early years (Kagan, 1998; Kagan et al., 1978). Some traits, such as social attitudes, are much less stable than temperament, especially during the impressionable late adolescent years (Krosnick & Alwin, 1989; Rekker et al., 2015). And older children and adolescents can learn new ways of coping. It is true that delinquent children later have higher rates of work problems, substance abuse, and crime, but many confused and troubled children blossom into mature, successful adults (Moffitt et al., 2002; Roberts et al., 2001; Thomas & Chess, 1986). Happily, life is a process of becoming.

In some ways, we *all* change with age. Most shy, fearful toddlers begin opening up by age 4. And after adolescence most people gradually become more conscientious, self-disciplined, agreeable, and self-confident (Lucas & Donnellan, 2011; Shaw et al., 2010; Van den Akker et al., 2014). Risk-prone adolescents tend to become more cautious adults (Mata et al., 2016). Indeed, many 20-year-old goof-offs have matured into 40-year-old business or cultural leaders. (If you are the former, you aren't done yet.)

Life requires *both* stability and change. Stability increasingly marks our personality as we age (Briley & Tucker-Drob, 2014). "As at 7, so at 70," says a Jewish proverb. And stability gives us our identity. But our ability to change gives us hope for a brighter future and lets us adapt and grow from experience.

IN YOUR EVERYDAY LIFE

Are you the same person you were as a preschooler? As an 8-year-old? As a 12-year-old? How are you different? How are you the same?

RETRIEVE & REMEMBER

ANSWERS IN APPENDIX E

1. Developmental researchers who consider how biological, psychological, and social-cultural forces interact are focusing on __________ and __________.
2. Developmental researchers who emphasize learning and experience are supporting __________; those who emphasize biological maturation are supporting __________.
3. What findings in psychology support (1) the stage theory of development and (2) the idea of stability in personality across the life span?

Prenatal Development and the Newborn

CONCEPTION

LOQ 3-2 How does conception occur? What are *chromosomes, DNA, genes*, and the human *genome?* And how do genes and the environment interact?

Nothing is more natural than a species reproducing itself, yet nothing is more wondrous. For you, the process began when your mother's ovary released a mature egg—a cell roughly the size of the period that ends this sentence. The 250 million or more sperm deposited by your father then began their frantic race upstream. Like space voyagers approaching a huge planet, the sperm approached a cell 85,000 times their own size. The small number reaching the egg released enzymes that ate away the egg's protective coating (**FIGURE 3.2a**). As soon as the one winning sperm broke through that coating (Figure 3.2b), the egg's surface blocked out the others. Before half a day passed, the egg nucleus and the sperm nucleus fused. The two became one. Consider it your most fortunate of moments. Among 250 million sperm, the one needed to make you, in combination with that one particular egg, won the race, and so also for each of your ancestors through all human history. Lucky you.

Contained within the new single cell is a master code. This code will interact with your experience, creating you—a being in many ways like all other humans, but in other ways like no other human. Each of your trillions of cells carries this code in its **chromosomes.** These threadlike structures contain **DNA (deoxyribonucleic acid). Genes** are pieces of DNA, and they are either active *(expressed)* or inactive. External influences can "turn on" genes much as a cup of hot water lets a teabag express its flavor. When turned on, your genes will provide the code for creating protein molecules, your body's building blocks. **FIGURE 3.3** summarizes the elements that make up your personal **heredity.**

Eye of Science/Science Source

(a)

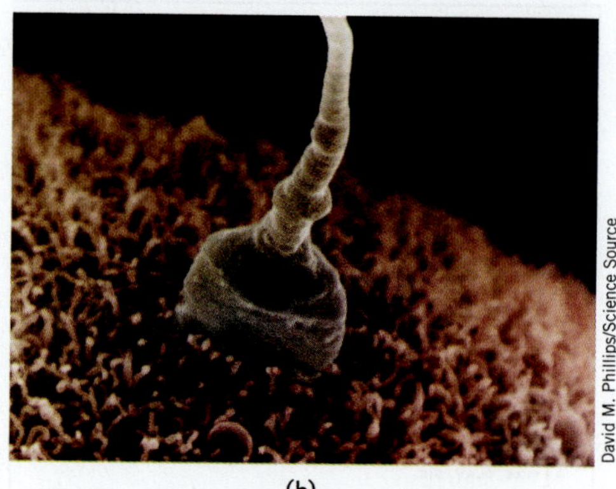

David M. Phillips/Science Source

(b)

FIGURE 3.2 Life is sexually transmitted (a) Sperm cells surround an egg. (b) As one sperm penetrates the egg's jellylike outer coating, a series of chemical events begins that will cause sperm and egg to fuse into a single cell. If all goes well, that cell will subdivide again and again to emerge 9 months later as a 37-trillion-cell human being.

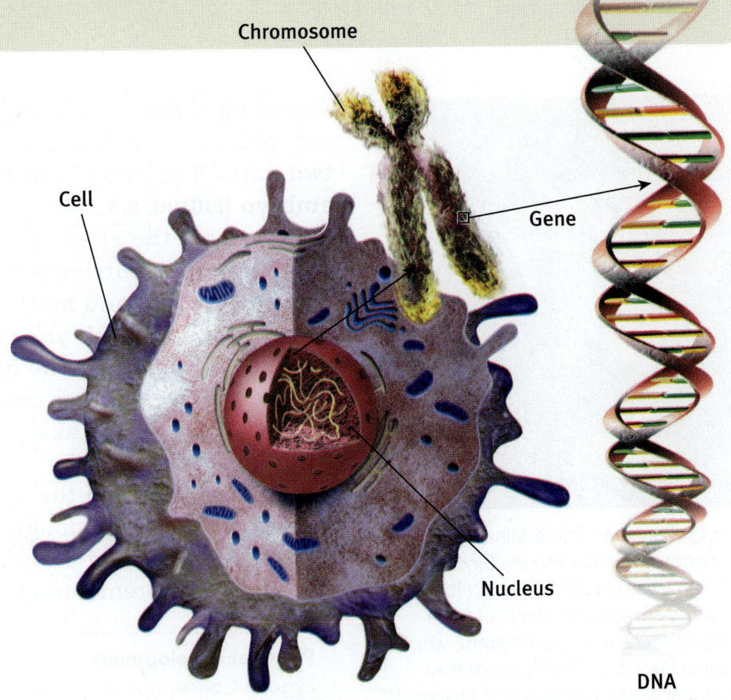

FIGURE 3.3 The life code The nucleus of every human cell contains chromosomes. Each is made up of two strands of DNA, connected in a double helix. Genes are DNA segments that, when expressed (turned on), direct the development of proteins that influence our individual development.

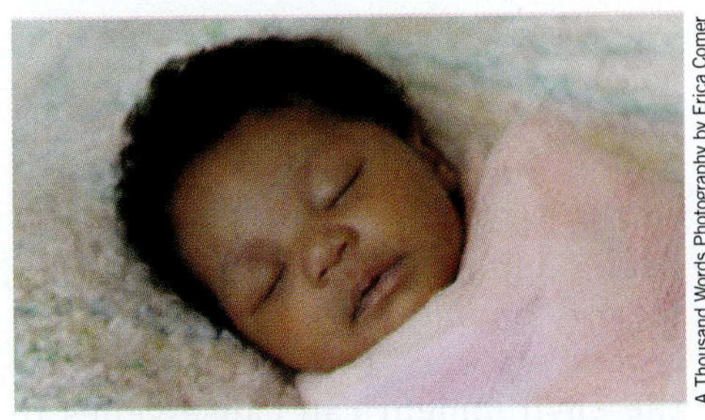
A Thousand Words Photography by Erica Comer

The nurture of nature Parents everywhere wonder: Will my baby grow up to be peaceful or aggressive? Successful or struggling at every step? What comes built in, and what is nurtured—and how? Research reveals that nature and nurture together shape our development—every step of the way.

Genetically speaking, every other human is close to being our identical twin. This shared genetic profile—our human **genome**—is what makes us humans, rather than chimpanzees, bananas, or tulips. "Your DNA and mine are 99.9 percent the same," noted Human Genome Project director, Francis Collins (2007). "At the DNA level, we are clearly all part of one big worldwide family."

> "We share half our genes with the banana."
> —Evolutionary biologist Robert May, president of Britain's Royal Society, 2001

The slight person-to-person variations found at particular gene sites in your DNA give clues to your uniqueness. We are each a one-of-a-kind package of looks, language, personality, interests, and cultural background. The genetic variations help explain why one person has a disease that another does not, why one person is tall and another short, why one is anxious and another calm. Most of our traits are influenced by many genes. How tall you are, for example, reflects the height of your face, the length of your leg bones, and so forth. Each of those is influenced by different genes. Traits such as intelligence, happiness, and aggressiveness are similarly influenced by a whole orchestra of genes (Holden, 2008). Indeed, one of the big take-home findings of today's genetics research is that there is no single gene that predicts your smarts, sexual orientation, or psychological health. Rather, our differing traits are influenced by "many genes of small effect" (Lee et al., 2018; Okbay et al., 2016; Plomin et al., 2016).

Our human differences are also shaped by our **environment**—by every external influence, from maternal nutrition while in the womb to social support while nearing the tomb. Your height, for example, may be influenced by your diet.

How do heredity and environment **interact?** Let's imagine two babies with two different sets of genes. Malia is a beautiful child and is also sociable and easygoing. Kalie is plain, shy, and cries constantly. Malia's pretty, smiling face attracts more affectionate and stimulating care. This in turn helps her develop into an even warmer and more outgoing person. Kalie's fussiness often leaves her caregivers tired and stressed. As the two children grow older, Malia, the more naturally outgoing child, often seeks activities and friends that increase her social confidence. Shy Kalie has few friends and becomes even more withdrawn.

chromosomes threadlike structures made of DNA molecules that contain the genes.

DNA (deoxyribonucleic acid) a molecule containing the genetic information that makes up the chromosomes.

genes the biochemical units of heredity that make up the chromosomes; segments of DNA.

heredity the genetic transfer of characteristics from parents to offspring.

genome the complete instructions for making an organism, consisting of all the genetic material in that organism's chromosomes.

environment every external influence, from prenatal nutrition to social support in later life.

interaction the interplay that occurs when the effect of one factor (such as environment) depends on another factor (such as heredity).

Our genetically influenced traits affect how others respond. And vice versa, *our environments trigger gene activity.* Nature and nurture interact.

The field of **epigenetics** explores the nature–nurture meeting place. *Epigenetics* means "in addition to" or "above and beyond" genetics. This field studies how the environment can cause genes to become either active *(expressed)* or inactive (not expressed). Genes can influence development, but the environment can switch genes on or off.

The molecules that trigger or block genetic expression are called *epigenetic marks.* When one of these molecules attaches to part of a DNA segment, it instructs the cell to ignore any gene present in that DNA stretch (**FIGURE 3.4**).

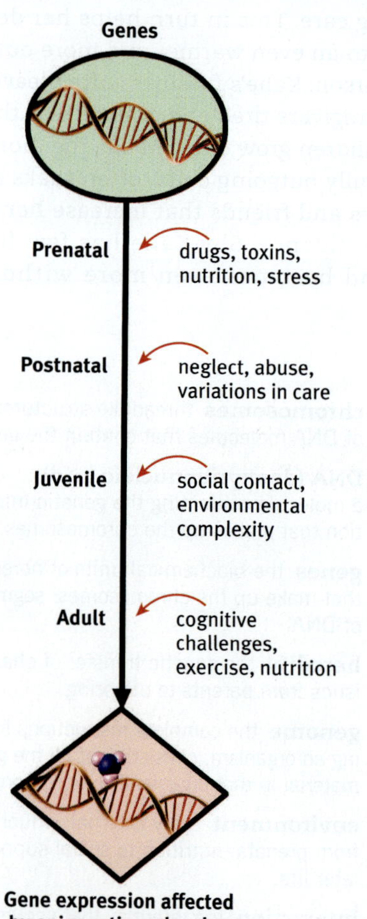

FIGURE 3.4 Beginning in the womb, life experiences lay down *epigenetic marks*—often organic molecules. These molecules can block the expression of any gene in the DNA segment they affect. (Research from Champagne, 2010.)

Adrian Wyld/The Canadian Press via AP

Lasting effects Canadian Prime Minister Justin Trudeau honored Senator Murray Sinclair with a humanitarian award in 2016. Sinclair led an in-depth study of the devastating effects of Canada's long-running residential school program, which removed Aboriginal Canadian children from their families. Psychologist Susan Pinker (2015) observed that the epigenetic effects of forced family separation "can play out, not only in the survivors of residential schools but in subsequent generations."

Diet, drugs, stress, and other experiences can affect these epigenetic molecules. Thus, from conception onward, heredity and experience dance together.

RETRIEVE & REMEMBER

ANSWERS IN APPENDIX E

4. Put the following cell structures in order from smallest to largest: nucleus, gene, chromosome.

PRENATAL DEVELOPMENT

LOQ 3-3 How does life develop before birth, and how do *teratogens* put prenatal development at risk?

How many fertilized eggs, called **zygotes,** survive beyond the first 2 weeks? Fewer than half (Grobstein, 1979; Hall, 2004). For the survivors, one cell becomes two, then four—each just like the first—until this cell division has produced some 100 identical cells within the first week. Then the cells begin to specialize. ("I'll become a brain, you become intestines!")

About 10 days after conception, the zygote attaches to the wall of the mother's uterus. So begins about 37 weeks of the closest human relationship. Near the beginning of this astonishing bodybuilding feat, the tiny clump of cells forms two parts. The inner cells become the **embryo** (**FIGURE 3.5**). Many of the outer cells become the *placenta,* the life-link that transfers nutrients and oxygen between embryo and mother. Over the next 6 weeks, the embryo's organs begin to form and function. The heart begins to beat. By 9 weeks after conception, an embryo looks unmistakably human. It is now a **fetus** (Latin for "offspring" or "young one"). During the sixth month, organs will develop enough to give the fetus a good chance of surviving and thriving if born prematurely.

Prenatal development
Zygote: Conception to 2 weeks
Embryo: 2 weeks through 8 weeks
Fetus: 9 weeks to birth

Remember: *Heredity and environment interact.* This is true even in the prenatal period. The placenta not only transfers nutrients and oxygen from mother to fetus, it also screens out many harmful substances. But some slip by. **Teratogens,** agents such as viruses and drugs, can damage an embryo or fetus. This is one reason pregnant women are advised not to drink alcoholic beverages or smoke cigarettes or marijuana (Saint Louis, 2017). A pregnant woman never drinks alone. When alcohol enters her bloodstream and that of her fetus, it reduces activity in both their central nervous systems.

Even light drinking, occasional binge drinking, or marijuana smoking can affect the fetal brain (Braun, 1996; CDC, 2018; Marjonen et al., 2015). Persistent heavy drinking puts the fetus at risk for birth defects, future behavior problems, and lower intelligence. For 1 in about 130 children worldwide and 1 in 30 in the United States, the effects are visible as *fetal alcohol spectrum disorder* (Lange et al., 2017; May et al., 2018). Its most serious form is **fetal alcohol syndrome (FAS),** which is marked by facial and mental abnormalities. The fetal damage may occur because alcohol has an epigenetic

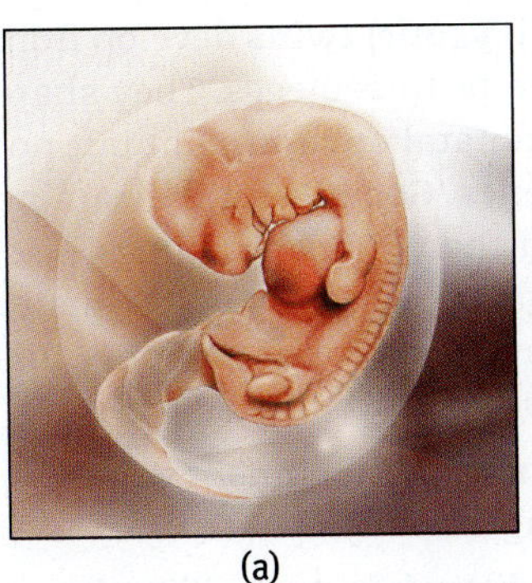
(a)

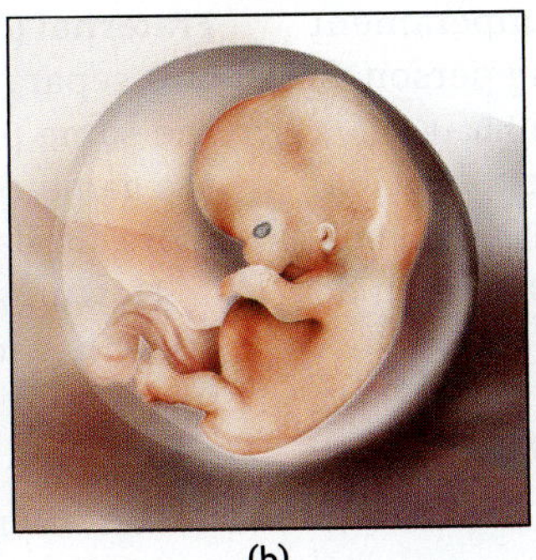
(b)

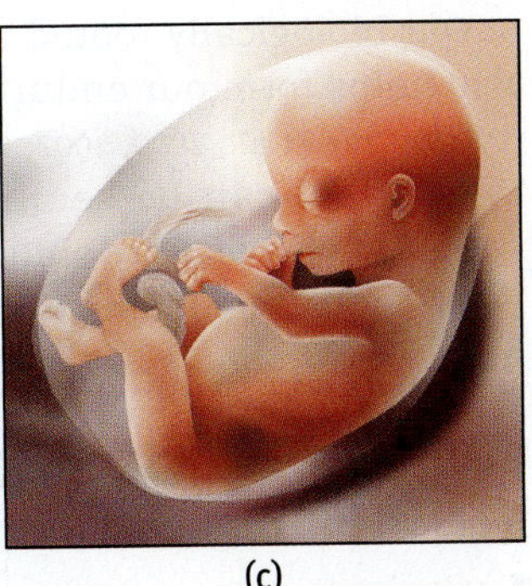
(c)

FIGURE 3.5 Prenatal development (a) The embryo grows and develops rapidly. At 40 days, the spine is visible and the arms and legs are beginning to grow. (b) By the start of the ninth week, when the fetal period begins, facial features, hands, and feet have formed. (c) As the fetus enters the sixteenth week, its 3 ounces could fit in the palm of your hand.

effect. It leaves chemical marks on DNA that switch genes to abnormal on or off states (Liu et al., 2009). Smoking cigarettes or marijuana during pregnancy also leaves epigenetic scars that may increase vulnerability to stress or addiction (Stroud et al., 2014; Szutorisz & Hurd, 2016). Some stress in early life prepares us to cope with later adversity. But substantial prenatal stress, including food scarcity, puts a child at increased risk for later health problems (Santavirta et al., 2018; Serpeloni et al., 2017).

Lightscapes Photography, Inc./Corbis/Glow Images

Alice DeWall

Prepared to feed and eat Like birds and other animals, we are predisposed to respond to our offspring's cries for food—even if we are in the middle of a 314-mile ultramarathon, as I [ND] was when my 18-month-old, Bevy, decided that only Daddy could feed her.

RETRIEVE & REMEMBER

ANSWERS IN APPENDIX E

5. The first two weeks of prenatal development is the period of the ____________. The period of the ____________ lasts from 9 weeks after conception until birth. The time between those two prenatal periods is considered the period of the ____________.

LaunchPad For an interactive review of prenatal development, see *Topic Tutorial: PsychSim6, Conception to Birth*. See also the 8-minute *Video: Prenatal Development.*

THE COMPETENT NEWBORN

LOQ 3-4 What are some abilities and traits of newborns?

Having survived prenatal hazards, we arrive as newborns with automatic **reflex** responses ideally suited for our survival. (Recall Chapter 2's discussion of the neural basis of reflexes.) New parents are often in awe of the finely tuned set of reflexes by which their baby gets food. When something touches their cheek, babies turn toward that touch, open their mouth, and actively *root* for a nipple. Finding one, they quickly close on it and begin *sucking*. (Failing to find satisfaction, the hungry baby may cry—a sound that parents find highly unpleasant, and very rewarding to relieve.) Other reflexes that helped our ancestors survive include the *startle* reflex (when arms and legs spring out, quickly followed by fist clenching and loud crying) and the surprisingly strong *grasping* reflex, both of which may have helped infants stay close to their caregivers.

As newborns, we search out sights and sounds linked with other humans. We turn our heads in the direction of human voices. As young infants, we also prefer to look at objects 8 to 12 inches away. Wonder of wonders, that just happens to be about the distance between a mother's eyes and those of her nursing infant (Maurer & Maurer, 1988). We gaze longer at a drawing of a face-like image (**FIGURE 3.6**). Even late-stage fetuses look more at face-like patterns in red lights shined through the womb (Reid et al., 2017).

We seem especially tuned in to that human who is our mother. Can newborns distinguish their own mother's smell in a sea of others? Indeed they can. Within days after birth, our brain has picked up and stored the smell of our mother's body (MacFarlane, 1978).

epigenetics the study of the molecular ways by which environments can influence gene expression (without a DNA change).

zygote the fertilized egg; it enters a 2-week period of rapid cell division and develops into an embryo.

embryo the developing human organism from about 2 weeks after fertilization through the second month.

fetus the developing human organism from 9 weeks after conception to birth.

teratogens [tuh-RAT-uh-jenz] agents, such as chemicals or viruses, that can reach the embryo or fetus during prenatal development and cause harm.

fetal alcohol syndrome (FAS) physical and mental abnormalities in children caused by a pregnant woman's heavy drinking. In severe cases, signs include a small, out-of-proportion head and abnormal facial features.

reflex a simple, automatic response to a sensory stimulus.

FIGURE 3.6 Newborns' preference for faces When shown these two images with the same three elements, newborns spent nearly twice as many seconds looking at the face-like image (Johnson & Morton, 1991). Newborns—average age 53 minutes in one study—have an apparently inborn preference for looking toward faces (Mondloch et al., 1999).

What's more, that smell preference lasts. One experiment was able to show this, thanks to some French nursing mothers who had used a chamomile-scented balm to prevent nipple soreness (Delaunay-El Allam et al., 2010). Twenty-one months later, their toddlers preferred playing with chamomile-scented toys! Other toddlers who had not sniffed the scent while breast feeding did not show this preference. (This makes us wonder: Will these children grow up to become devoted chamomile tea drinkers?)

So, even very young infants are competent. They smell and hear well. They see what they need to see. They are already using their sensory equipment to learn. Guided by biology and experience, those sensory and perceptual abilities will continue to develop steadily over the next months.

Yet, as most parents of multiple children will tell you, babies differ. One difference is in **temperament.** From the first weeks of life, some babies are *difficult* (irritable, intense, and unpredictable). Others are *easy* (cheerful, relaxed, and with predictable feeding and sleeping schedules) (Chess & Thomas, 1987). Temperament is genetically influenced (Fraley & Tancredy, 2012; Kandler et al., 2013). Differences in temperament appear in physical differences: Anxious, inhibited infants have high and variable heart rates. They become very aroused when facing new or strange situations (Kagan & Snidman, 2004; Roque et al., 2012).

Our biologically rooted temperament also helps form our enduring personality (McCrae et al., 2000, 2007; Rothbart, 2007). This effect can be seen in identical twins, who have more similar personalities—including temperament—than do fraternal twins.

TWIN AND ADOPTION STUDIES

LOQ 3-5 How do twin and adoption studies help us understand the effects of nature and nurture?

For about 1 in 270 sets of parents, pregnancy news brings a bonus. Detection of two heartbeats reveals that, during its early days of development, the zygote split into two (**FIGURE 3.7**). If all goes well, two genetically identical babies will emerge from their underwater world.

Identical (monozygotic) twins are nature's own human clones. They develop from a single fertilized egg, and they share the same genes. They also share the same uterus, and usually the same birth date and cultural history.

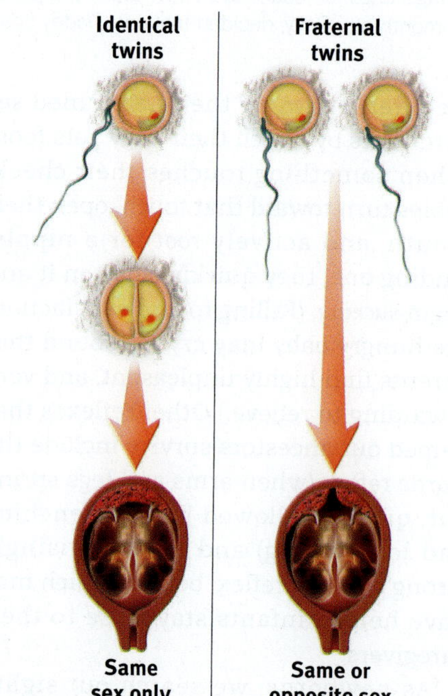

FIGURE 3.7 Same fertilized egg, same genes; different eggs, different genes Identical twins develop from a single fertilized egg, fraternal twins from two.

Fraternal (dizygotic) twins develop from two separate fertilized eggs. They share the same prenatal environment but not the same genes. Genetically, they are no more similar than ordinary siblings.

How might researchers use twins to study the influences of nature and nurture? To do so, they would need to

- vary the home environment while controlling heredity.
- vary heredity while controlling the home environment.

Happily for our purposes, nature has done this work for us.

LaunchPad See the *Video: Twin Studies* for a helpful tutorial animation.

Identical Versus Fraternal Twins

Identical twins have identical genes. Do these shared genes mean that identical twins also *behave* more similarly than fraternal twins (Bouchard, 2004)? Thousands of studies of nearly 15 million identical and fraternal twin pairs worldwide provide a consistent answer. Identical twins are more similar than fraternal twins in their abilities, personal traits, and interests (Polderman et al., 2015).

Next question: Could shared experiences rather than shared genes explain these similarities? Again, twin studies give some answers.

Separated Twins

In 1979, some time after divorcing, Jim Lewis awoke next to his second wife. Determined to make this marriage work, Jim left love notes around the house. As he lay there he thought about others he had loved, including his son, James Alan, and his faithful dog, Toy.

Jim loved building furniture in his basement woodworking shop, including a white bench circling a tree. Jim also liked to drive his Chevy, watch stock-car racing, and drink Miller Lite beer.

What was extraordinary about Jim Lewis, however, was that at that moment (we are not making this up) there was another man named Jim for whom all these things were also true.[1] This other Jim — Jim Springer — just happened, 38 years earlier, to have been Jim Lewis' womb-mate. Thirty-seven days after their birth, these genetically identical twins were separated and adopted. They grew up with no contact until the day Jim Lewis received a call from his genetic clone (who, having been told he had a twin, set out to find him).

One month later, the brothers became the first of 137 separated twin pairs tested by psychologist Thomas Bouchard and his colleagues (Miller, 2012c). Given tests measuring their personality, intelligence, heart rate, and brain waves, the Jim twins were virtually as alike as the same person tested twice. Their voice patterns were so similar that, hearing a playback of an earlier interview, Jim Springer guessed "That's me." Wrong—it was Jim Lewis.

This and other research on separated identical twins supports the idea that genes matter.

Twin similarities do not impress Bouchard's critics, however. If you spent hours with a complete stranger comparing your individual behaviors and life histories, wouldn't you also discover many coincidental similarities? Moreover, critics note, identical twins share an appearance and the responses it evokes, so they have probably had similar experiences. Bouchard replies that the life choices made by separated fraternal twins are not as dramatically similar as those made by separated identical twins.

[1] Actually, this description of the two Jims errs in one respect: Jim Lewis named his son James Alan. Jim Springer named his James Allan.

Derek Storm/Splash News/Newscom

Genetic space exploration In 2015, Scott Kelly (left) spent 340 days orbiting Earth in the International Space Station. His identical twin, Mark Kelly (right), remained on Earth. Both twins underwent the same physical and psychological testing. The study results will help scientists understand how genes and environment interact—in outer space and on Earth.

Biological Versus Adoptive Relatives

The separated-twin studies control heredity while varying environment. Nature's second type of real-life experiment — adoption — controls environment while varying heredity. Adoption creates two groups: genetic relatives (biological parents and siblings) and environmental relatives (adoptive parents and siblings). For any given trait we study, we can therefore ask three questions:

- How much do adopted children resemble their biological parents, who contributed their genes?
- How much do they resemble their adoptive parents, who contribute a home environment?
- While sharing a home environment, do adopted siblings come to share traits?

By providing children with loving, nurturing homes, adoption matters. Yet researchers asking these questions about *personality* agree on one stunning finding, based on studies of hundreds of adoptive families. *Nontwin siblings who grow up together, whether biologically related or not, do not much resemble one another in personality* (McGue & Bouchard, 1998; Plomin et al., 1988; Rowe, 1990). In traits such as outgoingness and agreeableness, for example, people who have been adopted are more similar to their biological parents than their caregiving adoptive parents.

As we discuss throughout this book, twin and adoption study results shed light on how nature and nurture interact to influence intelligence, disordered behavior, and many other traits.

RETRIEVE & REMEMBER

ANSWERS IN APPENDIX E

6. How do researchers use twin and adoption studies to learn about psychological principles?

Infancy and Childhood

As a flower develops in accord with its genetic instructions, so do we humans. **Maturation** — the orderly sequence of biological growth — dictates much of our shared path. Babies stand, then walk. Toddlers use nouns, then verbs. Severe deprivation or abuse can slow development, but genetic growth patterns exist from birth: They come "factory-installed" — they are inborn. Maturation (nature) sets the basic course of development; experience (nurture) adjusts it. Genes and scenes interact.

PHYSICAL DEVELOPMENT

LOQ 3-6 During infancy and childhood, how do the brain and motor skills develop?

Brain Development

In your mother's womb, your developing brain formed nerve cells at the explosive rate of nearly one-quarter million per minute. Your brain and your mental abilities developed together. On the day you were born, you had most of the brain

temperament a person's characteristic emotional reactivity and intensity.

identical (monozygotic) twins individuals who developed from a single fertilized egg that split in two, creating two genetically identical siblings.

fraternal (dizygotic) twins individuals who developed from separate fertilized eggs. They are genetically no closer than ordinary siblings, but shared a prenatal environment.

maturation biological growth processes leading to orderly changes in behavior, mostly independent of experience.

cells you would ever have. However, the wiring among these cells—your nervous system—was immature. After birth, these neural networks had a wild growth spurt, branching and linking in patterns that would eventually enable all your abilities. This rapid development helps explain why infant brain size increases rapidly in the early days after birth (Holland et al., 2014).

From ages 3 to 6, the most rapid brain growth was in your frontal lobes, the seat of reasoning and planning. During those years, your ability to control your attention and behavior developed rapidly (Garon et al., 2008; Thompson-Schill et al., 2009). The brain's association areas—those linked with thinking, memory, and language—were the last cortical areas to develop. As they did, your mental abilities surged (Chugani & Phelps, 1986; Thatcher et al., 1987). Fiber pathways supporting language and agility continued their rapid growth into puberty. Then, a use-it-or-lose-it *pruning process* began to shut down unused links and strengthen others (Paus et al., 1999; Thompson et al., 2000).

Your genes laid down the basic design of your brain, rather like the lines of a coloring book. Experience fills in the details (Kenrick et al., 2009). So how do early experiences shape the brain? Some fascinating experiments separated young rats into two groups (Renner & Rosenzweig, 1987; Rosenzweig, 1984). Rats in one group lived alone, with little to interest or distract them. The other rats shared a cage, complete with objects and activities that might exist in a natural "rat world" (**FIGURE 3.8**). Compared with the "loner" rats, those that lived in an enriched environment developed a heavier and thicker brain cortex.

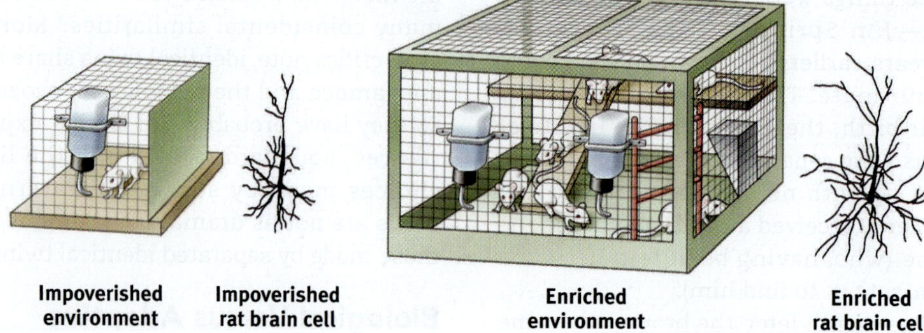

FIGURE 3.8 Experience affects brain development Researchers raised rats either alone, in an environment without playthings, or with other rats in an environment enriched with playthings changed daily (Rosenzweig et al., 1962). In 14 of 16 repetitions of this experiment, rats in the enriched environment developed significantly more cerebral cortex (relative to the rest of the brain's tissue) than did those in the impoverished environment.

The environment's effect was so great that if you viewed brief video clips of the rats, you could tell from their activity and curiosity whether they had lived in solitary confinement or in the enriched setting (Renner & Renner, 1993). After 60 days in the enriched environment, some rats' brain weight increased 7 to 10 percent. The number of brain synapse connections mushroomed by about 20 percent (Figure 3.8) (Kolb & Whishaw, 1998). The enriched environment literally increased brain power. In humans, too, lack of stimulation can slow brain and cognitive development (Farah, 2017).

Touching or massaging infant rats and premature human babies has similar benefits (Field, 2010; Sarro et al., 2014). In hospital intensive care units, medical staff now massage premature infants to help them develop faster neurologically, gain weight more rapidly, and go home sooner. Preemies who have had skin-to-skin contact with their mothers sleep better, experience less stress, and show better cognitive development 10 years later (Feldman et al., 2014).

Nature and nurture interact to sculpt our synapses. Brain maturation provides us with a wealth of neural connections. Experience—sights and smells, touches and tastes, music and movement—activates and strengthens some neural pathways while others weaken from disuse. Similar to paths through a forest, less-traveled neural pathways gradually disappear and popular ones are broadened (Gopnik et al., 2015).

We seem to have a **critical period** for some skills. During early childhood—while excess connections are still available—youngsters can most easily master another language. Lacking any exposure to spoken, written, or signed language before adolescence, a person will never master any language (see Chapter 8). Likewise, lacking visual experience during the early years, a person whose vision is restored by cataract removal will never achieve normal perceptions (more on this in Chapter 5) (Gregory, 1978; Wiesel, 1982). Without that early visual stimulation, the brain cells normally assigned to vision will die during the pruning process or be used for other purposes. For normal brain development, early stimulation is critical. The maturing brain's rule: Use it or lose it.

The brain's development does not, however, end with childhood. Thanks to the brain's amazing *plasticity*, our neural tissue is ever changing and reorganizing in response to new experiences. Throughout life, whether we are learning to text friends or write textbooks, we perform with increasing skill as our learning changes our brain tissue (Ambrose, 2010).

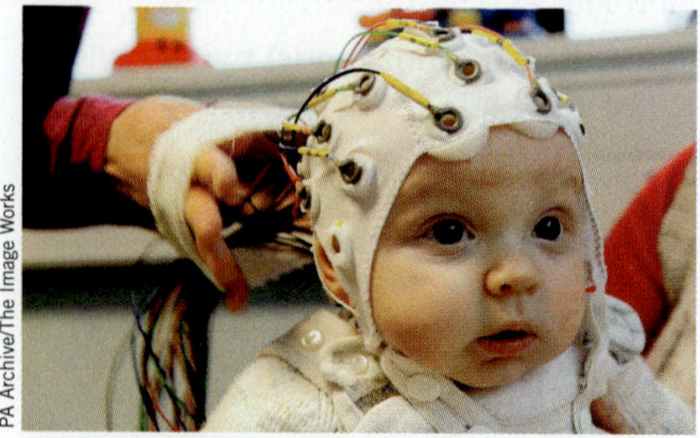

PA Archive/The Image Works

The baby experiment This electrode cap allows researchers to detect changes in brain activity triggered by different stimuli.

IMPROVE YOUR EVERYDAY LIFE

What skills did you practice the most as a child—sports, music, cooking, video gaming? How do you think this affected your brain development? How will you continue to develop your brain with new learning and new skills?

Motor Development

Babies gain control over their movements as their nervous system and muscles mature. Skills emerge, and with occasional exceptions, the motor development sequence is universal. Babies roll over before they sit unsupported. They usually crawl before they walk. The recommended infant *back to sleep position* (putting babies to sleep on their backs to reduce crib-death risk) has been associated with somewhat later crawling but not with later walking (Davis et al., 1998; Lipsitt, 2003).

There are, however, individual differences in timing. Consider walking. In the United States, 90 percent of all babies walk by age 15 months. But 25 percent walk by 11 months, and 50 percent within a week after their first birthday (Frankenburg et al., 1992). In some regions of Africa, the Caribbean, and India, caregivers often massage and exercise babies. This can speed up the process of learning to walk (Karasik et al., 2010).

Nevertheless, genes guide motor development. Identical twins typically begin walking on nearly the same day (Wilson, 1979). The rapid development of the cerebellum (at the back of the brain; see Chapter 2) helps create our eagerness to walk at about age 1. Maturation is likewise important for mastering other physical skills, including bowel and bladder control. Before a child's muscles and nerves mature, no amount of pleading or punishment will produce successful toilet training.

Physical development Sit, crawl, walk, run—the sequence of these motor development milestones is the same around the world, though babies reach them at varying ages.

RETRIEVE & REMEMBER

ANSWERS IN APPENDIX E

7. The biological growth process called ____________ explains why most children begin walking by about 12 to 15 months.

Brain Maturation and Infant Memory

Can you recall your third birthday? Most of us *consciously* recall little from before age 4. Psychologists call this blank space in our conscious memory *infantile amnesia*. But our brain was processing and storing information during that time. How do we know that? To see how developmental psychologists study thinking and learning in very young children, consider a surprise discovery.

In 1965, Carolyn Rovee-Collier was finishing her doctoral work in psychology. She was a new mom, whose colicky 2-month-old, Benjamin, could be calmed by moving a mobile hung above his crib. Weary of hitting the mobile, she strung a cloth ribbon connecting the mobile to Benjamin's foot. Soon, he was kicking his foot to move the mobile.

Thinking about her unintended home experiment, Rovee-Collier realized that, contrary to popular opinion in the 1960s, babies can learn. To know for sure that little Benjamin wasn't just a whiz kid, Rovee-Collier repeated the experiment with other infants (Rovee-Collier, 1989, 1999). Sure enough, they, too, soon kicked more when hitched to a mobile, both on the day of the experiment and the day after. They had learned the link between a moving leg and a moving mobile. If, however, she hitched them to a different mobile the next day, the infants showed no learning. Their actions indicated that they remembered the original mobile and recognized the difference. Moreover, when tethered to the familiar mobile a month later, they remembered the association and again began kicking.

Traces of forgotten childhood languages may also persist. One study tested English-speaking British adults who had spoken Hindi (an Indian language) or Zulu (an African language) in their childhood. Although they had no conscious memory of those languages, they could, up to age 40, relearn subtle Hindi or Zulu sound contrasts that other English speakers could *not* learn (Bowers et al., 2009). And Chinese adoptees living in Canada since age 1 process Chinese sounds as do fluent Chinese speakers, even if they have no conscious recollection of Chinese words (Pierce et al., 2014). We see our two-track mind at work here. What the conscious mind does not know and cannot express in words, the nervous system and our unconscious mind somehow remember.

IN YOUR EVERYDAY LIFE

What do you regard as your earliest memory? Now that you know about infantile amnesia (and you'll learn much more about memory in Chapter 7), has your opinion changed about the accuracy of that memory?

COGNITIVE DEVELOPMENT

LOQ 3-7 How did Piaget broaden our understanding of the way a child's mind develops, and how have today's researchers built on his work?

Somewhere on your journey from egghood to childhood, you became conscious. When was that? Psychologist Jean Piaget [pee-ah-ZHAY] spent a half-century searching for answers to such questions. He studied children's developing **cognition**—all the mental activities associated with thinking, knowing, remembering, and communicating.

critical period a period early in life when exposure to certain stimuli or experiences is needed for proper development.

cognition all the mental activities associated with thinking, knowing, remembering, and communicating.

Thanks partly to his pioneering work, we now understand that a child's mind is not a miniature model of an adult's. Children reason *differently,* in "wildly illogical ways about problems whose solutions are self-evident to adults" (Brainerd, 1996).

Piaget's interest in children's cognitive development began in 1920, when he was developing questions for children's intelligence tests in Paris. Looking over the test results, Piaget noticed something interesting. At certain ages, children made strikingly similar mistakes. Where others saw childish mistakes, Piaget saw developing intelligence at work.

Piaget's studies led him to believe that a child's mind develops through a series of stages. This upward march begins with the newborn's simple reflexes, and it ends with the adult's abstract reasoning power. Moving through these stages, Piaget believed, is like climbing a ladder. A child can't easily move to a higher rung without first having a firm footing on the one below.

Tools for thinking and reasoning differ in each stage. Thus, you can tell an 8-year-old that "getting an idea is like having a light turn on in your head," and the child will understand. A 2-year-old won't get the analogy. But an adult mind likewise can reason in ways that an 8-year-old won't understand.

Bill Anderson/Science Source

Jean Piaget (1896–1980) "If we examine the intellectual development of the individual or of the whole of humanity, we shall find that the human spirit goes through a certain number of stages, each different from the other" (1930).

Image Ideas/Getty Images

Christian L Birmele

FIGURE 3.9 A changing marriage schema Most people once had a *marriage* schema as a union between a man and a woman. Today, more than two dozen countries have legalized same-sex marriage.

Piaget believed that the force driving us up this intellectual ladder is our struggle to make sense of our experiences. His core idea was that "children are active thinkers, constantly trying to construct more advanced understandings of the world" (Siegler & Ellis, 1996). Part of this active thinking is building **schemas** — concepts or mental molds into which we pour our experiences (**FIGURE 3.9**).

To explain how we use and adjust our schemas, Piaget proposed two more concepts. First, we **assimilate** new experiences — we interpret them in terms of our current schemas (understandings). Having a simple schema for *dog,* for example, a toddler may call all four-legged animals *dogs.* But as we interact with the world, we also adjust, or **accommodate,** our schemas to incorporate information provided by new experiences. Thus, the child soon learns that the original dog schema is too broad and accommodates by refining the category.

IN YOUR EVERYDAY LIFE

Can you recall a time when you misheard some song lyrics because you assimilated them into your own schema? (For hundreds of examples of this, visit KissThisGuy.com.)

Piaget's Theory and Current Thinking

Piaget believed that children construct their understanding of the world as they interact with it. Their minds go through spurts of change, he believed, followed by greater stability as they move from one level to the next. In his view, cognitive development consisted of four major stages — *sensorimotor, preoperational, concrete operational,* and *formal operational.*

Sensorimotor Stage The **sensorimotor stage** begins at birth and lasts to nearly age 2. In this stage, babies take in the world through their senses and actions — through looking, hearing, touching, mouthing, and grasping. As their hands and limbs begin to move, they learn to make things happen.

Very young babies seem to live in the present. Out of sight is out of mind. In one test, Piaget showed an infant an appealing toy and then flopped his hat over it. Before the age of 6 months, the infant acted as if the toy no longer existed. Young infants lack **object permanence** — the awareness that objects continue to exist when out of sight (**FIGURE 3.10**). By about 8 months, infants begin to show that they do remember things they can no longer see. If you hide a toy, an 8-month-old will briefly look for it. Within another month or two, the infant will look for it even after several seconds have passed.

So does object permanence in fact blossom suddenly at 8 months, much as tulips blossom in spring? Today's researchers think not. They believe object permanence unfolds gradually, and they view development as more continuous than Piaget did.

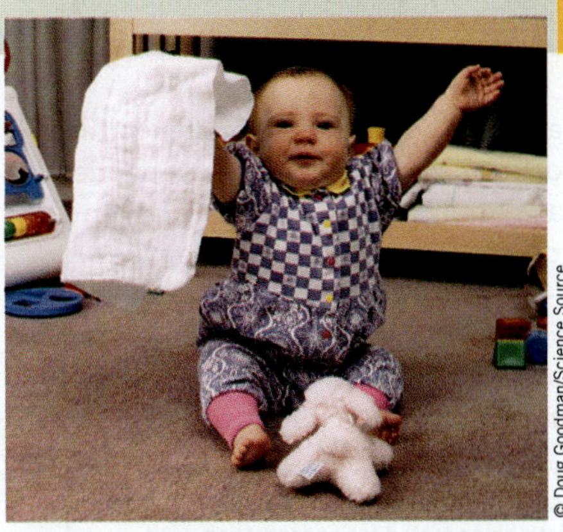
© Doug Goodman/Science Source

FIGURE 3.10 Object permanence Infants younger than 6 months seldom understand that things continue to exist when they are out of sight. But for this older infant, out of sight is definitely not out of mind.

They also think that young children are more competent than Piaget and his followers believed. Young children think like little scientists, testing ideas and learning from patterns (Gopnik et al., 2015). For example, infants seem to have an inborn grasp of simple physical laws—they have "baby physics." Like adults staring in disbelief at a magic trick (the "*Whoa!*" look), infants look longer at an unexpected, impossible, or unfamiliar scene—a car seeming to pass through a solid object. They also stare longer at a ball stopping in midair, or at an object that seems to magically disappear (Baillargeon, 2008; Shuwairi & Johnson, 2013; Stahl & Feigenson, 2015). Why do infants show this visual bias? Because impossible events violate infants' *expectations* (Baillargeon et al., 2016). Even as babies, we had a lot on our minds.

Preoperational Stage Piaget believed that until about age 6 or 7, children are in a **preoperational stage**—able to represent things with words and images, but too young to perform *mental operations* (such as imagining an action and mentally reversing it).

Conservation Consider a 5-year-old who tells you there is too much milk in a tall, narrow glass. "Too much" may become just right if you pour that milk into a short, wide glass. Focusing only on the height dimension, the child cannot perform the operation of mentally pouring the milk back into the tall glass. Before about age 6, said Piaget, young children lack the concept of **conservation**—the idea that the amount remains the same even if it changes shape (**FIGURE 3.11**).

Pretend Play Symbolic thinking and *pretend play* occur at an earlier age than Piaget supposed. One researcher showed children a model of a room and hid a miniature stuffed dog behind its miniature couch (DeLoache & Brown, 1987). The 2½-year-olds easily remembered where to find the miniature toy in the model,

schema a concept or framework that organizes and interprets information.

assimilation interpreting our new experiences in terms of our existing schemas.

accommodation adapting our current understandings (schemas) to incorporate new information.

sensorimotor stage in Piaget's theory, the stage (from birth to nearly 2 years of age) at which infants know the world mostly in terms of their sensory impressions and motor activities.

object permanence the awareness that things continue to exist even when not perceived.

preoperational stage in Piaget's theory, the stage (from about 2 to 6 or 7 years of age) in which a child learns to use language but cannot yet perform the mental operations of concrete logic.

conservation the principle (which Piaget believed to be a part of concrete operational reasoning) that properties such as mass, volume, and number remain the same despite changes in shapes.

Bianca Moscatelli/Worth Publishers

FIGURE 3.11 Piaget's test of conservation This visually focused preoperational child does not yet understand the principle of conservation. When the milk is poured into a tall, narrow glass, it suddenly seems like "more" than when it was in the shorter, wider glass. In another year or so, she will understand that the amount stays the same.

but that knowledge didn't transfer to the real world. They could not use the model to locate an actual stuffed dog behind a couch in a real room. Three-year-olds — only 6 months older — usually went right to the actual stuffed animal in the real room, showing they *could* think of the model as a symbol for the room.

LaunchPad For quick video examples of children being tested for conservation, visit *Concept Practice: Piaget and Conservation.*

Egocentrism Piaget also taught us that preschool children are **egocentric:** They have difficulty imagining things from another's point of view. Asked to "show Mommy your picture," 2-year-old Gabriella holds the picture up facing her own eyes. Told to hide, 3-year-old Gray puts his hands over his eyes, assuming that if he can't see you, you can't see him. Asked what he would do if he saw a bear, 3-year-old Grant replies, "We cover our eyes so the bears can't see us."

When a TV-watching preschooler blocks your view of the screen, the child probably assumes that you see what she sees. At this age, children simply are not yet able to take another's viewpoint. Even adolescents egocentrically overestimate how much others are noticing them (Lin, 2016). And adults may overestimate the extent to which others share their views. Have you ever mistakenly assumed that something would be clear to a friend because it was clear to you? Or sent an email mistakenly thinking that the receiver would "hear" your "just kidding" intent (Epley et al., 2004; Kruger et al., 2005)? As children, we were even more prone to such egocentrism.

Dave Myers

Egocentrism in action "Look, Granddaddy, a match!" So said my [DM's] granddaughter, Allie, at age 4, when showing me two memory game cards with matching pictures — that faced her.

Concrete Operational Stage By about age 7, said Piaget, children enter the **concrete operational stage.** Given concrete (physical) materials, they begin to grasp concepts such as conservation. Understanding that change in form does not mean change in quantity, they can mentally pour milk back and forth between glasses of different shapes. They also enjoy jokes that allow them to use this new understanding:

> Mr. Jones went into a restaurant and ordered a whole pizza for his dinner. When the waiter asked if he wanted it cut into 6 or 8 pieces, Mr. Jones said, "Oh, you'd better make it 6, I could never eat 8 pieces!" (McGhee, 1976)

Piaget believed that during the concrete operational stage, children become able to understand simple math and conservation. When my [DM's] daughter, Laura, was 6, I was astonished at her inability to reverse simple arithmetic. Asked, "What is 8 plus 4?" she required 5 seconds to compute "12," and another 5 seconds to then compute 12 minus 4. By age 8, she could answer a reversed question instantly.

Formal Operational Stage By age 12, said Piaget, our reasoning expands to include abstract thinking. We are no longer limited to purely concrete reasoning, based on actual experience. As children approach adolescence, many become capable of abstract *if . . . then* thinking: *If* this happens, *then* that will happen. Piaget called this new systematic reasoning ability **formal operational** thinking. (Stay tuned for more about adolescents' thinking abilities later in this chapter.) **TABLE 3.1** summarizes the four stages in Piaget's theory.

TABLE 3.1 Piaget's Stages of Cognitive Development

Typical Age Range	Stage and Description	Key Milestones
Birth to nearly 2 years	*Sensorimotor* Experiencing the world through senses and actions (looking, hearing, touching, mouthing, and grasping)	• Object permanence • Stranger anxiety
About 2 to 6 or 7 years	*Preoperational* Representing things with words and images; using intuitive rather than logical reasoning	• Pretend play • Egocentrism
About 7 to 11 years	*Concrete operational* Thinking logically about concrete events; grasping concrete analogies and performing arithmetical operations	• Conservation • Mathematical transformations
About 12 through adulthood	*Formal operational* Reasoning abstractly	• Abstract logic • Potential for mature moral reasoning

Image Source/Getty Images

Pretend play

Reflecting on Piaget's Theory

What remains of Piaget's ideas about the child's mind? Plenty. *Time* magazine singled him out as one of the twentieth century's 20 most influential scientists and thinkers. And a survey of British psychologists rated him as the last century's greatest psychologist (Psychologist, 2003). Piaget identified significant cognitive milestones and stimulated worldwide interest in how the mind develops. His emphasis was less on the ages at which children typically reach specific milestones than on their sequence. Studies around the globe, from Algeria to North America, have confirmed that human cognition unfolds basically in the sequence Piaget described (Lourenco & Machado, 1996; Segall et al., 1990).

However, today's researchers see development as more continuous than did Piaget. By detecting the beginnings of each type of thinking at earlier ages, they have revealed conceptual abilities Piaget missed. Moreover, they see formal logic as a smaller part of cognition than he did. Today, as part of our own cognitive development, we are adapting Piaget's ideas to accommodate new findings and our broader, cultural understandings.

Piaget's insights can nevertheless help teachers and parents understand young children. Remember this: Young children cannot think with adult logic and cannot take another's viewpoint. What seems simple and obvious to us—getting off a seesaw will cause a friend on the other end to crash—may never occur to a 3-year-old. Finally, accept children's cognitive immaturity as adaptive. It is nature's strategy for keeping children close to protective adults and providing time for learning and socialization (Bjorklund & Green, 1992).

RETRIEVE & REMEMBER

ANSWERS IN APPENDIX E

8. Object permanence, pretend play, conservation, and abstract logic are developmental milestones for which of Piaget's stages, respectively?

9. Identify each of the following developmental abilities (i–vi) with the correct cognitive developmental stage: (a) sensorimotor, (b) preoperational, (c) concrete operational, (d) formal operational.
   i. Thinking about abstract concepts, such as "freedom."
   ii. Enjoying imaginary play (such as dress-up).
   iii. Understanding that physical properties stay the same even when objects change form.
   iv. Having the ability to reverse math operations.
   v. Understanding that something is not gone for good when it disappears from sight, as when Mom "disappears" behind the shower curtain.
   vi. Having difficulty taking another's point of view (as when blocking someone's view of the TV).

LaunchPad For a 7-minute synopsis of Piaget's concepts, see the *Video: Cognitive Development.*

An Alternative Viewpoint: Vygotsky and the Social Child

LOQ 3-8 How did Vygotsky view children's cognitive development?

As Piaget was forming his theory of cognitive development, Russian psychologist Lev Vygotsky was also studying how children think and learn. Where Piaget emphasized how the child's mind grows through interaction with the *physical* environment, Vygotsky emphasized how the child's mind grows through interaction with the *social* environment. If Piaget's child was a young scientist, Vygotsky's was a young apprentice. By giving children new words and mentoring them, parents, teachers, and other children provide what we now call a temporary **scaffold** from which children can step to higher levels of thinking (Renninger & Granott, 2005; Wood et al., 1976). Children learn best when their social environment presents them with something in the sweet spot between too easy and too difficult. And it's important for all of us to remember that children are not empty containers waiting to be filled with knowledge. By building on what children already know, we can engage them with demonstrations and stimulate them to think for themselves.

Language, an important ingredient of social mentoring, provides the building blocks for thinking, noted Vygotsky. By age 7, children increasingly think in words and use words to solve problems. They do this, Vygotsky said, by internalizing their culture's language and relying on inner speech (Fernyhough, 2008). Parents who say, "No, no, Bevy!" when pulling their child's hand away from a cup of hot coffee are giving her a self-control tool. When Bevy later needs to resist temptation, she may likewise think, "No, no, Bevy!" Second graders who muttered to themselves while doing math problems grasped third-grade math better the following year (Berk, 1994). Whether out loud or silently, talking to themselves helps children control their behavior and emotions and to master new skills. (It helps adults, too. Adults who motivate themselves using self-talk—"You can do it!"—experience better performance [Kross et al., 2014].)

egocentrism in Piaget's theory, the preoperational child's difficulty taking another's point of view.

concrete operational stage in Piaget's theory, the stage of cognitive development (from about 7 to 11 years of age) at which children gain the mental operations that enable them to think logically about concrete events.

formal operational stage in Piaget's theory, the stage of cognitive development (normally beginning about age 12) at which people begin to think logically about abstract concepts.

scaffold in Vygotsky's theory, a framework that offers children temporary support as they develop higher levels of thinking.

Theory of Mind

LOQ 3-9 What does it mean to develop a *theory of mind,* and how is this impaired in those with *autism spectrum disorder?*

When Little Red Riding Hood realized her "grandmother" was really a wolf, she swiftly revised her ideas about the creature's intentions and raced away. Preschoolers develop this ability to read others' mental states when they begin forming a **theory of mind.**

When children can imagine another person's viewpoint, all sorts of new skills emerge. They can tease, because they now understand what makes a playmate angry. They can make nice, so may now be able to share with a sibling. Knowing what might make a parent buy a toy, they may try to persuade. Children who have an advanced ability to understand others' minds tend to be more helpful and well-liked (Imuta et al., 2016; Slaughter et al., 2015).

Between about ages 3 and 4½, children worldwide use their new theory-of-mind skills to realize that others may hold false beliefs (Callaghan et al., 2005; Rubio-Fernandez & Geurts, 2013; Sabbagh et al., 2006). One research team asked preschoolers what was inside a Band-Aid box (Jenkins & Astington, 1996). Expecting Band-Aids, the children were surprised to see that the box contained pencils. Then came the theory-of-mind question. Asked what a child who had never seen the box would think was inside, 3-year-olds typically answered "pencils." By age 4 to 5, children knew better. They anticipated their friends' false belief that the box would hold Band-Aids.

Children with **autism spectrum disorder (ASD),** a cognitive and social-emotional disorder, have an *impaired theory of mind* (Rajendran & Mitchell, 2007; Senju et al., 2009). They look less at others' eyes and have difficulty reading and remembering other people's thoughts and feelings (Baron-Cohen, 2017). Most children learn that another child's pouting mouth signals sadness, and that twinkling eyes mean happiness or mischief. A child with ASD—an estimated 1 in 66 Canadian and 1 in 59 U.S. children (Baio et al., 2018; Offner et al., 2018)—fails to understand these signals (Boucher et al., 2012; Frith & Frith, 2001).

ASD has differing levels of severity. "High-functioning" individuals generally have normal intelligence, and they often have an exceptional skill or talent in a specific area. But they lack social and communication skills and motivation, and they tend to become distracted by minor and unimportant stimuli (Clements et al., 2018; Remington et al., 2009). Those at the spectrum's most severe end struggle to use language.

Biological factors, including genetic influences and abnormal brain development, contribute to ASD (Colvert et al., 2015; Makin, 2015a; Tick et al., 2015). Childhood measles, mumps, and rubella (MMR) vaccinations do *not* (Taylor et al., 2014). Based on a fraudulent 1998 study—"the most damaging medical hoax of the last 100 years" (Flaherty, 2011)—some parents were misled into thinking that the childhood MMR vaccine increased risk of ASD. The unfortunate result was a drop in vaccination rates and an increase in cases of measles and mumps, putting those children and others who cannot be vaccinated at serious risk.

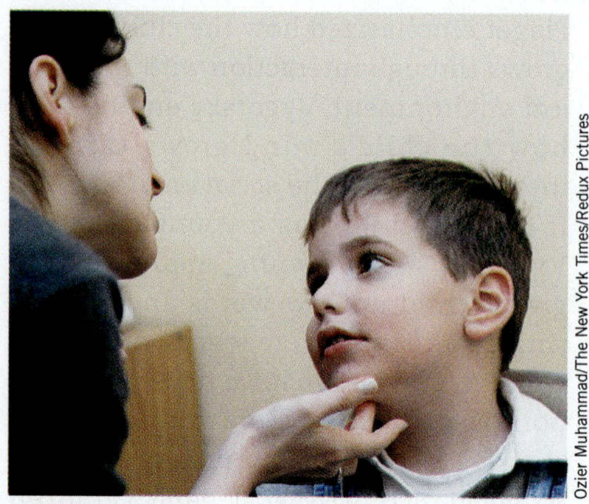
Ozier Muhammad/The New York Times/Redux Pictures

Autism spectrum disorder This speech-language pathologist is helping a boy with ASD learn to form sounds and words. ASD is marked by limited communication ability and difficulty understanding others' states of mind.

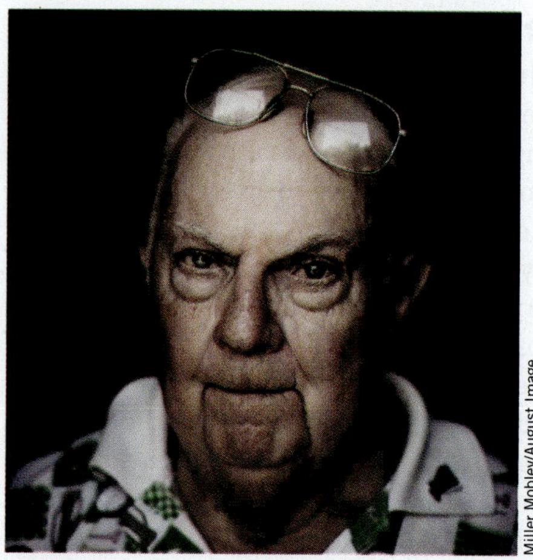
Miller Mobley/August Image

"Autism" case number 1 In 1943, Donald Gray Triplett, an "odd" child with unusual gifts and social weaknesses, was the first person to receive the diagnosis of "autism." (After a 2013 change in the diagnosis manual, his condition is now called *autism spectrum disorder.*) In 2016, at age 82, Triplett was still living in his family home and Mississippi town, where he often played golf (Atlas, 2016).

ASD gets diagnosed in about three boys for every girl, perhaps partly because girls could be more skilled in hiding ASD-related traits (Dean et al., 2017; Loomes et al., 2017). Psychologist Simon Baron-Cohen believes the imbalance is because boys more often than girls are "systemizers." They tend to understand things according to rules or laws, as in mathematical and mechanical systems. Girls, he thinks, are more often predisposed to be "empathizers." They tend to be better at reading facial expressions and gestures (van Honk et al., 2011). Whether male or female, those with ASD are systemizers who have more difficulty reading facial expressions (Baron-Cohen et al., 2015).

Why is reading faces so difficult for those with ASD? The underlying cause seems to be poor communication among brain regions that normally work together to let us take another's viewpoint. This effect appears to result from ASD-related genes interacting with the environment (State & Šestan, 2012). Children with ASD do make friends, but their peers may often find such relationships emotionally unsatisfying (Mendelson et al., 2016).

RETRIEVE & REMEMBER

ANSWERS IN APPENDIX E

10. What does *theory of mind* have to do with autism spectrum disorder?

SOCIAL DEVELOPMENT

From birth, most babies everywhere are social creatures, developing an intense bond with their caregivers. Infants come to prefer familiar faces and voices, then to coo and gurgle when given their attention. Have you ever wondered why tiny infants can happily be handed off to admiring visitors, but after a certain age pull back? By about 8 months, soon after object permanence emerges and children become mobile, a curious thing happens: They develop **stranger anxiety.** When handed to a stranger they may cry and reach back: "No! Don't leave me!" At about this age, children have schemas for familiar faces—mental images of how their caregivers should look. When the new face does not fit one of these remembered images, they become distressed (Kagan, 1984). Once again, we see an important principle: *The brain, mind, and social-emotional behavior develop together.*

Origins of Attachment

LOQ 3-10 How do the bonds of attachment form between caregivers and infants?

One-year-olds typically cling tightly to a caregiver when they are frightened or expect separation. Reunited after being apart, they often shower that special someone with smiles and hugs. This striking caregiver-infant **attachment** bond is a powerful survival impulse that keeps infants close. Infants normally become attached to people—typically their parents—who are comfortable and familiar. For many years, psychologists reasoned that infants grew attached to those who satisfied their need for nourishment. It made sense. But an accidental finding overturned this idea.

During the 1950s, University of Wisconsin psychologists Harry Harlow and Margaret Harlow bred monkeys for their learning studies. Shortly after birth, they separated the infants from their mothers and placed each infant in an individual cage with a cheesecloth baby blanket (Harlow et al., 1971). Then came a surprise: When their soft blankets were taken to be washed, the infant monkeys became distressed.

Imagine yourself as one of the Harlows, trying to figure out why the monkey infants were so intensely attached to their blankets. Psychologists believed that infants became attached to those who nourish them. Might comfort instead be the key? How could you test that idea? The Harlows decided to pit the drawing power of a food source against the contact comfort of the blanket by creating two artificial mothers. One was a bare wire cylinder with a wooden head and an attached feeding bottle. The other was a cylinder wrapped with terry cloth.

For the monkeys, it was no contest. They overwhelmingly preferred the comfy cloth mother (**FIGURE 3.12**). Like anxious infants clinging to their live mothers, the monkey babies would cling to their cloth mothers when anxious. When exploring their environment, they used her as a *secure base.* They acted as though they were attached to her by an invisible elastic band that stretched only so far before pulling them back. Researchers soon learned that other qualities—rocking, warmth, and feeding—made the cloth mother even more appealing.

Human infants, too, become attached to parents who are soft and warm and who rock, pat, and feed. Much parent-infant emotional communication occurs via touch, which can be either soothing (snuggles) or arousing (tickles) (Hertenstein et al., 2006). The human parent also provides a safe haven for a distressed child and a secure base from which to explore. People across the globe agree that the ideal mother "shows affection by touching" (Mesman et al., 2015). Such parental affection aids brain development and later cognitive ability (Davis et al., 2017).

PR INC/Science Source

FIGURE 3.12 The Harlows' mothers The infant monkeys much preferred contact with the comfortable cloth mother, even while feeding from the wire nourishing mother.

Attachment Differences

LOQ 3-11 Why do attachment differences matter, and how does an infant's ability to develop basic trust affect later relationships?

Children's attachments differ. To study these differences, Mary Ainsworth (1979) designed the *strange situation* experiment. She observed mother-infant pairs at home during their first six months.

theory of mind people's ideas about their own and others' mental states—about their feelings, perceptions, and thoughts, and the behaviors these might predict.

autism spectrum disorder (ASD) a disorder that appears in childhood and is marked by significant limitations in communication and social interaction, and by rigidly fixated interests and repetitive behaviors.

stranger anxiety the fear of strangers that infants commonly display, beginning by about 8 months of age.

attachment an emotional tie with others; shown in young children by their seeking closeness to caregivers and showing distress on separation.

Later she observed the 1-year-old infants in a strange situation (usually a laboratory playroom) with and without their mothers. Such research shows that about 60 percent of infants and young children display *secure attachment* (Moulin et al., 2014). In their mother's presence, they play comfortably, happily exploring their new environment. When she leaves, they become upset. When she returns, they seek contact with her.

Other infants show *insecure attachment,* marked by either anxiety or avoidance of trusting relationships. These infants are less likely to explore their surroundings. Anxiously attached infants may cling to their mother. When she leaves, they might cry loudly and remain upset. Avoidantly attached infants seem not to notice or care about her departure and return (Ainsworth, 1973, 1989; Kagan, 1995; van IJzendoorn & Kroonenberg, 1988).

Ainsworth and others found that sensitive, responsive mothers—those who noticed what their babies were doing and responded appropriately—had infants who were securely attached (De Wolff & van IJzendoorn, 1997). Insensitive, unresponsive mothers—mothers who attended to their babies when they felt like doing so but ignored them at other times—often had infants who were insecurely attached. The Harlows' monkey studies, with unresponsive artificial mothers, produced even more striking effects. When put in strange situations without their artificial mothers, the deprived infants were terrified (**FIGURE 3.13**).

Science Source

FIGURE 3.13 Social deprivation and fear In the Harlows' experiments, monkeys raised with artificial mothers were terror-stricken when placed in strange situations without those mothers.

Today's climate of greater respect for animal welfare would likely prevent such primate studies. Many now remember Harry Harlow as the researcher who tortured helpless monkeys. But others support the Harlows' work. "Harry Harlow, whose name has [come to mean] cruel monkey experiments, actually helped put an end to cruel child-rearing practices," said primatologist Frans de Waal (2011). Harry Harlow defended their methods: "Remember, for every mistreated monkey there exist a million mistreated children." He expressed the hope that his research would sensitize people to child abuse and neglect.

So, caring parents (and other caregivers) matter. But is attachment style the *result* of parenting? Or are other factors also at work?

Temperament and Attachment How does temperament affect attachment style? As we saw earlier in this chapter, temperament is genetically influenced.

Some babies tend to be *difficult*—irritable, intense, and unpredictable. Others are *easy*—cheerful, relaxed, and feeding and sleeping on predictable schedules (Chess & Thomas, 1987). Parenting studies that neglect such inborn differences, critics say, might as well be "comparing foxhounds reared in kennels with poodles reared in apartments" (Harris, 1998). To separate the effects of nature and nurture on attachment, we would need to vary parenting while controlling temperament. (Pause and think: If you were the researcher, how might you do this?)

One researcher's solution was to randomly assign 100 temperamentally difficult infants to two groups. Half of the 6- to 9-month-olds were in the experimental group, in which mothers received personal training in sensitive responding. The other half were in a control group, in which mothers did not receive this training (van den Boom, 1990, 1995). At 12 months of age, 68 percent of the infants in the first group were securely attached, as were only 28 percent of the control group infants. Other studies confirm that such programs can increase parental sensitivity and, to some extent, infant attachment security (Bakermans-Kranenburg et al., 2003; Van Zeijl et al., 2006). Nature and nurture interact.

Researchers have more often studied mother care than father care, but fathers are more than just mobile sperm banks. Nearly 100 studies worldwide have shown that a father's love and acceptance are comparable with a mother's love in predicting an offspring's health and well-being (Rohner & Veneziano, 2001).

Children's anxiety over separation from parents peaks at around 13 months, then gradually declines (Kagan, 1976). This happens whether they live with one parent or two, are cared for at home or in day care, live in North America, Guatemala, or the Kalahari Desert. As the power of early attachment relaxes, we humans begin to move out into a wider range of situations. We communicate with strangers more freely. And we stay attached emotionally to loved ones despite distance.

At all ages, we are social creatures. But as we mature, our secure base shifts—from parents to peers and partners (Cassidy & Shaver, 1999). We gain strength when someone offers, by words and actions, a safe haven: "I will be here. I am interested in you. Come what may, I will actively support you" (Crowell & Waters, 1994).

> **LaunchPad** Play the role of a researcher studying temperament and personality by engaging online with the activity *How Would You Know If Personality Runs in Our Genes?*

Attachment Styles and Later Relationships Developmental psychologist Erik Erikson (1902–1994), working with his wife, Joan Erikson (1902–1997), believed that securely attached children approach life with a sense of **basic trust**—a sense that the world is predictable and reliable. This lifelong attitude of trust rather than fear, they said, flows from children's interactions with sensitive, loving caregivers.

Do our early attachments form the foundation for adult relationships, including our comfort with *intimacy?*

Many researchers now believe they do (Birnbaum et al., 2006; Fraley et al., 2013). People who report that they had secure relationships with their parents tend to enjoy secure friendships (Gorrese & Ruggieri, 2012). Children with secure, responsive mothers tend to have good grades and strong friendships (Raby et al., 2014).

Feeling insecurely attached to others during childhood may take either of two main forms (Fraley et al., 2011). One is *anxious attachment,* in which people constantly crave acceptance but remain alert to signs of possible rejection. The other is *avoidant attachment,* in which people experience discomfort getting close to others and tend to keep their distance. An anxious attachment style can annoy relationship partners. An avoidant style decreases commitment and increases conflict (DeWall et al., 2011; Overall et al., 2015).

IN YOUR EVERYDAY LIFE

How has your upbringing affected your attachment style?

LaunchPad To consider how your own attachment style may be affecting your current relationships, engage online with the activity *Assess Your Strengths: What Is Your Attachment Style?*

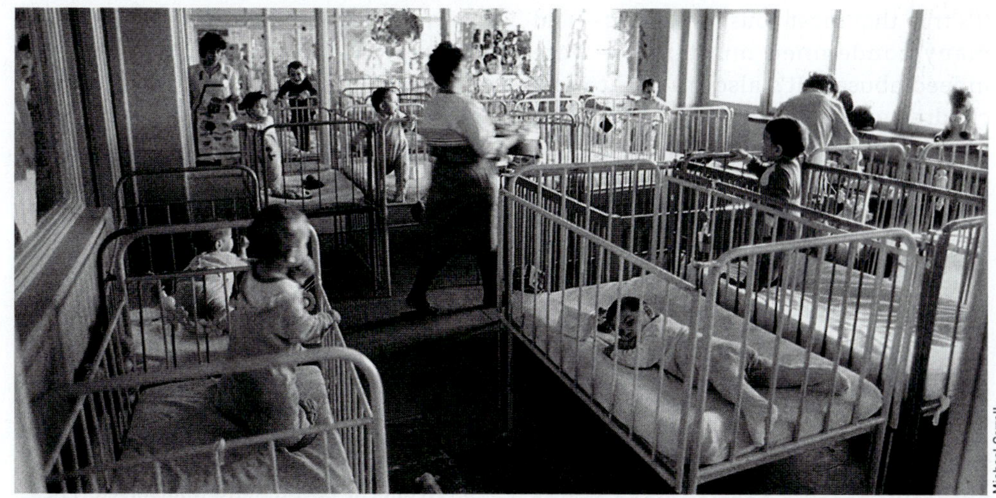

Michael Carroll

The deprivation of attachment In this 1980s Romanian orphanage, the 250 children between ages one and five outnumbered caregivers 15 to 1.

Deprivation of Attachment

If secure attachment fosters social trust, what happens when circumstances prevent a child from forming any attachments? In all of psychology, there is no sadder research literature. Some of these babies were raised in institutions without a regular caregiver's stimulation and attention. Others were locked away at home under conditions of abuse or extreme neglect. Most were withdrawn, frightened, even speechless. Those left in understaffed Romanian orphanages during the 1980s looked "frighteningly like Harlow's monkeys" (Carlson, 1995). When the deprived children were tested years later, they had impaired brain, cognitive, and social development compared with children assigned to quality foster care settings (Bick et al., 2015; Kennedy et al., 2016; Nelson et al., 2014). Dozens of studies have found that orphaned children generally fare better on later intelligence tests when raised in family homes from an early age (van IJzendoorn et al., 2008, 2017).

The Harlows' monkeys bore similar scars if raised in total isolation, without even an artificial mother. As adults, when placed with other monkeys their age, they either cowered in fright or lashed out in aggression. When they reached sexual maturity, most were incapable of mating. Females who did have babies were often neglectful, abusive, even murderous toward them.

In humans, too, the unloved sometimes become the unloving. Some 30 percent of those who have been abused do later abuse their own children. This is four times the U.S. national rate of child abuse (Dumont et al., 2007; Widom, 1989a,b). Childhood abuse victims have a doubled risk of later depression, more troubled adult romantic relationships, and poorer physical health (Jakubowski et al., 2018; Labella et al., 2018; Nanni et al., 2012). They are especially at risk for depression if they carry a gene variation that spurs stress-hormone production (Bradley et al., 2008). As we will see again and again, behavior and emotion arise from a particular environment interacting with particular genes.

Recall that, depending on our experience, genes may or may not be expressed (active). Epigenetics studies show that experience puts molecular marks on genes that influence their expression. Severe child abuse, for example, can affect the normal expression of genes (Lutz et al., 2017; Romens et al., 2015). Extreme childhood trauma can also leave footprints on the brain (Teicher & Samson, 2016). Normally placid golden hamsters that are repeatedly threatened and attacked while young grow up to be cowards when caged with same-sized hamsters, or bullies when caged with weaker ones (Ferris, 1996). Young children who are terrorized through bullying, physical abuse, sexual abuse, or wartime atrocities (being beaten, witnessing torture, and living in constant fear) often suffer other lasting wounds. They live at increased risk for health problems, psychological disorders, substance abuse, criminality, and, for women, earlier death (Chen et al., 2016; Lereya et al., 2015). Still, many children successfully survive abuse.

basic trust according to Erik Erikson, a sense that the world is predictable and trustworthy; said to be formed during infancy by appropriate experiences with responsive caregivers.

It's true that most abusive parents—and many condemned murderers—were indeed abused. It's also true that most children growing up in harsh conditions *don't* become violent criminals or abusive parents. Indeed, hardship short of trauma often boosts mental toughness (Seery, 2011). And though the hardship of growing up poor puts children at risk for some problems, growing up rich puts them at risk for others. Wealthy children are at greater risk for substance abuse, eating disorders, anxiety, and depression (Lund & Dearing, 2012; Luthar et al., 2013). Children who have coped with some adversity become hardier when facing future stresses (Ellis et al., 2017). So when you recall some adversity you have faced, consider the silver lining. Your coping may have strengthened your *resilience*—your tendency to bounce back and go on to lead a better life.

Parenting Styles

LOQ 3-12 What are the four main parenting styles?

Child-raising practices vary. Some parents are strict; some are lax. Some show little affection; some liberally hug and kiss. How do parenting differences affect children?

The most heavily researched aspect of parenting has been how, and to what extent, parents seek to control their children. Parenting styles can be described as a combination of two traits: how *responsive* and how *demanding* parents are (Kakinami et al., 2015). Investigators have identified four parenting styles (Baumrind, 1966, 1967; Steinberg, 2001):

1. ***Authoritarian*** parents are *coercive*. They set the rules and expect obedience: "Don't interrupt." "Keep your room clean." "Don't stay out late or you'll be grounded." "Why? Because I said so."
2. ***Permissive*** parents are *unrestraining*. They make few demands and use little punishment. They may be unwilling to set limits.
3. ***Negligent*** parents are *uninvolved*. They are neither demanding nor responsive. They are careless, inattentive, and do not seek a close relationship with their children.
4. ***Authoritative*** parents are *confrontive*. They are both demanding and responsive. They exert control by setting rules, but especially with older children, they encourage open discussion and allow exceptions.

For more on parenting styles and their associated outcomes, see Thinking Critically About: Parenting Styles.

Remember, too, that parenting doesn't happen in a vacuum. One of the forces that influences parenting styles is culture.

Robert Weber/The New Yorker Collection/The Cartoon Bank

"Thank you, Adrian. Parenting is a learning process, and your criticisms help."

IMPROVE YOUR EVERYDAY LIFE

What kinds of mistakes do you think parents of the past made? What mistakes do you think today's parents might be making, and that as a parent you would want to (or already try to) avoid?

Culture and Child Raising Culture, as we noted in Chapter 1, is the set of enduring behaviors, ideas, attitudes, values, and traditions shared by a group of people and handed down from one generation to the next (Brislin, 1988). In Chapter 4, we'll explore the effects of culture on gender. In later chapters, we'll consider the influence of culture on social interactions and psychological disorders. For now, let's look at the way that child-raising practices reflect cultural values.

Variations in child-raising values reflect cultural diversity, and changes over time. Do you prefer children who are independent, or children who comply with what others think? Compared with families in Asian cultures, families in Western cultures more often favor independence. "You are responsible for yourself." "Follow your conscience. Be true to yourself. Discover your gifts." In recent years, some Western parents have gone further, telling their children, "You are more special than other children" (Brummelman et al., 2015). Many with Western cultural values no longer prioritize obedience, respect, and sensitivity to others (Alwin, 1990; Remley, 1988). Western parents a generation ago were more likely to teach their children to: "Be true to your traditions. Be loyal to your heritage and country. Show respect toward your parents and other superiors." Cultures vary. And cultures change.

Children across place and time have thrived under various child-raising systems. Upper-class British parents traditionally handed off routine caregiving to nannies, then sent their 10-year-olds away to boarding school.

Stephen H. Reehl

Cultures vary Parents everywhere care about their children, but raise and protect them differently depending on the surrounding culture. In big cities, parents keep their children close. In smaller, close-knit communities, such as Scotland's Orkney Islands' town of Stromness, social trust has enabled parents to park their toddlers outside shops.

Thinking Critically About:
Parenting Styles—Too Hard, Too Soft, Too Uncaring, and Just Right?

LOQ 3-13 What outcomes are associated with each parenting style?

Researchers have identified four parenting styles,[1] which have been associated with varying outcomes.

1 Authoritarian parents

↕

Children with less social skill and self-esteem, and a brain that over-reacts when they make mistakes[2]

2 Permissive parents

↕

Children who are more aggressive and immature [3]

HOWEVER, Correlation ≠ Causation!

What other factors might explain this parenting-competence link?

- **Children's traits may influence parenting. Parental warmth and control vary somewhat from child to child, even in the same family.[6] Maybe socially mature, agreeable, easygoing children get greater trust and warmth from their parents? Twin studies have supported this possibility.[7]**
- **Some underlying third factor may be at work. Perhaps, for example, competent parents and their competent children share genes that make social competence more likely. Twin studies have also supported this possibility.[8]**

3 Negligent parents

↕

Children with poor academic and social outcomes[4]

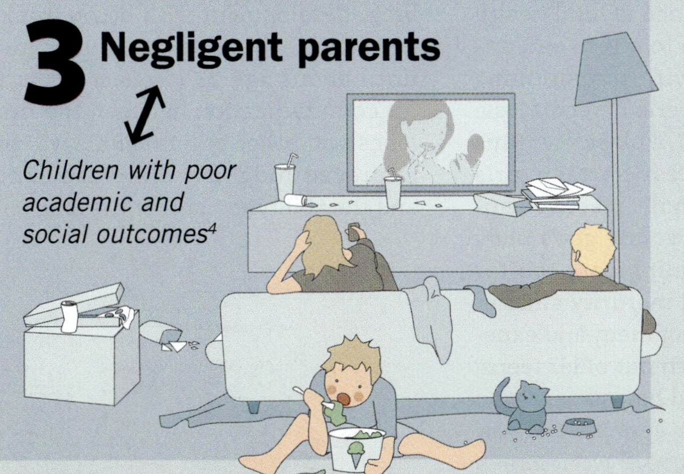

4 Authoritative parents

↕

Children with the highest self-esteem, self-reliance, self-regulation, and social competence[5]

1. Kakinami et al., 2015. 2. Meyer et al., 2015. 3. Luyckx et al., 2011. 4. Pinquart, 2015; Steinberg et al., 1994. 5. Baumrind, 1996, 2013; Buri et al.,1988; Coopersmith, 1967; Sulik et al., 2015. 6. Holden & Miller, 1999; Klahr & Burt, 2014. 7. Kendler, 1996. 8. South et al., 2008.

Those from Asian and African countries more often value emotional closeness. Many of these cultures encourage a strong sense of *family self,* which may mean that what shames the child shames the family, and what brings honor to the family brings honor to the self. Infants and toddlers may spend their days close to a family member (Morelli et al., 1992; Whiting & Edwards, 1988). In traditional African Gusii society, babies nursed freely but spent most of the day on their mother's or siblings' back, with lots of body contact but little face-to-face and language interaction. If the mother became pregnant again, the toddler was weaned and handed over to another family member. Westerners may wonder about the negative effects of the lack of verbal interaction, but then the Gusii may in turn have wondered about Western mothers pushing their babies around in strollers, carrying them in car seats, and putting them in playpens (Small, 1997).

In some rural villages in Senegal, cultural traditions discourage caregivers' talking with young children. Programs encouraging verbal interaction improved the children's language development one year later (Weber et al., 2017). But was it worth the cultural disruption? Such diversity in child raising cautions us against presuming that our culture's way is the only way to raise children successfully.

RETRIEVE & REMEMBER

ANSWERS IN APPENDIX E

11. The four parenting styles may be described as "too hard, too soft, too uncaring, and just right." Which parenting style goes with which of these descriptions, and how do children benefit from the "just right" style?

LaunchPad See the *Video: Correlational Studies* for a helpful tutorial animation about correlational research design.

Adolescence

During **adolescence** we morph from child to adult. Adolescence starts with a physical event—bodily changes that mark the beginning of sexual maturity. It ends with a social event—independent adult status. Thus, in cultures where teens are self-supporting, adolescence hardly exists. And in Western cultures, where sexual maturation is occurring earlier and independence later, adolescence is lengthening (Worthman & Trang, 2018).

PHYSICAL DEVELOPMENT

LOQ 3-14 How is *adolescence* defined, and how do physical changes affect developing teens?

Adolescence begins with **puberty,** the time when we mature sexually. Puberty follows a surge of hormones, which may intensify moods and which trigger a series of bodily changes outlined in Chapter 4.

The timing of puberty. Just as in the earlier life stages, we all go through the same *sequence* of changes in puberty. All girls, for example, develop breast buds and pubic hair before *menarche,* their first menstrual period. The *timing* of such changes is less predictable. Some girls start their growth spurt at 9, some boys as late as age 16. How do girls and boys experience early versus late maturation?

Early maturation can be a challenge. "Early maturing adolescents may be more likely to experience mental health problems attributable to stress and difficulties associated with transitioning through the pubertal period," report Josie Ullsperger and Molly Nikolas (2017). This vulnerability is greatest for teen girls and boys with emotionally reactive temperaments. Also, if a young girl's body and hormone-fed feelings are too far beyond her emotional maturity and her friends' physical development and experiences, she may search out older teens, suffer teasing or sexual harassment, and experience anxiety or depression (Alloy et al., 2016; Ge & Natsuaki, 2009; Weingarden & Renshaw, 2012).

The teenage brain. An adolescent's brain is a work in progress. These years are the time when unused neurons and their connections are *pruned* (Blakemore, 2008). What we don't use, we lose.

As teens mature, their frontal lobes also continue to develop. But frontal lobe maturation lags behind the development of the emotional limbic system. When puberty's hormonal surge combines with limbic system development and unfinished frontal lobes, it's no wonder teens feel stressed. Impulsiveness, risky behaviors, and emotional storms—slamming doors and turning up the music—happen (Casey & Caudle, 2013; Fuhrmann et al., 2015; Smith, 2018). Not yet fully equipped for making long-term plans and curbing impulses, young teens may give in to the lure of smoking or vaping. Teens typically know the risks of smoking, fast driving, and unprotected sex. They just, reasoning from their gut, weigh the benefits of risky behaviors more heavily (Reyna & Farley, 2006; Steinberg, 2010). Teens find rewards more exciting than adults do. They are like cars with giant gas pedals but tiny brake pedals (Chick, 2015) (**FIGURE 3.14**).

So, when Junior drives recklessly and academically self-destructs, should his parents reassure themselves that "he can't help it; his frontal cortex isn't yet fully grown"? They can at least take hope: The brain with which Junior begins his teens differs from the brain with which he will end his teens. Unless he slows his brain development with heavy drinking, his frontal lobes will continue maturing until about age 25 (Beckman, 2004). Better communication between the frontal lobes and other brain regions will bring improved judgment, impulse control, and the ability to plan for the long term.

"Young man, go to your room and stay there until your cerebral cortex matures."

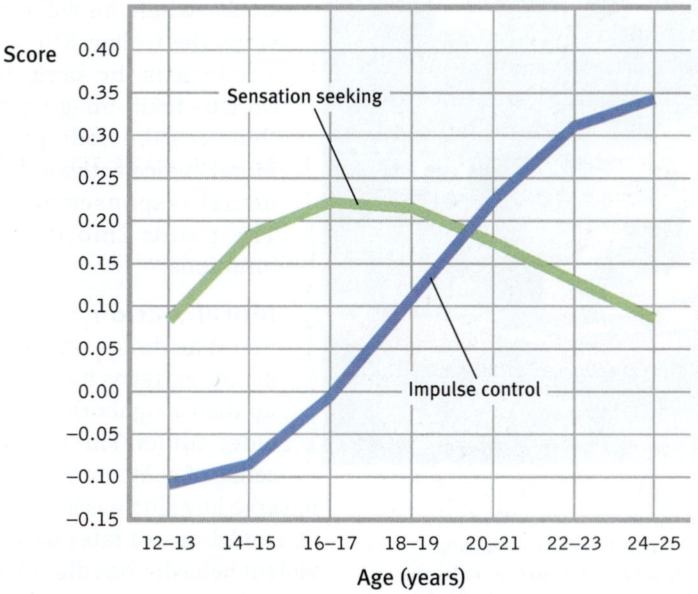

FIGURE 3.14 Impulse control lags reward seeking Surveys of more than 7000 American 12- to 24-year-olds reveal that sensation seeking peaks in the mid-teens. Impulse control develops more slowly as frontal lobes mature. (National Longitudinal Study of Youth and Children and Young Adults survey data presented by Steinberg, 2013.)

In 2004, the American Psychological Association (APA) joined seven other medical and mental health associations in filing U.S. Supreme Court briefs arguing against the death penalty for 16- and 17-year-olds. They presented evidence for the teen brain's immaturity "in areas that bear upon adolescent decision making." Brain scans of young teens reveal that frontal lobe immaturity is most evident among juvenile offenders and drug users (Shannon et al., 2011; Whelan et al., 2012). Teens are "less guilty by reason of adolescence," suggested psychologist Laurence Steinberg and law professor Elizabeth Scott (2003; Steinberg et al., 2009). In 2005, by a 5-to-4 margin, the Court agreed, declaring juvenile death penalties unconstitutional.

COGNITIVE DEVELOPMENT

LOQ 3-15 How did Piaget, Kohlberg, and later researchers describe cognitive and moral development during adolescence?

During the early teen years, *egocentrism* endures, and reasoning is often self-focused. Capable of thinking about their own and others' thinking, teens also begin imagining what others are thinking about *them* and develop an intense awareness of this *imaginary audience*. (They might worry less if they understood their peers' similar self-focus.) Teens also have a tendency to develop a *personal fable*—believing that they are unique and special and what happens to "most people" would never happen to them. "My vaping is just for fun; I would never end up an addicted smoker like my uncle."

Developing Reasoning Power

When adolescents achieve the intellectual peak Jean Piaget called *formal operations*, they apply their new abstract thinking tools to the world around them. They may debate human nature, good and evil, truth and justice. Having left behind the concrete images of early childhood, they may search for spirituality and a deeper meaning of life (Boyatzis, 2012; Elkind, 1970). Logically, they can now spot hypocrisy and detect inconsistencies in others' reasoning (Peterson et al., 1986). (Can you remember having a heated family debate? Did you perhaps even vow silently never to lose sight of your own ideals?)

Developing Morality

Two crucial tasks of childhood and adolescence are determining right from wrong and developing character—the psychological muscles for controlling impulses. To be a moral person is to *think* morally and *act* accordingly. Jean Piaget and Lawrence Kohlberg proposed that moral reasoning guides moral actions. A more recent view builds on psychology's game-changing recognition that much of our functioning occurs not on the "high road" of deliberate, conscious thinking but on the "low road" of unconscious, automatic thinking. Our morality provides another demonstration of our two-track mind.

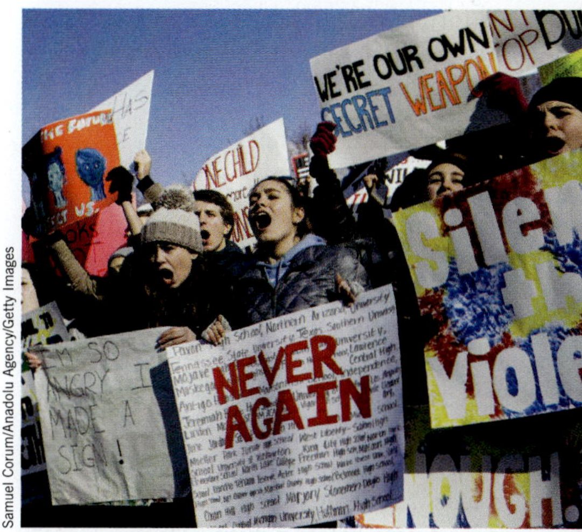

Samuel Corum/Anadolu Agency/Getty Images

Fed up with firearms After a 2018 mass shooting at a high school in Parkland, Florida, student survivors started the #NeverAgain movement to demand U.S. gun law reform. Hundreds of thousands of teens have since participated in school walkouts and marches, demonstrating their ability to think logically about abstract topics and to voice their ideals. According to Piaget, these teens are in the final cognitive stage, formal operations.

adolescence the transition period from childhood to adulthood, extending from puberty to independence.

puberty the period of sexual maturation, during which a person becomes capable of reproducing.

Moral Reasoning Piaget (1932) believed that children's moral judgments build on their cognitive development. Agreeing with Piaget, Lawrence Kohlberg (1981, 1984) sought to describe the development of *moral reasoning*, the thinking that occurs as we consider right and wrong. Kohlberg posed moral dilemmas—for example, should a person steal medicine to save a loved one's life? He then asked children, adolescents, and adults whether the action was right or wrong. He believed their answers would give evidence of stages of moral thinking. His findings led him to propose three basic levels of moral thinking: *preconventional, conventional,* and *postconventional* (**TABLE 3.2**). Kohlberg claimed these levels form a moral ladder. As with all stage theories, the sequence never changes. We begin on the bottom rung and rise to varying heights. At the postconventional level, we may place others' comfort above our own (Crockett et al., 2014). Kohlberg's critics have noted that his postconventional level is culturally limited. It appears mostly among people from large *individualist* societies that give priority to personal goals, rather than from *collectivist* societies that place more value on group goals (Barrett et al., 2016; Eckensberger, 1994). In more collectivist India, morality is less a matter of personal choice and more a role-related duty (Miller et al., 2017). With women tending to emphasize care for others in need over what is "fair," Kohlberg's theory can also be viewed as male-focused (Gilligan, 1982, 2015).

Luke Sharrett/Bloomberg via Getty Images

Moral reasoning Some Houston, Texas, residents faced a moral dilemma in 2017 when Hurricane Harvey caused disastrous flooding. Should they risk their lives to try to rescue family, friends, and neighbors in dangerously flooded areas? Their reasoning likely reflected different levels of moral thinking, even if they behaved similarly.

Moral Intuition According to psychologist Jonathan Haidt [pronounced HITE] (2002, 2006, 2010) much of our morality is rooted in *moral intuitions*—"quick gut feelings." In this view, the mind makes moral judgments quickly and automatically. Feelings of disgust or elation trigger moral reasoning, says Haidt.

Imagine seeing a runaway trolley headed for five people. All will certainly be killed unless you throw a switch that diverts the trolley onto another track, where it will kill one person. Should you throw the switch? Most say *Yes*. Kill one, save five.

Now imagine the same dilemma, with one change. This time, you must save the five by pushing a large stranger onto the tracks, where he will die as his body stops the trolley. Kill one, save five? The logic is the same, but most say No. One brain-imaging study showed that only the body-pushing type of moral choice activated emotion-area neural responses (Green et al., 2001). The point: Emotions feed moral intuitions.

Moral Action *Moral action* feeds moral attitudes. In service-learning programs, teens have tutored, cleaned up their neighborhoods, and assisted older adults. The result? The teens' sense of competence and their desire to serve have increased, school absenteeism and drop-out rates have dropped, and violent behavior has diminished (Andersen, 1998; Heller, 2014; Piliavin, 2003).

These programs also teach the self-discipline needed to restrain one's own impulses. Those who have learned to *delay gratification*—to live with one eye on the future—have become more socially responsible, academically successful, and productive (Daly et al., 2015; Funder & Block, 1989; Sawyer et al., 2015).

"The best time to plant a tree was 20 years ago. The second best time is now."
—Chinese proverb

In one of psychology's best-known experiments, Walter Mischel (2014) gave 4-year-olds a choice between one marshmallow now, or two marshmallows when he returned a few minutes later. The children who had the willpower to delay gratification went on to have higher

TABLE 3.2 Kohlberg's Levels of Moral Thinking Kohlberg posed moral dilemmas, such as: "Is it okay to steal medicine to save a loved one?"

Level (approximate age)	Focus	Example of Moral Reasoning
Preconventional morality (before age 9)	Self-interest; obey rules to avoid punishment or gain concrete rewards.	"If you steal the medicine, you will go to jail."
Conventional morality (early adolescence)	Uphold laws and rules to gain social approval or maintain social order.	"We are supposed to take care of our loved ones, so you should steal the drug."
Postconventional morality (adolescence and beyond)	Actions reflect belief in basic rights and self-defined ethical principles.	"People have a right to live."

"This might not be ethical. Is that a problem for anybody?"

college completion rates and incomes, and less often suffered addiction problems. A replication of this famous study confirmed that 4-year-olds who were able to delay gratification achieved more at age 15. But the difference was modest and partly due to family differences and higher intelligence among the less impulsive children (Watts et al., 2018). Yet the delay of gratification principle remains: Maturity and life success grow from the ability to say no to small pleasures now in order to enjoy greater pleasures later.

IN YOUR EVERYDAY LIFE

Think about a difficult decision you had to make in early adolescence and later regretted. What did you do? How would you do things differently now?

RETRIEVE & REMEMBER

ANSWERS IN APPENDIX E

12. According to Kohlberg, ___________ morality focuses on self-interest, ___________ morality focuses on self-defined ethical principles, and ___________ morality focuses on upholding laws and social rules.
13. How has Kohlberg's theory of moral reasoning been criticized?

SOCIAL DEVELOPMENT

LOQ 3-16 What are the social tasks and challenges of adolescence?

Erik Erikson (1963) believed that we must resolve a specific crisis at each stage of life. Thus, each stage has its own *psychosocial* task. Young children wrestle with issues of *trust,* then *autonomy* (independence), then *initiative.* School-age children strive for *competence*—feeling able and productive. The adolescent's task is to blend past, present, and future possibilities into a clearer sense of self. Adolescents wonder, "Who am I as an individual? What do I want to do with my life? What values should I live by? What do I believe in?" Such questions, said Erikson, are part of the adolescent's *search for identity* (**TABLE 3.3**).

TABLE 3.3 Erikson's Stages of Psychosocial Development

Stage (approximate age)	Issue	Description of Task
Infancy (to 1 year)	Trust vs. mistrust	If needs are dependably met, infants develop a sense of basic trust.
Toddlerhood (1 to 3 years)	Autonomy vs. shame and doubt	Toddlers learn to exercise their will and do things for themselves, or they doubt their abilities.
Preschool (3 to 6 years)	Initiative vs. guilt	Preschoolers learn to initiate tasks and carry out plans, or they feel guilty about their efforts to be independent.
Elementary school (6 years to puberty)	Competence vs. inferiority	Children learn the pleasure of applying themselves to tasks, or they feel inferior.
Adolescence (teen years into 20s)	Identity vs. role confusion	Teenagers work at refining a sense of self by testing roles and then integrating them to form a single identity, or they become confused about who they are.
Young adulthood (20s to early 40s)	Intimacy vs. isolation	Young adults struggle to form close relationships and to gain the capacity for intimate love, or they feel socially isolated.
Middle adulthood (40s to 60s)	Generativity vs. stagnation	Middle-aged people discover a sense of contributing to the world, usually through family and work, or they may feel a lack of purpose.
Late adulthood (late 60s and up)	Integrity vs. despair	Reflecting on their lives, older adults may feel a sense of satisfaction or failure.

© Oliver Rossi/ Corbis

Intimacy vs. isolation

Forming an Identity

To refine their sense of identity, adolescents in Western cultures usually try out different "selves" in different situations. They may act out one self at home, another with friends online, and still another at school. Sometimes separate worlds overlap. Do you remember having your friend world and family world bump into each other, and wondering, "Which self should I be? Which is the real me?" Most of us make peace with our various selves. In time, we blend them into a stable and comfortable sense of who we are—an **identity.**

For both adolescents and adults, our group identities are often formed by how we differ from those around us—in gender and sexual orientation, in age and relative wealth, in abilities and beliefs. When living in Britain, I [DM] become conscious of my Americanness. When spending time in Hong Kong, I [ND] become conscious of my minority White race. For international students, for those of a minority ethnic or religious group, for gay and transgender people, or for people with a disability, a **social identity** often forms around their distinctiveness. (We will learn more about how identity can collide with prejudice in Chapter 11.)

But not always. Erikson noticed that some adolescents bypass this period. Some forge their identity early, simply by taking on their parents' values and expectations. Others may adopt

identity our sense of self; according to Erikson, the adolescent's task is to solidify a sense of self by testing and blending various roles.

social identity the "we" aspect of our self-concept; the part of our answer to "Who am I?" that comes from our group memberships.

the identity of a particular peer group—jocks, preps, geeks, band kids, debaters.

"I don't think any of us like to be reduced to just one label." —Actor Riz Ahmed, 2016

Cultural values may influence teens' search for an identity. Traditional, more collectivist cultures teach adolescents who they are, rather than encouraging them to decide on their own. In individualist Western cultures, young people may continue to try out possible roles well into their late teen years, when many people begin attending college or working full time. Bicultural adolescents form complex identities as they work through their group memberships and their feelings about them (Marks et al., 2011).

During the early to mid-teen years, self-esteem typically falls and, for girls, depression scores often increase (Salk et al., 2017). As Chapter 9 will explain, teen depression and suicide rates have increased since the spread of social media and the peer comparisons they enable. If your life feels dull compared with all the fun your online friends are posting, be consoled: Most of your friends feel the same way (Deri et al., 2017).

Then, during the late teens and twenties, self-image bounces back, and self-esteem gender differences become small (Zuckerman et al., 2016). Agreeableness and emotional stability also increase during late adolescence and early adulthood (Klimstra et al., 2009; Lucas & Donnellan, 2011).

Erikson believed that adolescent identity formation (which continues into adulthood) is followed in young adulthood by a developing capacity for **intimacy,** the ability to form emotionally close relationships. With a clear and comfortable sense of who you are, said Erikson, you are ready for close relationships. Such relationships are, for most of us, a source of great pleasure.

LaunchPad For an interactive self-assessment of your own identity, see *Topic Tutorial: PsychSim6, Who Am I?*

Parent and Peer Relationships

LOQ 3-17 How do parents and peers influence adolescents?

As adolescents in Western cultures seek to form their own identities, they begin to pull away from their parents (Shanahan et al., 2007). The preschooler who can't be close enough to her mother, who loves to touch and cling to her, becomes the 14-year-old who wouldn't be caught dead holding hands with Mom. The transition occurs gradually, but this period is typically a time when parental influence wanes and peer influence grows. Adolescents even recognize their peers' faces more quickly than they do adult faces (while for children it's adult faces rather than other children's faces) (Picci & Scherf, 2016). As ancient Greek philosopher Aristotle long ago recognized, we humans are "the social animal." At all ages, but especially during childhood and the teen years, we seek to fit in with our groups and are influenced by them (Blakemore, 2018; Harris, 1998, 2002).

When researchers used a beeper to sample the daily experiences of American teens, they found them unhappiest when alone and happiest when with friends (Csikszentmihalyi & Hunter, 2003). Teens who start smoking typically have smoker friends who offer cigarettes (Liu et al., 2017). A *selection effect* partly influences this; those who smoke (or don't) may select as friends those who also smoke (or don't). Put two teens together and their brains become supersensitive to reward (Albert et al., 2013). This increased activation helps explain why teens take more driving risks when with friends than they do alone (Chein et al., 2011).

By adolescence, parent-child arguments occur more often, usually over ordinary things—household chores, bedtime, homework (Tesser et al., 1989). For a minority of families, these arguments lead to real splits and great stress (Steinberg & Morris, 2001). But most disagreements are at the level of harmless bickering. With sons, the issues often are behavior problems, such as acting out or hygiene. For daughters, the conflict commonly involves relationships, such as dating and friendships (Schlomer et al., 2011). In a survey of nearly 6000 adolescents—from Australia to Bangladesh to Turkey—most said they like their parents (Offer et al., 1988). They often reported, "We usually get along but . . ." (Galambos, 1992; Steinberg, 1987).

Positive parent-teen relations and positive peer relations often go hand in hand. High school girls who had the most affectionate relationships with their mothers tended also to enjoy the most intimate friendships with girlfriends (Gold & Yanof, 1985). And teens who felt close to their parents have tended to be healthy and happy and to do well in school (Resnick et al., 1997). But pause now to think critically. Look what happens if you state this association another way: Teens in trouble are more likely to have tense relationships with parents and other adults. Remember: *Correlations don't prove cause and effect.*

As we saw earlier, heredity does much of the heavy lifting in forming individual temperament and personality differences. Parents and peers influence teens' behaviors and attitudes.

When with peers, teens discount the future and focus more on immediate rewards (O'Brien et al., 2011). Most teens are herd animals. They talk, dress, and act more like their peers than their parents. What their friends are, they often become, and what "everybody's doing,"

Nine times out of ten, it's all about peer pressure.

they often do. Teens' social media use illustrates this. When viewing photos with many likes, teens not only prefer them but show increased activity in brain areas associated with reward processing and imitation (Sherman et al., 2016).

Both online and face-to-face, for those who feel bullied and excluded by their peers, the pain is acute. Most excluded teens "suffer in silence. . . . A small number act out in violent ways against their classmates" (Aronson, 2001). The pain of exclusion also persists. In one large study, those who were bullied as children showed poorer physical health and greater psychological distress 40 years later (Takizawa et al., 2014). Peer approval matters.

IN YOUR EVERYDAY LIFE

What are the most positive and the most negative things you remember about your own adolescence? Who do you credit or blame more—your parents or your peers?

How Much Credit or Blame Do Parents Deserve? Parents usually feel enormous satisfaction in their children's successes, and feel guilt or shame over their failures. They beam over the child who wins an award. They wonder where they went wrong with the child who is repeatedly called into the principal's office. Freudian psychiatry and psychology encouraged such ideas, blaming problems from asthma to schizophrenia on "bad mothering." Believing that parents shape their offspring as a potter molds clay, many people praise parents for their children's virtues and blame them for their children's vices.

But do parents really produce wounded future adults by being (take your pick from the toxic-parenting lists) overbearing—or uninvolved? Pushy—or weak? Overprotective—or distant? Should we then blame our parents for our failings, and ourselves for our children's failings? Or does all the talk of wounding fragile children through normal parental mistakes trivialize the brutality of real abuse? Are parents less like potters and more like gardeners who provide the soil for their children's natural growth (Gopnik, 2016)?

Frederick Breedon IV/Getty Images

Ryan Anson/Bloomberg/Getty Images

Adoption matters Country music singer Faith Hill and late Apple founder Steve Jobs both benefited from one of the biggest gifts of love: adoption.

Parents do matter. The power of parenting is clearest at the extremes: the abused who become abusive, the loved but firmly handled who become self-confident and socially competent. The power of the family environment also appears in the remarkable academic and vocational successes of many children of people who leave their home countries, such as those of refugees who fled war-torn Vietnam and Cambodia—successes attributed to close-knit, supportive, even demanding families (Caplan et al., 1992).

Yet in personality measures, shared environmental influences from the womb onward typically account for less than 10 percent of children's personality differences. In the words of Robert Plomin and Denise Daniels (1987; Plomin, 2011), "Two children in the same family are [apart from their shared genes] as different from one another as are pairs of children selected randomly from the population." To developmental psychologist Sandra Scarr (1993), this meant that "parents should be given less credit for kids who turn out great and blamed less for kids who don't." So, knowing that children's personalities are not easily sculpted by parental nurture, perhaps parents can relax and love their children for who they are.

The genetic leash may limit the family environment's influence on personality, but does it mean that adoptive parenting is a fruitless venture? No. As an adoptive parent, I [ND] find it heartening to know that parents do influence their children's attitudes, values, manners, politics, and faith (Kandler & Riemann, 2013). This was dramatically illustrated during World War II by separated identical twins Jack Yufe, a Jew, and Oskar Stöhr, a member of Germany's Hitler Youth. After later reuniting, Oskar mused to Jack: "If we had been switched, I would have been the Jew, and you would have been the Nazi" (Segal, 2005, p. 70).

Child neglect, abuse, and parental divorce are rare in adoptive homes, in part because adoptive parents are carefully screened. Despite a slightly greater risk of psychological disorder, most adopted children thrive, especially when adopted as infants (Benson et al., 1994; Wierzbicki, 1993). Seven in eight report feeling strongly attached to one or both adoptive parents. As children of self-giving parents, they themselves grow up to be more self-giving than average (Sharma et al., 1998). Many score higher than their biological parents and raised-apart biological siblings on intelligence tests, and most grow into happier and more stable adults (Kendler et al., 2015b; van IJzendoorn et al., 2005). *The bottom line:* Regardless of personality differences between parents and their adoptees, children benefit from adoption. Parenting—and the cultural environments in which parents place children—matters!

intimacy in Erikson's theory, the ability to form close, loving relationships; a primary developmental task in early adulthood.

The investment in raising a child buys many years of joy and love, but also of worry and irritation. Yet for most people who become parents, a child is one's biological and social legacy—one's personal investment in the human future. To paraphrase psychiatrist Carl Jung, we reach backward into our parents and forward into our children, and through their children into a future we will never see, but about which we must therefore care.

IN YOUR EVERYDAY LIFE

Do you know biological siblings who, despite having been raised together, have very different personalities? (Are you one of these siblings, perhaps?) Knowing what you do of their lives and upbringing, what do you think contributed to these differences?

RETRIEVE & REMEMBER

ANSWERS IN APPENDIX E

14. What is the *selection effect*, and how might it affect a teen's decision to join sports teams at school?

EMERGING ADULTHOOD

LOQ 3-18 What is *emerging adulthood?*

In the Western world, adolescence now roughly equals the teen years. At earlier times, and in other parts of the world today, this slice of life has been much smaller (Baumeister & Tice, 1986). Shortly after sexual maturity, teens would assume adult responsibilities and status. The event might be celebrated with an elaborate initiation—a public rite of passage. The new adult would then work, marry, and have children.

Where schooling became compulsory, independence was put on hold until after graduation. And as educational goals rose, so did the age of independence. Adolescents are now taking more time to finish their education, leave the nest, and establish careers. Today's adolescents also less often work for pay, drive, and have romantic attachments (Twenge & Park, 2019).

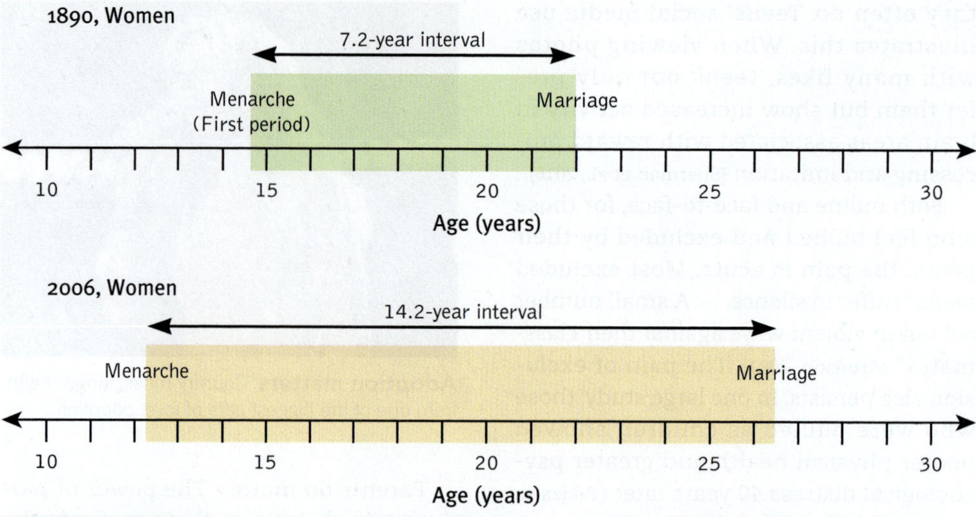

FIGURE 3.15 The transition to adulthood is being stretched from both ends In the 1890s, the average interval between a woman's first menstrual period and marriage, which typically marked a transition to adulthood, was about 7 years. By 2006, in industrialized countries, that gap had widened in well-off communities to about 14 years (Finer & Philbin, 2014; Guttmacher Institute, 1994). Although many adults are unmarried, later marriage combines with prolonged education and earlier menarche to help stretch out the transition to adulthood.

In 1960, three-quarters of all U.S. women and two-thirds of all U.S. men had, by age 30, finished school, left home, become financially independent, married, and had a child. In the early twenty-first century, fewer than half of 30-year-old women and one-third of men were meeting these five milestones (Henig, 2010). In 2016, 15 percent of 25- to 35-year-old Americans—double the 1981 proportion—were living in their parents' home (Fry, 2017).

As we noted, earlier puberty and delayed independence has widened the once-brief gap between child and adult (**FIGURE 3.15**). In well-off communities, the time from 18 to the mid-twenties is an increasingly not-yet-settled phase of life, now often called **emerging adulthood** (Arnett, 2006, 2007). No longer adolescents, these emerging adults—having not yet assumed adult responsibilities and independence—feel "in between." Those furthering their education or working may be setting their own goals and managing their own time. Yet they may still be living in their parents' home, unable to afford their own place and perhaps still emotionally dependent as well (Fry, 2017). Recognizing today's more gradually emerging adulthood, the U.S. government now allows children up to age 26 to remain on their parents' health insurance (Cohen, 2010).

"When I was your age, I was an adult."

IN YOUR EVERYDAY LIFE

What do you think makes a person an adult? Do you feel like an adult? Why or why not?

RETRIEVE & REMEMBER

ANSWERS IN APPENDIX E

15. Match the psychosocial development stage below (i–viii) with the issue that Erikson believed we wrestle with at that stage (a–h).

i. Infancy	a. Generativity vs. stagnation
ii. Toddlerhood	b. Integrity vs. despair
iii. Preschool	c. Initiative vs. guilt
iv. Elementary school	d. Intimacy vs. isolation
v. Adolescence	e. Identity vs. role confusion
vi. Young adulthood	f. Competence vs. inferiority
vii. Middle adulthood	g. Trust vs. mistrust
viii. Late adulthood	h. Autonomy vs. shame and doubt

Adulthood

The unfolding of our lives continues across the life span. Earlier in this chapter, we considered what we all share in life's early years. Making such statements about the adult years is much more difficult. If we know that James is a 1-year-old and Jamal is a 10-year-old, we can say a great deal about each child. Not so with adults who differ by a decade. A 20-year-old may be a parent who supports a child or a child who gets an allowance. A new mother may be 25 or 45. A boss may be 30 or 60.

Rick Doyle/Getty Images

Adult abilities vary widely George Blair was, at age 92, the world's oldest barefoot water skier. He is shown here in 2002 when he first set the record, at age 87. (He died in 2013 at age 98.)

Nevertheless, our life courses are in some ways similar. Physically, cognitively, and especially socially, we differ at age 60 from our 25-year-old selves. In the discussion that follows, we recognize these differences and use three terms: *early adulthood* (roughly twenties and thirties), *middle adulthood* (to age 65), and *late adulthood* (the years after 65). Remember, though, that within each of these stages, people vary in physical, psychological, and social development.

IN YOUR EVERYDAY LIFE

Imagining the future, how do you think you might change? How might you stay the same? In what ways do you most want to grow as a person?

PHYSICAL DEVELOPMENT

LOQ 3-19 What physical changes occur from early to late adulthood?

Early Adulthood

Our physical abilities—our muscular strength, reaction time, sensory keenness, and cardiac output—all crest by our mid-twenties. Like the declining daylight at summer's end, those physical abilities then begin to decline slowly. Athletes are often the first to notice. Baseball players peak at about age 27—with 60 percent of Most Valuable Player awardees since 1985 coming within 2 years of that age (Silver, 2012). But few of the rest of us notice. Unless our daily lives require top physical condition, we hardly perceive the early signs of decline.

Middle Adulthood

During early and middle adulthood, physical vigor has less to do with age than with a person's health and exercise habits. Sedentary 25-year-olds may find themselves huffing and puffing up two flights of stairs. Glancing out the window, they may see their physically fit 50-year-old neighbor jog by on a daily 4-mile run.

Physical decline is gradual, but as most athletes know, the pace of that decline gradually picks up. As a lifelong basketball player, I [DM] find myself increasingly not racing for that loose ball. The good news is that even diminished vigor is enough for normal activities.

Aging also brings a gradual decline in fertility. For a 35- to 39-year-old woman, the chance of getting pregnant after a single act of intercourse is only half that of a woman 19 to 26 (Dunson et al., 2002). Women experience **menopause** as the menstrual cycle ends, usually within a few years of age 50. There is no male menopause—no end of fertility or sharp drop in sex hormones. Men experience a more gradual decline in sperm count, testosterone level, and speed of erection and ejaculation.

Late Adulthood

Is old age "more to be feared than death" (Juvenal, Satires)? Or is life "most delightful when it is on the downward slope"

emerging adulthood a period from about age 18 to the mid-twenties, when many in Western cultures are no longer adolescents but have not yet achieved full independence as adults.

menopause the end of menstruation. In everyday use, it can also mean the biological transition a woman experiences from before until after the end of menstruation.

(Seneca, *Epistulae ad Lucilium*)? What is it like to grow old?

Although physical decline begins in early adulthood, we are not usually acutely aware of it until later in life. Vision changes. We have trouble seeing fine details, and our eyes take longer to adapt to changes in light levels. As the eye's pupil shrinks and its lens grows cloudy, less light reaches the *retina*—the light-sensitive inner portion of the eye. In fact, a 65-year-old retina receives only about one-third as much light as its 20-year-old counterpart (Kline & Schieber, 1985). Thus, to see as well as a 20-year-old when reading or driving, a 65-year-old needs three times as much light.

Aging also levies a tax on the brain. A small, gradual net loss of brain cells begins in early adulthood. By age 80, the brain has lost about 5 percent of its former weight. Some of the brain regions that shrink during aging are areas important for memory (Ritchie et al., 2015). No wonder older adults feel even older after taking a memory test. It's like "aging 5 years in 5 minutes," joked one research team (Hughes et al., 2013). The frontal lobes, which help restrain impulsivity, also shrink, which helps explain older people's occasional blunt questions ("Have you put on weight?") or inappropriate comments (von Hippel, 2007, 2015). Happily for us, there is still some plasticity in the aging brain. It partly compensates for what it loses by recruiting and reorganizing neural networks (Park & McDonough, 2013).

Up to the teen years, we process information with greater and greater speed (Fry & Hale, 1996; Kail, 1991). But compared with teens and young adults, older people take a bit more time to react, to solve perceptual puzzles, even to remember names (Bashore et al., 1997; Verhaeghen & Salthouse, 1997). At video games, most 70-year-olds are no match for a 20-year-old.

"I am still learning." —Michelangelo, 1560, at age 85

But there is good news. Studies of identical twin pairs—in which only one of the two exercised—show that exercise slows aging (Iso-Markku et al., 2016; Rottensteiner et al., 2015). Midlife and older adults who do more exercising and less sitting around tend to be mentally quick older adults (Hoang et al., 2016; Kramer & Colcombe, 2018). Physical exercise enhances muscles, bones, and energy while helping to prevent obesity and heart disease. It also stimulates *neurogenesis*—the development of new brain cells—and neural connections (Erickson et al., 2010; Pereira et al., 2007). That may help explain why sedentary older adults randomly assigned to aerobic exercise programs exhibited enhanced memory, sharpened judgment, and reduced risk of severe cognitive decline (Northey et al., 2018; Raji et al., 2016; Smith, 2016). In the aging brain, exercise reduces brain shrinkage (Gow et al., 2012).

Exercise also helps maintain the *telomeres,* which protect the ends of chromosomes, and even appears to slow the progression of Alzheimer's disease (Kivipelto & Håkansson, 2017; Loprinzi et al., 2015; Smith et al., 2014). (In Chapter 7, we'll see the devastating effects of Alzheimer's disease on the brain.) With age, telomeres wear down, much as the tip of a shoelace frays. Smoking, obesity, or stress can speed up this wear. We are more likely to rust from disuse than to wear out from overuse. Fit bodies support fit minds.

Muscle strength, reaction time, and stamina also diminish noticeably in late adulthood. The fine-tuned senses of smell, hearing, touch, and distance perception that we took for granted in our twenties and thirties will become distant memories. In later life, the stairs get steeper, the print gets smaller, and other people seem to mumble more.

For those growing older, there is both bad and good news about health. The bad news: The body's disease-fighting immune system weakens, putting older adults at higher risk for life-threatening ailments, such as cancer and pneumonia. The good news: Thanks partly to a lifetime's collection of antibodies, those over 65 suffer fewer short-term ailments, such as common flu and cold viruses. One study found they were half as likely as 20-year-olds and one-fifth as likely as preschoolers to suffer upper respiratory flu each year (National Center for Health Statistics, 1990). No wonder older workers have lower absenteeism rates (Rhodes, 1983).

For both men and women, sexual activity also remains satisfying, though less frequent, after middle age. When does sexual desire diminish? In one sexuality survey, age 75 was the point when most women and nearly half the men reported little sexual desire (DeLamater, 2012; DeLamater & Sill, 2005). In other surveys, 75 percent of respondents nevertheless reported being sexually active into their eighties. It seems that most older people sustain sexual satisfaction even as sexual frequency subsides (Forbes et al., 2017; Schick et al., 2010).

"The things that stop you having sex with age are exactly the same as those that stop you riding a bicycle (bad health, thinking it looks silly, no bicycle)." —Alex Comfort, *The Joy of Sex,* 2002

Nicole Bengiveno/The New York Times/Redux Pictures

Suiting up for old age A long life is a gift. To reach old age, it takes good genes, a nurturing environment, and a little luck. New technology allows you to put yourself in your elders' shoes. In these special suits, younger people can hear, see, and move like a typical 85-year-old.

COGNITIVE DEVELOPMENT

Aging and Memory

LOQ 3-20 How does memory change with age?

As we age, we remember some things well. Looking back in later life, adults asked to recall the one or two most important events over the last half-century tend to name events from their teens or twenties (Conway et al., 2005; Rubin et al., 1998). Whatever people experience around this time of life—the Vietnam war, the 9/11 terrorist attacks, the surprise election of Donald Trump—gets remembered (Pillemer, 1998; Schuman & Scott, 1989). Our teens and twenties are also the time when we experience many of our big "firsts"—our first date, first job, first day at college, first apartment.

Early adulthood is indeed a peak time for some types of learning and remembering. Consider one experiment in which 1205 people were invited to learn some names (Crook & West, 1990). They watched video clips in which 14 strangers said their names, using a common format: "Hi, I'm Larry." Even after a second and third replay of the introductions with more personal information, younger adults consistently remembered more names than older adults. How well older people remember depends in part on the task. When asked to *recognize* words they had earlier tried to memorize, older adults showed no memory decline. When asked to *recall* that information without clues, however, the decline was greater (**FIGURE 3.16**).

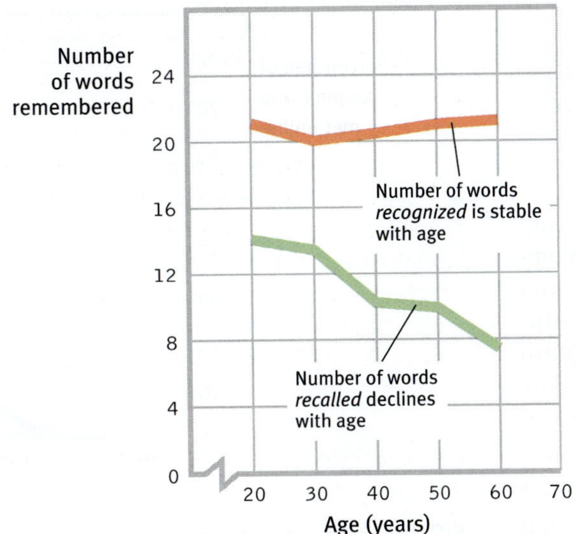

FIGURE 3.16 Recall and recognition in adulthood
(Data from Schonfield & Robertson, 1966.)

No matter how quick or slow we are, remembering seems also to depend on the type of information we are trying to retrieve. If the information is meaningless—nonsense syllables or unimportant events or experiences—then the older we are, the more errors we make. If the information is *meaningful*, older people's rich web of existing knowledge will help them to hold it. But they may take longer than younger adults to *produce* the words and things they know. Older adults also more often experience tip-of-the-tongue forgetting (Ossher et al., 2012). Quick-thinking game show winners are usually young or middle-aged adults (Burke & Shafto, 2004).

Chapter 8 explores another dimension of cognitive development: intelligence. As we will see, cross-sectional studies and longitudinal studies have identified mental abilities that do and do not change as people age. Age is less a predictor of memory and intelligence than is the nearness of a natural death, which does give a clue to someone's mental ability. In the last three or four years of life, and especially as death approaches, negative feelings and cognitive decline typically increase (Vogel et al., 2013; Wilson et al., 2007). Researchers call this near-death drop *terminal decline* (Backman & MacDonald, 2006). Our goals also shift. We're driven less to learn and more to connect socially (Carstensen, 2011).

Maintaining Mental Abilities

Psychologists who study the aging mind debate whether "brain-fitness" computer-based training programs can build "mental muscles" and hold off cognitive decline. Our brain remains plastic throughout life (Gutchess, 2014). So, can exercising our brain—with memory, visual tracking speed, and problem-solving exercises—prevent us from losing our minds? "At every point in life, the brain's natural plasticity gives us the ability to improve how our brains function," said one neuroscientist-entrepreneur (Merzenich, 2007). One study of cognitive training programs showed that they consistently improved scores on tests related to their training (Simons et al., 2016). Video game playing may also enhance people's attention (Bediou et al., 2018).

Based on such findings, some computer game makers have been marketing daily brain-exercise programs for older people. But researchers, after reviewing all the available studies, advise skepticism (Melby-Lervåg et al., 2016; Redick et al., 2017; Sala et al., 2018). As one researcher explained, "Play a video game and you'll get better at that video game, and maybe at very similar video games"—but not at driving a car or filling out your tax return (Hambrick, 2014). One recent experiment found that, compared with mere online video game playing, the prominent brain-training program, Luminosity, did not improve mental performance (Kable et al., 2017).

"I've been working out for six months, but all my gains have been in cognitive function."

SOCIAL DEVELOPMENT

LOQ 3-21 What are adulthood's two primary commitments, and how do chance events and the social clock influence us?

Adulthood's Commitments

Two basic aspects of our lives dominate adulthood. Erik Erikson called them *intimacy* (forming close relationships) and *generativity* (being productive and supporting future generations). Sigmund Freud (1935/1960) put it most simply: The healthy adult, he said, is one who can *love* and *work*.

Love We typically flirt, fall in love, and commit—one person at a time. Although some choose the platonic love of friends and family, most of us eventually pair up. "Pair-bonding is a trademark of the human animal," observed anthropologist Helen Fisher (1993). From an evolutionary perspective, this pairing makes sense. Parents who cooperated to nurture their children to maturity were more likely to have their gene-carrying children survive and reproduce.

Historically, couples have met at school, on the job, or through friends and family. Many couples now meet online (**FIGURE 3.17**). Romantic attraction can also be influenced by *chance events* (Bandura, 1982). Psychologist Albert Bandura (2005) recalled the true story of a book editor who came to one of Bandura's lectures on the "Psychology of Chance Encounters and Life Paths"—and ended up marrying the woman who happened to sit next to him.

Bonds of love are most satisfying and enduring when two adults share interests, values, and emotional and material support. One tie that binds couples is *self-disclosure*—revealing intimate aspects of ourselves to others (see Chapter 11). There also appears to be "vow power." Straight and gay relationships sealed with commitment more often endure (Balsam et al., 2008; Rosenfeld, 2014).

The chances that a marriage will last increase when couples marry after age

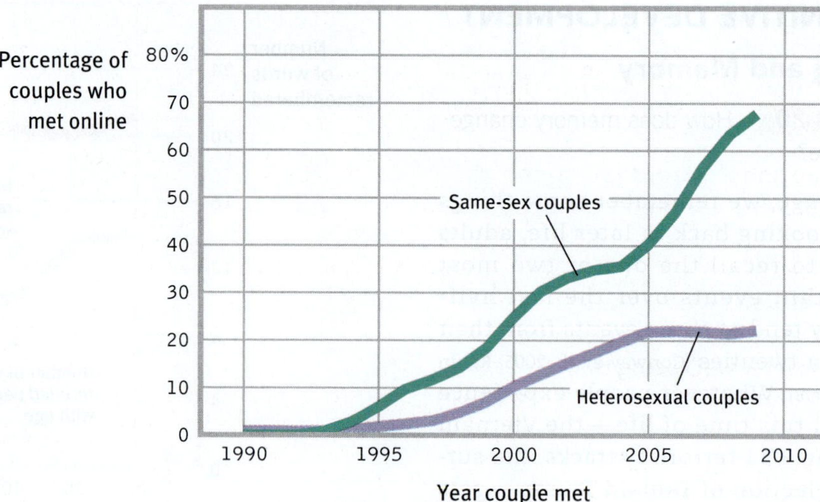

FIGURE 3.17 The changing way we meet our partners The internet's role is clear in an American survey of 2452 straight couples and 462 gay and lesbian couples. (Data from Rosenfeld, 2013; Rosenfeld & Thomas, 2012.)

20 and are well educated. Compared with their counterparts of 30 years ago, people in Western countries *are* better educated and marrying later (Wolfinger, 2015). These trends may help explain why the American divorce rate, which surged from 1960 to 1980, has since slightly declined. Canadian divorce rates since the 1980s have followed a similar pattern (Statistics Canada, 2011). Both men and women now expect more than an enduring bond when they marry. Most hope for a mate who is a wage earner, caregiver, intimate friend, and warm and responsive lover (Finkel, 2017).

Andersen Ross/Blend Images/Alamy

Love Intimacy, attachment, commitment—love by whatever name—is central to healthy and happy adulthood.

Might test-driving life together in a "trial marriage" reduce divorce risk? In one Gallup survey of American twenty-somethings, 62 percent thought it would (Whitehead & Popenoe, 2001). In reality, in Europe, Canada, and the United States, those living together before marriage (and especially before engagement) have had *higher* rates of divorce and marital troubles than those who have not lived together (Goodwin et al., 2010; Jose et al., 2010; Manning & Cohen, 2012; Stanley et al., 2010). Thus, in Europe and North America, "children born into cohabiting families are more likely to see their parents split by age 12" (Social Trends, 2017). Cohabiting couples tend to be initially less committed to the ideal of enduring marriage, and they become even less marriage-supporting while living together.

Nonetheless, the institution of marriage endures. Ninety-five percent of Americans have either married during their lifetime or want to (Newport & Wilke, 2013). And marriage is a predictor of happiness, sexual satisfaction, income, and physical and mental health (Scott et al., 2010; Wilcox & Wolfinger, 2017). Neighborhoods with high marriage rates typically have low rates of crime, delinquency, and emotional disorders among children. Between 1972 and 2016, surveys of nearly 58,000 Americans revealed that 40 percent of married adults were "very happy," compared with 23 percent of unmarried adults. Lesbian couples, too, report greater well-being than those who are single (Peplau & Fingerhut, 2007; Wayment & Peplau, 1995).

Often, love bears children. For most people, this most enduring of life changes is a happy event—one that adds meaning, joy, and occasional stress (Nelson et al., 2013; Witters, 2014). "I feel an overwhelming love for my children unlike anything I feel for anyone else," said 93 percent of American mothers in a national survey (Erickson & Aird, 2005). Many fathers feel the same. A few weeks after the birth of my first child, I [DM] was suddenly struck by a realization: "So *this* is how my parents felt about me!"

Children eventually leave home. This departure is a significant and sometimes difficult event. But for most people, an empty nest is a happy place (Adelmann et al., 1989; Gorchoff et al., 2008). Many parents experience a "postlaunch honeymoon," especially if they maintain close relationships with their children (White & Edwards, 1990). As Daniel Gilbert (2006) concluded, "The only known symptom of 'empty nest syndrome' is increased smiling."

LaunchPad Play the role of the researchers exploring the connection between parenting and happiness by engaging online with the activity *How Would You Know If Having Children Relates to Being Happier?*

Work Having work that fits your interests provides a sense of competence and accomplishment. For many adults, the answer to "Who are you?" depends a great deal on the answer to "What do you do?" Choosing a career path is difficult, especially during uncertain economic times. (See Appendix B: Psychology at Work for more on building work satisfaction.)

Hill Street Studios/Getty Images

© Jose Luis Pelaez Inc/ Blend Images/ Corbis

Job satisfaction and life satisfaction Work can provide us with a sense of identity and competence, and opportunities for accomplishment. Perhaps this is why challenging and interesting occupations enhance people's happiness.

For both men and women, there exists a **social clock**—a culture's definition of "the right time" to leave home, get a job, marry, have children, and retire. It's the expectation people have in mind when saying "I married early" or "I started college late." Today the clock still ticks but people feel freer to keep their own time.

"I am very curious. . . . I wouldn't still be working if I didn't find it exciting."
—99-year-old neuropsychologist Brenda Milner, 2017

Well-Being Across the Life Span

LOQ 3-22 What factors affect our well-being in later life?

To live is to grow older. This moment marks the oldest you have ever been and the youngest you will henceforth be. That means we all can look back with satisfaction or regret, and forward with hope or dread. When asked what they would have done differently if they could relive their lives, people most often answer, "taken my education more seriously and worked harder at it" (Kinnier & Metha, 1989; Roese & Summerville, 2005). Other regrets—"I should have told my father I loved him," "I regret that I never went to Europe"—have also focused less on mistakes made than on the things one *failed* to do (Gilovich & Medvec, 1995).

From the teens to midlife, people's sense of identity, confidence, and self-esteem typically grows stronger (Bleidorn et al., 2016; Huang, 2010). The popular image of the midlife crisis—an early-forties man who leaves his family for a younger romantic partner and a hot sports car—is more myth than reality (Hunter & Sundel, 1989; Mroczek & Kolarz, 1998). Although challenges inevitably arise in later life, until the very end the over-65 years are not notably unhappy. Self-esteem, for example, remains stable (Wagner et al., 2013). Gallup asked 658,038 people worldwide to rate their lives on a ladder from 0 ("the worst possible life") to 10 ("the best possible life"). Age—from 15 to over 90 years—gave no clue to life satisfaction (Morrison et al., 2014).

If anything, positive feelings, supported by better emotional control, tend to grow after midlife, and negative feelings decline (Stone et al., 2010; Urry & Gross, 2010). Compared with younger Chinese and American adults, older adults are *more* attentive to positive news (Isaacowitz,

social clock the culturally preferred timing of social events such as marriage, parenthood, and retirement.

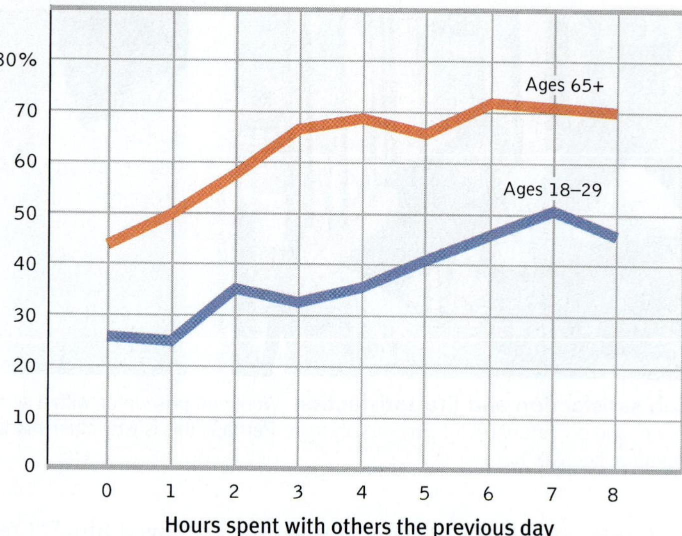

FIGURE 3.18 Humans are social creatures Both younger and older adults report greater happiness when spending time with others. (Note, this correlation could also reflect happier people being more social.) (Gallup survey data reported by Crabtree, 2011.)

2012; Wang et al., 2015a). Like people of all ages, older adults are happiest when not alone (**FIGURE 3.18**). Older adults experience fewer problems in their relationships—less attachment anxiety, stress, and anger (Chopik et al., 2013; Fingerman & Charles, 2010). With age, we become more stable and more accepting (Carstensen et al., 2011; Shallcross et al., 2013).

Throughout the life span, the bad feelings tied to negative events fade faster than the good feelings linked with positive events (Walker et al., 2003). This leaves most older people with the comforting feeling that life, on balance, has been mostly good (Mather, 2016). As the years go by, feelings mellow (Brose et al., 2015). Highs become less high, lows less low.

IMPROVE YOUR EVERYDAY LIFE

How will you look back on your life 10 years from now? What should you change so that someday you will recall your choices with satisfaction?

RETRIEVE & REMEMBER

ANSWERS IN APPENDIX E

16. Freud defined the healthy adult as one who is able to ________ and to ________.

Death and Dying

LOQ 3-23 How do people's responses to a loved one's death vary?

Warning: If you begin reading the next paragraph, you will die.

But of course, if you hadn't read this, you would still die in due time. Death awaits us all. Health, as has been said, is simply the slowest way to die.

Most of us will also have to cope with the death of a close relative or friend. Typically, the most difficult separation a person experiences is the death of a partner—a loss suffered by four times more women than men. Maintaining everyday engagements and relationships increases resilience in the face of such a loss (Infurna & Luthar, 2016).

"Love—why, I'll tell you what love is: It's you at 75 and her at 71, each of you listening for the other's step in the next room, each afraid that a sudden silence, a sudden cry, could mean a lifetime's talk is over." —Brian Moore, *The Luck of Ginger Coffey*, 1960

But for some people, grief is severe, especially when a loved one's death comes suddenly and before its expected time on the social clock. I [ND] experienced this firsthand when a tragic accident claimed the life of my 60-year-old mother. Such tragedies may trigger a year or more of memory-filled mourning. Eventually, this may give way to a mild depression (Lehman et al., 1987).

For some, the loss is unbearable. One study tracked more than 17,000 people who had suffered the death of a child under 18. In the five years following that death, 3 percent of them were hospitalized for the first time in a psychiatric unit. That is 67 percent higher than the rate recorded for parents who had not lost a child (Li et al., 2005).

Why do grief reactions vary so widely? Some cultures encourage public weeping and wailing. Others expect mourners to hide their emotions. In all cultures, some individuals grieve more intensely and openly. Some popular beliefs, however, are *not* confirmed by scientific studies:

- Those who immediately express the strongest grief do not purge their grief faster (Bonanno & Kaltman, 1999; Wortman & Silver, 1989). But grieving parents who try to protect their partner by "staying strong" and not discussing their child's death may actually prolong the grieving (Stroebe et al., 2013).
- Grief therapy and self-help groups offer support, but there is similar healing power in the passing of time, the support of friends, and the act of giving support and help to others (Baddeley & Singer, 2009; Brown et al., 2008; Neimeyer & Currier, 2009). After a spouse's death, those who talk often with others or who receive grief counseling adjust about as well as those who grieve more privately (Bonanno, 2009; Stroebe et al., 2005).
- Terminally ill and grief-stricken people do not go through identical stages, such as denial before anger (Friedman & James, 2008; Nolen-Hoeksema &

Larson, 1999). Given similar losses, some people grieve hard and long, others grieve less (Ott et al., 2007).

- Compared to what people *imagine* they would feel when facing death, those actually facing death due to terminal illness are more positive and less sad and despairing. In the researchers' words, "Meeting the grim reaper may not be as grim as it seems" (Goranson et al., 2017).

Facing death with dignity and openness helps people complete the life cycle with a sense of life's meaningfulness and unity—the sense that their existence has been good and that life and death are parts of an ongoing cycle. Although death may be unwelcome, life itself can be affirmed even at death. This is especially so for people who review their lives not with despair but with what Erik Erikson called a sense of *integrity*—a feeling that one's life has been meaningful and worthwhile.

Mick Stevens/The New Yorker Collection/The Cartoon Bank

"You never think it's going to happen to you."

RETRIEVE & REMEMBER

ANSWERS IN APPENDIX E

17. What are some of the most significant challenges and rewards of growing old?

CHAPTER 3 REVIEW Developing Through the Life Span

LEARNING OBJECTIVES

TEST YOURSELF *Answer these repeated Learning Objective Questions on your own (before checking the answers in Appendix D) to improve your retention of the concepts* (McDaniel et al., 2009, 2015).

Developmental Psychology's Major Issues

3-1: What are the three major issues studied by developmental psychologists?

Prenatal Development and the Newborn

3-2: How does conception occur? What are *chromosomes, DNA, genes*, and the human *genome?* And how do genes and the environment interact?

3-3: How does life develop before birth, and how do *teratogens* put prenatal development at risk?

3-4: What are some abilities and traits of newborns?

3-5: How do twin and adoption studies help us understand the effects of nature and nurture?

Infancy and Childhood

3-6: During infancy and childhood, how do the brain and motor skills develop?

3-7: How did Piaget broaden our understanding of the way a child's mind develops, and how have today's researchers built on his work?

3-8: How did Vygotsky view children's cognitive development?

3-9: What does it mean to develop a *theory of mind*, and how is this impaired in those with *autism spectrum disorder?*

3-10: How do the bonds of attachment form between caregivers and infants?

3-11: Why do attachment differences matter, and how does an infant's ability to develop basic trust affect later relationships?

3-12: What are the four main parenting styles?

3-13: What outcomes are associated with each parenting style?

Adolescence

3-14: How is *adolescence* defined, and how do physical changes affect developing teens?

3-15: How did Piaget, Kohlberg, and later researchers describe cognitive and moral development during adolescence?

3-16: What are the social tasks and challenges of adolescence?

3-17: How do parents and peers influence adolescents?

3-18: What is *emerging adulthood?*

Adulthood

3-19: What physical changes occur from early to late adulthood?

3-20: How does memory change with age?

3-21: What are adulthood's two primary commitments, and how do chance events and the social clock influence us?

3-22: What factors affect our well-being in later life?

3-23: How do people's responses to a loved one's death vary?

TERMS AND CONCEPTS TO REMEMBER

TEST YOURSELF Write down the definition in your own words, then check your answer.

developmental psychology, *p. 71*
cross-sectional study, *p. 71*
longitudinal study, *p. 71*
chromosomes, *p. 73*
DNA (deoxyribonucleic acid), *p. 73*
genes, *p. 73*
heredity, *p. 73*
genome, *p. 73*
environment, *p. 73*
interaction, *p. 73*
epigenetics, *p. 75*
zygote, *p. 75*
embryo, *p. 75*
fetus, *p. 75*
teratogens [tuh-RAT-uh-jenz], *p. 75*
fetal alcohol syndrome (FAS), *p. 75*
reflex, *p. 75*
temperament, *p. 77*
identical (monozygotic) twins, *p. 77*
fraternal (dizygotic) twins, *p. 77*
maturation, *p. 77*
critical period, *p. 79*
cognition, *p. 79*
schema, *p. 81*
assimilation, *p. 81*
accommodation, *p. 81*
sensorimotor stage, *p. 81*
object permanence, *p. 81*
preoperational stage, *p. 81*
conservation, *p. 81*
egocentrism, *p. 83*
concrete operational stage, *p. 83*
formal operational stage, *p. 83*
scaffold, *p. 83*
theory of mind, *p. 85*
autism spectrum disorder (ASD), *p. 85*
stranger anxiety, *p. 85*
attachment, *p. 85*
basic trust, *p. 87*
adolescence, *p. 91*
puberty, *p. 91*
identity, *p. 93*
social identity, *p. 93*
intimacy, *p. 95*
emerging adulthood, *p. 97*
menopause, *p. 97*
social clock, *p. 101*

CHAPTER TEST

TEST YOURSELF Answer the following questions on your own first, then check your answers in Appendix E.

1. How do cross-sectional and longitudinal studies differ?
2. The three major issues that interest developmental psychologists are nature/nurture, stability/change, and ________/________.
3. Although development is lifelong, there is stability of personality over time. For example,
   a. most personality traits emerge in infancy and persist throughout life.
   b. temperament tends to remain stable throughout life.
   c. few people change significantly after adolescence.
   d. people tend to undergo greater personality changes as they age.

4. The threadlike structures made largely of DNA molecules are called ________.

5. A small segment of DNA is called a ________.

6. Epigenetics is the study of the molecular ways by which ________________ trigger or block genetic expression.

7. Body organs first begin to form and function during the period of the ________; within 6 months, during the period of the ________, the organs are sufficiently functional to provide a good chance of surviving and thriving.

   a. zygote; embryo
   b. zygote; fetus
   c. embryo; fetus
   d. placenta; fetus

8. Chemicals that the placenta isn't able to screen out that may harm an embryo or fetus are called ________.

9. Stroke a newborn's cheek and the infant will root for a nipple. This illustrates

   a. a reflex.
   b. nurture.
   c. a preference.
   d. continuity.

10. Fraternal twins result when

    a. a single egg is fertilized by a single sperm and then splits.
    b. a single egg is fertilized by two sperm and then splits.
    c. two eggs are fertilized by two sperm.
    d. two eggs are fertilized by a single sperm.

11. ________ twins share the same DNA.

12. Adoption studies seek to understand genetic influences on personality. They do this mainly by

    a. comparing adopted children with nonadopted children.
    b. evaluating whether adopted children's personalities more closely resemble those of their adoptive parents or their biological parents.
    c. studying the effect of prior neglect on adopted children.
    d. studying the effect of children's age at adoption.

13. Between ages 3 and 6, the human brain experiences the greatest growth in the ________ lobes, which enable reasoning and planning.

14. Which of the following is true of motor-skill development?

    a. It is determined solely by genetic factors.
    b. The sequence, but not the timing, is universal.
    c. The timing, but not the sequence, is universal.
    d. It is determined solely by environmental factors.

15. Why can't people consciously recall learning to walk?

16. Use Piaget's first three stages of cognitive development to explain why young children are not just miniature adults in the way they think.

17. Although Piaget's stage theory continues to inform our understanding of children's thinking, many researchers believe that

    a. Piaget's stages begin earlier and development is more continuous than he realized.
    b. children do not progress as rapidly as Piaget predicted.
    c. few children progress to the concrete operational stage.
    d. there is no way of testing much of Piaget's theoretical work.

18. An 8-month-old infant who reacts to a new babysitter by crying and clinging to his father's shoulder is showing ________ ________.

19. In a series of experiments, the Harlows found that monkeys raised with artificial mothers tended, when afraid, to cling to their cloth mother rather than to a wire mother holding the feeding bottle. Why was this finding important?

20. From the very first weeks of life, infants differ in their characteristic emotional reactions, with some infants being intense and anxious, while others are easygoing and relaxed. These differences are usually explained as differences in ________.

21. Adolescence is marked by the onset of

    a. an identity crisis.
    b. puberty.
    c. separation anxiety.
    d. parent-child conflict.

22. According to Piaget, a person who can think logically about abstractions is in the ________ ________ stage.

23. In Erikson's stages, the primary task during adolescence is

    a. attaining formal operations.
    b. forging an identity.
    c. developing a sense of intimacy with another person.
    d. living independent of parents.

24. Some developmental psychologists refer to the period that occurs in some Western cultures from age 18 to the mid-twenties as _______________.

25. By age 65, a person would be most likely to experience a cognitive decline in the ability to

a. recall and list all the important terms and concepts in a chapter.

b. select the correct definition in a multiple-choice question.

c. recall their own birth date.

d. practice a well-learned skill, such as knitting.

26. Freud defined the healthy adult as one who is able to love and work. Erikson agreed, observing that the adult struggles to attain intimacy and _______________.

27. Contrary to what many people assume,

a. older people are significantly less happy than adolescents are.

b. people become less happy as they move from their teen years into midlife.

c. positive feelings tend to grow after midlife.

d. those whose children have recently left home—the empty nesters—have the lowest level of happiness of all groups.

Continue testing yourself with **LearningCurve** or **Achieve Read & Practice** to learn and remember most effectively.

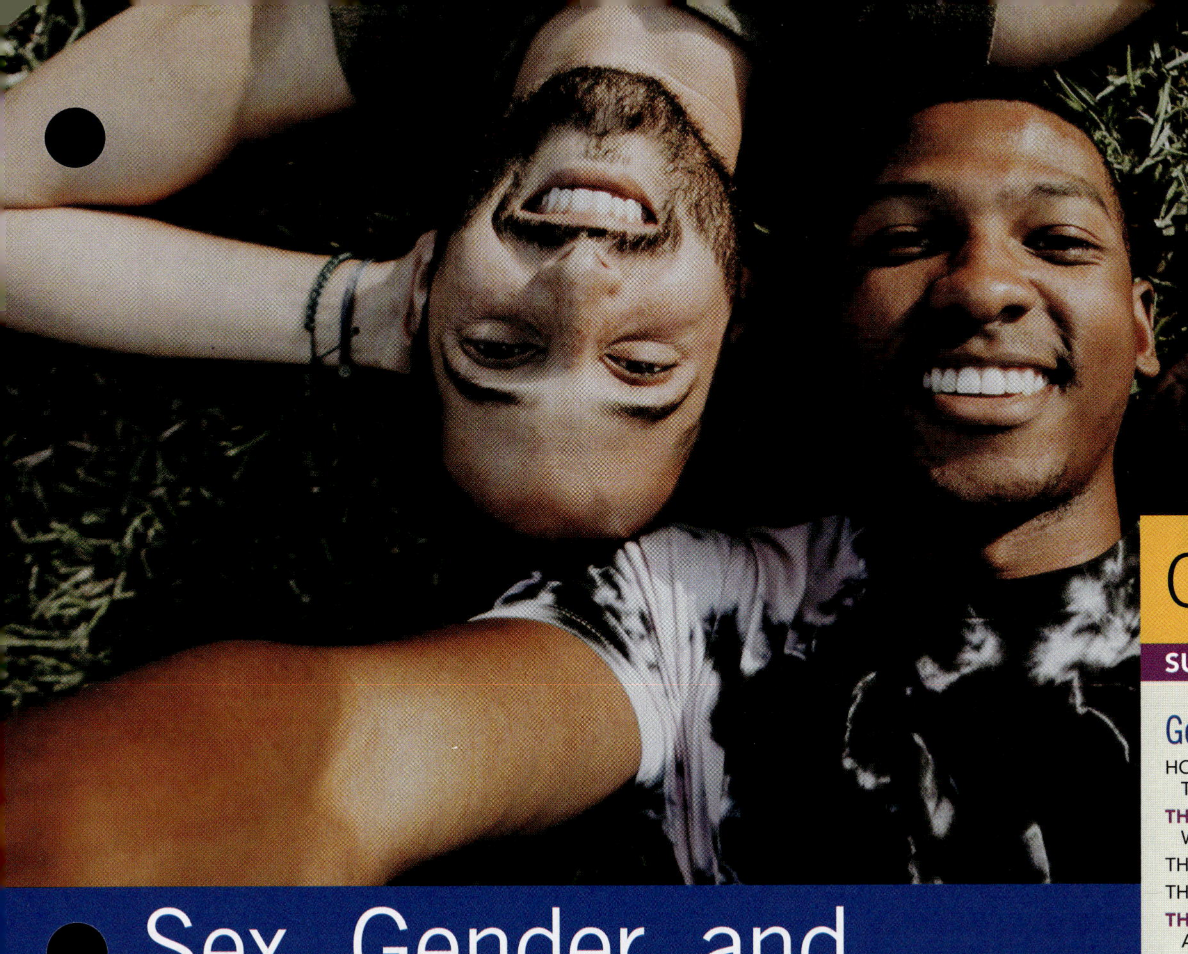
Rawpixel.com/Shutterstock

CHAPTER 4

Sex, Gender, and Sexuality

SURVEY THE CHAPTER

We humans can't resist the urge to organize our world into distinct categories. We divide people, who may reflect an ethnic mix, into "Black," "White," "Asian," or "Hispanic." We eagerly identify people as either male or female. When you were born, everyone wanted to know: "Is it a boy or a girl?" The answer described your birth-designated *sex*.

Most people's birth-designated sex also helps define their *gender*—their culture's expectations about what it means to be male or female. But there are exceptions. Occasionally people's *gender identity* differs from their assigned sex. This is the case for writer Jan Morris, who was born male. From an early age, she said, "I realized that I had been born into the wrong body, and should really be a girl" (Morris, 2015). After sex-reassignment surgery, British law (which forbade same-sex marriage) required Morris and her wife—who had "continued to live together in a remarkably strong marital bond"—to divorce. Years later, when same-sex marriage finally became legal, they remarried.

More recently, the public has followed the journey of Caitlyn Jenner, the Olympic decathlon champion whose transition from Bruce Jenner made headlines. Cases like those of Morris, Jenner, and many less-famous transgender people make us wonder: How do nature and nurture interact to form our unique gender identities? How are the genders alike, and how and why do they differ? This chapter explores these issues. We'll also gain insight about the psychology and biology of sexual attraction and intimacy. As part of the journey, we'll see how evolutionary psychologists explain our sexuality. And we will see examples of swiftly changing and sometimes controversial terminology and understandings.

Let's start at the beginning. What is gender, and how does it develop?

Gender Development

Learning Objective Question LOQ 4-1 How does the meaning of *gender* differ from the meaning of *sex?*

Simply said, your body defines your **sex**; your mind defines your **gender.** But your mind's understanding of gender arises from the interplay between your biology and your experiences (Eagly & Wood, 2013). Before we consider that interplay in more detail, let's take a closer look at some ways that males and females are both similar and different.

HOW ARE MALES AND FEMALES ALIKE? HOW DO THEY DIFFER?

LOQ 4-2 What are some of the ways males and females tend to be alike and to differ?

Whether male, female, or **intersex,** most of us receive 23 chromosomes from our mother and 23 from our father. Of those 46 chromosomes, 45 are typically *unisex*—the same for all sexes. Our similar biology helped our evolutionary ancestors face similar adaptive challenges. Both men and women needed to survive, reproduce, and avoid predators, and so today they are in most ways alike. Do you identify yourself as male, female, neither, or some combination of male and female? No matter your answer, you gave no clues to your vocabulary, happiness, or ability to see, hear, learn, and remember. Whatever our gender, we are, on average, similarly creative and intelligent. We feel the same emotions and longings (Hyde, 2014).

But in some areas, male and female traits do differ, and differences command attention. Some much-talked-about gender differences (like the difference in self-esteem) are actually quite modest (Zell et al., 2015). Others are more striking. The average girl enters puberty about a year earlier than the average boy, and her life expectancy is 5 years longer. She expresses emotions more freely, smiling and crying more. And in Facebook updates, she more often expresses "love" and being "sooo excited!!!" (Fischer & LaFrance, 2015; Schwartz et al., 2013). She can detect fainter odors, receives offers of help more often, and can become sexually re-aroused sooner after orgasm. She also has twice the risk of developing depression and anxiety and 10 times the risk of developing an eating disorder. Yet the average man is 4 times more likely to die by suicide or to develop an alcohol use disorder. His "more likely" list also includes autism spectrum disorder, color-deficient vision, and attention-deficit/hyperactivity disorder (ADHD). And as an adult, he is more at risk for antisocial personality disorder. Male or female, each has its own share of risks.

Gender similarities and differences appear throughout this book. For now, let's take a closer look at three gender differences. Although individuals vary greatly, the *average* male and female differ in aggression, social power, and social connectedness.

Aggression

To a psychologist, **aggression** is any physical or verbal act intended to hurt someone physically or emotionally (Bushman & Huesmann, 2010). Think of examples of aggressive people. Are most of them men? Likely yes. Men generally admit to more aggression, especially extreme physical violence (Wölfer & Hewstone, 2015; Yount et al., 2017). In romantic relationships between men and women, minor acts of physical aggression, such as slaps, are roughly equal, but the most violent acts are usually committed by men (Archer, 2000; Johnson, 2008).

Laboratory experiments confirm a gender difference in aggression. Men have been more willing to blast people with what they believed was intense and prolonged noise (Bushman et al., 2007). The gender gap also appears outside the laboratory. Who commits more violent crimes worldwide? Men do (Antonaccio et al., 2011; Caddick & Porter, 2012; Frisell et al., 2012). Men also take the lead in hunting, fighting, warring, and supporting war (Liddle et al., 2012; Wood & Eagly, 2002, 2007).

Amy Sancetta/AP Images

Deadly relational aggression Sladjana Vidovic was a high school student who died by suicide after suffering constant relational aggression by bullies.

Here's another question: Think of examples of people harming others by passing along hurtful gossip, or by shutting someone out of a social group or situation. Were most of those people men? Perhaps not. Those behaviors are acts of **relational aggression,** and women are slightly more likely than men to commit them (Archer, 2004, 2007, 2009).

Social Power

Imagine walking into a job interview. You sit down and peer across the table at your two interviewers. The unsmiling person on the left oozes self-confidence and independence and maintains steady eye contact. The person on the right gives you a warm, welcoming smile but makes less eye contact and seems to expect the other interviewer to take the lead.

Which interviewer is male?

If you said the person on the left, you're not alone. Around the world, from Nigeria to New Zealand, people have perceived gender differences in power (Williams & Best, 1990). For more on this topic, see Thinking Critically About: Gender Bias in the Workplace.

Social Connectedness

Whatever our gender, we all have a *need to belong* (more on this in Chapter 9). But males and females satisfy this need in different ways (Baumeister, 2010). Males tend to be *independent*. Even as children, males typically form large play groups that brim with activity and competition, with little intimate discussion (Rose & Rudolph, 2006). As adults, men enjoy side-by-side activities, and their conversations often focus on problem solving (Tannen, 1990; Wright, 1989). When asked a difficult question to which they don't know the answer—"Do you know why the sky is blue?"—men are more likely than women to invent an answer, rather than admit they don't know. Have you ever experienced this phenomenon, which researchers call the *male answer syndrome* (Giuliano et al., 1998)?

Scans of more than 1400 brains show no big male-female differences. "Human brains cannot be categorized into two distinct classes: male brain/female brain" (Joel et al., 2015). Brain scans do, however, suggest a subtle difference: A woman's brain, more than a man's, is wired in a way that enables social relationships (Ingalhalikar et al., 2013). This helps explain why females tend to be more *interdependent*. As children, they compete less and imitate social relationships more (Maccoby, 1990; Roberts, 1991). They usually play in small groups, often with one friend. As teens, girls spend less time alone and more time with friends (Wong & Csikszentmihalyi, 1991). Girls' and women's friendships are more intimate, with more conversation that explores relationships (Maccoby, 2002).

Anthony Asael/Danita Delimont Stock Photography

© 2/Rob Van Petten/Ocean/Corbis

Every man for himself, or "tend and befriend"? Gender differences in the way we interact with others begin to appear at a very young age.

Teen girls average twice as many daily texts as boys and, in late adolescence, spend more time on social networking sites (Lenhart, 2015a; Pryor et al., 2007, 2011). In one analysis of 10 million Facebook posts, women's status updates were as assertive as men's, but women used warmer words. Men more often swore or expressed anger (Park et al., 2016). And consider another big-data analysis, of more than 700 million words collected from Facebook messages: Men used more work-related words, and women used more family-related words (Schwartz et al., 2013).

Think about the last time you felt worried or hurt and wanted to talk with someone. Was that person male or female? At such times, most people turn to women. Both men and women have reported that their friendships with women are more intimate, enjoyable, and nurturing (Kuttler et al., 1999; Rubin, 1985; Sapadin, 1988). When stressed, women are also more likely than men to turn to others for support. They are said to *tend and befriend* (Tamres et al., 2002; Taylor, 2002).

Gender differences in both social connectedness and power are greatest in late adolescence and early adulthood—the prime years for dating and mating. By their teen years, girls become less assertive and more flirtatious, and boys appear more dominant and less expressive (Chaplin, 2015). In adulthood, after the birth of a first child, attitude and behavior differences often peak. Mothers especially may express more traditionally female attitudes and behaviors (Ferriman et al., 2009; Katz-Wise et al., 2010).

By age 50, most parenting-related gender differences subside. Men become less domineering and more empathic. Women—especially those with paid employment—become more assertive and self-confident (Kasen et al., 2006; Maccoby, 1998). Worldwide, fewer women than men work full-time for an employer (19 percent versus 33 percent). But, similar to men, women are more satisfied with their lives when employed rather than unemployed (Ryan, 2016).

Will McPhail/The Cartoon Bank/Conde Nast Publications

"I said, 'I wonder what it means,' not 'Tell me what it means.'"

sex in psychology, the biologically influenced characteristics by which people define *male*, *female*, and *intersex*.

gender in psychology, the behavioral characteristics that people associate with *boy, girl, man*, and *woman*. (See also *gender identity*.)

intersex possessing both male and female biological sexual characteristics at birth.

aggression any act intended to harm someone physically or emotionally.

relational aggression an act of aggression (physical or verbal) intended to harm a person's relationship or social standing.

Thinking Critically About:
Gender Bias in the Workplace

LOQ 4-3 What factors contribute to gender bias in the workplace?

Differences in PERCEPTION

Among politicians who seem power-hungry, women are less successful than men.[1]

She's so aggressive!
He's so take-charge!

Most political leaders are men:

Men held 77% of seats in the world's governing parliaments in 2018.[2]

People around the world tend to see men as more powerful.[3]

When groups form, whether as juries or companies, leadership tends to go to males.[4]

Differences in COMPENSATION

Women in traditionally male occupations have received less than their male colleagues.[5]

Medicine U.S. salary disparity between male and female physicians:[6]

$150,053 women

$211,526 men

Academia Female research grant applicants have received lower "quality of researcher" ratings and have been less likely to be funded.[7] (But as we will see, gender attitudes and roles are changing.)

Differences in FAMILY-CARE RESPONSIBILITY

U.S. mothers still do nearly **twice** as much child care as **fathers**.[8] In the workplace, women are less often driven by money and status, compromise more, and more often opt for reduced work hours.[9]

What else contributes to WORKPLACE GENDER BIAS?

Social norms

In most societies, men place more importance on power and achievement, and are socially dominant.[10]

Leadership styles

Men are more *directive*, telling people what to do and how to do it.

Women are more *democratic*, welcoming others' input in decision making.[11]

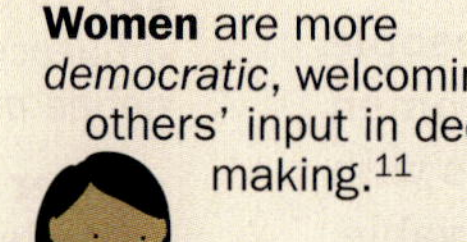

Interaction styles

Women are more likely to express support.[12]

Men are more likely to offer opinions.[12]

Everyday behavior

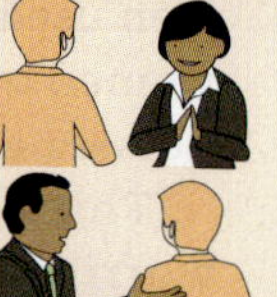

Women smile and apologize more than men.[13]

Men are more likely to talk assertively, interrupt, initiate touches, and stare.[13]

Yet GENDER ROLES VARY WIDELY across place and time.

Women are increasingly represented in leadership (now 50% of Canada's cabinet ministers) and in the workforce. In 1963, the Harvard Business School admitted its first women students. Among its Class of 2018, 41% were women.[14] In 1960, women were 6% of U.S. medical students. Today they are about half.[15]

1. Okimoto & Brescoll, 2010. 2. IPU, 2018. 3. Williams & Best, 1990. 4. Colarelli et al., 2006. 5. Willett et al., 2015. 6. Census Bureau, 2014. 7. van der Lee & Ellemers, 2015. 8. CEA, 2014; Parker & Wang, 2013; Pew, 2015. 9. Nikolova & Lamberton, 2016; Pinker, 2008. 10. Gino et al., 2015; Schwartz & Rubel-Lifschitz, 2009. 11. Eagly & Carli, 2007; van Engen & Willemsen, 2004. 12. Aries, 1987; Wood, 1987. 13. Leaper & Ayres, 2007; Major et al., 1990; Schumann & Ross, 2010. 14. HBS, 2018. 15. AAMC, 2014.

So, although women and men are more alike than different, there are some behavior differences between the average woman and man. Are such differences dictated by their biology? Shaped by their cultures and other experiences? Do we vary in how gender-conforming or nonconforming we are? Read on.

RETRIEVE & REMEMBER

ANSWERS IN APPENDIX E

1. __________ (Men/Women) are more likely to commit relational aggression, and __________ (men/women) are more likely to commit physical aggression.

THE NATURE OF GENDER

LOQ 4-4 How do sex hormones influence prenatal and adolescent sexual development?

Biology does not *dictate* gender, but it can influence our gender psychology in two ways:

- ***Genetically:*** We have differing *sex chromosomes.*
- ***Physiologically:*** We have differing concentrations of *sex hormones,* which trigger other anatomical differences.

These influences began to form you long before you were born.

Prenatal Sexual Development

Six weeks after you were conceived, you looked pretty much like everyone else. Then, as your genes kicked in, your biological sex became more apparent. If you are male or female, your mother's contribution to your twenty-third chromosome pair—the two sex chromosomes—was an **X chromosome.** It was your father's contribution that determined your birth sex. From him, you received the 1 chromosome out of the usual 46 that is not unisex—either another X chromosome, making you female, or a **Y chromosome,** making you male. There are other sexual development variations, as we will see shortly.

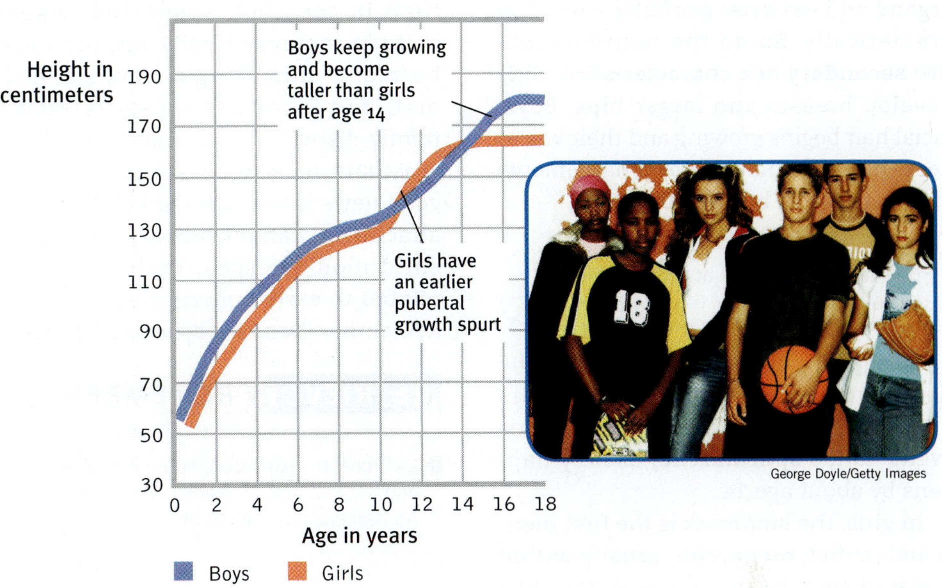

FIGURE 4.1 Height differences (Data from Tanner, 1978.)

About seven weeks after conception, a single gene on the Y chromosome throws a master switch. "Turned on," this switch triggers the testes to develop and to produce **testosterone,** the main *androgen* (male hormone) that promotes male sex organ development. (Females also have testosterone, but less of it.) Later, during the fourth and fifth prenatal months, sex hormones bathe the fetal brain and tilt its wiring toward female or male patterns (Hines, 2004; Udry, 2000).

Adolescent Sexual Development

During adolescence, we enter **puberty** and mature sexually. A surge of hormones triggers a two-year period of rapid physical development, beginning at about age 11 in girls and age 12 in boys, and visible male-female differences emerge. Hints of this upcoming puberty, such as enlarging testes, appear earlier (Herman-Giddens et al., 2012). A year or two before physical changes are visible, boys and girls often feel the first stirrings of sexual attraction (McClintock & Herdt, 1996).

Girls' slightly earlier entry into puberty can at first propel them to greater height than boys of the same age (**FIGURE 4.1**). But boys catch up when they begin puberty, and by age 14 they are usually taller than girls. During these growth spurts, the **primary sex characteristics**—the reproductive

X chromosome the sex chromosome found in both males and females. Females typically have two X chromosomes; males typically have one. An X chromosome from each parent produces a female child.

Y chromosome the sex chromosome found only in males. When paired with an X chromosome from the mother, it produces a male child.

testosterone the most important male sex hormone. Both males and females have it, but the additional testosterone in males stimulates the growth of the male sex organs during the fetal period, and the development of the male sex characteristics during puberty.

puberty the period of sexual maturation, when a person becomes capable of reproducing.

primary sex characteristics the body structures (ovaries, testes, and external genitalia) that make sexual reproduction possible.

organs and external genitalia—develop dramatically. So do the nonreproductive **secondary sex characteristics.** Girls develop breasts and larger hips. Boys' facial hair begins growing and their voices deepen. Pubic and underarm hair emerge in both girls and boys (**FIGURE 4.2**).

Pubertal boys may not at first like their sparse beard. (But then it grows on them.)

For boys, puberty's landmark is the first ejaculation, which often occurs during sleep (as a "wet dream"). This event, called **spermarche,** usually happens by about age 14.

In girls, the landmark is the first menstrual period, **menarche,** usually within a year of age 12½ (Anderson et al., 2003). Scientists have identified nearly 250 genes that predict when girls experience menarche (Day et al., 2017). But environment matters, too. Early menarche is more likely following stresses related to father absence, sexual abuse, insecure attachments, or a history of a mother's smoking during pregnancy (Richardson et al., 2018; Shrestha et al., 2011; Sung et al., 2016). Girls in various countries are developing breasts and reaching puberty earlier today than in the past. Suspected triggers include increased body fat, increased hormone-mimicking chemicals in the diet, and increased stress related to family disruption (Biro et al., 2010, 2012; Ellis et al., 2012; Herman-Giddens, 2013). But the good news is that a secure child-mother attachment can provide a buffer against childhood stresses, including those related to early puberty (Sung et al., 2016). Remember: *Nature and nurture interact.*

RETRIEVE & REMEMBER

ANSWERS IN APPENDIX E

2. Prenatal sexual development begins about __________ weeks after conception. Adolescence is marked by the onset of __________.

LaunchPad For a 7-minute discussion of gender development, see the *Video: Gender Development.*

Sexual Development Variations

Nature may blur the biological line between males and females. People who are intersex may be born with unusual combinations of male and female chromosomes, hormones, and anatomy. For example, a genetic male may be born with two or more X chromosomes as well as a Y chromosome *(Klinefelter syndrome)*, often resulting in sterility and small testes. Genetic females born with only one normal X chromosome *(Turner syndrome)* may not have menstrual periods, develop breasts, or be able to have children without reproductive assistance. Such individuals may struggle with their *gender identity*.

In the past, medical professionals often recommended *sex-reassignment surgery* to create a clear sex identity for such children. One study reviewed 14 cases of genetic boys who had undergone early sex-reassignment surgery and been raised as girls. Of those cases, 6 later identified as male, 5 were living as females, and 3 reported an unclear gender identity (Reiner & Gearhart, 2004).

In one famous case, a little boy lost his penis during a botched circumcision. His parents followed a psychiatrist's advice to raise him as a girl rather than as a damaged boy. So, with male chromosomes and hormones and a female upbringing, did nature or nurture form this child's gender identity? Although raised as a girl, "Brenda" Reimer was not

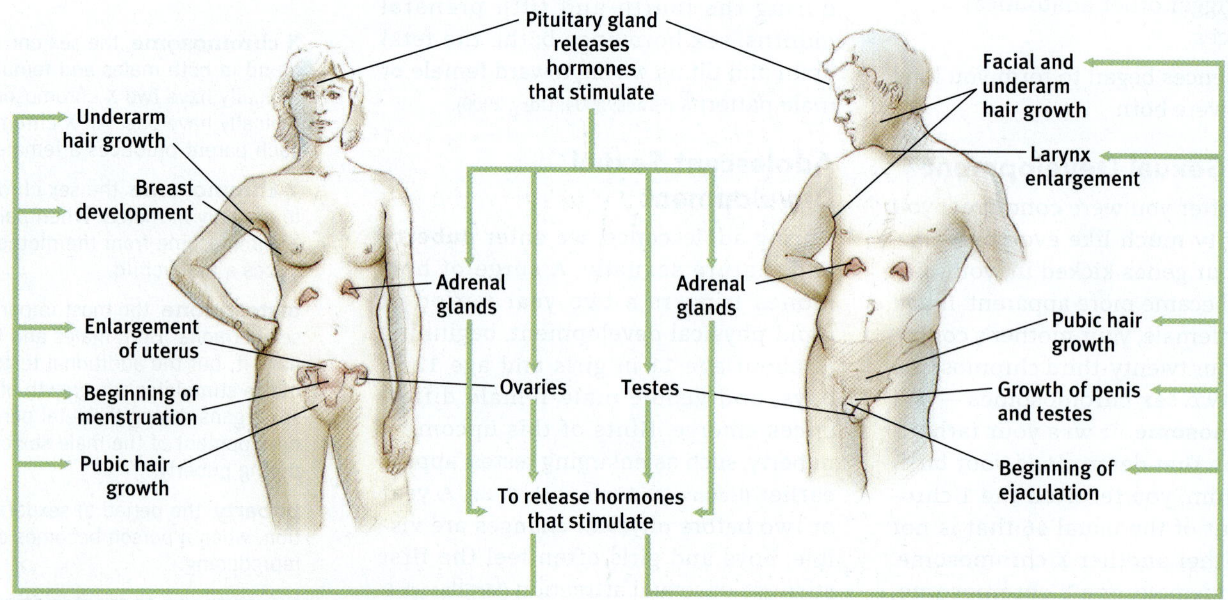

FIGURE 4.2 Body changes at puberty At about age 11 in girls and age 12 in boys, a surge of hormones triggers a variety of visible physical changes.

Michael Dalder/SEMENYA Reuters/Newscom

"I am who I am." Dramatic improvements in South African track star Caster Semenya's race times prompted the International Association of Athletics Federations to undertake sex testing in 2009. Semenya was reported to have physical characteristics not typically male or female. She was officially cleared to continue competing as a woman. Semenya declared, "God made me the way I am and I accept myself. I am who I am" (*YOU*, 2009). In 2016, she won an Olympic gold medal.

like most other girls. "She" didn't like dolls. She tore her dresses with rough-and-tumble play. At puberty she wanted no part of kissing boys. Finally, Brenda's parents explained what had happened, which led Brenda immediately to reject the assigned female identity. He underwent surgery to remove the breasts he developed from hormone therapy. He cut his hair and chose a male name, David. He eventually married a woman and became a stepfather. Sadly, he later died by suicide—but so did his identical twin brother, who also had been depressed (Colapinto, 2000). Today, experts generally recommend postponing surgery until a child's naturally developing physical appearance and gender identity become clear.

The bottom line: "Sex matters," concluded the National Academy of Sciences (2001). Sex-related genes and physiology "result in behavioral and cognitive differences between males and females." Yet environmental factors matter, too, as we will see next. Nature and nurture work together.

THE NURTURE OF GENDER

For many people, birth-designated sex and gender exist together in harmony. Biology draws the outline, and culture paints the details. The physical traits that define a newborn as male, female, or intersex are the same worldwide. But the gender traits that define how men (or boys) and women (or girls) should act, interact, and feel about themselves differ across time and place (Zentner & Eagly, 2015).

Gender Roles

LOQ 4-5 What are some of the cultural influences on gender roles?

Cultures shape our behaviors by defining how we ought to behave in a particular social position, or **role.** We can see this shaping power in **gender roles**—the social expectations that guide people's behavior as men or as women.

In just a thin slice of history, gender roles worldwide have undergone an extreme makeover. At the beginning of the twentieth century, only one country in the world—New Zealand—granted women the right to vote (Briscoe, 1997). Effective 2015, all countries granted that right. A century ago, American women could not vote in national elections, serve in the military, or divorce a husband without cause. If a woman worked for pay, she would more likely have been a seamstress than a surgeon. When asked to draw a scientist in the 1960s and 1970s, less than 1 percent of U.S. children drew a woman. In more recent studies, 25 percent did so (Miller et al., 2018).

Now, nearly half the U.S. workforce is female (DOL, 2015). In the STEM fields (science, technology, engineering, and mathematics), men still hold most faculty

Dinodia/The Image Works

The gendered tsunami In Sri Lanka, Indonesia, and India, the gendered division of labor helps explain the excess of female deaths from the 2004 tsunami. In some villages, 80 percent of those killed were women, who were mostly at home while the men were more likely to be at sea fishing or doing tasks elsewhere. Many women also died trying to save children and elderly relatives (Oxfam, 2005).

MARWAN NAAMANI/Getty Images

Driving change Thanks to the years-long efforts of Manal al-Sharif and other brave women activists, driving a car became a universal right for women in 2018 when Saudi Arabia finally lifted its ban.

secondary sex characteristics nonreproductive sexual traits, such as female breasts and hips, male voice quality, and body hair.

spermarche [sper-MAR-key] the first ejaculation.

menarche [meh-NAR-key] the first menstrual period.

role a set of expectations (norms) about a social position, defining how those in the position ought to behave.

gender role a set of expected behaviors, attitudes, and traits for men and for women.

positions and receive greater financial research support (Ceci et al., 2014; Sege et al., 2015; Sheltzer & Smith, 2014). Women still experience subtle sexism that discourages a STEM-related career (Kuchynka et al., 2018). But signs point to increases in supply and demand for women in the STEM fields. For example, U.S. women, compared with men, earn more college degrees and higher college grades. They also show equal competence at STEM-related activities, such as writing computer code (Keiser et al., 2016; Stoet & Geary, 2018; Terrell et al., 2017). When researchers invited U.S. professors to recommend candidates for STEM positions, most said they preferred hiring the highly talented women over the equally talented men (Williams & Ceci, 2015). This is good news for budding female scientists and engineers, who benefit from having capable and motivated female mentors and role models (Dennehy & Dasgupta, 2017; Moss-Racusin et al., 2018).

Take a minute to check your own gender expectations. Would you agree that "When jobs are scarce, men should have more rights to a job"? In the United States, Britain, and Spain, a little over 12 percent of adults agree. In Nigeria, Pakistan, and India, about 80 percent of adults agree (Pew, 2010). This question taps people's views on the idea that men and women should be treated equally. We're all human, but my, how our views differ. Northern European countries offer the greatest gender equity, Middle Eastern and North African countries the least (UN, 2015a).

> "You cannot put women and men on an equal footing. It is against nature." —Turkish President Recep Tayyip Erdoğan, 2014

Expectations about gender roles also factor into cultural attitudes about **sexual aggression.** In the United States, 2017 marked the beginning of a massive cultural shift in such attitudes, as a number of famous and powerful men, and a few women—in politics, movie-making, broadcasting, sports, academia—faced credible accusations. Many of these accusations came years after the incidents, prompting some to wonder about the nature of our memories for traumatic events. (See Chapter 7 for more on this topic.) Many American colleges and universities now require certain employees to report any student disclosure of sexual aggression to university officials, even without the victims' consent (Holland et al., 2018). (See Thinking Critically About: Sexual Aggression.)

> "#MeToo, Time's Up, the Women's March, these movements tell us that we need to have a critical discussion on women's rights, equality, and the power dynamics of gender. . . . Sexual harassment, for example—in business and in government—is a systemic problem and it is unacceptable. As leaders, we need to act to show that truly, time is up." —Canadian Prime Minister Justin Trudeau, 2018

Gender Identity

LOQ 4-7 How do we form our gender identity?

A *gender role* describes how others expect us to think, feel, and act. Our **gender identity,** when *binary* (involving only two options) is our sense of being male or female. Those with a *non-binary* gender identity may not feel male *or* female, or they may identify as some combination of male *and* female. How do we develop our gender identity?

Social learning theory assumes that we acquire our gender identity in childhood, by observing and imitating others' gender-linked behaviors and by being rewarded or punished for acting in certain ways. ("Tatiana, you're such a good mommy to your dolls"; "Big boys don't cry, Armand.") But some critics think there's more to gender identity than imitation and reward. They ask us to consider how much **gender typing**—taking on a traditional male or female role—varies from child to child (Tobin et al., 2010).

Parents do help to transmit their culture's views on gender. In one analysis of 43 studies, parents with traditional gender views were more likely to have gender-typed children who shared their expectations about how males and females should act (Tenenbaum & Leaper, 2002). When fathers share equally in housework, their daughters develop higher aspirations for work outside the home (Croft et al., 2014).

But no matter how much parents encourage or discourage traditional gender behavior, children may drift toward what feels right to them. Some organize themselves into "boy worlds" and "girl worlds," each guided by their understanding of the rules. Other children seem to prefer **androgyny:** A blend of male and female roles feels right to them. Androgyny has benefits. As adults, androgynous people are more adaptable. They are more flexible in their actions and in their career choices (Bem, 1993). From childhood onward, they tend to bounce back more easily from bad events, accept themselves, and experience less depression (Lam & McBride-Chang, 2007; Mosher & Danoff-Burg, 2008; Pauletti et al., 2017).

Feelings matter, but so does how we think. Early in life, we all form *schemas,* or concepts that help us make sense of our world. Our *gender schemas* organize our experiences of male-female characteristics and help us think about our gender identity, about who we are (Bem, 1987, 1993; Martin et al., 2002).

sexual aggression any physical or verbal behavior of a sexual nature that is intended to harm someone physically or emotionally. Can be expressed as either *sexual harassment* or *sexual assault.*

gender identity our sense of being male, female, neither, or some combination of male and female.

social learning theory the theory that we learn social behavior by observing and imitating and by being rewarded or punished.

gender typing the acquisition of a traditional masculine or feminine role.

androgyny displaying both traditionally masculine and traditionally feminine psychological characteristics.

Thinking Critically About:

Sexual Aggression

LOQ 4-6 What are the effects of sexual aggression? How have cultural views changed, and how can we reduce sexual aggression?

Definition of Sexual Aggression

Sexual harassment involves making unwanted sexual advances, obscene remarks, or requests for sexual favors.[1]

Sexual assault is "any type of sexual contact or behavior that occurs without the explicit consent of the recipient," such as unwanted touching, molestation, and attempted or completed rape.[2]

Victims

In the U.S., **81%** of women and **43%** of men report having experienced sexual aggression in their lifetime.[3]

Sexual aggression affects people of *all ethnic groups*.[4]

Nearly **70%** of rape victims are between the ages of 11 and 24.[4]

In a National School Climate survey, **8** out of **10** gay or lesbian adolescents reported experiencing sex-related harassment in the prior year.[5]

Effects on Well-Being

Thanks to human resilience, victims of sexual aggression often recover and lead healthy and meaningful lives. Yet many also suffer serious setbacks, including:

- Disrupted sleep[6]
- Poor physical health[7]
- Difficulty trusting new relationship partners[8]

Cultural Effects on Our Views

By Place:

Some cultures view victims of sexual aggression as guilty of disgracing their families. In India and Pakistan, male family members kill an unknown number of women—one source estimates 1000 annually in each country[9]—for dishonoring their families.

Over Time:

Changes in U.S. culture have made it less acceptable to blame victims of sexual aggression.

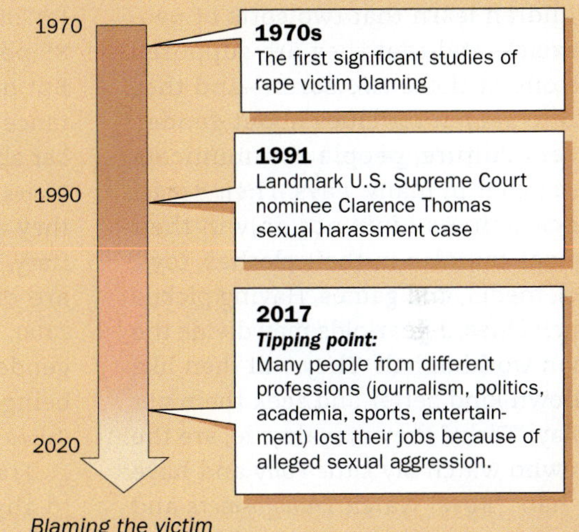

1970
1990
2020
1970s
The first significant studies of rape victim blaming
1991
Landmark U.S. Supreme Court nominee Clarence Thomas sexual harassment case

Tipping point:
Many people from different professions (journalism, politics, academia, sports, entertainment) lost their jobs because of alleged sexual aggression.
Blaming the victim becomes less acceptable.

How to Reduce Sexual Aggression

Therapy to treat sexual aggressors has not been very effective.[10] However, other, broader-based strategies do work:

Encourage victims to report their experiences to authority figures (parents, supervisors, law enforcement officials) and to share their experiences publicly.

Empower victims to take control of their situation and refuse to let their perpetrators dominate or manipulate them. Adjust social norms so that victims feel safe reporting their experiences.

Educate people about preventive bystander intervention strategies, such as "Green Dot," which has been shown to reduce sexual aggression in communities by as much as 20%.[11]

Person of the Year
TIME
The Silence Breakers
2017

THE INDIA POLIS STAR
Disgraced Dr. Nassar...sexual abuse
... Over 200 victims testify

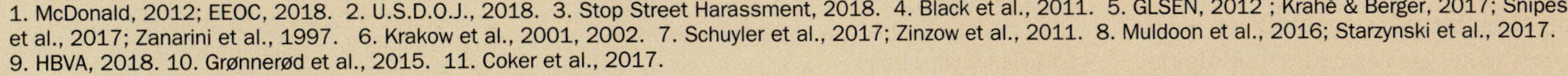
1. McDonald, 2012; EEOC, 2018. 2. U.S.D.O.J., 2018. 3. Stop Street Harassment, 2018. 4. Black et al., 2011. 5. GLSEN, 2012 ; Krahé & Berger, 2017; Snipes et al., 2017; Zanarini et al., 1997. 6. Krakow et al., 2001, 2002. 7. Schuyler et al., 2017; Zinzow et al., 2011. 8. Muldoon et al., 2016; Starzynski et al., 2017. 9. HBVA, 2018. 10. Grønnerød et al., 2015. 11. Coker et al., 2017.

As young children, we were "gender detectives" (Martin & Ruble, 2004). Before our first birthday, we knew the difference between a male and female voice or face (Martin et al., 2002). After we turned 2, language forced us to label the world in terms of gender. English classifies people as *he* and *she*. Other languages classify objects as masculine ("*le* train") or feminine ("*la* table").

Children learn that two sorts of people exist—and that they are supposed to be one of these two sorts—and they begin to search for clues about gender. In every culture, people communicate their gender in many ways. Their *gender expression* drops hints not only in their language but also in their clothes, toys, books, media, and games. Having picked up such clues, 3-year-olds may divide the human world in half. They will then like their own kind better and seek them out for play. "Girls," they may decide, are the ones who watch *My Little Pony* and have long hair. "Boys" watch *Transformers* and don't wear dresses. Armed with their newly collected "proof," they then adjust their behaviors to fit their concept of gender. These stereotypes are most rigid at about age 5 or 6. If the new neighbor is a girl, a 6-year-old boy may assume that he cannot share her interests. In a young child's life, gender looms large.

For people who identify as *cisgendered*, gender corresponds with birth sex. For those who identify as **transgender,** gender identity differs from what's typical for that person's birth-designated sex (APA, 2010; Bockting, 2014). From childhood onward, a person may feel like a male in a female body, or a female in a male body (Olson et al., 2015). Some transgender people experience profound distress from this conflict, increasing their risk for a diagnosis of *gender dysphoria* (McNeil et al., 2017; Mueller et al., 2017). Brain scans reveal that those (about 75 percent men) who seek medical sex-reassignment have some neural tracts that differ from those whose gender identity matches their birth-designated sex (Kranz et al., 2014; Van Kesteren et al., 1997). Biologist Robert Sapolsky (2015) explains: "It's not that [these] individuals think they are a different gender than they actually are. It's that they [are] stuck with bodies that are a different gender from who they actually are."

In most countries, it's not easy being transgender. In a national survey of lesbian, gay, bisexual, and transgender Americans, 71 percent saw "some" or "a lot" of social acceptance for gay men, and 85 percent said the same for lesbians. But only 18 percent saw similar acceptance for transgender people, who number about 1.4 million in the United States (Flores et al., 2016; Sandstrom, 2015). Although they are allowed to serve in the U.S. military, transgender recruits' applications are often delayed or rejected (Phillips, 2018). And in a survey of 27,175 transgender Americans, 46 percent reported being verbally harassed in the last year (James et al., 2016).

Transgender people may attempt to align their outward appearance and everyday lives with their internal gender identity. Such affirming of one's internal gender identity can help transgender people avoid depression and low self-esteem (Glynn et al., 2017). Note that *gender identity* is distinct from *sexual orientation* (the direction of one's sexual attraction). Transgender people may be sexually attracted to people of the other gender, the same gender, all genders, or to no one at all. Your sexual orientation, as some say, is who you fantasize going to bed *with;* your gender identity is who you go to bed *as*.

Axelle/Bauer-Griffin/Getty Images

Beloved son Chaz Bono, writer, musician, advocate, and actor, is the transgender son of singer and actor Cher, and the late musician and politician, Sonny Bono.

Natalie Behring

Legally non-binary In 2016, Jamie Shupe became the first legally-recognized non-binary American. Shupe struggled with a male birth-designated sex for 50 years. An attempted female transition didn't feel right, either. "I didn't have the. . . knowledge like I do now," Shupe explains, "that I could be other things" (Dake, 2016). After being granted the right to be identified as neither male nor female, Shupe declared, "I can be masculine, I can be feminine. I can do anything I want" (Hidden Brain, 2018).

An estimated 1 million Americans identify as transgender (Meerwijk & Sevelius, 2017). Roughly 30 percent in that group have broader non-binary gender identities—not strictly male or female but instead feeling a combination of male and female, or feeling neither male nor female (Barr et al., 2016; James et al., 2016; Mikalson et al., 2014).

IN YOUR EVERYDAY LIFE

How gender-typed are you? What has influenced your feelings of being male, female, neither, or some combination of male and female?

RETRIEVE & REMEMBER

ANSWERS IN APPENDIX E

3. What are gender roles, and what do their variations tell us about our human capacity for learning and adaptation?

LaunchPad For a 6.5-minute exploration of one pioneering transgender person's journey, see the *Video: Renée Richards—A Long Journey.*

Human Sexuality

As you've probably noticed, we can hardly talk about gender without talking about our sexuality. For all but the 1 percent of us considered **asexual** (Bogaert, 2004, 2015), dating and mating become a high priority from puberty on. Biologist Alfred Kinsey (1894–1956) pioneered the study of human sexuality (Kinsey et al., 1948, 1953). Kinsey and his colleagues' findings sparked debate and controversy. But they also paved the way for future research on the sexual behavior of men and women. Our sexual feelings and behaviors reflect both physiological and psychological influences.

In one British survey of 18,876 people (and in other surveys since), about 1 percent identified themselves as asexual, having "never felt sexually attracted to anyone at all" (Bogaert, 2004, 2015). People with an asexual orientation are, however, nearly as likely as others to report masturbating, noting that it feels good, reduces anxiety, or "cleans out the plumbing."

THE PHYSIOLOGY OF SEX

Unlike hunger, sex is not an actual *need.* (Without it, we may feel like dying, but we will not.) Yet sex is a part of life. Had this not been so for all of your biological ancestors, you would not be alive and reading these words. Sexual motivation is nature's clever way of making people procreate, thus enabling our species' survival. Life is sexually transmitted.

Hormones and Sexual Behavior

LOQ 4-8 How do hormones influence human sexual motivation?

Among the forces driving sexual behavior are the *sex hormones.* As we noted earlier, the main male sex hormone is *testosterone.* The main female sex hormones are the **estrogens,** such as *estradiol.* Sex hormones influence us at several points in the life span:

- During the prenatal period, they direct our sexual development.
- During puberty, a sex hormone surge ushers us into adolescence.
- After puberty and well into the late adult years, sex hormones facilitate sexual behavior.

In most mammals, sexual interest and fertility overlap. Females become sexually receptive when their estrogen levels peak at ovulation. By injecting female animals with estrogens, researchers can increase their sexual interest. Hormone injections do not affect male animals' sexual behavior as easily because male hormone levels are more constant. Nevertheless, male hamsters that have had their testosterone-making testes surgically removed gradually lose much of their interest in receptive females. They gradually regain it if injected with testosterone (Piekarski et al., 2009).

Hormones do influence human sexuality, but more loosely. Researchers are exploring and debating whether women's mating preferences change across the menstrual cycle, especially at ovulation, when both estrogens and testosterone rise (Haselton, 2018; Marcinkowska et al., 2018; Wood et al., 2014a). (Recall that women have testosterone, though less than men have.) Some evidence suggests that, among women with mates, sexual desire rises slightly at ovulation—a change men can sometimes detect in women's behaviors and voices (Haselton & Gildersleeve, 2011, 2016).

More than other mammalian females, women are responsive to their testosterone levels (Davison & Davis, 2011; van Anders, 2012). If a woman's natural testosterone level drops, as happens with removal of the ovaries or adrenal glands, her sexual interest may plummet (Davison & Davis, 2011; Lindau et al., 2007). And testosterone-replacement therapy can often restore sexual desire, arousal, and activity (Braunstein et al., 2005; Buster et al., 2005; Petersen & Hyde, 2011).

Testosterone-replacement therapy also increases sexual functioning in men with abnormally low testosterone levels (Khera et al., 2011). But normal ups and downs in testosterone levels (from man to man and hour to hour) have little effect on sexual drive (Byrne, 1982). In fact, male hormones sometimes vary in *response* to sexual stimulation (Escasa et al., 2011). One Australian study tested whether the presence of an attractive woman would affect heterosexual male skateboarders' performance. The result? Their testosterone surged, as did their riskier moves and crash landings (Ronay & von Hippel, 2010). Thus, sexual arousal can be a *cause* as well as a result of increased testosterone.

Large hormonal surges or declines do affect men's and women's sexual desire. These shifts take place at two predictable points in the life span, and sometimes at an unpredictable third point:

1. ***During puberty, the surge in sex hormones triggers development of sex characteristics and sexual interest.*** If puberty's hormonal surge is prevented, sex characteristics and sexual desire do not develop normally (Peschel & Peschel, 1987). This happened in Europe during the 1600s and 1700s, when boy sopranos were castrated to preserve their high voices for Italian opera.

transgender an umbrella term describing people whose gender identity or expression differs from that associated with their birth-designated sex.

asexual having no sexual attraction toward others.

estrogens sex hormones, such as estradiol, that contribute to female sex characteristics and are secreted in greater amounts by females than by males. Estrogen levels peak during ovulation. In nonhuman mammals, this promotes sexual receptivity.

2. ***In later life, sex hormone levels fall.*** Women experience menopause as their estrogen levels decrease; males experience a more gradual change (Chapter 3). Sex remains a part of life, but as hormone levels decline, sexual fantasies and intercourse decline as well (Leitenberg & Henning, 1995).
3. ***For some, surgery or drugs may cause hormonal shifts.*** After surgical castration, men's sex drive typically falls as testosterone levels decline sharply (Hucker & Bain, 1990). When male sex offenders took a drug that reduced their testosterone level to that of a boy before puberty, they also lost much of their sexual urge (Bilefsky, 2009; Money et al., 1983).

To recap, we might compare human sex hormones, especially testosterone, to the fuel in a car. Without fuel, a car will not run. But if the fuel level is at least adequate, adding more won't change how the car runs. This isn't a perfect comparison, because hormones and sexual motivation influence each other. But it does suggest that biology alone cannot fully explain human sexual behavior. Hormones are the essential fuel for our sex drive. But psychological stimuli turn on the engine, keep it running, and shift it into high gear. Let's now see just where that drive usually takes us.

RETRIEVE & REMEMBER

ANSWERS IN APPENDIX E

4. The primary female sex hormones are the ____________. The primary male sex hormone is ____________.

The Sexual Response Cycle

LOQ 4-9 What is the human *sexual response cycle,* and how do sexual dysfunctions and paraphilias differ?

As we noted in Chapter 1, science often begins by carefully observing behavior. Sexual behavior is no exception. In the 1960s, two researchers—gynecologist-obstetrician William Masters and his colleague, Virginia Johnson (1966)—made headlines with their observations of sexual behavior. They recorded the physiological responses of 382 female and 312 male volunteers who came to their lab to masturbate or have intercourse. (The volunteers were a somewhat atypical sample, consisting only of people able and willing to display arousal and orgasm while scientists observed.) The researchers identified a four-stage **sexual response cycle:**

1. ***Excitement:*** The genital areas fill with blood, causing a woman's clitoris and a man's penis to swell. A woman's vagina expands and secretes lubricant. Her breasts and nipples may enlarge.
2. ***Plateau:*** Excitement peaks as breathing, pulse, and blood pressure rates continue to rise. A man's penis becomes fully engorged—to an average 5.6 inches, among 1661 men who measured themselves for condom fitting (Herbenick et al., 2014). Some fluid—frequently containing enough live sperm to enable conception—may appear at its tip. A woman's vaginal secretion continues to increase, and her clitoris retracts. Orgasm feels imminent.
3. ***Orgasm:*** Muscles contract all over the body. Breathing, pulse, and blood pressure rates continue to climb. Men and women don't differ much in the delight they receive from sexual release. PET scans have shown that the same brain regions were active in men and women during orgasm (Holstege et al., 2003a,b).
4. ***Resolution:*** The body gradually returns to its unaroused state as genital blood vessels release their accumulated blood. For men, this happens relatively quickly if orgasm has occurred, relatively slowly otherwise. (It's like the nasal tickle that goes away rapidly if you have sneezed, slowly otherwise.) Men then enter a **refractory period,** a resting period that lasts from a few minutes to a day or more. During this time, they cannot achieve another orgasm. Women have a much shorter refractory period, enabling them to have more orgasms if restimulated during or soon after resolution.

As you learned in Chapter 2, there is also a *refractory period* in neural processing—the brief resting pause that occurs after a neuron has fired.

A nonsmoking 50-year-old male has about a 1-in-a-million chance of a heart attack during any hour. This increases to merely 2-in-a-million in the two hours during and following sex (with no increase for those who exercise regularly). Compared with risks associated with heavy exertion or anger (see Chapter 10), this risk seems not worth losing sleep (or sex) over (Jackson, 2009; Muller et al., 1996).

Sexual Dysfunctions and Paraphilias

Masters and Johnson had two goals: to describe the human sexual response cycle, and to understand and treat problems that prevent people from completing it. **Sexual dysfunctions** consistently impair sexual arousal or functioning at any point in this cycle. Some involve sexual motivation—the person lacks sexual energy and/or does not become aroused. For men, one common problem (and the subject of many TV commercials) is **erectile disorder,** an inability to have or maintain an erection. Another is *premature ejaculation,* reaching a sexual climax before the man or his partner wishes. For some women, pain during intercourse may prevent them from completing the sexual response cycle. Others may experience **female orgasmic disorder,** distress over rarely or never having an orgasm. In surveys of some 35,000 American women, about 4 in 10 reported a sexual problem, such as female orgasmic disorder or low desire. Most women who have reported sexual distress have connected it with their emotional relationship with their sexual partner (Bancroft et al., 2003).

Psychological and medical therapies can help people with sexual dysfunctions (Frühauf et al., 2013). Behaviorally oriented therapy, for example, can help men learn ways to control their urge to ejaculate, or help women learn to bring themselves to orgasm. Starting with the introduction of Viagra in 1998, erectile disorder has been routinely treated by taking a pill. Researchers have struggled to develop reliable drug treatments for *female sexual interest/arousal disorder.*

Sexual dysfunction involves problems with arousal or sexual functioning. People with **paraphilias** (mostly men) do experience sexual desire, but they direct it in unusual ways (Baur et al., 2016). The American Psychiatric Association (2013) only classifies such behavior as disordered if

- a person experiences distress from an unusual sexual interest or
- it entails harm or risk of harm to others.

The serial killer Jeffrey Dahmer had *necrophilia,* a sexual attraction to corpses. Those with *exhibitionism* derive pleasure from exposing themselves sexually to others, without consent. People with the paraphilic disorder *pedophilia* experience sexual arousal toward children who haven't entered puberty.

RETRIEVE & REMEMBER

ANSWERS IN APPENDIX E

5. Someone who is distressed by impaired sexual arousal may be diagnosed with a ____________. Exhibitionism would be considered a ____________.

LaunchPad To explore the stories of participants in a drug therapy program for sexual dysfunctions, see the 6-minute *Video: Sexual Dysfunctions and Their Treatments.*

Sexually Transmitted Infections

LOQ 4-10 How can sexually transmitted infections be prevented?

Every day, more than 1 million people worldwide acquire a *sexually transmitted infection* (*STI;* also called *STD,* for *sexually transmitted disease*) (WHO, 2013). Common STIs include chlamydia, gonorrhea, herpes simplex virus [HSV], and human papillomavirus [HPV] infection. "Compared with older adults," reports the Centers for Disease Control and Prevention (2016b), "sexually active adolescents aged 15–19 years and young adults aged 20–24 years are at higher risk." Teenage girls, for example, are at heightened risk because their anatomy is not fully mature and their level of protective antibodies is lower (Dehne & Riedner, 2005; Guttmacher Institute, 1994).

Condoms offer only limited protection against certain skin-to-skin STIs, such as herpes. But their ability to reduce other risks has saved lives (NIH, 2001). The effects were clear when Thailand promoted condom use by commercial sex workers. Over a 4-year period, condom use soared from 14 to 94 percent. During that time, the number of bacterial STIs plummeted from 410,406 to 27,362, a 93 percent reduction (WHO, 2000).

When used by people with an infected partner, condoms have also been 80 percent effective in preventing transmission of HIV (*human immunodeficiency virus*)—the virus that causes **AIDS** (Weller & Davis-Beaty, 2002; WHO, 2003). HIV can be transmitted by other means, such as needle sharing during drug use, but its sexual transmission is most common. Half of all those with HIV (and 1 in 5 Americans recently diagnosed with HIV) are women (CDC, 2018a). Because the virus is spread more easily from men to women, women's proportion of the worldwide AIDS population is growing.

Half of Americans with AIDS are between ages 30 and 49 (CDC, 2016). Given AIDS' long incubation period, this means that many were infected in their teens and twenties. In 2012, the death of 1.6 million people with AIDS worldwide left behind countless grief-stricken loved ones, including millions of orphaned children (UNAIDS, 2013). In sub-Saharan Africa, home to two-thirds of those with HIV, medical treatment to extend life and care for the dying is sapping social resources.

Having sex with one person means also partnering with that person's past partners—any one of whom might have unknowingly transmitted an STI. So, the first step in preventing STIs is knowing one's status, and sharing it with one's sexual partner.

THE PSYCHOLOGY OF SEX

LOQ 4-11 How do external and imagined stimuli contribute to sexual arousal?

Biological factors powerfully influence our sexual motivation and behavior. But despite our shared biology, human sexual motivation and behavior vary widely—over time, across place, and among individuals. So, social and psychological factors exert a great influence as well (**FIGURE 4.3**).

What motivates people to have sex? The 281 reasons study participants expressed ranged widely—from "to get closer to God" to "to get my boyfriend to shut up" (Buss, 2008; Meston & Buss, 2007). One thing is certain: Our most important sex organ may be the one resting above our shoulders. Our sophisticated brain enables sexual arousal both from what is real and from what is imagined.

sexual response cycle the four stages of sexual responding described by Masters and Johnson—excitement, plateau, orgasm, and resolution.

refractory period in human sexuality, a resting pause that occurs after orgasm, during which a person cannot achieve another orgasm.

sexual dysfunction a problem that consistently impairs sexual arousal or functioning.

erectile disorder inability to develop or maintain an erection due to insufficient blood flow to the penis.

female orgasmic disorder distress due to infrequently or never experiencing orgasm.

paraphilias sexual arousal from fantasies, behaviors, or urges involving nonhuman objects, the suffering of self or others, and/or nonconsenting persons.

AIDS (acquired immune deficiency syndrome) a life-threatening, sexually transmitted infection caused by the *human immunodeficiency virus (HIV).* AIDS depletes the immune system, leaving the person vulnerable to infections.

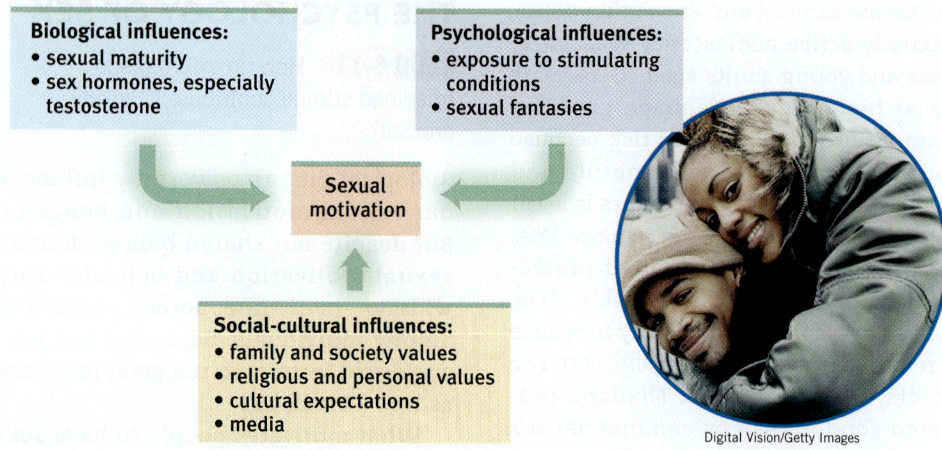

Digital Vision/Getty Images

FIGURE 4.3 Biopsychosocial influences on sexual motivation Our sexual motivation is influenced by biological factors, but psychological and social-cultural factors play an even bigger role.

External Stimuli

Men and women become aroused when they see, hear, or read erotic material (Heiman, 1975; Stockton & Murnen, 1992). In men more than in women, *feelings* of sexual arousal closely mirror their (more obvious) physical genital responses (Chivers et al., 2010).

People may find sexual arousal either pleasing or disturbing. (Those who wish to control their arousal often limit their exposure to arousing material, just as those wishing to avoid overeating limit their exposure to tempting food cues.) With repeated exposure to any stimulus, including an erotic stimulus, our response lessens—we *habituate*. During the 1920s, when Western women's hemlines rose to the knee, an exposed leg made hearts flutter. Today, many would barely notice.

Can exposure to sexually explicit material have lingering negative effects? Research indicates that it can, in three ways.

- ***Believing rape is acceptable*** Although some modern pornography portrays women in powerful roles, mostly it presents women as subservient sexual objects (Fritz & Paul, 2018; Jones, 2018). In some studies, people have viewed scenes in which women were forced to have sex and appeared to enjoy it. Those viewers were more accepting of the false idea that women want to be overpowered. Male viewers also expressed more willingness to hurt women and to commit rape after viewing these scenes (Allen et al., 1995, 2000; Foubert et al., 2011; Zillmann, 1989).
- ***Reducing satisfaction with a partner's appearance or with a relationship*** After viewing images or erotic films of sexually attractive women and men, people have judged an average person, their own partner, or their spouse as less attractive. And they have found their own relationship less satisfying (Kenrick & Gutierres, 1980; Lambert et al., 2012). Perhaps reading or watching erotica's unlikely scenarios creates expectations few men and women can fulfill.
- ***Desensitization*** Extensive online pornography viewing can desensitize young adults to normal sexuality. Repeated exposure to this distorted sexual world may contribute to lowered sexual desire and satisfaction, diminished brain activation in response to sexual images, and, for men, erectile problems (Wright et al., 2018). "Porn is messing with your manhood," argue Philip Zimbardo and colleagues (2016).

Imagined Stimuli

Sexual arousal and desire can also be products of our imagination. People left with no genital sensation after a spinal cord injury can still feel sexual desire (Willmuth, 1987).

Both men and women (about 95 percent of each) report having sexual fantasies. For a few women, these fantasies alone can produce orgasms (Komisaruk & Whipple, 2011). Men, regardless of sexual orientation, tend to have more frequent, more physical, and less romantic fantasies (Schmitt et al., 2012). They also prefer less personal and faster-paced sexual content in books and videos (Leitenberg & Henning, 1995).

Does fantasizing about sex indicate a sexual problem or dissatisfaction? *No.* If anything, sexually active people have *more* sexual fantasies.

Sexual Risk Taking and Teen Pregnancy

LOQ 4-12 What factors influence teenagers' sexual behaviors and use of contraceptives?

Sexual attitudes and behaviors vary dramatically across cultures and eras. "Sex between unmarried adults" is "morally unacceptable," agree 97 percent of Indonesians and 6 percent of Germans (Pew, 2014b). Thanks to decreased sexual activity and increased protection, American teen pregnancy rates are declining (CDC, 2016b, 2018f; Twenge et al., 2016b). What environmental factors and choices contribute to sexual risk taking among teens?

Communication About Birth Control

Many teens are uncomfortable discussing birth control with parents, partners, and peers. But teens who talk freely and openly with their parents and with their partner in an exclusive relationship are more likely to use contraceptives (Aspy et al., 2007; Milan & Kilmann, 1987).

"Condoms should be used on every conceivable occasion." —Anonymous

Impulsivity Among sexually active 12- to 17-year-old American girls, 72 percent said they regretted having had sex (Reuters, 2000). If passion overwhelms intentions to use contraceptives or to delay having sex, unplanned sexual activity may result in pregnancy (Ariely & Loewenstein, 2006; MacDonald & Hynie, 2008).

Alcohol Use Among older teens and young adults, most sexual hook-ups (casual encounters outside of a relationship) occur after alcohol use, often without knowing consent (Fielder et al., 2013; Garcia et al., 2013; Johnson & Chen, 2015). Those who use alcohol prior to sex are also less likely to use condoms (Kotchick et al., 2001). Alcohol disarms normal restraints by depressing the brain centers that control judgment, inhibition, and self-awareness.

Mass Media The more sexual content adolescents and young adults view or read, the more likely they are to perceive their peers as sexually active, to develop sexually permissive attitudes, to experience early intercourse, and to use condoms inconsistently (Escobar-Chaves et al., 2005; Kim & Ward, 2012; O'Hara et al., 2012, Parkes et al., 2013). These perceptions of peer norms (what "everybody else" is doing) influence teens' sexual behavior (Lyons et al., 2015; van de Bongardt et al., 2015). And they come in part from the popular media, which help write the **social scripts** that shape our views of how to act in certain situations.

Delaying Sex What are the characteristics of teens who delay having sex?

- ***High intelligence*** Teens with high rather than average intelligence test scores more often delay sex, partly because they consider possible negative consequences and are more focused on future achievements than on here-and-now pleasures (Harden & Mendle, 2011).
- ***Religious engagement*** Actively religious teens more often reserve sexual activity for adulthood or long-term relationships (Hull et al., 2011; Schmitt & Fuller, 2015; Štulhofer et al., 2011).
- ***Father presence*** Studies that followed hundreds of New Zealand and U.S. girls from age 5 to 18 found that having Dad around reduces the risk of teen pregnancy. A father's presence was linked to lower sexual activity before age 16 and to lower teen pregnancy rates (Ellis et al., 2003).
- ***Service learning participation*** American teens who volunteer as tutors or teachers' aides, or participate in community projects, have lower pregnancy rates than do comparable teens randomly assigned to control groups (Kirby, 2002; O'Donnell et al., 2002). Does service learning promote a sense of personal competence, control, and responsibility? Does it encourage more future-oriented thinking? Or does it simply reduce opportunities for unprotected sex? Researchers don't have those answers yet.

dpa/picture-alliance/Newscom

Keeping abreast of hypersexuality An analysis of the 60 top-selling video games found 489 characters, 86 percent of whom were males (like most of the game players). The female characters were much more likely than the male characters to be "hypersexualized"—partially nude or revealingly clothed, with large breasts and tiny waists (Downs & Smith, 2010). Such depictions can lead to unrealistic expectations about sexuality and contribute to the early sexualization of girls. The American Psychological Association suggests countering this by teaching girls to "value themselves for who they are rather than how they look" (APA, 2007).

IMPROVE YOUR EVERYDAY LIFE

What strategies could your community use to reduce teen pregnancy?

* * *

In the rest of this chapter, we will consider two special topics: *sexual orientation* (the direction of our sexual interests), and evolutionary psychology's explanation of our sexuality.

RETRIEVE & REMEMBER

ANSWERS IN APPENDIX E

6. What factors influence our sexual motivation and behavior?
7. Which THREE of the following five factors contribute to unplanned teen pregnancies?
   a. Alcohol use
   b. Higher intelligence level
   c. Father absence
   d. Mass media models
   e. Participating in service learning programs

Sexual Orientation

LOQ 4-13 What do we know about sexual orientation?

As noted earlier in this chapter, we express the *direction* of our sexual interest in our **sexual orientation**—our sexual attraction toward members of the other gender (*heterosexual* orientation), our own gender (*same-sex* orientation), male and female genders (*bisexual* orientation), or to no one at all (*asexual* orientation). For some people sexual attraction is not restricted to any sex or gender identity (*pansexual* orientation). We experience such attractions in our interests and fantasies (who appears in your imagination)?

social script a culturally modeled guide for how to act in various situations.

sexual orientation the direction of our sexual attractions, as reflected in our longings and fantasies.

Santiago Felipe/Getty Images

Pansexual identity Musician Roes (formerly known as Angel Haze) considers herself a "woman of color representing...pansexuality" and notes that "love is boundary-less" (Hoby, 2012; Symonds, 2014).

CULTURAL ATTITUDES AND PREVALENCE

Cultures vary in their attitudes toward same-sex attractions. "Should society accept homosexuality?" *Yes,* say 88 percent of Spaniards and 1 percent of Nigerians (Pew, 2013a). Women everywhere are more accepting than men. Yet whether a culture condemns or accepts same-sex unions, heterosexuality is most common and same-sex attraction and other variations exist. In most African countries, same-sex relationships are illegal. Yet the ratio of lesbian, gay, or bisexual people "is no different from other countries in the rest of the world," reports the Academy of Science of South Africa (2015). What is more, same-sex activity spans human history.

How many people have exclusively same-sex attractions? According to more than a dozen national surveys in Europe and the United States, about 3 or 4 percent of men and 2 percent of women (Chandra et al., 2011; Copen et al., 2016; Savin-Williams et al., 2012). But the percentages vary somewhat across surveys, with the percentage who feel comfortable self-reporting as lesbian, gay, bisexual, or transgender gradually increasing with increased social acceptance (Newport, 2018). Percentages are also slightly higher when reporting is anonymous (Copen et al., 2016). A larger number of Americans—13 percent of women and 5 percent of men—say they have had some same-sex sexual contact during their lives (Chandra et al., 2011). Psychologists have only begun to research the experiences of those who identify as pansexual. The American Psychological Association's Division 44, Society for the Psychology of Sexual Orientation and Gender Diversity, offers additional information and resources.

> In tribal cultures in which same-sex sexual behavior is expected of all boys before marriage, most men are heterosexual (Hammack, 2005; Money, 1987). As this illustrates, same-sex sexual *behavior* does not always indicate a same-sex sexual *orientation.*

What does it feel like to not be heterosexual in a majority heterosexual culture? If you are heterosexual, imagine that you have found "the one"—a perfect partner of the other sex. How would you feel if you weren't sure who you could trust with knowing you had these feelings? How would you react if you overheard people telling crude jokes about heterosexual people, or if most movies, TV shows, and advertisements showed only same-sex relationships? How would you like hearing that many people wouldn't vote for a political candidate who favors other-sex marriage? And how would you feel if children's organizations and adoption agencies thought you might not be safe or trustworthy because you're attracted to people of the other sex?

Facing such reactions, some people with same-sex attractions may at first try to ignore or deny their desires, hoping they will go away. But they don't. And these people may—particularly if they live in a region or a country that condemns same-sex attractions—conceal their orientation (Pachankis & Bränström, 2018). Especially during adolescence or when feeling rejected by their parents or peers, people may struggle against same-sex attractions. Without social support, gay and lesbian teens express greater anxiety and depression (Becker et al., 2014; Ross et al., 2018). They also have an increased risk of contemplating and attempting suicide (Lyons, 2015; Wang et al., 2012, 2015b). Some may try to change their orientation through psychotherapy, willpower, or prayer. But the feelings typically persist, as do those of heterosexual people—who are similarly unable to change (Haldeman, 1994, 2002; Myers & Scanzoni, 2005).

Today's psychologists view sexual orientation as neither willfully chosen nor willfully changed. In 1973, the American Psychiatric Association dropped homosexuality from its list of "mental illnesses." In 1993, the World Health Organization did the same, as did Japan's and China's psychiatric associations in 1995 and 2001. "Efforts to change sexual orientation are unlikely to be successful and involve some risk of harm," declared

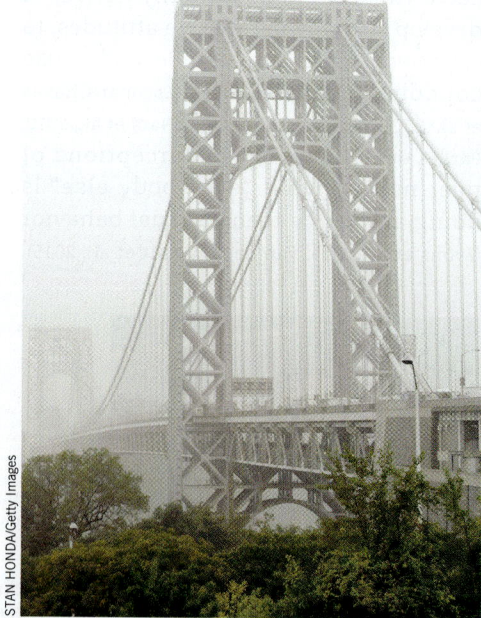

STAN HONDA/Getty Images

Driven to suicide In 2010, Rutgers University student Tyler Clementi jumped off this bridge after his roommate secretly filmed, shared, and tweeted about Clementi's intimate encounter with another man. Reports then surfaced of other gay teens who had reacted in a similarly tragic fashion after being taunted. Since 2010, Americans—especially those under 30—have been increasingly supportive of those with same-sex orientations.

a 2009 American Psychological Association report. Recognizing this, in 2016, Malta became the first European country to outlaw the controversial practice of "conversion therapy," which aims to change people's gender identities or sexual orientations. Several U.S. states have likewise banned conversion therapy with minors.

Sexual orientation in some ways is like handedness. Most people are one way, some the other. A smaller group experiences some form of ambidexterity. Regardless, the way we are endures, especially in men (Dickson et al., 2013; Norris et al., 2015). Women's sexual orientation tends to be less strongly felt and more fluid (Baumeister, 2000).

WHY DO WE DIFFER?

So, if we do not choose our sexual orientation and (especially for males) cannot change it, where do these feelings come from? In an early search for possible environmental influences on sexual orientation, Kinsey Institute investigators in the 1980s interviewed nearly 1000 lesbian/gay and 500 heterosexual people. They assessed almost every imaginable psychological cause of same-sex attraction—parental relationships, childhood sexual experiences, peer relationships, and dating experiences (Bell et al., 1981; Hammersmith, 1982). Their findings: Gay/lesbian people were no more likely than heterosexual people to have been smothered by maternal love or neglected by their father. And consider this: If "distant fathers" were more likely to produce gay sons, then shouldn't boys growing up in father-absent homes more often be gay? (They are not.) And shouldn't the rising number of such homes have led to a noticeable increase in the gay population? (It has not.) Most children raised by gay or lesbian parents display gender-typical behavior and are heterosexual (Farr et al., 2018; Gartrell & Bos, 2010). And they grow up with health and emotional well-being similar to (and sometimes better than) children with straight parents (Bos et al., 2016; Farr, 2017; Miller et al., 2017).

Environment likely contributes to sexual orientation—nature and nurture work together—but the inability to pin down specific environmental influences has led researchers to explore several lines of biological evidence:

- Same-sex attraction in other species,
- Brain differences,
- Genetic influences, and
- Prenatal influences.

Same-Sex Attraction in Other Species

In Boston's Public Gardens, caretakers solved the mystery of why a much-loved swan couple's eggs never hatched. Both swans were female. In New York City's Central Park Zoo, penguins Silo and Roy spent several years as devoted same-sex partners. Same-sex sexual behaviors have also been observed in several hundred other species, including grizzlies, gorillas, monkeys, flamingos, and owls (Bagemihl, 1999). Among rams, for example, some 7 to 10 percent display same-sex attraction by shunning ewes and seeking to mount other males (Perkins & Fitzgerald, 1997). Same-sex sexual behavior seems a natural part of the animal world.

LaunchPad See the *Video: Naturalistic Observation* for a helpful tutorial animation.

Boston Globe/Getty Images

Juliet and Juliet Boston's beloved swan couple, "Romeo and Juliet," were discovered actually to be, as are many other animal partners, a same-sex pair.

Brain Differences

Might the structure and function of gay and straight brains differ? Researcher Simon LeVay (1991) studied sections of the hypothalamus taken from deceased gay and straight people. (The hypothalamus is a brain structure linked to sexual behavior.) He found a cell cluster that was indeed reliably larger in straight men than in straight women and gay men.

It should not surprise us that brains differ with sexual orientation. Remember, *everything psychological is also biological.* But when did the brain difference begin? At conception? During childhood or adolescence? Did experience produce the difference? Or was it genes or prenatal hormones (or genes activating prenatal hormones)?

LeVay does not view this cell cluster as an "on-off button" for sexual orientation. Rather, he believes it is an important part of a brain pathway that is active during sexual behavior. He agrees that sexual behavior patterns could influence the brain's anatomy. Neural pathways in our brain do grow stronger with use. In fish, birds, rats, and humans, brain structures vary with experience—including sexual experience (Breedlove, 1997). But LeVay believes it is more likely that brain anatomy influences sexual orientation. His hunch seems confirmed by the discovery of a similar difference between male sheep that do and do not display same-sex attraction (Larkin et al., 2002; Roselli et al., 2002, 2004). Moreover, such differences seem to develop soon after birth, and perhaps even before birth (Rahman & Wilson, 2003).

> "Gay men simply don't have the brain cells to be attracted to women."
> —Simon LeVay, *The Sexual Brain*, 1993

Since LeVay's brain *structure* discovery, other researchers have reported additional differences in the way that gay and straight brains *function*. One is in an area of the hypothalamus that governs sexual arousal (Savic et al., 2005).

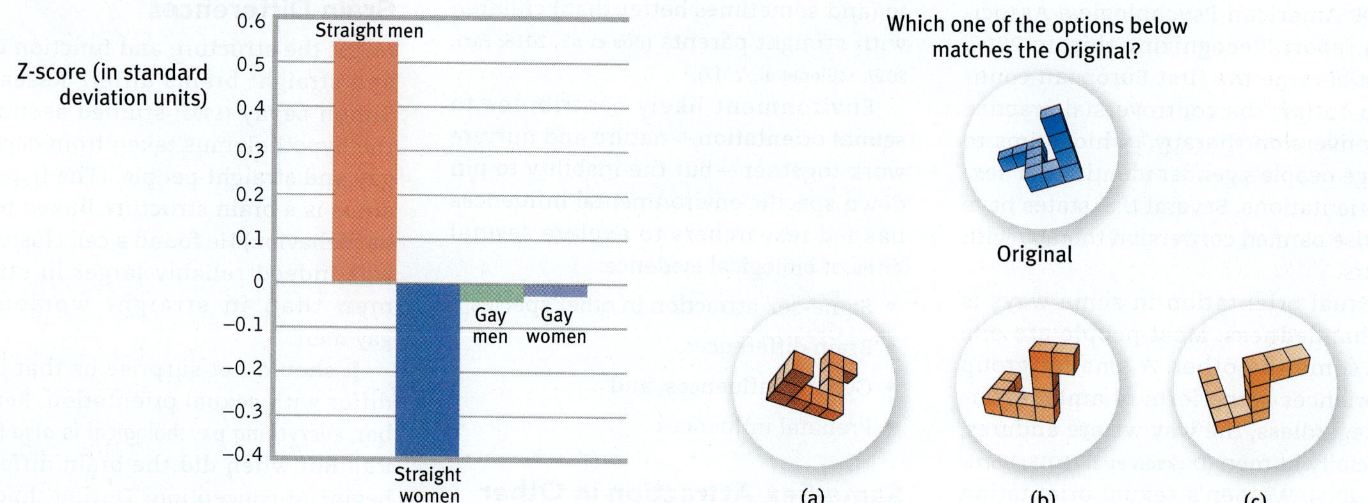

FIGURE 4.4 Spatial abilities and sexual orientation Which of the three figures can be rotated to match the Original figure?[1] Straight men tend to find this type of mental rotation task easier than do straight women, with gay men and women falling in between (see graph) (Rahman et al., 2004).

When straight women were given a whiff of a scent derived from men's sweat (which contains traces of male hormones), this area became active. Gay men's brains responded similarly to the men's scent. Straight men's brains did not. For them, only a female scent triggered the arousal response. In a similar study, lesbians' responses differed from those of straight women (Kranz & Ishai, 2006; Martins et al., 2005). Researcher Qazi Rahman (2015) sums it up: Compared with straight men and women, "gay men appear, on average, more 'female typical' in brain pattern responses and lesbian women are somewhat more 'male typical.'"

On several traits, the average gay man and gay woman fall midway between the average straight man and straight woman. Consider the gay-straight difference in spatial abilities. On mental rotation tasks such as the one in **FIGURE 4.4,** straight men tend to outscore straight women. And the scores of gay men and gay women fall in between (Boone & Hegarty, 2017).

Genetic Influences

Studies indicate that "about a third of variation in sexual orientation is attributable to genetic influences" (Bailey et al., 2016). Three lines of evidence suggest a genetic influence on sexual orientation.

- ***Same-sex orientation seems to run in families:*** Same-sex orientation appears more often in some families than in others (Mustanski & Bailey, 2003). Several studies have found that (1) gay men tend to have more gay relatives on their mother's than on their father's side, and (2) their heterosexual maternal relatives tend to produce more offspring than do the maternal relatives of heterosexual men (Camperio-Ciani et al., 2004, 2009; Camperio-Ciani & Pellizzari, 2012; VanderLaan et al., 2012; VanderLaan & Vasey, 2011).
- ***Gene and chromosome studies:*** In genetic studies of fruit flies, altering a single gene has changed the flies' sexual orientation and behavior (Dickson, 2005). In humans, it's likely that multiple genes, possibly interacting with other influences, shape human sexual orientation. In search of factors, researchers have studied the genes of 409 pairs of gay brothers and compared DNA from 1231 straight and 1077 gay men. They found links between sexual orientation and two genes on chromosomes 13 and 14, respectively. The first of those chromosome regions influences a brain area that varies in size with sexual orientation. The second is known to influence thyroid function, which has also been associated with sexual orientation (Sanders et al., 2015, 2017).
- ***Twin studies:*** Identical twins (who have identical genes) are somewhat more likely than fraternal twins (whose genes are not identical) to share a same-sex orientation (Alanko et al., 2010; Långström et al., 2010). However, sexual orientation differs in many identical twin pairs (especially female twins). This means that other factors besides genes must play a role. One such factor may be *epigenetic marks* that help distinguish gay and straight identical twins (Balter, 2015).

LaunchPad See the *Video: Twin Studies* for a helpful tutorial animation.

Prenatal Influences

Twins share not only genes, but also a prenatal environment. Recall that in the womb, sex hormones direct our male and female development. A critical period for human brain development occurs

[1]Answer: Figure (c).

in the second trimester (Ellis & Ames, 1987; Garcia-Falgueras & Swaab, 2010; Meyer-Bahlburg, 1995). Exposure to the hormone levels typically experienced by female fetuses during this period may predispose a person (female or male) later to become attracted to males. And female fetuses most exposed to testosterone are most likely later to exhibit gender-atypical traits and same-sex desires. The same is true for sheep (Money, 1987). "Prenatal sex hormones control the sexual differentiation of brain centers involved in sexual behaviors," noted Simon LeVay (2011, p. 216).

"Modern scientific research indicates that sexual orientation is . . . partly determined by genetics, but more specifically by hormonal activity in the womb." —Glenn Wilson and Qazi Rahman, *Born Gay: The Psychobiology of Sex Orientation*, 2005

A second important prenatal influence for males is the curious *older-brother effect*. Men with older brothers are somewhat more likely to be gay—about one-third more likely for each additional older brother (Blanchard, 2004, 2018; Bogaert, 2003). The odds of same-sex attraction are roughly 2 percent among first sons, and they rise to about 2.6 percent among second sons, 3.5 percent for third sons, and so on for each additional older brother (Bailey et al., 2016; see **FIGURE 4.5**). The older-brother effect seems to be biological. It does not occur among adopted brothers (Bogaert, 2006a). One possible explanation is that male fetuses may produce a substance that triggers a defensive response in the mother's immune system. After each pregnancy with a male fetus, antibodies in her system may grow stronger and may prevent the fetal brain from developing in a typical male pattern (Bogaert et al., 2018). Curiously, the older-brother effect is found only among right-handed men.

The point to remember: Taken together, the brain, genetic, and prenatal findings offer strong support for a biological explanation of sexual orientation, especially for men (LeVay, 2011; Rahman & Koerting, 2008). Our increasing understanding of the greater sexual fluidity of women suggests the need for more research on biopsychosocial influences (Diamond et al., 2017).

* * *

Those who believe sexual orientation is a lifestyle choice often oppose equal rights for people who are lesbian or gay. For example, in 2014 the president of Uganda signed a bill that made some same-sex sexual acts punishable by life in prison. To justify this, he declared that same-sex attraction is not inborn but rather is a matter of "choice" (Balter, 2014; Landau et al., 2014). Those who understand the inborn nature of sexual orientation—that it is shaped by the biological and prenatal influences outlined in this chapter—more likely favor "equal rights for homosexual and bisexual people" (Bailey et al., 2016).

"There is no sound scientific evidence that sexual orientation can be changed." —UK Royal College of Psychiatrists, 2009

Some of what you're reading about in this chapter may stretch your understandings or be surprising to you. Terms such as "non-binary gender identity" and "pansexual" were not common until recent years. Does this mean that people have changed, and these new terms and ideas are being created to reflect those changes? Actually, scientists believe that people have always experienced life on a continuum, with "normal" gender identity and sexual orientation ranging widely. People tend to fall somewhere on this broad spectrum and don't always fit neatly into a category as was once assumed. It is our understandings, not human nature, that have changed. And those understandings—and the associated terminology—are evolving faster than the science of sex and gender.

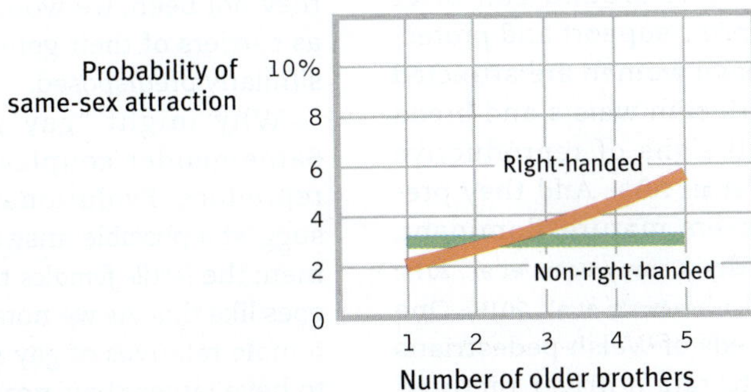

FIGURE 4.5 The older-brother effect These approximate curves depict a man's likelihood of same-sex attraction as a function of the number of biological (not adopted) older brothers he has (Blanchard, 2008a; Bogaert, 2006a). This correlation has been found in several studies, but only among right-handed men (as about 9 in 10 men are).

IMPROVE YOUR EVERYDAY LIFE

How has learning more about what contributes to sexual orientation and gender identity influenced your views? How might your new knowledge influence your interactions with people who identify as lesbian, gay, bisexual, transgender, or questioning/queer (LGBTQ)?

RETRIEVE & REMEMBER

ANSWERS IN APPENDIX E

8. Which THREE of the following five factors have researchers found to have an effect on sexual orientation?

    a. A domineering mother
    b. The size of a certain cell cluster in the hypothalamus
    c. Prenatal hormone exposure
    d. A distant or ineffectual father
    e. For right-handed men, having multiple older biological brothers

An Evolutionary Explanation of Human Sexuality

LOQ 4-14 How might an evolutionary psychologist explain male-female differences in sexuality and mating preferences?

Having faced many similar challenges throughout history, all genders have adapted in similar ways. We eat the same foods, avoid the same dangers, and perceive, learn, and remember in much the same way. When looking for a mate, we also prize many of the same traits—someone who is kind, honest, and intelligent. It is only in areas where we have faced differing adaptive challenges—most obviously in behaviors related to reproduction—that we differ, say **evolutionary psychologists.**

MALE-FEMALE DIFFERENCES IN SEXUALITY

And differ we do. Consider sex drives. Men and women are sexually motivated, some women more so than many men. Yet on average, who thinks more about sex? Hooks up more often? Masturbates more often? Views more pornography? The answers worldwide—*men, men, men,* and *men* (Baumeister et al., 2001; Hall et al., 2017; Lippa, 2009; Petersen & Hyde, 2010). Even among 65- to 80-year-old Americans, 12 percent of women and 50 percent of men reported being "very" or "extremely" interested in sex (Malani et al., 2018).

Many gender similarities and differences transcend sexual orientation. Compared with gay women, gay men (like straight men) report more responsiveness to visual sexual stimuli and more concern with their partner's physical attractiveness (Bailey et al., 1994; Doyle, 2005; Schmitt, 2007). Gay male couples also report having sex more often than do gay female couples (Peplau & Fingerhut, 2007). And (also like straight men) gay men report more interest in uncommitted sex (Schmitt, 2003).

> "It's not that gay men are oversexed; they are simply men whose male desires bounce off other male desires rather than off female desires." —Steven Pinker, *How the Mind Works*, 1997

NATURAL SELECTION AND MATING PREFERENCES

Natural selection is nature selecting traits and appetites that contribute to survival and reproduction. Thanks to random genetic mutations, our ancestors were born with varied traits, some of which helped them to survive and reproduce. Eventually, these characteristics became widespread. Evolutionary psychologists use this natural selection principle to explain how men and women differ more in the bedroom than in the boardroom. Our natural yearnings, they say, are our genes' way of reproducing themselves. "Humans are living fossils—collections of mechanisms produced by prior selection pressures" (Buss, 1995).

Why do women tend to be choosier than men when selecting sexual partners? Women have more at stake. To send her genes into the future, a woman must—at a minimum—conceive and protect a fetus growing inside her body for up to nine months, and may often nurse for an extended period following birth. And unlike men, women are limited in how many children they can have between puberty and menopause. No surprise, then, that heterosexual women prefer stick-around dads over likely cads. Partners who stick around can offer their joint offspring support and protection. Heterosexual women are attracted to tall men with slim waists and broad shoulders—all signs of reproductive success (Mautz et al., 2013). And they prefer men who seem mature, dominant, bold, and wealthy (Conroy-Beam et al., 2015; Fales et al., 2016; Lukaszewski et al., 2016). One study of hundreds of Welsh pedestrians asked people to rate a driver pictured at the wheel of a humble Ford Fiesta or a swanky Bentley. Men said a female driver was equally attractive in both cars. Women, however, found a male

driver more attractive if he was in the luxury car (Dunn & Searle, 2010).

The data are in, say evolutionists: Men pair widely; women pair wisely. And what traits do straight men find desirable?

For heterosexual men, some desired traits, such as a woman's smooth skin and youthful shape, cross place and time (Buss, 1994). Mating with such women might increase a man's chances of sending his genes into the future. And sure enough, men feel most attracted to women whose waist is roughly a third narrower than their hips—a sign of future fertility (Lewis et al., 2015; Perilloux et al., 2010). Even blind men show this preference for women with a low waist-to-hip ratio (Karremans et al., 2010).

There is a principle at work here, say evolutionary psychologists: Nature selects behaviors that increase genetic success. As mobile gene machines, we are designed to prefer whatever worked for our ancestors in their environments. They were predisposed to act in ways that would produce children, grandchildren, and beyond. Had they not been, we wouldn't be here. And as carriers of their genetic legacy, we are similarly predisposed.

Why might "gay genes" persist? Same-gender couples cannot usually reproduce. Evolutionary psychologists suggest a possible answer, at least for gay men: the *fertile females* theory. The theory goes like this. As we noted earlier, straight female relatives of gay men have tended to have larger-than-normal families. Perhaps, then, the genes that dispose women to be strongly attracted (or attractive) to men—and to have more children—also dispose some men to be attracted to men

Guillaume Horcajuelo/Epa/REX/Shutterstock

The mating game Evolutionary psychologists are not surprised that older men, and not just George Clooney (pictured with his wife, Amal Clooney, who is 16 years younger), often prefer younger women whose features suggest fertility.

(LeVay, 2011). Thus, there may actually be biological wisdom to genes that dispose some men to love other men.

LaunchPad To listen to experts discuss evolutionary psychology and sex differences, see the 4-minute *Video: Evolutionary Psychology and Sex Differences.*

CRITIQUING THE EVOLUTIONARY PERSPECTIVE

LOQ 4-15 What are the key criticisms of evolutionary explanations of human sexuality, and how do evolutionary psychologists respond?

Most psychologists agree that natural selection prepares us for survival and reproduction. But critics say there is a weakness in the reasoning evolutionary psychologists use to explain our mating preferences. Let's consider how an evolutionary psychologist might explain the findings in a startling study (Clark & Hatfield, 1989), and how a critic might object.

In this experiment, someone posing as a stranger approached people of the other sex and remarked, "I have been noticing you around campus. I find you to be very attractive." The "stranger" then asked a question, which was sometimes "Would you go to bed with me tonight?"

What percentage of men and women do you think agreed to this offer? An evolutionary explanation of genetic differences in sexuality would predict that women would be choosier than men in selecting their sexual partners. Indeed, not a single woman agreed—but 70 percent of the men did. A repeat of this study in France produced a similar result (Guéguen, 2011). The research seemed to support an evolutionary explanation.

Or did it? Critics note that evolutionary psychologists start with an effect—in this case, that men are more likely to accept casual sex offers—and work backward to explain what happened. What if research showed the opposite effect? If men refused an offer for casual sex, might we not reason that men who partner with one woman for life make better fathers, whose children more often survive?

Other critics ask why we should try to explain today's behavior based on decisions our ancestors made thousands of years ago. Don't cultural expectations also bend the genders? Behavior differences between men and women are smaller in cultures with greater gender equality (Eagly, 2009; Eagly & Wood, 1999). Such critics believe that *social learning theory* offers a better, more immediate explanation for these results. We all learn *social scripts* by watching and imitating others in our cultures. Women may learn that sexual encounters with strange men are dangerous, and that casual sex may not offer much sexual pleasure (Conley, 2011). This explanation of the study's effects proposes that women react to sexual encounters in ways that their modern culture teaches them. And men's reactions may reflect their learned social scripts: "Real men" take advantage of every opportunity to have sex.

A third criticism focuses on the social consequences of accepting an evolutionary explanation. Are heterosexual men truly hardwired to have sex with any woman who approaches them? If so, does this mean that men have no moral responsibility to remain faithful to their partners? Does this explanation excuse men's sexual aggression—"boys will be boys"—because of our evolutionary history?

Evolutionary psychologists agree that much of who we are is *not* hardwired. Our destiny is not written in our genes. "Evolution forcefully rejects a genetic determinism," insisted one research team (Confer et al., 2010). Evolutionary psychologists also remind us that men and women, having faced similar adaptive problems, are far more alike than different. Natural selection has prepared us to be flexible. We humans have a great capacity for learning and social progress. We adjust and respond to varied environments. We adapt and survive, whether we live in the Arctic or the desert.

Evolutionary psychologists also agree with their critics that some traits and behaviors, such as suicide, are hard to explain in terms of natural selection (Barash, 2012; Confer et al., 2010). But they ask us to remember evolutionary psychology's scientific goal: to explain behaviors and mental traits by offering testable predictions using principles of natural selection (Lewis et al., 2017). We may, for example, predict that people are more likely to perform favors for those who share their genes or can later return those favors. Is this true? (The answer is *Yes*.) And evolutionary psychologists remind us that the study of how we *came to be* need not dictate how we *ought to be*. Understanding our tendencies can help us overcome them.

IN YOUR EVERYDAY LIFE

Based on what you've learned so far, how do you think your genes, brain, hormones, and environment have worked together to influence *your* sexual development and sexual behavior?

RETRIEVE & REMEMBER

ANSWERS IN APPENDIX E

9. How do evolutionary psychologists explain male-female differences in sexuality?

10. What are the three main criticisms of the evolutionary explanation of human sexuality?

evolutionary psychology the study of how our behavior and mind have changed in adaptive ways over time due to natural selection.

natural selection the principle that inherited traits that better enable an organism to survive and reproduce in a particular environment will (in competition with other trait variations) most likely be passed on to subsequent generations.

LaunchPad To observe an experiment showing men's and women's attitudes toward casual sex, see the *Video: Openness to Casual Sex—A Study of Men Versus Women.* And for an interactive demonstration of evolutionary psychology and mating preferences, visit *Topic Tutorial: PsychSim6, Dating and Mating.*

Sex and Human Relationships

LOQ 4-16 What role do social factors play in our sexuality?

Scientific research on human sexuality does not aim to define the personal meaning of sex in our own lives. We could know every available fact about sex—that the initial spasms of male and female orgasm come at 0.8-second intervals, that systolic blood pressure rises some 60 points and respiration rate reaches 40 breaths per minute, that female nipples expand 10 millimeters at the peak of sexual arousal—but fail to understand the human significance of sexual intimacy.

Sexual desire motivates people to form intimate, committed relationships, which in turn enable satisfying sex (Birnbaum, 2018). In one national study that followed participants to age 30, later first sex predicted greater satisfaction in one's marriage or partnership (Harden, 2012). Another study of 2035 married people found that couples who reported being in a deeply committed relationship before having sex also reported greater relationship satisfaction and stability—and better sex than those who had sex very early in their relationship (Busby et al., 2010; Galinsky & Sonenstein, 2013). For both men and women, but especially for women, sex is more satisfying (with more orgasms and less regret) for those in a committed relationship, rather than a brief sexual hook-up (Armstrong et al., 2012; Bendixen et al., 2017; Dubé et al., 2017). Partners who share regular meals are more likely than one-time dinner companions to understand what seasoning touches suit each other's food tastes. So, too, with the touches of loyal partners who share a bed.

Sex is a socially significant act. Men and women can achieve orgasm alone. Yet most people find greater satisfaction after intercourse and orgasm with their loved one (Brody & Tillmann, 2006). Among newlyweds in one study, the "sexual afterglow" (lingering satisfaction after sex) lasted 48 hours and increased marital satisfaction (Meltzer et al., 2017). Sex at its human best is life uniting and love renewing.

Reflections on the Nature and Nurture of Sex, Gender, and Sexuality

LOQ 4-17 How do nature, nurture, and our own choices influence gender roles?

Our ancestral history helped form us as a species. Where there is variation, natural selection, and heredity, there will be evolution. Our genes form us. This is a great truth about human nature.

But our culture and experiences also shape us. If their genes and hormones predispose males to be more physically aggressive than females, culture can amplify this gender difference with norms that reward macho men and gentle women. If men are encouraged toward roles that demand physical power, and women toward more nurturing roles, each may act accordingly. By exhibiting the actions expected of those who fulfill such roles, men and women shape their own traits. Presidents in time typically become more presidential, servants more servile. Gender roles similarly shape us.

In many modern cultures, gender roles are merging. Brute strength has become less important for power and status (think "philanthrocapitalists" Priscilla Chan and Mark Zuckerberg). From 1965 to 2016, women soared from 9 percent to 47 percent of U.S. medical students (AAMC, 2014, 2016). In 1965, U.S. married women devoted eight times as many hours to housework as did their husbands. By 2012, this gap had shrunk to less than twice as many (Parker & Wang, 2013; Sayer, 2016). Such swift changes signal that biology does not fix gender roles.

If nature and nurture jointly form us, are we "nothing but" the product of nature and nurture? Are we rigidly determined?

We *are* the product of nature and nurture, but we're also an open system. Genes are all-pervasive but not all-powerful. People may reject their evolutionary role as transmitters of genes and choose not to reproduce. Culture, too, is all-pervasive but not all-powerful. People may defy peer pressures and resist social expectations.

Moreover, we cannot excuse our failings by blaming them solely on bad genes or bad influences. In reality, we are both creatures and creators of our worlds. So many things about us—including our gender roles—are the products of our genes and environments. Yet the stream that runs into the future flows through our present choices. Our decisions today design our environments tomorrow. We are the architects. Our hopes, goals, and expectations influence our destiny. And that is what enables cultures to vary and to change. Mind matters.

* * *

We know from our correspondence that some readers are troubled by the naturalism and evolutionism of contemporary science. They worry that a science of behavior (and evolutionary science in particular) will destroy our sense of the beauty, mystery, and spiritual significance of the human creature. For those concerned, we offer some reassuring thoughts.

When Isaac Newton explained the rainbow in terms of light of differing wavelengths, British poet John Keats feared that Newton had destroyed the rainbow's mysterious beauty. Yet, nothing about the science of optics need diminish our appreciation for the drama of a rainbow arching across a rain-darkened sky.

When Galileo assembled evidence that the Earth revolved around the Sun, not vice versa, he did not offer absolute proof for his theory. Rather, he offered an explanation that pulled together a variety of observations, such as the changing shadows cast by the Moon's mountains. His explanation eventually won the day because it described and explained things in a way that made sense, that hung together. Darwin's theory of evolution likewise offers an organizing principle that makes sense of many observations.

Many people of faith find the scientific idea of human origins fits with their own spirituality. In 2015, Pope Francis welcomed a science-religion dialogue, saying, "Evolution in nature is not inconsistent with the notion of creation, because evolution requires the creation of beings that evolve."

Meanwhile, many people of science are awestruck at the emerging understanding of the universe and the human creature. It boggles the mind—the entire universe popping out of a point some 14 billion years ago, and instantly inflating to cosmological size. Had the energy of this Big Bang been the tiniest bit less, the universe would have collapsed back on itself. Had it been the tiniest bit more, the result would have been a soup too thin to support life. Had gravity been a teeny bit stronger or weaker, or had the weight of a carbon proton been a wee bit different, our universe just wouldn't have worked.

What caused this almost-too-good-to-be-true, finely tuned universe? Why is there something rather than nothing? How did it come to be, in the words of Harvard-Smithsonian astrophysicist Owen Gingerich (1999), "so extraordinarily right, that it seemed the universe had been expressly designed to produce intelligent, sentient beings"? On such matters, a humble, awed, scientific silence is appropriate, suggested philosopher Ludwig Wittgenstein: "Whereof one cannot speak, thereof one must be silent" (1922, p. 189).

Rather than fearing science, we can welcome its enlarging our understanding and awakening our sense of awe. In a short 4 billion years, life on Earth has come from nothing to structures as complex as a 6-billion-unit strand of DNA and the incomprehensible intricacy of the human brain. Atoms no different from those in a rock somehow formed extraordinary, self-replicating, information-processing systems—us (Davies, 2007). Although we appear to have been created from dust, over eons of time, the end result is a priceless creature, one rich with potential beyond our imagining.

CHAPTER 4 REVIEW Sex, Gender, and Sexuality

LEARNING OBJECTIVES

TEST YOURSELF Answer these repeated Learning Objective Questions on your own (before checking the answers in Appendix D) to improve your retention of the concepts (McDaniel et al., 2009, 2015).

Gender Development

4-1: How does the meaning of *gender* differ from the meaning of *sex?*

4-2: What are some of the ways males and females tend to be alike and to differ?

4-3: What factors contribute to gender bias in the workplace?

4-4: How do sex hormones influence prenatal and adolescent sexual development?

4-5: What are some of the cultural influences on gender roles?

4-6: What are the effects of sexual aggression? How have cultural views changed, and how can we reduce sexual aggression?

4-7: How do we form our gender identity?

Human Sexuality

4-8: How do hormones influence human sexual motivation?

4-9: What is the human *sexual response cycle,* and how do sexual dysfunctions and paraphilias differ?

4-10: How can sexually transmitted infections be prevented?

4-11: How do external and imagined stimuli contribute to sexual arousal?

4-12: What factors influence teenagers' sexual behaviors and use of contraceptives?

Sexual Orientation

4-13: What do we know about sexual orientation?

An Evolutionary Explanation of Human Sexuality

4-14: How might an evolutionary psychologist explain male-female differences in sexuality and mating preferences?

4-15: What are the key criticisms of evolutionary explanations of human sexuality, and how do evolutionary psychologists respond?

Sex and Human Relationships

4-16: What role do social factors play in our sexuality?

Reflections on the Nature and Nurture of Sex, Gender, and Sexuality

4-17: How do nature, nurture, and our own choices influence gender roles?

TERMS AND CONCEPTS TO REMEMBER

TEST YOURSELF Write down the definition in your own words, then check your answer.

sex, *p.* 109
gender, *p.* 109
intersex, *p.* 109
aggression, *p.* 109
relational aggression, *p.* 109
X chromosome, *p.* 111
Y chromosome, *p.* 111
testosterone, *p.* 111
puberty, *p.* 111
primary sex characteristics, *p.* 111
secondary sex characteristics, *p.* 113
spermarche [sper-MAR-key], *p.* 113
menarche [meh-NAR-key], *p.* 113
role, *p.* 113
gender role, *p.* 113
sexual aggression, *p.* 114
gender identity, *p.* 114
social learning theory, *p.* 114
gender typing, *p.* 114
androgyny, *p.* 114
transgender, *p.* 117
asexual, *p.* 117
estrogens, *p.* 117
sexual response cycle, *p.* 119
refractory period, *p.* 119
sexual dysfunction, *p.* 119
erectile disorder, *p.* 119
female orgasmic disorder, *p.* 119
paraphilias, *p.* 119
AIDS (acquired immune deficiency syndrome), *p.* 119
social script, *p.* 121
sexual orientation, *p.* 121
evolutionary psychology, *p.* 127
natural selection, *p.* 127

CHAPTER TEST

TEST YOURSELF Answer the following questions on your own first, then check your answers in Appendix E.

1. In psychology, ________ is the biologically influenced characteristics by which people define male, female, and intersex. The behavioral characteristics that people associate with *boy, girl, man,* and *woman* is ________.

2. Females and males are very similar, but one way they differ is that

- **a.** females are more physically aggressive than males.
- **b.** males are more democratic than females in their leadership roles.
- **c.** as children, females tend to play in small groups, while males tend to play in large groups.
- **d.** females are more likely to die by suicide.

3. A fertilized egg will develop into a male if it receives a/n ________ chromosome from its father.

4. Primary sex characteristics relate to ________; secondary sex characteristics refer to ________.

- **a.** spermarche; menarche
- **b.** breasts and facial hair; ovaries and testes
- **c.** emotional maturity; hormone surges
- **d.** reproductive organs; nonreproductive traits

5. On average, girls begin puberty at about the age of ________, boys at about the age of ________.

6. A person born with a combination of male and female biological sexual characteristics is ________.

7. *Gender role* refers to our

- **a.** sense of being male, female, neither, or some combination of male and female.
- **b.** culture's expectations about the "right" way for males and females to behave.
- **c.** assigned birth sex—our chromosomes and anatomy.
- **d.** unisex characteristics.

8. Our sense of being male, female, neither, or some combination of male and female is known as our ________ ________.

9. A striking effect of hormonal changes on human sexual behavior is the

- **a.** end of sexual desire in men over 60.
- **b.** sharp rise in sexual interest at puberty.
- **c.** decrease in women's sexual desire at the time of ovulation.
- **d.** increase in testosterone levels in castrated males.

10. In describing the sexual response cycle, Masters and Johnson noted that

- **a.** a plateau phase follows orgasm.
- **b.** people experience a refractory period during which they cannot experience orgasm.
- **c.** the feeling that accompanies orgasm is stronger in men than in women.
- **d.** testosterone is released equally in women and men.

11. Using condoms during sex ________ (does/doesn't) reduce the risk of getting HIV and ________ (does/doesn't) fully protect against skin-to-skin STIs.

12. An example of an external stimulus that might influence sexual behavior is

- **a.** the level of testosterone in the bloodstream.
- **b.** the onset of puberty.
- **c.** a sexually explicit film.
- **d.** an erotic fantasy or dream.

13. Which factors have researchers so far found to be *unrelated* to the development of our sexual orientation?

14. How do evolutionary psychologists use the principle of *natural selection* to explain differences in mating preferences in men and women?

Continue testing yourself with **LearningCurve** or **Achieve Read & Practice** to learn and remember most effectively.

Huy Lam/Getty Images

Sensation and Perception

CHAPTER 5

SURVEY THE CHAPTER

"I have perfect vision," explains the writer and teacher Heather Sellers. Her vision may be perfect, but her perception is not. In her book *You Don't Look Like Anyone I Know,* she tells of awkward moments resulting from her lifelong *prosopagnosia*—face blindness (Sellers, 2010):

> In college, on a date at the Spaghetti Station, I returned from the bathroom and plunked myself down in the wrong booth, facing the wrong man. I remained unaware he was not my date even as my date (a stranger to me) accosted Wrong Booth Guy, and then stormed out. . . . I do not recognize myself in photos or videos. I can't recognize my stepsons in the soccer pick-up line; I failed to determine which husband was mine at a party, in the mall, at the market.

People sometimes see Sellers as snobby or cold. "Why did you walk past me?" a neighbor might later ask. Hoping to avoid offending others, Sellers sometimes fakes recognition. She smiles at people she passes, in case she knows them. Or she may pretend to know the person with whom she is talking. But there is an upside to these perception failures. When she runs into someone who previously irritated her, she typically feels no ill will. She doesn't recognize the person.

Unlike Sellers, most of us have a functioning area on the underside of our brain's right hemisphere that helps us recognize a familiar human face as soon as we detect it—in only one-seventh of a second (Jacques & Rossion, 2006). This ability is an example of a broader principle.

Nature's sensory gifts enable each animal to obtain essential information. Other examples:

- Human ears are most sensitive to sound frequencies that include human voices, especially a baby's cry.
- Frogs, which feed on flying insects, have cells in their eyes that fire only in response to small, dark, moving objects. A frog could starve to death knee-deep in motionless flies. But let one zoom by and the frog's "bug detector" cells snap awake. (As Kermit the Frog said, "Time's fun when you're having flies.")
- Male silkworm moths' odor receptors can detect one-billionth of an ounce of chemical sex attractant per second—released by a female one mile away (Sagan, 1977). That is why there continue to be silkworms.

In this chapter, we'll look more closely at what psychologists have learned about how we sense and perceive the world around us. We begin with some basic principles that apply to all our senses.

Basic Concepts of Sensation and Perception

Learning Objective Question LOQ 5-1 What are *sensation* and *perception?* What do we mean by *bottom-up processing* and *top-down processing?*

Sellers' curious mix of "perfect vision" and face blindness illustrates the distinction between *sensation* and *perception*. When she looks at a friend, her **sensation** is normal. Her **sensory receptors** detect the same information yours would, and they transmit that information to her brain. And her **perception**—the processes by which her brain organizes and interprets the sensory input—is *almost* normal. Thus, she may recognize people from their hair, walk, voice, or peculiar build, just not from their face. Her experience is much like the struggle any human would have trying to recognize a specific penguin.

Under normal circumstances, your sensory and perceptual processes work together to help you decipher the world around you.

- **Bottom-up processing** starts at your sensory receptors and works up to higher levels of processing.
- **Top-down processing** constructs perceptions from this sensory input by drawing on your experience and expectations.

As your brain absorbs the information in **FIGURE 5.1**, bottom-up processing enables your sensory systems to detect the lines, angles, and colors that form the flower and leaves. Using top-down processing, you interpret what your senses detect.

But how do you do it? How do you create meaning from the blizzard of sensory stimuli bombarding your body 24 hours a day? In its silent, cushioned, inner world, your brain floats in utter darkness. By itself, it sees nothing. It hears nothing. It feels nothing. *So, how does the world out there get in?*

© Sandro Del-Prete/www.sandrodelprete.com

FIGURE 5.1 What's going on here? Our sensory and perceptual processes work together to help us sort out complex images, including the hidden couple in Sandro Del-Prete's drawing, *The Flowering of Love*.

To phrase the question scientifically: How do we construct our representations of the external world? How do a campfire's flicker, crackle, and smoky scent activate pathways in our brain? And how, from this living neurochemistry, do we create our conscious experience of the fire's motion and temperature, its aroma and beauty? In search of answers, let's look at some processes that cut across all our sensory systems.

FROM OUTER ENERGY TO INNER BRAIN ACTIVITY

LOQ 5-2 What three steps are basic to all of our sensory systems?

Your sensory systems perform an amazing feat: They convert one form of energy into another. Vision processes light energy. Hearing processes sound waves. All your senses

- ***receive*** sensory stimulation, often using specialized receptor cells.
- ***transform*** that stimulation into neural impulses.
- ***deliver*** the neural information to your brain.

The process of converting one form of energy into another form that your brain can use is **transduction.** Transduction is rather like translation. It translates physical energy, such as light waves, into the brain's electrochemical language. Later in this chapter, we'll focus on individual sensory systems. How do we see? Hear? Feel pain? Taste? Smell? Keep our balance? In each case, we'll consider these three steps—receiving, transforming, and delivering the information to the brain. First, though, let's explore some strengths and weaknesses in our ability to detect and interpret stimuli in the sea of energy around us.

RETRIEVE & REMEMBER

ANSWERS IN APPENDIX E

1. What is the rough distinction between sensation and perception?

THRESHOLDS

LOQ 5-3 How do *absolute thresholds* and *difference thresholds* differ?

At this moment, we are being struck by X-rays and radio waves, ultraviolet and infrared light, and sound waves of very high and very low frequencies. To all of these we are blind and deaf. Other animals with differing needs detect a world beyond our human experience. Migrating birds stay on course aided by an internal magnetic compass. Bats and dolphins locate prey using sonar, bouncing sounds off objects. Bees navigate on cloudy days by detecting aspects of sunlight we cannot see.

Our senses open the shades just a crack, giving us only a tiny glimpse of the energy around us. But for our needs, this is enough.

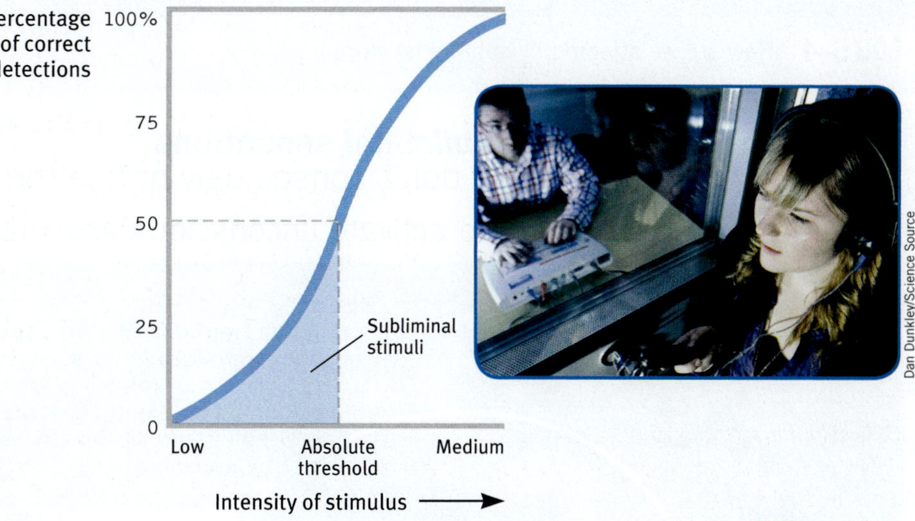

FIGURE 5.2 Absolute threshold Can I detect this sound? An *absolute threshold* is the intensity at which a person can detect a stimulus half the time. Hearing tests locate these thresholds for various frequencies.

Absolute Thresholds

To some kinds of stimuli we are amazingly sensitive. Standing atop a mountain on a dark, clear night, most of us could see a candle flame atop another mountain 30 miles away. We could feel the wing of a bee falling on our cheek. We could smell a single drop of perfume in a three-room apartment (Galanter, 1962).

Our awareness of these faint stimuli illustrates our **absolute thresholds.** To test your absolute threshold for sounds, a hearing specialist would send tones, at varying levels, into each of your ears and record whether you could hear each tone. The test results would show the point where, for any sound frequency, half the time you could detect the sound and half the time you could not. That 50-50 point would define your absolute threshold.

Stimuli you cannot detect 50 percent of the time are **subliminal**—below your absolute threshold (**FIGURE 5.2**). Can we be *controlled* by subliminal messages? (See Thinking Critically About: Subliminal Sensation and Subliminal Persuasion.)

LaunchPad For a helpful tutorial animation about experimental research methods, see the *Video: Experiments.*

Difference Thresholds

To function effectively, we need absolute thresholds low enough to allow us to detect important sights, sounds, textures, tastes, and smells. Many of life's important decisions also depend on our ability to detect small differences among stimuli. A musician must detect tiny differences when tuning an instrument. Parents must detect the sound of their own child's voice amid other children's voices. Even after two years in Scotland, all lamb *baa*s sounded alike to my [DM's] ears. But not to lamb mothers. After shearing, I observed, each ewe would streak directly to the *baa* of *her* lamb amid the chorus of other distressed lambs.

sensation the process by which our sensory receptors and nervous system receive and represent stimulus energies from our environment.

sensory receptors sensory nerve endings that respond to stimuli.

perception the process by which our brain organizes and interprets sensory information, transforming it into meaningful objects and events.

bottom-up processing analysis that begins with the sensory receptors and works up to the brain's integration of sensory information.

top-down processing information processing guided by higher-level mental processes, as when we construct perceptions drawing on our experience and expectations.

transduction changing one form of energy into another. In sensation, the transforming of stimulus energies (such as sights, sounds, and smells) into neural impulses our brain can interpret.

absolute threshold the minimum stimulus energy needed to detect a particular stimulus 50 percent of the time.

subliminal below a person's absolute threshold for conscious awareness.

Thinking Critically About:
Subliminal Sensation and Subliminal Persuasion

LOQ 5-4 How are we affected by subliminal stimuli?

We can be affected by *subliminal* sensations —stimuli so weak that we don't consciously notice them.

Researchers use **priming** to activate unconscious associations.

Participant views slides of people and offers either favorable or unfavorable ratings of each person.

BUT an instant before each slide appears, the trickster researcher subliminally flashes another image—either pleasant (for example, kittens), or unpleasant (for example, a werewolf).

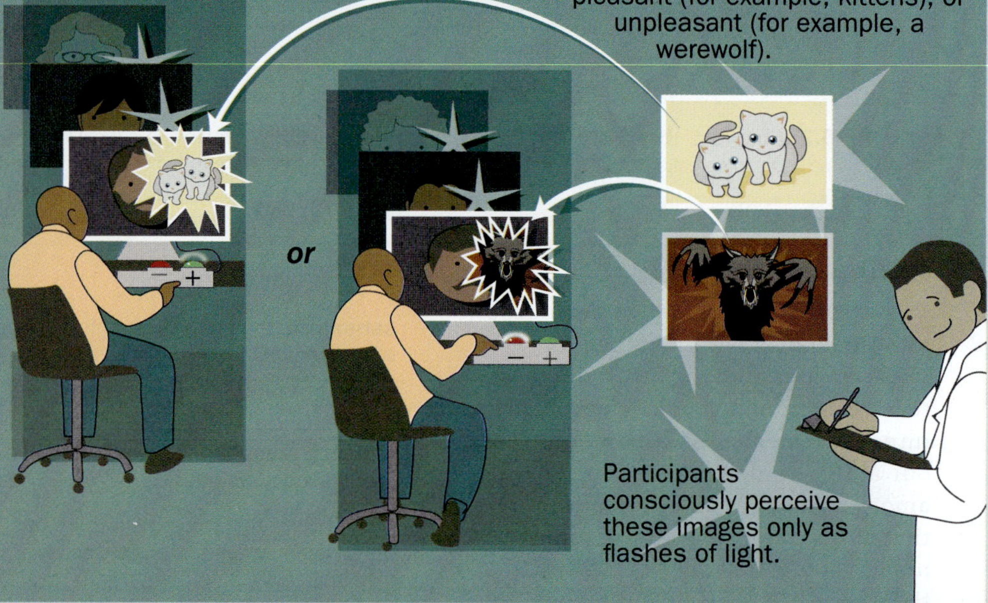

Participants consciously perceive these images only as flashes of light.

Will participants' ratings of the faces be affected?

Yes![1]

More **favorable** ratings of people

More **unfavorable** ratings of people

Our two-track mind: Priming happens even though the viewer's brain does not have time to consciously perceive the flashed images. We may evaluate a stimulus even when we are not consciously aware of it.[2]

So, we can be *primed*, but can we be *persuaded* by subliminal stimuli, for example to lose weight, stop smoking, or improve our memory?

Audio and video messages subliminally (without recipients' conscious awareness) announce:

"I am thin,"
"Cigarette smoke tastes bad,"
and
"I do well on tests. I have total recall of information."

Results from 16 experiments[3] showed no powerful, enduring influence on behavior. Not one of the recordings helped more than a placebo, which works only because we believe it will.

1. Krosnick et al., 1992. 2. Ferguson & Zayas, 2009. 3. Greenwald et al., 1991, 1992.

The LORD is my shepherd;
I shall not want.
He maketh me to lie down
in green pastures:
he leadeth me
beside the still waters.
He restoreth my soul:
he leadeth me
in the paths of righteousness
for his name's sake.
Yea, though I walk through the valley
of the shadow of death,
I will fear no evil:
for thou art with me;
thy rod and thy staff
they comfort me.
Thou preparest a table before me
in the presence of mine enemies:
thou anointest my head with oil,
my cup runneth over.
Surely goodness and mercy
shall follow me
all the days of my life:
and I will dwell
in the house of the LORD
for ever.

The difference threshold In this computer-generated copy of the Twenty-third Psalm, each line increases in size slightly. How many lines are required for you to experience a *just noticeable difference?*

The **difference threshold** (or the *just noticeable difference [jnd]*) is the minimum stimulus difference a person can detect half the time. That detectable difference increases with the size of the stimulus. If we listen to our music at 40 decibels, we might barely detect an added 5 decibels (the jnd). But if we increase the volume to 110 decibels, we probably won't detect an additional 5-decibel change.

In the late 1800s, German physician Ernst Weber noted something so simple and so useful that we still refer to it as **Weber's law.** It states that for an average person to perceive a difference, two stimuli must differ by a constant minimum *percentage* (not a constant *amount*). The exact percentage varies, depending on the stimulus. Two lights, for example, must differ in intensity by 8 percent. Two objects must differ in weight by 2 percent. And two tones must differ in frequency by only 0.3 percent (Teghtsoonian, 1971).

RETRIEVE & REMEMBER

ANSWERS IN APPENDIX E

2. Using sound as your example, show how these concepts differ: *absolute threshold, subliminal stimulation,* and *difference threshold.*

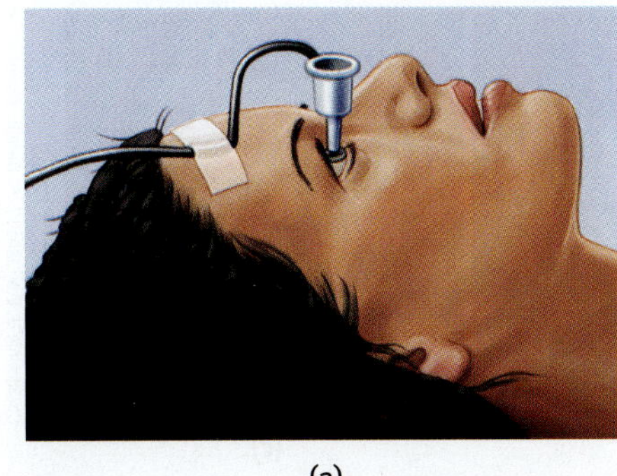

(a)

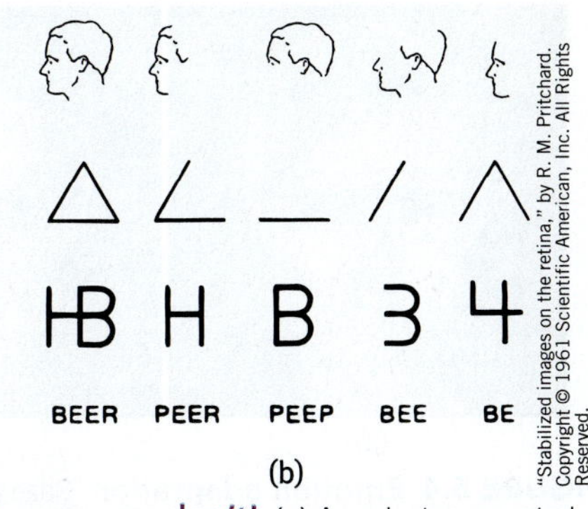

(b)

FIGURE 5.3 Sensory adaptation: Now you see it, now you don't! (a) A projector mounted on a contact lens makes the projected image move with the eye. (b) At first, the person sees the whole image. But thanks to sensory adaptation, her eye soon becomes accustomed to the unchanging stimulus. Rather than the full image, she begins to see fragments fading and reappearing.

SENSORY ADAPTATION

LOQ 5-5 What is the function of sensory adaptation?

Sitting down on the bus, you are overwhelmed by your seatmate's heavy perfume. You wonder how she can stand it, but within minutes you no longer notice. **Sensory adaptation** has come to your rescue. When constantly exposed to an unchanging stimulus we become less aware of it, because our nerve cells fire less frequently. (To experience sensory adaptation, roll up your sleeve. You will feel it—but only for a few moments.)

"We need above all to know about changes; no one wants or needs to be reminded 16 hours a day that his shoes are on." —Neuroscientist David Hubel (1979)

Why, then, if we stare at an object without flinching, does it *not* vanish from sight? Because, unnoticed by us, our eyes are always moving. This continual flitting from one spot to another ensures that stimulation on the eyes' receptors is always changing.

What if we actually could stop our eyes from moving? Would sights seem to vanish, as odors do? To find out, psychologists have designed clever instruments that maintain a constant image on the eye's inner surface. Imagine that we have fitted a volunteer, Mary, with such an instrument—a miniature projector mounted on a contact lens (**FIGURE 5.3a**). When Mary's eye moves, the image from the projector moves as well. So everywhere that Mary looks, the scene is sure to go.

If we project images through this instrument, what will Mary see? At first, she will see the complete image. But within a few seconds, as her sensory system begins to tire, things will get weird. Bit by bit, the image will vanish, only to reappear and then disappear—often in fragments (Figure 5.3b).

Although sensory adaptation reduces our sensitivity, it offers an important benefit. It frees us to focus on informative changes in our environment without

priming the activation, often unconsciously, of associations in our mind, thus setting us up to perceive, remember, or respond to objects or events in certain ways.

difference threshold the minimum difference between two stimuli required for detection 50 percent of the time. We experience the difference threshold as a *just noticeable difference* (or *jnd*).

Weber's law the principle that, to be perceived as different, two stimuli must differ by a constant minimum percentage (rather than a constant amount).

sensory adaptation reduced sensitivity in response to constant stimulation.

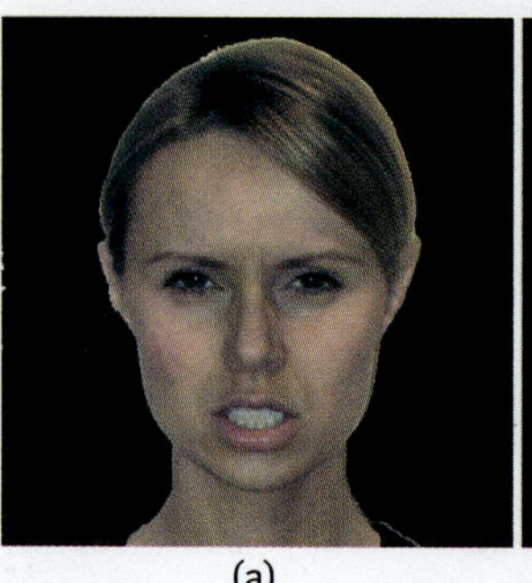
(a)
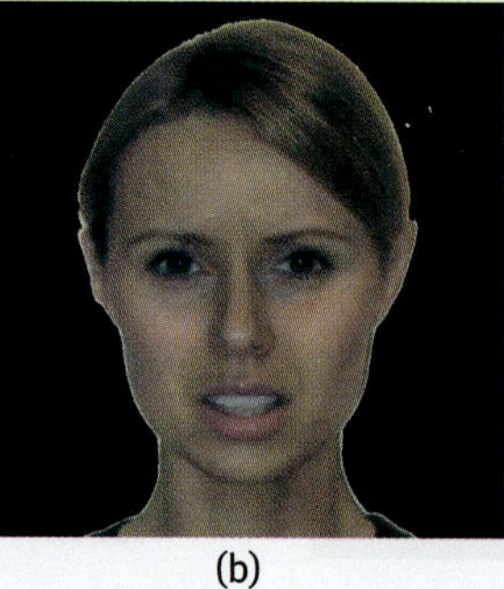
(b)
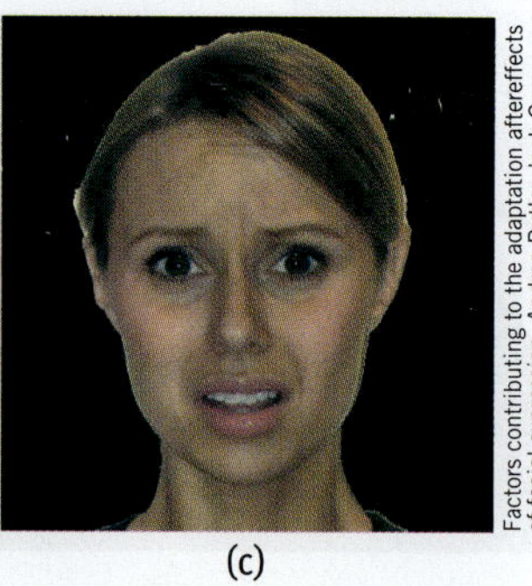
(c)

Factors contributing to the adaptation aftereffects of facial expression. Andrea Butler, Ipek Oruc, Christopher J. Fox, Jason J. S. Barton, *Brain Research*, 29 January 2008.

FIGURE 5.4 Emotion adaptation Gaze at the angry face in image (a) for 20 to 30 seconds, then look at the face in image (b)—looks scared, yes? Then gaze at the scared face in image (c) for 20 to 30 seconds, before returning to the image (b) face—now looks angry, yes? (From Butler et al., 2008.)

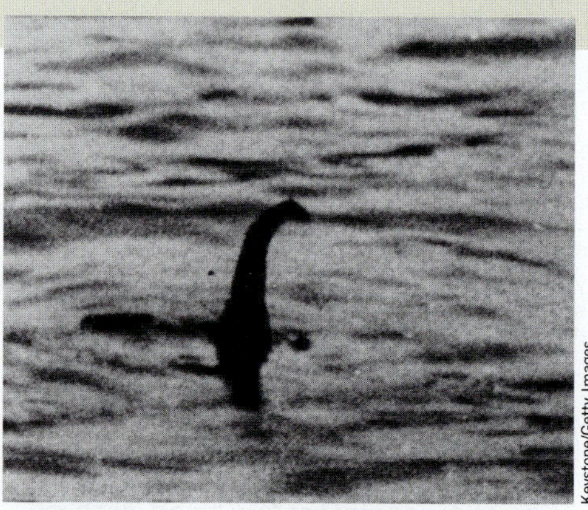

Keystone/Getty Images

FIGURE 5.5 Believing is seeing What do you perceive? Is this Nessie, the Loch Ness monster, or a log?

being distracted by background chatter. Technology companies understand the attention-grabbing power of changing stimulation. Our phone's new tweets, likes, snapchats, breaking news stories, and other background chatter are hard to ignore. As one of Instagram's founding engineers said, "There's always another hashtag to click on" (Alter, 2017).

Sensory adaptation even influences our perception of emotions. By creating a 50-50 morphed blend of an angry face and a scared face (**FIGURE 5.4b**), researchers showed that our visual system adapts to an unchanging facial expression (as in Figure 5.4a or 5.4c) by becoming less responsive to that expression (Butler et al., 2008). The effect is created by our brain, not by our retinas. How do we know this? Because the illusion also works when we view either image (a) or (c) with one eye, and image (b) with the other eye.

The point to remember: Our sensory system is alert to novelty; bore it with repetition and it frees our attention for more important things. *We perceive the world not exactly as it is, but as it is useful for us to perceive it.*

IN YOUR EVERYDAY LIFE

What types of sensory adaptation have you experienced in the last 24 hours?

RETRIEVE & REMEMBER

ANSWERS IN APPENDIX E

3. Why is it that after wearing shoes for a while, you cease to notice them (until questions like this draw your attention back to them)?

PERCEPTUAL SET

LOQ 5-6 How do our expectations, contexts, motivations, and emotions influence our perceptions?

To see is to believe. As we less fully appreciate, to believe is to see. Through experience, we come to expect certain results. Those expectations may give us a **perceptual set,** a set of mental tendencies and assumptions that affects, top-down, what we hear, taste, feel, and see. In 1972, a British newspaper published "the most amazing pictures ever taken"—of a lake "monster" in Scotland's Loch Ness. If this information creates in you the same expectations it did in most of the paper's readers, you, too, will see a monster in a similar photo in **FIGURE 5.5.** But when a skeptical researcher approached the photos with different expectations, he saw a curved tree limb—as had others the day the photo was shot (Campbell, 1986). What a difference a new perceptual set makes.

When shown the phrase

Mary had a
a little lamb

many people perceive what they expect and miss the repeated word. Did you?

Perceptual set also affects what we hear—"stuffy nose" or "stuff he knows"? Consider the kindly airline pilot who, on a takeoff run, looked over at his unhappy co-pilot and said, "Cheer up." Expecting to hear the usual "Gear up," the co-pilot promptly raised the wheels—before they left the ground (Reason & Mycielska, 1982). Or ask the little boy who loved the prelude to Major League Baseball games when people rose to sing to him: "José, can you see?"

Our expectations can influence our taste perceptions, too. In one experiment, preschool children, by a 6-to-1 margin, thought french fries tasted better when served in a McDonald's bag rather than a plain white bag (Robinson et al., 2007). Another experiment invited campus bar patrons at the Massachusetts Institute of Technology to sample free beer (Lee et al., 2006). When researchers added a few drops of vinegar to a brand-name beer and called it "MIT brew," the tasters preferred it—unless they had been told they were drinking vinegar-laced beer. In that case, they expected, and usually experienced, a worse taste. In both cases, people's past experiences (tastes they had enjoyed, and positive associations with respected institutions such as MIT) led them to form concepts, or *schemas,* that they then used to interpret new stimuli.

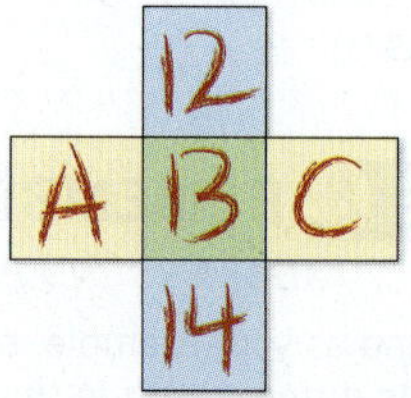

Do you perceive a number or a letter in the middle? If you read from left to right, you likely perceive a letter. But if you read from top to bottom, you may perceive the same center image as a number.

The New Yorker Collection, 2002, Leo Cullum from cartoonbank.com

FIGURE 5.6 Culture and context effects What is above the woman's head? In one classic study, most rural East Africans questioned said the woman was balancing a metal box or can on her head (a typical way to carry water at that time). They also perceived the family as sitting under a tree. Westerners, used to running water and boxlike houses with corners, were more likely to perceive the family as being indoors, with the woman sitting under a window (Gregory & Gombrich, 1973).

CONTEXT, MOTIVATION, AND EMOTION

Perceptual set influences how we interpret stimuli. But our immediate context, and the motivation and emotion we bring to a situation, also affect our interpretations.

Context Effects Social psychologist Lee Ross invited us to recall our own perceptions in different contexts: "Ever notice that when you're driving you hate . . . the way [pedestrians] saunter through the crosswalk, almost daring you to hit them, but when you're walking you hate drivers?" (Jaffe, 2004). People's expectations influence their perceptions constantly, whether about the hoodie-wearing teen *(Is it because of the rain or due to criminal intent?)* or the person coming close *(Is this a threat or a come-on?)*.

Some other examples of the power of context:

- When holding a gun, people become more likely to perceive another person as also gun-toting—a perception that has led to the shooting of some unarmed people who were actually holding their phone or wallet (Witt & Brockmole, 2012).
- Imagine hearing a noise interrupted by the words "eel is on the wagon." Likely you would actually perceive the first word as *wheel*. Given "eel is on the orange," you would more likely hear *peel*. In each case, the context creates an expectation that, top-down, influences our perception (Grossberg, 1995). Depending on our perceptual set, "rhapsody" may become "rap city," "sects" may become "sex," and "meteorologist" may be heard as the muscular "meaty urologist."
- Cultural context helps form our perceptions, so it's not surprising that people from different cultures view things differently, as in **FIGURE 5.6**.
- How is the woman in **FIGURE 5.7** feeling?

IMPROVE YOUR EVERYDAY LIFE

Can you think of a time when your expectations caused you to misperceive a person or a group's intentions? How might you use awareness of *context effects* to modify your expectations?

Motivation Motives give us energy as we work toward a goal. Like context, they can bias our interpretations of neutral stimuli:

- Desirable objects, such as a water bottle viewed by a thirsty person, seem closer than they really are (Balcetis & Dunning, 2010).
- A softball appears bigger when players are hitting well (Witt & Proffitt, 2005).

Emotion Other clever experiments have demonstrated that emotions can shove our perceptions in one direction or another:

- Hearing sad music can tilt the mind toward hearing a spoken word as *mourning* rather than *morning*, as *die* rather than *dye*, as *pain* rather than *pane* (Halberstadt et al., 1995).
- A hill seems less steep to people who feel others understand them (Oishi et al., 2013).
- When angry, people more often perceive neutral objects as guns (Baumann & DeSteno, 2010).

Craig Klomparens/Hope College

FIGURE 5.7 What emotion is this? (See Figure 5.8.)

perceptual set mental tendencies and assumptions that set us up to perceive one thing and not another.

FIGURE 5.8 Context makes clearer The Hope College volleyball team celebrates its national championship winning moment.

The point to remember: Much of what we perceive comes not just from what's "out there," but also from what's behind our eyes and between our ears. Through top-down processing, our experiences, assumptions, and expectations—and even our context, motivation, and emotions—can shape and color our views of reality.

* * *

The processes we've discussed so far are features shared by all our sensory systems. Let's turn now to the ways those systems are unique. We'll start with our most prized and complex sense, vision.

RETRIEVE & REMEMBER

ANSWERS IN APPENDIX E

4. Does *perceptual set* involve bottom-up or top-down processing? Why?

Vision: Sensory and Perceptual Processing

Your eyes receive light energy and *transduce* (transform) it into neural messages that your brain—in one of life's greatest wonders—then creates into what you consciously see. How does such a taken-for-granted yet remarkable thing happen?

LIGHT ENERGY AND EYE STRUCTURES

LOQ 5-7 What are the characteristics of the energy we see as visible light? What structures in the eye help focus that energy?

Light Energy: From the Environment Into the Brain

When you look at a bright red tulip, what strikes your eyes are not bits of the color red but pulses of energy that your visual system *perceives* as red. What we see as visible light is but a thin slice of the wide spectrum of electromagnetic energy shown in **FIGURE 5.9.** On one end of this spectrum are short gamma waves, no longer than the diameter of an atom. On the other end are mile-long waves of radio transmission. In between is the narrow band visible to us. Other portions

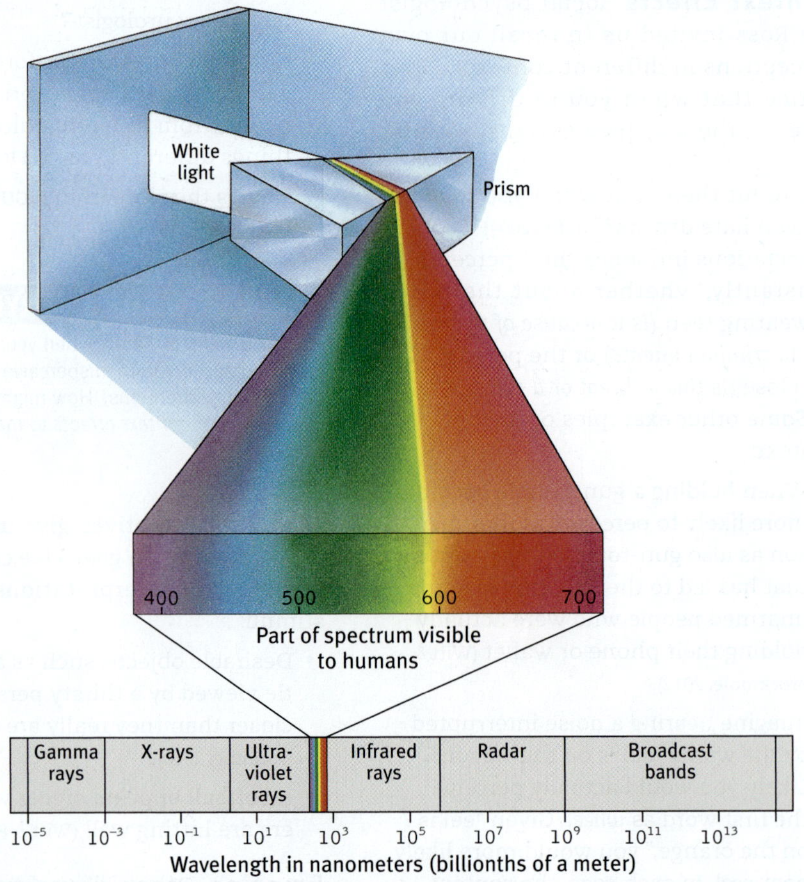

FIGURE 5.9 The wavelengths we see What we see as light is only a tiny slice of a wide spectrum of electromagnetic energy. The wavelengths visible to the human eye (shown enlarged) extend from the shorter waves of blue-violet light to the longer waves of red light.

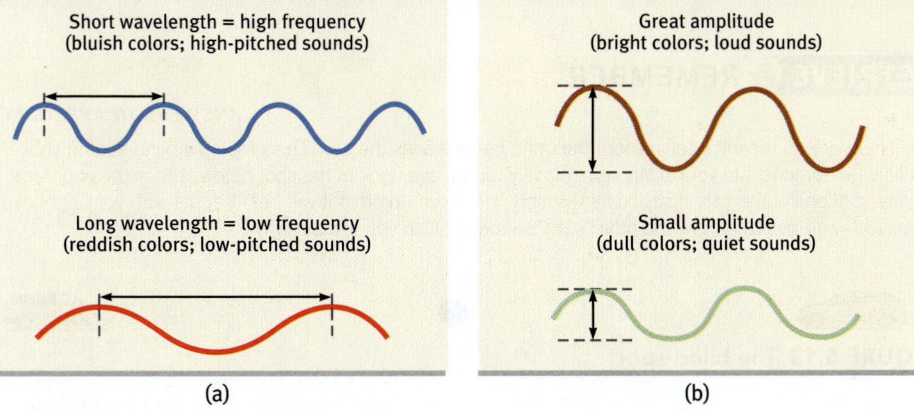

FIGURE 5.10 The physical properties of waves (a) Waves vary in *wavelength* (the distance between successive peaks). *Frequency,* the number of complete wavelengths that can pass a point in a given time, depends on the wavelength. The shorter the wavelength, the higher the frequency. Wavelength determines the perceived *color* of light (and also the *pitch* of sound). (b) Waves also vary in *amplitude,* the height from top to bottom. Wave amplitude influences the perceived *brightness* of colors (and also the *intensity* of sounds).

are visible to other animals. Bees, for instance, cannot see what we perceive as red (but can see ultraviolet light).

Light travels in waves, and the shape of those waves influences what we see. Light's **wavelength** is the distance from one wave peak to the next (**FIGURE 5.10a**). Wavelength determines **hue**—the color we experience, such as a tulip's red petals. A light wave's *amplitude,* or height, determines its **intensity**—the amount of energy the wave contains. Intensity influences *brightness* (Figure 5.10b).

To understand *how* we transform physical energy into color and meaning, we need to know more about vision's window—the eye.

The Eye

What color are your eyes? Asked this question, most people describe their *iris,* the doughnut-shaped ring of muscle that controls the size of your *pupil.* Your iris is so distinctive that iris-scanning technology can be used to confirm your identity. Your sensitive iris can also reveal some of your thoughts and emotions. The iris constricts when you feel disgust or are about to answer *No* (de Gee et al., 2014; Goldinger & Papesh, 2012). Imagine a sunny sky and your iris will constrict, making your pupil smaller; imagine a dark room and it will dilate (Laeng & Sulutvedt, 2014). And when you're feeling romantic, your iris dilates, enlarging your pupil and signaling your interest. But its main job is controlling the amount of light entering your eye.

Light enters the eye through the *cornea.* After passing through your pupil, light hits the transparent *lens* in your eye. The lens then focuses the light rays into an image on your eyeball's inner surface, the **retina.** For centuries, scientists knew that an image of a candle passing through a small opening will cast an upside-down, mirror image on a dark wall behind. They wondered how, if the eye's structure casts this sort of image on the retina (as in **FIGURE 5.11**), can we see the world right side up?

Eventually the answer became clear: The retina doesn't "see" a whole image. Rather, its millions of receptor cells take an image apart and rebuild it. Consider the four-tenths of a second a baseball batter takes to respond to a pitcher's fastball. The retina's millions of cells convert the particles of light energy from that fastball into neural impulses and forward those to the brain. The brain reassembles them into what the batter perceives—incoming fastball! Visual information processing moves through increasingly abstract levels, all at astonishing speed.

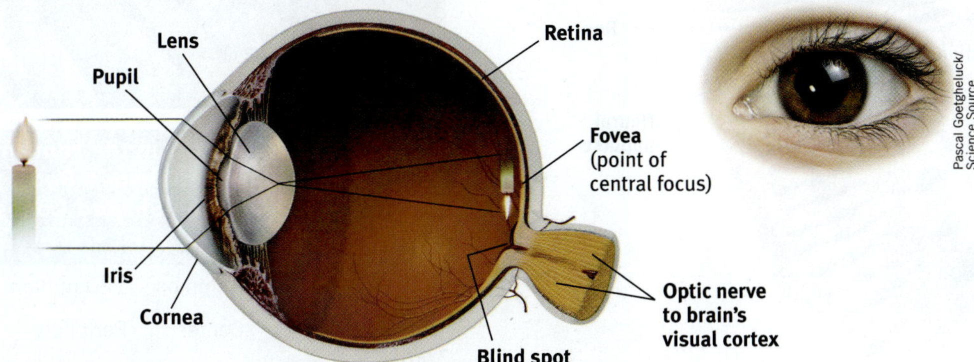

FIGURE 5.11 The eye Light rays reflected from a candle pass through the cornea, pupil, and lens. The curvature and thickness of the lens change to bring nearby or distant objects into focus on the retina. Rays from the top of the candle strike the bottom of the retina. Those from the left side of the candle strike the right side of the retina. The candle's image on the retina thus appears upside down and reversed.

wavelength the distance from the peak of one light wave or sound wave to the peak of the next.

hue the dimension of color that is determined by the wavelength of light; what we know as the color names *blue, green,* and so forth.

intensity the amount of energy in a light wave or sound wave, which influences what we perceive as brightness or loudness. Intensity is determined by the wave's amplitude (height).

retina the light-sensitive inner surface of the eye. Contains the receptor rods and cones plus layers of neurons that begin the processing of visual information.

INFORMATION PROCESSING IN THE EYE AND BRAIN

The Eye-to-Brain Pathway

LOQ 5-8 How do the rods and cones process information, and what path does information take from the eye to the brain?

Imagine that you could follow a single light-energy particle after it reached the retina. First, you would thread your way through your retina's sparse outer layer of cells. Then, reaching the very back of the eye, you would meet the retina's buried receptor cells, the **rods** and **cones** (FIGURE 5.12). There, you would see the light energy trigger chemical changes. That chemical reaction would spark neural signals in the nearby *bipolar cells.* You could then watch the bipolar cells activate neighboring *ganglion cells,* whose axons twine together like strands of a rope to form the **optic nerve.** After a momentary stopover at the thalamus, the information will fly on to the final destination, your visual cortex, in the occipital lobe at the back of your brain.

RETRIEVE & REMEMBER

ANSWERS IN APPENDIX E

5. There are no receptor cells where the optic nerve leaves the eye. This creates a blind spot in your vision. To demonstrate your blind spot, close your left eye, look at the spot below, and move your face away until one of the cars disappears. (Which one do you predict it will be?) Repeat with your right eye closed—and note that now the other car disappears. Can you explain why?

FIGURE 5.13 The blind spot

The optic nerve is an information highway from the eye to the brain. This nerve can send nearly 1 million messages at once through its nearly 1 million ganglion fibers. We pay a price for this high-speed connection. Your eye has a **blind spot,** with no receptor cells, where the optic nerve leaves the eye (FIGURE 5.13). Close one eye. Do you see a black hole? No, because, without seeking your approval, your brain will fill in the hole.

The retina's two types of light-sensitive photoreceptor cells, rods and cones, differ in where they're found and in what they do (TABLE 5.1). Cones cluster in and around the *fovea,* the retina's area of central focus. Many cones have their own hotline to the brain. One cone transmits its message to a single bipolar cell, which relays it to the visual cortex. These direct connections preserve the cones' precise information, making them better able to detect fine detail. Cones can detect white and enable you to perceive color—but not at night (Sabesan et al., 2016). In dim light, cones don't function well.

Rods, which unlike cones are located around the outer regions (the periphery) of your retina, remain sensitive in dim light. If cones are soloists, rods perform as a chorus. They enable black-and-white vision. Rods have no hotlines to

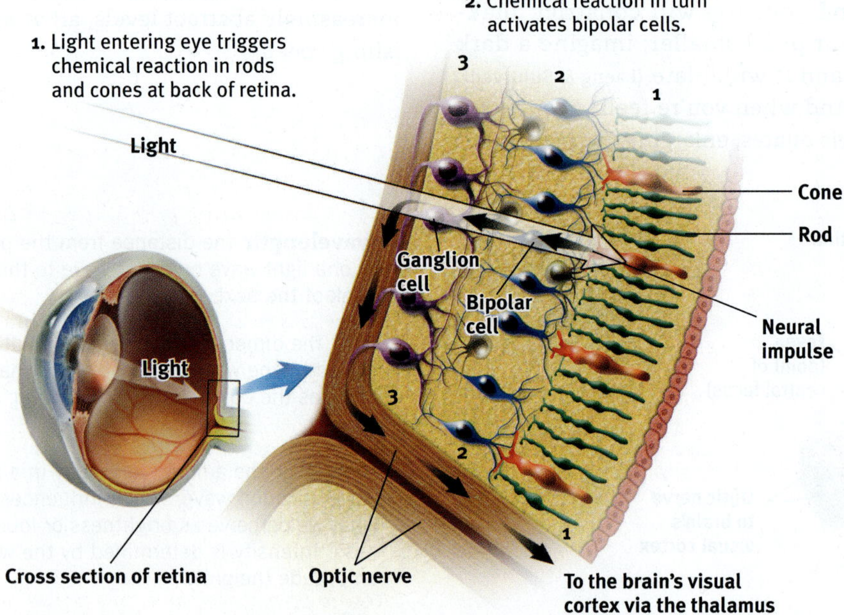
2. Chemical reaction in turn activates bipolar cells.
1. Light entering eye triggers chemical reaction in rods and cones at back of retina.
Light
3
2
1
Cone
Rod
Ganglion cell
Bipolar cell
Neural impulse
Light
3
2
1
Cross section of retina
Optic nerve
To the brain's visual cortex via the thalamus
3. Bipolar cells then activate the ganglion cells, whose combined axons form the optic nerve. This nerve transmits information (via the thalamus) to the brain.

FIGURE 5.12 The retina's reaction to light

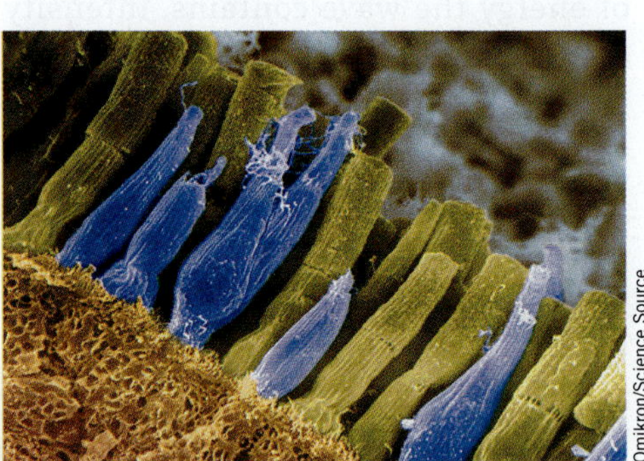
Omikron/Science Source

TABLE 5.1 Receptors in the Human Eye: Rod-Shaped Rods and Cone-Shaped Cones

	Cones	Rods
Number	6 million	120 million
Location in retina	Center	Periphery
Sensitivity in dim light	Low	High
Color sensitivity	High	Low
Detail sensitivity	High	Low

FIGURE 5.14 How many dots can you see at once? Look at or near any of the 12 black dots and you can see them, but not in your peripheral vision.

the brain. Several rods pool their faint energy output and funnel it onto a single bipolar cell, which sends the combined message to your brain. Cones and rods each provide a special sensitivity—cones to detail and color, and rods to faint light and peripheral motion.

Stop for a minute and experience the rod-cone difference. Pick a word in this sentence and stare directly at it, focusing its image on the cones in the center of your eye. Notice that words a few inches off to the side appear blurred? They lack detail because their image is striking your retina's outer regions, where most rods are found. Thus, when you drive or bike, rods help you detect a car in your peripheral vision well before you perceive its details. And in **FIGURE 5.14,** which has 12 black dots, you can see barely two at a time, with your brain filling in the less distinct peripheral input (Kitaoka, 2016, adapting Ninio & Stevens, 2000).

So, cones and rods each provide a special sensitivity, and do more than simply pass along electrical impulses. They begin processing sensory information by coding and analyzing it. (In a frog's eye, for example, those "bug detector" cells that fire when they respond to moving fly-like objects are found in the retina's third neural layer.) After this round of processing, information travels up your optic nerve, headed toward a specific location in your visual cortex. In an important stop on that journey, the optic nerve links up with neurons in the thalamus (**FIGURE 5.15**).

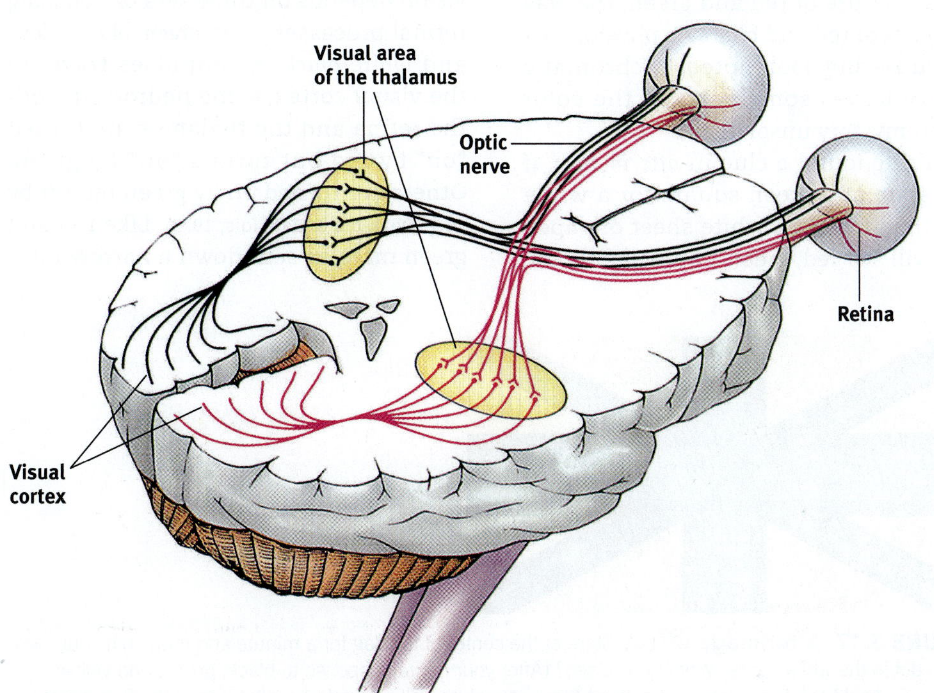

FIGURE 5.15 Pathway from the eyes to the visual cortex The retina's ganglion axons form the optic nerve. In the thalamus, these axons pass messages to other neurons that run to the visual cortex.

IN YOUR EVERYDAY LIFE

Consider your activities in the last hour. Which of them relied on your rods? Which relied on your cones? How would these activities be different—or impossible—without these cells' different abilities?

RETRIEVE & REMEMBER

ANSWERS IN APPENDIX E

6. Some night-loving (nocturnal) animals, such as toads, mice, rats, and bats, have impressive night vision thanks to having many more ____________ (rods/cones) than ____________ (rods/cones) in their retinas. These creatures probably have very poor ____________ (color/black-and-white) vision.

7. Cats are able to open their ____________ much wider than we can, which allows more light into their eyes so they can see better at night.

Color Processing

LOQ 5-9 How do we perceive color in the world around us?

We talk as though objects possess color: "A tomato is red." Recall the old question, "If a tree falls in the forest and no one hears it, does it make a sound?" We can ask the same of color: If no one sees the tomato, is it red?

The answer is No. First, the tomato is everything *but* red, because it *rejects* (reflects) the long wavelengths of red.

rods retinal receptors that detect black, white, and gray, and are sensitive to movement. Rods are necessary for peripheral and twilight vision, when cones don't respond.

cones retinal receptors that are concentrated near the center of the retina, and that function in daylight or well-lit conditions. Cones detect fine detail and give rise to color sensations.

optic nerve the nerve that carries neural impulses from the eye to the brain.

blind spot the point at which the optic nerve leaves the eye; this part of the retina is "blind" because it has no receptor cells.

Second, the tomato's color is our mental construction. As the famous physicist Sir Isaac Newton (1704) observed more than three centuries ago, "The [light] rays are not colored." Color, like all aspects of vision, lives not in the object itself but in the theater of our brain. Even while dreaming, we usually perceive things in color.

One of vision's most basic and intriguing mysteries is how we see the world in color. How, from the light energy striking your retina, does the brain construct your experience of so many colors?

Modern detective work on the mystery of color vision began in the nineteenth century, when German scientist Hermann von Helmholtz built on the insights of an English physicist, Thomas Young. They knew that any color can be created by combining the light waves of three primary colors—red, green, and blue. Young and von Helmholtz reasoned that the eye must therefore have three types of receptors, one for each color.

Years later, researchers confirmed the **Young-Helmholtz trichromatic (three-color) theory.** By measuring the response of various cones to different color stimuli, they confirmed that the retina does indeed have three types of color receptors. Each type is especially sensitive to the wavelengths of red, green, and blue. When light stimulates combinations of these cones, we see other colors. For example, the retina has no separate receptors especially sensitive to yellow. But when red and green wavelengths stimulate both red-sensitive and green-sensitive cones, we see yellow. Said differently, when your eyes see red and green without blue, your brain says *yellow*.

In Singapore, yellow taxis—which are strikingly visible—have had 9 percent fewer accidents than blue taxis (Ho et al., 2017).

By one estimate, we can see differences among more than 1 million color variations (Neitz et al., 2001). At least most of us can. Worldwide, about 1 in 12 men and 1 in 200 women have the genetically sex-linked condition of *color-deficient vision*. Most people who are "color-blind" are not actually blind to all colors. They simply have trouble perceiving the difference between red and green. They don't have three-color vision. Instead, perhaps unknown to them (because their lifelong vision *seems* normal), their retinas' red- or green-sensitive cones, or sometimes both, don't function properly (**FIGURE 5.16**).

(a)

(b)

BEN SOLOMON/The New York Times/Redux Pictures

FIGURE 5.16 Color-deficient vision The photo in image (a) shows how people with red-green deficiency perceived a 2015 football game. "For the 8 percent of American men like me that are Red-Green colorblind, this #JetsVsBills game is a nightmare to watch," tweeted one fan. "Everyone looks like they're on the same team," said another. The photo in image (b) shows how the game looked for those with normal color vision.

But why do people blind to red and green often still see yellow? And why does yellow appear to be a pure color, not a mixture of red and green, the way purple is of red and blue? As physiologist Ewald Hering soon noted, trichromatic theory leaves some parts of the color vision mystery unsolved.

Hering found a clue in *afterimages*. If you stare at a green square for a while and then look at a white sheet of paper, you will see red, green's opponent color. Stare at a yellow square and its opponent color, blue, will appear on the white paper. (To experience this, try the flag demonstration in **FIGURE 5.17**.) Hering proposed that color vision must involve two additional processes: one responsible for red-versus-green perception, and the other for blue-versus-yellow perception.

A century later, researchers confirmed Hering's hypothesis, now called the **opponent-process theory.** This concept is tricky, but here's the gist. Color vision depends on three sets of opposing retinal processes—*red-green*, *blue-yellow*, and *white-black*. As impulses travel to the visual cortex, some neurons in both the retina and the thalamus are turned "on" by red but turned "off" by green. Others are turned on by green but off by red (DeValois & DeValois, 1975). Like red and green marbles sent down a narrow tube,

FIGURE 5.17 Afterimage effect Stare at the center of the flag for a minute and then shift your eyes to the dot in the white space. What do you see? (After your neural response to black, green, and yellow tires, you should see their opponent colors.) Stare at a white wall and note how the size of the flag grows with the projection distance.

"red" and "green" messages cannot both travel at once. Red and green are thus opponents, so we see either red or green, not a reddish-green mixture. But red and blue travel in separate channels, so we are able to see a reddish-blue, or purple.

So how does opponent-process theory help us understand negative afterimages, as in the flag demonstration? Here's the answer (for the green changing to red):

- First, you stared at green bars, which tired your green response.
- Then you stared at a white area. White contains all colors, including red.
- Because you had tired your green response, only the red part of the green-red pairing fired normally.

The present solution to the mystery of color vision is therefore roughly this: *Color processing occurs in two stages.*

1. The retina's red-, green-, and blue-sensitive cones respond in varying degrees to different color stimuli, as the Young-Helmholtz trichromatic theory suggested.
2. The cones' responses are then processed by opponent-process cells, as Hering's opponent-process theory proposed.

Feature Detection

LOQ 5-10 What are *feature detectors,* and what do they do?

Scientists once compared the brain to a movie screen on which the eye projected images. Then along came David Hubel and Torsten Wiesel (1979), who showed that our visual processing system takes images apart and later reassembles them. Hubel and Wiesel received a Nobel Prize for their work on **feature detectors,** nerve cells in the occipital lobe's visual cortex that respond to a scene's specific features—to particular edges, lines, angles, and movements. These specialized neurons pass this specific information to other cortical areas, where teams of cells *(supercell clusters)* respond to more complex patterns, such as recognizing faces. The resulting brain activity varies depending on what's viewed. Thus, with the help of brain scans, "we can tell if a person is looking at a shoe, a chair, or a face" (Haxby, 2001).

One temporal lobe area by your right ear enables you to perceive faces and, thanks to a specialized neural network, to recognize them from many viewpoints (Connor, 2010). If stimulated in this *fusiform face area,* you might spontaneously see faces. As one participant said to the experimenter, "You just turned into someone else" (Koch, 2015). If this region is damaged, people still may recognize other forms and objects, but, like Heather Sellers, they cannot recognize familiar faces. How do we know this? In part because in laboratory experiments, researchers have used magnetic pulses to disrupt that brain area, producing a temporary loss of face recognition. The interaction between feature detectors and supercells provides instant analyses of objects in the world around us.

Parallel Processing

LOQ 5-11 How does the brain use parallel processing to construct visual perceptions?

One of the most amazing aspects of visual information processing is how the brain divides a scene into its parts. Using **parallel processing,** your brain assigns different teams of nerve cells the separate tasks of simultaneously processing a scene's movement, form, depth, and color (**FIGURE 5.18**). You then construct your perceptions by integrating *(binding)* the work of these different visual teams (Livingstone & Hubel, 1988).

Destroy or disable the neural workstation for a visual subtask and something

IN YOUR EVERYDAY LIFE

Does it surprise you to learn that colors don't "live" in the objects we perceive—that in fact, these objects are everything *but* the color we experience? If someone had asked you, "Is grass green?" before you read this section, how would you have responded?

RETRIEVE & REMEMBER

ANSWERS IN APPENDIX E

8. What are two key theories of color vision? Do they contradict each other, or do they make sense together? Explain.

LaunchPad For an interactive review of these color vision principles, visit *Topic Tutorial: PsychSim6, Colorful World.*

Patrick McDermott//Getty Images

Supercells score In this 2017 National Hockey League game, Alex Ovechkin (in red) instantly processed visual information about the positions and movements of three opponents. By using his pattern-detecting supercells, Ovechkin somehow managed to get the puck into the net.

Young-Helmholtz trichromatic (three-color) theory the theory that the retina contains three different types of color receptors—one most sensitive to red, one to green, one to blue. When stimulated in combination, these receptors can produce the perception of any color.

opponent-process theory the theory that opposing retinal processes (red-green, blue-yellow, white-black) enable color vision. For example, some cells are turned "on" by green and turned "off" by red; others are turned on by red and off by green.

feature detectors nerve cells in the brain's visual cortex that respond to specific features of a stimulus, such as shape, angles, or movement.

parallel processing processing many aspects of a stimulus or problem at once.

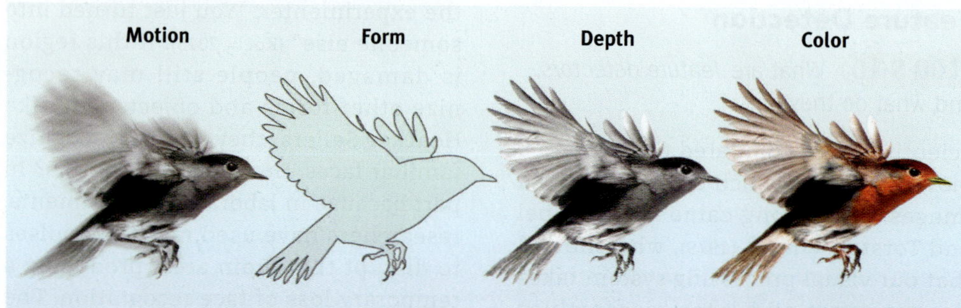
Motion
Form
Depth
Color

FIGURE 5.18 Parallel processing Studies of patients with brain damage suggest that the brain delegates the work of processing motion, form, depth, and color to different areas. After taking a scene apart, the brain integrates these parts into a whole perceived image. How does the brain do this? Vision researchers seek the answer to this *binding problem* (how the brain binds multiple sensory inputs into a single perception).

peculiar results, as happened to "Mrs. M." (Hoffman, 1998). After a stroke damaged areas near the rear of both sides of her brain, she could not perceive motion. People in a room seemed "suddenly here or there but I [had] not seen them moving." Pouring tea into a cup was a challenge because the fluid appeared frozen—she could not perceive it rising in the cup. Brain damage often reveals the importance of the astonishing parallel processing that operates, beyond our awareness, in our normal everyday life.

* * *

Think about the wonders of visual processing. As you read these words, the letters reflect light rays onto your retina, which then sends formless nerve impulses to several areas of your brain, which integrate the information and decode its meaning. The amazing result: We have transferred information across time and space, from our minds to yours (**FIGURE 5.19**). That all of this happens instantly, effortlessly, and continuously is awe-inspiring.

"I am . . . wonderfully made." —King David, Psalm 139:14

RETRIEVE & REMEMBER

ANSWERS IN APPENDIX E

9. What is the rapid sequence of events that occurs when you see and recognize a friend?

PERCEPTUAL ORGANIZATION

LOQ 5-12 What was the main message of Gestalt psychology, and how do *figure-ground* and *grouping* principles help us perceive forms?

Our understanding of how we organize and interpret sights into *meaningful* perceptions—a rose in bloom, a familiar face, a sunset—was advanced early in the twentieth century by a group of German psychologists. They noticed that people given a cluster of sensations tend to organize them into a **gestalt,** a German word meaning a "form" or a "whole." As we look straight ahead, we cannot separate the perceived scene into our left and right fields of view (each as seen with one eye closed). Our conscious perception is, at every moment, one whole, seamless scene. Consider **FIGURE 5.20.** The individual elements of this figure, called a *Necker cube,* are really nothing but eight blue circles, each with three white lines meeting near the center. What happens when we view all these elements together, though? The Necker cube nicely illustrates a famous saying

FIGURE 5.20 A Necker cube What do you see: circles with white lines, or a cube? If you stare at the cube, you may notice that it reverses location, moving the tiny X in the center from the front edge to the back. At times, the cube may seem to float forward, with circles behind it. At other times, the circles may become holes through which the cube appears, as though it were floating behind them. There is far more to perception than meets the eye. (From Bradley et al., 1976.)

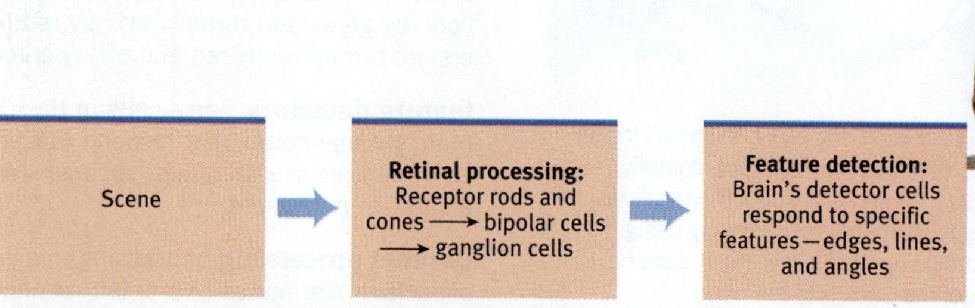
Scene
Retinal processing: Receptor rods and cones ⟶ bipolar cells ⟶ ganglion cells
Feature detection: Brain's detector cells respond to specific features—edges, lines, and angles
Parallel processing: Brain cell teams process combined information about motion, form, depth, and color
Recognition: Brain interprets the constructed image based on information from stored images—it's a tiger!

FIGURE 5.19 A simplified summary of visual information processing

of Gestalt psychologists: *In perception, the whole may exceed the sum of its parts.*

Over the years, the Gestalt psychologists demonstrated many principles we use to organize our sensations into perceptions. Underlying all of them is a basic truth: *Our brain does more than register information about the world.* Perception is not a picture printing itself on the brain. We filter incoming information and we *construct* perceptions. Mind matters.

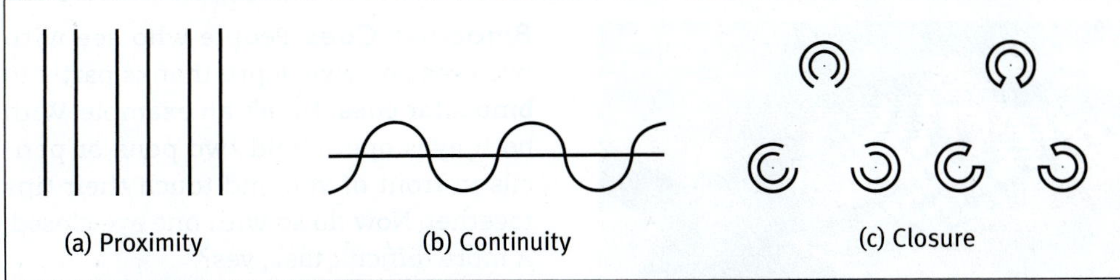

FIGURE 5.22 Three principles of grouping (a) Thanks to *proximity,* we group nearby figures together. We see not six separate lines, but three sets of two lines. (b) Through *continuity,* we perceive smooth, continuous patterns rather than discontinuous ones. This pattern could be a series of alternating semicircles, but we perceive it as two continuous lines—one wavy, one straight. (c) Using *closure,* we fill in gaps to create a complete, whole object. Thus, we assume that the circles on the left are complete but partially blocked by the (illusory) triangle. Add nothing more than little line segments to close off the circles and your brain may stop constructing a triangle.

How Do We Perceive Form?

Imagine designing one of today's video-computer systems that, like your eye-brain system, recognizes faces at a glance. What abilities does it need? To start with, the video-computer system needs to perceive **figure-ground**—to separate faces from their backgrounds. In our eye-brain system, this is our first perceptual task—perceiving any object (the *figure*) as distinct from its surroundings (the *ground*). As you read, the words are the figure; the white space is the ground. This perception applies to our hearing, too. As you hear voices at a party, the one you attend to becomes the figure; all others are part of the ground. Sometimes, the same stimulus can trigger more than one perception, as in **FIGURE 5.21,** where the figure-ground relationship continually reverses. First we see the vase (or the faces), then the faces (or the vase), but we always perceive a figure standing out from a ground.

While telling figure from ground, we (and our video-computer system) must also organize the figure into a *meaningful* form. Some basic features of a scene—such as color, movement, and light-dark contrast—we process instantly and automatically (Treisman, 1987). Our mind brings order and form to other stimuli by following certain rules for **grouping,** also identified by the Gestalt psychologists. These rules, which we apply even as infants and even in our touch perceptions, illustrate how the perceived whole differs from the sum of its parts (Gallace & Spence, 2011; Quinn et al., 2002; Rock & Palmer, 1990). See **FIGURE 5.22** for three examples.

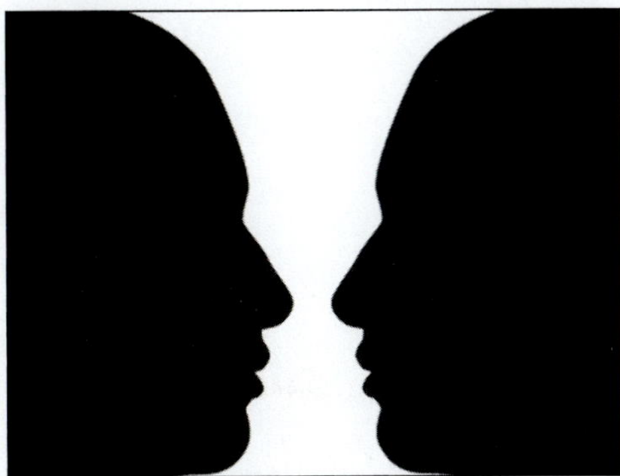

FIGURE 5.21 Reversible figure and ground

RETRIEVE & REMEMBER

ANSWERS IN APPENDIX E

10. In terms of perception, a band's lead singer would be considered __________ (figure/ground), and the other musicians would be considered __________ (figure/ground).
11. What do we mean when we say that, in perception, "the whole may exceed the sum of its parts"?

How Do We Perceive Depth?

LOQ 5-13 How do we use binocular and monocular cues to see in three dimensions, and how do we perceive motion?

Our eye-brain system performs many amazing tricks, but one of its best is **depth perception.** From the two-dimensional images falling on our retinas, our brain creates three-dimensional perceptions that, for example, let us estimate the distance of an oncoming car. How do we acquire this ability? Are we born with it? Do we learn it?

As psychologist Eleanor Gibson picnicked on the rim of the Grand Canyon, her scientific curiosity kicked in. She

Monika Skolimowska/AP Images

Creating three-dimensional perceptions from two dimensions Several of the world's cities slow traffic with illusory 3-D crosswalk paintings, thanks to artists Saumya Pandya Thakkar and Shakuntala Pandyaand, who created the first of these in India.

gestalt an organized whole. Gestalt psychologists emphasized our tendency to integrate pieces of information into meaningful wholes.

figure-ground the organization of the visual field into objects (the *figures*) that stand out from their surroundings (the *ground*).

grouping the perceptual tendency to organize stimuli into meaningful groups.

depth perception the ability to see objects in three dimensions, although the images that strike the retina are two-dimensional; allows us to judge distance.

FIGURE 5.23 Visual cliff Eleanor Gibson and Richard Walk devised this glass-covered miniature cliff to determine whether crawling infants and newborn animals can perceive depth.

wondered, *Would a toddler peering over the rim perceive the dangerous drop-off and draw back?* To answer that question and others, Gibson and Richard Walk (1960) designed a series of experiments using a **visual cliff**—a model of a cliff with a "drop-off" area that was covered by sturdy glass. They placed 6- to 14-month-olds on the edge of the "cliff" and had one of their parents coax the infants to crawl out onto the glass (**FIGURE 5.23**). Most infants refused to do so, indicating that they could perceive depth.

Had they *learned* to perceive depth? Crawling, no matter when it begins, seems to increase an infant's fear of heights (Adolph et al., 2014; Campos et al., 1992). But depth perception is also partly innate. Mobile newborn animals—even those with no visual experience (including young kittens, a day-old goat, and newly hatched chicks)—also refuse to venture across the visual cliff. Thus, biology prepares us to be wary of heights, and experience amplifies that fear.

If we were to build this ability to perceive depth into our video-computer system, what rules might enable it to convert two-dimensional images into a single three-dimensional perception? A good place to start would be the depth cues our brain receives from information supplied by one or both eyes.

Binocular Cues People who see with two eyes perceive depth thanks partly to **binocular cues.** Here's an example. With both eyes open, hold two pens or pencils in front of you and touch their tips together. Now do so with one eye closed. A more difficult task, yes?

We use binocular cues to judge the distance of nearby objects. One such cue is *convergence,* the inward angle of the eyes focusing on a near object. Another is **retinal disparity.** Because your eyes are about 2 inches apart, your retinas receive slightly different images of the world. By comparing these two images, your brain can judge how close an object is to you. The greater the disparity (difference) between the two retinal images, the closer the object. Try it. Hold your two index fingers, with the tips about half an inch apart, directly in front of your nose, and your retinas will receive quite different views. If you close one eye and then the other, you can see the difference. (You can also create a finger sausage, as in **FIGURE 5.24.**) At a greater distance—say, when you hold your fingers at arm's length—the disparity is smaller.

We could easily include retinal disparity in our video-computer system. Moviemakers sometimes film a scene with two cameras placed a few inches apart. Viewers then watch the film through glasses that allow the left eye to see only the image from the left camera, and the right eye to see only the image from the right camera. The resulting effect, as 3-D movie fans know, mimics or exaggerates normal retinal disparity, giving the perception of depth.

Monocular Cues How do we judge whether a person is 10 or 100 meters away? Retinal disparity won't help us here, because there won't be much difference between the images cast on our right and left retinas. At such distances, we depend on **monocular cues** (depth cues available to each eye separately). See **FIGURE 5.25** for some examples.

"I can't go on living with such lousy depth perception!"

Tom Cheney/New Yorker Cartoon/Cartoon Bank

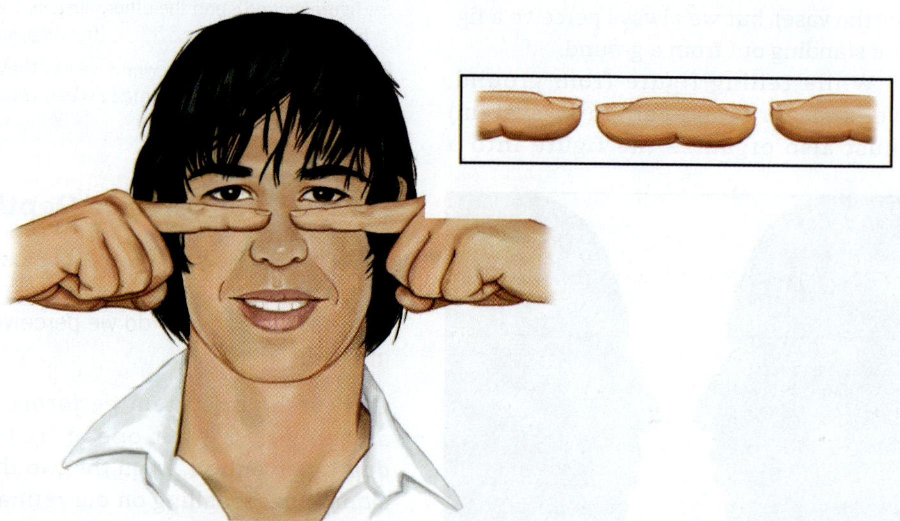

FIGURE 5.24 The floating finger sausage Hold your two index fingers about 5 inches in front of your eyes, with their tips half an inch apart. Now look beyond them and note the weird result. Move your fingers out farther and the retinal disparity—and the finger sausage—will shrink.

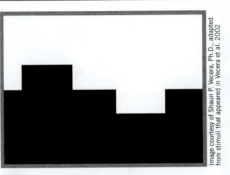

Relative height We perceive objects higher in our field of vision as farther away. Because we assume the lower part of a figure-ground illustration is closer, we perceive it as figure (Vecera et al., 2002). If upside down, the black will become ground, like a night sky.

Relative size If we assume two objects are similar in size, *most* people perceive the one that casts the smaller retinal image as farther away.

Interposition If one object partially blocks our view of another, we perceive it as closer.

Relative motion As we move, stable objects may also appear to move. If while riding on a bus you fix your gaze on some point—say, a house—the objects beyond the fixation point will appear to move with you. Objects in front of the point will appear to move backward. The farther an object is from the fixation point, the faster it will seem to move.

Fixation point

Direction of passenger's motion →

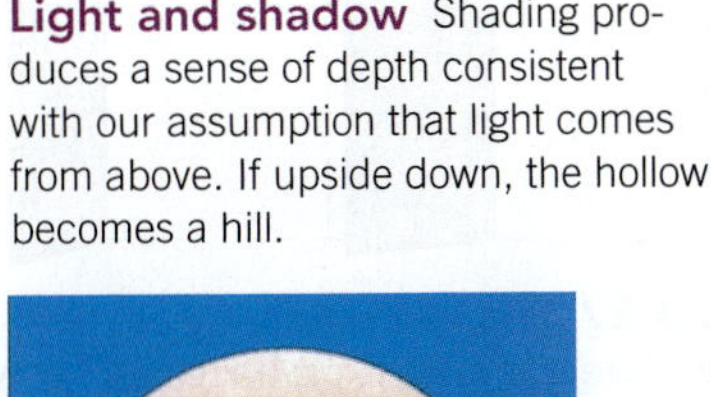

Light and shadow Shading produces a sense of depth consistent with our assumption that light comes from above. If upside down, the hollow becomes a hill.

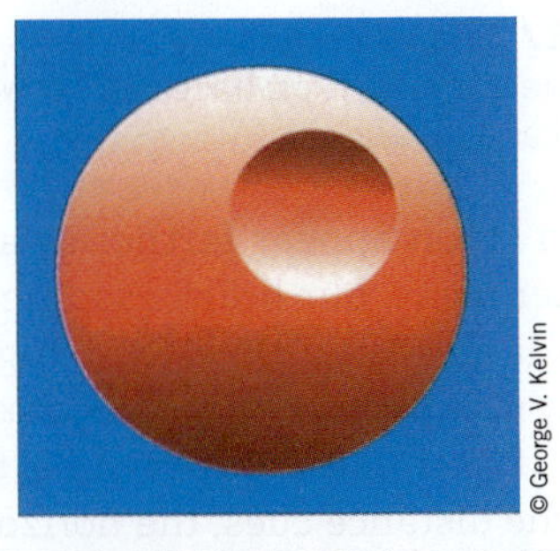

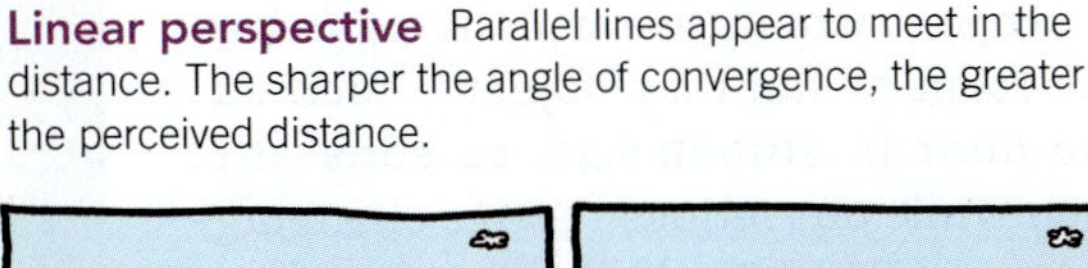

Linear perspective Parallel lines appear to meet in the distance. The sharper the angle of convergence, the greater the perceived distance.

FIGURE 5.25 Monocular depth cues

RETRIEVE & REMEMBER

ANSWERS IN APPENDIX E

12. How do we normally perceive depth?

LaunchPad Check your understanding of these cues by engaging online with *Concept Practice: Depth Cues.*

How Do We Perceive Motion?

Imagine that you could perceive the world as having color, form, and depth but that you could not see motion. You would be unable to bike or drive, and writing, eating, and walking would be a challenge.

Normally your brain computes motion based partly on its assumption that shrinking objects are moving away (not getting smaller) and enlarging objects are approaching. In young children, this ability to correctly perceive approaching (and enlarging) vehicles is not yet fully developed, which puts them at risk for pedestrian accidents (Wann et al., 2011).

It's not just children who have occasional difficulties with motion

visual cliff a laboratory device for testing depth perception in infants and young animals.

binocular cue a depth cue, such as retinal disparity, that depends on the use of two eyes.

retinal disparity a binocular cue for perceiving depth. By comparing images from the two eyes, the brain computes distance—the greater the disparity (difference) between the two images, the closer the object.

monocular cue a depth cue, such as interposition or linear perspective, available to either eye alone.

perception. Our adult brain is sometimes tricked into believing what it is not seeing. When large and small objects move at the same speed, the large objects appear to move more slowly. Thus, trains seem to move slower than cars, and jumbo jets seem to land more slowly than smaller jets.

Perceptual Constancy

LOQ 5-14 How do perceptual constancies help us construct meaningful perceptions?

So far, we have noted that our video-computer system must perceive objects as we do—as having a distinct form, location, and perhaps motion. Its next task is to recognize objects without being deceived by changes in their color, shape, or size. We call this *top-down* process **perceptual constancy.** This feat is an enormous challenge for a video-computer system.

Color Constancy Our experience of color depends on an object's *context.* This would be clear if you viewed an isolated tomato through a paper tube over the course of the day. As the light—and thus the tomato's reflected wavelengths—changed, the tomato's color would also seem to change. But if you discarded the paper tube and viewed the tomato as one item in a salad bowl, its perceived color would remain basically constant. This perception of consistent color is known as *color constancy.*

We see color thanks to our brain's ability to decode the meaning of the light reflected by an object *relative to the objects surrounding it.* **FIGURE 5.26** dramatically illustrates the ability of a blue object to appear very different in three different contexts. Yet we have no trouble seeing these disks as blue. Paint manufacturers have learned this lesson. Knowing that your perception of a paint color will be determined by other colors in your home, they offer trial samples you can test in that context. The take-home lesson: *Context governs our perceptions.*

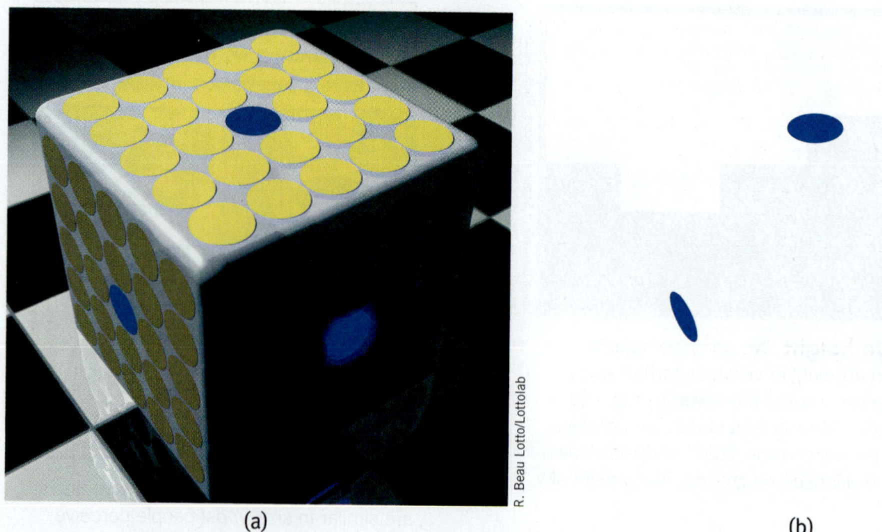

FIGURE 5.26 Color depends on context (a) Believe it or not, these three blue disks are identical in color. (b) Remove the surrounding context and see what results.

Shape and Size Constancies Thanks to *shape constancy,* we usually perceive the form of familiar objects, such as the door in **FIGURE 5.27,** as constant even while our retinas receive changing images of them. Thanks to *size constancy,* we perceive an object as having an unchanging size even while our distance from it varies. We assume a car is large enough to carry people, even when we see its tiny image from two blocks away. This assumption also shows the close connection between perceived *distance* and perceived *size.* Perceiving an object's distance gives us cues to its size. Likewise, knowing its general size—that the object is a car—provides us with cues to its distance.

> "Sometimes I wonder: Why is that Frisbee getting bigger? And then it hits me." —Anonymous

Even in size-distance judgments, however, we consider an object's context. This interplay between perceived size and perceived distance helps explain several well-known illusions, including the *Moon illusion.* The Moon looks up to 50 percent larger when near the horizon than when high in the sky. Can you imagine why? One reason is that monocular cues to an object's distance make

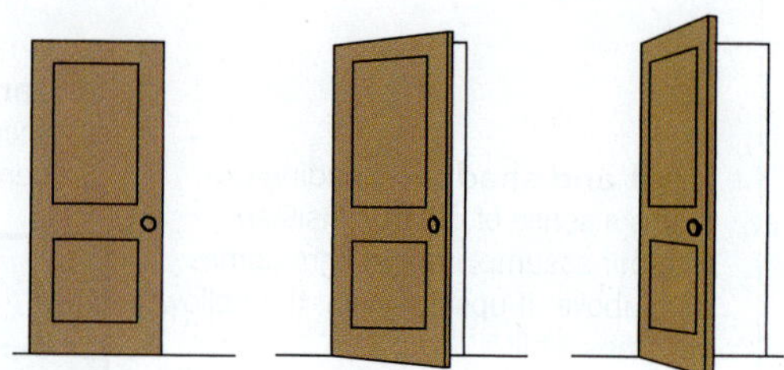

FIGURE 5.27 Shape constancy An opening door looks more and more like a trapezoid. Yet we still perceive it as a rectangle.

the horizon Moon appear farther away. If it's farther away, our brain assumes, it must be larger than the Moon high in the night sky (Kaufman & Kaufman, 2000). But again, if you use a paper tube to take away the distance cues, the horizon Moon will immediately seem smaller.

Mistaken judgments like these reveal the workings of our normally effective perceptual processes. The perceived relationship between distance and size is usually valid. But under special circumstances it can lead us astray.

Form perception, depth perception, motion perception, and perceptual constancies illuminate how we organize our visual experiences. Perceptual organization applies to our other senses, too. Listening to an unfamiliar language, we have trouble hearing where one word stops and the next one begins. Listening to our own language, we automatically hear distinct words. We even organize a string of letters—THEDOGATEMEAT—into words that make an understandable phrase, more likely "The dog ate meat" than "The do gate me at" (McBurney & Collings, 1984). Perception, however, is more than organizing stimuli. Perception also requires what would be another big challenge to our video-computer system: interpretation—finding meaning in what we perceive.

LaunchPad To experience more visual illusions, and to understand what they reveal about how you perceive the world, visit *Topic Tutorial: PsychSim6, Visual Illusions.*

PERCEPTUAL INTERPRETATION

The debate over whether our perceptual abilities spring from our nature or our nurture has a long history. To what extent do we *learn* to perceive? German philosopher Immanuel Kant (1724–1804) maintained that knowledge comes from our inborn ways of organizing sensory experiences. Psychology's findings support this idea. We do come equipped to process sensory information. But British philosopher John Locke (1632–1704) argued that through our experiences we also learn to perceive the world. Psychology also supports this idea. We do learn to link an object's distance with its size. So, just how important is experience? How much does it shape our perceptual interpretations?

Experience and Visual Perception

LOQ 5-15 What does research on restored vision, sensory restriction, and perceptual adaptation reveal about the effects of experience on perception?

Restored Vision and Sensory Restriction Writing to John Locke, a friend wondered what would happen if "a man *born* blind, and now adult, [was] taught by his *touch* to distinguish between a cube and a sphere." Could he, if made to see, visually distinguish the two? Locke's answer was *No,* because the man would never have *learned* to see the difference.

This question has since been put to the test with people who, though blind from birth, later gained sight (Gandhi et al., 2017; Gregory, 1978; von Senden, 1932). Most were born with cataracts—clouded lenses that allowed them to see only light and shadows, rather as a sighted person might see a foggy image through a Ping-Pong ball sliced in half. After cataract surgery, the patients could tell the difference between figure and ground, could sense colors, and distinguish faces from nonfaces. This suggests that we are born with these aspects of perception. But much as Locke supposed, they often could not visually recognize objects that were familiar by touch.

Seeking to gain more control than is provided by clinical cases, researchers have outfitted infant kittens and monkeys with goggles through which they could see only diffuse, unpatterned light (Wiesel, 1982). After infancy, when their vision was restored, the animals behaved much like humans born with cataracts. They could distinguish color and brightness but not form. Their eyes were healthy. Their retinas still sent signals to their visual cortex. But without early stimulation, their brain's cortical cells had not developed normal connections. Thus, the animals remained functionally blind to shape.

Marcio Jose Sanchez/AP Images

Learning to see At age 3, Mike May lost his vision in an explosion. Decades later, after a new cornea restored vision to his right eye, he got his first look at his wife and children. Alas, although signals were now reaching his visual cortex, it lacked the experience to interpret them. May could not recognize expressions, or faces, apart from features such as hair. Yet he can see an object in motion and has learned to navigate his world and to marvel at such things as dust floating in sunlight (Abrams, 2002; Gorlick, 2010).

Surgery on blind children in India reveals that those who are blind from birth can benefit from removal of cataracts. The younger they are, the more they will benefit (Chatterjee, 2015; Gandhi et al., 2014). For normal sensory and perceptual development, there is a *critical period*—a limited time when exposure to certain stimuli or experiences is required.

In humans and other animals, similar sensory restrictions later in life do no permanent harm. When researchers cover an adult animal's eye for several months, its vision will be unaffected after the eye patch is removed. When surgeons remove cataracts that developed during late adulthood, most people are thrilled at the return to normal vision.

Perceptual Adaptation Given a new pair of glasses, we may feel a little strange, even dizzy. Within a day or two, we adjust. Our **perceptual adaptation** to changed visual input makes the world seem normal again. But imagine wearing a far more dramatic pair of new glasses—one that shifts the apparent location of objects 40 degrees to the left. When you toss a ball to a friend, it sails off to the left. Walking forward to shake hands with someone, you veer to the left.

perceptual constancy perceiving objects as unchanging (having consistent color, shape, and size) even as illumination and retinal images change.

perceptual adaptation the ability to adjust to changed sensory input, including an artificially displaced or even inverted visual field.

Courtesy of Hubert Dolezal

Perceptual adaptation "Oops, missed," thought researcher Hubert Dolezal as he attempted a handshake while viewing the world through inverting goggles. Yet, believe it or not, kittens, monkeys, and humans can adapt to an upside-down world.

Could you adapt to this distorted world? Not if you were a baby chicken. When fitted with such lenses, baby chicks continue to peck where food grains *seem* to be (Hess, 1956; Rossi, 1968). But we humans adapt to distorting lenses quickly. Within a few minutes, your throws would again be accurate, your stride on target. Remove the lenses and you would experience an aftereffect. At first your throws would err in the *opposite* direction, sailing off to the right. But again, within minutes you would adjust.

Indeed, given an even more radical pair of glasses—one that literally turns the world upside down—you could still adapt. Psychologist George Stratton (1896) experienced this when he invented, and for eight days wore, a device that flipped left to right and up to down, making him the first person to experience a right-side-up retinal image while standing upright. The ground was up; the sky was down.

At first, when Stratton wanted to walk, he found himself searching for his feet, which were now "up." Eating was nearly impossible. He became nauseated and depressed. But he persisted, and by the eighth day he could comfortably reach for an object and, if his hands were in view, could walk without bumping into things. When Stratton finally removed the headgear, he readapted quickly. So did research participants who also later wore such gear—while riding a motorcycle, skiing the Alps, or flying an airplane (Dolezal, 1982; Kohler, 1962). By actively moving about in their topsy-turvy world, they adapted to their new context and learned to coordinate their movements.

So, do we learn to perceive the world? In part we do, as we constantly adjust to changed sensory input. Research on critical periods teaches us that early nurture sculpts what nature has provided. In less dramatic ways, nurture continues to do this throughout our lives. Experience guides, sustains, and maintains the pathways in our brain that enable our perceptions.

IN YOUR EVERYDAY LIFE

Consider someone you know (could be yourself) who has a visual disability of some kind. What sort of disruption in the visual process might cause that disability?

The Other Senses

For humans, vision is the major sense. More of our brain cortex is devoted to vision than to any other sense. Yet without hearing, touch, taste, smell, and body position and movement, our experience of the world would be vastly diminished.

HEARING

Like our other senses, our hearing—**audition**—helps us adapt and survive. Hearing provides information and enables relationships. People seem more thoughtful, competent, and likable when others can hear, not just read, their words (Schroeder & Epley, 2015, 2016). And hearing is pretty spectacular. It lets us communicate invisibly—we shoot unseen air waves across space and receive the same from others. Hearing loss is therefore the great invisible disability. To miss the hilarious joke is to be deprived of what others know, and sometimes to feel excluded. As a person with hearing loss, I [DM] know the feeling, and can understand why adults with significant hearing loss experience a doubled risk of depression (Li et al., 2014).

Most of us, however, can hear a wide range of sounds, and the ones we hear best are those in the range of the human voice. With normal hearing, we are remarkably sensitive to faint sounds, such as a child's whimper. (If our ears were only slightly more sensitive, we would hear a constant hiss from the movement of air molecules.) We also are acutely sensitive to sound differences. Among thousands of possible voices, we easily distinguish an unseen friend's. Moreover, hearing is fast. Your reaction to a sudden sound is at least 10 times faster than your response when you suddenly see something "from the corner of your eye, turn your head toward it, recognize it, and respond to it" (Horowitz, 2012). A fraction of a second after such events stimulate your ear's receptors, millions of neurons are working together to extract the essential features, compare them with past experience, and identify the sound (Freeman, 1991). For hearing as for seeing, we wonder: How do we do it?

Sound Waves: From the Environment Into the Brain

LOQ 5-16 What are the characteristics of the air pressure waves that we hear as sound?

Hit a piano key and you unleash the energy of sound waves. Moving molecules of air, each bumping into the next, create waves of compressed and expanded air, like ripples on a pond circling out from a tossed stone. Our ears detect these brief air pressure changes.

Like light waves, sound waves vary in shape. The height, or *amplitude*, of

Zdorov Kirill Vladimirovich/Shutterstock

sbarabu/Shutterstock

The sounds of music A violin's short, fast waves create a high pitch. The longer, slower waves of a cello or bass create a lower pitch. Differences in the waves' height, or amplitude, also create differing degrees of loudness. (To review the physical properties of light and sound waves, see Figure 5.10.)

sound waves determines their perceived *loudness*. Their **frequency** determines the **pitch** (the high or low tone) we experience. Long waves have low frequency—and low pitch. Short waves have high frequency—and high pitch. Sound waves produced by a referee's whistle are much shorter and faster than those produced by a truck horn.

We measure sounds in *decibels,* with zero decibels representing the lowest level detectable by human ears. Normal conversation registers at about 60 decibels. A whisper falls at about 20 decibels, and a jet plane passing 500 feet overhead registers at about 110 decibels. If prolonged, exposure to sounds above 85 decibels can produce hearing loss. Tell that to basketball fans at the University of Kentucky who, in 2017, broke the Guinness World Record for the noisiest indoor stadium at 126 decibels (WKYT, 2017). Hear today, gone tomorrow.

RETRIEVE & REMEMBER

ANSWERS IN APPENDIX E

13. The amplitude of a sound wave determines our perception of __________ (loudness/pitch).

14. The longer the sound waves are, the __________ (lower/higher) their frequency and the __________ (lower/higher) their pitch.

Decoding Sound Waves

LOQ 5-17 How does the ear transform sound energy into neural messages, and how do we locate sounds?

How does vibrating air trigger nerve impulses that your brain can decode as sounds?

The process begins when sound waves strike your *eardrum,* causing this tight membrane to vibrate (**FIGURE 5.28a**). In your **middle ear,** three tiny bones—the *hammer* (malleus), *anvil* (incus), and *stirrup* (stapes)—pick up the vibrations and transmit them to the **cochlea,** a snail-shaped tube in your **inner ear.**

The incoming vibrations then cause the cochlea's membrane-covered opening (the *oval window*) to vibrate, sending ripples through the fluid inside the cochlea (Figure 5.28b). The ripples bend the *hair cells* lining the *basilar membrane* on the cochlea's surface, much as wind bends wheat stalks in a field.

The hair cell movements in turn trigger impulses in nerve cells, whose axons combine to form the *auditory nerve*. The auditory nerve carries the impulses to your thalamus and then on to the *auditory cortex* in your brain's temporal lobe. From vibrating air, to tiny moving bones, to fluid waves, to electrical impulses to the brain: You hear!

What do you hear at www.tinyurl.com/YannyLaurel? With a unique, top-down hearing system, each of us may process the same sound differently. Some people hear *Yanny* and some hear *Laurel*—two rather different names.

Perhaps the most magical part of the hearing process is the hair cells—"quivering bundles that let us hear" thanks to their "extreme sensitivity and extreme speed" (Goldberg, 2007). A cochlea has 16,000 of these cells, which sounds like a lot until we compare that with an eye's 130 million or so receptors. But consider a hair cell's responsiveness. Deflect the tiny bundles of *cilia* on its tip by only the width of an *atom*, and the alert hair cell will trigger a neural response (Corey et al., 2004).

Damage to the cochlea's hair cell receptors or the auditory nerve can cause **sensorineural hearing loss** (or nerve deafness). With auditory nerve damage, people may hear sound but have trouble discerning what someone is saying (Liberman, 2015). Occasionally, disease

audition the sense or act of hearing.

frequency the number of complete wavelengths that pass a point in a given time (for example, per second).

pitch a tone's experienced highness or lowness; depends on frequency.

middle ear the chamber between the eardrum and cochlea containing three tiny bones—hammer (malleus), anvil (incus), and stirrup (stapes)—that concentrate the vibrations of the eardrum on the cochlea's oval window.

cochlea [KOHK-lee-uh] a coiled, bony, fluid-filled tube in the inner ear; sound waves traveling through the cochlear fluid trigger nerve impulses.

inner ear the innermost part of the ear, containing the cochlea, semicircular canals, and vestibular sacs.

sensorineural hearing loss hearing loss caused by damage to the cochlea's receptor cells or to the auditory nerve. The most common form of hearing loss (also called *nerve deafness*).

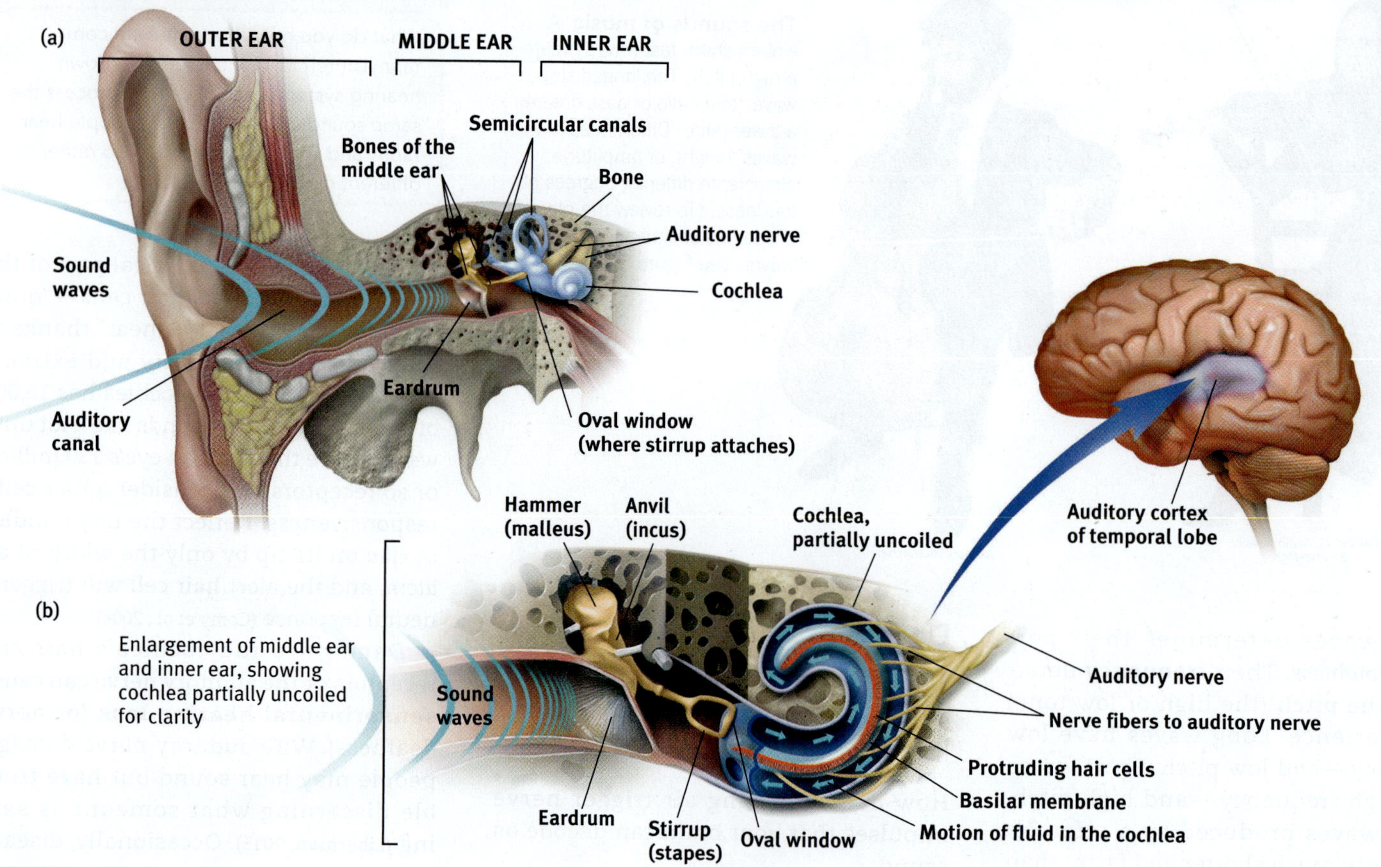

FIGURE 5.28 Hear here: How we transform sound waves into nerve impulses that our brain interprets (a) The outer ear funnels sound waves to the eardrum. The bones of the middle ear (hammer, anvil, and stirrup) amplify and relay the eardrum's vibrations through the oval window into the fluid-filled cochlea. (b) As shown in this detail of the middle ear and inner ear, the resulting pressure changes in the cochlear fluid cause the basilar membrane to ripple, bending the hair cells on its surface. Hair cell movements trigger impulses at the base of the nerve cells, whose fibers join together to form the auditory nerve. That nerve sends neural messages to the thalamus and on to the auditory cortex.

damages hair cell receptors, but more often the culprits are biological changes linked with heredity and aging, or prolonged exposure to ear-splitting noise or music. Sensorineural hearing loss is more common than **conduction hearing loss,** which is caused by damage to the mechanical system—the eardrum and middle ear bones—that conducts sound waves to the cochlea.

Hair cells have been compared to carpet fibers. Walk around on them and they will spring back. But leave a heavy piece of furniture on them and they may never rebound. As a general rule, any noise we cannot talk over (loud machinery, fans screaming at a sports event, music blasting at maximum volume) may be harmful, especially if repeated or long-lasting (Roesser, 1998). And if our ears ring after such experiences, we have been bad to our unhappy hair cells. As pain alerts us to possible bodily harm, ringing in the ears alerts us to possible hearing damage. It is hearing's version of bleeding.

Worldwide, 1.23 billion people are challenged by hearing loss (Global Burden of Disease, 2015). Since the early 1990s, teen hearing loss has risen by a third and affects 1 in 6 teens (Shargorodsky et al., 2010; Weichbold et al., 2012). Exposure to loud music, both live and through headphones, is a culprit: After three hours of a rock concert averaging 99 decibels, 54 percent of teens reported not hearing as well, and 1 in 4 had ringing in their ears (Derebery et al., 2012). Teen boys more than teen girls or adults blast themselves with loud volumes for long periods (Zogby, 2006). People who spend many hours behind a power mower, above a jackhammer, or in a loud club should wear earplugs, or they risk needing a hearing aid later.

Nerve deafness cannot be reversed. One way to restore hearing is a sort of bionic ear—a **cochlear implant.** Some 50,000 people, including some 30,000 children, receive these electronic devices each year (Hochmair, 2013). The implants translate sounds into electrical signals that, wired into the cochlea's nerves, transmit sound information to the brain. When given to deaf kittens and human infants, cochlear implants have seemed to trigger an "awakening" of brain areas normally used in hearing (Klinke et al., 1999; Sireteanu, 1999). They can help children become skilled in oral communication (especially if they receive them as preschoolers or ideally before age 1) (Dettman et al., 2007; Schorr et al., 2005). Hearing, like vision, has a critical period.

How Do We Locate Sounds?

Why don't we have one big ear—perhaps above our one nose? "All the better to hear you with," as the wolf said to Little Red Riding Hood. Our two ears are about 6 inches apart, and they pick up two slightly different messages (**FIGURE 5.29**). Say a car to your right honks. Your right ear will receive a more *intense* sound. It will also receive the sound slightly *sooner* than your left ear. Because sound travels 750 miles per hour, the intensity difference and the time lag will be very small—just 0.000027 second! Lucky for us, our supersensitive sound system can detect such tiny differences and locate the sound (Brown & Deffenbacher, 1979; Middlebrooks & Green, 1991).

FIGURE 5.29 How we locate sounds Sound waves strike one ear sooner and more intensely than the other. From this information, our nimble brain can compute the sound's location. As you might therefore expect, people who lose all hearing in one ear often have difficulty locating sounds.

LaunchPad For an interactive review of how we perceive sound, visit *Topic Tutorial: PsychSim6, The Auditory System.* For an animated test of your knowledge, engage online with *Concept Practice: The Auditory Pathway.*

TOUCH

LOQ 5-18 What are the four basic touch sensations, and how do we sense touch?

Touch, our tactile sense, is vital. From infancy to adulthood, affectionate touches promote our well-being (Jakubiak & Feeney, 2017). Right from the start, touch enables our development. Infant monkeys that are allowed to see, hear, and smell—but not touch—their mother become desperately unhappy (Suomi et al., 1976). Those separated by a screen with holes that allow touching are much less miserable. Premature human babies gain weight faster and go home sooner if they are stimulated by hand massage (Field et al., 2006). As adults, we still yearn to touch—to kiss, to stroke, to snuggle.

Humorist Dave Barry was perhaps right to joke that your skin "keeps people from seeing the inside of your body, which is repulsive, and it prevents your organs from falling onto the ground." But skin does much more. Our "sense of touch" is actually a mix of four basic and distinct skin senses: *pressure, warmth, cold,* and *pain.* Other skin sensations are variations of these four. For example, stroking side-by-side pressure spots creates a tickle. Repeated gentle stroking of a pain spot creates an itching sensation. Touching side-by-side cold and pressure spots triggers a sense of wetness (which you can experience by touching dry, cold metal).

Touch sensations involve more than feelings on our skin, however. A soft touch on the leg evokes a different cortical response when a straight man believes he was caressed by an attractive woman rather than by another man (Gazzola et al., 2012). Such responses show how quickly our thinking brain influences our sensory responses, as we can see in the ways we experience and respond to pain.

The precious sense of touch As William James wrote in his *Principles of Psychology* (1890), "Touch is both the alpha and omega of affection."

Pain—What Is It and How Can We Control It?

LOQ 5-19 What biological, psychological, and social-cultural influences affect our experience of pain? How do placebos, distraction, and hypnosis help control pain?

Be thankful for occasional pain. Pain is your body's way of telling you something has gone wrong. Drawing your attention to a burn or a sprain, pain orders you to change your behavior—"Stay off that ankle!" The rare people born without the ability to feel pain may experience severe injury or even early death. Without the discomfort that makes us shift positions, their joints can fail from excess strain.

conduction hearing loss a less common form of hearing loss, caused by damage to the mechanical system that conducts sound waves to the cochlea.

cochlear implant a device for converting sounds into electrical signals and stimulating the auditory nerve through electrodes threaded into the cochlea.

Jeff Riedel/Contour/Getty Images

"Pain is a gift." So said a doctor studying Ashlyn Blocker, who has a rare genetic mutation that prevents her from feeling pain. As a child, she ran around for two days on a broken ankle. She has put her hands on a hot machine and burned the flesh off. And she has reached into boiling water to retrieve a dropped spoon. "Everyone in my class asks me about it, and I say, 'I can feel pressure, but I can't feel pain.' *Pain!* I cannot feel it!" (Heckert, 2012).

Without the warnings of pain, infections can run wild and injuries can multiply (Neese, 1991).

Many more people live with chronic pain, which is rather like an alarm that won't shut off. Persistent backaches, arthritis, headaches, and cancer-related pain prompt two questions: What is pain? And how might we control it?

Understanding Pain Our feeling of pain reflects both *bottom-up* sensations and *top-down* cognition. Pain is a biopsychosocial event (Hadjistavropoulos et al., 2011). As such, pain experiences vary widely, from group to group and from person to person.

Biological Influences Pain is a physical event produced by your senses. But pain differs from some of your other sensations. No one type of stimulus triggers pain, the way light triggers vision. And no specialized receptors process pain signals, the way the rods and cones in your eyes react to light rays. Instead, you have sensory receptors called *nociceptors*, mostly in your skin, which detect hurtful temperatures, pressure, or chemicals.

Your experience of pain also depends in part on the genes you inherited and on your physical characteristics (Gatchel et al., 2007; Reimann et al., 2010). Women are more sensitive to pain than are men—and their senses of hearing and smell also tend to be more sensitive (Ruau et al., 2012; Wickelgren, 2009).

No pain theory can explain it all. But one useful model called the *gate-control theory* suggests that the spinal cord contains a "gate" that controls the transmission of pain messages to the brain (Melzack & Katz, 2013; Melzack & Wall, 1965, 1983). Small spinal cord nerve fibers conduct most pain signals, so an injury opens the gate and we feel pain. Large-fiber activity (through massage, electrical stimulation, or acupuncture) can close the pain gate.

But pain is not merely a physical event in which injured nerves send impulses to a specific brain or spinal cord area—like pulling on a rope to ring a bell. The brain can actually create pain, as it does in *phantom limb sensations* after a limb amputation. Without normal sensory input, the brain may misinterpret other neural activity. As a dreamer may see with eyes closed, so 7 in 10 such people feel pain or movement in limbs that no longer exist (Melzack, 1992, 2005).

Phantoms may haunt other senses, too. People with hearing loss often experience the sound of silence: *tinnitus*. This phantom sound of ringing in the ears is accompanied by auditory brain activity (Sedley et al., 2015). Those who lose vision to glaucoma, cataracts, diabetes, or macular degeneration may experience phantom sights—nonthreatening hallucinations (Ramachandran & Blakeslee, 1998). And damage to nerves in the systems for tasting and smelling can give rise to phantom tastes or smells, such as ice water that seems sickeningly sweet or fresh air that reeks of rotten food (Goode, 1999). The point to remember: *We see, hear, taste, smell, and feel pain with our brain, which can sense even without functioning senses.*

Psychological Influences One powerful influence on our perception of pain is the attention we focus on it. Athletes, focused on winning, may perceive pain differently and play through it.

We also seem to edit our *memories* of pain. The pain we experience may not be the pain we remember. In experiments, and after painful medical procedures or childbirth, people overlook how long a pain lasted. Their memory snapshots instead record two points: the *peak* moment of pain, and how much pain they felt at the *end*. In one experiment, people put one hand in painfully cold water for 60 seconds, and then the other hand in the same painfully cold water for 60 seconds, followed by a slightly less painful 30 seconds more (Kahneman et al., 1993). Which experience would you expect they recalled as most painful?

Curiously, when asked which trial they would prefer to repeat, most preferred the longer trial, with more net pain—but less pain at the end. Physicians have used this principle with patients undergoing colon exams—lengthening the discomfort by a minute, but lessening its intensity at the end (Kahneman, 1999). Patients experiencing this taper-down treatment later recalled the exam as less painful than did those whose pain ended abruptly. Endings matter.

Social-Cultural Influences Pain is a product of our attention, our expectations, and our culture (Gatchel et al., 2007; Reimann et al., 2010). Not surprisingly, then, our perception of pain varies with our social situation and our cultural traditions. We tend to feel more pain when others also seem to be experiencing pain (Symbaluk et al., 1997). The pain in sprain is mainly in the brain. When people feel empathy for another's pain, their own brain activity partly mirrors the activity of the actual brain in pain (Singer et al., 2004).

Controlling Pain If pain is where body meets mind—if pain is both a physical and a psychological event—then it should be treatable both physically and psychologically. Depending on the symptoms, pain control therapies may include drugs, surgery, acupuncture, electrical stimulation, massage, exercise, hypnosis, relaxation training, meditation, and thought distraction.

We have some built-in pain controls, too. Our brain releases a natural painkiller—*endorphins*—in response to severe pain or even vigorous exercise. Thus, when we are distracted from pain and soothed by endorphin release, the pain we experience may be greatly reduced. People who carry a gene that boosts the normal supply of endorphins are less bothered by pain, and their brain is less responsive to it (Zubieta et al., 2003). Others, who carry a gene that disrupts the neural pain circuit, may be unable to experience pain (Cox et al., 2006). Such discoveries point the way toward future pain medications that mimic these genetic effects.

"Pain is increased by attending to it."
—Charles Darwin, *The Expression of the Emotions in Man and Animals,* 1872

Reinhold Matay/AP Images

Distracted from the pain After a tackle in the first half of a competitive game, Mohammed Ali Khan (here playing for BK Häcken in white) said he "had a bit of pain" but thought it was "just a bruise." With his attention focused on the game, he played on. In the second half, he was surprised to learn that his leg was broken.

Placebos Even *placebos* can help, by dampening the central nervous system's attention and responses to painful experiences—mimicking painkilling drugs (Eippert et al., 2009; Wager & Atlas, 2013). After being injected in the jaw with a stinging saltwater solution, men in one experiment received a placebo. They had been told it would relieve pain, and it did—they immediately felt better. "Nothing" worked. The men's belief in the fake painkiller triggered their brain to respond by dispensing endorphins, as revealed by activity in an area that releases the natural painkillers (Scott et al., 2007; Zubieta et al., 2005).

Distraction When endorphins combine with distraction, amazing things can happen. Have you ever had a health care professional suggest that you focus on a pleasant image ("Think of a warm, comfortable environment") or perform some task ("Count backward by 3s")? Drawing attention away from the painful stimulation is an effective way to activate brain pathways that decrease pain and increase tolerance (Edwards et al., 2009). For burn victims receiving painful wound care, an even more effective distraction is escaping into a computer-generated 3-D world. Functional MRI (fMRI) scans reveal that playing in virtual reality reduces the brain's pain-related activity (Hoffman, 2004).

Hypnosis Better yet, research suggests, maximize pain relief by combining a placebo with distraction (Buhle et al., 2012), and amplify their effects with **hypnosis.** Imagine you are about to be hypnotized. The hypnotist invites you to sit back, fix your gaze on a spot high on the wall, and relax. You hear a quiet, low voice suggest, "Your eyes are growing tired . . . Your eyelids are becoming heavy . . . now heavier and heavier . . . They are beginning to close . . . You are becoming more deeply relaxed . . . Your breathing is now deep and regular . . . Your muscles are becoming more and more relaxed. Your whole body is beginning to feel like lead." After a few minutes of this *hypnotic induction,* you may experience hypnosis.

Hypnotists have no magical mind-control power; they merely focus

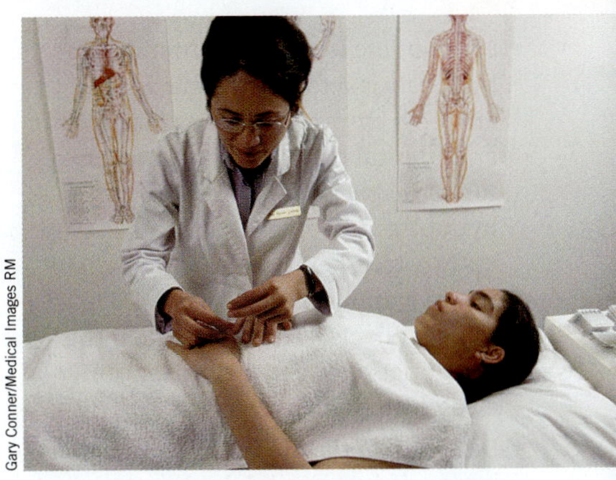

Gary Conner/Medical Images RM

Acupuncture: A jab well done This acupuncturist is attempting to help this woman gain relief from back pain by using needles on points of the patient's hand.

people's attention on certain images or behaviors. To some extent, we are all open to suggestion. But highly hypnotizable people—such as the 20 percent who can carry out a suggestion not to react to an open bottle of stinky ammonia—are especially suggestible and imaginative (Barnier & McConkey, 2004; Silva & Kirsch, 1992). Their brain also displays altered activity when under hypnosis (Jiang et al., 2016).

Can hypnosis relieve pain? *Yes.* In surgical experiments, hypnotized patients have required less medication, recovered sooner, and left the hospital earlier than unhypnotized control patients (Askay & Patterson, 2007; Hammond, 2008; Spiegel, 2007). Nearly 10 percent of us can become so deeply hypnotized that even major surgery can be performed without anesthesia. Half of us can gain at least some relief from hypnosis. The surgical use of hypnosis has flourished in Europe, where one Belgian medical team has performed more than 5000 surgeries with a combination of hypnosis, local anesthesia, and a mild sedative (Song, 2006). Hypnosis has also lessened some forms of chronic and disability-related pain (Adachi et al., 2014; Bowker & Dorstyn, 2016).

But how does hypnosis work? Psychologists have proposed two explanations.

hypnosis a social interaction in which one person (the hypnotist) suggests to another person (the subject) that certain perceptions, feelings, thoughts, or behaviors will spontaneously occur.

- ***Social influence theory*** contends that hypnosis is a form of social influence—a by-product of normal social and mental processes (Lynn et al., 1990, 2015; Spanos & Coe, 1992). In this view, hypnotized people, like actors caught up in a role, begin to feel and behave in ways appropriate for "good hypnotic subjects." They may allow the hypnotist to direct their attention away from pain.
- ***Dissociation theory*** proposes that hypnosis is a special dual-processing state of *dissociation*—a split between normal sensations and conscious awareness. Dissociation theory seeks to explain why, when no one is watching, hypnotized people may carry out **posthypnotic suggestions** (which are made during hypnosis but carried out after the person is no longer hypnotized) (Perugini et al., 1998). It also offers an explanation for why people hypnotized for pain relief may show brain activity in areas that receive sensory information, but not in areas that normally process pain-related information (Rainville et al., 1997).

Selective attention may also be at work (Chapter 2). Brain scans show that hypnosis increases activity in the brain's attention systems (Oakley & Halligan, 2013). Thus, hypnosis doesn't block the sensory input itself, but it may block our attention to those stimuli. This helps explain why injured soldiers, caught up in battle, may feel little or no pain until they reach safety.

IMPROVE YOUR EVERYDAY LIFE

What methods of pain control do you usually turn to when you need it? Has learning about these ways to control pain given you some new ideas about other effective strategies to try?

RETRIEVE & REMEMBER

ANSWERS IN APPENDIX E

15. Which of the following has NOT been proven to reduce pain?
   a. Distraction
   b. Hypnosis
   c. Phantom limb sensations
   d. Endorphins

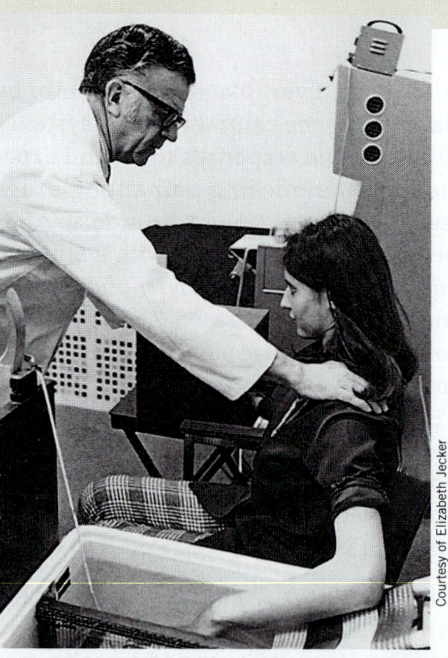

Courtesy of Elizabeth Jecker

Dissociation or social influence? This hypnotized woman being tested by famous researcher Ernest Hilgard showed no pain when her arm was placed in an ice bath. But asked to press a key if some part of her felt the pain, she did so. To Hilgard (1986, 1992), this was evidence of dissociation, or divided consciousness. The social influence perspective, however, maintains that people responding this way are caught up in playing the role of "good subject."

TASTE

LOQ 5-20 In what ways are our senses of taste and smell similar, and how do they differ?

Like touch, *gustation*—our sense of taste—involves several basic sensations. Taste's sensations were once thought to be *sweet, sour, salty,* and *bitter,* with all others stemming from a mixture of these four (McBurney & Gent, 1979). Then, as researchers searched for specialized nerve fibers for those four taste sensations, they discovered a fifth sensation—the savory, meaty taste of *umami*. You've likely experienced umami as the flavor enhancer monosodium glutamate (MSG).

Tastes give us pleasure, but they also help us survive. Pleasant tastes attracted our ancestors to foods rich in energy or protein (see **TABLE 5.2**). Unpleasant tastes warned them away from new foods that might be toxic. The taste preferences of today's 2- to 6-year-olds reflect this inherited biological wisdom. At this age, children are typically fussy eaters and often turn away from new meat dishes or bitter-tasting vegetables, such as spinach and brussels sprouts (Cooke et al., 2003). But learning—another tool in our early ancestors' survival kit—comes to the aid of frustrated parents across the globe. When given repeated small tastes of disliked new foods, children usually learn to accept them (Wardle et al., 2003). We come to like what we eat. German babies who were bottle-fed vanilla-flavored milk became adults with a striking preference for vanilla flavoring (Haller et al., 1999).

TABLE 5.2 The Survival Functions of Basic Tastes

Taste	Indicates
Sweet	Energy source
Salty	Sodium essential to physiological processes
Sour	Potentially toxic acid
Bitter	Potential poisons
Umami	Proteins to grow and repair tissue

Taste is a chemical sense. Look into a mirror and you'll see little bumps on the top and sides of your tongue. Each bump contains 200 or more taste buds. Each taste bud contains a pore that catches food chemicals and released neurotransmitters (Roper & Chaudhari, 2017). In each taste bud pore, 50 to 100 taste receptor cells project antenna-like hairs that sense food molecules. Some receptors respond mostly to sweet-tasting molecules, others to salty-, sour-, umami-, or bitter-tasting ones. Each receptor transmits its message to a matching partner cell in your brain's temporal lobe (Barretto et al., 2015).

It doesn't take much to trigger a taste response. If a stream of water is pumped across your tongue, the addition of a concentrated salty or sweet taste for only one-tenth of a second will get your attention (Kelling & Halpern, 1983). When a friend asks for "just a taste" of your sports drink, you can squeeze off your straw after a mere instant.

Taste receptors reproduce themselves every week or two, so if you burn your

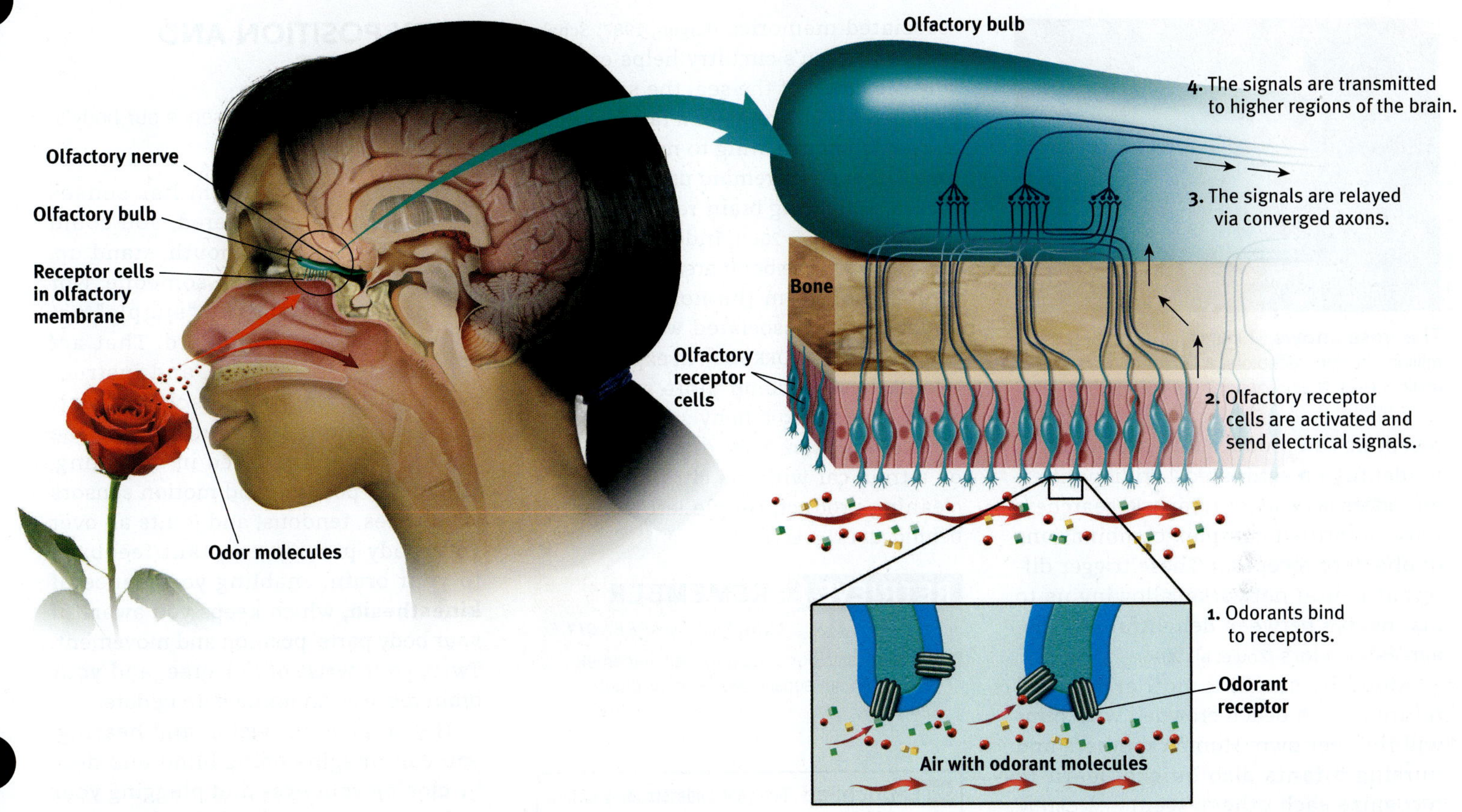
Olfactory nerve
Olfactory bulb
Receptor cells in olfactory membrane
Odor molecules
Olfactory bulb
4. The signals are transmitted to higher regions of the brain.
3. The signals are relayed via converged axons.
Bone
Olfactory receptor cells
2. Olfactory receptor cells are activated and send electrical signals.
1. Odorants bind to receptors.
Odorant receptor
Air with odorant molecules

FIGURE 5.30 The sense of smell To smell a flower, airborne molecules of its fragrance must reach receptors at the top of your nose. By sniffing, you swirl air up to those receptors, enhancing the aroma. The receptor cells send messages to the brain's olfactory bulb, which then sends them to the temporal lobe's primary smell cortex and to the parts of the limbic system involved in memory and emotion.

tongue, it hardly matters. However, as you grow older, it may matter more, because the number of taste buds in your mouth will decrease, as will your taste sensitivity (Cowart, 1981). (No wonder adults enjoy strong-tasting foods that children resist.) Smoking and alcohol can speed up the loss of taste buds.

There's more to taste than meets the tongue. Our expectations also influence what we taste. When told a sausage roll was "vegetarian," nonvegetarian people in one experiment judged it inferior to its identical partner labeled "meat" (Allen et al., 2008). In another experiment, hearing that a wine cost $90 rather than its real $10 price made it taste better and triggered more activity in a brain area that responds to pleasant experiences (Plassman et al., 2008).

SMELL

Inhale, exhale. Between birth's first inhale and death's last exhale, an average 500 million breaths of life-sustaining air bathe human nostrils in a stream of scent-laden molecules. The resulting experience of smell—*olfaction*—is strikingly intimate. With every breath, you inhale something of whatever or whoever it is you smell.

Smell, like taste, is a chemical sense. We smell something when molecules of a substance carried in the air reach a tiny cluster of receptor cells at the top of each nasal cavity (**FIGURE 5.30**). These 20 million olfactory receptors, waving like sea anemones on a reef, respond selectively—to the aroma of a cake baking, to a wisp of smoke, to a friend's fragrance. Instantly, they alert the brain through their axon fibers.

Being part of an old, primitive sense, olfactory neurons bypass the brain's sensory control center, the thalamus. Eons before our cerebral cortex had fully evolved, our mammalian ancestors sniffed for food—and for predators. They also smelled molecules called *pheromones*, secreted by other members of their species. Some pheromones serve as sexual attractants.

Odor molecules come in many shapes and sizes—so many, in fact, that it takes hundreds of different receptors, designed by a large family of genes, to recognize these molecules (Miller, 2004). We do not have one distinct receptor for each detectable odor. Instead, receptors on the surface of nasal cavity neurons work in different combinations to send messages to the brain, activating different patterns in the olfactory cortex (Buck & Axel, 1991). As the English alphabet's 26 letters can combine to form many words, so olfactory

posthypnotic suggestion a suggestion, made during a hypnosis session, to be carried out after the subject is no longer hypnotized; used by some clinicians to help control undesired symptoms and behaviors.

LAYNE BAILEY/AP Images

The nose knows Humans have some 20 million olfactory receptors. A bloodhound has 220 million (Herz, 2007).

receptors can produce different patterns to identify an estimated 1 trillion different odors (Bushdid et al., 2014). Researchers have identified complex combinations of olfactory receptors. These trigger different neural networks, allowing us to distinguish between delightful and disagreeable odors (Zou et al., 2016).

Aided by smell, a mother fur seal returning to a beach crowded with pups will find her own. Human mothers and nursing infants also quickly learn to recognize each other's scents (McCarthy, 1986). When women catch a whiff of their romantic partner's scent, their stress hormone levels drop (Hofer et al., 2018). And the brain knows what the nose doesn't like (Cook et al., 2017; Zou et al., 2016). When mice sniff a predator's scent, their brain instinctively sends signals to stress-related neurons (Kondoh et al., 2016). But a smell's appeal—or lack of it—depends in part on learned associations (Herz, 2001). In North America, people associate the smell of wintergreen with candy and gum, and they tend to like it. In Britain, wintergreen is often associated with medicine, and people find it less appealing.

Our sense of smell is less impressive than our senses of seeing and hearing. Looking out across a garden, we see its forms and colors in wonderful detail and hear a variety of birds singing. Yet we miss some of a garden's scents without sticking our nose directly into the blossoms. We also have trouble recalling odors by name. But we have a remarkable capacity to recognize long-forgotten smells and their associated memories (Engen, 1987; Schab, 1991). Our brain's circuitry helps explain why the smell of the sea, the scent of a perfume, or the aroma of a favorite relative's kitchen can bring to mind a happy time. Other odors remind us of traumatic events, activating brain regions related to fear (Kadohisa, 2013). Indeed, a hotline runs between the brain area that receives information from the nose and other brain centers associated with memory and emotion (**FIGURE 5.31**). In experiments, people have become more suspicious when exposed to a fishy smell (Lee et al., 2015; Lee & Schwarz, 2012). And when riding on a train car with the citrus scent of a cleaning product, people left less trash behind (de Lange et al., 2012).

RETRIEVE & REMEMBER

ANSWERS IN APPENDIX E

16. How does our system for sensing smell differ from our sensory systems for touch and taste?

LaunchPad Test your understanding of how we smell by engaging online with *Concept Practice: Sense of Smell.*

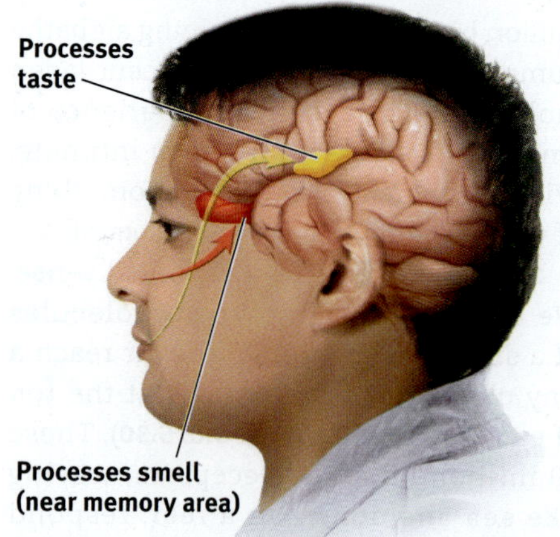

FIGURE 5.31 Taste, smell, and memory Information from the taste buds (yellow arrow) travels to an area between the frontal and temporal lobes of the brain. It registers in an area not far from where the brain receives information from our sense of smell, which interacts with taste. The brain's circuitry for smell (red area) also connects with areas involved in memory storage, which helps explain why a smell can trigger a memory.

BODY POSITION AND MOVEMENT

LOQ 5-21 How do we sense our body's position and movement?

Using only the five familiar senses we have so far considered, you could not put food in your mouth, stand up, or reach out and touch someone. Nor could you perform the "simple" act of taking one step forward. That act requires feedback from, and instructions to, some 200 muscles, and it engages brain power that exceeds the mental activity involved in reasoning. Millions of position and motion sensors in muscles, tendons, and joints all over your body provide constant feedback to your brain, enabling your sense of **kinesthesia,** which keeps you aware of your body parts' position and movement. Twist your wrist one degree, and your brain receives an immediate update.

If you have full vision and hearing, you can imagine being blind and deaf by closing your eyes and plugging your ears to experience the dark silence. But what would it be like to live without the benefits of kinesthesia? Ian Waterman of Hampshire, England, knows. At age 19, Waterman contracted a rare viral infection that destroyed the nerves enabling his sense of light touch and of body position and movement. People with this condition report feeling disconnected from their body, as though it is dead, not real, not theirs (Sacks, 1985). With long practice, Waterman has learned to walk and eat—by visually focusing on his limbs and directing them accordingly. But if the lights went out, he would crumple to the floor (Azar, 1998).

Vision interacts with kinesthesia for you, too. If you are able, stand with your right heel in front of your left toes. Easy. Now close your eyes and try again. Did you wobble?

A companion **vestibular sense** works hand in hand with kinesthesia to monitor your head's (and thus your body's) position and movement. Two structures in your inner ear join forces to help you maintain your balance. The first, your fluid-filled *semicircular canals,* look like a three-dimensional pretzel (Figure 5.28a). The second structure is the pair of calcium-crystal–filled *vestibular sacs.* When your head rotates or tilts, the movement of these organs stimulates hair-like receptors, which send messages to your cerebellum at the back of your brain, enabling you to sense your body position and maintain your balance.

If you twirl around and then come to an abrupt halt, it takes a few seconds for the fluid in your semicircular canals and for your kinesthetic receptors to return to their neutral state. The aftereffect fools your dizzy brain with the sensation that you're still spinning. This illustrates a principle underlying perceptual illusions: *Mechanisms that normally give us an accurate experience of the world can, under special conditions, fool us.* Understanding how we get fooled provides clues to how our perceptual system works.

Your vestibular sense is speedy. You might try this: Hold one of your thumbs in front of your face, then move it rapidly right to left and back. Notice how your vision isn't fast enough to track your thumb clearly. Now hold your thumb still and swivel your *head* from left to right. Surprise! Your thumb stays clear—because your vestibular system, which is tracking your head position, speedily moves the eyes. Head moves right, eyes move left. Vision is fast, but the vestibular sense is faster.

© Robert Kanavel

Bodies in space This high school competitive cheer team shows that by using information from the inner ears, the brain expertly monitors body position.

RETRIEVE & REMEMBER

ANSWERS IN APPENDIX E

17. Where are kinesthetic receptors and the vestibular sense receptors located?

© Albrecht Weisser/Westend61/Corbis

FIGURE 5.32 Sensory interaction Seeing the speaker forming the words in video chats makes those words easier to understand for hard-of-hearing listeners (Knight, 2004).

Sensory Interaction

LOQ 5-22 How does *sensory interaction* influence our perceptions, and what is *embodied cognition?*

We have seen that vision and kinesthesia interact. Actually, all our senses eavesdrop on one another (Rosenblum, 2013). This is **sensory interaction** at work. One sense can influence another.

Consider how smell sticks its nose into the business of taste. Hold your nose, close your eyes, and have someone feed you various foods. You may be unable to tell a slice of apple from a chunk of raw potato. A piece of steak may taste like cardboard. Without their smells, a cup of cold coffee and a glass of red wine may seem the same. A big part of taste is right under your nose. We normally inhale the aroma—which is why food tastes bland when you have a bad cold. Smell enhances our taste: A strawberry odor intensifies our perception of a drink's sweetness. Even touch can influence taste. Depending on its texture, a potato chip "tastes" fresh or stale (Smith, 2011). Smell + texture + taste = flavor. Yet flavor *feels* located in the mouth (Stevenson, 2014).

Hearing and vision may similarly interact. A tiny flicker of light is more easily seen if it is paired with a short burst of sound (Kayser, 2007). The reverse is also true: Soft sounds are more easily heard when paired with a visual cue (**FIGURE 5.32**). If I [DM], a person with hearing loss, watch a video with on-screen captions, I have no trouble hearing the words I see. But if I then decide I don't need the captions, and turn them off, I will quickly realize I do need them. The eyes guide the ears.

So our senses interact. But what happens if they disagree? What if our eyes *see* a speaker form one sound but our ears *hear* another sound? Surprise: Our brain may perceive a third sound that blends both inputs. Seeing mouth movements for *ga* while hearing *ba,* we may perceive *da.* This is known as the *McGurk effect,* after one of its discoverers (McGurk & MacDonald, 1976). For all of us, lip reading is part of hearing.

We have seen that our perceptions have two main ingredients: Our bottom-up sensations and our top-down cognitions (such as expectations, attitudes, thoughts, and memories). But

kinesthesia [kin-ehs-THEE-zhuh] our movement sense—our system for sensing the position and movement of individual body parts.

vestibular sense our sense of balance—our sense of body movement and position that enables our sense of balance.

sensory interaction the principle that one sense may influence another, as when the smell of food influences its taste.

TABLE 5.3 Summarizing the Senses

Sensory System	Source	Receptors	Key Brain Areas
Vision	Light waves striking the eye	Rods and cones in the retina	Occipital lobes
Hearing	Sound waves striking the outer ear	Cochlear hair cells (cilia) in the inner ear	Temporal lobes
Touch	Pressure, warmth, cold, harmful chemicals	Receptors (including pain-sensitive *nociceptors*), mostly in the skin, which detect pressure, warmth, cold, and pain	Somatosensory cortex
Taste	Chemical molecules in the mouth	Basic taste receptors for sweet, sour, salty, bitter, and umami	Frontal/temporal lobe border
Smell	Chemical molecules breathed in through the nose	Millions of receptors at top of nasal cavities	Olfactory bulb
Body position—kinesthesia	Any change in position of a body part, interacting with vision	Kinesthetic sensors in joints, tendons, and muscles	Cerebellum
Body movement—vestibular sense	Movement of fluids in the inner ear caused by head/body movement	Hair-like receptors in the ears' semicircular canals and vestibular sacs	Cerebellum

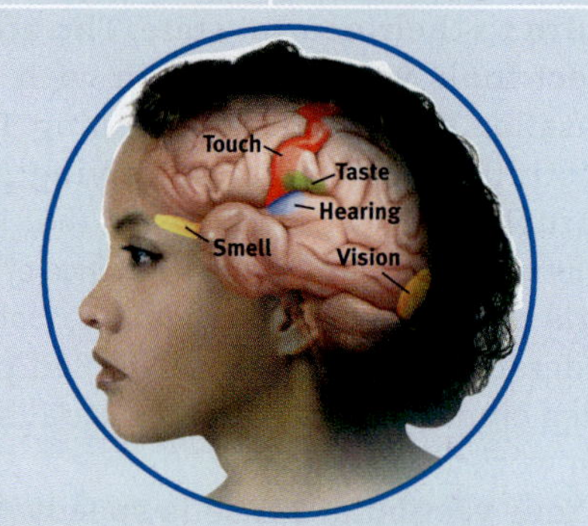

let's return to our starting point in this chapter. In everyday life, sensation and perception are two points on a continuum. We think from within a body. It's not surprising, then, that the brain circuits processing our bodily sensations may sometimes interact with brain circuits responsible for cognition. The result is **embodied cognition.** Here are two examples from some playful experiments.

- ***Judgments may mimic body sensations.*** Sitting at a wobbly desk and chair can make relationships seem less stable (Forest et al., 2015; Kille et al., 2013).
- ***Physical warmth may promote social warmth.*** After holding a warm drink rather than a cold one, people were more likely to rate someone more warmly, feel closer to them, and behave more generously (IJzerman & Semin, 2009; Williams & Bargh, 2008). On days when people feel physically warm, they feel socially warm and friendly (Fetterman et al., 2018). Want to perceive others and yourself as warmer? Try hot tea instead of iced tea.

As we attempt to decipher our world, our brain blends inputs from multiple channels. But in a few rare individuals, the brain circuits for two or more senses become joined in a condition called *synesthesia,* where one sort of sensation (such as hearing sound) produces another (such as seeing color). Early in life, "exuberant neural connectivity" produces some random associations among the senses, which later are normally—but not always—pruned (Wagner & Dobkins, 2011). Equipped with a brain that blends sensations, hearing music may activate color-sensitive cortex regions and trigger a sensation of color (Brang et al., 2008; Hubbard et al., 2005). Seeing the number 3 may evoke a taste or color sensation (Ward, 2003).

* * *

For a summary of our sensory systems, see **TABLE 5.3.**

IN YOUR EVERYDAY LIFE

When have you experienced a feeling that you think could be explained by embodied cognition?

LaunchPad Are you wondering how researchers test these kinds of questions? Play the role of researcher by engaging online with the activity: *How Would You Know If a Cup of Coffee Can Warm Up Relationships?*

ESP—Perception Without Sensation?

LOQ 5-23 What are the claims of ESP, and what have most research psychologists concluded after putting these claims to the test?

The river of perception is fed by streams of sensation, cognition, and emotion. If perception is the product of these three sources, what can we say about **extrasensory perception (ESP),** which claims that perception can occur *without* sensory input?

The answer depends in part on who you ask. Nearly half of all Americans surveyed believe we are capable of extrasensory perception and 41 percent believe in psychics (Gecewicz, 2018; Kim et al., 2015). The most testable and, for this chapter, most relevant ESP claims are

- *telepathy:* mind-to-mind communication.

- *clairvoyance:* perceiving remote events, such as a house on fire across the country.
- *precognition:* perceiving future events, such as an unexpected death in the next month.

Closely linked to these ESP claims is *psychokinesis,* or "mind moving matter," such as using mind power alone to raise a table or control the roll of a die. (The claim, also called *telekinesis,* is illustrated by the wry request, "Will all those who believe in psychokinesis please raise my hand?") In Britain, psychologists created a "mind machine" to see if festival visitors could influence or predict a coin toss (Wiseman & Greening, 2002). Using a touch-sensitive screen, people were given four attempts to call heads or tails, playing against a computer. By the time the experiment ended, nearly 28,000 people had predicted 110,959 tosses—with 49.8 percent correct.

Most research psychologists and scientists are skeptical of ESP claims. No greedy—or charitable—psychic has been able to make billions on the stock market. Where were the psychics the day before the 9/11 terrorist attacks? Why, despite a $50 million reward, could no psychic help locate Osama bin Laden afterward? And why, when the Chilean government consulted four psychics after a 2010 mine collapse trapped 33 miners, did those psychics sorrowfully decide "they're all dead" (Kraul, 2010)? Imagine their surprise when all 33 miners were rescued 69 days later.

What about the hundreds of visions offered by psychics working with the police? These have been no more accurate than guesses made by others (Nickell, 1994, 2005; Radford, 2010; Reiser, 1982). But their sheer volume increases the odds of an occasional correct guess, which psychics can then report to the media.

Are everyday people's "visions" any more accurate? Do our dreams predict the future, or do they only seem to do so when we recall or reconstruct them in light of what has already happened? Are our remembered visions merely revisions? After famed aviator Charles Lindbergh's baby son was kidnapped and murdered in 1932, but before the body was discovered, two psychologists invited people to report their dreams about the child (Murray & Wheeler, 1937). How many replied? 1300. How many accurately saw the child dead? 65. How many also correctly anticipated the body's location—buried among trees? Only 4. Although this number was surely no better than chance, to those 4 dreamers, the accuracy of their apparent prior knowledge must have seemed uncanny.

Given countless daily events, and given enough days, some stunning coincidences are sure to occur. By one careful estimate, chance alone would predict that more than a thousand times per day, someone on Earth will think of another person and then, within the next five minutes, learn of that person's death (Charpak & Broch, 2004). Thus, when explaining an astonishing event, we should "give chance a chance" (Lilienfeld, 2009). With enough time and enough people, the improbable becomes inevitable.

> A headline you've never seen: "Psychic wins lottery."

When faced with claims of mind reading or out-of-body travel or communication with the dead, how can we separate fiction from strange-but-true fact? Psychological science offers a simple answer: *Test claims to see if they work.* If they do, so much the better for the ideas. If they don't, so much the better for our skepticism.

How might we test ESP claims in a controlled, reproducible experiment? An experiment differs from a staged demonstration. In the laboratory, the experimenter controls what the "psychic" sees and hears. On stage, the "psychic" controls what the audience sees and hears.

Daryl Bem, a respected social psychologist, once joked that "a psychic is an actor playing the role of a psychic" (1984). Yet this one-time skeptic reignited hopes for scientific evidence of ESP with nine experiments that seemed to show people anticipating future events (Bem, 2011). In one, people guessed when an erotic scene would appear on a screen in one of two randomly selected positions. Participants guessed right 53.1 percent of the time, beating chance by a small but statistically significant margin.

Despite Bem's research surviving critical reviews by a top-tier journal, critics found the methods "badly flawed" (Alcock, 2011) or the statistical analyses "biased" (Wagenmakers et al., 2011). Others predicted the results could not be replicated by "independent and skeptical researchers" (Helfand, 2011).

Anticipating such skepticism, Bem made his research materials available to anyone who wishes to replicate his studies. Multiple attempts have met with minimal success, and the debate continues (Bem et al., 2014; Galak et al., 2012; Ritchie et al., 2012; Wagenmakers, 2014). Regardless, science is doing its work. It has been open to a finding that challenges its assumptions. Through follow-up research, it has assessed the reliability and validity of that finding. And that is how science sifts crazy-sounding ideas, leaving most on the historical waste heap while occasionally surprising us.

Will you marry me, live happily for 3 years, become bored, pretend to be taking a pottery class but actually be having an affair, then agree to go to marriage counseling to stay together for the sake of our hyperactive son, Derrick?

WHEN PSYCHICS PROPOSE

embodied cognition the influence of bodily sensations, gestures, and other states on cognitive preferences and judgments.

extrasensory perception (ESP) the controversial claim that perception can occur apart from sensory input; includes telepathy, clairvoyance, and precognition.

For 19 years, one skeptic, magician James Randi, offered $1 million "to anyone who proves a genuine psychic power under proper observing conditions" (Randi, 1999; Thompson, 2010). French, Australian, and Indian groups have made similar offers of up to 200,000 euros (CFI, 2003). Large as these sums are, the scientific seal of approval would be worth far more. To silence those who say there is no ESP, one need only produce a single person who can demonstrate a single, reproducible ESP event. (To silence those who say pigs can't talk would take but one talking pig.) So far, no such person has emerged.

***

Most of us will never know what it is like to see colorful music, to be incapable of feeling pain, or to be unable to recognize the faces of friends and family. But within ordinary sensation and perception lies much that is truly extraordinary. More than a century of research has revealed many secrets of sensation and perception. For future generations of researchers, though, there remain profound and genuine mysteries to solve.

RETRIEVE & REMEMBER

ANSWERS IN APPENDIX E

18. If an ESP event occurred under controlled conditions, what would be the next best step to confirm that ESP really exists?

LaunchPad Do you think you might have ESP? Test your skills by engaging online with *Assess Your Strengths: ESP and Critical Thinking.*

CHAPTER 5 REVIEW Sensation and Perception

LEARNING OBJECTIVES

TEST YOURSELF Answer these repeated Learning Objective Questions on your own (before checking the answers in Appendix D) to improve your retention of the concepts (McDaniel et al., 2009, 2015).

Basic Concepts of Sensation and Perception

5-1: What are *sensation* and *perception?* What do we mean by *bottom-up processing* and *top-down processing?*

5-2: What three steps are basic to all of our sensory systems?

5-3: How do *absolute thresholds* and *difference thresholds* differ?

5-4: How are we affected by subliminal stimuli?

5-5: What is the function of sensory adaptation?

5-6: How do our expectations, contexts, motivations, and emotions influence our perceptions?

Vision: Sensory and Perceptual Processing

5-7: What are the characteristics of the energy we see as visible light? What structures in the eye help focus that energy?

5-8: How do the rods and cones process information, and what path does information take from the eye to the brain?

5-9: How do we perceive color in the world around us?

5-10: What are *feature detectors,* and what do they do?

5-11: How does the brain use parallel processing to construct visual perceptions?

5-12: What was the main message of Gestalt psychology, and how do *figure-ground* and *grouping* principles help us perceive forms?

5-13: How do we use binocular and monocular cues to see in three dimensions, and how do we perceive motion?

5-14: How do perceptual constancies help us construct meaningful perceptions?

5-15: What does research on restored vision, sensory restriction, and perceptual adaptation reveal about the effects of experience on perception?

The Other Senses

5-16: What are the characteristics of the air pressure waves that we hear as sound?

5-17: How does the ear transform sound energy into neural messages, and how do we locate sounds?

5-18: What are the four basic touch sensations, and how do we sense touch?

5-19: What biological, psychological, and social-cultural influences affect our experience of pain? How do placebos, distraction, and hypnosis help control pain?

5-20: In what ways are our senses of taste and smell similar, and how do they differ?

5-21: How do we sense our body's position and movement?

Sensory Interaction

5-22: How does *sensory interaction* influence our perceptions, and what is *embodied cognition?*

ESP—Perception Without Sensation?

5-23: What are the claims of ESP, and what have most research psychologists concluded after putting these claims to the test?

TERMS AND CONCEPTS TO REMEMBER

TEST YOURSELF Write down the definition in your own words, then check your answer.

sensation, *p.* 133
sensory receptors, *p.* 133
perception, *p.* 133
bottom-up processing, *p.* 133
top-down processing, *p.* 133
transduction, *p.* 133
absolute threshold, *p.* 133
subliminal, *p.* 133
priming, *p.* 135
difference threshold, *p.* 135
Weber's law, *p.* 135
sensory adaptation, *p.* 135
perceptual set, *p.* 137
wavelength, *p.* 139
hue, *p.* 139
intensity, *p.* 139
retina, *p.* 139
rods, *p.* 141
cones, *p.* 141
optic nerve, *p.* 141
blind spot, *p.* 141
Young-Helmholtz trichromatic (three-color) theory, *p.* 143
opponent-process theory, *p.* 143
feature detectors, *p.* 143
parallel processing, *p.* 143
gestalt, *p.* 145
figure-ground, *p.* 145
grouping, *p.* 145
depth perception, *p.* 145
visual cliff, *p.* 147
binocular cue, *p.* 147
retinal disparity, *p.* 147
monocular cue, *p.* 147
perceptual constancy, *p.* 149
perceptual adaptation, *p.* 149
audition, *p.* 151
frequency, *p.* 151
pitch, *p.* 151
middle ear, *p.* 151
cochlea [KOHK-lee-uh], *p.* 151
inner ear, *p.* 151
sensorineural hearing loss, *p.* 151
conduction hearing loss, *p.* 153
cochlear implant, *p.* 153
hypnosis, *p.* 155
posthypnotic suggestion, *p.* 157
kinesthesia [kin-ehs-THEE-zhuh], *p.* 159
vestibular sense, *p.* 159
sensory interaction, *p.* 159
embodied cognition, *p.* 161
extrasensory perception (ESP), *p.* 161

CHAPTER TEST

TEST YOURSELF Answer the following questions on your own first, then check your answers in Appendix E.

1. Sensation is to ________ as perception is to ________.
a. absolute threshold; difference threshold
b. bottom-up processing; top-down processing
c. interpretation; detection
d. grouping; priming

2. The process by which we organize and interpret sensory information is called ________.

3. Subliminal stimuli are
a. too weak to be processed by the brain.
b. consciously perceived more than 50 percent of the time.
c. always strong enough to affect our behavior at least 75 percent of the time.
d. below our absolute threshold for conscious awareness.

4. Another term for *difference threshold* is the ________ ________ ________.

5. Weber's law states that for a difference to be perceived, two stimuli must differ by
a. a fixed or constant energy amount.
b. a constant minimum percentage.
c. a constantly changing amount.
d. more than 7 percent.

6. Sensory adaptation helps us focus on
a. visual stimuli.
b. auditory stimuli.
c. constant features of the environment.
d. important changes in the environment.

7. Our perceptual set influences what we perceive. This mental tendency reflects our
a. experiences, assumptions, and expectations.
b. sensory adaptation.
c. priming ability.
d. difference thresholds.

8. The characteristic of light that determines the color we experience, such as blue or green, is ________.

9. The amplitude of a light wave determines our perception of ________.
a. brightness.
b. color.
c. meaning.
d. distance.

10. The blind spot in your retina is located where
a. there are rods but no cones.
b. there are cones but no rods.
c. the optic nerve leaves the eye.
d. the bipolar cells meet the ganglion cells.

11. Cones are the eye's receptor cells that are especially sensitive to ________ light and are responsible for our ________ vision.
a. bright; black-and-white
b. dim; color
c. bright; color
d. dim; black-and-white

12. Two theories together account for color vision. The Young-Helmholtz trichromatic theory shows that the eye contains ________, and Hering's theory accounts for the nervous system's having ________.
   a. opposing retinal processes; three pairs of color receptors
   b. opponent-process cells; three types of color receptors
   c. three pairs of color receptors; opposing retinal processes
   d. three types of color receptors; opponent-process cells
13. What mental processes allow you to perceive a lemon as yellow?
14. The cells in the visual cortex that respond to certain lines, edges, and angles are called ________ ________.
15. The brain's ability to process many aspects of an object or a problem simultaneously is called ________ ________.
16. In listening to a concert, you attend to the solo instrument and perceive the orchestra as accompaniment. This illustrates the organizing principle of
   a. figure-ground.
   b. shape constancy.
   c. grouping.
   d. depth perception.
17. Our tendencies to fill in the gaps and to perceive a pattern as continuous are two different examples of the organizing principle called
   a. interposition.
   b. depth perception.
   c. shape constancy.
   d. grouping.
18. The visual cliff experiments suggest that
   a. infants have not yet developed depth perception.
   b. crawling human infants and very young animals perceive depth.
   c. we have no way of knowing whether infants can perceive depth.
   d. unlike other species, humans are able to perceive depth in infancy.
19. Depth perception underlies our ability to
   a. group similar items in a gestalt.
   b. perceive objects as having a constant shape or form.
   c. judge distances.
   d. fill in the gaps in a figure.
20. Two examples of ________ depth cues are interposition and linear perspective.
21. Perceiving a tomato as consistently red, despite lighting shifts, is an example of
   a. shape constancy.
   b. perceptual constancy.
   c. a binocular cue.
   d. continuity.
22. After surgery to restore vision, adults who had been blind from birth had difficulty
   a. recognizing objects by touch.
   b. recognizing objects by sight.
   c. distinguishing figure from ground.
   d. distinguishing between bright and dim light.
23. In experiments, people have worn glasses that turned their visual fields upside down. After a period of adjustment, they learned to function quite well. This ability is called ________ ________.
24. The snail-shaped tube in the inner ear, where sound waves are converted into neural activity, is called the ________.
25. What are the basic steps in transforming sound waves into perceived sound?
26. The sensory receptors that are found mostly in the skin and that detect hurtful temperatures, pressure, or chemicals are called ________.
27. The gate-control theory of pain proposes that
   a. special pain receptors send signals directly to the brain.
   b. the pain gate is controlled by the thalamus.
   c. small spinal cord nerve fibers conduct most pain signals, but large-fiber activity can close access to those pain signals.
   d. pain can often be controlled and managed effectively through the use of relaxation techniques.
28. How does the biopsychosocial approach explain our experience of pain? Provide examples.
29. We have specialized nerve receptors for detecting which five tastes? How did this ability aid our ancestors?
30. ________ is your sense of body position and movement. Your ________ ________ specifically monitors your head's movement, with sensors in the inner ear.
31. Why do you feel a little dizzy immediately after a roller-coaster ride?
32. A food's aroma can greatly enhance its taste. This is an example of
   a. sensory adaptation.
   b. synesthesia.
   c. kinesthesia.
   d. sensory interaction.
33. Which of the following types of ESP claims is supported by solid, replicable scientific evidence?
   a. Telepathy
   b. Clairvoyance
   c. Precognition
   d. None of these claims

Continue testing yourself with **LearningCurve** or **Achieve Read & Practice** to learn and remember most effectively.

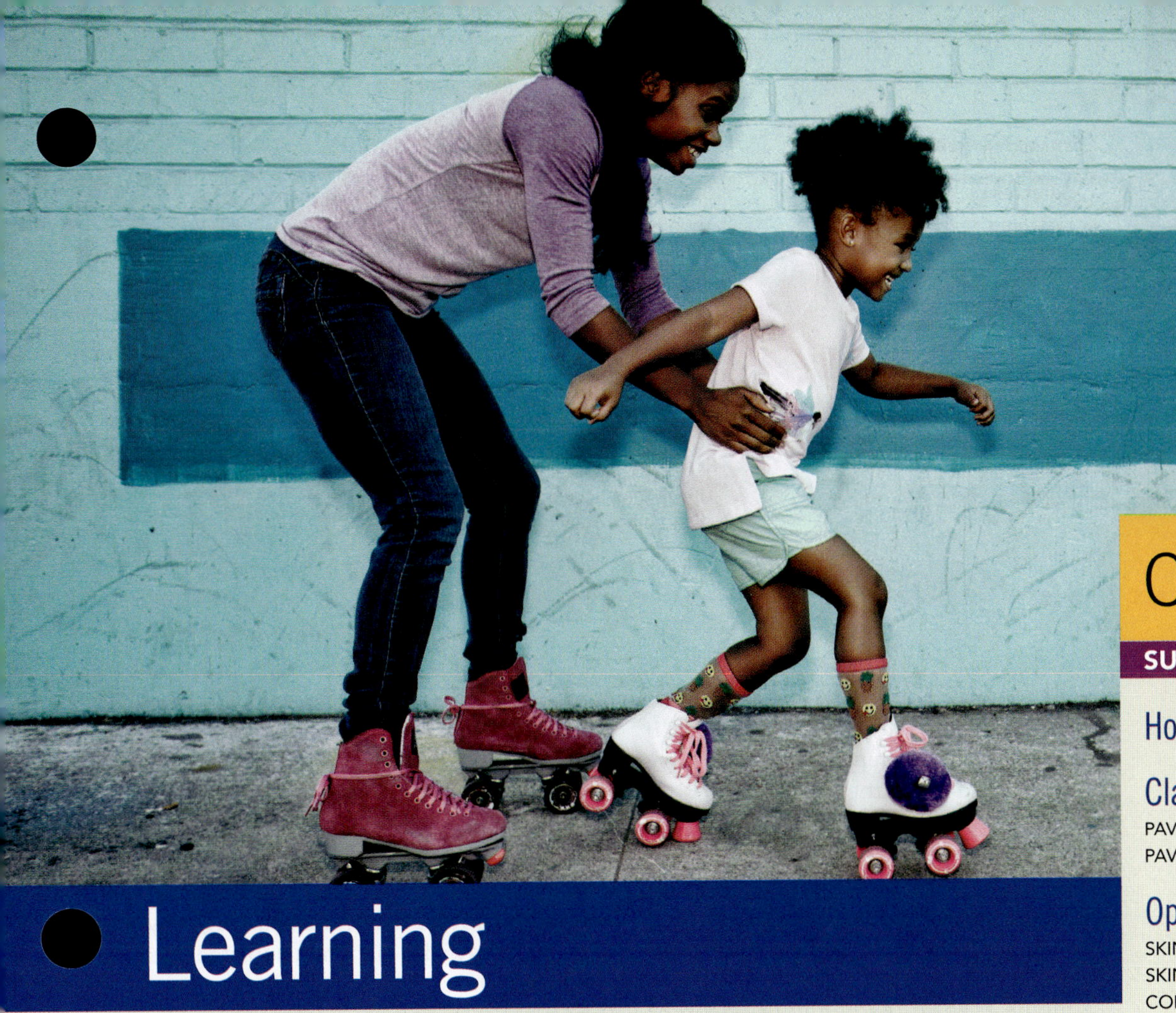
Peathegee Inc/Getty Images

CHAPTER 6

Learning

SURVEY THE CHAPTER

In the early 1940s, University of Minnesota graduate students Marian Breland and Keller Breland witnessed the power of a new learning technology. Their mentor, B. F. Skinner, would become famous for *shaping* rat and pigeon behaviors, by delivering well-timed rewards as the animals inched closer and closer to a desired behavior. Impressed by Skinner's results, the Brelands began shaping the behavior of cats, chickens, parakeets, turkeys, pigs, ducks, and hamsters (Bailey & Gillaspy, 2005). The company they formed spent the next half-century training more than 15,000 animals from 140 species. Their efforts helped pave the way for training animals to help humans, including police officers and people with vision loss or seizure disorders.

Like other animals, humans learn from experience. Indeed, nature's most important gift may be our *adaptability*—our capacity to learn new behaviors that help us cope with our changing world. We can learn how to build grass huts or snow shelters, submarines or space stations, and thereby adapt to almost any environment.

Oprah Winfrey is a living example of adaptability. Growing up in poverty with her grandmother, Winfrey wore dresses made of potato sacks. She was a constant target of racism. Beginning at age 9, she was molested by several family members, leading her to run away from home at age 13. She became pregnant at age 14, but her son died shortly after birth.

To overcome such tremendous adversity, Winfrey learned how to adapt to new situations. She joined her high school speech team and used this talent to win a college scholarship. After graduating, she moved to Chicago and took over as the host of a struggling show, transforming it into the most popular daytime talk show in America. "Education," Winfrey said, "is the key to unlocking the world, a passport to freedom."

Winfrey shows us how learning breeds hope. What is learnable we may be able to teach—a fact that encourages animal trainers, and also parents, educators, and coaches. What has been learned we may be able to change by new learning—an assumption underlying stress management and counseling programs. No matter how unhappy, unsuccessful, or unloving we are, we can learn and change.

No topic is closer to the heart of psychology than *learning,* the process of acquiring, through experience, new and relatively enduring information or behaviors. (Learning acquires information, and memory—our next chapter topic—retains it.) In earlier chapters we considered the learning of sleep patterns, of gender roles, of visual perceptions. In later chapters we will see how learning shapes our thoughts, our emotions, our personality, and our attitudes.

Two related events:

Result after repetition:

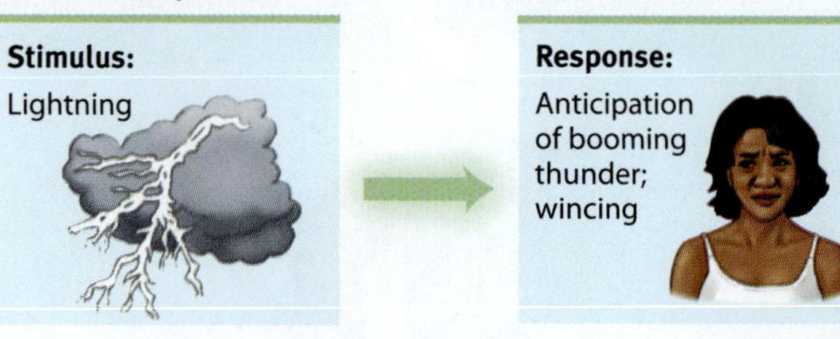

FIGURE 6.1
Classical conditioning

How Do We Learn?

Learning Objective Question LOQ 6-1

How do we define *learning,* and what are some basic forms of learning?

By **learning,** we humans adapt to our environments. We learn to expect and prepare for significant events such as the arrival of food or pain *(classical conditioning)*. We learn to repeat acts that bring good results and to avoid acts that bring bad results *(operant conditioning)*. We learn new behaviors by observing events and people, and through language, we learn things we have neither experienced nor observed *(cognitive learning)*. But *how* do we learn?

One way we learn is by *association.* Our minds naturally connect events that occur in sequence. Suppose you see and smell freshly baked bread, eat some, and find it satisfying. The next time you see and smell fresh bread, you will expect that eating it will again be satisfying. So, too, with sounds. If you associate a sound with a frightening consequence, hearing the sound alone may trigger your fear. As one 4-year-old said after watching a TV character get mugged, "If I had heard that music, I wouldn't have gone around the corner!" (Wells, 1981).

Learned associations also feed our habitual behaviors (Wood, 2017). Habits can form when we repeat behaviors in a given context—sleeping in the same comfy position in bed, biting our nails in class, eating buttery popcorn in a movie theater. As behavior becomes linked with the context, our next experience of that context will evoke our habitual response. Especially when our willpower is depleted, as when we're mentally fatigued, we tend to fall back on our habits—good or bad (Graybiel & Smith, 2014; Neal et al., 2013). To increase our self-control, to connect our resolutions with positive outcomes, the key is forming "beneficial habits" (Galla & Duckworth, 2015).

How long does it take to form a beneficial habit? To find out, researchers asked 96 university students to choose some healthy behavior, such as running before dinner or eating fruit with lunch, and to perform it daily for 84 days. The students also recorded whether the behavior felt automatic (something they did without thinking and would find hard not to do). When did the behaviors turn into habits? After about 66 days, on average (Lally et al., 2010). Is there something you'd like to make a routine or essential part of your life? Just do it every day for two months, or a bit longer for exercise, and you likely will find yourself with a new habit. This happened for both of us—with a midday workout [DM] or late afternoon run [ND] having long ago become an automatic daily routine.

Other animals also learn by association. To protect itself, the sea slug *Aplysia* withdraws its gill when squirted with water. If the squirts continue, as happens naturally in choppy water, the withdrawal response weakens. But if the sea slug repeatedly receives an electric shock just after being squirted, its protective response to the squirt instead grows stronger. The animal has learned that the squirt signals an upcoming shock.

Complex animals can learn to link outcomes with their own responses. An aquarium seal will repeat behaviors, such as slapping and barking, that prompt people to toss it a herring.

By linking two events that occur close together, the sea slug and the seal are exhibiting **associative learning.** The sea slug associated the squirt with an upcoming shock. The seal associated its slapping and barking with a herring treat. Each animal has learned something important to its survival: anticipating the immediate future.

This process of learning associations is *conditioning.* It takes two main forms:

- In *classical conditioning* (**FIGURE 6.1**), we learn to associate two stimuli and

(a) Action: Being polite (b) Consequence: Getting a treat (c) Behavior strengthened

FIGURE 6.2 Operant conditioning

thus to anticipate events. (A **stimulus** is any event or situation that evokes a response.) We learn that a flash of lightning will be followed by a crack of thunder, so when lightning flashes nearby, we start to brace ourselves. We associate stimuli that we do not control, and we respond automatically. This is called **respondent behavior.**

- In *operant conditioning,* we learn to associate an action (our behavior) and its consequence. Thus, we (and other animals) learn to repeat acts followed by good results (**FIGURE 6.2**) and to avoid acts followed by bad results. These associations produce **operant behaviors** (which operate on the environment to produce consequences).

Conditioning is not the only form of learning. Through **cognitive learning** we acquire mental information that guides our behavior. *Observational learning,* one form of cognitive learning, lets us learn from others' experiences. Chimpanzees, for example, sometimes learn behaviors merely by watching other chimpanzees. If one animal sees another solve a puzzle and gain a food reward, the observer may perform the trick more quickly. So, too, in humans: We look and we learn.

RETRIEVE & REMEMBER

ANSWERS IN APPENDIX E

1. Why are habits, such as having something sweet with that cup of coffee, so hard to break?

Classical Conditioning

For many people, the name Ivan Pavlov (1849–1936) rings a bell. His early twentieth-century experiments—now psychology's most famous research—are classics. The process he explored we justly call **classical conditioning.**

PAVLOV'S EXPERIMENTS

LOQ 6-2 What is *classical conditioning,* and how does it demonstrate associative learning?

For his studies of dogs' digestive system, Pavlov (who held a medical degree) earned Russia's first Nobel Prize. But Pavlov's novel experiments on learning, which consumed the last three decades of his life, earned this feisty, intense scientist his place in history (Todes, 2014).

Pavlov's new direction came when his creative mind focused on what seemed to others an unimportant detail. Without fail, putting food in a dog's mouth caused the animal to drool—to *salivate.* Moreover, the dog began salivating not only to the taste of the food but also to the mere sight of the food or the food dish. The dog even drooled to the sight of the person delivering the food or the sound of that person's approaching footsteps. At first, Pavlov considered these "psychic secretions" an annoyance. Then he realized they pointed to a simple but important form of learning.

Pavlov and his assistants tried to imagine what the dog was thinking and feeling as it drooled in anticipation of the food. This only led them into useless debates. So, to make their studies more objective, they experimented. To rule out other possible influences, they isolated the dog in a small room, placed it in a harness, and attached a device to

Macmillan Learning

Ivan Pavlov "Experimental investigation . . . should lay a solid foundation for a future true science of psychology" (1927).

learning the process of acquiring, through experience, new and relatively enduring information or behaviors.

associative learning learning that certain events occur together. The events may be two stimuli (as in classical conditioning) or a response and its consequence (as in operant conditioning).

stimulus any event or situation that evokes a response.

respondent behavior behavior that occurs as an automatic response to some stimulus.

operant behavior behavior that operates on the environment, producing a consequence.

cognitive learning the acquisition of mental information, whether by observing events, by watching others, or through language.

classical conditioning a type of learning in which we link two or more stimuli and anticipate events.

measure its saliva. Then, from the next room, they presented food. First, they slid in a food bowl. Later, they blew meat powder into the dog's mouth at a precise moment. Finally, they paired various **neutral stimuli (NS)**—events the dog could see or hear but didn't associate with food—with food in the dog's mouth. If a sight or sound regularly signaled the arrival of food, would the dog learn the link? If so, would it begin salivating in anticipation of the food?

The answers proved to be *Yes* and *Yes*. Just before placing food in the dog's mouth to produce salivation, Pavlov sounded a tone. After several pairings of tone and food, the dog got the message. Anticipating the meat powder, it began salivating to the tone alone. In later experiments, a buzzer, a light, a touch on the leg, even the sight of a circle set off the drooling.

A dog doesn't *learn* to salivate in response to food in its mouth. Rather, food in the mouth automatically, *unconditionally*, triggers this response. Thus, Pavlov called this drooling an **unconditioned response (UR).** And he called the food an **unconditioned stimulus (US).**

Salivating in response to a tone, however, is learned. Because it is *conditional* upon the dog's linking the tone with the food (**FIGURE 6.3**), we call this response the **conditioned response (CR).** The stimulus that used to be neutral (in this case, a previously meaningless tone that now triggers drooling) is the **conditioned stimulus (CS).** Remembering the difference between these two kinds of stimuli and responses is easy: Conditioned = learned; *un*conditioned = *un*learned.

If Pavlov's demonstration of associative learning was so simple, what did he do for the next three decades? What discoveries did his research factory publish in his 532 papers on salivary conditioning (Windholz, 1997)? He and his associates explored five major conditioning processes: *acquisition, extinction, spontaneous recovery, generalization,* and *discrimination*

Remember:
NS = Neutral Stimulus
US = Unconditioned Stimulus
UR = Unconditioned Response
CS = Conditioned Stimulus
CR = Conditioned Response

RETRIEVE & REMEMBER

ANSWERS IN APPENDIX E

2. An experimenter sounds a tone just before delivering an air puff that causes your eye to blink. After several repetitions, you blink to the tone alone. What is the NS? The US? The UR? The CS? The CR?

An unconditioned stimulus (US) produces an unconditioned response (UR).

A neutral stimulus (NS) produces no salivation response.

The US is repeatedly presented just after the NS. The US continues to produce a UR.

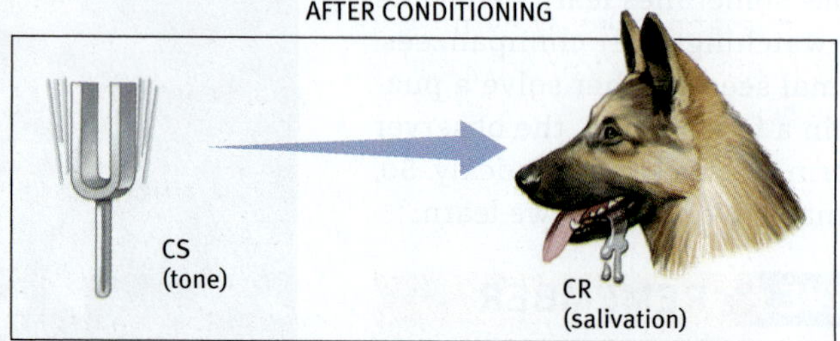

The previously neutral stimulus alone now produces a conditioned response (CR), thereby becoming a conditioned stimulus (CS).

FIGURE 6.3 Pavlov's classic experiment Pavlov presented a neutral stimulus (a tone) just before an unconditioned stimulus (food in mouth). The neutral stimulus then became a conditioned stimulus, producing a conditioned response.

Acquisition

LOQ 6-3 What parts do acquisition, extinction, spontaneous recovery, generalization, and discrimination play in classical conditioning?

Acquisition is the first stage in classical conditioning. This is the point when Pavlov's dogs learned the link between the NS (the tone, the light, the touch) and the US (the food). To understand this stage, Pavlov and his associates wondered: How much time should pass between presenting the neutral stimulus and the food? In most cases, not much—half a second usually works well.

What do you suppose would happen if the food (US) appeared before the tone (NS) rather than after? Would conditioning occur? Not likely. Conditioning usually won't occur when the NS follows the US. Remember: *Classical conditioning is biologically adaptive because it helps humans and other animals prepare for good or bad events.* To Pavlov's dogs, the originally neutral tone became a CS after signaling an important biological event—the arrival of food (US). To deer in the forest, the snapping of a twig (CS) may signal a predator's approach (US).

Research on male Japanese quail shows how a CS can signal another important biological event (Domjan, 1992, 1994, 2005). Just before presenting a sexually approachable female quail, the researchers turned on a red light. Over time, as the red light continued to announce the female's arrival, the light alone caused the male quail to become excited. They developed a preference for their cage's red-light district. When a female appeared, they mated with her more quickly and released more semen and sperm (Matthews et al., 2007). This capacity for classical conditioning supports reproduction.

Can objects, sights, and smells associated with sexual pleasure become conditioned stimuli for human sexual arousal, too? Indeed they can (Byrne, 1982; Hoffman, 2012). Onion breath does not usually produce sexual arousal (**FIGURE 6.4**). But when repeatedly paired with a passionate kiss, it can become a CS and do just that. The larger lesson: *Conditioning helps an animal survive and reproduce—by responding to cues that help it gain food, avoid dangers, locate mates, and produce offspring* (Hollis, 1997). Learning makes for yearning.

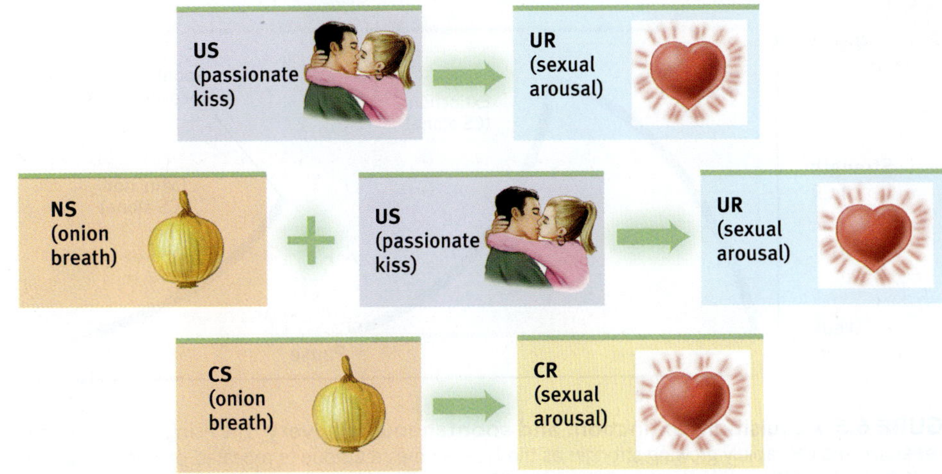

FIGURE 6.4 An unexpected CS Psychologist Michael Tirrell (1990) recalled: "My first girlfriend loved onions, so I came to associate onion breath with kissing. Before long, onion breath sent tingles up and down my spine. Oh what a feeling!"

IN YOUR EVERYDAY LIFE

Psychologist Michael Tirrell recalled coming to associate his girlfriend's onion breath with arousal. Can you remember ever experiencing something that would normally be neutral (or even unpleasant) that came to mean something special?

RETRIEVE & REMEMBER

ANSWERS IN APPENDIX E

3. Companies often pay to make their products visible in popular movies—such as when admired actors drink certain beverages. Based on classical conditioning principles, what might be an effect of this pairing?

Extinction and Spontaneous Recovery

What would happen, Pavlov wondered, if after conditioning, the CS occurred repeatedly without the US? If the tone sounded again and again, but no food appeared, would the tone still trigger drooling? The answer was mixed. The dogs salivated less and less, a reaction known as **extinction.** Extinction

neutral stimulus (NS) in classical conditioning, a stimulus that evokes no response before conditioning.

unconditioned response (UR) in classical conditioning, an unlearned, naturally occurring response (such as salivation) to an unconditioned stimulus (US) (such as food in the mouth).

unconditioned stimulus (US) in classical conditioning, a stimulus that unconditionally—naturally and automatically—triggers a response (UR).

conditioned response (CR) in classical conditioning, a learned response to a previously neutral (but now conditioned) stimulus (CS).

conditioned stimulus (CS) in classical conditioning, an originally neutral stimulus that, after association with an unconditioned stimulus (US), comes to trigger a conditioned response (CR).

acquisition in classical conditioning, the initial stage—when we link a neutral stimulus and an unconditioned stimulus so that the neutral stimulus begins triggering the conditioned response. (In operant conditioning, the strengthening of a reinforced response.)

extinction in classical conditioning, the weakening of a conditioned response when an unconditioned stimulus does not follow a conditioned stimulus. (In operant conditioning, the weakening of a response when it is no longer reinforced.)

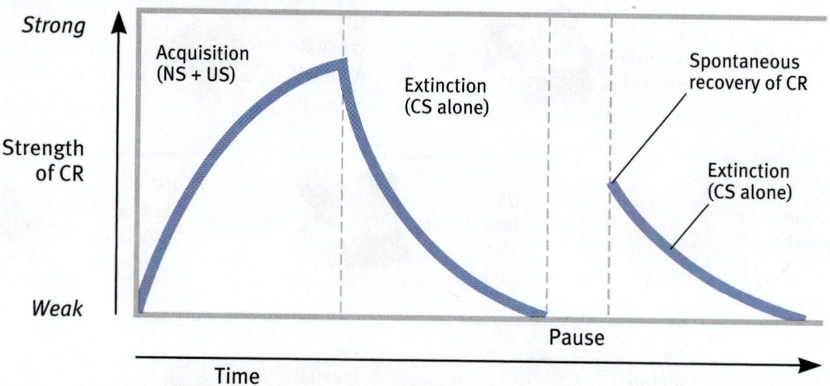

FIGURE 6.5 Acquisition, extinction, and spontaneous recovery The rising curve (simplified here) shows the CR rapidly growing stronger as the NS becomes a CS due to repeated pairing with the US *(acquisition)*. The CR then weakens rapidly as the CS is presented alone *(extinction)*. After a pause, the (weakened) CR reappears *(spontaneous recovery)*.

RETRIEVE & REMEMBER

ANSWERS IN APPENDIX E

5. What conditioning principle is influencing the snail's affections?

"I don't care if she's a tape dispenser. I love her."

is the drop-off in responses when a CS (tone) no longer signals an upcoming US (food). But if, after several hours' delay, Pavlov sounded the tone again, the dogs drooled in response. This **spontaneous recovery**—the reappearance of a (weakened) CR after a pause—suggested to Pavlov that extinction was *suppressing* the CR rather than eliminating it (**FIGURE 6.5**).

RETRIEVE & REMEMBER

ANSWERS IN APPENDIX E

4. The first step of classical conditioning, when an NS becomes a CS, is called __________. When a US no longer follows the CS, and the CR becomes weakened, this is called __________.

Generalization

Pavlov and his students noticed that a dog conditioned to the sound of one tone also responded somewhat to the sound of a new and different tone. Likewise, a dog conditioned to salivate when rubbed would also drool a bit when scratched or when touched on a different body part (Windholz, 1989). This tendency to respond similarly to stimuli that resemble the CS is called **generalization** (or *stimulus generalization*).

Generalization can be adaptive, as when toddlers who learn to fear moving cars also become afraid of moving trucks and motorcycles. And generalized fears can linger. For two months after being in a car collision, sensitized young drivers are less vulnerable to repeat collisions (O'Brien et al., 2017). Years after being tortured, one Argentine writer reported still flinching with fear at the sight of black shoes—his first glimpse of his torturers as they approached his cell (Timerman, 1980). This generalized fear response was also found in laboratory studies comparing abused and nonabused children (Pollak et al., 1998). In all these human examples, people's emotional reactions to one stimulus have generalized to similar stimuli.

Discrimination

Pavlov's dogs also learned to respond to the sound of a particular tone and *not* to other tones. One stimulus (tone) predicted the US, and the others did not. This learned ability to *distinguish* between a conditioned stimulus (which predicts the US) and other irrelevant stimuli is called **discrimination.** Being able to recognize differences is adaptive. Slightly different stimuli can be followed by vastly different results. When running alone, Aliyah has learned to avoid certain routes where she has experienced harassment. Facing a guard dog, your heart may race; facing a guide dog, it probably will not.

PAVLOV'S LEGACY

LOQ 6-4 Why is Pavlov's work important, and how is it being applied?

What remains today of Pavlov's ideas? A great deal. Most psychologists now agree that classical conditioning is a basic form of learning. Modern neuroscience has also supported Pavlov's ideas—by identifying neural circuits that link a conditioned stimulus (warning signal) with an upcoming unconditioned stimulus (threat) (Harnett et al., 2016). Judged with today's knowledge of the biological and cognitive influences on conditioning, some of Pavlov's ideas were incomplete. But if we see further than Pavlov did, it is because we stand on his shoulders.

Why does Pavlov's work remain so important? If he had merely taught us that old dogs can learn new tricks, his experiments would long ago have been forgotten. Why should we care that dogs can be conditioned to drool to the sound of a tone? The importance lies first in this finding: *Many other responses to many other stimuli can be classically conditioned in many other creatures*—in fact, in every species tested, from earthworms to fish to dogs to monkeys to people (Schwartz, 1984). Thus, classical conditioning is one way that virtually all animals learn to adapt to their environment.

Second, *Pavlov showed us how a process such as learning can be studied objectively.* He was proud that his methods were not based on guesswork about a dog's mind. The salivary response is a behavior we can measure in cubic centimeters of saliva. Pavlov's success therefore suggested a scientific model for how the young field of psychology might proceed. That model was to isolate the basic building blocks of complex behaviors and study them with objective laboratory procedures.

RETRIEVE & REMEMBER

ANSWERS IN APPENDIX E

6. If the aroma of a baking cake makes your mouth water, what is the US? The CS? The CR?

LaunchPad Play the role of an experimenter in classical conditioning research by visiting *Topic Tutorial: PsychSim6, Classical Conditioning.* And review Pavlov's classic work by watching a 3-minute re-creation of Pavlov's lab in the *Video: Pavlov's Discovery of Classical Conditioning.*

Classical Conditioning in Everyday Life

Other chapters in this text—on motivation and emotion, stress and health, psychological disorders, and therapy—show how Pavlov's principles can influence human health and well-being. Three examples:

- ***Medical treatments.*** Drugs given as cancer treatments can trigger nausea and vomiting. Patients may then develop classically conditioned nausea (and sometimes anxiety) to the sights, sounds, and smells associated with the clinic (Hall, 1997). Merely entering the clinic's waiting room or seeing the nurses can provoke these feelings (Burish & Carey, 1986).
- ***Drug cravings.*** Former drug users often feel a craving when they are again in the drug-using context. They associate particular people or places with previous highs. Thus, drug counselors advise their clients to steer clear of people and settings that may trigger these cravings (Siegel, 2005).
- ***Food cravings.*** Classical conditioning makes dieting difficult. Sugary substances evoke sweet sensations. Researchers have conditioned healthy volunteers to experience cravings after only one instance of eating a sweet food (Blechert et al., 2016). So, the next time you think "I can definitely eat just one donut," remember that it may cause you to crave more donuts in the future.

Does Pavlov's work help us understand our own emotions? John B. Watson thought so. He believed that human emotions and behaviors, though biologically influenced, are mainly a bundle of conditioned responses (1913). Working with an 11-month-old, Watson and his graduate student Rosalie Rayner (1920; Harris, 1979) showed how specific fears might be conditioned. Like most infants, "Little Albert" feared loud noises but not white rats. Watson and Rayner presented a white rat and, as Little Albert reached to touch it, struck a hammer against a steel bar just behind the infant's head. After seven repeats of seeing the rat and hearing the frightening noise, Albert burst into tears at the mere sight of the rat. Five days later, he reportedly generalized this startled fear reaction to the sight of a rabbit, a dog, and even a furry coat. Although a modern reanalysis questions Watson's evidence for Albert's conditioning, the case remains legendary (Powell & Schmaltz, 2017).

For years, people wondered what became of Little Albert. Detective work by Russell Powell and his colleagues (2014) found that the child of one of the campus hospital's wet nurses matched Little Albert's description. The child, William Albert Barger, went by Albert B.—precisely the name used by Watson and Rayner. This Albert was an easygoing person, though, perhaps coincidentally, he had an aversion to dogs. He died in 2007 without ever knowing of his role in psychology's history.

People also wondered what became of Watson. After losing his Johns Hopkins professorship over an affair with Rayner (whom he later married), he joined an advertising agency as the company's resident psychologist. There, he used his knowledge of associative learning in many successful advertising campaigns. One of them, for Maxwell House, helped make the "coffee break" an American custom (Hunt, 1993).

Some psychologists had difficulty repeating Watson and Rayner's findings with other children. (These experiments would be unethical by today's standards.) Nevertheless, Little Albert's learned fears led many psychologists to wonder whether each of us might be a walking storehouse of conditioned emotions. If so, might extinction procedures or new conditioning help us change our unwanted responses to emotion-arousing stimuli?

Comedian-writer Mark Malkoff extinguished his fear of flying by doing just that. With support from an airline, he faced his fear. Living on an airplane for 30 days and taking 135 flights, he spent 14 hours a day in the air (NPR, 2009). After a week and a half, Malkoff's fear had faded. Freed of his fear, Malkoff began playing games with fellow passengers. His favorite was the "toilet paper experiment": put one end of a roll in the toilet, unroll the rest down the aisle, and flush, sucking down the whole roll in 3 seconds. (Our [DM and ND's] advice: Don't try this at home!) In Chapter 14, we will see more examples of how psychologists use behavioral techniques such as *counterconditioning* to treat emotional disorders and promote personal growth.

spontaneous recovery the reappearance, after a pause, of an extinguished conditioned response.

generalization in classical conditioning, the tendency, after conditioning, to respond similarly to stimuli that resemble the conditioned stimulus. (In operant conditioning, *generalization* occurs when responses learned in one situation occur in other, similar situations.)

discrimination in classical conditioning, the learned ability to distinguish between a conditioned stimulus and similar stimuli that do not signal an unconditioned stimulus. (In operant conditioning, the ability to distinguish responses that are reinforced from similar responses that are not reinforced.)

RETRIEVE & REMEMBER

ANSWERS IN APPENDIX E

7. In Watson and Rayner's experiments, "Little Albert" learned to fear a white rat after repeatedly experiencing a loud noise as the rat was presented. In these experiments, what was the US? The UR? The NS? The CS? The CR?

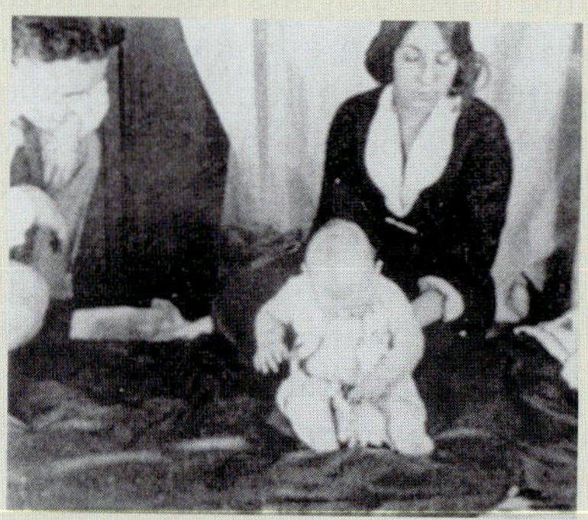

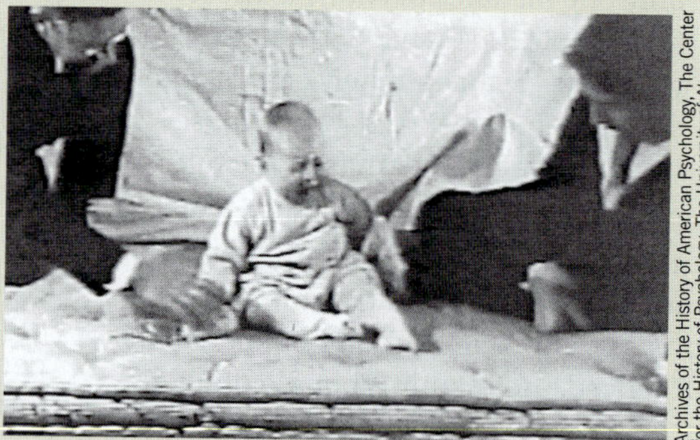

Archives of the History of American Psychology, The Center for the History of Psychology, The University of Akron

8. With classical conditioning, we learn associations between events we ________ (do/do not) control. With operant conditioning, we learn associations between our behavior and ________ (resulting/random) events.

LaunchPad See the *Video: Research Ethics* for a helpful tutorial animation.

Operant Conditioning

LOQ 6-5 What is *operant conditioning,* and how is operant behavior reinforced and shaped?

It's one thing to classically condition a dog to salivate to the sound of a tone, or a child to fear a white rat. But to teach an elephant to walk on its hind legs or a child to say *please,* we must turn to another type of learning—*operant conditioning.*

Classical conditioning and operant conditioning are both forms of associative learning. But their differences are straightforward:

- In *classical conditioning,* an animal (dog, child, sea slug) forms associations between two events it does not control. Classical conditioning involves *respondent behavior*—automatic responses to a stimulus (such as salivating in response to meat powder and later in response to a tone).
- In **operant conditioning,** animals associate their own actions with consequences. Actions followed by a rewarding event increase; those followed by a punishing event decrease. Behavior that *operates* on the environment to *produce* rewarding or punishing events is called *operant behavior.*

We can therefore distinguish our classical from our operant conditioning by asking two questions. *Are we learning associations between events we do not control* (classical conditioning)? *Or are we learning associations between our behavior and resulting events* (operant conditioning)?

SKINNER'S EXPERIMENTS

B. F. Skinner (1904–1990) was a college English major who had set his sights on becoming a writer. Then, seeking a new direction, he became a graduate student in psychology, and, eventually, modern *behaviorism's* most influential and controversial figure.

Skinner's work built on a principle that psychologist Edward L. Thorndike (1874–1949) called the **law of effect:** Rewarded behavior tends to be repeated (**FIGURE 6.6**). From this starting point, Skinner went on to develop experiments that would reveal principles of *behavior control.* By shaping pigeons' natural walking and pecking behaviors, for example, Skinner was able to teach them such unpigeon-like behaviors as walking in a figure 8, playing Ping-Pong, and keeping a missile on course by pecking at a screen target.

For his studies, Skinner designed an **operant chamber,** popularly known as a *Skinner box* (**FIGURE 6.7**). The box has a bar

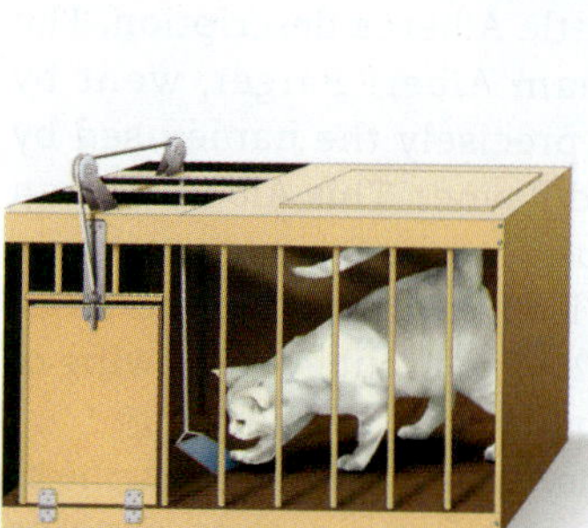

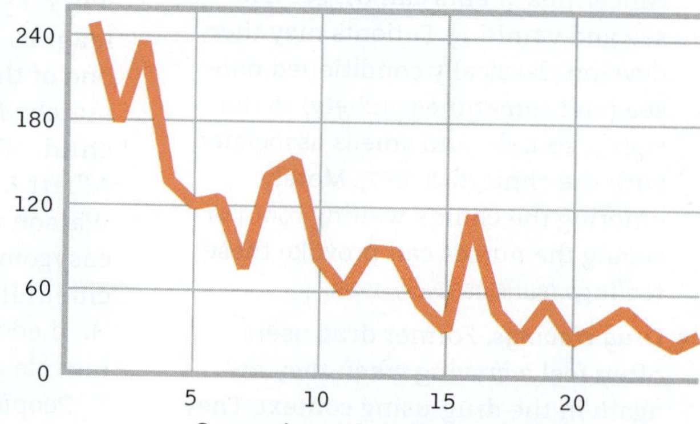

FIGURE 6.6 Cat in a puzzle box Thorndike used a fish reward to entice cats to find their way out of a puzzle box through a series of maneuvers. The cats' performance tended to improve with successive trials, illustrating Thorndike's *law of effect.* (Data from Thorndike, 1898.)

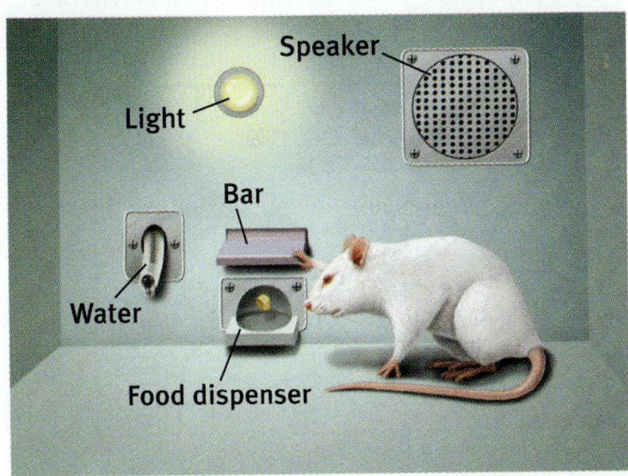

FIGURE 6.7 A Skinner box Inside the box, the rat presses a bar for a food reward. Outside, measuring devices (not shown here) record the animal's accumulated responses.

or button that an animal presses or pecks to release a food or water reward. It also has a device that records these responses. This creates a stage on which rats and other animals act out Skinner's concept of **reinforcement:** any event that strengthens (increases the frequency of) a preceding response. What is reinforcing depends on the animal and the conditions. For people, it may be praise, attention, or a paycheck. For hungry and thirsty rats, food and water work well. Skinner's experiments have done far more than teach us how to pull habits out of a rat. They have explored the precise conditions that foster efficient and enduring learning.

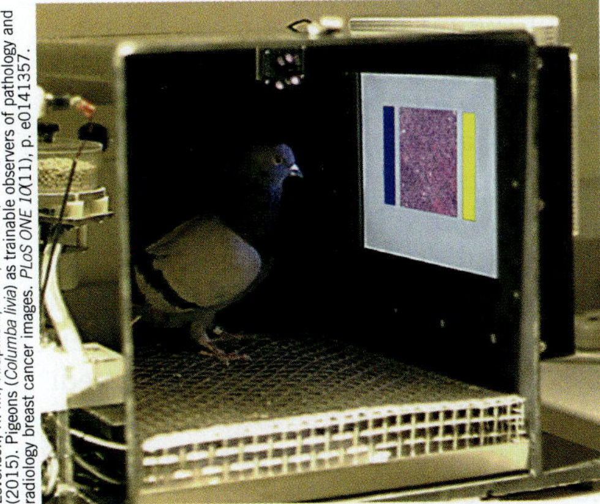

Levenson, R. M., Krupinski, E. A., Navarro, V. M., Wasserman, E. A. (2015). Pigeons (*Columba livia*) as trainable observers of pathology and radiology breast cancer images. *PLoS ONE 10*(11), p. e0141357.

Bird brains spot tumors After being rewarded with food when correctly spotting breast tumors, pigeons became as skilled as humans at discriminating cancerous from healthy tissue (Levenson et al., 2015). Other animals have been shaped to sniff out land mines or locate people amid rubble (La Londe et al., 2015).

Shaping Behavior

Imagine that you wanted to condition a hungry rat to press a bar. Like Skinner, you could tease out this action with **shaping,** gradually guiding the rat's actions toward the desired behavior. First, you would watch how the animal naturally behaves, so that you could build on its existing behaviors. You might give the rat a bit of food each time it approaches the bar. Once the rat is approaching regularly, you would give the treat only when it moves close to the bar, then closer still. Finally, you would require it to touch the bar to get food. By rewarding *successive approximations,* you reinforce only those responses that are ever-closer to the final desired behavior. By giving rewards only for desired behaviors and ignoring all other responses, researchers and animal trainers gradually shape complex behaviors.

We can also readily shape our own behavior. Let's say you want to get in shape to run your first 5K race. You set up a daily exercise plan that starts with a little jogging and works up to running 1 mile. Reaching this goal, you give yourself a nice reward. You do this again when you can run 1.5 miles, and again for every additional half mile—rewarding successive approximations of your target behavior.

Shaping can also help us understand what nonverbal organisms can perceive. Can a dog see red and green? Can a baby hear the difference between lower- and higher-pitched tones? If we can shape them to respond to one stimulus and not to another, then we know they can perceive the difference. Such experiments have even shown that some nonhuman animals can form concepts. When experimenters reinforced pigeons for pecking after seeing a human face, but not after seeing other images, the pigeons learned to recognize human faces (Herrnstein & Loveland, 1964). After being trained to discriminate among classes of events or objects—flowers, people, cars, chairs—pigeons were usually able to identify the category in which a new pictured object belonged (Bhatt et al., 1988; Wasserman, 1993).

Skinner noted that we continually reinforce and shape others' everyday behaviors, though we may not mean to do so. Erlinda's nagging annoys her mom, for example, but consider how Mom typically responds:

ERLINDA: *Could you take me to the mall?*

MOM: *(Continues checking her phone.)*

ERLINDA: *Mom, I need to go to the mall.*

MOM: *Uh, yeah, in a few minutes.*

ERLINDA: *MOM! The mall!*

MOM: *Show some manners! Okay, where are my keys . . .*

Erlinda's nagging is reinforced, because she gets something desirable—a trip to the mall. Mom's response is reinforced, because it ends something *aversive* (unpleasant)—Erlinda's nagging.

Or consider a teacher who sticks gold stars on a wall chart beside the names of children scoring 100 percent on spelling tests. As everyone can then see, some children always score 100 percent. The others, who take the same test and may have worked harder than the academic all-stars, get no stars. Using operant conditioning principles, what advice could you offer the teacher to help all students do their best work?

operant conditioning a type of learning in which a behavior becomes more probable if followed by a reinforcer or less probable if followed by a punisher.

law of effect Thorndike's principle that behaviors followed by favorable consequences become more likely, and that behaviors followed by unfavorable consequences become less likely.

operant chamber in operant conditioning research, a chamber (also known as a *Skinner box*) containing a bar or key that an animal can manipulate to obtain a food or water reinforcer; attached devices record the animal's rate of bar pressing or key pecking.

reinforcement in operant conditioning, any event that *strengthens* the behavior it follows.

shaping an operant conditioning procedure in which reinforcers guide actions closer and closer toward a desired behavior.

IN YOUR EVERYDAY LIFE

Can you recall a time when a teacher, coach, family member, or employer helped you learn something by shaping your behavior in little steps until you achieved your goal?

Types of Reinforcers

LOQ 6-6 How do positive and negative reinforcement differ, and what are the basic types of reinforcers?

Until now, we've mainly been discussing **positive reinforcement,** which strengthens responding by *presenting* a typically *pleasurable* stimulus immediately afterward. But, as the nagging Erlinda story shows us, there are two basic kinds of reinforcement (**TABLE 6.1**). **Negative reinforcement** strengthens a response by *reducing or removing* something *undesirable or unpleasant*. Erlinda's nagging was *positively* reinforced, because Erlinda got something desirable—a trip to the mall. Her mom's response (doing what Erlinda wanted) was *negatively* reinforced, because it got rid of something undesirable—Erlinda's nagging. Similarly, taking aspirin may relieve your headache, and hitting *snooze* will silence your irritating alarm. These welcome results provide negative reinforcement and increase the odds that you will repeat these behaviors. For those with drug addiction, the negative reinforcement of ending withdrawal pangs can be a compelling reason to resume using (Baker et al., 2004).

Note that *negative reinforcement is not punishment*. (Some friendly advice: Repeat the italicized words in your mind.) Rather, negative reinforcement—psychology's most misunderstood concept—*removes* a punishing event. Think of negative reinforcement as something that provides relief—from that nagging person, bad headache, or annoying alarm clock. *The point to remember:* Whether it works by getting rid of something we *don't* enjoy or by giving us something we *do* enjoy, *reinforcement is any consequence that strengthens behavior.*

RETRIEVE & REMEMBER

ANSWERS IN APPENDIX E

9. How is operant conditioning at work in this cartoon?

HI & LOIS © 1992 by King Features Syndicate, Inc. World Rights Reserved.

Will Burgess/Reuters/Newscom

Reinforcers vary with circumstances What is reinforcing (a heat lamp) to one animal (a cold meerkat) may not be to another (an overheated bear). What is reinforcing in one situation (a cold snap at the Taronga Zoo in Sydney) may not be in another (a sweltering summer day). Reinforcers also vary among humans. A chocolate treat that is reinforcing to Clarice might not be to Carlos (a vanilla-lover).

Primary and Conditioned Reinforcers

Getting food when hungry or having a painful headache go away is innately (naturally) satisfying. These **primary reinforcers** are unlearned. **Conditioned reinforcers,** also called *secondary reinforcers,* get their power through learned associations with primary reinforcers. If a rat in a Skinner box learns that a light reliably signals a food delivery, the rat will work to turn on the light. The light has become a secondary reinforcer linked with food. Our lives are filled with conditioned reinforcers—money, good grades, a pleasant tone of voice—each of which has been linked with a more basic reward—food, shelter, safety, social support.

Immediate and Delayed Reinforcers

In shaping experiments, rats are conditioned with immediate rewards. You want the rat to press the bar. So, when it sniffs the bar (a step toward the target behavior), you immediately give it a food pellet. If a distraction delays your giving the rat its prize, the rat won't learn to link the bar sniffing with the food pellet reward. Delays also decrease human learning. Students learn class material better when they complete frequent quizzes that provide them with immediate feedback (Healy et al., 2017).

But unlike rats, humans *can* respond to delayed reinforcers. We associate the paycheck at the end of the week, the good grade at the end of the term, the trophy at the end of the sports season with our earlier actions. Indeed, learning to control our impulses in order to achieve more valued rewards is a big step toward maturity (Logue, 1998a,b). Chapter 3

TABLE 6.1 Ways to Increase Behavior

Operant Conditioning Term	Description	Examples
Positive reinforcement	Add a desirable stimulus	Pet a dog that comes when you call it; pay someone for work done.
Negative reinforcement	Remove an aversive stimulus	Take painkillers to end pain; fasten seatbelt to end loud beeping.

"Oh, not bad. The light comes on, I press the bar, they write me a check. How about you?"

described a famous finding in which some children curbed their impulses and delayed gratification, choosing two marshmallows later over one now. Those impulse-controlled children later achieved greater educational and career success (Mischel, 2014). A modern study showed a similar (though weaker) relationship between delay of gratification and achievement later (Watts et al., 2018). The *bottom line*: It pays to delay.

Sometimes, however, small but immediate pleasures (the enjoyment of watching late-night TV, for example) are more attractive than big but delayed rewards (feeling rested for a big exam tomorrow). For many teens, the immediate gratification of impulsive, unprotected sex wins over the delayed gratification of safe sex or saved sex (Loewenstein & Furstenberg, 1991). And for too many of us, the immediate rewards of today's gas-guzzling vehicles, air travel, and air conditioning win over the bigger future consequences of climate change, rising seas, and extreme weather.

Reinforcement Schedules

LOQ 6-7 How do continuous and partial reinforcement schedules affect behavior?

In most of our examples, the desired response has been reinforced every time it occurs. But **reinforcement schedules** vary. With **continuous reinforcement**, learning occurs rapidly, which makes it the best choice for mastering a behavior. But there's a catch: Extinction also occurs rapidly.

TABLE 6.2 Schedules of Partial Reinforcement

	Fixed	Variable
Ratio	*Every so many:* reinforcement after every *nth* behavior, such as buy 10 coffees, get 1 free, or pay workers per product units produced	*After an unpredictable number:* reinforcement after a random number of behaviors, as when playing slot machines or fly fishing
Interval	*Every so often:* reinforcement for behavior after a fixed time, such as Tuesday discount prices	*Unpredictably often:* reinforcement for behavior after a random amount of time, as when checking our phone for a message

When reinforcement stops—when we stop delivering food after the rat presses the bar—the behavior soon stops (is *extinguished*). If a normally dependable candy machine fails to deliver a chocolate bar twice in a row, we stop putting money into it (although a week later we may exhibit *spontaneous recovery* by trying again).

Real life rarely provides continuous reinforcement. Salespeople don't make a sale with every pitch. But they persist because their efforts are occasionally rewarded. And that's the good news about **partial (intermittent) reinforcement** schedules, in which responses are sometimes reinforced, sometimes not. Learning is slower than with continuous reinforcement, but *resistance to extinction* is greater. Imagine a pigeon that has learned to peck a key to obtain food. If you gradually phase out the food delivery until it occurs only rarely, in no predictable pattern, the pigeon may peck 150,000 times without a reward (Skinner, 1953). Slot machines reward gamblers in much the same way—occasionally and unpredictably. And like pigeons, slot players keep trying, again and again. With intermittent reinforcement, hope springs eternal.

Lesson for parents: Partial reinforcement also works with children. What happens when we occasionally give in to children's tantrums for the sake of peace and quiet? We have intermittently reinforced the tantrums. This is the best way to make a behavior persist.

Skinner (1961) and his collaborators compared four schedules of partial reinforcement and their effects on behavior (**TABLE 6.2**).

Fixed-ratio schedules reinforce behavior after a set number of responses. Shoe stores may reward us with a free pair after every 10 purchased. In the laboratory, rats may be reinforced on a fixed ratio of, say, one food pellet for every 30 responses. Once conditioned, the rats

positive reinforcement increasing behaviors by presenting a pleasurable stimulus, such as food. A positive reinforcer is anything that, when *presented* after a response, strengthens the response.

negative reinforcement increasing behaviors by stopping or reducing aversive stimuli, such as an electric shock. A negative reinforcer is anything that, when *removed* after a response, strengthens the response. (*Note:* Negative reinforcement is *not* punishment.)

primary reinforcer an event that is innately reinforcing, often by satisfying a biological need.

conditioned reinforcer an event that gains its reinforcing power through its link with a primary reinforcer. (Also known as *secondary reinforcer.*)

reinforcement schedule a pattern that defines how often a desired response will be reinforced.

continuous reinforcement reinforcing a desired response every time it occurs.

partial (intermittent) reinforcement reinforcing a response only part of the time; results in slower acquisition but much greater resistance to extinction than does continuous reinforcement.

fixed-ratio schedule in operant conditioning, a reinforcement schedule that reinforces a response only after a specified number of responses.

will pause only briefly to munch on the pellet before returning to a high rate of responding.

Variable-ratio schedules provide reinforcers after an unpredictable number of responses. This unpredictable reinforcement is what slot-machine players and fly fishers experience. And it's what makes gambling and fly fishing so hard to extinguish even when they don't produce the desired results. Because reinforcers increase as the number of responses increases, variable-ratio schedules produce high rates of responding.

Fixed-interval schedules reinforce the first response after a fixed time period. Pigeons on a fixed-interval schedule peck more rapidly as the time for reinforcement draws near. People waiting for an important letter check more often as delivery time approaches. A cook peeks into the oven more frequently as the casserole comes close to completion. This produces a choppy stop-start pattern rather than a steady rate of response.

Variable-interval schedules reinforce the first response after unpredictable time intervals. At unpredictable times, a food pellet rewarded Skinner's pigeons for persistence in pecking a key. Like the longed-for message that finally rewards persistence in rechecking our phone, variable-interval schedules tend to produce slow, steady responding. This makes sense, because there is no knowing when the waiting will be over.

In general, response rates are higher when reinforcement is linked to the number of responses (a ratio schedule) rather than to time (an interval schedule). But responding is more consistent when reinforcement is unpredictable (a variable schedule) than when it is predictable (a fixed schedule).

Animal behaviors differ, yet Skinner (1956) contended that the reinforcement principles of operant conditioning are universal. It matters little, he said, what response, what reinforcer, or what species you use. The effect of a given reinforcement schedule is pretty much the same: "Pigeon, rat, monkey, which is which? It doesn't matter. . . . Behavior shows astonishingly similar properties."

RETRIEVE & REMEMBER

ANSWERS IN APPENDIX E

10. People who send spam email are reinforced by which schedule? Home bakers checking the oven to see if the cookies are done are reinforced on which schedule? Coffee shops that offer a free coffee drink after every 10 purchased are using which reinforcement schedule?

Punishment

LOQ 6-8 How does punishment differ from negative reinforcement, and how does punishment affect behavior?

Reinforcement increases a behavior; **punishment** does the opposite. A *punisher* is any consequence that *decreases* the frequency of the behavior it follows (**TABLE 6.3**). Swift and sure punishers can powerfully restrain unwanted behaviors. The rat that is shocked after touching a forbidden object and the child who is burned by touching a hot stove will learn not to repeat those behaviors.

Criminal behavior, much of it impulsive, is also influenced more by swift and sure punishers than by the threat of severe sentences (Darley & Alter, 2013). Thus, when Arizona introduced an exceptionally harsh sentence for first-time drunk drivers, the drunk-driving rate changed very little. But when Kansas City police started patrolling a high crime area to increase the swiftness and sureness of punishment, that city's crime rate dropped dramatically.

What do punishment studies imply for parenting? One analysis of over 160,000 children found that physical punishment rarely corrects unwanted behavior (Gershoff & Grogan-Kaylor, 2016). Many psychologists note five major drawbacks of physical punishment (Finkenauer et al., 2015; Gershoff et al., 2018; Marshall, 2002).

1. ***Punished behavior is suppressed, not forgotten. This temporary state may (negatively) reinforce parents' punishing behavior.*** The child swears, the parent swats, the child stops swearing when their parents are nearby, so the parents believe the punishment successfully stopped the behavior. No wonder spanking is a hit with so many parents—with 68 percent of American adults believing that a child sometimes needs a "good hard spanking" (Smith et al., 2017).
2. ***Physical punishment does not replace the unwanted behavior.*** Physical punishment may reduce or even eliminate unwanted behavior, but it does not provide direction for appropriate behavior. A child who is spanked for screaming in the car may stop yelling but continue to throw her food or steal her brother's toys.
3. ***Punishment teaches discrimination among situations.*** In operant conditioning, *discrimination* occurs when we learn that some responses, but not others, will be reinforced. Did the punishment effectively end the

TABLE 6.3 Ways to Decrease Behavior

Type of Punisher	Description	Examples
Positive punishment	Administer an aversive stimulus.	Spray water on a barking dog; give a traffic ticket for speeding.
Negative punishment	Withdraw a rewarding stimulus.	Take away a misbehaving teen's driving privileges; block a rude commenter on social media.

child's swearing? Or did the child simply learn that while it's not okay to swear around the house, it's okay elsewhere?

4. ***Punishment can teach fear.*** In operant conditioning, *generalization* occurs when our responses to similar stimuli are also reinforced. A punished child may associate fear not only with the undesirable behavior but also with the person who delivered the punishment or the place it occurred. Thus, children may learn to fear a punishing teacher and try to avoid school, or may become anxious (Gershoff et al., 2010). For such reasons, most European countries and 31 U.S. states now ban hitting children in public schools (EndCorporalPunishment.org). As of 2018, 53 countries had outlawed hitting by parents. A large survey in Finland, the second country to pass such a law, revealed that children born after the law passed were, indeed, less often slapped and beaten (Österman et al., 2014).

5. ***Physical punishment may increase aggression by modeling violence as a way to cope with problems.*** Studies find that spanked children are at increased risk for aggression (MacKenzie et al., 2013). We know, for example, that many aggressive delinquents and abusive parents come from abusive families (Straus et al., 1997).

Some researchers question this logic. Physically punished children may be more aggressive, they say, for the same reason that people who have undergone psychotherapy are more likely to suffer depression—because they had preexisting problems that triggered the treatments (Ferguson, 2013a; Larzelere, 2000; Larzelere et al., 2004). So, does spanking cause misbehavior, or does misbehavior trigger spanking? Correlations don't hand us an answer.

LaunchPad See the *Video: Correlational Studies* for a helpful tutorial animation.

David Strickler/The Image Works

Children see, children do? Children who often experience physical punishment tend to display more aggression.

The debate continues. Some researchers note that frequent spankings predict future aggression—even when studies control for preexisting bad behavior (Taylor et al., 2010a). Other researchers believe that lighter spankings pose less of a problem (Baumrind et al., 2002; Larzelere & Kuhn, 2005). That is especially so if physical punishment is used only as a backup for milder disciplinary tactics, and if it is combined with a generous dose of reasoning and reinforcing.

Parents of delinquent youths may not know how to achieve desirable behaviors without screaming, hitting, or threatening their children with punishment (Patterson et al., 1982). Training programs can help them translate dire threats ("Apologize right now or I'm taking that cell phone away!") into positive incentives ("You're welcome to have your phone back when you apologize"). Stop and think about it. Aren't many threats of punishment just as forceful, and perhaps more effective, when rephrased positively? Thus, "If you don't get your homework done, I'm not giving you money for a movie!" could be phrased more positively as . . . .

In classrooms, too, teachers can give feedback by saying "No, but try this . . ." and "Yes, that's it!" Such responses reduce unwanted behavior while reinforcing more desirable alternatives. Remember: *Punishment tells you what not to do; reinforcement tells you what to do.*

What punishment often teaches, said Skinner, is how to avoid it. The bottom line: *Most psychologists now favor an emphasis on reinforcement.* Notice people doing something right and affirm them for it.

RETRIEVE & REMEMBER

ANSWERS IN APPENDIX E

11. Fill in the blanks with one of the following terms: positive reinforcement (PR), negative reinforcement (NR), positive punishment (PP), and negative punishment (NP). We have provided the first answer (PR) for you.

Type of Stimulus	Give It	Take It Away
Desired (for example, a teen's use of the car)	1. PR	2.
Undesired/aversive (for example, an insult)	3.	4.

variable-ratio schedule in operant conditioning, a reinforcement schedule that reinforces a response after an unpredictable number of responses.

fixed-interval schedule in operant conditioning, a reinforcement schedule that reinforces a response only after a specified time has elapsed.

variable-interval schedule in operant conditioning, a reinforcement schedule that reinforces a response at unpredictable time intervals.

punishment an event that decreases the behavior it follows.

SKINNER'S LEGACY

LOQ 6-9 Why were Skinner's ideas controversial, and how might his operant conditioning principles be applied at school, at work, in sports, in parenting, and for self-improvement?

B. F. Skinner stirred a hornet's nest with his outspoken beliefs. He repeatedly insisted that external influences (not internal thoughts and feelings) shape behavior. He argued that brain science isn't needed for psychological science, saying that "a science of behavior is independent of neurology" (Skinner, 1938/1966, pp. 423–424). And he urged people to use operant conditioning principles to influence others' behavior at school, work, and home. Knowing that behavior is shaped by its results, he argued that we should use rewards to evoke more desirable behavior.

Skinner's critics objected, saying that by neglecting people's personal freedom and trying to control their actions, he treated them as less than human. Skinner's reply: External consequences already control people's behavior. So why not steer those consequences toward human betterment? Wouldn't reinforcers be more humane than the punishments used in homes, schools, and prisons? And if it is humbling to think that our history has shaped us, doesn't this very idea also give us hope that we can shape our future?

Macmillan Learning

B. F. Skinner "I am sometimes asked, 'Do you think of yourself as you think of the organisms you study?' The answer is yes. So far as I know, my behavior at any given moment has been nothing more than the product of my genetic endowment, my personal history, and the current setting" (1983).

LaunchPad Simulate operant conditioning and shaping by visiting *Topic Tutorial: PsychSim6, Operant Conditioning* and also *Topic Tutorial: PsychSim6, Shaping.*

Operant Conditioning in Everyday Life

In later chapters we will see how psychologists apply operant conditioning principles to help people reduce high blood pressure or gain social skills. Reinforcement techniques are also at work in schools, workplaces, and homes, and these principles can support our self-improvement as well (Flora, 2004).

At School More than 50 years ago, Skinner and others worked toward a day when "machines and textbooks" would shape learning in small steps, by immediately reinforcing correct responses. Such machines and texts, they said, would revolutionize education and free teachers to focus on each student's special needs. "Good instruction demands two things," said Skinner (1989). "Students must be told immediately whether what they do is right or wrong and, when right, they must be directed to the step to be taken next."

Skinner might be pleased to know that many of his ideals for education are now possible. Teachers used to find it difficult to pace material to each student's rate of learning, and to provide prompt feedback. Online adaptive quizzing, such as the LearningCurve and Achieve Read & Practice systems available with this text, do both. Students move through quizzes at their own pace, according to their own level of understanding. And they get immediate feedback on their efforts, including personalized study plans.

LaunchPad **Operant conditioning principles may be used to help us achieve our goals. What else affects our goal achievement? To find out, engage online with *Assess Your Strengths: How Might Your Willingness to Think of the Future Affect Your Ability to Achieve Long-Term Goals?***

At Work and in Sports Skinner's ideas also show up in the workplace. Knowing that reinforcers influence productivity, many organizations have invited employees to share the risks and rewards of company ownership. Others have focused on reinforcing a job well done. How might managers successfully motivate their employees, and coaches motivate their players? Make the reinforcement *immediate,* and reward specific, achievable behaviors, not vaguely defined "merit." People, unlike pigeons, also respond to delayed reinforcers. General Motors CEO Mary Barra understood. In 2015, she observed workers' high performance and awarded record bonuses that year (Vlasic, 2015). But rewards don't have to be monetary. An effective manager may simply walk the floor and sincerely praise people for good work, or write notes of appreciation for a completed project.

As Skinner said, "How much richer would the whole world be if the reinforcers in daily life were more effectively contingent on productive work?"

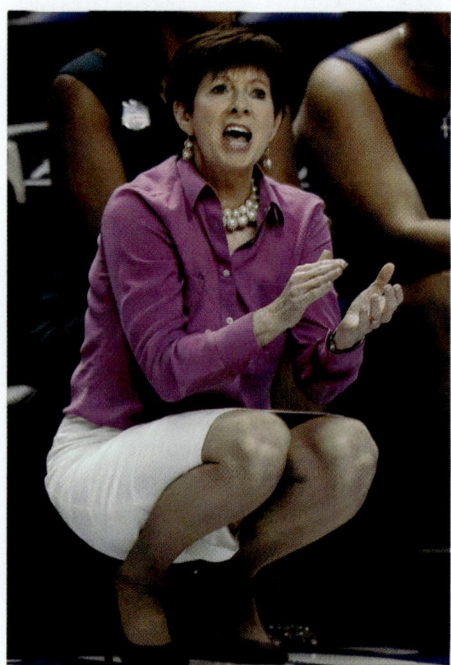

Chuck Burton/AP Images

Immediate reinforcement Muffet McGraw, the coach of Notre Dame's 2018 national championship women's basketball team, focuses on catching her players doing things right and applauds them for it on the spot.

In Parenting As we have seen, parents can learn from operant conditioning practices. Parent-training researchers remind us that by saying "Get ready for bed" and then caving in to protests or defiance, parents reinforce such whining and arguing. Exasperated, they may then yell or make threatening gestures. When the child, now frightened, obeys, that in turn reinforces the parents' angry behavior. Over time, a destructive parent-child relationship develops.

To disrupt this cycle, parents should remember the basic rule of shaping: *Notice people doing something right and affirm them for it.* Give children attention and other reinforcers when they are behaving *well* (Wierson & Forehand, 1994). Target a specific behavior, reward it, and watch it increase. When children misbehave or are defiant, do not yell at or hit them. Simply explain what they did wrong and take away the iPad, remove a misused toy, or give a brief time-out.

To Change Your Own Behavior Want to stop smoking? Eat less? Study or exercise more? To reinforce your own desired behaviors and extinguish the undesired ones, psychologists suggest applying operant conditioning in five steps.

1. ***State a realistic goal in measurable terms and announce it.*** You might, for example, aim to boost your study time by an hour a day. Share that goal with friends to increase your commitment and chances of success.
2. ***Decide how, when, and where you will work toward your goal.*** Take time to plan. Those who list specific steps showing how they will reach their goals become more focused on those goals and more often achieve them (Gollwitzer & Oettingen, 2012).
3. ***Monitor how often you engage in your desired behavior.*** You might log your current study time, noting under what conditions you do and don't study. (When we began writing textbooks, we each logged our time and were amazed to discover how much time we were wasting.)

"I wrote another five hundred words. Can I have another cookie?"

4. ***Reinforce the desired behavior.*** People's persistence toward long-term goals, such as New Year's resolutions to study or exercise more, is powered mostly by immediate rewards (Woolley & Fishbach, 2017). So to increase your study time, give yourself a reward (a snack or some activity you enjoy) only after you finish your extra hour of study. Agree with your friends that you will join them for weekend activities only if you have met your realistic weekly studying goal.
5. ***Reduce the rewards gradually.*** As your new behaviors become habits, give yourself a mental pat on the back instead of a cookie.

IMPROVE YOUR EVERYDAY LIFE

Think of a bad habit of yours. How could you use operant conditioning to break it?

RETRIEVE & REMEMBER

ANSWERS IN APPENDIX E

12. Joslyn constantly misbehaves at preschool even though her teacher scolds her repeatedly. Why does Joslyn's misbehavior continue, and what can her teacher do to stop it?

CONTRASTING CLASSICAL AND OPERANT CONDITIONING

LOQ 6-10 How does classical conditioning differ from operant conditioning?

Both classical and operant conditioning are forms of *associative learning* (**TABLE 6.4**). In both, we *acquire* behaviors that may later become *extinct* and then *spontaneously reappear.* We often *generalize* our responses but learn to *discriminate* among different stimuli.

Classical and operant conditioning also differ: Through classical conditioning, we associate different events that we don't control, and we respond automatically *(respondent behaviors).* Through operant conditioning, we link our behaviors—which act on our environment to produce rewarding or punishing events *(operant behaviors)*—with their consequences.

TABLE 6.4 Comparison of Classical and Operant Conditioning

	Classical Conditioning	Operant Conditioning
Basic idea	Learning associations between events we do not control.	Learning associations between our behavior and its consequences.
Response	Involuntary, automatic.	Voluntary, operates on environment.
Acquisition	Associating events; NS is paired with US and becomes CS.	Associating a response with a consequence (reinforcer or punisher).
Extinction	CR decreases when CS is repeatedly presented alone.	Responding decreases when reinforcement stops.
Spontaneous recovery	The reappearance, after a rest period, of an extinguished CR.	The reappearance, after a rest period, of an extinguished response.
Generalization	The tendency to respond to stimuli similar to the CS.	Responses learned in one situation occurring in other, similar situations.
Discrimination	Learning to distinguish between a CS and other stimuli that do not signal a US.	Learning that some responses, but not others, will be reinforced.

As we shall see next, our *biology* and our *thought processes* influence both classical and operant conditioning.

RETRIEVE & REMEMBER

ANSWERS IN APPENDIX E

13. Salivating in response to a tone paired with food is a(n) __________ behavior; pressing a bar to obtain food is a(n) __________ behavior.

LaunchPad Conditioning principles may also be applied in clinical settings. Play the role of a researcher exploring these applications by engaging online with the activity *How Would You Know If People Can Learn to Reduce Anxiety?*

Biology, Cognition, and Learning

From drooling dogs, running rats, and pecking pigeons, we have learned much about the basic processes of learning. But conditioning principles don't tell us the whole story. Our learning is the product of the interaction of biological, psychological, and social-cultural influences.

BIOLOGICAL LIMITS ON CONDITIONING

LOQ 6-11 What limits does biology place on conditioning?

Evolutionary theorist Charles Darwin proposed that *natural selection* favors traits that aid survival. In the middle of the twentieth century, researchers further showed that there are biological constraints (limits) on learning. Each species comes predisposed (biologically prepared) to learn those things crucial to its survival.

Biological Limits on Classical Conditioning

A discovery by John Garcia and Robert Koelling in the 1960s helped end a popular and widely held belief in psychology: that environments rule our behavior. Part of this idea was that almost any stimulus (whether a taste, sight, or sound) could serve equally well as a conditioned stimulus. Garcia and Koelling's work put that idea to the test and proved it wrong. They noticed that rats would avoid a taste—but not sights or sounds—associated with becoming sick, even hours later (1966). This response, which psychologists call *taste aversion*, makes adaptive sense. For rats, the easiest way to identify tainted food is to taste it. Taste aversion makes it tough to wipe out an invasion of "bait-shy" rats by poisoning. After being sickened by the bait, they are biologically prepared to avoid that taste ever after.

Humans, too, seem biologically prepared to learn some things rather than others. If you become violently ill four hours after eating a tainted hamburger, you will probably develop an aversion to the *taste* of hamburger. But you usually won't avoid the sight of the associated restaurant, its plates, the people you were with, or the music you heard there.

Though Garcia and Koelling's taste-aversion research began with the discomfort of some laboratory animals, it later enhanced the welfare of many others. In one taste-aversion study, coyotes and wolves were tempted into eating sheep carcasses laced with a sickening poison. Ever after, they avoided sheep meat (Gustavson et al., 1974, 1976). Two wolves penned with a live sheep seemed actually to fear it. These studies not only saved the sheep from their predators, but also saved the sheep-shunning coyotes and wolves from angry ranchers and farmers. In later experiments, conditioned taste aversion has successfully prevented baboons from raiding African gardens, raccoons from attacking chickens, and ravens and crows from feeding on crane eggs. In all these cases, research helped preserve both the prey and their predators (Dingfelder, 2010; Garcia & Gustavson, 1997).

Macmillan Learning

John Garcia As the laboring son of California farmworkers, Garcia attended school only in the off-season during his early childhood years. After entering junior college in his late twenties, and earning his Ph.D. in his late forties, he received the American Psychological Association's Distinguished Scientific Contribution Award "for his highly original, pioneering research in conditioning and learning." He was also elected to the National Academy of Sciences.

blickwinkel/Alamy

Animal taste aversion As an alternative to killing wolves and coyotes that preyed on sheep, some ranchers have sickened the animals with lamb laced with a drug to create a taste aversion.

Such research supports Darwin's principle that natural selection favors traits that aid survival. Our ancestors who readily learned taste aversions were unlikely to eat the same toxic food again and were more likely to survive and leave descendants. Nausea, like anxiety, pain, and other bad feelings, serves a good purpose. Like a car's low-fuel warning light, each alerts the body to a threat (Davidson & Riley, 2015; Neese, 1991).

RETRIEVE & REMEMBER

ANSWERS IN APPENDIX E

14. How did Garcia and Koelling's taste-aversion studies help disprove the belief that almost any stimulus (tastes, sights, sounds) could serve equally well as a conditioned stimulus?

Biological Limits on Operant Conditioning

Nature also sets limits on each species' capacity for operant conditioning. Science fiction writer Robert Heinlein

(1907–1988) said it well: "Never try to teach a pig to sing; it wastes your time and annoys the pig."

We most easily learn and retain behaviors that reflect our biological predispositions. Thus, using food as a reinforcer, you could easily condition a hamster to dig or to rear up, because these are among the animal's natural food-searching behaviors. But you won't be so successful if you use food to try to shape face washing and other hamster behaviors that normally have no link to food or hunger (Shettleworth, 1973). Similarly, you could easily teach pigeons to flap their wings to avoid being shocked, and to peck to obtain food. That's because fleeing with their wings and eating with their beaks are natural pigeon behaviors. However, pigeons have a hard time learning to peck to avoid a shock, or to flap their wings to obtain food (Foree & LoLordo, 1973). The principle: *Our biology predisposes us to learn associations that are naturally adaptive.*

Jeffery Jones/The Gallup Independent/AP Images

Natural athletes Animals can most easily learn and retain behaviors that draw on their biological predispositions, such as horses' inborn ability to move around obstacles with speed and agility.

LaunchPad To learn more about biology's influence on learning, engage online with *Concept Practice: Biologically Adaptive Associations.*

COGNITIVE INFLUENCES ON CONDITIONING

LOQ 6-12 How do cognitive processes affect classical and operant conditioning?

Cognition and Classical Conditioning

John B. Watson, the "Little Albert" researcher, was one of many psychologists who built on Ivan Pavlov's work. Pavlov and Watson shared many beliefs. They came to avoid "mentalistic" concepts (such as consciousness) that referred to inner thoughts, feelings, and motives (Watson, 1913). They also came to maintain that the basic laws of learning are the same for all animals—whether dogs or humans. Thus, the science of psychology should study how organisms respond to stimuli in their environments, said Watson. "Its theoretical goal is the prediction and control of behavior." This view—that psychology should be an objective science based on observable behavior—was called **behaviorism.** Behaviorism influenced North American psychology, especially during the first half of the twentieth century.

Later research has shown that Pavlov's and Watson's views of learning underestimated two important sets of influences. The first, as we have seen, is the way that biological predispositions limit our learning. The second is the effect of our *cognitive processes*—our thoughts, perceptions, and expectations—on learning.

The early behaviorists believed that rats' and dogs' learned behaviors were mindless mechanisms, so there was no need to consider cognition. But experiments have shown that animals can learn the *predictability* of an event (Rescorla & Wagner, 1972). If a shock always is preceded by a tone, and then may also be preceded by a light that accompanies the tone, a rat will react with fear to the tone but not to the light. Although the light is always followed by the shock, it adds no new information; the tone is a better predictor. It's as if the animal learns an *expectancy,* an awareness of how likely it is that the US will occur.

Macmillan Learning

John B. Watson Watson (1924) admitted to "going beyond my facts" when offering his famous boast: "Give me a dozen healthy infants, well-formed, and my own specified world to bring them up in and I'll guarantee to take any one at random and train him to become any type of specialist I might select—doctor, lawyer, artist, merchant-chief, and, yes, even beggar-man and thief, regardless of his talents, penchants, tendencies, abilities, vocations, and race of his ancestors."

Cognition matters in humans, too. For example, people being treated for alcohol use disorder may be given alcohol spiked with a nauseating drug. However, their *awareness* that the drug, not the alcohol, causes the nausea tends to weaken the association between drinking alcohol and feeling sick, making the treatment less effective. In classical conditioning, it is—especially with humans—not simply the CS-US pairing, but also the thought that counts.

Cognition and Operant Conditioning

B. F. Skinner acknowledged the biological underpinnings of behavior and the existence of private thought processes. Nevertheless, many psychologists criticized him for discounting cognition's importance.

A mere eight days before dying of leukemia in 1990, Skinner stood before those of us attending the American Psychological Association convention. In this final address, he still rejected the growing belief that presumed cognitive processes

behaviorism the view that psychology (1) should be an objective science that (2) studies behavior without reference to mental processes. Most research psychologists today agree with (1) but not with (2).

have a necessary place in the science of psychology and even in our understanding of conditioning. For Skinner, thoughts and emotions were behaviors that follow the same laws as other behaviors.

Nevertheless, the evidence of cognitive processes cannot be ignored. For example, rats exploring a maze, given no obvious rewards, seem to develop a **cognitive map**, a mental representation of the maze. In one study, when an experimenter placed food in the maze's goal box, these roaming rats ran the maze as quickly as (and even faster than) other rats that had always been rewarded with food for reaching the goal. Like people sightseeing in a new town, the exploring rats seemingly experienced **latent learning** during their earlier tours. Their latent learning became evident only when they had some reason to demonstrate it.

To sum up, **TABLE 6.5** compares the biological and cognitive influences on classical and operant conditioning.

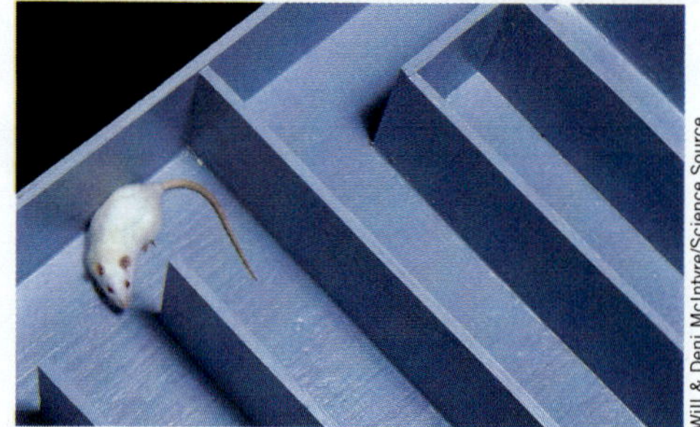

Will & Deni McIntyre/Science Source

Latent learning Animals, like people, can learn from experience, with or without reinforcement. In a classic experiment, rats in one group repeatedly explored a maze, always with a food reward at the end. Rats in another group explored the maze with no food reward. But once given a food reward at the end, rats in the second group thereafter ran the maze as quickly as (and even faster than) the always-rewarded rats (Tolman & Honzik, 1930).

IN YOUR EVERYDAY LIFE

Can you remember examples from your childhood of learning through *classical conditioning* (salivating at the sound or smell of some delicious food cooking in the kitchen?), *operant conditioning* (deciding not to repeat a behavior because you disliked its consequence?), and *cognitive learning* (repeating or avoiding what you watched someone else do)?

TABLE 6.5 Biological and Cognitive Influences on Conditioning

	Classical Conditioning	Operant Conditioning
Biological influences	Biological tendencies limit the types of stimuli and responses that can easily be associated. Involuntary, automatic.	Animals most easily learn behaviors similar to their natural behaviors; associations that are not naturally adaptive are not easily learned.
Cognitive influences	Thoughts, perceptions, and expectations can weaken the association between the CS and the US.	Animals may develop an expectation that a response will be reinforced or punished; latent learning may occur without reinforcement.

RETRIEVE & REMEMBER

ANSWERS IN APPENDIX E

15. Latent learning is an example of what important idea?

Learning by Observation

LOQ 6-13 What is *observational learning?*

Cognition supports **observational learning** (also called *social learning*), in which higher animals learn without direct experience, by watching and imitating others. A child who sees his sister burn her fingers on a hot stove learns, without getting burned himself, that hot stoves can burn us. We learn our native languages and all kinds of other specific behaviors by observing and imitating others, a process called **modeling.**

Picture this scene from an experiment by Albert Bandura, the pioneering researcher of observational learning (Bandura et al., 1961). A preschool child works on a drawing. In another part of the room, an adult builds with Tinkertoys. As the child watches, the adult gets up and for nearly 10 minutes pounds, kicks, and throws around the room a large, inflated Bobo doll, yelling, "Sock him in the nose. . . . Hit him down. . . . Kick him."

The child is then taken to another room filled with appealing toys. Soon the experimenter returns and tells the child she has decided to save these good toys "for the other children." She takes the now-frustrated child to a third room containing a few toys, including a Bobo doll. Left alone, what does the child do?

Compared with other children in the study, those who viewed the model's actions were much more likely to lash out at the doll. Apparently, observing the aggressive outburst lowered their inhibitions. But *something more* was also at work, for the children often imitated the very acts they had observed and used the very words they had heard (**FIGURE 6.8**).

Polaris/Newscom

Albert Bandura "The Bobo doll follows me wherever I go. The photographs are published in every introductory psychology text and virtually every undergraduate takes introductory psychology. I recently checked into a Washington hotel. The clerk at the desk asked, 'Aren't you the psychologist who did the Bobo doll experiment?' I answered, 'I am afraid that will be my legacy.' He replied, 'That deserves an upgrade. I will put you in a suite in the quiet part of the hotel'" (2005). A recent analysis of citations, awards, and textbook coverage identified Bandura—shown here receiving a 2016 U.S. National Medal of Science from President Obama—as the world's most eminent psychologist (Diener et al., 2014).

FIGURE 6.8 The famous Bobo doll experiment Notice how the children's actions directly imitate the adult's.

That "something more," Bandura suggested, was this: By watching models, we *vicariously* (in our imagination) experience what they are experiencing. Through *vicarious reinforcement* or *vicarious punishment,* we learn to anticipate a behavior's consequences in situations like those we are observing. We are especially likely to experience models' outcomes vicariously if we identify with them—if we perceive them as

- similar to ourselves.
- successful.
- admirable.

Functional MRI (fMRI) scans show that when people observe someone winning a reward, their own brain reward systems become active, much as if they themselves had won the reward (Mobbs et al., 2009). Even our learned fears may extinguish as we observe another safely navigating the feared situation (Golkar et al., 2013).

LaunchPad For 3 minutes of classic footage, see the *Video: Bandura's Bobo Doll Experiment.*

MIRRORS AND IMITATION IN THE BRAIN

LOQ 6-14 How may observational learning be enabled by neural mirroring?

In one of those quirky events that appear in the growth of science, researchers made an amazing discovery.

In 1991, on a hot summer day in Parma, Italy, a lab monkey awaited its researchers' return from lunch. The researchers had implanted a monitoring device in the monkey's brain, in a frontal lobe region important for planning and acting out movements. The device would alert the researchers to activity in that region. When the monkey moved a peanut into its mouth, for example, the device would buzz. That day, the monkey stared as one of the researchers entered the lab carrying an ice cream cone in his hand. As the researcher raised the cone to lick it, the monkey's monitor buzzed—as if the motionless monkey had itself made some movement (Blakeslee, 2006; Iacoboni, 2009). The same buzzing had been heard earlier, when the monkey watched humans or other monkeys move peanuts to their mouths.

This quirky event, the researchers believed, marked an amazing discovery: a previously unknown type of neuron (Rizzolatti et al., 2002, 2006). In their view, these **mirror neurons** provided a neural basis for everyday imitation and observational learning. When one monkey sees, these neurons mirror what another monkey does. (Other researchers continue to debate the existence and importance of mirror neurons and related brain networks [Fox et al. 2016; Gallese et al., 2011; Hickok, 2014; Iacoboni, 2009].)

It's not just monkey business. Imitation occurs in various animal species, but it is most striking in humans. Our catchphrases, fashions, ceremonies, foods, traditions, morals, and fads all spread by one person copying another. Children are natural imitators (Marshall & Meltzoff, 2014). From 8 to 16 months, infants come to imitate various novel gestures (Jones, 2007, 2017). By age 12 months, they begin looking where an adult is looking (Meltzoff et al., 2009). And by 14 months, children imitate acts modeled on TV (Meltzoff & Moore, 1997). Children see, children do.

"This instinct to humiliate, when it's modeled by someone in the public platform, by someone powerful, it filters down into everybody's life, because it . . . gives permission for other people to do the same thing." —Meryl Streep, U.S. Golden Globe Award speech, 2017

cognitive map a mental image of the layout of one's environment.

latent learning learning that is not apparent until there is an incentive to demonstrate it.

observational learning learning by observing others.

modeling the process of observing and imitating a specific behavior.

mirror neuron a neuron that fires when we perform certain actions and when we observe others performing those actions; a neural basis for imitation and observational learning.

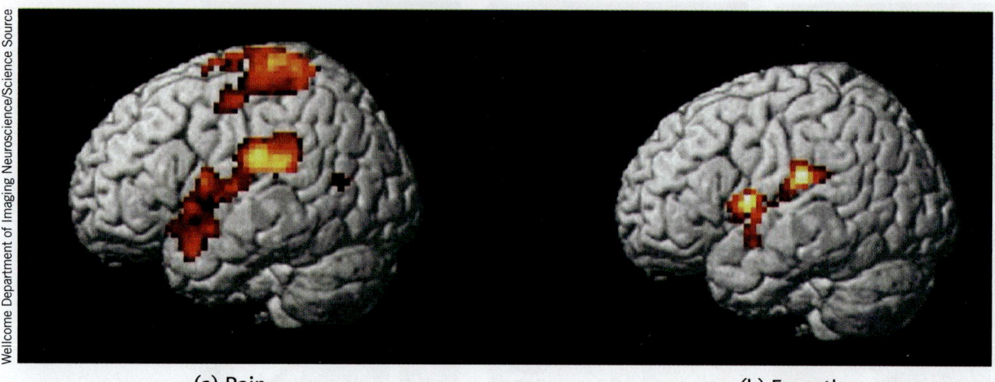

FIGURE 6.9 Experienced and imagined pain in the brain (a) In this fMRI scan, brain activity related to actual pain is mirrored in the brain of an observing loved one (Singer et al., 2004). (b) Empathy in the brain shows up in areas that process emotions, but not in the areas that register physical pain.

Because of our brain's responses, emotions are contagious. As we observe others' postures, faces, voices, and writing styles, we unconsciously mimic them. And by doing that, we grasp others' states of mind and we feel what they are feeling (Bernieri et al., 1994; Ireland & Pennebaker, 2010).

Seeing a loved one's pain, our faces mirror the loved one's emotion. And so do our brains (**FIGURE 6.9**). Even fiction reading may trigger such activity, as we indirectly experience the feelings and actions described (Mar & Oatley, 2008; Speer et al., 2009). In other experiments, reading about Harry Potter and his acceptance of people such as the "Mudbloods" reduced prejudice against immigrants, refugees, and gay people (Vezzali et al., 2015).

So real are these mental instant replays that we may remember an action we have observed as an action we have actually performed (Lindner et al., 2010). The bottom line: *Brain activity underlies our intensely social nature.*

OBSERVATIONAL LEARNING IN EVERYDAY LIFE

LOQ 6-15 What is the impact of prosocial modeling and of antisocial modeling?

The big news from Bandura's studies and the mirror-neuron research is that we look, we mentally imitate, and we learn. Models—in our family, our neighborhood, or the media we consume—may have effects, good and bad.

Prosocial Effects

The good news is that people's modeling of **prosocial** (positive, helpful) **behaviors** can have prosocial effects. Across many countries and dozens of studies, viewing prosocial TV, movies, and video games boosted later helping behavior (Coyne et al., 2018; Prot et al., 2014). Real people who model nonviolent, helpful behavior can also prompt similar behavior in others. After observing someone helping (assisting a woman with dropped books), people became more helpful, such as by assisting someone who dropped a dollar (Burger et al., 2015). India's Mahatma Gandhi and America's Martin Luther King, Jr., both drew on the power of modeling, making nonviolent action a powerful force for social change in both countries (Matsumoto et al., 2015). Parents are also powerful models. European Christians who risked their lives to rescue Jews from the Nazis usually had a close relationship with at least one parent who modeled a strong moral or humanitarian concern. This was also true for U.S. civil rights activists in the 1960s (London, 1970; Oliner & Oliner, 1988).

A model caregiver This girl is learning orphan-nursing skills, as well as compassion, by observing her mentor in this Humane Society program. As the sixteenth-century proverb states, "Example is better than precept."

Models are most effective when their actions and words are consistent. To encourage children to read, read to them and surround them with books and people who read. To increase the odds that your children will practice your religion, worship and attend religious activities with them. Sometimes, however, models say one thing and do another. Many parents seem to operate according to the principle "Do as I *say,* not as I do." Experiments suggest that children learn to do both (Rice & Grusec, 1975; Rushton, 1975). Exposed to a hypocrite, they tend to imitate the hypocrisy—by doing what the model did and saying what the model said.

IMPROVE YOUR EVERYDAY LIFE

Who has been a significant role model for you? What did you learn from observing this person? For whom are you a role model? How might you become a better role model for others?

Antisocial Effects

The bad news is that observational learning may also have *antisocial effects.* This helps us understand why abusive parents might have aggressive children, why children who are lied to become more likely to cheat and lie, and why many men who beat their wives had wife-battering fathers (Hays & Carver, 2014; Stith et al., 2000). Critics note that such aggressiveness could be genetic. But with monkeys, we know it can be environmental.

prosocial behavior positive, constructive, helpful behavior. The opposite of antisocial behavior.

In study after study, young monkeys separated from their mothers and subjected to high levels of aggression grew up to be aggressive themselves (Chamove, 1980). The lessons we learn as children are not easily unlearned as adults, and they are sometimes visited on future generations.

TV shows, movies, and online videos are sources of observational learning. While watching, children may "learn" that bullying is an effective way to control others, that free and easy sex brings pleasure without later misery or disease, or that men should be tough and women gentle. Some films glorify high-speed and risky driving. Do these films "teach" viewers that fast driving is acceptable? An analysis of nearly 200,000 speeding tickets showed a large increase in speeding tickets for the weekends following the release of *The Fast and the Furious* films (Jena et al., 2018).

And they have ample time to learn such lessons. During their first 18 years, most children in developed countries spend more time watching TV shows than they spend in school. In the United States, the average teen watches TV shows more than 4 hours a day; the average adult, 3 hours (Robinson & Martin, 2009; Strasburger et al., 2010).

Viewers are learning about life from a strange storyteller, one with a taste for violence. During one closely studied year, nearly 6 in 10 U.S. network and cable programs featured violence. Of those violent acts, 74 percent went unpunished, and the victims' pain was usually not shown. Nearly half the events were portrayed as "justified," and nearly half the attackers were attractive (Donnerstein, 1998). These conditions define the recipe for the *violence-viewing effect* described in many studies and recognized by most media researchers (Anderson et al., 2017; Bushman, 2018). (See Thinking Critically About: The Effects of Viewing Media Violence.)

Screen time's greatest effect may stem from what it displaces. Children and adults who spend several hours a day in front of a screen spend that many fewer hours in other pursuits—talking, studying, playing, reading, or socializing in real time with friends. What would you have done with your extra time if you had spent even half as many hours in front of a screen, and how might you therefore be different?

RETRIEVE & REMEMBER

ANSWERS IN APPENDIX E

16. Emily's parents and older friends all drive over the speed limit, but they advise her not to. Hannah's parents and friends drive within the speed limit, but they say nothing to deter her from speeding. Will Emily or Hannah be more likely to speed?

17. Match the examples (i–v) to the appropriate underlying learning principle (a–e):

i. Knowing the way from your bed to the bathroom in the dark
ii. Your little brother getting in a fight after watching a violent action movie
iii. Salivating when you smell brownies in the oven
iv. Disliking the taste of chili after becoming violently sick a few hours after eating chili
v. Your dog racing to greet you on your arrival home

a. Classical conditioning
b. Operant conditioning
c. Latent learning
d. Observational learning
e. Biological predispositions

Thinking Critically About:
The Effects of Viewing Media Violence

LOQ 6-16 What is the violence-viewing effect?

RIP
RIP

Introduction of TV in U.S. and Canada, 1957–1974 ↔ Doubling of homicide rate in U.S. and Canada[1]

Introduction of TV for White South Africans in 1975 ↔ Near-doubling of homicide rate in South Africa[1]

Heavy exposure to media violence for U.S. 9–11-year-olds ↔ Increased fighting, and more violent behavior later as teens[2]

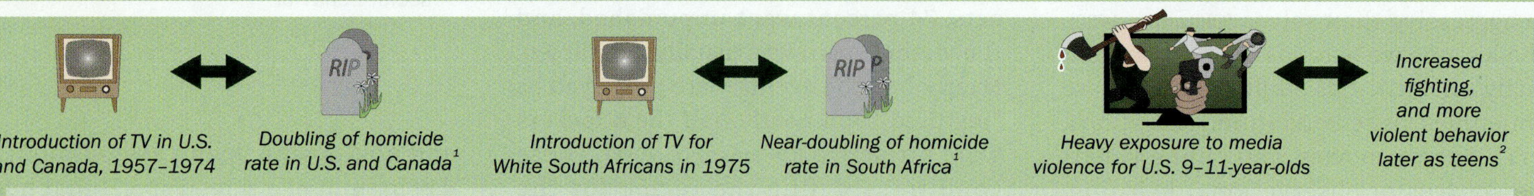

BUT, CORRELATION ≠ CAUSATION!

Experimental **studies have also found that media violence viewing can cause aggression:**

Viewing violence (compared to entertaining nonviolence) → participants react more cruelly when provoked. (Effect is strongest if the violent person is attractive, the violence seems justified and realistic, the act goes unpunished, and the viewer does not see pain or harm caused.)

What prompts the *violence-viewing effect*?

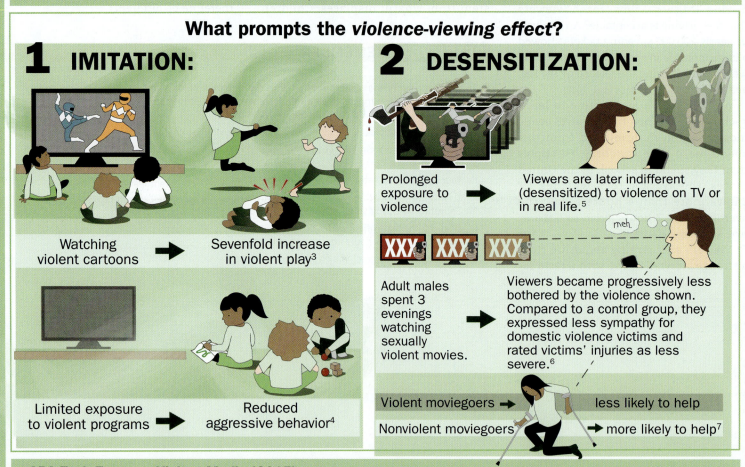

1 IMITATION:

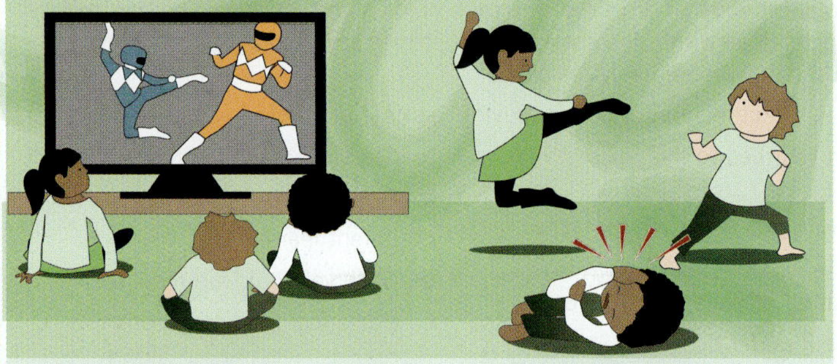

Watching violent cartoons → Sevenfold increase in violent play[3]

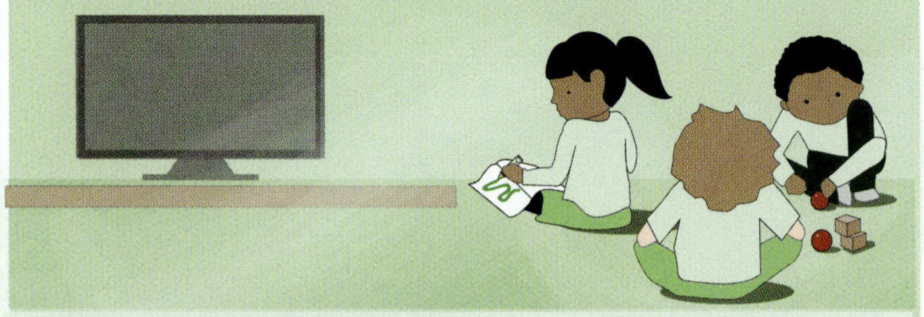

Limited exposure to violent programs → Reduced aggressive behavior[4]

2 DESENSITIZATION:

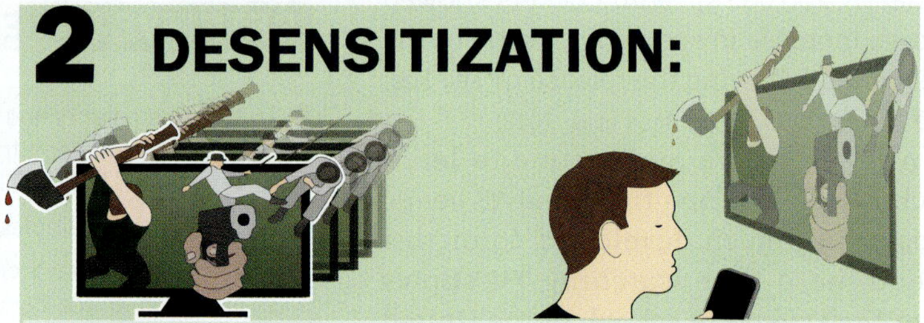

Prolonged exposure to violence → Viewers are later indifferent (desensitized) to violence on TV or in real life.[5]

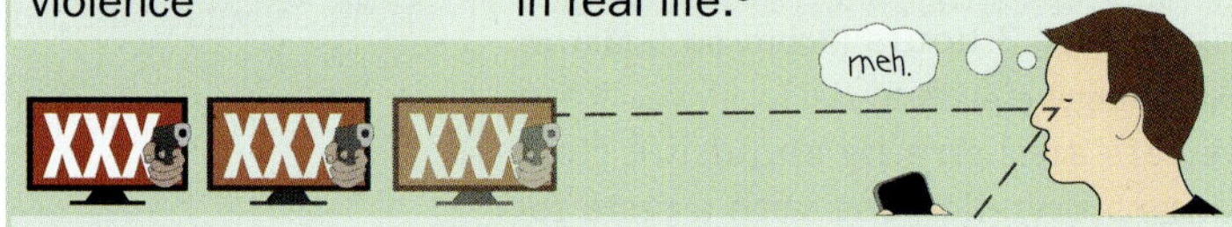

meh.
XXX
XXX
XXX

Adult males spent 3 evenings watching sexually violent movies. → Viewers became progressively less bothered by the violence shown. Compared to a control group, they expressed less sympathy for domestic violence victims and rated victims' injuries as less severe.[6]

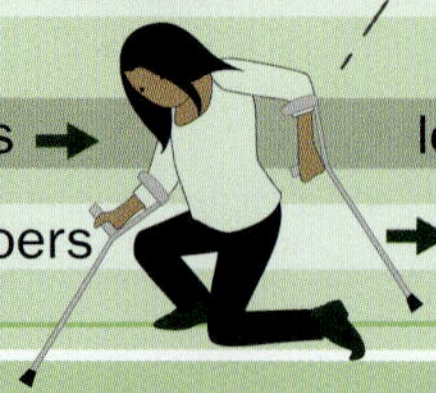

Violent moviegoers → less likely to help

Nonviolent moviegoers → more likely to help[7]

- **APA Task Force on Violent Media (2015)** found that the "research demonstrates a consistent relation between violent video game use and increases in aggressive behavior, aggressive cognitions, and aggressive affect, and decreases in prosocial behavior, empathy, and sensitivity to aggression."

- **American Academy of Pediatrics (2009)** has advised pediatricians that "media violence can contribute to aggressive behavior, desensitization to violence, nightmares, and fear of being harmed."

1. Centerwall, 1989. 2. Boxer at al., 2009; Gentile et al., 2011; Gentile & Bushman, 2012. 3. Boyatzis et al., 1995. 4. Christakis et al., 2013. 5. Fanti et al., 2009; Rule & Ferguson, 1986. 6. Mullin & Linz, 1995. 7. Bushman & Anderson, 2009.

LEARNING OBJECTIVES

TEST YOURSELF Answer these repeated Learning Objective Questions on your own (before checking the answers in Appendix D) to improve your retention of the concepts (McDaniel et al., 2009, 2015).

How Do We Learn?

6-1: How do we define *learning*, and what are some basic forms of learning?

Classical Conditioning

6-2: What is *classical conditioning*, and how does it demonstrate associative learning?

6-3: What parts do acquisition, extinction, spontaneous recovery, generalization, and discrimination play in classical conditioning?

6-4: Why is Pavlov's work important, and how is it being applied?

Operant Conditioning

6-5: What is *operant conditioning*, and how is operant behavior reinforced and shaped?

6-6: How do positive and negative reinforcement differ, and what are the basic types of reinforcers?

6-7: How do continuous and partial reinforcement schedules affect behavior?

6-8: How does punishment differ from negative reinforcement, and how does punishment affect behavior?

6-9: Why were Skinner's ideas controversial, and how might his operant conditioning principles be applied at school, at work, in sports, in parenting, and for self-improvement?

6-10: How does classical conditioning differ from operant conditioning?

Biology, Cognition, and Learning

6-11: What limits does biology place on conditioning?

6-12: How do cognitive processes affect classical and operant conditioning?

Learning by Observation

6-13: What is *observational learning?*

6-14: How may observational learning be enabled by neural mirroring?

6-15: What is the impact of prosocial modeling and of antisocial modeling?

6-16: What is the violence-viewing effect?

TERMS AND CONCEPTS TO REMEMBER

TEST YOURSELF Write down the definition in your own words, then check your answer.

learning, *p.* 167
associative learning, *p.* 167
stimulus, *p.* 167
respondent behavior, *p.* 167
operant behavior, *p.* 167
cognitive learning, *p.* 167
classical conditioning, *p.* 167
neutral stimulus (NS), *p.* 169
unconditioned response (UR), *p.* 169
unconditioned stimulus (US), *p.* 169
conditioned response (CR), *p.* 169
conditioned stimulus (CS), *p.* 169
acquisition, *p.* 169
extinction, *p.* 169
spontaneous recovery, *p.* 171
generalization, *p.* 171
discrimination, *p.* 171
operant conditioning, *p.* 173
law of effect, *p.* 173
operant chamber, *p.* 173
reinforcement, *p.* 173
shaping, *p.* 173
positive reinforcement, *p.* 175
negative reinforcement, *p.* 175
primary reinforcer, *p.* 175
conditioned reinforcer, *p.* 175
reinforcement schedule, *p.* 175
continuous reinforcement, *p.* 175
partial (intermittent) reinforcement, *p.* 175
fixed-ratio schedule, *p.* 175
variable-ratio schedule, *p.* 177
fixed-interval schedule, *p.* 177
variable-interval schedule, *p.* 177
punishment, *p.* 177
behaviorism, *p.* 181
cognitive map, *p.* 183
latent learning, *p.* 183
observational learning, *p.* 183
modeling, *p.* 183
mirror neuron, *p.* 183
prosocial behavior, *p.* 185

CHAPTER TEST

TEST YOURSELF Answer the following questions on your own first, then check your answers in Appendix E.

1. Learning is defined as "the process of acquiring, through experience, new and relatively enduring ________ or ________."

2. Two forms of associative learning are classical conditioning, in which we associate ________, and operant conditioning, in which we associate ________.
   a. two or more responses; a response and its consequence
   b. two or more stimuli; two or more responses
   c. two or more stimuli; a response and its consequence
   d. two or more responses; two or more stimuli

3. In Pavlov's experiments, the tone started as a neutral stimulus, and then became a(n) ________ stimulus.

4. Dogs have been taught to salivate to a circle but not to a square. This process is an example of ________.

5. After Watson and Rayner classically conditioned Little Albert to fear a white rat, the child later showed fear in response to a rabbit, a dog, and a furry coat. This illustrates
   a. extinction.
   b. generalization.
   c. spontaneous recovery.
   d. discrimination between two stimuli.

6. "Sex sells!" is a common saying in advertising. Using classical conditioning terms, explain how sexual images in advertisements can condition your response to a product.

7. Thorndike's law of effect was the basis for ________'s work on operant conditioning and behavior control.

8. One way to change behavior is to reward natural behaviors in small steps, as they get closer and closer to a desired behavior. This process is called ________.

9. Your dog is barking so loudly that it's making your ears ring. You clap your hands, the dog stops barking, your ears stop ringing, and you think to yourself, "I'll have to do that when he barks again." The end of the barking was for you a
   a. positive reinforcer.
   b. negative reinforcer.
   c. positive punishment.
   d. negative punishment.

10. How could your psychology instructor use negative reinforcement to encourage you to pay attention during class?

11. Reinforcing a desired response only some of the times it occurs is called ________ reinforcement.

12. A restaurant is running a special deal. After you buy four meals at full price, you will get a free appetizer. This is an example of a ________-________ schedule of reinforcement.
    a. fixed-ratio
    b. variable-ratio
    c. fixed-interval
    d. variable-interval

13. The partial reinforcement schedule that reinforces a response after unpredictable time periods is a ________-________ schedule.

14. An old saying notes that "a burnt child dreads the fire." In operant conditioning, the burning would be an example of a
    a. primary reinforcer.
    b. negative reinforcer.
    c. punisher.
    d. positive reinforcer.

15. Which research showed that conditioning can occur even when the unconditioned stimulus (US) does not immediately follow the neutral stimulus (NS)?
    a. The Little Albert experiment
    b. Pavlov's experiments with dogs
    c. Watson's behaviorism studies
    d. Garcia and Koelling's taste-aversion studies

16. Taste-aversion research has shown that some animals develop aversions to certain tastes but not to sights or sounds. This finding supports
    a. Pavlov's demonstration of generalization.
    b. Darwin's principle that natural selection favors traits that aid survival.
    c. Watson's belief that psychologists should study observable behavior, not mentalistic concepts.
    d. the early behaviorists' view that any organism can be conditioned to any stimulus.

17. Evidence that cognitive processes play an important role in learning comes in part from studies in which rats running a maze develop a ________ ________ of the maze.

18. Rats that explored a maze without any reward were later able to run the maze as well as other rats that had received food rewards for running the maze. The rats that had learned without reinforcement demonstrated ________ ________.

19. Children learn many social behaviors by imitating parents and other models. This type of learning is called ________ ________.

20. According to Bandura, we learn by watching models because we experience ________ reinforcement or ________ punishment.

21. Parents are most effective in getting their children to imitate them if
    a. their words and actions are consistent.
    b. they have outgoing personalities.
    c. one parent works and the other stays home to care for the children.
    d. they carefully explain why a behavior is acceptable in adults but not in children.

22. Some scientists believe that the brain has ________ neurons that enable observation and imitation.

23. Most experts agree that repeated viewing of media violence
    a. makes all viewers significantly more aggressive.
    b. has little effect on viewers.
    c. is a risk factor for viewers' increased aggression.
    d. makes viewers angry and frustrated.

Continue testing yourself with **LearningCurve** or **Achieve Read & Practice** to learn and remember most effectively.

LWA/Getty Images

CHAPTER 7

Memory

SURVEY THE CHAPTER

Imagine being unable to form new conscious memories. This was life for Henry Molaison (or H. M., as psychologists knew him until his 2008 death). In 1953, surgeons removed much of H. M.'s hippocampus in order to stop severe seizures. He remained intelligent and did daily crossword puzzles. Yet for his remaining 55 years he lived an unusual inner life. "I've known H. M. since 1962," reported one neuroscientist, "and he still doesn't know who I am" (Corkin, 2005, 2013). For about 20 seconds, he could keep something in mind. When distracted, he would lose what was just said or what had just occurred. Thus, he never could name the current U.S. president (Ogden, 2012).

My [DM's] father suffered a similar problem after a small stroke at age 92. His upbeat personality was unchanged. He enjoyed poring over family photo albums and telling stories about his pre-stroke life. But he could not tell me what day of the week it was, or what he'd had for dinner. Told repeatedly of his brother-in-law's recent death, he was surprised and saddened each time he heard the news.

Some disorders slowly strip away memory. *Alzheimer's disease* affects millions of people, usually later in life. What begins as difficulty remembering new information progresses into an inability to do everyday tasks. Complex speech becomes simple sentences. Family members and close friends become strangers. The brain's memory centers, once strong, become weak and wither away (Desikan et al., 2009). Over several years, people become unknowing and unknowable. Lost memory strikes at the core of our humanity, stealing joy, meaning, and companionship.

At the other extreme are people who win gold medals in memory competitions. When two-time World Memory champion Feng Wang was a 21-year-old college student, he didn't need help from his phone to remember his friends' numbers. The average person could parrot back a string of about 7—maybe even 9—numbers. Feng could reliably repeat up to 200, if they were read about 1 second apart in an otherwise silent room (Ericsson et al., 2017). At one competition, he even memorized 300 numbers!

Amazing? Yes, but consider your own impressive memory. You remember countless faces, places, and happenings; tastes, smells, and textures; voices, sounds, and songs. In one study, students listened to snippets—a mere four-tenths of a second—from popular songs. How often did they recognize the artist and song? More than 25 percent of the time (Krumhansl, 2010). We often recognize songs as quickly as we recognize familiar voices, faces, and places. In another experiment, people were exposed to 2800 images for only 3 seconds each. Later, viewing these and other images in a second round, they spotted the repeats with 82 percent accuracy (Konkle et al., 2010). Some super-recognizers display an extraordinary ability to recognize faces. Eighteen months after viewing a video of an armed robbery, one such police officer spotted and arrested the robber walking on a busy street (Davis et al., 2013).

How do we accomplish such memory feats? How can we remember things we have not thought about for years, yet forget the name of someone we just met? How are our memories stored in our brain? Why, when we ask you later in this chapter, will you be likely to have trouble recalling this sentence: *"The angry rioter threw the rock at the window"?* In this chapter, we'll consider these fascinating questions and more, including some tips on how we can improve our own memories.

IN YOUR EVERYDAY LIFE

Imagine having an injury that significantly impaired your memory. Now, imagine having a record-setting ability to remember, like Feng Wang. How would each condition affect your daily routine?

Studying Memory

Learning Objective Question LOQ 7-1

What is *memory,* and how do information-processing models help us study memory?

Be thankful for **memory**—your storehouse of accumulated learning. Your memory enables you to recognize family, speak your language, and find your way home. Your memory allows you to enjoy an experience and then mentally replay it to enjoy again. Without memory, you could not savor past achievements, nor feel guilt or anger over painful past events. You would instead live in an endless present, each moment fresh. Each person would be a stranger, every language foreign, every task—dressing, cooking, biking—a new challenge. You would even be a stranger to yourself, lacking that ongoing sense of self that extends from your distant past to your momentary present.

In Chapter 6, Sensation and Perception, we considered one of psychology's big questions: How does the world enter your brain? This chapter's related question: How does your brain pluck information from the world around you and store it for a lifetime of use? Said simply, how does your brain construct your memories?

To help clients imagine future buildings, architects create virtual models. Similarly, psychologists create memory models that, even if imperfect, help us think about how our brain forms and retrieves memories. An *information-processing model* compares human memory to a computer's operation. It assumes that, to remember something, we must

- *get information into our brain,* a process called **encoding.**
- *retain that information,* a process called **storage.**
- later *get the information back out,* a process called **retrieval.**

Let's **take a closer look.**

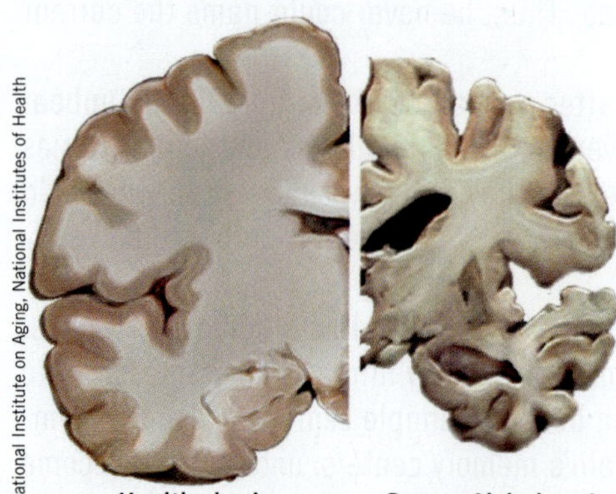

Extreme forgetting Alzheimer's disease severely damages the brain, and in the process strips away memory.

IN YOUR EVERYDAY LIFE

What has your memory system encoded, stored, and retrieved today?

AN INFORMATION-PROCESSING MODEL

LOQ 7-2 What is the three-stage information-processing model, and how has later research updated this model?

Richard Atkinson and Richard Shiffrin (1968; 2016) proposed that we form memories in three stages.

1. We first record to-be-remembered information as a fleeting **sensory memory.**
2. From there, we process information into **short-term memory,** where we encode it through *rehearsal.*
3. Finally, information moves into **long-term memory** for later retrieval.

This model has been updated with important newer concepts, including *working memory* and *automatic processing* (**FIGURE 7.1**).

Working Memory

In Atkinson and Shiffrin's original model, the second, short-term stage appeared to be a temporary shelf for holding recent thoughts and experiences. We now know that this **working-memory** stage is a scratchpad where your brain actively processes important information,

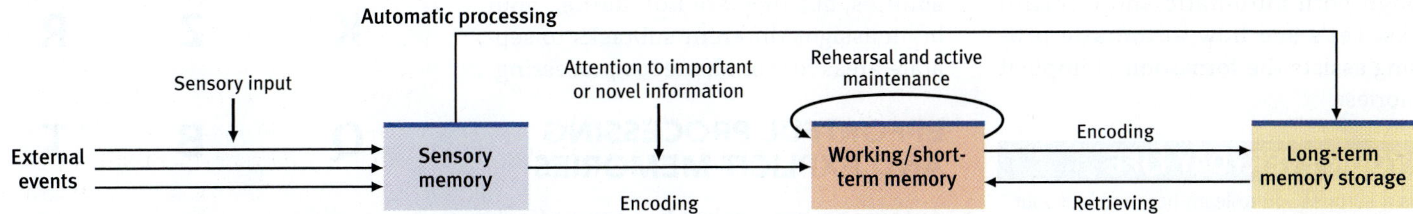

FIGURE 7.1 A modified three-stage processing model of memory Atkinson and Shiffrin's classic three-step model helps us to think about how memories are processed, but researchers now recognize other ways long-term memories form. For example, some information slips into long-term memory via a "back door," without our consciously attending to it *(automatic processing).* And so much active processing occurs in the short-term memory stage that many now prefer the term *working memory.*

making sense of new input and linking it with long-term memories. It also works in the opposite direction, processing already stored information. When you process verbal information, your *active* working memory connects new information to what you already know or imagine (Cowan, 2010, 2016; Kail & Hall, 2001). If you hear "eye-screem," you may encode it as *ice cream* or *I scream,* depending on both your experience and the context (snack shop or horror film).

For most of you, what you are reading enters your working memory through vision. You may also silently repeat the information using auditory rehearsal. Integrating these memory inputs with your existing long-term memory requires focused attention.

Without focused attention, information often fades. If you think you can look something up later, you attend to it less and forget it more quickly. In one experiment, people read and typed new information they would later need, such as "An ostrich's eye is bigger than its brain." If they knew the information would be available online, they invested less energy in remembering it, and they remembered it less well (Wegner & Ward, 2013). Online, out of mind.

RETRIEVE & REMEMBER

ANSWERS IN APPENDIX E

1. How does the *working memory* concept update the classic Atkinson-Shiffrin three-stage information-processing model?
2. What are two basic functions of working memory?

LaunchPad For a 14-minute explanation and demonstration of our memory systems, see the *Video: Models of Memory.*

Building Memories: Encoding

OUR TWO-TRACK MEMORY SYSTEM

LOQ 7-3 How do implicit and explicit memories differ?

As we have seen throughout this text, our mind operates on two tracks. This theme appears again in the way we process memories:

- On one track, information skips the Atkinson-Shiffrin stages and barges directly into storage, without our awareness. These **implicit** *(nondeclarative)* **memories** form without our conscious effort. Implicit memories, formed through **automatic processing,** bypass the conscious encoding track.
- On the second track, we process our **explicit** *(declarative)* **memories** of the facts and experiences we can consciously know and "declare." We encode explicit memories through conscious, **effortful processing.** The Atkinson-Shiffrin model helps us understand how this memory track operates (Figure 7.1).

Our two-track mind, then, helps us encode, retain, and recall information

memory the persistence of learning over time through the encoding, storage, and retrieval of information.

encoding the process of getting information into the memory system.

storage the process of retaining encoded information over time.

retrieval the process of getting information out of memory storage.

sensory memory the immediate, very brief recording of sensory information in the memory system.

short-term memory activated memory that holds a few items briefly (such as digits of a phone number while calling) before the information is stored or forgotten.

long-term memory the relatively permanent and limitless storehouse of the memory system. Includes knowledge, skills, and experiences.

working memory a newer understanding of short-term memory that adds conscious, active processing of incoming sensory information, and of information retrieved from long-term memory.

implicit memory retention of learned skills, or classically conditioned associations, without conscious awareness. (Also called *nondeclarative memory.*)

automatic processing unconscious encoding of everyday information, such as space, time, and frequency, and of well-learned information, such as word meanings.

explicit memory retention of facts and personal events you can consciously retrieve. (Also called *declarative memory.*)

effortful processing encoding that requires attention and conscious effort.

through both automatic and effortful tracks. Let's see how automatic processing assists the formation of implicit memories.

IN YOUR EVERYDAY LIFE

Does it surprise you to learn how much of your memory processing is automatic? What might life be like if *all* memory processing were effortful?

AUTOMATIC PROCESSING AND IMPLICIT MEMORIES

LOQ 7-4 What information do we process automatically?

Your implicit memories include automatic skills (such as how to ride a bike) and classically conditioned *associations*. If once attacked by a dog, years later you may, without recalling the conditioned association, automatically tense up when a dog approaches.

Without conscious effort, you also automatically process information about

- ***space.*** While studying, you often encode the place where certain material appears. Later, when you want to retrieve the information, you may visualize its location.
- ***time.*** While you are going about your day, your brain is working behind the scenes, jotting down the sequence of your day's events. Later, if you realize you've left your phone somewhere, you can call up that sequence and retrace your steps.
- ***frequency.*** Your behind-the-scenes mind also keeps track of how often things have happened, thus enabling you to realize, "This is the third time I've run into her today!"

Your two-track mind processes information efficiently. As one track automatically tucks away routine details, the other track focuses on conscious, effortful processing. This division of labor illustrates the **parallel processing** we've also seen in Chapter 2 and Chapter 5. Mental feats such as thinking, vision, and memory may seem to be single abilities, but they are not. Rather, your brain assigns different subtasks to separate areas for simultaneous processing.

EFFORTFUL PROCESSING AND EXPLICIT MEMORIES

Automatic processing happens effortlessly. When you see words in your language, you can't help but start to register their meaning. *Learning* to read was not automatic. You at first worked hard to pick out letters and connect them to certain sounds. But with experience and practice, your reading became automatic. Imagine now learning to read sentences in reverse:

.citamotua emoceb nac gnissecorp
luftroffE

At first, this requires effort, but with practice it becomes more automatic. We develop many skills in this way: driving, texting, and speaking a new language. With practice, these tasks become automatic.

Sensory Memory

LOQ 7-5 How does sensory memory work?

Sensory memory (recall Figure 7.1) is the first stage in forming explicit memories. A memory-to-be enters by way of the senses, feeding very brief images, echoes of sounds, and strong scents into our working memory. But sensory memory, like a lightning flash, is fleeting. How fleeting? In one experiment, people viewed three rows of three letters each for only one-twentieth of a second (**FIGURE 7.2**). Then the nine letters disappeared. How many letters could people recall? Only about half of them.

Was it because they had too little time to see them? *No.* People actually *could* see and recall all the letters, but only briefly (Sperling, 1960). We know this because the researcher sounded a tone immediately *after* flashing the nine letters. A high tone directed people to report the top row of letters; a medium tone, the middle row; a low tone, the bottom row. With these cues, they rarely missed a letter, showing that all nine were briefly available for recall.

K	Z	R
Q	B	T
S	G	N

FIGURE 7.2 Total recall—briefly

This fleeting sensory memory of the flashed letters was an *iconic memory*. For a few tenths of a second, our eyes retain a picture-image memory of a scene. Then our visual field clears quickly, and new images replace old ones. We also have a fleeting sensory memory of sounds. It's called *echoic memory,* because the sound echoes in our mind for 3 or 4 seconds.

Short-Term Memory Capacity

LOQ 7-6 What is our short-term memory capacity?

Recall that short-term memory refers to what we can briefly retain. The related idea of working memory also includes our active processing, as our brain makes sense of incoming information and links it with stored memories. What are the limits of what we can hold in this middle, short-term stage?

Memory researcher George Miller (1956) proposed that we can store about seven bits of information (give or take two) in this middle stage. Miller's Magical Number Seven is psychology's contribution to the list of magical sevens—the seven wonders of the world, the seven seas, the seven deadly sins, the seven colors of the rainbow, the seven musical scale notes, the seven days of the week—seven magical sevens. After Miller's 2012 death, his daughter recalled his best moment of golf: "He made the one and only hole-in-one of his life at the age of 77, on the seventh green . . . with a seven iron. He loved that" (quoted by Vitello, 2012).

Other research confirms that we can, if nothing distracts us, recall about seven bits of information. But the number varies by task; we tend to remember about six letters and only about five words (Baddeley et al., 1975; Cowan, 2015). How quickly do our short-term memories disappear? To find out, researchers asked people to remember groups of three consonants, such as *CHJ* (Peterson & Peterson, 1959). To prevent rehearsal, researchers distracted participants (asking them, for example, to start at 100 and begin counting aloud backward by threes). Without active processing, people's short-term memories of the consonants disappeared. After 3 seconds, they recalled the letters only about half the time. After 12 seconds, they seldom recalled them at all (**FIGURE 7.3**).

Working-memory capacity varies, depending on age and other factors. Young adults have greater working-memory capacity—the ability to juggle multiple items while processing information—than do children and older adults. This helps young adults to better retain information after sleeping and to solve problems creatively (De Dreu et al., 2012; Fenn & Hambrick, 2012; Wiley & Jarosz, 2012). But everyone does better and more efficient work when focused, without distractions, on one task at a time. *The bottom line:* It's probably a bad idea to try to watch a live stream, text your friends, and write a psychology paper all at the same time (Willingham, 2010)!

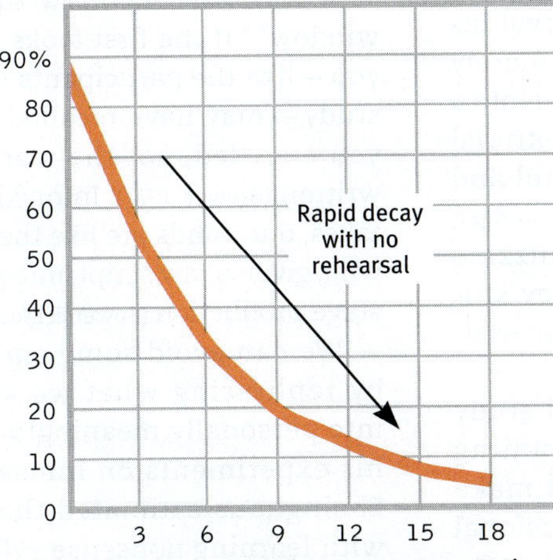

FIGURE 7.3 Short-term memory decay (Data from Peterson & Peterson, 1959; see also Brown, 1958.)

LaunchPad For a review of memory stages and a test of your own short-term memory capacity, visit *Topic Tutorial: PsychSim6, Short-Term Memory.*

Effortful Processing Strategies

LOQ 7-7 What are some effortful processing strategies that can help us remember new information?

Let's recap. To form a lasting explicit memory of a fact or an experience, it helps to *focus our attention* and *make a conscious effort* to remember. But our working-memory touchscreen has limited space, and images, sounds, and other distractions compete for our attention.

We can boost our ability to form new explicit memories by using specific effortful processing strategies, such as *chunking* and *mnemonics.*

- *Chunking*: When we **chunk** information, we organize items into familiar, manageable units (Thalmann et al., 2018). Glance for a few seconds at row 1 of **FIGURE 7.4**, then look away and try to draw those forms. Impossible, yes? But you can easily reproduce row 2, which is just as complex. And row 4 is probably much easier to remember than row 3, although both contain the same letters. As you can see, chunking information helps us to recall it more easily.

  Chunking usually occurs so naturally that we take it for granted. Try remembering 43 individual numbers and letters. It would be impossible, unless chunked into, say, seven meaningful chunks—such as "Try remembering 43 individual numbers and letters!" 😊

- *Mnemonics*: In ancient Greece, scholars and public speakers needed memory aids to help encode long passages and speeches. They developed **mnemonics,** which often rely on vivid imagery. We are particularly good at remembering mental pictures. Concrete words that create these mental images are easier to remember than abstract words (Akpinar & Berger, 2015). (When we quiz you later, which three of these words—*bicycle, void, cigarette, inherent, fire, process*—will you most likely recall?) Do you still recall the rock-throwing rioter sentence mentioned at the beginning of this chapter? If so, it is probably not only because of the meaning you encoded but also because the sentence painted a mental image.

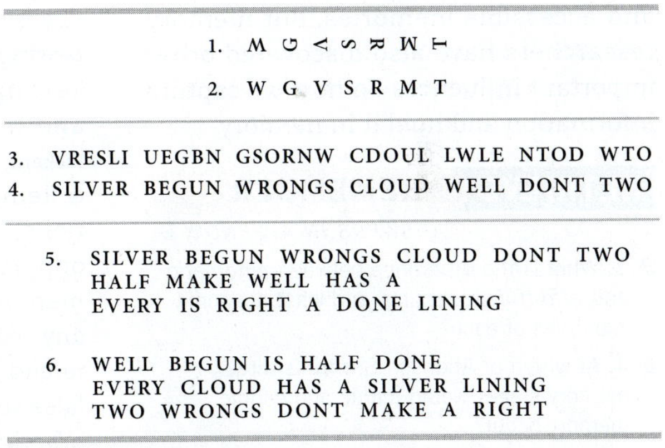

1. M G V S R M T

2. W G V S R M T

3. VRESLI UEGBN GSORNW CDOUL LWLE NTOD WTO
4. SILVER BEGUN WRONGS CLOUD WELL DONT TWO

5. SILVER BEGUN WRONGS CLOUD DONT TWO
HALF MAKE WELL HAS A
EVERY IS RIGHT A DONE LINING

6. WELL BEGUN IS HALF DONE
EVERY CLOUD HAS A SILVER LINING
TWO WRONGS DONT MAKE A RIGHT

FIGURE 7.4 Chunking effects Organizing information into meaningful units, such as letters, words, and phrases, helps us recall it more easily (Hintzman, 1978).

parallel processing processing many aspects of a stimulus or problem at once.

chunking organizing items into familiar, manageable units; often occurs automatically.

mnemonics [nih-MON-iks] memory aids, especially techniques that use vivid imagery and organizational devices.

Memory whizzes understand the power of such systems. Star performers in the World Memory Championships do not usually have exceptional intelligence. Rather, they are superior at using mnemonic strategies (Maguire et al., 2003b). Frustrated by his ordinary memory, science writer Joshua Foer wanted to see how much he could improve it. After a year of intense practice, he won the U.S. Memory Championship by memorizing a pack of 52 playing cards in under two minutes. How did Foer do it? He added vivid new details to memories of a familiar place—his childhood home. Each card, presented in any order, could then match up with the clear picture in his head. As the test subject of his own wild memory experiment, he learned the power of painting pretty pictures in his mind (Foer, 2011).

* * *

Effortful processing requires closer attention and effort, and chunking and mnemonics help us form meaningful and accessible memories. But memory researchers have also discovered other important influences on how we capture information and hold it in memory.

RETRIEVE & REMEMBER

ANSWERS IN APPENDIX E

- 3. What is the difference between *automatic* and *effortful* processing, and what are some examples of each?
- 4. At which of Atkinson-Shiffrin's three memory stages would iconic and echoic memory occur?

Spaced Study and Self-Assessment

LOQ 7-8 Why is cramming ineffective, and what is the *testing effect?* Why is it important to make new information meaningful?

We retain information better when our encoding is spread over time. Experiments have confirmed that this **spacing effect** *(distributed practice)* produces better long-term recall (Cepeda et al., 2006; Soderstrom et al., 2016). Cramming *(massed practice)* can produce speedy short-term learning and feelings of confidence. But as pioneering memory researcher Hermann Ebbinghaus (1850–1909) observed in 1885, those who learn quickly also forget quickly. You'll retain material better if, rather than cramming, you space your study, with reviewing time later. How much later? If you need to remember something 10 days from now, practice it again tomorrow. If you need to remember something 6 months from now, practice it again a month from now (Cepeda et al., 2008). The spacing effect is one of psychology's most reliable findings, and it extends to motor skills and online game performance (Stafford & Dewar, 2014). Memory researcher Henry Roediger (2013) sums it up: "Hundreds of studies have shown that distributed practice leads to more durable learning." Distributing your learning over several months, rather than over a shorter term, can help you retain information for a lifetime.

One effective way to distribute practice is *repeated self-testing,* often called the **testing effect** (Roediger & Karpicke, 2006, 2018). Testing does more than assess learning and memory; it improves them (Pan & Rickard, 2018). In this textbook, the Retrieve & Remember questions and Review sections, including the Chapter Tests, offer opportunities to improve learning and memory. Better to practice retrieval (as any exam will demand) than to merely reread material (which may lull you into a false sense of mastery). Happily, "retrieval practice (or testing) is [a] powerful and general strategy for learning" (Roediger, 2013). No wonder daily online quizzing improves introductory psychology students' course performance (Batsell et al., 2017; Pennebaker et al., 2013).

The point to remember: Spaced study and self-assessment beat cramming and rereading. Practice may not make perfect, but smart practice—occasional rehearsal with self-testing—makes for lasting memories.

Here is another sentence we will ask you about later: *The fish attacked the swimmer.*

Making New Information Meaningful

Spaced practice helps, but if new information is neither meaningful nor related to your experience, you will have trouble processing it. Imagine being asked to remember this passage (Bransford & Johnson, 1972):

> The procedure is actually quite simple. First you arrange things into different groups. Of course, one pile may be sufficient depending on how much there is to do. . . . After the procedure is completed one arranges the materials into different groups again. Then they can be put into their appropriate places. Eventually they will be used once more and the whole cycle will then have to be repeated. However, that is part of life.

When some students heard the paragraph you just read, without a meaningful context, they remembered little of it. Others were told the paragraph described doing laundry (something meaningful to them). They remembered much more of it—as you probably could now after rereading it.

Can you repeat the sentence about the angry rioter (from this chapter's opening section)?

Was the sentence "The angry rioter threw the rock *through* the window" or "The angry rioter threw the rock *at* the window"? If the first looks more correct, you—like the participants in the original study—may have recalled the meaning you encoded, not the words that were written (Brewer, 1977). In making such mistakes, our minds are like theater directors who, given a raw script, imagine a finished stage production (Bower & Morrow, 1990).

We can avoid some encoding errors by rephrasing what we see and hear into personally meaningful terms. From his experiments on himself, Hermann Ebbinghaus estimated that, compared with learning nonsense syllables, learning meaningful material required one-tenth the effort. As another memory researcher noted, "The time you spend thinking about material you are reading and relating it to previously stored material is about the most useful thing you can do in learning any new subject matter" (Wickelgren, 1977, p. 346).

What information do people most easily remember? Personally relevant information. This tendency, called the *self-reference effect*, is especially strong in individualist Western cultures (Symons & Johnson, 1997; Wagar & Cohen, 2003). In contrast, people in collectivist Eastern cultures remember self-relevant and family-relevant information equally well (Sparks et al., 2016).

The point to remember: You can profit from taking time to find personal meaning in what you are studying.

RETRIEVE & REMEMBER

ANSWERS IN APPENDIX E

5. Which strategies are better for long-term retention: cramming and rereading material, or spreading out learning over time and repeatedly testing yourself?

LaunchPad For suggestions on how to apply the *testing effect* to your own learning, watch my [DM's] 5-minute *Video: Make Things Memorable* in LaunchPad or at tinyurl.com/HowToRemember.

Memory Storage

LOQ 7-9 What is the capacity of long-term memory? Are our long-term memories processed and stored in specific locations?

In Arthur Conan Doyle's *A Study in Scarlet*, Sherlock Holmes offers a popular theory of memory capacity:

> I consider that a man's brain originally is like a little empty attic, and you have to stock it with such furniture as you choose. . . . It is a mistake to think that that little room has elastic walls and can distend to any extent. Depend upon it, there comes a time when for every addition of knowledge you forget something that you knew before.

Contrary to Holmes' "memory model," our capacity for storing long-term memories has no real limit. Many memories endure for a lifetime. Our brains are not like attics, which, once filled, can store more items only if we discard old ones. One research team, after studying the brain's neural connections, estimated its storage capacity as "in the same ballpark as the World Wide Web" (Sejnowski, 2016).

RETAINING INFORMATION IN THE BRAIN

I [DM] marveled at my aging mother-in-law, a retired pianist and organist. At age 88, her blind eyes could no longer read music. But let her sit at a keyboard and she could flawlessly play any of hundreds of hymns, including ones she had not thought of for 20 years. Where did her brain store those thousands of note patterns?

For a time, some surgeons and memory researchers marveled at what appeared to be vivid memories triggered by stimulating the brain during surgery. Did this prove that our whole past, not just well-practiced music, is "in there," just waiting to be relived? Further research disproved this idea. The vivid flashbacks were actually new creations of a stressed brain, not real memories (Loftus & Loftus, 1980). We do not store information in single, specific spots, as libraries store their books. As with perception, language, emotion, and much more, memory requires brain networks. Many parts of our brain interact as we encode, store, and retrieve information.

Explicit Memory System: The Hippocampus and Frontal Lobes

LOQ 7-10 What roles do the hippocampus and frontal lobes play in memory processing?

Separate brain regions process our explicit and implicit memories. We know this from scans of the brain in action, and from autopsies of people who suffered different types of memory loss.

Explicit, conscious memories are either **semantic** (facts and general knowledge) or **episodic** (experienced events). New explicit memories of these facts and episodes are laid down via the **hippocampus**, a limbic system neural center that is our brain's equivalent of a "save" button (**FIGURE 7.5**). As children mature, their hippocampus grows, enabling them to construct detailed memories (Keresztes et al., 2017). Brain scans reveal activity in the hippocampus and nearby brain networks as people form explicit memories of names, images, and events (Terada et al., 2017; Wang et al., 2014). Your hippocampus acts as a loading dock where your brain registers

spacing effect the tendency for distributed study or practice to yield better long-term retention than is achieved through massed study or practice.

testing effect enhanced memory after retrieving, rather than simply rereading, information. Also sometimes referred to as a *retrieval practice effect* or *test-enhanced learning*.

semantic memory explicit memory of facts and general knowledge; one of our two conscious memory systems (the other is *episodic memory*).

episodic memory explicit memory of personally experienced events; one of our two conscious memory systems (the other is *semantic memory*).

hippocampus a neural center located in the limbic system; helps process explicit (conscious) memories—of facts and events—for storage.

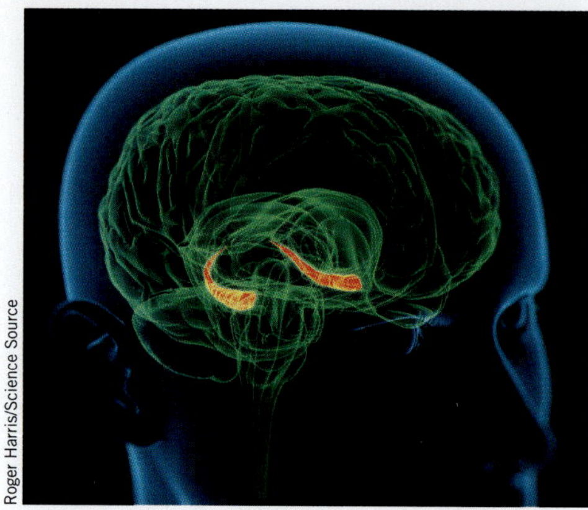

Roger Harris/Science Source

FIGURE 7.5 The hippocampus Explicit memories for facts and episodes are processed in the hippocampus (orange structures) and fed to other brain regions for storage.

and temporarily stores aspects of an event—its smell, feel, sound, and location. Then, like older files shifted to be archived, memories migrate to the cortex for storage. This storage process is called **memory consolidation.**

Your brain's right and left frontal lobes store different information. Recalling a password and holding it in working memory, for example, would activate your left frontal lobe. Calling up a visual image of last night's party would more likely activate your right frontal lobe.

Sleep supports memory consolidation. In one experiment, students who learned material in a study/sleep/restudy condition remembered material better, both a week and six months later, than did students who studied in the morning and restudied in the evening without intervening sleep (Mazza et al., 2016). During sleep, the hippocampus and brain cortex display rhythmic patterns of activity, as if they were talking to each other (Euston et al., 2007; Khodagholy et al., 2018). Researchers suspect that the brain is replaying the day's experiences as it transfers them to the cortex for long-term storage (Squire & Zola-Morgan, 1991). When our learning is distributed over days rather than crammed into a single day, we experience more sleep-induced memory consolidation. And that helps explain the spacing effect.

Tim Zurowski/All Canada Photos/Getty Images

Hippocampus hero One contender for champion memorist is a mere birdbrain—the Clark's Nutcracker—which can locate up to 6000 caches of pine seed it previously buried (Shettleworth, 1993).

Implicit Memory System: The Cerebellum and Basal Ganglia

LOQ 7-11 What roles do the cerebellum and basal ganglia play in memory processing?

You could lose your hippocampus and still—thanks to automatic processing—lay down *implicit* memories of newly conditioned associations and skills. Memory loss following brain damage left one patient unable to recognize her physician as, each day, he shook her hand and introduced himself. One day, after reaching for his hand, she yanked hers back, for the physician had pricked her with a tack in his palm. When he next introduced himself, she refused to shake his hand but couldn't explain why. Having been *classically conditioned,* she just wouldn't do it (LeDoux, 1996). Implicitly, she felt what she could not explain.

Your *cerebellum,* a brain region extending out from the rear of your brainstem, plays an important role in forming and storing memories created by classical conditioning. People with a damaged cerebellum cannot develop some conditioned reflexes. They can't, for example, link a tone with an oncoming puff of air, so they don't blink just before the puff, as anyone else would learn to do (Daum & Schugens, 1996; Green & Woodruff-Pak, 2000). Implicit memory formation needs the cerebellum.

Your memories of physical skills—walking, cooking, dressing—are also implicit memories. Your *basal ganglia,* deep brain structures involved in motor movement, help form your memories for these skills (Mishkin, 1982; Mishkin et al., 1997). If you have learned how to ride a bike, thank your basal ganglia.

Although not part of our conscious adult memory system, the reactions and skills we learned during infancy reach far into our future. Can you remember learning to talk and walk as a baby? If you cannot, you are not alone. As adults, our *conscious* memory of our first four years is largely blank, an experience called *infantile amnesia.* My [ND's] daughter, Bevy, enjoyed a visit to Hong Kong Disneyland at age 2, but as an adult she will have no conscious memory of that happy time. To form and store explicit memories, we need a command of language and a well-developed hippocampus. Before age 4, we don't have those memory tools.

RETRIEVE & REMEMBER

ANSWERS IN APPENDIX E

6. Which parts of the brain are important for *implicit* memory processing, and which parts play a key role in *explicit* memory processing?
7. Your friend has experienced brain damage in an accident. He can remember how to tie his shoes but has a hard time remembering anything you tell him during a conversation. How can implicit versus explicit information processing explain what's going on here?

The Amygdala, Emotions, and Memory

LOQ 7-12 How do emotions affect our memory processing?

Arousal can sear certain events into the brain (Birnbaum et al., 2004; McGaugh, 2015; Strange & Dolan, 2004). Excitement or stress (perhaps at a time you performed music or in a sport in front of a crowd) triggers your glands to produce stress hormones. By making more glucose energy available to fuel brain activity, stress hormones signal the brain that something important is happening. Stress hormones also focus memory. They provoke the *amygdala* (two limbic system, emotion-processing clusters) to boost activity in the brain's memory-forming areas (Buchanan, 2007; Kensinger, 2007) (**FIGURE 7.6**).

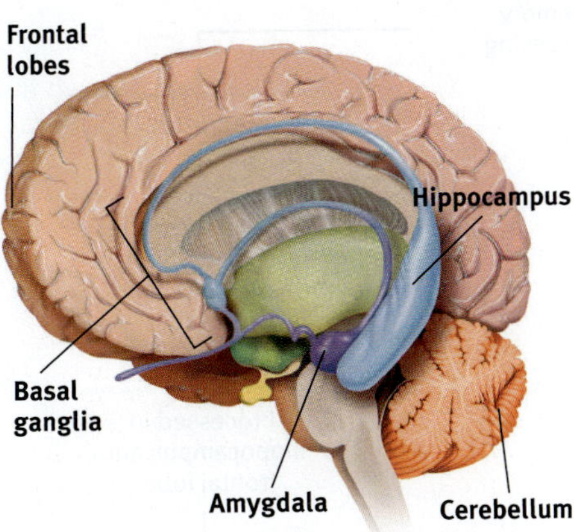

FIGURE 7.6 Review key memory structures in the brain
Frontal lobes and *hippocampus:* explicit memory formation
Cerebellum and *basal ganglia:* implicit memory formation
Amygdala: emotion-related memory formation

The resulting emotions often persist without our conscious awareness of what caused them, as one clever experiment demonstrated. The participants were patients with hippocampal damage, which left them unable to form new explicit memories. Researchers first showed them a sad film, and later a happy film. Although these viewers could not consciously recall the films, the sad or happy emotion lingered (Feinstein et al., 2010).

After a horrific experience—a school shooting, a house fire, a rape—vivid memories of the event may intrude again and again. The result is "stronger, more reliable memories" (McGaugh, 1994, 2003). The persistence of such memories is adaptive. They alert us to future dangers. By focusing our attention on the remembered, important event, they reduce our attention to minor details (Mather & Sutherland, 2012). Whatever captures our attention gets recalled well, at the expense of the surrounding context.

Why are some memories so much stronger than others? Emotion-triggered hormonal changes help explain why we long remember exciting or shocking events, such as our first kiss or our whereabouts when learning of a loved one's death. Psychologists call them **flashbulb memories.** It's as if the brain commands, "Capture this!" Where were you, for example, when you learned that Donald Trump was elected U.S. president? In a 2006 Pew survey, 95 percent of American adults said they could recall exactly where they were or what they were doing when they first heard the news of the 9/11 terrorist attacks. With time, some errors crept in (compared with earlier reports taken right afterward). Mostly, however, people's memories of 9/11 remained consistent over the next two to three years (Conway et al., 2009; Hirst et al., 2009).

Which is more important—your experiences or your memories of them?

Dramatic experiences remain clear in our memory in part because we rehearse them (Hirst & Phelps, 2016). We think about them and describe them to others. Memories of personally important experiences also endure (Storm & Jobe, 2012; Talarico & Moore, 2012). Compared with non-Catholics, devout Catholics recalled better the resignation of Pope Benedict XVI (Curci et al., 2015). Ditto for baseball fans' memories of their team's championship games (Breslin & Safer, 2011). When their team won, fans enjoyed recalling and recounting the victory, leading to longer-lasting memories.

LaunchPad For an 8-minute examination of emotion's effect on memory, see the *Video: The Role of Emotion.*

SYNAPTIC CHANGES

LOQ 7-13 How do changes at the synapse level affect our memory processing?

As you now think and learn about memory processes, your brain is changing. Activity in some brain pathways is increasing. Neural network connections are forming and strengthening. Changes are taking place at your *synapses*—the sites where nerve cells communicate with one another by means of chemical messengers (neurotransmitters). Experience alters the brain's neural networks (see Chapter 3).

Donna Ikenberry/Art Directors/Alamy

Memory slug The much-studied California sea slug, *Aplysia*, has increased our understanding of the neural basis of learning and memory.

To understand the power of the brain's memory centers, researchers Eric Kandel and James Schwartz (1982) recruited a seemingly unlikely candidate for research: the California sea slug. This simple animal's nerve cells are unusually large, enabling the researchers to observe how the neurons change during learning. Using mild electric shocks, they classically conditioned the sea slugs to withdraw their gills when squirted with water, much as we might jump at the sound of a firecracker. By observing the slugs' neural connections before and after this conditioning, Kandel and Schwartz pinpointed changes. As a slug learns, it releases more of the neurotransmitter *serotonin* into certain neurons. These cells' synapses then become more efficient at transmitting signals. Experience and learning can increase—even double—the number of synapses, even in slugs (Kandel, 2012). No wonder the brain area that processes spatial memory grows larger in London taxi driver trainees, too, as they learn to navigate the city's complicated maze of streets (Woolett & Maguire, 2011).

memory consolidation the neural storage of a long-term memory.

flashbulb memory a clear memory of an emotionally significant moment or event.

As synapses become more efficient, so do neural networks. Sending neurons now release their neurotransmitters more easily. Receiving neurons may grow additional receptor sites. This increased neural efficiency, called **long-term potentiation (LTP),** enables learning and memory (Lynch, 2002; Whitlock et al., 2006). Several lines of evidence confirm that LTP is a physical basis for memory:

- Drugs that block LTP interfere with learning (Lynch & Staubli, 1991).
- Drugs that mimic what happens during learning increase LTP (Harward et al., 2016).
- Rats given a drug that enhanced synaptic efficiency (LTP) learned to run a maze with half the usual number of mistakes (Service, 1994).

After LTP has occurred, an electric current passing through the brain won't erase old memories. Before LTP, however, the same current can wipe out very recent memories. This often happens when severely depressed people receive *electroconvulsive therapy (ECT)* (see Chapter 14). Sports concussions can also wipe out recent memories. Football players and boxers knocked unconscious typically have no memory of events just before the blow to the head (Yarnell & Lynch, 1970). Their working memory had no time to process the information into long-term memory before the shutdown.

Recently, I [DM] did a little test of memory consolidation. While on an operating table for a basketball-related tendon repair, I was given a face mask and soon could smell the anesthesia gas. "So how much longer will I be with you?" I asked the anesthesiologist. My last moment of memory was her answer: "About 10 seconds." My brain spent that 10 seconds consolidating a memory for her 2-second answer, but could not tuck any further memory away before I was out cold.

FIGURE 7.7 summarizes the brain's two-track memory processing and storage system for implicit (automatic) and explicit (effortful) memories. *The bottom line:* Learn something and you change your brain a little.

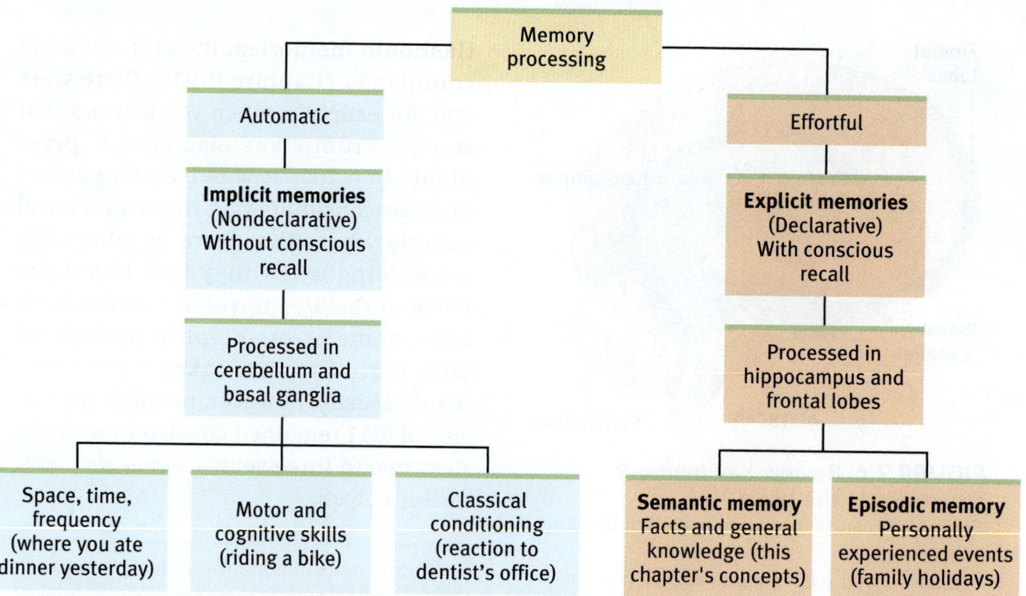

FIGURE 7.7 Our two memory systems

RETRIEVE & REMEMBER

ANSWERS IN APPENDIX E

8. Which brain area responds to stress hormones by helping to create stronger memories?
9. Increased efficiency at the synapses is evidence of the neural basis of learning and memory. This is called ____________ - ____________ ____________.

Retrieval: Getting Information Out

Remembering an event requires more than getting information into our brain and storing it there. To use that information, we must retrieve it. How do psychologists test whether learning has been retained over time? What triggers retrieval?

MEASURING RETENTION

LOQ 7-14 How do psychologists assess memory with recall, recognition, and relearning?

Memory is learning that persists over time. Three types of evidence indicate whether something has been learned and retained:

- **Recall**—*retrieving* information out of storage and into your conscious awareness. Example: a fill-in-the-blank question.
- **Recognition**—*identifying* items you previously learned. Example: a multiple-choice question.
- **Relearning**—*learning something more quickly* when you learn it a second or later time. Example: When you review the first weeks of course work to prepare for your final exam, it will be easier to relearn the material than it was to learn it originally.

Psychologists can measure these different forms of memory separately. The Wechsler Memory Scale, first developed by David Wechsler in 1945 and now in its fourth edition (WMS-IV), includes a global assessment of memory functioning. For class, your instructor may include a combination of fill-in-the-blank (recall) and multiple-choice (recognition) exam questions.

Long after you cannot *recall* most of your high school classmates, you may still be able to *recognize* their yearbook pictures and spot their names in a list of names. One research team found that people who had graduated 25 years earlier could not recall many of their old classmates, but they could recognize

Remembering things past Even if Taylor Swift and Bruno Mars had not become famous, their high school classmates would most likely still recognize them in these photos.

90 percent of their pictures and names (Bahrick et al., 1975).

Our recognition memory is quick and vast. "Is your friend wearing a new or old outfit?" *Old.* "Is this 5-second movie clip from a film you've ever seen?" *Yes.* "Have you read this textbook material before?" *No.* Before our mouth can form an answer to any of millions of such questions, our mind knows, and knows that it knows. And it's not just humans who have shown remarkable memory for faces. Sheep remember faces, too (**FIGURE 7.8**). And so has at least one fish species—as demonstrated by their spitting water at familiar faces to trigger a food reward (Newport et al., 2016).

FIGURE 7.8 Other animals also display face smarts After food rewards are repeatedly associated with some sheep faces, but not with others, sheep remember food-associated faces for two years (Kendrick & Feng, 2011).

Our response speed when recalling or recognizing information indicates memory strength, as does our speed at *relearning.* Memory explorer Ebbinghaus showed this long ago by studying his own learning and memory (**FIGURE 7.9**).

Put yourself in Ebbinghaus' shoes. How could you produce new items to learn? Ebbinghaus' answer was to form a big list of nonsense syllables by sandwiching a vowel between two consonants. Then, for a particular experiment, he would randomly select a sample of the syllables, practice them, and test himself. To get a feel for his experiments, rapidly read aloud the following list, repeating it eight times (from Baddeley, 1982). Then, without looking, try to recall the items:

JIH, BAZ, FUB, YOX, SUJ, XIR, DAX, LEQ, VUM, PID, KEL, WAV, TUV, ZOF, GEK, HIW.

The day after learning such a list, Ebbinghaus recalled only a few of the syllables. But were they entirely forgotten? No. The more often he practiced the list aloud on Day 1, the fewer times he would have to practice it to *relearn* it on Day 2. For students, this means that it helps to rehearse course material over time, even after you know it. Better to rehearse and *overlearn* than relax and remember too little.

The point to remember: Tests of recognition and of time spent relearning demonstrate that *we remember more than we can recall.*

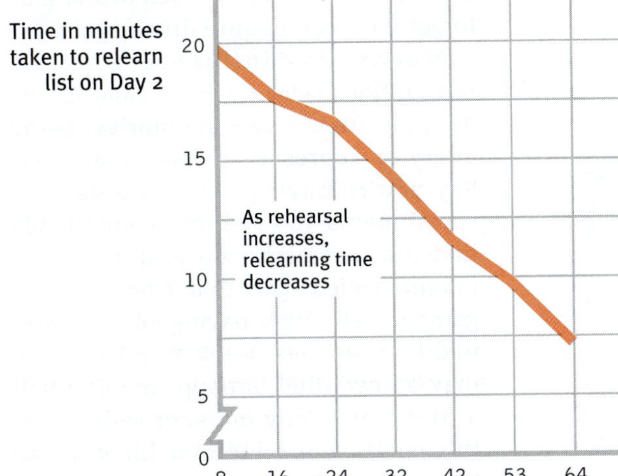

FIGURE 7.9 Ebbinghaus' retention curve The more times he practiced a list of nonsense syllables on Day 1, the less time he required to relearn it on Day 2. Speed of relearning is one measure of memory retention. (Data from Baddeley, 1982.)

RETRIEVE & REMEMBER

ANSWERS IN APPENDIX E

10. Multiple-choice questions test our ___________. Fill-in-the-blank questions test our ___________.

11. If you want to be sure to remember what you're learning for an upcoming test, would it be better to use *recall* or *recognition* to check your memory? Why?

long-term potentiation (LTP) an increase in a nerve cell's firing potential after brief, rapid stimulation. LTP is a neural basis for learning and memory.

recall memory demonstrated by retrieving information learned earlier, as on a fill-in-the-blank test.

recognition memory demonstrated by identifying items previously learned, as on a multiple-choice test.

relearning memory demonstrated by time saved when learning material again.

RETRIEVAL CUES

LOQ 7-15 How do external events, internal moods, and order of appearance affect memory retrieval?

Imagine a spider suspended in the middle of her web, held up by the many strands extending outward from her in all directions to different points. You could begin at any one of these anchor points and follow the attached strand to the spider.

Retrieving a memory is similar. Memories are held in storage by a web of associations, each piece of information connected to many others. Suppose you encode into your memory the name of the person sitting next to you in class. With that name, you will also encode other bits of information, such as your surroundings, mood, seating position, and so on. These bits serve as **retrieval cues,** anchor points for pathways you can follow to access your classmate's name when you need to recall it later. The more retrieval cues you've encoded, the better your chances of finding a path to the memory suspended in this web of information. We need memory for both our past (called *retrospective memory*) and for what actions may lie ahead (*prospective memory*). To remember to do something (say, to write a note tomorrow), one effective strategy is to mentally associate the act with a cue (leave a pen where you'll see it) (Rogers & Milkman, 2016).

The best retrieval cues come from associations you form at the time you encode a memory—smells, tastes, and sights that can call up your memory of the associated person or event. When trying to recall something, you may mentally place yourself in the original context. For most of us, that includes visual information. After losing his sight, British scholar John Hull (1990, p. 174) described his difficulty recalling such details:

> I knew I had been somewhere, and had done particular things with certain people, but where? I could not put the conversations . . . into a context. There was no background, no features against which to identify the place. Normally, the memories of people you have spoken to during the day are stored in frames which include the background.

LaunchPad For an 8-minute summary of how we access what's stored in our brain, see the *Video: Memory Retrieval.*

Priming

Often associations are activated without your awareness. Seeing or hearing the word *rabbit* can activate associations with *hare*, even though you may not recall having seen or heard *rabbit* (Bower, 1986) (**FIGURE 7.10**). Although this process, called **priming,** happens without your conscious awareness, it can influence your attitudes and your behavior.

Want to impress your friends with your new knowledge? Ask them three rapid-fire questions:

1. What color is snow?
2. What color are clouds?
3. What do cows drink?

If they answer *milk* to the third question, you have demonstrated priming.

Context-Dependent Memory

Have you noticed? Putting yourself back in the context where you earlier experienced something can prime your memory retrieval. Remembering, in many ways, depends on our environment (Palmer, 1989). When you visit your childhood home, old memories surface. When scuba divers listened to a word list in two different settings (either 10 feet underwater or sitting on the beach), they recalled more words when later tested in the same place where they first heard the list (Godden & Baddeley, 1975).

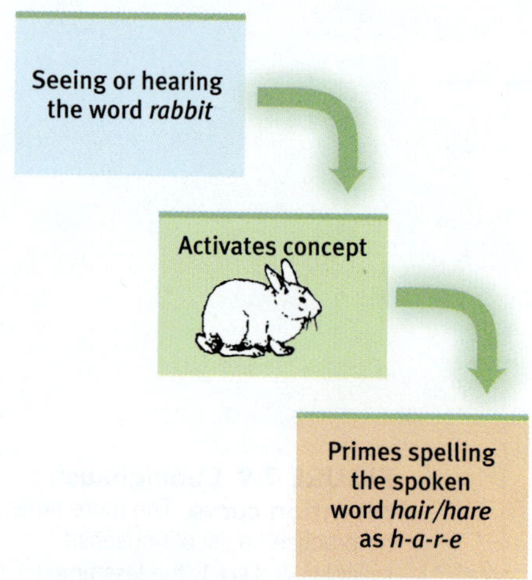

FIGURE 7.10 Priming associations unconsciously activates related associations

By contrast, experiencing something outside the usual setting can be confusing. Have you ever run into a former teacher in an unusual place, such as at the store? Maybe you recognized the person, but struggled to figure out who it was and how you were acquainted. The **encoding specificity principle** helps us understand how *specific* cues will most effectively trigger that memory. In new settings, you may not have the memory cues needed for speedy face recognition. Our memories are *context-dependent* and are affected by the cues we have associated with that context.

State-Dependent Memory

State-dependent memory is closely related to context-dependent memory. What we learn in one state—be it drunk or sober—may be more easily recalled when we are again in that state. What people learn when drunk they don't recall well in *any* state (alcohol disrupts memory storage). But they recall it slightly better when again drunk. Someone who hides money when drunk may forget the location until drunk again.

Moods also influence what we remember (Gaddy & Ingram, 2014). Being happy primes sweet memories. Being angry or depressed primes sour ones. Say you're having a terrible day. On social media you see that your friends had fun last night without you, your parents called *again* to ask how you are going to get a high-paying job, and your midterms are next week. Your bad mood may trigger other unhappy memories. If a friend or family member walks in at this point, your mind may fill with bad memories of that person.

"I can't remember what we're arguing about, either. Let's keep yelling, and maybe it will come back to us."

This tendency to recall events that fit our mood is called **mood-congruent memory.** If put in a great mood—whether under hypnosis or just by the day's events (a World Cup soccer victory for German participants in one study)—people recall the world through rose-colored glasses (DeSteno et al., 2000; Forgas et al., 1984; Schwarz et al., 1987). They recall their behaviors as competent and effective. They view other people as kind and giving. And they're sure happy events happen more often than unhappy ones.

Have you ever noticed that your current mood influences your perceptions of family members? In one study, adolescents' ratings of parental warmth in one week have offered few clues to how they would rate their parents six weeks later (Bornstein et al., 1991). When teens were down, their parents seemed cruel. As moods brightened, those devil parents became angels.

Mood effects on retrieval help explain why our moods persist. When happy, we recall happy events and see the world as a happy place, which prolongs our good mood. When depressed, we recall sad events, which darkens our view of current events. For those predisposed to depression, this process can help maintain a vicious, dark cycle. Moods magnify.

IMPROVE YOUR EVERYDAY LIFE

What sort of mood have you been in lately? How might spending a few minutes to focus on the positive aspects of your life color your memories, perceptions, and expectations?

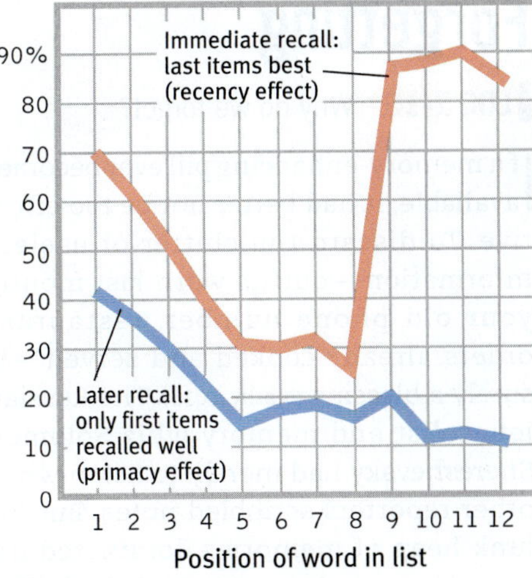

FIGURE 7.11 The serial position effect Immediately after Pope Francis made his way through this receiving line of special guests, he would probably have recalled the names of the last few people best *(recency effect).* But later he may have been able to recall the first few people best *(primacy effect).*

Serial Position Effect

Another memory-retrieval quirk, the **serial position effect,** explains why you may have large holes in your memory of a list of recent events. Imagine it's your first day in a new job, and your manager is introducing co-workers. As you meet each person, you silently repeat everyone's name, starting from the beginning. As the last person smiles and turns away, you hope you'll be able to greet your new co-workers by name the next day.

Don't count on it. Because you have spent more time rehearsing the earlier names than the later ones, those are the names you'll probably recall more easily the next day. In experiments, when people viewed a list of items (words, names, dates, even experienced odors or tastes) and immediately tried to recall them in any order, they fell prey to the serial position effect (Daniel & Katz, 2018; Reed, 2000). They briefly recalled the last items especially quickly and well (a *recency effect*), perhaps because those last items were still in working memory. But after a delay, when their attention was elsewhere, their recall was best for the first items (a *primacy effect*; see **FIGURE 7.11**).

RETRIEVE & REMEMBER

ANSWERS IN APPENDIX E

12. What is *priming?*

13. When tested immediately after viewing a list of words, we tend to recall the first and last items best. This is known as the ____________ ____________ effect.

LaunchPad For a simulated experiment showing the probability of recalling a specific item from a list, engage online with *Concept Practice: The Serial Position Effect.*

retrieval cue any stimulus (event, feeling, place, and so on) linked to a specific memory.

priming the activation, often unconsciously, of particular associations in memory.

encoding specificity principle the idea that cues and contexts specific to a particular memory will be most effective in helping us recall it.

mood-congruent memory the tendency to recall experiences that are consistent with your current good or bad mood.

serial position effect our tendency to recall best the last and first items in a list.

Forgetting

LOQ 7-16 Why do we forget?

If a memory-enhancing pill ever becomes available, it had better not be too effective. To discard the clutter of useless information—outfits worn last month, your old phone number, restaurant orders already cooked and served—is surely a blessing (Nørby, 2015). The Russian journalist and memory whiz Solomon Shereshevsky had merely to listen while other reporters scribbled notes. But his junk heap of memories dominated his conscious mind (Luria, 1968). He had difficulty thinking abstractly—generalizing, organizing, evaluating. So does Jill Price, whose incredibly accurate memory of her life's events since age 14 has been closely studied. She reports that her super-memory, called "highly superior autobiographical memory," interferes with her life, with one memory cuing another (McGaugh & LePort, 2014; Parker et al., 2006): "It's like a running movie that never stops." People like Price are prone to having their mind fill up with information that, once in memory storage, never leaves (Patihis, 2016). In such people, researchers have identified enlarged brain areas and increased brain activity in memory centers (Ally et al., 2013; LePort et al., 2012; Santangelo et al., 2018).

MEMORIES START TO FADE
Lightspring/Shutterstock

More often, however, our quirky memories fail us when we least expect it. My [DM's] own memory can easily call up such episodes as that wonderful first kiss with the woman I love, or trivial facts like the air mileage from London to Detroit. Then it abandons me when I discover that I have failed to encode, store, or retrieve a student's name or the spot where I left my hat.

As we process information, we sift, change, or lose most of it (**FIGURE 7.12**).

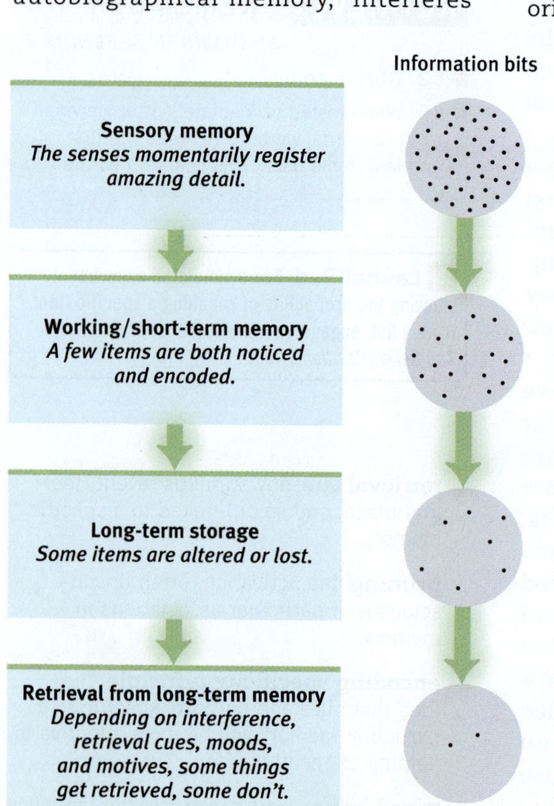
Information bits
Sensory memory
The senses momentarily register amazing detail.
Working/short-term memory
A few items are both noticed and encoded.
Long-term storage
Some items are altered or lost.
Retrieval from long-term memory
Depending on interference, retrieval cues, moods, and motives, some things get retrieved, some don't.

FIGURE 7.12 When do we forget? Forgetting can occur at any memory stage. When we process information, we filter, alter, or lose much of it.

FORGETTING AND THE TWO-TRACK MIND

For some, memory loss is severe and permanent, as it was for Henry Molaison (H. M.), whom you met earlier in this chapter. Molaison suffered from **anterograde amnesia**—he could recall his past, but he could not form *new* conscious memories. (Those who cannot recall their past—the old information stored in long-term memory—suffer from **retrograde amnesia**.) Neurologist Oliver Sacks described another patient, Jimmie, who was stuck in 1945, the year of his brain injury. When Jimmie gave his age as 19, Sacks set a mirror before him: "Look in the mirror and tell me what you see. Is that a 19-year-old looking out from the mirror?" (Sacks, 1985, pp. 26–27)

Jimmie turned pale, gripped the chair, cursed, then became frantic: "What's going on? What's happened to me? Is this a nightmare? Am I crazy? Is this a joke?" When his attention was directed to some children playing baseball, his panic ended, the dreadful mirror forgotten.

Sacks showed Jimmie a photo from *National Geographic*. "What is this?" he asked.

"It's the Moon," Jimmie replied.

"No, it's not," Sacks answered. "It's a picture of the Earth taken from the Moon."

"Doc, you're kidding! Someone would've had to get a camera up there!"

"Naturally."

"Hell! You're joking—how the hell would you do that?" Jimmie's wonder was that of a bright young man from the 1940s, amazed by his travel back to the future.

Careful testing of these unique people reveals something even stranger. Although they cannot recall new facts or anything they have done recently, they can learn new skills and can be classically conditioned. Shown hard-to-find figures in pictures (in the *Where's Waldo?* series), they can quickly spot them again later. They can find their way to the bathroom, though without being able to tell you where it is. They can master mirror-image writing, jigsaw puzzles, and even complicated *procedural* job skills (Schacter, 1992, 1996; Xu & Corkin, 2001). However, *they do all these things with no awareness of having learned them.*

Molaison and Jimmie lost their ability to form new explicit memories, but their automatic processing ability remained intact. They could learn *how* to do something, but they had no conscious recall of learning their new skill. Such sad case studies confirm that we have two distinct memory systems, controlled by different parts of the brain.

For most of us, forgetting is a less drastic process. Let's consider some of the reasons we forget.

LaunchPad For a helpful tutorial animation about this type of research method, see the *Video: Case Studies.*

ENCODING FAILURE

Much of what we sense we never notice, and what we fail to encode, we will never remember (**FIGURE 7.13**). Age can affect encoding ability. When young adults encode new information, areas of their brain jump into action. In older adults, these areas are slower to respond. Learning and retaining a new neighbor's name or mastering new technology becomes more of a challenge. This encoding lag helps explain age-related memory decline (Grady et al., 1995). (For more on aging's effect on memory, see Chapter 3.)

But no matter how young we are, we pay conscious attention to only a limited portion of the vast number of sights and sounds bombarding us. Consider: You have surely seen the Apple logo thousands of times. Can you draw it? In one study, only 1 of 85 UCLA students (including 52 Apple users) could do so accurately (Blake et al., 2015). Without encoding effort, many might-have-been memories never form.

STORAGE DECAY

Even after encoding something well, we may later forget it. That master of nonsense-syllable learning, Hermann Ebbinghaus, also studied how long memories last. After learning his lists of nonsense syllables, such as *YOX* and *JIH*, he measured how much he remembered

at various times, from 20 minutes to 30 days later. The result was his famous forgetting curve: *The course of forgetting is rapid at first, then levels off with time* (Wixted & Ebbesen, 1991).

People studying Spanish as a foreign language showed this forgetting curve for Spanish vocabulary (Bahrick, 1984). Compared with others who had just completed a high school or college Spanish course, people 3 years out of school had forgotten much of what they had learned. However, what they remembered then, they still basically remembered 25 and more years later. Their forgetting had leveled off (**FIGURE 7.14**).

One explanation for these forgetting curves is a gradual fading of the **memory trace,** which is a physical change in the brain as a memory forms. Researchers are getting closer to solving the mystery of the physical storage and decay of memories. But memories fade for many reasons, including other learning that disrupts our retrieval.

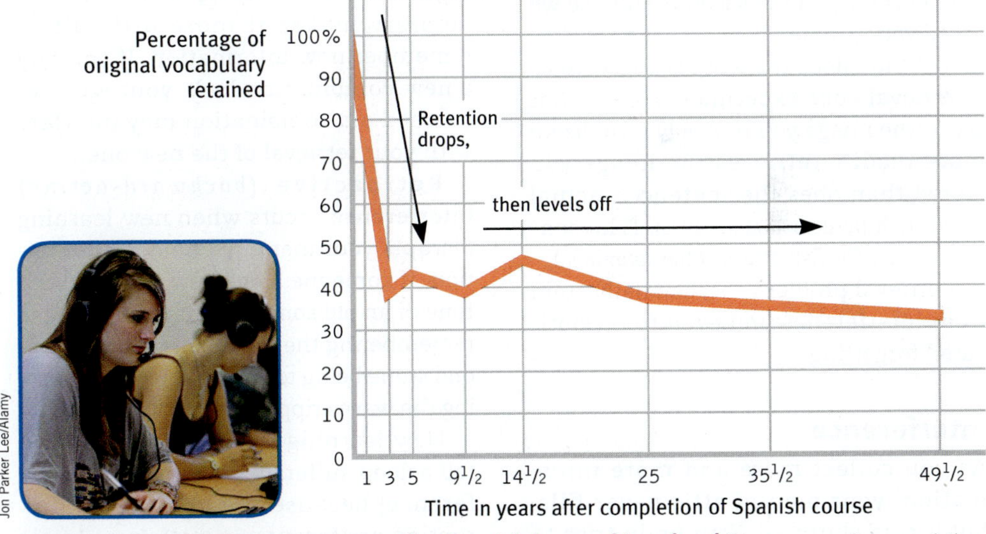

FIGURE 7.14 The forgetting curve for Spanish learned in school Three years after completing a Spanish course, people remembered much less than did those just completing the course, but not *much* less than long-ago students. (Data from Bahrick, 1984.)

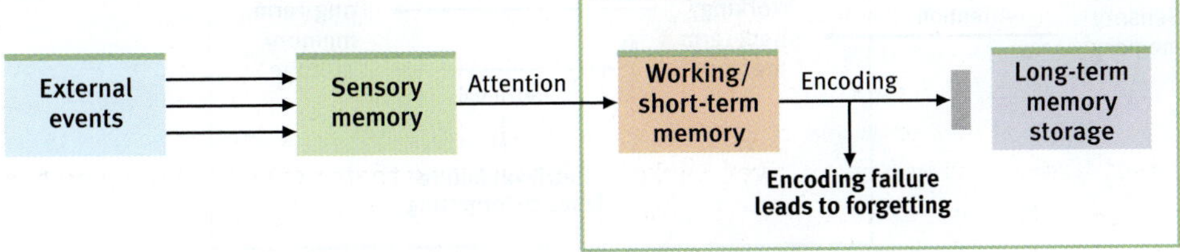

FIGURE 7.13 Forgetting as encoding failure We cannot remember what we have not encoded.

anterograde amnesia an inability to form new memories.

retrograde amnesia an inability to remember information from our past.

memory trace lasting physical change in the brain as a memory forms.

RETRIEVAL FAILURE

We can compare forgotten events to books you can't find in your local library. Some aren't available because they were never acquired (not encoded). Others have been discarded (stored memories decay).

But there is a third possibility. The book—or memory—may be out of reach because we don't have enough information to access it. For example, what causes frustrating "tip-of-the-tongue" forgetting? (Deaf people fluent in sign language may experience a parallel "tip-of-the-fingers" feeling [Thompson et al., 2005].) These are retrieval problems (**FIGURE 7.15**). Given retrieval cues (*It begins with an M*), you may easily retrieve the memory. Older adults more frequently have these frustrating tip-of-the-tongue experiences (Abrams, 2008; Salthouse & Mandell, 2013).

Here's a question to test your memory. Do you recall the second sentence we asked you to remember—about the swimmer? If not, does the word *shark* serve as a retrieval cue? Experiments show that *shark* (the image you probably visualized) more readily retrieves the image you stored than does the sentence's actual word, *fish* (Anderson et al., 1976). (The sentence was, *The fish attacked the swimmer.*)

Retrieval problems occasionally stem from interference and even from motivated forgetting.

Interference

As you collect more and more information, your mental attic never fills, but it gets cluttered. Your brain tries to keep things tidy. Using a new password weakens your memory of competing old passwords (Wimber et al., 2015). But sometimes the clutter wins, as new and old learning collide. **Proactive** *(forward-acting)* **interference** occurs when an older memory makes it more difficult to remember new information. If you buy a new combination lock, your well-rehearsed old combination may interfere with your retrieval of the new one.

Retroactive *(backward-acting)* **interference** occurs when new learning disrupts your memory of older information. If someone sings new words to the tune of an old song, you may have trouble remembering the original. Imagine a second stone being tossed in a pond, disrupting the waves rippling out from the first.

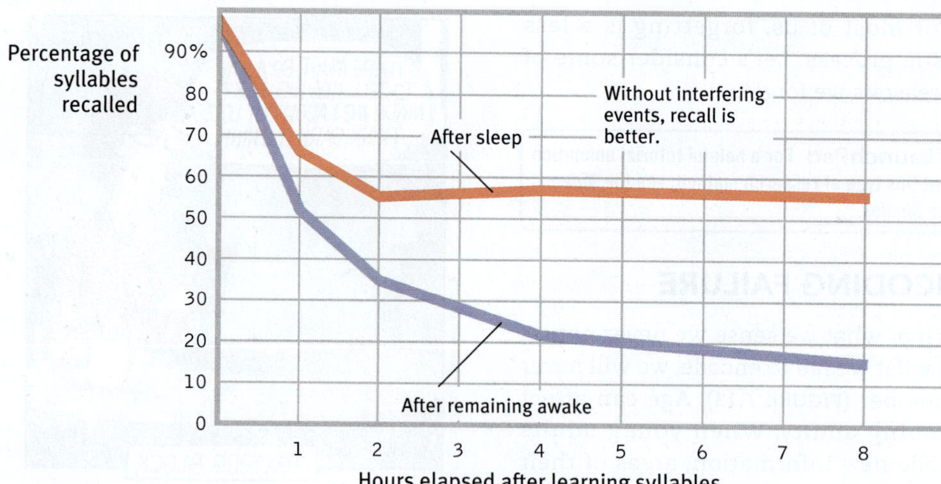

FIGURE 7.16 Retroactive interference People forgot more when they stayed awake and experienced other new material. (Data from Jenkins & Dallenbach, 1924.)

New learning in the hour before we fall asleep suffers less retroactive interference, because the chances of disruption are few (Mercer, 2015). In a classic experiment, two people each learned some nonsense syllables, day after day (Jenkins & Dallenbach, 1924). When they tried to recall them after a night's sleep, they could retrieve more than half the items. But when they learned the material and then stayed awake and were involved with other activities, they forgot more, and sooner (**FIGURE 7.16**).

The hour before sleep is a good time to commit information to memory (Scullin & McDaniel, 2010), but not the *seconds* just before sleep (Wyatt & Bootzin, 1994). And if you're considering learning *while* sleeping, forget it. We have little memory for information played aloud in the room during sleep, although our ears do register it (Wood et al., 1992).

Old and new information do not always compete. Knowing Spanish helped me [ND] pick up some Portuguese when I was in Brazil to watch the 2016 Olympics. This effect is called *positive transfer*.

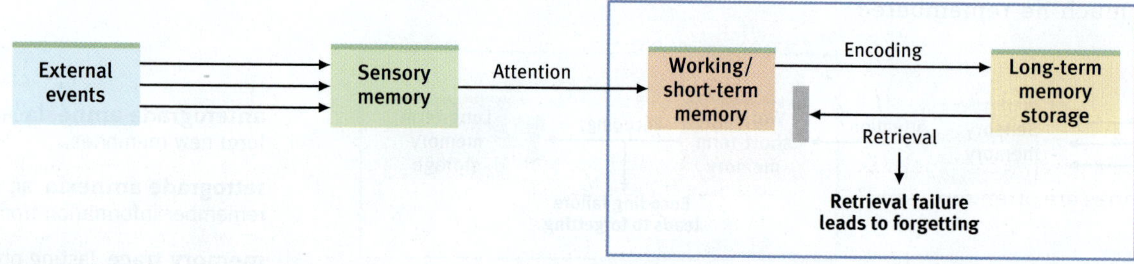

FIGURE 7.15 Retrieval failure Sometimes even stored information cannot be accessed, which leads to forgetting.

LaunchPad To experience a demonstration and explanation of interference effects on memory, visit *Topic Tutorial: PsychSim6, Forgetting.*

Motivated Forgetting

To remember our past is often to revise it. Years ago, the huge cookie jar in my [DM's] kitchen was jammed with freshly baked cookies. Still more were cooling across racks on the counter. A day later, not a crumb was left. Who had taken them? During that time, my wife, three children, and I were the only people in the house. So while memories were still fresh, I conducted a little memory test. Andy admitted wolfing down as many as 20. Peter thought he had eaten 15. Laura guessed she had stuffed her then-6-year-old body with 15 cookies. My wife, Carol, recalled eating 6. I remembered consuming 15 and taking 18 more to the office. We sheepishly accepted responsibility for 89 cookies. Still we had not come close; there had been 160.

Why were our estimates so far off? Was our cookie confusion an *encoding* problem? (Did we just not notice what we had eaten?) Was it a *storage* problem? (Might our memories of cookies, like Ebbinghaus' memory of nonsense syllables, have melted away almost as fast as the cookies themselves?) Or was the information still intact but not *retrievable* because it would be embarrassing to remember?

Sigmund Freud might have argued that our memory systems self-censored this information. He proposed that we **repress** painful or unacceptable memories to protect our self-concept and to minimize anxiety. But the repressed memory lingers, he believed, and can be retrieved by some later cue or during therapy. Repression was central to Freud's psychoanalytic theory and remains a popular idea. Indeed, an American study revealed that 81 percent of university students, and 60 to 90 percent of therapists (depending on their perspective), believe "traumatic memories are often repressed" (Patihis et al., 2014a,b). However, increasing numbers of memory researchers think repression rarely, if ever, occurs. Evidence of this is found even in the words people later remember. Victims of sexual assault, for example, succeed in forgetting neutral words (*salt, plant*), but they struggle to forget trauma-related words (*intercourse, assault*) (Blix & Brennen, 2011). Why do trauma victims retain their most upsetting memories? Trauma releases stress hormones that cause people to pay attention and remember a threat (Quaedflieg & Schwabe, 2017). Thus, people often have intrusive memories of the traumas they would most like to forget (Marks et al., 2018).

Stringer/Newscom/European Pressphoto Agency/Lages/PORTUGAL

Do people vividly remember—or repress—traumatic experiences? Imagine yourself several hours into Flight AT236 from Toronto to Lisbon. A fractured fuel line begins leaking. Soon the engines go silent. In the eerie silence, the pilots instruct you and the other terrified passengers to put on life jackets, and, when hearing the countdown to ocean impact, to assume a brace position. After minutes of descent, the pilot declares—above the passengers' screams and prayers—"About to go into the water." Death awaits.

But no! "We have a runway! We have a runway! Brace! Brace! Brace!" The plane makes a hard landing at an Azores airbase, averting death for you and the 305 other passengers and crew.

Among the passengers thinking, "I'm going to die" was psychologist Margaret McKinnon. Seizing the opportunity, she tracked down 15 of her fellow passengers to test their trauma memories. Did they repress the experience? *No.* All exhibited vivid, detailed memories. With trauma comes not repression, but, far more often, "robust" memory (McKinnon et al., 2015).

"Memory of traumatic events is stored differently in the brain. Some [details] . . . can be recalled in excruciating detail, as if the event just occurred, while others may be forgotten." —Jessica Henderson Daniel, president of the American Psychological Association, 2018

RETRIEVE & REMEMBER

ANSWERS IN APPENDIX E

14. What are three ways we forget, and how does each of these happen?
15. Freud believed (though many researchers doubt) that we ________ unacceptable memories to minimize anxiety.

Memory Construction Errors

LOQ 7-17 How do misinformation, imagination, and source amnesia influence our memory construction? How do we decide whether a memory is real or false?

Memory is not exact. Even people with exceptional memories, such as Feng Wang and Jill Price, sometimes make mistakes (Johnson, 2017; Patihis, 2018). Like scientists who infer a dinosaur's appearance from its remains, we infer our past from stored tidbits of information plus

proactive interference the forward-acting disruptive effect of older learning on the recall of *new* information.

retroactive interference the backward-acting disruptive effect of newer learning on the recall of *old* information.

repression in psychoanalytic theory, the basic defense mechanism that banishes from consciousness anxiety-arousing thoughts, feelings, and memories.

what we later imagined, expected, saw, and heard. We don't just retrieve memories; we reweave them (Gilbert, 2006). Our memories are like Wikipedia pages, capable of constant revision. When we "replay" a memory, we often replace the original with a slightly modified version (Hardt et al., 2010). Memory researchers call this **reconsolidation** (Elsey et al., 2018). So, in a sense, said Joseph LeDoux (2009), "your memory is only as good as your last memory. The fewer times you use it, the more [unchanged] it is." This means that, to some degree, all memory is false (Bernstein & Loftus, 2009b).

Despite knowing all this, I [DM] recently rewrote my own past. It happened at an international conference, where memory researcher Elizabeth Loftus (2012) showed us a handful of individual faces that we were later to identify, as if in a police lineup. Then she showed us some pairs of faces—one face we had seen earlier and one we had not—and asked us to identify the one we had seen. But one pair she had slipped in included *two* new faces, one of which was rather *like* a face we had seen earlier. Most of us understandably but wrongly identified this face as one we had previously seen. To climax the demonstration, when she showed us the originally seen face and the previously chosen wrong face, most of us picked the wrong face! As a result of our memory reconsolidation, we—an audience of psychologists who should have known better—had replaced the original memory with a false memory.

Clinical researchers have begun experimenting with memory reconsolidation in hopes of helping people forget unwanted memories. They ask people to recall a traumatic or negative experience and then disrupt the reconsolidation of that memory with a drug or a brief, painless electroconvulsive shock (Kroes et al., 2014; Lonergan et al., 2013; Treanor et al., 2017). Someday it might be possible to use memory reconsolidation in this way to erase a memory of a specific traumatic experience. Would you wish for this? If brutally assaulted, would you welcome having your memory of the attack and its associated fears deleted? To understand how to help or hinder memory reconsolidation, neuroscientists are working to identify relevant brain regions and neurochemicals (Bang et al., 2018).

MISINFORMATION AND IMAGINATION EFFECTS

In more than 200 experiments involving more than 20,000 people, Loftus has shown how eyewitnesses reconstruct their memories when questioned after a crime or accident. In one important study, two groups of people watched a film clip of a traffic accident and then answered questions about what they had seen (Loftus & Palmer, 1974). Those asked, "About how fast were the cars going when they *smashed* into each other?" gave higher speed estimates than those asked, "About how fast were the cars going when they *hit* each other?" A week later, when asked whether they recalled seeing any broken glass, people who had heard *smashed* in the leading (suggestive) version of the question were more than twice as likely to report seeing glass fragments (**FIGURE 7.17**). In fact, the film showed no broken glass.

In many follow-up experiments around the world, others have witnessed an event. Then they have received or not received misleading information about it. And then they have taken a memory test. The repeated result is a **misinformation effect**. Exposed to subtly misleading information, we tend to misremember (Brewin & Andrews, 2017; Loftus et al., 1992; Scoboria et al., 2017). Coke cans become peanut cans. Breakfast cereal becomes eggs. A clean-shaven man morphs into a man with a mustache. The human mind, it seems, comes with built-in Photoshopping software.

> "Memory is insubstantial. Things keep replacing it. Your batch of snapshots will both fix and ruin your memory. . . . You can't remember anything from your trip except the wretched collection of snapshots." —Annie Dillard, "To Fashion a Text," 1988

Just hearing a vivid retelling of an event may implant false memories. One experiment falsely suggested to some Dutch university students that, as children, they had become ill after eating spoiled egg salad (Geraerts et al., 2008). After absorbing that suggestion, they were less likely to eat egg salad sandwiches, both immediately and four months later.

Even repeatedly *imagining* fake actions and events can create false memories. Canadian university students were asked to recall two events from their past. One event actually happened; the other was a false event that involved committing a crime, such as assaulting someone with a weapon. Initially, none of the lawful students remembered breaking the law. But after repeated interviewing, 70 percent (more than in other studies) reported a detailed false memory of having committed the crime (Shaw & Porter, 2015; Wade et al., 2018). In real life, some people, after suggestive interviews, have vividly recalled murders they didn't commit (Aviv, 2017). People's lies can likewise

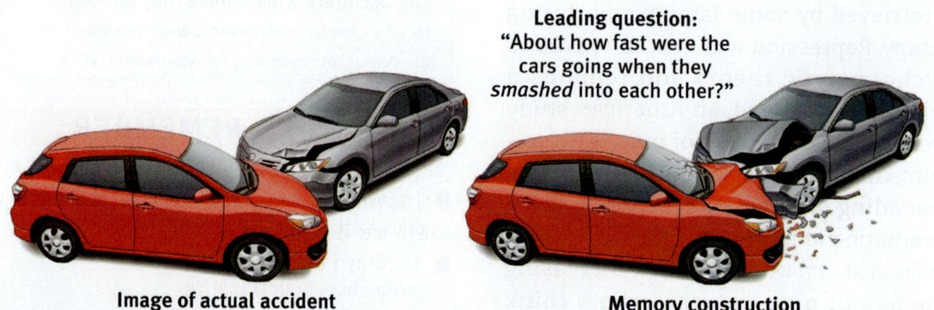
Leading question:
"About how fast were the cars going when they *smashed* into each other?"
Image of actual accident
Memory construction

FIGURE 7.17 Memory construction People who viewed a film clip of a car accident and later were asked a leading question recalled a more serious accident than they had witnessed (Loftus & Palmer, 1974).

change their own memories (Otgaar & Baker, 2018). Fibbing feeds falsehoods.

In experiments, researchers have altered photos from a family album to show some family members taking a hot-air balloon ride. After viewing these photos (rather than photos showing just the balloon), children "remembered" the faked experience. Days later, they reported even richer details of their false memories (Strange et al., 2008; Wade et al., 2002). Many people—39 percent in one survey—recall improbable (likely fictional) first memories from age 2 and before (Akhtar et al., 2018). And in British and Canadian university surveys, nearly one-fourth of students have reported personal memories that they later realized were not accurate (Foley, 2015; Mazzoni et al., 2010). *The bottom line:* Don't believe everything you remember.

Evan Agostini/Invision/AP

Was Alexander Hamilton a U.S. president? We often misuse familiar information. In one study, many people mistakenly recalled Alexander Hamilton—whose face appears on the U.S. $10 bill, and who is the subject of a popular Broadway musical by Lin-Manuel Miranda (shown here playing the starring role)—as a U.S. president (Roediger & DeSoto, 2016).

In 2015, *NBC Nightly News* anchor Brian Williams recounted a story about traveling in a military helicopter hit by a rocket-propelled grenade. But the event never happened as he described. The public branded him a liar, leading his bosses to fire him. Memory researchers, including Christopher Chabris, had a different opinion: "A lot of people don't appreciate the extent to which false memories can happen even when we are extremely confident in the memory" (2015).

SOURCE AMNESIA

What is the weakest part of a memory? Its source. Have you ever dreamed about an event and later wondered whether it really happened? Or remembered learning something on social media but then questioned whether it was real or false news? Or told a friend some gossip, only to learn you got the news from the friend? If so, you experienced **source amnesia**—you retained the memory of the event but not of its context. Source amnesia, along with the misinformation effect, is at the heart of many false memories. Authors, songwriters, and comedians sometimes suffer from it. They think an idea came from their own creative imagination, when in fact they are unintentionally plagiarizing something they earlier read or heard.

Even preschoolers experience source amnesia. In one study, "Mr. Science" engaged preschoolers in activities such as blowing up a balloon with baking soda and vinegar (Poole & Lindsay, 1995, 2001). Three months later, on three successive days, their parents read them a story. It described some things the children had experienced with Mr. Science and some they had not. When asked about an activity that was only in the story—"Did Mr. Science have a machine with ropes to pull?"—4 in 10 children spontaneously recalled engaging in the event.

Source amnesia also helps explain **déjà vu** (French for "already seen"). Two-thirds of us have experienced this fleeting, eerie sense that "I've been in this exact situation before." The key to déjà vu seems to be that we are familiar with a stimulus or one like it but can't recall where we ran into it before (Brown & Marsh, 2009; Cleary & Claxton, 2018). Normally, we experience a feeling of *familiarity* (thanks to temporal lobe processing) before we consciously remember details (thanks to hippocampus and frontal lobe processing). Sometimes, though, we may have a feeling of familiarity without conscious recall. As our amazing brain tries to make sense of this source amnesia, we get an eerie feeling that we're reliving some earlier part of our life.

"Do you ever get that strange feeling of vujà dé? Not déjà vu; vujà dé. It's the distinct sense that, somehow, something just happened that has never happened before. Nothing seems familiar. And then suddenly the feeling is gone. Vujà dé."—Comedian George Carlin, *Funny Times*, December 2001

RETRIEVE & REMEMBER

ANSWERS IN APPENDIX E

16. What—given the commonness of source amnesia—might life be like if we remembered all our waking experiences and all our dreams?

RECOGNIZING FALSE MEMORIES

We often are confident of our inaccurate memories. Because the misinformation effect and source amnesia happen outside our awareness, it is hard to separate false memories from real ones (Schooler et al., 1986). Perhaps you can recall describing

reconsolidation a process in which previously stored memories, when retrieved, are potentially altered before being stored again.

misinformation effect occurs when a memory has been corrupted by misleading information.

source amnesia faulty memory for how, when, or where information was learned or imagined.

déjà vu that eerie sense that "I've experienced this before." Cues from the current situation may unconsciously trigger retrieval of an earlier experience.

a childhood experience to a friend and filling in memory gaps with reasonable guesses. We all do it. After more retellings, those guessed details—now absorbed into your memory—may feel as real as if you had actually experienced them (Roediger et al., 1993). False memories, like fake diamonds, seem so real. False memories can be persistent. Imagine that we were to read aloud a list of words such as *candy, sugar, honey,* and *taste*. Later, we ask you to recognize those words in a larger list. If you are at all like the people in a famous experiment (Roediger & McDermott, 1995), you would err three out of four times—by falsely remembering a new but similar word, such as *sweet*. We more easily remember the *gist*—the general idea—than the words themselves.

False memories are contagious. When we hear others falsely remember events, we tend to make the same memory mistakes (Roediger et al., 2001). Your Facebook friend may misremember a shy classmate as acting rude, leading you to also mistakenly remember the classmate negatively. It's easy to see how false online stories can spread and become false memories.

Memory construction errors also help explain why some people have been sent to prison for crimes they never committed. Of 362 people who were later proven not guilty by DNA testing, 70 percent had been convicted because of faulty eyewitness identification (Innocence Project, 2018; Smalarz & Wells, 2015). "Hypnotically refreshed" memories of crimes often contain similar errors. If a hypnotist asks leading questions *(Did you hear loud noises?)*, witnesses may weave that false information into their memory of the event. Memory construction errors also seem to be at work in many "recovered" memories of childhood abuse. See Thinking Critically About: Can Memories of Childhood Sexual Abuse Be Repressed and Then Recovered?

IN YOUR EVERYDAY LIFE

Think of a memory you frequently recall. How might you have changed it without conscious awareness?

LaunchPad To participate in a simulated experiment on false memory formation, and to review related research, visit *Topic Tutorial: PsychSim6, Can You Trust Your Memory?*

CHILDREN'S EYEWITNESS RECALL

LOQ 7-19 How reliable are young children's eyewitness descriptions?

If memories can be sincere, yet sincerely wrong, how can jurors decide cases in which children's memories of sexual abuse are the only evidence?

Stephen Ceci (1993) thinks "it would be truly awful to ever lose sight of the enormity of child abuse." Yet Ceci and Maggie Bruck's (1993, 1995) studies have made them aware of how easily children's memories can be molded. For example, they asked 3-year-olds to show on anatomically correct dolls where a pediatrician had touched them. Of the children who had not received genital examinations, 55 percent pointed to either genital or anal areas.

In other experiments, the researchers studied the effect of suggestive interviewing techniques (Bruck & Ceci, 1999, 2004). In one study, children chose a card from a deck of possible happenings, and an adult then read the card to them. For example, "Think real hard, and tell me if this ever happened to you. Can you remember going to the hospital with a mousetrap on your finger?" In weekly interviews, the same adult repeatedly asked children to think about several real and fictitious events. After 10 weeks of this, a new adult asked the same questions. The stunning result: 58 percent of preschoolers produced false (often vivid) stories about one or more events they had never experienced (Ceci et al., 1994). Here's one:

> My brother Colin was trying to get Blowtorch [an action figure] from me, and I wouldn't let him take it from me, so he pushed me into the wood pile where the mousetrap was. And then my finger got caught in it. And then we went to the hospital, and my mommy, daddy, and Colin drove me there, to the hospital in our van, because it was far away. And the doctor put a bandage on this finger.

Given such detailed stories, professional psychologists who specialize in interviewing children could not reliably separate the real memories from the false ones. Nor could the children themselves. The child quoted above, reminded that his parents had told him several times that the mousetrap event never happened—that he had imagined it—protested. "But it really did happen. I remember it!"

We shouldn't forget that children can be accurate eyewitnesses. When a neutral person asks nonleading questions soon after the event, using words they understand, children often accurately recall what happened and who did it (Brewin & Andrews, 2017; Goodman & Quas, 2008; Pipe et al., 2004).

RETRIEVE & REMEMBER

ANSWERS IN APPENDIX E

17. Imagine being a jury member in a trial for a parent accused of sexual abuse based on a recovered memory. What insights from memory research should you share with the rest of the jury?

LaunchPad Consider how researchers have studied these issues by engaging online with the activity: *How Would You Know If People's Memories Are Accurate?*

Improving Memory

LOQ 7-20 How can you use memory research findings to do better in this course and in others?

Biology's findings benefit medicine. Botany's findings benefit agriculture. Can memory researchers' findings benefit your performance in class and on tests? You bet! Here, for easy reference, is a summary of research-based suggestions that can help you remember information when you need it. The SQ3R—Survey, Question, Read, Retrieve, Review—study technique introduced in Chapter 1 includes several of these strategies:

Rehearse repeatedly. To master material, remember the *spacing effect*—use *distributed (spaced) practice*. To learn a

Thinking Critically About:

Can Memories of Childhood Sexual Abuse Be Repressed and Then Recovered?

LOQ 7-18 Why have reports of repressed and recovered memories been so hotly debated?

Two Possible Tragedies:

1. **People doubt childhood sexual abuse survivors who tell their secret.**
2. **Innocent people are falsely accused,** as therapists prompt "recovered" memories of childhood sexual abuse:

"Victims of sexual abuse often have your symptoms. So maybe you were abused and *repressed* the memory. Let's see if I can help you recover the memory, by digging back and visualizing your trauma."

Misinformation effect and **source amnesia:** Adult client may form image of threatening person.

With *rehearsal* (repeated therapy sessions), the image grows more vivid.

Client is stunned, angry, and ready to confront or sue the remembered abuser.

Accused person is equally stunned and vigorously denies the accusation of long-ago abuse.

Professional organizations (including the American Medical, American Psychological, and American Psychiatric Associations) are working to find sensible common ground to resolve psychology's "memory war":[1]

- **Childhood sexual abuse happens** and can leave its victims at risk for problems ranging from sexual dysfunction to depression.[2] But there is no "survivor syndrome"—no group of symptoms that lets us spot victims of sexual abuse.[3]
- **Injustice happens.** Innocent people have been falsely convicted. And guilty people have avoided punishment by casting doubt on their truth-telling accusers.
- **Forgetting happens.** Children abused when very young may not have understood the meaning of their experience or remember it. Forgetting long-ago good and bad events is an ordinary part of everyday life.
- **Recovered memories are common.** Cued by a remark or an experience, we may recover pleasant or unpleasant memories of long-forgotten events. But does the unconscious mind forcibly repress painful experiences, and can these experiences be recovered by therapist-aided techniques?[4] Memories that surface naturally are more likely to be true.[5]
- **Memories of events before age 4 are unreliable.** Infantile amnesia results from not yet developed brain pathways. Most psychologists therefore doubt "recovered" memories of abuse during infancy.[6] The older a child was when suffering sexual abuse, and the more severe the abuse, the more likely it is to be remembered.[7x]
- **Memories "recovered" under hypnosis are especially unreliable.**
- **Memories, whether real or false, can be emotionally upsetting.** What was born of mere suggestion can become, like an actual event, a stinging memory that drives bodily stress.[8]

Psychologists question whether *repression* ever occurs.
(See Chapter 12 for more on this concept, which is central to Freud's theory.)

Traumatic experiences (witnessing a loved one's murder, being terrorized by a hijacker or rapist, losing everything in a natural disaster) → **TYPICALLY LEAD TO** → **vivid, persistent, haunting memories[9]**

1. Patihis et al., 2014a. 2. Freyd et al., 2007. 3. Kendall-Tackett et al., 1993. 4. McNally & Geraerts, 2009. 5. Geraerts et al., 2007. 6. Gore-Felton et al., 2000; Knapp & VandeCreek, 2000. 7. Goodman et al., 2003. 8. McNally, 2003, 2007. 9. Porter & Peace, 2007.

© Sigrid Olsson/PhotoAlto/Corbis

Thinking and memory What's the best way to retain new information? Think actively as you read. That includes rehearsing and relating ideas and making the material personally meaningful.

concept, give yourself many separate study sessions. Take advantage of life's little intervals—riding a bus, walking across campus, waiting for class to start. New memories are weak; if you exercise them they will strengthen. To memorize specific facts or figures, research has shown that you should "rehearse the name or number you are trying to memorize, wait a few seconds, rehearse again, wait a little longer, rehearse again, then wait longer still and rehearse yet again. The waits should be as long as possible without losing the information" (Landauer, 2001). Rehearsal will help you retain material. As the *testing effect* has shown, it pays to study actively. Mentally saying, writing, or typing information beats silently reading it (MacLeod & Bodner, 2017). This *production effect* explains why we so often learn best when teaching, or when rehearsing information out loud (Forrin & Macleod, 2018; Koh et al., 2018). But even just taking lecture notes by hand can help. That way you will summarize the material in your own words, which will lead to better retention than typing the lecture word for word on your laptop. For lectures, "the pen is mightier than the keyboard," note researchers Pam Mueller and Daniel Oppenheimer (2014).

> Laptop distraction? In one study of introductory psychology students, the average student spent one-third of the class hour browsing online. The greater the amount of time spent online, the poorer the exam performance (Ravizza et al., 2017).

Make the material meaningful. You can build a network of retrieval cues by forming as many associations as possible. Apply concepts to your own life; this text's *In* Your Everyday Life questions and *Improve* Your Everyday Life questions are a good way to do this. Form images. Understand and organize information. Relate material to what you already know or have experienced. As William James (1890) suggested, "Knit each new thing on to some acquisition already there." Mindlessly repeating someone else's words without taking the time to really understand what they mean won't supply many retrieval cues. On an exam, you may find yourself stuck when a question uses terms different from the ones you memorized.

Activate retrieval cues. Remember the importance of *context-dependent* and *state-dependent memory*. Mentally re-create the situation in which your original learning occurred. Imagine returning to the same location and being in the same mood. Jog your memory by allowing one thought to cue the next.

Use mnemonic devices. Make up a story that uses *vivid images* of the items. *Chunk* information for easier retrieval.

> In the discussion of mnemonics, we gave you six words and told you we would quiz you about them later. How many of those words can you now recall? Of these, how many are concrete, vivid-image words? How many describe abstract ideas?[1]

Minimize proactive and retroactive interference. Study before sleeping. Do not schedule back-to-back study times for topics that are likely to interfere with each other, such as Spanish and French.

Sleep more. During sleep, the brain reorganizes and *consolidates* information for long-term memory. Sleep deprivation disrupts this process (Frenda et al., 2014; Lo et al., 2016). Even 10 minutes of waking rest enhances memory of what we have read (Dewar et al., 2012). So, after a period of hard study, you might just sit or lie down for a few minutes before tackling the next subject.

Test your own knowledge, both to rehearse it and to find out what you don't yet know. The testing effect is real, and it is powerful. Don't become overconfident because you can *recognize* information. Test your *recall* using the Retrieve & Remember items found throughout each chapter, and the numbered Learning Objective Questions and Chapter Test questions at the end of each chapter. Outline sections using a blank page. Define the terms and concepts listed at each chapter's end before turning back to their definitions. Experts recommend retrieving a to-be-remembered item three times before you stop studying it (Miyatsu et al., 2018). Take practice tests; the online resources that accompany many texts, including LaunchPad and Achieve Read & Practice for this text, are a good source for such tests.

IMPROVE YOUR EVERYDAY LIFE

Which three of these study and memory strategies will be most important for you to start using to improve your own learning and retention?

RETRIEVE & REMEMBER

ANSWERS IN APPENDIX E

18. Which memory strategies can help you study smarter and retain more information?

[1] Bicycle, void, cigarette, inherent, fire, process.

CHAPTER 7 REVIEW Memory

LEARNING OBJECTIVES

TEST YOURSELF Answer these repeated Learning Objective Questions on your own (before checking the answers in Appendix D) to improve your retention of the concepts (McDaniel et al., 2009, 2015).

Studying Memory

7-1: What is *memory*, and how do information-processing models help us study memory?

7-2: What is the three-stage information-processing model, and how has later research updated this model?

Building Memories: Encoding

7-3: How do implicit and explicit memories differ?

7-4: What information do we process automatically?

7-5: How does sensory memory work?

7-6: What is our short-term memory capacity?

7-7: What are some effortful processing strategies that can help us remember new information?

7-8: Why is cramming ineffective, and what is the *testing effect?* Why is it important to make new information meaningful?

Memory Storage

7-9: What is the capacity of long-term memory? Are our long-term memories processed and stored in specific locations?

7-10: What roles do the hippocampus and frontal lobes play in memory processing?

7-11: What roles do the cerebellum and basal ganglia play in memory processing?

7-12: How do emotions affect our memory processing?

7-13: How do changes at the synapse level affect our memory processing?

Retrieval: Getting Information Out

7-14: How do psychologists assess memory with recall, recognition, and relearning?

7-15: How do external events, internal moods, and order of appearance affect memory retrieval?

Forgetting

7-16: Why do we forget?

Memory Construction Errors

7-17: How do misinformation, imagination, and source amnesia influence our memory construction? How do we decide whether a memory is real or false?

7-18: Why have reports of repressed and recovered memories been so hotly debated?

7-19: How reliable are young children's eyewitness descriptions?

Improving Memory

7-20: How can you use memory research findings to do better in this course and in others?

TERMS AND CONCEPTS TO REMEMBER

TEST YOURSELF Write down the definition in your own words, then check your answer.

memory, *p.* 191
encoding, *p.* 191
storage, *p.* 191
retrieval, *p.* 191
sensory memory, *p.* 191
short-term memory, *p.* 191
long-term memory, *p.* 191
working memory, *p.* 191
implicit memory, *p.* 191
automatic processing, *p.* 191
explicit memory, *p.* 191
effortful processing, *p.* 191
parallel processing, *p.* 193
chunking, *p.* 193
mnemonics [nih-MON-iks], *p.* 193
spacing effect, *p.* 195
testing effect, *p.* 195
semantic memory, *p.* 195
episodic memory, *p.* 195
hippocampus, *p.* 195
memory consolidation, *p.* 197
flashbulb memory, *p.* 197
long-term potentiation (LTP), *p.* 199
recall, *p.* 199
recognition, *p.* 199
relearning, *p.* 199
retrieval cue, *p.* 201
priming, *p.* 201
encoding specificity principle, *p.* 201
mood-congruent memory, *p.* 201
serial position effect, *p.* 201
anterograde amnesia, *p.* 203
retrograde amnesia, *p.* 203
memory trace, *p.* 203
proactive interference, *p.* 205
retroactive interference, *p.* 205
repression, *p.* 205
reconsolidation, *p.* 207
misinformation effect, *p.* 207
source amnesia, *p.* 207
déjà vu, *p.* 207

CHAPTER TEST

TEST YOURSELF Answer the following questions on your own first, then check your answers in Appendix E.

1. The psychological terms for taking in information, retaining it, and later getting it back out are ________, ________, and ________.
2. The concept of working memory
   a. clarifies the idea of short-term memory by focusing on the active processing that occurs in this stage.
   b. splits short-term memory into two substages—sensory memory and iconic memory.
   c. splits short-term memory into two types—implicit and explicit memory.
   d. clarifies the idea of short-term memory by focusing on space, time, and frequency.
3. Sensory memory may be visual (________ memory) or auditory (________ memory).
4. Our short-term memory for new information is limited to about ________ bits of information.
5. Memory aids that use visual imagery or other organizational devices are called ________.
6. The hippocampus seems to function as a
   a. temporary processing site for explicit memories.
   b. temporary processing site for implicit memories.
   c. permanent storage area for emotion-based memories.
   d. permanent storage area for iconic and echoic memories.
7. Hippocampus damage typically leaves people unable to learn new facts or recall recent events. However, they may be able to learn new skills, such as riding a bicycle, which is an ________ (explicit/implicit) memory.
8. Long-term potentiation (LTP) refers to
   a. emotion-triggered hormonal changes.
   b. the role of the hippocampus in processing explicit memories.
   c. an increase in a cell's firing potential.
   d. aging people's potential for learning.
9. A psychologist who asks you to write down as many objects as you can remember having seen a few minutes earlier is testing your ________.
10. Specific odors, visual images, emotions, or other associations that help us access a memory are examples of ________ ________.
11. When you feel sad, why might it help to look at pictures that reawaken some of your best memories?
12. When tested immediately after viewing a list of words, people tend to recall the first and last items more readily than those in the middle. When retested after a delay, they are most likely to recall
    a. the first items on the list.
    b. the first and last items on the list.
    c. a few items at random.
    d. the last items on the list.
13. When forgetting is due to encoding failure, information has not been transferred from
    a. the environment into sensory memory.
    b. sensory memory into long-term memory.
    c. long-term memory into short-term memory.
    d. short-term memory into long-term memory.
14. Ebbinghaus' forgetting curve shows that after an initial decline, memory for novel information tends to
    a. increase slightly.
    b. decrease noticeably.
    c. decrease greatly.
    d. level off.
15. You will experience less ________ (proactive/retroactive) interference if you learn new material in the hour before sleep than you will if you learn it before turning to another subject.
16. Freud proposed that painful or unacceptable memories are blocked from consciousness through a mechanism called ________.
17. One reason false memories form is our tendency to fill in memory gaps with our reasonable guesses and assumptions, sometimes based on misleading information. This tendency is an example of
    a. proactive interference.
    b. the misinformation effect.
    c. retroactive interference.
    d. the forgetting curve.
18. Eliza's family loves to tell the story of how she "stole the show" as a 2-year-old, dancing at her aunt's wedding reception. Even though she was so young, Eliza says she can recall the event clearly. How might Eliza have formed this memory?
19. We may recognize a face at a social gathering but be unable to remember how we know that person. This is an example of ________ ________.
20. When a situation triggers the feeling that "I've been here before," you are experiencing ________ ________.
21. Children can be accurate eyewitnesses if
    a. interviewers give the children hints about what really happened.
    b. a neutral person asks nonleading questions soon after the event.
    c. the children have a chance to talk with involved adults before the interview.
    d. interviewers use precise technical and medical terms.
22. Memory researchers involved in the study of memories of abuse tend to *disagree* with some therapists about which of the following statements?
    a. Memories of events that happened before age 4 are not reliable.
    b. We tend to repress extremely upsetting memories.
    c. Memories can be emotionally upsetting.
    d. Sexual abuse happens.

Continue testing yourself with **LearningCurve** or **Achieve Read & Practice** to learn and remember most effectively.

FatCamera/Getty Images

CHAPTER 8

Thinking, Language, and Intelligence

SURVEY THE CHAPTER

Throughout history, we humans have celebrated our wisdom and bemoaned our foolishness. Throughout this text, we likewise marvel at both our abilities and our errors. As our brain develops, our mind blossoms. We move from the amazing abilities of the newborn, to the logic of adolescence, to the wisdom of older age. Our sensory systems gather countless sensations, convert them into nerve impulses, and send them to multiple brain sites, forming meaningful perceptions. Meanwhile, our two-track mind is processing, interpreting, and storing vast amounts of information, with and without our awareness. Not bad for the meatloaf-sized three pounds of tissue jammed inside our skull.

Yet we are also sometimes simple-minded or error-prone. Our species is kin to the other animals, influenced by the same principles that produce learning in rats, pigeons, and even slugs. Sometimes our thinking fails us. We not-so-wise humans are easily fooled by perceptual illusions, fake psychic claims, and false memories.

In this chapter, we find more examples of these two images—the rational and irrational human. We will consider thinking, and how we use—and sometimes ignore or misuse—information about the world around us. We will look at our gift for language and why and how it develops. We will consider a century's research on intelligence—what it is and how (and why) we measure it. And we will reflect on how deserving we are of our species name, *Homo sapiens* ("wise human").

Thinking

CONCEPTS

Learning Objective Question LOQ 8-1

What is *cognition,* and what are the functions of concepts?

Psychologists who study **cognition** focus on the mental activities associated with thinking, knowing, remembering, and communicating information. One of these activities is forming **concepts**—mental groupings of similar objects, events, ideas, or people. The concept *chair* includes many items—a baby's high chair, a reclining chair, a dentist's chair—all for sitting.

Concepts simplify our thinking. Imagine life without them. We could not ask a child to "throw the ball" because there would be no concept of *throw* or *ball*. We could not say, "I want to earn money" because people aren't born with a concept of money. Concepts such as *ball* and *money* give us much information with little mental effort.

We often form our concepts by developing a **prototype**—a mental image or best example of a category (Rosch, 1978). People more quickly agree that "a crow is a bird" than that "a penguin is a bird." For most of us, the crow is the birdier bird; it more closely resembles our *bird* prototype. When something closely matches our prototype of a concept, we readily recognize it as an example of the concept.

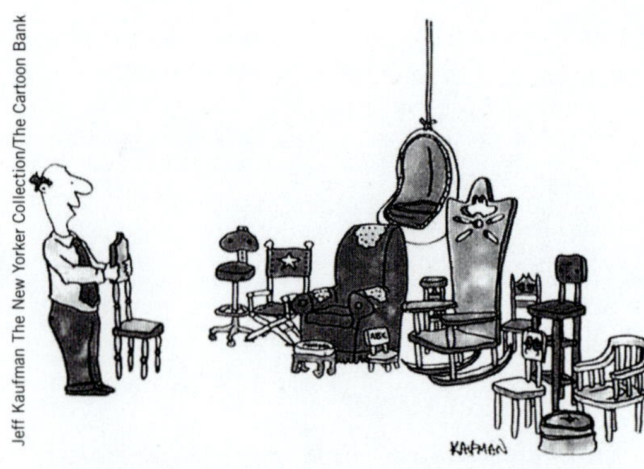

Jeff Kaufman The New Yorker Collection/The Cartoon Bank

"Attention, everyone! I'd like to introduce the newest member of our family."

Sometimes, though, our experiences don't match up neatly with our prototypes. When this happens, our category boundaries may blur. Is a 16-year-old female a girl or a woman? Is a whale a fish or a mammal? Is a tomato a fruit? Because a tomato fails to match our *fruit* prototype, we are slower to recognize it as a fruit.

Similarly, when symptoms don't fit one of our disease prototypes, we are slow to perceive an illness (Bishop, 1991). People whose heart attack symptoms (shortness of breath, exhaustion, a dull weight in the chest) don't match their *heart attack* prototype (sharp chest pain) may not seek help. Concepts speed and guide our thinking. But they don't always make us wise.

SOLVING PROBLEMS

LOQ 8-2 What cognitive strategies help us solve problems, and what tendencies work against us?

One tribute to our rationality is our impressive problem-solving skill. What's the best route around this traffic jam? How should we handle a friend's criticism? How, without our keys, can we get in the house?

Some problems we solve through *trial and error.* Thomas Edison tried thousands of light bulb filaments before stumbling upon one that worked. For other problems, we use **algorithms,** step-by-step procedures that guarantee a solution. But following the steps in an algorithm takes time and effort—sometimes a lot of time and effort. To find a word using the 10 letters in *SPLOYOCHYG,* for example, you could construct a list, with each letter in each of the 10 positions. But your list of 907,200 different combinations would be very long! In such cases, we often resort to **heuristics,** simpler thinking strategies. Thus, you might reduce the number of options in the *SPLOYOCHYG* example by grouping letters that often appear together (*CH* and *GY*) and avoiding rare combinations (such as *YY*). By using heuristics and then applying trial and error, you may hit on the answer. Have you guessed it?[1]

Sometimes we puzzle over a problem, with no feeling of getting closer to the answer. Then, suddenly the pieces fall together in a flash of **insight**—an abrupt, true-seeming, and often satisfying solution (Topolinski & Reber, 2010). Ten-year-old Johnny Appleton had one of these Aha! moments and solved a problem that had stumped many adults. How could they rescue a young robin that had fallen into a narrow, 30-inch-deep hole in a cement-block wall? Johnny's solution: Slowly pour in sand, giving the bird enough time to keep its feet on top of the constantly rising mound (Ruchlis, 1990). Insights aren't perfect, but they often lead to correct solutions (Danek & Salvi, 2018).

What happens in the brain when people experience these Aha! moments? Scans (EEGs or fMRIs) show bursts of activity associated with sudden flashes of insight (Kounios & Beeman, 2014). In one study, researchers asked people to think of a word that forms a compound word or phrase with each of three words in a set (such as *pine, crab,* and *sauce*). When people knew the answer, they were to press a button, which would sound a bell. (Need a hint? The word is a fruit.[2]) A sudden Aha! insight led to about half the solutions. Before the Aha! moment, the problem solvers' frontal lobes (involved in focusing attention) were active. Then, at the instant of discovery, there was a burst of activity in their right temporal lobe, just above the ear **(FIGURE 8.1)**.

Insight gives us a happy sense of satisfaction. The joy of a joke is similarly a sudden "I get it!" reaction to a double meaning or a surprise ending: "You don't need a parachute to skydive. You only need a parachute to skydive twice." Comedian Groucho Marx was a master at this: "I once shot an elephant in my pajamas. How he got into my pajamas I'll never know."

[1] Answer to SPLOYOCHYG problem: PSYCHOLOGY

[2] The word is apple: pineapple, crabapple, applesauce.

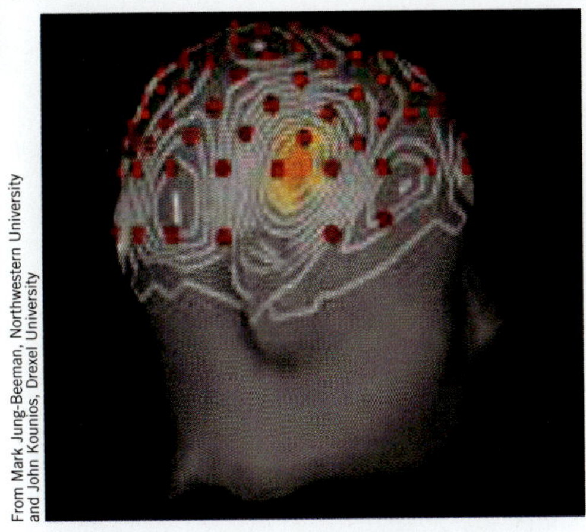

FIGURE 8.1 The Aha! moment A burst of right temporal lobe EEG activity (yellow area) accompanied insight solutions to word problems (Jung-Beeman et al., 2004). The red dots show placement of the EEG electrodes. The light gray lines show patterns of brain activity during insight.

Insightful as we are, other cognitive tendencies may lead us astray. **Confirmation bias,** for example, leads us to seek evidence *for* our ideas more eagerly than we seek evidence *against* them (Klayman & Ha, 1987; Skov & Sherman, 1986). Peter Wason (1960) demonstrated confirmation bias in a now-classic study. He gave students a set of three numbers (2-4-6) and told them the sequence was based on a rule. Their task was to guess the rule. (It was simple: Each number must be larger than the one before it.) Before giving their answers, students formed their own three-number sets, and Wason told them whether their sets worked with his rule. When they felt certain they had the rule, they could announce it. The result? Most students formed a wrong idea ("Maybe it's counting by twos") and then searched only for evidence confirming the wrong rule (by testing 6-8-10, 100-102-104, and so forth). They were seldom right but never in doubt.

In real life, this tendency can have grave results. Having formed a belief—that vaccines cause (or do not cause) autism spectrum disorder, that people can (or cannot) change their sexual orientation, that gun control fails (or does not fail) to save lives—we prefer information that supports our belief.

And once we get hung up on an incorrect view of a problem, it's hard to approach it from a different angle. This obstacle to problem solving is called **functional fixedness,** an inability to come to a fresh perspective. Can you solve the matchstick problem in **FIGURE 8.2**? (See the solution in **FIGURE 8.3.**)

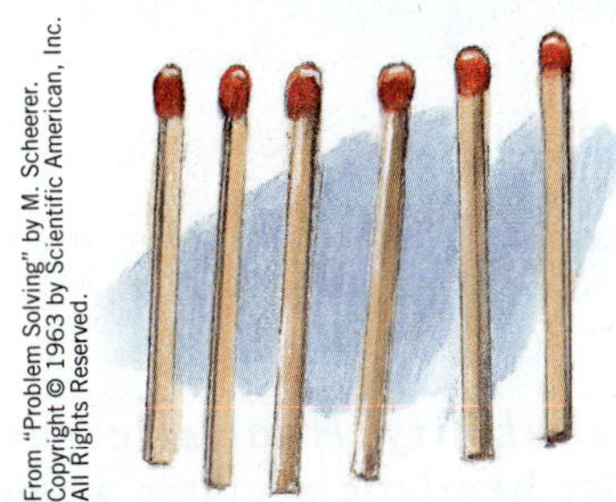

FIGURE 8.2 The matchstick problem How would you arrange six matches to form four equilateral triangles?

MAKING GOOD (AND BAD) DECISIONS AND JUDGMENTS

LOQ 8-3 What is *intuition,* and how can the representativeness and availability heuristics influence our decisions and judgments?

Each day we make hundreds of judgments and decisions. (*Should I take a jacket? Can I trust this person? Should I shoot the basketball or pass to the player who's hot?*) As we judge the odds and make our decisions, we seldom take the time and effort to reason systematically. We just follow our **intuition,** our fast, automatic, unreasoned feelings and thoughts. After interviewing leaders in government, business, and education, one social psychologist concluded that they often made decisions without considered thought and reflection. How did they usually reach their decisions? "If you ask, they are likely to tell you . . . they do it mostly *by the seat of their pants*" (Janis, 1986).

Two Quick But Risky Shortcuts

When we need to make snap judgments, *heuristics* enable quick thinking that often serves us well (Gigerenzer, 2015).

cognition all the mental activities associated with thinking, knowing, remembering, and communicating.

concept a mental grouping of similar objects, events, ideas, or people.

prototype a mental image or best example of a category. Matching new items to a prototype provides a quick and easy method for sorting items into categories (as when you compare a feathered creature to a prototypical bird, such as a crow).

algorithm a methodical, logical rule or procedure that guarantees you will solve a particular problem. Contrasts with the usually speedier—but also more error-prone—use of *heuristics.*

heuristic a simple thinking strategy that often allows you to make judgments and solve problems efficiently; usually speedier but also more error-prone than an *algorithm.*

insight a sudden realization of the solution to a problem; contrasts with strategy-based solutions.

confirmation bias a tendency to search for information that supports your preconceptions and to ignore or distort evidence that contradicts them.

functional fixedness in cognition, the inability to see a problem from a new perspective; an obstacle to problem solving.

intuition an effortless, immediate, automatic feeling or thought, as contrasted with explicit, conscious reasoning.

But as cognitive psychologists Amos Tversky and Daniel Kahneman (1974) showed, some intuitive mental shortcuts—the *representativeness* and *availability heuristics*—can lead even the smartest people into dumb decisions.[3]

The Representativeness Heuristic To judge the likelihood of something by intuitively comparing it to particular prototypes is to use the **representativeness heuristic.** Imagine someone who is short, slim, and likes to read poetry. Is this person more likely to be an Ivy League university English professor or a truck driver (Nisbett & Ross, 1980)?

Many people guess English professor—because the person better fits their prototype of nerdy professor than of truck driver. In doing so, they fail to consider the number of Ivy League English professors (fewer than 400) and truck drivers (3.5 million in the United States alone). Thus, even if the description is 50 times more typical of English professors than of truck drivers, the fact that there are about 7000 times more truck drivers means that the poetry reader is many times more likely to be a truck driver.

Or consider the questions one mother of two Black and three White teens asked other parents: "Do store personnel follow your children when they are picking out their Gatorade flavors? They didn't follow my White kids. . . . When your kids trick-or-treat dressed as a ninja and a clown, do they get asked who they are with and where they live, door after door? My White kids didn't get asked" (Roper, 2016). If people have a prototype—a stereotype—of delinquent Black teens, they may unconsciously use the representativeness heuristic when judging individuals. The result, even if unintended, is racism.

[3] Tversky and Kahneman's joint work on decision making received a 2002 Nobel Prize; sadly, only Kahneman was alive to receive the honor. As Kahneman wrote in a vignette for my [DM's] *Social Psychology* text, "Amos and I shared the wonder of together owning a goose that could lay golden eggs—a joint mind that was better than our separate minds."

FIGURE 8.3 Solution to the matchstick problem Were you, by chance, fixated on two-dimensional solutions? Solving problems often requires taking a new angle on the situation.

representativeness heuristic judging the likelihood of events in terms of how well they seem to represent, or match, particular prototypes; may lead us to ignore other relevant information.

availability heuristic judging the likelihood of events based on their availability in memory; if an event comes readily to mind (perhaps because it was vivid), we assume it must be common.

The Availability Heuristic The **availability heuristic** operates when we estimate how common an event is, *based on its mental availability.* Anything that makes information pop into mind—its vividness, recentness, or distinctiveness—can make it seem commonplace. Casinos know this. They entice us to gamble by broadcasting (infrequent) wins with flashing lights. The (far more frequent) big losses are invisible.

The availability heuristic distorts our judgments of risks. Who's scarier: toddlers or terrorists? Perhaps you'll change your answer, once you consider that armed toddlers killed more Americans than did feared foreign terrorists in 2015 and 2016 (Ingraham, 2016; LaCapria, 2015). If foreign terrorists were to kill 1000 people in the United States this year, Americans would be mighty afraid. Yet they would have reason to be 30 times more afraid of homicidal, suicidal, and accidental death by guns, which take more than 30,000 lives annually. *The bottom line:* We often fear the wrong things (see Thinking Critically About: The Fear Factor).

Dramatic outcomes make us gasp; probabilities we hardly grasp. Over 40 nations have sought to harness the positive power of vivid, memorable images by putting eye-catching warnings and graphic photos on cigarette packages (Riordan, 2013). This campaign has worked (Huang et al., 2013). Why? Because we reason emotionally—we overfeel and underthink. In 2015, an iconic photo of a Syrian child lying dead on a beach went viral. Red Cross donations to Syrian refugees were 55 times greater in response to that photo than in response to statistics describing the hundreds of thousands of other refugee deaths (Slovic et al., 2017).

"In creating these problems, we didn't set out to fool people. All our problems fooled us, too."—Amos Tversky (1985)

"Intuitive thinking [is] fine most of the time. . . . But sometimes that habit of mind gets us in trouble."—Daniel Kahneman (2005b)

Thinking Critically About:

The Fear Factor

LOQ 8-4 What factors exaggerate our fear of unlikely events?

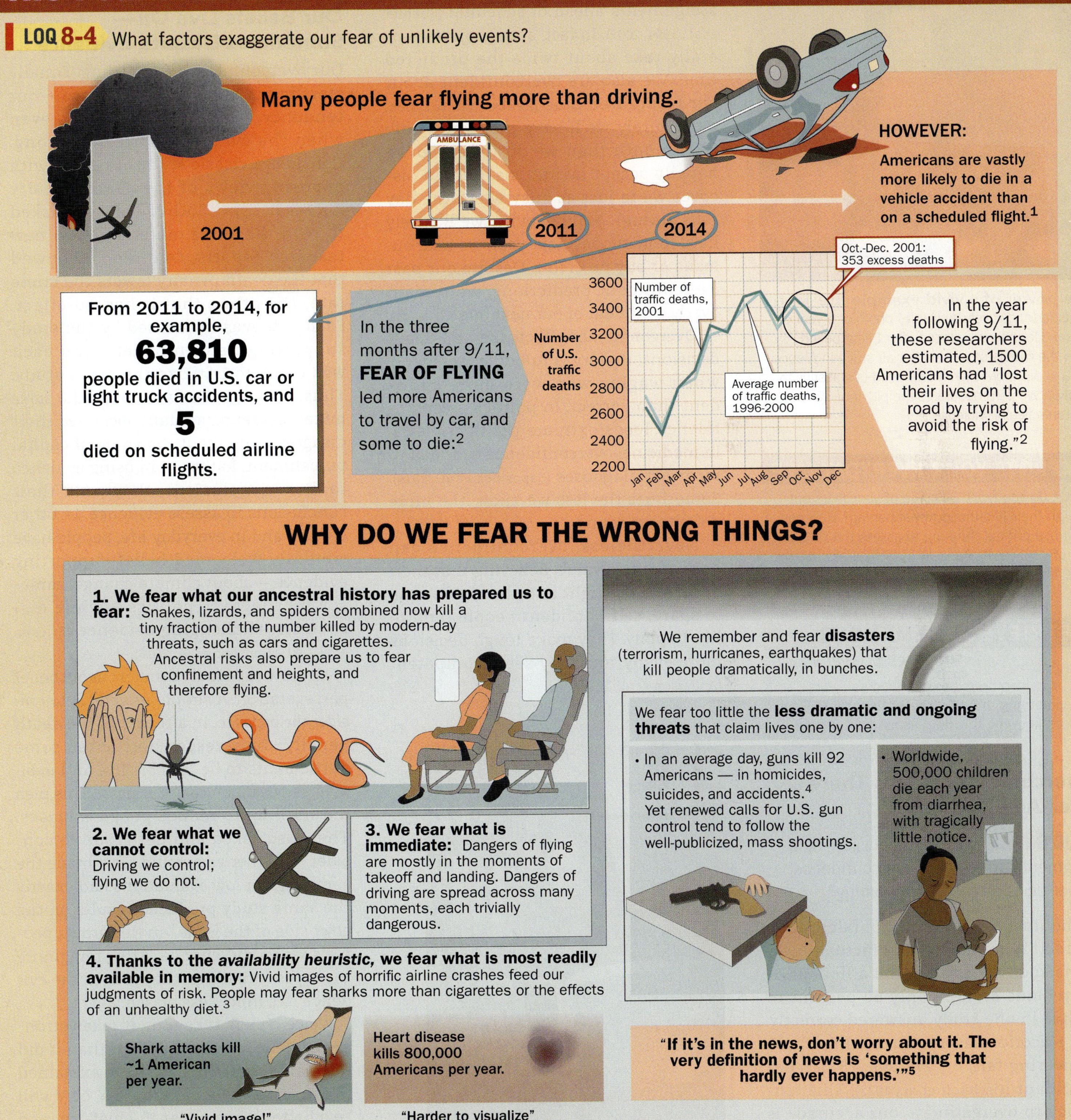

Many people fear flying more than driving.
AMBULANCE
2001
2011
2014
HOWEVER:
Americans are vastly more likely to die in a vehicle accident than on a scheduled flight.[1]
From 2011 to 2014, for example,
63,810
people died in U.S. car or light truck accidents, and
5
died on scheduled airline flights.
In the three months after 9/11, FEAR OF FLYING led more Americans to travel by car, and some to die:[2]
Number of U.S. traffic deaths
3600
3400
3200
3000
2800
2600
2400
2200
Jan Feb Mar Apr May Jun Jul Aug Sep Oct Nov Dec
Number of traffic deaths, 2001
Average number of traffic deaths, 1996-2000
Oct.-Dec. 2001: 353 excess deaths
In the year following 9/11, these researchers estimated, 1500 Americans had "lost their lives on the road by trying to avoid the risk of flying."[2]
WHY DO WE FEAR THE WRONG THINGS?
1. We fear what our ancestral history has prepared us to fear: Snakes, lizards, and spiders combined now kill a tiny fraction of the number killed by modern-day threats, such as cars and cigarettes. Ancestral risks also prepare us to fear confinement and heights, and therefore flying.
2. We fear what we cannot control: Driving we control; flying we do not.
3. We fear what is immediate: Dangers of flying are mostly in the moments of takeoff and landing. Dangers of driving are spread across many moments, each trivially dangerous.
4. Thanks to the availability heuristic, we fear what is most readily available in memory: Vivid images of horrific airline crashes feed our judgments of risk. People may fear sharks more than cigarettes or the effects of an unhealthy diet.[3]
Shark attacks kill ~1 American per year.
"Vivid image!"
Heart disease kills 800,000 Americans per year.
"Harder to visualize"
We remember and fear disasters (terrorism, hurricanes, earthquakes) that kill people dramatically, in bunches.
We fear too little the less dramatic and ongoing threats that claim lives one by one:
• In an average day, guns kill 92 Americans — in homicides, suicides, and accidents.[4] Yet renewed calls for U.S. gun control tend to follow the well-publicized, mass shootings.
• Worldwide, 500,000 children die each year from diarrhea, with tragically little notice.
"If it's in the news, don't worry about it. The very definition of news is 'something that hardly ever happens.'"[5]

1. National Safety Council, 2017. 2. Gaissmater & Gigerenzer, 2012; Gigerenzer, 2004, 2006. 3. Daley, 2011. 4. Xu et al., 2016. 5. Schneier, 2007.

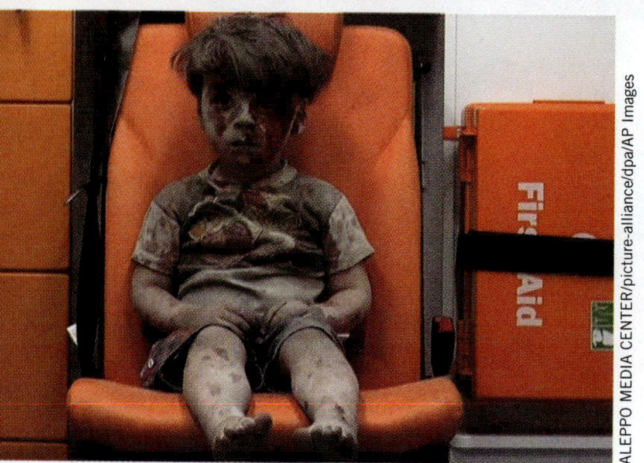

ALEPPO MEDIA CENTER/picture-alliance/dpa/AP Images

The power of a vivid example The unforgettable (cognitively available) photo of 5-year-old Omran Daqneesh—dazed after being pulled from the rubble of yet another air strike in Aleppo, Syria—did more than an armload of statistics to awaken Western nations to the plight of Syrian migrants fleeing violence.

IMPROVE YOUR EVERYDAY LIFE

What do you fear? Do some of your fears outweigh their likelihood of happening? How can you use critical thinking to assess the rationality of your fears—and to identify areas of your life where you need to take more precautions?

RETRIEVE & REMEMBER

ANSWERS IN APPENDIX E

1. Why can news be described as "something that hardly ever happens"? How does knowing this help us assess our fears?

Overconfidence: Was There Ever Any Doubt?

LOQ 8-5 How are our decisions and judgments affected by overconfidence, belief perseverance, and framing?

Sometimes we are more confident than correct. When answering factual questions such as "Is absinthe a liqueur or a precious stone?" only 60 percent of people in one study answered correctly. (It's a licorice-flavored liqueur.) Yet those answering felt, on average, 75 percent confident (Fischhoff et al., 1977). This tendency to overestimate our accuracy is **overconfidence.**

Classrooms are full of overconfident students who expect to finish assignments ahead of schedule (Buehler et al., 1994, 2002). In fact, such projects generally take about twice the predicted time. We also are overconfident about our future free time (Zauberman & Lynch, 2005). Surely we'll have more free time next month than we do today. So we happily accept invitations, only to discover we're just as busy when the day rolls around. And believing we'll surely have more money next year, we take out loans or buy on credit. Despite our past overconfident predictions, we remain overly confident of our next one.

Overconfidence affects life-and-death decisions. History is full of leaders who, when waging war, were more confident than correct. In politics, overconfidence feeds extreme political views. In medicine, overconfidence can lead to incorrect diagnoses (Saposnick et al., 2016). Sometimes the less we know, the more definite we sound.

Nevertheless, overconfidence can have adaptive value. Believing that their decisions are right and they have time to spare, self-confident people tend to live happily. They make tough decisions more easily, and they seem competent (Anderson et al., 2012).

Bianca Moscatelli/Worth Publishers

Predict your own behavior When will you finish reading this chapter?

Our Beliefs Live On—Sometimes Despite Evidence

Our overconfidence is startling. Equally startling is **belief perseverance**—our tendency to cling to our beliefs even when the evidence proves us wrong. Consider a classic study of people with opposing views of the death penalty (Lord et al., 1979). Both sides were asked to read the same material—two new research reports. One report showed that the death penalty lowers the crime rate; the other, that it has no effect. Each side was impressed by the study supporting its own beliefs, and each was quick to criticize the other study. Thus, showing the two groups the *same* mixed evidence actually *increased* their disagreement about the value of capital punishment. Rather than using evidence to draw conclusions, they used their conclusions to assess evidence. In other studies and in everyday life, people have similarly welcomed belief-supporting evidence—about climate change, same-sex marriage, or politics—while discounting challenging evidence (Friesen et al., 2015; Sunstein et al., 2016).

So how can smart thinkers avoid belief perseverance? A simple remedy is to *consider the opposite.* In a repeat of the death penalty study, researchers asked some participants to be "as *objective* and *unbiased* as possible" (Lord et al., 1984). This plea did nothing to reduce people's biases. They also asked another group to consider "whether you would have made the same high or low evaluations had exactly the same study produced results on the *other* side of the issue." In this group, people's views did change. After imagining the *opposite* findings, they judged the evidence in a much less biased way.

Once beliefs take root, it takes stronger evidence to change them than it did to create them. Once we have explained to ourselves why candidate X or Y will be a better commander-in-chief, we tend to ignore evidence that challenges our belief. Often, prejudice persists. Beliefs persevere.

IN YOUR EVERYDAY LIFE

Can you recall a time when contradictory information challenged one of your views? Was it hard for you to consider the opposite view? What caused you to change your thinking or keep your opinion?

Framing: Let's Put It This Way . . .

Framing—the way we present an issue—can be a powerful tool of persuasion. Working together, psychologists and economists have shown how the framing of options can **nudge** people toward beneficial decisions (Benartzi et al., 2017; Bohannon, 2016; Thaler & Sunstein, 2008).

- ***Saving for retirement.*** U.S. companies once required employees who wanted to contribute to a retirement plan to choose a lower take-home pay. Few employees opted in. But when a new law allowed companies to enroll their employees in the plan automatically, letting employees instead opt *out* if they chose, enrollments soared (Rosenberg, 2010). Britain's 2012 change to an opt-out framing similarly led to 5 million more retirement savers (Halpern, 2015).
- ***Making smart medical decisions.*** Imagine two surgeons explaining the risk of an upcoming surgery. One explains that during this type of surgery, 10 percent of people die. The other explains that 90 percent survive. The information is the same. The effect is not. In real-life surveys, patients and physicians overwhelmingly say the risk is greater when they hear that 10 percent *die* (Marteau, 1989; McNeil et al., 1988; Rothman & Salovey, 1997).
- ***Becoming an organ donor.*** In many European countries, as well as in the United States, people renewing their driver's license can decide whether to be organ donors. In some countries, the assumed answer is *Yes*, unless you opt out. Nearly 100 percent of the people in these opt-out countries agree to be donors. In countries where the assumed answer is *No*, most do *not* agree to be donors (Hajhosseini et al., 2013; Johnson & Goldstein, 2003). To nudge people to donate their organs, change the default option to helping humans.

The point to remember: Framing can nudge our attitudes and decisions.

The Perils and Powers of Intuition

LOQ 8-6 How do smart thinkers use intuition?

We have seen how our unreasoned thinking can plague our efforts to solve problems, assess risks, and make wise decisions. Moreover, these perils of intuition persist even when people are offered extra pay for thinking smart or when asked to justify their answers. And they persist even among those with high intelligence, including expert physicians, clinicians, and U.S. federal intelligence agents (Reyna et al., 2014; Shafir & LeBoeuf, 2002; Stanovich et al., 2013).

But psychological science is also revealing intuition's powers:

- ***Intuition is recognition born of experience.*** It is implicit (unconscious) knowledge—what we've learned and recorded in our brains but can't fully explain (Chassy & Gobet, 2011; Gore & Sadler-Smith, 2011). We see this ability to size up a situation and react in an eyeblink in chess masters playing speed chess, when they intuitively know the right move (Burns, 2004). We see it in the smart and quick judgments of seasoned nurses, firefighters, art critics, and car mechanics. We see it in skilled athletes who react without thinking. Indeed, conscious thinking may disrupt well-practiced movements, leading skilled athletes to choke under pressure, as when shooting free throws (Beilock, 2010). And we would see this instant intuition in you, too, for anything in which you have developed a deep and special knowledge, based on experience.
- ***Intuition is usually adaptive.*** Our fast and frugal heuristics let us intuitively assume that fuzzy-looking objects are far away—which they usually are, except on foggy mornings. Our learned associations surface as gut feelings, right or wrong. Seeing a stranger who looks like someone who has harmed or threatened us in the past, we may automatically react with distrust. Newlyweds' implicit, gut-level attitudes toward their new spouses likewise predict their future marital happiness (McNulty et al., 2013).
- ***Intuition is huge.*** Unconscious automatic influences are constantly affecting our judgments (Custers & Aarts, 2010). Imagine participating in this decision-making experiment (Strick et al., 2010). You've been assigned to one of three groups that will receive complex information about four apartment options. Those in the first group will state their choice immediately after reading the information. Those in the second group will analyze the information before choosing one of the options. Your group, the third, will consider the information but then be distracted for a time before giving your decision. Which group will make the smartest decision?

Did you guess the second group would make the best choice? Most people do, believing that the more complex the choice, the smarter it is to make decisions rationally rather than intuitively (Inbar et al., 2010). Actually, the third group made the

overconfidence the tendency to be more confident than correct—to overestimate the accuracy of our beliefs and judgments.

belief perseverance clinging to beliefs even after evidence has proven them wrong.

framing the way an issue is posed; framing can significantly affect decisions and judgments.

nudge framing choices in a way that encourages people to make decisions that support their personal well-being.

best choice in this real-life experiment. When making complex decisions, we benefit by letting a problem "incubate" while we attend to other things (Dijksterhuis & Strick, 2016). Facing a difficult decision involving a lot of facts, we're wise to gather all the information we can, and then say, "Give me some time *not* to think about this." Even sleeping on it can help. Thanks to our ever-active brain, nonconscious thinking (reasoning, problem solving, decision making, planning) is surprisingly wise (Creswell et al., 2013; Hassin, 2013; Lin & Murray, 2015).

Critics remind us, however, that with most complex tasks, deliberate, conscious thought helps (Newell, 2015; Nieuwenstein et al., 2015; Phillips et al., 2016). With many sorts of problems, smart thinkers may initially fall prey to an intuitive option but then reason their way to a better answer. Consider a random coin flip. If someone flipped a coin six times, which of the following sequences of heads (H) and tails (T) would seem most likely: HHHTTT or HTTHTH or HHHHHH?

If you're like most people, you intuitively believe HTTHTH would be the most likely random sequence (Kahneman & Tversky, 1972). Actually, each of these exact sequences is equally likely (or, you might say, equally unlikely).

The bottom line: Our two-track mind makes sweet harmony as smart, critical thinking listens to the creative whispers of our vast unseen mind and then evaluates evidence, tests conclusions, and plans for the future.

THINKING CREATIVELY

LOQ 8-7 What is *creativity,* and what fosters it?

Creativity is the ability to produce ideas that are both novel and valuable (Hennessey & Amabile, 2010). Consider Princeton mathematician Andrew Wiles' incredible, creative moment. Pierre de Fermat (1601–1665), a mischief-loving genius, dared scholars to match his solutions to various number theory problems. Three centuries later, one of those problems continued to baffle the greatest mathematical minds, even after a $2 million prize (in today's money) had been offered for cracking the puzzle.

PETER MUHLY/Getty Images

Industrious creativity When she accepted her Nobel Prize for Literature in 2013, author Alice Munro described creative writing as challenging work: "The part that's hardest is when you go over the story and realize how bad it is." Once the initial excitement wears off, Munro said, "that is when you really have to get to work."

Wiles had searched for the answer for more than 30 years and reached the brink of a solution. One morning in 1994, out of the blue, an "incredible revelation" struck him. "It was so . . . beautiful . . . so simple and so elegant. I couldn't understand how I'd missed it. . . . It was the most important moment of my working life" (Singh, 1997, p. 25).

Creativity like Wiles' requires a certain level of *aptitude* (ability to learn). But there is more to creativity than aptitude, or what intelligence tests reveal. Aptitude tests (such as the SAT) require **convergent thinking**—an ability to provide a single correct answer. Creativity tests (*How many uses can you think of for a brick?*) require **divergent thinking**—the ability to consider many different options and to think in novel ways.

Robert Sternberg and his colleagues (1988, 2003; Sternberg & Lubart, 1991, 1992) believe creativity has five ingredients.

1. ***Expertise***—a solid knowledge base—furnishes the ideas, images, and phrases we use as mental building blocks. The more blocks we have, the more novel ways we can combine them. Wiles' well-developed base of mathematical knowledge gave him access to many combinations of ideas and methods.
2. ***Imaginative thinking skills*** give us the ability to see things in novel ways, to recognize patterns, and to make connections. Wiles' imaginative solution combined two partial solutions.
3. ***A venturesome personality*** seeks new experiences, tolerates gray areas, takes risks, and stays focused despite obstacles. Wiles said he worked in near-isolation from the mathematics community, partly to stay focused and avoid distraction. This kind of focus and dedication is an enduring trait.
4. ***Intrinsic motivation*** (as explained in Chapter 9) arises internally rather than from external rewards or pressures (extrinsic motivation) (Amabile & Hennessey, 1992). Creative people seem driven by the pleasure and challenge of the work itself, not by meeting deadlines, impressing people, or making money. As Wiles said, "I was so obsessed by this problem that . . . I was thinking about it all the time—[from] when I woke up in the morning to when I went to sleep at night" (Singh & Riber, 1997).
5. ***A creative environment*** sparks, supports, and refines creative ideas. Colleagues are an important part of creative environments. In one study of 2026 leading scientists and inventors, the best known of them had challenging and supportive relationships with colleagues (Simonton, 1992). Many creative environments also minimize stress and foster focused awareness (Byron & Khazanchi, 2011). While on a retreat in a monastery, Jonas Salk solved a problem that led to the polio vaccine. Later, when he designed the Salk Institute, he provided quiet spaces where scientists could think and work without interruption (Sternberg, 2006).

Would you like some research-based tips to boost your own creative process?

TABLE 8.1 Comparing Cognitive Processes and Strategies

Process or Strategy	Description	Powers	Perils
Algorithm	Methodical rule or procedure	Guarantees solution	Requires time and effort
Heuristic	Simple thinking shortcut, such as the availability heuristic (which estimates likelihood based on how easily events come to mind)	Lets us act quickly and efficiently	Puts us at risk for errors
Insight	Sudden Aha! reaction	Provides instant realization of solution	May not happen
Confirmation bias	Tendency to search for support for our own views and ignore contradictory evidence	Lets us quickly recognize supporting evidence	Hinders recognition of contradictory evidence
Functional fixedness	Inability to view problems from a new angle	Focuses thinking	Hinders creative problem solving
Intuition	Fast, automatic feelings and thoughts	Is based on our experience; huge and adaptive	Can lead us to overfeel and underthink
Overconfidence	Overestimating the accuracy of our beliefs and judgments	Allows us to be happy and to make decisions easily	Puts us at risk for errors
Belief perseverance	Ignoring evidence that proves our beliefs are wrong	Supports our enduring beliefs	Closes our mind to new ideas
Framing	Wording a question or statement so that it evokes a desired response	Can influence others' decisions	Can produce a misleading result
Creativity	Ability to innovate valuable ideas	Produces new insights and products	May distract from structured, routine work

Try these:

- ***Develop your expertise.*** What do you care about most? What do you enjoy doing? Follow your passion by broadening your knowledge base and becoming an expert at your special interest.
- ***Allow time for ideas to hatch.*** Think hard on a problem, but then set it aside and come back to it later. During periods of inattention ("sleeping on a problem"), automatic processing can help associations to form (Zhong et al., 2008).
- ***Set aside time for your mind to roam freely.*** Creativity springs from "defocused attention" (Simonton, 2012a, b). So detach from attention-grabbing television, social networking, and video gaming. Jog, go for a long walk, or meditate. Serenity seeds spontaneity. "Time alone is . . . the font of creativity" says playwright and musician Lin-Manuel Miranda (Hainey, 2016).
- ***Experience other cultures and ways of thinking.*** Viewing life from a different perspective sometimes sets the creative juices flowing. Students who spend time in another country learn how to blend new norms with those of their home culture, which increases creativity (Godart et al., 2015; Lu et al., 2018). Even getting out of your neighborhood or embracing intercultural friendships fosters flexible thinking (Kim et al., 2013; Ritter et al., 2012).

* * *

TABLE 8.1 summarizes the cognitive processes and strategies discussed in this section.

creativity the ability to produce new and valuable ideas.

convergent thinking narrowing the available solutions to determine the single best solution to a problem.

divergent thinking expanding the number of possible solutions to a problem; creative thinking that branches out in different directions.

WELL, I TOLD YOU TO ADD YEAST TO YOUR SHAMPOO.

"For the love of God, is there a doctor in the house?"

Imaginative thinking Cartoonists often display creativity as they see things in new ways or make unusual connections.

RETRIEVE & REMEMBER

ANSWERS IN APPENDIX E

2. Match the process or strategy listed below (i–xi) with the description (a–k).

i. Algorithm
ii. Intuition
iii. Insight
iv. Heuristic
v. Functional fixedness
vi. Confirmation bias
vii. Overconfidence
viii. Creativity
ix. Framing
x. Belief perseverance
xi. Nudge

a. Inability to view problems from a new angle; focuses thinking but hinders creative problem solving
b. Step-by-step rule or procedure that guarantees a solution but requires time and effort
c. Your fast, automatic, effortless feelings and thoughts based on your experience; huge and adaptive but can lead you to overfeel and underthink
d. Simple thinking shortcut that lets you act quickly and efficiently but puts you at risk for errors
e. Sudden Aha! reaction that instantly reveals the solution
f. Tendency to search for support for your own views and to ignore evidence that opposes them
g. Holding on to your beliefs even after they are proven wrong; closing your mind to new ideas
h. Overestimating the accuracy of your beliefs and judgments; allows you to be happier and to make decisions more easily, but puts you at risk for errors
i. Wording a question or statement so that it produces a desired response; can mislead people and influence their decisions
j. The ability to produce novel and valuable ideas
k. Framing choices to encourage good decisions

DO OTHER SPECIES SHARE OUR COGNITIVE SKILLS?

LOQ 8-8 What do we know about thinking in other species?

Other species are surprisingly smart (de Waal, 2016). Neuroscientists have agreed that "nonhuman animals, including all mammals and birds" possess the *neural networks* "that generate consciousness" (Low, 2012). Consider, then, what animal brains can do.

Using Concepts and Numbers

Black bears have learned to sort pictures into animal and nonanimal categories, or concepts (Vonk et al., 2012). The great apes—a group that includes chimpanzees and gorillas—also form concepts, such as *cat* and *dog*. After monkeys have learned these concepts, certain frontal lobe neurons in their brains fire in response to new "cat-like" images, others to new "dog-like" images (Freedman et al., 2001). Even pigeons—mere birdbrains—can sort objects (pictures of cars, cats, chairs, flowers) into categories. Shown a picture of a never-before-seen chair, pigeons will reliably peck a key that represents *chairs* (Wasserman, 1995).

Until his death in 2007, Alex, an African Grey parrot, displayed jaw-dropping numerical skills. He categorized and named objects (Pepperberg, 2009, 2012, 2013). He could comprehend numbers up to 8. He could speak the number of objects. He could add two small clusters of objects and announce the sum. He could indicate which of two numbers was greater. And he gave correct answers when shown various groups of objects. Asked, for example, "What color four?" (meaning "What's the color of the objects of which there are four?"), he could speak the answer.

Displaying Insight

We are not the only creatures to display insight. Psychologist Wolfgang Köhler (1925) placed a piece of fruit and a long stick outside the cage of a chimpanzee named Sultan, beyond his reach. Inside the cage, Köhler placed a short stick, which Sultan grabbed, using it to try to reach the fruit. After several failed attempts, the chimpanzee dropped the stick and seemed to survey the situation. Then suddenly (as if thinking "Aha!"), Sultan jumped up and seized the short stick again. This time, he used it to pull in the longer stick, which he then used to reach the fruit. (For one example of a chimpanzee's use of foresight, see **FIGURE 8.4a.**)

Birds, too, have displayed insight. One experiment brought to life one of Aesop's fables (ancient Greek stories), in which a thirsty crow is unable to reach the water in a partly filled pitcher. See the crow's solution (exactly as in the fable) in

Tomas Persson, PLoS ONE.

(a)

Chris Bird & Nathan Emery

(b)

FIGURE 8.4 Animal talents (a) One male chimpanzee in Sweden's Furuvik Zoo was observed every morning collecting stones, which later in the day he used as ammunition to throw at visitors (Osvath & Karvonen, 2012). (b) Crows studied by Christopher Bird and Nathan Emery (2009) quickly learned to raise the water level in a tube and nab a floating worm by dropping in stones. Other crows have used twigs to probe for insects, and bent strips of metal to reach food.

Figure 8.4b. Other crows have fashioned wire or sticks for extracting food, such as insects in rotting logs (Rutz et al., 2016).

Transmitting Culture

Like humans, other animals invent behaviors and transmit cultural patterns to their observing peers and offspring (Boesch-Achermann & Boesch, 1993). Forest-dwelling chimpanzees select different tools for different purposes—a heavy stick for making holes, a light, flexible stick for fishing for termites, or a pointed stick for roasting marshmallows. (Just kidding: They don't roast marshmallows, but they have surprised us with their sophisticated tool use [Sanz et al., 2004].) Researchers have found at least 39 local customs related to chimpanzee tool use, grooming, and courtship (Whiten & Boesch, 2001). One group may slurp termites directly from a stick; another group may pluck them off individually. One group may break nuts with a stone, while their neighbors use a piece of wood. One chimpanzee discovered that tree moss could absorb water for drinking from a waterhole, and within six days, seven other observant chimpanzees began doing the same (Hobaiter et al., 2014). These transmitted behaviors, along with differing communication and hunting styles, are the chimpanzee version of cultural diversity.

Other Cognitive Skills

Great apes, dolphins, and elephants recognize themselves in a mirror, demonstrating self-awareness. Elephants also display their abilities to learn, remember, discriminate smells, empathize, cooperate, teach, and spontaneously use tools (Byrne et al., 2009). Chimpanzees have shown altruism, cooperation, and group aggression. Like humans, they may intentionally kill their neighbor to gain land, and they grieve over dead relatives (Anderson et al., 2010; Biro et al., 2010; Mitani et al., 2010).

So there is no question that other species display many remarkable cognitive skills. Are they also capable of what we humans call language, the topic we consider next?

Language

Imagine an alien species that could pass thoughts from one head to another merely by setting air molecules in motion between them. Actually, we are those creatures! When we speak, we send air-pressure waves banging against other people's eardrums as we transfer thoughts from our brain into theirs. We sometimes sit for hours "listening to other people make noise as they exhale, because those hisses and squeaks contain *information*" (Pinker, 1998). And depending on how you vibrate the air after opening your own mouth, you may get a scowl or a kiss.

Language is our spoken, written, or signed words, and the ways we meaningfully combine them. When I [DM] created this paragraph, my fingers on a keyboard triggered electronic signals that morphed into squiggles on a page. As you read these squiggles, they trigger nerve impulses that travel to areas of your brain that decode the meaning. Thanks to our shared language, information has just moved from my mind to yours. With language, we humans can transmit civilization's knowledge from one generation to the next. Many animals know little more than what they sense. Thanks to language, we know much that we've never seen and that our ancestors never knew.

LANGUAGE ACQUISITION AND DEVELOPMENT

We humans have an astonishing knack for language. Without blinking, we sample tens of thousands of words in our memory, effortlessly combine them with near-perfect syntax (ordering), and spew them out, three words a second (Vigliocco & Hartsuiker, 2002). We rarely form sentences in our minds before we speak them. We organize them on the fly as we speak. And while doing all this, we fine-tune our language to our social and cultural setting. (*How far apart should we stand? Is it okay to interrupt?*) Given how many ways we can mess up, it's amazing that we master this social dance. How and when does it happen?

Language Acquisition: How Do We Learn Language?

LOQ 8-9 How do we acquire language, and what is *universal grammar?*

Linguist Noam Chomsky has argued that language is an unlearned human trait, separate from other parts of human cognition. He believed that humans are born with a built-in readiness—a predisposition—to learn grammar rules. He called this predisposition *universal grammar*. This helps explain why preschoolers pick up language so readily and use grammar so well. It happens naturally—as naturally as birds learn to fly—that training hardly helps.

Other researchers note that children learn grammar as they discern patterns in the language they hear (Ibbotson & Tomasello, 2016). And even Chomsky agrees that we are not born with a built-in *specific* language or set of grammatical rules. The world's 6000+ languages are structurally more diverse than the universal grammar idea implies (Bergen, 2014). But they all have nouns, verbs, and adjectives as building blocks, and they use words in some common ways (Blasi et al., 2016; Futrell et al., 2015). Whatever language we experience as children, whether spoken or signed, we readily learn its specific grammar and vocabulary (Bavelier et al., 2003). And we start speaking mostly in nouns (*kitty, da-da*) rather than verbs and adjectives (Bornstein et al., 2004). Once again, biology and experience work together.

language our spoken, written, or signed words, and the ways we combine them to communicate meaning.

RETRIEVE & REMEMBER

ANSWERS IN APPENDIX E

3. What was researcher Noam Chomsky's explanation of language acquisition?

Language Development: When Do We Learn Language?

LOQ 8-10 What are the milestones in language development, and when is the critical period for learning language?

Make a quick guess: How many words did you learn in your native language between your first birthday and your high school graduation? Although you use only 150 words for about half of what you say, you probably learned about 60,000 words (Bloom, 2000; McMurray, 2007). That averages (after age 2) nearly 3500 words each year, or nearly 10 each day! How you did it—how those 3500 words could so far outnumber the roughly 200 words your schoolteachers consciously taught you each year—is one of the great human wonders.

Could you even now state the rules of *syntax* (the correct way to string words together to form sentences) for the language(s) you speak fluently? Most of us cannot. Yet before you were able to add 2 + 2, you were creating your own original sentences and applying these rules. As a preschooler, your ability to understand and speak your language(s) was so great it would put to shame college students struggling to learn a new language.

Receptive Language Children's language development moves from simplicity to complexity. Infants start without language (*in fantis* means "not speaking"). Yet by 4 months of age, babies can recognize differences in speech sounds (Stager & Werker, 1997). They can also read lips, preferring to look at a face that matches a sound. They can recognize that "*ah*" comes from wide open lips and "*ee*" from a mouth with corners pulled back (Kuhl & Meltzoff, 1982). Recognizing such differences marks the beginning of the development of babies' *receptive language,* their ability to understand what is said to and about them. At 7 months and beyond, they grow in their power to break language they hear into individual words—which adults find difficult when listening to an unfamiliar language.

TABLE 8.2 Summary of Language Development

Month (approximate)	Stage
4	Babbles many speech sounds ("ah-goo")
10	Babbling resembles household language ("ma-ma")
12	One-word speech ("Kitty!")
24	Two-word speech ("Get ball.")
24+	Rapid development into complete sentences

Productive Language Babies' *productive language,* their ability to produce words, matures after their receptive language. Before nurture molds babies' speech, nature allows a wide range of possible sounds in the **babbling stage,** around 4 months of age. In this stage, they seem to sample all the sounds they can make, such as *ah-goo.* Babbling is not an imitation of adult speech. We know this because babbling includes sounds from languages not spoken in the household. From this early babbling, a listener could not identify an infant as being, say, French, Korean, or Ethiopian.

By about 10 months old, infants' babbling has changed so that a trained ear can identify the household language (de Boysson-Bardies et al., 1989). Do deaf infants babble in sign language? They do, especially if they have deaf parents whose signing they observe (Petitto & Marentette, 1991). Without exposure to other languages, babies lose their ability to do what we (believe it or not) cannot—to discriminate and produce sounds and tones found outside their native language (Kuhl et al., 2014; Meltzoff et al., 2009; Pallier et al., 2001). Thus, by adulthood those who speak only English cannot discriminate certain sounds in Japanese speech. Nor can Japanese adults with no training in English hear the difference between the English *r* and *l*. For a Japanese-speaking adult, "*la-la-ra-ra*" may sound like the same syllable repeated.

Around their first birthday, most children enter the **one-word stage.** They know that sounds carry meanings. They begin to use sounds—usually only one barely recognizable syllable, such as *ma* or *da*—to communicate meaning. But family members learn to understand, and gradually the infant's language sounds more like the family's language. Across the world, baby's first words are often nouns that label objects or people (Tardif et al., 2008). At this one-word stage, a single word (*"Doggy!"*) may equal a sentence (*"Look at the dog out there!"*).

At about 18 months, children's word learning explodes, jumping from about a word each week to a word each day. By their second birthday, most have entered the **two-word stage** (**TABLE 8.2**). They start uttering two-word sentences in **telegraphic speech.** Like yesterday's telegrams that charged by the word (TERMS ACCEPTED. SEND MONEY), a 2-year-old's speech contains mostly nouns and verbs (*"Want juice"*). Also like telegrams, their speech follows rules of syntax, arranging words in a sensible order. English-speaking children typically place adjectives before nouns—*white house* rather than *house white.* Spanish reverses this order, as in *casa blanca.*

Moving out of the two-word stage, children quickly begin speaking in longer phrases (Fromkin & Rodman, 1983). By early elementary school, they understand complex sentences. They can enjoy a joke with a double meaning: "You never starve in the desert because of all the sand-which-is there."

Critical Periods What might happen if a child gets a late start on learning a language? This is not uncommon for children who have surgery to enable

Sidney Harris

"Got idea. Talk better. Combine words. Make sentences."

hearing, or who are adopted by a family in another country. For these late bloomers, language development follows the same sequence, though the pace is often faster (Ertmer et al., 2007; Snedeker et al., 2007). But there is a limit on how long language learning can be delayed.

Childhood seems to represent a *critical* (or "sensitive") *period* for mastering certain aspects of language before the language-learning window closes (Hernandez & Li, 2007; Lenneberg, 1967). That window closes gradually. Later-than-usual exposure to language—at age 2 or 3—unleashes their brain's idle language capacity, producing a rush of language. But there is no similar rush of learning if children are not exposed to either a spoken or a signed language until age 7. Such deprived children lose their ability to master *any* language. And children exposed to low-quality language—such as 4-year-olds in classrooms with 3-year-olds—often display less language skill (Ansari et al., 2015; Hirsh-Pasek et al., 2015).

The impact of early experience is evident in language learning in children who have been deaf from birth. More than 90 percent of such children have parents who are not deaf and who do not use sign language. These children typically are not exposed to sign language during their early years. Those who learn to sign as teens or adults can master basic words and learn to order them. But they are not as fluent as native signers in using and understanding subtle differences in **grammar** (Newport, 1990).

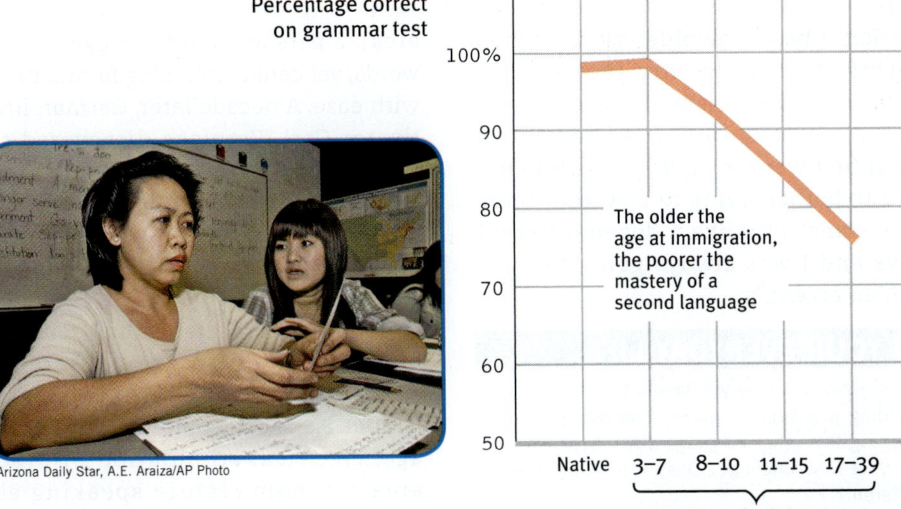

Arizona Daily Star, A.E. Araiza/AP Photo

FIGURE 8.5 Our ability to learn a new language diminishes with age Ten years after coming to the United States, Asian immigrants took an English grammar test. Although there is no sharply defined critical period for second language learning, those who arrived before age 8 understood American English grammar as well as native speakers did. Those who arrived later did not. (Data from Johnson & Newport, 1991.)

After the language window closes, even learning a second language becomes more difficult. Have you learned a second language as an adult? If so, you almost certainly speak it with the accent of your first, and likely with imperfect grammar (Hartshorne et al., 2018). This difficulty appeared in one study of U.S. immigrants from South Korea and China (Johnson & Newport, 1991). Their task was to read 276 English sentences, such as *"Yesterday the hunter shoots a deer,"* and to decide whether each sentence was grammatically correct or incorrect. All had lived in the United States for approximately 10 years. Some had arrived as very young children, others as adults. As **FIGURE 8.5** reveals, those who had learned their second language early

©Susan Meiselas / Magnum Photos

Creating a language Brought together as if on a desert island (actually a school), Nicaragua's young deaf children over time drew upon sign gestures from home to create their own Nicaraguan Sign Language, complete with words and intricate grammar. Our biological predisposition for language does not create language in a vacuum. But activated by a social context, nature and nurture work creatively together (Osborne, 1999; Sandler et al., 2005; Senghas & Coppola, 2001).

babbling stage the stage in speech development, beginning around 4 months, during which an infant spontaneously utters various sounds that are not all related to the household language.

one-word stage the stage in speech development, from about age 1 to 2, during which a child speaks mostly in single words.

two-word stage the stage in speech development, beginning about age 2, during which a child speaks mostly in two-word statements.

telegraphic speech the early speech stage in which a child speaks in compressed sentences, like a telegram—"want milk" or "Daddy go store"—using mostly nouns and verbs.

grammar in a language, a system of rules that enables us to communicate with and understand others.

learned it best. The older we are when moving to a new country, the harder it is to learn the new language and culture (Cheung et al., 2011; Hakuta et al., 2003). When I [ND] first went to Japan, I was told not even to bother trying to bow, that there were something like a dozen different bows and I was always going to "bow with an accent."

IN YOUR EVERYDAY LIFE

Consider a language you began to learn *after* learning your first language. How did your learning this other language differ from learning your first language? Does speaking it feel different?

RETRIEVE & REMEMBER

ANSWERS IN APPENDIX E

4. What is the difference between *receptive* language and *productive* language, and when do children normally hit these milestones in language development?
5. Why is it so difficult to learn a new language in adulthood?

THE BRAIN AND LANGUAGE

LOQ 8-11 What brain areas are involved in language processing and speech?

We think of speaking and reading, or writing and reading, or singing and speaking as merely different examples of the same general ability—language. But consider this curious finding: Damage to any one of several areas of the brain's cortex can impair language. Even more curious, some people with brain damage can speak fluently but cannot read (despite good vision). Others can understand what they read but cannot speak. Still others can write but not read, read but not write, read numbers but not letters, or sing but not speak. To sort out this puzzle required a lot of smart thinking by many different scientists, all seeking to answer the same question: How does the brain process language?

In 1865, French physician Paul Broca confirmed a fellow physician's observation that after damage to a specific area of the left frontal lobe (later called **Broca's area**), a person would struggle to *speak* words, yet could often sing familiar songs with ease. A decade later, German investigator Carl Wernicke discovered that after damage to a specific area of the left temporal lobe **(Wernicke's area),** people were unable to *understand* others' sentences and could speak only meaningless sentences.

Today's neuroscience has confirmed brain activity in Broca's and Wernicke's areas during language processing (**FIGURE 8.6**). For people with brain damage, electrical stimulation of Broca's area can help restore speaking abilities (Marangolo et al., 2016). But we also now know that the brain's processing of language is complex. Although you experience language as a single, unified stream, fMRI scans would show that your brain is busily multitasking and networking. Different brain networks are activated by nouns and verbs (or objects and actions); by different vowels; by stories of visual versus motor experiences; by who spoke and what was said; and by many other stimuli (Perrachione et al., 2011; Shapiro et al., 2006; Speer et al., 2009). Moreover, if you're lucky enough to be natively fluent in two languages, your brain processes them in similar areas (Kim et al., 2017). But if you learned a second language *after* the first, your brain processes them in different areas (Berken et al., 2015; Kovelman et al., 2014).

The point to remember: In processing language, as in other forms of information processing, the brain operates by dividing its mental functions—speaking, perceiving, thinking, remembering—into smaller tasks. Your conscious experience of reading this page *seems* to be one task. But thanks to your parallel processing, many different neural networks are pooling their work to give meaning to the words, sentences, and paragraphs (Fedorenko et al., 2016).

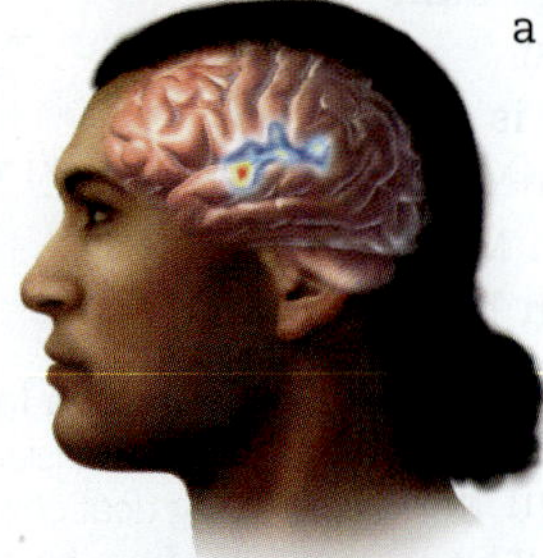

(a) Speaking words (Broca's area and the motor cortex)

(b) Hearing words (Wernicke's area and the auditory cortex)

FIGURE 8.6 Brain activity when speaking and hearing words

RETRIEVE & REMEMBER

ANSWERS IN APPENDIX E

6. ________ ________ is one part of the brain that, if damaged, might impair your ability to speak words. Damage to ________ ________ might impair your ability to understand language.

LaunchPad To review research on left and right hemisphere language processing—and to test your own processing speed—see *Topic Tutorial: PsychSim6, Dueling Hemispheres.*

THINKING WITHOUT LANGUAGE

LOQ 8-12 How can thinking in images be useful?

To turn on the cold water in your bathroom, in which direction do you turn the handle? To answer, you probably thought not in words but in images—perhaps a mental picture of your hand turning the faucet.

Indeed, we often think in images. Mental practice relies on thinking in images. One year after placing second in a worldwide piano competition, pianist Liu Chi Kung was imprisoned during China's cultural revolution. Soon after his release, after seven years without touching a piano, Liu was back on tour. The critics judged his playing to be better than ever, and his fans wondered how he had continued to develop without practice. "I did practice," said Liu, "every day. I rehearsed every piece I had ever played, note by note, in my mind" (Garfield, 1986).

One experiment on the benefits of mental rehearsal observed the University of Tennessee women's basketball team (Savoy & Beitel, 1996). Over 35 games, researchers tracked the team's skill at shooting free throws following standard physical practice or mental practice. After physical practice, the team scored about 52 percent of their shots. After mental practice, that score rose to 65 percent. During mental practice, players had repeatedly imagined making free throws under various conditions, including being "trash-talked" by the opposition. In a dramatic conclusion, Tennessee won that season's national championship game in overtime, thanks in part to their free-throw shooting.

Once you have learned a skill, even *watching* that skill happen triggers brain activity in the same areas that are active when you actually use the skill. As ballet dancers watch ballet videos, fMRI scans show their brain dancing along (Calvo-Merino et al., 2004). Just *imagining* a physical experience, such as pain, can have similar results. Imagined pain activates the same neural networks that are active during *actual* pain (Grèzes & Decety, 2001).

Can mental rehearsal also help you reach your academic goals? Definitely! One study demonstrated this with two groups of introductory psychology students facing a midterm exam one week later (Taylor et al., 1998). (Students who were not engaged in any mental rehearsal formed a third, control group.) The first group spent five minutes each day imagining themselves scanning the posted grade list, seeing their A, beaming with joy, and feeling proud. This daily *outcome simulation* had little effect, adding only 2 points to their average exam score. The second group spent five minutes each day imagining themselves effectively studying—reading the chapters, going over notes, eliminating distractions, declining an offer to go out. This daily *process simulation* paid off. In real life, this group began studying sooner, spent more time at it, and beat the other group's average score by 8 points.

The point to remember: To benefit from your fantasy time, it's better to imagine *how* to reach your goal than to focus on your desired destination.

IMPROVE YOUR EVERYDAY LIFE

How could you use mental practice to improve your performance in some area of your life? When could you use mental practice in your schoolwork, personal relationships, or hobbies?

RETRIEVE & REMEMBER

ANSWERS IN APPENDIX E

7. What is mental practice, and how can it help you to prepare for an upcoming event?

LaunchPad To experience your own thinking as (a) manipulating words and (b) manipulating images, see *Topic Tutorial: PsychSim6, My Head Is Spinning!*

DO OTHER SPECIES HAVE LANGUAGE?

LOQ 8-13 What do we know about other species' capacity for language?

Humans have long and proudly claimed that language sets us above all other animals. "When we study human language, we are approaching what some might call the 'human essence,' the qualities of mind that are, so far as we know, unique [to humans]" (Chomsky, 1972). Is it true that humans, alone, have language?

Some animals display basic language processing. Pigeons can learn the difference between words and nonwords, but they could never read this book (Scarf et al., 2016). Various monkey species sound different alarm cries for different predators: a barking call for a leopard, a cough for an eagle, and a chuttering for a snake. Hearing the leopard alarm, vervets climb the nearest tree. Hearing the eagle alarm, they rush into the bushes. Hearing the snake alarm, they stand up and scan the ground (Byrne, 1991; Clarke et al., 2015; Coye et al., 2015). To indicate multiple threats (eagle, leopard, falling tree, neighboring group), monkeys will combine 6 different calls into a 25-call sequence (Balter, 2010). But are such communications language?

Susanne Baus/AFP/Getty Images/Newscom

Comprehending canine Border collie Rico had a vocabulary of 200 human words. If asked to retrieve a toy with a name he had never heard, Rico would pick out a new toy from a group of familiar items (Kaminski et al., 2004). Hearing that name for the second time four weeks later, Rico more often than not would retrieve the same toy. Another border collie, Chaser, has set an animal record by learning 1000 object names (Pilley, 2013). Like a 3-year-old child, she can also categorize them by function and shape. She can "fetch a ball" or "fetch a doll."

Psychologists Allen Gardner and Beatrix Gardner (1969) were among the earliest to address this question in scientific experiments using sign language. In the late 1960s, they aroused enormous scientific and public interest with their work with Washoe, a young chimpanzee. After four years, Washoe could use 132 signs. By her life's end in 2007, she was using 250 signs (Metzler, 2011; Sanz et al., 1998).

During the 1970s, more and more reports came in. Some chimpanzees were stringing signs together to form sentences. Washoe, for example, signed "You me go out, please." Some word combinations seemed very creative—saying *water bird* for "swan" or *apple which-is orange* for "orange" (Patterson, 1978; Rumbaugh, 1977).

Broca's area a frontal lobe brain area, usually in the left hemisphere, that helps control language expression by directing the muscle movements involved in speech.

Wernicke's area a brain area, usually in the left temporal lobe, involved in language comprehension and expression.

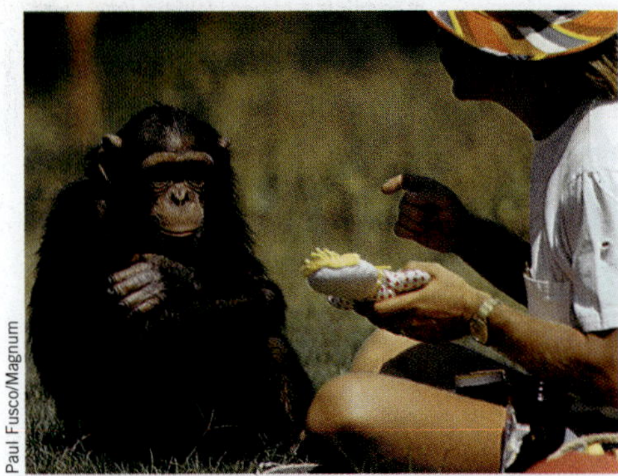

But is this language? Chimpanzees' ability to express themselves in American Sign Language (ASL) raises questions about the very nature of language. Here, the trainer is asking, "What is this?" The sign in response is "Baby." Does the response constitute language?

But by the late 1970s, other psychologists were growing skeptical. Were the chimps language champs or were the researchers chumps? Consider the skeptics' points:

- Ape vocabularies and sentences are simple, rather like those of a 2-year-old child. And apes gain their limited vocabularies only with great difficulty (Wynne, 2004, 2008). Speaking or signing children can easily soak up dozens of new words each week, and 60,000 by adulthood.
- Chimpanzees can make signs or push buttons in a sequence to get a reward. But pigeons, too, can peck a sequence of keys to get grain (Straub et al., 1979). The apes' signing might be nothing more than aping their trainers' signs and learning that certain arm movements produce rewards (Terrace, 1979).
- Studies of *perceptual set* (see Chapter 5) show that when information is unclear, we tend to see what we want or expect to see. Interpreting chimpanzee signs as language may have been little more than the trainers' wishful thinking (Terrace, 1979). When Washoe signed *water bird*, she may have been separately naming *water* and *bird*.
- "Give orange me give eat orange me eat orange . . ." is a far cry from the mastery of syntax in a 3-year-old's sentences (Anderson, 2004; Pinker, 1995). To the child, "You tickle" and "Tickle you" communicate different ideas. A chimpanzee, lacking human syntax, might use the same sequence of signs for both phrases.

Controversy can stimulate progress, as it did in this case. Studies of animal communication and the possibility of nonhuman language continued. An early and surprising finding was that Washoe's adopted son, Loulis, had picked up 68 signs, simply by observing Washoe and three other language-trained chimps signing together (Fouts, 1992, 1997). Even more stunning was a report that Kanzi, a bonobo with a reported 384-word vocabulary, could understand syntax in spoken English (Savage-Rumbaugh et al., 1993, 2009). Kanzi, who appears to have the receptive language ability of a human 2-year-old, has responded appropriately when asked, "Can you show me the light?" and "Can you bring me the [flash] light?" and "Can you turn the light on?" Given stuffed animals and asked—for the first time—to "make the dog bite the snake," he put the snake to the dog's mouth.

How should we interpret such studies? Are humans the only language-using species? If by *language* we mean verbal or signed expression of complex grammar, most psychologists would now agree that humans alone possess language. If we mean, more simply, an ability to communicate through a meaningful sequence of symbols, then apes are indeed capable of language.

One thing is certain. Studies of animal language and thinking have moved psychologists toward a greater appreciation of other species' remarkable abilities (Friend, 2004; Rumbaugh & Washburn, 2003; Wilson et al., 2014). In the past, many psychologists doubted that other species could plan, form concepts, count, use tools, or show compassion (Thorpe, 1974). Today, thanks to animal researchers, we know better. When communicating, chimps consider what others know—*Does my friend know a snake is nearby* (Crockford et al., 2017)? Nonhuman animals exhibit insight, show family loyalty, care for one another, and transmit cultural patterns across generations. Working out what this means for the moral rights of other animals is an unfinished task.

* * *

Thinking about other species' abilities brings us back to a question raised earlier in this chapter: Do we deserve the label *Homo sapiens*—wise human? Let's pause to give our species some midterm grades. On decision making and risk assessment, our smart but error-prone species might rate a B–. On problem solving, where humans are inventive yet subject to confirmation bias and functional fixedness, we would probably receive a better mark, perhaps a B+. On creativity and cognitive skills, our divergent thinking and quick (though sometimes faulty) heuristics would earn us an A. And when it comes to language and the processing that occurs outside of consciousness, the awestruck experts would surely award the human species an A+.

IN YOUR EVERYDAY LIFE

Can you think of a time when you believed an animal was communicating with you? How might you put that to a test?

RETRIEVE & REMEMBER

ANSWERS IN APPENDIX E

8. If your dog barks at a stranger at the door, does this qualify as language? What if the dog yips in a telltale way to let you know she needs to go out?

LaunchPad For examples of intelligent communication and problem solving among orangutans, elephants, and killer whales, see the 6-minute *Video: How Intelligent Are Animals?* See also the *Video: Case Studies* for a helpful tutorial animation on this type of research method.

Intelligence

Few topics have sparked more debate than the intelligence controversy. Does each of us have some natural general mental capacity (intelligence)? Can we express this capacity as a meaningful number? How much does intelligence vary within and between groups, and why? And can we measure intelligence without bias? In this section, we consider some findings from more than a century of research, as psychologists have searched for answers to these questions and more.

WHAT IS INTELLIGENCE?

LOQ 8-14 How do psychologists define *intelligence,* and what are the arguments for general intelligence *(g)?*

Intelligence is not a quality like height or weight, which has the same meaning in all generations, worldwide. People assign this term to the qualities that enable success in their own time and place (Sternberg & Kaufman, 1998). In Cameroon's equatorial forest, intelligence may be understanding the medicinal qualities of local plants. In a North American high school, it may be mastering difficult concepts in calculus or chemistry. In both places, **intelligence** is the ability to learn from experience, solve problems, and use knowledge to adapt to new situations.

You probably know some people with talents in science or history, and others gifted in athletics, art, music, or dance. You may also know a terrific artist who is stumped by the simplest math problem, or a brilliant math student with little talent for writing term papers. Are all these people intelligent? Could you rate their intelligence on a single scale? Or would you need several different scales?

Is Intelligence One General Ability?

Charles Spearman (1863–1945) believed we have one **general intelligence** (often shortened to *g*) that is at the heart of our smarts, from sailing the sea to sailing through school. People often have special, outstanding abilities, he noted, but those who score high in one area (such as verbal ability) typically score above average in other areas (such as spatial or reasoning ability).

Spearman's (1904) belief stemmed in part from his work with *factor analysis,* a statistical tool that identifies clusters of related items. In Spearman's view, mental abilities are much like physical abilities. Athleticism is not one thing, but many. The ability to run fast is distinct from the eye-hand coordination required to throw a ball on target. Yet there remains some tendency for good things to come packaged together. Running speed and throwing accuracy, for example, often correlate, thanks to general athletic ability. So, too, with intelligence—for humans worldwide (Warne & Burningham, 2019). Several distinct abilities tend to correlate enough to define a general intelligence factor (the common skill set we call the *g factor*). Or to say this in the language of contemporary neuroscience, we have many distinct neural networks that enable our many varied abilities. Our brain coordinates all that activity, and the result is *g* (Cole et al., 2015; Hampshire et al., 2012).

Theories of Multiple Intelligences

LOQ 8-15 How do Gardner's and Sternberg's theories of multiple intelligences differ, and what criticisms have they faced?

Other psychologists, particularly since the mid-1980s, have proposed that the definition of *intelligence* should be broadened, beyond the idea of academic smarts.

Gardner's Multiple Intelligences

Howard Gardner (1983, 2006, 2011; Davis et al., 2011) views intelligence as multiple abilities that come in different packages. Brain damage, he notes, may destroy one ability but leave others intact. He sees other evidence of multiple intelligences

Then Chin Wey/Xinhua News Agency/Newscom

Islands of genius: savant syndrome After a brief helicopter ride over Singapore followed by five days of drawing, British savant artist Stephen Wiltshire accurately reproduced a view of the city from memory.

in people with **savant syndrome.** These people have an island of brilliance but often score low on intelligence tests and may have limited or no language ability (Treffert, 2010). Some can render incredible works of art or music. Others can compute numbers almost instantly, or identify the day of the week of any given historical date (Miller, 1999).

About four in five people with savant syndrome are males. Many also have *autism spectrum disorder* (ASD), a developmental disorder. The late memory whiz Kim Peek (who did not have ASD) inspired the movie *Rain Man.* In 8 to 10 seconds, Peek could read and remember a page. During his lifetime, he memorized 9000 books, including Shakespeare's plays and the Bible.

intelligence the ability to learn from experience, solve problems, and use knowledge to adapt to new situations.

general intelligence (*g*) according to Spearman and others, underlies all mental abilities and is therefore measured by every task on an intelligence test.

savant syndrome a condition in which a person otherwise limited in mental ability has an exceptional specific skill, such as in computation or drawing.

FIGURE 8.7 Gardner's eight intelligences Gardner has also proposed existential intelligence (the ability to ponder deep questions about life) as a ninth possible intelligence.

He absorbed details of maps and could provide GPS-like travel directions within any major U.S. city. Yet he could not button his clothes, and he had little capacity for abstract concepts. Asked by his father at a restaurant to lower his voice, he slid down in his chair to lower his voice box. Asked for Lincoln's Gettysburg Address, he responded, "227 North West Front Street. But he only stayed there one night—he gave the speech the next day" (Treffert & Christensen, 2005).

Gardner has identified a total of eight *relatively independent intelligences*, including the verbal and mathematical aptitudes assessed by standardized tests (**FIGURE 8.7**). (Gardner [1999a] has also proposed a ninth possibility—*existential intelligence*—the ability to think in depth about deep questions in life.) Thus, the computer programmer, the poet, the street-smart adolescent, and the basketball team's play-making point guard exhibit different kinds of intelligence (Gardner, 1998). To Gardner, a general intelligence score is like the overall rating of a city—it tells you something but doesn't give you much specific information about the city's schools, streets, or nightlife.

> "You have to be careful, if you're good at something, to make sure you don't think you're good at other things that you aren't necessarily so good at. . . . Because I've been very successful at [software development] people come in and expect that I have wisdom about topics that I don't." —Bill Gates, 1998

LaunchPad To witness extraordinary savant ability in music, see the *Video: Savant Musical Skills.*

Sternberg's Three Intelligences Robert Sternberg (1985, 2011) agrees with Gardner that there is more to real-world success than traditional intelligence and that we have multiple intelligences. But Sternberg's *triarchic theory* proposes three, not eight or nine, intelligences:

- ***Analytical (academic problem-solving) intelligence*** is assessed by intelligence tests, which present well-defined problems having a single right answer.
- ***Creative intelligence*** is demonstrated in innovative smarts: the ability to adapt to new situations and generate novel ideas.
- ***Practical intelligence*** is required for everyday tasks that may be poorly defined and may have multiple solutions.

Gardner and Sternberg differ in some areas, but they agree on two important points: Multiple abilities can contribute to life success, and varieties of giftedness bring both spice to life and challenges for education. Trained to appreciate such variety, many teachers have applied multiple intelligence theories in their classrooms.

Donald Reilly The New Yorker Collection/The Cartoon Bank

"You're wise, but you lack tree smarts."

IN YOUR EVERYDAY LIFE

The concept of multiple intelligences assumes that the analytical school smarts measured by traditional intelligence tests are important, but that other abilities are also important. Different people have different gifts. What are yours?

Criticisms of Multiple Intelligence Theories Wouldn't it be nice if the world were so fair that a weakness in one area would be balanced by genius in another? Alas, say critics, the world is not fair (Ferguson, 2009; Scarr, 1989). Research using factor analysis confirms that there is a general intelligence factor: *g* matters (Johnson et al., 2008). It predicts performance on various complex tasks and in various jobs (Arneson et al., 2011; Gottfredson, 2002a,b, 2003a,b). Youths' intelligence test scores predict their income decades later (Zagorsky, 2007).

Even so, "success" is not a one-ingredient recipe. It also helps to have the luck of an advantaged home and school, and to have been born in a time and place where your talents matter.

TABLE 8.3 Comparing Theories of Intelligence

Theory	Summary	Strengths	Other Considerations
Spearman's general intelligence (g)	A basic intelligence predicts our abilities in many different academic areas.	Different abilities, such as verbal and spatial, do have some tendency to correlate.	Human abilities are too varied to be presented as a single general intelligence factor.
Gardner's multiple intelligences	Our abilities are best classified into eight or nine independent intelligences, which include a broad range of skills beyond traditional school smarts.	Intelligence is more than just verbal and mathematical skills. Other abilities are equally important to our human adaptability.	Should all our abilities be considered *intelligences?* Shouldn't some be called less vital *talents?*
Sternberg's triarchic theory	Our intelligence is best classified into three areas that predict real-world success: analytical, creative, and practical.	These three areas can be reliably measured.	These three areas may be less independent than Sternberg thought and may actually share an underlying *g* factor.
Emotional intelligence	Social intelligence contributes to life success. Emotional intelligence is a key aspect, consisting of perceiving, understanding, managing, and using emotions.	These four components predict social success and emotional well-being.	Does this stretch the concept of intelligence too far?

And though high intelligence may get you into a profession (via the schools and training programs that open doors), it won't make you successful once there. Success is a combination of talent and *grit*—your motivation and drive. Highly successful people tend also to be conscientious, well connected, and doggedly energetic. These qualities often translate into dedicated hard work.

Researchers report a *10-year rule:* Expert performers—in chess, dance, sports, computer programming, music, and medicine—have all spent about a decade in intense, daily practice (Ericsson & Pool, 2016; Simon & Chase, 1973). Becoming a professional musician or an elite athlete requires, first, native ability (Macnamara et al., 2014, 2016). But it also requires years of practice—about 11,000 hours on average, and *at least* 3000 hours (Campitelli & Gobet, 2011). (For more on how self-disciplined grit feeds success, see Chapter 9.) The recipe for success is a gift of nature plus a whole lot of nurture.

RETRIEVE & REMEMBER

ANSWERS IN APPENDIX E

9. How does the existence of savant syndrome support Gardner's theory of multiple intelligences?

Emotional Intelligence

LOQ 8-16 What four abilities make up emotional intelligence?

Social intelligence is the know-how involved in understanding social situations and managing ourselves successfully (Cantor & Kihlstrom, 1987). Psychologist Edward Thorndike first proposed the concept in 1920, noting that "the best mechanic in a factory may fail as a foreman for lack of social intelligence" (Goleman, 2006, p. 83).

A critical part of social intelligence, **emotional intelligence,** includes four abilities (Mayer et al., 2002, 2012, 2016):

- ***Perceiving*** emotions (recognizing them in faces, music, and stories)
- ***Understanding*** emotions (predicting them and how they may change and blend)
- ***Managing*** emotions (knowing how to express them in varied situations)
- ***Using*** emotions to facilitate adaptive or creative thinking

Emotionally intelligent people are both socially aware and self-aware. They avoid being hijacked by overwhelming depression, anxiety, or anger. They can read others' emotions and know what to say to soothe a grieving friend, encourage a workmate, and manage a conflict. They can delay gratification in favor of long-range rewards. Thus, emotionally intelligent people tend to succeed in career, marriage, and parenting situations where academically smarter, but emotionally less intelligent people may fail (Cherniss, 2010a,b; Czarna et al., 2016; Miao et al., 2016). They also tend to be happy and healthy (Sánchez-Álvarez et al., 2016; Schutte et al., 2007, 2016). Aware of these benefits, school-based programs have sought to increase teachers' and students' emotional intelligence (Castillo-Gualda et al., 2017; Nathanson et al., 2016).

* * *

TABLE 8.3 summarizes these theories of intelligence.

LaunchPad Engage online with *Concept Practice: Theories of Intelligence* to review different approaches to intelligence.

emotional intelligence the ability to perceive, understand, manage, and use emotions.

ASSESSING INTELLIGENCE

LOQ 8-17 What is an *intelligence test*, and how do achievement and aptitude tests differ?

An **intelligence test** assesses a person's mental aptitudes and compares them with those of others, using numerical scores. We can test people's mental abilities in two ways, depending on what we want to know.

- **Achievement tests** are designed to *reflect* what you have learned. Your final exam will measure what you learned in this class.
- **Aptitude tests** are designed to *predict* what you will be able to learn. If you took a college entrance exam, it was designed to predict your ability to do college work. Aptitude supports achievement: People who learn quickly also retain information better (Zerr et al., 2018).

So, how do psychologists design these tests, and why should we believe in the results?

IN YOUR EVERYDAY LIFE

What achievement or aptitude tests have you taken? In your opinion, how well did these tests assess what you'd learned or predict what you were capable of learning?

RETRIEVE & REMEMBER

ANSWERS IN APPENDIX E

10. An employer with a pool of applicants for a single available position is interested in testing each applicant's potential. To determine that, she should use an ___________ (achievement/aptitude) test. That same employer wishing to test the effectiveness of a new, on-the-job training program would be wise to use an ___________ (achievement/aptitude) test.

What Do Intelligence Tests Test?

LOQ 8-18 When and why were intelligence tests created, and how do today's tests differ from early intelligence tests?

Barely more than a century ago, psychologists began designing tests to assess people's mental abilities. Modern intelligence testing traces its birth to early twentieth-century France.

Alfred Binet: Predicting School Achievement With a new French law that required all children to attend school, officials knew that some children, including many newcomers to Paris, would need special classes. But how could the schools make fair judgments about children's learning potential? Teachers might assess children who had little prior education as slow learners. Or they might sort children into classes on the basis of their social backgrounds. To avoid such bias, France's minister of public education gave psychologist Alfred Binet the task of designing fair tests.

Binet and his student, Théodore Simon, began by assuming that all children follow the same course of intellectual development but that some develop more rapidly (Nicolas & Levine, 2012). A "dull" child should therefore score much like a typical younger child, and a "bright" child like a typical older child. Thus, their goal became measuring each child's **mental age,** the level of performance typically associated with a certain *chronological age* (age in years). Average 8-year-olds, for example, have a mental age of 8. An 8-year-old with a below-average mental age (perhaps performing at the level of a typical 6-year-old) would struggle with schoolwork considered normal for 8-year-olds.

Macmillan Learning

Alfred Binet (1857–1911) Adaptations of Binet's pioneering intelligence test were sometimes used to discriminate against immigrant and minority groups. But his intent was simply to match children with appropriate schooling.

Binet and Simon tested a variety of reasoning and problem-solving questions on Binet's two daughters, and then on "bright" and "backward" Parisian schoolchildren. The items they developed predicted how well French children would handle their schoolwork.

Binet hoped his test would be used to improve children's education. But he also feared it would be used to label children and limit their opportunities (Gould, 1981).

Lewis Terman: Measuring Innate Intelligence Binet's fears were realized soon after his death in 1911, when others adapted his tests for use as a numerical measure of inherited intelligence. Lewis Terman (1877–1956), a Stanford University professor, tried the Paris-developed questions and age norms with California kids. He adapted some of Binet's original items, added others, and established new age norms. He also extended the upper end of the test's range from age 12 to "superior adults." He gave his revision the name it still has today—the **Stanford-Binet.**

German psychologist William Stern's contribution to intelligence testing was the famous **intelligence quotient,** or **IQ.** The IQ was simply a person's mental age divided by chronological age and multiplied by 100 to get rid of the decimal point. Thus, an average child, whose mental age (8) and chronological age (8) are the same, has an IQ of 100. But an 8-year-old who answers questions at the level of a typical 10-year-old has an IQ of 125:

$$\text{IQ} = \frac{\text{mental age of 10}}{\text{chronological age of 8}} \times 100 = 125$$

The original IQ formula worked fairly well for children but not for adults. (Should a 40-year-old who does as well on the test as an average 20-year-old be assigned an IQ of only 50?) Most current intelligence tests, including the Stanford-Binet, no longer compute an IQ (though the term *IQ* still lingers in everyday vocabulary as short for "intelligence test score"). Instead, they assign a score that represents a test-taker's performance *relative to the average performance* (which is arbitrarily set at 100) of others the same age. Most people—about 68 percent of those taking an intelligence test—fall between 85 and 115. (We'll return to these figures shortly, in the discussion of the *normal curve*.)

Terman assumed that intelligence tests revealed a fixed mental capacity present from birth. He also assumed that some ethnic groups were naturally more intelligent than others. And he supported the controversial *eugenics* movement—the much-criticized nineteenth- and twentieth-century movement that proposed measuring human traits and using the results to encourage only smart and fit people to reproduce. Abuses of the early intelligence tests serve to remind us that science can reflect the scientist's values. Behind a screen of scientific objectivity, ideology sometimes lurks.

David Wechsler: Testing Separate Strengths Psychologist David Wechsler created what is now the most widely used individual intelligence test, the **Wechsler Adult Intelligence Scale (WAIS).** There is a version for school-age children (the *Wechsler Intelligence Scale for Children* [WISC]), and another for preschool children (Evers et al., 2012). The 2008 WAIS edition (with a new version anticipated in 2020) consists of 15 subtests, broken into verbal and performance areas. Here is a sample:

- *Similarities*—reasoning the commonality of two objects or concepts ("In what way are wool and cotton alike?")
- *Vocabulary*—naming pictured objects, or defining words ("What is a guitar?")
- *Block design*—visual abstract processing ("Using the four blocks, make one just like this.")
- *Letter-number sequencing*—on hearing a series of numbers and letters ("R-2-C-1-M-3"), repeating the numbers in ascending order, and then the letters in alphabetical order.

The WAIS yields both an overall intelligence score and separate scores for verbal comprehension, perceptual reasoning, working memory, and processing speed. In such ways, this test helps realize Binet's aim: to identify those who could benefit from special educational opportunities for improvement.

Richard T. Nowitz/Getty Images

Matching patterns Block-design puzzles test visual abstract processing ability. Wechsler's individually administered intelligence test comes in forms suited for adults and children.

RETRIEVE & REMEMBER

ANSWERS IN APPENDIX E

- 11. What did Binet hope to achieve by establishing a child's mental age?
- 12. What is the IQ of a 4-year-old with a mental age of 5?

LaunchPad To learn more about the promise and perils of intelligence testing, watch the *Video: Locking Away the "Feebleminded"—A Shameful History.* And to test your own performance on simulated WAIS subtasks, see *Concept Practice: Wechsler Intelligence Tasks.*

Three Tests of a "Good" Test

LOQ 8-19 What is a *normal curve*, and what does it mean to say that a test has been standardized and is reliable and valid?

To be widely accepted, a psychological test must be *standardized*, *reliable*, and *valid*. The Stanford-Binet and Wechsler tests meet these requirements.

Was the Test Standardized? The number of questions you answer correctly on an intelligence test would reveal almost nothing. To know how well you performed, you would need some basis for comparison. That's why test-makers give new tests to a representative sample of people. The scores from this pretested group become the basis for future comparisons. If you then take the test following the same procedures, your score will be meaningful when compared with others. This process is called **standardization.**

One way to compare scores is to graph them. For many human attributes—height, weight, or mental aptitude—people's scores tend to form a bell-shaped pattern

intelligence test a method for assessing an individual's mental aptitudes and comparing them with those of others, using numerical scores.

achievement test a test designed to assess what a person has learned.

aptitude test a test designed to predict a person's future performance; *aptitude* is the capacity to learn.

mental age a measure of intelligence test performance devised by Binet; the level of performance typically associated with children of a certain chronological age. Thus, a child who does as well as an average 8-year-old is said to have a mental age of 8.

Stanford-Binet the widely used American revision (by Terman at Stanford University) of Binet's original intelligence test.

intelligence quotient (IQ) defined originally as the ratio of mental age *(ma)* to chronological age *(ca)* multiplied by 100 (thus, IQ = *ma*/*ca* × 100). On contemporary intelligence tests, the average performance for a given age is assigned a score of 100.

Wechsler Adult Intelligence Scale (WAIS) the WAIS and its companion versions for children are the most widely used intelligence tests; they contain verbal and performance (nonverbal) subtests.

standardization defining uniform testing procedures and meaningful scores by comparison with the performance of a pretested group.

called the *bell curve,* or **normal curve.** The curve's highest point is the average score. Moving out from the average, toward either extreme, we find fewer and fewer people.

On an intelligence test, the average score has a value of 100 (**FIGURE 8.8**). For both the Stanford-Binet and the Wechsler tests, your score would indicate whether your performance fell above or below that average. A score of 130, for example, would indicate that only 2.5 percent of all test-takers had scores higher than yours. About 95 percent of all people score within 30 points above or 30 points below 100.

Is the Test Reliable? Knowing where you stand in comparison to a standardization group still won't say much about your intelligence unless the test has **reliability.** A reliable test gives consistent scores, no matter who takes the test or when they take it. To check a test's reliability, researchers test many people many times. They may retest people using the same test, test with alternative forms of the test, or split the test in half and see whether odd-question scores and even-question scores agree. If the two sets of scores generally agree—if they *correlate*—the test is reliable. The higher the correlation, the more reliable the test.

The tests we have considered—the Stanford-Binet, the WAIS, and the WISC—all are very reliable after early childhood. In retests, sometimes decades later, people's scores generally are similar to the first score (Deary et al., 2009; Lyons et al., 2017).

Is the Test Valid? A **valid** test measures or predicts what it promises. A test can be reliable but not valid. Imagine buying a tape measure with faulty markings. If you use it to measure people's heights, your results will be very reliable. No matter how many times you measure, people's heights will be the same. But your faulty height results will not be valid.

We expect intelligence tests to have **predictive validity:** They should predict future performance, and to some extent, they do. The predictive power of aptitude tests is fairly strong in the early school years (Roth et al., 2015). But later it weakens.

LaunchPad Watch the *Video: Correlational Studies* for a helpful tutorial animation.

High and Low Scorers—How Do They Differ?

LOQ 8-20 What are the traits of people with extremely low and high intelligence scores?

One way to glimpse the validity and significance of any test is to compare people who score at the two extremes of the normal curve. As Figure 8.8 shows, about 5 percent of intelligence test-takers score at the extremes—2.5 percent higher than 130, and 2.5 percent lower than 70. If a test is valid, the two extreme groups should differ noticeably. On intelligence tests, they do.

The Low Extreme **Intellectual disability** (formerly called *mental retardation*) is a developmental condition that is apparent before age 18. It sometimes has a known physical cause. *Down syndrome,* for example, is a disorder of varying intellectual and physical severity caused by an extra copy of chromosome 21 in the person's genetic makeup. People diagnosed with a mild intellectual disability—those just below the 70 score—may be able to live independently.

To be diagnosed with an intellectual disability, a person must meet two criteria:

1. An intelligence test score indicating performance that is in the lowest 3 percent of the population, or about 70 or below (Schalock et al., 2010).
2. Difficulty adapting to the normal demands of independent living, as expressed in three areas, or skills: *conceptual* (language, reading, and concepts of money, time, and number); *social* (interpersonal skills, being socially responsible, following basic rules and laws, avoiding being victimized); and *practical* (health and personal care, occupational skill, and travel). In mild forms, intellectual disability, like normal intelligence, results from a combination of genetic and environmental factors (Reichenberg et al., 2016).

The High Extreme Children whose intelligence test scores indicate extraordinary academic gifts mostly thrive. In one famous project begun in 1921, Lewis Terman studied more than 1500 California schoolchildren with IQ scores over 135. These high-scoring children (later called the "Termites") were healthy,

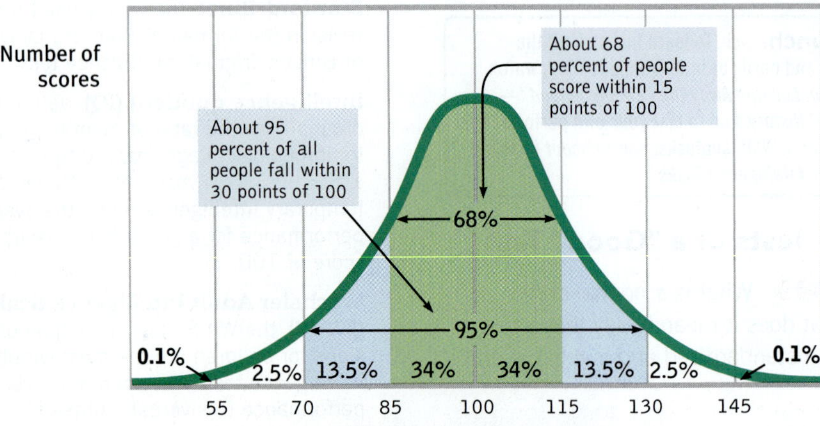

FIGURE 8.8 The normal curve Scores on aptitude tests tend to form a normal, or bell-shaped, curve around an average score. For the Wechsler scale, for example, the average score is 100.

Richard Bailey/Getty Images

Integrated intelligence Many U.S. classrooms combine children with differing intellectual abilities, providing additional support services as needed.

well-adjusted, and unusually successful academically (Friedman & Martin, 2012; Koenen et al., 2009; Lubinski, 2009a). Their success continued over the next seven decades. Most attained high levels of education, and many were doctors, lawyers, professors, scientists, and writers (Austin et al., 2002; Holahan & Sears, 1995).

Other studies have focused on young people who aced the SAT. One group of 1650 math whizzes had at age 13 scored in the top 1 percent of their age group. By their fifties, those individuals had claimed 681 patents (Lubinski et al., 2014). Another group of 13-year-old verbal aptitude high scorers were by age 38 twice as likely as the math stars to have become humanities professors or written a novel (Kell et al., 2013). Among Americans in general, about 1 percent earn doctorates. But for the 12- and 13-year-olds who scored in the top hundredth of 1 percent among those of their age taking the SAT, 63 percent have done so (Lubinski, 2009b).

Jean Piaget, the twentieth century's most famous developmental psychologist, might have felt right at home with these whiz kids. By age 15, he was already publishing scientific articles on mollusks (Hunt, 1993).

Barbara Smaller The New Yorker Collection/The Cartoon Bank

"Zach is in the gifted-and-talented-and-you're-not class."

Among the high-scoring whiz kids in national searches for precocious youth were Google co-founder Sergey Brin, Facebook's Mark Zuckerberg, and musician Stefani Germanotta (Lady Gaga) (Clynes, 2016). Another became a professional poker player with $100,000+ annual earnings (Lubinski, 2016).

RETRIEVE & REMEMBER

ANSWERS IN APPENDIX E

13. What are the three requirements that a psychological test must meet in order to be widely accepted? Explain.

THE NATURE AND NURTURE OF INTELLIGENCE

Intelligence runs in families. But why? Are our intellectual abilities mostly inherited? Or are they molded by our environment?

Heredity and Intelligence

LOQ 8-21 What is *heritability?* What do twin and adoption studies tell us about the nature and nurture of intelligence?

Heritability is the portion of the *variation among individuals in a group* that we can assign to genes. Estimates of the heritability of intelligence range from 50 to 80 percent (Madison et al., 2016; Plomin et al., 2016; Plomin & von Stumm, 2018). Does this mean that we can assume that 50 percent of *your* intelligence is due to your genes, and the rest to your environment? No. Heritability is a tricky concept. *The important point to remember:* Heritability never applies to an *individual,* only to *why people in a group differ from one another.*

The heritability of intelligence varies from study to study. To see why, consider humorist Mark Twain's fantasy of raising boys in barrels until age 12, feeding them through a hole. Let's take his joke a step further and say we'll give all those boys an intelligence test at age 12. Since their *environments* were all equal, any differences in their test scores could only be due to their heredity. In this "study," heritability would be 100 percent. But what if a mad scientist cloned 100 genetically identical boys and raised them in drastically different environments (some in barrels and others in mansions)? In this case, their *heredity* would be equal, so any test-score differences could only be due to their environment. The environmental effect would be 100 percent, and heritability would be zero.

normal curve the bell-shaped curve that describes the distribution of many physical and psychological attributes. Most scores fall near the average, and fewer and fewer scores lie near the extremes.

reliability the extent to which a test yields consistent results, as assessed by the consistency of scores on two halves of the test, on alternative forms of the test, or on retesting.

validity the extent to which a test measures or predicts what it is supposed to. (See also *predictive validity.*)

predictive validity the success with which a test predicts the behavior it is designed to predict.

intellectual disability a condition of limited mental ability, indicated by an intelligence test score of 70 or below and difficulty adapting to the demands of life. (Formerly referred to as *mental retardation.*)

heritability the proportion of variation among people in a group that we can attribute to genes. The heritability of a trait may vary, depending on the population and the environment.

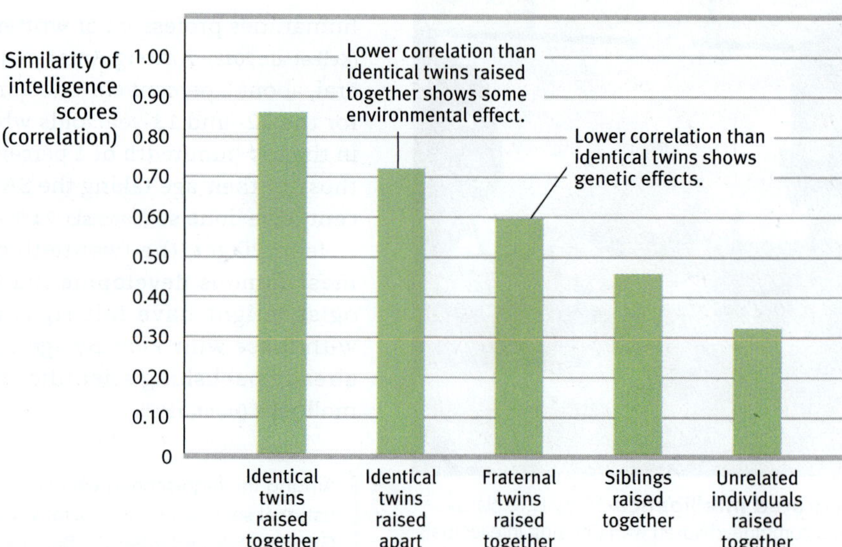

FIGURE 8.9 Intelligence: nature and nurture The most genetically similar people have the most similar intelligence scores. Remember: 1.00 indicates a perfect correlation; zero indicates no correlation at all. (Data from McGue et al., 1993.)

In real life, we can't clone people to study the effects of heredity and environment. But as we noted in Chapter 3, nature has done that work for us. Identical twins share the same genes. Do they also share the same mental abilities? As you can see from **FIGURE 8.9**, which summarizes many studies, the answer is *Yes*. Even when identical twins are adopted by two different families, their intelligence test scores are very similar. When they grow up together, their scores are nearly as similar as those of one person taking the same test twice (Haworth et al., 2009; Lykken, 2006; Plomin et al., 2016). Identical twins are also very similar in specific talents, such as music, math, and sports.

Although genes matter, there is no known "genius" gene. When 100 researchers pooled their data on 269,867 people, all the gene variations analyzed accounted for only about 5 percent of the differences in educational achievement (Savage et al., 2018). Another analysis of genes from 1.1 million people accounted for about 12 percent of their educational attainment differences (Lee et al., 2018). The search for smart genes continues, but this much is clear: Many, many genes contribute to intelligence. Intelligence is thus like height (Johnson, 2010). More than 50 specific gene variations account for only 5 percent of our individual height differences. What matters for intelligence (as for height, personality, sexual orientation, schizophrenia, or just about any human trait) is the *combination* of many genes (Sniekers et al., 2017).

RETRIEVE & REMEMBER

ANSWERS IN APPENDIX E

14. A check on your understanding of heritability: If environments become more equal, the heritability of intelligence will
a. increase.
b. decrease.
c. be unchanged.

Environment and Intelligence

Fraternal twins are genetically no more alike than other siblings. But they usually share an environment and are often treated more alike. So are their intelligence test scores more alike than those of other siblings? *Yes*—as Figure 8.9 shows. So environment does have some effect.

Adoption studies help us assess the influence of environment. Seeking to untangle genes and environment, researchers have compared the intelligence test scores of adopted children with those of their

- ***biological parents*** (who provided their genes).
- ***adoptive parents*** (who provided their home environment).
- ***adoptive siblings*** (who shared that home environment).

Several studies suggest that a shared environment exerts a modest influence on intelligence test scores.

- Adoption from poverty into middle-class homes enhances children's intelligence test scores (Nisbett et al., 2012). One large Swedish study looked at this effect among children adopted into wealthier families with more educated parents. The adopted children's test scores were higher, by an average of 4.4 points, than those of their not-adopted biological siblings (Kendler et al., 2015a).
- Adoption of mistreated or neglected children also enhances their intelligence scores (Almas et al., 2017).
- The intelligence scores of "virtual twins"—same-age, unrelated children adopted as infants and raised together as siblings—correlate at a level higher than chance: +0.28 (Segal et al., 2012).

So during childhood, adoptive siblings' test scores correlate modestly. What do you think happens as the years go by and adopted children settle in with their adoptive families? Would you expect the shared-environment effect to grow stronger, and the shared-gene effect to shrink?

If you said *Yes*, we have a surprise for you. Adopted children's intelligence test scores resemble those of their biological parents much more than their adoptive families (Loehlin, 2016). And over time, adopted children's verbal ability scores become even more like those of their biological parents (**FIGURE 8.10**). Mental ability similarities between adopted children and their adoptive families *lessen* with age. Who would have guessed?

Genetic influences become more apparent as we accumulate life experience. Identical twins' similarities, for example, continue or increase into their eighties (Deary et al., 2012).

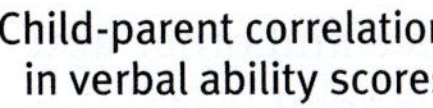
LaunchPad For a helpful tutorial animation, watch the *Video: Twin Studies.* Then try to predict the correlation of intelligence scores in *Concept Practice: Studying Twins and Adopted Children.*

Gene-Environment Interactions

LOQ 8-22 How can environmental influences affect cognitive development?

Genes and experience together weave the fabric of intelligence. (Recall from Chapter 3 that *epigenetics* is the field that studies this nature–nurture meeting place.) With mental abilities, as with physical abilities, *our genes shape the experiences that shape us.* If you have a natural aptitude for sports, you will probably play more often than others (getting more practice, coaching, and experience). Or, if you have a natural aptitude for academics, you will more likely stay in school, read books, and ask questions—all of which will increase your brain power. The same would be true for your identical twin—who might, not just for genetic reasons, also become a strong performer. In these gene-environment interactions, small genetic advantages can trigger social experiences that multiply your original skills (Sauce & Matzel, 2018).

Sometimes, however, environmental conditions work in reverse, depressing physical or cognitive development. Severe deprivation leaves footprints on the brain, as J. McVicker Hunt (1982) observed in one Iranian orphanage.

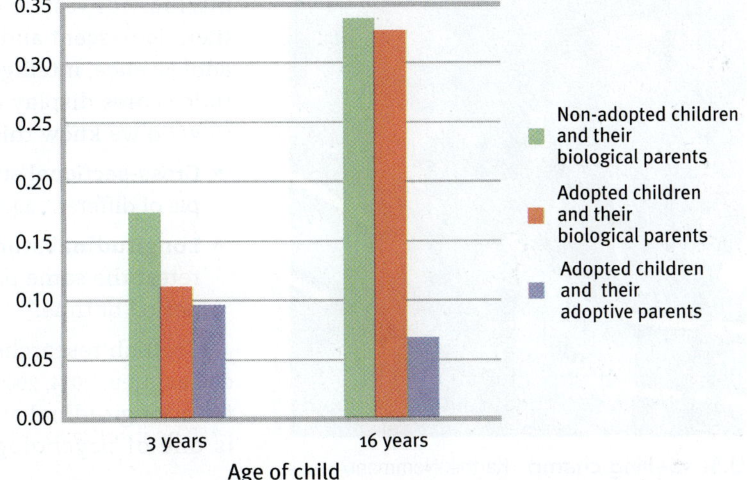

FIGURE 8.10 In verbal ability, whom do adopted children resemble? As the years went by in their adoptive families, children's verbal ability scores became more like their *biological* parents' scores. (Data from Plomin & DeFries, 1998.)

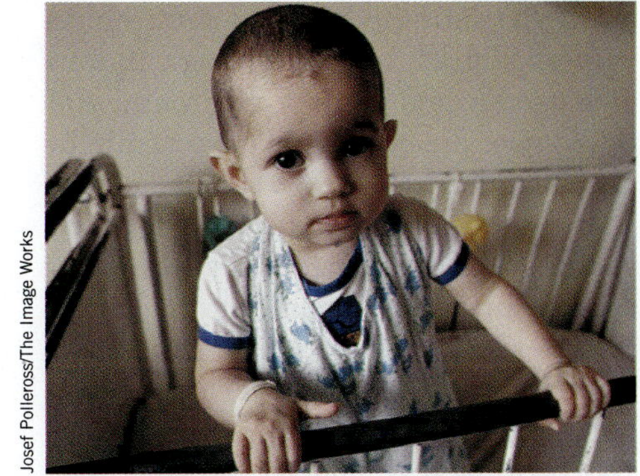
Josef Polleross/The Image Works

Devastating neglect Some Romanian orphans, such as this child in the Leaganul Pentru Copii orphanage in 1990, had minimal interaction with caregivers and suffered delayed development.

The typical child Hunt observed there could not sit up unassisted at age 2 or walk at age 4. The little care infants received was not in response to their crying, cooing, or other behaviors, so the children developed little sense of personal control over their environment. They were instead becoming passive "glum lumps." Extreme deprivation was crushing native intelligence—a finding confirmed by other studies of children raised in poorly run orphanages in Romania and elsewhere (Nelson et al., 2009, 2013; van IJzendoorn et al., 2008).

Aware of both the dramatic effects of early experiences and the impact of early intervention, Hunt began a training program for the Iranian caregivers, teaching them to play language-fostering games with 11 infants. They imitated the babies' babbling. They engaged them in vocal follow-the-leader. And, finally, they taught the infants sounds from the Persian language. The results were dramatic. By 22 months of age, the infants could name more than 50 objects and body parts. They so charmed visitors that most were adopted—an impressive new success rate for the orphanage.

Hunt's findings are an extreme case of a more general finding: The poor environmental conditions that accompany poverty can depress cognitive development and produce stresses that worsen cognitive performance (Heberle & Carter, 2015; Tuerk, 2005). And this may help explain another finding: Where environments vary widely, as they do among children of less-educated parents, environmental differences are more predictive of intelligence scores (Tucker-Drob & Bates, 2016).

If extreme conditions—sensory deprivation, social isolation, poverty—can slow normal brain development, could the reverse also be true? Could an "enriched" environment amplify normal brain development? Most experts are doubtful (Bruer, 1999; DeLoache et al., 2010; Reichert et al., 2010). There is no recipe for fast-forwarding a normal infant into a genius. All babies should have normal exposure to sights, sounds, and speech. Beyond that, developmental psychologist Sandra Scarr's (1984) verdict is still widely shared: "Parents who are very concerned about providing special educational lessons for their babies are wasting their time." Later in childhood, however, some forms of enrichment can pay intelligence-score dividends (Protzko et al., 2013).

Growth Mindset Schooling and intelligence interact, and both enhance later income (Ceci & Williams, 1997, 2009). But what we accomplish with our intelligence depends also on our own beliefs and motivation. One analysis of 72,431 undergraduates found that study motivation and study skills rivaled aptitude and previous grades as predictors of academic achievement (Credé & Kuncel, 2008). Motivation can even affect intelligence test performance. Studies show that, when promised money for doing well, adolescents score higher on such tests (Duckworth et al., 2011).

These observations would not surprise psychologist Carol Dweck (2012a,b, 2015, 2018). She reports that believing that intelligence is changeable fosters a *growth mindset*—a focus on learning and growing. Dweck teaches young teens that the brain is like a muscle, growing stronger with use. Receiving praise for *effort* and for tackling challenges, rather than for being smart or accomplished, helps teens understand the link between hard work and success (Gunderson et al, 2013). Although a growth mindset doesn't alter intelligence, it can make children and youth more resilient when others frustrate them (Paunesku et al., 2015; Yeager et al., 2013, 2014, 2016a). But researchers caution against blaming struggling individuals for their circumstances (Ikizer & Blanton, 2016). Sometimes people need more than the power of positive thinking to overcome their harsh conditions.

More than 300 studies confirm that ability + opportunity + motivation = success in fields from sports to science to music (Ericsson et al., 2007). High school students' math achievements and college students' grades reflect their aptitude but also their self-discipline, their belief in the power of effort, and a curious "hungry mind" (Murayama et al., 2013; Richardson et al., 2012; von Stumm et al., 2011). And consider: Between 2008 and 2018, youth of South Asian heritage won all nine U.S. national spelling bee contests. This achievement was likely influenced by a cultural belief that strong effort energizes you and brings success (Rattan et al., 2012; Savani & Job, 2017). To reach your potential, the formula is simple: Believe in your ability to learn, and apply yourself with sustained effort.

So, environmental influences can foster or diminish cognitive skills. But what is the general trend? On our journey from womb to tomb, does our intelligence change or remain stable?

Jacquelyn Martin/AP Images

U.S. spelling champ Karthik Nemmani, 14, won the 2018 Scripps National Spelling Bee. What was Karthik's winning word? "koinonia."

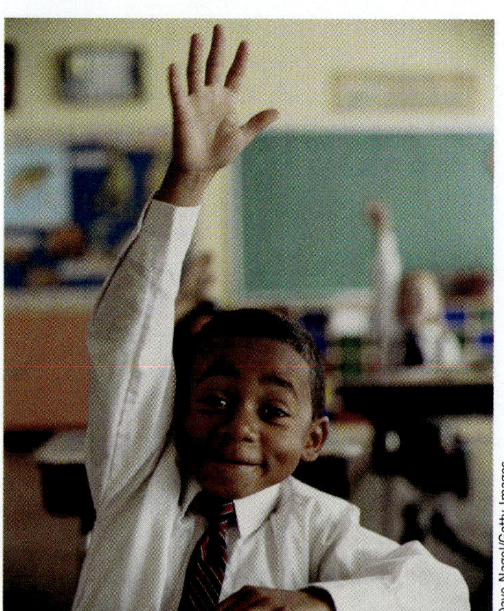
Dave Nagel/Getty Images

A hungry mind

IMPROVE YOUR EVERYDAY LIFE

Are you working to the potential reflected in your standardized test scores? What, other than your aptitude, is affecting your school performance?

INTELLIGENCE ACROSS THE LIFE SPAN

Stability or Change?

LOQ 8-23 How stable are intelligence test scores over the life span?

Intelligence endures. By age 4, children's intelligence test scores begin to predict their adolescent and adult scores. By late adolescence, intelligence and other aptitude scores display remarkable stability. How do we know this?

- **Cross-sectional studies** compare people of different ages with one another.
- **Longitudinal studies** restudy and retest the same people over a long period of time.[4]

Scottish researcher Ian Deary and his colleagues (2004, 2009b, 2013) set a record for a longitudinal study, and their story is one of psychology's great tales. On

[4] For more on these research methods, see Appendix A, Statistical Reasoning in Everyday Life.

June 1, 1932, Scotland did what no other nation has done before or since. To identify working-class children who would benefit from further education, the government gave every child born in Scotland in 1921 an intelligence test—87,498 eleven-year-olds in all.

On June 1, 1997, sixty-five years later to the day, Patricia Whalley, the wife of Deary's co-worker, Lawrence Whalley, discovered the test results on dusty storeroom shelves at the Scottish Council for Research in Education, not far from Deary's Edinburgh University office. "This will change our lives," Deary replied when Whalley told him the news. And so it has, with dozens of studies of the stability and the predictive capacity of these early test results. One study, for example, retested 542 survivors from the 1932 test group at age 80 (Deary et al., 2004). The result? After nearly 70 years of varied life experiences, the correlation between the test-takers' two sets of scores was striking **(FIGURE 8.11).** Ditto when 106 survivors were retested at age 90 (Deary et al., 2013).

Higher-scoring children and adults tend to live healthier and longer lives (Calvin et al., 2017; Stephan et al., 2018). Why might this be the case? Deary (2008) has proposed four possible explanations:

- Intelligence gives people better access to more education, better jobs, and a healthier environment.
- Intelligence encourages healthy living: less smoking, better diet, more exercise.
- Prenatal events or early childhood illnesses can influence both intelligence and health.
- A "well-wired body," as evidenced by fast reaction speeds, may foster both intelligence and longer life.

So, intelligence scores are strikingly *stable.* And high intelligence is a predictor of health and long life. Yet, with age, our knowledge and our mental agility change, as we see next.

RETRIEVE & REMEMBER

ANSWERS IN APPENDIX E

15. Researcher A wants to study how intelligence changes over the life span. Researcher B wants to study the intelligence of people who are now at various life stages. Which researcher should use the cross-sectional method, and which the longitudinal method?

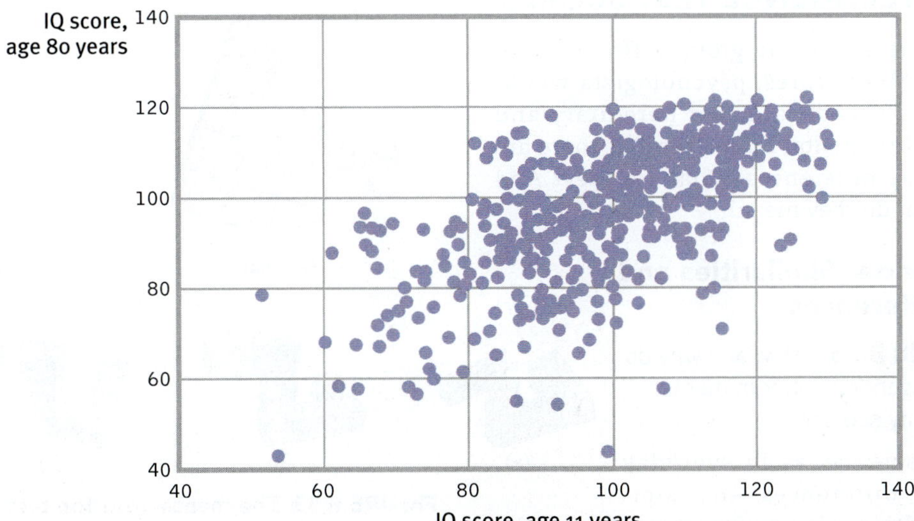

FIGURE 8.11 Intelligence endures When Ian Deary and his colleagues retested 80-year-old Scots, using an intelligence test they had taken as 11-year-olds, their scores across seven decades correlated +0.66, as shown here. (Data from Deary et al., 2004.) When 106 survivors were again retested at age 90, the correlation with their age 11 scores was +0.54 (Deary et al., 2013).

LaunchPad Watch the *Video: Longitudinal and Cross-Sectional Studies* for a helpful tutorial animation.

Crystallized and Fluid Intelligence

LOQ 8-24 What are *crystallized* and *fluid intelligence,* and how does aging affect them?

Does intelligence increase, decrease, or remain constant as we age? The answer to that question depends on the task and the type of ability it represents.

- **Crystallized intelligence**—our accumulated knowledge, as reflected in vocabulary and word-power tests—*increases* as we age, up to old age.
- **Fluid intelligence**—our ability to reason speedily and abstractly, as when solving unfamiliar logic problems—*decreases* beginning in the twenties and thirties. It declines slowly until about age 75 or so, and then more rapidly, especially after age 85 (Cattell, 1963; Deary & Ritchie, 2016; Salthouse, 2009, 2013).

With age we lose and we win. We lose recall memory and processing speed, but we gain vocabulary and knowledge **(FIGURE 8.12).** In older adulthood, our social reasoning skills increase. We are better able to see many different viewpoints, to appreciate the limits of knowledge, and to offer helpful wisdom in times of conflict (Grossmann et al., 2010).

cross-sectional study research that compares people of different ages at the same point in time.

longitudinal study research that follows and retests the same people over time.

crystallized intelligence your accumulated knowledge and verbal skills; tends to increase with age.

fluid intelligence your ability to reason speedily and abstractly; tends to decrease with age, especially during late adulthood.

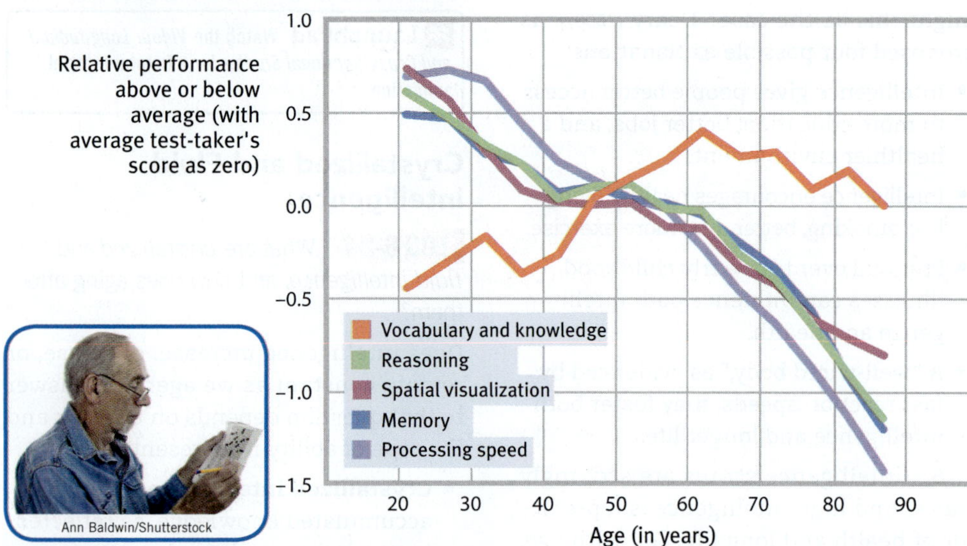

FIGURE 8.12 With age, we lose and we win. Studies reveal that word power grows with age, while fluid intelligence declines. (Data from Salthouse, 2010.)

© Randy Glasbergen

"We're looking for someone with the wisdom of a 50-year-old, the experience of a 40-year-old, the drive of a 30-year-old, and the payscale of a 20-year-old."

Our decisions also become less distorted by negative emotions such as anxiety, depression, or anger (Blanchard-Fields, 2007; Carstensen & Mikels, 2005).

These life-span differences in mental abilities help explain why older adults are less likely to embrace new technologies (Charness & Boot, 2009; Pew, 2017). They also help explain some curious findings about creativity. Mathematicians and scientists produce much of their most creative work during their late twenties or early thirties, when fluid intelligence is at its peak (Jones et al., 2014). Prose authors, historians, and philosophers, who depend more on crystallized intelligence, tend to produce their best work in their forties, fifties, and beyond (Simonton, 1988, 1990).

LaunchPad Play the role of a researcher studying these issues by engaging online with the activity ***How Would You Know If Intelligence Changes With Age?***

GROUP DIFFERENCES IN INTELLIGENCE TEST SCORES

If there were no group differences in aptitude scores, psychologists would have less debate over hereditary and environmental influences. But there are group differences. What are they? And what do they mean?

Gender Similarities and Differences

LOQ 8-25 How and why do the genders differ in mental ability scores?

In science, as in everyday life, differences—not similarities—excite interest. Men's self-estimated intelligence is often higher than women's self-estimated intelligence, which may fuel a false perception that men are smarter than women (Furnham, 2016). In truth, our intelligence differences are minor. For example, in the 1932 testing of all Scottish 11-year-olds, boys' intelligence scores averaged 100.5 and girls' 100.6 (Deary et al., 2003). As far as *g* is concerned, boys and girls, men and women, are the same.

Yet most people find differences more newsworthy. In cultures where both boys and girls benefit from schooling, girls outpace boys in spelling, verbal fluency, and locating objects (Voyer & Voyer, 2014). They are better emotion detectors and are more sensitive to touch, taste, and color (Halpern et al., 2007). In math computation and overall math performance, girls and boys hardly differ (Else-Quest et al., 2010; Hyde & Mertz, 2009; Lindberg et al., 2010).

On complex math problems, boys outperform girls. But the most reliable male edge appears in spatial ability tests like the one shown in **FIGURE 8.13** (Maeda & Yoon, 2013; Palejwala & Fine, 2015). (To solve the problem, you must quickly rotate three-dimensional objects in your mind.) Males' mental ability scores (and brains) also vary more than females'.

Which one of the options below matches the Original?

(a)

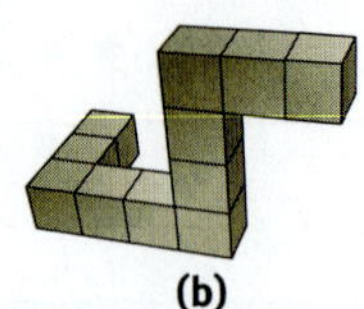

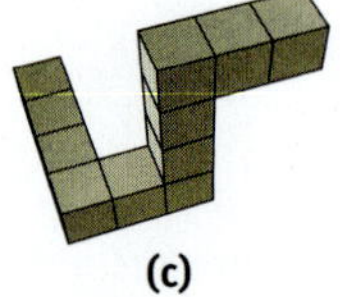

FIGURE 8.13 The mental rotation test These kinds of items are often found on spatial abilities tests. See answer below.[5]

[5] The correct answer is c.

"That's an excellent suggestion, Miss Triggs. Perhaps one of the men would like to suggest it."

Worldwide, boys outnumber girls at both the low and high extremes (Ball et al., 2017; Brunner et al., 2013). Boys, for example, are more often found in special education classes, but also among those scoring very high on the SAT math test.

Psychologist Steven Pinker (2005) has argued the evolutionary perspective — that biology affects gender differences in life priorities (women's somewhat greater interest in people versus men's in money and things), in risk-taking (with men more reckless), and in math reasoning and spatial abilities. Such differences are, he noted, observed across cultures, stable over time, influenced by prenatal hormones, and observed in genetic boys raised as girls.

Maryam Mirzakhani/Getty Images

Minding the math gap In 2014, Iranian math professor Maryam Mirzakhani (1977–2017) became the first woman to win math's most admired award, the Fields Medal. What was her advice to people who want to know more about math? Practice patience. "The beauty of mathematics," Mirzakhani said, "only shows itself to more patient followers" (*The Guardian*, 2014).

But social expectations and opportunities also construct gender by shaping interests and abilities (Crawford et al., 1995; Eccles et al., 1990). In Asia and Russia, teen girls have outperformed boys in an international science exam. In North America and Britain, boys have scored higher (Fairfield, 2012). More gender-equal cultures, such as Sweden and Iceland, exhibit little of the gender math gap found in gender-unequal cultures, such as Turkey and Korea (Guiso et al., 2008; Kane & Mertz, 2012). And since the 1970s, as gender equity has increased in the United States, the boy-to-girl ratio among 12- to 14-year-olds with very high SAT math scores has declined from 13 to 1 to 3 to 1 (Makel et al., 2016; Nisbett et al., 2012). As we have seen in so many areas of life, experience matters.

Racial and Ethnic Similarities and Differences

LOQ 8-26 How and why do racial and ethnic groups differ in mental ability scores?

Fueling the group-differences debate are two other disturbing but scientifically agreed-upon facts:

- Racial and ethnic groups differ in their average intelligence test scores.
- High-scoring people (and groups) are more likely to achieve high levels of education and income.

There are many group differences in average intelligence test scores. New Zealanders of European descent outscore native Maori New Zealanders. Israeli Jews outscore Israeli Arabs. Most Japanese outscore most Burakumin, a stigmatized Japanese minority. And White Americans have outscored Black Americans. This Black-White difference seems to have shrunk in recent years, especially among children (Dickens & Flynn, 2006; Nisbett et al., 2012).

One more agreed-upon fact is that *group* differences provide little basis for judging individuals. Worldwide, women outlive men by four years, but knowing that you are a woman or a man won't tell us much about how long you will live.

We have seen that heredity contributes to *individual* differences in intelligence. But group differences in a heritable trait may be entirely environmental, as in our earlier boys-in-barrels versus boys-in-mansions example. Consider one of nature's experiments: Allow some children to grow up hearing their culture's dominant language, while others, born deaf, do not. Then give both groups an intelligence test rooted in the dominant language. The result? No surprise. Those with expertise in the dominant language will score higher than those who were born deaf (Braden, 1994; Steele, 1990; Zeidner, 1990).

Might racial and ethnic gaps be similarly environmental? Consider:

Genetics research reveals that under the skin, we humans are remarkably alike. Despite some racial variation, such as in health risks, the average genetic difference between two Icelandic villagers or between two Kenyans greatly exceeds the group difference between Icelanders and Kenyans (Cavalli-Sforza et al., 1994; Rosenberg et al., 2002). Moreover, looks can deceive. Light-skinned Europeans and dark-skinned Africans are genetically closer than are dark-skinned Africans and dark-skinned Aboriginal Australians.

Larry Williams/Getty Images

Race is not a neatly defined biological category. Many social scientists think *race* is no longer a meaningful term. They view race primarily as a social category without well-defined physical boundaries. Each racial group, they point out, blends seamlessly into its geographical neighbors (Helms et al., 2005; Smedley & Smedley, 2005). In one genetic analysis of more than 160,000 people living in the United States, most with less than 28 percent African ancestry said they were White; those with more than 28 percent mostly said they were African-American (Byrc et al., 2015). Moreover, with increasingly mixed ancestries, fewer and fewer people fit neatly into any one category, and more and more identify themselves as multiracial (Pauker et al., 2009).

Within the same populations, there are generation-to-generation differences in test scores. Test scores of today's better-fed, better-educated, and more test-prepared populations exceed the scores of 1930s populations (Flynn, 2012, 2018; Pietschnig & Voracek, 2015; Trahan et al., 2014). The scores of the two generations differ by a greater margin than the score difference between today's U.S. Whites and U.S. Blacks. The average intelligence test performance of today's sub-Saharan Africans is the same as that of British adults in 1948 (Wicherts et al., 2010). No one credits genetics for such generation-to-generation differences.

Schools and culture matter. Countries whose economies create a large wealth gap between rich and poor also tend to have a large rich-versus-poor intelligence test score gap (Nisbett, 2009). Moreover, educational policies (such as kindergarten attendance, school discipline, and instructional time per year) predict national differences in intelligence and knowledge tests (Lynn & Vanhanen, 2012; Rindermann & Ceci, 2009). One analysis of 600,000 students showed that each additional year of school predicted 1 to 5 additional IQ points (Ritchie & Tucker-Drob, 2018). Staying in school secures superior smarts.

Math achievement, aptitude test differences, and especially grades may reflect conscientiousness more than competence (Poropat, 2014). Asian students, who have outperformed North American students on such tests, have also spent 30 percent more time in school and much more time in and out of school studying math (Geary et al., 1996; Larson & Verma, 1999; Stevenson, 1992). Women in college and university similarly outperform equally able men, thanks partly to their greater conscientiousness (Keiser et al., 2016).

In different eras, different ethnic groups have experienced golden ages—periods of remarkable achievement. Twenty-five hundred years ago, it was the Greeks and the Egyptians, then the Romans. In the eighth and ninth centuries, genius seemed to reside in the Arab world. Five hundred years ago, the Aztec Indians and peoples of Northern Europe took the lead. Today, many people notice Asian technological genius and Jewish cultural success. Cultures rise and fall over centuries. The gene pool changes more slowly.

PIUS UTOMI EKPEI/Getty Images

World Scrabble champs In 2015, Team Nigeria was the top country in the World Scrabble Championship. Five of its six members finished among the top 50 contestants, including Wellington Jighere, center, the individual world Scrabble champion.

RETRIEVE & REMEMBER

ANSWERS IN APPENDIX E

16. The heritability of intelligence scores will be greater in a society marked by equal opportunity than in a society with great differences in citizens' wealth and status. Why?

Are Intelligence Tests Biased?

LOQ 8-27 Are intelligence tests biased or unfair? What is *stereotype threat,* and how does it affect test-takers' performance?

Knowing there are group differences in intelligence test scores leads us to wonder whether those differences are built into the tests. Are intelligence tests biased? The answer depends on how we define *bias*.

The *scientific* meaning of *bias* hinges only on a test's validity. A valid intelligence test should predict future behavior for all groups of test-takers, not just for some. For example, if the SAT accurately predicted the college achievement of women but not that of men, then the test would be biased. Almost all psychologists agree that in this scientific sense, the major U.S. aptitude tests are *not* biased (Berry & Zhao, 2015; Neisser et al., 1996; Wigdor & Garner, 1982). Their predictive validity is roughly the same, regardless of gender, race, ethnicity, or socioeconomic level. If an intelligence test score of 95 predicts slightly below-average grades, that rough prediction usually applies equally to all groups of test-takers.

But in everyday language, we may consider a test "biased" if scores will be influenced by test-takers' cultural experiences. If we use "biased" in this popular sense, then yes, intelligence tests may be considered unfair (even if scientifically unbiased). Why? Because they measure the test-takers' developed abilities, which reflect, in part, their education and experiences. Some researchers therefore recommend culture-neutral questions—such as those that assess people's ability to learn novel words, sayings, and analogies—to enable *culture-fair* aptitude tests (Fagan & Holland, 2007, 2009).

As you've seen in so many contexts in this text, expectations and attitudes influence perceptions and behaviors. For intelligence test-makers, expectations can introduce bias. And for intelligence test-takers, expectations and attitudes can become self-fulfilling prophecies.

Test-Takers' Expectations In one study, equally capable men and women took a difficult math test. The women did not do as well as the men—except when they had been led to expect that women usually do as well as men on the test (Spencer et al., 1997). Otherwise, something affected their performance. There was a "threat in the air" (Spencer et al., 2016). This self-fulfilling **stereotype threat** appeared again when Black students were reminded of their race just before taking verbal aptitude tests and performed worse (Steele et al., 2002). Negative stereotypes may undermine people's academic potential (Grand, 2016; Nguyen & Ryan, 2008; Walton & Spencer, 2009). If you worry that your group or "type" often doesn't do well on a certain kind of test or task, your self-doubts and self-monitoring may hijack your working memory and impair attention, performance, and learning (Hutchison et al., 2013; Inzlicht & Kang, 2010; Rydell et al., 2010).

Stereotype threat helps explain why Blacks have scored higher when tested by Blacks than when tested by Whites (Danso & Esses, 2001). And it gives us insight into why women have scored higher on math tests with no male test-takers present, and why men would rather stay in traditionally feminine jobs (primary school teacher, child protection worker) when they perform their duties without highly competent women present (Doyle & Voyer, 2016; Kalokerinos et al., 2018). From such studies, some researchers have concluded that making students believe they probably won't succeed can function as a stereotype and weaken performance. Remedial "minority support" programs may sometimes have this effect (Steele, 1995, 2010).

Other research teams have demonstrated benefits of self-affirmation exercises (Cohen & Sherman, 2014; Goyer et al., 2017; Harackiewicz et al., 2014, 2016). Programs that challenge disadvantaged university students to believe in their potential, think positively about their diverse life experiences, increase their sense of belonging, or focus on the idea that intelligence is not fixed have had good results. Students' grades were markedly higher, and their dropout rates lower (Layous et al., 2017; Sarrasin et al., 2018; Townsend et al., 2019; Yeager et al., 2016b).

RETRIEVE & REMEMBER

ANSWERS IN APPENDIX E

17. What is the difference between a test that is culturally biased and a test that is scientifically biased?

18. What psychological principle helps explain why women tend to perform more poorly when they believe their online chess opponent is male?

* * *

Perhaps, then, these should be our goals for tests of mental abilities. First, *we should realize the benefits Alfred Binet foresaw*—to enable schools to recognize who might profit most from early intervention. Second, we must *remain alert to Binet's wish* that intelligence test scores not be misinterpreted as literal measures of a person's worth and potential. Third, we must *remember that the competence that general intelligence tests sample is important*. It helps enable success in some life paths. Without such tests, those who decide on jobs and admissions would rely more on other considerations, such as personal opinion. But these tests reflect only one important aspect of personal competence (Stanovich et al., 2013, 2014a,b). Our rationality, practical intelligence, and emotional intelligence matter, too, as do other forms of creativity, talent, and character.

The point to remember: There are many ways of being successful. Our differences are variations of human adaptability. Life's great achievements result not only from abilities (and fair opportunity) but also from motivation. Competence + Diligence = Accomplishment.

What time is it now? When you were reading about overconfidence, did you underestimate or overestimate how quickly you would finish the chapter?

LaunchPad To explore how you perceive your own intelligence, engage online with the activity ***Assess Your Strengths: What Is Your Theory of Intelligence, and How Is That Affecting Your Success?***

stereotype threat a self-confirming concern that you will be judged based on a negative stereotype.

CHAPTER 8 REVIEW Thinking, Language, and Intelligence

LEARNING OBJECTIVES

TEST YOURSELF Answer these repeated Learning Objective Questions on your own (before checking the answers in Appendix D) to improve your retention of the concepts (McDaniel et al., 2009, 2015).

Thinking

8-1: What is *cognition,* and what are the functions of concepts?

8-2: What cognitive strategies help us solve problems, and what tendencies work against us?

8-3: What is *intuition,* and how can the representativeness and availability heuristics influence our decisions and judgments?

8-4: What factors exaggerate our fear of unlikely events?

8-5: How are our decisions and judgments affected by overconfidence, belief perseverance, and framing?

8-6: How do smart thinkers use intuition?

8-7: What is *creativity,* and what fosters it?

8-8: What do we know about thinking in other species?

Language

8-9: How do we acquire language, and what is *universal grammar?*

8-10: What are the milestones in language development, and when is the critical period for learning language?

8-11: What brain areas are involved in language processing and speech?

8-12: How can thinking in images be useful?

8-13: What do we know about other species' capacity for language?

Intelligence

8-14: How do psychologists define *intelligence,* and what are the arguments for general intelligence *(g)?*

8-15: How do Gardner's and Sternberg's theories of multiple intelligences differ, and what criticisms have they faced?

8-16: What four abilities make up emotional intelligence?

8-17: What is an *intelligence test,* and how do achievement and aptitude tests differ?

8-18: When and why were intelligence tests created, and how do today's tests differ from early intelligence tests?

8-19: What is a *normal curve,* and what does it mean to say that a test has been standardized and is reliable and valid?

8-20: What are the traits of people with extremely low and high intelligence scores?

8-21: What is *heritability?* What do twin and adoption studies tell us about the nature and nurture of intelligence?

8-22: How can environmental influences affect cognitive development?

8-23: How stable are intelligence test scores over the life span?

8-24: What are *crystallized* and *fluid intelligence,* and how does aging affect them?

8-25: How and why do the genders differ in mental ability scores?

8-26: How and why do racial and ethnic groups differ in mental ability scores?

8-27: Are intelligence tests biased or unfair? What is *stereotype threat,* and how does it affect test-takers' performance?

TERMS AND CONCEPTS TO REMEMBER

TEST YOURSELF Write down the definition in your own words, then check your answer.

cognition, *p. 215*
concept, *p. 215*
prototype, *p. 215*
algorithm, *p. 215*
heuristic, *p. 215*
insight, *p. 215*
confirmation bias, *p. 215*
functional fixedness, *p. 215*
intuition, *p. 215*
representativeness heuristic, *p. 216*
availability heuristic, *p. 216*
overconfidence, *p. 219*
belief perseverance, *p. 219*
framing, *p. 219*
nudge, *p. 219*
creativity, *p. 221*
convergent thinking, *p. 221*
divergent thinking, *p. 221*
language, *p. 223*
babbling stage, *p. 225*
one-word stage, *p. 225*
two-word stage, *p. 225*
telegraphic speech, *p. 225*
grammar, *p. 225*
Broca's area, *p. 227*
Wernicke's area, *p. 227*
intelligence, *p. 229*
general intelligence (*g*), *p. 229*
savant syndrome, *p. 229*
emotional intelligence, *p. 231*

intelligence test, *p. 233*
achievement test, *p. 233*
aptitude test, *p. 233*
mental age, *p. 233*
Stanford-Binet, *p. 233*
intelligence quotient (IQ), *p. 233*
Wechsler Adult Intelligence Scale (WAIS), *p. 233*
standardization, *p. 233*
normal curve, *p. 235*
reliability, *p. 235*
validity, *p. 235*
predictive validity, *p. 235*
intellectual disability, *p. 235*
heritability, *p. 235*
cross-sectional study, *p. 239*
longitudinal study, *p. 239*
crystallized intelligence, *p. 239*
fluid intelligence, *p. 239*
stereotype threat, *p. 243*

CHAPTER TEST

TEST YOURSELF Answer the following questions on your own first, then check your answers in Appendix E.

1. A mental grouping of similar things is called a ________.
2. The most systematic procedure for solving a problem is a(n) ________.
3. Oscar describes his political beliefs as "strongly liberal," but he is interested in exploring opposing viewpoints. How might he be affected by confirmation bias and belief perseverance?
4. A major obstacle to problem solving is functional fixedness, which is a(n)
   a. tendency to base our judgments on vivid memories.
   b. tendency to wait for insight to occur.
   c. inability to view a problem from a new perspective.
   d. rule of thumb for judging the likelihood of an event in terms of our mental image of it.
5. Terrorist attacks made Americans more fearful of being victimized by terrorism than of other, greater threats. Such exaggerated fear after dramatic events illustrates the ________ heuristic.
6. When consumers respond more positively to ground beef described as "75 percent lean" than to the same product labeled "25 percent fat," they have been influenced by ________.
7. Which of the following is NOT a characteristic of a creative person?
   a. Expertise
   b. Extrinsic motivation
   c. A venturesome personality
   d. Imaginative thinking skills
8. According to Chomsky, humans have a built-in predisposition to learn grammar rules; he called this trait ________ ________.
9. Children reach the one-word stage of speech development at about
   a. 4 months.
   b. 6 months.
   c. 1 year.
   d. 2 years.
10. When young children speak in short phrases using mostly verbs and nouns, this is referred to as ________ ________.
11. Most researchers agree that apes can
    a. communicate through symbols.
    b. reproduce most human speech sounds.
    c. master language in adulthood.
    d. surpass a human 3-year-old in language skills.
12. Charles Spearman suggested we have one ________ ________ underlying success across a variety of intellectual abilities.
13. The existence of savant syndrome seems to support
    a. Sternberg's distinction among three types of intelligence.
    b. criticism of multiple intelligence theories.
    c. Gardner's theory of multiple intelligences.
    d. Thorndike's view of social intelligence.
14. Sternberg's three types of intelligence are ________, ________, and ________.
15. Emotionally intelligent people tend to
    a. seek immediate gratification.
    b. understand their own emotions but not those of others.
    c. understand others' emotions but not their own.
    d. succeed in their careers.
16. The IQ of a 6-year-old with a measured mental age of 9 would be
    a. 67.
    b. 133.
    c. 86.
    d. 150.

17. The Wechsler Adult Intelligence Scale (WAIS) is best able to tell us

a. what part of an individual's intelligence is determined by genetic inheritance.

b. whether the test-taker will succeed in a job.

c. how the test-taker compares with other adults in vocabulary and arithmetic reasoning.

d. whether the test-taker has specific skills for music and the performing arts.

18. The Stanford-Binet, the Wechsler Adult Intelligence Scale, and the Wechsler Intelligence Scale for Children yield consistent results, for example on retesting. In other words, these tests have high ________.

19. To say that the heritability of intelligence is about 50 percent means that 50 percent of

a. an individual's intelligence is due to genetic factors.

b. the similarities between two groups of people are attributable to genes.

c. the variation in intelligence within a group of people is attributable to genetic factors.

d. an individual's intelligence is due to each parent's genes.

20. The strongest support for heredity's influence on intelligence is the finding that

a. identical twins, but not other siblings, have nearly identical intelligence test scores.

b. the correlation between intelligence test scores of fraternal twins is not higher than that for other siblings.

c. similarity of mental abilities between adopted siblings increases with age.

d. children in impoverished families have similar intelligence scores.

21. The environmental influence that has the clearest, most profound effect on intellectual development is

a. exposing normal infants to enrichment programs before age 1.

b. growing up in an economically disadvantaged home.

c. being raised in conditions of extreme deprivation.

d. being an identical twin.

22. Which of the following is NOT a possible explanation for the fact that more intelligent people tend to live longer, healthier lives?

a. Intelligence makes it easier to access more education, better jobs, and a healthier environment.

b. Intelligence encourages a more health-promoting lifestyle.

c. Intelligent people have slower reaction times, so are less likely to put themselves at risk.

d. Prenatal events or early childhood illnesses could influence both intelligence and health.

23. Use the concepts of crystallized and fluid intelligence to explain why writers tend to produce their most creative work later in life, while scientists often hit their peak much earlier.

24. ________ ________ can lead to poor performance on tests by undermining test-takers' belief that they can do well on the test.

Continue testing yourself with **LearningCurve** or **Achieve Read & Practice** to learn and remember most effectively.

Thomas Barwick/Getty Images

Motivation and Emotion

CHAPTER 9

SURVEY THE CHAPTER

How well I [DM] remember asking my first discussion question in a new introductory psychology class. Several hands rose, along with one left foot. The foot belonged to Chris Klein, who was the unlikeliest person to have made it to that class. At birth, Chris suffered oxygen deprivation that required 40 minutes of CPR. "One doctor wanted to let him go," recalled his mother.

The result was severe cerebral palsy. With damage to the brain area that controls muscle movement, Chris can't contain his constantly moving hands. He cannot feed, dress, or care for himself. And he cannot speak. But what Chris can control are his keen mind and his left foot. With that blessed foot, he operates the joystick on his motorized wheelchair. Using his left big toe, he can type sentences, which his communication system can store, send, or speak. And Chris is motivated — very motivated.

When Chris was a high school student in suburban Chicago, three teachers doubted he would be able to leave home for college. Yet he persisted, and, with much support, attended Hope College. Five years later, as his left foot drove him across the stage to receive his diploma, his admiring classmates gave him a spontaneous standing ovation.

Today, Chris is an inspirational speaker for schools, churches, and community events, giving "a voice to those that have none, and a helping hand to those with disabilities." He is writing a book, *Lessons from the Big Toe.* And he has found love and married.

Few of us face Chris Klein's challenges. But we all seek to direct our energy in ways that will produce satisfaction and success. We are moved by our feelings along the way, and we inspire them in others. We are pushed by biological motives, such as hunger, and by social ones, such as the needs to belong and to achieve. Chris Klein's fierce will to live, learn, and love highlights the close ties between our own *motivations* and *emotions,* which energize, direct, and enrich our lives.

Katie Green/MLIVE.COM/Barcroft

A motivated man: Chris Klein To see and hear Chris presenting his story, visit tinyurl.com/ChrisPsychStudent.

Motivational Concepts

Learning Objective Question LOQ 9-1

What is *motivation,* and what are three key perspectives that help us understand motivated behaviors?

Our **motivations** arise from the interplay between nature (the bodily "push") and nurture (the "pulls" from our personal experiences, thoughts, and culture). Our motives drive our behavior. That is usually, but not always, for the better. Those with *substance abuse disorder,* for example, may be driven to satisfy harmful cravings instead of those for food, safety, and social support.

Let's consider three perspectives that psychologists have used to understand motivated behaviors.

DRIVES AND INCENTIVES

Drive-reduction theory makes three assumptions:

- We have **physiological needs,** such as the need for food or water.
- If a need is not met, it creates a *drive,* an aroused, motivated state, such as hunger or thirst.
- That drive pushes us to reduce the need by, say, eating or drinking.

Need (food, water)

Drive (hunger, thirst)

Drive-reducing behaviors (eating, drinking)

FIGURE 9.1 Drive-reduction theory Drive-reduction motivation arises from *homeostasis*—our body's natural tendency to maintain a steady internal state. Thus, if we are water-deprived, our thirst drives us to drink to restore the body's normal state.

The goal of this three-step process (**FIGURE 9.1**) is **homeostasis,** our body's natural tendency to maintain a steady internal state. (*Homeostasis* means "staying the same.") For example, our body regulates its temperature in a way similar to a room's thermostat. Both systems monitor temperature and feed information to a control device. If the room's temperature cools, the control device switches on the furnace. Likewise, if our body's temperature cools, our blood vessels narrow to conserve warmth, and we search for warmer clothes or a warmer environment.

We also are pulled by **incentives**—environmental stimuli that attract or repel us, depending on our individual learning histories. Such stimuli (when positive) increase our dopamine levels, causing our underlying drives (such as for food or sex) to become active impulses (Hamid et al., 2016). And the more these impulses are satisfied and reinforced, the stronger the drive may become. If you are hungry, the aroma of good food will motivate you. Whether that aroma comes from roasted peanuts or toasted ants will depend on your culture and experience. Incentives can also be negative. If teasing others on social media results in our being unfollowed or unfriended, that negative incentive may motivate us to change our behavior.

When there is both a need and an incentive, we feel strongly driven. You've skipped lunch and you can smell pizza baking in your friend's kitchen. You will feel a strong drive to satisfy your hunger, and the baking pizza will be a powerful incentive that will motivate your actions.

For each motive, we can therefore ask, "How are we *pushed* by our inborn bodily needs and *pulled* by incentives in the environment?"

AROUSAL THEORY

We are much more than calm homeostatic systems, however. When we are aroused, we are physically energized, or tense. Some motivated behaviors actually *increase* rather than decrease arousal. Well-fed animals with no clear, need-based drive will leave a safe shelter to explore and gain information. Curiosity drives monkeys to monkey around trying to figure out how to unlock a latch that opens nothing, or how to open a window that allows them to see outside their room (Butler, 1954). Curiosity drives newly mobile infants to check out every corner of the house. It drove curious students, in one experiment, to click on pens to see whether they did or didn't deliver an electric shock (Hsee & Ruan, 2016). It drives the scientists whose work this text discusses. And it strongly drives some individuals, such as mountain adventurer George Mallory. Asked why he wanted to climb Mount Everest, Mallory famously answered, "Because it is there." Those who, like Mallory, enjoy high arousal are most likely to enjoy intense music, novel foods, and risky behaviors (Roberti et al., 2004; Zuckerman, 1979, 2009).

We humans hunger for information (Biederman & Vessel, 2006). When we find that all our biological needs have been met, we feel bored and seek stimulation to increase our arousal. Why might people seek to increase their arousal? Moderate arousal and even anxiety can be motivating. For example, it can lead to higher levels of math achievement (Wang et al., 2015c). Yet *too* much stimulation or stress motivates us to look for ways to decrease arousal. Arousal theory describes this search for the right arousal level, a search that energizes and directs our behavior.

Science Source

Glenn Swier

Driven by curiosity Young monkeys and children are fascinated by the unfamiliar. Their drive to explore maintains an optimum level of arousal and is one of several motives that do not fill any immediate physiological need.

Two early twentieth-century psychologists studied the relationship of arousal to performance. They identified the **Yerkes-Dodson law:** *Moderate arousal leads to optimal performance* (Yerkes & Dodson, 1908). When taking an exam, it pays to be moderately aroused—alert but not trembling with nervousness. (If you're already nervous, remember that caffeine or nicotine may make you even more jumpy.) Between bored low arousal and anxious hyperarousal lies a well-lived life. Optimal arousal levels depend on the task, with more difficult tasks requiring lower arousal for best performance (Hembree, 1988).

IN YOUR EVERYDAY LIFE

Does boredom ever motivate you to do things just to figure out something new? When was the last time that happened, and what did you find?

RETRIEVE & REMEMBER

ANSWERS IN APPENDIX E

1. Performance peaks at lower levels of arousal for difficult tasks, and at higher levels for easy or well-learned tasks. (a) How might this affect marathon runners? (b) How might this affect anxious test-takers facing a difficult exam?

A HIERARCHY OF NEEDS

Some needs are more important than others. At this moment, with your needs for air and food hopefully satisfied, other motives—such as your desires to learn and to achieve—are energizing and directing your behavior. But if you were deprived of nourishment, your hunger would take over your thoughts. Deprived of air, your hunger would disappear.

Abraham Maslow (1970) viewed human motives as a pyramid—a **hierarchy of needs** (FIGURE 9.2). At the pyramid's base are physiological needs, such as for food. Only after these needs are met, said Maslow (1971), do we try to meet our need for safety, and then to satisfy our needs to give and receive love and to enjoy self-esteem. At the peak of the pyramid are self-transcendence needs.

Self-transcendence needs
Need to find meaning and identity beyond the self

Self-actualization needs
Need to live up to our fullest and unique potential

Esteem needs
Need for self-esteem, achievement, competence, and independence; need for recognition and respect from others

Belongingness and love needs
Need to love and be loved, to belong and be accepted; need to avoid loneliness and separation

Safety needs
Need to feel that the world is organized and predictable; need to feel safe, secure, and stable

Physiological needs
Need to satisfy hunger and thirst

Lionsgate/Photofest © Lionsgate

FIGURE 9.2 Maslow's hierarchy of needs Reduced to semistarvation by their rulers, inhabitants of Suzanne Collins' fictional nation, Panem, hunger for food and survival. *Hunger Games* heroine Katniss Everdeen (played by Jennifer Lawrence) expresses higher-level needs for actualization and transcendence, and in the process inspires the nation.

motivation a need or desire that energizes and directs behavior.

drive-reduction theory the idea that a physiological need creates an aroused state (a drive) that motivates us to satisfy the need.

physiological need a basic bodily requirement.

homeostasis a tendency to maintain a balanced or constant internal state; the regulation of any aspect of body chemistry, such as blood glucose, around a particular level.

incentive a positive or negative environmental stimulus that motivates behavior.

Yerkes-Dodson law the principle that performance increases with arousal only up to a point, beyond which performance decreases.

hierarchy of needs Maslow's pyramid of human needs; at the base are physiological needs. These basic needs must be satisfied before higher-level safety needs, and then psychological needs, become active.

At the *self-actualization* level, people seek to realize their own potential. At the very top is *self-transcendence,* which Maslow proposed near the end of his life. At this level, some people strive for meaning, purpose, and identity in a way that is *transpersonal*—beyond *(trans)* the self (Koltko-Rivera, 2006).

"Do you feel your life has an important purpose or meaning?" When Gallup asked this of people in 132 countries, 91 percent answered Yes (Oishi & Diener, 2014). We sense meaning when we experience our life as having *purpose* (goals), *significance* (value), and *coherence* (sense). These feelings may be nourished by strong social connections, a religious faith, an orderly world, and social status (King et al., 2016; Martela & Steger, 2016). People's sense of life's meaning predicts their psychological and physical well-being, and their ability to delay gratification (Heine et al., 2006; Van Tongeren et al., 2018). Meaning matters.

There are exceptions to Maslow's hierarchy. For example, people have starved themselves to make a political statement. Nevertheless, some needs are indeed more basic than others. In poorer nations, money—and the food and shelter it buys—more strongly predicts feelings of well-being. In wealthy nations, social connections (such as home-life satisfaction) better predict well-being (Oishi et al., 1999).

Let's take a closer look now at three specific motives: the basic-level motive, *hunger,* and two higher-level needs, the *need to belong* and the need to *achieve.* As you read about these motives, watch for ways that incentives (the psychological "pull") interact with bodily needs (the biological "push") (**TABLE 9.1**).

TABLE 9.1 Classic Motivation Theories

Theory	Its Big Idea
Drive-reduction theory	Physiological needs (such as hunger and thirst) create an aroused state that drives us to reduce the need (for example, by eating or drinking).
Arousal theory	Our need to maintain an optimal level of arousal motivates behaviors that meet no physiological need (such as our yearning for stimulation and our hunger for information).
Maslow's hierarchy of needs	We prioritize survival-based needs and then social needs more than the needs for esteem and meaning.

IN YOUR EVERYDAY LIFE

Consider your own experiences in terms of Maslow's hierarchy of needs. Do you remember experiencing hunger or thirst that displaced your concern for other, higher-level needs? Do you usually feel safe? Loved? Confident? How often do you feel you are able to address what Maslow called "self-actualization" needs? What about "self-transcendence" needs?

RETRIEVE & REMEMBER

ANSWERS IN APPENDIX E

2. After hours of driving alone in an unfamiliar city, you finally see a diner. Although it looks deserted and a little creepy, you stop because you are *really* hungry and thirsty. How would Maslow's hierarchy of needs explain your behavior?

LaunchPad **To test your understanding of the hierarchy of needs, engage online with *Concept Practice: Building Maslow's Hierarchy.***

Hunger

Those who have tried to restrict their eating know that physiological needs are powerful. This was vividly demonstrated when Ancel Keys and his research team (1950) did a now-classic study with volunteers (who participated as an alternative to military service). After feeding 200 men normally for three months, researchers halved the food intake for 36 of them. The effects soon became visible. Without thinking about it, these men began conserving energy. They appeared sluggish and dull. Eventually, their body weights stabilized about 25 percent below their starting weights.

"Never hunt when you're hungry."

As Maslow might have guessed, the men became obsessed with food. They talked about it. They daydreamed about it. They collected recipes, read cookbooks, and feasted their eyes on tasty but forbidden food. Focused on their unmet basic need, they lost interest in sex and social activities. One man reported, "If we see a show, the most interesting [parts are] scenes where people are eating. I couldn't laugh at the funniest picture in the world, and love scenes are completely dull." As journalist Dorothy Dix (1861–1951) observed, "Nobody wants to kiss when they are hungry."

Motives can capture our consciousness. When we're hungry, thirsty, fatigued, or sexually aroused, little else may seem to matter. (You may recall from Chapter 7 a parallel effect of our current good or bad mood on our memories.) In one experiment, people were given money to bid for foods. When hungry, people *over*bid for snacks they were told they could eat later when they would be full. When full, people *under*bid for snacks they were told they could eat later when they would be hungry (Fisher & Rangel, 2014). It's hard to imagine what we're not feeling! *Motives matter mightily.*

THE PHYSIOLOGY OF HUNGER

LOQ 9-2 What physiological factors cause us to feel hungry?

Deprived of a normal food supply, Keys' volunteers were clearly hungry. But what triggers hunger? Is it the pangs of an empty stomach? So it seemed to A. L. Washburn. Working with Walter Cannon, Washburn agreed to swallow a balloon that was attached to a recording device (Cannon & Washburn, 1912) (**FIGURE 9.3**).

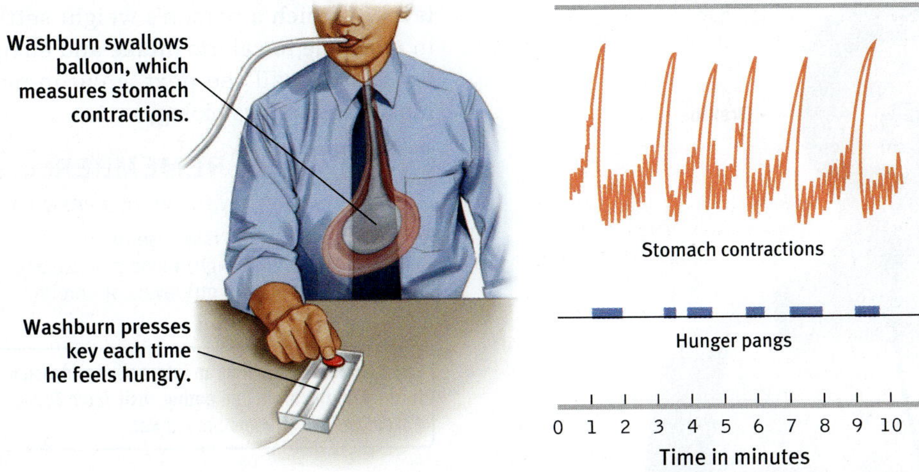

FIGURE 9.3 Monitoring stomach contractions (Information from Cannon, 1929.)

When inflated to fill his stomach, the balloon tracked his stomach contractions. Washburn supplied information about his *feelings* of hunger by pressing a key each time he felt a hunger pang. The discovery: When Washburn felt hungry, he was indeed having stomach contractions.

Can hunger exist without stomach pangs? To answer that question, researchers removed some rats' stomachs and created a direct path to their small intestines (Tsang, 1938). Did the rats continue to eat? Indeed they did. Some hunger similarly persists in humans whose stomachs have been removed to treat ulcers or cancer. So the pangs of an empty stomach cannot be the *only* source of hunger. What else might trigger hunger?

Body Chemistry and the Brain

Your body is keeping tabs on the energy it takes in and the energy it uses. This balancing act enables you to maintain a stable body weight. A major source of energy in your body is the **glucose** circulating in your bloodstream. If your blood glucose level drops, you won't consciously feel the lower blood sugar. But your brain, which automatically monitors your blood chemistry and your body's internal state, will trigger your feeling of hunger.

How does the brain sound the alarm? The work is done by several neural areas, some housed deep in the brain within the *hypothalamus* (**FIGURE 9.4**). This neural traffic intersection includes areas that influence eating. In one neural network (called the *arcuate nucleus*), a center pumps out appetite-stimulating hormones, and another center pumps out appetite-suppressing hormones. When researchers stimulate this appetite-enhancing center, well-fed animals will begin to eat. If they destroy the area, even starving animals lose interest in food. The opposite occurs when the appetite-suppressing area is stimulated: The animal will stop eating. Destroy this area and animals can't stop eating and will become obese (Duggan & Booth, 1986; Hoebel & Teitelbaum, 1966).

Blood vessels connect the hypothalamus to the rest of the body, so it can respond to our current blood chemistry and other incoming information. One of its tasks is monitoring levels of appetite hormones, such as *ghrelin,* a hunger-arousing hormone secreted by an empty stomach. When people have surgery for severe *obesity,* surgeons seal off or remove part of the stomach. The remaining stomach then produces much less ghrelin, reducing the person's appetite and making food less tempting (Ammori, 2013; Lemonick, 2002; Scholtz et al., 2013). Other appetite hormones include *orexin, insulin, leptin,* and PYY. **FIGURE 9.5** describes how they influence your feelings of hunger.

You can also blame your brain for weight regain (Cornier, 2011). The interaction of appetite hormones and brain activity suggests that the body has a "weight thermostat." When semistarved rats fall below their normal weight, this system signals their bodies to restore the lost weight. It's like fat cells cry out, "Feed me!" and start grabbing glucose from the bloodstream (Ludwig & Friedman, 2014). Hunger increases and energy output decreases. If body weight rises—as happens when rats are force-fed—hunger decreases and energy output increases.

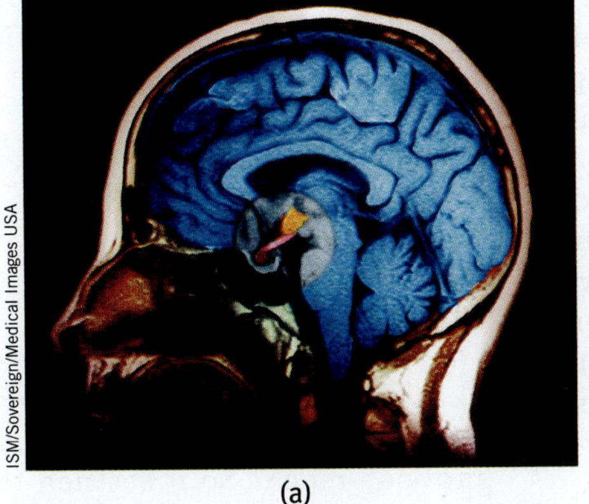

ISM/Sovereign/Medical Images USA

(a)

Voisin/Phanie/Science Source

(b)

FIGURE 9.4 The hypothalamus (a) The hypothalamus (colored orange) performs various body maintenance functions, including control of hunger. The hypothalamus responds to our current blood chemistry and to incoming neural information about the body's state. (b) The fat mouse on the left has nonfunctioning receptors in the appetite-suppressing part of the hypothalamus.

glucose the form of sugar that circulates in the blood and provides the major source of energy for body tissues. When its level is low, we feel hunger.

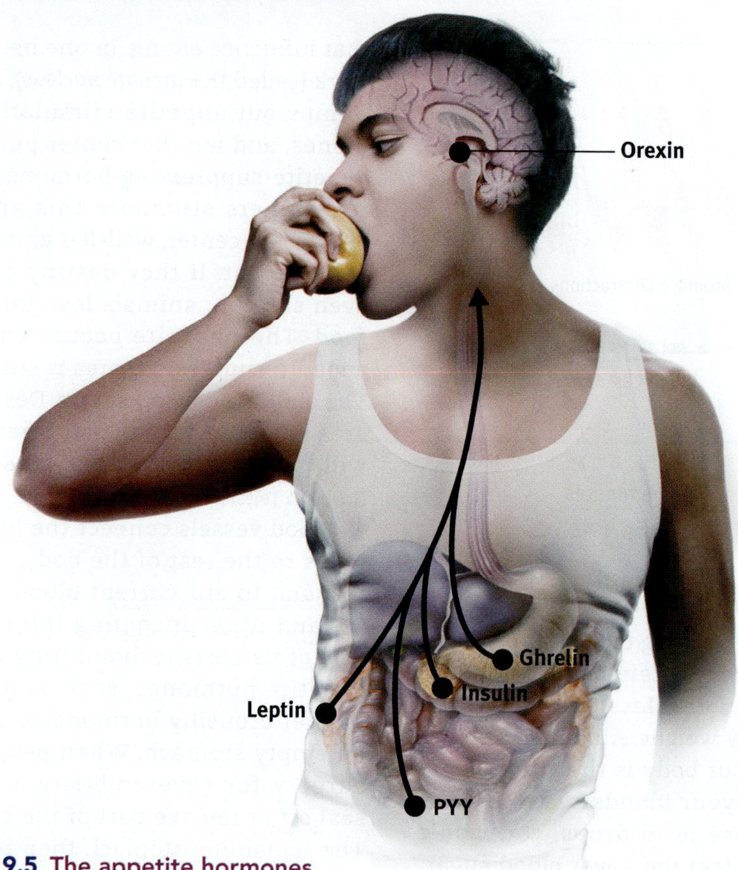

FIGURE 9.5 The appetite hormones

Increases appetite

- *Ghrelin:* Hormone secreted by empty stomach; sends "I'm hungry" signals to the brain.
- *Orexin:* Hunger-triggering hormone secreted by hypothalamus.

Decreases appetite

- *Insulin:* Hormone secreted by pancreas; controls blood glucose.
- *Leptin:* Protein hormone secreted by fat cells; when abundant, causes brain to increase metabolism and decrease hunger.
- *PYY:* Digestive tract hormone; sends "I'm *not* hungry" signals to the brain.

In this way, rats (and humans) tend to hover around a stable weight, or **set point,** influenced in part by heredity (Keesey & Corbett, 1983; Müller et al., 2010).

We humans (and other species, too) vary in our **basal metabolic rate,** our resting rate of energy use for maintaining basic body functions. But we share a common response to decreased food intake: Our basal metabolic rate drops. So it did for the participants in Keys' experiment. After 24 weeks of semistarvation, they stabilized at three-quarters of their normal weight, even though they were taking in only *half* their previous calories. How did they achieve this dieter's nightmare? They reduced the amount of energy they were using—partly by being less active, but partly because their basal metabolic rate dropped by 29 percent.

Some researchers have suggested that the idea of a biologically *fixed* set point is too rigid to explain why slow, steady changes in body weight can alter a person's set point (Assanand et al., 1998), or why, when we have unlimited access to various tasty foods, we tend to overeat and gain weight (Raynor & Epstein, 2001). Thus, many researchers prefer the looser term *settling point* to indicate the level at which a person's weight settles in response to caloric intake and energy use. As we will see next, environment matters as well as biology.

RETRIEVE & REMEMBER

ANSWERS IN APPENDIX E

3. Hunger occurs in response to __________ (low/high) blood glucose and __________ (low/high) levels of ghrelin.

LaunchPad For an interactive and visual tutorial on the brain and eating, visit *Topic Tutorial: PsychSim6, Hunger and the Fat Rat.*

THE PSYCHOLOGY OF HUNGER

LOQ 9-3 How do cultural and situational factors affect our taste preferences and eating habits?

Our hunger is pushed by our body chemistry and brain activity. Yet there is more to hunger than meets the stomach. This was strikingly apparent when researchers tested two patients who had no memory for events occurring more than a minute ago (Rozin et al., 1998). If offered a second lunch 20 minutes after eating a normal lunch, both patients readily ate it . . . and usually a third meal offered 20 minutes after they finished the second. This suggests that one part of our decision to eat is our memory of the time of our last meal. As time passes, we think about eating again, and that thought triggers feelings of hunger. Psychological influences on eating behavior affect all of us at some point.

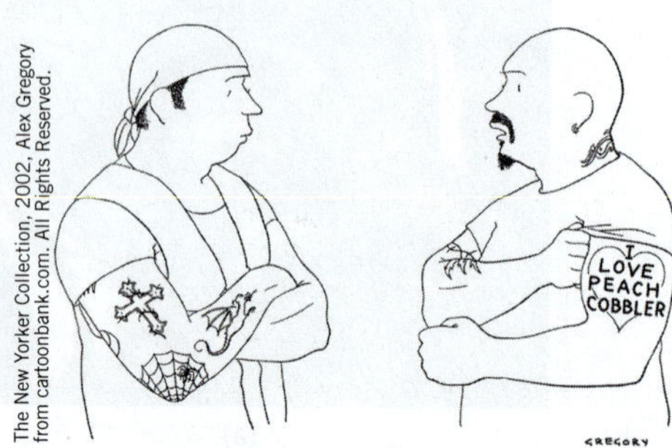

"Never get a tattoo when you're drunk and hungry."

IN YOUR EVERYDAY LIFE

Do you usually eat only when your body sends hunger signals? How much does the sight or smell of delicious food tempt you even when you're full?

Taste Preferences: Biology and Culture

Both body cues and environment influence our feelings of hunger and what we hunger for—our taste preferences. When feeling tense or depressed, do you crave starchy, carbohydrate-laden foods? High-carb foods, such as pasta, chips, and sweets, help boost levels of the neurotransmitter serotonin, which has calming effects. When dieting and stressed, both rats and many humans find it extra rewarding to scarf cookies (Boggiano et al., 2005; Sproesser et al., 2014).

Our preferences for sweet and salty tastes are genetic and universal. Other taste preferences are learned. People given highly salted foods, for example, develop a liking for excess salt (Beauchamp, 1987). People who become violently ill after eating a particular food often develop a dislike of it. (The frequency of children's illnesses provides many chances for them to learn to avoid certain foods.)

Our culture teaches us what foods are delicious. Many Asian people enjoy *durian*, a fruit that's been described as smelling like "turpentine and onions, garnished with a gym sock" (Sterling, 2003). Asians are often repulsed by what many Westerners love—"the rotted bodily fluid of an ungulate" (a.k.a. cheese, some varieties of which have the same bacteria and odor as stinky feet) (Herz, 2012).

We also may learn to prefer some tastes because they are adaptive. In hot climates, where food spoils more quickly, recipes often include spices that slow the growth of bacteria (**FIGURE 9.6**). India averages nearly 10 spices per meat recipe, Finland 2 spices. Pregnancy-related food aversions—and the nausea associated with them—peak about the tenth week, when the developing embryo is most vulnerable to toxins. Thus, many pregnant women avoid potentially harmful foods and other substances, such as alcoholic and caffeinated beverages (Forbes et al., 2018; Gaskins et al., 2018).

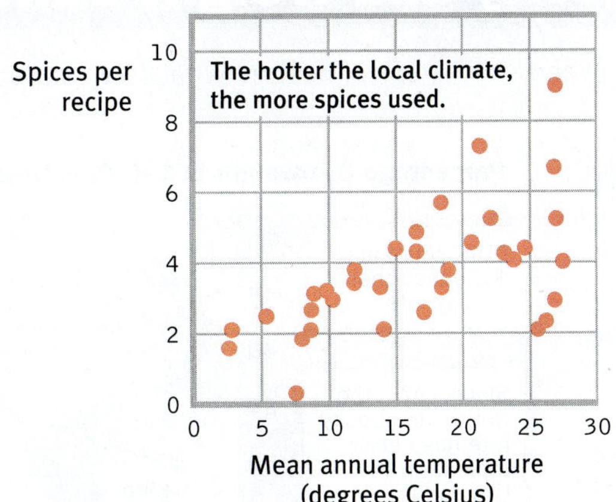

FIGURE 9.6 Hot cultures like hot spices

Rats tend to avoid unfamiliar foods (Sclafani, 1995). So do we, especially those that are animal-based. This surely was adaptive for our ancestors by protecting them from potentially toxic substances.

Tempting Situations

Would it surprise you to know that situations also control your eating? Some examples:

- ***Friends and food*** Do you eat more when eating with others? Most of us do (Herman et al., 2003; Hetherington et al., 2006). The presence of others tends to amplify our natural behavior tendencies. (This is *social facilitation* and you'll hear more about it in Chapter 11.)
- ***Serving size*** Researchers studied the effects of portion size by offering people varieties of free snacks (Geier et al., 2006). For example, in an apartment building's lobby, they laid out full or half pretzels, big or little Tootsie Rolls, or a small or large serving scoop by a bowl of M&M'S. Their consistent result: Offered a supersized portion, people put away more calories. Larger portions prompt bigger bites, which may increase intake by decreasing oral exposure time (Herman et al., 2015). Portion size matters.
- ***Stimulating selections*** Food variety promotes eating. Offered a dessert buffet, people eat more than they do when choosing a portion from one favorite dessert. And they take more of easier-to-reach foods on buffet lines (Marteau et al., 2012). For our early ancestors, eating more when foods were abundant and varied was adaptive. Consuming a wide range of vitamins and minerals and storing fat offered protection later, during winter cold or famine. When bad times hit, they could eat less, hoarding their small food supply until winter or famine ended (Polivy et al., 2008; Remick et al., 2009).
- ***Nudging nutrition*** One research team quadrupled carrots taken by offering schoolchildren carrots before they picked up other foods in a lunch line (Redden et al., 2015). Such "nudges" show how psychological science can improve your everyday life.

* * *

To consider how hunger and other factors affect our risk for **obesity,** see Thinking Critically About: The Challenges of Obesity and Weight Control. And for tips on shedding unwanted weight, see **TABLE 9.2**

set point the point at which your "weight thermostat" may be set. When your body falls below this weight, increased hunger and a lowered metabolic rate may combine to restore lost weight.

basal metabolic rate the body's resting rate of energy output.

obesity defined as a body mass index (BMI) measurement of 30 or higher, which is calculated from our weight-to-height ratio. (Individuals who are *overweight* have a BMI of 25 or higher.)

Thinking Critically About:

The Challenges of Obesity and Weight Control

LOQ 9-4 How does obesity affect physical and psychological health? What factors are involved in weight management?

Obesity and Its Health Effects

Obesity is associated with:

- **physical health risks**, including diabetes, high blood pressure, heart disease, gallstones, arthritis, and certain types of cancer.[1]
- **increased depression**, especially among women.[2]
- **bullying,** outranking race and sexual orientation as the biggest reason for youth bullying in Western cultures.[3]

Percentage Overweight in 195 Countries Studied[4]

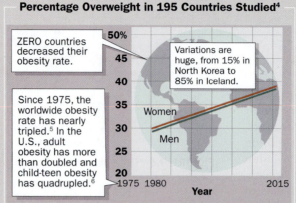

ZERO countries decreased their obesity rate.

Variations are huge, from 15% in North Korea to 85% in Iceland.

Since 1975, the worldwide obesity rate has nearly tripled.[5] In the U.S., adult obesity has more than doubled and child-teen obesity has quadrupled.[6]

50% 45 40 35 30 25 20

Women

Men

1975 1980 2015

Year

Body Mass Index (BMI)

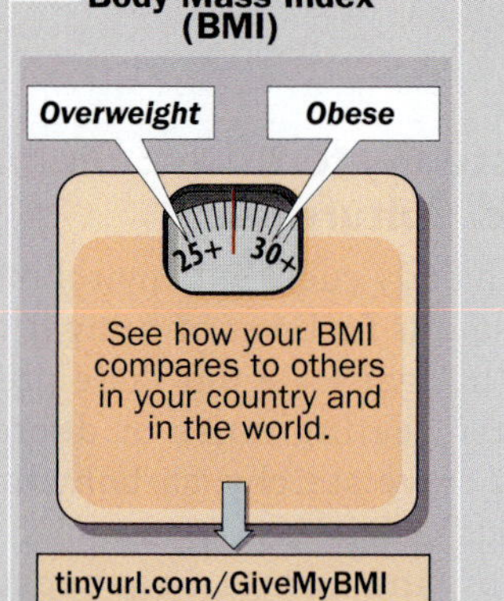

How Did We Get Here?

Does obesity reflect a simple lack of willpower, as some people presume?[7] ***No.*** Many factors contribute to obesity.

Physiology Factors

Storing fat was adaptive.

- This ideal form of stored energy carried our ancestors through periods of famine. People in some impoverished places still find heavier bodies attractive, as plumpness signals affluence and status.[8]
- In food-rich countries, the drive for fat has become dysfunctional.[9]

Set point and metabolism matter.

- Fat (lower metabolic rate than muscle) requires less food intake to maintain than it did to gain.
- If weight drops below *set point/settling point*, the brain triggers more hunger and a slowed metabolism.
- Body perceives STARVATION; adapts by burning fewer calories. Most dieters in the long run regain what they lose on weight-loss programs.[10]
  - 30 weeks of competition on *The Biggest Loser* ➡ 6 years later ➡ Only 1 of 14 contestants kept the weight off. On average they regained 70% of what they lost, and their metabolism remained slow.[11]

Genes influence us.

- Lean people seem naturally disposed to move about, burning more calories than energy-conserving overweight people, who tend to sit still longer.[12]
- Adoptive siblings' body weights are uncorrelated with one another or with their adoptive parents, instead resembling their biological parents' weight.[13]
- Identical twins have closely similar weights, even if raised apart.[14] Much lower *fraternal* twin weight correlation suggests genes explain 2/3 of our varying body mass.[15]
- More than 100 genes have been identified as each affecting weight in some small way.[16]

Environmental Factors

- **Sleep loss** makes us more vulnerable to obesity.[17]

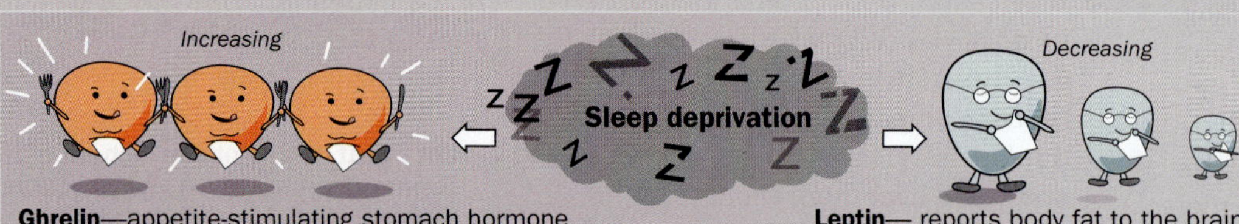

- **Social influences:** Our own odds of becoming obese triple if a close friend becomes obese.[18]
- **Food and activity levels:** Worldwide, we eat more and move less, with 31% of adults (including 43% of Americans and 25% of Europeans) now sedentary—averaging <20 minutes per day of moderate activity such as walking.[19]

NOTE: With weight, as with intelligence and other characteristics, there can be high levels of *heritability* (genetic influence on *individual* differences) without heredity explaining *group* differences. Genes mostly determine why one person today is heavier than another. Environment mostly determines why people today are heavier than people were 50 years ago.

1. Kitahara et al., 2014. 2. de Wit et al., 2010; Luppino et al., 2010. 3. Puhl et al., 2015. 4. GBD, 2017. 5. NCD, 2016. 6. Flegal et al., 2010, 2012, 2016. 7. NORC, 2016b. 8. Furnham & Baguma, 1994; Nettle et al., 2017; Swami, 2015. 9. Hall, 2016. 10. Mann et al., 2015. 11. Fothergill et al., 2016. 12. Levine et al., 2005. 13. Grilo & Pogue-Geile, 1991. 14. Hjelmborg et al., 2008; Plomin et al., 1997. 15. Maes et al., 1997. 16. Akiyama et al., 2017. 17. Keith et al., 2006; Nedeltcheva et al., 2010; Taheri, 2004; Taheri et al., 2004. 18. Christakis & Fowler, 2007. 19. Hallal et al., 2012.

TABLE 9.2 Tips for Weight Management

For those wishing to lose weight, researchers recommend medical guidance, along with these tips:

- ***Begin only if you feel motivated and self-disciplined.*** Permanent weight loss usually requires a lifelong change in eating habits combined with increased exercise.
- ***Exercise and get enough sleep.*** Especially when supported by 7 to 8 hours of sleep a night, exercise empties fat cells, builds muscle, speeds up metabolism, helps lower your settling point, and reduces stress and stress-induced craving for carbohydrate-rich comfort foods (Bennett, 1995; Ruotsalainen et al., 2015; Thompson et al., 1982). Among *Biggest Loser* competitors, exercise predicted less weight regain (Kerns et al., 2017).
- ***Minimize exposure to tempting food cues.*** Food shop on a full stomach. Keep tempting foods out of your home, and tuck away special-occasion foods. You can't eat it if you can't reach it.
- ***Limit variety and eat healthy foods.*** Given more variety, people consume more. So, eat simple meals with vegetables, fruits, and whole grains. Healthy fats, such as those found in olive oil and fish, help regulate appetite (Taubes, 2001, 2002). Water- and vitamin-rich veggies can fill the stomach with few calories. Better crispy greens than Krispy Kremes.
- ***Reduce portion sizes.*** Offered more, people consume more.
- ***Don't starve all day and eat one big meal at night.*** This common eating pattern slows metabolism. Moreover, those who eat a balanced breakfast are, by late morning, more alert and less fatigued (Spring et al., 1992).
- ***Beware of the binge.*** Drinking alcohol or feeling anxious or depressed can unleash the urge to eat (Herman & Polivy, 1980). And men especially should note that eating slowly can lead to eating less (Martin et al., 2007).
- ***Before eating with others, decide how much you want to eat.*** Eating with friends can distract us from monitoring our own eating (Ward & Mann, 2000).
- ***Remember, most people occasionally lapse.*** A lapse need not become a collapse.
- ***Chart your progress online.*** Those who record and disclose their progress toward a goal more often achieve it (Harkin et al., 2016).
- ***Connect to a support group.*** Join with others, either face-to-face or online, to share goals and progress updates (Freedman, 2011).

IMPROVE YOUR EVERYDAY LIFE

Have you or your loved ones ever tried unsuccessfully to lose weight? What happened? What weight-loss strategies might have been more successful?

RETRIEVE & REMEMBER

ANSWERS IN APPENDIX E

4. After an 8-hour hike without food, your long-awaited favorite dish is placed in front of you, and your mouth waters in anticipation. Why?
5. Why can two people of the same height, age, and activity level maintain the same weight, even if one of them eats much less than the other does?

LaunchPad For a 7-minute review of hunger, see the *Video: Hunger and Eating.*

The Need to Belong

LOQ 9-5 What evidence points to our human need to belong?

Imagine yourself like the fictional Robinson Crusoe, dropped on an island . . . alone . . . for the rest of your life. Food, shelter, and comfort are yours—but there is not a single fellow human around, no way to connect with loved ones, no story but your own. Would you savor the stress-free serenity?

Probably not. We are what the ancient Greek philosopher Aristotle called the *social animal*. Cut off from friends or family—alone in prison or in a new school or in a foreign land—most people feel keenly their lost connections with important others. Although some people

Photodisc/Getty Images

are more social than others, this deep **need to belong** is a key human motivation (Baumeister & Leary, 1995).

"We must love one another or die." —W. H. Auden, "September 1, 1939"

THE BENEFITS OF BELONGING

Social bonds boosted our ancestors' chances of survival. These bonds motivated caregivers to keep children close, protecting them from threats (Esposito et al., 2013). As adults, those who formed attachments were more likely to survive and reproduce and co-nurture their offspring to maturity. To be "wretched" literally means, in its Middle English origin (*wrecched*), to be without kin nearby.

Survival also was supported by cooperation. In solo combat, our ancestors were not the toughest predators. But as

need to belong the need to build and maintain relationships and to feel part of a group.

hunters, they learned that eight hands were better than two. As food gatherers, they gained protection from threats by traveling in groups. Those who felt a need to belong survived and reproduced most successfully, and their genes now rule.

People in every society on Earth belong to groups and, as Chapter 11 explains, prefer and favor "us" over "them." Having a *social identity*—feeling part of a group—boosts people's health and well-being (Allen et al., 2015; Greenaway et al., 2015, 2016). We feel included, accepted, and loved, and our self-esteem rides high. Indeed, *self-esteem* is a measure of how valued and accepted we feel (Leary, 2012). According to **self-determination theory,** we strive to satisfy three needs: *competence, autonomy,* and *relatedness* (Deci & Ryan, 2012; Ryan & Deci, 2000). One analysis of 200,000 people from nearly 500 studies concluded that "self-determination is key to explaining human motivation" (Howard et al., 2017, p. 1346). To feel capable, free, and connected is to enjoy a good life.

Small wonder, then, that our social behavior so often aims to increase our feelings of belonging, and that spending more time with friends and family increases happiness (Li & Kanazawa, 2016; Rohrer et al., 2018). To win friendship and avoid rejection, we generally conform to group standards. We monitor our behavior, hoping to make a good impression. We spend billions on clothes, cosmetics, and diet and fitness aids—all motivated by our search for love and acceptance.

Thrown together in groups at school, at work, or at camp, we behave like magnets, moving closer, forming bonds. Parting, we feel distress. We promise to stay in touch and to come back for reunions. By drawing a sharp circle around "us," the need to belong feeds both deep attachments to those inside the circle (loving families, faithful friendships, and team loyalty) and hostilities toward those outside (teen gangs, ethnic rivalries, and fanatic nationalism).

VINCENT YU/AP Images

The need to connect Six days a week, women from the Philippines work as domestic helpers in thousands of Hong Kong households. On Sundays, they throng to the central business district to picnic, dance, sing, talk, and laugh. "Humanity could stage no greater display of happiness," reported one observer (*Economist,* 2001).

Even when bad relationships end, people suffer. In one 16-nation survey, and in repeated U.S. surveys, separated and divorced people have been half as likely as married people to say they are "very happy" (Inglehart, 1990; NORC, 2016a). Divorce also predicts earlier mortality. Data from more than 600 million (!) people in 24 countries reveal that, compared with married people, separated and divorced people are at greater risk for early death (Shor et al., 2012). As one data scientist noted, "[A happy marriage] is perhaps as important as not smoking, which is to say: huge" (Ungar, 2014).

Children who move through a series of foster homes also know the fear of being alone. After repeated breaks in budding relationships, children may have difficulty forming deep attachments (Oishi & Schimmack, 2010). The evidence is clearest at the extremes, as we saw in Chapter 3. Children who grow up in institutions without a sense of belonging to anyone, or who are locked away at home and severely neglected, often become withdrawn, frightened, even speechless.

No matter how secure our early years were, we all experience anxiety, loneliness, jealousy, or guilt when something threatens or dissolves our social ties. Many of life's best moments occur when close relationships begin: making a new friend, falling in love, having a baby. And many of life's worst moments happen when close relationships end (Beam et al., 2016). At such times, we may feel life is empty, pointless, and we may overeat to fill that emptiness (Yang et al., 2016). For those moving alone to new places, the stress and loneliness can be depressing. The second Syrian refugee family settling in a town generally has an easier adjustment than the first.

LaunchPad Consider your own need to belong by engaging with the activity *Assess Your Strengths: How Strong Is Your Need to Belong, and How Can You Strengthen Your Feelings of Belonging?* And work on improving your relationships with the activity *Assess Your Strengths: How Strong Is Your Relationship, and How Might You Increase Its Strength?*

THE PAIN OF BEING SHUT OUT

Can you recall feeling excluded, ignored, or shunned? Perhaps your texts went unanswered, or you were ignored or unfriended online. Perhaps others gave you the silent treatment, avoided you, looked away, mocked you, or shut you out in some other way. This is **ostracism**—social exclusion (Williams, 2007, 2009). Worldwide, humans use many forms of ostracism—exile, imprisonment, solitary confinement—to punish, and therefore control, social behavior. For children, even a brief time-out in isolation can be punishing. Among prisoners, half of all suicides occur among those experiencing the extreme exclusion of solitary confinement (Goode, 2012).

Being shunned threatens our need to belong (Vanhalst et al., 2015; Wirth et al., 2010). Lea, a lifelong victim of the silent treatment by her mother and grandmother, described the effect. "It's the meanest thing you can do to someone, especially if you know they can't fight back. I never should have been born." Like Lea,

Enduring the pain of ostracism White cadets at the United States Military Academy at West Point ostracized Henry Flipper for years, hoping he would drop out. Somehow he resisted their cruelty, and in 1877 he became the first African-American West Point graduate.

people often respond to ostracism with initial efforts to restore their acceptance, followed by depressed mood, and finally leading to withdrawal. Prisoner William Blake (2013) has spent more than a quarter-century in solitary confinement. "I cannot fathom how dying any death could be harder and more terrible than living through all that I have been forced to endure," he observed. To many, social exclusion is a sentence worse than death.

> "How can we subject prisoners to unnecessary solitary confinement, knowing its effects, and then expect them to return to our communities as whole people? It doesn't make us safer. It's an affront to our common humanity." —U.S. President Barack Obama, 2016

Rejected and powerless, excluded people may seek new friends. Or they may turn hostile. Ostracism breeds disagreeableness, which leads to further ostracism (Hales et al., 2016). College students were made to feel rejected in one series of experiments (Gaertner et al., 2008; Twenge et al., 2001).[1] Some students were told that people they had met didn't want them in a group that was forming. Still others heard good news: "Everyone chose you as someone they'd like to work with." How did students react after being told they weren't wanted? They were much more likely to engage in self-defeating behaviors and to act in mean or aggressive ways (blasting people with noise, for example). These findings may help us understand school shooters, who often experience social rejection (Leary et al., 2003). When a Texas high school student experienced romantic rejection in 2018, he shot and killed the girl who rejected him and nine other students and teachers (BBC, 2018).

Ostracism is a real pain. Brain scans show increased activity in areas that also activate in response to physical pain (Lieberman & Eisenberger, 2015; Rotge et al., 2015). That helps explain some other surprising findings. The pain reliever acetaminophen (as in Tylenol), taken to relieve physical pain, also lessens *social* pain (DeWall et al., 2010). Ditto for marijuana, which dulls both physical and social pain (Deckman et al., 2014). Psychologically, we seem to experience social pain with the same emotional unpleasantness that marks physical pain. And across cultures, we use the same words (for example, *hurt, crushed*) for physical and social pain (MacDonald & Leary, 2005).

The opposite of ostracism—feeling loved—activates brain areas associated with rewards and satisfaction. Loved ones activate a brain region that dampens feelings of physical pain (Eisenberger et al., 2011). In one experiment, university students felt markedly less pain when looking at their beloved's picture, rather than at someone else's photo (Younger et al., 2010).

The bottom line: Social isolation and rejection foster depressed moods or emotional numbness, and they can trigger aggression (Bernstein & Claypool, 2012; Gerber & Wheeler, 2009). They can put us at risk for mental decline and ill health (Cacioppo et al., 2015). Thus, the World Health Organization (2017) lists the connection to family, friends, and community as a "determinant of health." To overcome feelings of social isolation and rejection, nurture strong relationships with family and friends, and engage actively in new groups.

[1] The researchers later *debriefed* and reassured the participants.

IN YOUR EVERYDAY LIFE

Have there been times when you felt lonely or ostracized? How might spending quality time with family and friends, or engaging in group activities help you cope next time?

RETRIEVE & REMEMBER

ANSWERS IN APPENDIX E

6. How have students reacted in studies when they were made to feel rejected and unwanted? What helps explain these results?

CONNECTING AND SOCIAL NETWORKING

LOQ 9-6 How does social networking influence us?

As social creatures, we live for connection. Researcher George Vaillant (2013) was asked what he had learned from studying 238 Harvard University men from the 1930s to the end of their lives. He replied, "Happiness is love." A South African Zulu saying captures the idea: *Umuntu ngumuntu ngabantu*—"a person is a person through other persons."

Mobile Networks and Social Media

Look around and see humans connecting: talking, tweeting, texting, posting, chatting, social gaming, emailing. The changes in how we connect have been fast and vast.

- *Mobile phones:* By 2016's end, 95 percent of the world's 7.5 billion people lived in an area covered by a mobile-cellular network (ITU, 2016). Ninety-five percent of American teens have access to a smartphone (Anderson & Jiang, 2018).

self-determination theory the theory that we feel motivated to satisfy our needs for competence, autonomy, and relatedness.

ostracism deliberate social exclusion of individuals or groups.

- ***Texts and instant messaging:*** The average American sends and receives 94 texts/messages per day (Burke, 2018). Half of 18- to 29-year-olds check their phone multiple times per hour, and "can't imagine . . . life without [it]" (Newport, 2015; Saad, 2015). Worldwide in 2017, more than 15 million texts were sent each minute (Domo, 2018).
- ***The internet:*** In 2015, 68 percent of adults around the world used the internet (Poushter, 2016). A survey of 90,000 people from 31 countries found that 6 percent showed signs of "internet addiction" (Cheng & Li, 2014).
- ***Social networking:*** Four in 10 entering American college students use social networking sites at least six hours per week (Eagan et al., 2017). With our friends online, it's hard to avoid social networks. Check in or miss out.

The Net Result: Social Effects of Social Networking

By connecting like-minded people, the internet serves as a social amplifier. In times of social crisis or personal stress, it provides information and supportive connections. The internet can also function as a matchmaker. (I [ND] can attest to this. I met my wife online.) Although dating websites are not adept at matchmaking, they do expand the pool of potential matches (Joel et al., 2017).

But social media also leads people to compare their lives with others (who are mostly showing themselves having fun or doing well). This "social comparison" can trigger envy and depressed feelings (Verduyn et al., 2017). As smartphones became widespread after 2010—with increasing time spent web surfing, texting, gaming, and on social media—teens experienced decreasing face-to-face communications and sleep, and increased loneliness, depression, and suicide (Twenge, 2017). More than 10 hours of screen time per week predicts less teen happiness (Twenge et al., 2018). Many U.S. teens understand such risks, with 54 percent

Alex Gregory The New Yorker Collection/The Cartoon Bank

"Look, until there's a Tinder for Pandas, we have to meet the old-fashioned way: being locked in a room together by scientists."

saying they have too much screen time, and two-thirds of their parents saying the same (Jiang, 2018).

Online networking is double-edged: Nature has designed us for face-to-face relationships, and those who spend hours online are *less* likely to know and draw help from their real-world neighbors. But it does help us connect with friends, stay in touch with extended family, and find support when facing challenges (Pew, 2009; Pinker, 2014; Rainie et al., 2011). When used in moderation, social networking predicts longer life (Hobbs et al., 2016).

Does Electronic Communication Stimulate Healthy Self-Disclosure?

Self-disclosure is sharing ourselves—our joys, worries, and weaknesses—with others. As we will see in Chapter 10, confiding in others can be a healthy way of coping with day-to-day challenges.

Liam Francis Walsh The New Yorker Collection/The Cartoon Bank

"The women on these dating sites don't seem to believe I'm a prince."

When communicating electronically rather than face-to-face, we often are less focused on others' reactions. We are less self-conscious and thus less inhibited. Sometimes this is taken to an extreme, as when bullies hound a victim, hate groups post messages promoting bigotry, or people send photos of themselves they later regret. More often, however, the increased self-disclosure serves to deepen friendships (Valkenburg & Peter, 2009).

Does Social Networking Promote Narcissism? **Narcissism** is self-esteem gone wild. Narcissistic people are self-important, self-focused, and self-promoting. To measure your narcissistic tendencies, you might rate your agreement with personality test items such as "I like to be the center of attention." People who agree with such statements tend to have high narcissism scores—and they are especially active on social networking sites (Liu & Baumeister, 2016). They collect more superficial "friends." They post more staged, glamorous selfies. They retaliate more against negative comments. And, not surprisingly, they *seem* more narcissistic to strangers (Buffardi & Campbell, 2008; Weiser, 2015).

For narcissists, social networking sites are more than a gathering place; they are a feeding trough. In one study, college students were *randomly assigned* either to edit and explain their online profiles for 15 minutes, or to use that time to study and explain a Google Maps routing (Freeman & Twenge, 2010). After completing their tasks, all were tested. Who then scored higher on a narcissism measure? Those who had spent the time focused on themselves.

LaunchPad See the *Video: Random Assignment* for a helpful tutorial animation.

Maintaining Balance and Focus

It will come as no surprise that excessive online socializing and gaming have been associated with lower grades and with increased anxiety and depression

Self-esteem or narcissism? Social networking can help people share self-relevant information and stay connected with family and friends. But social networking can also feed narcissistic tendencies and reward self-glamorizing photo posting.

(Brooks, 2015; Lepp et al., 2014; Walsh et al., 2013). In one U.S. survey, 47 percent of the heaviest users of the internet and other media were receiving mostly C grades or lower, as were just 23 percent of the lightest users (Kaiser Family Foundation, 2010). Brain scans reveal a smaller *amygdala* (an emotion-control center) among extremely heavy social media users, making them similar in this way to people with substance use disorder (He et al., 2018).

In today's world, it can be challenging to maintain a healthy balance between our real-world and online time. Experts offer some practical suggestions:

- ***Monitor your time.*** Keep track of how you use your time. Then ask yourself, "Does my time use reflect my priorities? Am I spending more time online than I intended? Does it interfere with my school or work performance or my relationships?"
- ***Monitor your feelings.*** Ask yourself, "Am I emotionally distracted by my online interests? When I disconnect and move to another activity, how do I feel?"
- ***"Hide" from your more constantly posting online friends when necessary.*** And in your own postings, practice the golden rule. Before you post, ask yourself, "Is this something I'd care about reading if someone else posted it?"
- ***When studying, get in the habit of checking your phone less often.*** Selective attention—the flashlight of your mind—can be in only one place at a time. When we try to do two things at once, we don't do either one of them very well (Willingham, 2010). If you want to study or work productively, resist the temptation to always be available. Disable sound alerts, vibration, and pop-ups. (To reduce distraction, I [ND] am writing this chapter while using an app that blocks distracting websites.)
- ***Refocus by taking a nature walk.*** People learn better after a peaceful walk in a park, which—unlike a walk on a busy street—refreshes our capacity for focused attention (Berman et al., 2008).

As psychologist Steven Pinker (2010a) said, "The solution is not to bemoan technology but to develop strategies of self-control, as we do with every other temptation in life."

"It keeps me from looking at my phone every two seconds."

IMPROVE YOUR EVERYDAY LIFE

Do your connections on social media increase your sense of belonging? Sometimes, do they make you feel lonely? Which of the strategies discussed will you find most useful to maintain balance and focus?

RETRIEVE & REMEMBER

ANSWERS IN APPENDIX E

7. Social networking tends to ________ (strengthen/weaken) your relationships with people you already know, and ________ (increase/decrease) your self-disclosure.

Achievement Motivation

LOQ 9-7 What is *achievement motivation,* and what are some ways to encourage achievement?

Some motives seem to have little obvious survival value. Reality TV stars may be motivated to attract ever more social media followers, politicians to achieve ever more power, daredevils to seek ever greater thrills. Motives vary across cultures. In an *individualist* culture, employees may work to receive an "employee of the month" award; in a *collectivist* culture, they may strive to join a company's hardest-working team. The more we achieve, the more we may need to achieve. Psychologist Henry Murray (1938) defined **achievement motivation** as a desire for significant accomplishment, for mastering skills or ideas, for control, and for attaining a high standard.

Achievement motivation matters. One famous study followed the lives of 1528 California children whose intelligence test scores were in the top 1 percent.

narcissism excessive self-love and self-absorption.

achievement motivation a desire for significant accomplishment, for mastery of skills or ideas, for control, and for attaining a high standard.

Forty years later, researchers compared those who were most and least successful professionally. What did the researchers discover? A motivational difference. The most successful were more ambitious, energetic, and persistent. As children, they had more active hobbies. As adults, they participated in more groups and sports (Goleman, 1980). Gifted children are able learners. Accomplished adults are tireless doers. Most of us are energetic doers when starting and when finishing a project. It's easiest—have you noticed?—to get stuck in the middle. That's when high achievers keep going (Bonezzi et al., 2011). People with high achievement motivation tend to have greater financial success, healthy social relationships, and good physical and mental health (Steptoe & Wardle, 2017).

In some studies of both secondary school and university students, self-discipline has surpassed intelligence test scores in predicting school performance, attendance, and graduation honors. For school performance, "discipline outdoes talent," concluded researchers Angela Duckworth and Martin Seligman (2005, 2006).

"Genius is 1% inspiration and 99% perspiration." —Thomas Edison (1847–1931)

Discipline focuses and refines talent. By their early twenties, top violinists have fiddled away thousands of lifetime practice hours—in fact, double the practice time of other violin students aiming to be teachers (Ericsson 2001, 2006, 2007). Similarly, a study of outstanding scholars, athletes, and artists found that all were highly motivated and self-disciplined. They dedicated hours every day to the pursuit of their goals (Bloom, 1985). These achievers became superstars through daily discipline, not just natural talent. Great achievement, it seems, mixes a spoonful of inspiration with a bucket of perspiration.

Duckworth (2016) has a name for passionate dedication to an ambitious, long-term goal: **grit.** Other researchers see grit as similar to conscientiousness (Credé et al., 2016; Ion et al., 2017; Schmidt et al., 2018). But they agree on this: Passion and perseverance fuel gritty goal-striving, which can produce great achievements (Jachimowicz et al., 2018). As the saying goes, "If you want to look good in front of thousands, you have to outwork thousands in front of nobody."

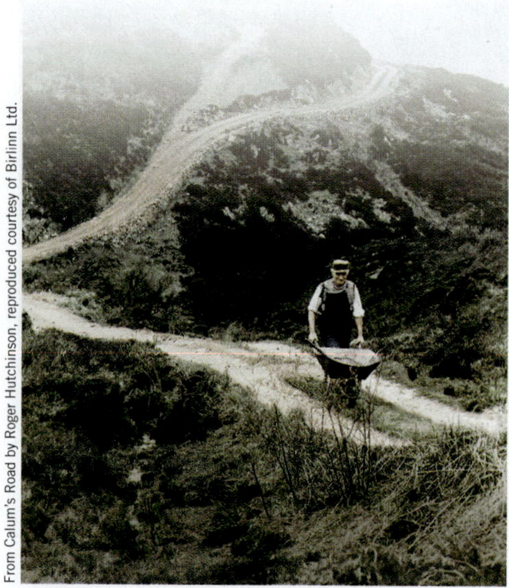

Calum's road: What grit can accomplish
Having spent his life on the Scottish island of Raasay, farming a small patch of land, tending its lighthouse, and fishing, Malcolm ("Calum") MacLeod (1911–1988) felt anguished. His local government repeatedly refused to build a road that would enable vehicles to reach his north end of the island. With the once-flourishing population there having dwindled to two—MacLeod and his wife—he responded with heroic determination. One spring morning in 1964, MacLeod, then in his fifties, gathered an ax, a chopper, a shovel, and a wheelbarrow. By hand, he began to transform the existing footpath into a 1.75-mile road (Miers, 2009).

"With a road," a former neighbor explained, "he hoped new generations of people would return to the north end of Raasay," restoring its culture (Hutchinson, 2006). Day after day he worked through rough hillsides, along hazardous cliff faces, and over peat bogs. Finally, 10 years later, he completed his supreme achievement. The road, which the government has since surfaced, remains a visible example of what vision plus determined grit can accomplish. It bids us each to ponder: What "roads"—what achievements—might we, with sustained effort, build in the years before us?

INTRINSIC AND EXTRINSIC MOTIVATION

Although intelligence is distributed like a *bell-shaped curve* (with the scores of most people of similar ability clustered together in the middle), achievements are not. This tells us that achievement involves much more than raw ability. That is why it pays to know how best to engage people's motivations to achieve. Promising people a reward for an enjoyable task can backfire. Excessive rewards can destroy **intrinsic motivation**—the desire to perform a behavior effectively for its own sake. In experiments, rewarding children with toys or candy for reading shortens the time they spend reading (Marinak & Gambrell, 2008). It is as if they think, "If I have to be bribed into doing this, it must not be worth doing!"

To sense the difference between intrinsic motivation and **extrinsic motivation** (behaving in certain ways that gain external rewards or avoid threatened punishment), think about your experience in this course. Like most students, you probably want to earn a high grade. But what motivates your actions to achieve your goal? Do you feel pressured to finish this reading before a deadline? Are you worried about your grade? Eager for the credits that will count toward graduation? If *Yes,* then you are extrinsically motivated (as, to some extent, all students must be). Do you also find the material interesting? Does learning it make you feel more competent? If there were no grade at stake, might you be curious enough to want to learn the material for its own sake? If *Yes,* intrinsic motivation also fuels your efforts.

People who focus on their work's meaning and significance not only do better work but ultimately earn more extrinsic rewards (Wrzesniewski et al., 2014). Kids with greater-than-average academic intrinsic motivation—who love learning for its own sake—go on to perform better in school, take more challenging classes, and earn more advanced degrees (Fan &

Williams, 2018; Gottfried et al., 2006). Extrinsic rewards work well when people perform tasks that don't naturally inspire complex, creative thinking (Hewett & Conway, 2015). They're also effective when used to signal a job well done (rather than to bribe or control someone) (Boggiano et al., 1985)."Most improved player" awards, for example, can boost feelings of competence and increase enjoyment of a sport. When applied correctly, rewards can improve performance and spark creativity (Eisenberger & Aselage, 2009; Henderlong & Lepper, 2002). And the rewards that often follow academic achievement, such as access to scholarships and a variety of jobs, can have long-lasting benefits.

HOW CAN WE MOTIVATE PERSONAL SUCCESS?

Organizational psychologists seek ways to engage and motivate ordinary people doing ordinary jobs (see Appendix B: Psychology at Work). Indeed, each of us can adopt some research-based strategies for achieving our goals:

1. ***Do make that resolution.*** Challenging goals motivate achievement (Harkin et al., 2016). Concrete goals—"finish that psychology paper by Tuesday"—direct attention and motivate persistence.
2. ***Announce the goals to friends and family.*** We're more likely to follow through after making a public commitment.
3. ***Develop an action plan.*** Be specific about when, where, and how you'll progress toward your goal. People who flesh out goals with detailed plans become more focused and more likely to succeed (Gollwitzer & Oettingen, 2012). Better to center on small steps—the day's running goal, say—than to fantasize about the marathon.
4. ***Create short-term rewards that support long-term goals.*** Although delayed rewards motivate us to set goals, immediate rewards best predict our persistence toward them (Woolley & Fishbach, 2017).
5. ***Monitor and record progress.*** If striving for more exercise, use a wearable fitness tracker such as a Fitbit. And it's even more motivating when progress is shared with others rather than kept secret (Harkin et al., 2016).
6. ***Create a supportive environment.*** When trying to eat healthily, keep junk food out of the cupboards. Decrease portion sizes. When focusing on a project, hole up in the library. When sleeping, stash the phone. Such "situational self-control strategies" prevent tempting impulses (Duckworth et al., 2016).
7. ***Transform the hard-to-do behavior into a must-do habit.*** Habits form when we repeat behaviors in a given context (Chapter 6). As our behavior becomes linked with the context, our next experience of that context prompts our habitual response. Forming "beneficial habits" increases self-control, which helps us connect our resolutions with positive outcomes (Galla & Duckworth, 2015). Do something every day for about two months and see it become an ingrained habit.

To achieve important life goals, we often know what to do. We *know* that a full night's sleep boosts our alertness, energy, and mood. We *know* that exercise lessens depression and anxiety, builds muscle, and strengthens our heart and mind. We *know* that what we put into our body—junk food or balanced nutrition, addictive substances or clean air—affects our health and life expectancy. Sometimes it's hard to stay motivated. But we can achieve our goals by taking these seven steps—resolving, announcing, planning, rewarding, monitoring, controlling, and persistently acting.

IMPROVE YOUR EVERYDAY LIFE

What goal would you like to achieve? How might you use the seven strategies offered in this section to meet that goal?

RETRIEVE & REMEMBER

ANSWERS IN APPENDIX E

8. What have researchers found to be an even better predictor of school performance than intelligence test scores?

Emotion: Arousal, Behavior, and Cognition

LOQ 9-8 What are the three parts of an emotion, and what theories help us to understand our emotions?

Motivated behavior is often connected to powerful emotions. My [DM's] own need to belong was unforgettably disrupted one day when I went to a huge store and brought along Peter, my toddler first-born child. As I set Peter down on his feet for a moment so I could do some paperwork, a passerby warned, "You'd better be careful or you'll lose that boy!" Not more than a few breaths later, I turned and found no Peter beside me. With mild anxiety, I looked around one end of the store aisle. No Peter in sight. With slightly more anxiety, I peered around the other side. No Peter there, either. Now, with my heart pounding, I circled the neighboring counters. Still no Peter anywhere.

Courtesy of David Myers

grit in psychology, passion and perseverance in the pursuit of long-term goals.

intrinsic motivation the desire to perform a behavior well for its own sake.

extrinsic motivation the desire to perform a behavior to receive promised rewards or avoid threatened punishment.

As anxiety turned to panic, I began racing up and down the store aisles. He was nowhere to be found. Seeing my alarm, the store manager used the public-address system to ask customers to assist in looking for a missing child. Soon after, I passed the customer who had warned me. "I told you that you were going to lose him!" he now scolded. With visions of kidnapping (strangers routinely admired that beautiful child), I braced for the possibility that my neglect had caused me to lose what I loved above all else, and — dread of all dreads — that I might have to return home and face my wife without our only child. Never before or since have I felt such panic.

But then, as I passed the customer service counter yet again, there he was, having been found and returned by some obliging customer! In an instant, the arousal of terror spilled into ecstasy. Clutching my son, with tears suddenly flowing, I found myself unable to speak my thanks and stumbled out of the store awash in grateful joy.

Where do such emotions come from? Why do we have them? What are they made of? Emotions don't exist just to give us interesting experiences. They are our body's adaptive response, supporting our survival. When we face challenges, emotions focus our attention and energize our action (Cyders & Smith, 2008). Our heart races. Our pace quickens. All our senses go on high alert. Receiving unexpected good news, we may find our eyes tearing up. We raise our hands in triumph. We feel joy and a newfound confidence.

As my panicked search for Peter illustrates, **emotions** are a mix of

- *bodily arousal* (heart pounding),
- *expressive behaviors* (quickened pace), and
- *conscious experience* (Is this a kidnapping?) *and feelings* (fear, panic, joy).

The puzzle for psychologists is fitting these three pieces together. To do that, we need answers to two big questions:

1. A chicken-and-egg debate: Does your bodily arousal come *before* or *after* your emotional feelings? (Did I first notice my racing heart and faster step, and then feel terror about losing Peter? Or did my sense of fear come first, stirring my heart and legs to respond?)
2. How do *thinking* (cognition) and *feeling* interact? Does cognition always come before emotion? (Did I think about a kidnapping threat before I reacted emotionally?)

Early theories of emotion, as well as current research, have tried to answer these questions. The psychological study of emotion began with the first question: How do bodily responses relate to emotions? Two of the earliest emotion theories offered different answers.

JAMES-LANGE THEORY: AROUSAL COMES BEFORE EMOTION

Common sense tells most of us that we cry because we are sad, lash out because we are angry, tremble because we are afraid. But to psychologist William James, an early explorer of human feelings, this commonsense view of emotion had things backward. Rather, "We feel sorry because we cry, angry because we strike, afraid because we tremble" (1890, p. 1066). James' idea was also proposed by Danish physiologist Carl Lange, and so is called the **James-Lange theory.** James and Lange would have guessed that I noticed my racing heart and then, shaking with fright, felt the whoosh of emotion — that my feeling of fear *followed* my body's response.

CANNON-BARD THEORY: AROUSAL AND EMOTION HAPPEN AT THE SAME TIME

Physiologist Walter Cannon (1871–1945) disagreed with James and Lange. Does a racing heart signal fear, anger, or love? The body's responses — heart rate, perspiration, and body temperature — are too similar to *cause* the different emotions, said Cannon. He and another physiologist, Philip Bard, concluded that our bodily responses and experienced emotions occur simultaneously. So, according to the **Cannon-Bard theory,** my heart began pounding *as* I experienced fear. The emotion-triggering stimulus traveled to my sympathetic nervous system, causing my body's arousal. *At the same time,* it traveled to my brain's cortex, causing my awareness of my emotion. My pounding heart did not cause my feeling of fear, nor did my feeling of fear cause my pounding heart. Bodily responses and experienced emotions are separate.

But are they really independent of each other? The Cannon-Bard theory has been challenged by studies of people with severed spinal cords, including a survey of 25 injured World War II soldiers (Hohmann, 1966). Those with *lower-spine injuries,* who had lost sensation only in their legs, reported little change in their emotions' intensity. Those with *high spinal cord injury,* who could feel nothing below the neck, did report changes. Some reactions were much less intense than before the injuries. Anger, one man with a high spinal cord injury confessed, "just

MATT SULLIVAN/REUTERS/Newscom

Joy expressed is joy felt According to the James-Lange theory, we don't just smile because we share our teammates' joy. We also share the joy because we are smiling with them.

doesn't have the heat to it that it used to. It's a mental kind of anger." Other emotions, those expressed mostly in body areas above the neck, were felt *more* intensely. These men reported increases in weeping, lumps in the throat, and getting choked up when saying goodbye, worshipping, or watching a touching movie. Such evidence has led some researchers to view feelings as "mostly shadows" of our bodily responses and behaviors (Damasio, 2003).

But our emotions also involve cognition (Averill, 1993; Barrett, 2006, 2017). Here we arrive at psychology's second big emotion question: How do thinking and feeling interact? Whether we fear the man behind us on a dark street depends entirely on whether or not we interpret his actions as threatening.

SCHACHTER-SINGER TWO-FACTOR THEORY: AROUSAL + LABEL = EMOTION

Stanley Schachter and Jerome Singer (1962) demonstrated that how we *appraise* (interpret) our experiences also matters. Our physical reactions and our thoughts (perceptions, memories, and interpretations) together create emotion. In their **two-factor theory,** emotions therefore have two ingredients: *physical arousal* and *cognitive appraisal*. An emotional experience, they argued, requires a conscious interpretation of arousal.

Sometimes our arousal spills over from one event to the next, influencing our response. Imagine arriving home after a fast run and finding a message that you got a longed-for job. With arousal lingering from the run, will you feel more excited than you would be if you heard this news after staying awake all night studying?

To explore this *spillover effect*, Schachter and Singer injected college men with the hormone *epinephrine*, which triggers feelings of arousal. But the trickster researchers told one group of men that the drug would just help test their eyesight. Picture yourself as a participant. After receiving the injection, you go to a waiting room. You find yourself with another person (actually someone working with the experimenters) who is acting either joyful or irritated. As you observe this accomplice, you begin to feel your heart race, your body flush, and your breathing become more rapid. If you had been in the group who were told to expect these effects from the injection, what would you feel? In the actual experiment, these volunteers felt little emotion—because they correctly assumed their arousal was caused by the drug. But if you had been told the injection would help assess your eyesight, what would you feel? Perhaps you would react as this group of participants did. They "caught" the apparent emotion of the other person in the waiting room. They became happy if the accomplice was acting joyful, and testy if the accomplice was acting irritated.

We can experience a stirred-up state as one emotion or another, depending on how we interpret and label it. Dozens of experiments have demonstrated this effect, and it continues to influence modern emotion research (MacCormack & Lindquist, 2016; Reisenzein, 1983; Sinclair et al., 1994). As one happiness researcher noted, "Feelings that one interprets as fear in the presence of a sheer drop may be interpreted as lust in the presence of a sheer blouse" (Gilbert, 2006).

The point to remember: Arousal fuels emotion; cognition channels it.

OLEG POPOV/REUTERS/Newscom

The spillover effect Arousal from a soccer match can fuel anger, which can descend into rioting or other violent confrontations.

LaunchPad For a 4-minute demonstration of the relationship between arousal and cognition, see the *Video: Emotion = Arousal Plus Interpretation.*

ZAJONC, LEDOUX, AND LAZARUS: EMOTION AND THE TWO-TRACK BRAIN

Is the heart always subject to the mind? Must we *always* interpret our arousal before we can experience an emotion? No, said Robert Zajonc [ZI-yence] (1923–2008). He argued that we actually have many emotional reactions apart from, or even before, our interpretation of a situation (1980, 1984). Can you recall liking something or someone immediately, without knowing why? These reactions often reflect the automatic processing that takes place in our two-track mind.

Our emotional responses are the final step in a process that can follow two different pathways in our brain, both via the thalamus. Some emotions, especially our more complex feelings, like hatred and love, travel a "high road" to the brain's cortex (**FIGURE 9.7a**). There, we analyze and label information before we order a response via the amygdala.

emotion a response of the whole organism, involving (1) bodily arousal, (2) expressive behaviors, and (3) conscious experience.

James-Lange theory the theory that our experience of emotion occurs when we become aware of our physiological responses to an emotion-arousing stimulus.

Cannon-Bard theory the theory that an emotion-arousing stimulus simultaneously triggers (1) physiological responses and (2) the subjective experience of emotion.

two-factor theory Schachter and Singer's theory that to experience emotion we must (1) be physically aroused and (2) cognitively label the arousal.

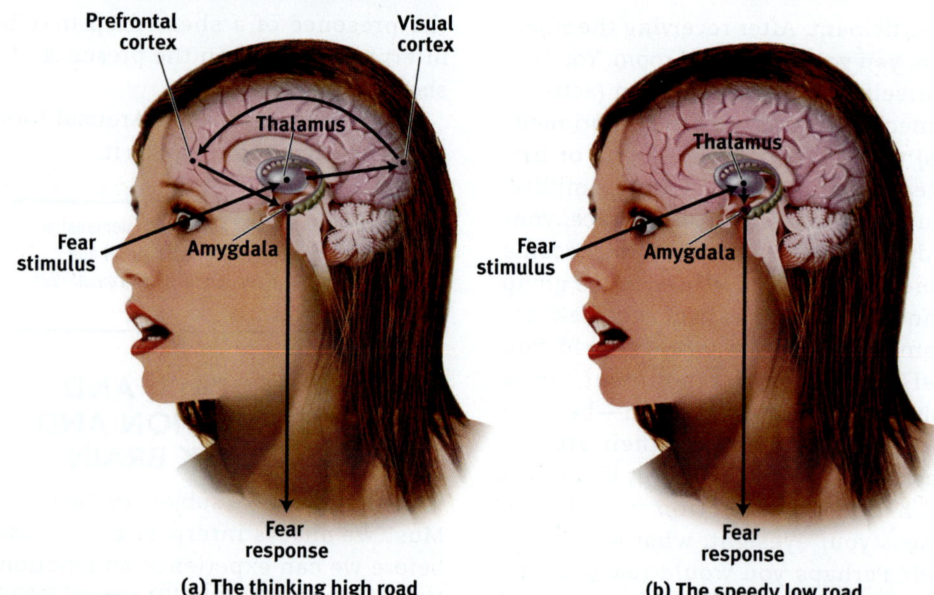

FIGURE 9.7 The brain's pathways for emotions The two-track brain processes sensory input on two different pathways. (a) Some input travels to the cortex (via the thalamus) for analysis and is then sent to the amygdala. (b) Other input travels directly to the amygdala (via the thalamus) for an instant emotional reaction.

But sometimes our emotions (especially simple likes, dislikes, and fears) take what Joseph LeDoux (2002, 2015) has called the more direct "low road." This neural shortcut bypasses the cortex (Figure 9.7b). Following the low road, a fear-provoking stimulus travels from the eye or the ear directly to the amygdala. This shortcut enables our greased-lightning emotional response (*Life in danger!*) before our brain interprets the exact source of danger. Like speedy reflexes (that also operate separately from the brain's thinking cortex), the amygdala's reactions are so fast that we may not be aware of what's happened (Dimberg et al., 2000). A conscious fear experience then occurs as we become aware that our brain has detected danger (LeDoux & Brown, 2017).

The amygdala's structure makes it easier for our feelings to hijack our thinking than for our thinking to rule our feelings (LeDoux & Armony, 1999). It sends more neural projections up to the cortex than it receives back. In the forest, we can jump when we hear rustling in nearby bushes and leave it to our cortex (via the high road) to decide later whether the sound was made by a snake or by the wind. Such experiences support Zajonc's and LeDoux's belief that *some* of our emotional reactions involve no deliberate thinking.

Emotion researcher Richard Lazarus (1991, 1998) agreed that our brain processes vast amounts of information without our conscious awareness, and that some emotional responses do not require *conscious* thinking. Much of our emotional life operates via the automatic, speedy low road. But he wondered: How would we *know* what we are reacting to if we did not in some way appraise the situation? The appraisal may be effortless and we may not be conscious of it, but it is still a mental function. To know whether a stimulus is good or bad, the brain must have some idea of what it is (Storbeck et al., 2006). Thus, said Lazarus, emotions arise when we *appraise* an event as harmless or dangerous. We appraise the sound of the rustling bushes as the presence of a threat. Then we learn that it was "just the wind."

Let's sum up (see also **TABLE 9.3**). As Zajonc and LeDoux have demonstrated, some simple emotional responses involve no conscious thinking. When I [ND] see a big spider trapped behind glass, I experience fear, even though I *know* the spider can't hurt me. Such responses are difficult to alter by changing our thinking. Within a fraction of a second, we may automatically perceive one person as more likable or trustworthy than another (Willis & Todorov, 2006). This instant appeal can even influence our political decisions if we vote (as many people do) for the candidate we *like* over the candidate expressing positions closer to our own (Westen, 2007).

TABLE 9.3 Summary of Emotion Theories

Theory	Explanation of Emotions	Example
James-Lange	Our awareness of our specific bodily responses to emotion-arousing stimuli.	We observe our heart racing after a threat and then feel afraid.
Cannon-Bard	Bodily responses and simultaneous subjective experience.	Our heart races at the same time that we feel afraid.
Schachter-Singer Two-Factor	Two factors: general arousal and a conscious cognitive label.	We may interpret our arousal as fear or excitement, depending on the context.
Zajonc's; LeDoux's	Some embodied responses happen instantly, without conscious appraisal.	We automatically feel startled by a sound in the forest before labeling it as a threat.
Lazarus'	Cognitive appraisal ("Is it dangerous or not?")—sometimes without our awareness—defines emotion.	The sound is "just the wind."

But other emotions—including depressive moods and complex feelings, like hatred and love—are greatly affected by our interpretations, memories, and expectations. For these emotions, we have more conscious control. When we feel emotionally overwhelmed, we can change our interpretations (Gross, 2013). Such *reappraisal* often reduces distress and the corresponding amygdala response (Buhle et al., 2014; Denny et al., 2015). Reappraisal of stress not only reduces worry, it also helps students achieve higher exam scores (Jamieson et al., 2016). So don't stress about your stress. Embrace it, and approach your next exam with this mindset: "Stress evolved to help maintain my focus and solve problems."

RETRIEVE & REMEMBER

ANSWERS IN APPENDIX E

9. According to the Cannon-Bard theory, (a) our *physiological response* to a stimulus (for example, a pounding heart), and (b) the *emotion we experience* (for example, fear) occur ___________ (simultaneously/sequentially). According to the James-Lange theory, (a) and (b) occur ___________ (simultaneously/sequentially).
10. According to Schachter and Singer, two factors lead to our experience of an emotion: (a) physiological arousal and (b) ___________ appraisal.
11. Emotion researchers have disagreed about whether emotional responses occur in the absence of cognitive processing. How would you characterize the approach of each of the following researchers: Zajonc, LeDoux, Lazarus, Schachter, and Singer?

Embodied Emotion

Whether you are falling in love or grieving a loved one's death, you need little convincing that emotions involve the body. Feeling without a body is like breathing without lungs. Some physical responses are easy to notice; others happen without your awareness. Indeed, many take place at the level of your brain's neurons.

THE BASIC EMOTIONS

LOQ 9-9 What are some basic emotions?

When surveyed, most emotion scientists agreed that anger, fear, disgust, sadness, and happiness are basic human emotions (Ekman, 2016). Carroll Izard (1977) isolated 10 basic emotions: joy, interest-excitement, surprise, sadness, anger, disgust, contempt, fear, shame, and guilt. Most are present in infancy (**FIGURE 9.8**). Other researchers believe that pride and love are also basic emotions (Shaver et al., 1996; Tracey & Robins, 2004). But Izard has argued that they are combinations of the basic 10, with love, for example, being a mixture of joy and interest-excitement. Do our different emotions have distinct arousal footprints? (In other words, does our body know the difference between fear and anger?) Before answering that question, let's review what happens in your autonomic nervous system when your body becomes aroused.

EMOTIONS AND THE AUTONOMIC NERVOUS SYSTEM

LOQ 9-10 What is the link between emotional arousal and the autonomic nervous system?

As we saw in Chapter 2, in a crisis, the *sympathetic division* of your *autonomic nervous system (ANS)* mobilizes your body for action (**FIGURE 9.9**). It triggers your adrenal glands to release stress hormones. To provide energy, your liver pours extra sugar into your bloodstream.

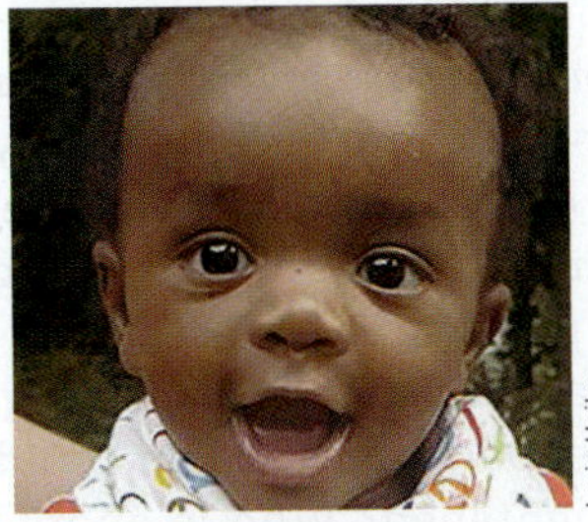

Lorie Hailey

(a) Joy (mouth forming smile, cheeks lifted, twinkle in eye)

Patrick Donehue/Science Source

(b) Anger (brows drawn together and downward, eyes fixed, mouth squarish)

© Emma Kim/cultura/Corbis

(c) Interest (brows raised or knitted, mouth softly rounded, lips may be pursed)

FIGURE 9.8 Some naturally occurring infant emotions To identify the emotions generally present in infancy, Carroll Izard analyzed the facial expressions of infants.

lina aidukaite/Getty Images

(d) Disgust (nose wrinkled, upper lip raised, tongue pushed outward)

Samuel Borges Photography/Shutterstock

(e) Surprise (brows raised, eyes widened, mouth rounded in oval shape)

bendao/Getty Images

(f) Sadness (brows' inner corners raised, mouth corners drawn down)

Vladimir Godnik/Getty Images

(g) Fear (brows level, drawn in and up, eyelids lifted, mouth corners retracted)

Autonomic Nervous System Controls Physiological Arousal

Sympathetic division (arousing)		Parasympathetic division (calming)
Pupils open wider	EYES	Pupils get smaller
Decreases	SALIVATION	Increases
Perspires	SKIN	Dries
Increases	RESPIRATION	Decreases
Speeds up	HEART	Slows
Slows	DIGESTION	Speeds up
Increased stress hormones	ADRENAL GLANDS	Decreased stress hormones
Reduced	IMMUNE SYSTEM FUNCTIONING	Enhanced

FIGURE 9.9 Emotional arousal In a crisis, the autonomic nervous system's sympathetic system arouses us. When the danger passes, the parasympathetic division calms us.

To help burn the sugar, your breathing rate increases to supply needed oxygen. Your heart rate and blood pressure increase. Your digestion slows, allowing blood to move away from your internal organs and toward your muscles. With blood sugar driven into the large muscles, running becomes easier. Your pupils open wider, letting in more light. To cool your stirred-up body, you perspire. If you were wounded, your blood would clot more quickly.

After your next crisis, think of this: Without any conscious effort, your body's response to danger is wonderfully coordinated and adaptive—preparing you for *fight* or *flight*. When the crisis passes, the *parasympathetic division* of your ANS gradually calms your body, as stress hormones slowly leave your bloodstream.

IN YOUR EVERYDAY LIFE

Can you think of a recent time when you noticed your body's reactions to an emotionally charged situation, such as a tense social setting, or perhaps before an important test or game? How would you describe your sympathetic nervous system's responses?

LaunchPad To review and then check your understanding of the ANS in action, engage online with *Concept Practice: The Autonomic Nervous System.*

THE PHYSIOLOGY OF EMOTIONS

LOQ 9-11 How do our body states relate to specific emotions?

Imagine conducting an experiment, measuring the body's responses to different emotions. In each room, participants watch one of four movies: a horror film, an anger-provoking film, a sexually arousing film, or an utterly boring movie. From the control center, you are tracking participants' physical responses, measuring perspiration, pupil size, breathing, and heart rate. Do you think you could tell who is frightened? Who is angry? Who is sexually aroused? Who is bored?

With training, you could probably pick out the bored viewer. But spotting the bodily differences among fear, anger, and sexual arousal would be much more difficult (Siegel et al., 2018). Different emotions can share common biological signatures.

"No one ever told me that grief felt so much like fear. I am not afraid, but the sensation is like being afraid. The same fluttering in the stomach, the same restlessness, the yawning. I keep on swallowing." —C. S. Lewis, *A Grief Observed*, 1961

Despite similar bodily responses, sexual arousal, fear, and anger *feel* different to us, and they often *look* different to others. We may appear "paralyzed with fear" or "ready to explode."

With the help of sophisticated laboratory tools, researchers have pinpointed some subtle indicators of different emotions (Lench et al., 2011). The finger temperatures and hormone secretions that accompany fear do sometimes differ from those that accompany rage (Ax, 1953; Levenson, 1992). When guppies get grumpy, their eye color changes from silver to black (Heathcote et al., 2018). Fear and joy stimulate different facial muscles. When fearful, your brow muscles tense. When joyful, muscles in your cheeks and under your eyes pull into a smile (Witvliet & Vrana, 1995).

Brain scans and EEGs reveal that some emotions also have distinct brain circuits (Dixon et al., 2017; Panksepp, 2007). When you experience negative emotions such as disgust, your right frontal cortex is more active than your left frontal cortex. People who are prone to depression, or who have generally negative perspectives, also show more activity in their right frontal lobe (Harmon-Jones et al., 2002).

Thinking Critically About:

Lie Detection

LOQ 9-12 How effective are polygraphs in using body states to detect lies?

Polygraphs measure emotion-linked autonomic arousal, as reflected in changed breathing, heart rate, and perspiration. Can we use these results to detect lies?

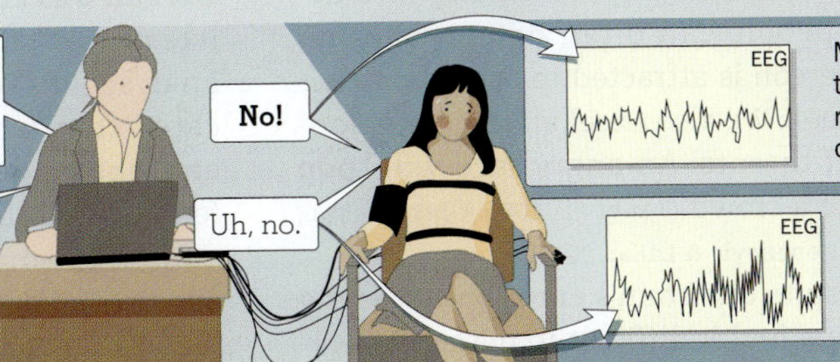

In the last 20 years, have you ever taken something that didn't belong to you?
No!
Did you ever steal anything from your previous employer?
Uh, no.
EEG
EEG

Many people tell a little white lie in response to this *control question*, prompting elevated arousal readings that give the examiner a baseline for comparing responses to other questions.

This person shows greater arousal in response to the *critical question* than she did to the control question, so the examiner may infer she is lying.

But is it true that *only a thief* becomes nervous when denying a theft?

1. We have similar bodily arousal in response to anxiety, irritation, and guilt. So, is she really guilty, or just anxious?
2. **Many innocent people do get tense and nervous when accused of a bad act.** (Many rape victims, for example, have "failed" these tests because they had strong emotional reactions while telling the truth about the rapist.[1])

About one-third of the time, polygraph test results are ***just wrong***.[2]

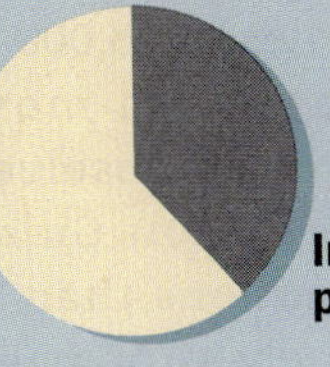

Judged innocent by polygraph — Judged guilty by polygraph

If these polygraph experts had been the judges, more than one-third of the innocent would have been declared guilty, and nearly one-fourth of the guilty would have gone free.

The CIA and other U.S. agencies have spent millions of dollars testing tens of thousands of employees. Yet the U.S. National Academy of Sciences (2002) has reported that "no spy has ever been caught [by] using the polygraph."

***The Concealed Information Test* is more effective**. Innocent people are seldom wrongly judged to be lying.

Questions focus on specific crime-scene details known only to the police and the guilty person.[3] (If a camera and computer had been stolen, for example, only a guilty person should react strongly to the brand names of the stolen items.)

1. Lykken, 1991. 2. Kleinmuntz & Szucko, 1984. 3. Ben-Shakhar & Elaad, 2003; Verschuere & Meijer, 2014; Vrij & Fisher, 2016.

Scary thrills Intense, happy excitement and panicky fear involve similar physiological arousal, which allows us to flip rapidly between the two emotions.

Gary Dobner/Alamy

One not-unhappy wife reported that her husband, who had lost part of his right frontal lobe in brain surgery, became less irritable and more affectionate (Goleman, 1995). My [DM's] father, after a right-hemisphere stroke at age 92, lived the last two years of his life with happy gratitude and nary a complaint or negative emotion.

When you experience positive moods—when you are enthusiastic, energized, and happy—your left frontal lobe will be more active. Increased left frontal lobe activity is found in people with positive personalities—from jolly infants to alert, energetic, and persistently goal-directed adults (Davidson & Begley, 2012; Urry et al., 2004). When you're happy and you know it, your brain will surely show it.

To sum up, we can't easily see differences in emotions from tracking heart rate, breathing, and perspiration. But facial expressions and brain activity can vary from one emotion to another. So do we, like Pinocchio, give off telltale signs when we lie? Can a so-called *lie detector*—a **polygraph**—reveal lies? For more on that question, see Thinking Critically About: Lie Detection.

polygraph a machine often used in attempts to detect lies that measures emotion-linked changes in perspiration, heart rate, and breathing.

RETRIEVE & REMEMBER

ANSWERS IN APPENDIX E

12. How do the two divisions of the autonomic nervous system affect our emotional responses?

LaunchPad To see how skilled you are at lie detection, visit *Topic Tutorial: PsychSim6, Catching Liars.*

Expressed and Experienced Emotion

Expressive behavior implies emotion. Dolphins, with smiles seemingly plastered on their faces, appear happy. To decipher people's emotions we read their body language, listen to their voice tones, and study their faces. Does this nonverbal language vary with culture, or is it the same everywhere? And do our expressions influence what we feel?

DETECTING EMOTION IN OTHERS

LOQ 9-13 How do we communicate nonverbally? How do women and men differ in these abilities?

All of us communicate without words. Westerners "read" a firm handshake as evidence of an outgoing, expressive personality (Chaplin et al., 2000). A glance can communicate intimacy, while darting eyes may signal anxiety (Kleinke, 1986; Perkins et al., 2012). Passionate love typically drives people to spend time—lots of time—gazing into each other's eyes (Bolmont et al., 2014; Rubin, 1970). Would such gazes stir loving feelings between strangers? To find out, researchers asked male-female (and presumed heterosexual) pairs of strangers to gaze intently for 2 minutes either at each other's hands or into each other's eyes. After separating, the eye gazers reported feeling a tingle of attraction and affection (Kellerman et al., 1989).

Our brain is an amazing detector of subtle expressions, helping most of us read nonverbal cues fairly well. We are adept at detecting a hint of a smile (Maher et al., 2014). Shown 10 seconds of video from the end of a speed-dating interaction, people can often detect whether one person is attracted to the other (Place et al., 2009). We also excel at detecting nonverbal threats. An angry face will "pop out" of a crowd (Fox et al., 2000; Öhman et al., 2001; Stjepanovic & LaBar, 2018).

Despite our brain's emotion-detecting skill, we find it difficult to detect deceiving expressions. The behavioral differences between liars and truth tellers are too slight for most of us to detect (Hartwig & Bond, 2011). One summary of many studies of sorting truth from lies found that people were just 54 percent accurate—barely better than a coin toss (Bond & DePaulo, 2006). Are experts more skilled at spotting lies? No. Virtually no one—save perhaps police professionals in high-stakes situations—beats chance by much, not even when detecting children's lies (Gongola et al., 2017; O'Sullivan et al., 2009; ten Brinke et al., 2016).

Some of us more than others are skilled at reading emotions. In one study, people named the emotion displayed in brief film clips. The clips showed portions of a person's emotionally expressive face or body, sometimes accompanied by a garbled voice (Rosenthal et al., 1979). For example, one 2-second scene—a "thin slice" of behavior—revealed only the face of an upset woman. After watching the scene, viewers stated whether the woman was criticizing someone for being late or was talking about her divorce. An analysis of 176 "thin slice" studies indicated that women outperform men at emotion detection (Hall et al., 2016). The female advantage emerges early in development. Female infants, children, and adolescents have outperformed males in many studies (McClure, 2000).

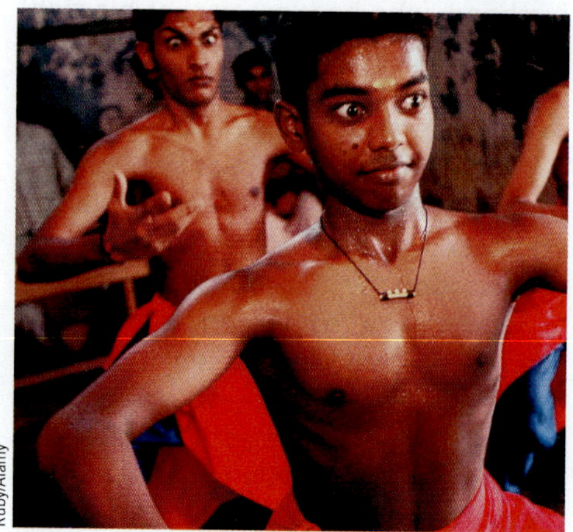

Ruby/Alamy

A silent language of emotion Hindu classic dance uses the face and body to effectively convey 10 different emotions (Hejmadi et al., 2000).

Women's skill at decoding emotions may help explain why women tend to respond with and express greater emotion, especially positive emotions (Fischer & LaFrance, 2015; McDuff et al., 2017). In studies of 23,000 people from 26 cultures, women more than men have reported themselves open to feelings (Costa et al., 2001). Girls also express stronger emotions than boys do, hence the extremely strong perception (nearly all 18- to 29-year-old Americans in one survey) that emotionality is "more true of women" (Chaplin & Aldao, 2013; Newport, 2001).

One exception: Quickly—imagine an angry face. What gender is the person? If you're like 3 in 4 Arizona State University students, you imagined a male (Becker et al., 2007). And when a gender-neutral face was made to look angry, most people perceived it as male. If the face was smiling, they were more likely to perceive it as female (**FIGURE 9.10**). Anger strikes most people as a more masculine emotion.

Are there gender differences in empathy? If you have *empathy,* you identify with others. You consider things from their point of view. You imagine being in their skin. You appraise a situation as they do, rejoicing with those who rejoice and weeping with those who weep (Wondra & Ellsworth, 2015). In surveys, women are far more likely than men to describe themselves as empathic. But measures of body responses, such as one's heart rate while seeing another's distress, reveal a much smaller gender gap (Eisenberg & Lennon, 1983; Rueckert et al., 2010).

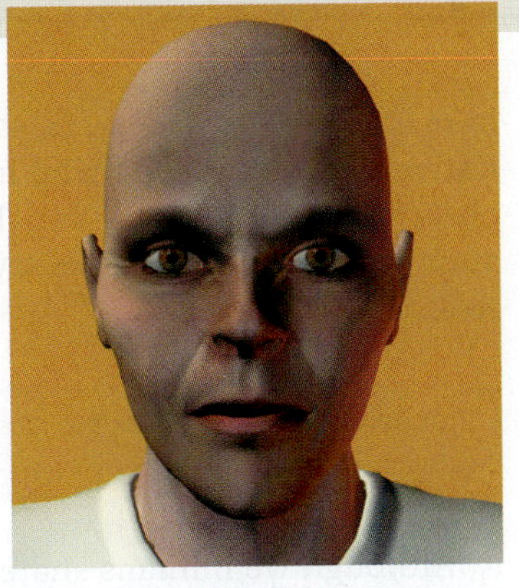

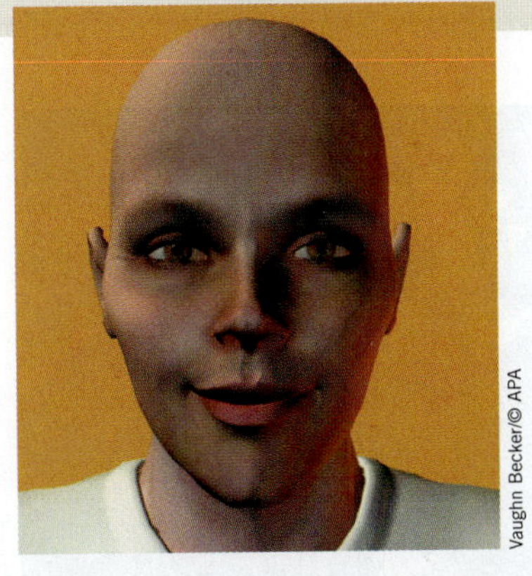

Vaughn Becker/© APA

FIGURE 9.10 Male or female? Researchers manipulated a gender-neutral face. People were more likely to see the face as male when it wore an angry expression and as female when it wore a smile (Becker et al., 2007).

Nevertheless, females are also more likely to *express* empathy—to display more emotion when observing others' emotions. As **FIGURE 9.11** shows, this gender difference was clear when men and women watched film clips that were sad (children with a dying parent), happy (slapstick comedy), or frightening (a man nearly falling off the ledge of a tall building) (Kring & Gordon, 1998; Vigil, 2009). Women also more deeply experience upsetting emotional events, such as viewing pictures of mutilations. (Brain scans show more activity in areas sensitive to emotion.) Women tend to remember the scenes better three weeks later, too (Canli et al., 2002).

RETRIEVE & REMEMBER

ANSWERS IN APPENDIX E

13. __________ (Women/Men) report experiencing emotions more deeply, and they tend to be more adept at reading nonverbal behavior.

CULTURE AND EMOTION

LOQ 9-14 How are gestures and facial expressions of emotion understood within and across cultures?

The meaning of *gestures* varies from culture to culture. U.S. President Richard Nixon learned this while traveling in Brazil. He made the North American "A-OK" sign before a welcoming crowd, not knowing it was a crude insult in that country. In 1968, North Korea publicized photos of supposedly happy officers from a captured U.S. Navy spy ship. In the photo, three men had raised their middle fingers, telling their captors—who didn't recognize the cultural gesture—it was a "Hawaiian good luck sign" (Fleming & Scott, 1991).

Do *facial expressions* also have different meanings in different cultures? To find out, researchers showed photographs of some facial expressions to people in different parts of the world and asked them to guess the emotion (Ekman, 1994, 2016; Ekman & Friesen, 1975; Ekman et al., 1987; Izard, 1977, 1994). You can try this matching task yourself by pairing the six emotions with the six faces in **FIGURE 9.12.**

Regardless of your cultural background, you probably did pretty well. A smile's a smile the world around. Ditto for laughter and sadness. (People around the world can discriminate real from fake laughs [Bryant et al., 2018].) Other emotional expressions are less universally recognized (Crivelli et al., 2016a; Jack et al., 2012). But there is no culture where people frown when they are happy. We do slightly better when judging emotional displays from our own culture (Crivelli et al., 2016b; Elfenbein & Ambady, 2002; Laukka et al., 2016). Nevertheless, the outward signs of emotion are generally the same across cultures.

Do these shared emotional categories reflect shared *cultural* experiences, such as movies and TV programs that are seen around the world? Apparently not. Paul Ekman and Wallace Friesen (1971) asked isolated people in New Guinea to respond to such statements as, "Pretend your child has died." When North American undergraduates viewed the recorded responses, they easily read the New Guineans' facial reactions.

So we can say that facial muscles speak a fairly universal language. This discovery would not have surprised Charles Darwin (1809–1882). In *The Expression of the Emotions in Man and*

"Now, that wasn't so hard, was it?"

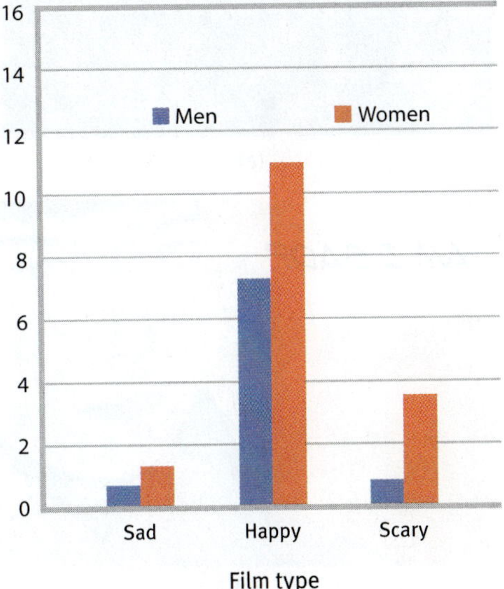

FIGURE 9.11 Gender and expressiveness Male and female film viewers did not differ dramatically in self-reported emotions or physiological responses. But the women's faces *showed* much more emotion. (Data from Kring & Gordon, 1998.)

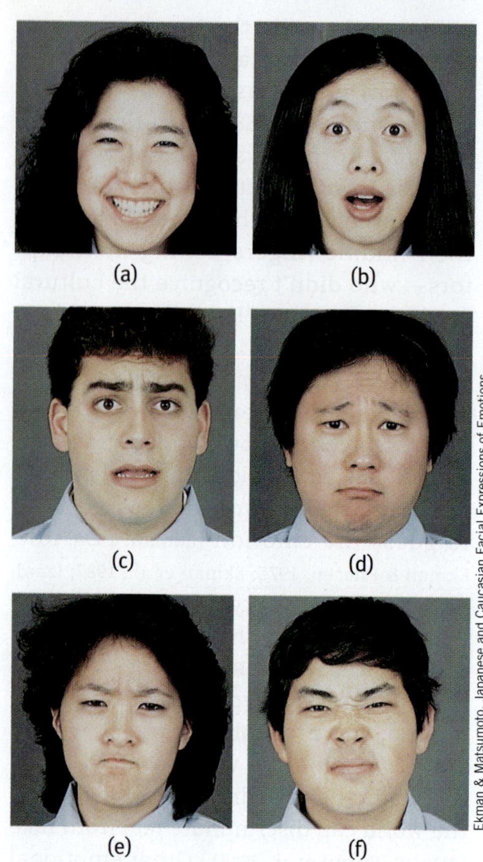

Ekman & Matsumoto, Japanese and Caucasian Facial Expressions of Emotions

FIGURE 9.12 Culture-specific or culturally universal expressions? As people of differing cultures, do our faces speak differing languages? Which face expresses disgust? Anger? Fear? Happiness? Sadness? Surprise?[2] (From Matsumoto & Ekman, 1989.)

Animals (1872), Darwin argued that in prehistoric times, before our ancestors communicated in words, they communicated threats, greetings, and submission with facial expressions. Such expressions helped them survive and became part of our shared heritage (Hess & Thibault, 2009). A sneer, for example, retains elements of an animal's baring its teeth in a snarl. Emotional expressions may enhance our survival in other ways, too. Surprise raises our eyebrows and widens our eyes, helping us take in more information. Disgust wrinkles our nose, closing out foul odors.

Scott Olson/Getty Images

Universal emotions No matter where on Earth you live, you have no trouble recognizing the joy experienced by Chicago Cubs fans over their 2016 World Series victory following a 108-year wait.

Smiles are social as well as emotional events. Olympic gold medalists typically don't smile when they are awaiting their award ceremony. But they wear broad grins when interacting with officials and when facing the crowd and cameras (Fernández-Dols & Ruiz-Belda, 1995). Even natively blind athletes, who have never observed smiles, display social smiles in such situations (Matsumoto & Willingham, 2006, 2009).

> "For news of the heart, ask the face."
> —Guinean proverb

Although we humans share a universal facial language for some emotions, it has been adaptive for us to interpret faces in particular contexts (**FIGURE 9.13**). People judge an angry face set in a frightening situation as afraid, and a fearful face set in a painful situation as pained (Carroll & Russell, 1996). Movie directors harness this tendency by creating scenes and soundtracks that amplify our perceptions of particular emotions.

Smiles are also cultural events, with *display rules* on how *much* emotion to express. In the United States, people of

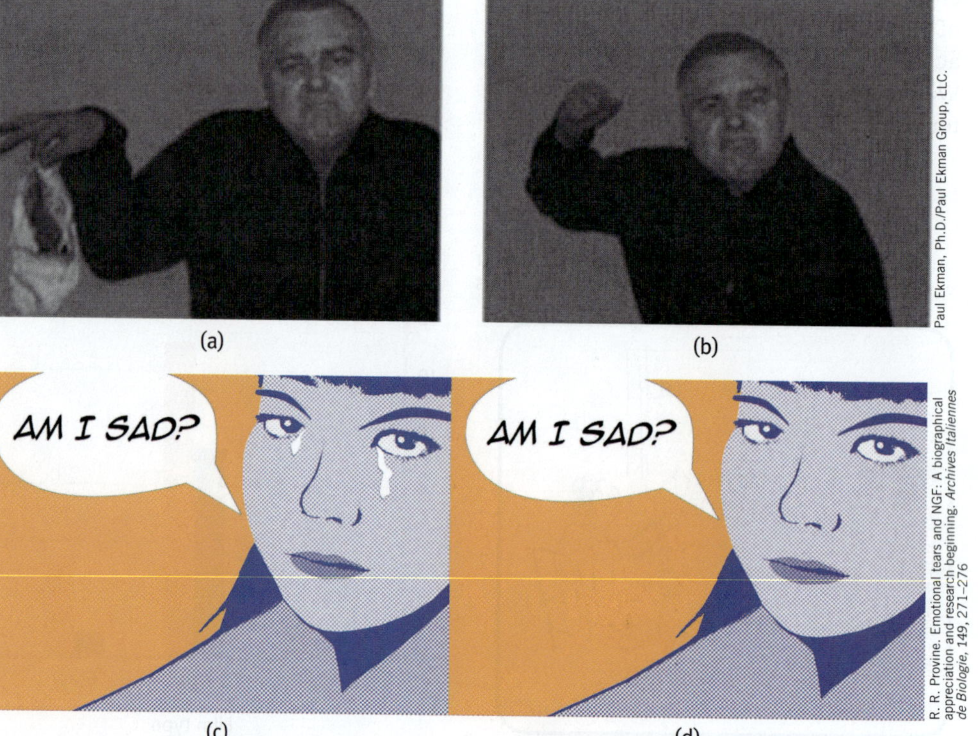

Paul Ekman, Ph.D./Paul Ekman Group, LLC.

R. R. Provine. Emotional tears and NGF: A biographical appreciation and research beginning. *Archives Italiennes de Biologie*, 149, 271–276

FIGURE 9.13 We read faces in context Whether we perceive the man as (a) disgusted or (b) angry depends on which body his face appears on (Aviezer et al., 2008). Tears on a woman's face in (c) make her expression seem sadder than in (d) (Provine et al., 2009).

[2] (a) happiness, (b) surprise, (c) fear, (d) sadness, (e) anger, (f) disgust.

FIGURE 9.14 Culture and smiling Former U.S. Vice President Joe Biden's broad smile and Chinese President Xi Jinping's more reserved one illustrate a cultural difference in facial expressiveness.

European descent tend to display excitement; in China, people are more likely to emphasize calmness (Tsai et al., 2006). These cultural differences shape facial expressiveness (Tsai et al., 2016). Compared with their counterparts in China, where calmness is emphasized, European-American leaders express broad smiles over six times more frequently in their official photos (**FIGURE 9.14**). If we're happy and we know it, our culture will surely teach us how to show it.

RETRIEVE & REMEMBER

ANSWERS IN APPENDIX E

14. Are people more likely to differ culturally in their interpretations of facial expressions, or of gestures?

LaunchPad For a 4-minute demonstration of our universal facial language, see the *Video: Emotions and Facial Expression.*

THE EFFECTS OF FACIAL EXPRESSIONS

LOQ 9-15 How do facial expressions influence our feelings?

As famed psychologist William James (1890) struggled with feelings of depression and grief, he came to believe that we can control our emotions by going "through the outward movements" of any emotion we want to experience. "To feel cheerful," he advised, "sit up cheerfully, look around cheerfully, and act as if cheerfulness were already there."

Was James right? Can our outward expressions and movements trigger our inner feelings and emotions? You can test his idea: Fake a big grin. Now scowl. Can you feel the "smile therapy" difference? Participants in dozens of experiments have felt a difference. For example, researchers tricked students into making a frowning expression by asking them to contract certain muscles and to pull their brows together (Laird, 1974, 1984; Laird & Lacasse, 2014). (The students thought they were helping the researchers attach facial electrodes.) The result? The students reported feeling a little angry.

So, too, for other basic emotions. For example, people reported feeling more fear than anger, disgust, or sadness when made to construct a fearful expression (Duclos et al., 1989). (They were told, "Raise your eyebrows. And open your eyes wide. Move your whole head back, so that your chin is tucked in a little bit, and let your mouth relax and hang open a little.") This **facial feedback effect** has been found many times, in many places, for many basic emotions (**FIGURE 9.15**).

facial feedback effect the tendency of facial muscle states to trigger corresponding feelings such as fear, anger, or happiness.

Just activating one of the smiling muscles by holding a pen in the teeth (rather than gently between the lips, which produces a neutral expression) makes stressful situations less upsetting (Kraft & Pressman, 2012). When happy we smile, and when smiling we become happier (unless we're distracted by being videoed [Marsh et al., 2019; Noah et al., 2018; Strack, 2016]).

So, your face is more than a billboard that displays your feelings; it also feeds your feelings. Scowl and the whole world scowls back. No wonder some depressed patients reportedly feel better after between-the-eyebrows Botox injections

RETRIEVE & REMEMBER

ANSWERS IN APPENDIX E

FIGURE 9.15 How to make people smile without telling them to smile Do as Kazuo Mori and Hideko Mori (2009) did with students in Japan: Attach rubber bands to the sides of the face with adhesive bandages, and then run them either over the head or under the chin.

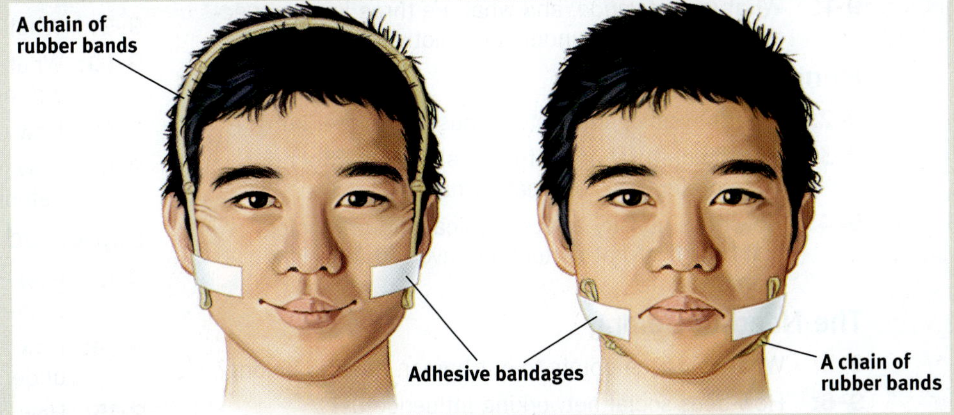

15. (a) Based on the *facial feedback effect,* how might students report feeling when the rubber bands raise their cheeks as though in a smile? (b) How might students report feeling when the rubber bands pull their cheeks downward?

that freeze their frown muscles (Parsaik et al., 2016). Botox paralysis of the frowning muscles also slows people's reading of sadness- or anger-related sentences, and it slows activity in emotion-related brain circuits (Havas et al., 2010; Hennenlotter et al., 2008). The opposite happens when Botox paralyzes laughter muscles: People feel more depressed (Lewis, 2018).

Other studies have noted a similar *behavior feedback effect* (Carney et al., 2015; Flack, 2006). Try it. Walk for a few minutes with short, shuffling steps, keeping your eyes downcast. Now walk around taking long strides, with your arms swinging and your eyes looking straight ahead. Can you feel your mood shift? Or when angry, lean back in a reclined sitting position and feel the anger lessen (Krahé et al., 2018). Going through the motions awakens the emotions.

You can use your understanding of feedback effects to become more empathic—to feel what others feel. See what happens if you let your own face mimic another person's expression. Acting as another acts helps us feel what another feels (Vaughn & Lanzetta, 1981). Indeed, natural mimicry of others' emotions helps explain why emotions are contagious (Dimberg et al., 2000; Neumann & Strack, 2000; Peters & Kashima, 2015). Positive, upbeat Facebook posts create a ripple effect, leading Facebook friends to also express more positive emotions (Kramer, 2012).

IMPROVE YOUR EVERYDAY LIFE

Imagine a situation in which you would like to change the way you feel. How could you do so by altering your facial expressions or the way you carry yourself? In what other settings could you apply your knowledge of these feedback effects?

* * *

We have seen how our motivated behaviors, triggered by the forces of nature and nurture, often go hand in hand with emotional responses. Our psychological emotions likewise come equipped with physical reactions. Nervous about an upcoming date, we feel stomach butterflies. Anxious over public speaking, we head for the bathroom. Smoldering over a family conflict, we get a splitting headache. Negative emotions and the prolonged high arousal that may accompany them can tax the body and harm our health. You'll hear more about this in Chapter 10. In that chapter, we'll also take a closer look at the emotion of happiness.

CHAPTER 9 REVIEW Motivation and Emotion

LEARNING OBJECTIVES

TEST YOURSELF Answer these repeated Learning Objective Questions on your own (before checking the answers in Appendix D) to improve your retention of the concepts (McDaniel et al., 2009, 2015).

Motivational Concepts

9-1: What is *motivation,* and what are three key perspectives that help us understand motivated behaviors?

Hunger

9-2: What physiological factors cause us to feel hungry?

9-3: How do cultural and situational factors affect our taste preferences and eating habits?

9-4: How does obesity affect physical and psychological health? What factors are involved in weight management?

The Need to Belong

9-5: What evidence points to our human need to belong?

9-6: How does social networking influence us?

Achievement Motivation

9-7: What is *achievement motivation,* and what are some ways to encourage achievement?

Emotion: Arousal, Behavior, and Cognition

9-8: What are the three parts of an emotion, and what theories help us to understand our emotions?

Embodied Emotion

9-9: What are some basic emotions?

9-10: What is the link between emotional arousal and the autonomic nervous system?

9-11: How do our body states relate to specific emotions?

9-12: How effective are polygraphs in using body states to detect lies?

Expressed and Experienced Emotion

9-13: How do we communicate nonverbally? How do women and men differ in these abilities?

9-14: How are gestures and facial expressions of emotion understood within and across cultures?

9-15: How do facial expressions influence our feelings?

TERMS AND CONCEPTS TO REMEMBER

TEST YOURSELF Write down the definition in your own words, then check your answer.

motivation, *p.* 249
drive-reduction theory, *p.* 249
physiological need, *p.* 249
homeostasis, *p.* 249
incentive, *p.* 249
Yerkes-Dodson law, *p.* 249
hierarchy of needs, *p.* 249
glucose, *p.* 251
set point, *p.* 253
basal metabolic rate, *p.* 253
obesity, *p.* 253
need to belong, *p.* 255
self-determination theory, *p.* 257
ostracism, *p.* 257
narcissism, *p.* 259
achievement motivation, *p.* 259
grit, *p.* 261
intrinsic motivation, *p.* 261
extrinsic motivation, *p.* 261
emotion, *p.* 263
James-Lange theory, *p.* 263
Cannon-Bard theory, *p.* 263
two-factor theory, *p.* 263
polygraph, *p.* 267
facial feedback effect, *p.* 271

CHAPTER TEST

TEST YOURSELF Answer the following questions on your own first, then check your answers in Appendix E.

1. An example of a physiological need is ________. An example of a psychological drive is ________.
   a. hunger; a "push" to find food
   b. a "push" to find food; hunger
   c. curiosity; a "push" to reduce arousal
   d. a "push" to reduce arousal; curiosity
2. Danielle walks into a friend's kitchen, smells cookies baking, and begins to feel very hungry. The smell of baking cookies is a(n) ________ (incentive/drive).
3. ________ theory attempts to explain behaviors that do NOT reduce physiological needs.
4. With a challenging task, such as taking a difficult exam, performance is likely to peak when arousal is
   a. very high.
   b. moderate.
   c. very low.
   d. absent.
5. According to Maslow's hierarchy of needs, our most basic needs are physiological, including the need for food and water; just above these are ________ needs.
   a. safety
   b. self-esteem
   c. belongingness
   d. self-transcendence
6. Journalist Dorothy Dix once remarked, "Nobody wants to kiss when they are hungry." Which motivation theory best supports her statement?
7. According to the concept of ________ point, our body maintains itself at a particular weight level.
8. Which of the following is a genetically predisposed response to food?
   a. An aversion to eating cats and dogs
   b. An interest in novel foods
   c. A preference for sweet and salty foods
   d. An aversion to carbohydrates
9. Blood sugar provides the body with energy. When it is ________ (low/high), we feel hungry.
10. The rate at which your body expends energy while at rest is referred to as the ________ ________ rate.
11. Obese people often struggle to lose weight permanently. This is due to several factors, including the fact that
    a. it takes more energy to maintain weight than it did to gain it.
    b. the set point of obese people is lower than average.
    c. with dieting, metabolism increases.
    d. there is a genetic influence on body weight.
12. Sanjay eats a diet high in processed foods, fat, and sugar. He knows he may gain weight, but he figures it's no big deal because he can simply lose it in the future. How would you evaluate Sanjay's plan?
13. Which of the following is NOT evidence supporting the view that humans are strongly motivated by a need to belong?
    a. Students who rated themselves as "very happy" also tended to have satisfying close relationships.
    b. Social exclusion—such as exile or solitary confinement—is considered a severe form of punishment.
    c. As adults, adopted children tend to resemble their biological parents.
    d. Children who are extremely neglected become withdrawn, frightened, and sometimes even speechless.

14. What are some ways to manage our social networking time successfully?

15. If we want to increase our chance of success in achieving a new goal, such as stopping smoking, we ________ (should/should not) announce the goal publicly, and we ________ (should/should not) share with others our progress toward achieving that goal.

16. The ________-________ theory of emotion maintains that our emotional experience occurs after our awareness of a physiological response.

17. Assume that after returning from an hour-long run, you receive a letter saying that your scholarship application has been approved. The two-factor theory of emotion would predict that your physical arousal will

a. weaken your happiness.

b. intensify your happiness.

c. transform your happiness into relief.

d. have no particular effect on your happiness.

18. Zajonc and LeDoux have maintained that some emotional reactions occur before we have had the chance to consciously label or interpret them. Lazarus noted the importance of how we appraise events. These psychologists differ in the emphasis they place on ________ in emotional responses.

a. physical arousal

b. the hormone epinephrine

c. cognitive processing

d. learning

19. What does a polygraph measure, and why are its results questionable?

20. When people are induced to assume fearful expressions, they often report feeling some fear. This response is known as the ________ ________ effect.

21. Aiden has a bad cold and finds himself shuffling to class with his head down. How might his posture (as well as his cold) affect his emotional well-being?

Continue testing yourself with **LearningCurve** or **Achieve Read & Practice** to learn and remember most effectively.

Disability Images/Huntstock, Inc.

CHAPTER 10

Stress, Health, and Human Flourishing

For many students, the transition to college (or back to college) is not easy. College is a happy time, but it presents challenges. Debt piles up. Deadlines loom. New relationships form, and sometimes fail. Family demands continue. Big exams or class presentations make you tense. You become glued to social media, fearful of missing important social opportunities. Stuck in traffic, late to class or work, your mood may turn sour. It's enough to give you a headache or disrupt your sleep. No wonder 8 in 10 Americans say they frequently or sometimes experience stress in their daily lives (Saad, 2017).

Other times, major stressful events strike without warning. Imagine being 21-year-old Ben Carpenter on the world's wildest and fastest wheelchair ride. As he crossed an intersection on a sunny summer afternoon in 2007, the light changed. A large truck, whose driver didn't see him, moved into the intersection. As they bumped, Ben's wheelchair handles got stuck in the truck's grille. Off they went, the driver unable to hear Ben's cries for help. As Ben clutched his wheelchair, his heart raced, his hands sweated, and his breathing sped up. His mind tried to cope with the loss of control.

They sped down the highway about an hour from my [DM's] home. Passing motorists caught the bizarre sight of a truck pushing a wheelchair at 50 miles per hour and started calling 911. (The first caller: "You are not going to believe this. There is a semitruck pushing a guy in a wheelchair on Red Arrow highway!") Lucky for Ben, one passerby was an undercover police officer. Pulling a quick U-turn, he followed the truck to its destination a couple of miles from where the wild ride had started, and informed the disbelieving driver that he had a passenger hooked in his grille. "It was very scary," said Ben.

Stress can sometimes be extreme, as Ben experienced. But life transitions and everyday stressors, like the ones you might experience as a student, produce similar (though weaker) physical and psychological responses. And, as we will see, all stress — from the catastrophic to the everyday — can harm our health.

In this chapter we explore stress — what it is, how it affects us, and how we can reduce it. Then we'll take a close look at happiness — an important measure of whether we are flourishing. Let's begin with some basic terms.

Stress: Some Basic Concepts

Learning Objective Question LOQ 10-1

How does our appraisal of an event affect our stress reaction, and what are the three main types of stressors?

Stress is a slippery concept. In everyday life, we may use the word to describe threats or challenges ("Ben was under a lot of stress") or to describe our responses to those events ("Ben experienced acute stress"). Psychologists use more precise terms. The challenge or event (Ben's terrifying truck ride) is a *stressor*. Ben's physical and emotional responses are a *stress reaction*. And the process by which he interprets the threat is *stress*.

Thus, **stress** is the process of appraising an event as threatening or challenging, and responding to it (Lazarus, 1998). If you have prepared for an important math test, you may welcome it as a challenge. You will be aroused and focused, and you will probably do well (**FIGURE 10.1**).

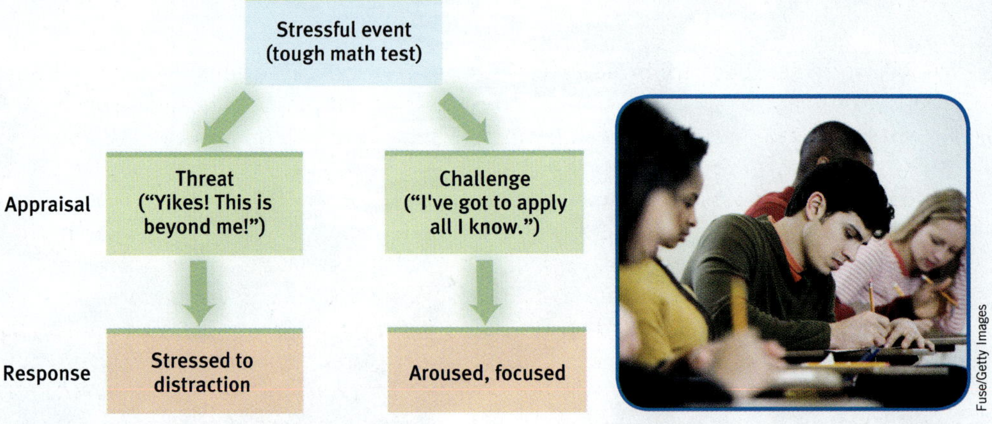

FIGURE 10.1 Stress appraisal The events of our lives flow through a psychological filter. How we appraise an event influences how much stress we experience and how effectively we respond.

Championship athletes, successful entertainers, motivated students, and great teachers and leaders all thrive and excel when aroused by a challenge (Blascovich & Mendes, 2010; Wang et al., 2015a).

Stressors that we appraise as threats, not challenges, can instead lead to strong negative reactions. If prevented from preparing for your math test, you will appraise the test as a threat, and your response will be distress.

What is your perceived stress level? Take the self-test in **FIGURE 10.2** to find out. (Worried about your stress levels?

Perceived Stress Scale

The questions in this scale ask about your feelings and thoughts *during the last month.* In each case, indicate how often you felt or thought a certain way.

0	1	2	3	4
Never	**Almost never**	**Sometimes**	**Fairly often**	**Very often**

In the last month...

1. ___ ...how often have you been upset because of something that happened unexpectedly?
2. ___ ...how often have you felt that you were unable to control the important things in your life?
3. ___ ...how often have you felt nervous and "stressed"?
4. ___ ...how often have you felt confident about your ability to handle your personal problems?
5. ___ ...how often have you felt that things were going your way?
6. ___ ...how often have you found that you could not cope with all the things you had to do?
7. ___ ...how often have you been able to control irritations in your life?
8. ___ ...how often have you felt that you were on top of things?
9. ___ ...how often have you been angered because of things that were outside of your control?
10. ___ ...how often have you felt difficulties were piling up so high that you could not overcome them?

SCORING:

- First, reverse your scores for questions 4, 5, 7, and 8. On these four questions, change the scores like this: 0 = 4, 1 = 3, 2 = 2, 3 = 1, 4 = 0.
- Next, add up your scores to get a **total score**.
- Scores range from 0 to 40, with higher scores indicating higher perceived stress.
- Scores ranging from 0-13 would be considered *low perceived stress.*
- Scores ranging from 14-26 would be considered *moderate perceived stress.*
- Scores ranging from 27-40 would be considered *high perceived stress.*

Scale data from Cohen, S., Kamarck, T., Mermelstein, R. (1983). A global measure of perceived stress. *Journal of Health and Social Behavior, 24,* 385-396.

FIGURE 10.2 Perceived Stress Scale

We will consider ways to reduce stress later in this chapter.)

Extreme or prolonged stress can harm us. Stress can trigger risky decisions and unhealthy behaviors (Cohen et al., 2016; Starcke & Brand, 2016). Pregnant women with overactive stress systems tend to have shorter pregnancies, which pose health risks for their infants (Guardino et al., 2016). Demanding jobs that mentally exhaust workers also risk their physical health (Huang et al., 2010).

So there is an interplay between our head and our health. Before we explore that interplay, let's take a closer look at types of stressors and stress reactions.

STRESSORS—THINGS THAT PUSH OUR BUTTONS

Stressors fall into three main types: catastrophes, significant life changes, and daily hassles (including social stress). All can be toxic—they can increase our risk of disease and death.

Catastrophes

Catastrophes are large-scale disasters such as earthquakes, floods, wildfires, and storms. Even though we often give aid and comfort to one another after such events, the damage to emotional and physical health is significant. In surveys taken in the three weeks after the 9/11 terrorist attacks, for example, 58 percent of Americans said they were experiencing greater than average arousal and anxiety (Silver et al., 2002). And those who watched a lot of 9/11 television footage had worse health outcomes two to three years later (Silver et al., 2013). The 2011 terrorist attacks in Norway triggered a similar uptick in health issues, from heart problems to suicides (Strand et al., 2016).

Significant Life Changes

During catastrophes, misery often has company. But during significant life changes, we may experience stress alone. Even happy life changes, such as graduating from college or marrying the love of your life, can be stressful. So can other personal events—leaving home, having a loved one die, taking on student debt, losing a job, or getting divorced. Many life changes happen during young adulthood. The stress of those years was clear in a survey that asked, "Are you trying to take on too many things at once?" Who reported the highest stress levels? Women and younger adults (APA, 2009). About half of people in their twenties, but only one-fifth of those over 65, reported experiencing stress during "a lot of the day yesterday" (Newport & Pelham, 2009).

How does stress related to life changes affect our health? Long-term studies indicate that people recently widowed, fired, or divorced are more disease-prone (Dohrenwend et al., 1982; Sbarra et al., 2015; Strully, 2009). In one study of 96,000 widowed people, their risk of death doubled in the week following their partner's death (Kaprio et al., 1987). Experiencing a cluster of crises (perhaps losing a job and an important relationship while falling behind in schoolwork) puts one even more at risk.

Daily Hassles

Events don't have to remake our lives to cause stress. Stress also comes from *daily hassles*—dead cell phones, lost keys, irritating housemates, and too many things to do (Lazarus, 1990; Pascoe & Richman, 2009; Ruffin, 1993). When daily stressful feelings linger, they often predict poor physical health years later (Leger et al., 2018).

Some people simply shrug off such hassles. Others find them hard to ignore. This is especially the case for those who wake up each day facing housing problems, unreliable child care, budgets that won't stretch to the next payday, and poor health. Poverty and inequality can likewise take a toll on physical and mental well-being (Piazza et al., 2013; Sapolsky, 2018; Sin et al., 2015). Prejudice-related stress, like other stress, can harm our psychological and physical health (Benner et al., 2018; Pascoe & Richman, 2009). Many transgender and gender nonconforming people experience stress due to stigma and discrimination (Valentine & Shipherd, 2019). People with a same-sex sexual orientation who face frequent prejudice in their communities die, on average, 12 years sooner than do those who live in more accepting communities (Hatzenbueler et al., 2014).

Scott Olson/Getty Images

A hurricane of stress and destruction Unpredictable large-scale events trigger significant levels of stress-related ills. Hurricane Michael raged across northern Florida in 2018, killing at least 43 people and destroying thousands of homes and other structures. My [ND's] in-laws experienced the devastation first-hand, losing their home and other possessions. When an earthquake struck Los Angeles in 1994, sudden-death heart attacks increased fivefold. Most occurred in the first two hours after the quake and near its center and were unrelated to physical exertion (Muller & Verrier, 1996).

STRESS REACTIONS—FROM ALARM TO EXHAUSTION

LOQ 10-2 How does the body respond to stress?

Our response to stress is part of a unified mind-body system. Walter Cannon (1929) first realized this in the 1920s. He found that extreme cold, lack of oxygen, and emotion-arousing events all trigger an outpouring of stress hormones from the adrenal glands. When your brain sounds an alarm, your *sympathetic nervous system* (Chapter 2) responds. It increases your heart rate and respiration, diverts blood from your digestive

stress the process by which we perceive and respond to certain events, called *stressors*, that we appraise as threatening or challenging.

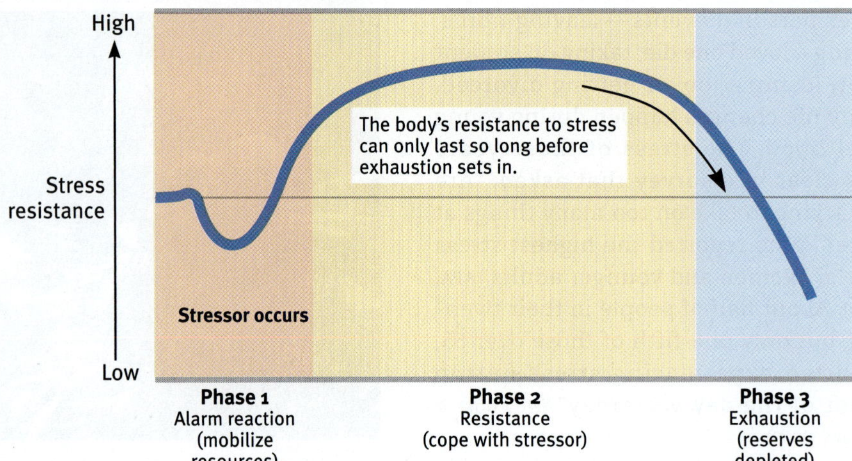

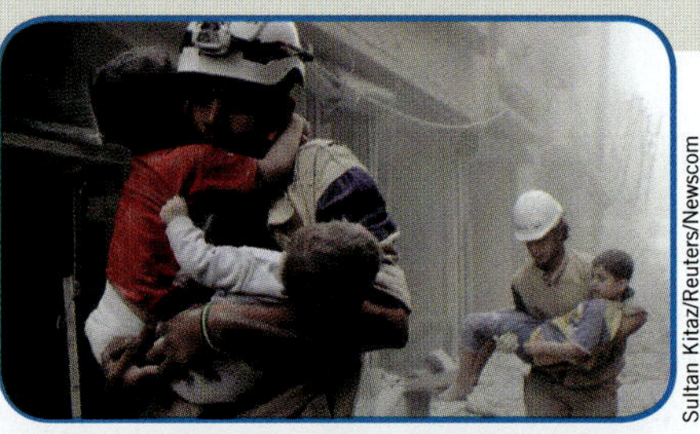

Sultan Kitaz/Reuters/Newscom

Sebastiano Tomada/Getty Images

FIGURE 10.3 Selye's general adaptation syndrome Due to the ongoing conflict, Syria's White Helmets (volunteer rescuers) are perpetually in "alarm reaction" mode, rushing to pull victims from the rubble after each fresh attack. As their resistance depletes, they risk exhaustion.

organs to your skeletal muscles, dulls your feeling of pain, and releases sugar and fat from your body's stores. All this prepares your body for the wonderfully adaptive **fight-or-flight response** (see Figure 9.9 in Chapter 9). The sympathetic nervous system helps more with immediate threats (a poisonous snake nearby) than with distant threats (future climate change). By fighting or fleeing, we increase our chances of survival.

Hans Selye (1936, 1976) extended Cannon's findings. His studies of animals' reactions to various stressors, such as electric shock and surgery, helped make stress a major concept in both psychology and medicine. Selye discovered that the body's adaptive response to stress was so general that it was like a single burglar alarm that sounds, no matter what intrudes. He named this response the **general adaptation syndrome (GAS),** and he saw it as a three-stage process. Here's how those stages, or phases, might look if you suffered a physical or emotional trauma:

- In *Phase 1,* you have an ***alarm reaction,*** as your sympathetic nervous system suddenly activates. Your heart rate soars. Blood races to your skeletal muscles. You feel the faintness of shock.
- During *Phase 2,* ***resistance,*** your temperature, blood pressure, and respiration remain high. With your resources mobilized, you are ready to resist the trauma—to fight back. Your adrenal glands pump stress hormones into your bloodstream. You are fully engaged, summoning all your resources to meet the challenge.
- In *Phase 3,* constant stress causes ***exhaustion.*** As time passes, with no relief from stress, your reserves begin to run out. Your body copes well with temporary stress, but prolonged stress can damage it. You become more vulnerable to illness or even, in extreme cases, collapse and death.

Syria's civil war has taken a toll on the health of its refugees (Al Ibraheem et al., 2017; **FIGURE 10.3**). And former prisoners of war, who experienced constant stress and suffering, develop shorter *telomeres* protecting the chromosome ends. That may explain why, compared with noncaptive soldiers, former war prisoners tend to die sooner (Solomon et al., 2014, 2017).

We respond to stress in other ways, too. One response is common after a loved one's death: Withdraw. Pull back. Conserve energy. Faced with an extreme disaster, such as a car sinking in a body of water, some people become paralyzed by fear. They stay strapped in their seatbelt instead of swimming to safety. Another response, found often among women, is to give and receive support (Lim & DeSteno, 2016; Taylor, 2006; von Dawans et al., 2019). Perhaps you have participated in this **tend-and-befriend response** by contributing help after a natural disaster.

"We sleep afraid, we wake up afraid, and leave our homes afraid." —15-year-old girl's Facebook post, describing her family's daily life in war-torn Yemen (al-Asaadi, 2016)

Streeter Lecka/Getty Images

Friendly foes Olympic marathoners Kara Goucher and Shalane Flanagan are athletic rivals, but they also happen to be good friends. Tending and befriending helps them cope with the similar stressors they endure as professional athletes and perform their best. During the 2012 London Olympic Marathon, they battled intense rain and physical pain and finished within 1 second of each other.

FIGURE 10.4 A simplified view of immune responses Four types of cells fuel our immune system:

- *B lymphocytes* (white blood cells) release antibodies that fight bacterial infections.
- *T lymphocytes* (white blood cells) attack cancer cells, viruses, and foreign substances.
- *Macrophage cells* ("big eaters") identify, pursue, and ingest harmful invaders and worn-out cells.
- *Natural killer cells* (NK cells) attack diseased cells (such as those infected by viruses or cancer).

Intruders!
Romariolen/Shutterstock
Is it a bacterial infection?
Is it a cancer cell, virus, or other "foreign substance"?
Is it some other harmful intruder, or perhaps a worn-out cell needing to be cleaned up?
Are there diseased cells (such as those infected by viruses or cancer) that need to be cleared out?
Possible Responses:

Send in: *B lymphocytes,* which fight bacterial infections. (This one is shown in front of a macrophage.)

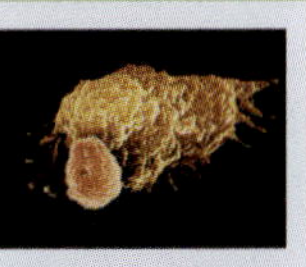
CNRI/Science Source

Send in: *T lymphocytes,* which attack cancer cells, viruses, and foreign substances.

NIBSC/Science Source

Send in: *macrophage cells* ("big eaters"), which attack harmful invaders and worn-out cells. (This one is engulfing tuberculosis bacteria.)

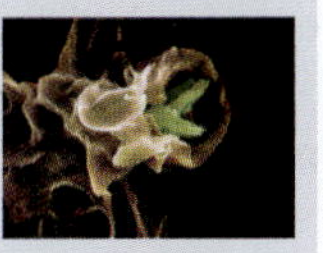
SPL/Science Source

Send in: *natural killer cells* (NK cells), which attack diseased cells. (These two are attacking a cancer cell.)

Eye of Science/ Science Source

It often pays to spend our physical and mental resources in fighting or fleeing an external threat. But we do so at a cost. When our stress is momentary, the cost is small. When stress persists, we may pay a much higher price: lowered resistance to infections and other threats to mental and physical health.

RETRIEVE & REMEMBER

ANSWERS IN APPENDIX E

1. The stress response system: When alerted to a negative, uncontrollable event, our ____________ nervous system arouses us. Heart rate and respiration ____________ (increase/decrease). Blood is diverted from digestion to the skeletal ____________. The body releases sugar and fat. All this prepares the body for the ____________-____________-____________ response.

Stress Effects and Health

LOQ 10-3 How does stress influence our immune system?

How do you try to stay healthy? Avoid sneezers? Get extra rest? Wash your hands? You should add stress management to that list. Why? Because, as we have seen throughout this text, everything psychological is also biological. Stress is no exception. Stress contributes to high blood pressure and headaches. Stress also leaves us less able to fight off disease. To manage stress, we need to understand these connections.

The field of **psychoneuroimmunology** studies our mind-body interactions (Kiecolt-Glaser, 2009; Kipnis, 2018). That mouthful of a word makes sense when said slowly. Your emotions *(psycho)* affect your brain *(neuro)*, which controls the endocrine hormones that influence your disease-fighting *immune* system. And this field is the study *(ology)* of those interactions. Let's start by focusing on the immune system.

Your immune system resembles a complex security system. When it functions properly, it keeps you healthy by capturing and destroying bacteria, viruses, and other invaders. Four types of cells carry out these search-and-destroy missions (**FIGURE 10.4**).

Your age, nutrition, genetics, body temperature, and stress all influence your immune system's activity. When your immune system doesn't function properly, it can err in two directions:

1. Responding too strongly, it may attack the body's own tissues, causing some forms of arthritis or an allergic reaction. Women have stronger immune systems than men do, making them less likely to get infections. But this very strength also puts women at higher risk for self-attacking diseases, such as lupus and multiple sclerosis (Nussinovitch & Schoenfeld, 2012; Schwartzman-Morris & Putterman, 2012).
2. Underreacting, the immune system may allow a bacterial infection to flare, a dormant herpes virus to erupt,

fight-or-flight response an emergency response, including activity of the sympathetic nervous system, that mobilizes energy and activity for attacking or escaping a threat.

general adaptation syndrome (GAS) Selye's concept of the body's adaptive response to stress in three stages—alarm, resistance, exhaustion.

tend-and-befriend response under stress, people (especially women) often provide support to others *(tend)* and bond with and seek support from others *(befriend)*.

psychoneuroimmunology the study of how psychological, neural, and endocrine processes combine to affect our immune system and health.

or cancer cells to multiply. Surgeons may deliberately suppress a patient's immune system to protect transplanted organs (which the body treats as foreign invaders).

A flood of stress hormones can also suppress the immune system. In laboratories, immune suppression appears when animals are stressed by physical restraints, unavoidable electric shocks, noise, crowding, cold water, social defeat, or separation from their mothers (Maier et al., 1994). In one such study, monkeys were housed with new roommates—three or four new monkeys—each month for six months (Cohen et al., 1992). If you know the stress of adjusting to even one new roommate, you can imagine how trying it would be to repeat this experience monthly. By the experiment's end, the socially stressed monkeys' immune systems were weaker than those of other monkeys left in stable groups.

Human immune systems react similarly. Three examples:

- ***Surgical wounds heal more slowly in stressed people.*** In one experiment, two groups of dental students received punch wounds (small holes punched in the skin). Punch-wound healing was 40 percent slower in the group wounded three days before a major exam than in the group wounded during summer vacation (Kiecolt-Glaser et al., 1998).
- ***Stressed people develop colds more readily.*** Researchers dropped a cold virus into people's noses (**FIGURE 10.5**). Among those living stress-filled lives, 47 percent developed colds. Among those living relatively free of stress, only 27 percent did (Cohen et al., 2003, 2006; Cohen & Pressman, 2006).
- ***Stress can speed the course of disease.*** As its name tells us, *AIDS (acquired immune deficiency syndrome)* is an immune disorder, caused by the *human immunodeficiency virus (HIV)*. Stress cannot give people AIDS. But an analysis of 33,252 participants from around the world found that stress and negative emotions sped the transition from HIV infection to AIDS. And stress predicted a faster decline in those with AIDS (Chida & Vedhara, 2009). The greater the stress that HIV-infected people experienced, the faster their disease progressed.

The stress effect on immunity makes sense. It takes energy to track down invaders, produce swelling, and maintain fevers (Maier et al., 1994). Stress hormones drain this energy away from the disease-fighting lymphocytes. When you are ill, your body demands less activity and more sleep, in part to cut back on the energy your muscles usually use. Stress does the opposite. During an aroused fight-or-flight reaction, your stress responses draw energy away from your disease-fighting immune system and send it to your muscles and brain (see Figure 9.9 in Chapter 9). This competing energy need leaves you more open to illness.

Those experiencing the stress of depression tend to age faster and die sooner (McIntosh & Relton, 2018). Even within twin pairs, the less happy one tends to die first (Saunders et al., 2018).

The bottom line: Stress gets under the skin. It does not make us sick. But it does reduce our immune system's ability to function, and that leaves us less able to fight infection.

Let's look now at how stress might affect cancer and heart disease.

RETRIEVE & REMEMBER

ANSWERS IN APPENDIX E

- 2. The field of ___________ studies mind-body interactions, including the effects of psychological, neural, and endocrine functioning on the immune system and overall health.
- 3. What general effect does stress have on our health?

STRESS AND CANCER

Stress does not create cancer cells. In a healthy, functioning immune system, lymphocytes, macrophages, and NK cells search out and destroy cancer cells and cancer-damaged cells. If stress weakens the immune system, might this weaken a person's ability to fight off cancer? To find out, researchers implanted tumor cells in rodents. Next, they exposed some of the rodents to uncontrollable stress (for example, inescapable shocks). Compared with their unstressed counterparts, the stressed rodents developed cancer more often, experienced tumor growth sooner, and grew larger tumors (Sklar & Anisman, 1981).

Does this stress-cancer link apply to humans? The results are generally the same (Lutgendorf & Andersen, 2015). Some studies have found that people are at increased risk for cancer within a year after experiencing significant stress or grief. In one large study, the risk of colon cancer was 5.5 times greater among people with a history of workplace stress

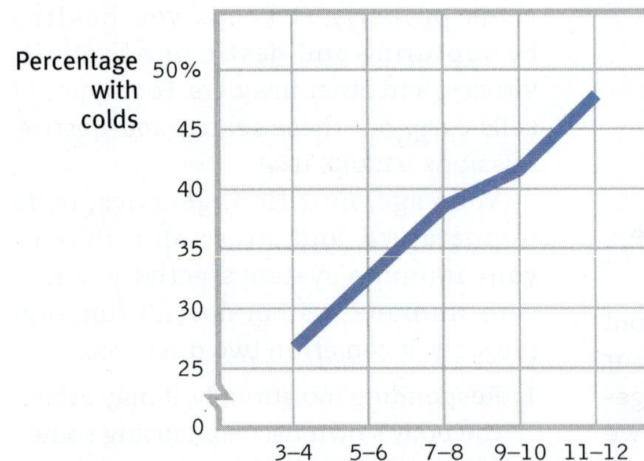

FIGURE 10.5 Stress and colds People with the highest life stress scores were also most vulnerable when exposed to an experimentally delivered cold virus (Cohen et al., 1991).

than among those who did not report such problems. The difference was not due to group differences in age, smoking, drinking, or physical characteristics (Courtney et al., 1993). But other studies have found no link between stress and human cancer risk (Edelman & Kidman, 1997; Fox, 1998; Petticrew et al., 1999, 2002). Concentration camp survivors and former prisoners of war, for example, do not have elevated cancer rates. Overstating the link between attitudes and cancer may lead some patients to blame themselves for their illness.

"I didn't give myself cancer." —Mayor Barbara Boggs Sigmund (1939–1990), Princeton, New Jersey

It's important enough to repeat: *Stress does not create cancer cells.* At worst, stress may affect their growth by weakening the body's natural defenses against multiplying cancer cells (Lutgendorf et al., 2008; Nausheen et al., 2010; Sood et al., 2010). Although a relaxed, hopeful state may enhance these defenses, we should be aware of the thin line that divides science from wishful thinking. For cancer patients who are depressed, treating the depression typically improves quality of life—but it does not increase survival rates (Mulick et al., 2018). The powerful biological processes at work in advanced cancer are not likely to be completely derailed by avoiding stress or maintaining a relaxed but determined spirit (Anderson, 2002).

LaunchPad For a 7-minute demonstration of the links between stress, cancer, and the immune system, see the *Video: Fighting Cancer—Mobilizing the Immune System.*

STRESS AND HEART DISEASE

LOQ 10-4 How does stress increase coronary heart disease risk?

Imagine a world where you wake up each day, eat your breakfast, and check the news. Among the headlines, you see that four 747 jumbo jet airplanes crashed again yesterday, killing another 1642 passengers. You finish your breakfast, grab your bag, and head out the door. It's just an average day.

Replace airplane crashes with **coronary heart disease,** the United States' leading cause of death, and you have reentered reality. About 630,000 Americans die annually from heart disease (CDC, 2017). In the amount of time it takes you to read this page (about 3 minutes), three Americans will die from a heart-disease event (Heron, 2018). Heart disease occurs when the blood vessels that nourish the heart muscle gradually close. High blood pressure and a family history of the disease increase the risk. So do smoking, obesity, an unhealthy diet, physical inactivity, and a high cholesterol level.

© PhotoSpin, Inc/Alamy

Stress and personality also play a big role in heart disease. The more psychological trauma people experience, the more their bodies generate *inflammation,* which is associated with heart and other health problems, including depression (Haapakoski et al., 2015; O'Donovan et al., 2012). Kids who experience extremely stressful events—physical or sexual abuse, for example—have a 40 percent greater risk of adult heart disease (Jakubowksi et al., 2018). Plucking a hair and measuring its level of *cortisol* (a stress hormone) can help indicate whether a child has experienced prolonged stress or predict whether an adult will have a future heart attack (Karlén et al., 2015; Pereg et al., 2011; Vliegenthart et al., 2016).

The Effects of Personality

In a classic study, Meyer Friedman, Ray Rosenman, and their colleagues measured the blood cholesterol level and clotting speed of 40 U.S. male tax accountants during unstressful and stressful times of year (Friedman & Ulmer, 1984). From January through March, the accountants showed normal results. But as the accountants began scrambling to finish their clients' tax returns before the April 15 filing deadline, their cholesterol and clotting measures rose to dangerous levels. In May and June, with the deadline passed, their health measures returned to normal. For these men, stress predicted heart attack risk.

So, are some of us at high risk of stress-related coronary disease? To answer this question, the researchers launched a *longitudinal study* of more than 3000 healthy men, aged 35 to 59. They interviewed each man for 15 minutes, noting his work and eating habits, manner of talking, and other behavioral patterns. Some of the men were competitive, hard-driving, impatient, time-conscious, super-motivated, verbally aggressive, and easily angered. These men were labeled **Type A.** The roughly equal number who were more easygoing they called **Type B.**

Nine years later, 257 men in the study had suffered heart attacks, and 69 percent of them were Type A. Moreover, not one of the "pure" Type Bs—the most mellow and laid-back of their group—had suffered a heart attack.

As often happens in science, this exciting discovery provoked enormous public interest. But after that initial honeymoon period, researchers wanted to know more. Was the finding reliable? If so, what exactly is so toxic about the Type A profile: Time-consciousness? Competitiveness? Anger? Further research revealed the answer. Type A's toxic core is negative emotions—especially anger. When these people are threatened or challenged by

coronary heart disease the clogging of the vessels that nourish the heart muscle; the leading cause of death in the United States and many other countries.

Type A Friedman and Rosenman's term for competitive, hard-driving, impatient, verbally aggressive, and anger-prone people.

Type B Friedman and Rosenman's term for easygoing, relaxed people.

a stressor, they react aggressively. As their often-active sympathetic nervous system redistributes blood flow to the muscles, it pulls blood away from internal organs. The liver, which normally removes cholesterol and fat from the blood, can't do its job. Excess cholesterol and fat continue to circulate in the blood and are deposited around the heart. Our heart and mind interact.

Hundreds of other studies of young and middle-aged men and women confirm that people who react with anger over little things are the most coronary-prone (Chida & Hamer, 2008; Chida & Steptoe, 2009). In Western cultures, suppressing negative emotions only heightens the risk (Kitayama et al., 2015; Kupper & Denollet, 2007). Rage "seems to lash back and strike us in the heart muscle" (Spielberger & London, 1982).

IN YOUR EVERYDAY LIFE

Do you think you are Type A, Type B, or somewhere in between? In what ways has this been helpful to you, and in what ways has this been a challenge?

RETRIEVE & REMEMBER

ANSWERS IN APPENDIX E

4. Which component of the Type A personality has been linked most closely to coronary heart disease?

LaunchPad See the *Video: Longitudinal and Cross-Sectional Studies* for a helpful tutorial animation about these types of research studies.

The Effects of Pessimism and Depression

Pessimism, the tendency to judge a glass as half empty instead of half full, increases the risk for heart attack (Pänkäläinen et al., 2016). One longitudinal study of 1306 men (ages 40 to 90) measured pessimism levels. Those who reported higher levels of pessimism were more than twice as likely as optimists to develop heart disease (Kubzansky et al., 2001) (**FIGURE 10.6**).

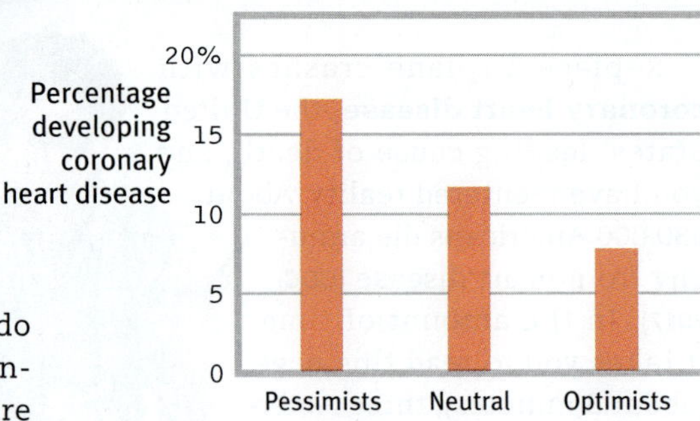

FIGURE 10.6 Pessimism and heart disease (Data from Kubzansky et al., 2001.)

Many studies show that depression, too, can be lethal (Wulsin et al., 1999). Three examples:

- Nearly 4000 English adults (ages 52 to 79) provided mood reports from a single day. Compared with those in a good mood on that day, those in a depressed mood were twice as likely to be dead five years later (Steptoe & Wardle, 2011).
- In a U.S. survey of 164,102 adults, those who had experienced a heart attack were twice as likely to report also having been depressed at some point in their lives (Witters & Wood, 2015).
- People with high scores for depression in the years following a heart attack were four times more likely than their low-scoring counterparts to develop further heart problems (Frasure-Smith & Lesperance, 2005).

Jason LaVeris/Getty Images

A broken heart? The day after the death of her beloved daughter, Carrie Fisher (right), actress Debbie Reynolds (left) also died. People wondered: Did grief-related depression and stress hormones contribute to Reynolds' stroke (Carey, 2016)?

It is still unclear why depression poses such a serious risk for heart disease, but this much seems clear: Depression is disheartening.

LaunchPad To play the role of a researcher studying these issues, engage online with the activity *How Would You Know If Stress Increases Risk of Disease?*

* * *

Stress can affect our health in many ways. (See Thinking Critically About: Stress and Health.) The stress-illness connection is a price we pay for the benefits of stress. Stress enriches our lives. It arouses and motivates us. An unstressed life would not be challenging, productive, or even safe.

Coping With Stress

LOQ 10-6 What are two basic ways that people cope with stress?

Stressors are unavoidable. That's the reality we live with. One way we can develop our strengths and protect our health is to learn better ways to **cope** with our stress.

We need to find new ways to feel, think, and act when we are dealing with stressors. We address some stressors directly, with **problem-focused coping.** For example, if our impatience leads to a family fight, we may go directly to that family member to work things out. We tend to use problem-focused strategies when we feel a sense of control over a situation and think we can change the circumstances, or at least change ourselves to deal with the circumstances more capably.

We turn to **emotion-focused coping** when we cannot—or *believe* we cannot—change a situation. If, despite our best efforts, we cannot get along with a family member, we may relieve stress by confiding in friends and reaching out for support and comfort.

Emotion-focused strategies can benefit our long-term health, as when we

Thinking Critically About:
Stress and Health

LOQ 10-5 So, does stress *cause* illness?

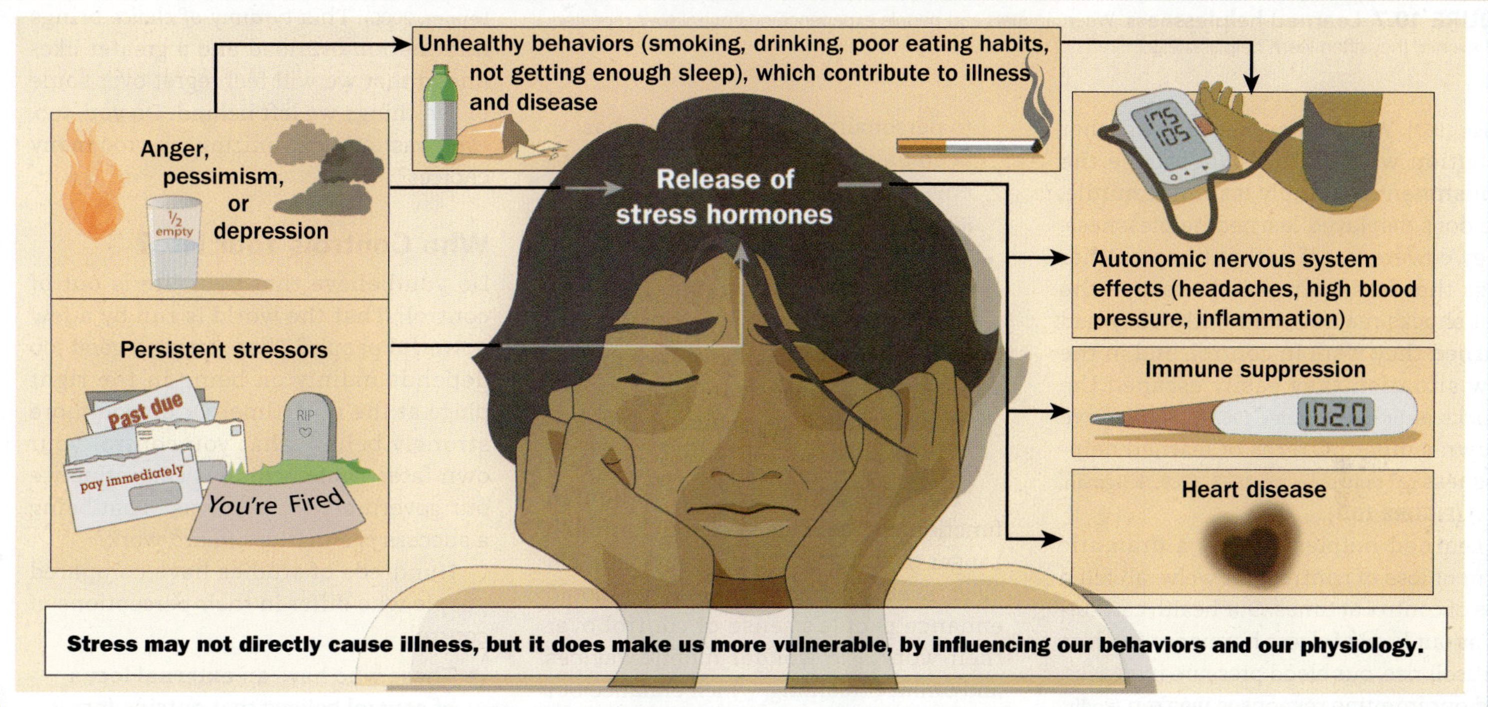
Unhealthy behaviors (smoking, drinking, poor eating habits, not getting enough sleep), which contribute to illness and disease
Anger, pessimism, or depression
1/2 empty
Release of stress hormones
Persistent stressors
Past due
pay immediately
RIP
You're Fired
Autonomic nervous system effects (headaches, high blood pressure, inflammation)
175 105
Immune suppression
102.0
Heart disease
Stress may not directly cause illness, but it does make us more vulnerable, by influencing our behaviors and our physiology.

attempt to gain emotional distance from a damaging relationship or keep busy with hobbies to avoid thinking about an old addiction. But some emotion-focused strategies can harm our health, as when we respond to a stressful situation by eating unhealthy comfort foods.

Our success in coping depends on several factors. Let's look at four of them: personal control, an optimistic outlook, social support, and finding meaning in life's ups and downs.

RETRIEVE & REMEMBER

ANSWERS IN APPENDIX E

5. To cope with stress when we feel in control of our world, we tend to use ___________(emotion/problem)-focused strategies. To cope with stress when we believe we cannot change a situation, we tend to use ___________(emotion/problem)-focused strategies.

PERSONAL CONTROL, HEALTH, AND WELL-BEING

LOQ 10-7 How does our sense of control influence stress and health?

Personal control refers to how much we perceive having control over our environment. Psychologists study the effect of personal control (or any personality factor) in two ways:

1. They *correlate* people's feelings of control with their behaviors and achievements.
2. They *experiment*, by raising or lowering people's sense of control and noting the effects.

Any of us may feel helpless, hopeless, and depressed after experiencing a series of bad events beyond our control. For some animals and people, a series of uncontrollable events creates a state of **learned helplessness,** with feelings of passive resignation. In one series of experiments, dogs were strapped in a harness and given repeated shocks, with no opportunity to avoid them (Seligman &

coping reducing stress using emotional, cognitive, or behavioral methods.

problem-focused coping attempting to reduce stress directly—by changing the stressor or the way we interact with that stressor.

emotion-focused coping attempting to reduce stress by avoiding or ignoring a stressor and attending to emotional needs related to our stress reaction.

personal control our sense of controlling our environment rather than feeling helpless.

learned helplessness the hopelessness and passive resignation an animal or person learns when unable to avoid repeated aversive events.

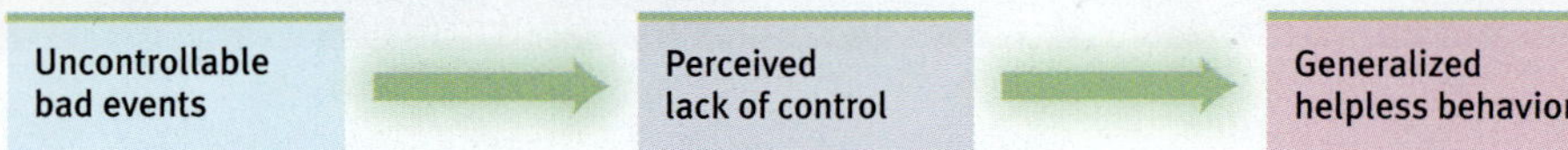

FIGURE 10.7 Learned helplessness When animals and people experience no control over repeated bad events, they often learn helplessness.

Maier, 1967). When later placed in another situation where they *could* escape the punishment by simply leaping a hurdle, the dogs displayed learned helplessness. They cowered as if without hope. Other dogs that had been able to escape the first shocks reacted differently. They had learned they were in control, and in the new situation they easily escaped the shocks (Seligman & Maier, 1967). People have shown similar patterns of learned helplessness (Abramson et al., 1978, 1989; Seligman, 1975) (**FIGURE 10.7**).

Learned helplessness is a dramatic form of loss of control. But we've all felt a loss of control at times. Our health can suffer as our level of stress hormones (such as cortisol) rise, our blood pressure increases, and our immune responses weaken (Rodin, 1986; Sapolsky, 2005). One study found these effects among nurses, who reported their workload and their level of personal control on the job. The greater their workload, the higher their cortisol level and blood pressure—but *only* among nurses who reported little control over their environment (Fox et al., 1993). Stress effects have also been observed among captive animals. Those in captivity are more prone to disease than their wild counterparts, which have more control over their lives (Roberts, 1988). Similar effects are found when humans are crowded together in high-density neighborhoods, prisons, and even college dorms (Fleming et al., 1987; Fuller et al., 1993; Ostfeld et al., 1987). Feelings of control drop, and stress hormone levels and blood pressure rise.

In many cases, increasing control has noticeably improved health and morale (Humphrey et al., 2007; Ng et al., 2012; Ruback et al., 1986). These efforts have included:

- Allowing prisoners to move chairs and control room lights and the TV.
- Having workers participate in decision making. Simply allowing people to personalize their workspace has been linked with a 55 percent higher engagement with their work (Krueger & Killham, 2006).
- Offering nursing home residents choices about their environment. In one famous study, 93 percent of nursing home patients who were encouraged to exert more control became more alert, active, and happy (Rodin, 1986).

"Perceived control is basic to human functioning," concluded researcher Ellen Langer (1983, p. 291). "For the young and old alike," she suggested, environments should enhance people's sense of control over their world. No wonder mobile devices and online streaming, which enhance our control of the content and timing of our entertainment, are so popular.

Google has incorporated these principles effectively. Each week, Google employees can spend 20 percent of their working time on projects they find personally interesting. This Innovation Time Off program has increased employees' personal control over their work environment. It has also paid off: Gmail was developed this way.

The power of personal control also appears at the national level. People thrive when they live in conditions of personal freedom and empowerment. For example, citizens of stable democracies report higher levels of happiness (Inglehart et al., 2008).

So, some freedom and control are better than none. But does ever-increasing choice breed ever-happier lives? Some researchers suggest that today's Western cultures offer an "excess of freedom"—too many choices. The result can be decreased life satisfaction, increased depression, or even behavior paralysis (Schwartz, 2000, 2004). In one study, people offered a choice of one of 30 brands of jam or chocolate were less satisfied with their decision than were others who had chosen from only 6 options (Iyengar & Lepper, 2000). This *tyranny of choice* brings information overload and a greater likelihood that we will feel regret over some of the things we left behind. Do you, too, ever waste time agonizing over too many choices?

Who Controls Your Life?

Do you believe that your life is out of control? That the world is run by a few powerful people? That getting a good job depends mainly on being in the right place at the right time? Or do you more strongly believe that you control your own fate? That each of us can influence our government's decisions? That being a success is a matter of hard work?

Hundreds of studies have compared people who differ in their perceptions of control:

- Those who have an **external locus of control** believe that outside forces control their fate.
- Those who have an **internal locus of control** believe they control their own destiny.

Adrees Latif/Reuters/Newscom

Loss of control In 2018, new immigration policies meant that thousands of immigrating children were separated from their parents at the southern U.S. border. Children taken from parents and held in detention camps lose a sense of control over their own fate. Psychological research suggests that such extreme stress may make these children vulnerable to future physical and psychological problems.

Does it matter which view we hold? In study after study comparing people with these two viewpoints, the "internals" have achieved more in school and work, acted more independently, enjoyed better health, and felt less depressed (Lefcourt, 1982; Ng et al., 2006). In longitudinal research on more than 7500 people, those who had expressed a more internal locus of control at age 10 exhibited less obesity, lower blood pressure, and less distress at age 30 (Gale et al., 2008). By contrast, in one study of more than 1200 Israeli individuals exposed to missile attacks, those with an external locus of control experienced the most *posttraumatic stress* symptoms (Hoffman et al., 2016).

Compared with their parents' generation, today's young Americans more often express an external locus of control (Twenge et al., 2004). This shift may help explain an associated increase in rates of depression and other psychological disorders in young people (Twenge et al., 2010b).

Another way to say that we believe we are in control of our own life is to say we have *free will*. Studies show that people who believe they have free will learn better, persist, and perform better at work, and behave more helpfully (Job et al., 2010; Li et al., 2018; Stillman et al., 2010). They tend to enjoy making decisions, oppose behavior-restricting government regulations, and favor punishing rule breakers (Clark et al., 2014; Feldman et al., 2014; Hannikainen et al., 2016). Belief in free will also predicts another type of control known as *willpower* or *self-control*—which we turn to next.

Coping With Stress by Boosting Self-Control

Google trusted its belief in the power of personal control, and the company and its employees reaped the benefits. Could we reap similar benefits by actively managing our own behavior? One place to start might be increasing our **self-control**—the ability to control impulses and delay immediate gratification. Strengthening our self-control may not pay off with a Gmail invention, but self-control has been linked to health and well-being (Moffitt et al., 2011; Smithers et al., 2018). People with more self-control earn higher incomes, get better grades, and enjoy good health (Bub et al., 2016; Keller et al., 2016; Moffitt et al., 2011). In studies of American, Asian, and New Zealander children, self-control outdid intelligence test scores in predicting future academic and life success (Duckworth & Seligman, 2005; Poulton et al., 2015; Wu et al., 2016).

LatitudeStock - Brian Fairbrother/Getty Images

Extreme self-control Our ability to exert self-control increases with practice, and some of us have practiced more than others! A number of performing artists make their living as very convincing human statues, as does this performer on The Royal Mile in Edinburgh, Scotland.

Strengthening self-control is an important key to coping with stress. Doing so requires attention and energy—similar to strengthening a muscle. It's easy to form bad habits, but it takes hard work to break them. With frequent practice in overcoming unwanted urges, people have been better able to manage their anger, dishonesty, smoking, and impulsive spending (Beames et al., 2017; Wang et al., 2017a).

Self-control varies over time. Like a muscle, it tends to weaken after use, recover after rest, and grow stronger with exercise (Baumeister & Vohs, 2016). Does exercising willpower temporarily gobble up the mental energy we need for self-control on other tasks (Grillon et al., 2015; Luethi et al., 2016; Vohs et al., 2012)? In one famous experiment, hungry people who had spent some of their willpower resisting tempting chocolate chip cookies then abandoned a frustrating task sooner than did others (Baumeister et al., 1998a). Although some researchers debate the reliability of this "depletion effect" (Hagger et al., 2016), the big lesson of self-control remains: Develop self-discipline, and your self-control can help you lead a healthier, happier, and more successful life (Baumeister et al., 2018; Tuk et al., 2015). Delaying a little fun now can lead to big rewards later.

IMPROVE YOUR EVERYDAY LIFE

How much control do you have over your life? What changes could you make to increase your sense of control?

LaunchPad Test your own self-control with *Assess Your Strengths: How Much Self-Control Do You Have, and Why Is This Worth Working to Increase?* Then consider research-based strategies for improving your self-control by watching my [ND's] 7-minute *Video: Self-Control—Our Greatest Inner Strength,* available in LaunchPad or at tinyurl.com/DeWallSelf-Control.

IS THE GLASS HALF FULL OR HALF EMPTY?

LOQ 10-8 How do optimists and pessimists differ, and why does our outlook on life matter?

Another part of coping with stress is our outlook—how we perceive the world. **Optimists** agree with statements such

external locus of control the perception that outside forces beyond our personal control determine our fate.

internal locus of control the perception that we control our own fate.

self-control the ability to control impulses and delay short-term gratification for greater long-term rewards.

optimism the anticipation of positive outcomes. Optimists are people who expect the best and expect their efforts to lead to good things.

as, "In uncertain times, I usually expect the best" (Scheier & Carver, 1992). Optimists expect to have control, to cope well with stressful events, and to enjoy good health (Aspinwall & Tedeschi, 2010; Boehm & Kubzansky, 2012; Hernandez et al., 2015). **Pessimists,** as noted earlier, don't share these expectations. They expect things to go badly (Aspinwall & Tedeschi, 2010; Carver et al., 2010; Rasmussen et al., 2009). And when bad things happen, pessimists believe they knew it all along. They lacked the necessary skills ("I can't do this"). The situation prevented them from doing well ("There is nothing I can do about it"). They expected the worst and their expectations were fulfilled.

Optimism, like a feeling of personal control, pays off. Optimists respond to stress with smaller increases in blood pressure, and they recover more quickly from heart bypass surgery. And during the stressful first few weeks of classes, U.S. law school students who were optimistic ("It's unlikely that I will fail") enjoyed better moods and stronger immune systems (Segerstrom et al., 1998). When American dating couples wrestle with conflicts, optimists and their partners see each other as engaging constructively. They tend to feel more supported and satisfied with the resolution and with their relationship (Srivastava et al., 2006). Optimism also predicts well-being and success elsewhere, including in China and Japan (Qin & Piao, 2011).

Sam Gross The New Yorker Collection/The Cartoon Bank

"We just haven't been flapping them hard enough."

Is an optimistic outlook related to living a longer life? Possibly. One research team followed 70,021 nurses over time. Those scoring in the top quarter on optimism were nearly 30 percent less likely to have died than those scoring in the bottom quarter (Kim et al., 2017). Even greater optimism-longevity differences have been found in studies of Finnish men and American Vietnam War veterans (Everson et al., 1996; Phillips et al., 2009).

The optimism–long-life correlation also appeared in a famous study of 180 American Catholic nuns. At about 22 years of age, each of these women had written a brief autobiography. In the decades that followed, they lived similar lifestyles. Those who had expressed happiness, love, and other positive feelings in their autobiographies lived an average of seven years longer than did the more negative nuns (Danner et al., 2001). By age 80, only 24 percent of the most positive-spirited had died, compared with 54 percent of those expressing few positive emotions.

Optimism runs in families, so some people truly are born with a sunny, hopeful outlook. If one identical twin is optimistic, the other often will be as well (Bates, 2015; Mosing et al., 2009). One genetic marker of optimism is a gene that enhances the social-bonding hormone *oxytocin,* which in humans is released, for example, by cuddling, massage, and breast feeding (Campbell, 2010; Saphire-Bernstein et al., 2011).

Positive thinking pays dividends, but so does a dash of realism (Schneider, 2001). Realistic anxiety over possible *future* failures—worrying about being able to pay a bill on time, or fearing you will do badly on an exam—can cause you to try extra hard to avoid failure (Goodhart, 1986; Norem, 2001; Showers, 1992). Students concerned about failing an upcoming exam may study more, and therefore outperform equally able but more confident peers. This may help explain the impressive academic achievements of some Asian-American students. Compared with European-Americans, these students express somewhat greater pessimism (Chang, 2001). Success requires enough optimism to provide hope and enough pessimism to keep you on your toes.

Rubberball/Mark Andersen/Getty Images

Laughter among friends is good medicine Laughter arouses us, massages muscles, and then leaves us feeling relaxed (Robinson, 1983). Humor (though not hostile sarcasm) may defuse stress, ease pain, and strengthen immune activity (Ayan, 2009; Berk et al., 2001; Dunbar et al., 2011; Kimata, 2001). People who laugh a lot have also tended to have lower rates of heart disease (Clark et al., 2001).

Excessive optimism can blind us to real risks (Tenney et al., 2015). More than 1000 studies have shown how our natural positive thinking bias can lead to "unrealistic optimism" (Shepperd et al., 2015; Weinstein, 1980). Most students exhibit such unrealistic optimism: They believe they are more likely than their classmates to get a high-paying job and own a nice home, and less likely to have a heart attack or get cancer (Waters et al., 2011). If overconfident of our ability to control an impulse such as the urge to smoke, we are more likely to expose ourselves to temptations—and to fail (Nordgren et al., 2009). Blinded by optimism, people young and old echo the statement famed basketball player Magic Johnson made (1992) after contracting HIV: "I didn't think it could happen to me."

SOCIAL SUPPORT

LOQ 10-9 How do social support and finding meaning in life influence health?

Which of these factors has the strongest association with poor health: smoking 15 cigarettes daily, being obese, being inactive, or lacking strong social connections? This is a trick question, because each factor has a roughly similar impact (Cacioppo & Patrick, 2008). That's right! *Social support*—feeling liked and encouraged by intimate friends and family—promotes both happiness and health. It helps you cope with stress. Not having this support can affect your health as much as smoking nearly a pack per day.

International investigations that followed thousands of people over several years reached similar conclusions. Although *individualist* (individual-focused) and *collectivist* (group-focused) cultures vary in how much value they place on social support, it is universally related to greater happiness (Brannan et al., 2013; Chu et al., 2010; Rueger et al., 2016). People supported by close relationships are also less likely to die early (Shor et al., 2013). These relationships may be with friends, family, fellow students or workers, members of our faith community, or some other support group.

Happy marriages bathe us in social support and promote longevity (VanderWeele, 2017). One seven-decade-long study found that at age 50, healthy aging is better predicted by a good marriage than by a low cholesterol level (Vaillant, 2002). On the flip side, divorce is a predictor of poor health. In one analysis of 600 million people in 24 countries, separated and divorced people were more likely to die early (Shor et al., 2012). But it's less marital status than marital *quality* that predicts health—to about the same extent as a healthy diet and physical activity do (Robles, 2015; Smith & Baucom, 2017).

Social support helps us fight illness in at least two ways. First, it calms our cardiovascular system, which lowers blood pressure and stress hormone levels (Baron et al., 2016; Hostinar et al., 2014; Uchino et al., 1996, 2017). To see if social support might calm people's response to threats, one research team subjected happily married women, while lying in an fMRI machine, to the threat of electric shock to an ankle (Coan et al., 2006). During the experiment, some women held their husband's hand. Others held a stranger's hand or no hand at all. While awaiting the occasional shocks, the women's brains reacted differently. Those who held their husband's hand had less activity in threat-responsive areas. This soothing benefit was greatest for women reporting the highest-quality marriages. People with supportive marriages also had below-average stress hormone levels 10 years later (Slatcher et al., 2015). Even pets can help buffer stress (Siegel, 1990).

Social support helps us cope with stress in a second way. It helps us fight illness by fostering stronger *immune functioning*. We have seen that stress puts us at risk for disease by stealing disease-fighting energy from our immune system. Social support seems to reboot our immune system. In one series of studies, research participants with strong support systems showed greater resistance to cold viruses (Cohen, 2004; Cohen et al., 1997). After inhaling nose drops

Pets are friends, too Pets can provide social support. Having a pet may increase the odds of survival after a heart attack, relieve depression among people with AIDS, and lower blood pressure and other coronary risk factors (Allen, 2003; McConnell et al., 2011; Wells, 2009). To lower blood pressure, pets are no substitute for effective drugs and exercise. But for people who enjoy animals, and especially for those who live alone, pets are a healthy pleasure (Reis et al., 2017).

pessimism the anticipation of negative outcomes. Pessimists are people who expect the worst and doubt that their goals will be achieved.

loaded with a cold virus, two groups of healthy volunteers were isolated and observed for five days. (In these experiments, the more than 600 participants were well-paid volunteers.) Age, race, sex, and health habits being equal, those with close social ties were least likely to catch a cold. People whose daily life included frequent hugs likewise experienced fewer cold symptoms and less symptom severity (Cohen et al., 2015). The cold fact: The effect of social ties is nothing to sneeze at!

When we are trying to cope with stressors, social ties can tug us toward or away from our goal. Are you trying to exercise more, drink less, quit smoking, or eat better? If so, think about whether your social network can help or hinder you.

FINDING MEANING

Catastrophes and significant life changes can leave us confused and distressed as we try to make sense of what happened. At such times, an important part of coping with stress is finding meaning in life—some redeeming purpose in our suffering (Guo et al., 2013; Taylor, 1983). Unemployment is very threatening, but it may free up time to spend with children. The loss of a loved one may force us to expand our social network. A heart attack may trigger a shift toward healthy, active living. Some have argued that the search for meaning is fundamental. We constantly seek to maintain meaning when our expectations are not met (Heine el al., 2006). As psychiatrist Viktor Frankl (1962), who survived a Nazi concentration camp, observed, "Life is never made unbearable by circumstances, but only by lack of meaning and purpose."

Close relationships offer an opportunity for "open heart therapy"—a chance to confide painful feelings and sort things out (Frattaroli, 2006). Talking about things that push our buttons may arouse us in the short term. But in the long term, it calms us (Lieberman et al., 2007; Mendolia & Kleck, 1993; Niles et al., 2015). After we gain distance from a stressful event, talking or writing about the experience helps us make sense of it and find meaning in it (Esterling et al., 1999). In one study, 33 Holocaust survivors spent two hours recalling their experiences, many in intimate detail never before disclosed (Pennebaker et al., 1989). Those who were most self-disclosing had the most improved health 14 months later. Another study surveyed surviving spouses of people who had committed suicide or died in car accidents. Those who bore their grief alone had more health problems than those who could share it with others (Pennebaker & O'Heeron, 1984). Confiding is good for the body and the soul.

The mood boost When energy or spirits are sagging, few things reboot the day better than exercising, as I [DM] can confirm from my noontime biking and basketball, and as I [ND] can confirm from my running.

IN YOUR EVERYDAY LIFE

Can you remember a time when you felt better after discussing a problem with a loved one, or even after playing with your pet? How did doing so help you to cope?

Managing Stress Effects

Having a sense of control, nurturing an optimistic outlook, building our social support, and finding meaning can help us *experience* less stress and thus improve our health. What do we do when we cannot avoid stress? At such times, we need to *manage* our stress. Aerobic exercise, relaxation, meditation, and religious engagement have helped people gather inner strength and lessen stress effects.

AEROBIC EXERCISE

LOQ 10-10 How well does aerobic exercise help us manage stress and improve well-being?

It's hard to find a medicine that works for most people most of the time. But **aerobic exercise**—sustained activity that increases heart and lung fitness—is one of these rare near-perfect "medicines." Estimates vary, but some studies suggest that exercise adds to your quantity of life—about *seven hours longer life for every exercise hour* (Lee et al., 2017; Mandsager et al., 2018; Zahrt & Crum, 2017)—and your quality of life, with more energy, better mood, and stronger relationships (Flueckiger et al., 2016; Hogan et al., 2015; Wiese et al., 2018). Go for a daily jog or swim, and you can expect to live both longer and happier.

Throughout this book, we have revisited one of psychology's basic themes: Heredity and environment interact. Physical activity can weaken the influence of genetic risk factors for obesity. In one analysis of 45 studies, that risk fell by 27 percent (Kilpeläinen et al., 2012). Exercise also helps fight heart disease. It strengthens your heart, increases blood flow, keeps blood vessels open, lowers overall blood pressure, and reduces the hormone and blood pressure reaction to stress (Ford, 2002; Manson, 2002). Compared with inactive adults, people who exercise suffer about half as many heart attacks (Evenson et al., 2016; Visich & Fletcher, 2009). Dietary fat contributes to clogged arteries, but exercise makes our muscles hungry for those fats and helps clean them out of our arteries (Barinaga, 1997).

People who do aerobic exercise at least three times a week manage stress better, have more self-confidence and energy, and feel less depressed and tired than their inactive peers (Rebar et al., 2015; Smits et al., 2011). A study of 1.44 million Americans and Europeans found that exercise predicted "lower risks of many cancer types" (Moore et al., 2016). Going from active exerciser to couch potato can increase risk for depression—by 51 percent in two years for the women in one study (Wang et al., 2011). Among people with depression, getting off the couch and into a more physically active life reduces depressive symptoms (Kvam et al., 2016; Snippe et al., 2016).

But we could state these observations another way: Stressed and depressed people exercise less. It's that old correlation problem again—cause and effect are not clear. To sort out cause and effect, researchers experiment. They may *randomly assign* people either to an aerobic exercise group or to a control group. Next, they measure whether aerobic exercise (compared with a control activity not involving exercise) produces a change in stress, depression, anxiety, or some other health-related outcome. In one such experiment (McCann & Holmes, 1984), researchers randomly assigned mildly depressed female college students to one of three groups:

- Group 1 completed an aerobic exercise program.
- Group 2 completed a relaxation program.
- Group 3 functioned as a pure control group and did not complete any special activity.

As **FIGURE 10.8** shows, 10 weeks later the women in the aerobic exercise program reported the greatest decrease in depression. Many of them had, quite literally, run away from their troubles.

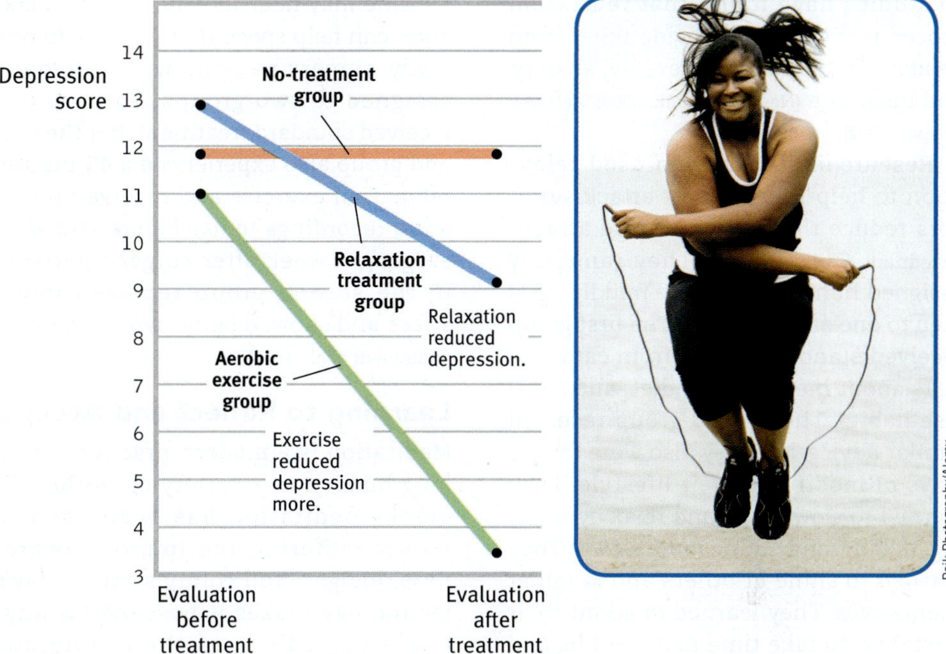

FIGURE 10.8 Aerobic exercise reduces mild depression (Data from McCann & Holmes, 1984.)

Another experiment randomly assigned depressed people to an exercise group, an antidepressant group, or a placebo pill group. Again, exercise diminished depression levels. And it did so as effectively as antidepressants, with longer-lasting effects (Hoffman et al., 2011). Aerobic exercise counteracts depression in two ways. First, it increases arousal. Second, it does naturally what some prescription drugs do chemically: It increases the brain's serotonin activity.

More than 150 other studies have confirmed that exercise reduces depression and anxiety. What is more, toned muscles filter out a depression-causing toxin (Agudelo et al., 2014). Aerobic exercise has therefore taken a place, along with antidepressant drugs and psychotherapy, on the list of effective treatments for depression and anxiety (Arent et al., 2000; Berger & Motl, 2000; Dunn et al., 2005).

LaunchPad See the *Video: Random Assignment* for a helpful tutorial animation about this important part of effective research design.

RELAXATION AND MEDITATION

LOQ 10-11 In what ways might relaxation and meditation influence stress and health?

Sit with your back straight, getting as comfortable as you can. Breathe a deep, single breath of air through your nose. Now exhale that air through your mouth as slowly as you can. As you exhale, repeat a focus word, phrase, or prayer—something from your own belief system. Do this five times. Do you feel more relaxed?

Why Relaxation Is Good

Like aerobic exercise, relaxation can improve our well-being. Did you notice in Figure 10.8 that women in the relaxation treatment group also experienced reduced depression? More than

aerobic exercise sustained exercise that increases heart and lung fitness; also helps reduce depression and anxiety.

60 studies have found that relaxation procedures can also provide relief from headaches, high blood pressure, anxiety, and insomnia (Nestoriuc et al., 2008; Stetter & Kupper, 2002).

Researchers have even used relaxation to help Type A heart attack survivors reduce their risk of future attacks (Friedman & Ulmer, 1984). They randomly assigned hundreds of these middle-aged men to one of two groups. The first group received standard advice from cardiologists about medications, diet, and exercise habits. The second group received similar advice, but they also were taught ways of modifying their lifestyle. They learned to slow down and relax by walking, talking, and eating more slowly. They learned to smile at others and laugh at themselves. They learned to admit their mistakes, to take time to enjoy life, and to renew their religious faith. The training paid off spectacularly (**FIGURE 10.9**). During the next three years, the lifestyle modification group had half as many repeat heart attacks as did the first group. A British study spanning 13 years supported this finding. High-risk people trained to modify their thinking and lifestyle similarly showed a halved death rate (Eysenck & Grossarth-Maticek, 1991).

Time may heal all wounds, but relaxation can help speed that process. In one study, surgery patients were randomly assigned to two groups. Both groups received standard treatment, but the second group also experienced a 45-minute relaxation exercise and received relaxation recordings to use before and after surgery. A week after surgery, patients in the second group reported lower stress and showed better wound healing (Broadbent el al., 2012).

Learning to Reflect and Accept

Meditation is a modern practice with a long history. In a variety of world religions, meditation has been used to reduce suffering and improve awareness, insight, and compassion. Today's technology makes it possible for anyone — regardless of their religious beliefs — to practice meditation. Apps such as Headspace and Calm offer users free, guided meditation techniques.

Why might you want to try meditation? Numerous studies have confirmed the psychological benefits of different types of meditation (Goyal et al., 2014; Rosenberg et al., 2015; Sedlmeier et al., 2012). One type, **mindfulness meditation,** has found a new home in

Djomas/Shutterstock

stress management programs. If you were taught this practice, you would relax and silently attend to your inner state, without judging it (Brown et al., 2016; Kabat-Zinn, 2001). You would sit down, close your eyes, and mentally scan your body from head to toe. Zooming in on certain body parts and responses, you would remain aware and accepting. You would also pay attention to your breathing, attending to each breath as if it were a material object.

Practicing mindfulness may lessen anxiety and depression (Goyal et al., 2014). In one study of 1140 people, some received mindfulness-based therapy for several weeks. Others did not. Levels of anxiety and depression were lower among those who received the therapy (Hofmann et al., 2010). Mindfulness practices have also been linked with improved sleep, helpfulness, and immune system functioning (Donald et al., 2018; Gong et al., 2016; Rosenkranz et al., 2013; Sedlmeier et al., 2012).

Some researchers caution that mindfulness has been over-hyped (Hafenbrock & Vohs, 2018; Van Dam et al., 2018). Mere solitude can similarly relax us and reduce stress (Nguyen et al., 2018). But the positive results make us wonder: What's going on in the brain as we practice mindfulness? Correlational and experimental studies offer three explanations. Mindfulness

- ***strengthens connections among brain regions.*** The affected regions are those associated with focusing our attention, processing what we see and

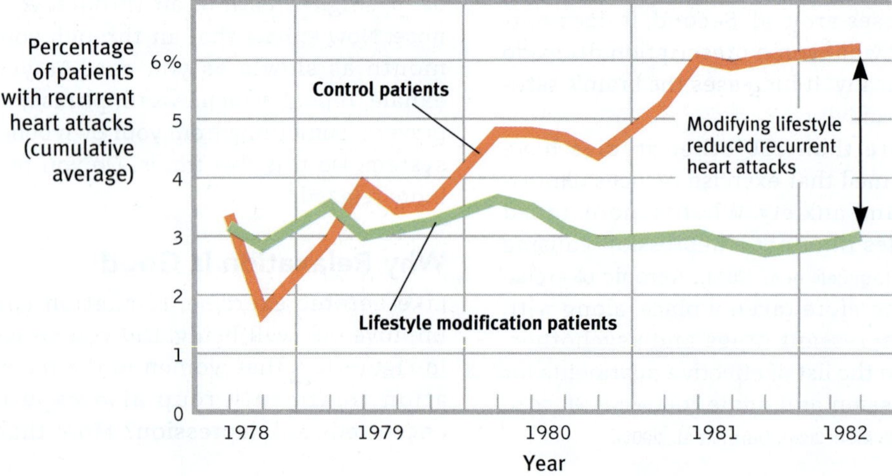

FIGURE 10.9 Recurrent heart attacks and lifestyle modification The San Francisco Recurrent Coronary Prevention Project offered counseling from a cardiologist to survivors of heart attacks. Those who were also guided in modifying their Type A lifestyle suffered fewer repeat heart attacks. (Data from Friedman & Ulmer, 1984.)

hear, and being reflective and aware (Berkovich-Ohana et al., 2014; Ives-Deliperi et al., 2011; Kilpatrick et al., 2011).

- ***activates brain regions associated with more reflective awareness*** (Davidson et al., 2003; Way et al., 2010). When labeling emotions, mindful people show less activation in the amygdala, a brain region associated with fear, and more activation in the prefrontal cortex, which aids emotion regulation (Creswell et al., 2007; Gotink et al., 2016).
- ***calms brain activation in emotional situations.*** This lower activation was clear in one study in which participants watched two movies—one sad, one neutral. Those in the control group, who were not trained in mindfulness, showed strong differences in brain activation when watching the two movies. Those who had received mindfulness training showed little change in brain response to the two movies (Farb et al., 2010). Emotionally unpleasant images also trigger weaker electrical brain responses in mindful people than in their less mindful counterparts (Brown et al., 2013). A mindful brain is strong, reflective, and calm.

Exercise and meditation are not the only routes to healthy relaxation. Massage helps relax both premature infants (Chapter 3) and those suffering pain (Chapter 5), and it also helps reduce depression (Hou et al., 2010).

IMPROVE YOUR EVERYDAY LIFE

What strategies have you used to manage stress in your life? How well have they worked? What other strategies could you try?

FAITH COMMUNITIES AND HEALTH

LOQ 10-12 Does religious involvement relate to health?

A wealth of studies has revealed another curious correlation, called the *faith factor* (Koenig et al., 2012; VanderWeele, 2018). Religiously active people tend to live longer than those who are not religiously active. In one 16-year study, researchers tracked 3900 Israelis living in one of two groups of communities (Kark et al., 1996). The first group contained 11 religiously orthodox collective settlements. The second group contained 11 matched, nonreligious collective settlements. The researchers found that "belonging to a religious collective was associated with a strong protective effect" not explained by age or economic differences. In every age group, religious community members were about half as likely to have died as were those in the nonreligious community. Another study followed 74,534 nurses over 20 years. When controlling for various health risk factors, those who attended religious services more than weekly were a third less likely to have died than were non-attenders, and were much less likely to have died by suicide (Li et al., 2016; VanderWeele et al., 2016). In obituaries, mention of a religious affiliation predicted 7.5 years of additional life compared with no religious affiliation (Wallace et al., 2018).

How should we interpret such findings? Without the ability to randomly assign people to be religious or nonreligious, how can researchers explore the faith-health connection further? Remember, first, that correlation does not mean causation. What other factors might explain these protective effects? Here's one possibility: Women are more religiously active than men, and women outlive men. Does religious involvement reflect this gender-longevity link? No. Although the religiosity-longevity correlation is stronger among women, it also appears among men (McCullough et al., 2000; McCullough & Laurenceau, 2005). In study after study—some lasting 28 years, and some studying more than 20,000 people—the faith factor holds (Chida et al., 2009; Hummer et al., 1999; Schnall et al., 2010). And it holds after researchers control for age, sex, race, ethnicity, education, and region. In one study, this effect translated into a life expectancy of 83 years for those who regularly attended religious services, and 75 years for nonattenders.

Does this mean that nonattenders who start attending services and change nothing else will live longer? Again, the answer is *No.* But we can say that religious involvement *predicts* health and longevity, just as nonsmoking and exercise do. Religiously active people have demonstrated healthier immune functioning, fewer hospital admissions, and, for people with AIDS, fewer stress hormones and longer survival (Ironson et al., 2002; Koenig & Larson, 1998; Lutgendorf et al., 2004).

Barbara Smaller

"We don't have a time-out chair in our Classroom Community. That's our mindfulness chair."

mindfulness meditation a reflective practice in which people attend to current experiences in a nonjudgmental and accepting manner.

Can you imagine why religiously active people might be healthier and live longer than others (**FIGURE 10.10**)? Here are three factors that help explain the correlation:

- ***Healthy behaviors*** Religion promotes self-control (DeWall et al., 2014; McCullough & Willoughby, 2009). This helps explain why religiously active people tend to smoke and drink much less and to have healthier lifestyles (Islam & Johnson, 2003; Koenig & Vaillant, 2009; Masters & Hooker, 2013; Park, 2007). In one Gallup survey of 550,000 Americans, 15 percent of the very religious were smokers, compared with 28 percent of the nonreligious (Newport et al., 2010). But healthy lifestyles are not the complete answer. In studies that have controlled for unhealthy behaviors, such as inactivity and smoking, about 75 percent of the life-span difference remained (Musick et al., 1999).
- ***Social support*** If you think of the religiosity factor as a drug, its strongest active ingredient is social support. Those who belong to a faith community participate in a support network. When misfortune strikes, religiously active people can turn to each other. In the 20-year nurses study, for example, religious people's social support was the best predictor of their good health. Moreover, religion encourages marriage, another predictor of health and longevity. In the Israeli religious settlements, for example, divorce was almost nonexistent.
- ***Positive emotions*** Even after controlling for social support, unhealthy behaviors, gender, and preexisting health problems, studies have found that religiously engaged people tend to live longer (Chida et al., 2009). Researchers speculate that a third set of influences helps protect religiously active people from stress and enhance their well-being (**FIGURE 10.11**). Religiously active people have a stable worldview, a sense of hope for the long-term future, and feelings of ultimate acceptance. They may also benefit from the relaxed meditation of prayer or other religious observances. Taken together, these positive emotions, expectations, and practices may have a protective effect on well-being.

AlisaNata/Shutterstock

Getty Images/Fuse

Sura Nualpradid/Shutterstock

casejustin/Shutterstock

Georgios Kollidas/Alamy

Georgios Kollidas/Shutterstock

ppart/Shutterstock

* * *

Let's summarize what we've learned so far: Sustained emotional reactions to stressful events can be damaging. However, some qualities and influences can help us cope with life's challenges by making us emotionally and physically stronger. These include a sense of control, an optimistic outlook, relaxation, healthy habits, social support, and a sense of meaning.

In the remainder of this chapter, we'll take a closer look at our pursuit of happiness and how it relates to our human flourishing.

Risk of dying in any given year relative to others (100% = same annual risk of dying as others)

	Men	Women
Not smoking	~55%	~59%
Regular exercise	~73%	~65%
Weekly religious attendance	~76%	~54%

FIGURE 10.10 Predictors of longer life: Not smoking, frequent exercise, and regular religious attendance One 28-year study followed more than 5200 adults (Oman et al., 2002; Strawbridge, 1999; Strawbridge et al., 1997). Controlling for age and education, the researchers found that not smoking, regular exercise, and religious attendance all predicted a lowered risk of death in any given year. Women attending weekly religious services, for example, were only 54 percent as likely to die in a typical study year as were nonattenders.

RETRIEVE & REMEMBER

ANSWERS IN APPENDIX E

6. What are some of the tactics we can use to successfully manage the stress we cannot avoid?

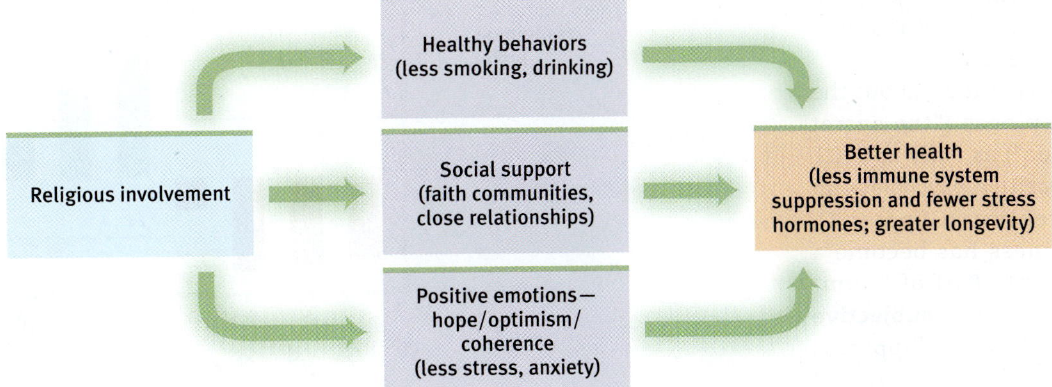

FIGURE 10.11 Possible explanations for the correlation between religious involvement and health/longevity

LaunchPad To check your understanding of the best ways to handle stress, engage online with *Concept Practice: Methods of Managing Stress.*

Happiness

LOQ 10-13 What are the causes and consequences of happiness?

In *The How of Happiness* (2008), psychologist Sonja Lyubomirsky tells the true story of Randy. By any measure, Randy lived a hard life. His dad and best friend both died by suicide. Growing up, his mother's boyfriend treated him poorly. Randy's first wife was unfaithful, and they divorced. Despite these setbacks, Randy is a happy person whose endless optimism can light up a room. He remarried and enjoys being a stepfather to three boys. His work life is rewarding. Randy says he survived his life stressors by seeing the "silver lining in the cloud."

Overcoming serious challenges, as Randy did, people may feel a stronger sense of self-esteem and a deeper sense of purpose. Tough challenges, especially early in life, can foster personal growth and emotional **resilience** (Seery, 2011).

Are you a person who makes everyone around you smile and laugh? Have you, like Randy, bounced back from serious challenges and become stronger because of it? Our state of happiness or unhappiness colors our thoughts and our actions. Happy people perceive the world as safer. Their eyes are drawn toward emotionally positive information (Raila et al., 2015). They are more decisive and cooperate more easily. They experience more career success (Walsh et al., 2018). They live healthier and more energized and satisfied lives (Boehm et al., 2015; De Neve et al., 2013; Mauss et al., 2011; Stellar et al., 2015). And they are more generous (Boenigk & Mayr, 2016).

The simple conclusion: *Moods matter.* We all get gloomy sometimes. When that happens, life as a whole may seem depressing and meaningless. Let your mood brighten and your thinking broadens, becoming more playful and creative (Baas et al., 2008; Forgas, 2008; Fredrickson, 2013).

This helps explain why young adults' happiness helps predict their life course. In one study, which surveyed thousands of U.S. college students in 1976 and restudied them at age 37, happy students had gone on to earn significantly more money than their less-happy-than-average peers (Diener et al., 2002). In another, the happiest 20-year-olds were not only more likely to marry, but also less likely to divorce (Stutzer & Frey, 2006). When we are happy, our relationships, self-image, and hopes for the future also seem more promising.

Moreover—and this is one of psychology's most consistent findings—when we feel happy we become more helpful. Psychologists call it the **feel-good, do-good phenomenon** (Salovey, 1990). Happiness doesn't just feel good, it does good. In study after study, a mood-boosting experience (finding money, succeeding on a challenging task, recalling a happy event) has made people more likely to give money, pick up someone's dropped papers, volunteer time, and do other good deeds.

The reverse is also true: Doing good promotes feeling good. One survey of more than 200,000 people in 136 countries found that, pretty much everywhere, people report feeling happier after spending money on others rather than themselves (Aknin et al., 2013; Dunn et al., 2014). Why does doing good feel so good? One reason is that it strengthens our social relationships (Aknin et al., 2015; Yamaguchi et al., 2015). Some happiness coaches and instructors harness this

resilience the personal strength that helps most people cope with stress and recover from adversity and even trauma.

feel-good, do-good phenomenon our tendency to be helpful when in a good mood.

force by asking their clients to perform a daily "random act of kindness" and to record how it made them feel.

William James was writing about the importance of happiness ("the secret motive for all [we] do") as early as 1902. With the rise of *positive psychology* in the twenty-first century (Chapter 1), the study of happiness has become a main area of research. Part of happiness research is the study of **subjective well-being**—our feelings of happiness (sometimes defined as a high ratio of positive to negative feelings) or our sense of satisfaction with life. This information, combined with objective measures of well-being, such as a person's physical and economic condition, helps us make more informed quality-of-life judgments.

LaunchPad To assess your own well-being and consider ways to improve it, engage online with *Assess Your Strengths: How Satisfied Are You With Your Life, and How Could You Be More Satisfied?*

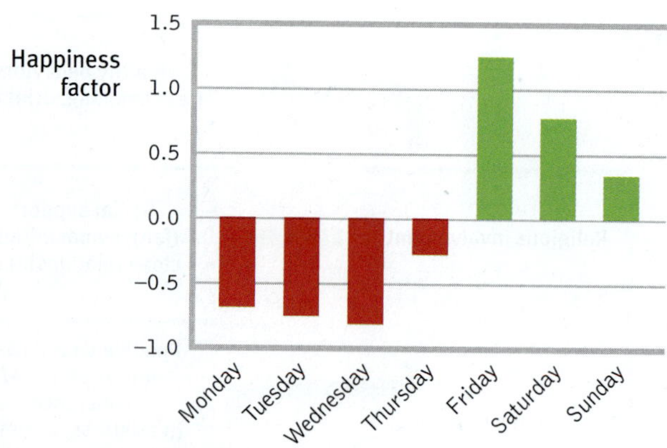

FIGURE 10.12 Using science to track happy days Adam Kramer (2010) tracked positive and negative emotion words in many "billions" (the exact number is proprietary information) of status updates of U.S. Facebook users between September 7, 2007, and November 17, 2010.

THE SHORT LIFE OF EMOTIONAL UPS AND DOWNS

Are some days of the week happier than others? In what may be psychology's biggest-ever data sample, one social psychologist (Kramer, 2010—at my [DM's] request and in cooperation with Facebook) did a *naturalistic observation* of emotion words in *billions* of status updates. After eliminating exceptional days, such as holidays, he tracked the frequency of positive and negative emotion words by day of the week. The days with the most positive moods? Friday and Saturday (**FIGURE 10.12**). Similar analyses of questionnaire responses and 59 million Twitter messages found Friday to Sunday the week's happiest days (Golder & Macy, 2011; Helliwell & Wang, 2015, Young & Lim, 2014). For you, too?

Over the long run, our emotional ups and downs tend to balance out, even over the course of the day. Positive emotion rises over the early to middle part of most days and then drops off (Kahneman et al., 2004; Watson, 2000). So, too, with day-to-day moods. A stressful event—an argument, a sick child, a car problem—triggers a bad mood. No surprise there. But by the next day, the gloom nearly always lifts (Affleck et al., 1994; Bolger et al., 1989; Stone & Neale, 1984). If anything, people tend to bounce back from a bad day to a *better*-than-usual good mood the following day.

Worse events—the loss of a spouse or a job—can drag us down for longer periods (Infurna & Luthar, 2016a). But eventually, our bad mood usually ends. We may feel that our heart has broken during a romantic breakup, but in time the wound heals.

Grief over the loss of a loved one or anxiety after a severe trauma can linger. But usually, even tragedy is not permanently depressing. People who become blind or paralyzed may not completely recover their previous well-being, but those with an agreeable personality usually recover near-normal levels of day-to-day happiness (Boyce & Wood, 2011; Hall et al., 1999). So do those who count their blessings and remain optimistic in the wake of a school shooting or terrorist bombing (Birkeland et al., 2016; Vieselmeyer et al., 2017). Even if you become paralyzed, explained psychologist Daniel Kahneman (2005a), "you will gradually start thinking of other things, and the more time you spend thinking of other things, the less miserable you are going to be." Contrary to what many people believe, even most patients "locked" in a motionless body report a mostly positive outlook and no wish to die (Bruno et al., 2008, 2011; Chaudhary et al., 2017; Nizzi et al., 2012). The surprising reality: *We overestimate the duration of our emotions and underestimate our resilience—our ability to bounce back.*

LaunchPad See the *Video: Naturalistic Observation* for a helpful tutorial animation about this type of research design.

CAN MONEY BUY HAPPINESS?

Would you be happier if you made more money? In a 2006 Gallup poll, 73 percent of Americans thought they would be. How important is "Being very well off financially"? "Very important" or "essential," say 82 percent of entering U.S. college students (Eagen et al., 2016). But can money truly buy happiness?

Effects of Income and Inequality

Money does buy happiness, up to a point. People in rich countries are happier than those in poor countries (Diener & Tay, 2015). Having enough money to eat, to have a sense of control over your life, and to treat yourself to something special once in a while predicts greater happiness (Fischer & Boer, 2011; Ruberton et al., 2016). This is especially true for people during their midlife working years (Cheung & Lucas, 2015). Money's power to buy happiness also depends on your current income. A 10 percent wage increase does a lot more for someone making $10,000 per year than for someone making $100,000. But once we have enough money for comfort and security, piling up more and more matters less and less (Jebb et al., 2018).

"But on the positive side, money can't buy happiness—so who cares?"

Consider: During the last 60 years, the average U.S. citizen's buying power almost tripled—enabling larger homes and twice as many cars per person, not to mention tablets and smartphones. Did it also buy more happiness? As FIGURE 10.13 shows, Americans have become no happier. In 1957, some 35 percent said they were "very happy," as did slightly fewer—33 percent—in 2014. Ditto China, where living standards have risen but happiness and life satisfaction have not (Davey & Rato, 2012; Graham et al., 2018). These findings lob a bombshell at modern materialism: *Economic growth in wealthy countries has provided no apparent boost to people's morale or social well-being.*

Why is this? One reason is that economic growth has produced rising *inequality*, which predicts unhappiness.

subjective well-being self-perceived happiness or satisfaction with life. Used along with measures of objective well-being (for example, physical and economic indicators) to judge our quality of life.

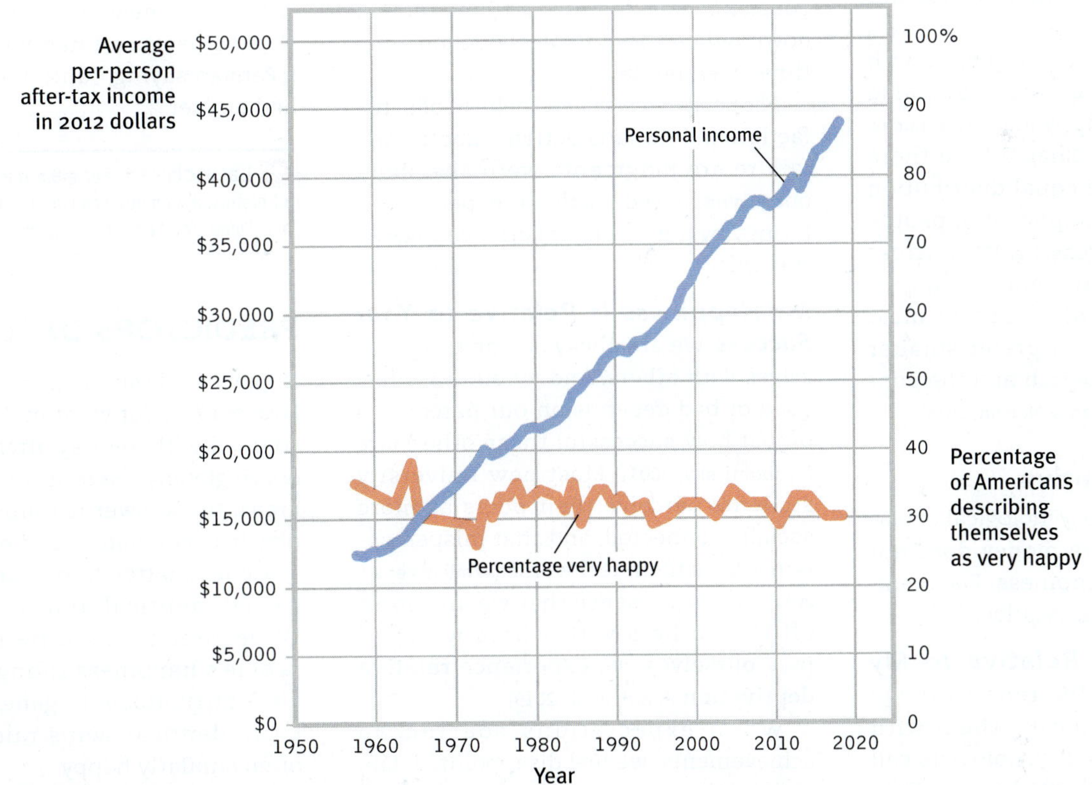

FIGURE 10.13 Does money buy happiness? It surely helps us to avoid certain types of pain. But although average buying power has nearly tripled since the 1950s, Americans' reported happiness has remained almost unchanged. (Happiness data from National Opinion Research Center surveys; income data from *Historical Statistics of the United States and Economic Indicators.*)

"Researchers say I'm not happier for being richer, but do you know how much researchers make?"

In many countries, including the United States, the rising economic tide has lifted the yachts faster than the rowboats (World Inequality Lab, 2018). Countries and states with greater inequality tend also to experience more ill health, social problems, and mental disorder (Burkhauser et al., 2016; Payne, 2017; Wilkinson & Pickett, 2017a,b). Times and places with greater income inequality have also tended to be less happy (Cheung & Lucas, 2016; Graafland & Lous, 2018). Where there is growth with more equal distribution (often government-supported), people more often flourish (Cheung, 2018). Across the world, we seem to understand this. Regardless of their political party, most people say they would prefer smaller pay gaps between the rich and the poor (Arsenio, 2018; Kiatpongsan & Norton, 2014).

Happiness Is Relative

There are two other psychological explanations for why more money does not usually buy more happiness. Each suggests that happiness is relative.

My Happiness Is Relative to My Own Experience We tend to judge new events by comparing them with our past experiences. Psychologists call this the **adaptation-level phenomenon.** Our past experiences act as *neutral* levels—sounds that seem neither loud nor soft, temperatures that seem neither hot nor cold, events that seem neither pleasant nor unpleasant. We then notice and react to variations up or down from these levels. Have you noticed how a chilly fall day, after summer, feels colder than the same temperature in late winter?

So, could we ever create a permanent social paradise? Probably not (Campbell, 1975; Di Tella et al., 2010). People who have experienced a recent windfall—from the lottery, an inheritance, or a surging economy—typically feel joy and satisfaction (Diener & Oishi, 2000; Gardner & Oswald, 2007). You would, too, if you woke up tomorrow with all your wishes granted. Wouldn't you love to live in a world with no bills, no ills, and perfect grades? But eventually, you would adapt to this new normal. Before long, you would again sometimes feel joy and satisfaction (when events exceed your expectations), sometimes feel let down (when they fall below), and sometimes feel neutral.

The point to remember: Feelings of satisfaction and dissatisfaction, success and failure are judgments we make about ourselves, based partly on expectations formed by our recent experience (Rutledge et al., 2014).

My Happiness Is Relative to Your Success We are always comparing ourselves with others. And whether we feel good or bad depends on our perception of just how successful those others are (Lyubomirsky, 2001). Most new university students perceive their peers as more socially connected, and that misperception makes them feel worse (Whillans et al., 2017). When we sense that we are worse off than others with whom we compare ourselves, we experience **relative deprivation** (Smith et al., 2019).

When expectations soar above achievements, we feel disappointed. Life satisfaction suffers when people with low incomes compare themselves to those with higher incomes. Nevertheless, once people reach a moderate income level, further increases buy smaller increases in happiness. Why? Because as people climb the ladder of success, they mostly compare themselves with local peers who are at or above their current level (Gruder, 1977; Suls & Tesch, 1978; Zell & Alicke, 2010).

Just as comparing ourselves with those who are better off creates envy, so counting our blessings as we compare ourselves with those worse off boosts our contentment. In one study, university women considered others' suffering (Dermer et al., 1979). They viewed vivid images of how grim city life could be in 1900. They imagined and then wrote about various personal tragedies, such as being burned and disfigured. Later, the women expressed greater satisfaction with their own lives. Similarly, when mildly depressed people have read about someone who was even more depressed, they felt somewhat better (Gibbons, 1986). "I cried because I had no shoes," states a Persian saying, "until I met a man who had no feet."

LaunchPad For a 6.5-minute examination of historical and modern views of happiness, see the *Video: The Search for Happiness.*

PREDICTORS OF HAPPINESS

Happy people share many characteristics (**TABLE 10.1**). But what makes one person so filled with joy, day after day, and others so gloomy? Here, as in so many other areas, the answer is found in the interplay between nature and nurture.

Genes matter. In one analysis of over 55,000 identical and fraternal twins, 36 percent of the differences among people's happiness ratings was heritable—attributable to genes (Bartels, 2015). Even identical twins raised apart are often similarly happy.

But our personal history and our culture matter, too. On the personal level, as we saw earlier, our emotions tend to

TABLE 10.1 Happiness Is . . .

Researchers Have Found That Happy People Tend to	However, Happiness Seems Not Much Related to Other Factors, Such as
Have high self-esteem (in individualist countries).	Age.
Be optimistic, outgoing, and agreeable.	Gender (women are more often depressed, but also more often joyful).
Have close, positive, and lasting relationships.	Physical attractiveness.
Have work and leisure that engage their skills.	
Have an active religious faith (especially in more religious cultures).	
Sleep well and exercise.	

Information from Batz-Barbarich et al., 2018; De Neve & Cooper, 1998; Diener et al., 2003, 2011; Headey et al., 2010; Lucas et al., 2004; Myers, 1993, 2000; Myers & Diener, 1995, 1996; Steel et al., 2008. Veenhoven, 2014, 2015 offers a database of 13,000+ correlates of happiness at WorldDatabaseofHappiness.eur.nl

balance around a level defined by our experiences. On the cultural level, groups vary in the traits they value. Self-esteem matters more in Western cultures, which value individualism. Social acceptance and harmony matter more in communal cultures that stress family and community, such as Japan (Diener et al., 2003; Fulmer et al., 2010; Uchida & Kitayama, 2009).

Depending on our genes, our outlook, and our recent experiences, our happiness seems to vary around a "happiness set point." Some of us seem ever upbeat; others, more negative. Even so, our satisfaction with life can change (Lucas & Donnellan, 2007). As researchers studying human strengths will tell you, happiness rises and falls, and we can control some of the factors that make us more or less happy (Layous & Lyubomirsky, 2014; Nes et al., 2010).

If we can enhance our happiness on an *individual* level, could we use happiness research to refocus our *national* priorities? Many psychologists believe we could. Many political leaders agree: 43 nations have begun measuring their citizens' well-being (Diener et al., 2015). Happy societies are not only prosperous, but also places where people trust one another, feel free, and enjoy close relationships (Helliwell et al., 2013; Oishi & Schimmack, 2010a). Thus, in debates about economic inequality, tax rates, divorce laws, health care, and city planning, people's psychological well-being can be a consideration. Such measures may help guide nations toward policies that decrease stress, foster human flourishing, and promote "the pursuit of happiness."

Scientifically Proven Ways to Have a Happier Life

Your happiness, like your cholesterol level, is genetically influenced. Yet as cholesterol is also influenced by diet and exercise, so happiness is to some extent under your personal control (Nes, 2010; Sin & Lyubomirsky, 2009). Here are some research-based suggestions for improving your mood, building your personal strengths, and increasing your satisfaction with life.

Take control of your time. Happy people feel in control of their lives. To master your use of time, set goals and divide them into daily aims. We all tend to overestimate how much we will accomplish in any given day. The good news is that we generally underestimate how much we can accomplish in a year, given just a little daily progress.

Act happy. Research shows that people who are manipulated into a smiling expression feel better. So put on a happy face. Talk as if you feel positive self-esteem, are optimistic, and are outgoing. We can often act our way into a happier state of mind.

Seek work and leisure that engage your skills. Happy people often are in a zone called *flow*—absorbed in tasks that challenge but don't overwhelm them. Passive forms of leisure (watching TV) often provide less flow experience than exercising, socializing, or expressing artistic interests.

Buy experiences rather than things. For those struggling financially, an education that enables greater earnings can reduce stress and increase control. For those with the means to do so, money buys more happiness when spent on experiences. This is especially true of socially shared experiences that you look forward to, enjoy, remember, and talk about later (Caprariello & Reis, 2013; Kumar & Gilovich, 2013, 2015; Lee et al., 2018). As pundit Art Buchwald said, "The best things in life aren't things."

Join the "movement" movement. Aerobic exercise can relieve mild depression and anxiety as it promotes health and energy. Sound minds reside in sound bodies.

Give your body the sleep it wants. Happy people live active lives yet reserve time for renewing, refreshing sleep. Sleep debt results in fatigue, reduced alertness, and gloomy moods. Sleep now, smile later.

Give priority to close relationships. Compared with unhappy people, happy people engage in meaningful conversations (Milek et al., 2018). Resolve to nurture your closest

adaptation-level phenomenon our tendency to form judgments (of sounds, of lights, of income) relative to a neutral level defined by our past experiences.

relative deprivation the perception that we are worse off relative to those with whom we compare ourselves.

relationships by not taking your loved ones for granted. Give them the sort of kindness and affirmation you give others. Relationships matter.

Focus and find meaning beyond self. Reach out to those in need. Perform acts of kindness. Happiness increases helpfulness, but doing good also makes us feel good. We feel happier when our life has meaning and purpose.

Challenge your negative thinking. Reframe "I failed" to "I can learn from this." Remind yourself that stuff happens, and that in a month or a year, this bad experience may not seem like that big a deal.

Count your blessings and record your gratitude. Keeping a gratitude journal heightens well-being (Davis et al., 2016). Take time to savor positive experiences and achievements, and to appreciate why they occurred (Sheldon & Lyubomirsky, 2012). Express your gratitude to others (Dickens, 2017).

Nurture your spiritual self. Meditation helps us stay steady, emotionally. And for many people, faith provides a support community, a reason to focus beyond self, and a sense of purpose and hope. That helps explain why people active in faith communities report greater-than-average happiness and often cope well with crises.

IMPROVE YOUR EVERYDAY LIFE

Were you surprised by any of the findings related to happiness? What things might you change in your life to increase your own happiness?

RETRIEVE & REMEMBER

ANSWERS IN APPENDIX E

7. Which of the following factors does NOT predict self-reported happiness?
   a. Age
   b. Personality traits
   c. Sleep and exercise
   d. Active religious faith

CHAPTER 10 REVIEW Stress, Health, and Human Flourishing

LEARNING OBJECTIVES

TEST YOURSELF Answer these repeated Learning Objective Questions on your own (before checking the answers in Appendix D) to improve your retention of the concepts (McDaniel et al., 2009, 2015).

Stress: Some Basic Concepts

10-1: How does our appraisal of an event affect our stress reaction, and what are the three main types of stressors?

10-2: How does the body respond to stress?

Stress Effects and Health

10-3: How does stress influence our immune system?

10-4: How does stress increase coronary heart disease risk?

10-5: So, does stress *cause* illness?

Coping With Stress

10-6: What are two basic ways that people cope with stress?

10-7: How does our sense of control influence stress and health?

10-8: How do optimists and pessimists differ, and why does our outlook on life matter?

10-9: How do social support and finding meaning in life influence health?

Managing Stress Effects

10-10: How well does aerobic exercise help us manage stress and improve well-being?

10-11: In what ways might relaxation and meditation influence stress and health?

10-12: Does religious involvement relate to health?

Happiness

10-13: What are the causes and consequences of happiness?

TERMS AND CONCEPTS TO REMEMBER

TEST YOURSELF Write down the definition in your own words, then check your answer.

stress, *p. 277*
fight-or-flight response, *p. 279*
general adaptation syndrome (GAS), *p. 279*
tend-and-befriend response, *p. 279*
psychoneuroimmunology, *p. 279*
coronary heart disease, *p. 281*
Type A, *p. 281*
Type B, *p. 281*
coping, *p. 283*
problem-focused coping, *p. 283*
emotion-focused coping, *p. 283*
personal control, *p. 283*
learned helplessness, *p. 283*
external locus of control, *p. 285*
internal locus of control, *p. 285*
self-control, *p. 285*
optimism, *p. 285*
pessimism, *p. 287*
aerobic exercise, *p. 289*
mindfulness meditation, *p. 291*
resilience, *p. 293*
feel-good, do-good phenomenon, *p. 293*
subjective well-being, *p. 295*
adaptation-level phenomenon, *p. 297*
relative deprivation, *p. 297*

CHAPTER TEST

TEST YOURSELF Answer the following questions on your own first, then check your answers in Appendix E.

1. The number of short-term illnesses and stress-related psychological disorders was higher than usual in the months following an earthquake. Such findings suggest that
   a. daily hassles have adverse health consequences.
   b. experiencing a very stressful event increases a person's vulnerability to illness.
   c. the amount of stress a person feels is directly related to the number of stressors experienced.
   d. daily hassles don't cause stress, but catastrophes can be toxic.
2. Which of the following is NOT one of the three main types of stressors?
   a. Catastrophes
   b. Significant life changes
   c. Daily hassles
   d. Pessimism
3. Selye's general adaptation syndrome (GAS) consists of an alarm reaction followed by ________, then ________.
4. When faced with stress, women are more likely than men to exhibit the ________-and-________ response.
5. Stress can suppress the ________ ________ by prompting a decrease in the release of lymphocytes, the cells that ordinarily attack bacteria, viruses, cancer cells, and other foreign substances.
6. Research has shown that people are at increased risk for cancer a year or so after experiencing depression, helplessness, or grief. In describing this link, researchers are quick to point out that
   a. accumulated stress causes cancer.
   b. anger is the negative emotion most closely linked to cancer.
   c. stress does not create cancer cells, but it weakens the body's natural defenses against them.
   d. feeling optimistic about chances of survival increases the likelihood of a cancer patient's recovery.
7. A Chinese proverb warns, "The fire you kindle for your enemy often burns you more than him." How is this true of Type A individuals?
8. When faced with a situation over which you feel you have little control, you are more likely to turn to ________ (emotion/problem)-focused coping.
9. Research has shown that a dog will respond with learned helplessness if it has received repeated shocks and has had
   a. the opportunity to escape.
   b. no control over the shocks.
   c. pain or discomfort.
   d. no food or water prior to the shocks.
10. When elderly patients take an active part in managing their own care and surroundings, their morale and health tend to improve. Such findings indicate that people do better when they experience an ________ (internal/external) locus of control.

11. People who have close relationships are less likely to die prematurely than those who do not, supporting the idea that

a. social ties can be a source of stress.

b. gender influences longevity.

c. Type A behavior is responsible for many premature deaths.

d. social support has a beneficial effect on health.

12. Because it triggers the release of mood-boosting neurotransmitters such as serotonin, ________ exercise raises energy levels and helps alleviate depression and anxiety.

13. Research on the faith factor has found that

a. pessimists tend to be healthier than optimists.

b. our expectations influence our feelings of stress.

c. religiously active people tend to outlive those who are not religiously active.

d. religious engagement promotes social isolation and repression.

14. One of the most consistent findings of psychological research is that happy people are also

a. more likely to express anger.

b. generally luckier than others.

c. concentrated in the wealthier nations.

d. more likely to help others.

15. After moving to a new apartment, you find the street noise irritatingly loud, but after a while it no longer bothers you. This reaction illustrates the

a. relative deprivation principle.

b. adaptation-level phenomenon.

c. feel-good, do-good phenomenon.

d. importance of mindfulness meditation.

16. A philosopher observed that we cannot escape envy, because there will always be someone more successful, more accomplished, or richer with whom to compare ourselves. In psychology, this observation is embodied in the ________ ________ principle.

Continue testing yourself with **LearningCurve** or **Achieve Read & Practice** to learn and remember most effectively.

Jessica Lia/Getty Images

Social Psychology

CHAPTER 11

SURVEY THE CHAPTER

On a winter day in 1569, Dirk Willems faced a moment of decision. He had just escaped from prison, where he was facing torture and death for belonging to a persecuted religious minority. Willems fled across an ice-covered pond in Asperen, Holland, with his stronger and heavier jailer close behind. Then, suddenly, the jailer fell through the ice. Unable to climb out, he pleaded for Willems' help to escape the icy waters.

Rather than racing to freedom, Willems acted with ultimate selflessness: He turned back and rescued his pursuer. The jailer, following orders, took Willems back to prison where, a few weeks later, Willems was burned alive. For his martyrdom, Asperen has a street named in honor of its folk hero (Toews, 2004).

What drives groups to feel and act so heartlessly toward those, like Willems, who differ from them? What motivates people, such as his jailer, to carry out unfair orders? What inspired the selflessness of Willems' response, and of so many who have died trying to save others?

We are social animals. We cannot live for ourselves alone. We like and we love, and, sometimes, we dislike and we hate. Your life is connected by "a thousand fibres," through which "run your actions as causes, and return to you as effects" (Melvill, 1855). In this chapter, we explore many of these connections and see how social psychologists study them.

Mennonite Library and Archives/ Bethel Colleg

An etching of Dirk Willems by Dutch artist Jan Luyken (From *The Martyrs Mirror,* 1685.)

What Is Social Psychology's Focus?

Learning Objective Question LOQ 11-1 What are three main focuses of social psychology?

Social psychologists use *scientific methods* to study how we *think about, influence,* and *relate to* one another. We all want to understand why people act as they do. Personality psychologists (Chapter 12) study the personal traits and processes that explain why, in a given situation, *different people* may act differently. (Would you have acted as Willems did, helping his jailer out of the icy water?) Social psychologists study the social forces that explain why *the same person* acts differently in *different situations.* (Might Willems' jailer have released him under other circumstances?)

Social Thinking

When we try to explain people's actions, our search for answers often leaves us with two choices. We can attribute behavior to a person's stable, enduring traits. Or we can attribute behavior to the situation (Heider, 1958). Our explanations, or *attributions,* affect our feelings and actions.

THE FUNDAMENTAL ATTRIBUTION ERROR

LOQ 11-2 How does the fundamental attribution error describe how we tend to explain others' behavior compared with our own?

In class, we notice that Jill seldom talks. Over coffee, Jack talks nonstop. That must be the sort of people they are, we decide. Jill must be shy and Jack outgoing. Are they? Perhaps. People do have enduring personality traits. But often our explanations are wrong. We fall prey to the **fundamental attribution error:** We overestimate the influence of personality and underestimate the influence of situations. In class, Jack may be as quiet as Jill. Catch Jill at a party and you may hardly recognize your quiet classmate.

Researchers demonstrated this tendency in an experiment with college students (Napolitan & Goethals, 1979). Students talked, one at a time, with a woman who acted either cold and critical or warm and friendly. Before the talks, researchers told half the students that the woman's behavior would be normal and natural. They told the other half the truth—that they had instructed her to *act* friendly or unfriendly.

Did hearing the truth affect students' impressions of the woman? Not at all! If the woman acted friendly, both groups decided she really was a warm person. If she acted unfriendly, both decided she really was a cold person. In other words, they attributed her behavior to her personal traits, *even when they were told that her behavior was part of the experimental situation.*

To see how easily we make the fundamental attribution error, answer this question: Is your psychology instructor shy or outgoing? If you're tempted to answer "outgoing," remember that you know your instructor from one situation—the classroom, where teaching demands talking. Outside the classroom, professors seem less professorial, students less studious.

Culture affects our attributions. Westerners more often attribute behavior to people's personal traits. People in Japan are more sensitive to the power of situations (Miyamoto & Kitayama, 2018). In experiments in which people were asked to view scenes, such as a big fish swimming amid smaller fish and underwater plants, Americans focused more on the attributes of the big fish. Japanese viewers focused on the scene—the situation (Chua et al., 2005; Nisbett, 2003).

Whose behavior also matters. When we explain *our own* behavior, we are sensitive to how behavior changes with the situation (Idson & Mischel, 2001). We also are sensitive to the power of the situation when we explain the behavior of people we have seen in many different contexts. So, when are we most likely to commit the fundamental attribution error? The odds are highest when a stranger acts badly. Having never seen this enraged person in other situations, we assume he must be an angry person. But outside the stadium, that fan screaming at the referee may be a great neighbor and a good father.

Could we broaden our awareness of our own behavior by taking another person's view? Researchers tested this idea by using separate cameras to reverse the perspectives of *actor* and *observer.* They filmed two people interacting, and then showed each person a replay of their interaction—filmed from the other person's perspective. Sure enough, this reversed participants' attributions of the behaviors. Seeing the world from the actor's perspective, the observers credited their own behavior more to their *disposition* (personal character), much as an observer typically would (Lassiter & Irvine, 1986; Storms, 1973).

Two important exceptions to our usual view of our own actions: Our deliberate and *admirable* actions we often attribute to our own good reasons, not to the situation (Malle, 2006; Malle et al., 2007). And as we age, we tend to attribute our younger selves' behavior mostly to our traits (Pronin & Ross, 2006). In 5 or 10 years, your current self may seem like another person.

Keith Srakocic/AP Images

Personal versus situational attributions Should the 2018 slaughter of 11 Jewish worshippers at Pittsburgh's Tree of Life synagogue be attributed to the shooter's hateful disposition? To America's gun culture? (The shooter reportedly used 4 of his 10 guns.) Or to both? And to what should we attribute the compassion of the emergency room nurse—a Jew and the son of a rabbi—who treated the hate-spewing shooter (Flynn, 2018)?

The way we explain others' actions, attributing them to the person or the situation, can have important real-life effects (Fincham & Bradbury, 1993; Fletcher et al., 1990). Does a warm greeting reflect friendliness or romantic interest? Are a candidate's promises sincere or to be forgotten post-election? Does a manager's acid-tongued remark reflect a job threat or just a bad day? Attributions matter.

Do you explain poverty or unemployment to social circumstances, or to personal traits and bad choices? In Britain, India, Australia, and the United States, political conservatives have tended to attribute responsibility to the personal traits of the poor and unemployed (Dunn, 2018; Furnham, 1982; Pandey et al., 1982; Wagstaff, 1982; Zucker & Weiner, 1993). "People make their choices. Anybody who tries hard can get ahead." In experiments, those who reflect on the power of choice—either by recalling their own choices or taking note of another's choices—are more likely to think that inequality just comes down to effort (Savani & Rattan, 2012). Those not asked to consider the power of choice are more likely to blame past and present situations.

The point to remember: Our attributions—to someone's personal traits or to the situation—have real consequences.

LaunchPad For a quick interactive tutorial, engage online with *Concept Practice: Making Attributions.*

ATTITUDES AND ACTIONS

LOQ 11-3 What is an *attitude,* and how do attitudes and actions affect each other?

Attitudes are feelings, often based on our beliefs, that can influence how we respond to particular objects, people, and events. If we *believe* someone is mean, we may *feel* dislike for the person and *act* unfriendly.

The traffic between our attitudes and our actions is two-way. Our attitudes affect our actions. Hateful attitudes feed violent behavior. And our actions affect our attitudes (much as our emotional expressions affect our emotions).

Attitudes Affect Actions

Attitudes affect our behavior, but other factors, including the situation, also influence behavior. For example, in votes requiring politicians to state their support or opposition publicly, situational pressures can control the outcome. Politicians may vote as their supporters demand, despite privately disagreeing with those demands (Nagourney, 2002).

When are attitudes most likely to affect behavior? Under these conditions (Glasman & Albarracin, 2006):

- External influences are minimal.
- The attitude is stable.
- The attitude is specific to the behavior.
- The attitude is easily recalled.

One experiment used vivid, easily recalled information to convince White sun-tanning college students that repeated tanning put them at risk for future skin cancer. One month later, 72 percent of the participants, and only 16 percent of those in a "waitlist" control group, had lighter skin (McClendon & Prentice-Dunn, 2001). Changed attitudes (about skin cancer risk) changed behavior (less tanning).

Matthias Hangst/Getty Images

FIGURE 11.1 Attitudes follow behavior Cooperative actions, such as those performed by people on sports teams (including Germany, shown here celebrating a World Cup victory), feed mutual liking. Such attitudes, in turn, promote positive behavior.

Actions Affect Attitudes

We also come to believe in what we have stood up for. Many streams of evidence confirm that *attitudes follow behavior* (**FIGURE 11.1**).

Foot-in-the-Door Phenomenon How would you react if someone got you to act against your beliefs? Would you change your beliefs? Many people do. During the Korean war, many U.S. prisoners were held in Chinese communist camps. The captors gained prisoners' cooperation in various activities,

social psychology the scientific study of how we think about, influence, and relate to one another.

fundamental attribution error the tendency, when analyzing others' behavior, to overestimate the influence of personal traits and underestimate the influence of the situation.

attitude feelings, often based on our beliefs, that predispose us to respond in a particular way to objects, people, and events.

ranging from simple tasks (to gain privileges) to more serious actions (false confessions, informing on other prisoners, and revealing U.S. military information). After doing so, the prisoners sometimes adjusted their beliefs to be more consistent with their public acts (Lifton, 1961). When the war ended, 21 prisoners chose to stay with the communists. Some others returned home convinced that communism was good for Asia (though not actually "brainwashed," as has often been said).

The Chinese captors succeeded in part thanks to the **foot-in-the-door phenomenon.** They knew that people who agree to a small request will find it easier to agree later to a larger one. The Chinese began with harmless requests, such as copying a trivial statement. Gradually, they made bigger demands (Schein, 1956). The next statement to be copied might contain a list of the flaws of capitalism. Then, to gain privileges, the prisoners would move up to participating in group discussions, writing self-criticisms, and, finally, uttering public confessions. The point is simple. To get people to agree to something big, start small and build (Cialdini, 1993). A trivial act makes the next act easier. Telling a small lie paves the way to telling a bigger lie. Fibbers may become frauds. Give in to a temptation and the next temptation becomes harder to resist.

Experiments also reveal a *door-in-the-face* effect: Approach someone with an unreasonable request ("Could you volunteer daily for the next two weeks?"). After you get turned down (the door in the face), a smaller follow-up request becomes more acceptable ("Could you volunteer for the next 30 minutes?").

In dozens of experiments, researchers have coaxed people into acting against their attitudes or violating their moral standards, with the same result. Doing becomes believing. After giving in to an order to harm an innocent victim—by making nasty comments or delivering presumed electric shocks—people begin to look down on their victim. After speaking or writing in support of a position they have doubts about, they begin to believe their own words.

Fortunately, the principle that attitudes follow behavior works for good deeds as well. It has helped boost charitable contributions and blood donations. After U.S. schools were desegregated and the 1964 Civil Rights Act was passed, White Americans expressed lower levels of racial prejudice. And as Americans in different regions came to *act* more alike—thanks to more uniform national standards against discrimination—they began to *think* more alike. Experiments confirm the point: *Moral actions strengthen moral convictions.*

IMPROVE YOUR EVERYDAY LIFE

Do you have an attitude or tendency you would like to change? Using the attitudes-follow-behavior principle, how might you go about changing that attitude?

Role-Playing Affects Attitudes How many new **roles** have you adopted recently? Becoming a college student is a new role. Perhaps you've started a new job, or a new relationship, or even become engaged or married. At first, your behaviors may have felt phony, because you were acting a role. Soldiers may at first feel they are playing war games. Newlyweds may feel they are "playing house." Before long, however, what began as play-acting in the theater of life becomes *you.* (This fact is reflected in the Alcoholics Anonymous advice: "Fake it until you make it.")

Role-playing was dramatized in one famous, controversial study in which male college students volunteered to spend time in a mock prison (Zimbardo, 1972). Stanford psychologist Philip Zimbardo randomly assigned some volunteers to be guards. He gave them uniforms, clubs, and whistles and instructed them to enforce rules. Others became prisoners, locked in barren cells and forced to wear humiliating outfits.

Paul Burns/Blend Images/Alamy

New nurse Pulling on scrubs for the first time can feel like playing dress-up. But over time that role defines the players, as they jump in to the day-to-day work and follow the social cues in their new environment.

For a day or two, the volunteers self-consciously played their roles. But then, reported Zimbardo, most guards developed negative attitudes and "became tyrannical," devising cruel and degrading routines. One by one, the prisoners broke down, rebelled, or became passively resigned. After only six days, Zimbardo called off the study.

Critics question the reliability of Zimbardo's results (Griggs, 2014). Others argue that Zimbardo stage-managed the experiment to get his predicted results, and that the volunteers for a "prison experiment" would have had above-average levels of aggressiveness and authoritarianism (Bartels et al., 2016; Haslam et al., 2018; Reicher et al., 2018). But this much Zimbardo and his critics agree on: The Stanford study was more a *demonstration* of toxic behavior than a true experiment (Haney et al., 2018). It demonstrated the power of the situation—of how an authority figure can shape people's identities and behaviors (Haslam et al., 2019). Yet people differ. In real-life atrocity-producing situations, some people have given in to the situation and others have not (Haslam & Reicher, 2007, 2012; Mastroianni & Reed, 2006; Zimbardo, 2007). Person and situation interact.

Cognitive Dissonance: Relief From Tension We have seen that actions can affect attitudes, sometimes turning prisoners into collaborators and role players into believers. But why? One explanation is that when we become aware of a mismatch between our attitudes and actions, we experience mental discomfort, or *cognitive dissonance*. To relieve this mental tension, according to Leon Festinger's **cognitive dissonance theory,** we often bring our attitudes into line with our actions.

Dozens of experiments have tested cognitive dissonance theory. Many have made people feel responsible for behavior that clashed with their attitudes. As a participant in one of these experiments, you might agree for a small sum of money to help a researcher by writing an essay supporting something you don't believe in (perhaps a tuition increase). Feeling responsible for your written statements (which don't reflect your attitudes), you would probably feel dissonance, especially if you thought an administrator would be reading your essay. How could you reduce the uncomfortable tension? One way would be to start believing your phony words. It's as if we tell ourselves, "If I chose to do it (or say it), I must believe in it." Thus, we may change our attitudes to help justify the act.

The attitudes-follow-behavior principle can also help us become better people. We cannot control all our feelings, but we can influence them by altering our behavior. (Recall from Chapter 9 the emotional effects of facial expressions and of body postures.) If we are depressed, we can alter our attributions and explain events in more positive terms, with more self-acceptance and fewer self-put-downs. If we are unloving, we can become more loving. We can do thoughtful things, express affection, and give support. Act as if you like someone, and you soon may. What we do we become.

The point to remember: Not only can we think ourselves into action, we can act ourselves into a way of thinking.

RETRIEVE & REMEMBER

ANSWERS IN APPENDIX E

1. Driving to school one snowy day, Marco narrowly misses a car that slides through a red light. "Slow down! What a terrible driver," he thinks to himself. Moments later, Marco himself slips through an intersection and yelps, "Wow! These roads are awful. The city plows need to get out here." What social psychology principle has Marco just demonstrated? Explain.
2. How do our attitudes and our actions affect each other?
3. When people act in a way that is not in keeping with their attitudes, and then change their attitudes to match those actions, __________ __________ theory attempts to explain why.

LaunchPad To check your understanding of cognitive dissonance, engage online with *Concept Practice: Cognitive Dissonance.*

PERSUASION

LOQ 11-4 How do *peripheral route persuasion* and *central route persuasion* differ?

Knowing that public attitudes affect public policies, people on both sides of any debate aim to *persuade*. Persuasion efforts generally take two forms:

- **Peripheral route persuasion** uses attention-getting cues to trigger speedy, emotion-based judgments. One experiment gave some people information showing that vaccines do not cause autism (which they do not); others were shown photos of unvaccinated children suffering mumps, measles, or rubella, along with a parent's description of measles. Only those given the vivid disease images and parental experience became more supportive of vaccines (Horne et al., 2015). Endorsements by beautiful or famous people also can influence people, whether to choose a political candidate or to buy the latest personal care product. When environmental activist and actor Cate Blanchett urges action to counter climate change, or when Pope Francis (2015) states that "Climate change is a global problem with grave implications," they hope to harness their appeal for peripheral route persuasion.
- **Central route persuasion** offers evidence and arguments that aim to trigger careful thinking. To persuade buyers to purchase a new gadget, an ad might list all the latest features. Effective arguments to act on climate change have focused on the accumulating greenhouse gases, melting arctic ice, rising world temperatures and seas, and increasing extreme weather (van der Linden et al., 2015). Central route persuasion works well for people who are naturally analytical or involved in an issue. And because it is more thoughtful and less superficial, it is more durable.

We often want to persuade others to agree with our own way of thinking. For more on effective persuasion strategies, see Thinking Critically About: How to Be Persuasive.

foot-in-the-door phenomenon the tendency for people who have first agreed to a small request to comply later with a larger request.

role a set of expectations *(norms)* about a social position, defining how those in the position ought to behave.

cognitive dissonance theory the theory that we act to reduce the discomfort (dissonance) we feel when two of our thoughts (cognitions) clash. For example, when we become aware that our attitudes and our actions don't match, we may change our attitudes so that we feel more comfortable.

peripheral route persuasion occurs when people are influenced by unimportant cues, such as a speaker's attractiveness.

central route persuasion occurs when interested people's thinking is influenced by considering evidence and arguments.

Thinking Critically About:

How to Be Persuasive

LOQ 11-5 How can we share our views more effectively?

Would you like to be persuasive with those whose views differ from yours?

Do not:

Loudly argue your position before listening. Yelling backfires.

Humiliate people, or imply that they are ignorant. Insults breed defensiveness.

^%*&#!!
idiot
Stupid
#&#!!

Bore people with complex and forgettable information.

Therefore, with that said, direct your attention to this very dull and wonky and boring statistic that you will never remember. Now, however, on the other hand, here are yet more data points that are even more dry and overly complicated than the last... Let us continue...

Do:

Identify your shared values or goals, such as, "We all want to graduate, yes? Find a better job? Let's study for the test before we take time off to hang out."

Appeal to others' admirable motives. Relate your aims to their yearnings.[1] For example:

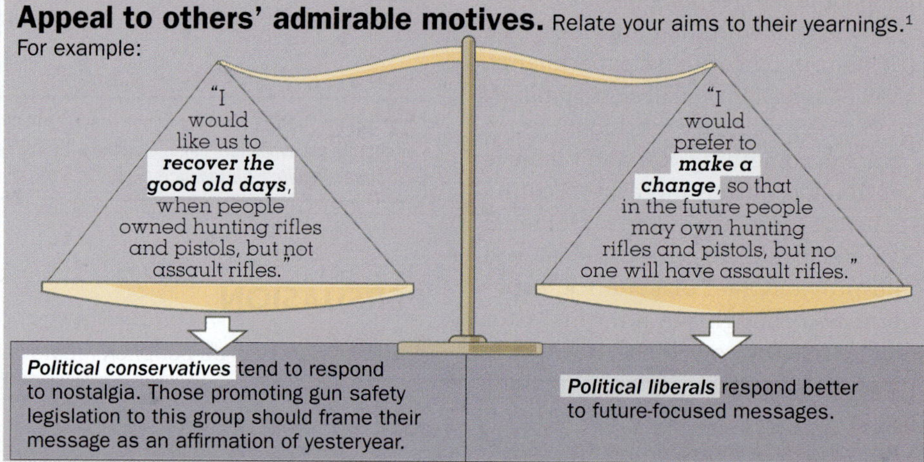

"I would like us to ***recover the good old days***, when people owned hunting rifles and pistols, but not assault rifles."
"I would prefer to ***make a change***, so that in the future people may own hunting rifles and pistols, but no one will have assault rifles."

Political conservatives tend to respond to nostalgia. Those promoting gun safety legislation to this group should frame their message as an affirmation of yesteryear.

Political liberals respond better to future-focused messages.

Make your message vivid. People remember dramatic visual examples well. Pictures of unvaccinated children suffering from preventable diseases, or hungry children starving speak to the heart as well as the head.

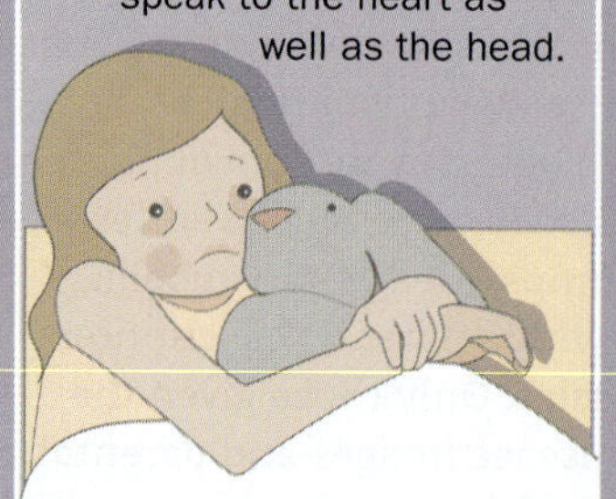

Repeat your message. People often come to believe repeated falsehoods, but they also tend to believe oft-repeated truths.

Science
Science
Evidence-based
Science
Evidence-based
Consider alternatives
Science
Evidence-based
Evidence-based
Consider alternatives
Science

Engage your audience in restating your message or, better yet, acting on it. Engage them in actively owning it—not just passively listening.

1. Lammers & Baldwin, 2018.

IMPROVE YOUR EVERYDAY LIFE

Have you found yourself using any of these ineffective persuasive strategies? How might you improve your approach the next time you are having an important discussion?

RETRIEVE & REMEMBER

ANSWERS IN APPENDIX E

4. What are some evidence-based ways to effectively persuade others?

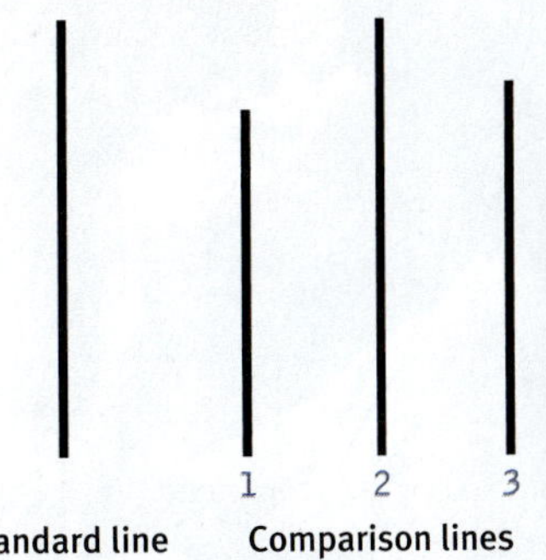

William Vendivert/Scientific American

FIGURE 11.2 Asch's conformity experiments Which of the three comparison lines is equal to the standard line? What do you suppose most people would say after hearing five others say, "Line 3"? In this photo from one of Asch's experiments, the student in the center shows the severe discomfort that comes from disagreeing with the responses of other group members (in this case, accomplices of the experimenter).

Social Influence

Social psychology's great lesson is the enormous power of social influence. We adjust our views to match the desires of those around us. We follow orders. We behave as others in our group behave. On campus, workout clothes are the dress code. On New York's Wall Street, business suits are the norm. Let's examine the pull of these social strings. How strong are they? How do they operate? When do we break them?

CONFORMITY AND OBEDIENCE

LOQ 11-6 What do experiments on conformity and obedience reveal about the power of social influence?

Fish swim in schools. Birds fly in flocks. And humans, too, tend to go with their group—to do what it does and think what it thinks. Behavior is influenced by *social contagion*. If one of us laughs, coughs, yawns, scratches an itch, stares at the sky, or checks our phone, others will often do the same (Holle et al., 2012). Even just reading about yawning increases people's yawning (Provine, 2012), as perhaps you've now noticed?

© Dave Coverly/speedbump.com

Researchers have referred to this social contagion as a *chameleon effect* (likening it to a chameleon lizard's ability to take on the color of its surroundings), capturing it in a clever experiment (Chartrand & Bargh, 1999). They had students work in a room beside another person (actually an *accomplice* working for the experimenters). Sometimes the accomplices rubbed their own face. Sometimes they shook their foot. Sure enough, students tended to rub their face with the face-rubbing person and shake their foot with the foot-shaking person.

Social contagion is not confined to behavior. We human chameleons also take on the emotional tones of those around us—their expressions, postures, and voice tones—and even their grammar (Ireland & Pennebaker, 2010). Just hearing someone reading a neutral text in either a happy- or sad-sounding voice creates *mood contagion* in listeners (Neumann & Strack, 2000).

This natural mimicry enables us to *empathize*—to feel what others feel. This helps explain why we feel happier around happy people than around depressed people. The more we mimic, the greater our empathy, and the more people tend to like us (Chartrand & van Baaren, 2009; Lakin et al., 2008). We tend to mimic those we like, and to like those who mimic us (Kämpf et al., 2018). Just going for a walk with someone—perhaps someone with whom you disagreed—not only synchronizes your movements but increases rapport and empathy (Webb et al., 2017).

Group Pressure and Conformity

To study **conformity**—adjusting our behavior or thinking toward some group standard—Solomon Asch (1955) designed a simple test. As a participant in what you believe is a study of visual perception, you arrive in time to take a seat at a table with five other people. The experimenter asks the group members to state, one by one, which of three comparison lines is identical to a standard line. You see clearly that the answer is Line 2, and you wait your turn to say so. Your boredom begins to show when the next set of lines proves equally easy.

Now comes the third trial, and the correct answer seems just as clear-cut (**FIGURE 11.2**). But the first person gives what strikes you as a wrong answer: "Line 3." When the second person and then the third and fourth give the same wrong answer, you sit up straight and squint. When the fifth person agrees with the first four, you feel your heart begin to pound. The experimenter

conformity adjusting our behavior or thinking to coincide with a group standard.

then looks to you for your answer. Torn between the agreement voiced by the five others and the evidence of your own eyes, you feel tense and suddenly unsure of yourself. You wait a bit before answering, wondering whether you should suffer the pain of being the oddball. What answer do you give?

In Asch's experiments, college students experienced this conflict. Answering questions alone, they were wrong less than 1 percent of the time. But what happened when several others—accomplices—answered incorrectly? More than one-third of the time, these "intelligent and well-meaning" college students were then "willing to call white black" by going along with the group.

Experiments reveal that we are more likely to conform when we

- are made to feel incompetent or insecure.
- are in a group with at least three people.
- are in a group in which everyone else agrees. (If just one other person disagrees, we will almost surely disagree.)
- admire the group's status and attractiveness.
- have not already committed ourselves to any response.
- know that others in the group will observe our behavior.
- are from a culture that strongly encourages respect for social standards.

"Have you ever noticed how one example—good or bad—can prompt others to follow? How one illegally parked car can give permission for others to do likewise? How one racial joke can fuel another?" —Marian Wright Edelman, *The Measure of Our Success*, 1994

Why do we so often do as others do and think as they think? Why, when asked controversial questions, are students' answers more similar when they raise their hands and more varied when they use anonymous electronic clickers (Stowell et al., 2010)? Why do we clap when others clap, eat as others eat, believe what others believe, even see what others see? Sometimes it's to avoid rejection or to gain social approval (Williams & Sommer, 1997). In such cases, we are responding to **normative social influence.** We are sensitive to social norms—understood rules for accepted and expected behavior—because the price we pay for being different can be severe (Calcutt et al., 2019). But sometimes we conform because we want to be accurate. We are responding to **informational social influence** when we accept others' opinions about reality, as when reading online movie and restaurant reviews.

Gerda & Helmut Schill/Anzenber/Redux

Tattoos: Yesterday's nonconformity, today's conformity?

Is conformity good or bad? Conformity can be bad—leading people to agree with falsehoods or go along with bullying. Or it can be good—leading people to give more generously after observing others' generosity (Nook et al., 2016).

Our values are influenced by our culture (as we'll discuss in Chapter 12). Western Europeans and people in most English-speaking countries tend to prize *individualism* (emphasizing an independent self). People in many Asian, African, and Latin American countries place a higher value on *collectivism* (emphasizing group standards). Experiments across 17 countries have found lower conformity rates in individualist cultures (Bond & Smith, 1996).

IN YOUR EVERYDAY LIFE

How have you found yourself conforming, or perhaps "conforming to nonconformity" this week? In what ways have you seen others identifying themselves with those of the same culture or subculture?

RETRIEVE & REMEMBER

ANSWERS IN APPENDIX E

5. Which of the following strengthens conformity to a group?
   a. Finding the group attractive
   b. Feeling secure
   c. Coming from an individualist culture
   d. Having already decided on a response
6. Despite her mother's pleas to use a more comfortable backpack, Antonia insists on trying to carry all of her books to school in an oversized purse the way her fashionable friends all seem to do. Antonia is affected by what type of social influence?

LaunchPad To review the classic conformity studies and experience a simulated experiment, visit *Topic Tutorial: PsychSim6, Everybody's Doing It!*

Obedience

Social psychologist Stanley Milgram (1963, 1974), a high school classmate of Phillip Zimbardo and later a student of Solomon Asch, knew that people often give in to social pressure. But what about outright commands? Would they respond as did those who carried out Holocaust atrocities? (Some of Milgram's family members had suffered in Nazi concentration camps.) To find out, he undertook what have become social psychology's most famous and controversial experiments.

Imagine yourself as one of the nearly 1000 people, mostly men, who took part in Milgram's 20 experiments. You have responded to an ad for participants in a Yale University psychology study of the effect of punishment on learning. Professor Milgram's assistant asks you and another person to draw slips from a hat to see who will be the "teacher" and who will be the "learner." You draw the "teacher" slip (unknown to you,

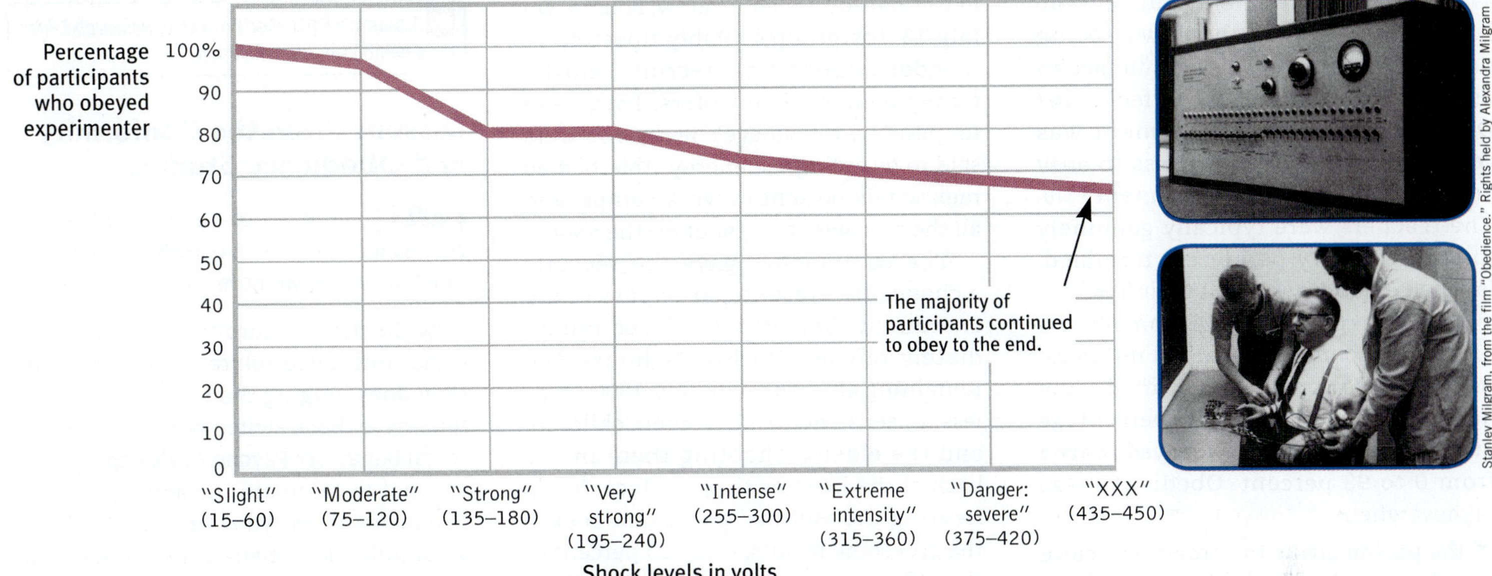

FIGURE 11.3 Milgram's follow-up obedience experiment In a repeat of the earlier experiment, 65 percent of the adult male "teachers" fully obeyed the experimenter's commands to continue. They did so despite the "learner's" earlier mention of a heart condition and despite hearing increasingly agonized cries of protest after they administered what they thought were greater and greater voltages. (Data from Milgram, 1974.)

both slips say "teacher"). The supposed "learner" is led to a nearby room and strapped into a chair. From the chair, wires run through the wall to a shock machine. You sit down in front of the machine and are given your task: Teach and then test the learner on a list of word pairs. If the learner gives a wrong answer, you are to flip a switch to deliver a brief electric shock. For the first wrong answer, you will flip the switch labeled "15 Volts—Slight Shock." With each additional error, you will move to the next higher voltage. The researcher demonstrates by flipping the first switch. Lights flash and an electric buzzing fills the air.

The experiment begins, and you deliver the shocks after the first and second wrong answers. If you continue, you hear the learner grunt when you flick the third, fourth, and fifth switches. After you flip the eighth switch ("120 Volts—Moderate Shock"), the learner cries out that the shocks are painful. After the tenth switch ("150 Volts—Strong Shock"), he begins shouting: "Get me out of here! I won't be in the experiment anymore! I refuse to go on!" You draw back, but the experimenter prods you. "Please continue—the experiment requires that you continue." You resist, but the experimenter insists, "It is absolutely essential that you continue," or "You have no other choice, you *must* go on."

If you obey, you hear the learner shriek in agony as you continue to raise the shock level after each new error. After the 330-volt level, the learner falls silent. Still, the experimenter pushes you toward the final, 450-volt switch. Ask the question, he says, and if no correct answer is given, administer the next shock level.

Would you follow an experimenter's commands to shock someone? At what level would you refuse to obey? Previously, Milgram had asked nonparticipants what they would do. Most were sure they would stop playing such a sadistic-seeming role soon after the learner first indicated pain, certainly before he shrieked in agony. Forty psychiatrists agreed with that prediction. Were the predictions accurate? Not even close. When Milgram actually conducted the experiment with men aged 20 to 50, he was amazed. More than 60 percent followed orders—right up to the last switch. When he ran a new study, with 40 new teachers and a learner who complained of a "slight heart condition," the results were the same. A full 65 percent of the new teachers obeyed every one of the experimenter's commands, right up to 450 volts (**FIGURE 11.3**). In 10 later studies, women obeyed at rates similar to men's (Blass, 1999).

Were Milgram's results a product of the 1960s American mindset? No. In a more recent replication, 70 percent of the participants obeyed up to the 150-volt point (only a modest reduction from Milgram's 83 percent at that level) (Burger, 2009). A Polish research team found 90 percent obedience to the same level (Doliński et al., 2017). And in a French reality TV show replication, 81 percent of people, egged on by a cheering audience, obeyed and tortured a screaming victim (Beauvois et al., 2012).

normative social influence influence resulting from a person's desire to gain approval or avoid disapproval.

informational social influence influence resulting from a person's willingness to accept others' opinions about reality.

Did Milgram's teachers figure out the hoax—that no real shock was being delivered and the learner was in fact an assistant only pretending to feel pain? Did they realize the experiment was really testing their willingness to obey commands to inflict punishment? No. The teachers were typically genuinely distressed. They perspired, trembled, laughed nervously, and bit their lips.

In later experiments, Milgram discovered some conditions that did influence people's behavior. When he varied some details of the situation, the percentage of participants who fully obeyed ranged from 0 to 93 percent. Obedience was highest when

- the person giving the orders was close at hand and was perceived to be a legitimate authority figure.
- the authority figure was supported by a respected, well-known institution (Yale University).
- the victim was depersonalized or at a distance, even in another room. Similarly, many soldiers in combat either do not fire their rifles at an enemy they can see or do not aim them properly. Such refusals to kill are rarer among those who kill from a distance. (Veterans who operated remotely piloted drones have suffered stress, though much less posttraumatic stress than have on-the-ground Afghanistan and Iraq war veterans [Miller, 2012a].)
- there were no role models for defiance. (Teachers did not see any other participant disobey the experimenter.)

The power of legitimate, close-at-hand authorities is dramatically apparent in stories of those who followed orders to carry out the Nazis' Holocaust atrocities. Obedience alone does not explain the Holocaust; anti-Semitic ideology produced eager killers as well (Fenigstein, 2015; Mastroianni, 2015). But obedience was a factor. In the summer of 1942, nearly 500 middle-aged German reserve police officers were dispatched to German-occupied Jozefow, Poland. On July 13, the group's visibly upset commander informed his recruits, mostly family men, of their orders. They were to round up the village's Jews, who were said to be aiding the enemy. Able-bodied men would be sent to work camps, and all the rest were to be shot on the spot.

The commander gave the recruits a chance to refuse to participate in the executions. Only about a dozen immediately refused. Within 17 hours, the remaining 485 officers killed 1500 helpless citizens, including women, children, and the elderly, shooting them in the back of the head as they lay face down. Hearing the victims' pleas and seeing the gruesome results, some 20 percent of the officers did eventually disobey. They did so either by missing their victims or by hiding until the slaughter was over (Browning, 1992). In real life, as in Milgram's experiments, those who resisted were the minority.

> "I was only following orders." —Adolf Eichmann, director of Nazi deportation of Jews to concentration camps

A different story played out in the French village of Le Chambon. There, villagers openly defied orders to cooperate with the "New Order." They sheltered French Jews and sometimes helped them escape across the Swiss border. The villagers' Protestant ancestors had themselves been persecuted. Their pastors had been teaching them to "resist whenever our adversaries will demand of us obedience contrary to the orders of the Gospel" (Rochat, 1993). Ordered by police to give a list of sheltered Jews, the head pastor modeled defiance. "I don't know of Jews, I only know of human beings." At great personal risk, the people of Le Chambon made a commitment to defy. They suffered from poverty and were punished for their disobedience. But they drew support from their beliefs, their role models, their interactions with one another, and their own early actions. They remained defiant to the war's end.

LaunchPad See the *Video: Research Ethics* for a helpful tutorial animation.

Lessons From the Conformity and Obedience Studies

LOQ 11-7 What do the social influence studies teach us about ourselves? How much power do we have as individuals?

How do the laboratory experiments on social influence relate to everyday life? How does judging the length of a line or flipping a shock switch relate to everyday social behavior? Psychology's experiments aim not to re-create the actual, complex behaviors of everyday life but to explore what influences them. Solomon Asch and Stanley Milgram devised experiments that forced a familiar choice: Do I remain true to my own standards, even when they conflict with the expectations of others?

In Milgram's experiments and their modern replications, participants were also torn. Should they respond to the pleas of the victim or the orders of the experimenter? Their moral sense warned them not to harm another. But that same sense also prompted them to obey the experimenter and to be a good research participant. With kindness and obedience on a collision course, obedience usually won.

These experiments demonstrated that strong social influences can make people conform to falsehoods or give in to cruelty. Milgram saw this as the most basic lesson of his work. "Ordinary people, simply doing their jobs, and without any particular hostility on their part, can become agents in a terrible destructive process" (1974, p. 6).

Using the foot-in-the-door technique, Milgram began with a little tickle of electricity and advanced step by step. To those throwing the switches, the small action became justified, making the next act tolerable.

In any society, great evils often grow out of people's acceptance of lesser evils. The Nazi leaders suspected that most German civil servants would resist shooting or gassing Jews directly.

But they found them willing to handle the paperwork of the Holocaust (Silver & Geller, 1978). Milgram found a similar reaction in his experiments. When he asked 40 men to give the learning test while someone else delivered the shocks, 93 percent agreed. Cruelty does not require devilish villains. All it takes is ordinary people corrupted by an evil situation. Ordinary students may follow orders to haze newcomers to their group. Ordinary employees may follow orders to produce and market harmful products. Ordinary soldiers may follow orders to torture prisoners (Lankford, 2009). Among people abducted into a violent group, those forced to perpetrate violence are most likely to then identify with the group (Littman, 2018). Attitudes follow behavior.

In Jozefow and Le Chambon, as in Milgram's experiments, those who resisted usually did so early. After the first acts of obedience or resistance, attitudes began to follow and justify behavior.

What have social psychologists learned about the power of the individual? *Social control* (the power of the situation) and *personal control* (the power of the individual) interact. Much as water dissolves salt but not sand, so rotten situations turn some people into bad apples while others resist (Johnson, 2007).

When feeling pressured, some people react by doing the opposite of what is expected (Brehm & Brehm, 1981). The power of one or two individuals to sway majorities is *minority influence* (Moscovici, 1985). One research finding repeatedly stands out. When you are the minority, you are far more likely to sway the majority if you hold firmly to your position and don't waffle. This tactic won't make you popular, but it may make you influential, especially if your self-confidence stimulates others to consider why you react as you do. Even when a minority's influence is not yet visible, people may privately develop sympathy for the minority position and rethink their views (Wood et al., 1994).

The powers of social influence are enormous, but so are the powers of the committed individual. Were this not so,

JEFF KOWALSKY/Getty Images

The power of one After former gymnast Rachel Denhollander went public with her report of childhood sexual molestation by former U.S. Gymnastics doctor Lawrence Nassar, she suffered six months of public shaming, with her "sexual assault . . . wielded like a weapon against" her. But eventually more than 300 other women stepped forward to publicly testify to similar abuse, and Nassar was jailed for life (Correa & Louttit, 2018). After Denhollander concluded her testimony, Judge Rosemarie Aquilina said, "You made this happen. You are the bravest person I've ever had in my courtroom" (Macur, 2018).

Rosa Parks' refusal to sit at the back of the bus would not have ignited the U.S. civil rights movement. Social forces matter. But individuals matter, too.

RETRIEVE & REMEMBER

ANSWERS IN APPENDIX E

- 7. Psychology's most famous obedience experiments, in which most participants obeyed an authority figure's demands to inflict presumed painful, dangerous shocks on an innocent participant, were conducted by social psychologist ______________ ______________.
- 8. Which four situations have researchers found to be most likely to encourage obedience in participants?

GROUP INFLUENCE

LOQ 11-8 How does the presence of others influence our actions, via social facilitation, social loafing, and deindividuation?

Imagine standing in a room, holding a fishing pole. Your task is to wind the reel as fast as you can. On some occasions you wind in the presence of another participant who is also winding as fast as possible. Will the other's presence affect your own performance?

In one of social psychology's first experiments, Norman Triplett (1898) found that adolescents would wind a fishing reel faster in the presence of someone doing the same thing. He and later social psychologists studied how the presence of others affects our behavior. Group influences operate both in simple groups—one person in the presence of another—and in more complex groups.

Social Facilitation

Triplett's finding—of stronger performance in others' presence—is called **social facilitation.** But later studies revealed that the presence of others strengthens our most *likely* response—the correct one on an easy task, an incorrect one on a difficult task. Why? Because when others observe us, we become aroused, and this arousal amplifies our reactions.

The energizing effect of an enthusiastic audience helps explain the home-team advantage. Studies of more than a quarter-million college and professional athletic events in various countries show that the home-team advantage—which has been 54 percent in Major League Baseball games, 60 percent in National Basketball Association games, and 63 percent in English Premier League soccer games—is real (Allen & Jones, 2014; Jamieson, 2010; Moskowitz & Wertheim, 2011).

The point to remember: What you do well, you are likely to do even better in front of an audience, especially a friendly audience. What you normally find difficult may seem all but impossible when you are being watched.

Social facilitation also helps explain a funny effect of crowding. Comedians know that a "good house" is a full one.

social facilitation in the presence of others, improved performance on simple or well-learned tasks, and worsened performance on difficult tasks.

Hope College

Social facilitation Skilled athletes often find they are "on" before an audience. What they do well, they do even better when people are watching.

What they may not know is that crowding triggers arousal. Comedy routines that are mildly amusing in an uncrowded room seem funnier in a densely packed room (Aiello et al., 1983; Freedman & Perlick, 1979). When seated close to one another, people like a friendly person even more and an unfriendly person even less (Schiffenbauer & Schiavo, 1976; Storms & Thomas, 1977). So, to increase the socializing at your next event, choose a room or set up seating that will just barely hold all your guests.

Social Loafing

Does the presence of others have the same arousal effect when we perform a task as a group? In a team tug-of-war, do we exert more, less, or the same effort as in a one-on-one tug-of-war? If you said "less," you're right. In one experiment, students who believed three others were also pulling behind them exerted only 82 percent as much effort as when they knew they were pulling alone (Ingham et al., 1974). And consider what happened when blindfolded people seated in a group clapped or shouted as loudly as they could while hearing (through headphones) other people clapping or shouting (Latané, 1981). In one round of noise-making, the participants believed the researchers could identify their individual sounds. In another round, they believed their clapping and shouting was blended with other people's. When they thought they were part of a group effort, the participants produced about one-third less noise than when clapping "alone."

This lessened effort is called **social loafing** (Jackson & Williams, 1988; Latané, 1981). Experiments in the United States, India, Thailand, Japan, China, and Taiwan have found social loafing on various tasks, but it was especially common among men in individualist cultures (Karau & Williams, 1993). What causes social loafing? When people act as part of a group, they may

- ***feel less accountable,*** so worry less about what others think.
- ***view individual contributions as unneeded*** (Harkins & Szymanski, 1989; Kerr & Bruun, 1983).
- ***overestimate their own contributions,*** downplaying others' efforts (Schroeder et al., 2016).
- ***free ride on others' efforts.*** Unless highly motivated, group members may slack off (as you've probably noticed in work on group assignments), especially when they share equally in the benefits regardless of how much they contribute.

IMPROVE YOUR EVERYDAY LIFE

What steps could you take to reduce social loafing in your next group project assignment?

Deindividuation

We've seen that the presence of others can arouse people, or it can make them feel less responsible. But sometimes the presence of others does both, triggering behavior that can range from a food fight to vandalism or rioting. This process of losing self-awareness and self-restraint is called **deindividuation.** It often occurs when group participation makes people feel *aroused* and *anonymous*. In one experiment, some female students

Jessica Kourkounis/Reuters/Newscom

Deindividuation In the excitement that followed the Philadelphia Eagles winning their first National Football League Super Bowl in 2018, some fans, disinhibited by social arousal and the anonymity provided by their "underdog" masks, became destructive.

dressed in Ku Klux Klan–style hoods that concealed their identity. Others in a control group did not wear the hoods. Those wearing hoods delivered twice as much presumed electric shock to a victim (Zimbardo, 1970).

Deindividuation thrives in many different settings. Internet anonymity unleashes bullying and hate speech (Chetty & Alathur, 2018; Kowalski et al., 2018; Zych et al., 2018). Online trolls, illustrating the dark side of free speech, report enjoying abusing others (Buckels et al., 2014; Sest & March, 2017). They might never say, "you're disgusting" to someone's face, but they can hide behind their anonymity online. Tribal warriors wearing face paints or masks have been more likely than those with exposed faces to kill, torture, or mutilate captured enemies (Watson, 1973). When we shed self-awareness and self-restraint—whether in a mob, at a concert, at a ball game, or at worship—we become more responsive to the group experience, bad or good. For a comparison of social facilitation, social loafing, and deindividuation, see **TABLE 11.1.**

TABLE 11.1 Behavior in the Presence of Others: Three Phenomena

Phenomenon	Social context	Psychological effect of others' presence	Behavioral effect
Social facilitation	Individual being observed	Increased arousal	Amplified dominant behavior, such as doing better what one does well (or doing worse what is difficult)
Social loafing	Group projects	Diminished feelings of responsibility when not individually accountable	Decreased effort
Deindividuation	Group setting that fosters arousal and anonymity	Reduced self-awareness	Lowered self-restraint

Group Polarization

LOQ 11-9 How can group interaction enable group polarization?

We live in an increasingly polarized world. In 1990, a one-minute speech in the U.S. Congress would enable you to guess the speaker's party just 55 percent of the time; by 2009, partisanship was evident 83 percent of the time (Gentzkow et al., 2016). In 2016, for the first time in survey history, most U.S. Republicans and Democrats reported having "*very* unfavorable" views of the other party (Doherty & Kiley, 2016). And a record 77 percent of Americans perceived their nation as divided (Jones, 2016). A powerful principle helps us understand this increasing polarization: The beliefs and attitudes we bring to a group grow stronger as we discuss them with like-minded others. This process, called **group polarization,** can have positive results, as when low-prejudice students become even more accepting while discussing racial issues. As George Bishop and I [DM] discovered, it can also have negative results (**FIGURE 11.4**), as when high-prejudice students who discuss racial issues become *more* prejudiced (Myers & Bishop, 1970). Our repeated finding: Like minds polarize.

Group polarization can feed extremism and even suicide terrorism. The terrorist mentality emerges slowly (McCauley, 2002; McCauley & Segal, 1987; Merari, 2002). As group members interact in isolation (sometimes with other "brothers" and "sisters" in camps or in prisons), their views grow more and more extreme. Increasingly, they divide the world into "us" against "them" (Chulov, 2014; Moghaddam, 2005).

"Dear Satan, thank you for having my internet news feeds tailored especially for ME!" —Comedian Steve Martin, 2016

The internet offers a connected global world, yet also provides an easily accessible medium for group polarization. When I [DM] got my start in social psychology with experiments on group polarization, I never imagined the potential power of polarization in *virtual* groups. With news feeds and retweets, we fuel one another with information—and misinformation—and click on content we agree with (Bakshy et al., 2015; Barberá et al., 2015). American Cesar Sayoc, who in 2018 sent over a dozen pipe bombs to prominent Democrats and their perceived supporters, had vented his partisan resentments on the internet, which "echoed them back. It validated and cultivated them. It took something dark and colored it darker still" (Bruni, 2018).

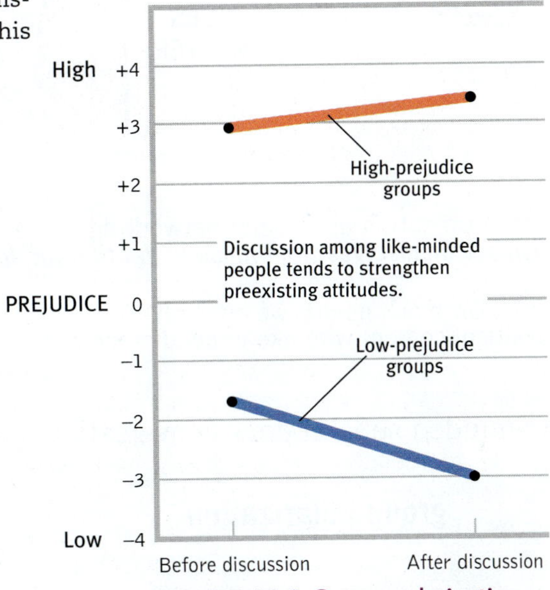

FIGURE 11.4 Group polarization

"Groups tend to be more immoral than individuals." —Martin Luther King, Jr., "Letter from Birmingham Jail," 1963

Mindful of the viral false news phenomenon, tech companies are working on ways to promote media literacy. (For more on the internet's role in group polarization, see Thinking Critically About: The Internet as Social Amplifier.)

NO EXIT © Andy Singer
TECHNOLOGY'S A MIXED BAG
SOCIAL MEDIA HELPS ME CONNECT WITH OTHER GAY AND BISEXUAL KIDS AND FEEL LESS ISOLATED IN MY SMALL TOWN.
SOCIAL MEDIA HELPS ME CONNECT WITH NAZIS AND WHITE SUPREMACISTS AND FEEL LESS ISOLATED IN MY SMALL TOWN.
SINGER

Technology is a Mixed Bag by Andy Singer, Politicalcartoons.com

social loafing the tendency for people in a group to exert less effort when pooling their efforts toward attaining a common goal than when individually accountable.

deindividuation the loss of self-awareness and self-restraint occurring in group situations that foster arousal and anonymity.

group polarization strengthening of a group's preexisting attitudes through discussions within the group.

Thinking Critically About:

The Internet as Social Amplifier

LOQ 11-10 What role does the internet play in group polarization?

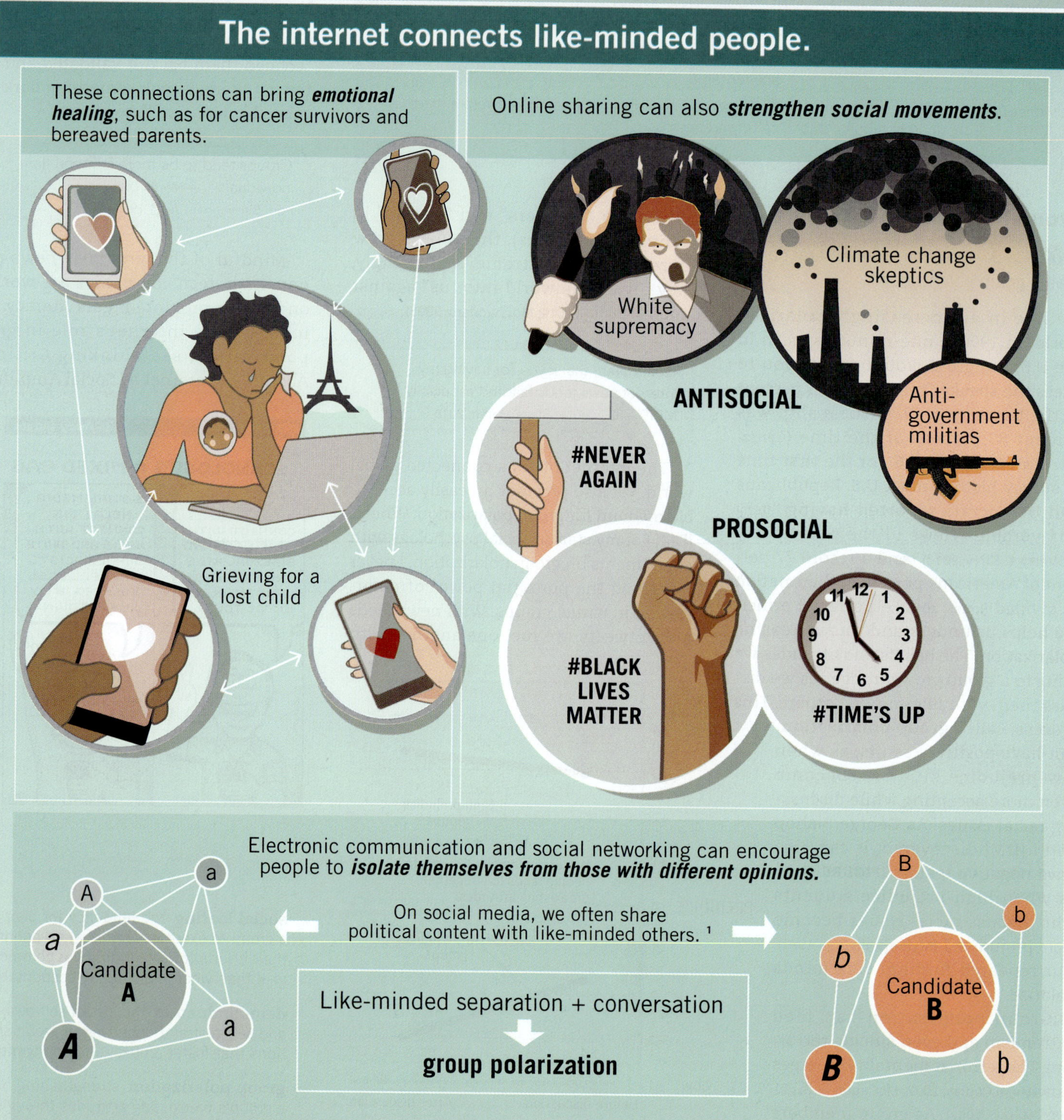

The internet connects like-minded people.
These connections can bring ***emotional healing***, such as for cancer survivors and bereaved parents.
Grieving for a lost child
Online sharing can also ***strengthen social movements***.
White supremacy
Climate change skeptics
ANTISOCIAL
Anti-government militias
#NEVER AGAIN
PROSOCIAL
#BLACK LIVES MATTER
#TIME'S UP
Electronic communication and social networking can encourage people to ***isolate themselves from those with different opinions.***
On social media, we often share political content with like-minded others.[1]
Candidate A
A
a
Candidate B
B
b
Like-minded separation + conversation
group polarization

1. Bakshy et al., 2015; Barberá et al., 2015.

Groupthink

LOQ 11-11 How can group interaction enable groupthink?

Does group influence ever distort important national decisions? It can and it does. In one famous decision, it led to what is now known as the Bay of Pigs fiasco. In 1961, U.S. President John F. Kennedy and his advisers decided to invade Cuba with 1400 CIA-trained Cuban exiles. When the invaders were easily captured and quickly linked to the U.S. government, the president wondered aloud, "How could I have been so stupid?"

Reading a historian's account of the ill-fated blunder, social psychologist Irving Janis (1982) found some clues in the invasion's decision-making process. The morale of the popular and recently elected president and his advisers was soaring. Their confidence was almost unlimited. To preserve the good feeling, group members with differing views kept quiet, especially after President Kennedy voiced his enthusiasm for the scheme. Since no one spoke strongly against the idea, everyone assumed the support was unanimous. **Groupthink** was at work: The desire for harmony had replaced realistic judgment.

Later studies showed that groupthink—fed by overconfidence, conformity, self-justification, and group polarization—contributed to other fiascos as well. Among them were the failure to anticipate the 1941 Japanese attack on Pearl Harbor; the U.S. space shuttle *Challenger* explosion (Esser & Lindoerfer, 1989); and the Iraq war, launched on the false idea that Iraq had weapons of mass destruction (U.S. Senate Select Committee on Intelligence, 2004).

How can we prevent groupthink? Leaders can welcome open debate, invite experts' critiques of developing plans, and assign people to identify possible problems.

The point to remember: Two heads are often better than one, especially when we encourage independent thinking and open debate.

IN YOUR EVERYDAY LIFE

How have you been influenced by group polarization on social media recently?

RETRIEVE & REMEMBER

ANSWERS IN APPENDIX E

9. What is *social facilitation,* and why does it improve performance with a well-learned task?
10. People tend to exert less effort when working with a group than they would alone, which is called __________ __________.
11. You are organizing a meeting of fiercely competitive political candidates and their supporters. To add to the fun, friends have suggested handing out masks of the candidates' faces for supporters to wear. What effect might these masks have?
12. When like-minded groups discuss a topic, and the result is the strengthening of the preexisting opinion, this is called __________ __________.
13. When a group's desire for harmony overrides its realistic analysis of other options, __________ has occurred.

Social Relations

We have sampled how we *think about* and *influence* one another. Now we come to social psychology's third focus—how we *relate* to one another. What are the roots of prejudice? What causes people sometimes to hate and harm, and at other times to love and help? How can we transform the closed fists of aggression into the open arms of compassion? We will ponder the bad and the good: from prejudice and aggression to attraction, altruism, and peacemaking.

PREJUDICE

LOQ 11-12 What are the three parts of *prejudice*? How do explicit and implicit prejudice differ?

Prejudice means "prejudgment." It is an unfair and usually negative attitude toward some group and its members—often people of a particular racial or ethnic group, gender, sexual orientation, or belief system. Remember that attitudes are feelings, influenced by beliefs, that predispose us to act in certain ways. The ingredients in prejudice's three-part mixture are

- *negative emotions,* such as hostility or fear.
- **stereotypes,** which are generalized beliefs about a group of people. Our stereotypes sometimes reflect reality. As Texas Senator Ted Cruz (2018) explained, "It's a stereotype that Texans like barbecue. It also happens that pretty much all Texans like barbeque." But stereotypes often overgeneralize or exaggerate—as when liberals and conservatives overestimate the extremity of each other's views, or Christians and atheists misperceive each other's values (Graham et al., 2012; Simpson & Rios, 2016).
- a *predisposition* to **discriminate**—to act in negative and unfair ways toward members of the group. Sometimes prejudice is obvious. Other times it is more subtle, taking the form of *microaggressions,* such as race-related traffic stops, a reluctance to choose a train seat next to someone of a different race, or longer Uber wait times and less Airbnb acceptance for people with African-American names (Edelman et al., 2017; Ge et al., 2016; Wang et al., 2011).

To feel dislike for an obese person is to be prejudiced. To reject a qualified obese job candidate is to discriminate.

groupthink the mode of thinking that occurs when the desire for harmony in a decision-making group overrides a realistic appraisal of alternatives.

prejudice an unfair and usually negative attitude toward a group and its members. Prejudice generally involves negative feelings, stereotyped beliefs, and a predisposition to discriminatory action.

stereotype a generalized (sometimes accurate but often overgeneralized) belief about a group of people.

discrimination unfair negative behavior toward a group or its members.

Explicit and Implicit Prejudice

Again and again, we have seen that our brain processes thoughts, memories, and attitudes on two different tracks. Sometimes that processing is *explicit*—on the radar screen of our awareness. More often, it is *implicit*—below the radar. In 2015, the U.S. Supreme Court, in upholding the Fair Housing Act, recognized implicit bias research, noting that "unconscious prejudices" can cause discrimination even when people do not consciously intend to discriminate.

> "Cleanse me from my hidden faults."
> —Psalm 19:12

Psychologists study implicit prejudice by

- ***testing for unconscious group associations.*** Tests in which people quickly pair a person's image with a trait demonstrate that even people who deny any racial prejudice may hold negative associations (Banaji & Greenwald, 2013). Millions of people have taken the Implicit Association Test (as you can, too, at Implicit.Harvard.edu). During the #BlackLivesMatter movement after the 2013 Trayvon Martin killing, implicit pro-White prejudice declined (Sawyer & Gampa, 2018). Nevertheless, critics question the test's reliability and caution against using it to assess or label individuals (Oswald et al., 2013, 2015). But defenders argue that implicit biases predict behaviors ranging from simple acts of friendliness to the evaluation of work quality (Greenwald et al., 2015; Jost, 2019).
- ***evaluating bodily responses.*** Even people who consciously express little prejudice may give off telltale signals as their body responds selectively to an image of a person from another ethnic group. Neuroscientists can detect signals of implicit prejudice in the viewer's facial-muscle responses and in brain activity in the emotion-processing amygdala (Cunningham et al., 2004; Eberhardt, 2005; Stanley et al., 2008).

Targets of Prejudice

LOQ 11-13 What groups are frequent targets of prejudice?

Racial and Ethnic Prejudice Americans' expressed racial attitudes have changed dramatically. "Marriage between Blacks and Whites" was approved by 4 percent of Americans surveyed in 1958 and 87 percent in 2013 (Newport, 2013a). Six in ten Americans—double the number in most European countries—now agree that "an increasing number of people of many different races, ethnic groups, and nationalities in our country makes it a better place to live" (Drake & Poushter, 2016). Such acceptance of diversity increases intergroup contact, which benefits everyone. For example, one analysis of 9 million papers and 6 million scientists demonstrated that ethnically diverse scientific teams produced the most influential research (AlShebli et al., 2018).

Yet as open interracial prejudice wanes, *subtle* prejudice lingers. People with darker skin tones experience greater criticism and more accusations of immoral behavior (Alter et al., 2016). And although many people *say* they would feel upset with someone making racist (or homophobic) comments, they often respond indifferently when actually hearing prejudice-laden language (Kawakami et al., 2009).

Rex Features via AP Images

Implicit bias? Does implicit bias research—used increasingly by police organizations and companies in diversity training programs in the United States and beyond—help us understand the 2013 death of Trayvon Martin (shown here 7 months before he was killed)? As he walked alone to his father's fiancée's house in a gated Florida neighborhood, a suspicious resident confronted and shot him. Commentators wondered: Had Martin been an unarmed White teen, would he have been perceived and treated the same way?

As noted, prejudice is not just subtle, but often unconscious (implicit). An Implicit Association Test found 9 in 10 White respondents taking longer to identify pleasant words (such as *peace* and *paradise*) as "good" when presented with Black-sounding names (such as *Latisha* and *Darnell*) than they did with White-sounding names (such as *Katie* and *Ian*). Moreover, people who more quickly associate good things with White names or faces also are the quickest to perceive anger and apparent threat in Black faces (Hugenberg & Bodenhausen, 2003). A greater association of pleasant words with European-American than with African-American names has also been observed in more than 800 billion internet words (Caliskan et al., 2017).

Our perceptions can also reflect implicit bias. In 1999, Amadou Diallo, who was Black, was stopped as he approached his doorway by police officers looking for a rapist. When he pulled out his wallet, the officers, perceiving a gun, riddled his body with 19 bullets from 41 shots. In one analysis of 59 unarmed suspect shootings in Philadelphia over seven years, 49 involved the misidentification of an object (such as a phone) or movement (such as pants tugging). Black suspects were more than twice as likely to be misperceived as threatening, even by Black officers (Blow, 2015). Across the United States, nearly 40 percent of the unarmed people shot and killed by police during 2015 and 2016 were Black (*Washington Post*, 2017).

> Phones in our pocket have increased public awareness of the everyday challenges of "living while Black." There was a public outcry when two Black men seated in a Starbucks coffee shop, awaiting the start of a business meeting, were filmed being wrongfully arrested for trespassing. As one of the men, Donte Robinson, later noted, "It's time to pay attention and understand what's really going on. We do want a seat at the table" (AP, 2018). Starbucks later closed all of its U.S. stores for four hours for racial bias training.

To better understand tragic shootings, researchers have simulated them (Correll et al., 2007, 2015; Plant & Peruche, 2005; Sadler et al., 2012a). They asked viewers to press buttons quickly to "shoot" or not shoot men who suddenly appeared on screen. Some of the on-screen men held a gun. Others held a harmless object, such as a flashlight or bottle. People (both Blacks and Whites, including police officers) more often shot Black men holding the harmless object (**FIGURE 11.5**).

Gender Prejudice Expressed gender prejudice has also declined sharply. Although women worldwide still represent nearly two-thirds of illiterate adults, and 30 percent have experienced intimate partner violence, 65 percent of all people now say it is very important that women have the same rights as men (UN, 2015b; WHO, 2016; Zainulbhai, 2016).

Nevertheless, both implicit and explicit gender prejudice and discrimination persist. Consider:

- ***Pay.*** In Western countries, we pay more to those (usually men) who care for our streets than to those (usually women) who care for our children.
- ***Leadership.*** From 2007 through 2016, male directors of 1000 popular films (the top 100 for each year) outnumbered female directors by 24 to 1 (Smith et al., 2017).
- ***Respect.*** People more often refer to men (including male instructors) by their last name and women by their first name (Atir & Ferguson, 2018).
- ***Perceived intelligence.*** Gender bias even applies to beliefs about intelligence: Despite equality between males and females in intelligence test scores, people tend to perceive their fathers as more intelligent than their mothers and their sons as brighter than their daughters (Furnham, 2016).

Unwanted female infants are no longer left out on a hillside to die of exposure, as was the practice in ancient Greece. Yet the normal male-to-female newborn ratio (105-to-100) doesn't explain what has been estimated as the world's 163 million (say that number slowly) "missing women" (Hvistendahl, 2011). In many places, sons are valued more than daughters. In China and India, which together have 50 million more males than females under age 20, many bachelors will be without mates (Denyer & Gowen, 2018; Gupta, 2017). A shortage of women also contributes to increased crime, violence, prostitution, and trafficking of women (Brooks, 2012).

> "Until I was a man, I had no idea how good men had it at work. . . . The first time I spoke up in a meeting in my newly low, quiet voice and noticed that sudden, focused attention, I was so uncomfortable that I found myself unable to finish my sentence." —Thomas Page McBee, 2016, after transitioning from female to male

LGBTQ Prejudice In most of the world, gay, lesbian, and transgender people cannot openly and comfortably disclose who they are and whom they love (Katz-Wise & Hyde, 2012; UN, 2011). Although by 2018 two dozen countries had allowed same-sex marriage, dozens more had laws criminalizing same-sex relationships.

Explicit anti-LGBTQ prejudice persists, even in countries with legal protections in place. When experimenters sent thousands of responses to employment ads, those whose past activities included "Treasurer, Progressive and Socialist Alliance" received more replies than did those that specified "Treasurer, Gay and Lesbian Alliance" (Agerström et al., 2012; Bertrand & Mullainathan, 2004; Drydakis, 2009, 2015). Other evidence has appeared in national surveys of LGBTQ Americans:

- 39 percent reported having been "rejected by a friend or family member" because of their sexual orientation or gender identity (Pew, 2013b).
- 58 percent reported being "subject to slurs or jokes" (Pew, 2013b).
- 54 percent reported having been harassed at school and at work (Grant et al., 2011b; James et al., 2016).

Belief Systems Prejudice Prejudice can center on particular beliefs, including religious beliefs. For example, in the aftermath of the 9/11 terrorist attacks, the Iraq and Afghanistan wars, and much political fear mongering, many non-Muslim Americans developed irrational fear and anger toward *all* Muslims (and those they *thought* might be Muslim). (The reality since 2001: U.S. attacks by homegrown White supremacists and other non-Muslim extremists were nearly twice as likely [Shane, 2015].) As a result, nearly half of Muslim Americans have reported personally experiencing discrimination in the last year—more than double the average among Catholics and Protestants (Gallup, 2016).

(a) © Inti St Clair/Blend Images/Corbis

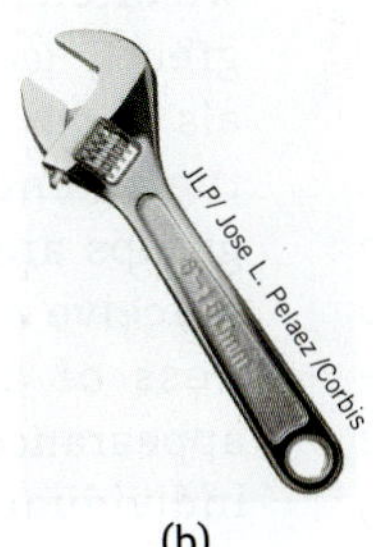

(b)

(c)

FIGURE 11.5 Race primes perceptions In experiments, people viewed (a) a White or Black face, immediately followed by (b) a flashed gun or hand tool, which was then followed by (c) a masking screen. Participants were more likely to misperceive a tool as a gun when it was preceded by a Black rather than White face (Payne, 2006).

Roots of Prejudice

LOQ 11-14 What are some social, emotional, and cognitive roots of prejudice? What are some ways to combat prejudice?

Prejudice springs from a culture's divisions, the heart's passions, and the mind's natural workings.

Social Inequalities and Divisions

When some people have money, power, and prestige and others do not, the "haves" usually develop attitudes that justify things as they are. The **just-world phenomenon** assumes that good is rewarded and evil is punished. From this it is but a short and sometimes automatic leap to assume that those who succeed must be good and those who suffer must be bad. Such reasoning enables the rich to see both their own wealth and the poor's misfortune as justly deserved. When slavery existed in the United States, slaveholders developed attitudes—that slaves were lazy, ignorant, and irresponsible—that "justified" enslaving them. Stereotypes rationalize inequalities.

Victims of discrimination may react in ways that feed prejudice through the classic *blame-the-victim* dynamic (Allport, 1954). Do the circumstances of poverty breed a higher crime rate? If so, that higher crime rate can be used to justify discrimination against those who live in poverty.

Dividing the world into "us" and "them" can result in conflict, racism, and war, but it also provides benefits. Thus, we cheer for our groups, kill for them, die for them. Indeed, we define who we are—our *social identity*—partly in terms of our groups (Greenaway et al., 2016; Hogg, 1996, 2006; Turner, 1987, 2007). When Margarita identifies herself as a woman, an American, a political Independent, a Hudson Community College student, a Catholic, and a part-time letter carrier, she knows who she is, and so do we. Mentally drawing a circle defines "us," the **ingroup.** But the social definition of who we are also states who we are not. People outside that circle are "them," the **outgroup.** An **ingroup bias**—a favoring of our own group—soon follows. In experiments, people, beginning early in childhood, have favored their own group (just created by a simple coin toss) when dividing rewards (Tajfel, 1982; Wilder, 1981; Wynn et al., 2018). Across 17 countries, ingroup bias appears more as ingroup favoritism than as harm to the outgroup (Romano et al., 2017). Discrimination is triggered less by outgroup hostility than by ingroup networking and mutual support—such as hiring a friend's child at the expense of other candidates (Greenwald & Pettigrew, 2014).

Robert Mankoff The New Yorker Collection/ The Cartoon Bank

We have inherited our Stone Age ancestors' need to belong, to live and love in groups. There was safety in solidarity: Whether hunting, defending, or attacking, 10 hands were better than 2. Evolution prepared us, when encountering strangers, to make instant judgments: friend or foe? This urge to distinguish enemies from friends, and to dehumanize or "otherize" those not like us, predisposes prejudice against strangers (Kteily & Bruneau, 2017; Whitley, 1999). Many high school students form cliques—jocks, preps, nerds—and insult those outside their own group. Even chimpanzees have been seen to wipe clean the spot where they were touched by a chimpanzee from another group (Goodall, 1986).

Negative Emotions

Negative emotions feed prejudice. When facing threats, people cling more tightly to their ingroup. As fears of terrorism heighten patriotism, they also produce loathing and aggression toward those who appear to threaten (Pyszczynski et al., 2002, 2008). **Scapegoat theory** proposes that when things go wrong, finding someone to blame can provide a target for our negative emotions. During and after the heated 2016 U.S. presidential election, hate crime reports rose, and then rose again in 2017 (FBI, 2018; Levin et al., 2018). Why did such hate crimes rise following the 2016 U.S. presidential election? One reason may be greater acceptance of prejudice toward the groups that then-candidate Donald Trump had targeted during the campaign, such as Muslims and immigrants (Crandall et al., 2018). "Fear and anger create aggression, and aggression against citizens of different ethnicity or race creates racism and, in turn, new forms of terrorism," noted Philip Zimbardo (2001).

Evidence for the scapegoat theory of prejudice comes in two forms: (1) Economically frustrated people tend to express heightened prejudice. Racial prejudice intensifies during economic downturns (Bianchi et al., 2018). (2) Experiments that create temporary frustration intensify prejudice. Students who experience failure or are made to feel insecure often restore their self-esteem by insulting a rival school or another person (Cialdini & Richardson, 1980; Crocker et al., 1987). This may boost our own sense of status; a rival's misfortune sometimes provides a twinge of pleasure. By contrast, those made to feel loved and supported become more open to and accepting of others who differ (Mikulincer & Shaver, 2001).

Cognitive Shortcuts

Stereotyped beliefs are a by-product of how we cognitively simplify the world. To help understand the world around us, we frequently form categories. We all categorize people by gender, ethnicity, race, age, and many other characteristics. But when we categorize people into groups, we often stereotype. We recognize how greatly *we* differ from other individuals in *our* groups. But we overestimate the extent to which members of other groups are alike (Bothwell et al., 1989). We perceive *outgroup homogeneity*—sameness of attitudes, personality, and appearance. Our greater recognition for individual own-race faces—called the **other-race effect** (or *cross-race effect* or *own-race bias*)—emerges during infancy, between 3 and 9 months of age (Anzures

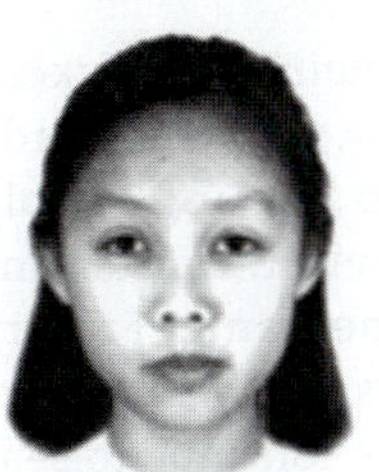
100% Chinese

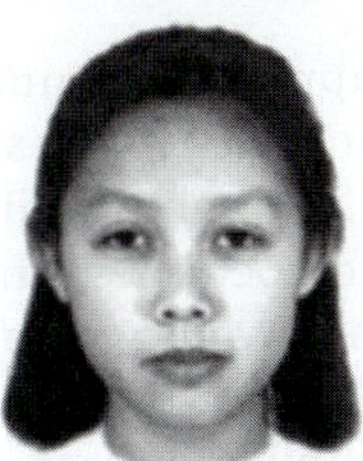
80% Chinese
20% Caucasian

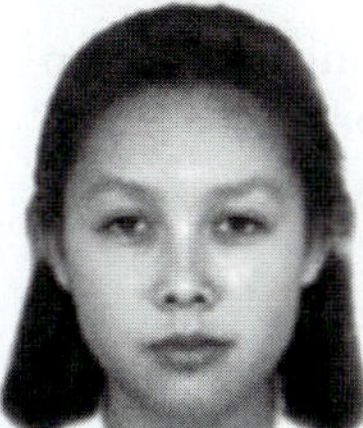
60% Chinese
40% Caucasian

40% Chinese
60% Caucasian

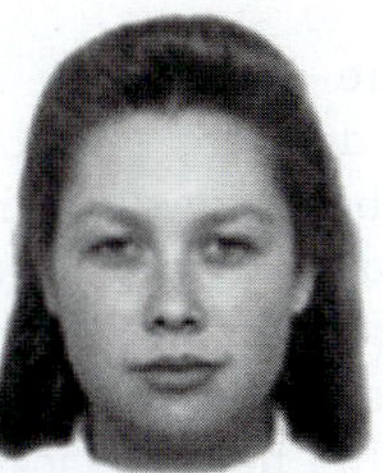
20% Chinese
80% Caucasian

100% Caucasian

FIGURE 11.6 Categorizing mixed-race people When New Zealanders quickly classified 104 photos by race, those of European descent more often than those of Chinese descent classified the ambiguous middle two as Chinese (Halberstadt et al., 2011).

et al., 2013; Telzer et al., 2013). (We also have an *own-age bias*—better recognition memory for faces of our own age group [Rhodes & Anastasi, 2012]).

Sometimes, however, people don't fit easily into our racial categories. If so, they are often assigned to their minority identity. This may happen because, after learning the features of a familiar racial group, the observer's *selective attention* is drawn to the distinctive features of the less-familiar minority. Researchers illustrated this by showing New Zealanders blended Chinese-Caucasian faces (Halberstadt et al., 2011). Compared with participants of Chinese descent, European-descent New Zealanders more readily classified ambiguous faces as Chinese (see **FIGURE 11.6**). With effort and with experience, people get better at recognizing individual faces from another group (Hugenberg et al., 2010; Young et al., 2012).

YOU'RE BOB? SORRY, YOU RESEARCHERS ALL LOOK ALIKE TO ME.

Remembering Vivid Cases As we saw in Chapter 8, we also simplify our world by employing *heuristics*—mental shortcuts that enable snap judgments. The *availability heuristic* is the tendency to estimate the frequency of an event by how readily it comes to mind. Vivid cases come to mind easily, so it's no surprise that they feed our stereotypes. In a classic experiment, researchers showed two groups of University of Oregon students lists containing information about 50 men (Rothbart et al., 1978). The first group's list included 10 men arrested for *nonviolent* crimes, such as forgery. The second group's list included 10 men arrested for *violent* crimes, such as assault. Later, both groups were asked how many men on their list had committed *any* sort of crime. The second group overestimated the number. Violent crimes form vivid memories (**FIGURE 11.7**).

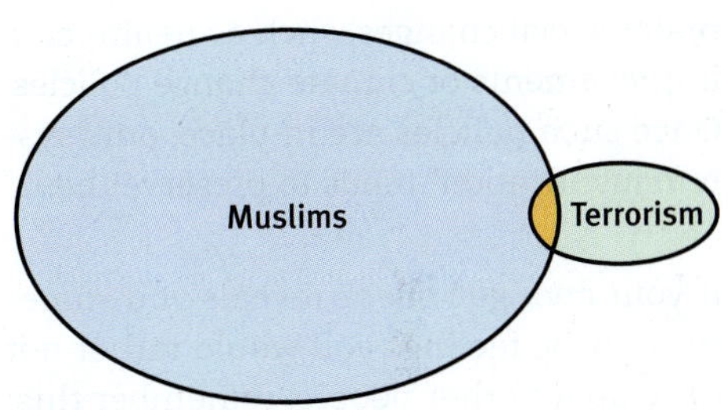

FIGURE 11.7 Vivid cases feed stereotypes Global terrorism has created, in many minds, an exaggerated stereotype of Muslims as terrorism-prone. Actually, reported a U.S. National Research Council panel on terrorism (which offered this inexact illustration), most terrorists are *not* Muslim.

Victim Blaming As we noted earlier, people often justify their prejudices by blaming victims. If the world is just, they assume, people must get what they deserve. As one German civilian is said to have remarked when visiting the Bergen-Belsen concentration camp shortly after World War II, "What terrible criminals these prisoners must have been to receive such treatment."

Hindsight bias amplifies victim blaming (Carli & Leonard, 1989). Have you ever heard people say that rape victims, abused spouses, or people with AIDS got what they deserved? In one experiment, two groups were given a detailed account of a date (Janoff-Bulman et al., 1985). The first group's account reported that the date ended with the woman being raped. Members of that group perceived the woman's behavior as at least partly to blame, and in hindsight, they thought, "She should have known better."

just-world phenomenon the tendency to believe that the world is just and people therefore get what they deserve and deserve what they get.

ingroup "us"—people with whom we share a common identity.

outgroup "them"—those perceived as different or apart from our ingroup.

ingroup bias the tendency to favor our own group.

scapegoat theory the theory that prejudice offers an outlet for anger by providing someone to blame.

other-race effect the tendency to recall faces of one's own race more accurately than faces of other races.

The second group, given the same account with the rape ending deleted, did not perceive the woman's behavior as inviting rape. In the first group, hindsight bias promoted a blame-the-victim mentality. Blaming the victim also serves to reassure people that it couldn't happen to them.

People also have a basic tendency to justify their culture's social systems (Jost et al., 2009; Kay et al., 2009). This natural conservatism makes it difficult to legislate major social changes, such as health care improvements or climate change policies. Once such policies are in place, our "system justification" tends to preserve them.

* * *

If your own gut-check reveals you sometimes have feelings you would rather not have about other people, remember this: It is what we *do* with our feelings that matters. By monitoring our feelings and actions, by replacing old habits with new ones, and by seeking out new friendships, we can work to free ourselves from prejudice.

IMPROVE YOUR EVERYDAY LIFE

What are some examples of ingroup bias in your own life, and in your community? How can you help break down barriers that you or others may face?

RETRIEVE & REMEMBER

ANSWERS IN APPENDIX E

14. When prejudice causes us to blame an innocent person for a problem, that person is called a ___________.

LaunchPad To review attribution research and experience a simulation of how stereotypes form, visit *Topic Tutorial: PsychSim6, Not My Type.* And for a 6.5-minute synopsis of the social and cognitive psychology of prejudice, see the *Video: Prejudice.*

AGGRESSION

In psychology, **aggression** is any verbal or physical behavior intended to harm someone, whether it is passing along a vicious rumor or engaging in a physical attack.

Aggressive behavior emerges when biology interacts with experience. For a gun to fire, the trigger must be pulled. With some people, as with hair-trigger guns, it doesn't take much to trip an explosion. Let's look first at some biological factors that influence our thresholds for aggressive behavior. Then we'll turn to the psychological and social-cultural factors that pull the trigger.

The Biology of Aggression

LOQ 11-15 What biological factors make us more likely to be aggressive?

Is aggression an unlearned instinct? The wide variation from culture to culture, era to era, and person to person argues against that idea. But biology does *influence* aggression at three levels—genetic, biochemical, and neural.

Genetic Influences Genes influence aggression. We know this because animals have been bred for aggressiveness—sometimes for sport, sometimes for research. The effect of genes also appears in human *twin studies* (Kendler et al., 2015; Miles & Carey, 1997). If one identical twin admits to "having a violent temper," the other twin will often independently admit the same. Fraternal twins are much less likely to respond similarly. Researchers continue to search for genetic markers, or predictors, in those who commit the most violence (Ficks & Waldman, 2014). One is already well known and is carried by half the human race: the Y chromosome.

Gilbert Laurie/Getty Images

Do guns in the home save or take more lives? "Personal safety/protection" is the number one reason U.S. gun owners give for firearm ownership (Swift, 2013). Yet firearm ownership often backfires: In 2017, 39,773 Americans died from firearm injuries; 2 in 3 were suicides (CDC, 2018e). Over the last half-century more than 1.5 million Americans have suffered nonwar firearm deaths—more than all war deaths in American history (Jacobson, 2015). Compared with people of the same sex, race, age, and neighborhood, those who keep a gun in the home have been twice as likely to be murdered and three times as likely to die by suicide (Anglemyer et al., 2014; Stroebe, 2013). States and countries with high gun ownership rates also tend to have high gun death rates (VPC, 2016).

LaunchPad See LaunchPad's *Video: Twin Studies* for a helpful tutorial animation.

Biochemical Influences Our genes engineer our individual nervous systems, which operate electrochemically. The hormone testosterone, for example, circulates in the bloodstream and influences the neural systems that control aggression. A raging bull becomes a gentle giant when castration reduces its testosterone level. And when injected with testosterone, gentle, castrated mice once again become aggressive.

In humans, high testosterone is associated with irritability, assertiveness, impulsiveness, and low tolerance for frustration. Drugs that sharply reduce testosterone levels subdue men's aggressive tendencies. As men age,

Donald Reilly The New Yorker Collection/The Cartoon Bank

"It's a guy thing."

Chris Courteau/AGE Fotostock

A lean, mean fighting machine—the testosterone-laden female hyena The hyena's unusual embryology pumps testosterone into female fetuses. The result is revved-up young female hyenas who seem born to fight.

their testosterone levels—and their aggressiveness—diminish. Hormonally charged, aggressive 17-year-olds mature into quieter and gentler 70-year-olds.

Another drug that sometimes circulates in the bloodstream—alcohol—unleashes aggressive responses to frustration. Aggression-prone people are more likely to drink, and when intoxicated they are more likely to become violent (White et al., 1993). Alcohol is a disinhibitor—it slows the brain activity that controls judgment and inhibitions. Under its influence, people may interpret certain acts, such as being bumped in a crowd, as provocations and react aggressively (Bègue et al., 2010; Giancola & Gorman, 2007). Alcohol has been a factor in 73 percent of homicides in Russia and 57 percent in the United States (Landberg & Norström, 2011). Alcohol's effects are both biological and psychological. Just *thinking* you've been drinking alcohol can increase aggression (Bègue et al., 2009). But so, too, does unknowingly drinking an alcohol-laced beverage.

Neural Influences There is no one spot in the brain that controls aggression. Aggression is a complex behavior, and it occurs in particular contexts. But animal and human brains have neural systems that, given provocation, will either inhibit or facilitate aggression (Dambacher et al., 2015; Falkner et al., 2016; Moyer, 1983). Consider:

- Researchers implanted a radio-controlled electrode in the brain of the domineering leader of a caged monkey colony. The electrode was in an area that, when stimulated, inhibits aggression. When researchers placed the control button for the electrode in the colony's cage, one small monkey learned to push it every time the boss became threatening.
- A neurosurgeon implanted an electrode in the brain of a mild-mannered woman to diagnose a disorder. The electrode was in her amygdala, within her limbic system. Because the brain has no sensory receptors, she did not feel the stimulation. But at the flick of a switch, she snarled, "Take my blood pressure. Take it now," then stood up and began to strike the doctor.
- Studies of violent criminals have revealed diminished activity in the frontal lobes, which help control impulses. If the frontal lobes are damaged, inactive, disconnected, or not yet fully mature, aggression may be more likely (Amen et al., 1996; Davidson et al., 2000; Raine, 2013).

Psychological and Social-Cultural Influences on Aggression

LOQ 11-16 What psychological and social-cultural factors may trigger aggressive behavior?

Biological factors influence how easily aggression is triggered. But what psychological and social-cultural factors spark aggression?

Aversive Events Suffering sometimes builds character. In laboratory experiments, however, those made miserable have often made others miserable (Berkowitz, 1983, 1989). Aversive stimuli—hot temperatures, physical pain, personal insults, foul odors, cigarette smoke, crowding, and a host of others—can evoke hostility. Even hunger can feed anger—making people "hangry" (Bushman et al., 2014). A prime example of this reaction is the **frustration-aggression principle.** Frustration creates anger, which can spark aggression. The frustration-aggression link was illustrated in one analysis of 27,667 hit-by-pitch Major League Baseball incidents between 1960 and 2004 (Timmerman, 2007). Pitchers were most likely to hit batters when the previous batter had hit a home run, the current batter had hit a home run the last time at bat, or the pitcher's teammate had been hit by a pitch in the previous half-inning. A separate study found a similar link between rising temperatures and the number of hit batters (Reifman et al., 1991; see **FIGURE 11.8**).

In the wider world, many studies have found that throughout history, higher temperatures have predicted increased violent crime, spousal abuse, wars, and revolutions (Anderson et al., 1997; Hsiang et al., 2013). One projection, based on the available data, estimates that global warming of 4 degrees Fahrenheit (about 2 degrees Celsius) could induce tens of thousands of additional assaults and murders (Anderson & Delisi, 2011; Miles-Novelo & Anderson, 2019). When overheated, we think, feel, and act more aggressively. And that's before the added violence inducement from climate-change–related drought, poverty, food insecurity, and migration.

LaunchPad How have researchers studied these concepts? Play the role of a researcher by designing one of these studies in the activity *How Would You Know If Hot Temperatures Cause Aggression?*

Reinforcement and Modeling Aggression may naturally follow aversive events, but learning can alter natural reactions. As Chapter 6 points out, we learn when our behavior is reinforced, and we learn by watching others. Children whose aggression successfully intimidates other children may become bullies. Animals that have successfully

aggression any act intended to harm someone physically or emotionally.

frustration-aggression principle the principle that frustration—the blocking of an attempt to achieve some goal—creates anger, which can generate aggression.

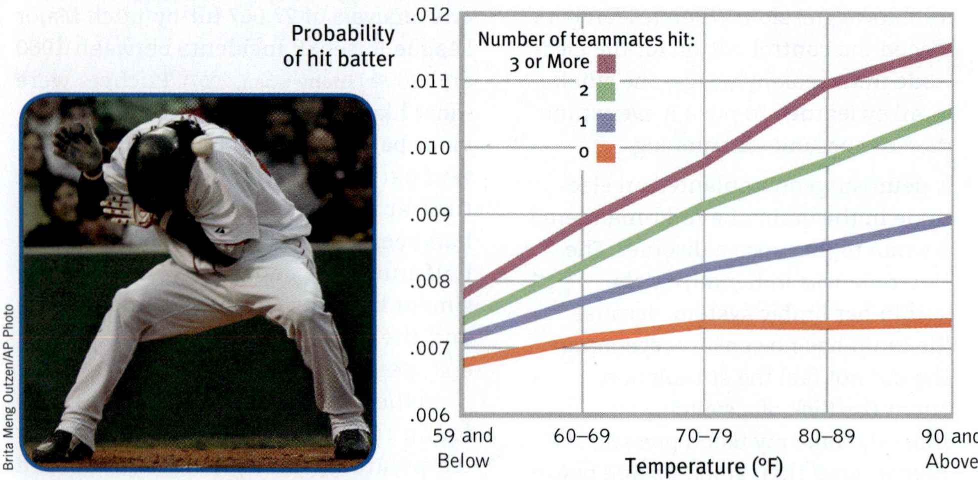

FIGURE 11.8 Temperature and retaliation Researchers looked for occurrences of batters hit by pitches during 4,566,468 pitcher-batter matchups across 57,293 Major League Baseball games since 1952 (Larrick et al., 2011). The probability of a hit batter increased if one or more of the pitcher's teammates had been hit, and also with temperature.

fought to get food or mates become increasingly ferocious. To foster a kinder, gentler world, we had best model and reward sensitivity and cooperation from an early age, perhaps by training parents to discipline without modeling violence.

Parent-training programs often advise parents to avoid modeling violence by not screaming and hitting when frustrated by their children's bad behavior. Instead, parents should reinforce desirable behaviors and frame statements positively. ("When you put your toys away, you can go play," rather than "If you don't put your toys away, you'd better watch out.")

Different cultures model, reinforce, and evoke different tendencies toward violence. Between 1882 and 1926, American lynch mobs in Georgia murdered 514 people. The best predictors of this collective violence were cultural norms that encouraged and supported lynching (Ritchey & Ruback, 2018). Some cultures also encourage people to fight to defend their honor (Nowak et al., 2016). "Culture of honor" states (such as some in the U.S. South) have had higher rates of students bringing weapons to school and of school shootings (Brown et al., 2009). Crime rates have also been higher (and happiness lower) in times and places marked by a great income gap between rich and poor (Messias et al., 2011; Oishi et al., 2011; Wilkinson & Pickett, 2009). And fathers matter. High rates of violence and youth imprisonment have been found in cultures and families with minimal or no father care (Harper & McLanahan, 2004; Triandis, 1994).

Media Models for Violence Parents are not the only aggression models. Television, films, video games, and the internet offer supersized portions of violence. An adolescent boy faced with a real-life challenge may "act like a man"—at least an action-film man—by intimidating or eliminating the threat. Media violence teaches us **social scripts**—culturally provided mental files for how to act in certain situations. As more than 100 studies confirm, we sometimes imitate what we've viewed. Watching media depictions of risk-glorifying behaviors (dangerous driving, extreme sports, unprotected sex) increases real-life risk-taking (Fischer et al., 2011). Watching violent behaviors (murder, robbery) can increase real-life aggressiveness (Anderson et al., 2017).

Music lyrics also write social scripts. In one study, German university men who listened to woman-hating song lyrics poured the most hot chili sauce for a woman to consume. A follow-up study found that listening to man-hating song lyrics had a similar effect on women (Fischer & Greitemeyer, 2006).

Repeatedly watching pornography—even nonviolent pornography—makes sexual aggression seem less serious (Harris, 1994). In one experiment, undergraduates viewed six brief films each week for six weeks (Zillmann & Bryant, 1984). Some viewed sexually explicit films; others viewed films with no sexual content. Three weeks later, both groups, after reading a newspaper report about a man convicted of raping a female hitchhiker, suggested an appropriate prison term. Participants who viewed the sexually explicit films recommended sentences only half as long as those recommended by the control group. In other studies that explored pornography's effects on aggression toward relationship partners, pornography consumption predicted both self-reported aggression and participants' willingness to administer laboratory noise blasts to their partner (Lambert et al., 2011; Peter & Valkenburg, 2016). Pornography acts mostly by adding fuel to a fire: It heightens risk of sexual aggression primarily among aggression-prone men (Malamuth, 2018).

Pornography with violent sexual content can also increase men's readiness to actually *behave* aggressively toward women. As a statement by 21 social scientists noted, "Pornography that portrays sexual aggression as pleasurable for the victim increases the acceptance of the use of coercion in sexual relations" (Surgeon General, 1986). Contrary to much popular opinion, viewing such scenes does not provide an outlet for bottled-up impulses. Rather, said the statement, "in laboratory studies measuring short-term effects, exposure to violent pornography increases punitive behavior toward women."

Do Violent Video Games Teach Social Scripts for Violence? Experiments worldwide indicate that playing positive games produces positive effects (Greitemeyer & Mügge, 2014; Prot et al., 2014). For example, playing the classic video game *Lemmings*, where a goal was to help others, increased real-life helping. So, might a parallel effect occur after playing games that enact violence? Violent video games became an issue for public debate after teenagers in more than a dozen places seemed to mimic the carnage in the shooter games they had so often played (Anderson, 2004, 2013).

Such violent mimicry makes us wonder: What are the effects of actively role-playing aggression? Does it cause people to become less sensitive to violence and more open to violent acts? Nearly 400 studies of 130,000 people offer some answers (Anderson et al., 2010a; Calvert et al., 2017; Prescott et al., 2018). Violent video game playing tends to make us less sensitive to cruelty (Arriaga et al., 2015). It also primes us to respond aggressively when provoked. Video games can prime aggressive thoughts, decrease empathy, and increase aggression. Adolescents and university students who spend the most hours playing violent video games have also tended to be the most physically aggressive (Anderson & Dill, 2000; Exelmans et al., 2015). For example, they more often acknowledged having hit or attacked someone else. And people randomly assigned to play a game involving bloody murders with groaning victims (rather than to play nonviolent games) became more hostile. On a follow-up task, they also were more likely to blast intense noise at a fellow student. Studies of young adolescents reveal that those who play a lot of violent video games see the world as more hostile (Bushman, 2016; Exelmans et al., 2015; Gentile, 2009). Compared with nongaming kids, they get into more arguments and fights and get worse grades.

> "Study finds exposure to violent children causes increased aggression in video game characters." —The [humorous] *Onion*, March 6, 2017

Ah, but is this merely because naturally hostile kids are drawn to such games? Apparently not. Comparisons of gamers and nongamers who scored low on hostility measures revealed a difference in the number of fights reported. Almost 4 in 10 violent-game players had been in fights, compared with only 4 in 100 of the nongaming kids (Anderson, 2004). Some researchers believe that, due partly to the more active participation and rewarded violence of game play, violent video games have even greater effects on aggressive behavior and cognition than do violent TV shows and movies (Anderson & Warburton, 2012).

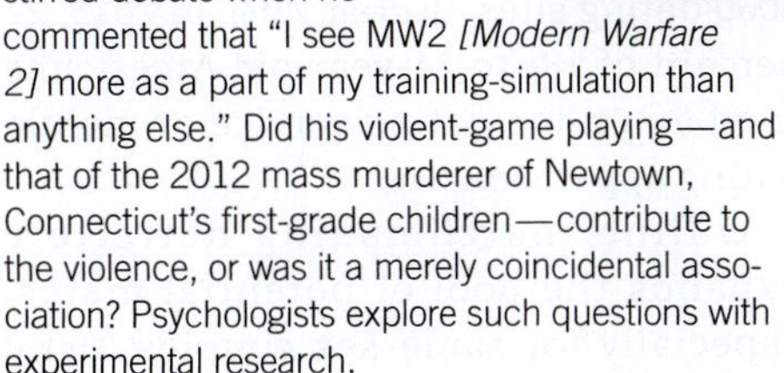

Coincidence or contributor? In 2011, Norwegian Anders Behring Breivik bombed government buildings in Oslo, then shot and killed 69 more people, mostly teens, at a youth camp. As a player of first-person shooter games, Breivik stirred debate when he commented that "I see MW2 *[Modern Warfare 2]* more as a part of my training-simulation than anything else." Did his violent-game playing—and that of the 2012 mass murderer of Newtown, Connecticut's first-grade children—contribute to the violence, or was it a merely coincidental association? Psychologists explore such questions with experimental research.

AFP/Getty Images

Other researchers are unimpressed by such findings (Ferguson, 2013b, 2014, 2015). They note that from 1996 to 2006, video game sales increased, yet youth violence declined. They argue that other factors—depression, family violence, peer influence—better predict aggression. The focused fun of game playing can also satisfy basic needs for a sense of competence, control, and social connection (Granic et al., 2014).

* * *

To sum up, research reveals biological, psychological, and social-cultural influences on aggressive behavior. Complex behaviors, including violence, have many causes, making any single explanation an oversimplification. Asking what causes violence is therefore like asking what causes cancer. Aspects of our biology, our psychology, and our social environment interact. Like so much else, aggression is a biopsychosocial phenomenon.

A happy concluding note: Historical trends suggest that the world is becoming less violent over time (Pinker, 2011). That people vary over time and place reminds us that environments differ. Yesterday's plundering Vikings have become today's peace-promoting Scandinavians. Like all behavior, aggression arises from the interaction of persons and situations.

IN YOUR EVERYDAY LIFE

In what ways have you been affected by social scripts for aggression? Have your viewing and gaming habits influenced your social scripts for aggression?

RETRIEVE & REMEMBER

ANSWERS IN APPENDIX E

15. What biological, psychological, and social-cultural influences interact to produce aggressive behaviors?

ATTRACTION

Pause a moment to think about your relationships with two people—a close friend, and someone who has stirred your romantic feelings. These special sorts of attachments help us cope with all other relationships. What is the psychological chemistry that binds us together in friendship and love? Social psychology suggests some answers.

The Psychology of Attraction

LOQ 11-17 Why do we befriend or fall in love with some people but not others?

We endlessly wonder how we can win others' affection and what makes our own affections flourish or fade. Does familiarity breed contempt or affection? Do birds of a feather flock together, or do opposites attract? Is it what's inside that counts, or does physical attractiveness matter, too? To explore these questions, let's consider three ingredients of our liking for one another: proximity, physical attractiveness, and similarity.

social script a culturally modeled guide for how to act in various situations.

Proximity Before friendships become close, they must begin. Proximity—geographic nearness—is friendship's most powerful predictor. Proximity can provide opportunities for aggression. But much more often it breeds liking (and sometimes even marriage) among those who live in the same neighborhood, sit nearby in class, work in the same office, share the same parking lot, or eat in the same dining hall. Look around. Mates first must meet.

Proximity breeds liking partly because of the **mere exposure effect.** Repeated exposure to novel visual stimuli increases our liking for them. By age 3 months, infants prefer photos of the race they most often see—usually their own (Kelly et al., 2007). Familiarity with a face also makes it look happier (Carr et al., 2017). Mere exposure increases our liking not only for familiar faces, but also for familiar nonsense syllables, geometric figures, and Chinese characters, and for the letters of our own name (Moreland & Zajonc, 1982; Nuttin, 1987; Zajonc, 2001). Mere exposure even increases *unconscious* liking of nonsense syllables—strings of letters presented so quickly our minds don't consciously process them (Van Dessel et al., 2019). So, up to a point (after which the effect wears off), familiarity feeds fondness (Bornstein, 1989, 1999; Montoya et al., 2017).

This would come as no surprise to the young Taiwanese man who wrote more than 700 letters to his girlfriend, urging her to marry him. She did marry—the mail carrier (Steinberg, 1993).

Modern Matchmaking If you have not found a romantic partner in your immediate proximity, should you cast a wider net? Millions search for love on one of 8000 dating sites (Hatfield, 2016). In 2015, 27 percent of 18- to 24-year-old Americans tried an online dating service or mobile dating app (Smith, 2016).

Online matchmaking definitely expands the pool of potential mates, especially for same-sex couples (Finkel et al., 2012a,b; Rosenfeld & Thomas, 2012). How effective is the matchmaking? Compared with those formed in person, internet-formed friendships and relationships are, on average, slightly more likely to last and be satisfying (Bargh & McKenna, 2004; Bargh et al., 2002; Cacioppo et al., 2013). Small wonder that some 10 million Americans are using online matchmaking (Statista, 2018). By one estimate, online dating has recently been responsible for about a fifth of U.S. marriages (Crosier et al., 2012).

Speed dating pushes the search for romance into high gear. In a process pioneered by a matchmaking Jewish rabbi, people meet a succession of would-be partners, either in person or via webcam (Bower, 2009). After a 3- to 8-minute conversation, people move on to the next person. (In an in-person heterosexual meeting, one group—usually the women—remains seated while the other group circulates.) Those who want to meet again can arrange for future contacts.

Emily Flake/Conde Nast/The Cartoon Bank

". . . and if anyone here suspects that the algorithm that put these two together might be flawed, speak now. . . ."

For researchers, speed dating offers a unique opportunity for studying influences on our first impressions of potential romantic partners. Some recent findings:

- ***People who fear rejection often provoke it.*** After a 3-minute speed date, those who most feared rejection were least often selected for a follow-up date (McClure & Lydon, 2014).
- ***Given more options, people make more superficial choices.*** When people meet lots of potential partners, they focus on more easily assessed characteristics, such as height and weight (Lenton & Francesconi, 2010, 2012).
- ***Men wish for future contact with more of their speed dates; women tend to be choosier.*** This gender difference disappears if the conventional roles

(a)

(b)

Jeffrey Mayer/Getty Images

Which is the real Sofía Vergara? The mere exposure effect applies even to ourselves. Because the human face is not perfectly symmetrical, the face we see in the mirror is not the same face our friends see. Most of us prefer the familiar mirror image, while our friends like the reverse (Mita et al., 1977). The person actor Sofía Vergara sees in the mirror each morning is shown in (b), and that's the photo she would probably prefer.

are reversed, so that men stay seated while women circulate (Finkel & Eastwick, 2009).

- *Compatibility is hard to predict.* In two speed-dating studies, participants answered more than 100 self-report measures beforehand. Alas, nothing predicted successful matches (Joel et al., 2017).

John Shearer/Getty Images; Bennett Raglin/Getty Images

Extreme makeover In affluent, beauty-conscious cultures, increasing numbers of people, such as celebrity Kylie Jenner, have turned to cosmetic procedures to change their looks.

Physical Attractiveness So proximity offers contact. What most affects our first impressions? The person's sincerity? Intelligence? Personality? The answer is physical appearance. This finding is unnerving for those of us taught that "beauty is only skin deep" and "appearances can be deceiving."

In one early study, researchers randomly matched new students for heterosexual blind dates in a Welcome Week dance (Walster et al., 1966). Before the dance, the researchers gave each student several personality and aptitude tests, and they rated each student's physical attractiveness. The couples then danced and talked for more than two hours and then took a brief break to rate their dates. What predicted whether they liked each other? Only one thing: appearance. Both the men and the women liked good-looking dates best. Women are more likely than men to say that another's looks don't affect them (Jonason et al., 2015; Lippa, 2007). But studies show that a man's looks do affect women's behavior (Eastwick et al., 2014a,b). In speed-dating experiments, as in Tinder swipes, attractiveness influences first impressions for both sexes (Belot & Francesconi, 2006; Finkel & Eastwick, 2008).

William Haefeli The New Yorker Collection/The Cartoon Bank

"I'd like to meet the algorithm that thought we'd be a good match."

Physical attractiveness also predicts how often people date and how popular they feel. We perceive attractive people as healthier, happier, more sensitive, more successful, and more socially skilled (Eagly et al., 1991; Feingold, 1992; Hatfield & Sprecher, 1986).

For those of us who find the importance of looks unfair and short-sighted, three other findings may be reassuring:

- People's attractiveness seems surprisingly unrelated to their self-esteem and happiness (Diener et al., 1995; Major et al., 1984). Unless we have just compared ourselves with superattractive people, few of us (thanks, perhaps, to the mere exposure effect) view ourselves as unattractive (Thornton & Moore, 1993).
- Strikingly attractive people are sometimes suspicious that praise for their work is simply a reaction to their looks. Less attractive people have been more likely to accept praise as sincere (Berscheid, 1981).
- For couples who were friends before lovers—who became romantically involved long after first meeting—looks matter less (Hunt et al., 2015). With slow-cooked love, values and interests matter more.

Beauty is also in the eye of the culture. Hoping to look attractive, people across the globe have pierced and tattooed their bodies, lengthened their necks, bound their feet, artificially lightened or darkened their skin and hair, dieted, and exercised. Cultural ideals also change over time. For women in the United States, for example, the soft, voluptuous Marilyn Monroe ideal of the 1950s has been replaced by today's lean yet busty ideal.

Do any aspects of heterosexual attractiveness cross place and time? Yes. As we noted in Chapter 4, men in many cultures, from Australia to Zambia, judge women as more attractive if they have a youthful, fertile appearance, suggested by a low waist-to-hip ratio (Karremans et al., 2010; Perilloux et al., 2010; Platek & Singh, 2010). Women feel attracted to healthy-looking men, but especially to those who seem mature, dominant, masculine, and wealthy (Gallup & Frederick, 2010; Gangestad et al., 2010). But faces matter, too. When people rate opposite-sex faces and bodies separately, the face tends to be the better predictor of overall physical attractiveness (Currie & Little, 2009; Peters et al., 2007).

mere exposure effect the tendency for repeated exposure to novel stimuli to increase our liking of them.

Sean Caffrey/Getty Images

Blend Images/Alamy

svetikd/Getty Images

What is "attractive"? The answer varies by culture and over time. Yet some adult physical features, such as a healthy appearance and a relatively symmetrical face, seem attractive everywhere.

Our feelings also influence our attractiveness judgments. Imagine two people: One is honest, humorous, and polite. The other is rude, unfair, and abusive. Which one is more attractive? Most people perceive the person with the appealing traits as more attractive (Lewandowski et al., 2007). Or imagine being paired with a stranger of the sex you find attractive, who listens intently to your self-disclosures. Might you feel a twinge of sexual attraction toward that empathic person? Student volunteers did, in several experiments (Birnbaum & Reis, 2012). Our feelings influence our perceptions.

In a Rodgers and Hammerstein musical of the fairy tale, Prince Charming asks Cinderella, "Do I love you because you're beautiful, or are you beautiful because I love you?" Chances are it's both. As we see our loved ones again and again, we notice their physical imperfections less, and their attractiveness grows more obvious (Beaman & Klentz, 1983; Gross & Crofton, 1977). Shakespeare said it in *A Midsummer Night's Dream:* "Love looks not with the eyes, but with the mind." Come to love someone and watch beauty grow. Love sees loveliness.

Similarity So you've met someone, and your appearance has made a decent first impression. What influences whether you will become friends? As you get to know each other, will the chemistry be better if you are opposites or if you are alike?

It makes a good story—extremely different types liking or loving each other: unlikely friends Frog and Toad in Arnold Lobel's books, unlikely couple Hermione and Ron in the Harry Potter series. These stories delight us by expressing what we seldom experience. In real life, opposites retract (Montoya & Horton, 2013; Rosenbaum, 1986). Birds that flock together usually are of a feather. Tall people typically find true love with other tall people; short people show a soft spot for other short people (Yengo et al., 2018). Compared with randomly paired people, friends and couples are far more likely to share attitudes,

© Dave Coverly/speedbump.com

Similarity attracts; perceived dissimilarity does not.

beliefs, and interests (and, for that matter, age, religion, race, education, intelligence, smoking behavior, and economic status). Moreover, people feel attracted to people when discovering they share a rare attitude—perhaps their liking of an unusual hobby or musician (Alves, 2018). Journalist Walter Lippmann was right to suppose that love lasts "when the lovers love many things together, and not merely each other."

Proximity, attractiveness, and similarity are not the only forces that influence attraction. We also like those who like us. This is especially true when our self-image is low. When we believe someone likes us, we feel good and respond warmly. Our warm response in turn leads them to like us even more (Curtis & Miller, 1986). To be liked is powerfully rewarding.

Indeed, all the findings we have considered so far can be explained by a simple *reward theory of attraction.* We will like those whose behavior is rewarding to us, including those who are both able and willing to help us achieve our goals (Montoya & Horton, 2014). When people live or work in close proximity, it requires less time and effort to develop the friendship and enjoy its benefits. When people are attractive, they are aesthetically pleasing, and associating with them can be socially rewarding. When people share our views, they reward us by confirming our beliefs.

IN YOUR EVERYDAY LIFE

To what extent have your closest relationships been affected by proximity, physical attractiveness, and similarity?

RETRIEVE & REMEMBER

ANSWERS IN APPENDIX E

16. People tend to marry someone who lives or works nearby. This is an example of proximity and the ____________ ____________ ____________ in action.

17. How does being physically attractive influence others' perceptions?

LaunchPad Test your own ability to improve your relationships by engaging online with the activity *Assess Your Strengths: Are You a "Skilled Opener," and How Does This Affect Your Relationships?*

Romantic Love

LOQ 11-18 How does romantic love typically change as time passes?

Sometimes people move from first impressions to friendship to the more intense, complex, and mysterious state of romantic love. If love endures, *passionate love* will mellow into a lingering *companionate love* (Hatfield, 1988).

Passionate Love **Passionate love** mixes something new with something positive (Aron et al., 2000; Coulter & Malouff, 2013). We intensely desire to be with our partner, and seeing our partner stimulates blood flow to a brain region linked to craving and obsession (Acevedo et al., 2012; Hatfield et al., 2015).

The *two-factor theory of emotion* (Chapter 9) explains the intense, positive absorption of passionate love (Hatfield, 1988). That theory makes two assumptions:

- Emotions have two ingredients—*physical arousal* plus *cognitive appraisal*.
- Arousal from any source can enhance an emotion, depending on how we interpret and label the arousal.

In one famous experiment, researchers studied men crossing two bridges above British Columbia's rocky Capilano River (Dutton & Aron, 1974, 1989). One, a swaying footbridge, was 230 feet (70 meters) above the rocks. The other was low and solid. As the men came off each bridge, an attractive young woman working for the researchers asked them to fill out a short questionnaire. She then offered her phone number in case they wanted to hear more about her project. Which men accepted the number and later called the woman? Far more of those who had just crossed the high bridge—which left their hearts pounding. To experience a stirred-up state and to associate some of that feeling with a desirable person is to experience the pull of passion. Adrenaline makes the heart grow fonder. Sexual desire + a growing attachment = the passion of romantic love.

2430/Getty Images

Love is an ancient thing This 5000- to 6000-year-old "Romeo and Juliet" young couple was unearthed locked in embrace, near Rome.

Companionate Love Passionate romantic love seldom endures. The intense absorption in the other, the thrill of the romance, the giddy "floating on a cloud" feeling typically fade. Are the French correct in saying that "love makes the time pass and time makes love pass"? Sometimes. But as love matures, it typically becomes a steadier **companionate love**—a deep, affectionate attachment (Hatfield, 1988). Like a passing storm, the flood of passion-feeding hormones (testosterone, dopamine, adrenaline) gives way. But another hormone, *oxytocin,* remains, supporting feelings of trust, calmness, and bonding with the mate. This shift from passion to attachment may be adaptive (Reis & Aron, 2008). Passionate love often produces children, whose survival is aided by the parents' waning obsession with each other.

In the most satisfying of marriages, attraction and sexual desire endure, minus the obsession of early-stage romance (Acevedo & Aron, 2009). Indeed, failure to appreciate passionate love's limited half-life can doom a relationship (Berscheid et al., 1984). Recognizing the short duration of passionate love, some societies judge such feelings a poor reason for marrying. Better, these cultures say, to search (or have someone search on your behalf) for a partner who shares your background and interests. Cultures where people rate love as less important for marriage do have lower divorce rates (Levine et al., 1995).

One key to a satisfying and enduring relationship is **equity,** as both partners receive in proportion to what they give (Gray-Little & Burks, 1983; Van Yperen & Buunk, 1990). In one national survey, "sharing household chores" ranked third, after "faithfulness" and a "happy sexual relationship," on a list of nine things Americans associated with successful marriages. As the Pew Research Center (2007) summarized, "I like hugs. I like kisses. But what I really love is help with the dishes."

Equity's importance extends beyond marriage. Mutually sharing one's self and possessions, making decisions together, giving and getting emotional support, promoting and caring about each other's welfare—all these acts are at the core of every type of loving relationship (Sternberg & Grajek, 1984). It's true for lovers, for parent and child, and for close friends.

passionate love an aroused state of intense positive absorption in another, usually present at the beginning of romantic love.

companionate love the deep affectionate attachment we feel for those with whom our lives are intertwined.

equity a condition in which people receive from a relationship in proportion to what they give to it.

Sharing includes **self-disclosure,** revealing intimate details about ourselves — our likes and dislikes, our dreams and worries, our proud and shameful moments. As one person reveals a little, the other returns the gift. The first then reveals more, and on and on, as friends or lovers move to deeper intimacy (Baumeister & Bratslavsky, 1999).

One study marched some student pairs through 45 minutes of increasingly self-disclosing conversation—from "What is the greatest accomplishment of your life?" to "When did you last cry in front of another person? By yourself?" Other pairs spent the time with small-talk questions, such as "What was your high school like?" (Aron et al., 1997). By the experiment's end, those experiencing the escalating intimacy felt much closer to their conversation partner than did the small-talkers. Likewise, after dating couples spent 45 minutes answering such questions, they felt increased love (Welker et al., 2014).

In the mathematics of love, self-disclosing intimacy + mutually supportive equality = enduring companionate love.

RETRIEVE & REMEMBER

ANSWERS IN APPENDIX E

18. How does the two-factor theory of emotion help explain *passionate love?*
19. Two vital components for maintaining *companionate love* are __________ and __________-__________.

ALTRUISM

LOQ 11-19 What is *altruism*? When are we most—and least—likely to help?

Altruism is an unselfish concern for the welfare of others, such as Dirk Willems displayed when he rescued his jailer. Willems fits the definition of a hero—moral, courageous, and protective of those in need (Kinsella et al., 2015). Consider another heroic example of altruism, which took place in a New York City subway station.

Subway hero Wesley Autrey and his children

Construction worker Wesley Autrey and his 6- and 4-year-old daughters were waiting for their train when they saw a nearby man collapse in a convulsion. The man then got up, stumbled to the platform's edge, and fell onto the tracks. With train headlights approaching, Autrey later recalled, "I had to make a split-second decision" (Buckley, 2007). His decision, as his girls looked on in horror, was to leap onto the track, push the man off the rails and into a foot-deep space between them, and lie on top of him. As the train screeched to a halt, five cars traveled just above his head, leaving grease on his knitted cap. When Autrey cried out, "I've got two daughters up there. Let them know their father is okay," the onlookers erupted into applause.

Such selfless goodness made New Yorkers proud to call that city home. Another New York story, four decades earlier, had a different ending. In 1964, a stalker repeatedly stabbed Kitty Genovese, then raped her as she lay dying outside her Queens, New York, apartment at 3:30 a.m. "Oh, my God, he stabbed me!" Genovese screamed into the early morning stillness. "Please help me!" Windows opened and lights went on as some neighbors heard her screams. Her attacker fled. Then he returned to stab and rape her again. Until it was too late, no one called police or came to her aid.

Bystander Intervention

In an emergency, some people intervene, as Wesley Autrey did, but others fail to offer help. Why do some people become heroes while others just stand and watch? Social psychologists John Darley and Bibb Latané (1968b) believed three conditions were necessary for bystanders to help. They must *notice* the incident, *interpret* it as an emergency, and *assume responsibility* for helping (**FIGURE 11.9**).

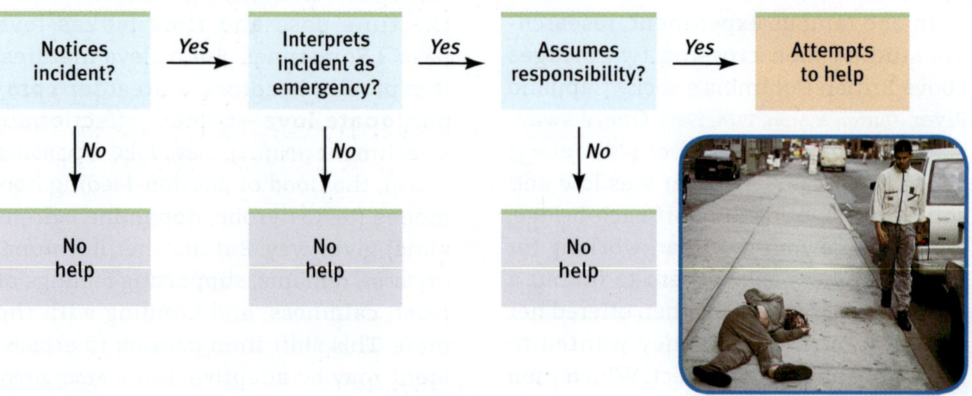

FIGURE 11.9 The decision-making process for bystander intervention Before helping, we must first notice an emergency, then correctly interpret it, and then assume responsibility. (Data from Darley & Latané, 1968b.)

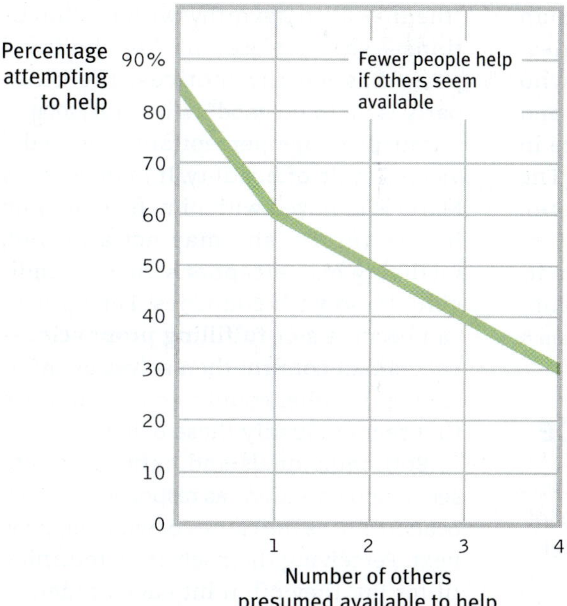

FIGURE 11.10 Responses to a simulated emergency When people thought they alone heard the calls for help from a person they believed to be having an epileptic seizure, they usually helped. But when they thought four others were also hearing the calls, fewer than one-third responded. (Data from Darley & Latané, 1968a.)

At each step, the presence of others can turn people away from the path that leads to helping. One of Darley and Latané's experiments staged a fake emergency as students in separate laboratory rooms took turns speaking over an intercom. Only the person whose microphone was switched on could be heard. When his turn came, one student (actually an accomplice) pretended to have an epileptic seizure, and he called for help (1968a).

How did the others react? As **FIGURE 11.10** shows, those who believed only they could hear the victim—and therefore thought they alone were responsible for helping him—usually went to his aid. Students who thought others could also hear the victim's cries were more likely to do nothing. When more people shared responsibility for helping—when no one person was clearly responsible—each listener was less likely to help. Indeed, this contributes to "global bystander nonintervention" as millions of far-away people die of hunger, disease, and genocide (Pittinsky & Diamante, 2015). And this helps explain bystander inaction in some horrific incidents broadcast on Facebook Live.

Hundreds of additional experiments have confirmed this **bystander effect.** For example, researchers and their assistants took 1497 elevator rides in three cities and "accidentally" dropped coins or pencils in front of 4813 fellow passengers (Latané & Dabbs, 1975). When alone with the person in need, 40 percent helped; in the presence of five other bystanders, only 20 percent helped.

Observations of behavior in thousands of situations—relaying an emergency phone call, aiding a stranded motorist, donating blood, picking up dropped books, contributing money, giving time, and more—show that the odds of our helping someone depend on the characteristics of that person, the situation, and our own internal state. The odds of helping are highest when

- the person appears to need and deserve help.
- the person is in some way similar to us.
- the person is a woman.
- we have just observed someone else being helpful.
- we are not in a hurry.
- we are in a small town or rural area.
- we are feeling guilty.
- we are focused on others and not preoccupied.
- we are in a good mood.

This last result, that happy people are helpful people, is one of psychology's most consistent findings. As poet Robert Browning (1868) observed, "Oh, make us happy and you make us good!" It doesn't matter how we are cheered. Whether by being made to feel successful and intelligent, by thinking happy thoughts, by finding money, or even by receiving a posthypnotic suggestion, we become more generous and more eager to help (Carlson et al., 1988).

So happiness breeds helpfulness. But it's also true that helpfulness breeds happiness. Helping those in need activates brain areas associated with reward (Harbaugh et al., 2007; Kawamichi et al., 2015). That helps explain a curious finding: People who give money away are happier than those who spend it almost entirely on themselves. In one experiment, researchers gave people an envelope with cash and instructions. Some were told to spend it on themselves, while others were told to spend it on others (Dunn et al., 2008; Dunn & Norton, 2013). Which group was happiest at the day's end? It was, indeed, those assigned to the spend-it-on-others condition.

IN YOUR EVERYDAY LIFE

Imagine being a newcomer needing directions at a busy bus terminal. What could you do to increase the odds that someone will assist you, and what sort of person would be most likely to offer help?

RETRIEVE & REMEMBER

ANSWERS IN APPENDIX E

20. Why didn't anybody help Kitty Genovese? What social psychology principle did this incident illustrate?

LaunchPad To test your understanding of emergency helping, engage online with *Concept Practice: When Will People Help Others?*

self-disclosure revealing intimate aspects of ourselves to others.

altruism unselfish concern for the welfare of others.

bystander effect the tendency for any given bystander to be less likely to give aid if other bystanders are present.

Norms for Helping

LOQ 11-20 How do social norms explain helping behavior?

Why do we help? Sometimes we go to the aid of another because we have been socialized to do so, through norms that prescribe how we *ought* to behave (Everett et al., 2015). Two such norms are the *reciprocity norm* and the *social-responsibility norm.*

The **reciprocity norm** is the expectation that we should return help, not harm, to those who have helped us. Those for whom we do favors will often return favors. With similar others, the reciprocity norm motivates us to give (in favors, gifts, or social invitations) about as much as we receive. Sometimes it means paying it forward, as happened in one experiment when people who were generously treated became more likely to be generous to a stranger (Tsvetkova & Macy, 2014). Returning favors feels good, so we tend to find the reciprocity norm a pleasant way to help others (Hein et al., 2016).

The reciprocity norm kicked in after Dave Tally, a Tempe, Arizona, homeless man, found $3300 in a backpack an Arizona State University student had lost on his way to buy a used car (Lacey, 2010). Tally could have used the cash for food, shelter, and much-needed bike repairs. Instead, he turned the backpack in to the social service agency where he volunteered. To reciprocate Tally's help, the backpack's owner thanked him with a cash reward. Hearing about Tally's self-giving deeds, dozens of others also sent him money and job offers.

The **social-responsibility norm** is the expectation that we should help those who depend on us. So, we help young children and others who cannot give back as much as they receive. Europeans are most welcoming of asylum seekers who are most vulnerable — those, for example, who have been tortured or have no surviving family (Bansak et al., 2016). Many world religions encourage their followers to practice the social-responsibility norm, and sometimes this leads to prosocial behavior. Between 2006 and 2008, Gallup polls sampled more than 300,000 people across 140 countries, comparing the "highly religious" (who said religion was important to them and who had attended a religious service in the prior week) to the less religious. The highly religious, despite being poorer, were about 50 percent more likely to report having "donated money to a charity in the last month" and to have volunteered time to an organization (Pelham & Crabtree, 2008).

FROM CONFLICT TO PEACE

LOQ 11-21 What social processes fuel conflict? How can we transform feelings of prejudice and conflict into behaviors that promote peace?

Positive social norms encourage generosity and enable group living. But conflicts often divide us. One response to recent global conflict- and scarcity-driven mass migrations has been increasing nationalism and nativism (favoring native-born citizens over newcomers). Moreover, *every day,* the world continues to spend almost $5 billion for arms and armies — money that could be used for needed housing, nutrition, education, and health care. Knowing that wars begin in human minds, psychologists have wondered: What in the human mind causes destructive conflict? How might the perceived threats of our differences be replaced by a spirit of cooperation?

To a social psychologist, a **conflict** is the perception that actions, goals, or ideas are incompatible. The elements of conflict are much the same, whether partners arguing, political groups feuding, or nations at war. In each situation, conflict may seed positive change, or be a destructive process that can produce results no one wants.

Enemy Perceptions

Psychologists have noticed a curious tendency: People in conflict form evil images of one another. These distorted images are so similar that we call them **mirror-image perceptions.** As we see "them" — untrustworthy, with evil intentions — so "they" see us. "My political party has worthy motives; the other party is up to no good" (Waytz et al., 2014).

Mirror-image perceptions can feed a vicious cycle of hostility. If Juan believes Maria is annoyed with him, he may snub her. In return, she may act annoyed, justifying his perceptions. As with individuals, so with countries. Perceptions can become **self-fulfilling prophecies—** beliefs that confirm themselves by influencing the other country to react in ways that seem to justify those beliefs.

Both individuals and nations tend to see their own actions as responses to provocation, not as the causes of what happens next. Perceiving themselves as returning tit for tat, they often hit back harder, as University College London volunteers did in one experiment (Shergill et al., 2003). After feeling pressure on their own finger, they were to use a mechanical device to press on another volunteer's finger. Although told to reciprocate with the same amount of pressure, they typically responded with about 40 percent more force than they had just experienced. Gentle touches soon escalated to hard presses. Volunteers felt confident that they were responding in kind, and their partners were the ones upping the pressure — much as when each child after a fight claims that "I just touched him, but he hit me!"

The point is not that truth must lie midway between two such views; one may be more accurate. The point is that enemy perceptions often form mirror images. Moreover, as enemies change, so do perceptions. In American minds and media, the "bloodthirsty, cruel, treacherous" Japanese of World War II became "intelligent, hardworking, self-disciplined, resourceful allies" (Gallup, 1972).

Promoting Peace

How can we change perceptions and make peace? Can contact and cooperation transform the anger and fear fed by prejudice and conflict into peace-promoting attitudes? Research indicates that, in some cases, they can.

Contact Does it help to put two conflicting parties into close contact? It depends. Negative contact increases *dis*liking (Graf et al., 2014; Paolini et al., 2014). But positive contact—especially noncompetitive contact between parties with equal status, such as fellow store clerks—typically helps. Initially prejudiced co-workers of different races have, in such circumstances, usually come to accept one another. Across a quarter-million people studied in 38 nations, friendly contact with ethnic minorities, older, and LGBTQ people, and (especially) people with disabilities has usually led to more positive and empathic attitudes (Paluck et al., 2018; Pettigrew & Tropp, 2011; Tropp & Barlow, 2018). Some examples:

- In both Germany and the United States, people in states with the most immigrants are the most supportive of immigrants; in states with few immigrants there is greater fear of immigrants (Myers, 2018).
- Straight, cisgender people's attitudes toward gay and transgender people are influenced not only by what they know but also by *whom* they know (Brown, 2017; Collier et al., 2012). In surveys, the reason people most often give for becoming more supportive of same-sex marriage is "having friends, family, or acquaintances who are gay or lesbian" (Pew, 2013). And in the United States, where 87 percent of people now say they know someone who is gay, attitudes toward gay people have become much more positive (Pew, 2016).
- Friendly interracial contact, say between Blacks and Whites as roommates, improves attitudes toward others of the different race, and toward other racial groups, too (Gaither & Sommers, 2013; Tausch et al., 2010).

However, contact is not always enough. In many schools, ethnic groups segregate themselves in lunchrooms and on school grounds (Alexander & Tredoux, 2010; Clack et al., 2005; Schofield, 1986). People in each group often think they would welcome more contact with the other group, but they assume the other group does not share their interest (Richeson & Shelton, 2007). When these mirror-image untruths are corrected, friendships can form and prejudices melt.

> "Most of us have overlapping identities which unite us with very different groups. We *can* love what we are, without hating what—and who—we are *not*. We can thrive in our own tradition, even as we learn from others." —Nobel Peace Prize lecture, UN Secretary-General Kofi Annan, 2001

Cooperation To see if enemies could overcome their differences, researcher Muzafer Sherif (1966) manufactured a conflict. He separated 22 boys into two separate camp areas. Then he had the two groups compete for prizes in a series of activities. Before long, each group became intensely proud of itself and hostile to the other group's "sneaky," "smart-alecky stinkers." Food wars broke out. Cabins were ransacked. Fistfights had to be broken up by camp counselors. Brought together, the two groups avoided each other, except to taunt and threaten. Little did they know that within a few days, they would be friends.

Sherif accomplished this reconciliation by giving them **superordinate goals—**shared goals that could be achieved only through cooperation. When he arranged for the camp water supply to "fail," all 22 boys had to work together to restore the water. To rent a movie in those pre-Netflix days, they all had to pool their resources. To move a stalled truck, everyone had to combine their strength, pulling and pushing together. Sherif used shared predicaments and goals to turn enemies into friends. What reduced conflict was not mere contact, but *cooperative* contact.

Critics suggest that Sherif's research team encouraged the conflict, hoping the study would illustrate their expectations about socially toxic competition and socially beneficial cooperation (Perry, 2018). Yet shared predicaments have powerfully unifying effects. Children and youth exposed to war, and minority group members facing rejection or discrimination, have likewise developed strong ingroup identification (Bauer et al., 2014; Ramos et al., 2012). Such experiences build strong bonds (though they can also bring insensitivity to the pain experienced by those in the outgroup) (Levy et al., 2016).

Grant Hindsley/AP Photo

Superordinate goals override differences Cooperative efforts to achieve shared goals are an effective way to break down social barriers.

At such times, cooperation can lead people to define a new, inclusive group that dissolves their former subgroups (Dovidio & Gaertner, 1999). If this were a social psychology experiment, you might seat members of two groups not on opposite sides, but alternately around a table. Give them a new, shared name. Have them work together. Then watch "us" and "them" become "we."

If superordinate goals and shared threats help bring rival groups together, might this principle bring diverse students together? Could cooperative learning in classrooms create interracial friendships, while also enhancing

reciprocity norm an expectation that people will help, not hurt, those who have helped them.

social-responsibility norm an expectation that people will help those needing their help.

conflict a perceived incompatibility of actions, goals, or ideas.

mirror-image perceptions mutual views often held by conflicting groups, as when each side sees itself as ethical and peaceful and views the other side as evil and aggressive.

self-fulfilling prophecy a belief that leads to its own fulfillment.

superordinate goals shared goals that override differences among people and require their cooperation.

Rosiland Beckton

Strangers coming together When a family got stuck in a Florida rip current, no less than 80 of their fellow beachgoers formed a human chain, rescuing them. Said one of the witnesses, Rosalind Beckton: "All races & ages join[ed] together to save lives" (AP, 2017).

student achievement? Experiments with teens from 11 countries confirm that the answer to both questions is *Yes* (Roseth et al., 2008). In the classroom as in the sports arena, members of multi-ethnic groups who work together on projects typically come to feel friendly toward one another. Knowing this, thousands of teachers have made multi-ethnic cooperative learning part of their classroom experience.

The power of cooperative activity to make friends of former enemies has led psychologists to urge increased international exchange and cooperation. Some experiments have found that simply imagining the shared threat of climate change reduces international hostilities (Pyszczynski et al., 2012). From Brazilian tribes to European countries, formerly conflicting groups have managed to build interconnections, interdependence, and a shared social identity as they seek common goals (Fry, 2012). Let us then engage in mutually beneficial trade, working together to protect our common destiny on this fragile planet and becoming more aware that our hopes and fears are shared. By taking such steps, we can change misperceptions that drive us apart and instead join together in a common cause based on common interests. As working toward shared goals reminds us, we are more alike than different.

Byron Buck

Polarized Americans finding common ground In local communities across the United States, mediators are helping "red" (conservative) and "blue" (liberal) citizens discover their common ground and form friendships (see Better-Angels.org).

> "Conflict resolution . . . sometimes gets lost in the shuffle of shouting polarities. . . . Just deal with it. Just do it. Just make it better wherever you find it." —Folk singer Buffy Sainte-Marie, 2017

IMPROVE YOUR EVERYDAY LIFE

Do you regret not getting along with a family member or arguing with a friend? Do you have some ideas now about how you might be able to resolve such conflicts, now or in the future?

RETRIEVE & REMEMBER

ANSWERS IN APPENDIX E

- 21. Why do sports fans tend to feel a sense of satisfaction when their archrival team loses? Do such feelings, in other settings, make conflict resolution more challenging?
- 22. What are two ways to reconcile conflicts and promote peace?

CHAPTER 11 REVIEW Social Psychology

LEARNING OBJECTIVES

TEST YOURSELF Answer these repeated Learning Objective Questions on your own (before checking the answers in Appendix D) to improve your retention of the concepts (McDaniel et al., 2009, 2015).

What Is Social Psychology's Focus?

11-1: What are three main focuses of social psychology?

Social Thinking

11-2: How does the fundamental attribution error describe how we tend to explain others' behavior compared with our own?

11-3: What is an *attitude,* and how do attitudes and actions affect each other?

11-4: How do *peripheral route persuasion* and *central route persuasion* differ?

11-5: How can we share our views more effectively?

Social Influence

11-6: What do experiments on conformity and obedience reveal about the power of social influence?

11-7: What do the social influence studies teach us about ourselves? How much power do we have as individuals?

11-8: How does the presence of others influence our actions, via social facilitation, social loafing, and deindividuation?

11-9: How can group interaction enable group polarization?

11-10: What role does the internet play in group polarization?

11-11: How can group interaction enable groupthink?

Social Relations

11-12: What are the three parts of *prejudice?* How do explicit and implicit prejudice differ?

11-13: What groups are frequent targets of prejudice?

11-14: What are some social, emotional, and cognitive roots of prejudice? What are some ways to combat prejudice?

11-15: What biological factors make us more likely to be aggressive?

11-16: What psychological and social-cultural factors may trigger aggressive behavior?

11-17: Why do we befriend or fall in love with some people but not others?

11-18: How does romantic love typically change as time passes?

11-19: What is *altruism?* When are we most—and least—likely to help?

11-20: How do social norms explain helping behavior?

11-21: What social processes fuel conflict? How can we transform feelings of prejudice and conflict into behaviors that promote peace?

TERMS AND CONCEPTS TO REMEMBER

TEST YOURSELF Write down the definition in your own words, then check your answer.

social psychology, *p.* 303
fundamental attribution error, *p.* 303
attitude, *p.* 303
foot-in-the-door phenomenon, *p.* 305
role, *p.* 305
cognitive dissonance theory, *p.* 305
peripheral route persuasion, *p.* 305
central route persuasion, *p.* 305
conformity, *p.* 307
normative social influence, *p.* 309
informational social influence, *p.* 309
social facilitation, *p.* 311
social loafing, *p.* 313
deindividuation, *p.* 313
group polarization, *p.* 313
groupthink, *p.* 315
prejudice, *p.* 315
stereotype, *p.* 315
discrimination, *p.* 315
just-world phenomenon, *p.* 319
ingroup, *p.* 319
outgroup, *p.* 319
ingroup bias, *p.* 319
scapegoat theory, *p.* 319
other-race effect, *p.* 319
aggression, *p.* 321
frustration-aggression principle, *p.* 321
social script, *p.* 323
mere exposure effect, *p.* 325
passionate love, *p.* 327
companionate love, *p.* 327
equity, *p.* 327
self-disclosure, *p.* 329
altruism, *p.* 329
bystander effect, *p.* 329
reciprocity norm, *p.* 331
social-responsibility norm, *p.* 331
conflict, *p.* 331
mirror-image perceptions, *p.* 331
self-fulfilling prophecy, *p.* 331
superordinate goals, *p.* 331

CHAPTER TEST

TEST YOURSELF Answer the following questions on your own first, then check your answers in Appendix E.

1. A study indicated that most teen boys and girls believe the women they see in online porn are experiencing real sexual pleasure (Jones, 2018). But the situation—being in front of the camera—suggests the women are acting their role. Social psychologists might explain the teens' misperception as the ________ ________ error.
2. We tend to agree to a larger request more readily if we have already agreed to a small request. This tendency is called the __________-__________-__________-__________ phenomenon.
3. Jamala's therapist has suggested that Jamala should "act as if" she is confident, even though she feels insecure and shy. Which social psychological theory would best support this suggestion, and what might the therapist be hoping to achieve?
4. Celebrity endorsements in advertising often lead consumers to purchase products through __________ (central/peripheral) route persuasion.
5. Researchers have found that a person is most likely to conform to a group if
   a. the group members have diverse opinions.
   b. the person feels competent and secure.
   c. the person admires the group's status.
   d. no one else will observe the person's behavior.

6. In Milgram's experiments, the rate of obedience was highest when
   a. the "learner" was at a distance from the "teacher."
   b. the "learner" was close at hand.
   c. other "teachers" refused to go along with the experimenter.
   d. the "teacher" disliked the "learner."
7. Dr. Huang, a popular music professor, delivers fascinating lectures on music history but gets nervous and makes mistakes when describing exam statistics in front of the class. Why does his performance vary by task?
8. In a group situation that fosters arousal and anonymity, a person sometimes loses self-consciousness and self-control. This phenomenon is called ___________.
9. Sharing our opinions with like-minded others tends to strengthen our views, a phenomenon referred to as ___________ ___________.
10. Prejudice toward a group involves negative feelings, a tendency to discriminate, and overly generalized beliefs referred to as ___________.
11. If several well-publicized murders are committed by members of a particular group, we may tend to react with fear and suspicion toward all members of that group. In other words, we
    a. blame the victim.
    b. overgeneralize from vivid, memorable cases.
    c. view the world as just.
    d. rationalize inequality.
12. The other-race effect occurs when we assume that other groups are ___________ (more/less) homogeneous than our own group.
13. Evidence of a biochemical influence on aggression is the finding that
    a. aggressive behavior varies widely from culture to culture.
    b. animals can be bred for aggressiveness.
    c. stimulation of an area of the brain's limbic system produces aggressive behavior.
    d. a higher-than-average level of the hormone testosterone is associated with violent behavior in males.
14. When those who feel frustrated become angry and aggressive, this is referred to as the ___________-___________ ___________.
15. Studies show that parents of delinquent young people tend to use physical force to enforce discipline. This suggests that aggression can be
    a. learned through direct rewards.
    b. triggered by exposure to violent media.
    c. learned through observation of aggressive models.
    d. caused by hormone changes at puberty.
16. Social scientists studying the effects of pornography have mostly agreed that violent pornography
    a. has little effect on most viewers.
    b. is the primary cause of reported and unreported rapes.
    c. leads viewers to be more accepting of coercion in sexual relations.
    d. has no effect, other than short-term arousal and entertainment.
17. Heterosexual pornography most directly influences men's aggression toward women when the following is true:
    a. Viewing time is lengthy.
    b. Eroticism is portrayed.
    c. Sexual violence is portrayed.
    d. The actors are attractive.
18. The more familiar a stimulus becomes, the more we tend to like it. This exemplifies the ___________ ___________ effect.
19. A happy couple celebrating their fiftieth wedding anniversary is likely to experience deep ___________ love, even though their ___________ love has probably decreased over the years.
20. After vigorous exercise you meet an attractive person, and you are suddenly seized by romantic feelings for that person. This response supports the two-factor theory of emotion, which assumes that emotions, such as passionate love, consist of physical arousal plus
    a. a reward.
    b. proximity.
    c. companionate love.
    d. our interpretation of that arousal.
21. Due to the bystander effect, a particular bystander is less likely to give aid if
    a. the victim is similar to the bystander in appearance.
    b. no one else is present.
    c. other people are present.
    d. the incident occurs in a deserted or rural area.
22. Our enemies often have many of the same negative impressions of us as we have of them. This exemplifies the concept of ___________-___________ perceptions.
23. One way of resolving conflicts and fostering cooperation is by giving rival groups shared goals that help them override their differences. These are called ___________ goals.

Continue testing yourself with **LearningCurve** or **Achieve Read & Practice** to learn and remember most effectively.

Alan Becker/Getty Images

Personality

CHAPTER 12

SURVEY THE CHAPTER

Lady Gaga dazzles millions with her unique musical arrangements, tantalizing outfits, and provocative performances. In shows around the world, Lady Gaga's most predictable feature is her unpredictability. She has worn a meat dress to an award show, sported 16-inch heels to meet with U.S. President Barack Obama (who later described the interaction as "a little intimidating"), and inspired U.S. Academy Award viewers in 2019 when she and Bradley Cooper performed *Shallow.*

Yet even Lady Gaga exhibits distinctive and enduring ways of thinking, feeling, and behaving. Her fans and critics alike can depend on her openness to new experiences and the energy she gets from the spotlight. And they can also rely on her painstaking dedication to her music and performances. She describes her high school self as "very dedicated, very studious, and very disciplined." Now, in adulthood, she shows similar self-discipline. Winning an Oscar in 2019, Lady Gaga said, "I've worked hard for a long time. It's not about winning. What it's about is not giving up." This chapter focuses on the ways we all demonstrate unique and persistent patterns of thinking, feeling, and behaving—our *personality.*

Much of this book deals with personality. Earlier chapters considered biological influences on personality; personality development across the life span; how personality relates to learning, motivation, emotion, and health; and social influences on personality. The next chapter will study disorders of personality. This chapter focuses on personality itself—what it is and how researchers study it.

We begin with two historically important theories of personality that have become part of Western culture: Sigmund Freud's *psychoanalytic theory* and the *humanistic theories*. These sweeping perspectives on human nature laid the foundation for later personality theorists and for what this chapter presents next: newer scientific explorations of personality. We'll look at the traits that define our uniqueness. We'll see how biology, psychology, and environment together influence personality. Finally, we'll note how our concept of self—that sense of "Who I am"—helps organize our thoughts, feelings, and behaviors.

What Is Personality?

Learning Objective Question LOQ 12-1 What is *personality*, and what theories inform our understanding of personality?

Psychologists have varied ways to view and study **personality**—our characteristic pattern of thinking, feeling, and acting. Sigmund Freud's *psychoanalytic theory* proposed that childhood sexuality and unconscious motivations influence personality. The *humanistic theories* focused on our inner capacities for growth and self-fulfillment. Later theorists built upon these two broad perspectives. *Trait theories* examine characteristic patterns of behavior *(traits)*. *Social-cognitive theories* explore the interaction between people's traits (including their thinking) and their social context. Let's begin with Freud's work, and its modern-day descendant, *psychodynamic theories*.

Psychodynamic Theories

Psychodynamic theories of personality view human behavior as a lively (dynamic) interaction between the conscious and unconscious mind, and they consider our related motives and conflicts. These theories came from Sigmund Freud's **psychoanalysis**—his theory of personality and the associated treatment techniques. Freud's work was the first to focus clinical attention on our unconscious mind.

FREUD'S PSYCHOANALYTIC PERSPECTIVE: EXPLORING THE UNCONSCIOUS

LOQ 12-2 How did Sigmund Freud's treatment of psychological disorders lead to his view of the unconscious mind?

Freud is not psychology's most important figure, but he is definitely the most famous. Ask 100 people on the street to name a deceased psychologist, suggested Keith Stanovich (1996, p. 1), and "Freud would be the winner hands down." His influence lingers in books, movies, and psychological therapies. Who was Freud, what did he teach, and why do we still study his work?

Like all of us, Sigmund Freud was a product of his times. The late nineteenth century was a time of great discovery and scientific advancement, but also of sexual suppression and male dominance. Men's and women's roles were clearly defined, with male superiority assumed and only male sexuality generally acknowledged (discreetly). These assumptions influenced Freud's thinking about personality. He believed that psychological troubles resulted from men's and women's unresolved conflicts with their expected roles.

Sigmund Freud (1856–1939) "I was the only worker in a new field."

Macmillan Learning

After graduating from the University of Vienna medical school, Freud specialized in nervous disorders. Before long, he began hearing complaints that made no medical sense. One patient had lost all feeling in one hand. Yet there is no nerve pathway that, if damaged, would numb the entire hand and nothing else. Freud wondered: What could cause such disorders? His search for the answer led in a direction that would challenge our self-understanding.

Could these strange disorders have mental rather than physical causes? Freud decided they could. Many meetings with patients led to Freud's "discovery" of the **unconscious**. In Freud's view, this deep well keeps unacceptable thoughts, wishes, feelings, and memories hidden away so thoroughly that we are unaware of them. But despite our best efforts, bits and pieces seep out. Thus, according to Freud, patients might have an odd loss of feeling in their hand because they have an unconscious fear of touching their genitals. Or their unexplained blindness might be caused by unconsciously not wanting to see something that makes them anxious.

Basic to Freud's theory was this belief that the mind is mostly hidden. Below the surface lies a large unconscious region where unacceptable passions and thoughts lurk. Freud believed we *repress* these unconscious feelings and ideas. We block them from awareness because admitting them would be too unsettling. Nevertheless, he said, these repressed feelings and ideas powerfully influence us.

For Freud, nothing was ever accidental. He saw the unconscious seeping not only into people's upsetting symptoms but also, in disguised forms, into their work, their beliefs, and their daily habits. He also glimpsed the unconscious in slips of the tongue and pen, as when a financially stressed patient, not wanting any large pills, said, "Please do not give me any bills, because I cannot swallow them." (Today we call these

"Good morning, beheaded—uh, I mean beloved."

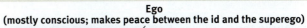

"Freudian slips.") He believed jokes, too, were expressions of repressed sexual and aggressive tendencies traveling in disguise. And dreams, he said, were the "royal road to the unconscious." He thought the dreams we remember are really censored versions of our unconscious wishes.

Hoping to unlock the door to the unconscious, Freud first tried hypnosis, but with poor results. He then turned to **free association**, telling patients to relax and say whatever came to mind, no matter how unimportant or embarrassing. Freud believed that free association would trace a path from the troubled present into a patient's distant past. The chain of thought would lead back to the patient's unconscious, the hiding place of painful past memories, often from childhood. His goal was to find these forbidden thoughts and release them.

Personality Structure

LOQ 12-3 What was Freud's view of personality?

Freud believed that human personality arises from a conflict between impulse and restraint. He argued that people are born with aggressive, pleasure-seeking urges. As we become socialized, we internalize social restraints against these urges. Personality is the result of our efforts to resolve basic conflict—to express these impulses in ways that bring satisfaction without guilt or punishment.

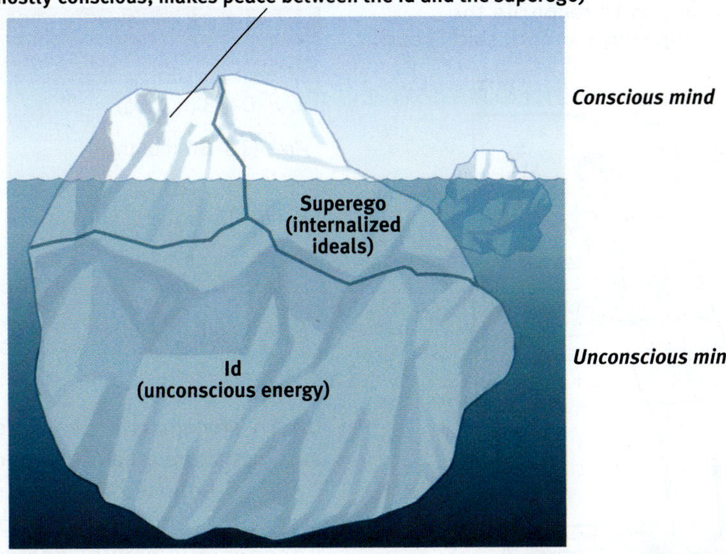

FIGURE 12.1 Freud's idea of the mind's structure Icebergs hide most of their bulk beneath the surface of the water. Psychologists often use this image to illustrate Freud's idea that the mind is mostly hidden beneath the conscious surface of our awareness. Note that the *id* is totally unconscious, but *ego* and *superego* operate both consciously and unconsciously. Like the interconnected parts of a frozen iceberg, the id, ego, and superego also interact.

To understand the mind's conflicts, Freud proposed three interacting systems: the *id*, *ego*, and *superego*. Psychologists have found it useful to view the mind's structure as an iceberg (**FIGURE 12.1**).

The **id** stores unconscious energy. It tries to satisfy our basic drives to survive, reproduce, and act aggressively. The id operates on the *pleasure principle:* It seeks immediate gratification. To understand the id's power, think of newborn infants crying out the moment they feel a need, wanting satisfaction now. Or think of people who abuse drugs, partying now rather than sacrificing today's temporary pleasure for future success and happiness (Fernie et al., 2013; Friedel et al., 2014; Keough et al., 1999).

The mind's second part, the **ego**, operates on the *reality principle*. The ego is the conscious mind. It tries to satisfy the id's impulses in realistic ways that will bring long-term benefits rather than pain or destruction.

As the ego develops, the young child learns to cope with the real world. Around age 4 or 5, Freud theorized, a child's ego begins to recognize the

personality an individual's characteristic pattern of thinking, feeling, and acting.

psychodynamic theories theories that view personality with a focus on the unconscious and the importance of childhood experiences.

psychoanalysis Freud's theory of personality that attributes thoughts and actions to unconscious motives and conflicts; the techniques used in treating psychological disorders by seeking to expose and interpret unconscious tensions.

unconscious according to Freud, a reservoir of mostly unacceptable thoughts, wishes, feelings, and memories. According to contemporary psychologists, information processing of which we are unaware.

free association in psychoanalysis, a method of exploring the unconscious in which the person relaxes and says whatever comes to mind, no matter how unimportant or embarrassing.

id a reservoir of unconscious psychic energy that, according to Freud, strives to satisfy basic sexual and aggressive drives. The id operates on the *pleasure principle*, demanding immediate gratification.

ego the largely conscious, "executive" part of personality that, according to Freud, balances the demands of the id, the superego, and reality. The ego operates on the *reality principle*, satisfying the id's desires in ways that will realistically bring pleasure rather than pain.

The ego struggles to reconcile the demands of superego and id, said Freud.

"Fifty is plenty." "Hundred and fifty."

TABLE 12.1 Freud's Psychosexual Stages	
Stage	**Focus**
Oral (0–18 months)	Pleasure centers on the mouth—sucking, biting, chewing
Anal (18–36 months)	Pleasure focuses on bowel and bladder elimination; coping with demands for control
Phallic (3–6 years)	Pleasure zone is the genitals; coping with incestuous sexual feelings
Latency (6 years to puberty)	A phase of dormant sexual feelings
Genital (puberty on)	Maturation of sexual interests

demands of the **superego**, the voice of our moral compass, or *conscience*. The superego forces the ego to consider not only the real but also the ideal. It focuses on how one *ought* to behave in a perfect world. It judges actions and produces positive feelings of pride or negative feelings of guilt.

As you may have guessed, the superego's demands often oppose the id's. It is the ego's job to reconcile the two. As the personality's "executive," the ego juggles the impulsive demands of the id, the restraining demands of the superego, and the real-life demands of the external world.

LaunchPad To review Freud's components of personality, take advantage of the online *Concept Practice: Freud's Personality Structure.*

Personality Development

LOQ 12-4 What developmental stages did Freud propose?

Freud believed that personality forms during life's first few years. He was convinced that children pass through a series of **psychosexual stages**, from oral to genital (**TABLE 12.1**). In each stage, the id's pleasure-seeking energies focus on an *erogenous zone*, a distinct pleasure-sensitive area of the body.

Freud believed that during the third stage, the *phallic stage*, boys develop unconscious sexual desires for their mother. They also feel jealousy and hatred for their father, who is a rival for their mother's attention. He believed these feelings cause boys to feel guilty and to fear punishment, perhaps by castration, from their father. Freud called this cluster of feelings the **Oedipus complex** after the Greek legend of Oedipus, whose failure to understand his unconscious desires led him to unknowingly kill his father and marry his mother. Some psychoanalysts in Freud's era believed that girls experience a parallel *Electra complex* (named after a mythological plotting daughter).

Children learn to cope with these feelings by repressing them, said Freud. They identify with the "rival" parent and try to become like him or her. It's as though something inside the child decides, "If you can't beat 'em, join 'em." This **identification** process strengthens children's superegos as they take on many of their parents' values. Freud believed that identification with the same-sex parent provides what psychologists now call our *gender identity*—our sense of being male, female, neither, or some combination of male and female.

Other conflicts could arise at other childhood stages. But whatever the stage, unresolved conflicts can cause trouble in adulthood. The result, Freud believed, would be **fixation**, locking the person's pleasure-seeking energies at the unresolved stage. A child who is either orally overindulged or orally deprived (perhaps by abrupt, early weaning) might become stalled at the oral stage, for example. As an adult, this orally fixated person might continue to seek oral gratification by smoking or excessive eating. In such ways, Freud suggested, the twig of personality is bent at an early age.

"I heard that as soon as we become aware of our sexual impulses, whatever they are, we'll have to hide them."

"Oh, for goodness' sake! Smoke!"

TABLE 12.2 Six Defense Mechanisms

Freud believed that *repression*, the basic mechanism that banishes anxiety-arousing impulses, enables other defense mechanisms, six of which are listed here.

Defense Mechanism	Unconscious Process Employed to Avoid Anxiety-Arousing Thoughts or Feelings	Example
Regression	Retreating to an earlier psychosexual stage, where some psychic energy remains fixated	A little boy reverts to the oral comfort of thumb sucking in the car on the way to his first day of school.
Reaction formation	Switching unacceptable impulses into their opposites	Repressing angry feelings, a person displays exaggerated friendliness.
Projection	Disguising one's own threatening impulses by attributing them to others	"The thief thinks everyone else is a thief" (an El Salvadoran saying).
Rationalization	Offering self-justifying explanations in place of the real, more threatening unconscious reasons for one's actions	A habitual drinker says she drinks with her friends "just to be sociable."
Displacement	Shifting sexual or aggressive impulses toward a more acceptable or less threatening object or person	A little girl kicks the family dog after her mother puts her in a time-out.
Denial	Refusing to believe or even perceive painful realities	A partner denies evidence of his loved one's affair.

Nacivet/Getty Images

Regression

Defense Mechanisms

LOQ 12-5 How did Freud think people defended themselves against anxiety?

Anxiety, said Freud, is the price we pay for civilization. As members of social groups, we must control our sexual and aggressive impulses, not act them out. Sometimes the ego fears losing control of this inner war between the id and superego, which results in a dark cloud of generalized anxiety. We feel unsettled, but we don't know why.

Freud proposed that the ego distorts reality in an effort to protect itself from anxiety. **Defense mechanisms** help achieve this goal by disguising threatening impulses and preventing them from reaching consciousness (**TABLE 12.2**). Note that, for Freud, *all defense mechanisms function indirectly and unconsciously*. Just as the body unconsciously defends itself against disease, so also does the ego unconsciously defend itself against anxiety. For example, **repression** banishes anxiety-arousing wishes and feelings from consciousness. According to Freud, *repression underlies all of the other defense mechanisms*. However, because repression is often incomplete, repressed urges may appear as symbols in dreams or as slips of the tongue in casual conversation.

RETRIEVE & REMEMBER

ANSWERS IN APPENDIX E

1. According to Freud's ideas about the three-part personality structure, the ___________ operates on the *reality principle* and tries to balance demands in a way that produces long-term pleasure rather than pain; the ___________ operates on the *pleasure principle* and seeks immediate gratification; and the ___________ represents the voice of our internalized ideals (our *conscience*).
2. In the psychoanalytic view, conflicts unresolved during one of the psychosexual stages may lead to ___________ at that stage.
3. Freud believed that our defense mechanisms operate ___________ (consciously/unconsciously) and defend us against ___________.

THE NEO-FREUDIAN AND LATER PSYCHODYNAMIC THEORISTS

LOQ 12-6 Which of Freud's ideas did his followers accept or reject?

Freud's writings sparked intense debate. Remember that Freud lived at a time when people seldom talked about sex,

superego the part of personality that, according to Freud, represents internalized ideals and provides standards for judgment (the conscience) and for future goals.

psychosexual stages the childhood stages of development (oral, anal, phallic, latency, genital) during which, according to Freud, the id's pleasure-seeking energies focus on distinct erogenous zones.

Oedipus [ED-uh-puss] **complex** according to Freud, a boy's sexual desires toward his mother and feelings of jealousy and hatred for the rival father.

identification the process by which, according to Freud, children incorporate their parents' values into their developing superegos.

fixation in psychoanalytic theory, a lingering focus of pleasure-seeking energies at an earlier psychosexual stage, in which conflicts were unresolved.

defense mechanisms in psychoanalytic theory, the ego's protective methods of reducing anxiety by unconsciously distorting reality.

repression in psychoanalytic theory, the basic defense mechanism that banishes from consciousness the thoughts, feelings, and memories that arouse anxiety.

and certainly not unconscious sexual desires for one's parent. So it's no surprise that Freud was harshly criticized. In a letter to a trusted friend, Freud wrote, "In the Middle Ages, they would have burned me. Now they are content with burning my books" (Jones, 1957). Despite the controversy, Freud attracted followers. Several young, ambitious physicians formed an inner circle around the strong-minded Freud. These *neo-Freudians,* such as Alfred Adler, Karen Horney [HORN-eye], and Carl Jung [Yoong], adopted Freud's interviewing techniques and accepted his basic ideas:

- Personality has three parts: id, ego, and superego.
- The unconscious is key.
- Personality forms in childhood.
- We use defense mechanisms to ward off anxiety.

But the neo-Freudians differed from Freud in two important ways. First, they placed more emphasis on the role of the *conscious* mind. Second, they doubted that sex and aggression were all-consuming motivations. Instead, they tended to emphasize loftier motives and social interactions.

Jung believed that we have a **collective unconscious**, a common group of images, or *archetypes*, that developed from our species' universal experiences. Jung said that the collective unconscious explains why, for many people, spiritual concerns are deeply rooted and why people in different cultures share certain myths and images. Most of today's psychologists disagree with the idea of inherited experiences. But they do believe that our shared evolutionary history shaped some universal dispositions, and that experience can leave *epigenetic* marks affecting gene expression (Neel et al., 2016).

Some of Freud's ideas have been incorporated into the diverse perspectives that make up modern psychodynamic theory. Theorists and clinicians who study personality from a psychodynamic perspective assume, with Freud and with much support from today's psychological science, that much of our mental life is unconscious. They believe we often struggle with inner conflicts among our wishes, fears, and values, and respond defensively. And they agree that childhood shapes our personality and ways of becoming attached to others. But in other ways, they differ from Freud. "Most contemporary [psychodynamic] theorists and therapists are not wedded to the idea that sex is the basis of personality," noted psychologist Drew Westen (1996). They "do not talk about ids and egos, and do not go around classifying their patients as oral, anal, or phallic characters."

LaunchPad For a helpful 9-minute overview, view the *Video: Psychodynamic Theories of Personality.*

ASSESSING UNCONSCIOUS PROCESSES

LOQ 12-7 What are *projective tests*, how are they used, and what criticisms have they faced?

Personality tests reflect the basic ideas of particular personality theories. So, what might be the assessment tool of choice for someone working in the Freudian tradition?

To find a way into the unconscious mind, you would need a sort of "psychological X-ray." The test would have to see through the top layer of social politeness, revealing hidden conflicts and impulses. **Projective tests** aim to provide this view by asking test-takers to describe an ambiguous image or tell a story about it. The image itself has no real meaning, but what the test-takers say about it offers a glimpse into their unconscious. (Recall that in Freudian theory, *projection* is a defense mechanism that disguises threatening impulses by "seeing" them in other people.) The **Thematic Apperception Test (TAT)** is one such test. The TAT has been used to assess *achievement motivation* (Schultheiss et al., 2014). Shown a daydreaming boy, those who imagine he is fantasizing about an achievement are presumed to be projecting their own goals.

"We don't see things as they are; we see things as we are." —The Talmud

Macmillan Learning

Alfred Adler (1870–1937) Adler believed that childhood feelings of insecurity can drive behavior, triggering strivings for power and superiority. Adler coined the term *inferiority complex.*

Macmillan Learning

Karen Horney (1885–1952) Horney proposed that children's feelings of dependency give rise to feelings of helplessness and anxiety. These feelings trigger adult desires for love and security. Horney believed Freud's views of personality showed a masculine bias.

Macmillan Learning

Carl Jung (1875–1961) Jung shared Freud's view of the power of the unconscious. He also proposed a human *collective unconscious*, derived from our species' experiences in the distant past. Today's psychology rejects the idea that experiences can be inherited.

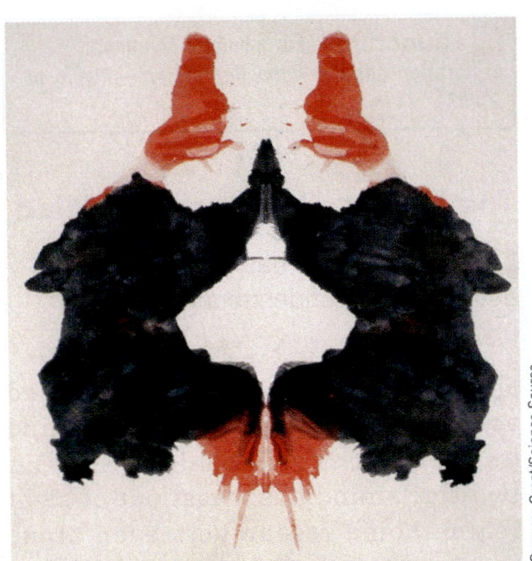

FIGURE 12.2 The Rorschach test In this projective test, people tell what they see in a series of symmetrical inkblots. Some who use this test are confident that the interpretation of ambiguous images will reveal unconscious aspects of the test-taker's personality.

The most famous projective test, the **Rorschach inkblot test,** was introduced in 1921. Swiss psychiatrist Hermann Rorschach [ROAR-shock] based it on a game he and his friends played as children. They would drip ink on paper, fold it, and then say what they saw in the resulting blot (Sdorow, 2005). The assumption is that what you see in a series of 10 inkblots reflects your inner feelings and conflicts. Do you see predatory animals or weapons in **FIGURE 12.2**? Perhaps you have aggressive tendencies.

Is this a reasonable assumption? Let's see how well the Rorschach test measures up to the two primary criteria of a good test (Chapter 8):

- ***Reliability*** (consistency of results): Raters trained in different Rorschach scoring systems show little agreement (Sechrest et al., 1998).
- ***Validity*** (predicting what it's supposed to): The Rorschach test is not very successful at predicting behavior or at discriminating between groups (for example, identifying who is suicidal and who is not). Inkblot results have inaccurately diagnosed many healthy adults as disordered (Wood, 2003; Wood et al., 2006).

The Rorschach test has neither much reliability nor great validity. But some clinicians value it as a source of suggestive leads, an icebreaker, or a revealing interview technique. Thus, the Rorschach test appears to have "the dubious distinction of being simultaneously the most cherished and most reviled of all psychological assessment instruments" (Hunsley & Bailey, 1999, p. 266).

EVALUATING FREUD'S PSYCHOANALYTIC PERSPECTIVE AND MODERN VIEWS OF THE UNCONSCIOUS

LOQ 12-8 How do today's psychologists view Freud's psychoanalysis?

"Many aspects of Freudian theory are indeed out of date, and they should be: Freud died in 1939, and he has been slow to undertake further revisions," observed one researcher (Westen, 1998). In Freud's time, there were no neurotransmitter or DNA studies. Decades of scientific breakthroughs in human development, thinking, and emotion were yet to come. Criticizing Freud's theory by comparing it with today's thinking is like criticizing the Ford Model T by comparing it with the Tesla Model S. How tempting it always is to judge the past from the perspective of our present.

But Freud's admirers and his critics agree that recent research contradicts many of his specific ideas. Developmental psychologists now see our development as lifelong, not fixed in childhood. They doubt that infant brain networks are mature enough to process emotional trauma in the ways Freud assumed. Some think Freud overestimated parental influence and underestimated peer influence (and child abuse). They also doubt that conscience and gender identity form as the child resolves the Oedipus complex at age 5 or 6. Our gender identity develops much earlier, and those who become strongly masculine or feminine do so even without a same-sex parent present. And they note that Freud's ideas about childhood sexuality arose from his female patients' stories of childhood sexual abuse. Some scholars suggest Freud doubted those stories, instead believing they reflected childhood sexual wishes and conflicts (Esterson, 2001; Powell & Boer, 1994).

Modern dream researchers disagree with Freud's idea that dreams disguise unfulfilled wishes lurking in our unconscious (Chapter 2). And slips of the tongue can be explained as competition between similar word choices in our memory network. Someone who says, "I don't want to do that—it's a lot of brothel" may simply be blending *bother* and *trouble* (Foss & Hakes, 1978).

"I remember your name perfectly but I just can't think of your face." — Oxford professor W. A. Spooner (1844–1930), famous for his linguistic flip-flops (*spoonerisms*).

Searching the nearly 300,000 emails I [DM] have received since 2000, I see that (among other such hilarities) friends have written me about their experience on "Wisconsin Pubic Radio" and about accessibility in "pubic venues." And I [ND] recently received an email supporting a new policy for the "general pubic." Such mistakes are likely mere random typos, concludes one big data analysis of typing errors (Stephens-Davidowitz, 2017).

collective unconscious Carl Jung's concept of a shared, inherited group of memories from our species' history.

projective test a personality test, such as the Rorschach or TAT, that provides ambiguous images designed to trigger projection of the test-taker's unconscious thoughts or feelings.

Thematic Apperception Test (TAT) a projective test in which people express their inner feelings and interests through the stories they make up about ambiguous scenes.

Rorschach inkblot test the most widely used projective test; a set of 10 inkblots, designed by Hermann Rorschach; seeks to identify people's inner feelings by analyzing their interpretations of the blots.

Psychology's strength comes from its use of the same scientific method that biologists, chemists, and physicists use to test their theories. Psychologists must ask the same question about Freud's theory that they ask about other theories. Remember that a good theory organizes observations and predicts behaviors or events (Chapter 1). How does Freudian theory stand up to the scientific tests?

Freud's theory rests on few objective observations, and it has produced few hypotheses to verify or reject. For Freud, his own interpretations of patients' free associations, dreams, and slips—sometimes selected to support his theory—were evidence enough. Moreover, say the critics, Freud's theory offers after-the-fact explanations of behaviors and traits, but it fails to predict them. There is also no way to disprove this theory. If you feel angry when your mother dies, you illustrate Freud's theory because "your unresolved childhood dependency needs are threatened." If you do not feel angry, you again illustrate his theory because "you are repressing your anger." That, say critics, "is like betting on a horse after the race has been run" (Hall & Lindzey, 1978, p. 68).

Freud's supporters object. To criticize Freudian theory for not making testable predictions is, they say, like criticizing baseball for not being an aerobic exercise—something it was never intended to be. Freud never claimed that psychoanalysis was predictive science. He merely claimed that, looking back, psychoanalysts could find meaning in their clients' mental state (Rieff, 1979).

Freud's supporters also note that some of his ideas *are* enduring. It was Freud who drew our attention to the unconscious and the irrational, when such ideas were not popular. Today, many researchers study our irrationality (Ariely, 2010; Thaler, 2015). Psychologist Daniel Kahneman (in 2002) and behavioral economist Richard Thaler (in 2017) each won Nobel Prizes for their studies of our faulty decision making. Freud also drew our attention to the importance of human sexuality. He made us aware of the tension between our biological impulses and our social well-being. He challenged our self-righteousness, pointed out our self-protective defenses, and reminded us of our potential for evil.

Modern Research Challenges the Idea of Repression

Psychoanalytic theory hinges on the assumption that our mind often *represses* offending wishes. Repression supposedly banishes emotions into the unconscious until they resurface, like long-lost books in a dusty attic. Some psychodynamic followers extended repression to explain apparently lost and recovered memories of childhood traumas (Boag, 2006; Cheit, 1998; Erdelyi, 2006). In one survey, 88 percent of university students believed that painful experiences commonly get pushed out of awareness and into the unconscious (Garry et al., 1994).

Today's memory researchers find that we sometimes preserve our self-esteem by ignoring threatening information (Green et al., 2008). Yet they also find that repression is rare, even in response to terrible trauma. Even those who have witnessed a parent's murder or survived Nazi death camps retain their unrepressed memories of the horror (Helmreich, 1992, 1994; Malmquist, 1986; Pennebaker, 1990). This led one prominent personality researcher to conclude, "Dozens of formal studies have yielded not a single convincing case of repression in the entire literature on trauma" (Kihlstrom, 2006).

Some researchers believe that extreme, prolonged stress, such as the stress some severely abused children experience, might disrupt memory by damaging the hippocampus (Schacter, 1996). But the far more common reality is that high stress and associated stress hormones *enhance* memory. Indeed, rape, torture, and other traumatic events haunt survivors, who experience unwanted flashbacks. They are seared onto the soul. "You see the babies," said Holocaust survivor Sally H. (1979). "You see the screaming mothers. You see hanging people. You sit and you see that face there. It's something you don't forget."

LaunchPad For a helpful 13-minute exploration, see the *Video: Repression—Reality or Myth?*

The Modern Unconscious Mind

LOQ 12-9 How has modern research developed our understanding of the unconscious?

Freud was right that we have limited access to all that goes on in our mind (Erdelyi, 1985, 1988, 2006; Kihlstrom, 1990). Our two-track mind has a vast out-of-sight realm. Some researchers even argue that "most of a person's everyday life is determined by unconscious thought processes" (Bargh & Chartrand, 1999). (Perhaps, for example, you can recall being sad or mad without consciously knowing why.)

But the unconscious mind studied by cognitive researchers today is not the place Freud thought it was for storing our censored anxiety-producing thoughts and seething passions. Rather, it is a part of our two-track mind, where information processing occurs without our awareness. To these researchers, the unconscious also involves

- the *right-hemisphere brain activity* that enables the split-brain patient's left hand to carry out an instruction the patient cannot verbalize (Chapter 2).
- the *parallel processing* of different aspects of vision and thinking, and the *schemas* that automatically control our perceptions and interpretations (Chapter 5).
- the *implicit memories* that operate without our conscious recall, even among those with amnesia (Chapter 7).
- the *emotions* we experience instantly, before conscious analysis (Chapter 9).
- the *stereotypes* and *implicit prejudice* that automatically and unconsciously influence how we process information about others (Chapter 11).

More than we realize, we fly on autopilot. Unconscious processing happens constantly. Like an enormous ocean, the unconscious mind is huge.

Research also supports two of Freud's defense mechanisms. One study demonstrated *reaction formation* (trading unacceptable impulses for their opposite). Men who reported strong anti-gay attitudes experienced greater physiological arousal (measured erections) when watching videos of gay men having sex, even though they said the films did not make them sexually aroused (Adams et al., 1996). Likewise, some evidence suggests that people who unconsciously identify as gay—but who consciously identify as straight—report more negative attitudes toward gays (Weinstein et al., 2012).

Freud's *projection* (attributing our own threatening impulses to others) has also been confirmed. People do tend to see their traits, attitudes, and goals in others (Baumeister et al., 1998b; Maner et al., 2005). Today's researchers call this the *false consensus effect*—the tendency to overestimate the extent to which others share our beliefs and behaviors. People who binge-drink or break speed limits tend to think many others do the same. However, neuroscience research shows that projection doesn't work exactly as Freud supposed. It seems motivated less by suppressing our sexual and aggressive impulses, as Freud imagined, than by our need to maintain a positive self-image (Welborn et al., 2017).

IN YOUR EVERYDAY LIFE

What understandings and impressions of Freud did you bring to this course? Are you surprised to find that some of his ideas have value, or that others have been called into question?

RETRIEVE & REMEMBER

ANSWERS IN APPENDIX E

4. What big ideas have survived from Freud's psychoanalytic theory? In what ways has Freud's theory been criticized?
5. Which elements of traditional psychoanalysis have modern-day *psychodynamic* theorists and therapists retained, and which elements have they mostly left behind?

Humanistic Theories

LOQ 12-10 How did humanistic psychologists view personality, and what was their goal in studying personality?

By the 1960s, some personality psychologists decided that their field needed fresh ideas and a new direction. They thought Freud's views were too negative. They were equally uncomfortable with the strict behaviorism of John Watson and B. F. Skinner (Chapter 6), judging it to be too mechanical. This movement helped produce *humanistic psychologists* such as Abraham Maslow and Carl Rogers. They shifted the focus from disorders born out of dark conflicts to emphasizing ways *healthy* people strive for self-determination and self-realization. In contrast to behaviorism's objective laboratory experiments, they asked people to report their own experiences and feelings.

ABRAHAM MASLOW'S SELF-ACTUALIZING PERSON

Abraham Maslow proposed that human motivations form a pyramid-shaped **hierarchy of needs** (Chapter 9). At the base are bodily needs. If those are met, we become concerned with the next-higher level of need, for personal safety. If we feel secure, we then seek to love and to be loved. With our love needs satisfied, we seek *self-esteem* (feelings of self-worth). Having achieved self-esteem, we strive for the top-level needs for **self-actualization** and **self-transcendence**. These motives, at the pyramid's peak, involve reaching our full potential.

Maslow (1970) formed his ideas by studying healthy, creative people rather than clinical cases of troubled people. His description of self-actualization grew out of his study of people, such as Abraham Lincoln, who had lived meaningful and productive lives. They were self-aware and self-accepting. They were open and spontaneous. They were loving and caring. They didn't worry too much about other people's opinions. Yet they were not self-centered. Curious about the world, they embraced uncertainties and stretched themselves to seek out new experiences (Compton, 2018; Kashdan, 2009). Once they focused their energies on a particular task, they often regarded that task as their life mission, or "calling" (Hall & Chandler, 2005). Most enjoyed a few deep relationships rather than many shallow ones. Many had been moved by spiritual or personal *peak experiences* that were beyond normal consciousness.

Maslow considered these to be mature adult qualities. These healthy people had outgrown their mixed feelings toward their parents. They had "acquired enough courage to be unpopular, to be unashamed about being openly virtuous."

Macmillan Learning

Abraham Maslow (1908–1970) "Any theory of motivation that is worthy of attention must deal with the highest capacities of the healthy and strong person as well as with the defensive maneuvers of crippled spirits" (*Motivation and Personality*, 1970, p. 33).

hierarchy of needs Maslow's pyramid of human needs; at the base are physiological needs. These basic needs must first be satisfied before people can fulfill their higher-level safety needs and then psychological needs.

self-actualization according to Maslow, the psychological need that arises after basic physical and psychological needs are met and self-esteem is achieved; the motivation to fulfill our potential.

self-transcendence according to Maslow, the striving for identity, meaning, and purpose beyond the self.

CARL ROGERS' PERSON-CENTERED PERSPECTIVE

Carl Rogers agreed that people have self-actualizing tendencies. Rogers' *person-centered perspective* held that people are basically good. Like plants, we are primed to reach our potential if we are given a growth-promoting environment. Rogers (1980) believed that such an environment provides

- *Acceptance.* If we are accepting, we offer **unconditional positive regard.** This is an attitude of total acceptance. We value a person even knowing the person's failings. We all find it a huge relief to drop our pretenses, confess our worst feelings, and discover that we are still accepted. In a good marriage, a close family, or an intimate friendship, we are free to be ourselves without fearing what others will think.
- *Genuineness.* If we are genuine to another person, we are open with our own feelings. We drop our false fronts and are transparent and self-disclosing.
- *Empathy.* If we are empathic, we share another's feelings and reflect that person's meanings back to them. "Rarely do we listen with real understanding, true empathy," said Rogers. "Yet listening, of this very special kind, is one of the most potent forces for change that I know."

Acceptance, genuineness, and empathy are, Rogers believed, the water, sun, and nutrients that enable people to grow like vigorous oak trees. For "as persons are accepted and prized, they tend to develop a more caring attitude toward themselves" (Rogers, 1980, p. 116). As persons are empathically heard, "it becomes possible for them to listen more accurately to the flow of inner experiencing."

Rogers called for acceptance, genuineness, and empathy in the relationship between therapist and client. But he also believed that these three qualities nurture growth between any two human beings — between leader and group member, teacher and student, manager and staff member, parent and child, friend and friend.

A father *not* offering unconditional positive regard.

Pat Byrnes The New Yorker Collection/The Cartoon Bank

"Just remember, son, it doesn't matter whether you win or lose—unless you want Daddy's love."

Writer Calvin Trillin (2006) recalled an example of parental acceptance and genuineness at a camp for children with severe disorders, where his wife, Alice, worked. L., a "magical child," had genetic diseases that meant she had to be tube-fed and could walk only with difficulty. Alice wondered "what this child's parents could have done . . . to make her the most optimistic, most enthusiastic, most hopeful human being I had ever encountered." One day Alice spotted a note that L. received from her mom: "If God had given us all of the children in the world to choose from, L., we would only have chosen you." Inspired, Alice approached a co-worker. "Quick. Read this," she whispered. "It's the secret of life."

Maslow and Rogers would have smiled knowingly. For them, a central feature of personality is one's **self-concept**—all the thoughts and feelings we have in response to the question, "Who am I?" If our self-concept is positive, we tend to act and perceive the world positively. If it is negative—if in our own eyes we fall far short of our *ideal self*—we feel dissatisfied and unhappy. A worthwhile goal for therapists, parents, teachers, and friends is therefore to help others know, accept, and be true to themselves, said Rogers.

Macmillan Learning

Carl Rogers (1902–1987) "The curious paradox is that when I accept myself just as I am, then I can change" (*On Becoming a Person*, 1961).

DYLAN MARTINEZ/REUTERS/Newscom

The picture of empathy Being open and sharing confidences is easier when the listener shows real understanding. Within such relationships we can relax and fully express our true selves.

IN YOUR EVERYDAY LIFE

Think back to a conversation you had when you knew someone was just waiting for their turn to speak instead of listening to you. Now consider the last time someone heard you with empathy. How did those two experiences differ?

LaunchPad To consider how this theory applies to your own life, try the online *Assess Your Strengths: What Is Your Self-Concept?*

ASSESSING THE SELF

LOQ 12-11 How did humanistic psychologists assess a person's sense of self?

Humanistic psychologists sometimes assessed personality by asking people to fill out questionnaires that would evaluate their self-concept. One questionnaire, inspired by Carl Rogers, asked people to describe themselves both as they would *ideally* like to be and as they *actually* are. When the ideal and the actual self are nearly alike, said Rogers, the self-concept is positive. Assessing his clients' personal growth during therapy, he looked for closer and closer ratings of actual and ideal selves.

Some humanistic psychologists believed that any standardized assessment of personality, even a questionnaire, is depersonalizing. Rather than forcing the person to respond to narrow categories, these humanistic psychologists presumed that interviews and intimate conversation would provide a better understanding of each person's unique experiences. Some researchers believe our identity may be revealed using the *life story approach*—collecting a rich narrative detailing each person's unique life history (Adler et al., 2016; McAdams & Guo, 2015). A lifetime of stories can show more of a person's complete identity than can the responses to a few questions.

EVALUATING HUMANISTIC THEORIES

LOQ 12-12 How have humanistic theories influenced psychology? What criticisms have they faced?

Just as Freudian concepts have seeped into modern culture, humanistic psychology has had a far-reaching impact. Maslow's and Rogers' ideas have influenced counseling, education, child raising, and management. And they laid the groundwork for today's scientific *positive psychology* subfield (Chapter 1).

These theorists have also influenced—sometimes in unintended ways—much of today's popular psychology. Is a positive self-concept the key to happiness and success? Do acceptance and empathy nurture positive feelings about ourselves? Are people basically good and capable of improving? Many would answer *Yes, Yes,* and *Yes*. In 2006, U.S. high school students reported notably higher self-esteem and greater expectations of future career success than did students living in 1975 (Twenge & Campbell, 2008). When you hear talk about the importance of "loving yourself," you can give some credit to the humanistic theorists.

Many psychologists have criticized the humanistic perspective. First, said the critics, its concepts are vague and based on the theorists' personal opinions, rather than on scientific methods. Consider Maslow's description of self-actualizing people as open, spontaneous, loving, self-accepting, and productive. Is this a scientific description? Or is it merely a description of Maslow's own values and ideals, as viewed in his own personal heroes (Smith, 1978)? Imagine another theorist who began with a different set of heroes—perhaps the French military conqueror Napoleon and U.S. President Donald Trump. This theorist might describe self-actualizing people as "not deterred by others' opinions," "motivated to achieve," and "comfortable with power."

Other critics objected to the attitudes that humanistic psychology encourages. Rogers (1985), for example, said, "The only question which matters is, 'Am I living in a way which is deeply satisfying to me, and which truly expresses me?'" (quoted by Wallach & Wallach, 1985). Imagine working on a group project with people who refuse to complete any task that is not deeply satisfying or does not truly express their identity. Such attitudes could lead to self-indulgence, selfishness, and a lack of moral restraint (Campbell & Specht, 1985; Wallach & Wallach, 1983).

Humanistic psychologists have replied that a secure, nondefensive self-acceptance is the important first step toward loving others. Indeed, people who recall feeling liked and accepted by a romantic partner—for who they are, not just for their achievements—report being happier in their relationships and acting more kindly toward their partner (Gordon & Chen, 2010).

A final criticism has been that humanistic psychology fails to appreciate our human capacity for evil (May, 1982). Faced with global climate change, overpopulation, terrorism, and the spread of nuclear weapons, we may be paralyzed by either of two ways of thinking. One is a naive optimism that denies the threat ("People are basically good; everything will work out"). The other is a dark despair ("It's hopeless; why try?"). Action requires enough realism to fuel concern and enough optimism to provide hope. Humanistic psychology, said the critics, encourages the needed hope but not the equally necessary realism about threats.

RETRIEVE & REMEMBER

ANSWERS IN APPENDIX E

- 6. How did the *humanistic theories* provide a fresh perspective?
- 7. What does it mean to be *empathic?* How about *self-actualized?* Which humanistic psychologists used these terms?

Trait Theories

LOQ 12-13 How do psychologists use traits to describe personality?

Freudian and humanistic theories shared a common goal: Explain how our personality develops. They focused

unconditional positive regard a caring, accepting, nonjudgmental attitude, which Carl Rogers believed would help people develop self-awareness and self-acceptance.

self-concept all our thoughts and feelings about ourselves, in answer to the question, "Who am I?"

on the forces that act upon us. **Trait** researchers, led by the work of Gordon Allport (1897–1967), have been less concerned with *explaining* traits than with *describing* them. They define personality as a *stable and enduring pattern of behavior,* such as Lady Gaga's self-discipline and openness to new experiences. These traits help describe her personality.

EXPLORING TRAITS

Imagine that you've been hired by an online dating service. Your job is to construct a questionnaire for a new app that will help people describe themselves to potential partners. With millions of people using such services each year, the need to understand and incorporate psychological science grows more important (Finkel et al., 2012a,b). What personality traits would give you the best sense for each person filling out your questionnaire? You might begin by thinking of how we describe a pizza. We place a pizza along several trait dimensions. It's small, medium, or large; it has one or more toppings; it has a thin or thick crust. By likewise placing people on trait dimensions, we can begin to describe them.

Basic Factors

An even better way to identify our personality is to identify **factors**—clusters of behavior tendencies that occur together (McCabe & Fleeson, 2016). People who describe themselves as outgoing may also say that

"Hello. This is Dial-a-Grump. What the hell do you want?"

they like excitement and practical jokes and dislike quiet reading. This cluster of behaviors reflects a basic factor, or trait—in this case, *extraversion.*

So how many traits will be just the right number for success with your dating questionnaire? If psychologists Hans Eysenck and Sybil Eysenck [EYE-zink] had been hired to do your job, they would have said two. They believed that we can reduce many normal human variations to two basic dimensions: *Extraversion–introversion* and *emotional stability–instability* (**FIGURE 12.3**). People in 35 countries, from China to Uganda to Russia, have taken the Eysenck Personality Questionnaire. The extraversion and emotionality factors emerged as basic personality dimensions (Eysenck, 1990, 1992).

Biology and Personality

Recall from the twin and adoption studies in Chapter 3 that our genes have much to say about the *temperament* and behavioral style that shape our personality. Children's shyness, for example, seems related to differences in their autonomic nervous systems. Those with a reactive autonomic nervous system respond to stress with greater anxiety and inhibition (Kagan, 2010) (see Thinking Critically About: The Stigma of Introversion).

Brain activity appears to vary with personality as well. Brain-activity scans suggest that extraverts seek stimulation because their normal brain arousal is relatively low. Also, a frontal lobe area involved in restraining behavior is less active in extraverts than in introverts (Johnson et al., 1999).

Personality differences among dogs are as obvious to researchers as they are to dog owners. Such differences (in energy, affection, reactivity, and curious intelligence) are as evident, and as consistently judged, as personality differences among humans (Gosling et al., 2003; Jones & Gosling, 2005). Monkeys, bonobos, chimpanzees, orangutans, sea lions, and even birds and fish also

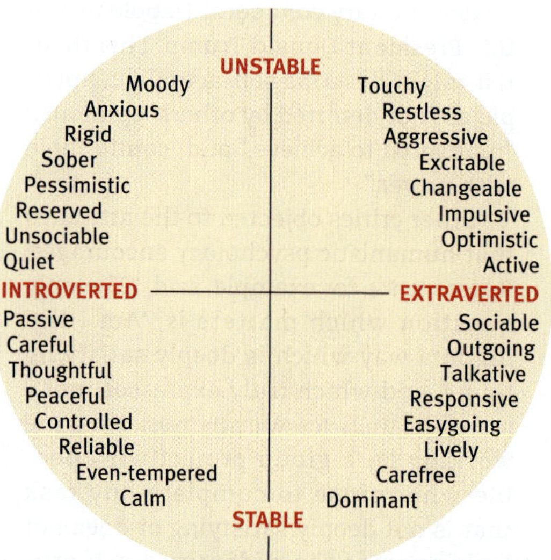

FIGURE 12.3 Two personality dimensions Mapmakers can tell us a lot by using two axes (north–south and east–west). Two primary personality factors (extraversion–introversion and stability–instability) are similarly useful as axes for describing personality variation. Varying combinations define other, more specific traits (Eysenck & Eysenck, 1963). Some accomplished actors, such as Emma Watson, are introverts—particularly capable of solitary study to become each character they portray. Successful comedians, such as Stephen Colbert, are often natural extraverts, or pretend to be.

Thinking Critically About:
The Stigma of Introversion

LOQ 12-14 What are some common misunderstandings about introversion?

Western cultures are hard on introverts:

Superheroes tend to be extraverted. Black Panther unites five tribes of people with his engaging strength of character. Take-charge Elastigirl saves the day in *The Incredibles*.

87% of Westerners want to be more extraverted.[2]

Being introverted seems to imply that we don't have the "right stuff."[3]

What do job interviewers want in their employees? Extraversion outranks most other personality traits.[1]

Elite U.S. colleges and universities show a bias in selecting extraverts.[4]

What is introversion?

Introverts tend to gain energy from time alone, and may find social interactions exhausting. Extraverts, by contrast, tend to draw energy from time spent with others.

Introverts are not "shy." (Shy people remain quiet because they fear others will evaluate them negatively.)

Introverted people seek low levels of stimulation from their environment because they're sensitive. For example, when given lemon juice, introverted people salivated more than extraverted people.[5]

Introversion has many benefits:

- Introverted leaders outperform extraverted leaders in some contexts, such as when their employees voice new ideas and challenge existing norms.[6]
- Introverts handle conflict well. In response, they seek solitude rather than revenge.[7]
- Many introverts have flourished, including Bill Gates, Mother Teresa, and Oprah Winfrey. "A true extravert," Winfrey explains, "gets energy,... feeds off people,... and I get sucked dry."[8]

1. Kluemper et al., 2015; Salgado & Moscoso, 2002. 2. Hudson & Roberts, 2014. 3. Cain, 2012. 4. Zimmerman, 2018. 5. Corcoran, 1964. 6. Grant et al., 2011a. 7. Ren et al., 2016. 8. OWN, 2018.

have stable personalities (Ciardelli et al., 2017; Latzman et al., 2015; Pennisi, 2016; Weiss et al., 2017). Through selective breeding, researchers can produce bold or shy birds. Both personality types have their place in natural history. In lean years, bold birds are more likely to find food; in abundant years, shy birds feed with less risk.

Octopus personality Otto the octopus loves getting attention from visitors to his German aquarium. But when the aquarium closes during the winter, Otto seems to get bored and plays pranks. He has juggled hermit crabs, squirted water at staff members, and broken his light by spraying it with water.

RETRIEVE & REMEMBER

ANSWERS IN APPENDIX E

8. Which two primary dimensions did Hans Eysenck and Sybil Eysenck propose for describing personality variation?

ASSESSING TRAITS

LOQ 12-15 What are *personality inventories?*

It helps to know that a potential date is an introvert or an extravert, or even that the person is emotionally stable or unstable. But wouldn't you like more information about the test-taker's personality before matching people as romantic partners? The **Minnesota Multiphasic Personality Inventory (MMPI)** might help. **Personality inventories**, including the famous MMPI, are long sets of questions covering a wide range of feelings and behaviors. Although the MMPI was originally developed to identify emotional disorders, it also assesses people's personality traits. Whereas most projective tests (such as the Rorschach) are scored subjectively, personality inventories are scored objectively. Objectivity does not, however, guarantee validity. People taking the MMPI for employment purposes can give the answers they know will create a good

trait a characteristic pattern of behavior or a tendency to feel and act in certain ways, as assessed by self-report inventories and peer reports.

factor a cluster of behavior tendencies that occur together.

Minnesota Multiphasic Personality Inventory (MMPI) the most widely researched and clinically used of all personality tests. Originally developed to identify emotional disorders (still considered its most appropriate use), this test is now used for many other screening purposes.

personality inventory a questionnaire (often with *true-false* or *agree-disagree* items) on which people respond to items designed to gauge a wide range of feelings and behaviors; used to assess selected personality traits.

impression. But in so doing they may also score high on a *lie scale* that assesses faking (as when people respond *False* to a universally true statement, such as "I get angry sometimes"). In other cases, the MMPI can be used to identify people pretending to have a disorder in order to avoid their work or other responsibilities (Chmielewski et al., 2017). The objectivity of the MMPI has contributed to its popularity and its translation into more than 100 languages.

LaunchPad Might astrology hold the secret to our personality traits? Play the role of a researcher testing this question by engaging online with the activity *How Would You Know If Astrologers Can Describe People's Personality?*

THE BIG FIVE FACTORS

LOQ 12-16 Which traits seem to provide the most useful information about personality variation?

Today's trait researchers rely on five factors (called the *Big Five*) to understand personality: *openness, conscientiousness, extraversion, agreeableness,* and *neuroticism* (emotional stability versus instability) (**TABLE 12.3**) (Costa & McCrae, 2011; Soto & John, 2017). Work by Paul Costa, Robert McCrae, and others shows that where we fall on these five dimensions reveals much of what there is to say about our personality. Some clinical psychologists have begun to use the Big Five to understand personality disorders, schizophrenia, and other types of dysfunction (Ohi et al., 2016; Widiger et al., 2016).

As the dominant model in personality psychology, Big Five research has explored various questions:

- ***How stable are these traits?*** One research team analyzed people's traits in adolescence and again 50 years later (Damian et al., 2018). Participants' personalities remained generally stable, but most showed signs of the *maturity principle*: They became more conscientious and agreeable and less neurotic (emotionally unstable) (Klimstra et al., 2018; Milojev & Sibley, 2017; Rohrer et al., 2018). Compared with Americans, the Japanese—who tend to adapt their personality to their environment—change more over time on all Big Five traits (Chopik & Kitayama, 2018).
- ***Do self-ratings on these traits match others' ratings?*** Family and friends' ratings of our Big Five trait levels resemble the ratings we give ourselves (Finnigan & Vazire, 2018; Luan et al., 2019).
- ***Do we inherit these traits?*** Roughly 40 percent of our individual differences on the Big Five can be credited to our genes (Vukasović & Bratko, 2015).
- ***Do these traits reflect differing brain structure?*** The size and thickness of brain tissue correlates with several Big Five traits (DeYoung & Allen, 2019; Li et al., 2017; Riccelli et al., 2017). For example, those who score high on conscientiousness tend to have a larger frontal lobe area that aids in planning and controlling behavior. Brain connections also influence the Big Five traits (Toschi et al., 2018). People high in neuroticism have brains that are wired to experience stress intensely (Shackman et al., 2016; Xu & Potenza, 2012).
- ***Do these traits reflect birth order?*** After controlling for other variables such as family size, are first-born children, for example, more conscientious and agreeable? Contrary to popular opinion, several massive studies failed to find any association between birth order and personality (Damian & Roberts, 2015; Harris, 2009; Rohrer et al., 2015).
- ***How well do these traits apply to various cultures?*** The Big Five dimensions describe personality in various cultures reasonably well (Fetvadjiev et al., 2017; Kim et al., 2018; Schmitt et al., 2007). After studying people from 50 cultures, Robert McCrae and 79 co-researchers concluded that "features of personality traits are common to all human groups" (2005).
- ***Do the Big Five traits predict our actual behaviors?*** Yes. Conscientiousness and agreeableness predict workplace success (Sackett & Walmsley, 2014). Agreeable people tend to help others and avoid criminal behavior (Habashi et al., 2016; Walters, 2018). Our traits also appear in our language patterns. In text messaging, extraversion predicts use of personal pronouns *(we, our, us)*. Neuroticism predicts negative-emotion words (Holtgraves, 2011).

To describe your personality, try the brief self-assessment in **FIGURE 12.4**. If you work the Big Five traits into your dating questionnaire, your mission should be accomplished—if people act the same way at all times and in all situations, that is. Do they?

TABLE 12.3 The "Big Five" Personality Factors

Researchers use self-report inventories and peer reports to assess and score the Big Five personality factors.
(*Memory tip:* Picturing an **OCEAN** will help you recall these.)

Practical, prefers routine, conforming	***O**penness*	Imaginative, prefers variety, independent
Disorganized, careless, impulsive	***C**onscientiousness*	Organized, careful, disciplined
Retiring, sober, reserved	***E**xtraversion*	Sociable, fun-loving, affectionate
Ruthless, suspicious, uncooperative	***A**greeableness*	Soft-hearted, trusting, helpful
Calm, secure, self-satisfied	***N**euroticism* (emotional stability vs. instability)	Anxious, insecure, self-pitying

Aaron Foster/Getty Images

Information from McCrae & Costa (1986, 2008).

How Do You Describe Yourself?

Describe yourself as you generally are now, not as you wish to be in the future. Describe yourself as you honestly see yourself, in relation to other people you know of the same sex and roughly the same age. Use the scale below to enter a number for each statement. Then, use the scoring guide at the bottom to see where you fall on the spectrum for each of the Big Five traits.

1	2	3	4	5
Very Inaccurate	Moderately Inaccurate	Neither Accurate Nor Inaccurate	Moderately Accurate	Very Accurate

1. ___Am the life of the party
2. ___Sympathize with others' feelings
3. ___Get stressed out easily
4. ___Am always prepared
5. ___Am full of ideas
6. ___Start conversations
7. ___Take time out for others
8. ___Follow a schedule
9. ___Worry about things
10. ___Have a vivid imagination

SCORING GUIDE SORTED BY BIG FIVE PERSONALITY TRAITS

Openness: statements 5, 10
Conscientiousness: statements 4, 8
Extraversion: statements 1, 6
Agreeableness: statements 2, 7
Neuroticism: statements 3, 9

How to score:
Separate your responses by each Big Five personality trait, as noted at left, and divide by two to obtain your score for each trait. So, for example, for the "Agreeableness" trait let's say you scored 3 for statement 2 ("Sympathize with others' feelings") and 4 for statement 7 ("Take time out for others"). That means on a scale from 1 to 5, your overall score for the "Agreeableness" trait is 3 + 4 = 7 ÷ 2 = 3.5.

Scale data from Goldberg, L. R. (1992). The development of markers for the Big-Five factor structure. *Psychological Assessment, 4*, 26–42.

FIGURE 12.4 The Big Five self-assessment

Tom Pennington/Getty Images

KENA BETANCUR/Getty Images

How do you vote? Let me count the likes Researchers can use your Facebook likes to predict your Big Five traits, your opinions, and your political attitudes (Youyou et al., 2015). Companies gather these "big data" for advertisers (who then personalize the ads you see). They do the same for political candidates, who can target you with persuasive messages (Matz et al., 2017). In 2016, one firm, Cambridge Analytica, reportedly harvested the Facebook profiles and likes of 87 million people. Information on individual voters' inferred political leanings and personality types was then fed to door-to-door campaigners for Donald Trump (Grassegger & Krogerus, 2017).[1]

[1] Facebook now protects the privacy of user likes.

IN YOUR EVERYDAY LIFE

Before trying the self-assessment in Figure 12.4, where would you have placed yourself on the Big Five personality dimensions? Where might your family and friends place you? Did the actual results surprise you, and do you think these results would surprise them?

RETRIEVE & REMEMBER

ANSWERS IN APPENDIX E

9. What are the *Big Five* personality factors, and why are they scientifically useful?

LaunchPad For a review of the Big Five, engage online with *Concept Practice: The Big Five Personality Traits.*

EVALUATING TRAIT THEORIES

LOQ 12-17 Does research support the consistency of personality traits over time and across situations?

To be useful indicators of personality, traits would have to persist over time and across situations. Friendly people, for example, would have to act friendly at different times and places. In some ways, our personality seems stable. Cheerful, friendly children tend to become cheerful, friendly adults. But it's also true that a fun-loving jokester can suddenly turn serious and respectful at a job interview. New situations and major life events can shift the personality traits we express. Transitioning from high school to college or the workforce may make us more agreeable, conscientious, and open-minded, and less neurotic (emotionally unstable) (Bleidorn et al., 2018).

The Person-Situation Controversy

Many researchers have studied personality stability over the life span. A group of 152 long-term *(longitudinal)* studies compared initial trait scores with scores for the same traits seven years later. These comparisons were done for several different age groups, and for each group, the scores were positively correlated.

But the correlations were strongest for comparisons done in adulthood. For young children, the correlation between early and later scores was +0.3. For college students, the correlation was +0.54. For 70-year-olds, the correlation was +0.73. (Remember that 0 indicates no relationship, and +1.0 would mean that one score perfectly predicts the other.)

As we grow older, our personality traits stabilize. Interests may change—the devoted collector of tropical fish may become a devoted gardener. Careers may change—the determined salesperson may become a determined social worker. Relationships may change—the hostile son may become a hostile husband. But most people recognize their personality as just who they are.

The consistency of specific *behaviors* from one situation to the next is another matter. People are not always predictable. What relationship would you expect to find between being conscientious in one situation (say, showing up for class on time) and being conscientious in another (say, avoiding unhealthy foods)? If you've noticed how outgoing you are in some situations and how reserved you are in others, perhaps you said, "Very little." That's what researchers have found—only a small correlation (Mischel, 1968; Sherman et al., 2015). This inconsistency in behaviors also makes personality test scores weak predictors of behaviors. People's scores on an extraversion test, for example, do not neatly predict how sociable they actually will be on any given occasion.

If we remember such results, we will be more careful about labeling other people (Mischel, 1968). We will recognize how difficult it is to predict whether someone is likely to violate parole, commit suicide, or be an effective employee. Years in advance, science can tell us the phase of today's Moon. A day in advance, meteorologists can often predict the weather. But we are much further from being able to predict how *you* will feel and act tomorrow.

Does this mean that psychological science has nothing meaningful to say

It's not just personality that stabilizes with age.

about personality traits? *No!* Remember that traits do a good job at predicting people's *average* behavior (outgoingness, happiness, carelessness) over *many* situations (Epstein, 1983a,b). This tendency to express similar traits in varied situations occurs worldwide, from the United States to Venezuela to Japan (Locke et al., 2017).

Even when we try to restrain them, our traits may assert themselves. During my [DM] noontime pickup basketball games with friends, I keep vowing to cut back on my jabbering and joking. But without fail, the irrepressible chatterbox reoccupies my body moments later. And I [ND] have a similar experience whenever I buy groceries. Somehow, I always end up chatting with the cashier!

Our personality traits lurk in some unexpected places, such as our

- ***music preferences.*** Your playlist reveals something of your personality. Classical, jazz, blues, and folk music lovers tend to be open to experience and verbally intelligent. Extraverts tend to prefer upbeat and energetic music. Country, pop, and religious music lovers tend to be cheerful, outgoing, and conscientious (Langmeyer et al., 2012; Nave et al., 2018; Rentfrow & Gosling, 2003, 2006).
- ***written communications.*** Have you ever felt you could detect others' personality from their writing voice? You are right!! What a cool finding!!! 😊 People's writings—even their brief tweets and Facebook posts—often express their extraversion, self-esteem, and agreeableness (Orehek & Human, 2017; Park et al., 2015; Pennebaker, 2011). "Off to meet a friend. Woohoo!!!" posted one Facebook user who had scored high on extraversion (Kern et al., 2014). Extraverts also use more adjectives.
- ***online and personal spaces.*** Online profiles, websites, and avatars are also a canvas for self-expression. People who seemed most likeable on Facebook or Twitter also seemed most likeable in person (Qiu et al., 2012; Weisbuch et al., 2009). Even mere photos, with their associated clothes, expressions, and postures, can give clues to personality and how people act in person (Gunyadin et al., 2017; Naumann et al., 2009). Our living and working spaces also help us express our identity. They all offer clues to our extraversion, agreeableness, conscientiousness, and openness (Back et al., 2010; Fong & Mar, 2015; Gosling, 2008).

In unfamiliar, formal situations—perhaps as a guest in the home of a person from another culture—our traits remain hidden as we carefully attend to social cues. In familiar, informal situations—just hanging out with friends—we feel more relaxed, and our traits emerge (Buss, 1989). In these informal situations, our expressive styles—our animation, manner of speaking, and gestures—are impressively

Gary Houlder/Getty Images

Room with a cue Even at "zero acquaintance," people can catch a glimpse of others' personality from looking at their online and personal spaces. So, what's your read on this person?

consistent. Viewing "thin slices" of someone's behavior—such as seeing a photo for a mere fraction of a second, or seeing several 2-second clips of a teacher in action—can tell us a lot about the person's basic personality traits (Ambady, 2010; Tackett et al., 2016).

To sum up, we can say that the immediate situation powerfully influences our behavior, *especially when the situation makes clear demands* (Cooper & Withey, 2009). We can better predict drivers' behavior at traffic lights from knowing the color of the lights than from knowing the drivers' personalities. Averaging our behavior across many occasions does, however, reveal distinct personality traits. Traits exist, and they leave tracks in our lives. We differ. And our differences matter.

IN YOUR EVERYDAY LIFE

How do you think your own personality traits shine through in your music preferences, communication style, and online and personal spaces?

RETRIEVE & REMEMBER

ANSWERS IN APPENDIX E

10. How well do personality test scores predict our behavior? Explain.

LaunchPad For a demonstration of trait research, view the 8-minute *Video: Trait Theories of Personality.*

Social-Cognitive Theories

LOQ 12-18 How do social-cognitive theorists view personality development, and how do they explore behavior?

RECIPROCAL INFLUENCES

So, our personal traits interact with our environment to influence our behavior. Albert Bandura (1986, 2006, 2008) called this process **reciprocal determinism**. "Behavior, internal personal factors, and environmental influences," he said, "all operate as interlocking determinants of each other" (**FIGURE 12.5**).

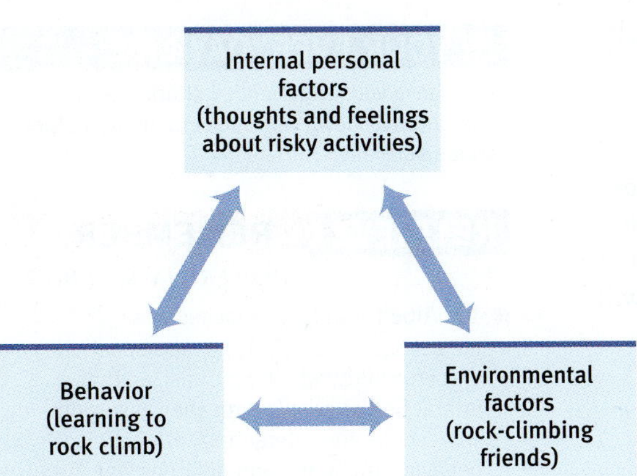

FIGURE 12.5 Reciprocal determinism

The **social-cognitive perspective** on personality that Bandura proposed is especially focused on the many ways our individual traits and thoughts interact with our social world as we move from one situation to another. We bring a lot to any social situation we enter. We bring our past learning, often picked up through conditioning or by observing others. We bring our **self-efficacy**—our expectations about whether we will succeed in (and attempt) new challenges (Bandura, 1977, 2018). We also bring our ways of thinking about specific situations. But situations themselves place different demands on us. Most of us know the general social rules for acceptable behavior at a grandparent's funeral, for example. We also know that a different set of rules outlines what's acceptable at a friend's New Year's Eve party. In the end, our behavior in any situation is in part the result of our own characteristics and in part the result of the situation.

Roughly speaking, the outside influences on behavior are the focus of *social psychology* (Chapter 11), and the inner influences are the focus of *personality psychology.* In actuality, behavior always depends on the interaction of persons with situations.

We can see this interaction in people's relationships. For example, Rosa's past romantic experiences (her behaviors) influence her romantic attitudes (internal factor), which affect how she now responds to Ryan (environmental factor).

Consider three specific ways in which individuals and environments interact:

1. ***Different people choose different environments.*** What school do you attend? What do you read? What career will you pursue? What shows do you watch? What music do you listen to? What social media do you use? With whom do you enjoy spending time? All these choices are part of an environment you are choosing, based partly on your personality (Denissen et al., 2018). And the environments we choose then shape us. People with inflated self-esteem post frequent selfies in online environments, for example, where they can receive the public attention and praise they crave. This leads to even greater self-love (Halpern et al., 2016).
2. ***Our personalities shape how we interpret and react to events.*** If we perceive the world as threatening, we will watch for threats and be prepared

reciprocal determinism the interacting influences of behavior, internal personal factors, and environment.

social-cognitive perspective a view of behavior as influenced by the interaction between persons (and their thinking) and their social context.

self-efficacy our sense of competence and effectiveness.

to defend ourselves. Anxious people tend to attend and react strongly to relationship threats (Campbell & Marshall, 2011).

3. ***Our personalities help create situations to which we react.*** How we view and treat people influences how they then treat us. If we expect that others will not like us, our bragging and other efforts to win their approval might actually cause them to reject us (Scopelliti et al., 2015).

In addition to the interaction of internal personal factors, the environment, and our behaviors, we also experience *gene-environment interaction* (Chapter 3). Our genetically influenced traits evoke certain responses from others, which may nudge us in one direction or another. In one well-replicated classic study, those with the interacting factors of (1) having a specific gene associated with aggression, and (2) being raised in a difficult environment were most likely to demonstrate adult antisocial behavior (Byrd & Manuck, 2014; Caspi et al., 2002).

In such ways, we are both the products and the architects of our environments. Boiling water turns an egg hard and a noodle soft. Academic challenges turn one person into a success and another toward collapse (Harms et al., 2006). At every moment, our behavior is influenced by our biology, our social and cultural experiences, and our thought processes and traits (**FIGURE 12.6**).

IN YOUR EVERYDAY LIFE

How have your experiences shaped your personality? How has your personality helped shape your environment?

RETRIEVE & REMEMBER

ANSWERS IN APPENDIX E

11. Albert Bandura proposed the ____________-____________ perspective on personality, which emphasizes the interaction of people with their environment. To describe the interacting influences of behavior, thoughts, and environment, he used the term ____________ ____________.

LaunchPad To explore the influence of the person-environment interaction on behavior, engage online with *Concept Practice: Reciprocal Determinism.*

ASSESSING BEHAVIOR IN SITUATIONS

To predict behavior, social-cognitive psychologists often observe behavior in realistic situations. Military and educational organizations and many Fortune 500 companies use such strategies (Bray & Byham, 1991, 1997; Eurich et al., 2009). AT&T has observed prospective managers doing simulated managerial work. Many colleges assess nursing students' potential by observing their clinical work, and evaluate potential faculty members' teaching abilities by observing them teach. Most American cities with populations of 50,000 or more have used such strategies in evaluating police officers and firefighters (Lowry, 1997).

Gustavo Caballero/Getty Images

If you can't stand the heat . . . On the Food Network's *Chopped*, contestants are pitted against one another in stressful situations. The episodes presume a valid point: People's behavior in job-relevant situations helps predict their job performance.

These procedures exploit the principle that the best way to predict future behavior is neither a personality test nor an interviewer's intuition; rather, *it is the person's past behavior patterns in similar situations* (Lyons et al., 2011; Mischel, 1981; Schmidt & Hunter, 1998).

EVALUATING SOCIAL-COGNITIVE THEORIES

LOQ 12-19 What criticisms have social-cognitive theorists faced?

Social-cognitive theories of personality emphasize how situations affect, and are affected by, individuals. More than other personality theories (**TABLE 12.4**), they build from psychological research on learning and cognition.

Critics charge that social-cognitive theories focus so much on the situation that they fail to appreciate the person's inner traits. They note that in many instances our unconscious motives, our emotions, and our traits shine through. Personality traits have been shown to predict behavior at work, in love, and at play. Consider Percy Ray Pridgen and Charles Gill. Each faced the same situation: They had jointly won a $90 million lottery jackpot (Harriston, 1993). When Pridgen learned of the winning numbers, he began trembling uncontrollably, huddled with a friend behind a bathroom door while confirming the win, and then sobbed. When Gill heard the news, he told his wife and then went to sleep.

Biological influences:
- genetically determined temperament
- autonomic nervous system reactivity
- brain activity

Psychological influences:
- learned responses
- unconscious thought processes
- expectations and interpretations

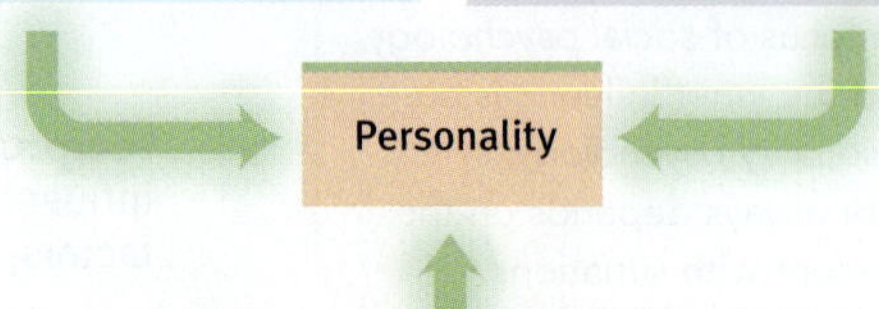

Social-cultural influences:
- childhood experiences
- situational factors
- cultural expectations
- social support

FIGURE 12.6 The biopsychosocial approach to the study of personality

TABLE 12.4 Comparing the Major Personality Theories

Personality Theory	Key Proponents	Assumptions	View of Personality	Personality Assessment Methods
Psychoanalytic	Freud	Emotional disorders spring from unconscious dynamics, such as unresolved sexual and other childhood conflicts, and fixation at various developmental stages. Defense mechanisms fend off anxiety.	Personality consists of pleasure-seeking impulses (the id), a reality-oriented executive (the ego), and an internalized set of ideals (the superego).	Free association, projective tests, dream analysis
Psychodynamic	Adler, Horney, Jung	The unconscious and conscious minds interact. Childhood experiences and defense mechanisms are important.	The dynamic interplay of conscious and unconscious motives and conflicts shapes our personality.	Projective tests, therapy sessions
Humanistic	Maslow, Rogers	Rather than focusing on disorders born out of dark conflicts, it's better to emphasize how healthy people may strive for self-realization.	If our basic human needs are met, we will strive toward self-actualization. In a climate of unconditional positive regard, we can develop self-awareness and a more realistic and positive self-concept.	Questionnaires, therapy sessions
Trait	Allport; Costa; Eysenck, H.; Eysenck, S.; McCrae	We have certain stable and enduring characteristics, influenced by genetic predispositions.	Scientific study of traits has isolated important dimensions of personality, such as the Big Five traits (openness, conscientiousness, extraversion, agreeableness, and neuroticism).	Personality inventories
Social-Cognitive	Bandura	Our traits interact with the social context to produce our behaviors.	Conditioning and observational learning interact with cognition to create behavior patterns. Our behavior in one situation is best predicted by considering our past behavior in similar situations.	Observing behavior in realistic situations

RETRIEVE & REMEMBER

ANSWERS IN APPENDIX E

12. What is the best way to predict a person's future behavior?

LaunchPad To review the perspectives and methods discussed in this chapter, engage online with *Concept Practice: Comparing Personality Theories.*

Exploring the Self

LOQ 12-20 Why has psychology generated so much research on the self? How important is self-esteem to our well-being?

Our personality feeds our sense of **self**. Asked to consider "Who I am," people draw on their distinctive and enduring ways of thinking, feeling, and acting. The self—the organizer of our thoughts, feelings, and actions—occupies the center of personality.

Consider the concept of *possible selves* (Markus & Nurius, 1986; Rathbone et al., 2016). Your possible selves include your visions of the self you dream of becoming—the rich self, the successful self, the loved and admired self. Your possible selves also include the self you fear becoming—the unemployed self, the academically failed self, the lonely and unpopular self. Possible selves motivate us to lay out specific goals that direct our energy effectively and efficiently (Landau et al., 2014). Middle school students whose families struggle financially are more likely to earn high grades if they have a clear vision of themselves succeeding in school (Duckworth et al., 2013).

"The first step to better times is to imagine them." —Chinese fortune cookie

Carried too far, our self-focus can lead us to fret that others are noticing and evaluating us. One of our favorite psychology experiments demonstrated this **spotlight effect** by having Cornell University students put on T-shirts

self your image and understanding of who you are; in modern psychology, the idea that this is the center of personality, organizing your thoughts, feelings, and actions.

spotlight effect overestimating others' noticing and evaluating our appearance, performance, and blunders (as if we presume a spotlight shines on us).

Timothy Large/Shutterstock and © Trinity Mirror/Mirrorpix/Alamy

featuring soft-rock star Barry Manilow, then enter a room with other students. Feeling self-conscious, the T-shirt wearers guessed that nearly half their peers would take note of the shirt as they walked in. In reality, only 23 percent did (Gilovich, 1996). *The point to remember:* We stand out less than we imagine, even with dorky clothes or bad hair, and even after a blunder like setting off a library alarm (Gilovich & Savitsky, 1999; Savitsky et al., 2001).

To turn down the spotlight's brightness, we can use two strategies. The first is simply to know and remember the spotlight effect. Public speakers perform better if they understand that their natural nervousness is hardly noticeable (Savitsky & Gilovich, 2003). The second is to take the audience's perspective. When we imagine audience members empathizing with our situation, we tend to expect we will not be judged as harshly (Epley et al., 2002).

IMPROVE YOUR EVERYDAY LIFE

What possible selves do you dream of—or fear—becoming? How might you use these imagined selves to motivate you now?

THE BENEFITS OF SELF-ESTEEM

If we like our self-image, we probably have high **self-esteem**. This feeling of high self-worth will translate into more restful nights and less pressure to conform. We'll be more persistent at difficult tasks. We'll feel less shy, anxious, and lonely, and, in the future, we'll be more successful and just plain happier (Greenberg, 2008; Orth & Robins, 2014; Swann et al., 2007). Our self-esteem grows from new experiences and achievement, and therefore changes as we age (Hutteman et al., 2015). Self-esteem often increases dramatically from adolescence to middle adulthood, continuing to climb until peaking between ages 50 and 60 (Bleidorn et al., 2016; Orth et al., 2018; von Soest et al. 2018).

Self-esteem is a household word. College students even report wanting high self-esteem more than food or sex (Bushman et al., 2011). But most research challenges the idea that high self-esteem is "the armor that protects kids" from life's problems (Baumeister, 2015; Baumeister & Vohs, 2018; Dawes, 1994; Leary, 1999; Seligman, 1994, 2002). Problems and failures lower self-esteem. So, maybe self-esteem simply reflects reality. Maybe it's a side effect of meeting challenges and getting through difficulties. Maybe kids with high self-esteem do better in school because doing better in school raises their self-esteem. Maybe self-esteem is a gauge that reports the state of our relationships with others (Reitz et al., 2016). If so, isn't pushing the gauge artificially higher with empty compliments much like forcing a car's low-fuel gauge to display "full"?

If feeling good *follows* doing well, then giving praise in the absence of good performance may actually harm people. After receiving weekly self-esteem-boosting messages, struggling students earned *lower* than expected grades (Forsyth et al., 2007). Other research showed that giving people random rewards hurt their productivity. Martin Seligman (2012) reported that "when good things occurred that weren't earned, like nickels coming out of slot machines, it did not increase people's well-being. It produced helplessness. People gave up and became passive."

There is, however, an important *effect* of low self-esteem. People who feel negatively about themselves also tend to behave negatively toward others (Amabile, 1983; Baumgardner et al., 1989; Pelham, 1993). Deflating a person's self-esteem produces similar effects. Researchers have temporarily lowered people's self-esteem—for example, by telling them they did poorly on a test or by insulting them. These participants were then more likely to insult others or to express racial prejudice (vanDellen et al., 2011; van Dijk et al., 2011; Ybarra, 1999). Self-image threat even increases unconscious racial bias (Allen & Sherman, 2011).

But inflated self-esteem can also cause problems. When studying insult-triggered aggression, researchers found that "conceited, self-important individuals turn nasty toward those who puncture their bubbles of self-love" (Baumeister, 2001; Rasmussen, 2016). **Narcissistic** people (more often men) forgive others less, take a game-playing approach to their romantic relationships, and engage in sexually forceful behavior (Blinkhorn et al., 2015; Bushman et al., 2003; Grijalva et al., 2015). They typically make good first impressions, which wane over time as their arrogance and bragging get old (Czarna et al., 2016; Leckelt et al., 2015). They crave others' admiration, are active on social media, and often become enraged

Dear diary,
Sorry to
bother you again.
LOW SELF-ESTEEM

Mike Twohy/The New Yorker Collection/The Cartoon Bank

when criticized (Geukes et al., 2016; Gnambs & Appel, 2018; Krizan & Herlache, 2018). Many had parents who told them they were superior to others (Brummelman et al., 2015).

SELF-SERVING BIAS

LOQ 12-21 What evidence reveals self-serving bias, and how do defensive and secure self-esteem differ?

Imagine dashing to class, hoping not to miss the first few minutes. But you arrive five minutes late, huffing and puffing. As you sink into your seat, what thoughts go through your mind? Do you go through a negative door, thinking, "I'm such a loser"? Or do you go through a positive door, telling yourself, "At least I made it to class" and "I really tried to get here on time"?

Personality psychologists have found that most people choose the second door, which leads to positive self-thoughts. We have a good reputation with ourselves. We show a **self-serving bias**—a readiness to perceive ourselves favorably (Myers, 2010). Consider these two findings:

People accept more responsibility for good deeds than for bad, and for successes than for failures. When athletes succeed, they credit their own talent. When they fail, they blame poor weather, bad luck, lousy officials, or the other team's amazing performance. Most students who receive poor exam grades blame the exam or the instructor, not themselves. On insurance forms, drivers have explained accidents in such words as "As I reached an intersection, a hedge sprang up, obscuring my vision, and I did not see the other car" and "A pedestrian hit me and went under my car." The question "What have I done to deserve this?" is one we usually ask of our troubles, not our successes. Although a self-serving bias can lead us to avoid uncomfortable truths, it can also motivate us to approach difficult tasks with confidence instead of despair (Tomaka et al., 1992; von Hippel & Trivers, 2011). Indeed, one analysis of 299 studies showed that having an unrealistically positive self-view predicted better emotional well-being (Dufner et al., 2018).

PEANUTS

Andrews McMeel Syndication

Most people see themselves as better than average. Compared with most other people, how moral are you? How easy to get along with? Where would you rank yourself, from the 1st to the 99th percentile? Most people put themselves well above the 50th percentile, the middle of the pack. This better-than-average effect appears for nearly any common, socially desirable behavior. Two in three Americans believe they have above average levels of intelligence (Heck et al., 2018). Most U.S. business executives say they are more ethical than the average executive. And at least 90 percent of business managers and college professors rate their performance as superior to that of their average peer. This self-serving bias is weaker in Asia, where people tend to value modesty (Church et al., 2014; Falk et al., 2009a). Yet self-serving biases have been observed worldwide: among Dutch, Australian, and Chinese students; Japanese drivers; Indian Hindus; and French people of most walks of life. In every one of 53 countries surveyed, people expressed self-esteem above the midpoint of the most widely used scale (Schmitt & Allik, 2005). Brain scans reveal that the more people judge themselves as better than average, the less brain activity they show in regions that enable self-reflection (Beer & Hughes, 2010).

Most people even see themselves as more immune than others to self-serving bias (Pronin, 2007). That's right, people believe they are above average at not believing they are above average. (Isn't psychology fun?) We also are quicker to believe flattering descriptions of ourselves than unflattering ones, and we are impressed with psychological tests that make us look good.

"If you are like most people, then like most people, you don't know you're like most people. Science has given us a lot of facts about the average person, and one of the most reliable of these facts is the average person doesn't see herself as average." —Daniel Gilbert, *Stumbling on Happiness*, 2006

Self-serving bias often underlies conflicts, such as blaming a partner for relationship problems or an assistant for work problems. All of us tend to see our own group as superior (whether it's our school, our state or country, or our ethnic group). Although there are 50 U.S. states, the average American thinks their home state made 18 percent of the contributions to U.S. history (Putnam et al., 2018). (If people perceived each state equally, they would think their home state contributed 2 percent to U.S. history.) Ethnic pride fueled Nazi horrors and Rwandan genocide. No wonder religion and literature so often warn against the perils of self-love and pride.

self-esteem our feelings of high or low self-worth.

narcissism excessive self-love and self-absorption.

self-serving bias our readiness to perceive ourselves favorably.

If the self-serving bias is so common, why do so many people put themselves down? For four reasons:

1. Some negative thoughts—"How could I have been so stupid!"—*protect us from repeating mistakes.*
2. Self put-downs are sometimes meant to *prompt positive feedback*. Saying "No one likes me" may at least get you "But not everyone has met you!"
3. Put-downs can help *prepare us for possible failure*. The coach who talks about the superior strength of the upcoming opponent makes a loss understandable, a victory noteworthy.
4. We often put down *our old selves,* not our current selves (Wilson & Ross, 2001). Chumps yesterday, but champs today: "At 18, I was a jerk; today I'm more sensitive."

Despite our self-serving bias, all of us some of the time (and some of us much of the time) do feel inferior. As we saw in Chapter 10, this often happens when we compare ourselves with those who are a step or two higher on the ladder of status, looks, income, or ability. Olympians who win silver medals, barely missing gold, show greater sadness on the award podium compared with the bronze medal winners (Medvec et al., 1995). The more deeply and frequently we have such feelings, the more unhappy or even depressed we become. Positive self-esteem predicts happiness and *persistence after failure* (Baumeister et al., 2003). So maybe it helps that, for most people, thinking has a naturally positive bias.

Researchers have shown the value of separating self-esteem into two categories—*defensive* and *secure* (Kernis, 2003; Lambird & Mann, 2006; Ryan & Deci, 2004).

- ***Defensive self-esteem is fragile.*** Its goal is to sustain itself, which makes failures and criticism feel threatening. Defensive people may respond to such perceived threats with anger or aggression (Crocker & Park, 2004; Donnellan et al., 2005).
- ***Secure self-esteem is sturdy.*** It relies less on other people's evaluations. If we feel accepted for who we are, and not for our looks, wealth, or fame, we are free of pressures to succeed. We can focus beyond ourselves, losing ourselves in relationships and purposes larger than ourselves (Crocker & Park, 2004). Secure self-esteem thus leads to greater quality of life. Such findings are in line with humanistic psychology's ideas about the benefits of a healthy self-image.

RETRIEVE & REMEMBER

ANSWERS IN APPENDIX E

13. What are the positive and negative effects of high self-esteem?

14. The tendency to accept responsibility for success and blame circumstances or bad luck for failure is called ___________-___________ ___________.

15. ___________ (Secure/Defensive) self-esteem is linked to angry and aggressive behavior. ___________ (Secure/Defensive) self-esteem is a healthier self-image that allows us to focus beyond ourselves and enjoy a higher quality of life.

CULTURE AND THE SELF

LOQ 12-22 How do individualist and collectivist cultures differ in their values and goals?

The meaning of *self* varies from culture to culture. How much of your identity is defined by your social connections? Your answer may depend on your culture, and whether it gives greater priority to the *independent self* or to the *interdependent self.*

If you are an **individualist**, you have an independent sense of "me," and an awareness of your unique personal convictions and values. Individualists prioritize personal goals. They define their identity mostly in terms of personal traits. They strive for personal control and individual achievement.

Individualists do share the human need to belong. They seek out and join groups. But being more self-contained, individualists also move in and out of social groups more easily. They change relationships, towns, and jobs with ease.

Over the past several decades, individualism has increased (Grossman & Varnum, 2015; Santos et al., 2017). American high school and college students in 2012 reported greater interest in obtaining benefits for themselves and lower concern for others than ever before (Twenge et al., 2012). People in competitive, individualist cultures have more personal freedom (**TABLE 12.5**). They take more pride in personal achievements, are less geographically bound to their families, and enjoy more privacy. People in individualist cultures also demand more romance and personal fulfillment in marriage. In one survey, "keeping romance alive" was rated as important to a good marriage by 78 percent of U.S. women but only 29 percent of Japanese women (*American Enterprise*, 1992).

If you are a **collectivist**, your identity may be closely tied to family, groups, and loyal friends. These connections define who you are. *Group identifications* provide a sense of belonging and a set of values. Collectivists have deep attachments to their groups—their family, clan, company, or country. Elders receive respect. For example, Chinese law states that parents aged 60 or above can sue their

Sam Harrel/Newscom/ZUMA Press/Fairbanks/AK/U.S.

Collectivist culture Although the United States is largely individualist, many cultural subgroups remain collectivist. This is true for many Alaska Natives, who demonstrate respect for tribal elders, and whose identity springs largely from their group affiliations.

TABLE 12.5 Value Contrasts Between Individualism and Collectivism

Concept	Individualism	Collectivism
Self	Independent (identity from individual traits)	Interdependent (identity from belonging to groups)
Life task	Discover and express your own uniqueness	Maintain connections, fit in, perform your role
What matters	Me—personal achievement and fulfillment; rights and liberties; self-esteem	Us—group goals and solidarity; social responsibilities and relationships; family duty
Coping method	Change reality	Adjust to reality
Morality	Defined by the individual (self-based)	Defined by social networks (duty-based)
Relationships	Many, often temporary or casual; confrontation is acceptable	Few, close, and enduring; harmony is valued
Attributing behavior	Behavior reflects the individual's personality and attitudes	Behavior reflects social norms and roles

Information from Thomas Schoeneman (1994) and Harry Triandis (1994).

" I'D LIKE a DECAFFACINNO FRAPPA CHAPPA DAPPA DINGO ICE BLENDED LAST OF THE MOCCA-HICANS VANILLA ICE ICE BETTER LATTE' THAN NEVER SMOOTHIE WITH a SHOT OF SELF-EXPRESSO."
hickerson

Cartoon by Buddy Hickerson

The tolerance of a Starbucks barista is severely tested.

sons and daughters if they fail to provide "for the elderly, taking care of them and comforting them, and cater[ing] to their special needs."

Individualist motto: "The squeaky wheel gets the grease."
Collectivist motto: "The quacking duck gets shot."

Collectivists are like athletes who take more pleasure in their team's victory than in their own performance. They find satisfaction in advancing their groups' interests, even when at the expense of personal needs. They preserve group spirit by avoiding direct confrontation, blunt honesty, and uncomfortable topics. They value humility, not self-importance (Bond et al., 2012). Instead of dominating conversations, collectivists hold back and display shyness when meeting strangers (Cheek & Melchior, 1990). Given the priority on "we," not "me," that super-customized latte that feels so soothing to a North American might sound selfishly demanding in Seoul (Kim & Markus, 1999).

A question: What do you think of people who willingly change their behavior to suit different people and situations? People in individualist countries (for example, the United States and Brazil) typically describe such people as "dishonest," "untrustworthy," and "insincere" (Levine, 2016). In traditionally collectivist countries (China, India, and Nepal, for example), people more often describe them as "mature," "honest," "trustworthy," and "sincere."

People vary within cultures, too. Southern Chinese farmers typically grow rice, a crop that requires group cooperation and builds collectivist values. Northern Chinese farmers often grow wheat, a crop that involves individual effort and leads to more individualist values. These differences lead people from Southern and Northern China to adopt different ways of thinking, feeling, and acting (Dong et al., 2019; Obschonka et al., 2018; Talhelm et al., 2014). In one clever study, researchers moved chairs together in Starbucks coffeehouses across China to block the aisle. They observed who acted like a typical individualist—controlling the environment and moving the chair out of the way—and who acted like a typical collectivist—adapting to the environment and squeezing through the chairs (Talhelm et al., 2018). Compared with the more collectivist Southern Chinese, the Northern Chinese were more likely to move the chair.

* * *

From Freud's psychoanalysis and Maslow's and Rogers' humanistic perspective, to the trait and social-cognitive theories, to today's study of the self, our understanding of personality has come a long way! This is a good base from which to explore Chapter 13's questions: How and why do some people suffer from disordered thinking and emotions?

IN YOUR EVERYDAY LIFE

Do you consider yourself to be more of a collectivist or an individualist? How do you think this sense of self has influenced your behavior, emotions, and thoughts?

RETRIEVE & REMEMBER

ANSWERS IN APPENDIX E

16. How do people in individualist and collectivist cultures differ?

individualism giving priority to our own goals over group goals and defining our identity in terms of personal traits rather than group membership.

collectivism giving priority to the goals of our group (often our extended family or work group) and defining our identity accordingly.

LEARNING OBJECTIVE QUESTIONS

TEST YOURSELF Answer these repeated Learning Objective Questions on your own (before checking the answers in Appendix D) to improve your retention of the concepts (McDaniel et al., 2009, 2015).

What Is Personality?

12-1: What is *personality,* and what theories inform our understanding of personality?

Psychodynamic Theories

12-2: How did Sigmund Freud's treatment of psychological disorders lead to his view of the unconscious mind?

12-3: What was Freud's view of personality?

12-4: What developmental stages did Freud propose?

12-5: How did Freud think people defended themselves against anxiety?

12-6: Which of Freud's ideas did his followers accept or reject?

12-7: What are *projective tests,* how are they used, and what criticisms have they faced?

12-8: How do today's psychologists view Freud's psychoanalysis?

12-9: How has modern research developed our understanding of the unconscious?

Humanistic Theories

12-10: How did humanistic psychologists view personality, and what was their goal in studying personality?

12-11: How did humanistic psychologists assess a person's sense of self?

12-12: How have humanistic theories influenced psychology? What criticisms have they faced?

Trait Theories

12-13: How do psychologists use traits to describe personality?

12-14: What are some common misunderstandings about introversion?

12-15: What are *personality inventories?*

12-16: Which traits seem to provide the most useful information about personality variation?

12-17: Does research support the consistency of personality traits over time and across situations?

Social-Cognitive Theories

12-18: How do social-cognitive theorists view personality development, and how do they explore behavior?

12-19: What criticisms have social-cognitive theorists faced?

Exploring the Self

12-20: Why has psychology generated so much research on the self? How important is self-esteem to our well-being?

12-21: What evidence reveals self-serving bias, and how do defensive and secure self-esteem differ?

12-22: How do individualist and collectivist cultures differ in their values and goals?

TERMS AND CONCEPTS TO REMEMBER

TEST YOURSELF Write down the definition in your own words, then check your answer.

CHAPTER TEST

TEST YOURSELF Answer the following questions on your own first, then check your answers in Appendix E.

1. According to Freud's view of personality structure, the "executive" system, the ________, seeks to gratify the impulses of the ________ in more acceptable ways.
   a. id; ego
   b. ego; superego
   c. ego; id
   d. id; superego
2. Freud proposed that the development of the "voice of our moral compass" is related to the ________, which internalizes ideals and provides standards for judgments.
3. According to the psychoanalytic view of development, we all pass through a series of psychosexual stages, including the oral, anal, and phallic stages. Conflicts unresolved at any of these stages may lead to
   a. dormant sexual feelings.
   b. fixation at that stage.
   c. unconscious blocking of impulses.
   d. a distorted gender identity.
4. Freud believed that defense mechanisms are unconscious attempts to distort or disguise reality, all in an effort to reduce our ________.
5. Freud believed that we may block painful or unacceptable thoughts, wishes, feelings, or memories from consciousness through an unconscious process called ________.
6. In general, neo-Freudians such as Adler and Horney accepted many of Freud's views but placed more emphasis than he did on
   a. development throughout the life span.
   b. the collective unconscious.
   c. the role of the id.
   d. social interactions.
7. Modern-day psychodynamic theorists and therapists agree with Freud about
   a. the existence of unconscious mental processes.
   b. the Oedipus complex.
   c. the predictive value of Freudian theory.
   d. the superego's role as the executive part of personality.
8. ________ tests ask test-takers to respond to an ambiguous image by describing it or telling a story about it.
9. Which of the following is NOT part of the contemporary view of the unconscious?
   a. Repressed memories of anxiety-provoking events
   b. Schemas that influence our perceptions and interpretations
   c. Stereotypes that affect our information processing
   d. Instantly activated emotions and implicit memories of learned skills
10. Maslow's hierarchy of needs proposes that we must satisfy basic physiological and safety needs before we seek ultimate psychological needs, such as self-actualization. Maslow based his ideas on
    a. Freudian theory.
    b. his experiences with patients.
    c. a series of laboratory experiments.
    d. his study of healthy, creative people.
11. How might Freud and Rogers differ in their explanations of how environment influences the development of a criminal?
12. The total acceptance Rogers advocated as part of a growth-promoting environment is called ________ ________ ________.
13. ________ theories of personality focus on describing characteristic behavior patterns, such as agreeableness or extraversion.
14. The most widely used personality inventory is the
    a. Extraversion–Introversion Scale.
    b. Person–Situation Inventory.
    c. MMPI.
    d. Rorschach.
15. Which of the following is NOT one of the Big Five personality factors?
    a. Conscientiousness
    b. Anxiety
    c. Extraversion
    d. Agreeableness
16. Our scores on personality tests best predict
    a. our behavior on a specific occasion.
    b. our average behavior across many situations.
    c. behavior involving a single trait, such as conscientiousness.
    d. behavior that depends on the situation or context.

17. The social-cognitive perspective proposes that our personality is shaped by a process called reciprocal determinism, as internal factors, environmental factors, and behaviors interact. An example of an environmental factor is

a. the presence of books in a home.

b. a preference for outdoor play.

c. the ability to read at a fourth-grade level.

d. the fear of violent action on television.

18. Critics say that ________-________ personality theory is very sensitive to an individual's interactions with particular situations, but that it gives too little attention to the person's enduring traits.

19. The tendency to overestimate others' attention to and evaluation of our appearance, performance, and mistakes is called the ________ ________.

20. Researchers have found that low self-esteem tends to be linked with life problems. How should this link be interpreted?

a. Life problems cause low self-esteem.

b. The answer isn't clear because the link is correlational and does not indicate cause and effect.

c. Low self-esteem leads to life problems.

d. Because of the self-serving bias, we must assume that external factors cause low self-esteem.

21. A fortune cookie advises, "Love yourself and happiness will follow." Is this good advice?

22. Individualist cultures tend to value ________; collectivist cultures tend to value ________.

a. interdependence; independence

b. independence; interdependence

c. solidarity; uniqueness

d. duty; fulfillment

Continue testing yourself with **LearningCurve** or **Achieve Read & Practice** to learn and remember most effectively.

coldsnowstorm/Getty Images

CHAPTER 13

Psychological Disorders

SURVEY THE CHAPTER

I felt the need to clean my room . . . and would spend four to five hours at it. I would take every book out of the bookcase, dust and put it back . . . I couldn't stop.

Marc, diagnosed with obsessive-compulsive disorder (from Summers, 1996)

Whenever I get depressed it's because I've lost a sense of self. I can't find reasons to like myself. I think I'm ugly. I think no one likes me.

Greta, diagnosed with depression (from Thorne, 1993, p. 21)

Voices, like the roar of a crowd, came. I felt like Jesus; I was being crucified.

Stuart, diagnosed with schizophrenia (from Emmons et al., 1997)

Now and then, all of us feel, think, or act in ways that may resemble a psychological disturbance. We get anxious, depressed, withdrawn, or suspicious, just less intensely and more briefly. So it's no wonder that we sometimes see ourselves in the mental illnesses we study. "To study the abnormal is the best way of understanding the normal," said William James (1842–1910).

Personally or through friends or family, many of us will know the confusion and pain of unexplained physical symptoms, irrational fears, or a feeling that life is not worth living. Worldwide, 1.1 billion people suffer from mental or substance use disorders (James et al., 2018). In a survey of first-year university students in eight countries, 1 in 3 reported a mental health problem during the prior year (Alonso et al., 2018). This is higher than the U.S. National Institute of Mental Health's estimate that 1 in 5 adult Americans currently have a "mental, behavioral, or emotional disorder (excluding developmental and substance use disorders)" or have had one within the past year (2015; **TABLE 13.1**). And, although rates and symptoms vary by culture, two of these disorders — major depressive disorder and schizophrenia — occur worldwide (Baumeister & Härter, 2007; Jablensky, 1999; Susser & Martines-Ales, 2018). This chapter examines these and other disorders. First, though, let's address some basic questions.

TABLE 13.1 Percentage of Americans Reporting Selected Psychological Disorders "in the Past Year"

Psychological Disorder	Percentage
Depressive disorders or bipolar disorder	9.3
Phobia of specific object or situation	8.7
Social anxiety disorder	6.8
Attention-deficit/hyperactivity disorder (ADHD)	4.1
Posttraumatic stress disorder (PTSD)	3.5
Generalized anxiety disorder	3.1
Schizophrenia	1.1
Obsessive-compulsive disorder	1.0

Data from: National Institute of Mental Health, 2015.

What Is a Psychological Disorder?

Most of us would agree that someone who is depressed and stays mostly in bed for three months has a psychological disorder. But what about a grieving father who can't resume his usual social activities three months after his child has died? Where do we draw the line between understandable grief and clinical depression? Between fear and a phobia? Between abnormality and normality?

In their search for answers, theorists and clinicians ask:

- How should we *define* psychological disorders?
- How should we *understand* disorders? How do underlying biological factors contribute to disorder? How do troubling environments influence our well-being? And how do these effects of nature and nurture interact?
- How should we *classify* psychological disorders? How can we use labels to guide treatment without negatively judging people or excusing their behavior?

DEFINING PSYCHOLOGICAL DISORDERS

Learning Objective Question LOQ 13-1 How should we draw the line between normality and disorder?

A **psychological disorder** is a syndrome (a collection of symptoms) marked by a "clinically significant disturbance in an individual's cognitions, emotion regulation, or behavior" (American Psychiatric Association, 2013).

Such thoughts, emotions, or behaviors are *dysfunctional* or *maladaptive*—they interfere with normal day-to-day life. An intense fear of spiders may be abnormal, but if it doesn't interfere with your life, it is not a disorder. Believing that your home must be thoroughly cleaned every weekend is not a disorder. But when cleaning rituals interfere with work and leisure, as Marc's uncontrollable rituals did, they may be signs of a disorder. Occasional sad moods that persist and become disabling may likewise signal a psychological disorder.

Distress often accompanies such dysfunction. Marc, Greta, and Stuart were all distressed by their thoughts, behaviors, or emotions.

The diagnosis of specific disorders has varied from culture to culture and even over time in the same culture. The American Psychiatric Association stopped classifying homosexuality as a disorder in 1973. By that point, most mental health workers no longer considered same-sex attraction as inherently dysfunctional or distressing. (Despite this cultural progress, American children and adolescents who identify as transgender or gender nonconforming are still at risk, being seven times more likely than their peers to be diagnosed with a psychological disorder [Becerra-Culqui et al., 2018]). On the other hand, high-energy children, who might have been viewed as normal youngsters running a bit wild in the 1970s, may today receive a diagnosis of **attention-deficit/hyperactivity disorder (ADHD).** One 10-year study in Sweden found children's attentional behaviors unchanging, while national ADHD diagnoses increased fivefold (Rydell et al., 2018). Times change, and research and clinical practices change, too. (See Thinking Critically About: ADHD—Normal High Energy or Disordered Behavior?)

Francois Dubourdeau/Skydive East Tennessee

(a)

Carol Beckwith

(b)

Culture and normality Young American men may plan elaborate invitations for big events, as did this student (a) who appealed (successfully) to his date for prom. Young men of the West African Wodaabe tribe (b) traditionally put on decorative makeup and costumes to attract women. Each culture may view the other's behavior as abnormal.

psychological disorder a syndrome marked by a clinically significant disturbance in a person's cognitions, emotion regulation, or behavior.

attention-deficit/hyperactivity disorder (ADHD) a psychological disorder marked by extreme inattention and/or hyperactivity and impulsivity.

Thinking Critically About:

ADHD—Normal High Energy or Disordered Behavior?

LOQ 13-2 Why is there controversy over attention-deficit/hyperactivity disorder?

Diagnosis in the U.S.

11%[1] 4- to 17-year-olds

2.5%[2] adults

Twice as often in BOYS as in girls

Symptoms

- inattention and distractibility[3]
- hyperactivity[4]
- impulsivity

SKEPTICS note:

Energetic child + boring school = ADHD overdiagnosis

- Children are not designed to sit for hours in chairs inside.
- The youngest children in a class tend to be more fidgety—and more often diagnosed.[5]
- Older students may seek out stimulant ADHD prescription drugs–"good-grade pills."[6]
- What are the long-term effects of drug treatment?
- Why the increase in ADHD diagnoses and drugs?[7]

A+ Excellent Work

SUPPORTERS note:

- More diagnoses reflect increased awareness.
- "ADHD is a real neurobiological disorder whose existence should no longer be debated."[8]
- ADHD is associated with abnormal brain structure, abnormal brain activity patterns, and future risky or antisocial behavior.[9]

Causes?

- May co-exist with a learning disorder or with defiant and temper-prone behavior.
- May be genetic.[10]

Treatment

- Stimulant drugs (Ritalin and Adderall) calm hyperactivity, and increase ability to sit and focus.[11] So do behavior therapy and aerobic exercise.[12]
- Psychological therapies help with the distress of ADHD.[13]

The bottom line:

Extreme inattention, hyperactivity, and impulsivity can derail social, academic, and work achievements. These symptoms can be treated with medication and other therapies. But the debate continues over whether normal high energy is too often diagnosed as a psychiatric disorder, and whether there is a cost to the long-term use of stimulant drugs in treating ADHD.

1. Schwarz & Cohen, 2013. 2. Simon et al., 2009. 3. Martel et al., 2016. 4. Kofler et al., 2016. 5. Chen et al., 2016. 6. Schwarz, 2012. 7. Ellison, 2015; Hales et al., 2018; Sayal et al., 2017. 8. World Federation for Mental Health, 2005. 9. Barkley et al., 2002; Hoogman et al., 2017. 10. Nikolas & Burt, 2010; Poelmans et al., 2011; Volkow et al., 2009; Williams et al., 2010. 11. Barbaresi et al., 2007. 12. Cerrillo-Urbina et al., 2015; Pelham et al., 2016. 13. Fabiano et al., 2008.

RETRIEVE & REMEMBER

ANSWERS IN APPENDIX E

1. A lawyer is distressed by feeling the need to wash her hands 100 times a day. She has little time left to meet with clients, and her colleagues are wondering about her competence. Her behavior would probably be labeled disordered, because it is __________, that is, it interferes with her day-to-day life.

UNDERSTANDING PSYCHOLOGICAL DISORDERS

LOQ 13-3 How do the medical model and the biopsychosocial approach influence our understanding of psychological disorders?

The way we view a problem influences how we try to solve it. In earlier times, people often thought that strange behaviors were evidence of strange forces at work. Had you lived during the Middle Ages, you might have said, "The devil made her do it." To drive out demons, "mad" people were sometimes caged or given "therapies" such as beatings, genital mutilations, removal of teeth or lengths of intestine, or transfusions of animal blood (Farina, 1982).

Reformers such as Philippe Pinel (1745–1826) in France opposed such brutal treatments. Madness is not demonic possession, he insisted, but a sickness of the mind caused by severe stress and inhumane conditions. Curing the sickness requires *moral treatment,* including boosting patients' morale by unchaining them and talking with them. He and others worked to replace brutality with gentleness, isolation with activity, and filth with clean air and sunshine.

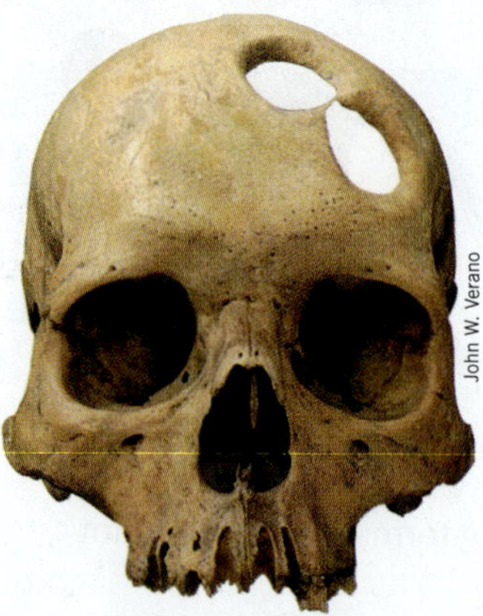

Yesterday's "therapy" Through the ages, psychologically disordered people have received brutal treatments. The holes drilled in the skull of this Stone Age patient may have been an attempt to release evil spirits and cure a mental disorder. Did the patient survive the "cure"?

In some places, cruel treatments for mental illness—including chaining people to beds or locking them in spaces with wild animals—linger even today. In response, the World Health Organization has launched a plan to transform hospitals worldwide "into patient-friendly and humane places with minimum restraints" (WHO, 2014).

The Medical Model

A medical breakthrough around 1900 prompted a new perspective on mental disorders. Researchers discovered that syphilis, a sexually transmitted infection, invades the brain and distorts the mind. This discovery triggered an eager search for physical causes of other mental disorders, and for treatments that would cure them. Hospitals replaced madhouses, and the **medical model** of mental disorders was born. This model is reflected in words we still use today. We speak of the mental *health* movement. A mental *illness* needs to be *diagnosed* on the basis of its *symptoms.* It needs to be treated through *therapy,* which may include *treatment* in a psychiatric *hospital.* The medical perspective has been energized by more recent discoveries that abnormal brain structures and biochemistry contribute to many disorders (Insel & Cuthbert, 2015). A growing number of clinical psychologists now work in medical hospitals, where they collaborate with physicians to determine how the mind and body operate together.

The Biopsychosocial Approach

To call psychological disorders "sicknesses" tilts research heavily toward the influence of biology and away from the influence of our personal histories and social and cultural surroundings. But as we have seen throughout this text, our behaviors, our thoughts, and our feelings are formed by the interaction of our biology, our psychology, and our social-cultural environment. As individuals, we differ in the amount of stress we experience and in the ways we cope with stress. Cultures also differ in the sources of stress they produce and in their traditional ways of coping. We are physically embodied and socially embedded.

Latin America, for example, lays claim to *susto,* a condition marked by severe anxiety, restlessness, and a fear of black magic. In Japanese culture, people may experience *taijin kyofusho*—social anxiety about physical appearance, combined with a readiness to blush and a fear of eye contact. The eating disorder *bulimia nervosa* occurs mostly in food-abundant Western cultures. Such disorders may share an underlying dynamic (such as anxiety) while differing in the typical culture-specific symptoms (an eating problem or a type of fear). Even disordered aggression may have varying explanations in different cultures. In Malaysia, *amok* describes a sudden outburst of violent behavior (as in the English phrase "run amok").

Two other disorders—depression and schizophrenia—occur worldwide. From Asia to Africa and across the Americas, schizophrenia's symptoms often include irrational and incoherent speech. Such disorders reflect genes and physiology, as well as internal psychological dynamics and social-cultural circumstances.

The biopsychosocial approach reminds us that mind and body work as one. Negative emotions contribute to physical illness, and abnormal physical processes contribute to negative emotions. The biopsychosocial approach gave rise to the *vulnerability-stress model,* in which individual characteristics combine with environmental stressors to influence the likelihood of a psychological disorder (Monroe & Simons, 1991; Zuckerman, 1999). Research on **epigenetics** (literally "in addition to genetics") supports this model by showing how our

DNA and our environment interact. In one environment, a gene will be *expressed*, but in another, it may lie dormant. For some, that will be the difference between developing a disorder or not developing it.

RETRIEVE & REMEMBER

ANSWERS IN APPENDIX E

2. Are psychological disorders universal or culture-specific? Explain with examples.
3. What is the biopsychosocial approach, and why is it important in our understanding of psychological disorders?

CLASSIFYING DISORDERS—AND LABELING PEOPLE

LOQ 13-4 How and why do clinicians classify psychological disorders, and why do some psychologists criticize the use of diagnostic labels?

In biology, classification creates order and helps us communicate. To say that an animal is a "mammal" tells us a great deal—that it is likely to be warm-blooded, have hair or fur, and produce milk to feed its young. In psychiatry and psychology, classification also tells us a great deal. To classify a person's disorder as "schizophrenia" implies that the person speaks in a disorganized way, has bizarre beliefs, shows either little emotion or inappropriate emotion, or is socially withdrawn. "Schizophrenia" is a quick way of describing a complex set of behaviors.

But diagnostic classification does more than give us a thumbnail sketch of a person's disordered behavior, thoughts, or feelings. In psychiatry and psychology, classification also attempts to *predict* a disorder's future course, *suggest* appropriate treatment, and *prompt research* into its causes. To study a disorder, we must first name and describe it.

In the United States and many other countries, the most common tool for describing disorders and estimating how often they occur is the American Psychiatric Association's *Diagnostic and Statistical Manual of Mental Disorders,* now in its fifth edition (**DSM-5**).[1] Physicians and mental health workers use the detailed listings in the DSM-5 to guide medical diagnoses and treatment. For example, a person may be diagnosed with and treated for *insomnia disorder* if he or she meets *all* the criteria in **TABLE 13.2.** The DSM-5 includes diagnostic codes from the World Health Organization's *International Classification of Diseases* (ICD), which are required for insurance coverage. This also makes it easy to track worldwide trends in psychological disorders.

In the DSM-5, some diagnostic labels changed. The conditions formerly called "autism" and "Asperger's syndrome" were combined under the label *autism spectrum disorder* (see Chapter 3). "Mental retardation" became *intellectual disability.* New disorder categories, such as *hoarding disorder* and *binge-eating disorder,* were added.

In real-world tests *(field trials)* assessing the reliability of the new DSM-5 categories, some diagnoses have fared well and others have fared poorly (Freedman et al., 2013). Clinician agreement on adult *posttraumatic stress disorder* and childhood *autism spectrum disorder,* for example, was near 70 percent. (If one psychiatrist or psychologist diagnosed someone with one of these disorders, there was a 70 percent chance that another mental health worker would independently give the same diagnosis.) But for *antisocial personality disorder* and *generalized anxiety disorder,* agreement was closer to 20 percent.

Critics have long faulted the DSM manual for casting too wide a net and bringing "almost any kind of behavior within the compass of psychiatry" (Eysenck et al., 1983). Some now worry that the DSM-5's even wider net will extend the pathologizing of everyday life—for example, by turning normal bereavement grief and distress into a *depressive disorder* and childish fidgeting into ADHD (Frances, 2013, 2014). Others respond that relentless bereavement-related depression and enduring hyperactivity are genuine disorders (Kamp & Due, 2018; Kendler, 2011; Kupfer, 2012).

[1] Many examples in this chapter were drawn from case studies in a previous DSM edition.

TABLE 13.2 Insomnia Disorder
• Feeling unsatisfied with amount or quality of sleep (trouble falling asleep, staying asleep, or returning to sleep)
• Sleep disruption causes distress or diminished everyday functioning
• Happens three or more nights each week
• Occurs during at least three consecutive months
• Happens even with sufficient sleep opportunities
• Independent from other sleep disorders (such as narcolepsy)
• Independent from substance use or abuse
• Independent from other mental disorders or medical conditions

Information from: American Psychiatric Association, 2013.

A new classification approach that builds upon the DSM is the U.S. National Institute of Mental Health's Research Domain Criteria (RDoC) project (Insel et al., 2010; NIMH, 2017). The RDoC framework organizes disorders according to behaviors and brain activity, aiming to study them with "the power of modern research approaches in genetics, neuroscience, and behavioral science" (Insel & Lieberman, 2013).

Other critics of classification register a more basic complaint. Diagnostic labels can be subjective, or even personal opinions disguised as scientific judgments. Labels can create stigma. Once we label a person, we view that person differently (Bathje & Pryor, 2011; Farina, 1982; Sadler et al., 2012b). Labels can change reality by putting us on alert for evidence that confirms our view. If we hear that a new co-worker is mean, we may treat her suspiciously.

medical model the concept that diseases, in this case psychological disorders, have physical causes that can be *diagnosed, treated,* and, in most cases, *cured,* often through treatment in a *hospital.*

epigenetics the study of the molecular ways by which environments can influence gene expression (without a DNA change).

DSM-5 the American Psychiatric Association's *Diagnostic and Statistical Manual of Mental Disorders,* Fifth Edition; a widely used system for classifying psychological disorders.

She may in turn respond to us as a mean person would. Ditto if we're led to believe that someone is smart. Teachers who were told certain students were "gifted" then acted in ways that brought out the creative behaviors they expected (Snyder, 1984). Labels can be self-fulfilling.

The biasing power of labels was clear in a classic, controversial study. David Rosenhan (1973) and seven others went to hospital admissions offices, complaining (falsely) of "hearing voices" saying *empty, hollow,* and *thud*. Apart from this complaint and giving false names and occupations, they answered questions truthfully. All eight of these healthy people were misdiagnosed with disorders.

Should we be surprised? Surely not. As one psychiatrist noted, if someone swallows blood, goes to an emergency room, and spits it up, we wouldn't blame the doctor for diagnosing a bleeding ulcer. But what followed the diagnoses was startling. Until being released an average of 19 days later, these eight "patients" showed no other symptoms. Yet after analyzing their (quite normal) life histories, clinicians were able to "discover" the causes of their disorders, such as having mixed emotions about a parent.

Labels matter. When people in another experiment watched recorded interviews, those told that they were watching job applicants perceived the people as normal (Langer & Abelson, 1974; Langer & Imber, 1980). Others, who were told they were watching cancer or psychiatric patients, perceived them as "different from most people." One therapist described the person being interviewed as "frightened of his own aggressive impulses," a "passive, dependent type," and so forth. People tend to stigmatize those with psychological disorders (Angermeyer & Dietrich, 2006; Corrigan & Watson, 2002; Pachankis et al., 2018; Weiner et al., 1988). The stigma of mental illness can cause people to hide their symptoms and to avoid seeking treatment (Corrigan, 2004; Nam et al., 2018).

The power of labels is just as real outside the laboratory. Getting a job or finding a place to rent can be a challenge for people recently released from a psychiatric hospital. Label someone as "mentally ill" and people may fear them as potentially violent. That reaction is fading as people better understand that psychological disorders are not failures of character. Public figures have helped foster this understanding by speaking openly about their own struggles with disorders such as anxiety, depression, and substance abuse—and about how beneficial it was to seek help, receive a diagnosis, and get better through treatment.

Despite their risks, diagnostic labels have benefits. They help mental health professionals communicate about their cases and study the causes and treatments of disorders. Clients are often relieved to learn that their suffering has a name and that they are not alone in experiencing their symptoms.

In the rest of this chapter, we will discuss some of the major disorders classified in the DSM-5. In Chapter 14, we will consider their *treatment*.

GRETCHEN ERTL/The New York Times/ReduxPictures

Struggles and recovery During his campaign, Boston Mayor Marty Walsh spoke openly about his past struggles with alcohol. His honesty helped him reduce stigma and win in 2014 and again in 2017.

> Old stereotypes are slowly being replaced in media portrayals of psychological disorders and disordered behavior. The superhero character of Tony Stark in the *Iron Man* and *Avengers* movies has a backstory of posttraumatic stress disorder. *Black Swan* (2010) dramatized a lead character suffering a delusional disorder. *A Single Man* (2009) depicted depression.

IN YOUR EVERYDAY LIFE

Do you know someone (perhaps even yourself) who has been diagnosed with a psychological disorder? How do you think a diagnostic label has helped or hurt this person?

RETRIEVE & REMEMBER

ANSWERS IN APPENDIX E

4. What is the value, and what are the dangers, of labeling individuals with disorders?

LaunchPad To test your ability to form diagnoses, try ***Topic Tutorial: PsychSim6, Classifying Disorders.***

Anxiety Disorders, OCD, and PTSD

Anxiety is part of life. Have you ever felt anxious when speaking in front of a class, peering down from a high ledge, or waiting to learn the results of a final exam? We all feel anxious at times. We may occasionally feel enough anxiety to avoid making eye contact or talking with someone—"shyness," we call it. Fortunately for most of us, our uneasiness is not intense and persistent. Some, however, are especially prone to fear the unknown and to notice and remember perceived threats—as if living while horror movie background music plays (Gorka et al., 2017; Mitte, 2008). When our brain's danger-detection system becomes overly active, we are at greater risk for an *anxiety disorder,* and for two other disorders that involve anxiety: *obsessive-compulsive disorder (OCD)* and *posttraumatic stress disorder.*[2]

[2] OCD and PTSD were formerly classified as anxiety disorders, but the DSM-5 now classifies them separately.

ANXIETY DISORDERS

LOQ 13-5 How do generalized anxiety disorder, panic disorder, and phobias differ? How do anxiety disorders differ from the ordinary worries and fears we all experience?

The **anxiety disorders** are marked by distressing, persistent anxiety or by maladaptive behaviors that reduce anxiety. For example, people with *social anxiety disorder* become extremely anxious in social settings where others might judge them, such as parties, class presentations, or even eating in a public place. One university student experienced heart palpitations, tremors, blushing, and sweating when giving a presentation, taking an exam, or meeting an authority figure, and also feared that he would embarrass himself. He avoided parties, phone calls, and other social contacts. By staying home he avoided the anxious feelings, but it was maladaptive. Avoiding others prevented him from learning to cope with the world and left him feeling lonely (Leichsenring & Leweke, 2017).

Let's take a closer look at three other anxiety disorders:

- ***generalized anxiety disorder,*** in which a person is, for no obvious reason, continually tense and uneasy;
- ***panic disorder,*** in which a person experiences *panic attacks*—sudden episodes of intense dread—and fears the next attack; and
- ***phobias,*** in which a person feels intensely and irrationally afraid of something.

Generalized Anxiety Disorder

For two years, Tom, a 27-year-old electrician, was bothered by dizziness, sweating palms, and an irregular heartbeat. He felt on edge and sometimes found himself shaking. Tom was fairly successful at hiding his symptoms from his family and co-workers. But he allowed himself few other social contacts, and sometimes he had to leave work. Neither his family doctor nor a neurologist was able to find any physical problem.

Tom's unfocused, out-of-control, agitated feelings suggest **generalized anxiety disorder,** which is marked by excessive and uncontrollable worry that persists for six months or more. People with this condition (two-thirds are women) worry continually. They are often jittery, on edge, and sleep-deprived (McLean & Anderson, 2009). They become fixated on potential threats (Pergamin-Hight et al., 2015). Concentration suffers, as everyday worries demand continual attention. Their *autonomic nervous system* arousal may leak out through furrowed brows, twitching eyelids, trembling, sweating, or fidgeting.

Those affected usually cannot identify, relieve, or avoid their anxiety. To use Sigmund Freud's term, the anxiety is *free-floating* (not linked to a specific stressor or threat). Generalized anxiety disorder and depression often go hand in hand, but even without depression, this disorder tends to be disabling (Hunt et al., 2004; Moffitt et al., 2007). Moreover, it may lead to physical problems, such as high blood pressure.

Panic Disorder

At some point, many of us will experience a terrifying panic attack—a minutes-long feeling of intense fear that something horrible is about to happen. Irregular heartbeat, chest pains, shortness of breath, choking, trembling, or dizziness may accompany the fear. One woman recalled suddenly feeling

> hot and as though I couldn't breathe. My heart was racing and I started to sweat and tremble and I was sure I was going to faint. Then my fingers started to feel numb and tingly and things seemed unreal. It was so bad I wondered if I was dying and asked my husband to take me to the emergency room. By the time we got there (about 10 minutes) the worst of the attack was over and I just felt washed out (Greist et al., 1986).

For the 3 percent of people with **panic disorder,** panic attacks are recurrent. These anxiety tornados strike suddenly, do their damage, and disappear, but they are not forgotten. After experiencing even a few panic attacks, people may come to fear the fear itself. Those having (or observing) a panic attack often misread the symptoms as an impending heart attack or other serious physical ailment. Smokers have at least a doubled risk of a panic attack and greater symptoms when they do have an attack (Knuts et al., 2010; Zvolensky & Bernstein, 2005). Because nicotine is a stimulant, lighting up doesn't lighten up.

The constant fear of another attack can lead people with panic disorder to avoid situations where panic might strike. Their avoidance may lead to a separate and additional diagnosis of *agoraphobia*—fear or avoidance of public situations from which escape might be difficult. People with agoraphobia may avoid being outside the home, in a crowd, or at a coffee shop.

Dia Dipasupil/Getty Images

Panic on the prowl As a youthful star in the *Twilight* movies, Kristen Stewart experienced frequent anxiety. "I would have panic attacks," she said. "I literally always had a stomach ache" (Lapidos, 2016). Being open and honest about her anxiety helped. "It opened my life up, and I'm so much happier."

anxiety disorders psychological disorders characterized by distressing, persistent anxiety or maladaptive behaviors that reduce anxiety.

generalized anxiety disorder an anxiety disorder in which a person is continually tense, fearful, and in a state of autonomic nervous system arousal.

panic disorder an anxiety disorder marked by unpredictable minutes-long episodes of intense dread in which a person may experience terror and accompanying chest pain, choking, or other frightening sensations; often followed by worry over a possible next attack.

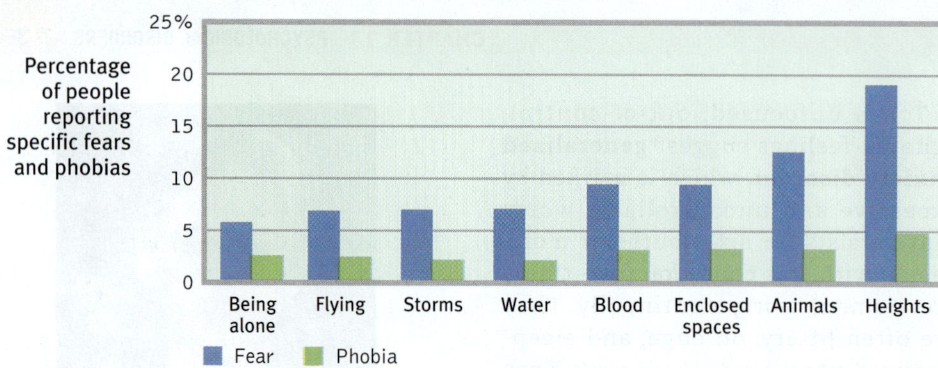

FIGURE 13.1 Some common specific fears Researchers surveyed Dutch people to identify the most common events or objects they feared. A strong fear becomes a phobia if it provokes a compelling but irrational desire to avoid the dreaded object or situation. (Data from Depla et al., 2008.)

Phobias

We all live with some fears. People with **phobias** are consumed by a persistent, irrational fear and avoidance of some object or situation. *Specific phobias* may focus on particular animals, insects, heights, blood, or enclosed spaces (**FIGURE 13.1**). Many people avoid the triggers (such as high places) that arouse their fear. Marilyn, an otherwise healthy and happy 28-year-old, so feared thunderstorms that she felt anxious as soon as a weather forecaster mentioned possible storms later in the week. If she would be alone when a storm was forecast, she often stayed with a close relative. During a storm, she hid from windows and buried her head to avoid seeing the lightning.

RETRIEVE & REMEMBER

ANSWERS IN APPENDIX E

5. Unfocused tension, apprehension, and arousal are symptoms of ___________ ___________ disorder.
6. Those who experience unpredictable periods of terror and intense dread, accompanied by frightening physical sensations, may be diagnosed with ___________ disorder.
7. If a person is focusing anxiety on specific feared objects, activities, or situations, that person may have a ___________.

OBSESSIVE-COMPULSIVE DISORDER (OCD)

LOQ 13-6 What is *OCD?*

As with the anxiety disorders, we can see aspects of our own behavior in **obsessive-compulsive disorder (OCD)**. *Obsessive thoughts* (recall Marc's focus on cleaning his room) are unwanted and seemingly unending. *Compulsive behaviors* are responses to those thoughts (cleaning and cleaning and cleaning).

Have you ever felt a bit anxious about how your place will appear to others and found yourself checking and cleaning one last time before your guests arrived? Or, perhaps worried about an upcoming exam, you caught yourself lining up your study materials "just so" before you began studying? Our everyday lives are full of little rehearsals and fussy behaviors. But they cross the fine line between normality and disorder when they *persistently interfere* with everyday life and cause us distress. Checking if you locked your door is normal; checking 10 times is not. Washing your hands is normal; washing so often that your skin becomes raw is not. Although people know their anxiety-fueled obsessive thoughts are irrational, the thoughts can become so haunting, and the compulsive rituals so senselessly time-consuming, that effective functioning becomes impossible.

Michael Campanella/WireImage/Getty Images

Thriving with OCD Music star Justin Timberlake says support from his family and a sense of humor have helped him cope with the challenges of obsessive-compulsive disorder.

Some people experience other OCD-related disorders, such as *hoarding disorder* (cluttering one's space with acquired possessions one can't part with), *body dysmorphic disorder* (preoccupation with perceived body defects), *trichotillomania* (hair pulling), or *excoriation disorder* (excessive skin-picking).

LaunchPad For an eye-opening, 7-minute snapshot of one woman's challenges with compulsive rituals, see the *Video: Obsessive-Compulsive Disorder—A Young Mother's Struggle.*

POSTTRAUMATIC STRESS DISORDER (PTSD)

LOQ 13-7 What is *PTSD?*

While serving overseas, one soldier, Jesse, saw the killing "of children and women. It was just horrible for anyone to experience." Back home, he suffered "real bad flashbacks" (Welch, 2005).

Jesse is not alone. In one study of 103,788 veterans returning from Iraq and Afghanistan, 25 percent were diagnosed with a psychological disorder (Seal et al., 2007). Some had *traumatic brain injuries (TBI)*, but the most frequent diagnosis was **posttraumatic stress disorder (PTSD).** Survivors of accidents, disasters, refugee displacement, and violent and sexual assaults (including an estimated two-thirds of prostitutes) have also experienced PTSD symptoms (Brewin et al., 1999; Guo et al., 2017; Reebs et al., 2017). Typical symptoms include recurring haunting memories and nightmares, laser-focused attention to and avoidance of possible threats, social withdrawal, jumpy anxiety, and trouble sleeping (Germain, 2013; Hoge et al., 2007; Yuval et al., 2017).

Many of us will experience a traumatic event. And many will display *survivor resiliency*—by recovering after severe stress (Bonanno, 2004, 2005; Infurna & Luthar, 2016b). Although philosopher Friedrich Nietzsche's (1889) idea that "what does

Chip Somodevilla/Getty Images

PTSD from Parkland In the 2018 Parkland, Florida school shooting, Samantha Fuentes (at right) witnessed friends dying, and shrapnel struck her face and legs. She later reported PTSD symptoms, including a fear of returning to the school and jumping at the sound of a slammed door. Two other student survivors died by apparent suicide in 2019, including one who had been diagnosed with PTSD (Mazzei, 2019).

not kill me makes me stronger" is not true for all, about half of trauma victims experience *posttraumatic growth* (more on this in Chapter 14) (Wu et al., 2019). Tears may turn into triumphs.

Why do 5 to 10 percent of people develop PTSD (Bonanno et al., 2011)? One factor seems to be the amount of trauma-related emotional distress: The higher the distress, the greater the risk for posttraumatic symptoms (King et al., 2015; Ozer et al., 2003). Some examples:

- Among American military personnel in Afghanistan, 7.6 percent of combatants developed PTSD, compared with 1.4 percent of noncombatants (McNally, 2012).
- Among survivors of the 9/11 terrorist attacks on New York's World Trade Center, the rates of subsequent PTSD diagnoses for those who had been inside were double the rates of those who had been outside (Bonanno et al., 2006).

What else can influence PTSD development after a trauma? Some people may, thanks to their genes, have a more sensitive emotion-processing limbic system that floods their bodies with stress hormones (Duncan et al., 2017; Kosslyn, 2005). Another factor is gender. After a traumatic event, women experience PTSD more often than do men (Olff et al., 2007; Ozer & Weiss, 2004).

Some psychologists believe PTSD has been overdiagnosed (Dobbs, 2009; McNally, 2003). Too often, say critics, PTSD gets stretched to include normal stress-related bad memories and dreams. And some well-intentioned procedures—such as "debriefing" people by asking them to revisit the experience and vent their emotions—may worsen stress reactions (Bonanno et al., 2010; Wakefield & Spitzer, 2002). Other research shows that reliving traumas through media coverage sustains the stress response (Holman et al., 2014). Nevertheless, people diagnosed with PTSD can benefit from other therapies, some of which are discussed in Chapter 14.

RETRIEVE & REMEMBER

ANSWERS IN APPENDIX E

8. Those who express anxiety through unwanted repetitive thoughts or actions may have a(n) ____________-____________ disorder.

9. Those with symptoms of recurring memories and nightmares, hypervigilance, avoidance, social withdrawal, jumpy anxiety, numbness of feeling, and/or insomnia for weeks after a traumatic event may be diagnosed with ____________ ____________ disorder.

UNDERSTANDING ANXIETY DISORDERS, OCD, AND PTSD

LOQ 13-8 How do conditioning, cognition, and biology contribute to the feelings and thoughts that mark anxiety disorders, OCD, and PTSD?

Anxiety is both a feeling and a thought—a doubt-laden self-appraisal. How do these anxious feelings and thoughts arise? Few psychologists now interpret anxiety the way Sigmund Freud did. His psychoanalytic theory (Chapter 12) proposed that, beginning in childhood, people *repress* certain impulses, ideas, and feelings. Freud believed that this submerged mental energy sometimes leaks out in odd symptoms, such as anxious hand washing. Most psychologists today believe that three modern perspectives—conditioning, cognition, and biology—are more helpful.

Conditioning

Conditioning happens when we learn to associate two or more things that occur together (see Chapter 6). Through *classical conditioning,* our fear responses can become linked with formerly neutral objects and events. To understand the link between learning and anxiety, researchers have given lab rats unpredictable electric shocks (Schwartz, 1984). The rats, like assault victims who report feeling anxious when returning to the scene of the crime, learned to be uneasy in their lab environment. The lab became a cue for fear.

Such research helps explain how anxious or traumatized people learn to associate their anxiety with certain cues (Bar-Haim et al., 2007; Duits et al., 2015). In one survey, 58 percent of those with social anxiety disorder said their symptoms began after a traumatic event (Ost & Hugdahl, 1981). Anxiety or an anxiety-related disorder is more likely to develop when bad events happen unpredictably and uncontrollably (Field, 2006; Mineka & Oehlberg, 2008). Even a single painful or frightening event may trigger a full-blown phobia, thanks to two processes: classical conditioning's *stimulus generalization* and operant conditioning's *reinforcement.*

Stimulus generalization occurs when a person experiences a fearful event and later develops a fear of similar events. I [ND] was once watching a terrifying movie about spiders, *Arachnophobia,*

phobia an anxiety disorder marked by a persistent, irrational fear and avoidance of a specific object, activity, or situation.

obsessive-compulsive disorder (OCD) a disorder characterized by unwanted repetitive thoughts (obsessions), actions (compulsions), or both.

posttraumatic stress disorder (PTSD) a disorder characterized by haunting memories, nightmares, hypervigilance, avoidance of trauma-related stimuli, social withdrawal, jumpy anxiety, numbness of feeling, and/or insomnia lingering for four weeks or more after a traumatic experience.

when a severe thunderstorm struck and the theater lost power. For months, I experienced anxiety at the sight of spiders or cobwebs. Those fears eventually disappeared, but sometimes fears linger and grow. Marilyn's thunderstorm phobia may have similarly generalized after a terrifying or painful experience during a thunderstorm.

Reinforcement helps maintain learned fears and anxieties. Anything that enables us to avoid or escape a feared situation can reinforce maladaptive behaviors. Fearing a panic attack, we may decide not to leave the house. Reinforced by feeling calmer, we are likely to repeat that behavior in the future (Antony et al., 1992). Compulsive behaviors operate similarly. If washing your hands relieves your feelings of anxiety, you may wash your hands again when those feelings return.

Cognition

Learning is more than just conditioning. *Cognition*—our thoughts, memories, interpretations, and expectations—plays a role in many kinds of learning, including what we learn to fear. In one form of cognitive learning, we learn by observing others. Consider wild monkeys' fear of snakes. Why do nearly all monkeys raised in the wild fear snakes, unlike lab-raised monkeys? Surely, most wild monkeys do not actually suffer snake bites. Do they learn their fear through observation? To find out, one researcher experimented (Mineka, 1985, 2002). Her study focused on six monkeys raised in the wild (all strongly fearful of snakes) and their lab-raised offspring (none fearing snakes). The young monkeys repeatedly observed their parents or peers refusing to reach for food in the presence of a snake. Can you predict what happened? The young monkeys also developed a strong fear of snakes. When they were retested three months later, their learned fear persisted. We humans similarly learn many fears by observing others (Helsen et al., 2011; Olsson et al., 2007).

Our interpretations and expectations also shape our reactions. People with anxiety-related disorders tend to be *hypervigilant*. They *attend* more to threatening stimuli. They more often *interpret* unclear stimuli as threatening (Everaert et al., 2018). A pounding heart signals a heart attack. A lone spider near the bed indicates an infestation. An everyday disagreement with a partner or boss spells doom. And they more often *remember* threatening events (Van Bockstaele et al., 2014). Anxiety is especially common when people cannot switch off such intrusive thoughts and perceive a loss of control and a sense of helplessness (Franklin & Foa, 2011).

HemeraTechnologies/PhotoObjects.net/360/Getty Images

IN YOUR EVERYDAY LIFE

What is a fear that you have learned? How were conditioning or cognition involved?

Biology

Conditioning and cognition can't explain all aspects of anxiety disorders, OCD, and PTSD. Our biology also plays a role.

Genes Genes matter. Among monkeys, fearfulness runs in families. A monkey reacts more strongly to stress if its close biological relatives have sensitive, high-strung temperaments (Suomi, 1986).

So, too, with people. Some of us have genes that make us like orchids—fragile, yet capable of beauty under favorable circumstances. Others of us are like dandelions—hardy and able to thrive in varied circumstances (Ellis & Boyce, 2008; Pluess & Belsky, 2013). Twins in general are not at higher risk for any disorder. But if one identical twin has an anxiety disorder, the other is also at risk (Polderman et al., 2015). Even when raised separately, identical twins may develop similar phobias (Carey, 1990; Eckert et al., 1981). One pair of separated identical twins independently became so afraid of water that each would wade into the ocean backward and only up to her knees. Researchers have found genes associated with OCD (Mattheisen et al., 2015; Taylor, 2013) and others associated with typical anxiety disorder symptoms (Hovatta et al., 2005).

But experience affects whether a gene will be expressed. A history of child abuse can leave tracks in the brain, increasing the chances that a genetic vulnerability to a disorder such as PTSD will be expressed (Mehta et al., 2013; Zannas et al., 2015).

The Brain Anxiety-related disorders all involve biological events. Traumatic experiences alter our brain, paving fear pathways that become easy inroads for more fear experiences (Armony et al., 1998).

Generalized anxiety disorder, panic attacks, phobias, OCD, and PTSD express themselves biologically as overarousal of brain areas involved in impulse control and habitual behaviors. These disorders reflect a brain danger-detection system gone hyperactive—producing anxiety when little danger exists. In OCD, for example, when the brain detects that something is wrong, it seems to generate

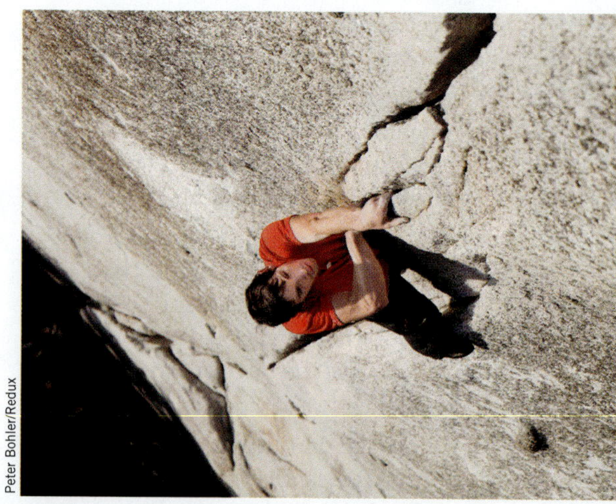

Peter Bohler/Redux

Fearless The biological perspective helps us understand why most people are more fearful of heights than Alex Honnold, shown here in 2017 becoming the first person to free solo climb (no safety ropes) Yosemite National Park's massive El Capitan granite wall. (The documentary about this feat, *Free Solo*, won a 2019 Oscar.)

a mental hiccup of repeating thoughts or actions (Gehring et al., 2000). Brain scans show elevated activity in specific brain areas during behaviors such as compulsive hand washing, checking, organizing, or hoarding (Insel, 2010; Mataix-Cols et al., 2004, 2005). Scientists are searching for specific brain cells that contribute to anxiety, with the goal of helping people to control it (Jimenez et al., 2018).

Natural Selection No matter how fearful or fearless we are, we humans seem biologically prepared to fear the threats our ancestors faced—spiders and snakes, enclosed spaces and heights, storms and darkness. Those who did not fear these threats were less likely to survive and leave descendants. Our Stone Age fears are easy to condition and hard to extinguish (Davey, 1995; Öhman, 1986). Britain has only one poisonous snake species, but Britons often fear snakes. We have these fears at very young ages. Nine-month-old infants attend more to sounds signaling ancient threats (hisses, thunder) than they do to today's dangers (a bomb exploding, breaking glass) (Erlich et al., 2013). Even some of our modern fears (such as of flying) may have their roots in our evolutionary past (of confinement and heights).

Our phobias focus on dangers our ancestors faced. Our compulsive acts typically exaggerate behaviors that helped them survive. Grooming had survival value. Gone wild, it becomes compulsive hair pulling. So, too, with washing up, which becomes ritual hand washing. And checking territorial boundaries becomes checking and rechecking already locked doors (Rapoport, 1989). Although natural selection shaped our behaviors, when taken to an extreme, these behaviors can interfere with daily life.

RETRIEVE & REMEMBER

ANSWERS IN APPENDIX E

10. Researchers believe that conditioning and cognition are aspects of learning that contribute to anxiety-related disorders. What *biological* factors contribute to these disorders?

TABLE 13.3 When Is Drug Use a Disorder?

According to the American Psychiatric Association, a person may be diagnosed with *substance use disorder* when drug use continues despite significant life disruption. Resulting brain changes may persist after quitting use of the substance (thus leading to strong cravings when exposed to people and situations that trigger memories of drug use). The severity of substance use disorder varies from *mild* (two to three of the indicators listed below) to *moderate* (four to five indicators) to *severe* (six or more indicators).
(*Source:* American Psychiatric Association, 2013.)

Diminished Control
1. Uses more substance, or for longer, than intended.
2. Tries unsuccessfully to regulate use of substance.
3. Spends much time acquiring, using, or recovering from effects of substance.
4. Craves the substance.
Diminished Social Functioning
5. Use disrupts commitments at work, school, or home.
6. Continues use despite social problems.
7. Causes reduced social, recreational, and work activities.
Hazardous Use
8. Continues use despite hazards.
9. Continues use despite worsening physical or psychological problems.
Drug Action
10. Experiences tolerance (needing more substance for the desired effect).
11. Experiences withdrawal when attempting to end use.

Substance Use Disorders

TOLERANCE AND ADDICTION

LOQ 13-9 What are *substance use disorders?*

Do you rely on caffeine pick-me-ups, such as coffee or energy drinks, to keep you going? Caffeine is usually harmless in small doses. But it still qualifies as a **psychoactive drug,** a chemical substance that changes perceptions and mood. Most of us manage to use some of these substances—even alcohol and painkillers—in moderation, without disrupting our lives. But sometimes, drug use crosses the line between moderation and **substance use disorder.** This happens when we continue to crave and use a substance that is significantly disrupting our life or putting us at risk physically (**TABLE 13.3**). Substance use disorders can endanger relationships, job and school performance, and our own and others' safety.

The DSM-5 also created separate categories for *substance/medication-induced* disorders (APA, 2018). A substance/medication-induced disorder occurs when drug use causes cognitive, emotional, and behavioral changes that resemble a

psychoactive drug a chemical substance that alters perceptions and mood.

substance use disorder a disorder characterized by continued substance craving and use despite significant life disruption and/or physical risk.

psychological disorder. The substance or medication use *induces* (brings about) the disorder. These disorders can include sexual dysfunctions and OCD, as well as bipolar, depressive, anxiety, psychotic, sleep, and neurocognitive disorders.

The three major categories of psychoactive drugs are *depressants, stimulants,* and *hallucinogens*. All do their work at the brain's synapses. They stimulate, inhibit, or mimic the activity of the brain's own chemical messengers, the neurotransmitters. But our reaction to psychoactive drugs depends on more than their *biological* effects. *Psychological* influences, including a user's expectations, and *cultural* traditions also play a role (Scott-Sheldon et al., 2012; Ward, 1994). If one culture assumes that a particular drug produces good feelings (or aggression or sexual arousal), and another does not, each culture may find its expectations fulfilled. Later, in the discussions of particular drugs, we'll take a closer look at the interaction of biopsychosocial forces. But first, to consider what contributes to the disordered use of various substances, see Thinking Critically About: Tolerance and Addiction.

TYPES OF PSYCHOACTIVE DRUGS

Depressants

LOQ 13-11 What are *depressants,* and what are their effects?

Depressants are drugs such as alcohol, barbiturates (tranquilizers), and opiates that calm (depress) neural activity and slow body functions.

Alcohol True or false? Alcohol is a depressant in large amounts but is a stimulant in small amounts. *False*. In any amount, alcohol is a depressant—it reduces neural activity and slows body functions.

Slowed Neural Functions Low doses of alcohol may, indeed, enliven a drinker, but they do so by acting as a *disinhibitor*. Alcohol slows activity in a part of the brain that controls judgment and inhibitions. As a result, the urges we would feel if sober are the ones we will more likely act upon when intoxicated. Alcohol is an equal-opportunity drug. It increases helpful tendencies, as when tipsy restaurant patrons leave big tips, or social drinkers bond as a group (Fairbairn & Sayette, 2014; Lynn, 1988). And it increases harmful tendencies, as when sexually aroused men become more aggressive. When drinking, both men and women are more disposed to casual sex (Claxton et al., 2015; Johnson & Chen, 2015).

Even the *belief* that we have consumed alcohol can influence our judgment. In one classic experiment (supposedly a study on "alcohol and sexual stimulation"), researchers gave college male volunteers either an alcoholic or a nonalcoholic drink (Abrams & Wilson, 1983). (Both drinks had a strong taste that masked any alcohol.) After watching an erotic movie clip, the men who *thought* they had consumed alcohol were more likely to report having strong sexual fantasies and feeling guilt free—whether they had actually consumed it or not. When people *believe* that alcohol affects social behavior in certain ways, and *believe* that they have been drinking alcohol, they will behave accordingly (Scott-Sheldon et al., 2012). In 14 "intervention studies," college drinkers taught that point came away with lower positive expectations of alcohol, and drank less the following month (Scott-Sheldon et al., 2014). *The point to remember:* Alcohol's effect lies partly in that powerful sex organ, the mind.

Alcohol also produces a sort of short-sightedness by focusing our attention on arousing situations (perhaps an attractive person or some apparent insult). The combination of lowered inhibitions and altered perceptions can reduce self-awareness and distract attention from future consequences (Giancola et al., 2010; Hull & Bond, 1986; Steele & Josephs, 1990).

Memory Disruption Sometimes, people drink to forget their troubles—a broken relationship, a lost game, a failed exam. And forget they do. Why? Because alcohol disrupts long-term memory processing. It does so in part by suppressing REM sleep, which helps fix the day's experiences into permanent memories. Thus, people recovering from a night of heavy drinking may have blackouts—unable to recall who they met the night before, or what they said or did.

Heavy drinking can have long-term effects on the brain. In rats, at a development period corresponding to human adolescence, binge drinking contributes to the death of nerve cells and reduces the birth rates of new nerve cells. It also impairs the growth of synaptic connections (Crews et al., 2006, 2007).

Slowed Body Functions Alcohol slows sympathetic nervous system activity. In low doses, it relaxes the drinker. In larger doses, it causes reactions to slow, speech to slur, and skilled performance to decline.

Alcohol is a potent sedative, especially when paired with lack of sleep. Add these physical effects to lowered inhibitions, and the result can be deadly. Worldwide, several hundred thousand lives are lost each year in alcohol-related accidents and violent crime. When sober, most drinkers believe that driving under the influence of alcohol is wrong, and insist they would not do so. When drunk, people aren't aware of how drunk they are (Moore et al., 2016). Most will drive home from a bar, even if given a Breathalyzer test and told they are intoxicated (Denton & Krebs, 1990; MacDonald et al., 1995).

tolerance a dwindling effect with regular use of the same dose of a drug, requiring the user to take larger and larger doses before experiencing the drug's effect.

withdrawal the discomfort and distress that follow ending the use of an addictive drug or behavior.

depressants drugs (such as alcohol, barbiturates, and opiates) that reduce (depress) neural activity and slow body functions.

Thinking Critically About:

Tolerance and Addiction

LOQ 13-10 What roles do tolerance and addiction play in substance use disorders, and how has the concept of *addiction* changed?

Tolerance

With continued use of alcohol and some other drugs (but not marijuana), users develop **tolerance** as their brain chemistry adapts to offset the drug effect (*neuroadaptation*). To experience the same effect, users require larger and larger doses, which increase the risk of becoming *addicted* and developing a *substance use disorder*.

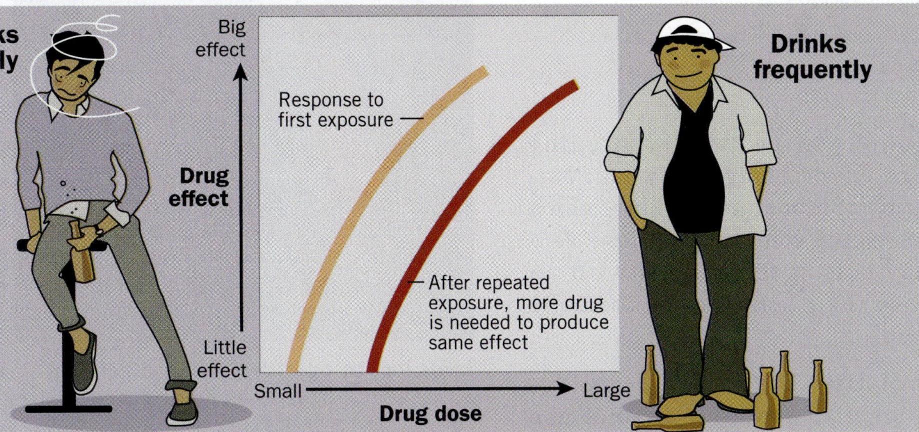

Addiction

Caused by ever-increasing doses of most psychoactive drugs (including prescription painkillers). Prompts user to crave the drug, to continue use despite adverse consequences, and to struggle when attempting to **withdraw** from it. These behaviors suggest a substance use disorder. Once in the grip of addiction, people *want* the drug more than they *like* the drug.[1]

4% of the world's people have an alcohol use disorder.[2]

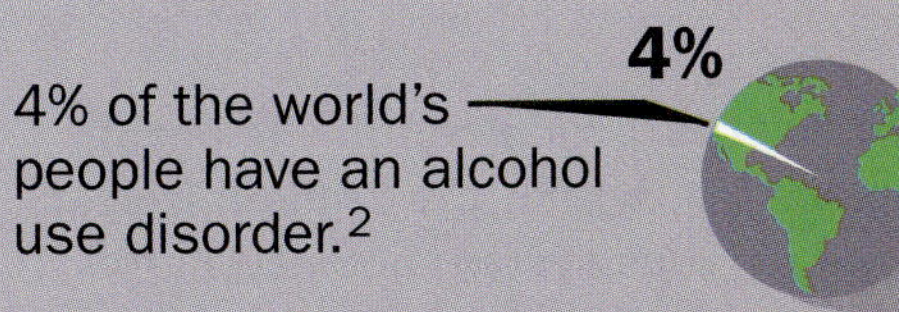

The lifetime odds of getting hooked after using various drugs:

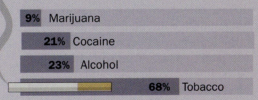

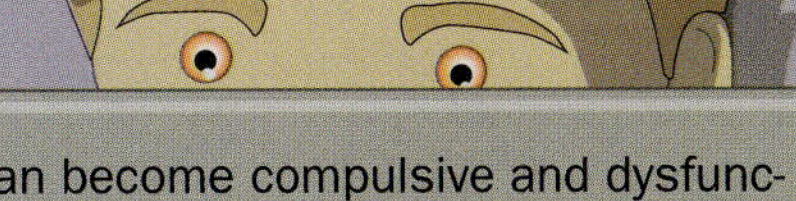

Source: National Epidemiologic Survey on Alcohol and Related Conditions[3]

Therapy or group support, such as from Alcoholics Anonymous, may help. It also helps to believe that addictions are controllable and that people can change. Many people do voluntarily stop using addictive drugs, without any treatment. Most ex-smokers have kicked the habit on their own.[4]

Behavior Addictions

Psychologists try to avoid using "addiction" to label driven, excessive behaviors such as eating, work, sex, and accumulating wealth.

Yet some behaviors can become compulsive and dysfunctional—similar to problematic alcohol and drug use.[5] Behavior addictions include *gambling disorder. Internet gaming disorder* is also now a diagnosable condition.[6] Such users display a consistent inability to resist logging on and staying on, even when this excessive use impairs their work and relationships. One international study of 19,000 gamers found that 1 in 3 had at least one symptom of the disorder. But fewer than 1 percent met criteria for a diagnosis.[7]

Psychological and drug therapies may be "highly effective" for problematic internet use.[8]

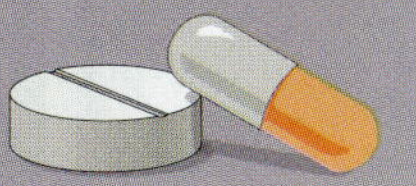

1. Berridge et al., 2009; Robinson & Berridge, 2003. 2. WHO, 2014b. 3. Lopez-Quintero et al., 2011. 4. Newport, 2013b. 5. Gentile, 2009; Griffiths, 2001; Hoeft et al., 2008. 6. WHO, 2018b. 7. Przybylski et al., 2017. 8. Winkler et al., 2013.

RETRIEVE & REMEMBER

ANSWERS IN APPENDIX E

- 11. What is the process that generally leads to drug tolerance?
- 12. Can someone become "addicted" to shopping?

Alcohol can be life threatening when heavy drinking follows an earlier period of moderate drinking, which suppresses the vomiting response. People may poison themselves with an overdose their body would normally throw up.

Alcohol Use Disorder *Alcoholism* is the popular name for **alcohol use disorder,** which can shrink the brain and contribute to premature death (Kendler et al., 2016). Its symptoms are tolerance, withdrawal, and a drive to continue using alcohol despite significant problems associated with that use. Girls and young women are especially vulnerable because they have less of a stomach enzyme that digests alcohol (Wuethrich, 2001). They can become addicted to alcohol more quickly than boys and young men. They also suffer lung, brain, and liver damage at lower consumption levels (CASA, 2003). With heavy drinking having increased among women, these gender differences have grown, with life-or-death consequences: Canadian women's risk for alcohol-related death between 2001 and 2017 grew at five times the rate of men's (Tam, 2018) (**FIGURE 13.2**).

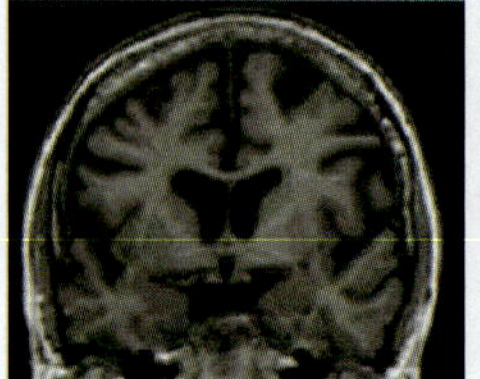
Scan of woman with alcohol use disorder
(a)

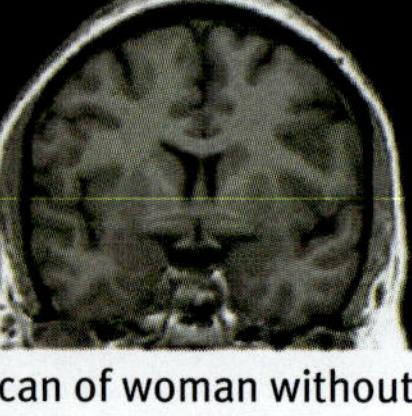
Scan of woman without alcohol use disorder
(b)

Daniel Hommer, NIAAA, NIH, HHS

FIGURE 13.2 Disordered drinking shrinks the brain MRI scans show brain shrinkage in women with alcohol use disorder (a) compared with women in a control group (b).

Theo Wargo/Getty Images

Jerod Harris/Getty Images

Lives lost to opioids Prince and Tom Petty are among the tens of thousands who have died of tragic, accidental opioid overdoses in recent years. Both musicians had been prescribed narcotic painkillers for chronic pain conditions.

Barbiturates Like alcohol, the **barbiturate** drugs, which are *tranquilizers,* depress nervous system activity. Barbiturates such as Nembutal, Seconal, and Amytal are sometimes prescribed to induce sleep or reduce anxiety. In larger doses, they can impair memory and judgment. If combined with alcohol, the total depressive effect on body functions can lead to death. This sometimes happens when people take a sleeping pill after an evening of heavy drinking.

Opiates The **opiates**—opium and its offshoots—also depress nervous system activity. Opiates include *heroin* and also its medically prescribed substitute, *methadone*. They also include pain-relief *narcotics* such as codeine, OxyContin, and morphine (and its powerful synthetic counterpart, fentanyl). As pleasure replaces pain and anxiety, the user's pupils constrict, breathing slows, and *lethargy* (a feeling of extreme relaxation and a lack of energy) sets in. Those who become addicted to this short-term pleasure may pay a long-term price: a gnawing craving for another fix, a need for progressively larger doses (as tolerance develops), and the extreme discomfort of withdrawal. When repeatedly flooded with an artificial opiate, the brain eventually stops producing *endorphins,* its own feel-good opiates. If the artificial opiate is then withdrawn, the brain will lack the normal level of these natural painkillers. Those who cannot or choose not to endure this state may pay an ultimate price—death by overdose. Between 2013 and 2017, the U.S. rate of overdose opioid deaths increased almost *ten times* to 43,036 (NIDA, 2018; NSC, 2019). "For the first time in U.S. history, a person is more likely to die from an accidental opioid overdose than from a motor vehicle crash," reported the National Safety Council in 2019.

RETRIEVE & REMEMBER

ANSWERS IN APPENDIX E

- 13. Alcohol, barbiturates, and opiates are all in a class of drugs called ____________.

Stimulants

LOQ 13-12 What are *stimulants,* and what are their effects?

A **stimulant** excites neural activity and speeds up body functions. Pupils dilate. Heart and breathing rates increase. Blood-sugar levels rise, reducing appetite. Energy and self-confidence also rise.

Stimulants include caffeine, nicotine, and the more powerful cocaine, amphetamines, methamphetamine (also known as *speed*), and Ecstasy. People use stimulants to feel alert, lose weight, or boost mood or athletic performance.

Some students resort to stimulants in hopes of boosting their grades, despite the fact that they offer little or no benefit (Ilieva et al., 2015; Teter et al., 2018). Stimulants can be addictive, as many know from the fatigue, headaches, irritability, and depression that result from missing their usual dose (Silverman et al., 1992). A mild dose of caffeine typically lasts three or four hours, which—if taken in the evening—may impair sleep.

IMPROVE YOUR EVERYDAY LIFE

Have you ever relied on caffeinated drinks to stay awake for a late-night study session, and then struggled to fall asleep afterward? How do you think this pattern affects your next-day class or work performance? How might you plan your study sessions to avoid relying on caffeine? (The student preface at the beginning of this book has some great time management tips.)

Nicotine One of the most addictive stimulants is **nicotine,** found in tobacco products. Is nicotine at least as addictive as heroin and cocaine? *Yes.*

Tobacco products include cigarettes, cigars, chewing tobacco, pipe tobacco, snuff, and—most recently—e-cigarettes. U.S. high school students use e-cigarettes more than traditional cigarettes (Johnston et al., 2018). Inhaling e-cigarette vapor ("vaping") gives users a jolt of nicotine without cancer-causing tar. E-cigarettes deliver other toxic chemicals, however, and can increase one's chances of using conventional cigarettes (Barrington-Trimis et al., 2016; Farsalinos et al., 2014). Their sales have boomed: Between 2013 and 2018, youth e-cigarette use quadrupled (CDC, 2018b). In 2018, 1 in 5 American high school students reported currently using e-cigarettes (CDC, 2018b). Teen use has prompted legal restrictions as well as investigations, including one by the U.S. Food and Drug Administration to determine whether e-cigarette companies target teenage users (Richtel & Kaplan, 2018).

Attempts to quit tobacco use even within the first weeks often fail (DiFranza, 2008). And, as with other addictions, users develop *tolerance*. Those who attempt to quit will experience nicotine-withdrawal symptoms—craving, insomnia, anxiety, irritability, and distractibility. When trying to focus on a task, their mind wanders at three times the normal rate (Sayette et al., 2010). And to make all this go away, all it takes is a single inhale.

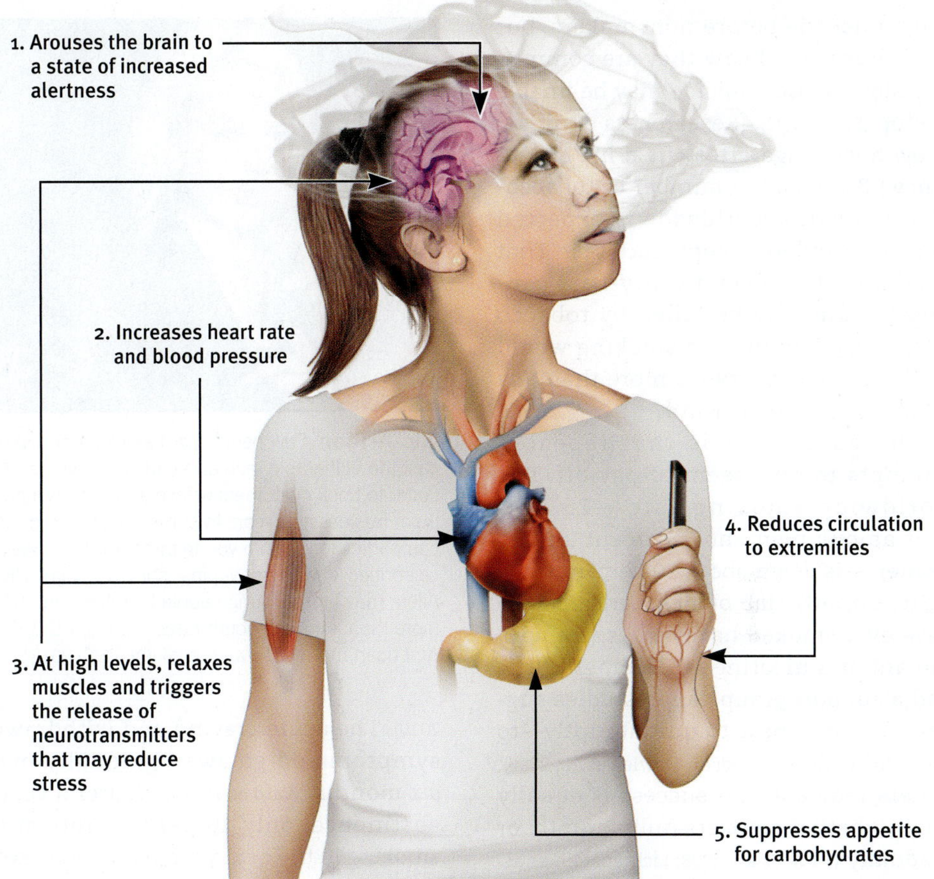
1. Arouses the brain to a state of increased alertness
2. Increases heart rate and blood pressure
3. At high levels, relaxes muscles and triggers the release of neurotransmitters that may reduce stress
4. Reduces circulation to extremities
5. Suppresses appetite for carbohydrates

FIGURE 13.3 Physiological effects of nicotine Nicotine reaches the brain within 7 seconds, twice as fast as intravenous heroin. Within minutes, the amount in the blood soars.

With that inhale, a rush of nicotine signals the central nervous system to release a flood of neurotransmitters (**FIGURE 13.3**). Epinephrine and norepinephrine diminish appetite and boost alertness and mental efficiency. Dopamine and other neurotransmitters calm anxiety and reduce sensitivity to pain (Ditre et al., 2011; Gavin, 2004). No wonder some ex-users, under stress, resume their habit. Some 1 million Americans did so after the 9/11 terrorist attacks (Pesko, 2014). Relapse is also a greater risk for people experiencing major depressive disorder (Zvolensky et al., 2015).

Cigarette smoking is the leading cause of preventable death in the United States, killing 480,000 people per year (CDC, 2018d). Although 3 in 4 cigarette smokers wish they could stop, each year fewer than 1 in 7 will be successful (Newport, 2013b). Smokers die, on average, at

alcohol use disorder (popularly known as *alcoholism*) alcohol use marked by tolerance, withdrawal, and a drive to continue problematic use.

barbiturates drugs that depress central nervous system activity, reducing anxiety but impairing memory and judgment.

opiates opium and its derivatives, such as morphine and heroin; depress neural activity, temporarily lessening pain and anxiety.

stimulants drugs (such as caffeine, nicotine, and the more powerful cocaine, amphetamines, methamphetamine, and Ecstasy) that excite neural activity and speed up body functions.

nicotine a stimulating and highly addictive psychoactive drug in tobacco products.

least a decade before nonsmokers, but even those who know they are committing slow-motion suicide may be unable to stop (Saad, 2002). (Researchers don't yet know how e-cigarettes affect life expectancy.) By 2030, the number of tobacco-related deaths worldwide is expected to reach 8 million people *each year*. That means that 1 *billion* twenty-first century people may be killed by tobacco (WHO, 2012). Eliminating smoking would increase life expectancy more than any other preventive measure.

The good news is that repeated attempts to quit seem to pay off. The worldwide smoking rate—25 percent among men and 5 percent among women—is down about 30 percent since 1990 (GBD, 2017). Half of all Americans who have ever smoked have quit, some with the aid of a nicotine replacement drug and a support group. Some studies suggest that it is best to quit abruptly—to go "cold turkey" (Lindson-Hawley et al., 2016). Others indicate that success is equally likely whether smokers quit abruptly or gradually (Fiore et al., 2008; Lichtenstein et al., 2010). The acute craving and withdrawal symptoms do go away gradually over six months (Ward et al., 1997). After a year's abstinence, only 10 percent return to smoking in the next year (Hughes et al., 2008).

VYPE/MEGA/Newscom

Nic-A-Teen Few people start smoking or vaping past the vulnerable teen and early-adult years. Eager to hook customers whose addiction will give them business for years to come, tobacco product companies focus on a young target market. Seeing celebrities smoking or vaping, such as singer Lily Allen, may tempt young people to imitate. In 2017, more than a third of youth-rated (G, PG, PG-13) American movies showed smoking (CDC, 2018c).

RETRIEVE & REMEMBER

ANSWERS IN APPENDIX E

14. What withdrawal symptoms should your friend expect when she finally decides to quit vaping?

Cocaine **Cocaine** is a powerful and addictive stimulant derived from the coca plant. The recipe for Coca-Cola originally included a coca extract, creating a cocaine tonic intended for tired elderly people. Between 1896 and 1905, Coke was indeed "the real thing." But no longer. Today, cocaine is snorted, injected, or smoked (sometimes as *crack cocaine*). It enters the bloodstream quickly, producing a rush of *euphoria*—feelings of great happiness and well-being. Those feelings continue until the brain's supply of the neurotransmitters dopamine, serotonin, and norepinephrine drops off (**FIGURE 13.4**). Then, within the hour, a crash of agitated depression follows. Many regular cocaine users chasing this high become addicted.

Cocaine use may heighten reactions, such as aggression (Licata et al., 1993). It may

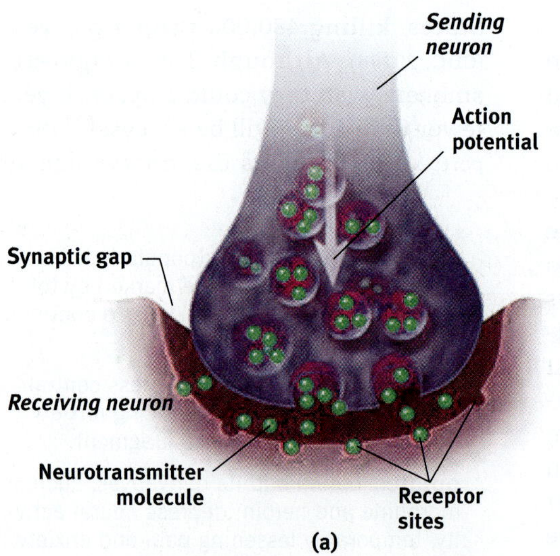

(a)

Neurotransmitters carry a message from a sending neuron across a synapse to receptor sites on a receiving neuron.

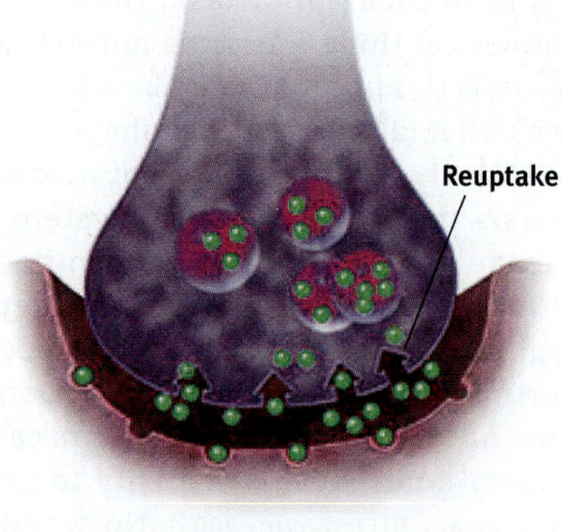

(b)

The sending neuron normally reabsorbs excess neurotransmitter molecules, a process called *reuptake*.

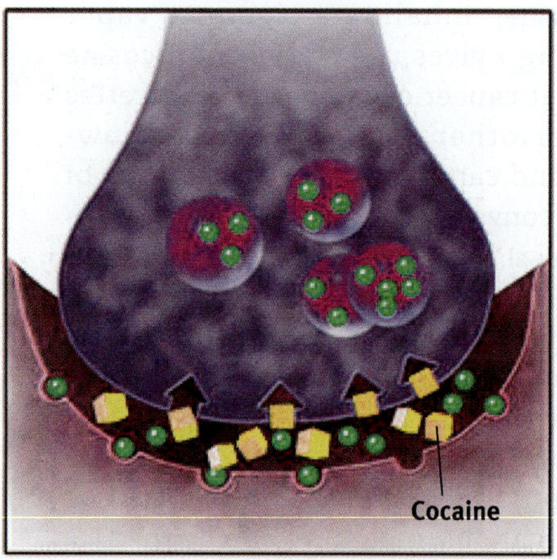

(c)

By binding to the sites that normally reabsorb neurotransmitter molecules, cocaine blocks reuptake of dopamine, norepinephrine, and serotonin (Ray & Ksir, 1990). The extra neurotransmitter molecules therefore remain in the synapse, intensifying their normal mood-altering effects and producing a euphoric rush. When the cocaine level drops, the absence of these neurotransmitters produces a crash.

FIGURE 13.4 Cocaine euphoria and crash

also lead to emotional disturbances, suspiciousness, convulsions, cardiac arrest, or respiratory failure. Cocaine use is nevertheless powerfully rewarding (Keramati et al., 2017). Its psychological effects depend in part on the dosage and form consumed, but the situation and the user's expectations and personality also play a role. Given a placebo, cocaine users who *thought* they were taking cocaine often had a cocaine-like experience (Van Dyke & Byck, 1982).

Methamphetamine **Amphetamines** stimulate neural activity. As body functions speed up, the user's energy rises and mood soars. Amphetamines are the parent drug for the highly addictive **methamphetamine,** which is chemically similar but has greater effects (NIDA, 2002, 2005). Methamphetamine triggers the release of the neurotransmitter dopamine, which stimulates brain cells that enhance energy and mood. Eight or so hours of heightened energy and mood then follow. Aftereffects may include irritability, insomnia, high blood pressure, seizures, social isolation, depression, and occasional violent outbursts (Homer et al., 2008). Over time, methamphetamine may reduce the brain's normal output of dopamine.

Ecstasy **Ecstasy** is the street name for **MDMA** (methylenedioxymethamphetamine, also known in its powdered form as *Molly*). This powerful drug is both a stimulant and a mild hallucinogen. (*Hallucinogens* distort perceptions and lead to false sensory images, as we'll see next.) Ecstasy is an amphetamine derivative that triggers the brain's release of dopamine. But its major effect is releasing stored serotonin and blocking its reuptake, thus prolonging serotonin's feel-good flood (Braun, 2001). Users feel the effect about a half-hour after taking an Ecstasy pill. For three or four hours, they experience high energy and emotional elevation. In a social setting, they will feel intimately connected to the people around them. ("I love everyone!")

Ecstasy's popularity first soared in the late 1990s as a "club drug" taken at nightclubs and all-night dance parties (Landry, 2002). There are, however, reasons not to be ecstatic about Ecstasy. One is its ability to cause dehydration. With prolonged dancing, this effect can lead to severe overheating, increased blood pressure, and death. Long-term, repeated use can also damage serotonin-producing neurons. Serotonin does more than just make us feel happy. It helps regulate our body rhythms (including sleep), our disease-fighting immune system, and our memory and other cognitive functions (Laws & Kokkalis, 2007; Pacifici et al., 2001; Schilt et al., 2007; Wagner et al., 2012). Ecstasy interferes with all these functions. The decreased serotonin output can be permanent and can lead to a permanently depressed mood (Croft et al., 2001; McCann et al., 2001; Roiser et al., 2005). Ecstasy delights for the night but darkens our tomorrows.

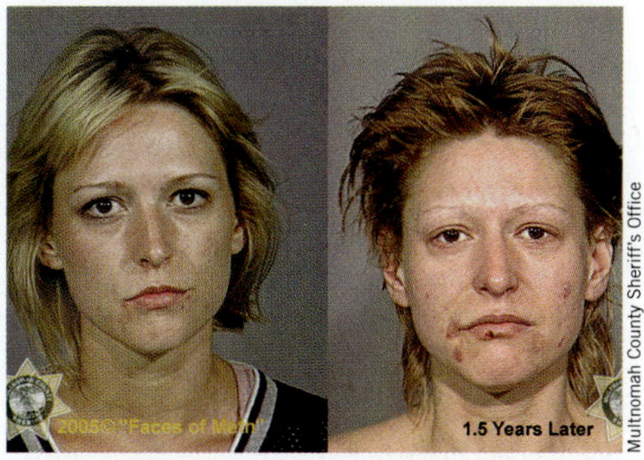

Dramatic drug-induced decline In the 18 months between these two mug shots, this woman's methamphetamine addiction led to obvious physical changes.

Hallucinogens

LOQ 13-13 What are *hallucinogens,* and what are their effects?

Hallucinogens distort perceptions and call up sensory images (such as sounds or sights) without any input from the senses. This helps explain why these drugs are also called *psychedelics,* meaning "mind-manifesting." Some are synthetic. The best-known synthetic hallucinogens are MDMA (Ecstasy) and LSD. Others, such as psilocybin and the mild hallucinogen marijuana, are natural substances.

Whether provoked to hallucinate by drugs, loss of oxygen, or extreme sensory deprivation, the brain hallucinates in basically the same way (Siegel, 1982). The experience typically begins with simple geometric forms, such as a spiral. Then come more meaningful images, which may be seen as part of a tunnel-like vision; others may be replays of past emotional experiences. Brain scans of people on an LSD (or *acid*) trip reveal that their visual cortex becomes hypersensitive and strongly connected to their brain's emotion centers (Carhart-Harris et al., 2016). As the hallucination peaks, people frequently feel separated from their body and experience dreamlike scenes. Their sense of self dissolves, as does the border between themselves and the external world (Lebedev et al., 2015).

These sensations are strikingly similar to the **near-death experience.** This altered state of consciousness is reported by about 10 to 15 percent of those revived from cardiac arrest (Agrillo, 2011; Greyson, 2010; Parnia et al., 2014).

cocaine a powerful and addictive stimulant derived from the coca plant; temporarily increases alertness and produces feelings of euphoria.

amphetamines drugs (such as *methamphetamine*) that stimulate neural activity, causing speeded-up body functions and associated energy and mood changes.

methamphetamine a powerfully addictive drug that stimulates the central nervous system with speeded-up body functions and associated energy and mood changes; over time, reduces baseline dopamine levels.

Ecstasy (MDMA) a synthetic stimulant and mild hallucinogen. Produces euphoria and social intimacy, but with short-term health risks and longer-term harm to serotonin-producing neurons and to mood and cognition.

hallucinogens psychedelic ("mind-manifesting") drugs, such as LSD, that distort perceptions and trigger sensory images in the absence of sensory input.

near-death experience an altered state of consciousness reported after a close brush with death (such as cardiac arrest); often similar to drug-induced hallucinations.

NUMAX3D/Shutterstock

FIGURE 13.5 Near-death vision or hallucination? People under the influence of hallucinogenic drugs often see "a bright light in the center of the field of vision. . . . The location of this point of light create[s] a tunnel-like perspective" (Siegal, 1977). This is very similar to others' near-death experiences.

Many describe visions of tunnels (**FIGURE 13.5**), bright lights, a replay of old memories, and out-of-body sensations (Siegel, 1980). Oxygen deprivation and other insults to the brain can produce what one philosopher-neuroscientist, Patricia Churchland (2013, p. 70), calls "neural funny business." During epileptic seizures and migraines, for example, people sometimes experience hallucinations of geometric patterns (Billock & Tsou, 2012). Solitary sailors and polar explorers have reported profound mystical experiences while enduring monotony, isolation, and cold (Suedfeld & Mocellin, 1987).

LSD In 1943, chemist Albert Hofmann reported perceiving "an uninterrupted stream of fantastic pictures, extraordinary shapes with an intense, kaleidoscopic play of colors" (Siegel, 1984). Hofmann had created and accidentally ingested **LSD (lysergic acid diethylamide).** LSD, like Ecstasy, interferes with the serotonin neurotransmitter system. An LSD trip can take users to unexpected places. Emotions may vary from euphoria to detachment to panic, depending in part on the person's mood and expectations.

Marijuana Marijuana leaves and flowers contain **THC** (delta-9-tetrahydrocannabinol). Whether smoked (getting to the brain in a mere 7 seconds) or eaten (traveling at a slower, unpredictable pace), THC produces a mix of effects. Synthetic marijuana (*K-2*, also called *Spice*) mimics THC but can have harmful side effects (agitation, hallucinations) (Fattore, 2016; Sherif et al., 2016).

Marijuana is usually classified as a mild hallucinogen, because it increases sensitivity to colors, sounds, tastes, and smells. But like the depressant alcohol, it relaxes, disinhibits, and may produce a euphoric high. And, like alcohol, it impairs motor coordination, perceptual skills, and reaction time, so it interferes with driving and the safe operation of other machines. "THC causes animals to misjudge events," reported Ronald Siegel (1990, p. 163). "Pigeons wait too long to respond to buzzers or lights that tell them food is available for brief periods; and rats turn the wrong way in mazes."

Marijuana and alcohol also differ. The body eliminates alcohol within hours, while THC and its by-products linger in the body for more than a week. Regular users may experience a less abrupt withdrawal, and achieve a high with smaller-than-usual amounts. This is the opposite of typical tolerance, in which repeat users need larger doses for the same effect.

After considering more than 10,000 scientific reports, the U.S. National Academies of Sciences, Engineering, and Medicine (2017) concluded that marijuana use

- reduces chronic pain and chemotherapy-related nausea,
- is not associated with tobacco-related diseases, such as lung cancer and damaged airways,
- predicts increased risk of traffic accidents, chronic bronchitis, psychosis, social anxiety disorder, and suicidal thoughts, and
- likely contributes to impaired attention, learning, and memory, and possibly to academic underachievement.

A marijuana user's experience can vary with the situation. If the person feels anxious or depressed, marijuana may intensify these feelings. The more often the person uses marijuana, the greater the risk of anxiety, depression, or opioid addiction (Huckins, 2017; Olfson et al., 2017; Volkow et al., 2016).

Some countries and U.S. states have passed laws legalizing marijuana possession. Greater legal acceptance helps explain why Americans' marijuana use nearly doubled between 2013 and 2016, from 7 to 13 percent (McCarthy, 2016).

* * *

TABLE 13.4 summarizes the psychoactive drugs discussed in this section. With the exception of marijuana, all trigger negative aftereffects that offset their immediate positive effects and grow stronger with repetition. This helps explain both tolerance and withdrawal.

RETRIEVE & REMEMBER

ANSWERS IN APPENDIX E

"How curiously [pleasure] is related to what is thought to be its opposite, pain! . . . Wherever the one is found, the other follows up behind." (Plato, *Phaedo,* fourth century B.C.E.)

15. How does this pleasure-pain description apply to the repeated use of psychoactive drugs?

LaunchPad To review the basic psychoactive drugs and their actions, and to play the role of experimenter as you administer drugs and observe their effects, visit *Topic Tutorial: PsychSim6, Your Mind on Drugs.*

UNDERSTANDING SUBSTANCE USE DISORDERS

LOQ 13-14 What biological, psychological, and social-cultural factors help explain why some people abuse mind-altering drugs?

Substance use by North American youth increased during the 1970s. Then, with increased drug education and a shift toward more realistic and less glamorous media portrayals of the effects of drugs, substance use declined sharply (except for

TABLE 13.4 A Guide to Selected Psychoactive Drugs

Drug	Type	Pleasurable Effects	Negative Aftereffects
Alcohol	Depressant	Initial high followed by relaxation and disinhibition	Depression, memory loss, organ damage, impaired reactions
Heroin	Depressant	Rush of euphoria, relief from pain	Depressed physiology, agonizing withdrawal
Caffeine	Stimulant	Increased alertness and wakefulness	Anxiety, restlessness, and insomnia in high doses; uncomfortable withdrawal
Nicotine	Stimulant	Arousal and relaxation, sense of well-being	Heart and lung disease, cancer
Cocaine	Stimulant	Rush of euphoria, confidence, energy	Cardiovascular stress, suspiciousness, depressive crash
Methamphetamine	Stimulant	Euphoria, alertness, energy	Irritability, insomnia, hypertension, seizures
Ecstasy (MDMA)	Stimulant; mild hallucinogen	Emotional elevation, disinhibition	Dehydration, overheating, depressed mood, impaired cognitive and immune functioning
LSD	Hallucinogen	Visual "trip"	Risk of panic
Marijuana (THC)	Mild hallucinogen	Enhanced sensation, relief of pain, distortion of time, relaxation	Impaired learning and memory, increased risk of psychological disorders

a small, brief rebound in the mid-1980s). After the early 1990s, the cultural antidrug voice softened, and drugs for a time were again glamorized in music and films. Even so, drug use among high school students has been holding fairly steady (**FIGURE 13.6**).

For many adolescents, occasional drug use represents thrill seeking. Yet why do some adolescents, but not others, become regular drug users? In search of answers, researchers have tried to sort out biological, psychological, and social-cultural influences.

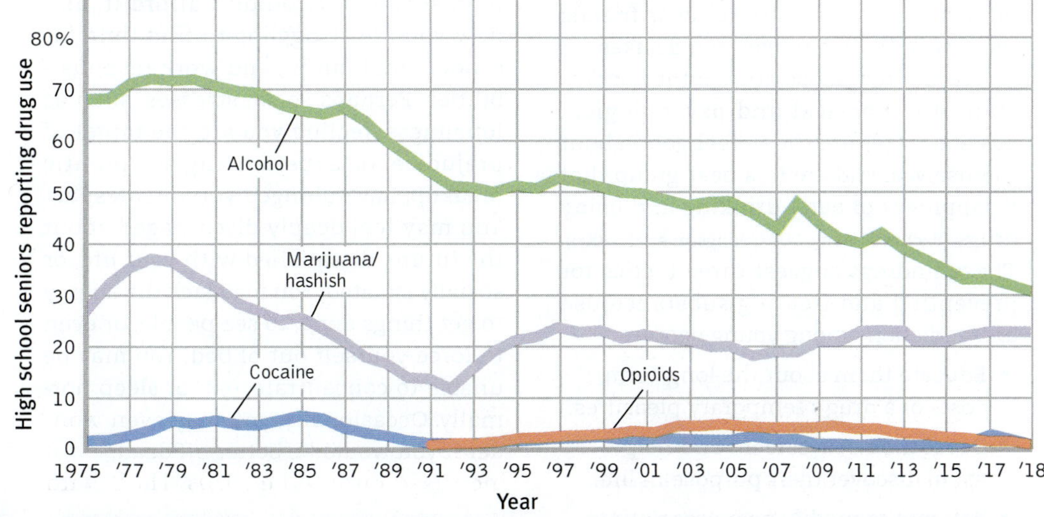

FIGURE 13.6 Trends in high school seniors' drug use The percentage of U.S. twelfth graders who said they had used alcohol or marijuana during the past 30 days largely declined from the late 1970s to the 1990s, when it partially rebounded for a few years. Reported cocaine use has declined since the mid-1980s, and opioid use peaked in 2009. (Data from Johnston et al., 2019; Miech et al., 2016.)

Biological Influences

Are some of us biologically vulnerable to particular drugs? Evidence indicates we are (Crabbe, 2002):

- If an identical rather than a fraternal twin is diagnosed with alcohol use disorder, the other twin also has an increased risk for alcohol problems (Kendler et al., 2002). In marijuana use, too, identical twins more closely resemble each other than do fraternal twins.
- Researchers have identified genes associated with alcohol use disorder, and are seeking genes that contribute to nicotine addiction (Stacey et al., 2012). These culprit genes seem to produce deficiencies in the brain's natural dopamine reward system.
- Large studies of adopted people, twins, and siblings found evidence of both genetic and environmental influences. Adoptees with drug-abusing *biological parents* were at doubled risk of drug abuse. But those with a drug-abusing *adoptive sibling* also had a doubled risk of drug abuse (Kendler et al., 2012; Maes et al., 2016). So, what might those environmental influences be?

Psychological and Social-Cultural Influences

Throughout this text, you have seen that *biological, psychological, and social-cultural influences interact to influence behavior.* So, too, with problematic drug use. One psychological factor that has appeared in studies of youth and young adults is a

LSD (lysergic acid diethylamide) a powerful hallucinogenic drug; also known as acid.

THC the major active ingredient in marijuana; triggers a variety of effects, including mild hallucinations.

feeling that life is meaningless and directionless (Newcomb & Harlow, 1986). This feeling is common among school dropouts trying to make their way in life without job skills, without privilege, and with little hope.

Sometimes, a psychological influence is obvious. Many heavy users of alcohol, marijuana, and cocaine have experienced significant stress or failure and are depressed. Girls with a history of depression, eating disorders, or sexual or physical abuse are at risk for substance addiction. So are youth undergoing school or neighborhood transitions (CASA, 2003; Logan et al., 2002). By temporarily dulling the pain of self-awareness, psychoactive drugs may offer a way to avoid coping with depression, anger, anxiety, or insomnia. The relief may be temporary, but as Chapter 6 explains, behavior is often controlled more by its immediate consequences than by its later ones.

Rates of substance use also vary across cultural and ethnic groups. Among actively religious people, alcohol and other substance addiction rates have been low, with extremely low rates among Orthodox Jews, Mormons, Mennonites, and the Amish (DeWall et al., 2014; Salas-Wright et al., 2012). African-American teens' rates of drinking, smoking, and cocaine use are sharply lower than among other U.S. teens (Johnston et al., 2007).

Substance use can also have social roots. Adolescents, self-conscious and often thinking the world is watching them, are especially vulnerable. Smoking and vaping usually begin in early adolescence. Teens may first light up to imitate glamorous celebrities, to project a mature image, to handle stress, or to get the social reward of acceptance by other users (Cin et al., 2007; DeWall & Pond, 2011; Tickle et al., 2006).

Peers influence attitudes about substance use. They throw the parties and provide (or don't provide) the drugs. If teens' friends abuse drugs, odds are that they will, too. If the friends do not, the opportunity may not even arise.

Adolescents' expectations—what they *believe* their friends are doing and favoring—matter, too. One study surveyed

SNAPSHOTS

Once upon a time, peer pressure caused Bob to start smoking.

Twenty years later, it forces him to quit.

©Jason Love

sixth-graders in 22 U.S. states. How many believed their friends had smoked marijuana? About 14 percent. How many of those friends said they had smoked it? Only 4 percent (Wren, 1999). College students have similar misperceptions. Drinking dominates social occasions partly because students overestimate their fellow students' enthusiasm for alcohol and underestimate their view of its risks (Moreira et al., 2009; Prentice & Miller, 1993; Self, 1994). As always with correlations, the traffic between friends' drug use and our own may be two-way. Our friends influence us, but we also select as friends those who share our likes and dislikes.

Teens rarely abuse drugs if they understand the physical and psychological costs, do well in school, feel good about themselves, and are in a peer group that disapproves of early drinking and using drugs (Bachman et al., 2007; Hingson et al., 2006). These findings suggest three tactics for preventing and treating substance use and addiction among young people:

- Educate them about the long-term costs of a drug's temporary pleasures.
- Boost their self-esteem and help them discover their purpose in life.
- Attempt to modify peer associations or to "inoculate" youth against peer pressures by training them in refusal skills.

IN YOUR EVERYDAY LIFE

Think of a friend or family member who is addicted to nicotine. What do you think would be most effective to say to that person to convince them to try to quit?

RETRIEVE & REMEMBER

ANSWERS IN APPENDIX E

16. Studies have found that people who begin drinking in their early teens are much more likely to develop alcohol use disorder than are those who begin at age 21 or after. What possible explanations might there be for this correlation?

Major Depressive Disorder and Bipolar Disorder

LOQ 13-15 How do major depressive disorder and bipolar disorder differ?

In the past year, have you at some time "felt so depressed that it was difficult to function"? If so, you were not alone. In one national survey, 31 percent of American college students answered *Yes* (ACHA, 2009).

Attending college is often exciting, but it can also be stressful. Perhaps you wanted to attend college right out of high school but couldn't afford it, and now you are struggling to find time for school amid family and work responsibilities. Perhaps social stresses, such as loneliness, feeling you are the target of prejudice, or experiencing a romantic breakup, have plunged you into despair. You may feel deeply discouraged about the future, dissatisfied with your life, or socially isolated. You may lack the energy to get things done, to see people, or even to force yourself out of bed. You may be unable to concentrate, eat, or sleep normally. Occasionally, you may even wonder if you would be better off dead.

"Depression is a silent, slow motion tsunami of dark breaking over me." —Effy Redman, "Waiting for Depression to Lift," 2017

Depression makes sense from an evolutionary perspective. To feel bad in reaction to very sad events is to be in touch with reality. At such times, depression is like a car's low-fuel light—a warning signal that we should stop and take appropriate measures. Biologically speaking, life's purpose is survival and reproduction, not happiness. Just as coughing, vomiting, and various forms of pain protect our body from danger, so depression protects us. It slows us down, prompting us, when losing a relationship or blocked from a goal, to conserve energy (Beck & Bredemeier, 2016; Gershon et al., 2016). It defuses aggression, reduces risk taking, and focuses our mind (Allen & Badcock, 2003; Andrews & Thomson, 2009a). As one social psychologist warned, "If someone offered you a pill that would make you permanently happy, you would be well advised to run fast and run far. Emotion is a compass that tells us what to do, and a compass that is perpetually stuck on NORTH is worthless" (Gilbert, 2006).

There is sense to suffering. After reassessing our life, we may redirect our energy in more promising ways. Even mild sadness helps people process and recall faces more accurately (Hills et al., 2011). They also tend to be better at critical thinking (and less easily fooled), pay more attention to details, and make better decisions (Forgas, 2009, 2017). Bad moods can serve good purposes.

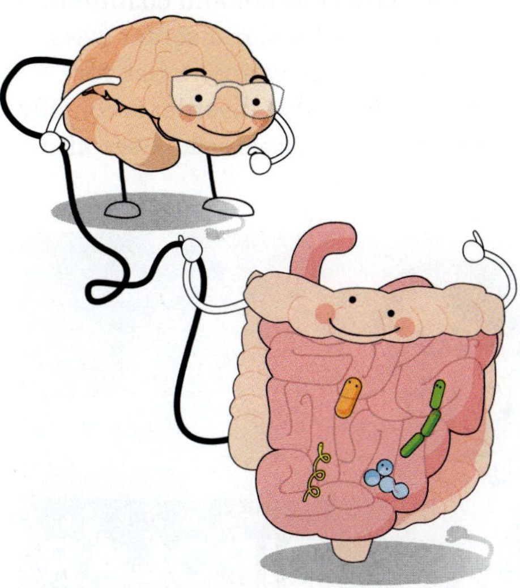

Minding the gut Does food affect mood? Digestive system bacteria produce neurotransmitters that influence emotions. Although some researchers think the gut-mood relationship is over-hyped, healthy, diverse gut microbes do at least correlate with a reduced risk of anxiety, depression, and PTSD (Hemmings et al., 2017; Hooks et al., 2019; Liu, 2017).

TABLE 13.5 Diagnosing Major Depressive Disorder

The DSM-5 classifies major depressive disorder as the presence of at least five of the following symptoms over a 2-week period of time (minimally including depressed mood or reduced interest) (American Psychiatric Association, 2013).
• Depressed mood most of the time
• Dramatically reduced interest or enjoyment in most activities most of the time
• Significant challenges regulating appetite and weight
• Significant challenges regulating sleep
• Physical agitation or lethargy
• Feeling listless or with much less energy
• Feeling worthless, or feeling unwarranted guilt
• Problems in thinking, concentrating, or making decisions
• Thinking repetitively of death and suicide

Sometimes, however, depression becomes seriously maladaptive. Let's look more closely at *major depressive disorder,* a state of hopelessness and lethargy lasting several weeks or months, and *bipolar disorder,* alternating states of depression and overexcited hyperactivity.

IMPROVE YOUR EVERYDAY LIFE

Has student life ever made you feel depressed or anxious? What advice would you have for new students (perhaps that you wish someone had given to you)?

MAJOR DEPRESSIVE DISORDER

Joy, contentment, sadness, and despair are different points on a continuum, points at which any of us may be found at any given moment. The difference between a blue mood after bad news and **major depressive disorder** is like the difference between breathing heavily after a hard run and being chronically exhausted (see **TABLE 13.5**). To sense what major depressive disorder feels like, imagine combining the anguish of grief with the exhaustion you would feel after pulling an all-nighter.

Depression is the number-one reason people seek mental health services. Indeed, the World Health Organization declared depression "the leading cause of disability worldwide" (WHO, 2017a). In one survey conducted in 21 countries, 4.6 percent of people interviewed were experiencing moderate or severe depression (Thornicroft et al., 2017). So were 1 in 10 U.S. adults, at some point during the prior year, according to another survey (Hasin et al., 2018).

Persistent depressive disorder is similar to major depressive disorder, but with milder symptoms that last a much longer period of time (American Psychiatric Association, 2013).

Some people's depression seems to have a *seasonal pattern,* returning each winter. When asked, "Have you cried today?" Americans in one survey said *Yes* twice as often in the winter (*Time*/CNN, 1994). Although the DSM-5 recognizes a seasonal pattern in major depressive disorder and bipolar disorder, some researchers question the idea of a seasonal pattern (LoBello, 2017; Traffanstedt et al., 2016).

major depressive disorder a disorder in which a person experiences, in the absence of drug use or a medical condition, two or more weeks with five or more symptoms, at least one of which must be either (1) depressed mood or (2) loss of interest or pleasure.

BIPOLAR DISORDER

Our genes dispose some of us, more than others, to respond emotionally to good and bad events (Whisman et al., 2014). In **bipolar disorder,** people bounce from one emotional extreme to the other (week to week, rather than day to day or moment to moment). When a depressive episode ends, a euphoric, overly talkative, wildly energetic, and excessively optimistic state called **mania** follows. But before long, the mood either returns to normal or plunges again into depression.

Recording artist Mariah Carey

Writer Virginia Woolf

Creativity and bipolar disorder There have been many creative artists, composers, writers, and musical performers with bipolar disorder. Some struggle secretly, as did Mariah Carey for 17 years. Others, like Virginia Woolf, have died by suicide.

If depression is living in slow motion, mania is fast forward. During the manic phase, people with bipolar disorder feel little need for sleep and show fewer sexual inhibitions. Feeling extreme optimism and self-esteem, they find advice irritating. Yet they need protection from their own poor judgment, which may lead to reckless spending or unsafe sex. Thinking fast feels good, but it also increases risk taking (Chandler & Pronin, 2012; Pronin, 2013).

Bipolar disorder may be associated with creativity (Taylor, 2017). Classical composer George Frideric Handel (1685–1759), who many believe suffered from a mild form of bipolar disorder, composed his nearly four-hour-long *Messiah* during three weeks of intense, creative energy (Keynes, 1980). Bipolar disorder strikes more often among people who rely on emotional expression and vivid imagery, such as poets and artists, and less often among those who rely on precision and logic, such as architects, designers, and journalists (Jamison, 1993, 1995; Kaufman & Baer, 2002; Ludwig, 1995).

Bipolar disorder is much less common than major depressive disorder, but is often more dysfunctional. It is also a potent predictor of suicide (Schaffer et al., 2015). Unlike major depressive disorder, for which women are at highest risk, bipolar disorder afflicts as many men as women. The diagnosis has risen among adolescents, whose mood swings, sometimes prolonged, may range from raging to bubbly. In the decade between 1994 and 2003, bipolar diagnoses in Americans under age 20 showed an astonishing 40-fold increase—from an estimated 20,000 to 800,000 (Carey, 2007; Flora & Bobby, 2008; Moreno et al., 2007). The DSM-5 classifications have, however, begun to reduce the number of child and adolescent bipolar diagnoses. Some of those who are persistently irritable and who have frequent and recurring behavior outbursts will now instead be diagnosed with *disruptive mood dysregulation disorder* (Faheem et al., 2017).

UNDERSTANDING MAJOR DEPRESSIVE DISORDER AND BIPOLAR DISORDER

LOQ 13-16 How can the biological and social-cognitive perspectives help us understand major depressive disorder and bipolar disorder?

From thousands of studies of the causes, treatment, and prevention of major depressive disorder and bipolar disorder, researchers have pulled out some common threads. Here, we focus primarily on major depressive disorder. Any theory of depression must explain a number of findings (Lewinsohn et al., 1985, 1998, 2003).

- ***Behavioral and cognitive changes accompany depression.*** People trapped in a depressed mood are inactive and feel alone, empty, and without a bright or meaningful future (Bullock & Murray, 2014; Khazanoy & Ruscio, 2016; Smith & Rhodes, 2014). They more often recall negative information and expect negative outcomes (my team will lose, my grades will fall, my love will fail).
- ***Depression is widespread.*** Worldwide, 350 million people have major depressive disorder and 60 million people have bipolar disorder (WHO, 2017a). Globally, women's risk for major depressive disorder is roughly double men's (Kuehner, 2017; see also

Bipolar disorder Artist Abigail Southworth illustrated her experience of bipolar disorder.

FIGURE 13.7). In one survey of more than 100,000 American youth, 14 percent of boys and 36 percent of girls experienced depression by age 17 (Breslau et al., 2017).

Women are generally more vulnerable to disorders involving internal states, such as depression, anxiety, and inhibited sexual desire. Women experience more situations that increase their risk for depression, such as receiving less pay for equal work, juggling multiple roles, and caring for children and elderly family members (Freeman & Freeman, 2013). Men's disorders tend to be more external—alcohol use disorder, and disorders related to antisocial conduct and lack of impulse control. Women often get sadder than men do; men often get madder than women do.

- ***Most major depressive episodes end on their own.*** Although therapy often speeds recovery, most people recover from depression and return to normal even without professional help. The black cloud of depression comes and, after sustained struggle, it often goes. But for about half of these people, the depression returns (Curry et al., 2011; Klein & Kotov, 2016). For about 20 percent, the condition will be chronic (Klein, 2010). An enduring recovery is more likely if: The first episode strikes later in life, there were no previous episodes, the person experiences minimal physical or psychological stress, and there is ample social support (Fuller-Thomson et al., 2016).
- ***Work and relationship stresses often precede depression.*** A significant loss or trauma—a loved one's death, a lost job, a marriage breakup, or a physical assault—increases one's risk of depression (Kendler et al., 2008; Monroe & Reid, 2009; Orth et al., 2009). So does moving to a new culture, especially for young people who have not yet formed an identity (Zhang et al., 2013). And childhood abuse doubles a person's risk of adult depression (Nelson et al., 2017). One long-term study tracked depression rates in 2000 people (Kendler, 1998). Among those who had experienced no stressful life event in the preceding month, the risk of depression was less than 1 percent. Among those who had experienced three such events in that month, the risk was 24 percent. Combating depression often means replacing stressors with meaningful, supportive relationships and activities (Heinz et al., 2018).
- ***Compared with generations past, depression strikes earlier (now often in the late teens) and affects more people.*** Although teen depression rates have recently leveled off, this earlier onset has been true in Canada, England, France, Germany, Italy, Lebanon, New Zealand, Puerto Rico, Taiwan, and the United States (Cross-National Collaborative Group, 1992; Kessler et al., 2010; Olfson et al., 2015). In North America, young adults are three times more likely than their grandparents to report having recently—or ever—suffered depression. This increase may reflect a cultural difference of today's young adults' greater openness about mental health.

Life after depression J. K. Rowling, author of the Harry Potter books, reported suffering acute depression—a "dark time," with suicidal thoughts—between ages 25 and 28. It was a "terrible place," she said, but it formed a foundation that allowed her "to come back stronger" (McLaughlin, 2010).

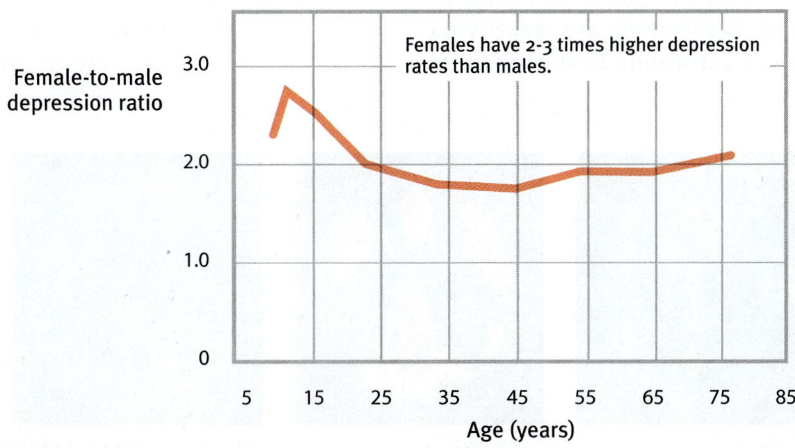

FIGURE 13.7 Female-to-male depression ratio, worldwide Compared with males, females have twice the risk of depression and a tripled rate during early adolescence (Salk et al., 2017). For many girls, the early teen years are a tough time.

bipolar disorder a disorder in which a person alternates between the hopelessness and weariness of depression and the overexcited state of mania. (Formerly called *manic-depressive disorder.*)

mania a hyperactive, wildly optimistic state in which dangerously poor judgment is common.

Armed with facts, today's researchers propose biological and cognitive explanations of depression, which are often combined in a biopsychosocial perspective.

"'Where did anxiety come from?' / Anxiety is the cousin visiting from out-of-town [that] depression felt obligated to bring to the party." —spoken-word poet Sabrina Benaim, "Explaining My Depression to My Mother," 2017

RETRIEVE & REMEMBER

ANSWERS IN APPENDIX E

17. The gender gap in depression refers to the finding that ___________ (men's/women's) risk of depression is roughly double that of ___________ (men's/women's).

LaunchPad For a 9-minute story about one young man's struggle with depression, see the *Video: Depression.*

Biological Influences

Depression is a whole-body disorder. It involves genetic predispositions and biochemical imbalances, as well as negative thoughts and a dark mood.

Genes Major depressive disorder and bipolar disorder run in families. The risk of being diagnosed with one of these disorders increases if your parent or sibling has the disorder (Sullivan et al., 2000; Weissman et al., 2016). If one identical twin is diagnosed with major depressive disorder, the chances are about 1 in 2 that at some time the other twin will be, too. If one identical twin has bipolar disorder, the chances of a similar diagnosis for the co-twin are even higher—7 in 10—even for twins raised apart (DiLalla et al., 1996). Summarizing the major twin studies, two research teams independently estimated the *heritability*—the extent to which individual depression differences are attributable to genes—of major depressive disorder at 40 percent (Kendler et al., 2018; Polderman et al., 2015; see also **FIGURE 13.8**).

To tease out the genes that put people at risk for depression, researchers may use *linkage analysis*. First, geneticists find

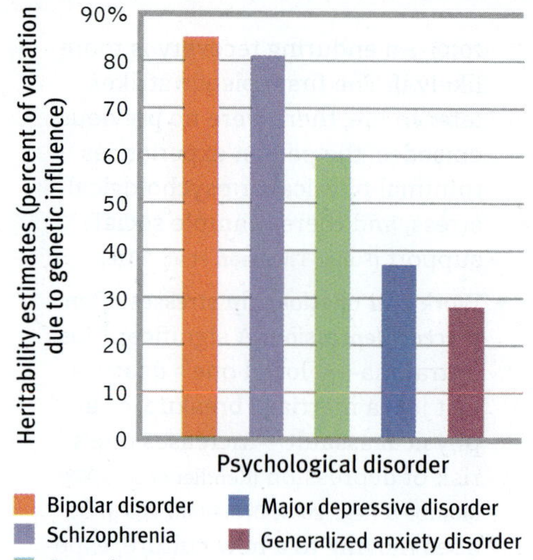

FIGURE 13.8 The heritability of various psychological disorders Using data from multiple studies of identical and fraternal twins, researchers estimated the heritability of bipolar disorder, schizophrenia, anorexia nervosa, major depressive disorder, and generalized anxiety disorder (Bienvenu et al., 2011).

families in which the disorder appears across several generations. Next, the researchers look for differences in DNA from affected and unaffected family members. Linkage analysis points them to a chromosome neighborhood; "a house-to-house search is then needed to find the culprit gene" (Plomin & McGuffin, 2003). But depression is a complex condition. Many genes work together, producing a mosaic of small effects that interact with other factors to put some people at greater risk. Researchers are identifying culprit gene variations that may open the door to more effective drug therapy (Sullivan et al., 2018).

Brain Activity Scanning devices offer a window into the brain's activity during depressed and manic states. During depression, brain activity slows. During mania, it increases (**FIGURE 13.9**). Depression can cause the brain's reward centers to become less active (Miller et al., 2015; Stringaris et al., 2015). During positive emotions, reward centers become more active (Davidson et al., 2002; Heller et al., 2009; Robinson et al., 2012).

At least two neurotransmitter systems are at work during these periods of brain inactivity and hyperactivity. Norepinephrine increases arousal and boosts mood. It is scarce during depression and overabundant during mania. Serotonin is also scarce or inactive during depression (Carver et al., 2008).

In Chapter 14, we will see how drugs that relieve depression tend to make more norepinephrine or serotonin available to the depressed brain. Repetitive physical exercise, such as jogging, which increases serotonin, can have a similar effect (Airan et al., 2007; Harvey et al., 2018; Ilardi, 2009). To get away from a bad mood, some people have used their own two feet.

Psychological and Social Influences

Biological influences contribute to depression, but as we have so often seen, nature and nurture interact. Our

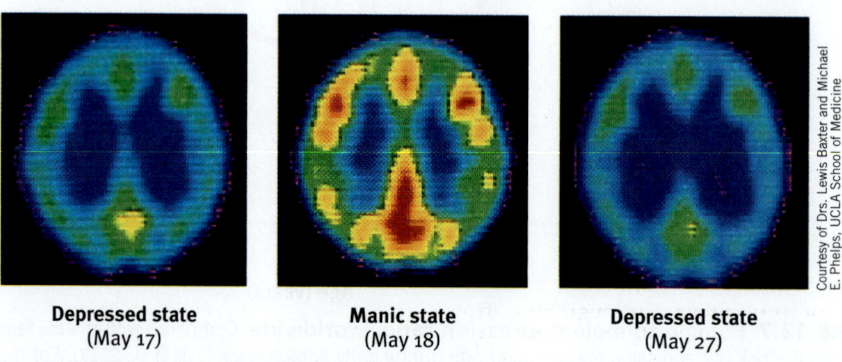

FIGURE 13.9 The ups and downs of bipolar disorder These top-facing PET scans show that brain energy consumption rises and falls with the patient's emotional switches. Red areas are where the brain rapidly consumes *glucose*, an important energy source.

life experiences—diet, drugs, stress, and other environmental influences—lay down *epigenetic marks,* molecular genetic tags that can turn certain genes on or off. Animal studies suggest that long-lasting epigenetic influences may play a role in depression (Nestler, 2011).

Thinking matters, too. The *social-cognitive perspective* explores how people's assumptions and expectations influence what they perceive. Many depressed people see life through dark glasses of low self-esteem (Orth et al., 2016). They have intensely negative views of themselves, their situation, and their future. Listen to Norman, a college professor, recalling his depression (Endler, 1982, pp. 45–49):

> I [despaired] of ever being human again. I honestly felt subhuman, lower than the lowest vermin. Furthermore, I . . . could not understand why anyone would want to associate with me, let alone love me. . . . I was positive that I was a fraud and a phony and that I didn't deserve my Ph.D. . . . I must have conned a lot of people.

Expecting the worst, depressed people magnify bad experiences and minimize good ones (Wenze et al., 2012). Their *self-defeating beliefs* and *negative explanatory style* feed their depression.

Negative Thoughts, Negative Moods, and Gender Why are women nearly twice as vulnerable as men to depression, and twice as likely to take antidepressant drugs (Pratt et al., 2017)? Women may respond more strongly to stress (Hankin & Abramson, 2001; Mazure et al., 2002; Nolen-Hoeksema, 2001, 2003). Do you agree or disagree with the statement, "I feel frequently overwhelmed by all I have to do"? In a survey of students entering American colleges, 38 percent of the women agreed (Pryor et al., 2006). Only 17 percent of the men agreed. (Did your answer fit that pattern?)

This higher risk may relate to women's tendency to *ruminate*—to overthink, fret, or brood (Nolen-Hoeksema, 2003; Spinhoven et al., 2018). Staying focused on a problem can be adaptive, thanks to the continuous firing of an attention-sustaining area of the brain (Altamirano et al., 2010; Andrews & Thomson, 2009a,b). But relentless, self-focused rumination can distract us, increase negative emotions, and disrupt daily activities (Johnson et al., 2016; Leary, 2018; Yang et al., 2017). Comparisons can also feed misery. While Wynton is happily playing video games, lonely Latifa scrolls through her social media feed and sees Maria having a blast at a party, Angelique enjoying a family vacation, and Tyra looking super in a swimsuit. In response, Latifa broods: "My life is terrible."

> "I think I, like a lot of people, have that type of brain where I find it interesting or fulfilling to worry about something." —Comedian Maria Bamford

Why do life's unavoidable failures lead only some people to become depressed? The answer lies partly in their *explanatory style*—who or what they blame for their failures (or credit for their successes). Think how you might feel if you failed a test. If you can blame someone else ("What an unfair test!"), you are more likely to feel angry. If you blame yourself, you probably will feel stupid and depressed.

I NEVER KNOW WHAT TO SAY TO PEOPLE.
NO ONE WANTS TO BE AROUND ME.
WILL I EVER GET A JOB?!
DO I SMELL BAD? I'M SO UGLY.

Rumination runs wild It's normal to think about our flaws. Sometimes, we do more than that and *ruminate:* We dwell constantly on negative thoughts, particularly negative thoughts about ourselves. Rumination makes it difficult to believe in ourselves and solve problems. People sometimes seek therapy to reduce their rumination.

Depression-prone people respond to bad events in an especially self-focused, self-blaming way (Huang, 2015; LeMoult & Gotlib, 2018; Mor & Winquist, 2002). As **FIGURE 13.10** illustrates, they explain bad events in terms that are *stable, global,* and *internal.*

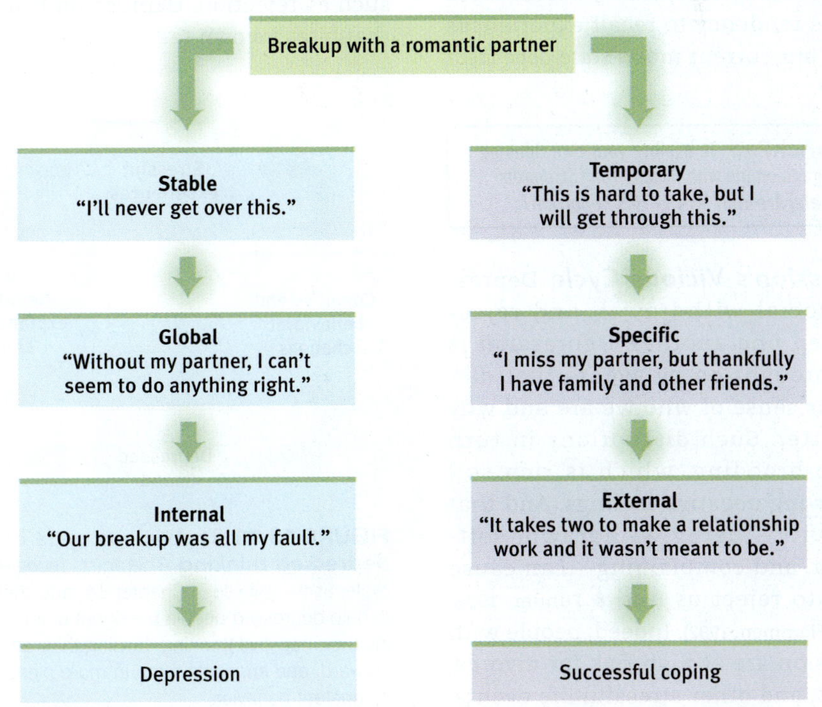

Breakup with a romantic partner
Stable
"I'll never get over this."
Global
"Without my partner, I can't seem to do anything right."
Internal
"Our breakup was all my fault."
Depression
Temporary
"This is hard to take, but I will get through this."
Specific
"I miss my partner, but thankfully I have family and other friends."
External
"It takes two to make a relationship work and it wasn't meant to be."
Successful coping

FIGURE 13.10 Explanatory style and depression

Self-defeating beliefs may arise from *learned helplessness*, the hopelessness and passive resignation humans and other animals learn (as we saw in Chapter 10) when they experience uncontrollable painful events (Maier & Seligman, 2016). Pessimistic, overgeneralized, self-blaming attributions may create a depressing sense of hopelessness (Abramson et al., 1989; Groß et al., 2017). As researcher Martin Seligman has noted, "A recipe for severe depression is preexisting pessimism encountering failure" (1991, p. 78).

Critics point out a chicken-and-egg problem nesting in the social-cognitive explanation of depression. Which comes first? The pessimistic explanatory style or the depressed mood? The negative explanations *coincide* with a depressed mood, and they are *indicators* of depression (Barnett & Gotlib, 1988). But do they *cause* depression, any more than a speedometer's reading causes a car's speed? Before or after being depressed, people's thoughts are less negative. Perhaps a depressed mood *triggers* negative thoughts. Temporarily putting people in a bad or sad mood does make their memories, judgments, and expectations more pessimistic. Memory researchers call this tendency to recall experiences that fit our current mood *state-dependent memory*.

LaunchPad To explore your own thinking style, engage online with *Assess Your Strengths: How Hopeful Are You? Why Is This Important?*

Depression's Vicious Cycle Depression, social withdrawal, and rejection feed one another. Depression is often brought on by events that disrupt our sense of who we are and why we matter. Such disruptions in turn lead to brooding, which is rich soil for growing negative feelings. And that negativity—being withdrawn, self-focused, and complaining—can cause others to reject us (Furr & Funder, 1998; Gotlib & Hammen, 1992). Indeed, people with depression are at high risk for divorce, job loss, and other stressful life events.

"You should never engage in unsupervised introspection."

New losses and stress then plunge the already depressed person into even deeper misery. Misery may love another's company, but company does not love another's misery.

We can now assemble pieces of the depression cycle (**FIGURE 13.11**): (1) Stressful experiences interpreted through (2) a brooding, negative explanatory style create (3) a hopeless, depressed state that (4) hampers the way the person thinks and acts. These thoughts and actions in turn fuel (1) further stressful experiences such as rejection. Depression is a snake that bites its own tail.

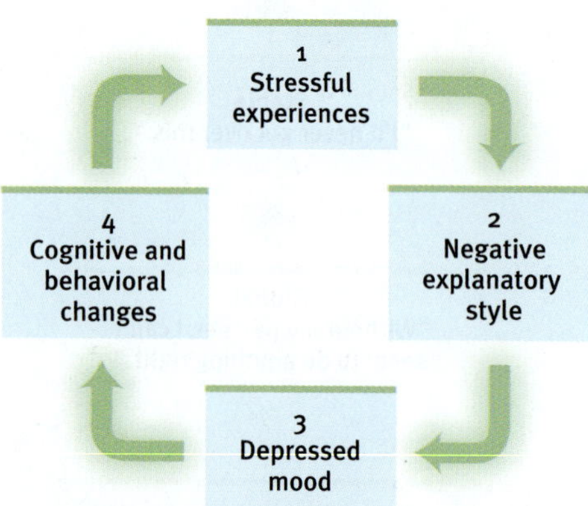

FIGURE 13.11 The vicious cycle of depressed thinking Therapists recognize this cycle, as we will see in Chapter 14, and they work to help depressed people break out of it by changing their negative thinking, turning their attention outward, and engaging them in more pleasant and competent behavior.

It is a cycle we can all recognize. Britain's Prime Minister Winston Churchill called depression a "black dog" that periodically hounded him. American President Abraham Lincoln was so withdrawn and brooding as a young man that his friends feared he might take his own life (Kline, 1974). Olympic swimming gold medalists Michael Phelps and Grant Hackett have both battled anxiety and depression (Crouse, 2017). As their lives remind us, people can and do struggle through depression. Most regain their capacity to love, to work, to hope, and even to succeed at the highest levels.

RETRIEVE & REMEMBER

ANSWERS IN APPENDIX E

18. What does it mean to say that "depression is a whole-body disorder"?

Schizophrenia

During their most severe periods, people with **schizophrenia** live in a private inner world, preoccupied with the strange ideas and images that haunt them. The word itself means "split" *(schizo)* "mind" *(phrenia)*. But in this disorder, the mind is not split into multiple personalities. Rather, the mind has suffered a split from reality that shows itself in disturbed perceptions and beliefs, disorganized speech, and diminished, inappropriate emotions. Schizophrenia is the chief example of a **psychotic disorder,** a group of disorders marked by irrationality, distorted perceptions, and lost contact with reality.

As you can imagine, these traits profoundly disrupt relationships and make it difficult to hold a job. When people with schizophrenia live in a supportive environment and receive medication, more than 40 percent will enjoy periods of normal life lasting a year or more (Jobe & Harrow, 2010). But only 1 in 7 will have a full and enduring recovery (Jääskeläinen et al., 2013).

SYMPTOMS OF SCHIZOPHRENIA

LOQ 13-17 What patterns of perceiving, thinking, and feeling characterize schizophrenia?

People with schizophrenia display symptoms that are *positive (inappropriate* behaviors are *present)* or *negative (appropriate* behaviors are *absent)*. Those with positive symptoms may experience disturbed perceptions, talk in disorganized and deluded ways, or exhibit inappropriate laughter, tears, or rage. Those with negative symptoms may have an absence of emotion in their voice, an expressionless face, or an unmoving—mute and rigid—body.

Disturbed Perceptions and Beliefs

People with schizophrenia sometimes *hallucinate*—they see, hear, feel, taste, or smell things that exist only in their minds. Most often, the hallucinations are voices, which sometimes make insulting remarks or give orders. The voices may tell the person that she is bad or that she must burn herself with a cigarette lighter. Imagine your own reaction if a dream broke into your waking consciousness, making it hard to separate your experience from your imagination. When the unreal seems real, the resulting perceptions are at best bizarre, at worst terrifying.

Hallucinations are false *perceptions*. People with schizophrenia also have disorganized, fragmented thinking often distorted by **delusions,** which are false *beliefs*. If they have *paranoid* delusions, they may believe they are being threatened or pursued.

One cause of disorganized thinking may be a breakdown in *selective attention* (Chapter 2). Normally, we have a remarkable ability to give our undivided attention to one set of sensory stimuli while filtering out others. People with schizophrenia are easily distracted by tiny, unrelated stimuli, such as the grooves on a brick or tones in a voice. But dozens of other cognitive differences are also associated with this disorder (Reichenberg & Harvey, 2007).

"Immediately, every sight, every sound, every smell coming at you carries equal weight; every thought, feeling, memory, and idea presents itself to you with an equally strong and demanding intensity." —Elyn R. Saks, *The Center Cannot Hold*, 2007

Disorganized Speech

Imagine trying to communicate with Maxine, a young woman whose thoughts spill out in no logical order. Her biographer, Susan Sheehan (1982, p. 25), observed her saying aloud to no one in particular, "This morning, when I was at Hillside [Hospital], I was making a movie. I was surrounded by movie stars. . . . I'm Mary Poppins. Is this room painted blue to get me upset? My grandmother died four weeks after my eighteenth birthday."

Jumbled ideas may make no sense even within sentences, forming what is known as *word salad*. One young man begged for "a little more allegro in the treatment," and suggested that "liberationary movement with a view to the widening of the horizon" will "ergo extort some wit in lectures."

Art by someone diagnosed with schizophrenia Commenting on the kind of artwork shown here (from Craig Geiser's 2010 art exhibit in Michigan), poet and art critic John Ashbery wrote: "The lure of the work is strong, but so is the terror of the unanswerable riddles it proposes."

Diminished and Inappropriate Emotions

The expressed emotions of schizophrenia are often utterly inappropriate, split off from reality (Kring & Caponigro, 2010). Maxine laughed after recalling her grandmother's death. On other occasions, she cried when others laughed, or became angry for no apparent reason. Others with schizophrenia lapse into an emotionless *flat affect* of no apparent feeling. For example, monetary perks fail to provide the normal brain reward center activation (Radua et al., 2015). Most also have an *impaired theory of mind*—they have difficulty reading other people's facial expressions and state of mind (Green & Horan, 2010; Kohler et al., 2010). Unable to understand others' mental states, those with schizophrenia struggle to feel sympathy and compassion (Bonfils et al., 2016). These emotional traits occur early in the illness and have a genetic basis (Bora & Pantelis, 2013). *Motor behavior* may also be inappropriate, ranging from remaining motionless for hours to senseless, compulsive actions (such as continually rocking or rubbing an arm) to severe and dangerous agitation.

ONSET AND DEVELOPMENT OF SCHIZOPHRENIA

LOQ 13-18 How do *acute schizophrenia* and *chronic schizophrenia* differ?

This year, 1 in 100 people will join an estimated 21 million others worldwide who have schizophrenia (WHO, 2017c). This disorder knows no national boundaries,

schizophrenia a disorder characterized by delusions, hallucinations, disorganized speech, and/or diminished, inappropriate emotional expression.

psychotic disorders a group of disorders marked by irrational ideas, distorted perceptions, and a loss of contact with reality.

delusion a false belief, often of persecution or grandeur, that may accompany psychotic disorders.

and typically strikes as young people are maturing into adulthood. Men tend to be diagnosed more often than women, and to be struck earlier and more severely (Aleman et al., 2003; Eranti et al., 2013; Picchioni & Murray, 2007).

For some, schizophrenia appears suddenly. Recovery is much more likely when a previously well-adjusted person develops the disorder, called **acute schizophrenia,** seemingly as a rapid reaction to particular life stresses. People with acute schizophrenia more often have positive symptoms that respond to drug therapy (Fenton & McGlashan, 1991, 1994; Fowles, 1992).

When schizophrenia is a slow-developing process, called **chronic schizophrenia,** recovery is doubtful (Harrison et al., 2001; Jääskeläinen et al., 2013). This was the case with Maxine, whose schizophrenia developed gradually, emerging from a long history of social inadequacy and poor school performance (MacCabe et al., 2008). Social withdrawal, a negative symptom, is often found among those with chronic schizophrenia (Kirkpatrick et al., 2006). Men more often exhibit negative symptoms and chronic schizophrenia (Räsänen et al., 2000).

UNDERSTANDING SCHIZOPHRENIA

Schizophrenia is one of the most heavily researched psychological disorders. Most studies now link it with abnormal brain tissue and genetic predispositions. Schizophrenia is a disease of the brain made visible in symptoms of the mind.

Brain Abnormalities

LOQ 13-19 What brain abnormalities are associated with schizophrenia?

What sorts of brain abnormalities might explain schizophrenia? Biochemical imbalances? Abnormal brain activity? Problems with brain structures or functions? Researchers are taking a close look at all of these.

Scientists have long known that strange behavior can have strange chemical causes. Have you ever heard the phrase "as mad as a hatter"? It is often thought to refer to the psychological decline of British hatmakers whose brains, it was later discovered, were slowly poisoned by the mercury-laden felt material (Smith, 1983). Could schizophrenia symptoms have a similar biochemical key?

One possible answer emerged when researchers examined schizophrenia patients' brains after death. They found an excess number of *dopamine* receptors (Seeman et al., 1993; Wong et al., 1986). What could this mean? Perhaps a high level of dopamine could intensify brain signals, creating positive symptoms such as hallucinations and paranoia (Maia & Frank, 2017). Sure enough, other evidence confirmed this idea. Drugs that block dopamine receptors often lessen the positive symptoms of schizophrenia. Drugs that increase dopamine levels, such as nicotine, amphetamines, and cocaine, sometimes intensify them (Basu & Basu, 2015; Farnia et al., 2014). But there's more to schizophrenia than abnormal brain chemistry.

Brain scans show that abnormal brain activity and brain structures accompany schizophrenia. Some people with schizophrenia have abnormally low activity in the brain's frontal lobes, which help us reason, plan, and solve problems (Morey et al., 2005; Pettegrew et al., 1993; Resnick, 1992). Others have an unusual corpus callosum, the band of nerve fibers through which the right and left hemispheres communicate (Arnedo et al., 2015).

One study took PET scans of brain activity while people with schizophrenia were hallucinating (Silbersweig et al., 1995). When patients heard a voice or saw something, their brain became vigorously active in several core regions. One was the thalamus, the structure that filters incoming sensory signals and transmits them to the brain's cortex. Another PET scan study of people with paranoia found increased activity in the amygdala, a fear-processing center (Epstein et al., 1998).

In schizophrenia, areas of the brain called ventricles become enlarged and fill with fluid; cerebral tissue also shrinks (Goldman et al., 2009; van Haren et al., 2016). These brain differences may be

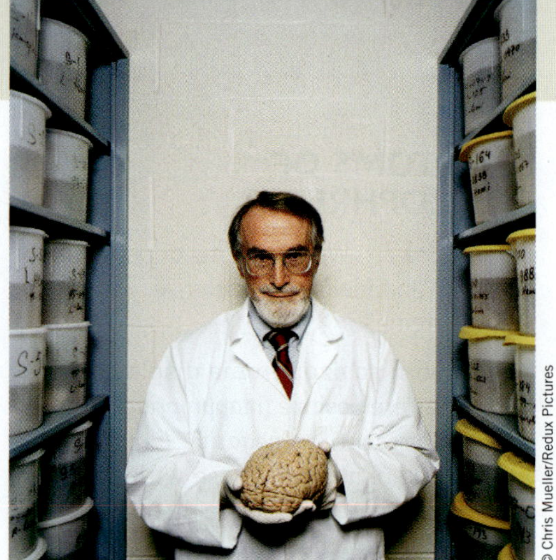

Storing and studying brains Psychiatrist E. Fuller Torrey has collected the brains of hundreds of people who died as young adults and suffered disorders such as schizophrenia and bipolar disorder.

inherited. If one identical twin's brain shows the abnormalities, the odds are at least 1 in 2 that the other twin's brain will also have them (van Haren et al., 2012). Some studies have even found brain abnormalities in people who *later* developed this disorder (Karlsgodt et al., 2010). The greater the shrinkage, the more severe the thought disorder (Collinson et al., 2003; Nelson et al., 1998; Shenton, 1992). Schizophrenia also tends to involve a loss of neural connections across the brain network (Bohlken et al., 2016; Kambeitz et al., 2016).

The bottom line: Schizophrenia involves not one isolated brain abnormality but problems with several brain regions and their interconnections (Andreasen, 1997, 2001; Arnedo et al., 2015).

Prenatal Environment and Risk

LOQ 13-20 What prenatal events are associated with increased risk of developing schizophrenia?

What causes these brain abnormalities seen in people with schizophrenia? Some researchers blame mishaps during prenatal development or delivery (Fatemi & Folsom, 2009; Walker et al., 2010). Risk factors include low birth weight, mother's diabetes, father's older age, and lack of oxygen during delivery (King et al., 2010). Famine may also increase risks. People conceived during the peak of World War II's Dutch famine developed schizophrenia at twice the normal rate. Those conceived during the famine of 1959 to 1961 in eastern China also displayed this doubled rate (St. Clair et al., 2005; Susser et al., 1996).

Let's consider another possible culprit. Might a midpregnancy viral infection impair fetal brain development (Brown & Patterson, 2011)? To test this fetal-virus idea, scientists have asked these questions:

- ***Are people at increased risk of schizophrenia if, during the middle of their fetal development, their country experienced a flu epidemic?*** The repeated answer is *Yes* (Mednick et al., 1994; Murray et al., 1992; Wright et al., 1995).
- ***Are people who are born in densely populated areas, where viral diseases spread more readily, at greater risk for schizophrenia?*** The answer, confirmed in a study of 1.75 million Danes, is *Yes* (Jablensky, 1999; Mortensen, 1999).
- ***Are people born during the winter and spring months—after the fall-winter flu season—also at increased risk?*** The answer is again *Yes* (Fox, 2010; Schwartz, 2011; Torrey & Miller, 2002; Torrey et al., 1997).
- ***In the Southern Hemisphere, where the seasons are the reverse of the Northern Hemisphere, are the months of above-average pre-schizophrenia births similarly reversed?*** Again, the answer is *Yes*. In Australia, people born between August and October are at greater risk. But people born in the Northern Hemisphere who *later* move to Australia still have a greater risk if they were born between January and March (McGrath et al., 1995; McGrath & Welham, 1999).
- ***Are mothers who report being sick with influenza or who experience extreme stress during pregnancy more likely to bear children who develop schizophrenia?*** *Yes* and *yes*. In one study of nearly 8000 women, being sick with influenza during pregnancy increased the schizophrenia risk from the customary 1 percent to about 2 percent. But that increase applied only to mothers who were infected during their second trimester (Brown et al., 2000). Another study of 200,000 Israeli mothers showed that exposure to terror attacks during pregnancy doubled their children's risk of schizophrenia (Weinstein et al., 2018).
- ***Does blood drawn from pregnant women whose offspring develop schizophrenia suggest a viral infection?*** In several studies—including one that collected blood samples from some 20,000 pregnant women—the answer has again been *Yes* (Brown et al., 2004; Buka et al., 2001; Canetta et al., 2014).

These converging lines of evidence suggest that fetal-virus infections contribute to the development of schizophrenia. This finding strengthens the U.S. government recommendation that "pregnant women need a flu shot" (CDC, 2014b).

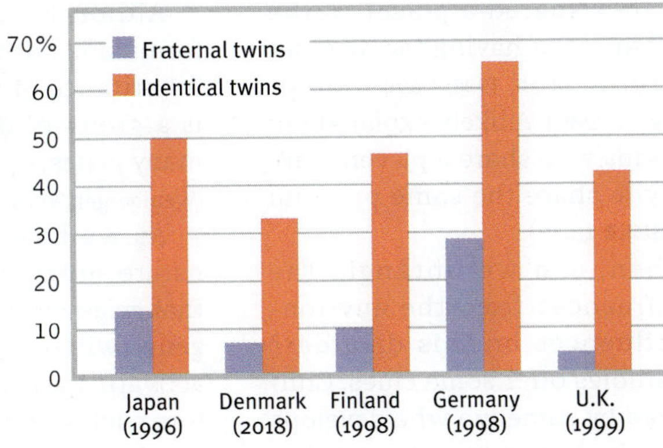

FIGURE 13.12 Risk of developing schizophrenia The lifetime risk of developing schizophrenia increases by how closely a person is related to someone having this disorder. Across countries, barely more than 1 in 10 fraternal twins, but some 5 in 10 identical twins, share a schizophrenia diagnosis. (Data from Gottesman, 2001; Hilker et al., 2018.)

Genetics and Risk

LOQ 13-21 How do genes influence schizophrenia?

Fetal-virus infections may increase the odds that a child will develop schizophrenia. But many women get the flu during their second trimester of pregnancy, and only 2 percent of their children develop schizophrenia. Why does prenatal exposure to the flu virus put some children at risk but not others? Might some people be more genetically vulnerable to this disorder? *Yes*. The 1-in-100 odds of any one person being diagnosed with schizophrenia become about 1 in 10 among those who have a sibling or parent with the disorder. If the affected sibling is an identical twin, the odds are close to 1 in 2 (**FIGURE 13.12**). Those odds are unchanged even when the twins are raised apart (Plomin et al., 1997). (Only about a dozen such cases are on record.)

But wait! Identical twins also share a prenatal environment. So, is it possible that shared germs as well as shared genes produce identical twin similarities? There is some evidence that supports this idea.

About two-thirds of identical twins also share a placenta and the blood it supplies. Other identical twins have two separate placentas. Sharing a placenta raises the odds of later sharing a schizophrenia diagnosis. If identical twins had separate placentas, the chances are

acute schizophrenia (also called *reactive schizophrenia*) a form of schizophrenia that can begin at any age, frequently occurs in response to a traumatic event, and from which recovery is much more likely.

chronic schizophrenia (also called *process schizophrenia*) a form of schizophrenia in which symptoms usually appear by late adolescence or early adulthood. As people age, psychotic episodes last longer and recovery periods shorten.

1 in 10. If they shared a placenta, the co-twin's chances of having the disorder are 6 in 10 (Davis et al., 1995; Davis & Phelps, 1995; Phelps et al., 1997). A likely explanation: Identical twins who share a placenta are more likely to share the same prenatal viruses (**FIGURE 13.13**).

How, then, can we untangle the genetic influences from the environmental influences on this disorder? Adoption studies offer some clues. Children adopted by someone who develops schizophrenia do not "catch" the disorder. Rather, adopted children have a higher risk if one of their *biological* parents has schizophrenia (Gottesman, 1991). Genes matter.

The search is on for specific genes that, in some combination, might lead to schizophrenia-inducing brain abnormalities. The largest genetic studies of schizophrenia involve scientists analyzing worldwide data from the genomes of tens of thousands of people with and without schizophrenia (Pardiñas et al., 2018; Schizophrenia Working Group, 2014). They have found 145 genome locations linked with this disorder. Some genes influence the activity of dopamine and other brain neurotransmitters. Others affect the production of *myelin,* a fatty substance that coats the axons of nerve cells and lets impulses travel at high speed through neural networks.

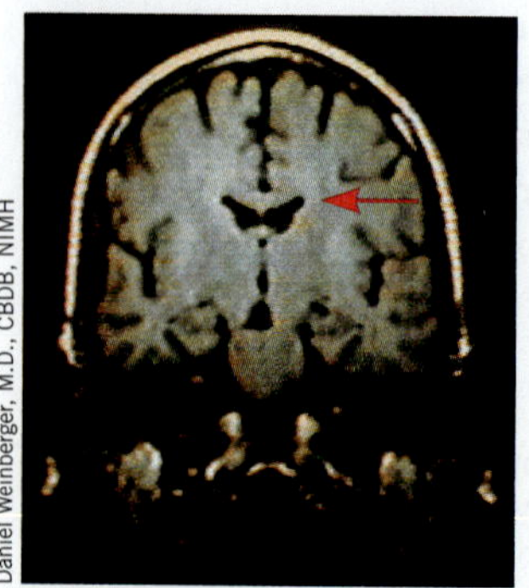

(a) No schizophrenia

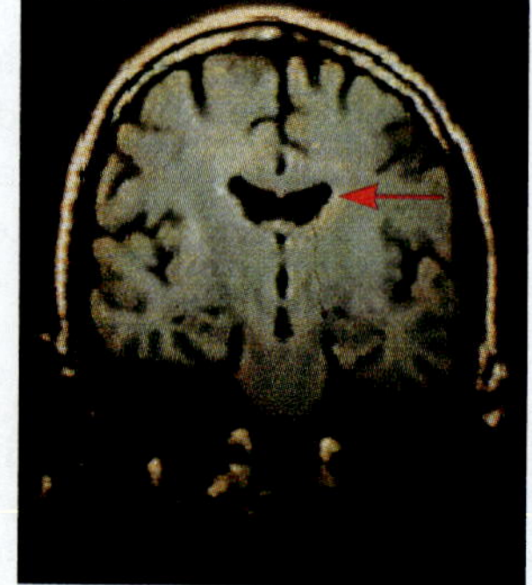

(b) Schizophrenia

Daniel Weinberger, M.D., CBDB, NIMH

FIGURE 13.13 Schizophrenia in only one identical twin When twins differ, only the brain of the one with schizophrenia typically has enlarged, fluid-filled cranial cavities (b) (Suddath et al., 1990). The difference between the twins implies some nongenetic factor, such as a virus or stress, is also at work.

Although genes matter, the genetic formula is not as straightforward as the inheritance of eye color. Schizophrenia is a group of disorders, influenced by many genes, each with very small effects (Weinberger, 2019).

As we have seen again and again, nature and nurture interact. Recall again that *epigenetic* factors influence whether genes will be expressed. Like hot water activating a tea bag, environmental factors such as viral infections, nutritional deprivation, and maternal or severe life stress can "turn on" the genes that put some of us at higher risk for this disorder. Identical twins' differing histories in the womb and beyond explain why only one may develop a disorder (Dempster et al., 2013; Walker et al., 2010). Our heredity and our life experiences work together. Neither hand claps alone.

LaunchPad To review a common research design for studying genetic influences, see the helpful tutorial animation *Video: Twin Studies.* Then take the role of a researcher studying these issues by engaging online with the activity *How Would You Know If Schizophrenia Is Inherited?*

* * *

Few of us can relate to the strange thoughts, perceptions, and behaviors of schizophrenia. Sometimes our thoughts jump around, but we rarely talk nonsensically. Occasionally, we feel unjustly suspicious of someone, but we do not believe the world is plotting against us. Often our perceptions err, but rarely do we see or hear things that are not there. We feel regret after laughing at someone's misfortune, but we rarely giggle in response to our own bad news. At times we just want to be alone, but we do not retreat into fantasy worlds. However, millions of people around the world do talk strangely, suffer delusions, hear nonexistent voices, see things that are not there, laugh or cry at inappropriate times, or withdraw into private imaginary worlds. The quest to solve the cruel puzzle of schizophrenia therefore continues, more vigorously than ever.

IN YOUR EVERYDAY LIFE

Can you recall a time when you heard something or someone casually (and inaccurately) described as "schizophrenic"? Now that you know more about this disorder, how might you correct such descriptions?

RETRIEVE & REMEMBER

ANSWERS IN APPENDIX E

19. A person with schizophrenia who has ________ (positive/negative) symptoms may have an expressionless face and toneless voice.

20. What factors contribute to the onset and development of schizophrenia?

LaunchPad For an 8-minute description of how clinicians define and treat schizophrenia, see the *Video: Schizophrenia—New Definitions, New Therapies.*

Other Disorders

EATING DISORDERS

LOQ 13-22 What are the three main eating disorders, and how do biological, psychological, and social-cultural influences make people more vulnerable to them?

Our bodies are naturally disposed to maintain a steady weight, storing energy in case food becomes unavailable. But psychological influences can overwhelm biological wisdom. Nowhere is this more painfully clear than in eating disorders.

- In **anorexia nervosa,** people—usually female adolescents, but some women, men, and boys as well—starve themselves. Anorexia often begins as an attempt to lose weight, but the dieting becomes a self-sustaining habit (Steinglass et al., 2018). Even when far below normal weight, the self-starved person feels fat, fears being fat, and focuses obsessively on losing weight, sometimes exercising excessively.

- In **bulimia nervosa**, a cycle of repeated episodes of binge eating alternates with behaviors to compensate, such as vomiting, laxative use, fasting, or excessive exercise. Unlike anorexia, bulimia is marked by weight shifts within or above normal ranges, making this disorder easier to hide. Binge-purge eaters are preoccupied with food (craving sweet and high-fat foods) and fearful of becoming overweight. They experience bouts of guilt, depression, and anxiety, especially during and following binges (Hinz & Williamson, 1987; Johnson et al., 2002).
- Those with **binge-eating disorder** engage in significant bouts of bingeing, followed by remorse. But they do not purge, fast, or exercise excessively.

At some point during their lifetime, about 2.6 million Americans (0.8 percent) meet DSM-5-defined criteria for anorexia, 2.6 million (0.8 percent) for bulimia, and 2.7 million (0.85 percent) for binge-eating disorder (Udo & Grilo, 2019). Anorexia, bulimia, and binge-eating disorder can be deadly. They harm the body and mind, resulting in shorter life expectancy and greater risk of suicide and nonsuicidal self-injury (Cucchi et al., 2016; Fichter & Quadflieg, 2016; Mandelli et al., 2018).

Sibling rivalry gone awry Twins Maria and Katy Campbell competed as children to see who could be thinner. Maria described her anorexia nervosa as "like a ball and chain around my ankle that I can't throw off" (Foster, 2011).

Understanding Eating Disorders

So, how can we explain eating disorders? Heredity matters. Identical twins share these disorders more often than fraternal twins do (Culbert et al., 2009; Klump et al., 2009; Root et al., 2010). Scientists are searching for culprit genes. Data from 15 studies indicate that having a gene that reduces available serotonin adds 30 percent to a person's risk of anorexia or bulimia (Calati et al., 2011).

But environment also matters. Families of those with anorexia tend to be competitive, high-achieving, and protective (Ahrén et al., 2013; Berg et al., 2014; Yates, 1989, 1990). And people with eating disorders often have low self-esteem, set impossible standards, fret about falling short of expectations, and worry about how others perceive them (Culbert et al., 2015; Farstad et al., 2016; Yiend et al., 2014). Some of these factors also predict teen boys' pursuit of extremely large muscles (Karazsia et al., 2017; Ricciardelli & McCabe, 2004).

Our environment includes our culture and our history. Ideal shapes vary across culture and time. In countries with high poverty rates, plump may mean prosperity and thin may signal poverty or illness (Knickmeyer, 2001; Swami et al., 2010).

Bigger less often seems better in Western cultures, where the rise in eating disorders over the last half of the twentieth century coincided with a dramatic increase in women having a poor body image (Feingold & Mazzella, 1998). Those most vulnerable to eating disorders have also been those (usually women or gay men) who most idealize thinness and have the greatest body dissatisfaction

"Up until that point, Bernice had never once had a problem with low self-esteem."

(Feldman & Meyer, 2010; Kane, 2010; Stice et al., 2010). Part of the pressure stems from images of unnaturally thin models and celebrities (Tovee et al., 1997). One former model recalled walking into a meeting with her agent, starving and with her organs failing due to anorexia (Caroll, 2013). Her agent's greeting: "Whatever you are doing, keep doing it."

Should it surprise us, then, that women who view such images often feel ashamed, depressed, and dissatisfied with their own bodies (Myers & Crowther, 2009; Tiggeman & Miller, 2010)? In one study, researchers tested media influences by

anorexia nervosa an eating disorder in which a person (usually an adolescent female) maintains a starvation diet despite being significantly underweight; sometimes accompanied by excessive exercise.

bulimia nervosa an eating disorder in which a person's binge eating (usually of high-calorie foods) is followed by inappropriate weight-loss-promoting behavior, such as vomiting, laxative use, fasting, or excessive exercise.

binge-eating disorder significant binge-eating episodes, followed by distress, disgust, or guilt, but without the behavior to compensate that marks bulimia nervosa.

giving some adolescent girls (but not others) a 15-month subscription to a teen fashion magazine (Stice et al., 2001). Vulnerable magazine readers (girls who felt dissatisfied, idealized thinness, and lacked social support) showed increased body dissatisfaction and eating disorder tendencies.

Some critics point out that there's much more to body dissatisfaction and anorexia than media effects (Ferguson et al., 2011). Peer influences, such as teasing and harassment, also matter. Nevertheless, the sickness of today's eating disorders stems in part from today's weight-obsessed culture—a culture that says "fat is bad" in countless ways.

Most people diagnosed with an eating disorder improve, as did 2 in 3 women with anorexia nervosa or bulimia nervosa in one long-term study (Eddy et al., 2017). Prevention is also possible. By teaching body acceptance, interactive programs reduce the risk of eating disorders (Beintner et al., 2012; Melioli et al., 2016; Vocks et al., 2010). By combating cultural learning, those at risk may instead live long and healthy lives.

RETRIEVE & REMEMBER

ANSWERS IN APPENDIX E

21. People with __________ (anorexia nervosa/bulimia nervosa) continue to want to lose weight even when they are underweight. Those with __________ __________ (anorexia nervosa/bulimia nervosa) tend to have a weight that fluctuates within or above normal ranges.

DISSOCIATIVE DISORDERS

LOQ 13-23 What are *dissociative disorders,* and why are they controversial?

Among the most bewildering disorders are the rare **dissociative disorders.** The person's conscious awareness is said to become separated—*dissociated*—from painful memories, thoughts, and feelings. In this state, people may suddenly lose their memory or change their identity, often in response to an overwhelmingly stressful situation.

Dissociative Identity Disorder

Dissociation itself is not so rare. Any one of us may have a fleeting sense of being unreal, of being separated from our body, of watching ourselves as if in a movie. But a massive dissociation of self from ordinary consciousness occurs in **dissociative identity disorder (DID).** At different times, two or more distinct identities seem to control the person's behavior, each with its own voice and mannerisms. Thus, the person may be prim and proper one moment, loud and flirtatious the next. Typically, the original identity denies any awareness of the other(s).

Understanding Dissociative Identity Disorder Skeptics find it suspicious that DID has such a short history. Between 1930 and 1960, the number of North American DID diagnoses was 2 per decade. By the 1980s, when the DSM contained the first formal code for this disorder, the number had exploded to more than 20,000 (McHugh, 1995a). The average number of displayed identities also mushroomed—from 3 to 12 per patient (Goff & Simms, 1993). And although diagnoses have been increasing in countries where DID has been publicized, the disorder is much less prevalent outside North America (Lilienfeld, 2017).

Skeptics have also asked if DID could be an extension of our normal capacity for identity shifts. Perhaps dissociative identities are simply a more extreme version of the varied "selves" we normally present—to our friends, say, versus our grandparents. Are clinicians who discover multiple identities merely triggering role playing by fantasy-prone people in a particular social context (Giesbrecht et al., 2008, 2010; Lynn et al., 2014; Merskey, 1992)? After all, clients do not enter therapy saying, "Allow me to introduce myselves." Rather, charge the critics, some therapists go fishing for multiple identities: "Have you ever felt like another part of you does things you can't control?" "Does this part of you have a name? Can I talk to the angry part of you?" Once clients permit a therapist to talk, by name, "to the part of you that says those angry things," they begin acting out the fantasy. Like actors who lose themselves in their roles, vulnerable people may "become" the parts they are acting out. The result may be the experience of another self.

Other researchers and clinicians believe DID is a real disorder. They cite findings of distinct brain and body states associated with differing identities (Putnam, 1991). Brain scans show shrinkage in areas that aid memory

Multiple identities in the movies Chris Sizemore's story, told in the book and movie *The Three Faces of Eve,* gave early visibility to what is now called dissociative identity disorder. This controversial disorder continues to influence modern media, as in the 2019 movie *Glass,* where James McAvoy's character displays 24 different identities.

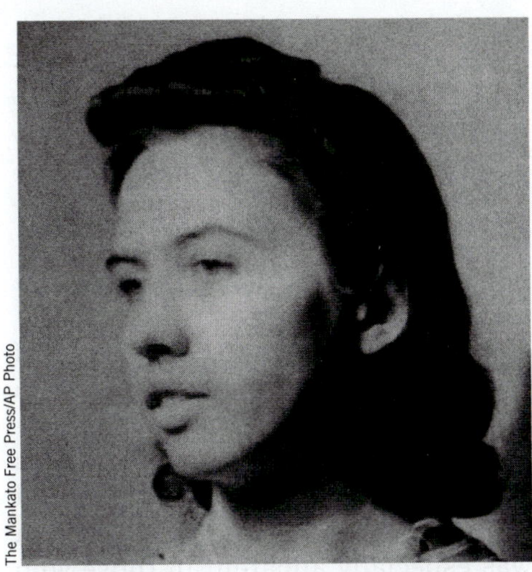

The Mankato Free Press/AP Photo

Widespread dissociation Shirley Mason was a psychiatric patient diagnosed with dissociative identity disorder. Her life formed the basis of the bestselling book, *Sybil* (Schreiber, 1973), and of two movies. The book and movies' popularity fueled North America's dramatic rise in DID diagnoses. Audio recordings revealed that Mason's psychiatrist manipulated her and that she actually did not have the disorder (Nathan, 2011).

and threat detection (Vermetten et al., 2006). Increased activity appears in brain areas linked with the control and inhibition of traumatic memories (Elzinga et al., 2007).

Both the psychodynamic and the learning perspectives have interpreted DID symptoms as ways of coping with anxiety. Some psychodynamic theorists see them as defenses against the anxiety caused by unacceptable impulses. In this view, a second identity could allow the discharge of forbidden impulses. Learning theorists see dissociative disorders as behaviors reinforced by anxiety reduction.

Some clinicians include dissociative disorders under the umbrella of posttraumatic stress disorder—a natural, protective response to traumatic experiences during childhood (Brand et al., 2016). Many people being treated for DID recall suffering physical, sexual, or emotional abuse as children (Gleaves, 1996; Lilienfeld et al., 1999). In one study of 12 murderers diagnosed with DID, 11 had suffered severe abuse, even torture, in childhood (Lewis et al., 1997). One had been set afire by his parents. Another had been used in child pornography and was scarred from being made to sit on a stove burner. Critics wonder, however, whether vivid imagination or therapist suggestion contributes to such recollections (Kihlstrom, 2005). The scientific debate continues.

IN YOUR EVERYDAY LIFE

Do you ever flip between displays of different aspects of your identity depending on the situation? How is your experience similar to and different from the described symptoms of dissociative identity disorder?

RETRIEVE & REMEMBER

ANSWERS IN APPENDIX E

22. The psychodynamic and learning perspectives agree that dissociative identity disorder symptoms are ways of dealing with anxiety. How do their explanations differ?

PERSONALITY DISORDERS

LOQ 13-24 What are the three clusters of personality disorders? What biological and psychological factors are associated with antisocial personality disorder?

There is little debate about the reality of **personality disorders.** These inflexible and enduring behavior patterns interfere with a person's ability to function socially. The ten disorders in DSM-5 tend to form three clusters, characterized by

- ***anxiety,*** such as a fearful sensitivity to rejection that predisposes the withdrawn *avoidant personality disorder.*
- ***eccentric or odd behaviors,*** such as actions prompted by the magical thinking of *schizotypal personality disorder.*
- ***dramatic or impulsive behaviors,*** such as the unstable, attention-getting *borderline personality disorder,* the self-focused and self-inflating *narcissistic personality disorder,* and—what we next discuss as an in-depth example—the callous, and often dangerous, *antisocial personality disorder.*

Antisocial Personality Disorder

The most troubling and heavily researched personality disorder is **antisocial personality disorder.** People with this disorder, typically male, can display symptoms by age 8. Their lack of conscience becomes plain before age 15, as they begin to lie, steal, fight, or display unrestrained sexual behavior (Cale & Lilienfeld, 2002). They behave impulsively and then feel and fear little (Fowles & Dindo, 2009). Not all children with these traits become antisocial adults. Those who do (about half) will generally act in violent or otherwise criminal ways, be unable to keep a job, and, if they have a spouse or children, behave irresponsibly toward them (Farrington, 1991). People with antisocial personality (sometimes called *sociopaths* or *psychopaths*) may show lower *emotional intelligence*—the ability to understand, manage, and perceive emotions (Ermer et al., 2012).

Antisocial traits, such as fearlessness and dominance, can be adaptive and do not necessarily lead to criminal behavior. If channeled in more productive directions, fearlessness may lead to athletic stardom, adventurism, or courageous heroism (Costello et al., 2018; Smith et al., 2013). Patient S. M., a 49-year-old woman with

dissociative disorders controversial, rare disorders in which conscious awareness becomes separated (dissociated) from previous memories, thoughts, and feelings.

dissociative identity disorder (DID) a rare dissociative disorder in which a person exhibits two or more distinct and alternating identities. (Formerly called *multiple personality disorder.*)

personality disorders inflexible and enduring behavior patterns that impair social functioning.

antisocial personality disorder a personality disorder in which a person (usually a man) exhibits a lack of conscience for wrongdoing, even toward friends and family members; may be aggressive and ruthless or a clever con artist.

No remorse Bruce McArthur, a 66-year-old landscaper in Toronto, shown here in a courtroom sketch, was convicted in 2019 of killing eight people over an 8-year span. He often targeted men who were gay, homeless, or immigrants, storing their remains in boxes at his job sites. McArthur exhibited the extreme lack of remorse that marks antisocial personality disorder.

amygdala damage, showed fearlessness and impulsivity but also heroism. She gave a man in need her only coat and scarf, and donated her hair to the Locks of Love charity after befriending a child with cancer (Lilienfeld et al., 2017). Lacking a sense of social responsibility, however, the same disposition may produce a cool con artist or killer (Lykken, 1995).

Do all criminals have antisocial personality disorder? Definitely not. Most criminals show responsible concern for their friends and family members.

Understanding Antisocial Personality Disorder Antisocial personality disorder is woven of both biological and psychological strands. No single gene codes for a complex behavior such as crime. There is, however, a genetic tendency toward a fearless and uninhibited life. Twin and adoption studies reveal that biological relatives of people with antisocial and unemotional tendencies are at increased risk for antisocial behavior (Frisell et al., 2012; Kendler et al., 2015b).

Genetic influences and negative environmental factors (such as childhood abuse, family instability, or poverty) can work together to help wire the brain (Dodge, 2009). This gene-environment combination also occurs in chimpanzees, which, like humans, vary in antisocial tendencies (Latzman et al., 2017). The genetic vulnerability of those with antisocial and unemotional tendencies appears as low arousal. Awaiting events that most people would find unnerving, such as electric shocks or loud noises, they show little bodily arousal (Hare, 1975; Hoppenbrouwers et al., 2016). Long-term studies show that their stress hormone levels were lower than average as teenagers, before committing any crime (**FIGURE 13.14**). And those who were slow to develop conditioned fears at age 3 were also more likely to commit a crime later in life (Gao et al., 2010).

Other brain activity differences appear in studies of antisocial criminals. Shown photographs that would produce an emotional response in most people (such as a man holding a knife to a woman's throat), antisocial criminals' heart rate and perspiration responses are lower than normal, and brain areas that typically respond to emotional stimuli are less active (Harenski et al., 2010; Kiehl & Buckholtz, 2010). Other studies have found that people with antisocial criminal tendencies have a smaller-than-normal amygdala, an emotion-controlling part of the brain (Pardini et al., 2014). They also display a hyper-reactive dopamine reward system that predisposes their impulsive drive to do something rewarding, despite the consequences (Buckholtz et al., 2010).

One study compared PET scans of 41 murderers' brains with those from people of similar age and sex. The murderers' frontal lobe, an area that helps control impulses, displayed reduced activity (Raine, 1999, 2005). This reduction was especially apparent in those who murdered impulsively. In a follow-up study, researchers found that violent repeat offenders had 11 percent less frontal lobe tissue than normal (Raine et al., 2000). This helps explain another finding: People with antisocial personality disorder fall far below normal in aspects of thinking, such as planning,

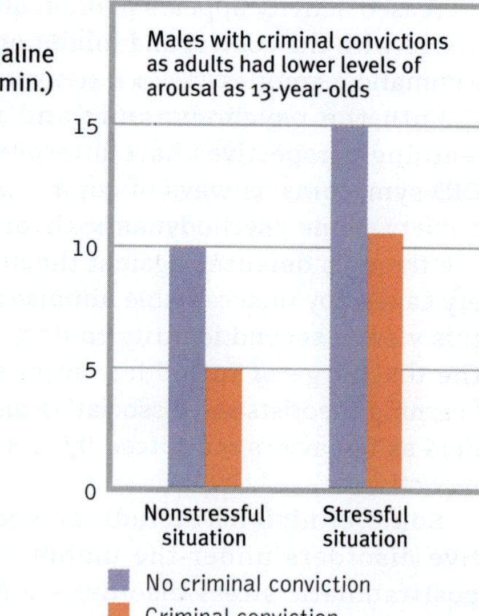

FIGURE 13.14 Cold-blooded arousability and risk of crime Levels of the stress hormone adrenaline were measured in two groups of 13-year-old Swedish boys. In both stressful and nonstressful situations, those who would later be convicted of a crime as 18- to 26-year-olds showed relatively low arousal. (Data from Magnusson, 1990.)

organization, and inhibition, which are all frontal lobe functions (Morgan & Lilienfeld, 2000). Such data remind us: Everything psychological is also biological.

RETRIEVE & REMEMBER

ANSWERS IN APPENDIX E

23. How do biological and psychological factors contribute to antisocial personality disorder?

Risk of Harm to Self and Others

People with psychological disorders are more likely to harm themselves. Are they also more likely to harm others?

UNDERSTANDING SUICIDE

LOQ 13-25 What factors increase the risk of suicide, and what do we know about nonsuicidal self-injury?

Each year some 800,000 despairing people worldwide—more than 2000 a day—will choose a permanent solution to what might have been a temporary problem (WHO, 2018a). A death by suicide will likely occur in the 40-odd seconds it takes you to read this paragraph. Men die of suicide 3.3 times more often than women in the United States and 1.8 times more often globally (WHO, 2018b). LGBTQ youth facing an unsupportive environment, including family or peer rejection, are also at increased risk of attempting suicide (Goldfried, 2001; Haas et al., 2011; Hatzenbuehler, 2011; Testa et al., 2017).

The risk of suicide is at least five times greater for those who have been depressed than for the general population (Bostwick & Pankratz, 2000). People seldom elect suicide while in the depths of depression, when energy and will are lacking. The risk increases when they begin to rebound and become capable of following through (Chu et al., 2016).

Suicide is not generally an act of hostility or revenge. People—especially older adults—may choose death as an alternative to current or future suffering, a way to switch off unendurable pain and relieve a perceived burden on family members. "People desire death when two fundamental needs are frustrated to the point of extinction," noted one suicide researcher: "The need to belong with or connect to others, and the need to feel effective with or to influence others" (Joiner, 2006, p. 47). Suicidal urges typically arise when people feel like they don't belong or are a burden to others, when they feel trapped by a seemingly inescapable situation, or when they feel incapable of experiencing joy (Chu et al., 2018; Ducasse et al., 2018; Taylor et al., 2011). Thus, suicide rates increase with unemployment during economic recessions (DeFina & Hannon, 2015; Reeves et al., 2014). Suicidal thoughts may also increase when perfectionist people are driven to achieve a goal—to become thin or straight or rich—and fall short (Chatard & Selimbegović, 2011; Smith et al., 2018).

Between 1999 and 2016, U.S. suicide rates increased about 20 percent (NIMH, 2018). The U.S. teen suicide rate rose even more, up a third since 2010 (Twenge et al., 2018a). What cultural shift may help explain rising suicide? Phone use has increased and face-to-face time with friends has decreased. Studies indicate that over time, increasing social media use predicts increased unhappiness, while unhappiness does not lead to more social media use. But stay tuned. Critics argue that the social media effect on unhappiness, although real, is small (Orben & Baukney-Przybylski, 2019).

Looking back, families and friends may recall signs that they believe should have forewarned them—verbal hints, giving possessions away, a sudden mood change, or withdrawal and preoccupation with death (Bagge et al., 2017). But few who talk or think of suicide (a number that includes one-third of all adolescents and college students) actually attempt it. Of those Americans who do attempt it, only about 1 in 25 will die (AAS, 2009). Although most attempts fail, the risk of eventual death by suicide is seven times greater among those who have attempted suicide than those who have not (Al-Sayegh et al., 2015).

Each year, about 45,000 Americans kill themselves—about two-thirds using guns. (Drug overdoses account for about 80 percent of suicide attempts, but only 14 percent of suicide fatalities.) States with high gun ownership, and weaker gun safety laws, are states with high suicide rates, even after controlling for poverty and urbanization (Anestis & Anestis, 2015; Anestis et al., 2015; Miller et al., 2002, 2016; Tavernise, 2013). Thus, although U.S. gun owners often keep a gun to feel safer, the increased risk of suicide and homicide indicates that a gun in the home *increases* the odds of a family member dying (Vyse, 2016).

How can we be helpful to someone who is talking suicide—who says, for example, "I wish I could just end it all" or "I hate my life; I can't go on"? If people write such things online, you can anonymously contact the safety teams at various social media websites (including Facebook, Twitter, Instagram, YouTube, and Tumblr). If a friend or family member talks suicide, you can

1. *listen* and empathize;
2. *connect* the person with the campus counseling center, with the Suicide Prevention Lifeline (1-800-273-TALK) or Crisis Text Line (by texting HOME to 741741) in the United States, or with their counterparts in other countries (such as CrisisServicesCanada.ca); and
3. *protect* someone who appears at immediate risk by seeking help from a doctor, the nearest hospital emergency room, or 911. Better to share a secret than to attend a funeral.

NONSUICIDAL SELF-INJURY

Self-harm takes many forms. Some people—most commonly adolescents and females—may engage in *nonsuicidal self-injury (NSSI)* (Mercado et al., 2017). Those who engage in NSSI cut or burn their skin, hit themselves, pull their hair out, poison themselves, insert objects under their nails or skin, or tattoo themselves (Fikke et al., 2011).

Why do people hurt themselves? They tend to experience bullying and harassment (van Geel et al., 2015). They are generally less able to tolerate and regulate emotional distress (Hamza et al., 2015). And they are often extremely self-critical (Cha et al., 2016). Through NSSI, they may

- gain relief from intense negative thoughts through the distraction of pain.
- attract attention and possibly get help.
- relieve guilt by punishing themselves.
- get others to change their negative behavior (bullying, criticism).
- fit in with a peer group.

Does NSSI lead to suicide? Usually not. Those who engage in NSSI are typically suicide gesturers, not suicide attempters (Nock & Kessler, 2006). But NSSI is a risk factor for suicidal thoughts and future suicide attempts, especially when coexisting with bipolar disorder (Runeson et al., 2016; Willoughby et al., 2015). If people do not find help, their nonsuicidal behavior may escalate to suicidal thoughts and, finally, to suicide attempts.

ADREES LATIF/REUTERS/Newscom

Mental health and mass shootings Following the 2012 Newtown, Connecticut, slaughter of 26 schoolchildren and adults, and again following the 2018 Parkland, Florida, massacre of 17 youth and adults, people wondered: Could mental health screenings prevent such tragedies? Could people with psychological disorders who are violence-prone (a tiny percentage) be identified in advance by mental health workers and prevented from gun ownership? It turns out that in 85 percent of U.S. mass killings between 1982 and 2017, the killer had no known prior contact with mental health professionals. Most homicide "is committed by healthy people in the grip of everyday emotions using guns" (Friedman, 2017).

DOES DISORDER EQUAL DANGER?

LOQ 13-26 What is the relationship between psychological disorders and violent acts?

Movies and television sometimes portray people with psychological disorders as homicidal, and news of mass killings reinforce public perceptions that people with psychological disorders are dangerous (Barry et al., 2013; Jorm et al., 2012). "People with mental illness are getting guns and committing these mass shootings," said U.S. Speaker of the House Paul Ryan (Editorial Board, *The New York Times*, 2015). In one survey, 84 percent of Americans agreed that "increased government spending on mental health screening and treatment" would be a "somewhat" or "very" effective "approach to preventing mass shootings at schools" (Newport, 2012). That was U.S. President Donald Trump's assumption in the aftermath of the 2018 Parkland, Florida, school massacre. He proposed opening more mental hospitals that could house would-be mass murderers: "When you have some person like this, you can bring them into a mental institution."

Do disorders actually increase risk of violence? And can clinicians predict who is likely to do harm? *No* and *no*. Most violent criminals are not mentally ill, and most mentally ill people are not violent (Skeem et al., 2016; Verdolini et al., 2018). Moreover, clinical prediction of violence is unreliable.

The few people with disorders who do commit violent acts tend to be those who experience threatening delusions and hallucinated voices that command them to act, who have suffered a financial crisis or lost relationship, or who abuse substances (Douglas et al., 2009; Elbogen, 2016; Fazel et al., 2009, 2010). Searching to explain terrible acts, we may suspect mental illness. Yet the offenders are often "ordinary" people with no obvious disorder.

People with disorders also are more likely to be *victims* than perpetrators of violence (Marley & Bulia, 2001). According to the U.S. Surgeon General's Office (1999, p. 7), "there is very little risk of violence or harm to a stranger from casual contact with an individual who has a mental disorder." *The bottom line:* Psychological disorders only rarely lead to violent acts. Thus, focusing gun restrictions only on mentally ill people is unlikely to significantly reduce gun violence (Friedman, 2012).

Better predictors of violence are use of alcohol or drugs, previous violence, gun availability, and—as in the case of the repeatedly head-injured and ultimately homicidal National Football League player Aaron Hernandez—brain damage (Belson, 2017). The mass-killing shooters do have one more thing in common: They tend to be young males. Said one psychologist,

"We could avoid two-thirds of all crime simply by putting all able-bodied young men in a cryogenic sleep from the age of 12 through 28" (Lykken, 1995).

IN YOUR EVERYDAY LIFE

Why do you think people often believe those with psychological disorders are dangerous?

* * *

The findings described in this chapter make clear the need for research and treatment to help the growing number of people, especially teenagers and young adults, who suffer the pain of a psychological disorder. Although mindful of their pain, we can also be encouraged by the many successful people who have pursued brilliant careers while enduring psychological difficulties. Eighteen of them were U.S. presidents, according to one psychiatric analysis of their biographies (Davidson et al., 2006). The bewilderment, fear, and sorrow caused by psychological disorders are real. But, as Chapter 14 shows, hope, too, is real.

CHAPTER 13 REVIEW Psychological Disorders

LEARNING OBJECTIVES

TEST YOURSELF Answer these repeated Learning Objective Questions on your own (before checking the answers in Appendix D) to improve your retention of the concepts (McDaniel et al., 2009, 2015).

What Is a Psychological Disorder?

13-1: How should we draw the line between normality and disorder?

13-2: Why is there controversy over attention-deficit/hyperactivity disorder?

13-3: How do the medical model and the biopsychosocial approach influence our understanding of psychological disorders?

13-4: How and why do clinicians classify psychological disorders, and why do some psychologists criticize the use of diagnostic labels?

Anxiety Disorders, OCD, and PTSD

13-5: How do generalized anxiety disorder, panic disorder, and phobias differ? How do anxiety disorders differ from the ordinary worries and fears we all experience?

13-6: What is *OCD?*

13-7: What is *PTSD?*

13-8: How do conditioning, cognition, and biology contribute to the feelings and thoughts that mark anxiety disorders, OCD, and PTSD?

Substance Use Disorders

13-9: What are *substance use disorders?*

13-10: What roles do tolerance and addiction play in substance use disorders, and how has the concept of *addiction* changed?

13-11: What are *depressants,* and what are their effects?

13-12: What are *stimulants,* and what are their effects?

13-13: What are *hallucinogens,* and what are their effects?

13-14: What biological, psychological, and social-cultural factors help explain why some people abuse mind-altering drugs?

Major Depressive Disorder and Bipolar Disorder

13-15: How do major depressive disorder and bipolar disorder differ?

13-16: How can the biological and social-cognitive perspectives help us understand major depressive disorder and bipolar disorder?

Schizophrenia

13-17: What patterns of perceiving, thinking, and feeling characterize schizophrenia?

13-18: How do *acute schizophrenia* and *chronic schizophrenia* differ?

13-19: What brain abnormalities are associated with schizophrenia?

13-20: What prenatal events are associated with increased risk of developing schizophrenia?

13-21: How do genes influence schizophrenia?

Other Disorders

13-22: What are the three main eating disorders, and how do biological, psychological, and social-cultural influences make people more vulnerable to them?

13-23: What are *dissociative disorders,* and why are they controversial?

13-24: What are the three clusters of personality disorders? What biological and psychological factors are associated with antisocial personality disorder?

Risk of Harm to Self and Others

13-25: What factors increase the risk of suicide, and what do we know about nonsuicidal self-injury?

13-26: What is the relationship between psychological disorders and violent acts?

TERMS AND CONCEPTS TO REMEMBER

TEST YOURSELF *Write down the definition in your own words, then check your answer.*

psychological disorder, *p. 362*
attention-deficit/hyperactivity disorder (ADHD), *p. 362*
medical model, *p. 365*
epigenetics, *p. 365*
DSM-5, *p. 365*
anxiety disorders, *p. 367*
generalized anxiety disorder, *p. 367*
panic disorder, *p. 367*
phobia, *p. 369*
obsessive-compulsive disorder (OCD), *p. 369*
posttraumatic stress disorder (PTSD), *p. 369*
psychoactive drug, *p. 371*
substance use disorder, *p. 371*
tolerance, *p. 372*
withdrawal, *p. 372*
depressants, *p. 372*
alcohol use disorder, *p. 375*
barbiturates, *p. 375*
opiates, *p. 375*
stimulants, *p. 375*
nicotine, *p. 375*
cocaine, *p. 377*
amphetamines, *p. 377*
methamphetamine, *p. 377*
Ecstasy (MDMA), *p. 377*
hallucinogens, *p. 377*
near-death experience, *p. 377*
LSD (lysergic acid diethylamide), *p. 379*
THC, *p. 379*
major depressive disorder, *p. 381*
bipolar disorder, *p. 383*
mania, *p. 383*
schizophrenia, *p. 387*
psychotic disorders, *p. 387*
delusion, *p. 387*
acute schizophrenia, *p. 389*
chronic schizophrenia, *p. 389*
anorexia nervosa, *p. 391*
bulimia nervosa, *p. 391*
binge-eating disorder, *p. 391*
dissociative disorders, *p. 393*
dissociative identity disorder (DID), *p. 393*
personality disorders, *p. 393*
antisocial personality disorder, *p. 393*

CHAPTER TEST

TEST YOURSELF Answer the following questions on your own first, then check your answers in Appendix E.

1. Two major disorders that are found worldwide are schizophrenia and ________ ________ ________.
2. Anna is embarrassed that it takes her several minutes to parallel park her car. She usually gets out of the car once or twice to inspect her distance, both from the curb and from the nearby cars. Should she worry about having a psychological disorder?
3. A therapist says that psychological disorders are sicknesses, and people with these disorders should be treated as patients in a hospital. This therapist's belief reflects the ________ model.
4. Many psychologists reject the disorder-as-illness view and instead argue that other factors may also be involved—for example, the person's level of stress and ways of coping with it. This view represents the ________ approach.
   a. medical
   b. epigenetics
   c. biopsychosocial
   d. diagnostic
5. Most psychologists and psychiatrists use ________ to classify psychological disorders.
   a. DSM descriptions and codes
   b. in-depth client histories
   c. input from clients' family and friends
   d. the theories of Pinel, Rosenhan, and others
6. A feeling of intense dread that can be accompanied by chest pains, choking sensations, or other frightening sensations is called
   a. an obsession.
   b. a compulsion.
   c. a panic attack.
   d. a specific phobia.
7. Anxiety that takes the form of an irrational and maladaptive fear and ________ of a specific object, activity, or situation is called a ________.
8. Marina became consumed with the need to clean the entire house and refused to participate in any other activities. Her family consulted a therapist, who diagnosed her as having ________ - ________ disorder.
9. The learning perspective proposes that phobias are
   a. the result of individual genetic makeup.
   b. a way of repressing unacceptable impulses.
   c. conditioned fears.
   d. a symptom of having been abused as a child.
10. After continued use of a psychoactive drug, the drug user needs to take larger doses to get the desired effect. This is referred to as ________.
11. The depressants include alcohol, barbiturates,
    a. and opiates.
    b. cocaine, and morphine.
    c. caffeine, nicotine, and marijuana.
    d. and amphetamines.
12. Why might alcohol make a person more helpful *or* more aggressive?
13. Long-term use of Ecstasy can
    a. depress sympathetic nervous system activity.
    b. deplete the brain's supply of epinephrine.
    c. deplete the brain's supply of dopamine.
    d. damage serotonin-producing neurons.
14. Near-death experiences are strikingly similar to the experiences evoked by ________ drugs.
15. Use of marijuana
    a. impairs motor coordination, perception, and reaction time.
    b. inhibits people's emotions.
    c. leads to dehydration and overheating.
    d. stimulates brain cell development.
16. An important psychological contributor to drug use is
    a. inflated self-esteem.
    b. the feeling that life is meaningless and directionless.
    c. a genetic predisposition.
    d. overprotective parents.
17. Rates of bipolar disorder in the United States rose dramatically between 1994 and 2003, especially among
    a. middle-aged women.
    b. middle-aged men.
    c. people 20 and over.
    d. people 19 and under.
18. Treatment for depression often includes drugs that increase supplies of the neurotransmitters ________ and ________.
19. Psychologists who emphasize the importance of negative perceptions, beliefs, and thoughts in depression are working within the ________-________ perspective.
20. A person with positive symptoms of schizophrenia is most likely to experience
    a. a mute and rigid body.
    b. delusions.
    c. withdrawal.
    d. flat emotion.

21. People with schizophrenia may hear voices urging self-destruction, an example of a(n) ________.

22. Valencia exclaimed, "The weather has been so schizophrenic lately: It's hot one day and freezing the next!" In addition to being insensitive to those with schizophrenia, this comparison is inaccurate. Why?

23. Chances for recovery from schizophrenia are best when

a. onset is sudden, in response to stress.

b. deterioration occurs gradually, during childhood.

c. no environmental causes can be identified.

d. there is a detectable brain abnormality.

24. Which of the following statements is true of bulimia nervosa?

a. People with bulimia continue to want to lose weight even when they are underweight.

b. Bulimia is marked by weight fluctuations within or above normal ranges.

c. Those with bulimia are equally likely to be male or female.

d. If one twin is diagnosed with bulimia, the chances of the other twin sharing the disorder are greater if they are fraternal rather than identical twins.

25. Dissociative identity disorder is controversial because

a. dissociation is quite rare.

b. it was reported frequently in the 1920s but is rarely reported today.

c. it is almost never reported outside North America.

d. its symptoms are nearly identical to those of obsessive-compulsive disorder.

26. A personality disorder, such as antisocial personality, is characterized by

a. depression.

b. hallucinations.

c. inflexible and enduring behavior patterns that impair social functioning.

d. an elevated level of autonomic nervous system arousal.

27. PET scans of murderers' brains have revealed

a. higher-than-normal activation in the frontal lobes.

b. lower-than-normal activation in the frontal lobes.

c. more frontal lobe tissue than normal.

d. no differences in brain structures or activity.

28. ________ (Women/men) are more likely than ________ (women/men) to die by suicide.

Continue testing yourself with **LearningCurve** or **Achieve Read & Practice** to learn and remember most effectively.

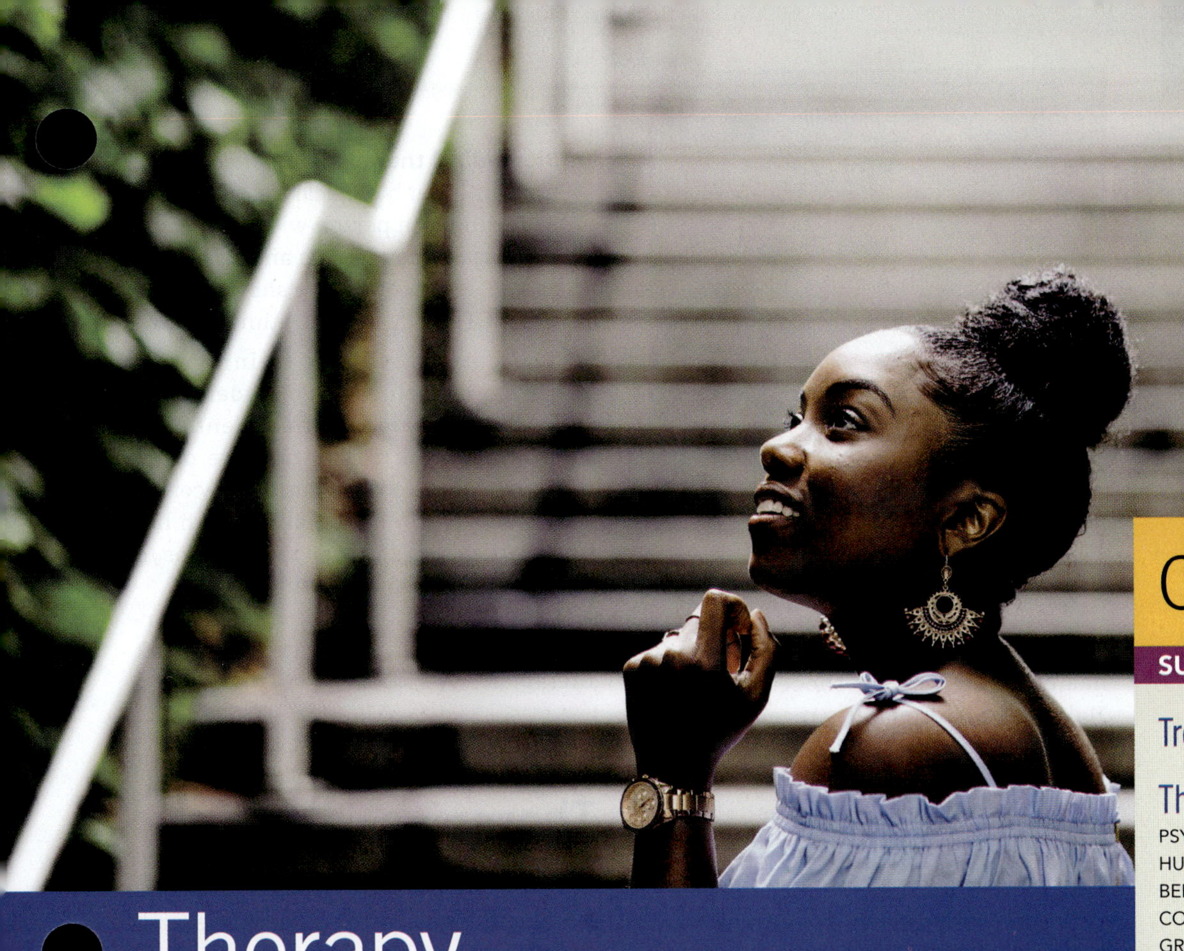

CHAPTER 14

Therapy

SURVEY THE CHAPTER

Kay Redfield Jamison is both an award-winning clinical psychologist and a world expert on the emotional extremes of bipolar disorder. She knows her subject firsthand:

> For as long as I can remember, I was frighteningly, although wonderfully, beholden to moods . . . as a child, as a young girl . . . as an adolescent. . . . Caught up in the cycles of manic-depressive illness [now known as bipolar disorder] by the time I began my professional life, I became, both by necessity and intellectual [choice], a student of moods (1995, pp. 4–5).

Jamison's life was blessed with times of intense sensitivity and passionate energy. But like her father's, it was at other times an emotional roller coaster. Reckless spending, racing conversation, and sleeplessness alternated with swings into "the blackest caves of the mind."

Then, "in the midst of utter confusion," she made a life-changing decision. Risking professional embarrassment, she made an appointment with a therapist, a psychiatrist she would visit weekly for years to come.

> He kept me alive a thousand times over. He saw me through madness, despair, wonderful and terrible love affairs, disillusionments and triumphs, recurrences of illness, an almost fatal suicide attempt, the death of a man I greatly loved, and the enormous pleasures and [frustrations] of my professional life. . . . He was very tough, as well as very kind. . . . Even though he understood more than anyone how much I felt I was losing . . . by taking medication, he never [lost] sight of the overall perspective of how costly, damaging, and life threatening my illness was. . . . Although I went to him to be treated for an illness, he taught me . . . the total beholdenness of brain to mind and mind to brain (pp. 87–89).

Actor Kerry Washington and singer Katy Perry have also shared openly about the benefits of psychotherapy. "I've been going to therapy for about five years," Perry says, "and I think it has really helped my mental health incredibly" (Chen, 2017). Catherine, Duchess of Cambridge—commonly known as Kate Middleton—has advocated to reduce the stigma surrounding mental illness and therapy: "We need to help young people and their parents understand that it's not a sign of weakness to ask for help" (Holmes, 2015).

This chapter explores some of the healing options available to therapists and the people who seek their help. We begin by exploring and evaluating *psychotherapies,* and then focus on *biomedical therapies* and preventing disorders.

Treating Psychological Disorders

Learning Objective Question LOQ 14-1

How do psychotherapy and the biomedical therapies differ?

The long history of efforts to treat psychological disorders has included a strange mix of harsh and gentle methods. Would-be healers have cut holes in people's heads and restrained, bled, or "beat the devil" out of them. But they also have given warm baths and massages and placed people in sunny and peaceful settings. They have given them drugs. And they have talked with them about childhood experiences, current feelings, and maladaptive thoughts and behaviors.

The transition to gentler methods began when reformers such as Philippe Pinel (1745–1826), Dorothea Dix (1802–1887), and others pushed for more humane treatments and for constructing mental hospitals. Their efforts largely paid off. Since the 1950s, the introduction of effective drug therapies and community-based treatment programs has emptied most of those hospitals. Today, 1 in 5 Americans receives some form of outpatient mental health therapy (Olfson et al., 2019).

Macmillan Learning

Dorothea Dix "I . . . call your attention to the state of the Insane Persons confined within this Commonwealth, in cages." (*Memorial to the Legislature of Massachusetts, 1843*)

Modern Western therapies fall into two main categories.

- In **psychotherapy,** a trained therapist uses psychological techniques to assist someone seeking to overcome difficulties and achieve personal growth. The therapist may explore a client's early relationships, encourage the client to adopt new ways of thinking, or coach the client in replacing old behaviors with new ones.

The history of treatment Visitors to eighteenth-century mental hospitals paid to gawk at patients, as though they were viewing zoo animals. William Hogarth's (1697–1764) painting captured one of these visits to London's St. Mary of Bethlehem hospital (commonly called Bedlam).

- **Biomedical therapy** offers medications or other biological treatments. For example, a person with severe depression may receive antidepressants, electroconvulsive shock therapy (ECT), or deep brain stimulation.

The care provider's training and expertise, as well as the disorder itself, influence the choice of treatment. Psychotherapy and medication are often combined. Kay Redfield Jamison received psychotherapy in her meetings with her psychiatrist, and she took medications to control her wild mood swings.

Let's look first at the psychotherapy options for those treated with "talk therapies."

The Psychological Therapies

Among the dozens of psychotherapies, we will focus on the most influential. Each is built on one or more of psychology's major theories: psychodynamic, humanistic, behavioral, and cognitive. Most of these techniques can be used one-on-one or in groups. Psychotherapists often combine multiple methods. Indeed, many psychotherapists describe their approach as **eclectic,** using a blend of therapies.

PSYCHOANALYSIS AND PSYCHODYNAMIC THERAPIES

LOQ 14-2 What are the goals and techniques of psychoanalysis, and how have they been adapted in psychodynamic therapy?

The first major psychological therapy was Sigmund Freud's **psychoanalysis.** Although few clinicians today practice therapy as Freud did, his work deserves discussion. It helped form the foundation for treating psychological disorders, and it continues to influence modern therapists working from the *psychodynamic* perspective.

The Goals of Psychoanalysis

Freud believed that in therapy, people could achieve healthier, less anxious living by releasing the energy they had previously devoted to id-ego-superego conflicts (Chapter 12). Freud assumed that we do not fully know ourselves. He believed that there are threatening things we *repress*—things we do not want to know, so we disown or deny them.

Freud's therapy aimed to bring patients' repressed feelings into conscious awareness. By helping them reclaim their unconscious thoughts and feelings, the therapist *(analyst)* would also help them gain *insight* into the origins of their disorders. This insight could in turn inspire them to take responsibility for their own growth.

The Techniques of Psychoanalysis

Psychoanalytic theory emphasizes the power of childhood experiences to mold us. Thus, psychoanalysis is historical reconstruction. It aims to unearth the past in the hope of loosening its bonds on the present. After trying and discarding hypnosis as a possible excavating tool, Freud turned to *free association.*

Imagine yourself as a patient using free association. You begin by relaxing, perhaps by lying on a couch. The psychoanalyst, who sits out of your line of vision, asks you to say aloud whatever comes to mind. At one moment, you're relating a childhood memory. At another, you're describing a dream or recent experience.

It sounds easy, but soon you notice how often you edit your thoughts as you speak. You pause for a second before describing an embarrassing thought. You skip things that seem trivial, off point, or shameful. Sometimes your mind goes blank, unable to remember important details. You may joke or change the subject to something less threatening.

To an analyst, these mental blips are blocks that indicate **resistance.** They hint that anxiety lurks and you are defending against sensitive material. The analyst will note your resistance and then provide insight into its meaning. If offered at the right moment, this **interpretation**—of, say, your not wanting to call, text, or message your mother—may reveal the underlying wishes, feelings, and conflicts you are avoiding. The analyst may also offer an explanation of how this resistance fits with other pieces of your psychological puzzle, including those based on an analysis of your dream content.

Multiply that one session by dozens and your relationship patterns will surface in your interactions with your analyst. You may find you have strong positive or negative feelings for your analyst. The analyst may suggest you are **transferring** feelings, such as dependency or mingled love and anger, that you experienced in earlier relationships with family members or other important people. By exposing such feelings, you may gain insight into your current relationships.

Relatively few U.S. therapists now offer traditional psychoanalysis. Much of its underlying theory is not supported by scientific research (Chapter 12). Analysts' interpretations cannot be proven or disproven. And psychoanalysis takes considerable time and money, often years of several expensive sessions per week. Some of these problems have been addressed in the modern *psychodynamic perspective* that has evolved from psychoanalysis.

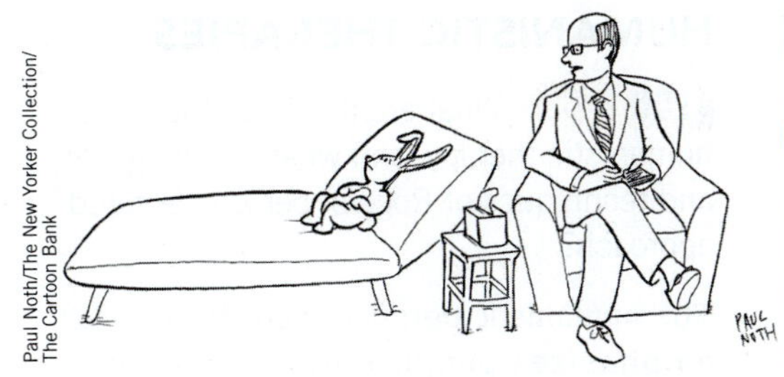

Paul Noth/The New Yorker Collection/The Cartoon Bank

"I'm more interested in hearing about the eggs you're hiding from yourself."

RETRIEVE & REMEMBER

ANSWERS IN APPENDIX E

1. In psychoanalysis, when patients experience strong feelings for their therapist, this is called ___________. Patients are said to demonstrate anxiety when they put up mental blocks around sensitive memories, indicating ___________. The therapist will attempt to provide insight into the underlying anxiety by offering a(n) ___________ of the mental blocks.

Psychodynamic Therapy

Although influenced by Freud's ideas, **psychodynamic therapists** don't talk much about id-ego-superego conflicts.

psychotherapy treatment involving psychological techniques; consists of interactions between a trained therapist and someone seeking to overcome psychological difficulties or achieve personal growth.

biomedical therapy prescribed medications or procedures that act directly on the person's physiology.

eclectic approach an approach to psychotherapy that uses techniques from various forms of therapy.

psychoanalysis Sigmund Freud's therapeutic technique. Freud believed that the patient's free associations, resistances, dreams, and transferences—and the analyst's interpretations of them—released previously repressed feelings, allowing the patient to gain self-insight.

resistance in psychoanalysis, the blocking from consciousness of anxiety-laden material.

interpretation in psychoanalysis, the analyst's noting of supposed dream meanings, resistances, and other significant behaviors and events in order to promote insight.

transference in psychoanalysis, the patient's transfer to the analyst of emotions linked with other relationships (such as love or hatred for a parent).

psychodynamic therapy therapy deriving from the psychoanalytic tradition; views individuals as responding to unconscious forces and childhood experiences, and seeks to enhance self-insight.

Instead, they try to help people understand their current symptoms by focusing on important relationships, including childhood experiences and the therapist-client relationship. "We can have loving feelings and hateful feelings toward the same person," observed one psychodynamic therapist, and "we can desire something and also fear it" (Shedler, 2009). Client-therapist meetings take place once or twice a week (rather than several times weekly) and often for only a few weeks or months. Rather than lying on a couch, out of the therapist's line of vision, clients meet with their therapist face-to-face.

In these meetings, clients explore and gain perspective on defended-against thoughts and feelings. One therapist illustrated this with the case of a young man who had told women that he loved them, when he knew that he didn't (Shapiro, 1999, p. 8). But later, with his wife, who wished he would say that he loved her, he found he *couldn't* do that—"I don't know why, but I can't."

> ***Therapist:*** *Do you mean, then, that if you could, you would like to?*
>
> ***Patient:*** *Well, I don't know. . . . Maybe I can't say it because I'm not sure it's true. Maybe I don't love her.*

Further interactions revealed that the client could not express real love because it would feel "mushy" and "soft" and therefore unmanly. He was "in conflict with himself, and . . . cut off from the nature of that conflict." The therapist noted that with such patients, who are estranged from themselves, therapists using psychodynamic techniques "are in a position to introduce them to themselves. We can restore their awareness of their own wishes and feelings, and their awareness, as well, of their reactions against those wishes and feelings" (Shapiro, 1999, p. 8). Thus, without embracing all aspects of Freud's theory, psychodynamic therapists aim to help people gain insight into unconscious dynamics that arise from their life experience.

HUMANISTIC THERAPIES

LOQ 14-3 What are the basic themes of humanistic therapy, and what are the goals and techniques of Rogers' person-centered approach?

The *humanistic* perspective (Chapter 12) emphasizes people's innate potential for self-fulfillment. Not surprisingly, humanistic therapies attempt to reduce the inner conflicts that interfere with natural development and growth. To achieve this goal, humanistic therapists try to give clients new insights. Indeed, because they share this goal, humanistic and psychodynamic therapies are often referred to as **insight therapies.** But humanistic therapies differ from psychodynamic therapies in many other ways:

- Humanistic therapists aim to boost people's self-fulfillment by helping them grow in self-awareness and self-acceptance.
- Promoting growth, not curing illness, is the therapy focus. Thus, those in therapy have become "clients" or just "persons" rather than "patients" (a change many other therapists have adopted).
- The path to growth is taking immediate responsibility for one's feelings and actions, rather than uncovering hidden causes.
- Conscious thoughts are more important than unconscious thoughts.
- The present and future are more important than the past. Therapy thus focuses on exploring feelings as they occur, rather than on gaining insights into the childhood origins of those feelings.

All these themes are present in a widely used humanistic technique developed by Carl Rogers (1902–1987). **Person-centered therapy** focuses on the person's conscious self-perceptions. In this *nondirective therapy,* the client leads the discussion. The therapist listens, without judging or interpreting, and refrains from directing the client toward certain insights.

Rogers (1961, 1980) believed that most people already possess the resources for growth. He encouraged therapists to foster growth by exhibiting acceptance, genuineness, and empathy. By being *accepting,* therapists may help clients feel freer and more open to change. By being *genuine,* therapists hope to encourage clients to likewise express their true feelings. By being *empathic,* therapists try to sense and reflect their clients' feelings, helping clients experience a deeper self-understanding and self-acceptance (Hill & Nakayama, 2000). As Rogers (1980, p. 10) explained,

> Hearing has consequences. When I truly hear a person and the meanings that are important to him at that moment, hearing not simply his words, but him, and when I let him know that I have heard his own private personal meanings, many things happen. There is first of all a grateful look. He feels released. He wants to tell me more about his world. He surges forth in a new sense of freedom. He becomes more open to the process of change.
>
> I have often noticed that the more deeply I hear the meanings of the person, the more there is that happens. Almost always, when a person realizes he has been deeply heard, his eyes moisten. I think in some real sense he is weeping for joy. It is as though he were saying, "Thank God, somebody heard me. Someone knows what it's like to be me."

To Rogers, "hearing" was **active listening.** The therapist echoes, restates, and seeks clarification of what the client expresses (verbally or nonverbally). The therapist also acknowledges those expressed feelings. Active listening is now an accepted part of counseling practices in many schools, colleges, and clinics. Counselors listen attentively. They interrupt only to restate and confirm feelings, to accept what was said, or to check their understanding of something.

Michael Rougier/Getty Images

Active listening Carl Rogers (right) empathized with a client during this group therapy session.

In the following brief excerpt, note how Rogers tried to provide a psychological mirror that would help the client see himself more clearly (Meador & Rogers, 1984, p. 167):

> **Rogers:** *Feeling that now, hm? That you're just no good to yourself, no good to anybody. Never will be any good to anybody. Just that you're completely worthless, huh?—Those really are lousy feelings. Just feel that you're no good at all, hm?*
>
> **Client:** *Yeah.* (Muttering in low, discouraged voice) *That's what this guy I went to town with just the other day told me.*
>
> **Rogers:** *This guy that you went to town with really told you that you were no good? Is that what you're saying? Did I get that right?*
>
> **Client:** *M-hm.*
>
> **Rogers:** *I guess the meaning of that if I get it right is that here's somebody that meant something to you and what does he think of you? Why, he's told you that he thinks you're no good at all. And that just really knocks the props out from under you.* (Client weeps quietly.) *It just brings the tears.* (Silence of 20 seconds)
>
> **Client:** (Rather defiantly) *I don't care though.*
>
> **Rogers:** *You tell yourself you don't care at all, but somehow I guess some part of you cares because some part of you weeps over it.*

Can a therapist be a perfect mirror, without selecting and interpreting what is reflected? Rogers granted that no one can be *totally* nondirective. Nevertheless, he said, the therapist's most important contribution is to accept and understand the client. Given a nonjudgmental, grace-filled environment that provides **unconditional positive regard,** people may accept even their worst traits and feel valued and whole.

How can we improve communication in our own relationships by listening more actively? Three Rogerian hints may help:

1. ***Summarize.*** Check your understanding by repeating the other person's statements in your own words.
2. ***Invite clarification.*** "What might be an example of that?" may encourage the person to say more.
3. ***Reflect feelings.*** "It sounds frustrating" might mirror what you're sensing from the person's body language and emotional intensity.

IN YOUR EVERYDAY LIFE

Think of your closest friends. Do they tend to express more empathy than those you feel less close to? How have your own active-listening skills changed as you've gotten older?

LaunchPad To learn more about how therapists may use these approaches, see the *Video: Psychodynamic and Humanistic Therapies.*

BEHAVIOR THERAPIES

LOQ 14-4 How does the basic assumption of behavior therapy differ from the assumptions of psychodynamic and humanistic therapies? What techniques are used in exposure therapies and aversive conditioning?

The insight therapies assume that self-awareness and psychological well-being go hand in hand.

- Psychodynamic therapies assume people's problems will lessen as they gain insight into their unresolved and unconscious tensions.
- Humanistic therapies assume people's problems will lessen as they get in touch with their feelings.

Behavior therapies, however, take a different approach. Rather than searching beneath the surface for inner causes, behavior therapists assume that problem behaviors *are* the problems. (You can become aware of why you are highly anxious during exams and still

insight therapies therapies that aim to improve psychological functioning by increasing a person's awareness of underlying motives and defenses.

person-centered therapy a humanistic therapy, developed by Carl Rogers, in which the therapist uses techniques such as *active listening* within an accepting, genuine, empathic environment to facilitate clients' growth. (Also called *client-centered therapy.*)

active listening empathic listening in which the listener echoes, restates, and seeks clarification. A feature of Rogers' person-centered therapy.

unconditional positive regard a caring, accepting, nonjudgmental attitude, which Carl Rogers believed would help clients develop self-awareness and self-acceptance.

behavior therapy therapy that applies learning principles to the elimination of unwanted behaviors.

What's the nature of the trouble, and when did it begin?
Let's drive it around and see what happens.
FREUDIAN
BEHAVIOR THERAPIST

Sidney Harris/ScienceCartoonsPlus.com

be anxious.) By harnessing the power of learning principles, behavior therapists offer clients useful tools for getting rid of unwanted behaviors. They view phobias, for example, as learned behaviors. So why not replace them with new, constructive behaviors learned through classical or operant conditioning?

Classical Conditioning Techniques

One cluster of behavior therapies draws on principles developed in Ivan Pavlov's early twentieth-century conditioning experiments (Chapter 6). As Pavlov and others showed, we learn various behaviors and emotions through *classical conditioning*. If we're attacked by a dog, we may thereafter have a conditioned fear response when other dogs approach. (Our fear generalizes, and all dogs become conditioned stimuli.)

Could other unwanted responses also be explained by conditioning? If so, might reconditioning be a solution? Learning theorist O. H. Mowrer thought so. He developed a successful conditioning therapy for chronic bed-wetters, using a liquid-sensitive pad connected to an alarm. If the sleeping child wets the bed pad, moisture triggers the alarm, waking the child. After a number of trials, the child associates bladder relaxation with waking. In three out of four cases, the treatment was effective and the success boosted the child's self-image (Christophersen & Edwards, 1992; Houts et al., 1994).

Let's broaden the discussion. What triggers your worst fear responses? Public speaking? Flying? Tight spaces? Circus clowns? Whatever the trigger, do you think you could unlearn your fear responses? With new conditioning, many people have. An example: The fear of riding in an elevator is often a learned negative response to the stimulus of being confined in a tight space. Therapists have successfully **counterconditioned** people with a fear of confined spaces. They pair the trigger stimulus (the enclosed space of the elevator) with a new response (relaxation) that cannot coexist with fear.

To replace unwanted responses with new responses, therapists may use *exposure therapies* and *aversive conditioning*.

Exposure Therapies

Picture the animal you fear the most. Maybe it's a snake, a spider, or even a cat or a dog. For 3-year-old Peter, it was a rabbit. To rid Peter of his fear of rabbits and other furry objects, psychologist Mary Cover Jones had a plan: Associate the fear-evoking rabbit with the pleasurable, relaxed response associated with eating.

As Peter began his midafternoon snack, she introduced a caged rabbit on the other side of the huge room. Peter, eagerly munching on his crackers and slurping his milk, hardly noticed the furry animal. Day by day, Jones moved the rabbit closer and closer. Within two months, Peter was holding the rabbit in his lap, even stroking it while he ate. His fear of other furry objects had subsided as well. It had been *countered*, or replaced, by a relaxed state that could not coexist with fear (Fisher, 1984; Jones, 1924).

Unfortunately for many who might have been helped by Jones' counterconditioning procedures, her story of Peter and the rabbit did not enter psychology's lore when it was reported in 1924. More than 30 years later, psychiatrist Joseph Wolpe (1958; Wolpe & Plaud, 1997) refined Jones' counterconditioning technique into the **exposure therapies** used today. These therapies, in a variety of ways, try to change people's reactions by repeatedly exposing them to stimuli that trigger unwanted responses. We all experience this process in everyday life. Someone who has moved to a new apartment may be annoyed by loud traffic sounds nearby—but only for a while. With repeated exposure, the person adapts. So, too, with people who have fear reactions to specific events, such as people with PTSD (Thompson et al., 2018). Exposed repeatedly to the situation that once terrified them, they can learn to react less anxiously (Barrera et al., 2013; Foa & McLean, 2016; Langkaas et al., 2017).

One exposure therapy widely used to treat phobias is **systematic desensitization.** You cannot be anxious and relaxed at the same time. Therefore, if you can repeatedly relax when facing anxiety-provoking stimuli, you can gradually eliminate your anxiety. The trick is to proceed gradually. Imagine you fear public speaking. A behavior therapist first helps you to create a list of speaking situations that trigger increasing levels of anxiety. Yours might range from mildly anxiety-provoking situations (perhaps speaking up in a small group of friends) to panic-provoking situations (having to address a large audience).

The therapist then trains you in *progressive relaxation*. You learn to release tension in one muscle group after another, until you feel comfortable and relaxed. The therapist then asks you to imagine, with your eyes closed, a mildly anxiety-arousing situation—perhaps a mental image of having coffee with a group of friends and trying to decide whether to speak up. If imagining the scene causes you to feel any anxiety, you are told to signal by raising your finger. Seeing the signal, the therapist instructs you to switch off the mental image and go back to deep relaxation. This imagined scene is repeatedly paired with relaxation until you feel no trace of anxiety.

The therapist then moves to the next item in your anxiety hierarchy, again using relaxation techniques to desensitize you to each imagined situation. After several sessions, you move to actual situations and practice what you had only imagined before. You begin with

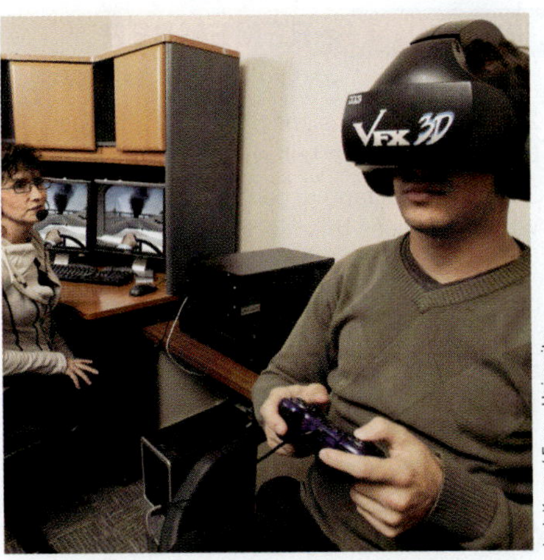

Jack Kearse/ Emory University

William Britten /E+/Getty Images

Virtual reality exposure therapy Within the confines of a room, virtual reality technology exposes people to vivid simulations of feared stimuli, such as walking across a rickety bridge high off the ground.

counterconditioning behavior therapy procedures that use classical conditioning to evoke new responses to stimuli that are triggering unwanted behaviors; includes *exposure therapies* and *aversive conditioning.*

exposure therapies behavioral techniques, such as *systematic desensitization* and *virtual reality exposure therapy,* that treat anxieties by exposing people (in imaginary or actual situations) to the things they fear and avoid.

systematic desensitization a type of exposure therapy that associates a pleasant, relaxed state with gradually increasing, anxiety-triggering stimuli. Commonly used to treat phobias.

virtual reality exposure therapy a counterconditioning technique that treats anxiety through creative electronic simulations in which people can safely face their greatest fears, such as airplane flying, spiders, or public speaking.

aversive conditioning associates an unpleasant state (such as nausea) with an unwanted behavior (such as drinking alcohol).

relatively easy tasks and gradually move to more anxiety-filled ones. Conquering your anxiety in an actual situation, not just in your imagination, raises your self-confidence (Foa & Kozak, 1986; Williams, 1987). Eventually, you may even become a confident public speaker.

Some anxiety-arousing situations (such as fears of flying, heights, particular animals, and public performances) may be too expensive, difficult, or embarrassing to re-create. In such cases, the therapist may recommend **virtual reality exposure therapy.** You would don a head-mounted display unit that projects a lifelike three-dimensional virtual world tailored to your particular fear. If you fear spiders, for example, you could look at a computer-generated, three-dimensional tarantula located on a table, and step-by-step over time walk toward it, place your hand on the table, and ultimately experience the "crawling" sensations as you "hold" the spider. If you fear social interactions, you could experience simulated stressful situations, such as entering a roomful of people. In controlled studies, people treated with virtual reality exposure therapy have experienced significant relief from real-life fear and social anxiety (Anderson et al., 2017; Freeman et al., 2018; Minns et al., 2019).

Aversive Conditioning An exposure therapy helps you learn what you *should* do. It enables a more relaxed, positive response to an upsetting *harmless* stimulus.

Aversive conditioning helps you learn what you *should not* do. It creates a negative (aversive) response to a *harmful* stimulus.

The aversive conditioning procedure is simple. It associates the unwanted behavior with *unpleasant* feelings. Is nail biting the problem? The therapist might suggest painting the fingernails with a yucky-tasting nail polish (Baskind, 1997). Is alcohol use disorder the problem? The therapist may offer the client appealing drinks laced with a drug that produces severe nausea. If that therapy links alcohol with violent nausea, the person's reaction to alcohol may change from positive to negative (**FIGURE 14.1**).

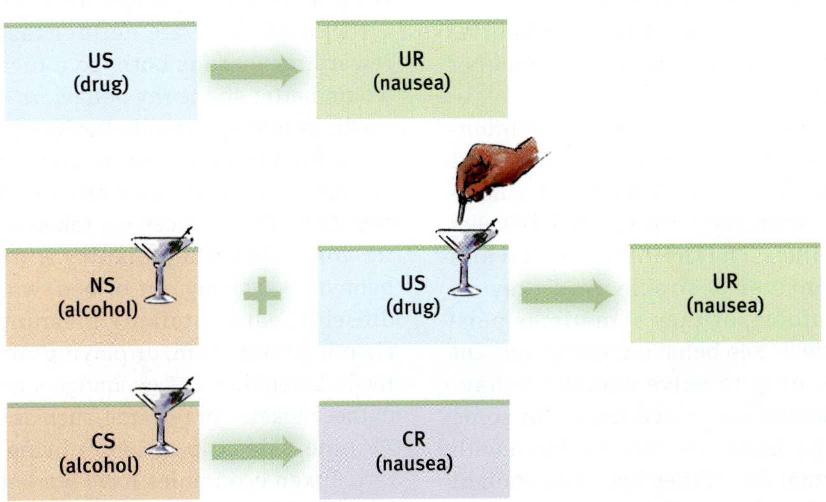

FIGURE 14.1 Aversion therapy for alcohol use disorder After repeatedly drinking an alcoholic beverage mixed with a drug that produces severe nausea, some people with a history of alcohol use disorder develop at least a temporary conditioned aversion to alcohol. (Remember: US is unconditioned stimulus, UR is unconditioned response, NS is neutral stimulus, CS is conditioned stimulus, and CR is conditioned response.)

Does aversive conditioning work? In the short run it may. In one classic study, 685 patients with alcohol use disorder completed an aversion therapy program (Wiens & Menustik, 1983). Over the next year, they returned for several booster treatments that paired alcohol with sickness. At the end of that year, 63 percent were not drinking alcohol. But after three years, only 33 percent were alcohol free.

Aversive conditioning has a built-in problem: Our thoughts can override conditioning processes (Chapter 6). People know that the alcohol-nausea link exists only in certain situations. This knowledge limits aversive conditioning's effectiveness. Thus, therapists often combine aversive conditioning with other treatments.

Operant Conditioning Techniques

LOQ 14-5 What is the basic idea of operant conditioning therapies?

If you swim, you know fear. Through trial, error, and instruction, you learned how to put your head underwater without suffocating, how to pull your body through the water, and perhaps even how to dive safely. Operant conditioning shaped your swimming. You were reinforced for safe, effective behaviors. And you were naturally punished, as when you swallowed water, for improper swimming behaviors.

Remember a basic operant conditioning concept: Consequences drive our voluntary behaviors (Chapter 6). Knowing this, therapists can practice *behavior modification*. They reinforce behaviors they consider desirable. And they do not reinforce, or they sometimes punish, undesirable behavior. Using operant conditioning to solve specific behavior problems has raised hopes for some seemingly hopeless cases. Children with intellectual disabilities have been taught to care for themselves. Socially withdrawn children with autism spectrum disorder (ASD) have learned to interact. People with schizophrenia have learned how to behave more rationally. In each case, therapists used positive reinforcers to *shape* behavior. In a step-by-step manner, they rewarded behaviors that came closer and closer to the desired behaviors.

In extreme cases, treatment must be intensive. One study worked with 19 withdrawn, uncommunicative three-year-olds with ASD. For two years, 40 hours each week, the children's parents attempted to shape their behavior (Lovaas, 1987). They positively reinforced desired behaviors and ignored or punished aggressive and self-abusive behaviors. The combination worked wonders for some children. By first grade, 9 of the 19 were functioning successfully in school and exhibiting normal intelligence. In a control group (not receiving this treatment), only one child showed similar improvement. Later studies focused on positive reinforcement—the effective part of this early intensive behavioral intervention (Reichow, 2012).

Not everyone finds the same things rewarding. Hence, the rewards used to modify behavior vary. Some people may respond well to attention or praise. Others require concrete rewards, such as food. Even then, certain foods won't work as reinforcements for everyone. I [ND] find chocolate neither tasty nor rewarding. Pizza is both, so a nice slice would better shape my behaviors. (What might best shape your behaviors?)

To modify behavior in institutional settings, therapists may create a **token economy.** People receive a token or plastic coin when they display a desired behavior—getting out of bed, washing, dressing, eating, talking meaningfully, cleaning their room, or playing cooperatively. Later, they can exchange a number of these tokens for rewards, such as candy, TV time, a day trip, or better living quarters. Token economies have worked well in group homes, classrooms, and correctional institutions, and among people with various disabilities (Matson & Boisjoli, 2009).

RETRIEVE & REMEMBER

ANSWERS IN APPENDIX E

- 2. What are the *insight therapies,* and how do they differ from behavior therapies?
- 3. Some maladaptive behaviors are learned. What hope does this fact provide?
- 4. Exposure therapies and aversive conditioning are applications of ____________ conditioning. Token economies are an application of ____________ conditioning.

COGNITIVE THERAPIES

LOQ 14-6 What are the goals and techniques of the cognitive therapies and of cognitive-behavioral therapy?

People with specific fears and problem behaviors may respond to behavior therapy. But how might behavior therapists modify the wide assortment of behaviors that accompany depressive disorders? Or treat people with generalized anxiety disorder, where unfocused anxiety doesn't lend itself to a neat list of anxiety-triggering situations? The *cognitive revolution* that has greatly influenced other areas of psychology during the last half-century has influenced therapy as well.

The **cognitive therapies** assume that *our thinking colors our feelings* (**FIGURE 14.2**). Between an event and our response lies the mind. Self-blaming and overgeneralized explanations of bad events feed depression (Chapter 13). If depressed, we may interpret a suggestion as criticism, disagreement as dislike, praise as flattery, friendliness as pity. Dwelling on such thoughts can sustain our bad mood. Cognitive therapies aim to help people break out of depression's vicious cycle by adopting new ways of perceiving and interpreting events (Kazdin, 2015).

"Life does not consist mainly, or even largely, of facts and happenings. It consists mainly of the storm of thoughts that are forever blowing through one's mind." —Mark Twain (1835–1910)

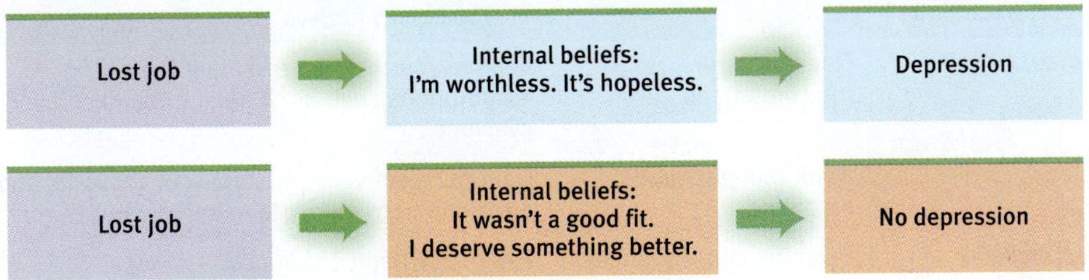

FIGURE 14.2 A cognitive perspective on psychological disorders The person's emotional reactions are produced not directly by the event, but by the person's thoughts in response to the event.

Beck's Therapy for Depression

In the late 1960s, a woman left a party early. Things had not gone well. She felt disconnected from the other party-goers and assumed no one liked her. A few days later, she visited cognitive therapist Aaron Beck. Rather than go down the traditional path to her childhood, Beck challenged her thinking. After she then listed a dozen people who did like her, Beck realized that challenging people's automatic negative thoughts could be therapeutic. And thus was born his cognitive therapy (Spiegel, 2015).

Depressed people don't see the world through rose-colored glasses. They perceive the world as full of loss, rejection, and abandonment. In daily life, they may be overly attentive to potential threats, and this ongoing focus gives rise to anxiety (MacLeod & Clarke, 2015). In therapy, they often recall and rehearse their own failings and worst impulses (Kelly, 2000).

Aaron Beck developed cognitive therapy to show depressed clients the irrational nature of their thinking, and to reverse their negative views of themselves, their situations, and their futures. With this technique, gentle questioning seeks to reveal irrational thinking and then to persuade people to remove the dark glasses through which they view life (Beck et al., 1979, pp. 145–146):

> **Client:** *I agree with the descriptions of me but I guess I don't agree that the way I think makes me depressed.*
>
> **Beck:** *How do you understand it?*
>
> **Client:** *I get depressed when things go wrong. Like when I fail a test.*
>
> **Beck:** *How can failing a test make you depressed?*
>
> **Client:** *Well, if I fail I'll never get into law school.*
>
> **Beck:** *So failing the test means a lot to you. But if failing a test could drive people into clinical depression, wouldn't you expect everyone who failed the test to have a depression? . . . Did everyone who failed get depressed enough to require treatment?*
>
> **Client:** *No, but it depends on how important the test was to the person.*
>
> **Beck:** *Right, and who decides the importance?*
>
> **Client:** *I do.*
>
> **Beck:** *And so, what we have to examine is your way of viewing the test (or the way that you think about the test) and how it affects your chances of getting into law school. Do you agree?*
>
> **Client:** *Right.*
>
> **Beck:** *Do you agree that the way you interpret the results of the test will affect you? You might feel depressed, you might have trouble sleeping, not feel like eating, and you might even wonder if you should drop out of the course.*
>
> **Client:** *I have been thinking that I wasn't going to make it. Yes, I agree.*
>
> **Beck:** *Now what did failing mean?*
>
> **Client:** (tearful) *That I couldn't get into law school.*
>
> **Beck:** *And what does that mean to you?*
>
> **Client:** *That I'm just not smart enough.*
>
> **Beck:** *Anything else?*
>
> **Client:** *That I can never be happy.*
>
> **Beck:** *And how do these thoughts make you feel?*
>
> **Client:** *Very unhappy.*
>
> **Beck:** *So it is the meaning of failing a test that makes you very unhappy. In fact, believing that you can never be happy is a powerful factor in producing unhappiness. So, you get yourself into a trap—by definition, failure to get into law school equals "I can never be happy."*

We often think in words. Therefore, getting people to change what they say to themselves is an effective way to change their thinking. Have you ever studied hard for an exam but felt extremely anxious before taking it? Many well-prepared students make matters worse with self-defeating thoughts: "This exam is going to be impossible. Everyone else seems so relaxed and confident. I wish I were better prepared. I'm so nervous I'll forget everything." Psychologists call this relentless, overgeneralized, self-blaming behavior *catastrophizing*.

To change such negative self-talk, cognitive therapists teach people to alter their thinking in stressful situations (Meichenbaum, 1977, 1985). Sometimes it may be enough simply to say more positive things to yourself. "Relax. The exam may be hard, but it will be hard for everyone else, too. I studied harder than most people. Besides, I don't need a perfect score to get a good grade." After learning to "talk back" to negative thoughts, depression-prone children, teens, and college students have shown a greatly reduced rate of future depression (Reivich et al., 2013; Seligman et al., 2009). Ditto for anxiety (Kodal et al., 2018; Krueze et al., 2018; Rith-Najarian

token economy an operant conditioning procedure in which people earn a token for exhibiting a desired behavior and can later exchange tokens for privileges or treats.

cognitive therapy therapy that teaches people new, more adaptive ways of thinking; based on the assumption that thoughts intervene between events and our emotional reactions.

et al., 2018). To a large extent, it is the thought that counts. (For a sampling of commonly used cognitive therapy techniques, see **TABLE 14.1**.)

TABLE 14.1 Selected Cognitive Therapy Techniques

Aim of Technique	Technique	Therapists' Directives
Reveal beliefs	Question your interpretations	Explore your beliefs, revealing faulty assumptions such as "I need to be liked by everyone."
	Rank thoughts and emotions	Gain perspective by ranking your thoughts and emotions from mildly to extremely upsetting.
Test beliefs	Examine consequences	Explore difficult situations, assessing possible consequences and challenging faulty reasoning.
	Decatastrophize thinking	Work through the actual worst-case consequences of the situation you face (it is often not as bad as imagined). Then determine how to cope with the real situation you face.
Change beliefs	Take appropriate responsibility	Challenge total self-blame and negative thinking, noting aspects for which you may be truly responsible, as well as aspects that aren't your responsibility.
	Resist extremes	Develop new ways of thinking and feeling to replace maladaptive habits. For example, change from thinking "I am a total failure" to "I got a failing grade on that paper, and I can make these changes to succeed next time."

PEANUTS

IMPROVE YOUR EVERYDAY LIFE

Have you ever struggled to reach a goal at school or work because of your own self-defeating thoughts? How could you challenge those thoughts?

LaunchPad To learn more about how cognitive therapy can be used to help those with anxiety, see the *Video: Cognitive Therapies.*

Cognitive-Behavioral Therapy

"The trouble with most therapy," said therapist Albert Ellis (1913–2007), "is that it helps you to feel better. But you don't get better. You have to back it up with action, action, action." **Cognitive-behavioral therapy (CBT)** takes a combined approach to depression and other disorders. This widely practiced *integrative* therapy aims to alter not only the way clients *think* but also the way they *act*. Like other cognitive therapies, CBT seeks to make people aware of their irrational negative thinking and to replace it with new ways of thinking. And like other behavior therapies, it trains people to practice a more positive approach in everyday settings.

Anxiety, depressive disorders, and bipolar disorder share a common problem: emotion regulation (Aldao & Nolen-Hoeksema, 2010; Szkodny et al., 2014). In cognitive-behavioral therapy, people learn to make more realistic appraisals and, as homework, to practice behaviors that are incompatible with their problem (Kazantzis & Dattilio, 2010; Kazantzis et al., 2010; Moses & Barlow, 2006). A person might keep a log of daily situations associated with negative and positive emotions and attempt to engage more in activities that lead to feeling good. Those who fear social situations might learn to shut down negative thoughts that trigger social anxiety and practice approaching people.

CBT effectively treats people with obsessive-compulsive disorder (Öst et al., 2015). In one classic study, people with obsessive-compulsive disorder learned to prevent their compulsive behaviors by relabeling their obsessive thoughts (Schwartz et al., 1996). Feeling the urge to wash their hands again, they would tell themselves, "I'm having a compulsive urge." They would explain to themselves that the hand-washing urge was a result of their brain's abnormal activity, which they had previously viewed in PET scans. Then, instead of giving in, they would spend 15 minutes in some enjoyable alternative behavior—practicing an instrument, taking a walk, gardening. This helped "unstick" the brain by shifting attention and engaging other brain areas. For two or three months, the weekly therapy sessions continued, with relabeling and refocusing practice at home. By the study's end, most participants' symptoms had diminished, and their PET scans revealed normalized brain activity.

Many other studies confirm CBT's effectiveness for treating anxiety, depression, eating disorders, and ADHD (Brown et al., 2018; Knouse et al., 2017; Linardon et al., 2017). Even online or app-guided CBT quizzes and exercises—therapy without a face-to-face therapist—have helped alleviate insomnia, depression, and anxiety (Andrews et al., 2018; Carlbring et al., 2018; Ebert et al., 2018). By offering flexible, affordable, and effective treatments, online CBT can reach members of disadvantaged groups who may struggle to attend face-to-face therapy sessions (Sheeber et al., 2017).

A newer CBT variation, *dialectical behavior therapy (DBT)*, helps change harmful and even suicidal behavior patterns (Linehan et al., 2015; McCauley et al., 2018; Mehlum et al., 2016). *Dialectical* means "opposing," and this therapy attempts to make peace

between two opposing forces—acceptance and change. Therapists create an accepting and encouraging environment, helping clients feel they have an ally who will offer them constructive feedback and guidance. In individual sessions, clients learn new ways of thinking that help them tolerate distress and regulate their emotions. They also receive training in social skills and in mindfulness meditation (see Chapter 10), which helps alleviate depression (Gu et al., 2015; Kuyken et al., 2016). Group training sessions offer additional opportunities to practice new skills in a social context, with further practice as homework.

Cognitive-behavioral therapy for eating disorders aided by journaling Cognitive-behavioral therapists guide people with eating disorders toward new ways of explaining their good and bad food-related experiences (Linardon et al., 2017). By recording positive events and how she has enabled them, this woman may become more mindful of her self-control and more optimistic.

RETRIEVE & REMEMBER

ANSWERS IN APPENDIX E

5. How do the humanistic and cognitive therapies differ?
6. What is *cognitive-behavioral therapy,* and what sorts of problems does this therapy best address?

GROUP AND FAMILY THERAPIES

LOQ 14-7 What are the aims and benefits of group and family therapies?

So far, we have focused mainly on therapies in which one therapist treats one client. Most therapies (though not traditional psychoanalysis) can also occur in small groups.

Group therapy does not provide the same degree of therapist involvement with each client. However, it offers other benefits:

- ***It saves therapists' time and clients' money,*** and often is no less effective than individual therapy (Burlingame et al., 2016).
- ***It offers a social laboratory for exploring social behaviors and developing social skills.*** Therapists frequently suggest group therapy when clients' problems stem from their interactions with others, as when families have conflicts or an individual's behavior distresses others. The therapist guides people's interactions as they confront issues and try out new behaviors.
- ***It enables clients to see that others share their problems.*** It can be a relief to find that others, despite their calm appearance, share your struggles, your troubling feelings, and your potentially harmful thoughts (Ooi et al., 2016).
- ***It provides feedback as clients try out new ways of behaving.*** Hearing that you look confident, even though you feel anxious and self-conscious, can be very reassuring.

Family therapy This type of therapy often acts as a preventive mental health strategy and may include marriage therapy, as shown here at a retreat for U.S. military families. The therapist helps family members understand how their ways of relating to one another create problems. The treatment's emphasis is not on changing the individuals, but on changing their relationships and interactions.

One special type of group interaction, **family therapy,** assumes that no person is an island. We live and grow in relation to others, especially our family. We struggle to find an identity outside of our family, but we also need to connect with our family emotionally. These two opposing tendencies can create stress for the individual and the family. This helps explain why therapists tend to view families as systems, in which each person's actions trigger reactions from others. To change negative interactions, the therapist often attempts to guide family members toward positive relationships and improved communication.

cognitive-behavioral therapy (CBT) a popular integrative therapy that combines cognitive therapy (changing self-defeating thinking) with behavior therapy (changing behavior).

group therapy therapy conducted with groups rather than individuals, providing benefits from group interaction.

family therapy therapy that treats people in the context of their family system. Views an individual's unwanted behaviors as influenced by, or directed at, other family members.

LaunchPad To study and remember the aims and techniques of different psychotherapies, review *Concept Practice: Types of Therapies and Therapists.* Assess your ability to recognize excerpts from each type with *Topic Tutorial: PsychSim6, Mystery Therapist.*

Evaluating Psychotherapies

Many Americans have great confidence in psychotherapy's effectiveness. "Seek counseling" or "Ask your mate to find a therapist," advice columnists often urge. Before 1950, psychiatrists were the primary providers of mental health care. Today, many others have joined their ranks. Clinical and counseling psychologists offer psychotherapy, and so do clinical social workers; pastoral, marital, abuse, and school counselors; and psychiatric nurses.

Psychotherapy takes an enormous amount of time, money, and effort. A critical thinker might wonder: Is the faith that millions of people worldwide place in psychotherapy justified? The question, though simply put, is not simply answered.

IS PSYCHOTHERAPY EFFECTIVE?

LOQ 14-8 Does psychotherapy work? How can we know?

Imagine that a loved one, knowing that you're studying psychology, has asked for your help. She's been feeling depressed, and she's thinking about making an appointment with a therapist. She wonders: Does psychotherapy really work? You've promised to gather some answers. Where will you start? Who decides whether psychotherapy is effective? Clients? Therapists? Friends and family members?

Clients' Perceptions

If clients' glowing comments were the only measuring stick, your job would be easy. Most clients believe that psychotherapy is effective. Consider 2900 *Consumer Reports* readers who rated their experiences with mental health professionals (1995; Kotkin et al., 1996; Seligman, 1995). How many were at least "fairly well satisfied"? Almost 90 percent (as was Kay Redfield Jamison, as we saw at this chapter's beginning). Among those who recalled feeling *fair* or *very poor* when beginning therapy, 9 in 10 now were feeling *very good, good,* or at least *so-so.* We have their word for it—and who should know better?

We should not dismiss clients' self-reports. But critics point out some reasons for skepticism:

- ***People often enter therapy in crisis.*** Life ebbs and flows. When the crisis passes, people may credit therapy for their improvement.
- ***Clients believe treatment will be effective.*** The *placebo effect* is the healing power of positive expectations.
- ***Clients generally speak kindly of their therapists.*** Even if their problems remain, clients "work hard to find something positive to say. The therapist had been very understanding, the client had gained a new perspective, he learned to communicate better, his mind was eased, anything at all so as not to have to say treatment was a failure" (Zilbergeld, 1983, p. 117).
- ***Clients want to believe the therapy was worth the effort.*** If you invested dozens of hours and lots of money in something, wouldn't you be motivated to find something positive about it? Psychologists call this *effort justification.*

© Jon Carter/Cartertoons
SO HOW LONG HAVE YOU WANTED TO BE A THERAPIST?
THAT'S WHAT I WOULD LIKE TO ASK YOU.
ED WAS IN THERAPY FOR BELIEVING HE WAS A THERAPIST.

Jon Carter/Cartoonstock

Feng Li/Getty Images

Trauma These women were mourning the tragic loss of lives and homes in the 2010 earthquake in China. Those who suffer through such trauma may benefit from counseling, though many people recover on their own or with the help of supportive relationships with family and friends. "Life itself still remains a very effective therapist," noted psychodynamic therapist Karen Horney (*Our Inner Conflicts,* 1945).

LaunchPad To consider the impact of clients' belief in the treatment, see the *Video: Therapeutic Effectiveness—The Placebo Effect.*

Clinicians' Perceptions

If clinicians' perceptions were proof of therapy's effectiveness, we would have even more reason to celebrate. Case studies of successful treatment abound. The problem is that clients justify entering psychotherapy by emphasizing their unhappiness and justify leaving by emphasizing their well-being. Therapists treasure compliments from those clients saying good-bye or later expressing their gratitude. But they hear little from clients who experience only temporary relief and seek out new therapists for their recurring problems. Thus, therapists are most aware of the failures of *other* therapists. The same person, suffering from the same recurring anxiety, depression, or marital difficulty, may be a "success" story in several therapists' files.

Moreover, therapists, like the rest of us, are vulnerable to cognitive errors. *Confirmation bias* can lead them to unconsciously seek evidence that confirms their beliefs and to ignore contradictory evidence. *Illusory correlations* can lead them to perceive associations that don't really exist (Lilienfeld et al., 2015).

Outcome Research

If clients' and therapists' most sincere ratings of their experiences can't inform us about psychotherapy's effectiveness, how can we know what to expect? What types of people and problems are helped, and by what type of psychotherapy?

In search of answers, psychologists have turned to the well-traveled path of controlled research. Similar research in the 1800s transformed the field of medicine when skeptical physicians began to realize that many patients were dying despite receiving fashionable treatments (bleeding, purging), and many others were getting better on their own. Sorting fact from superstition required observing patients and recording outcomes with and without a particular treatment. Typhoid fever patients, for example, often improved after being bled, convincing most doctors that the treatment worked. Then came the shock. A control group was given mere bed rest, and after five weeks of fever, 70 percent improved. The study showed that bleeding was worthless (Thomas, 1992).

A similar shock—and a spirited debate—followed in the twentieth century, when British psychologist Hans Eysenck (1952) summarized 24 studies of psychotherapy outcomes. He found that two-thirds of those receiving psychotherapy for disorders not involving hallucinations or delusions improved markedly. To this day, no one disputes that optimistic estimate. But there was a catch. Eysenck also reported similar improvement among people who were *untreated*, such as those on treatment waiting lists. With or without psychotherapy, he said, roughly two-thirds improved noticeably. Time was a great healer.

Later research revealed shortcomings in Eysenck's analyses. His sample was small—only 24 outcome studies in 1952, compared with hundreds available today. The best of these studies are *randomized clinical trials*, in which researchers randomly assign people on a waiting list to therapy or to no therapy. Later, they evaluate everyone and compare the outcomes, with tests and assessments by others who don't know whether therapy was given.

Therapists welcomed the result when the first statistical digest combined the results of 475 of these investigations (Smith et al., 1980). The outcome for the average therapy client was better than that for 80 percent of the untreated people (**FIGURE 14.3**). Mary Lee Smith and her colleagues summed it up: "Psychotherapy benefits people of all ages as reliably as schooling educates them, medicine cures them, or business turns a profit" (p. 183).

Dozens of such summaries have echoed the results of the earlier outcome studies: *Those not undergoing therapy often improve, but those undergoing therapy are more likely to improve—and to improve more quickly and with less risk of relapse* (Kolovos et al., 2017; Weisz et al., 2017). And some people with depression or anxiety have sudden reductions in their symptoms between their treatment sessions. These "sudden gains" offer hope for long-term improvement (Aderka et al., 2012; Wucherpfennig et al., 2017).

So, psychotherapy is a good investment of time and money. Like prenatal care, psychotherapy reduces long-term health care costs (Chisholm et al., 2016; Ising et al., 2015). One digest of 91 studies showed that after seeking psychotherapy, clients' search for other medical treatment dropped by 16 percent (Chiles et al., 1999).

It's good to know that psychotherapy, in general, is somewhat effective. But distressed people—and those paying for their therapy—really want a different question answered. How effective are *particular* treatments for *specific* problems? So, what can we tell these people?

WHICH PSYCHOTHERAPIES WORK BEST?

LOQ 14-9 Are some psychotherapies more effective than others for specific disorders?

The early statistical summaries and surveys did not find that any one type of psychotherapy was generally better than others (Smith & Glass, 1977; Smith et al., 1980). Later studies have similarly found that clients can benefit from psychotherapy regardless of their clinicians' experience, training, supervision, and licensing

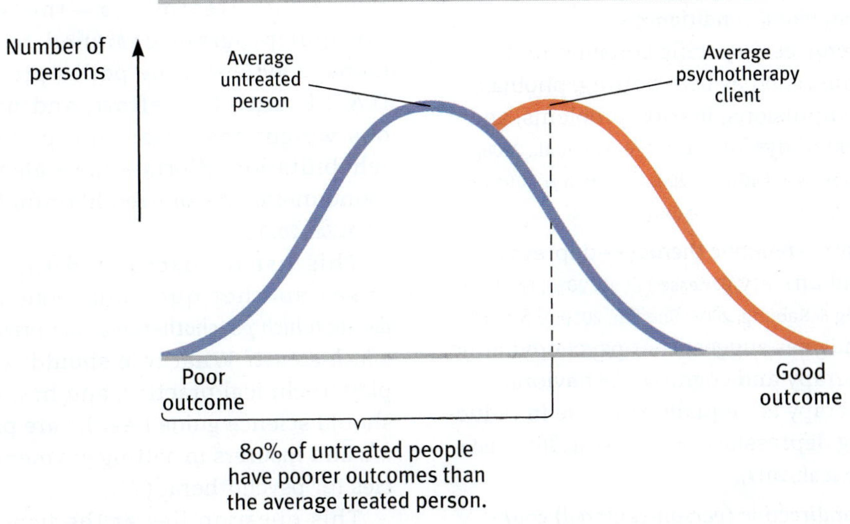

FIGURE 14.3 Treatment versus no treatment In 475 studies, the outcome for the average therapy client was better than that for 80 percent of the untreated people. (Data from Smith et al., 1980.)

(Cuijpers, 2017; Kivlighan et al., 2015; Wampold et al., 2017). A *Consumer Reports* survey confirmed this result (Seligman, 1995). Were clients treated by a psychiatrist, psychologist, or social worker? Were they seen in a group or individual context? Did the therapist have extensive or relatively limited training and experience? It didn't matter. Clients seemed equally satisfied.

So, was the dodo bird in *Alice in Wonderland* right: "Everyone has won and all must have prizes"? Not quite. One general finding emerges from the studies. The more specific the problem, the greater the hope that psychotherapy might solve it (Singer, 1981; Westen & Morrison, 2001). Those who experience phobias or panic, who are unassertive, or who are frustrated by sexual performance problems can hope for improvement. Those with less-focused problems, such as depression and anxiety, usually benefit in the short term but often relapse later. There often is also an overlapping or *comorbidity* of disorders.

Nevertheless, some forms of therapy do get prizes for effectively treating *particular* problems:

- ***Cognitive and cognitive-behavioral therapies***—anxiety, posttraumatic stress disorder, insomnia, and depression (Qaseem et al., 2016; Scaini et al., 2016; Tolin, 2010).
- ***Behavioral conditioning therapies***—specific behavior problems, such as bed-wetting, phobias, compulsions, marital problems, and sexual dysfunctions (Baker et al., 2008; Hunsley & DiGiulio, 2002; Shadish & Baldwin, 2005).
- ***Psychodynamic therapy***—depression and anxiety (Driessen et al., 2010; Leichsenring & Rabung, 2008; Shedler, 2010b). Some analyses suggest that psychodynamic therapy and cognitive-behavioral therapy are equally effective in reducing depression (Driessen et al., 2017; Steinert et al., 2017).
- ***Nondirective (person-centered) counseling***—mild to moderate depression (Cuijpers et al., 2012).

But no prizes would go to certain other psychotherapies (Arkowitz & Lilienfeld, 2006; Lilienfeld et al., 2015). We would all be wise to avoid approaches that have no scientific support, such as

- ***energy therapies,*** which propose to manipulate the client's invisible "energy fields."
- ***recovered-memory therapies,*** which aim to unearth "repressed memories" of early childhood abuse (Chapter 7).
- ***rebirthing therapies,*** which reenact the supposed trauma of a client's birth.
- ***conversion therapies,*** which aim to enable those with same-sex attractions to change their sexual orientation.

As with some medical treatments, some psychological treatments are not only ineffective but also harmful. The American Psychiatric Association and British Psychological Society have warned against conversion therapies, which aim to "repair" "something that is not a mental illness and therefore does not require therapy," declared APA president Barry Anton (2015). "There is insufficient scientific evidence that [conversion therapies] work, and they have the potential to harm the client." Citing this evidence, as of 2019, 15 U.S. states and Washington, DC, had banned conversion therapy for minors (Gold, 2019). Other treatments—the Scared Straight program designed to tame teenage violence, the police-promoted D.A.R.E. anti-drug effort, and numerous weight-reduction and pedophile rehabilitation efforts—have also been found ineffective or even harmful (Walton & Wilson, 2018).

This list of discredited therapies raises another question. *Who should decide which psychotherapies get prizes and which do not?* What role should science play in clinical practice, and how much should science guide health care providers and insurers in setting payment policies for psychotherapy?

This question lies at the heart of a controversy—some call it psychology's civil war. On one side are research psychologists who use scientific methods to extend the list of well-defined therapies with proven results in aiding people with various disorders. They worry that many clinicians "give more weight to their personal experience than to science" (Baker et al., 2008).

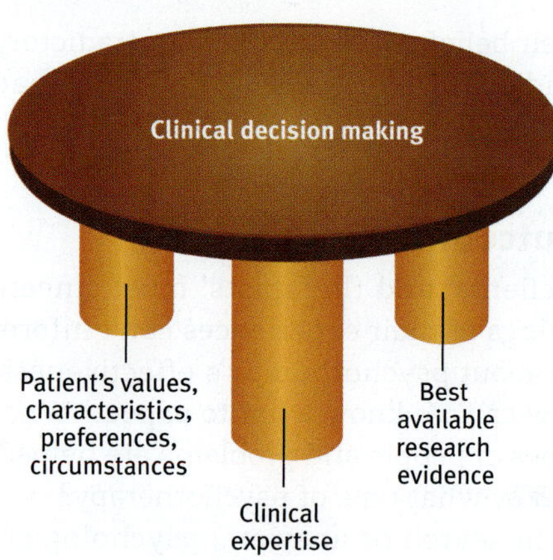

FIGURE 14.4 Evidence-based practice Ideal clinical decision making can be visualized as a three-legged stool, upheld by research evidence, clinical expertise, and knowledge of the client.

On the other side are the nonscientist therapists who view their practices as more art than science. They view psychotherapy as something that cannot be described in a manual or tested in an experiment. People are too complex and psychotherapy is too intuitive for a one-size-fits-all approach, many therapists say.

Between these two camps stand the science-oriented clinicians calling for **evidence-based practice** (**FIGURE 14.4**), which has been endorsed by the American Psychological Association and others (2006; Lilienfeld et al., 2013). Therapists using this approach make informed decisions based on research evidence, clinical expertise, and their knowledge of the client. Increasingly, insurer and government support for mental health services requires evidence-based practice.

RETRIEVE & REMEMBER

ANSWERS IN APPENDIX E

7. Therapy is most likely to be helpful for those with problems that __________ (are/are not) well defined.
8. What is *evidence-based practice?*

HOW DO PSYCHOTHERAPIES HELP PEOPLE?

LOQ 14-10 What three elements are shared by all forms of psychotherapy?

Why have studies found little correlation between therapists' training and experience and clients' outcomes? One answer seems to be that all psychotherapies offer three basic benefits (Frank, 1982; Wampold, 2007). They all offer *hope for demoralized people; a new perspective on oneself and the world;* and *an empathic, trusting, caring relationship.*

- ***Hope for demoralized people*** Many people seek therapy because they feel anxious, depressed, self-disapproving, and unable to turn things around. What any psychotherapy offers is hope—an expectation that, with commitment from the therapy seeker, things can and will get better. By harnessing the person's own healing powers, this belief, apart from any therapy technique, can improve morale, create feelings of inner strength, and reduce symptoms (Corrigan, 2014; Meyerhoff & Rohan, 2016).
- ***A new perspective*** Every psychotherapy offers people a possible explanation of their symptoms. Armed with a believable fresh perspective, people may approach life with a new attitude, open to making changes in their behaviors and their views of themselves.
- ***An empathic, trusting, caring relationship*** No matter what technique they use, effective therapists are empathic. They seek to understand the client's experiences. They communicate care and concern. And they earn trust through respectful listening, reassurance, and guidance. These qualities were clear in recorded therapy sessions from 36 recognized master therapists (Goldfried et al., 1998). Some took a cognitive-behavioral approach. Others used psychodynamic principles. Although the master therapists used different approaches, they showed some striking behavioral *similarities.* They helped clients evaluate themselves, connect different aspects of their life, and gain insight into their interactions with others. The emotional bond between therapist and client—the **therapeutic alliance**—helps explain why empathic, caring therapists are especially effective (Klein et al., 2003; Wampold, 2001).

Mort Gerberg The New Yorker Collection/The Cartoon Bank

"The thing is, you have to really want to change."

These three basic benefits—hope, a fresh perspective, and an empathic, caring relationship—help us understand why *paraprofessionals* (briefly trained caregivers) can assist so many troubled people so effectively (Bryan & Arkowitz, 2015; Christensen & Jacobson, 1994). They are an important part of what self-help and support groups offer their members. And they also are part of what traditional healers have offered (Jackson, 1992). Healers everywhere—special people to whom others disclose their suffering, whether psychiatrists or shamans—have listened in order to understand. And they have empathized, reassured, advised, consoled, interpreted, and explained (Torrey, 1986). Such qualities may explain why people who feel supported by close relationships—who enjoy the fellowship and friendship of caring people—have been less likely to seek therapy (Frank, 1982; O'Connor & Brown, 1984).

* * *

To recap, people who seek psychotherapy usually improve. So do many of those who do not undergo psychotherapy, and that is a tribute to our human resourcefulness and our capacity to care for one another. Nevertheless, though the therapist's orientation and experience appear not to matter much, people who receive some psychotherapy usually improve more than those who do not. People with clear-cut, specific problems tend to improve the most.

IN YOUR EVERYDAY LIFE

Based on what you've read, would you seek therapy if you were experiencing a problem? Why or why not? If you've already undergone therapy, does what you've learned influence your feelings about the experience?

RETRIEVE & REMEMBER

ANSWERS IN APPENDIX E

9. Those who undergo psychotherapy are __________ (more/less) likely to show improvement than those who do not undergo psychotherapy.

HOW DOES OUR DIVERSITY INFLUENCE PSYCHOTHERAPY?

LOQ 14-11 What personal factors influence the client-therapist relationship?

All psychotherapies offer hope. Nearly all psychotherapists try to enhance their clients' sensitivity, openness, personal responsibility, and sense of purpose (Jensen & Bergin, 1988). But in matters of culture, values, and personal identity, psychotherapists differ from one another and may differ from their clients (Delaney et al., 2007; Kelly, 1990).

These differences can create a mismatch—for example, when a therapist from one culture interacts with a client from another. In North America, Europe, and Australia, for example, most

evidence-based practice clinical decision making that integrates the best available research with clinical expertise and patient characteristics and preferences.

therapeutic alliance a bond of trust and mutual understanding between a therapist and client, who work together constructively to overcome the client's problem.

psychotherapists reflect their culture's *individualism*, which often gives priority to personal desires and identity. Clients with a *collectivist* perspective, as found in many Asian cultures, may assume people will be more mindful of social and family responsibilities, harmony, and group goals. These clients may have trouble relating to therapists who ask them to think only of their individual well-being (Markus & Kitayama, 1991).

Cultural differences help explain some groups' reluctance to use mental health services. People living in "cultures of honor" prize being strong and tough. They may feel that seeking mental health care is an admission of weakness (Brown et al., 2014b). And some cultural groups tend to be both reluctant to seek therapy and quick to leave it (Broman, 1996; Chen et al., 2009; Sue et al., 2009). In one experiment, Asian-American clients matched with counselors who shared their cultural values (rather than mismatched with those who did not) perceived more counselor empathy and felt more alliance with the counselor (Kim et al., 2005).

Client-therapist mismatches may also stem from other personal differences. Highly religious people may prefer and benefit from therapists who share their values and beliefs (Masters, 2010; Pearce et al., 2015). Likewise, therapists' attitudes toward people who identify as lesbian, gay, bisexual, transgender, or questioning/queer (LGBTQ) can affect the client-therapist relationship. Transgender people, for example, may seek out therapists who have affirming attitudes toward them (Bettergarcia & Israel, 2018).

FINDING A MENTAL HEALTH PROFESSIONAL

LOQ 14-12 What should a person look for when selecting a therapist?

Life for everyone is marked by a mix of calm and stress, blessings and losses, good moods and bad. So when should we seek a mental health professional's help? APA offers these common trouble signals:

- Feelings of hopelessness
- Deep and lasting depression
- Self-destructive behavior, such as substance abuse
- Disruptive fears
- Sudden mood shifts
- Thoughts of suicide
- Compulsive rituals, such as hand washing
- Sexual difficulties
- Hearing voices or seeing things that others don't experience

In looking for a psychotherapist, you may want to have a preliminary meeting with two or three. Your college counseling center is a great starting point. Colleges hire qualified therapists and offer some free services, which you find by browsing their web page or visiting in person. You can also ask your physician or walk-in clinic for a referral, or see whether your insurance company provides a listing of participating therapists. Many people use the internet to search for therapists and receive online help via one of the more than 10,000 mental health smartphone apps (Kocsis, 2018; Levin et al., 2018).

In your in-person or online meeting, you can describe your problem and learn each therapist's treatment approach. You can ask questions about the therapist's values, credentials (**TABLE 14.2**), and fees. And you can assess your own feelings about each therapist. The emotional bond between therapist and client is perhaps the most important factor in effective therapy.

The APA recognizes the importance of a strong therapeutic alliance and it welcomes diverse therapists who can relate well to diverse clients. It accredits programs that provide training in cultural sensitivity (for example, to differing values, communication styles, and language) and that recruit underrepresented cultural groups.

The Biomedical Therapies

Psychotherapy is one way to treat psychological disorders. The other is *biomedical therapy*. Biomedical treatments

TABLE 14.2 Therapists and Their Training

Type	Description
Clinical psychologists	Most are psychologists with a Ph.D. (includes research training) or Psy.D. (focuses on therapy) supplemented by a supervised internship and, often, post-doctoral training. About half work in agencies and institutions, half in private practice.
Psychiatrists	Psychiatrists are physicians who specialize in the treatment of psychological disorders. Not all psychiatrists have had extensive training in psychotherapy, but as M.D.s or D.O.s they can prescribe medications. Thus, they tend to see those with the most serious problems. Many have their own private practice.
Clinical or psychiatric social workers	A two-year master of social work graduate program plus post-graduate supervision prepares some social workers to offer psychotherapy, mostly to people with everyday personal and family problems. About half have earned the National Association of Social Workers' designation of clinical social worker.
Counselors	Marriage and family counselors specialize in problems arising from family relations. Clergy provide counseling to countless people. Abuse counselors work with substance abusers, spouse and child abusers, and victims of abuse. Mental health and other counselors may be required to have a two-year master's degree.

can change the brain's chemistry with drugs; affect its circuitry with electrical stimulation, magnetic impulses, or psychosurgery; or influence its responses with lifestyle changes.

Are you surprised to see *lifestyle changes* in this list? We find it convenient to talk of separate psychological and biological influences, but everything psychological is also biological. Thus, our lifestyle—our exercise, nutrition, relationships, recreation, relaxation, religious or spiritual engagement, and service to others—affects our mental health (Schuch et al., 2016; Walsh, 2011). (See Thinking Critically About: Therapeutic Lifestyle Change.)

Every thought and feeling depends on the functioning brain. Every creative idea, every moment of joy or anger, every period of depression emerges from the electrochemical activity of the living brain. Some psychologists consider even psychotherapy to be a biological treatment, because changing the way we think and behave is a brain-changing experience (Kandel, 2013). When psychotherapy relieves behaviors associated with obsessive-compulsive disorder or schizophrenia, PET scans reveal a calmer brain (Habel et al., 2010; Schwartz et al., 1996).

IMPROVE YOUR EVERYDAY LIFE

Which lifestyle changes are most important for *you* to make to improve your mental health?

RETRIEVE & REMEMBER

ANSWERS IN APPENDIX E

10. What are some examples of lifestyle changes people can make to enhance their mental health?

DRUG THERAPIES

LOQ 14-14 What are the drug therapies? How do double-blind studies help researchers evaluate a drug's effectiveness?

By far, the most widely used biomedical treatments today are the drug therapies. Most drugs for anxiety and depression are prescribed by primary care providers, followed by psychiatrists and, in some states, psychologists. People have a choice whether to follow medical advice and take their prescribed mental health drugs. In very rare cases, people are required to take certain medications in order to reduce their risk of harm to themselves or others.

Since the 1950s, drug researchers have written a new chapter in the treatment of people with severe disorders. Hundreds of thousands have been liberated from hospital confinement. Thanks to drug therapies and local community mental health programs, today's resident population of U.S. state and county mental hospitals has dropped to a small fraction of what it was 70 years ago.

Almost any new treatment, including drug therapy, is greeted by an initial wave of enthusiasm as many people apparently improve. But that enthusiasm often diminishes on closer examination. To judge the effectiveness of any new drug, researchers also need to know:

- Do untreated people also improve? If so, how many, and how quickly?
- Is recovery due to the drug or to the placebo effect? When patients or mental health workers expect positive results, they may see what they expect, not what really happens. Even mere exposure to advertising about a drug's supposed effectiveness can increase its effect (Kamenica et al., 2013).

Peter C. Vey/The New Yorker Collection

"If this doesn't help you don't worry, it's a placebo."

To control for these influences, drug researchers give half the patients the drug, and the other half a similar-appearing placebo. Because neither the staff nor the patients know who gets which, this is called a *double-blind technique*. The good news: In double-blind studies, several types of drugs effectively treat psychological disorders.

* * *

The four most common drug treatments for psychological disorders are *antipsychotic drugs, antianxiety drugs, antidepressant drugs,* and *mood-stabilizing medications*. Let's consider each of these in more detail.

Antipsychotic Drugs

Accidents sometimes launch revolutions. In this instance, an accidental discovery launched a treatment revolution for people with *psychoses*. The discovery was that some drugs used for other medical purposes calmed the hallucinations or delusions that are part of these patients' split from reality. First-generation **antipsychotic drugs,** such as chlorpromazine (sold as Thorazine), reduced responsiveness to irrelevant stimuli. Thus, they provided the most help to schizophrenia patients experiencing symptoms such as auditory hallucinations and paranoia (Leucht et al., 2017). (Antipsychotic drugs are less effective in changing the schizophrenia symptoms of apathy and withdrawal.)

How do antipsychotic drugs work? They mimic certain neurotransmitters. Some block the activity of dopamine by occupying its receptor sites. This finding reinforces the idea that an overactive dopamine system contributes to schizophrenia. Further support for this idea comes from a side effect of another drug. L-dopa is a drug sometimes given to

antipsychotic drugs drugs used to treat schizophrenia and other forms of severe thought disorders.

Thinking Critically About:
Therapeutic Lifestyle Change

LOQ 14-13 Why is therapeutic lifestyle change considered an effective biomedical therapy, and how does it work?

LIFESTYLE (exercise, nutrition, relationships, recreation, service to others, relaxation, and religious or spiritual engagement)

influences our BRAIN AND BODY

affects our MENTAL HEALTH[1]

Our shared history has prepared us to be physically active and socially engaged.

Our ancestors hunted, gathered, and built in groups.

Modern researchers have found that outdoor activity in a natural environment reduces stress and promotes health.[2]

APPLICATION TO THERAPY

Training seminars promote therapeutic lifestyle change.[3] Small groups of people with depression undergo a 12-week training program with the following goals:

Aerobic exercise, 30 minutes a day, at least three times weekly (increases fitness and vitality, stimulates endorphins)

Regular aerobic exercise rivals the healing power of antidepressant drugs.[4]

Adequate sleep, with a goal of 7 to 8 hours per night.

A complete night's sleep boosts immunity and increases energy, alertness, and mood.[5]

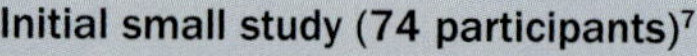

Light exposure, 15 to 30 minutes each morning with a light box (amplifies arousal, influences hormones)

Social connection, with less alone time and at least two meaningful social engagements weekly (helps satisfy the human need to belong)

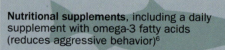

Reducing rumination, by identifying and redirecting negative thoughts (enhances positive thinking)

Nutritional supplements, including a daily supplement with omega-3 fatty acids (reduces aggressive behavior)[6]

Initial small study (74 participants)[7]

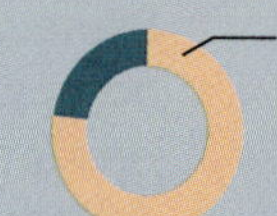

77% of those who completed the program experienced relief from depressive symptoms.

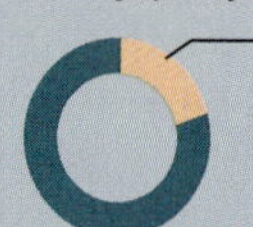

Only 19% of those assigned to a treatment-as-usual control group showed similar results.

Future research will try to identify which parts of the treatment produce the therapeutic effect.

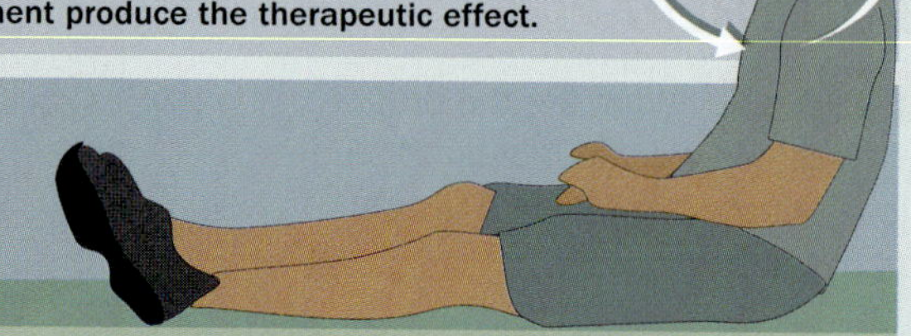

The biomedical therapies assume that mind and body are a unit: Affect one and you will affect the other.

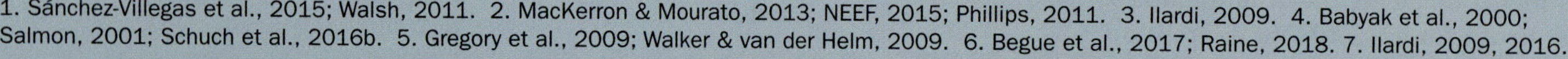

1. Sánchez-Villegas et al., 2015; Walsh, 2011. 2. MacKerron & Mourato, 2013; NEEF, 2015; Phillips, 2011. 3. Ilardi, 2009. 4. Babyak et al., 2000; Salmon, 2001; Schuch et al., 2016b. 5. Gregory et al., 2009; Walker & van der Helm, 2009. 6. Begue et al., 2017; Raine, 2018. 7. Ilardi, 2009, 2016.

people with Parkinson's disease to boost their production of dopamine, which is too low. L-dopa raises dopamine levels, but can you guess its occasional side effect? If you guessed hallucinations, you're right.

Do antipsychotic drugs also have side effects? *Yes,* and some are powerful. They may produce sluggishness, tremors, and twitches similar to those of Parkinson's disease (Kaplan & Saddock, 1989). Long-term use of antipsychotics can also produce *tardive dyskinesia,* with involuntary movements of the facial muscles (such as grimacing), tongue, and limbs. Although not more effective in controlling schizophrenia symptoms, many of the newer-generation antipsychotics (such as risperidone and olanzapine) work best for those with severe symptoms and have fewer of these effects (Furukawa et al., 2015). These drugs may, however, increase the risk of obesity and diabetes (Buchanan et al., 2010; Tiihonen et al., 2009).

Antipsychotics, combined with life-skills programs and family support, have given new hope to many people with schizophrenia (Goff et al., 2017; Guo et al., 2010). Hundreds of thousands of patients have left the wards of mental hospitals and returned to work and to near-normal lives (Leucht et al., 2003). New computer programs can help clinicians identify which people with schizophrenia will benefit from specific antipsychotic medications (Lee et al., 2018).

Elyn Saks, a University of Southern California law professor, knows what it means to live with schizophrenia. Thanks to her treatment, which combines an antipsychotic drug and psychotherapy, "Now I'm mostly well. I'm mostly thinking clearly. I do have episodes, but it's not like I'm struggling all of the time to stay on the right side of the line" (Sacks, 2007).

Antianxiety Drugs

Like alcohol, **antianxiety drugs,** such as Xanax or Ativan, depress central nervous system activity (and so should not be used in combination with alcohol). Some antianxiety drugs have been successfully used in combination with psychological therapy to treat anxiety disorders, obsessive-compulsive disorder, and posttraumatic stress disorder. They calm anxiety as the person learns to cope with frightening situations and fear-triggering stimuli.

Some critics fear that antianxiety drugs may reduce symptoms without resolving underlying problems, especially when used as an ongoing treatment. "Popping a Xanax" at the first sign of tension can provide immediate relief, which may reinforce a person's tendency to take drugs when anxious. Antianxiety drugs can also be addictive. Regular users who stop taking these drugs may experience increased anxiety, insomnia, and other withdrawal symptoms.

Antidepressant Drugs

The **antidepressant drugs** were named for their ability to lift people up from a state of depression. These drugs are now also increasingly used to treat anxiety disorders, obsessive-compulsive disorder, and posttraumatic stress disorder (Wetherell et al., 2013). Many of these drugs work by increasing the availability of norepinephrine or serotonin. These neurotransmitters elevate arousal and mood and are scarce when a person experiences feelings of depression or anxiety.

The most commonly prescribed drugs in this group, including Prozac and its cousins Zoloft and Paxil, lift spirits by prolonging the time serotonin molecules remain in the brain's synapses. They do this by partially blocking the normal reuptake process (see Figure 2.4 in Chapter 2). These drugs are called *selective serotonin reuptake inhibitors (SSRIs)* because they slow (inhibit) the synaptic vacuuming up (reuptake) of serotonin.

SSRIs begin to influence neurotransmission within hours. But their full psychological effect may take four weeks, possibly because these drugs promote the birth of new brain cells (Becker & Wojtowicz, 2007; Jacobs, 2004). With those at risk of suicide, researchers are also exploring the possibility of quicker-acting antidepressants such as ketamine, an anesthetic that acts as an opioid (Canuso et al., 2018; Domany et al., 2019; Williams et al., 2018).

Drugs are not the only way to lift our mood. Aerobic exercise often calms people who feel anxious and energizes those who feel depressed. Regular physical activity boosts teen mental health (Beauchamp et al., 2018). And for adults in every part of the world, exercise predicts a lower risk of future depression (Schuch et al., 2018). Cognitive therapy, by helping people reverse their habitual negative thinking style, can boost drug-aided relief from depression and reduce posttreatment relapses (Amick et al., 2015). Some clinicians attack depression (and anxiety) from both below and above (Cuijpers et al., 2010; Hollon et al., 2014; Kennard et al., 2014). They use antidepressant drugs (which work, bottom-up, on the emotion-forming limbic system) together with cognitive-behavioral therapy (which works, top-down, to change thought processes).

People with depression often improve after a month on antidepressant drugs. But after allowing for natural recovery and the placebo effect, how big is the drug effect? The effect is consistent but, critics argue, not very big (Cipriani et al., 2018; Kirsch et al., 1998, 2014, 2016). In double-blind clinical trials, placebos produced improvement comparable to about 75 percent of the active drug's effect. For those with severe depression, the placebo effect is less and the added drug benefit somewhat greater (Fournier et al., 2010; Kirsch et al., 2008; Olfson & Marcus, 2009).

antianxiety drugs drugs used to control anxiety and agitation.

antidepressant drugs drugs used to treat depression, anxiety disorders, obsessive-compulsive disorder, and posttraumatic stress disorder. (Several widely used antidepressant drugs are *selective serotonin reuptake inhibitors—SSRIs.)*

Given that antidepressants often have unwanted side effects, and that aerobic exercise and cognitive-behavioral therapy are also effective antidotes to mild or moderate depression, one researcher recommends more limited antidepressant use: "If they are to be used at all, it should be as a last resort" (Kirsch, 2016). *The bottom line:* If you're concerned about your mental health, consult with a mental health professional to determine the best treatment for you.

LaunchPad To play the role of a clinical researcher exploring these questions, engage online with the activity *How Would You Know How Well Antidepressants Work?*

Mood-Stabilizing Medications

In addition to antipsychotic, antianxiety, and antidepressant drugs, psychiatrists have *mood-stabilizing drugs* in their arsenal. One of them, Depakote, was originally used to treat epilepsy. It was also found effective in controlling the manic episodes associated with bipolar disorder. Another, the simple salt *lithium*, effectively levels the emotional highs and lows of this disorder. In the 1940s, Australian physician John Cade administered lithium to a patient with severe mania and the patient became perfectly well in less than a week (Snyder, 1986). Although we do not understand why, lithium works. About 7 in 10 people with bipolar disorder benefit from a long-term daily dose of this cheap salt (Solomon et al., 1995). Their risk of suicide is about one-sixth that of people with bipolar disorder who are not taking lithium (Oquendo et al., 2011). Kay Redfield Jamison (1995, pp. 88–89) described the effect:

> Lithium prevents my seductive but disastrous highs, diminishes my depressions, clears out the wool and webbing from my disordered thinking, slows me down, gentles me out, keeps me from ruining my career and relationships, keeps me out of a hospital, alive, and makes psychotherapy possible.

RETRIEVE & REMEMBER

ANSWERS IN APPENDIX E

11. How do researchers determine if particular drug therapies are effective?
12. The drugs given most often to treat depression are called __________. Schizophrenia is often treated with __________ drugs.

BRAIN STIMULATION

LOQ 14-15 How are brain stimulation and psychosurgery used in treating specific disorders?

Electroconvulsive Therapy

Another biomedical treatment, **electroconvulsive therapy (ECT),** manipulates the brain by shocking it. When ECT was first introduced in 1938, the wide-awake patient was strapped to a table and jolted with electricity to the brain. The procedure, which produced convulsions and brief unconsciousness, gained a barbaric image. Although that image lingers, today's ECT is much kinder and gentler, and no longer "convulsive." The patient receives a general anesthetic and a muscle relaxant (to prevent bodily convulsions). A psychiatrist then delivers a brief electrical pulse, which triggers a 30- to 60-second brain seizure. Within 30 minutes, the patient awakens and remembers nothing of the treatment or of the preceding hours.

Would you agree to ECT for yourself or a loved one? The decision might be difficult, but the treatment works. Surprising as it may seem, study after study confirms that ECT can effectively treat severe depression in patients who have not responded to drug therapy (Fink, 2009; Medda et al., 2015; Ross et al., 2018a). After three such sessions each week for two to four weeks, 70 percent or more of those receiving today's ECT improve markedly. They show less memory loss than with earlier versions of ECT and no apparent brain damage (HMHL, 2007). ECT also reduces suicidal thoughts and is credited with saving many from suicide (Kellner et al., 2006). The *Journal of the American Medical Association*'s conclusion: "The results of ECT in treating severe depression are among the most positive treatment effects in all of medicine" (Glass, 2001).

How does ECT relieve severe depression? After more than 75 years, no one knows for sure. One patient compared ECT to the smallpox vaccine, which was saving lives before we knew how it worked. Perhaps the brief electric current calms neural centers where overactivity produces depression. Some research indicates that ECT stimulates neurogenesis (new neurons) and new synaptic connections (Joshi et al., 2016; Rotheneichner et al., 2014; Wang et al., 2017b).

No matter how impressive the results, the idea of electrically shocking a person's brain still strikes many as barbaric, especially given our ignorance about why ECT works. Moreover, the mood boost may not last long. Many ECT-treated patients eventually relapse back into depression, although relapses are somewhat fewer for those who also receive antidepressant drugs or who do aerobic exercise (Rosenquist et al., 2016; Salehi et al., 2016). *The bottom line:* In the minds of many psychiatrists and patients, ECT is a lesser evil than severe depression's anguish and risk of suicide. As one psychologist reported after ECT relieved his deep depression, "A miracle had happened in two weeks" (Endler, 1982).

LaunchPad To witness the powerful effects of ECT, see the *Video: Electroconvulsive Therapy.*

Alternative Neurostimulation Therapies

Three other neural stimulation techniques—mild cranial electrical stimulation, magnetic stimulation, and deep brain stimulation—also aim to treat the depressed brain (**FIGURE 14.5**).

Transcranial Electrical Stimulation In contrast to ECT, which produces a brain seizure with about 800 milliamps of electricity, *transcranial direct current stimulation (tDCS)* administers a weak 1- to 2-milliamp current to the scalp. Skeptics argue that such a current is too weak

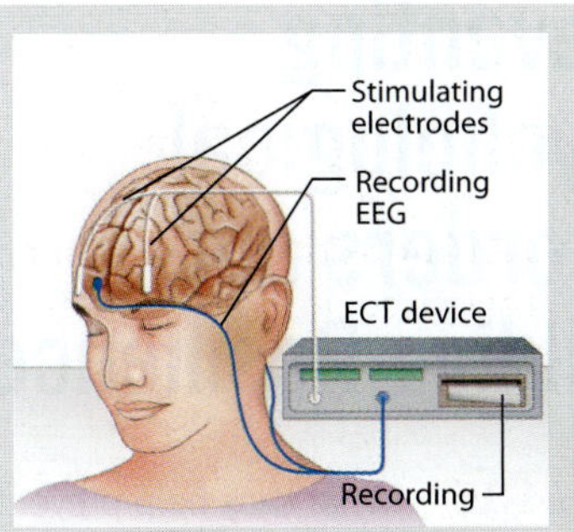

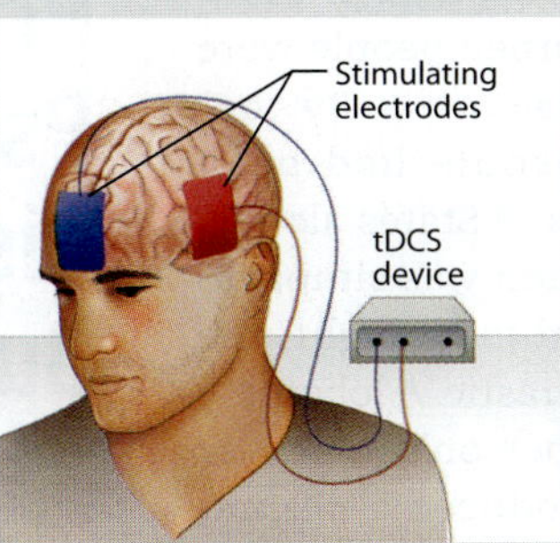

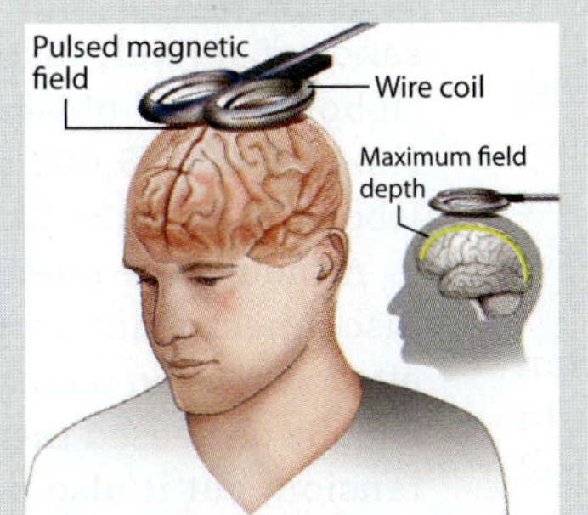

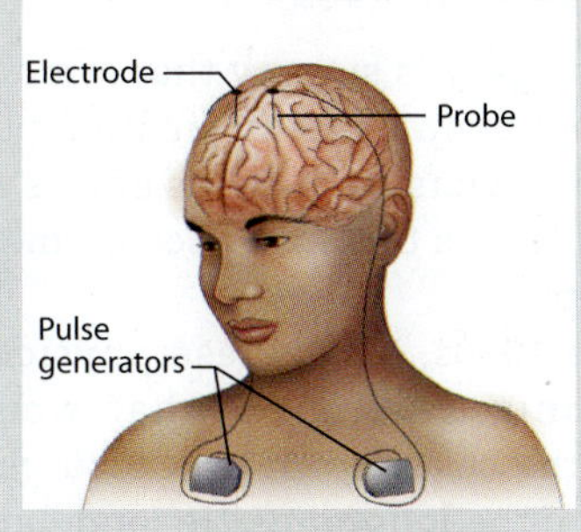

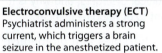

Electroconvulsive therapy (ECT) Psychiatrist administers a strong current, which triggers a brain seizure in the anesthetized patient.

Transcranial direct current stimulation (tDCS) Psychiatrist applies a weak current to the scalp.

Transcranial magnetic stimulation (TMS) Psychiatrist sends a painless magnetic field through the skull to the surface of the cortex to alter brain activity.

Deep brain stimulation (DBS) Psychiatrist stimulates electrodes implanted in "sadness centers" to calm those areas.

FIGURE 14.5 A stimulating experience Today's neurostimulation therapies apply strong or mild electricity, or magnetic energy, either to the skull's surface or directly to brain neurons.

to penetrate to the brain (Underwood, 2016). But research suggests that tDCS is a modestly effective depression and schizophrenia treatment (Bell & DeWall, 2018; Jeon et al., 2018; Koops et al., 2018).

Magnetic Stimulation Depressed moods also sometimes improve when a painless procedure—called **transcranial magnetic stimulation (TMS)**—is performed on wide-awake patients over several weeks. Repeated pulses surging through a magnetic coil held close to the skull can stimulate or suppress activity in areas of the cortex. Like tDCS (and unlike ECT), the TMS procedure produces no memory loss or other serious side effects, aside from possible headaches.

Results are mixed. Some studies have found that, for 30 to 40 percent of people with depression, TMS works (Becker et al. 2016; Brunoni et al., 2017; Taylor et al., 2017). TMS also reduces some symptoms of schizophrenia, such as loss of motivation and social interest (Osoegawa et al., 2018). How it works is unclear. One possible explanation is that the stimulation energizes the brain's left frontal lobe, which is relatively inactive during depression (Helmuth, 2001). Repeated stimulation may cause nerve cells to form new functioning circuits through the process of long-term potentiation. (For more on long-term potentiation, see Chapter 7.) Another possible explanation is a placebo effect—people benefit because they *believe* TMS will work (Yesavage et al., 2018).

Deep Brain Stimulation Other patients whose depression has resisted both drugs and ECT have benefited from an experimental treatment pinpointing a brain depression center. *Deep brain stimulation (DBS)* manipulates the depressed brain by means of a pacemaker that activates implanted electrodes in brain areas that feed negative emotions and thoughts (Lozano et al., 2008; Mayberg et al., 2005). The stimulation inhibits activity in those brain areas. Does DBS work? Multiple studies show that DBS causes large reductions in depressive symptoms (Kisely et al., 2018). Fifteen new National Institutes of Health-funded studies of DBS will soon shed more light on its effectiveness (Underwood, 2017).

electroconvulsive therapy (ECT) a biomedical therapy for severely depressed patients in which a brief electric current is sent through the brain of an anesthetized patient.

transcranial magnetic stimulation (TMS) the application of repeated pulses of magnetic energy to the brain; used to stimulate or suppress brain activity.

Helen Mayberg, M.D. PsychiatricNeuroimaging and Therapeutics, The Mayberg Lab atEmory University, Atlanta, GA/V. J. Wedeen and L.L.Wald/Athinoula A. Martinos Center For Biomedical Imaging and The Human Connectome Project, Boston,MA

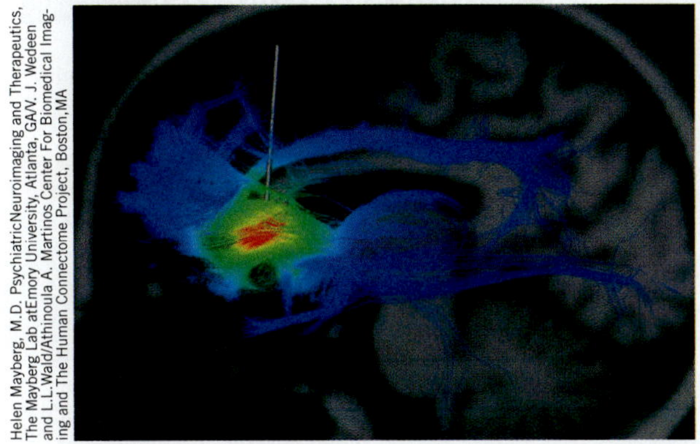

Jared Siskin/Patrick McMullan/Getty Images

A depression switch? By comparing the brains of patients with and without depression, researcher Helen Mayberg identified a brain area (highlighted in red) that appears active in people who are depressed or sad, and whose activity may be calmed by deep brain stimulation.

PSYCHOSURGERY

Psychosurgery is surgery that removes or destroys brain tissue in an attempt to change behaviors. Because its effects are irreversible, it is the least-used biomedical therapy.

In the 1930s, Portuguese physician Egas Moniz developed what would become the best-known psychosurgical operation: the **lobotomy.** He (and, later, other neurosurgeons) used it to calm uncontrollably emotional and violent patients. This crude but easy procedure took only about 10 minutes:

- Step 1. Shock the patient into a coma.
- Step 2. Hammer an icepick-like instrument through the top of each eye socket and into the brain.
- Step 3. Wiggle the instrument to cut nerves connecting the frontal lobes with the emotion-controlling centers of the inner brain.

New York Times Co./Getty Images

Failed lobotomy This 1940 photo shows Rosemary Kennedy (center) at age 22 with brother (and future U.S. president) John and sister Jean. A year later her father approved a lobotomy that doctors suggested would control her reportedly violent mood swings. The procedure left her confined to a hospital with an infantile mentality for the next 63 years, until her death in 2005.

Between 1936 and 1954, tens of thousands of severely disturbed people were "lobotomized" (Valenstein, 1986). By that time, some 35,000 people had been lobotomized in the United States alone.

Although the intention was simply to disconnect emotion from thought, the effect was often more drastic. A lobotomy usually decreased the person's misery or tension, but it also produced a permanently lethargic, immature, uncreative person. During the 1950s, when calming drugs became available, psychosurgery became scorned—as in the saying sometimes attributed to satirist Dorothy Parker that "I'd rather have a free bottle in front of me than a pre-frontal lobotomy."

Today, lobotomies are history. More precise micropsychosurgery is sometimes used in extreme cases. For example, if a patient suffers uncontrollable seizures, surgeons can deactivate the specific nerve clusters that cause or transmit the convulsions. MRI-guided precision surgery is also occasionally done to cut the circuits involved in severe major depressive disorder and obsessive-compulsive disorder (Carey, 2009, 2011; Kim et al., 2018; Sachdev & Sachdev, 1997). Because these procedures cannot be reversed, neurosurgeons perform them only as a last resort.

* * *

TABLE 14.3 summarizes the therapies discussed in this chapter.

IN YOUR EVERYDAY LIFE

What were your impressions of biomedical therapies before reading this chapter? Are any of your views different now? Why or why not?

RETRIEVE & REMEMBER

ANSWERS IN APPENDIX E

13. Severe depression that has not responded to other therapy may be treated with __________ __________, which can cause brain seizures and memory loss. More moderate neural stimulation techniques designed to help alleviate depression include __________ direct current stimulation, __________ magnetic stimulation, and __________ __________ stimulation.

Preventing Psychological Disorders and Building Resilience

LOQ 14-16 What may help prevent psychological disorders, and why is it important to develop resilience?

Psychotherapies and biomedical therapies tend to locate the cause of psychological disorders within the person. We assume that people who act cruelly must be cruel and that people who act "crazy" must be "sick." We label people to separate them from "normal" folks. We try to treat "abnormal" people by giving them insight into their problems, by changing their thinking, by helping them gain control with drugs.

But there is another viewpoint. We could interpret many psychological disorders as understandable responses to a disturbing and stressful society. According to this view, it is not just the person who needs treatment, but also the person's social context. Better to prevent problems by reforming an unhealthy situation, and by developing people's coping skills, than to wait for and treat problems.

PREVENTIVE MENTAL HEALTH

A story about the rescue of a drowning person from a rushing river illustrates prevention. Having successfully given first aid to the first victim, the rescuer spots another struggling person and pulls her out, too. After a half-dozen repetitions, the rescuer suddenly turns and starts running away while the river sweeps yet another person into view. "Aren't you going to rescue that guy?" asks a bystander. "No way," the rescuer replies. "I'm going upstream to find out what's pushing all these people in."

TABLE 14.3 Comparing Therapeutic Approaches

Therapy	Presumed Problem	Therapy Aim	Therapy Technique
Psychodynamic	Unconscious conflicts from childhood experiences	Reduce anxiety through self-insight.	Interpret clients' memories and feelings.
Person-centered	Barriers to self-understanding and self-acceptance	Enable growth via unconditional positive regard, acceptance, genuineness, and empathy.	Listen actively and reflect clients' feelings.
Behavior	Dysfunctional behaviors	Learn adaptive behaviors; extinguish problem ones.	Use classical conditioning (via exposure or aversion therapy) or operant conditioning (as in token economies).
Cognitive	Negative, self-defeating thinking	Promote healthier thinking and self-talk.	Train people to dispute negative thoughts and attributions.
Cognitive-behavioral	Self-harmful thoughts and behaviors	Promote healthier thinking and adaptive behaviors.	Train people to counter self-harmful thoughts and to act out their new ways of thinking.
Group and family	Stressful relationships	Heal relationships.	Develop an understanding of family and other social systems, explore roles, and improve communication.
Therapeutic lifestyle change	Stress and unhealthy lifestyle	Restore healthy biological state.	Alter lifestyle through adequate exercise, sleep, nutrition, and other changes.
Drug therapies	Neurotransmitter malfunction	Control symptoms of psychological disorders.	Alter brain chemistry through drugs.
Brain stimulation	Depression (ECT is used only for severe, treatment-resistant depression)	Alleviate depression, especially when it is unresponsive to drugs or other forms of therapy.	Stimulate brain through electroconvulsive shock, mild electrical stimulation, magnetic pulses, or deep brain stimulation.
Psychosurgery	Brain malfunction	Relieve severe disorders.	Remove or destroy brain tissue.

Preventive mental health care is upstream work. It aims to prevent psychological casualties by identifying and wiping out the conditions that cause them. Poverty, meaningless work, constant criticism, unemployment, racism, and sexism can undermine people's sense of competence, personal control, and self-esteem (Albee, 1986, 2006). Such stresses increase the risk of depression, alcohol use disorder, and suicide.

To prevent psychological casualties we should, said psychologist George Albee, support programs that control or eliminate these stressful situations. We eliminated smallpox not by treating the afflicted but by vaccinating the healthy. We conquered yellow fever by controlling mosquitoes. Better to drain the swamps than just swat the mosquitoes.

Preventing psychological problems means empowering those who have learned an attitude of helplessness and changing environments that breed loneliness. It means renewing fragile family ties. It means boosting parents' and teachers' skills at nurturing children's competence and belief in their abilities. It means using positive psychology interventions to enhance human flourishing. One intervention taught adolescents that personality isn't fixed — people can change — and reduced their incidence of future depression by 40 percent (Miu & Yeager, 2015). This result is no fluke: Preventive therapies have consistently reduced the risk for depression (Breedvelt et al., 2018).

In short, "everything aimed at improving the human condition, at making life more fulfilling and meaningful, may be considered part of primary prevention of mental or emotional disturbance" (Kessler & Albee, 1975, p. 557). Prevention can sometimes provide a double payoff. People with a strong sense of life's meaning are more engaging socially (Stillman et al., 2011). If we can strengthen people's sense of meaning in life, we may also lessen their loneliness as they grow into more engaging companions.

Among the upstream prevention workers are *community psychologists*. Mindful of how people interact with their environment, they focus on creating environments that support psychological health. Through their research and social action, community psychologists aim to empower people and to enhance their competence, health, and well-being.

psychosurgery surgery that removes or destroys brain tissue in an effort to change behavior.

lobotomy a psychosurgical procedure once used to calm uncontrollably emotional or violent patients. The procedure cut the nerves connecting the frontal lobes to the emotion-controlling centers of the inner brain.

Horst Faas/AP Images

Nancy Kaszerman/ZUMA Press/Newscom

Resilient growth from prisoner to politician Before becoming a U.S. senator, John McCain (1936–2018) spent more than five years as a Vietnam War prisoner. He was regularly beaten and tortured, which left him permanently unable to lift his arms above his head. Yet he found strength in reflecting positively on his experience. "I put the war behind me when I left," he said. "The memories I have are of the wonderful people I had the privilege of serving with" (Myre, 2000). When diagnosed with brain cancer in 2017, his daughter Meghan tweeted that "The one of us who is most confident and calm is my father."

resilience the personal strength that helps most people cope with stress and recover from adversity and even trauma.

posttraumatic growth positive psychological changes as a result of struggling with extremely challenging circumstances and life crises.

BUILDING RESILIENCE

Preventive mental health includes efforts to build individuals' **resilience**—the ability to cope with stress and recover from adversity.

Faced with extreme suffering or trauma, some people experience lasting harm, some experience stable resilience, and some actually experience growth (Myers, 2019). In the aftermath of the September 11 terror attacks, many New Yorkers demonstrated resilience. This was especially true for those who enjoyed supportive close relationships and who had not recently experienced other stressful events (Bonanno et al., 2007). More than 9 in 10 New Yorkers, although stunned and grief-stricken by 9/11, did *not* have a dysfunctional stress reaction. Among those who did, the stress symptoms were mostly gone by the following January (Person et al., 2006). Even most combat-stressed veterans, most political rebels who have survived torture, and most people with spinal cord injuries do not later exhibit posttraumatic stress disorder (Bonanno et al., 2012; Mineka & Zinbarg, 1996).

Struggling with challenging crises can lead to **posttraumatic growth.** Many cancer survivors have reported a greater appreciation for life, more meaningful relationships, increased personal strength, changed priorities, and a richer spiritual life (Tedeschi & Calhoun, 2004). Out of even our worst experiences, some good can come, especially when we can imagine new possibilities (Roepke, 2015; Roepke & Seligman, 2015). Through preventive efforts, such as community building and personal growth, fewer of us will fall into the rushing river of psychological disorders. Suffering can beget new sensitivity and strength.

RETRIEVE & REMEMBER

ANSWERS IN APPENDIX E

14. What is the difference between preventive mental health and psychological or biomedical therapy?

LaunchPad Consider ways to build your own resilience by engaging online with *Assess Your Strengths: How Resilient Are You, and Why Should You Build More Resilience?*

* * *

That brings us to the end of this book. Your introduction to psychological science is complete. Navigating through the waters of psychological science has taught us—and you, too?—about our moods and memories, about the inner nooks and crannies of our unconscious, about how our biology and culture shape us. Our hope, as your guides on this tour, is that you have shared some of our fascination, grown in your understanding and compassion, and sharpened your critical thinking. We also hope you enjoyed the ride.

With every good wish in your future endeavors,

David Myers
DavidMyers.org

Nathan DeWall
NathanDeWall.com

LEARNING OBJECTIVES

TEST YOURSELF Answer these repeated Learning Objective Questions on your own (before checking the answers in Appendix D) to improve your retention of the concepts (McDaniel et al., 2009, 2015).

Treating Psychological Disorders

14-1: How do psychotherapy and the biomedical therapies differ?

The Psychological Therapies

14-2: What are the goals and techniques of psychoanalysis, and how have they been adapted in psychodynamic therapy?

14-3: What are the basic themes of humanistic therapy, and what are the goals and techniques of Rogers' person-centered approach?

14-4: How does the basic assumption of behavior therapy differ from the assumptions of psychodynamic and humanistic therapies? What techniques are used in exposure therapies and aversive conditioning?

14-5: What is the basic idea of operant conditioning therapies?

14-6: What are the goals and techniques of the cognitive therapies and of cognitive-behavioral therapy?

14-7: What are the aims and benefits of group and family therapies?

Evaluating Psychotherapies

14-8: Does psychotherapy work? How can we know?

14-9: Are some psychotherapies more effective than others for specific disorders?

14-10: What three elements are shared by all forms of psychotherapy?

14-11: What personal factors influence the client-therapist relationship?

14-12: What should a person look for when selecting a therapist?

The Biomedical Therapies

14-13: Why is therapeutic lifestyle change considered an effective biomedical therapy, and how does it work?

14-14: What are the drug therapies? How do double-blind studies help researchers evaluate a drug's effectiveness?

14-15: How are brain stimulation and psychosurgery used in treating specific disorders?

Preventing Psychological Disorders and Building Resilience

14-16: What may help prevent psychological disorders, and why is it important to develop resilience?

TERMS AND CONCEPTS TO REMEMBER

TEST YOURSELF Write down the definition in your own words, then check your answer.

psychotherapy, *p.* 403
biomedical therapy, *p.* 403
eclectic approach, *p.* 403
psychoanalysis, *p.* 403
resistance, *p.* 403
interpretation, *p.* 403
transference, *p.* 403
psychodynamic therapy, *p.* 403
insight therapies, *p.* 405
person-centered therapy, *p.* 405
active listening, *p.* 405
unconditional positive regard, *p.* 405
behavior therapy, *p.* 405
counterconditioning, *p.* 407
exposure therapies, *p.* 407
systematic desensitization, *p.* 407
virtual reality exposure therapy, *p.* 407
aversive conditioning, *p.* 407
token economy, *p.* 409
cognitive therapy, *p.* 409
cognitive-behavioral therapy (CBT), *p.* 411
group therapy, *p.* 411
family therapy, *p.* 411
evidence-based practice, *p.* 415
therapeutic alliance, *p.* 415
antipsychotic drugs, *p.* 417
antianxiety drugs, *p.* 419
antidepressant drugs, *p.* 419
electroconvulsive therapy (ECT), *p.* 421
transcranial magnetic stimulation (TMS), *p.* 421
psychosurgery, *p.* 423
lobotomy, *p.* 423
resilience, *p.* 424
posttraumatic growth, *p.* 424

CHAPTER TEST

TEST YOURSELF Answer the following questions on your own first, then check your answers in Appendix E.

1. A therapist who helps clients search for the unconscious roots of their problem and offers interpretations of their behaviors, feelings, and dreams, is drawing from
   a. psychoanalysis.
   b. humanistic therapies.
   c. person-centered therapy.
   d. behavior therapy.
2. ________ therapies are designed to help individuals discover the unconscious thoughts and feelings that guide their motivation and behavior.
3. Compared with psychoanalysts, humanistic therapists are more likely to emphasize
   a. hidden or repressed feelings.
   b. childhood experiences.
   c. psychological disorders.
   d. self-fulfillment and growth.
4. A therapist who restates and clarifies the client's statements is practicing the technique of ________ ________.
5. The goal of behavior therapy is to
   a. identify and treat the underlying causes of the problem.
   b. improve learning and insight.
   c. eliminate the unwanted behavior.
   d. improve communication and social sensitivity.
6. Behavior therapies often use ________ techniques, such as systematic desensitization and aversive conditioning, to encourage clients to produce new responses to old stimuli.
7. The technique of ________ ________ teaches people to relax in the presence of progressively more anxiety-provoking stimuli.
8. After a near-fatal car accident, Rico developed such an intense fear of driving on the freeway that he takes lengthy alternative routes to work each day. Which psychological therapy might best help Rico overcome his phobia, and why?
9. At a treatment center, people who display a desired behavior receive coins that they can later exchange for other rewards. This is an example of a(n) ________ ________
10. Cognitive therapy has been especially effective in treating
    a. nail biting.
    b. phobias.
    c. alcohol use disorder.
    d. depression.
11. ________ - ________ therapy helps people to change their self-defeating ways of thinking and to act out those changes in their daily behavior.
12. In family therapy, the therapist assumes that
    a. only one family member needs to change.
    b. each person's actions trigger reactions from other family members.
    c. dysfunctional family behaviors are based largely on genetic factors.
    d. therapy is most effective when clients are treated apart from the family unit.
13. The most enthusiastic or optimistic view of the effectiveness of psychotherapy comes from
    a. outcome research.
    b. randomized clinical trials.
    c. reports of clinicians and clients.
    d. a government study of treatment for depression.
14. Studies show that ________ therapy is the most effective treatment for most psychological disorders.
    a. behavior
    b. humanistic
    c. psychodynamic
    d. no one type of
15. What are the three components of evidence-based practice?
16. How does the placebo effect bias clients' attitudes about the effectiveness of various therapies?
17. Some antipsychotic drugs, used to calm people with schizophrenia, can have unpleasant side effects, most notably
    a. hyperactivity.
    b. convulsions and momentary memory loss.
    c. sluggishness, tremors, and twitches.
    d. paranoia.

18. Drugs such as Xanax and Ativan, which depress central nervous system activity, can become addictive when used as ongoing treatment. These drugs are referred to as ________ drugs.

19. A simple salt that often brings relief to patients suffering the highs and lows of bipolar disorder is ________.

20. When drug therapies have not been effective, electroconvulsive therapy (ECT) may be used as treatment, largely for people with
    a. severe obsessive-compulsive disorder.
    b. severe depression.
    c. schizophrenia.
    d. anxiety disorders.

21. An approach that seeks to identify and alleviate conditions that put people at high risk for developing psychological disorders is called
    a. deep brain stimulation.
    b. the mood-stabilizing perspective.
    c. natural recovery.
    d. preventive mental health.

Continue testing yourself with **LearningCurve** or **Achieve Read & Practice** to learn and remember most effectively.

APPENDIX A

Statistical Reasoning in Everyday Life

SURVEY THE APPENDIX

Describing Data

MEASURES OF CENTRAL TENDENCY
MEASURES OF VARIATION
CORRELATION: A MEASURE OF RELATIONSHIPS

Significant Differences

WHEN IS AN OBSERVED DIFFERENCE RELIABLE?
THINKING CRITICALLY ABOUT: CROSS-SECTIONAL AND LONGITUDINAL STUDIES
WHEN IS AN OBSERVED DIFFERENCE SIGNIFICANT?

Statistics are important tools in psychological research. But accurate statistical understanding benefits everyone. To be an educated person today is to be able to apply simple statistical principles to everyday reasoning. We needn't memorize complicated formulas to think more clearly and critically about data.

Off-the-top-of-the-head estimates often misread reality and mislead the public. Someone throws out a big, round number. Others echo it, and before long the big, round number becomes public misinformation. Two examples:

- ***Ten percent of people are gay or lesbian.*** Or is it 2 to 4 percent, as suggested by various national surveys (Chapter 4)?
- ***We ordinarily use only 10 percent of our brain.*** Or is it closer to 100 percent (Chapter 2)?

If you find an attention-grabbing headline presented without evidence—that nationally there are one million teen pregnancies, two million homeless seniors, or three million alcohol-related car accidents—you can be pretty sure that someone is guessing. If they want to emphasize the problem, they will be motivated to guess big. If they want to minimize the problem, they will guess small. *The point to remember:* Use critical thinking when presented with big, round, undocumented numbers.

When setting goals, we love big, round numbers. We're far more likely to want to lose 20 pounds than 19 or 21 pounds. And batters try to improve their batting average shortly before the season's end, making them nearly four times more likely to finish with a .300 average than with a .299 average (Pope & Simonsohn, 2011).

Statistical illiteracy also feeds needless health scares (Gigerenzer, 2010). In the 1990s, the British press reported a study showing that women taking a particular contraceptive pill had a 100 percent increased risk of blood clots that could produce strokes. The story went viral, causing thousands of women to stop taking the pill. What resulted? A wave of unwanted pregnancies and an estimated 13,000 additional abortions (which also are associated with increased blood clot risk). Distracted by big, round numbers, few people focused on the study's actual findings: A 100 percent increased risk, indeed—but only from 1 in 7000 to 2 in 7000. Such false alarms underscore the need to think critically, to teach statistical reasoning, and to present statistical information more transparently.

"Figures can be misleading—so I've written a song which I think expresses the real story of the firm's performance this quarter."

Describing Data

Learning Objective Question LOQ A-1

How do we describe data using three measures of central tendency, and what is the relative usefulness of the two measures of variation?

Once researchers have gathered their data, they may organize that data using *descriptive statistics*. One way to do this is to convert the data into a simple *bar graph*, as in **FIGURE A.1,** which displays a distribution of different brands of trucks still on the road after a decade. When reading statistical graphs such as this one, take care. It's easy to design a graph to make a difference look big (Figure A.1a) or small (Figure A.1b). The secret lies in how you label the vertical scale (the *y-axis*).

The point to remember: Think smart. When interpreting graphs, consider the scale labels and note their *range*.

IN YOUR EVERYDAY LIFE

Think of a time when you used statistics to make a point—maybe in class, in a paper, or in a discussion with a friend or family member. Looking back, how did you know the data you cited were reliable?

RETRIEVE & REMEMBER

ANSWERS IN APPENDIX E

FIGURE A.1 Read the scale labels

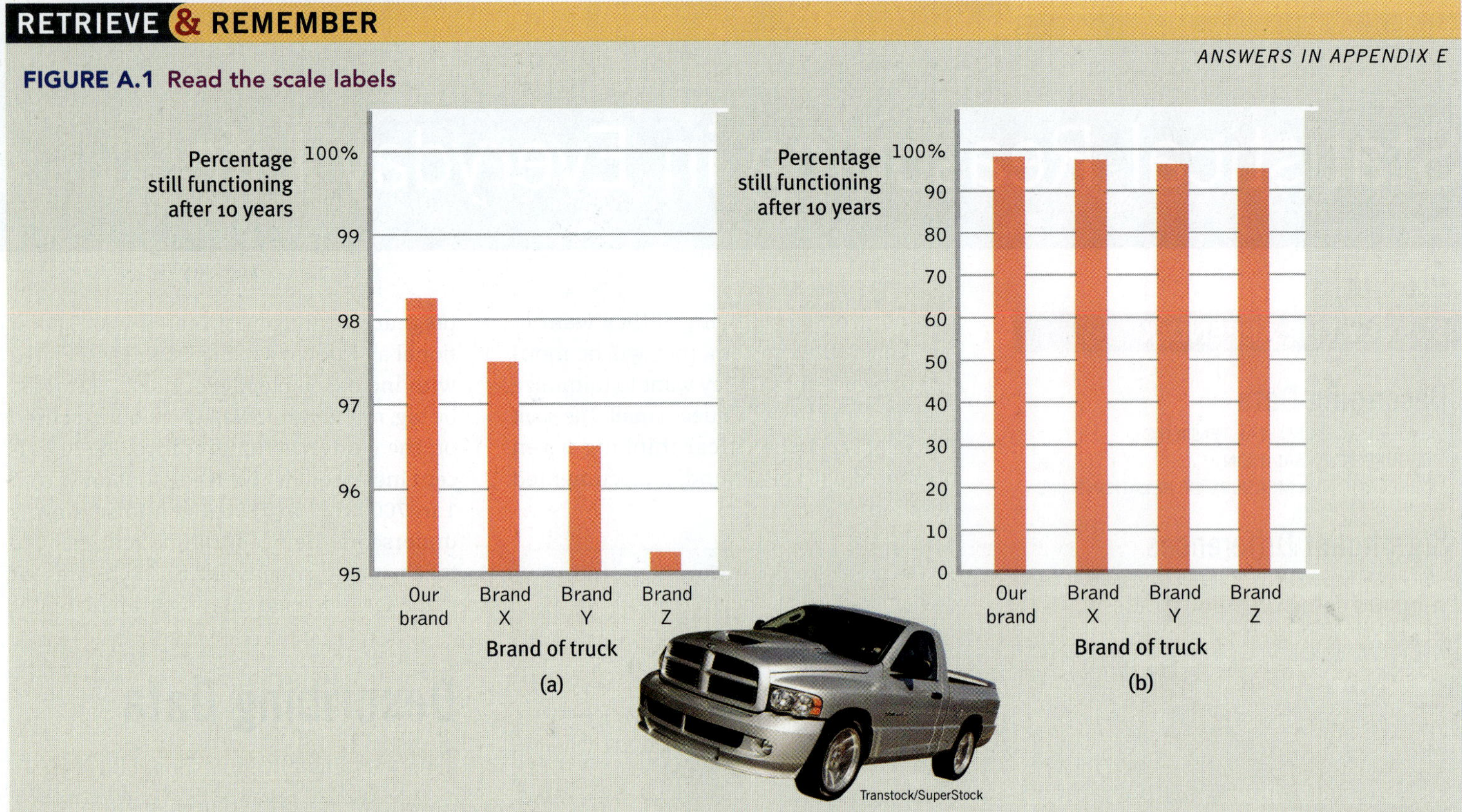

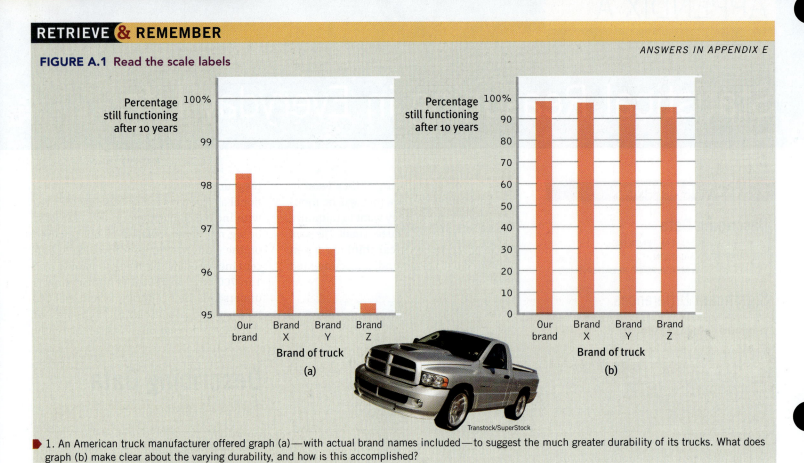

Transtock/SuperStock

1. An American truck manufacturer offered graph (a)—with actual brand names included—to suggest the much greater durability of its trucks. What does graph (b) make clear about the varying durability, and how is this accomplished?

MEASURES OF CENTRAL TENDENCY

The next step is to summarize the data using a *measure of central tendency,* a single score that represents a whole set of scores. The simplest measure is the **mode,** the most frequently occurring score or scores. The most familiar is the **mean,** or arithmetic average—the total sum of all the scores divided by the number of scores. The midpoint—the 50th percentile—is the **median.** On a divided highway, the median is the middle. So, too, with data: If you arrange all the scores in order from the highest to the lowest, half will be above the median and half will be below it.

"The average person has one ovary and one testicle."

Measures of central tendency neatly summarize data. But consider what happens to the mean when a distribution is lopsided—when it's *skewed* by a few way-out scores. With income data, for example, the mode, median, and mean often tell very different stories (**FIGURE A.2**). This happens because the mean is biased by a few extreme incomes. When Amazon founder Jeff Bezos sits down in a small café, its average (mean) customer instantly becomes a billionaire. But median customer wealth remains unchanged. Understanding this, you can see why, according to the 2010 U.S. Census, nearly 65 percent of U.S. households have "below average" income. The bottom half of earners receive much less than half of the total national income. So, most Americans make less than the mean. Mean and median tell different true stories.

The point to remember: Always note which measure of central tendency is reported. If it is a mean, consider whether a few atypical scores could be distorting it.

MEASURES OF VARIATION

Knowing the value of an appropriate measure of central tendency can tell us a great deal. But the single number omits other information. It helps to know something about the amount of *variation* in the data—how similar or diverse the scores are. Averages derived from scores with low variability are more reliable than averages based on scores with high variability. Consider a basketball player who scored between 13 and 17 points in each of the season's first 10 games. Knowing this, we would be more confident that she would score near 15 points in her next game than if her scores had varied from 5 to 25 points.

The **range** of scores—the gap between the lowest and highest—provides only a crude estimate of variation. In an otherwise similar group, a couple of extreme scores, such as the $950,000 and $1,420,000 incomes in Figure A.2, will create a deceptively large range.

The more useful standard for measuring how much scores deviate (differ) from one another is the **standard deviation.** It better gauges whether scores are packed together or dispersed, because it uses information

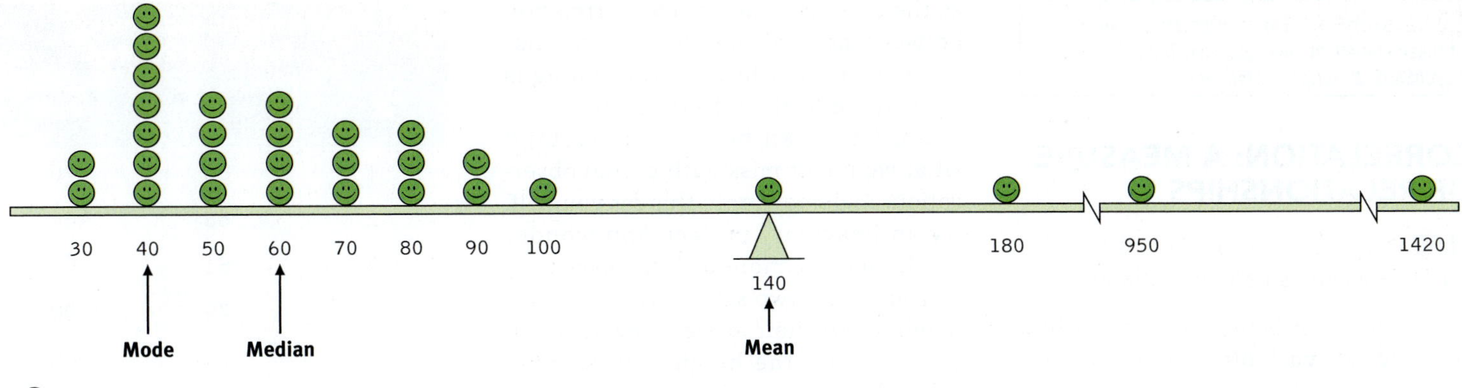

FIGURE A.2 A skewed distribution This graphic representation of the distribution of a village's incomes illustrates the three measures of central tendency—mode, median, and mean. Note how just a few high incomes make the mean—the fulcrum point that balances the incomes above and below—deceptively high.

from each score. The computation[1] assembles information about how much individual scores differ from the mean, which can be very telling. Let's say test scores from Class A and Class B both have the same mean (75 percent correct), but very different standard deviations (5.0 for Class A and 15.0 for Class B). Have you ever had test experiences like that—where two-thirds of your classmates in one course score in the 70 to 80 percent range, with scores in another course more spread out (two-thirds between 60 and 90 percent)? The standard deviation, as well as the mean score, tell us about how each class is faring.

You can grasp the meaning of the standard deviation if you consider how scores naturally tend to be distributed. Large numbers of data—heights, intelligence scores, life expectancy (though not incomes)—often form a symmetrical, *bell-shaped* distribution. Most cases fall near the mean, and fewer cases fall near either extreme. This bell-shaped distribution is so typical that we call the curve it forms the **normal curve.**

As **FIGURE A.3** shows, a useful property of the normal curve is that roughly 68 percent of the cases fall within one standard deviation on either side of the mean. About 95 percent of cases fall within two standard deviations. Thus, as Chapter 8 notes, about 68 percent of people taking an intelligence test will score within ±15 points of 100. About 95 percent will score within ±30 points.

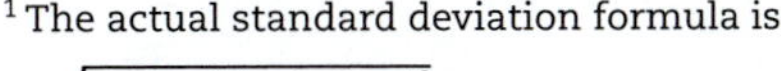
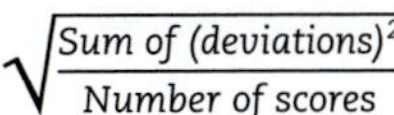

[1] The actual standard deviation formula is:

$$\sqrt{\frac{\textit{Sum of (deviations)}^2}{\textit{Number of scores}}}$$

RETRIEVE & REMEMBER

ANSWERS IN APPENDIX E

2. The average of a distribution of scores is the ________. The score that shows up most often is the ________. The score right in the middle of a distribution (half the scores above it; half below) is the ________. We determine how much scores vary around the average in a way that includes information about the ________ of scores (difference between highest and lowest) by using the ________ ________ formula.

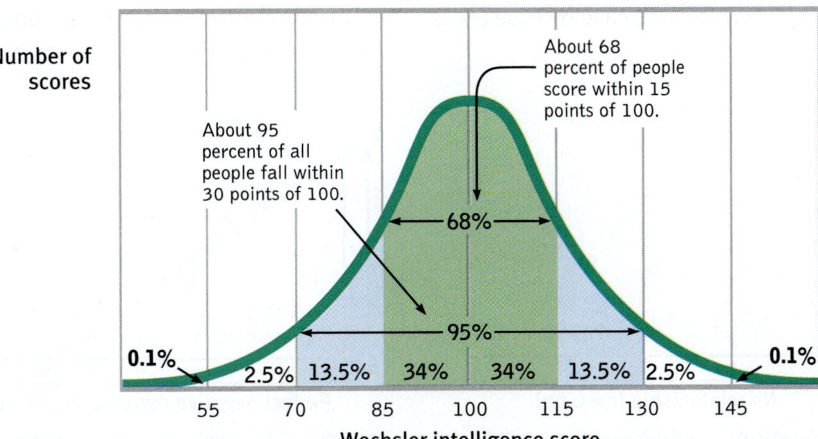

FIGURE A.3 The normal curve Scores on aptitude tests tend to form a normal, or bell-shaped, curve. For example, the most commonly used intelligence test, the Wechsler Adult Intelligence Scale, calls the average score 100.

mode the most frequently occurring score(s) in a distribution.

mean the arithmetic average of a distribution, obtained by adding the scores and then dividing by the number of scores.

median the middle score in a distribution; half the scores are above it and half are below it.

range the difference between the highest and lowest scores in a distribution.

standard deviation a computed measure of how much scores vary around the mean score.

normal curve a symmetrical, bell-shaped curve that describes the distribution of many types of data; most scores fall near the mean (about 68 percent fall within one standard deviation of it) and fewer and fewer near the extremes. (Also called a *normal distribution.*)

LaunchPad For an interactive review of these statistical concepts, visit *Topic Tutorial: PsychSim6, Descriptive Statistics.*

CORRELATION: A MEASURE OF RELATIONSHIPS

LOQ A-2 How do correlations measure relationships between variables?

Throughout this book, we often ask how strongly two **variables** are related: For example, how closely related are the personality test scores of identical twins? How well do intelligence test scores predict career achievement? How much do people's depressive symptoms predict their anxiety?

As we learned in Chapter 1, describing behavior is a first step toward predicting it. When naturalistic observation and surveys reveal that one trait or behavior accompanies another, we say the two *correlate*. A **correlation coefficient** is a statistical measure of relationship. In such cases, **scatterplots** can be very revealing.

Each dot in a scatterplot represents the values of two variables. The three scatterplots in **FIGURE A.4** illustrate the range of possible correlations—from a perfect positive to a perfect negative. (Perfect correlations rarely occur in the real world.) A correlation is positive if two sets of scores, such as for height and weight, tend to rise or fall together.

Saying that a correlation is "negative" says nothing about its strength. A correlation is negative if two sets of scores relate inversely, one set going up as the other goes down. The correlation between people's height and the distance from their head to the ceiling is strongly (perfectly, in fact) negative.

Statistics can help us understand what we might miss with casual observation. To demonstrate this for yourself, try an imaginary project. You wonder if tall men are more or less easygoing, so you collect two sets of scores: men's heights and their anxiety levels. First, you measure the heights of 20 men. Second, you have them complete an anxiety test, with scores ranging from 0 *(extremely calm)* to 100 *(highly anxious)*.

With all the relevant data right in front of you (**TABLE A.1**), can you tell whether the correlation between height and anxiety is positive, negative, or close to zero?

Comparing the columns in Table A.1, most people detect very little relationship between height and anxiety. In fact, the correlation in this imaginary example is positive (+0.63), as we can see if we display the data as a scatterplot (**FIGURE A.5**).

If we fail to see a relationship when data are presented as systematically as in Table A.1, how much less likely are we to notice them in everyday life? To see what is right in front of us, we sometimes need statistical illumination. We can easily see evidence of gender discrimination when given statistically summarized information about job level, seniority, performance, gender, and salary. But we often see no discrimination when the same information dribbles in, case by case (Twiss et al., 1989).

TABLE A.1 Height and Anxiety Scores of 20 Men

Person	Height in Inches	Anxiety Score
1	80	75
2	63	66
3	61	60
4	79	90
5	74	60
6	69	42
7	62	42
8	75	60
9	77	81
10	60	39
11	64	48
12	76	69
13	71	72
14	66	57
15	73	63
16	70	75
17	63	30
18	71	57
19	68	84
20	70	39

The point to remember: Correlation coefficients tell us nothing about cause and effect, but they can help us see

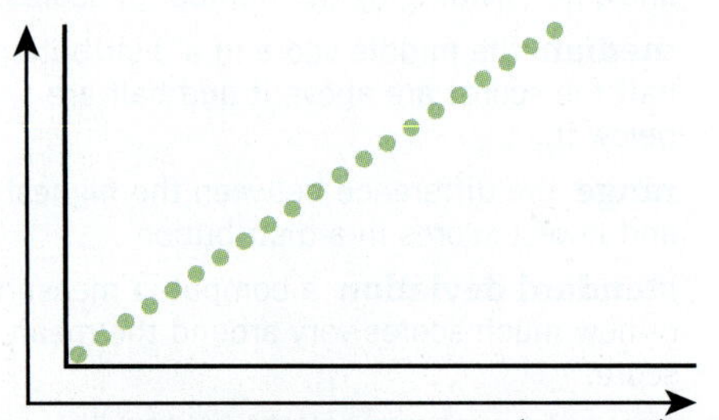
Perfect positive correlation ($r = +1.00$)

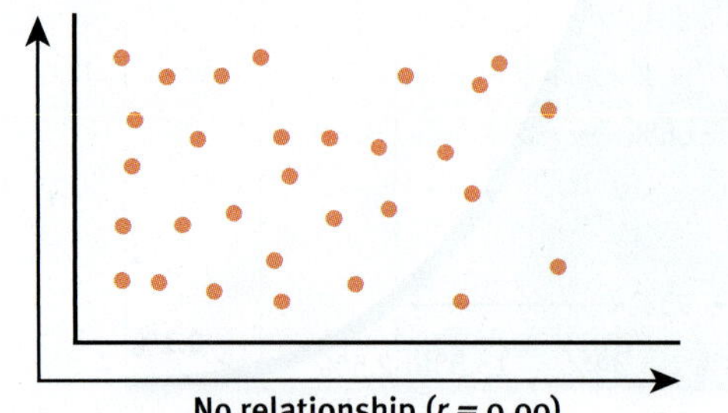
No relationship ($r = 0.00$)

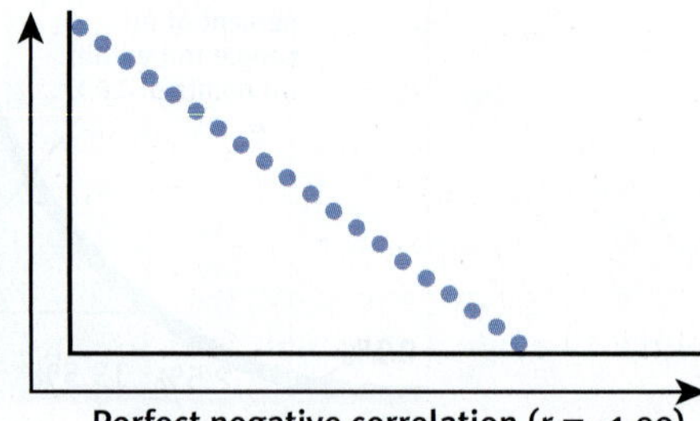
Perfect negative correlation ($r = -1.00$)

FIGURE A.4 Scatterplots, showing patterns of correlation Correlations—abbreviated r—can range from +1.00 (scores for one variable increase in direct proportion to scores for another), to 0.00 (no relationship), to −1.00 (scores for one variable decrease precisely as scores for the other rise).

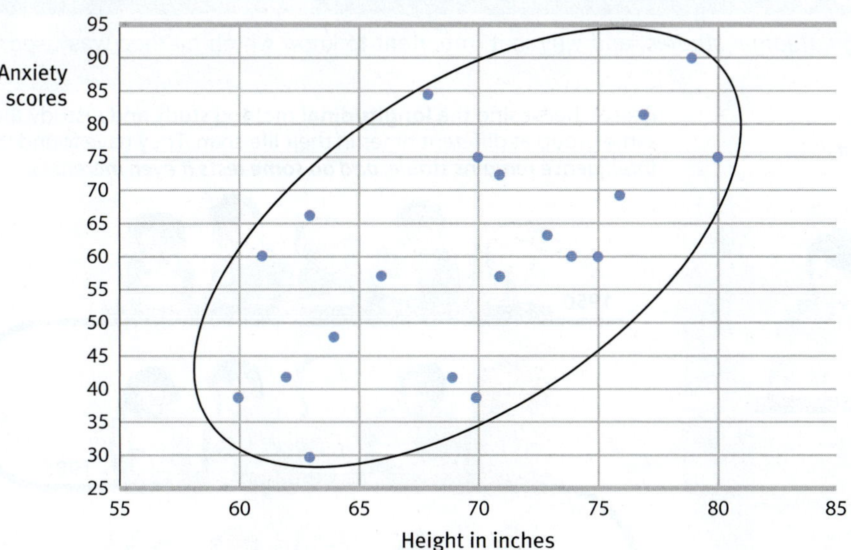

FIGURE A.5 Scatterplot for height and anxiety This display of data from 20 imagined men (each represented by a data point) reveals an upward slope, indicating a positive correlation. The considerable scatter of the data indicates the correlation is much lower than +1.00.

the world more clearly by revealing the extent to which two things relate.

LaunchPad For an animated tutorial on correlations, engage online with *Concept Practice: Positive and Negative Correlations.* See also the *Video: Correlational Studies* for another helpful tutorial animation.

Illusory Correlations and Regression Toward the Mean

LOQ A-3 What are *illusory correlations*, and what is *regression toward the mean?*

Correlations not only make clear the relationships we might otherwise miss; they also keep us from falsely observing nonexistent relationships. When we believe there is a relationship between two things, we are likely to notice and recall instances that confirm our belief. If we believe that dreams are forecasts of actual events, we may notice and recall confirming instances more than disconfirming instances. The result is an **illusory correlation.**

Illusory correlations can feed an illusion of control—that chance events are subject to our personal control. Gamblers, remembering their lucky rolls, may come to believe they can influence the roll of the dice by again throwing gently for low numbers and hard for high numbers. The illusion that uncontrollable events correlate with our actions is also fed by a statistical phenomenon called **regression toward the mean.** Average results are more typical than extreme results. Thus, after an unusual event, things tend to return toward their average level; extraordinary happenings tend to be followed by more ordinary ones.

"Once you become sensitized to it, you see regression everywhere." –Psychologist Daniel Kahneman (1985)

The point may seem obvious, yet we regularly miss it: We sometimes attribute what may be a normal regression (the expected return to normal) to something we have done. Consider two examples:

- Students who score much lower or higher on an exam than they usually do are likely, when retested, to return to their average.
- Unusual ESP subjects who defy chance when first tested nearly always lose their "psychic powers" when retested.

Failure to recognize regression is the source of many superstitions and of some ineffective practices as well. After scolding an employee for poorer-than-usual performance, a manager may—when the employee regresses to normal—feel rewarded by the "improvement." After lavishing praise for an exceptionally fine performance, the manager may be disappointed when the employee's behavior again migrates back toward his or her average. Ironically, then, regression toward the average can mislead us into feeling rewarded after criticizing others ("That criticism really made him work harder!") and feeling punished after praising them ("All those compliments made him slack off!") (Tversky & Kahneman, 1974).

The point to remember: When a fluctuating behavior returns to normal, fancy explanations for why it does so are probably wrong. Regression toward the mean is probably at work.

RETRIEVE & REMEMBER

ANSWERS IN APPENDIX E

3. You hear the school basketball coach telling her friend that she rescued her team's winning streak by yelling at the players after an unusually bad first half. What is another explanation of why the team's performance improved?

variable anything that can vary and is feasible and ethical to measure.

correlation coefficient a statistical index of the relationship between two things (from –1.00 to +1.00).

scatterplot a graphed cluster of dots, each of which represents the values of two variables. The slope of the points suggests the direction of the relationship between the two variables. The amount of scatter suggests the strength of the correlation (little scatter indicates high correlation).

illusory correlation perceiving a relationship where none exists, or perceiving a stronger-than-actual relationship.

regression toward the mean the tendency for extreme or unusual scores or events to fall back (regress) toward the average.

Thinking Critically About:
Cross-Sectional and Longitudinal Studies

LOQ A-5 What are *cross-sectional studies* and *longitudinal studies*, and why is it important to know which method was used?

Researchers using the **cross-sectional** method study different age groups at one time. They have found that ***mental ability declines with age.***[1]

Comparing 70-year-olds and 30-year-olds means not only comparing two different people but also two different eras. These researchers were comparing:

- generally less-educated people (born in the early 1900s) with better-educated people (born after 1950).
- people raised in large families with people raised in smaller families.
- people from less-affluent families with people from more-affluent families.

Researchers using the **longitudinal** method study and restudy the same group at different times in their life span. They have found that ***intelligence remains stable, and on some tests it even increases.***[2]

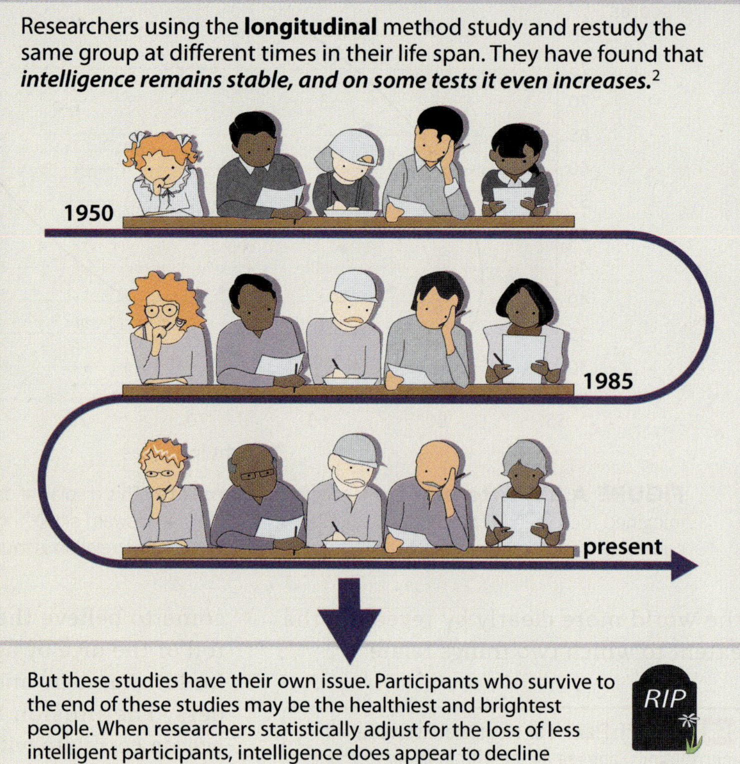

But these studies have their own issue. Participants who survive to the end of these studies may be the healthiest and brightest people. When researchers statistically adjust for the loss of less intelligent participants, intelligence does appear to decline somewhat in later life, especially after age 85.[3]

RIP

1. Wechsler, 1972. 2. Salthouse, 2004, 2010; Schaie & Geiwitz, 1982. 3. Brayne et al., 1999.

Significant Differences

LOQ A-4 How do we know whether an observed difference can be generalized to other populations?

Data are "noisy." The average score in one group could conceivably differ from the average score in another group not because of any real difference, but merely because of chance fluctuations in the people sampled. How confidently, then, can we *infer* that an observed difference is not just a fluke—a chance result from the research sample? For guidance, we can ask whether the observed difference between the two groups is reliable and statistically significant. These *inferential statistics* help us determine if results describe a larger population (all those in a group being studied).

WHEN IS AN OBSERVED DIFFERENCE RELIABLE?

In deciding when it is safe to generalize from a sample, we should keep three principles in mind:

1. ***Representative samples are better than biased (unrepresentative) samples.*** The best basis for generalizing is from a representative sample of cases, not from the exceptional and memorable cases one finds at the extremes. Research never randomly samples the whole human population. Thus, it pays to keep in mind what population a study has sampled. (To see how an unrepresentative sample can lead you astray, see Thinking Critically About: Cross-Sectional and Longitudinal Studies.)
2. ***Less-variable observations are more reliable than those that are more variable.*** As we noted earlier in the example of the basketball player whose game-to-game points were consistent, an average is more reliable when it comes from scores with low variability.
3. ***More cases are better than fewer cases.*** An eager prospective student visits two universities, each for a day. At the first, the student randomly attends two classes and finds both instructors to be witty and engaging. At the second, the two sampled instructors seem dull and uninspiring. Returning home, the student (discounting the small sample size of only two teachers at each institution) tells friends about the "great teachers" at the first school, and the

PEANUTS

"bores" at the second. Again, we know it but we ignore it: *Averages based on many cases are more reliable* (less variable) than averages based on only a few cases. When psychological studies fail to replicate, it is often because they do not have enough cases to yield reliable results (Stanley et al., 2018). More cases make for a more reliable average.

The point to remember: Smart thinkers are not overly impressed by a few anecdotes. Generalizations based on a few unrepresentative cases are unreliable.

LaunchPad Watch the ***Video: Longitudinal and Cross-Sectional Studies*** for a helpful tutorial animation.

WHEN IS AN OBSERVED DIFFERENCE SIGNIFICANT?

Let's say you compared men's and women's scores on a laboratory test of aggression. You found that men behaved more aggressively than women. But individuals differ. How likely is it that your observed gender difference was just a fluke? Statistical testing estimates the probability of the result occurring by chance.

Here is the underlying logic: When averages from two samples are each reliable measures of their respective populations (as when each is based on many observations that have small variability), then their *difference* is probably reliable as well. (Example: The less the variability in men's and in women's aggression scores, the more confidence we would have that your observed gender difference is reliable.) And when the difference between the sample averages is *large,* we have even more confidence that the difference between them reflects a real difference in their populations.

In short, when sample averages are reliable, and when the difference between them is relatively large, we say the difference has **statistical significance.** This means that the observed difference is probably not due to chance variation between the samples.

In judging statistical significance, psychologists are conservative. They are like juries who must presume innocence until guilt is proven. For most psychologists, proof beyond a reasonable doubt means not making much of a finding unless the probability (*p*-value) of it occurring by chance is less than 5 percent ($p < .05$).

When learning about research, you should remember that, given large enough samples, a difference between them may be "statistically significant" yet have little *practical* significance. For example, comparisons of intelligence test scores among hundreds of thousands of first-born and later-born individuals indicate a highly significant tendency for first-born individuals to have higher average scores than their later-born siblings (Rohrer et al., 2015; Zajonc & Markus, 1975). But because the scores differ only slightly, the "significant" difference has little practical importance.

The point to remember: Statistical significance indicates the *likelihood* that a result could have happened by chance. But this does not say anything about the *importance* of the result.

IMPROVE YOUR EVERYDAY LIFE

Can you think of a situation where you were fooled by a writer or speaker's attempts to persuade you with statistics? What have you learned in this appendix that will be most helpful in the future to avoid being misled?

RETRIEVE & REMEMBER

ANSWERS IN APPENDIX E

4. Can you solve this puzzle?

   The registrar's office at the University of Michigan has found that usually about 100 students in Arts and Sciences have perfect marks at the end of their first term. However, only about 10 to 15 students graduate with perfect marks. What do you think is the most likely explanation for the fact that there are more perfect marks after one term than at graduation (Jepson et al., 1983)?

5. ________ statistics summarize data, while ________ statistics determine if data can be generalized to other populations.

LaunchPad For a 9.5-minute summary of psychology's scientific research strategies, see the ***Video: Research Methods.***

cross-sectional study research that compares people of different ages at the same point in time.

longitudinal study research that follows and retests the same people over time.

statistical significance a statistical statement of how likely it is that an obtained result occurred by chance.

Statistical Reasoning in Everyday Life

LEARNING OBJECTIVES

TEST YOURSELF Answer these repeated Learning Objective Questions on your own (before checking the answers in Appendix D) to improve your retention of the concepts (McDaniel et al., 2009, 2015).

Describing Data

A-1: How do we describe data using three measures of central tendency, and what is the relative usefulness of the two measures of variation?

A-2: How do correlations measure relationships between variables?

A-3: What are *illusory correlations,* and what is *regression toward the mean?*

Significant Differences

A-4: How do we know whether an observed difference can be generalized to other populations?

A-5: What are *cross-sectional studies* and *longitudinal studies,* and why is it important to know which method was used?

TERMS AND CONCEPTS TO REMEMBER

TEST YOURSELF Write down the definition in your own words, then check your answer.

mode, *p. A-3*
mean, *p. A-3*
median, *p. A-3*
range, *p. A-3*
standard deviation, *p. A-3*
normal curve, *p. A-3*
variable, *p. A-5*
correlation coefficient, *p. A-5*
scatterplot, *p. A-5*
illusory correlation, *p. A-5*
regression toward the mean, *p. A-5*
cross-sectional study, *p. A-7*
longitudinal study, *p. A-7*
statistical significance, *p. A-7*

APPENDIX A TEST

TEST YOURSELF Answer the following questions on your own first, then check your answers in Appendix E.

1. Which of the three measures of central tendency is most easily distorted by a few very high or very low scores?
   a. The mode
   b. The mean
   c. The median
   d. They are all equally vulnerable to distortion from atypical scores.
2. The standard deviation is the most useful measure of variation in a set of data because it tells us
   a. the difference between the highest and lowest scores in the set.
   b. the extent to which the sample being used deviates from the bigger population it represents.
   c. how much individual scores differ from the mode.
   d. how much individual scores differ from the mean.
3. Another name for a bell-shaped distribution, in which most scores fall near the middle and fewer scores fall at each extreme, is a ____________ ____________.
4. In a ____________ correlation, the scores rise and fall together; in a(n) ____________ correlation, one score falls as the other rises.
   a. positive; negative
   b. positive; illusory
   c. negative; weak
   d. strong; weak
5. If a study revealed that high self-esteem people were less anxious than low self-esteem people, this would suggest that the correlation between self-esteem and anxiety is ____________ (positive/negative).

6. A ____________ provides a visual representation of the direction and the strength of a relationship between two variables.

7. How can regression toward the mean influence our interpretation of events?

8. In ____________ -____________ studies, a characteristic is assessed across different age groups at the same time.

9. When sample averages are ____________ and the difference between them is ____________, we can say the difference has statistical significance.

   a. reliable; large

   b. reliable; small

   c. due to chance; large

   d. due to chance; small

Continue testing yourself with **LearningCurve** or **Achieve Read & Practice** to learn and remember most effectively.

APPENDIX B

Psychology at Work

SURVEY THE APPENDIX

Work and Life Satisfaction
FLOW AT WORK
FINDING YOUR OWN FLOW, AND MATCHING INTERESTS TO WORK

Industrial-Organizational Psychology

Organizational Psychology
SATISFACTION AND ENGAGEMENT AT WORK
EFFECTIVE LEADERSHIP

For many people, to live is to work. Work supports us, giving us food, water, and shelter. Work connects us, meeting our social needs. Work helps define us, satisfying our self-esteem needs. Meeting people and wondering about their identity, we may ask, "So, what do you do?"

We vary in our job satisfaction. How will you feel the day you leave the workforce? Will you sadly bid your former employer farewell? Or will you gladly bid your former employer good riddance? Few of us will look back and say we have followed a predictable career path. We will have changed jobs, some of us often. The trigger for those changes may have been shifting needs in the economy. Rapid technological change has made some jobs disappear, with new ones taking their place — not always smoothly. Or it may have been a desire for better pay, happier on-the-job relationships, or more fulfilling work. What factors influence our perceptions of work as an activity marked by frustration versus *flow?* You might view your job as a necessary chore *or* a meaningful calling. You may also approach your job as an opportunity to do the bare minimum *or* to maximize your potential. Let's take a look at how psychologists can help explain why some jobs are more rewarding than others.

The jobs people do: Columnist Gene Weingarten (2002) noted that sometimes a humorist knows "when to just get out of the way." Here are some sample job titles from the U.S. Department of Labor's ***Dictionary of Occupational Titles:*** animal impersonator, human projectile, banana ripening-room supervisor, impregnator, impregnator helper, dope sprayer, finger waver, rug scratcher, egg smeller, bottom buffer, cookie breaker, brain picker, hand pouncer, bosom presser, and mother repairer.

Work and Life Satisfaction

FLOW AT WORK

Learning Objective Question LOQ B-1
What is *flow?*

Across various occupations, attitudes toward work tend to fall into one of three categories (Wrzesniewski & Dutton, 2001). Some people view their work as a *job*, an unfulfilling but necessary way to make money. Others view their work as a *career*. Their present position may not be ideal, but it is at least a rung on a ladder leading to increasingly better options. The third group views their work as a *calling*. For them, work is a fulfilling and socially useful activity. Of all these groups, those who see their work as a calling report the highest satisfaction with their work and their lives (Dik & Duffy, 2012). For example, physicians who find meaning in their work tend to avoid burnout and enjoy their careers (Levin et al., 2017).

These findings would not surprise Mihaly Csikszentmihalyi [chick-SENT-me-hi] (1990, 1999). He observed that quality of life increases when we are purposefully engaged. Between the anxiety of being overwhelmed and stressed, and the apathy of being underwhelmed and bored, lies a zone in which we experience **flow**. In this intense, focused state, our skills are totally engaged, and we may lose our awareness of self and time. When was the last time you experienced flow? Perhaps you can recall being in a zoned-out flow state while on social media or playing an online game. If so, then perhaps you can sympathize with the two airline pilots who in 2009 were so focused on their laptops that they missed their control tower's messages. The pilots flew 150 miles past their Minneapolis destination — and lost their jobs.

Csikszentmihalyi came up with the flow concept while studying artists who spent hour after hour wrapped up in a project. After painting or sculpting for hours as if

flow a completely involved, focused state, with lowered awareness of self and time; results from full engagement of our skills.

Jacob Ammentorp Lund/iStock/Getty Images

Life disrupted Playing and socializing online are ever-present sources of distraction. It takes energy to resist checking our phones, and time to refocus mental concentration after each disruption. Such frequent interruptions disrupt flow, so it's a good idea to instead schedule regular breaks for checking our devices.

nothing else mattered, they finished and appeared to move on. The artists seemed driven less by external rewards—money, praise, promotion—than by the internal rewards for creating the work. They do what they love, and love what they do. Nearly 200 other studies confirm that *intrinsic motivation* (Chapter 9) enhances performance (Cerasoli et al., 2014).

Fascinated, Csikszentmihalyi broadened his observations. He studied dancers, chess players, surgeons, writers, parents, mountain climbers, sailors, and farmers. His research included Australians, North Americans, Koreans, Japanese, and Italians. Participants ranged in age from the teen years to the golden years. A clear principle emerged: It's exhilarating to flow with an activity that fully engages our skills (Fong et al., 2015). Flow experiences boost our sense of self-esteem, competence, and well-being. Idleness may sound like bliss, but purposeful work enriches our lives. Busy people are happier (Hsee et al., 2010; Robinson & Martin, 2008). One research team interrupted some 5000 people on about a quarter-million occasions (using a phone app), and found people's minds wandering 47 percent of the time. They were, on average, happier when their mind was *not* wandering (Killingsworth & Gilbert, 2010). A focused mind is a happy mind.

FINDING YOUR OWN FLOW, AND MATCHING INTERESTS TO WORK

Want to identify your own path to flow? You can start by pinpointing your strengths and the types of work that may prove satisfying and successful. Marcus Buckingham and Donald Clifton (2001) suggested asking yourself four questions:

1. What activities give me pleasure? Bringing order out of chaos? Playing host? Helping others? Challenging sloppy thinking?
2. What activities leave me wondering, "When can I do this again?" rather than, "When will this be over?"
3. What sorts of challenges do I relish? And which do I dread?
4. What sorts of tasks do I learn easily? And which do I struggle with?

You may find your skills engaged and time flying when teaching or selling or writing or cleaning or consoling or creating or repairing. If an activity feels good, if it comes easily, if you look forward to it, then look deeper. You'll see your strengths at work (Buckingham, 2007). For a free (requires registration) assessment of your own strengths, take the "Brief Strengths Test" at AuthenticHappiness.sas.upenn.edu.

The U.S. Department of Labor also offers a career interest questionnaire through its Occupational Information Network (O*NET). At MyNextMove.org/explore/ip you will need about 10 minutes to respond to 60 items, indicating how much you would like or dislike activities ranging from building kitchen cabinets to playing a musical instrument. You will then receive feedback on how strongly your responses reflect six interest types (Holland, 1996):

- *Realistic* (hands-on doers)
- *Investigative* (thinkers)
- *Artistic* (creators)
- *Social* (helpers, teachers)
- *Enterprising* (persuaders, deciders)
- *Conventional* (organizers)

Finally, depending on how much training you are willing to complete, you will be shown occupations that fit your interest pattern (selected from a national database of 900+ occupations).

Do what you love and you will love what you do. A career counseling science aims, first, to assess people's differing values, personalities, and, especially, *interests*, which are remarkably stable and predictive of future life choices and outcomes (Dik & Rottinghaus, 2013; Stoll et al., 2017). (Your job may change, but your interests today will likely still be your interests in 10 years.) Second, it aims to alert people to well-matched careers—careers with a good *person-environment fit*. It pays to have a personality that fits your job. People who are highly open earn more if they hold jobs that demand openness (actors), whereas people who are highly conscientious earn more if they work in jobs that require conscientiousness (financial managers) (Denissen et al., 2018).

"Find a job you love, and you'll never work another day of your life." —Popular saying expressed in a Facebook hiring video, 2016

One study assessed 400,000 high school students' interests and then followed them over time. The take-home finding: "Interests uniquely predict academic and career success over and above cognitive ability and personality" (Rounds & Su, 2014). Sixty other studies confirm the point both for students in school and workers on the job: Interests predict both performance and persistence (Nye et al., 2012). Lack of job fit can fuel frustration, resulting in unproductive and even hostile work behavior (Harold et al., 2016). One fee-based online service, jobZology.com, was developed by *industrial-organizational psychologists* to put career counseling science into action. First, it assesses people's interests, values, personalities, and workplace culture preferences. It then suggests occupations and connects them to job listings.

IMPROVE YOUR EVERYDAY LIFE

What have you discovered about your own strengths and about the kind of career you might see yourself pursuing?

RETRIEVE & REMEMBER

ANSWERS IN APPENDIX E

1. What is the value of finding flow in our work?

Industrial-Organizational Psychology

LOQ B-2 What are industrial-organizational psychology's three key areas of study?

In developed nations, work has expanded, from farming to manufacturing to *knowledge work*. More and more work is *outsourced* to temporary employees and consultants, or to workers telecommuting from off-site workplaces (Allen, T. D. et al., 2015). (The two-author team for this book and its teaching package is aided immeasurably by a team of people in a dozen cities, from Alberta to Florida.)

As work has changed, have our attitudes toward our work also changed? Has our satisfaction with work increased or decreased? What has happened to the *psychological contract*—that two-way feeling of duty between workers and employers? How can psychologists help organizations make work more satisfying and productive? These are among the questions that fascinate **industrial-organizational (I/O) psychologists** as they apply psychology's principles to the workplace (**TABLE B.1**).

Human factors psychology, now a distinct field allied with I/O psychology, explores how machines and environments can best be designed to fit human abilities. The I/O psychology subfield of **personnel psychology** applies psychology's methods and principles to selecting, placing, training, and evaluating workers. **Organizational psychology** is the primary focus of this appendix. This I/O subfield considers an organization's goals, work environments, and management styles, and their influence on worker motivation, satisfaction, and productivity.

TABLE B.1 I/O Psychology and Human Factors Psychology at Work

As scientists, consultants, and management professionals, industrial-organizational (I/O) psychologists may be found helping organizations to resolve work-family conflicts, build employee retention, address organizational spirit, or promote teamwork. Human factors psychologists contribute to human safety and improved designs.

Personnel Psychology: Maximizing Human Potential	Organizational Psychology: Building Better Organizations
Developing training programs to increase job seekers' success **Selecting and placing employees** • Developing and testing assessment tools for selecting, placing, and promoting workers • Analyzing job content • Optimizing worker placement **Training and developing employees** • Identifying needs • Designing training programs • Evaluating training programs **Appraising performance** • Developing guidelines • Measuring individual performance • Measuring organizational performance	**Developing organizations** • Analyzing organizational structures • Increasing worker satisfaction and productivity • Easing organizational change **Enhancing quality of work life** • Expanding individual productivity • Identifying elements of satisfaction • Redesigning jobs • Balancing work and nonwork life in an era of social media, smartphones, and rapid technological change **Human Factors Psychology** • Designing optimum work environments • Optimizing person-machine interactions • Developing systems technologies

Information from the Society of Industrial and Organizational Psychology. For more information about I/O psychology and related job opportunities, visit SIOP.org.

(Left to right) Hope College; Lorie Hailey; Danielle Slevens; Kathryn Brownson; Trish Morgan; Don Probert; Anna Munroe; Stephanie Ellis; Jeff Brune; Laura Burden.

The modern workforce The editorial team that guides the development of this book and its resources works both in-house and from far-flung places. In column 1: Nancy Fleming in Massachusetts, Kathryn Brownson in Michigan, and Anna Munroe in New York. In column 2: Lorie Hailey in Kentucky, Trish Morgan in Alberta, Carlise Stembridge in Minnesota, and Laura Burden in New York. In column 3: Danielle Slevens in Massachusetts, Betty Probert in Florida, and Christine Brune in Washington, DC.

industrial-organizational (I/O) psychology the application of psychological concepts and methods to human behavior in workplaces.

human factors psychology a field of psychology allied with I/O psychology that explores how people and machines interact and how machines and physical environments can be made safe and easy to use.

personnel psychology an I/O psychology subfield that helps with job seeking, and with employee recruitment, selection, placement, training, appraisal, and development.

organizational psychology an I/O psychology subfield that examines organizational influences on worker satisfaction and productivity and facilitates organizational change.

JOB RECRUITER: "Why did you leave your last job?"
JOB CANDIDATE: "It was something my boss said."
RECRUITER: "What did he say?"
CANDIDATE: "You're fired."

—Joke adapted from ZoomInfo blog

Organizational Psychology

Organizational psychologists help motivate employees and keep them engaged. Organizational psychologists also explore effective leadership.

SATISFACTION AND ENGAGEMENT AT WORK

LOQ B-3 Why are organizational psychologists interested in employee satisfaction and engagement?

Organizational psychologists know that everyone wins when workers are satisfied with their jobs. For employees, satisfaction with work, and with one's work-life balance, feeds overall satisfaction with life (Bowling et al., 2010). Lower job stress (sometimes enabled by telecommuting) supports better health (Allen et al., 2015) (Chapter 10).

How do employers benefit from worker satisfaction? Positive moods can translate into greater creativity, persistence, and helpfulness (Ford et al., 2011; Jeffrey et al., 2014; Shockley et al., 2012). The correlation between individual job satisfaction and performance is modest but real (Judge et al., 2001; Ng et al., 2009; Parker et al., 2003). One analysis tracked 4500 employees at 42 British manufacturing companies. The most productive workers were those who found their work environments satisfying (Patterson et al., 2004). In the United States, *Fortune's* "100 Best Companies to Work For" have also produced much higher-than-average returns for their investors (Yoshimoto & Frauenheim, 2018).

Courtesy of New Lanark Trust

Doing well while doing good—"The Great Experiment" At the end of the 1700s, the New Lanark, Scotland, cotton mill had more than 1000 workers. Many were children drawn from Glasgow's poorhouses. They worked 13-hour days and lived in grim conditions.

On a visit to Glasgow, Welsh-born Robert Owen—an idealistic young cotton-mill manager—chanced to meet and marry the mill owner's daughter. Owen and some partners purchased the mill and on the first day of the 1800s began what he called "the most important experiment for the happiness of the human race that had yet been instituted at any time in any part of the world" (Owen, 1814). The abuse of child and adult labor was, he observed, producing unhappy and inefficient workers. Owen showed *transformational leadership* (discussed later in this appendix) when he undertook numerous innovations: a nursery for preschool children, education for older children (with encouragement rather than corporal punishment), Sundays off, health care, paid sick days, unemployment pay for days when the mill could not operate, and a company store selling goods at reduced prices. He also designed a goals- and worker-assessment program that included detailed records of daily productivity and costs but with "no beating, no abusive language."

The financial success fueled a reform movement for better working and living conditions. By 1816, with decades of profitability still ahead, Owen believed he had demonstrated "that society may be formed so as to exist without crime, without poverty, with health greatly improved, with little if any misery, and with intelligence and happiness increased a hundredfold." Although that vision has not been fulfilled, Owen's great experiment laid the groundwork for employment practices that have today become accepted in much of the world.

Consider a huge study of more than 198,000 employees (Harter et al., 2002). These people were employed in nearly 8000 business units of 36 large companies, including some 1100 bank branches, 1200 stores, and 4200 teams or departments. The study focused on links between various measures of organizational success and employee engagement—the extent of workers' involvement, enthusiasm, and identification with their organizations (**TABLE B.2**). The researchers found

TABLE B.2 Three Types of Employees

Engaged:	working with passion and feeling a profound connection to their company or organization.
Not engaged:	putting in the time but investing little passion or energy in their work.
Actively disengaged:	unhappy workers undermining what their colleagues accomplish.

Information from Gallup via Crabtree, 2005.

that *engaged* workers (compared with not-engaged workers, who are just putting in their time) know what's expected of them, have what they need to do their work, feel fulfilled in their work, have regular opportunities to do what they do best, perceive that they are part of something significant, and have opportunities to learn and develop. They also found that business units with engaged employees have more loyal customers, less turnover, higher productivity, and greater profits.

What percentage of employees are engaged? One massive study of 6.4 million people in 159 countries showed that only about 15 percent of workers reported being engaged (Gallup, 2017). Engagement—feeling involved in and enthusiastic about one's work—is highest among people who have knowledge-based jobs, such as those that require a college degree. By furthering your education, you'll increase your chances of having an engaging career.

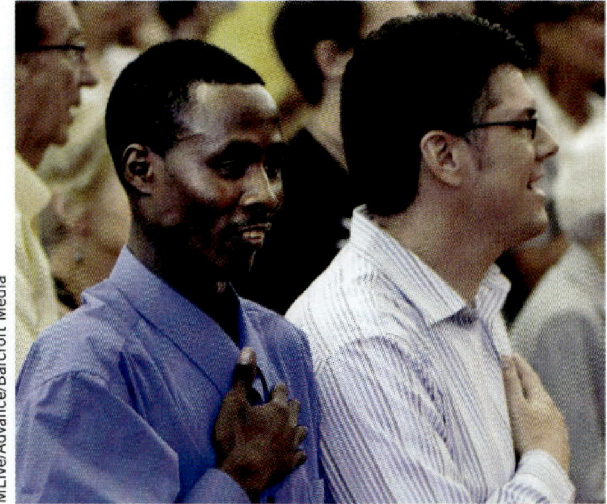

MLive/Advance/Barcroft Media

An engaged employee Mohamed Mamow, left, was joined by his employer in saying the Pledge of Allegiance as he became a U.S. citizen. Mamow and his wife met in a Somali refugee camp. Since then, he has supported his family by working as a machine operator. Mindful of his responsibility—"I don't like to lose my job. I have a responsibility for my children and my family"—he would arrive for work a half hour early and tend to every detail on his shift. "He is an extremely hard-working employee," noted his employer, and "a reminder to all of us that we are really blessed" (Roelofs, 2010).

But what causal arrows explain this correlation between business success and employee morale and engagement? Does success boost morale, or does high morale boost success? In a follow-up longitudinal study of 142,000 workers, researchers found that, over time, employee attitudes predicted future business success (more than the other way around) (Harter et al., 2010). Many other studies confirm that happy workers tend to be good workers (Ford et al., 2011; Seibert et al., 2011; Shockley et al., 2012). One analysis compared companies with top-quartile versus below-average employee engagement levels. Over a three-year period, earnings grew 2.6 times faster for the companies with highly engaged workers (Ott, 2007). It pays to have engaged employees.

EFFECTIVE LEADERSHIP

LOQ B-4 How can leaders be most effective?

Engaged employees don't just happen. They often have effective **leaders**—people who motivate and influence them to enable their group's success, and who engage their interests and loyalty. Such leaders figure out people's natural talents, adjust roles to suit their abilities, and develop those talents into great strengths (**FIGURE B.1**). Great managers support employees' well-being, explain

tdub_video/Getty Images

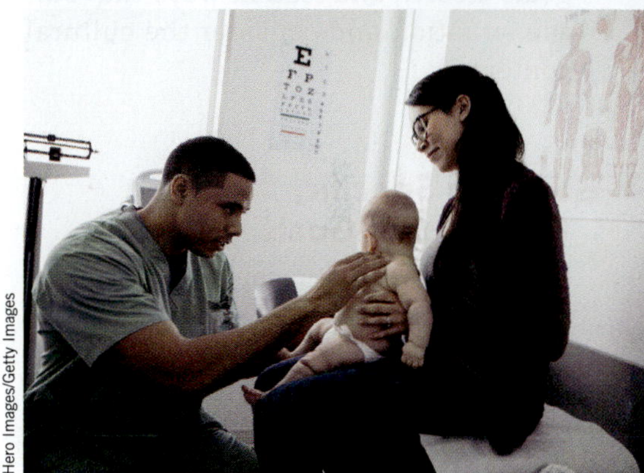

Hero Images/Getty Images

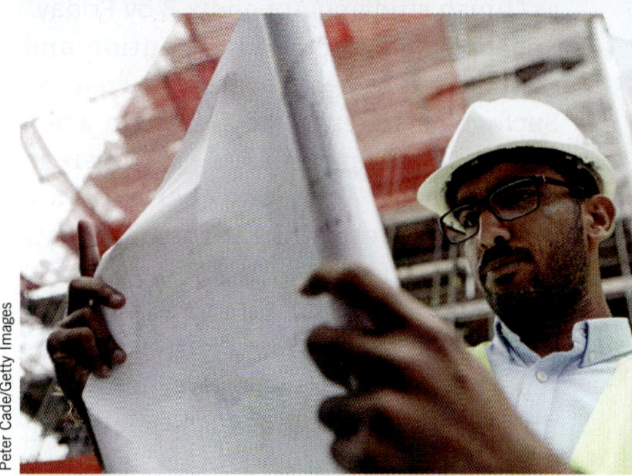

Peter Cade/Getty Images

Task significance People find their work meaningful and engaging when it has task significance—when they view their work as benefiting others (Allan, 2017).

leadership an individual's ability to motivate and influence others to contribute to their group's success.

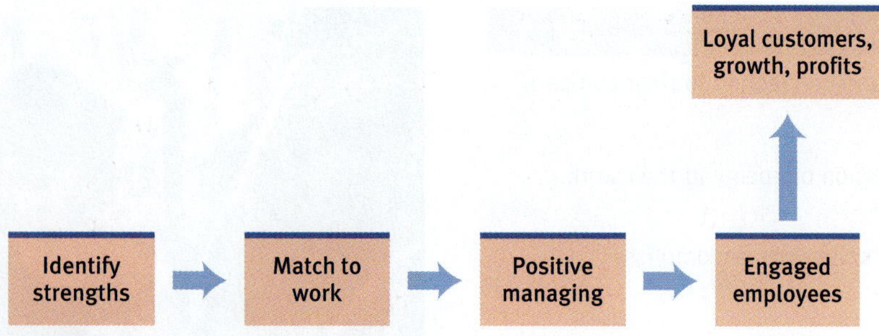

FIGURE B.1 On the right path The Gallup organization offers this path to organizational success. (Information from Fleming, 2001.)

goals clearly, and lead in ways that suit the situation and consider the cultural context.

Setting Specific, Challenging Goals

In study after study, people merely asked to do their best do not do so. Good managers know that a better way to motivate higher achievement is to set specific, challenging goals. For example, you might state your own current goal in this course as "finish studying Appendix B by Friday." Specific goals focus our attention and stimulate us to persist and to be creative. Such goals are especially effective when workers or team members participate in setting them. Achieving goals that are challenging yet within our reach boosts our self-evaluation (White et al., 1995).

Goals motivate achievement, especially when combined with progress reports (Harkin et al., 2016). For many people, a landmark in time—a special birthday, the new year or new school term, graduation, a new job, a new decade of life—spurs personal goal setting (Alter & Hershfield, 2014; Dai et al., 2014). Action plans that break large goals into smaller steps (*subgoals*) and specify *implementation intentions*—when, where, and how to achieve those steps—increase the chances of completing a project on time (Fishbach et al., 2006; Gollwitzer & Sheeran, 2006).

Through a task's ups and downs, we best sustain our mood and motivation when we focus on immediate goals (such as daily study) rather than distant goals (such as a course grade). Better to have our nose to the grindstone than our eye on the ultimate prize (Houser-Marko & Sheldon, 2008). Thus, before beginning each new edition of this book, our author-editor team *manages by objectives*—we agree on target dates for completion of each chapter draft. If we focus on achieving each of these short-term goals, then the prize—an on-time book—takes care of itself. So, to motivate high productivity, effective leaders work with people to define explicit goals, subgoals, and implementation plans, and then provide feedback on progress.

Choosing an Appropriate Leadership Style

Effective leaders of laboratory groups, work teams, and large corporations often have *charisma*—an ability to influence others while making them comfortable (Goethals & Allison, 2014; Tshkay et al., 2018). Charismatic people have the capacity to inspire others' loyalty and to focus their enthusiasm (Grabo & van Vugt, 2016).

Charisma can bolster leadership, especially when combined with practical managerial skills (Vergauwe et al., 2018). What other qualities help? Leadership styles vary, depending both on the qualities of the leader and the demands of the situation. In some situations (think of a commander leading troops into battle), a *directive* style may be needed (Fiedler, 1981). In other situations, the strategies that work on the battlefield may smother creativity. If developing a comedy show, for example, a leader might get better results using a *democratic* style that welcomes team member creativity.

Leaders differ in the personal qualities they bring to the job. Some excel at **task leadership**—by setting standards, organizing work, and focusing attention on goals. To keep the group centered on its mission, task leaders typically use a directive style. This style can work well if the leader gives good directions (Fiedler, 1987).

Other managers excel at **social leadership.** They explain decisions, help group members solve their conflicts, and build teams that work well together (Evans & Dion, 1991; Pfaff et al., 2013). Social leaders, many of whom are women, often have a democratic style. They share authority and welcome team members' opinions. Social leadership and team-building increases morale and productivity (Shuffler et al., 2011, 2013). We usually feel more satisfied and motivated, and perform better, when we can participate in decision making (Cawley et al., 1998; Pereira & Osburn, 2007). Moreover, when members are sensitive to one another and participate equally, groups solve problems with greater "collective intelligence" (Woolley et al., 2010).

In one study of morale at 50 Dutch firms, firms with the highest morale ratings had chief executives who inspired their colleagues "to transcend their own self-interests for the sake of the collective" (de Hoogh et al., 2004). This ability to motivate others to fully commit themselves to a group's mission is *transformational leadership*. Transformational leaders are often natural extraverts. They set their standards high, and they inspire others to share their vision. They pay attention to other people (Bono & Judge, 2004). The frequent result is a workforce that is more engaged, trusting, and effective (Turner et al., 2002).

Women more than men tend to be transformational leaders. This may help explain why companies with women in top management positions have tended to enjoy superior financial results (Eagly, 2007, 2013). That tendency has held even after researchers controlled for variables such as company size.

Studies in India, Taiwan, and Iran suggest that effective managers—whether in coal mines, banks, or government offices—often exhibit a high degree of *both* task and social leadership (Smith & Tayeb, 1989). As achievement-minded people, effective managers certainly care about how well people do their work. Yet they are sensitive to their workers' needs. That sensitivity is often repaid by worker loyalty. Workers in family-friendly organizations that offer flexible hours report feeling greater job satisfaction and loyalty to their employers (Butts et al., 2013; Roehling et al., 2001). Over time, U.S. senators who practice common virtues (humility, wisdom, courage) become more influential in leadership roles than do those who practice manipulation and intimidation (ten Brinke et al., 2016). Social virtues work.

Three other elements can make for effective leadership:

- ***Positive reinforcement*** Effective leadership often builds on a basic principle of *operant conditioning:* To teach a behavior, catch a person doing something right and reinforce it. It sounds simple, but many managers are like parents who, when a child brings home a near-perfect school report card, focus on the one low grade in a troublesome biology class and ignore the rest. "Sixty-five percent of Americans received NO praise or recognition in the workplace last year" reported the Gallup organization (2004).
- ***Fulfilling the need to belong*** A work environment that satisfies employees' need to belong is energizing. Employees who enjoy high-quality colleague relationships engage their work with more vigor (Carmeli et al., 2009). Gallup researchers have asked more than 15 million employees worldwide if they have a "best friend at work." The 30 percent who do "are *seven times* as likely to be engaged in their jobs" as those who don't, researchers report (Rath & Harter, 2010). And, as we noted earlier, positive, engaged employees are a mark of thriving organizations.
- ***Participative management*** Employee participation in decision making is common in Sweden, Japan, the United States, and elsewhere (Cawley et al., 1998; Sundstrom et al., 1990). Workers given a chance to voice their opinion and be part of the decision-making process have responded more positively to the final decision (van den Bos & Spruijt, 2002). They also feel more empowered, and are likely, therefore, to be more creative and committed (Hennessey & Amabile, 2010; Seibert et al., 2011).

The ultimate in employee participation is the employee-owned company. One such company in my [DM's] town is the Fleetwood Group, a thriving 115-employee manufacturer of educational furniture and wireless communication devices. Every employee owns part of the company, and as a group they own 100 percent. The more years employees work, the more they own, yet no one owns more than 5 percent. Like every corporate president, Fleetwood's president works for his stockholders—who also just happen to be his employees.

As a company that endorses faith-inspired "respect and care for each team member-owner," Fleetwood is free to place people above profits. Thus, when orders lagged during a recession, the employee-owners decided that job security meant more than profits. So the company paid otherwise idle workers to do community service, such as answering phones at nonprofit agencies and building Habitat for Humanity houses. Employee ownership attracts and retains talented people, which for Fleetwood has meant company success.

The power of positive coaching Football coach Pete Carroll, who led the University of Southern California to two national championships and the Seattle Seahawks to a Super Bowl championship, has combined positive enthusiasm and fun workouts with "a commitment to a nurturing environment that allows people to be themselves while still being accountable to the team" (Trotter, 2014). "It shows you can win with positivity," noted former Seahawks defensive star Richard Sherman. "It's literally all positive reinforcement," said teammate Jimmy Graham (Belson, 2015).

Cultural Influences on Leadership Styles

LOQ B-5 What cultural influences need to be considered when choosing an effective leadership style?

I/O psychology sprang from North American roots. So, how well do its leadership principles apply to cultures worldwide?

task leadership goal-oriented leadership that sets standards, organizes work, and focuses attention on goals.

social leadership group-oriented leadership that builds teamwork, resolves conflict, and offers support.

AJ_Watt/Getty Images

Effective leaders + satisfying work = engaged employees

One worldwide investigation, Project GLOBE (Global Leadership and Organizational Behavior Effectiveness), has studied cultural variations in leadership expectations (House et al., 2001). Some cultures, for example, encourage collective sharing of resources and rewards; others are more individualist. Some cultures minimize and others highlight traditional gender roles. Some cultures prioritize being friendly, caring, and kind, and others encourage a "me-first" attitude. The program's first research phase studied 17,300 leaders of 950 organizations in 61 countries (Brodbeck et al., 2008; Dorfman et al., 2012). One finding: Leaders who fulfill expectations, such as by being directive in some cultures or participative in others, tend to be successful. Cultures shape leadership and what makes for leadership success.

Nevertheless, some leader behaviors are universally effective. From its massive study of nearly 50,000 business units in 45 countries, Gallup observed that thriving companies tend to focus on identifying and enhancing employee *strengths* (rather than punishing their weaknesses). Doing so predicts increased employee engagement, customer satisfaction, and profitability (Rigoni & Asplund, 2016a,b). *Strengths-based* leadership pays dividends, supporting happier, more creative, more productive employees in workplaces with less absenteeism and turnover (Amabile & Kramer, 2011; De Neve et al., 2013).

Moreover, the same principles affect student satisfaction, retention, and future success (Larkin et al., 2013; Ray & Kafka, 2014). Students who feel supported by caring friends and mentors tend to persist and ultimately succeed during school and after graduation.

IMPROVE YOUR EVERYDAY LIFE

In what type of leadership role do you think you would most excel? If you already have leadership experience, how could you grow to become a more effective leader?

RETRIEVE & REMEMBER

ANSWERS IN APPENDIX E

2. What characteristics are important for *transformational leaders?*

APPENDIX B REVIEW Psychology at Work

LEARNING OBJECTIVES

TEST YOURSELF Answer these repeated Learning Objective Questions on your own (before checking the answers in Appendix D) to improve your retention of the concepts (McDaniel et al., 2009, 2015).

Work and Life Satisfaction

B-1: What is *flow?*

Industrial-Organizational Psychology

B-2: What are industrial-organizational psychology's three key areas of study?

Organizational Psychology

B-3: Why are organizational psychologists interested in employee satisfaction and engagement?

B-4: How can leaders be most effective?

B-5: What cultural influences need to be considered when choosing an effective leadership style?

TERMS AND CONCEPTS TO REMEMBER

TEST YOURSELF Write down the definition in your own words, then check your answer.

flow, *p. B-1*

industrial-organizational (I/O) psychology, *p. B-3*

human factors psychology, *p. B-3*

personnel psychology, *p. B-3*

organizational psychology, *p. B-3*

leadership, *p. B-5*

task leadership, *p. B-7*

social leadership, *p. B-7*

APPENDIX B TEST

TEST YOURSELF Answer the following questions on your own first, then check your answers in Appendix E.

1. People who view their work as a calling often experience _______, a focused state of consciousness, with lowered awareness of themselves and of time.
2. What are industrial-organizational psychology's three key areas of study?
3. ________ psychologists study job seeking, and the recruitment, selection, placement, training, appraisal, and development of employees; ________ ________ psychologists focus on how people and machines interact, and on optimizing devices and work environments.
4. What type of goals will best help you stay focused and motivated to do your finest work in this class?
5. Research indicates that women are often social leaders. They are also more likely than men to have a ________ leadership style.
6. Effective managers often exhibit
   a. only task leadership.
   b. only social leadership.
   c. both task and social leadership, depending on the situation and the person.
   d. task leadership for building teams and social leadership for setting standards.

Continue testing yourself with **LearningCurve** or **Achieve Read & Practice** to learn and remember most effectively.

APPENDIX C

Career Fields in Psychology

Jennifer Zwolinski *University of San Diego*

What can you do with a degree in psychology? Lots!

As a psychology major, you will graduate with a scientific mindset and an awareness of basic principles of human behavior (biological mechanisms, nature–nurture interactions, life-span development, cognition, psychological disorders, social interaction). This background will prepare you for success in many areas, including business, the helping professions, health services, marketing, law, sales, and teaching. You may even go on to graduate school for specialized training to become a psychology professional. This appendix provides an overview of some of psychology's key career fields.[1] For more detailed information, see ***Pursuing a Psychology Career*** in LaunchPad (LaunchPadWorks.com), where you can learn more about the many interesting options available to those with bachelor's, master's, and doctoral degrees in psychology.

If you are like most psychology students, you may be unaware of the wide variety of specialties and work settings available in psychology (Terre & Stoddart, 2000). To date, the American Psychological Association (APA) has 54 divisions (**TABLE C.1**) that represent the popular subfields and interest groups of APA members. APA Division 2 (Society for the Teaching of Psychology) offers an excellent career exploration resource for those interested in learning about the hundreds of career

TABLE C.1 APA Divisions by Number and Name

No.	Division	No.	Division
1.	Society for General Psychology	31.	State, Provincial and Territorial Psychological Association Affairs
2.	Society for the Teaching of Psychology	32.	Society for Humanistic Psychology
3.	Society for Experimental Psychology and Cognitive Science	33.	Intellectual and Developmental Disabilities/ Autism Spectrum Disorder
4.	*There is no active Division 4.*	34.	Society for Environmental, Population and Conservation Psychology
5.	Quantitative and Qualitative Methods	35.	Society for the Psychology of Women
6.	Society for Behavioral Neuroscience and Comparative Psychology	36.	Society for the Psychology of Religion and Spirituality
7.	Developmental Psychology	37.	Society for Child and Family Policy and Practice
8.	Society for Personality and Social Psychology	38.	Society for Health Psychology
9.	Society for the Psychological Study of Social Issues (SPSSI)	39.	Society for Psychoanalysis and Psychoanalytic Psychology
10.	Society for the Psychology of Aesthetics, Creativity and the Arts	40.	Society for Clinical Neuropsychology
11.	There is no active Division *11.*	41.	American Psychology-Law Society
12.	Society of Clinical Psychology	42.	Psychologists in Independent Practice
13.	Society of Consulting Psychology	43.	Society for Couple and Family Psychology
14.	Society for Industrial and Organizational Psychology	44.	Society for the Psychology of Sexual Orientation and Gender Diversity
15.	Educational Psychology	45.	Society for the Psychological Study of Culture, Ethnicity and Race
16.	School Psychology	46.	Society for Media Psychology and Technology
17.	Society of Counseling Psychology	47.	Society for Sport, Exercise and Performance Psychology
18.	Psychologists in Public Service	48.	Society for the Study of Peace, Conflict and Violence: Peace Psychology Division
19.	Society for Military Psychology	49.	Society of Group Psychology and Group Psychotherapy
20.	Adult Development and Aging	50.	Society of Addiction Psychology
21.	Applied Experimental and Engineering Psychology	51.	Society for the Psychological Study of Men and Masculinities
22.	Rehabilitation Psychology	52.	International Psychology
23.	Society for Consumer Psychology	53.	Society of Clinical Child and Adolescent Psychology
24.	Society for Theoretical and Philosophical Psychology	54.	Society of Pediatric Psychology
25.	Behavior Analysis	55.	American Society for the Advancement of Pharmacotherapy
26.	Society for the History of Psychology	56.	Trauma Psychology
27.	Society for Community Research and Action: Division of Community Psychology		
28.	Psychopharmacology and Substance Abuse		
29.	Society for the Advancement of Psychotherapy		
30.	Society of Psychological Hypnosis		

Source: American Psychological Association

[1] Although this text covers the world of psychology for students in many countries, this appendix draws primarily from available U.S. data. Its descriptions of psychology's career fields are, however, also applicable in many other countries.

options available for students with an undergraduate degree in psychology.

The following paragraphs (arranged alphabetically) describe some of psychology's main career fields, most of which require a graduate degree in psychology.

CLINICAL PSYCHOLOGISTS promote psychological health in individuals, groups, and organizations. Some clinical psychologists specialize in specific psychological disorders. Others treat a range of disorders, from adjustment difficulties to severe psychopathology. Clinical psychologists often provide therapy but may also engage in research, teaching, assessment, and consultation. Clinical psychologists work in a variety of settings, including private practice, industry, mental health service organizations, schools, universities, legal systems, medical systems, counseling centers, government agencies, correctional facilities, nonprofit organizations, and military services.

To become a clinical psychologist, you will need to earn a doctorate from a clinical psychology program. The APA sets the standards for clinical psychology graduate programs, offering accreditation (official recognition) to those who meet their standards. In all U.S. states, clinical psychologists working in independent practice must obtain a license to offer services such as therapy and testing.

AP Photo

Community care Community psychologists in Haiti have helped residents work through the ongoing emotional challenges that followed the devastating 2010 earthquake and the widely destructive 2016 hurricane.

COGNITIVE PSYCHOLOGISTS study thought processes and focus on such topics as perception, language, attention, problem solving, memory, judgment and decision making, forgetting, and intelligence. Research interests include designing computer-based models of thought processes and identifying biological correlates of cognition. As a cognitive psychologist, you might work as a professor, industrial consultant, or human factors specialist in an educational or business setting.

COMMUNITY PSYCHOLOGISTS move beyond focusing on specific individuals or families and deal with broad problems of mental health in community settings. These psychologists believe that human behavior is powerfully influenced by the interaction between people and their physical, social, political, and economic environments. They seek to promote psychological health by enhancing environmental settings—focusing on preventive measures and crisis intervention, with special attention to the problems of underserved groups and ethnic minorities. Some community psychologists collaborate with professionals in other areas, such as public health, with a shared emphasis on prevention. As a community psychologist, your work settings could include federal, state, and local departments of mental health, corrections, and welfare. You might conduct research or help evaluate research in health service settings, serve as an independent consultant for a private or government agency, or teach and consult as a college or university faculty member.

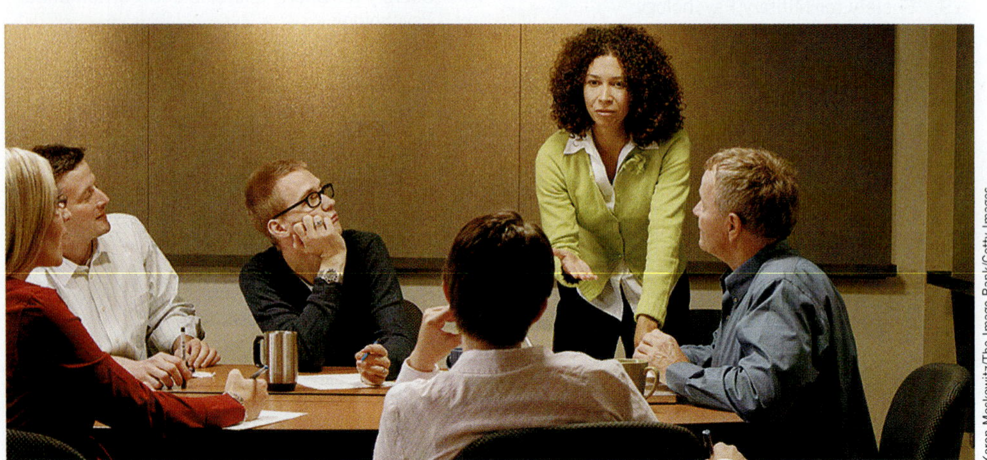

Karen Moskowitz/The Image Bank/Getty Images

Cognitive consulting Cognitive psychologists may advise businesses on how to operate more effectively by understanding the human factors involved.

COUNSELING PSYCHOLOGISTS help people adjust to life transitions or make lifestyle changes. Although similar to clinical psychologists, counseling psychologists typically help people with adjustment problems rather than severe psychopathology. Like clinical psychologists, counseling psychologists conduct therapy and provide assessments to individuals and groups. As a counseling psychologist, you would likely emphasize your clients' strengths, helping them to use their own skills, interests, and abilities to cope during transitions. You might find yourself working in an academic setting as a faculty member or administrator or in a university counseling center, community mental health center, business, or private practice. As with clinical psychology, if you plan to work in independent practice you will need to obtain a state license to provide counseling services to the public.

DEVELOPMENTAL PSYCHOLOGISTS conduct research on age-related behavioral changes and apply their scientific knowledge to educational, child-care, policy, and related settings. As a developmental psychologist, you would investigate change across a broad range of topics, including the biological, psychological, cognitive, and social aspects of development. Developmental psychology informs a number of applied fields, including educational psychology, school psychology, child psychopathology, and gerontology. The field also informs public policy in areas such as education and child-care reform, maternal and child health, and attachment and adoption. You would probably specialize in a specific stage of the life span, such as infancy, childhood, adolescence, or middle or late adulthood. Your work setting could be an educational institution, day-care center, youth group program, or senior center.

EDUCATIONAL PSYCHOLOGISTS are interested in the psychological processes involved in learning. They study the relationship between learning and physical and social environments, and they develop strategies for enhancing the learning process. As an educational psychologist working in a university psychology department or school of education, you might conduct basic research on topics related to learning, or develop innovative methods of teaching to enhance the learning process. You might design effective tests, including measures of aptitude and achievement. You might be employed by a school or government agency or charged with designing and implementing effective employee-training programs in a business setting.

ENVIRONMENTAL PSYCHOLOGISTS study the interaction of individuals with their natural and built (urban) environments. They are interested in how we influence and are affected by these environments. As an environmental psychologist, you might study wildlife conservation, the impact of urbanization on health, or cognitive factors involved in sustainable lifestyle choices. Environmental psychologists tend to address these kinds of questions by working with other professionals as part of an interdisciplinary team. As an environmental psychologist, you might work in a consulting firm, an academic setting, the nonprofit sector, or the government.

EXPERIMENTAL PSYCHOLOGISTS are a diverse group of scientists who investigate a variety of basic behavioral processes in humans and other animals. Prominent areas of experimental research include comparative methods of science, motivation, learning, thought, attention, memory, perception, and language. Most experimental psychologists identify with a particular subfield, such as cognitive psychology, depending on their interests and training. Experimental research methods are not limited to the field of experimental psychology; many other subfields rely on experimental methodology to conduct studies. As an experimental psychologist, you would most likely work in an academic setting, teaching courses and supervising students' research in addition to conducting your own research. Or you might be employed by a research institution, zoo, business, or government agency.

FORENSIC PSYCHOLOGISTS apply psychological principles to legal issues. They conduct research on the interface of law and psychology, help to create public policies related to mental health, help law enforcement agencies in criminal investigations, or consult on jury selection and deliberation processes. They also provide assessment to assist the legal community. Although most forensic psychologists are clinical psychologists, many have expertise in other areas of psychology, such as social or cognitive psychology. Some also hold law degrees. As a forensic psychologist, you might work in a university psychology department, law school, research organization, community mental health agency, law-enforcement agency, court, or correctional setting.

HEALTH PSYCHOLOGISTS are researchers and practitioners concerned with psychology's contribution to promoting health and preventing disease. As applied psychologists or clinicians, they may help individuals lead healthier lives by designing, conducting, and evaluating programs to stop smoking, lose weight, improve sleep, manage pain, prevent the spread of sexually transmitted infections, or treat psychosocial problems associated with chronic and terminal illnesses. As researchers and clinicians, they identify conditions and practices associated with health and illness to help create effective interventions. In public service, health psychologists study and work to improve government policies and health care systems. As a health psychologist, you could be employed in a hospital, medical school, rehabilitation center, public health agency, college or university, or, if you are also a clinical psychologist, in private practice.

INDUSTRIAL-ORGANIZATIONAL (I/O) PSYCHOLOGISTS study the relationship between people and their working environments. They may develop new ways to increase productivity, improve personnel selection, or promote job satisfaction in an organizational setting. Their interests include organizational structure and change, consumer

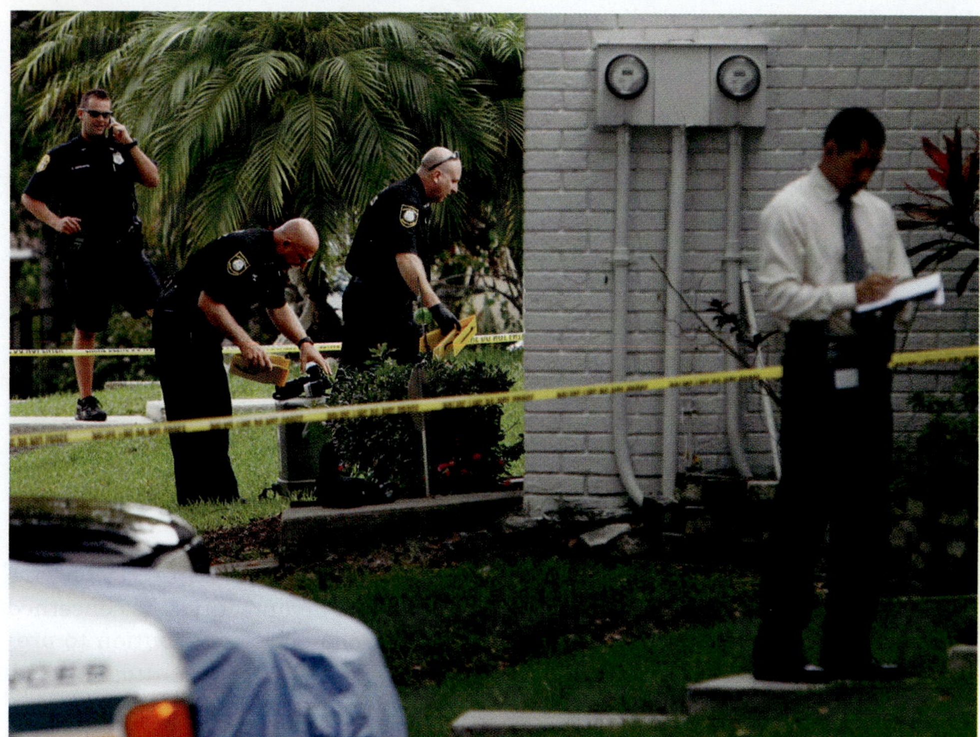

Criminal investigation Forensic psychologists may be called on to assist police officers who are investigating a crime scene, as is the case here after a shooting in Florida. Most forensic work, however, occurs in the lab and for the judicial system.

Assessing and supporting children School psychologists may find themselves working with children individually or in groups. They receive interdisciplinary training in mental health assessment and behavior analysis, research methods and design, and special needs education. They work primarily in schools, but also in a range of other settings, including pediatric hospitals, mental health centers, and correctional facilities.

behavior, and personnel selection and training. As an I/O psychologist, you might conduct workplace training or provide organizational analysis and development. You may find yourself working in business, industry, the government, or a college or university. Or you may be self-employed as a consultant or work for a management consulting firm. (For more on I/O psychology, see Appendix B, Psychology at Work.)

NEUROPSYCHOLOGISTS investigate the relationship between neurological processes (structure and function of the brain and nervous system) and behavior. As a neuropsychologist you might assess, diagnose, or treat central nervous system disorders, such as Alzheimer's disease or stroke. You might also evaluate individuals for evidence of head injuries; specific learning, disorders; and neurodevelopmental disorders, such as autism spectrum disorder and attention-deficit/hyperactivity disorder (ADHD). If you are a *clinical neuropsychologist*, you might work in a hospital's neurology, neurosurgery, or psychiatric unit. Neuropsychologists also work in academic settings, where they conduct research and teach.

PSYCHOMETRIC AND QUANTITATIVE PSYCHOLOGISTS study the methods and techniques used to acquire psychological knowledge. A psychometric psychologist may update existing neurocognitive or personality tests or devise new tests for use in clinical and school settings or in business and industry. These psychologists also administer, score, and interpret such tests. Quantitative psychologists collaborate with researchers to design, analyze, and interpret the results of research programs. As a psychometric or quantitative psychologist, you would need to be well trained in research methods, statistics, and computer technology. You would most likely be employed by a university or college, a testing company, a private research firm, or a government agency.

REHABILITATION PSYCHOLOGISTS are researchers and practitioners who work with people who have lost optimal functioning after an accident, illness, or other event. As a rehabilitation psychologist, you would probably work in a medical rehabilitation institution or hospital. You might also work in a medical school, university, or state or federal vocational rehabilitation agency, or in private practice serving people with physical disabilities.

SCHOOL PSYCHOLOGISTS are involved in the assessment of and intervention for children in educational settings. They diagnose and treat cognitive, social, and emotional problems that may negatively influence children's learning or overall functioning at school. As a school psychologist, you would collaborate with teachers, parents, and administrators, making recommendations to improve student learning. You would work in an academic setting, a pediatric hospital, a mental health center, or a correctional facility.

SOCIAL PSYCHOLOGISTS are interested in our interactions with others. Social psychologists study how our beliefs, feelings, and behaviors are affected by and influence other people. They study topics such as attitudes, aggression, prejudice, interpersonal attraction, group behavior, and leadership. As a social psychologist, you would probably be a college or university faculty member. You might also work in organizational consultation, market research, or an applied psychology field, such as social neuroscience. Some social psychologists work for hospitals, federal agencies, social networking sites, or businesses performing applied research.

Phil Walter/Getty Images

Cricket cures Sport psychologists often work directly with athletes to help them improve their performance. Here, a sport psychologist consults with Brendon McCullum, a record-breaking athlete who played international cricket for New Zealand.

SPORT PSYCHOLOGISTS study the psychological factors that influence, and are influenced by, participation in sports and other physical activities. Their professional activities include coach education and athlete preparation, as well as research and teaching. Sport psychologists who also have a clinical or counseling degree can apply those skills to working with individuals with psychological problems, such as anxiety or substance use disorder, that might interfere with optimal performance. As a sport psychologist, if you were not working in an academic or research setting, you would most likely work as part of a team or an organization or in a private capacity.

* * *

So, the next time someone asks you what you will do with your psychology degree, tell them you have a lot of options. You might use your acquired skills and understanding to get a job and succeed in any number of fields, or you might pursue graduate school and then career opportunities in associated professions. In any case, what you have learned about behavior and mental processes will surely enrich your life (Hammer, 2003).

APPENDIX D

Complete Chapter Reviews

CHAPTER 1

Psychology's Roots, Critical Thinking, and Self-Improvement Tools

PSYCHOLOGY IS A SCIENCE

1-1 How is psychology a science? How does critical thinking feed a scientific attitude, and smarter thinking for everyday life?

- Psychology's findings, based on a scientific approach, are the result of careful observation and testing. Sifting sense from nonsense requires a scientific attitude.
- *Critical thinking* is smart thinking. It challenges our beliefs and triggers new ways of thinking. Critical thinking feeds a scientific attitude by preparing us to examine assumptions, consider the source, uncover hidden values, weigh evidence, and test conclusions.

1-2 What are the three key elements of the scientific attitude, and how do they support scientific inquiry?

- These three key elements of the scientific attitude make modern science possible:
  - Curiosity triggers new ideas. When put to the test, can an idea's predictions be confirmed?
  - Skepticism encourages attention to the facts. Skeptical testing can reveal which claim best matches the facts.
  - Humility helps us discard predictions that can't be verified by research. Researchers must be willing to be surprised and follow new ideas.

1-3 How has psychology's focus changed over time?

- Wilhelm Wundt established the first psychological laboratory in Germany in 1879, and studied the basic elements of mental experience.
- Two early schools of thought in psychology were *structuralism* and *functionalism*.
- Early researchers defined psychology as "the science of mental life." This definition was revised under the influence of the *behaviorists* in the 1920s to the "scientific study of observable behavior."
- Behaviorism was one of psychology's two major forces well into the 1960s. However, the second major force of psychoanalytic psychology, along with the influences of *humanistic psychology* and *cognitive psychology*, revived interest in the study of mental processes.
- *Psychology* is now defined as "the science of behavior and mental processes."

1-4 What are psychology's current perspectives, and what are some of its subfields?

- Psychology's current perspectives include neuroscience, evolutionary, behavior genetics, psychodynamic, behavioral, cognitive, and social-cultural.
- Psychology's subfields include biological, developmental, cognitive, personality, social, health, and industrial-organizational.
- Psychologists may conduct basic research to increase the field's knowledge base or applied research to solve practical problems.

1-5 How do psychologists use the biopsychosocial approach, and how can it help us understand our diverse world?

- Behavior is a *biopsychosocial* event. The biological, psychological, and social-cultural levels of analysis each offer valuable insight into behavior and mental processes.
- Psychologists use the biopsychosocial approach to understand our diversity as groups and as individuals. Federal funding agencies, for example, now expect researchers to examine gender differences. Today's research also increasingly reaches beyond the WEIRD (Western, Educated, Industrial, Rich, and Democratic) cultures. Psychologists study both how individuals differ and how they share a common human kinship.

1-6 What are we learning about *dual processing* from psychological science?

- We operate with a two-track mind *(dual processing)*. Our brains process a surprising amount without our awareness, which affects our thinking, memory, perception, language, and attitudes.

1-7 How is psychology also a helping profession?

- Psychology is a science, but also a profession that helps people thrive. Four types of helping professionals are *counseling psychologists*, *clinical psychologists*, *psychiatrists*, and *community psychologists*.

1-8 What is *positive psychology?*

- Psychology's traditional focus on understanding and treating troubles has expanded with *positive psychology's* call for more research on human flourishing. Using scientific methods, it aims to discover and promote traits that help people to thrive.

THE NEED FOR PSYCHOLOGICAL SCIENCE

1-9 How does our everyday thinking sometimes lead us to a wrong conclusion?

- Our everyday thinking can lead us astray because of three human tendencies:
  - *Hindsight bias* (the I-knew-it-all-along phenomenon) is believing, after learning the outcome, that we would have foreseen it.
  - Overconfidence is our readiness to be more confident than correct.
  - We perceive order in random events due to our natural eagerness to make sense of our world.
- These tendencies lead us to overestimate our gut feelings and common sense, and then come to the wrong conclusion.

1-10 Why is it so easy to believe untruths?

- In our modern "post-truth" culture, our emotions, beliefs, and group identities may color our judgments, prevent our acceptance of objective facts, and prompt us to accept only what confirms our views. Misinformation may spread as a result of repetition and memorable examples.
- By embracing critical thinking and a scientific mindset, we can actively seek information and usually then know what really is so.

HOW DO PSYCHOLOGISTS ASK AND ANSWER QUESTIONS?

1-11 How do theories advance psychological science?

- Psychological *theories* are explanations using principles that organize observations and predict behaviors or events.
- Theories generate *hypotheses*—predictions that can be tested using descriptive, correlational, or experimental methods.
- Research results may confirm the theory, or lead to its rejection or revision.
- The precise language used in *operational definitions* allows *replication* by others. If others achieve similar results, confidence in the conclusion will be greater. *Preregistration* of research plans benefits psychological science by encouraging openness and transparency.

1-12 How do psychologists use case studies, naturalistic observations, and surveys to observe and describe behavior, and why is random sampling important?

- *Case studies* study one person or group in depth, in the hope of revealing things true of us all.
- *Naturalistic observation* studies examine behavior in naturally occurring situations without trying to change or control the situation.
- *Surveys* study many people in less depth, using *random sampling* to fairly represent the *population* being studied so that findings can be generalized.

1-13 What does it mean when we say two things are correlated, and what are positive and negative correlations?

- *Correlations* tell us how well one thing predicts another (using a measure called a correlation coefficient), but not whether one thing caused the other, or whether some third factor was involved.
- In a positive correlation, both things increase or decrease together. In a negative correlation, one thing increases as the other decreases. Correlations range from +1.00 (a perfect positive correlation) through 0 (no correlation) to −1.00 (a perfect negative correlation).

1-14 Why do correlations enable prediction but not cause-effect explanation?

- Correlations enable prediction because they show how two things are related—positively, negatively, or not at all. Correlations can suggest the possibility of a cause-effect relationship, but cannot prove the direction of the influence. A third variable may explain the correlation.

1-15 How do experiments clarify or reveal cause-effect relationships?

- *Experiments* create a controlled, simplified version of reality to discover cause-effect relationships.
- Psychologists manipulate one or more factors (*independent variables*) while controlling others. The researchers can then measure changes in other factors (*dependent variables*). Experiments minimize *confounding variables* (preexisting differences between groups) through *random assignment*.
- Experiments allow researchers to compare *experimental group* results with *control group* results. Experiments may use a *double-blind procedure* to control for the *placebo effect* and researcher bias.

1-16 How would you know which research design to use?

- Psychological scientists must design studies and choose research methods that will best provide meaningful results. After choosing a research question, psychologists determine the most appropriate research design (an experiment, for example) and how to set it up most effectively. (The Immersive Learning "How Would You Know?" activities in LaunchPad allow you to play the role of the researcher, making choices about the best ways to test interesting questions.)

1-17 How can simplified laboratory experiments help us understand general principles of behavior?

- Studying specific examples in controlled environments can reveal important general principles. These general principles, not the specific findings, may help explain many everyday behaviors.

PSYCHOLOGY'S RESEARCH ETHICS

1-18 Why do psychologists study animals, and what ethical guidelines safeguard human and animal research participants? How do psychologists' values influence what they study and how they apply their results?

- Research on animals advances our understanding of other species and sometimes benefits them directly. Animal experimentation also advances our understanding of ourselves and may help solve human problems. Government agencies, professional associations, and funding agencies have established standards for animals' well-being.
- Professional ethical standards and other legal guidelines, enforced by ethics committees, protect human participants. The ethics codes of the American Psychological Association (APA) and British Psychological Society (BPS) outline standards for safeguarding human participants' well-being, including obtaining their *informed consent* and *debriefing* them later.
- Psychologists' values influence their choice of research topics, their theories and observations, their labels for behavior, and their professional advice. Psychology's principles have been used mainly to enlighten and to achieve positive ends.

USE PSYCHOLOGY TO IMPROVE YOUR LIFE AND BECOME A BETTER STUDENT

1-19 How can psychological principles help you learn, remember, and thrive?

- Psychology is a tool through which we can learn about others and ourselves. Use psychology to Think, Consider, and Improve. Think critically, consider other voices and ideas, and use psychology's evidence-based principles to improve your everyday life.
- The *testing effect* shows that learning and memory are enhanced by actively retrieving, rather than simply rereading, previously studied material. The SQ3R study method—survey, question, read, retrieve, and review—applies principles derived from memory research and can help you learn and remember material.
- Psychological research has shown that people who live happy, thriving lives

(1) manage their time to get a full night's sleep; (2) make space for exercise; (3) set long-term goals, with daily aims; (4) have a growth mindset; and (5) prioritize relationships.

- Four additional study tips are (1) distribute your study time; (2) learn to think critically; (3) process class information actively; and (4) overlearn.

CHAPTER 2

The Biology of Behavior and Consciousness

THE POWER OF PLASTICITY

2-1 How do biology and experience enable neural plasticity?

- Everything psychological is simultaneously biological. The links between biology and behavior are a key part of the biopsychosocial approach.
- Our brain's *plasticity* allows us to build new neural pathways as we adjust to new experiences. Our brain is a work in progress, changing with the focus and practice we devote to new things.
- Neural plasticity is strongest in childhood, but it continues throughout life.

NEURAL COMMUNICATION

2-2 What are the parts of a neuron, and what is an *action potential?*

- *Neurons* (nerve cells), the basic building blocks of the nervous system, consist of a *cell body* and its branching fibers.
- A neuron has *dendrites* (extensions of the cell body) that receive and integrate messages, and an *axon* that sends messages to other neurons or to muscles and glands. Some axons are encased in a myelin sheath, which enables faster communication. *Glial cells* provide myelin, and they support, nourish, and protect neurons; they also play a role in learning, thinking, and memory.
- An *action potential* is a nerve impulse—a brief electrical charge that travels down an axon.

2-3 How do neurons communicate?

- Neurons transmit information in a chemistry-to-electricity process, sending action potentials down their axons. They receive incoming excitatory or inhibitory signals through their dendrites and cell body.
- Neurons fire in an *all-or-none response* when combined incoming signals are strong enough to pass a minimum *threshold*. A brief *refractory period* follows.
- The response triggers a release of chemical messengers *(neurotransmitters)* across the tiny gap *(synapse)* separating a sending neuron from a receiving cell.

2-4 How do neurotransmitters affect our mood and behavior?

- Specific neurotransmitters, such as serotonin and dopamine, travel designated pathways in the brain. Neurotransmitters affect particular behaviors and emotions, such as hunger, learning, movement, and arousal.
- *Endorphins* are natural *opiates* released in response to pain and intense exercise.
- Drugs and other chemicals affect brain chemistry at synapses.

THE NERVOUS SYSTEM

2-5 What are the two major divisions of the nervous system, and what are their basic functions?

- The *nervous system's* two major divisions are the *central nervous system (CNS)*—the brain and spinal cord—and the *peripheral nervous system (PNS)*—the sensory and motor neurons connecting the CNS to the rest of the body.
- *Interneurons* communicate within the brain and spinal cord and between *motor neurons* and *sensory neurons.*
- In the PNS, the *somatic nervous system* controls voluntary movements of the skeletal system. The *autonomic nervous system (ANS)* controls the involuntary muscles and the glands. The subdivisions of the ANS are the *sympathetic nervous system* (which arouses) and the *parasympathetic nervous system* (which calms).
- In the CNS, the brain's individual neurons form work groups called neural networks. The spinal cord is a two-way system connecting the PNS and the brain, with some nerve fibers bringing information from the senses to the brain, and others carrying motor-control information to the body parts. A *reflex* illustrates the spinal cord's work.

THE ENDOCRINE SYSTEM

2-6 How does the endocrine system transmit information and interact with the nervous system?

- The *endocrine system* is the body's slower information system. Its glands secrete *hormones* into the bloodstream, which influence brain and behavior.
- In times of stress or danger, the autonomic nervous system (ANS) activates the *adrenal glands'* fight-or-flight response.
- The *pituitary* (the endocrine system's master gland) triggers other glands, including sex glands, to release hormones, which then affect the brain and behavior. This complex feedback system reveals the interplay between the nervous and endocrine systems.

THE BRAIN

2-7 What are some techniques for studying the brain?

- To study the brain, researchers consider the effects of brain damage.
- Researchers use *EEG* and *MEG* recordings and *PET* and *fMRI* (functional MRI) scans to reveal brain activity.
- They also use *MRI* scans to reveal brain structures.

2-8 What structures make up the brainstem, and what are the functions of the brainstem, thalamus, reticular formation, and cerebellum?

- The *brainstem,* the oldest part of the brain, controls automatic survival functions.
- The brainstem's base is the *medulla,* which controls heartbeat and breathing. Just above the medulla, the pons helps coordinate movements and control sleep.
- The *thalamus,* sitting at the top of the brainstem, acts as the brain's sensory control center.
- The *reticular formation* controls arousal.
- The *cerebellum,* attached to the rear of the brainstem, helps process sensory input, coordinate muscle movement, and enable nonverbal learning and memory.

2-9 What are the structures and functions of the limbic system?

- The *limbic system* is linked to emotions, drives, and memory, and its neural centers include the amygdala, hypothalamus, and hippocampus:
  - The *amygdala* is involved in aggressive and fearful responses.
  - The *hypothalamus* monitors various bodily maintenance activities, is linked to emotion and reward, and triggers the pituitary to influence other glands of the endocrine system.
  - The *hippocampus* helps process explicit (conscious) memories.

2-10 What are the four lobes of the cerebral cortex, and where are they located?

- The *cerebral cortex* has two hemispheres, and each hemisphere has four lobes:
  - The *frontal lobes* (just behind the forehead) are involved in speaking, muscle movements, planning, and judging.
  - The *parietal lobes* (top-rear of the head) receive sensory input for touch and body position.
  - The *occipital lobes* (back of the head) receive input from the visual fields.
  - The *temporal lobes* (above the ears) receive input from the ears.

2-11 What are the functions of the motor cortex, somatosensory cortex, and association areas?

- The *motor cortex* (at the rear of the frontal lobes) controls voluntary muscle movement.
- The *somatosensory cortex* (at the front of the parietal lobes) registers and processes body touch and movement sensations.
- The cerebral cortex is mostly *association areas*, which are involved primarily in higher-level functions, such as learning, remembering, thinking, and speaking. Higher-level functions require the coordination of many brain areas.

2-12 Do we really use only 10 percent of our brain?

- Association areas, vast in humans, interpret, integrate, and act on sensory information and link it with stored memories. More intelligent animals have larger association areas.
- Evidence from brain damage shows that the neurons in association areas are busy with higher mental functions, so a bullet would not land in an "unused" area.

2-13 How does the brain modify itself after some kinds of damage?

- The brain's plasticity allows it to modify itself after some types of damage, especially early in life.
- The brain often attempts self-repair by reorganizing existing tissue. *Neurogenesis*, less common, is the formation of new neurons.

2-14 What is a *split brain*, and what does it reveal about the functions of our two brain hemispheres?

- The *corpus callosum* (a large band of nerve fibers) normally connects the two brain hemispheres. If surgically severed (for example, to treat severe epilepsy), a *split brain* results.
- Split-brain research shows that in most people, the hemispheres are specialized, though they work together in a normal brain. The left hemisphere usually specializes in verbal processing. The right hemisphere excels at making inferences, fine-tuning speech, and orchestrating our self-awareness.

BRAIN STATES AND CONSCIOUSNESS

2-15 What do we mean by *consciousness*, and how does selective attention direct our perceptions?

- *Consciousness* is our awareness of ourselves and our environment. To understand consciousness, *biological psychologists* study the links between biological (genetic, neural, hormonal) and psychological processes. In *cognitive neuroscience*, people from many fields join forces to study the brain activity linked with cognition.
- We process information at a conscious level (*sequential processing* of whatever requires focused attention) and at an unconscious level (*parallel processing* of routine business).
- We *selectively attend* to, and process, a very limited portion of incoming information, blocking out much and often shifting the spotlight of our attention from one thing to another.
- Focused intently on one task, we often display *inattentional blindness* to other events and *change blindness* (a form of inattentional blindness) to changes around us.

2-16 What is the *circadian rhythm*, and what are the stages of our nightly sleep cycle?

- The *circadian rhythm* is our internal biological clock; it regulates our daily cycles of alertness and sleepiness.
- Nightly *sleep* cycles every 90 minutes through recurring stages:
  - NREM-1 (or N1) sleep is the brief, near-waking sleep with irregular brain waves we enter (after leaving the *alpha waves* of being awake and relaxed); *hallucinations* (sensations such as falling or floating) may occur.
  - NREM-2 (or N2) sleep, in which we spend about half of our sleep time, includes characteristic bursts of rhythmic brain waves; this stage lengthens as the night goes on.
  - NREM-3 (or N3) sleep is deep sleep in which large, slow *delta waves* are emitted; this stage shortens as the night goes on.
  - *REM* (rapid eye movement, or *R*) *sleep* is described as a paradoxical sleep stage because of internal arousal but external calm (near paralysis). It includes most dreaming and, for younger adults, lengthens as the night goes on.

2-17 How do our sleep patterns differ? What five theories describe our need to sleep?

- Age, genetic, and social-cultural factors affect sleep patterns.
- Psychologists suggest five possible reasons why sleep evolved:
  - Sleep may have played a protective role in human evolution by keeping people safe during potentially dangerous periods.
  - Sleep helps restore and repair the immune system, brain tissue, and damaged neurons.
  - Sleep helps strengthen neural connections for learning and for building enduring memories.
  - Sleep promotes creative problem solving the next day.
  - During deep sleep, the pituitary gland secretes a growth hormone necessary for muscle development.

2-18 How does sleep loss affect us, and what are the major sleep disorders?

- Sleep loss causes fatigue and irritability, and impairs concentration, productivity, and memory consolidation. It can also lead to depression, obesity, joint inflammation, poor academic outcomes, a suppressed immune system, and slowed performance (with greater vulnerability to accidents).
- The major sleep disorders are *insomnia* (recurring problems in falling or staying asleep); *narcolepsy* (sudden, uncontrollable sleepiness, sometimes lapsing directly into REM sleep); *sleep apnea* (the repeated stopping of breathing while asleep); and sleepwalking, sleeptalking, and *night terrors*.

2-19 What do we dream about, and what are five explanations of *why* we dream?

- Our *dreams* often include ordinary events and everyday experiences, but with a vivid, emotional, and often bizarre flavor. Most dreams are bad dreams—of personal failures, dangers, or misfortunes.

- There are five major views of the function of dreams:
  - Freud's wish fulfillment: Dreams provide a psychic "safety valve," with *manifest content* (story line) acting as a censored version of *latent content* (underlying meaning that gratifies our unconscious wishes).
  - Information processing: Dreams help us sort out the day's events and consolidate them in memory.
  - Physiological function: Regular brain stimulation may help us develop and preserve neural pathways in the brain.
  - Neural activation: The brain attempts to make sense of neural static by weaving it into a story line.
  - Cognitive development: Dreams reflect dreamers' cognitive development—their knowledge and understanding.
- Most sleep theorists agree that REM sleep and its associated dreams serve an important function, as shown by the *REM rebound* that occurs following REM deprivation in humans and other species.

CHAPTER 3

Developing Through the Life Span

DEVELOPMENTAL PSYCHOLOGY'S MAJOR ISSUES

3-1 What are the three major issues studied by developmental psychologists?

- *Developmental psychologists* often use *cross-sectional* and *longitudinal studies* to study physical, cognitive, and social changes throughout the life span, with a focus on three major issues:
  - Nature and nurture—how our genetic inheritance (our nature) interacts with our experiences (our nurture) to influence our development.
  - Continuity and stages—which parts of development are gradual and continuous and which change relatively abruptly.
  - Stability and change—which traits persist through life and which change as we age.

PRENATAL DEVELOPMENT AND THE NEWBORN

3-2 How does conception occur? What are *chromosomes, DNA, genes,* and the human *genome?* And how do genes and the environment interact?

- At conception, one sperm cell fuses with one egg cell.
- *Genes* are the basic units of *heredity* that make up *chromosomes,* the threadlike coils of *DNA*. The human *genome* is the shared genetic profile that distinguishes humans from other species.
- The *interaction* between heredity and *environment* influences development. *Epigenetics* is the study of environmental influences on gene expression (making genes active or inactive) that occur without a DNA change.

3-3 How does life develop before birth, and how do *teratogens* put prenatal development at risk?

- From conception to 2 weeks, the *zygote* is in a period of rapid cell development.
- By 6 weeks, the *embryo's* body organs begin to form and function.
- By 9 weeks, the *fetus* is recognizably human.
- *Teratogens* are potentially harmful agents that can pass through the placenta and harm the developing embryo or fetus, as happens with *fetal alcohol syndrome*.

3-4 What are some abilities and traits of newborns?

- Newborns' sensory systems and *reflexes* aid their survival and social interactions with adults.
- Newborns smell and hear well, see what they need to see, and begin using their sensory equipment to learn.
- Inborn *temperament*—emotional reactivity and intensity—heavily influences our developing personality.

3-5 How do twin and adoption studies help us understand the effects of nature and nurture?

- *Identical (monozygotic) twins* develop from a single fertilized egg that splits into two; *fraternal (dizygotic) twins* develop from two separate fertilized eggs.
- Studies of separated identical twins allow researchers to maintain the same genes while testing the effects of different home environments. Studies of adoptive families let researchers maintain the same home environment while studying the effects of genetic differences.

INFANCY AND CHILDHOOD

3-6 During infancy and childhood, how do the brain and motor skills develop?

- Most brain cells form before birth. With *maturation* and experience, their interconnections multiply rapidly and become more complex. A pruning process strengthens heavily used links and weakens unused ones (but due to plasticity, our neural tissue is ever changing and reorganizing in response to new experiences). We seem to have a *critical period* for some skills, such as language.
- Complex motor skills—sitting, standing, walking—develop in a predictable sequence. Timing may vary with individual maturation and with culture.
- We have few conscious memories of events occurring before age 4, a blank space in our conscious memory that psychologists call infantile amnesia.

3-7 How did Piaget broaden our understanding of the way a child's mind develops, and how have today's researchers built on his work?

- As he studied children's *cognitive* development, Jean Piaget proposed that they actively construct and modify an understanding of the world through the processes of *assimilation* and *accommodation*. They form *schemas* that help them organize their experiences.
- Piaget believed children construct an understanding of the world by interacting with it while moving through four cognitive stages:
  - *Sensorimotor stage*—first two years; *object permanence* develops.
  - *Preoperational stage*—about age 2 to 6 or 7; preschoolers are *egocentric* and unable to perform simple logical operations.
  - *Concrete operational stage*—about 7 to 11 years; mastery of *conservation* and simple math.
  - *Formal operational stage*—about age 12 and up; reasoning expands to abstract thinking.

3-8 How did Vygotsky view children's cognitive development?

- Lev Vygotsky's studies of child development focused on the ways a child's mind grows by interacting with the social environment. Parents and other caregivers provide temporary *scaffolds* from which children can step to higher levels of thinking.

3-9 What does it mean to develop a *theory of mind,* and how is this impaired in those with *autism spectrum disorder?*

- As preschoolers, most children begin to develop a *theory of mind,* a sense of their own and others' mental states. Children with *autism spectrum disorder (ASD)* have trouble understanding others' states of mind. They look less at others' eyes and have difficulty reading and remembering other people's thoughts and feelings.

3-10 How do the bonds of attachment form between caregivers and infants?

- Infants develop *stranger anxiety* soon after object permanence.
- Infants form *attachments* with caregivers who satisfy nutritional needs but, more importantly, who are comfortable, familiar, and responsive.

3-11 Why do attachment differences matter, and how does an infant's ability to develop basic trust affect later relationships?

- Attachment styles differ (secure or insecure) due to the child's individual temperament and the responsiveness of the child's caregivers.
- Securely attached children develop *basic trust* and tend to have healthier adult relationships.
- Neglect or abuse can disrupt the attachment process and put children at risk for physical, psychological, and social problems.

3-12 What are the four main parenting styles?

- Parenting styles—authoritarian, permissive, negligent, and authoritative—reflect how responsive and how demanding parents are.
- Child-raising practices reflect both individual and cultural values.

3-13 What outcomes are associated with each parenting style?

- Children with the highest self-esteem, self-reliance, self-regulation, and social competence tend to have authoritative parents. Less positive outcomes are associated with authoritarian, permissive, and negligent parents.
- However, correlation does not equal causation (it's possible that children with positive characteristics are more likely to bring out positive parenting methods).

ADOLESCENCE

3-14 How is *adolescence* defined, and how do physical changes affect developing teens?

- *Adolescence,* the transition period from childhood to adulthood, begins with *puberty,* a time of sexual maturation.
- The brain's frontal lobes mature during adolescence and the early twenties, enabling improved judgment, impulse control, and long-term planning.

3-15 How did Piaget, Kohlberg, and later researchers describe cognitive and moral development during adolescence?

- In Jean Piaget's view, the capacity for formal operations (abstract reasoning) develops in adolescence, and this development is the basis for moral judgment.
- Lawrence Kohlberg proposed a stage theory of moral thinking: preconventional morality (self-interest), conventional morality (gaining others' approval or doing one's duty), and postconventional morality (basic rights and self-defined ethical principles). Kohlberg's critics note that the postconventional level is culturally limited (representing morality only from the perspective of an individualist society) and male-focused (since women more often emphasize care for those in need over what is "fair").
- Other researchers believe that morality lies in moral intuition and moral action as well as thinking. Life success can grow from the ability to delay gratification.

3-16 What are the social tasks and challenges of adolescence?

- Erik Erikson proposed eight stages of psychosocial development across the life span. He believed we need to achieve trust, autonomy, initiative, competency, identity (in adolescence), *intimacy* (in young adulthood), generativity, and integrity.
- Each life stage has its own psychosocial task, with the chief task of adolescence being solidifying one's sense of self, one's *identity.* This often means trying out a number of different roles. *Social identity* is the part of the self-concept that comes from a person's group memberships.

3-17 How do parents and peers influence adolescents?

- During adolescence, parental influence diminishes and peer influence increases, in part because of the selection effect—the tendency to choose similar others as friends.
- Parents influence our manners, attitudes, values, faith, and politics. Language and other behaviors are shaped by peer groups, as children adjust to fit in.

3-18 What is *emerging adulthood?*

- *Emerging adulthood* is the period from age 18 to the mid-twenties, when many young people in Western cultures are no longer adolescents but have not yet achieved full independence as adults.

ADULTHOOD

3-19 What physical changes occur from early to late adulthood?

- Muscular strength, reaction time, sensory abilities, and cardiac output begin to slightly decline in the late twenties. The decline accelerates through middle adulthood (to age 65) and late adulthood (after 65), varying considerably with personal health and exercise habits.
- Women's fertility ends with *menopause* around age 50; men experience a more gradual decline.
- In late adulthood, the immune system also weakens, but healthful habits may enable good health even in later life.

3-20 How does memory change with age?

- Recall begins to decline, especially for meaningless information. Recognition memory remains strong. Cognitive decline typically increases with the nearness of a natural death.

3-21 What are adulthood's two primary commitments, and how do chance events and the social clock influence us?

- Adulthood's two major commitments are love and work (Erikson's intimacy and generativity).
- Chance encounters affect many of our important decisions, such as our choice of romantic partners.
- The *social clock* is a culture's expected timing for social events such as marriage, parenthood, and retirement. Many people in Western cultures today feel freer about keeping their own time.

3-22 What factors affect our well-being in later life?

- Most older people retain a sense of well-being, partly due to the tendency to focus more on positive emotions and memories.

• People over 65 report as much happiness and satisfaction with life as younger people do.

3-23 How do people's responses to a loved one's death vary?

• Normal grief reactions vary widely. People do not grieve in predictable stages.

• Death of a loved one is much harder to accept when it comes before its expected time.

• Life can be affirmed even at death, especially for those who experience what Erikson called a sense of integrity—a feeling that one's life has been meaningful.

CHAPTER 4

Sex, Gender, and Sexuality

GENDER DEVELOPMENT

4-1 How does the meaning of *gender* differ from the meaning of *sex?*

• *Gender* refers to the behavioral characteristics that people associate with *boy, girl, man,* and *woman*. *Sex* refers to the biologically influenced characteristics by which people define *male, female,* and *intersex*. Our understanding of gender arises from the interplay between our biology and our experiences.

4-2 What are some of the ways males and females tend to be alike and to differ?

• Males and females are more alike than different, thanks to similar genetic makeup—they see, hear, learn, and remember similarly.

• Male-female differences include age of onset of puberty, life expectancy, emotional expressiveness, and onset of certain disorders.

• Men admit to more *aggression* than women do, and they are more likely to be physically aggressive. Women are slightly more likely than men to commit *relational aggression*.

• In most societies, men have more social power.

• Males tend to be independent, while females tend to be interdependent. Women often focus more on social connectedness than do men, and they "tend and befriend."

4-3 What factors contribute to gender bias in the workplace?

• Gender bias in the workplace is seen in such differences as perception, compensation, and child-care responsibility.

• Social norms, interaction styles, and everyday behaviors also contribute. Men's leadership style tends to be directive, whereas women's is more democratic.

4-4 How do sex hormones influence prenatal and adolescent sexual development?

• Both sex chromosomes and sex hormones influence development.

• The twenty-third pair of chromosomes determines sex, with the mother contributing an *X chromosome* and the father contributing either an X chromosome (for a female baby) or a Y *chromosome* (for a male baby). A Y chromosome triggers additional *testosterone* release and the formation of male sex organs.

• During *puberty*, both *primary* and *secondary sex characteristics* develop.

• Individuals who are *intersex* are born with unusual combinations of male and female chromosomes, hormones, and anatomy.

4-5 What are some of the cultural influences on gender roles?

• *Gender roles* describe how others expect us to act and vary depending on cultural expectations, which change over time and place.

• Gender roles worldwide have changed dramatically in the last century. Gender equity is greatest in the Northern European countries and lowest in the Middle Eastern and North African countries.

• Expectations about gender roles also influence cultural attitudes about *sexual aggression*.

4-6 What are the effects of sexual aggression? How have cultural views changed, and how can we reduce sexual aggression?

• Sexual aggression, which includes sexual harassment and sexual assault, can disrupt sleep, harm health, and make it difficult to trust new relationship partners.

• Cultural views of sexual aggression differ across time and place, with some cultures continuing to blame victims, but changes in the United States over the last half-century have made victim-blaming less acceptable.

• Therapy for sexual aggressors has not proven effective, but we may reduce sexual aggression by empowering victims, encouraging people to report and share their experiences, and educating communities about preventive bystander intervention strategies.

4-7 How do we form our gender identity?

• *Social learning theory* proposes that we learn our *gender identity*—our sense of being male, female, neither, or some combination of male and female—as we learn other things: through reinforcement, punishment, and observation. But critics argue that cognition also plays a role, because modeling and rewards cannot explain variation in *gender typing*.

• Some children organize themselves into "boy worlds" and "girl worlds"; others prefer *androgyny*.

• For people who identify as *cisgender*, gender identity corresponds with birth-assigned sex. For those who identify as *transgender*, gender identity differs from what's typical for that person's birth-assigned sex. Transgender people may be sexually attracted to people of the other gender, the same gender, all genders, or to no one at all.

HUMAN SEXUALITY

4-8 How do hormones influence human sexual motivation?

• The female *estrogen* and male *testosterone* hormones influence human sexual behavior less directly than they influence sexual behavior in other species.

• These hormones direct sexual development in the prenatal period, trigger development of sexual characteristics and interest in adolescence, and help activate sexual behavior from puberty to late adulthood.

• Women's sexuality is more responsive to testosterone level than to estrogen level. Short-term shifts in testosterone level are normal in men, partly in response to stimulation.

4-9 What is the human *sexual response cycle*, and how do sexual dysfunctions and paraphilias differ?

• William Masters and Virginia Johnson described four stages in the human *sexual response cycle:* excitement, plateau, orgasm (which involves similar feelings and brain activity in males and females), and resolution. Males then enter a *refractory period* in which renewed arousal and orgasm are impossible.

• *Sexual dysfunctions* are problems that consistently impair sexual arousal or functioning at any point in this cycle. They include *erectile disorder* and *female orgasmic disorder,* and can often be successfully treated by behaviorally oriented therapy or drug therapy.

• *Paraphilias* are considered disordered if a person experiences distress from an unusual sexual interest or if it entails harm or risk of harm to others.

4-10 How can sexually transmitted infections be prevented?

• Safe-sex practices help prevent sexually transmitted infections (STIs).

• Condoms are especially effective in preventing transmission of HIV, the virus that causes AIDS.

• The first step in preventing STIs is knowing one's status and sharing it with one's sexual partner.

4-11 How do external and imagined stimuli contribute to sexual arousal?

• Erotic material and other external stimuli can trigger sexual arousal in men and women.

• Viewing sexually coercive material can lead to increased acceptance of violence toward women. Viewing sexually explicit materials can cause people to perceive their partners as comparatively less appealing and to devalue their relationships.

• Imagined stimuli (fantasies) help trigger sexual arousal.

4-12 What factors influence teenagers' sexual behaviors and use of contraceptives?

• Teen sexuality varies from culture to culture and era to era.

• Factors contributing to teen pregnancy include minimal communication about birth control with parents, partners, and peers; impulsive sexual behavior, with passion overwhelming self-control; alcohol use; and mass media influences and *social scripts*.

• High intelligence, religious engagement, father presence, and participation in service learning programs have been predictors of teen sexual restraint.

SEXUAL ORIENTATION

4-13 What do we know about sexual orientation?

• *Sexual orientation* is our sexual attraction toward members of the other gender (heterosexual orientation), our own gender (same-sex orientation), male and female genders (bisexual orientation), all genders (pansexual orientation), or to no one at all (*asexual* orientation).

• About 3 or 4 percent of men and 2 percent of women have exclusively same-sex attractions.

• There is no evidence that environmental influences determine sexual orientation.

• Evidence for biological influences includes same-sex attraction in many animal species; brain and trait differences between gay people and straight people; genetic influences; and prenatal influences.

AN EVOLUTIONARY EXPLANATION OF HUMAN SEXUALITY

4-14 How might an evolutionary psychologist explain male-female differences in sexuality and mating preferences?

• *Evolutionary psychologists* attempt to understand how *natural selection* (how nature selects traits and appetites that contribute to survival and reproduction) has shaped behaviors found in all people.

• They reason that men's attraction to multiple healthy, fertile-appearing partners increases their chances of spreading their genes widely. In contrast, women tend to be choosier than men because of their need to incubate and nurse babies. Women increase their own and their children's chances of survival by searching for mates with the potential for long-term investment in their joint offspring.

4-15 What are the key criticisms of evolutionary explanations of human sexuality, and how do evolutionary psychologists respond?

• Critics argue that evolutionary psychologists (1) start with an effect and work backward to an explanation, (2) do not recognize social and cultural influences, and (3) relieve people from taking responsibility for their sexual behavior.

• Evolutionary psychologists respond that understanding our predispositions can help us overcome them. They recognize the importance of social and cultural influences, but they also cite the value of testable predictions based on evolutionary principles.

SEX AND HUMAN RELATIONSHIPS

4-16 What role do social factors play in our sexuality?

• Scientific research on human sexuality does not aim to define the personal meaning of sex in our own lives, which is influenced by many social factors. Sex is a socially significant act. Intimacy expresses our social nature, and sex at its human best is life uniting and love renewing.

REFLECTIONS ON THE NATURE AND NURTURE OF SEX, GENDER, AND SEXUALITY

4-17 How do nature, nurture, and our own choices influence gender roles?

• Our ancestral history helped form us as a species. Our genes form us, but our culture and experiences also shape us. Nature and nurture interact in the development of our gender-related traits and our mating behaviors. We are both the creatures and creators of our worlds, with our own hopes, goals, and expectations directing our future.

CHAPTER 5

Sensation and Perception

BASIC CONCEPTS OF SENSATION AND PERCEPTION

5-1 What are *sensation* and *perception?* What do we mean by *bottom-up processing* and *top-down processing?*

• *Sensation* is the process by which our sensory receptors and nervous system receive and represent information and transmit it to the brain. *Perception* is the process by which our brain organizes and interprets that information.

• *Bottom-up processing* is analysis that begins with the *sensory receptors* and works up to the brain. *Top-down processing* is information processing guided by higher-level mental processing, such as when we construct perceptions by filtering information through our experience and expectations.

5-2 What three steps are basic to all of our sensory systems?

• Our senses (1) receive sensory stimulation (often using specialized receptor cells); (2) transform that stimulation into neural impulses; and (3) deliver the neural information to the brain. *Transduction* is the process of converting one form of energy into another.

5-3 How do *absolute thresholds* and *difference thresholds* differ?

- Our *absolute threshold* for any stimulus is the minimum stimulation needed for us to be consciously aware of it 50 percent of the time.
- A *difference threshold* (also called the just noticeable difference, or jnd) is the minimum change needed to detect a difference between two stimuli 50 percent of the time.
- *Weber's law* states that two stimuli must differ by a constant minimum percentage (rather than a constant minimum amount).

5-4 How are we affected by subliminal stimuli?

- We do sense some stimuli *subliminally*—less than 50 percent of the time—and can be affected by these sensations. But although we can be *primed*, subliminal stimuli have no powerful, enduring influence on behavior.

5-5 What is the function of sensory adaptation?

- Our diminished sensitivity to constant or routine odors, sounds, and touches *(sensory adaptation)* focuses our attention on informative changes in our environment.

5-6 How do our expectations, contexts, motivations, and emotions influence our perceptions?

- Perception is influenced by our *perceptual set*—our mental predisposition to perceive one thing and not another.
- Our expectations, learning (including the schemas we have developed), context, motivation, and emotion can also affect our perceptions.

VISION: SENSORY AND PERCEPTUAL PROCESSING

5-7 What are the characteristics of the energy we see as visible light? What structures in the eye help focus that energy?

- The visible light we experience is just a thin slice of the broad spectrum of electromagnetic energy.
- The *hue* (blue, green, and so forth) we perceive in a light depends on its *wavelength*, and its brightness depends on its *intensity*.
- Light entering the eye through the pupil is focused by the lens on the *retina*—the inner surface of the eye.

5-8 How do the rods and cones process information, and what path does information take from the eye to the brain?

- The retina's light- and movement-sensitive *rods* and color-sensitive *cones* convert the light energy into neural impulses.
- After processing by bipolar and ganglion cells in the eyes' retina, neural impulses travel through the *optic nerve* to the thalamus and on to the visual cortex.

5-9 How do we perceive color in the world around us?

- According to the *Young-Helmholtz trichromatic (three-color) theory*, the retina contains three types of color receptors. Contemporary research has found three types of cones, each most sensitive to the wavelengths of one of the three primary colors of light (red, green, or blue).
- According to the *opponent-process theory*, there are three additional color processes (red-versus-green, blue-versus-yellow, black-versus-white). Contemporary research has confirmed that, on the way to the brain, neurons in the retina and the thalamus code the color-related information from the cones into pairs of opponent colors.
- These two theories, and the research supporting them, show that color processing occurs in two stages.

5-10 What are *feature detectors*, and what do they do?

- In the visual cortex, specialized nerve cells called *feature detectors* respond to specific features of the visual stimulus, such as shape, angle, or movement.

5-11 How does the brain use parallel processing to construct visual perceptions?

- Through *parallel processing*, the brain handles many aspects of vision (movement, form, depth, and color) simultaneously. You then construct your perceptions by integrating (binding) the results of these different visual teams.

5-12 What was the main message of Gestalt psychology, and how do *figure-ground* and *grouping* principles help us perceive forms?

- Gestalt psychologists showed that the brain organizes bits of sensory information into *gestalts*, or meaningful forms. In pointing out that the whole may exceed the sum of its parts, they noted that we filter sensory information and construct our perceptions.
- To recognize an object, we must first perceive it as distinct (see it as a *figure*) from its surroundings (the *ground*). We bring order and form to sensory input by organizing it into meaningful groups, following such rules as proximity, continuity, and closure.

5-13 How do we use binocular and monocular cues to see in three dimensions, and how do we perceive motion?

- Humans and many other species perceive depth at, or very soon after, birth. We transform two-dimensional retinal images into three-dimensional *depth perceptions* that allow us to see objects in three dimensions and to judge distance.
- *Binocular cues*, such as *retinal disparity*, are depth cues that rely on information from both eyes.
- *Monocular cues* (such as relative size, interposition, relative height, relative motion, linear perspective, and light and shadow) let us judge depth using information transmitted by only one eye.
- As objects move, we assume that shrinking objects are moving away and enlarging objects are approaching. The brain computes motion imperfectly, with young children especially at risk of incorrectly perceiving approaching hazards such as vehicles.

5-14 How do perceptual constancies help us construct meaningful perceptions?

- *Perceptual constancy* is our ability to recognize an object regardless of the changing image it casts upon our retinas due to its changing color, brightness, shape, and size. Our brain constructs our experience of an object's color or brightness through comparisons with other surrounding objects.
- Knowing an object's size gives us clues to its distance; knowing its distance gives clues about its size, but we sometimes misread monocular distance cues and reach the wrong conclusions, as in the Moon illusion.

5-15 What does research on restored vision, sensory restriction, and perceptual adaptation reveal about the effects of experience on perception?

- Experience guides our perceptual interpretations. People blind from birth who gain sight after surgery lack the experience to visually recognize shapes and forms.

- Sensory restriction research indicates that there is a critical period for some aspects of sensory and perceptual development. Without early stimulation, the brain's neural organization does not develop normally.
- Given eyeglasses that shift the world slightly to the left or right or turn it upside down, people can, through *perceptual adaptation,* learn to move about with ease.

THE OTHER SENSES

5-16 What are the characteristics of the air pressure waves that we hear as sound?

- Sound waves vary in amplitude (perceived as loudness) and in *frequency* (perceived as *pitch*—a tone's highness or lowness).
- Sound energy is measured in decibels.

5-17 How does the ear transform sound energy into neural messages, and how do we locate sounds?

- Through a mechanical chain of events, sound waves travel from the outer ear through the auditory canal, causing tiny vibrations in the eardrum. The bones of the *middle ear* transmit the vibrations to the fluid-filled *cochlea* in the *inner ear,* causing waves of movement in hair cells lining the basilar membrane. This movement triggers nerve cells to send signals along the auditory nerve to the thalamus and then to the brain's auditory cortex.
- *Sensorineural hearing loss* (or nerve deafness) results from damage to the cochlea's hair cells or their associated nerves. *Conduction hearing loss* results from damage to the mechanical system that transmits sound waves to the cochlea. *Cochlear implants* can restore hearing for some people.
- Small differences in the loudness and timing of the sounds received by each ear allow us to locate sounds.

5-18 What are the four basic touch sensations, and how do we sense touch?

- Our sense of touch is actually several senses—pressure, warmth, cold, and pain—that combine to produce other sensations, such as "itchy" or "wet."

5-19 What biological, psychological, and social-cultural influences affect our experience of pain? How do placebos, distraction, and hypnosis help control pain?

- Pain reflects bottom-up sensations and top-down processes. It is the sum of our biological, psychological, and cultural influences.
- The gate-control theory of pain suggests that a spinal cord "gate" controls the transmission of pain messages to the brain, with small fibers conducting most pain signals and large fibers able to close the pain gate. Pain treatments often combine physical and psychological elements. Combining a placebo with distraction, and amplifying the effect with *hypnosis* (which increases our response to suggestions), can help relieve pain. *Posthypnotic suggestion* is used by some clinicians to help control undesired symptoms and behavior.

5-20 In what ways are our senses of taste and smell similar, and how do they differ?

- Both taste and smell are chemical senses.
- Taste's five basic sensations are sweet, sour, salty, bitter, and umami. Taste receptors in the taste buds carry messages to matching partner cells in the brain.
- There are no basic sensations for smell (olfaction). Some 20 million olfactory receptor cells for smell, located at the top of each nasal cavity, send messages to the brain's olfactory bulb. It then sends them to the temporal lobe's primary smell cortex and to the parts of the limbic system involved in memory and emotion.

5-21 How do we sense our body's position and movement?

- Through *kinesthesia,* we sense the position and movement of our body parts.
- We monitor our head's (and therefore our body's) position and movement, and maintain our balance, with our *vestibular sense.* This sense relies on the semicircular canals and vestibular sacs to sense the tilt or rotation of our head.

SENSORY INTERACTION

5-22 How does *sensory interaction* influence our perceptions, and what is *embodied cognition?*

- *Sensory interaction* is the influence of one sense on another. This occurs, for example, when the smell of a favorite food enhances its taste.
- *Embodied cognition* is the influence of bodily sensations, gestures, and other states on cognitive preferences and judgments.

ESP—PERCEPTION WITHOUT SENSATION?

5-23 What are the claims of ESP, and what have most research psychologists concluded after putting these claims to the test?

- The three most testable forms of *extrasensory perception (ESP)* are telepathy (mind-to-mind communication), clairvoyance (perceiving remote events), and precognition (perceiving future events).
- Researchers have not been able to replicate (reproduce) ESP effects under controlled conditions.

CHAPTER 6

Learning

HOW DO WE LEARN?

6-1 How do we define *learning,* and what are some basic forms of learning?

- *Learning* is the process of acquiring new and relatively enduring information or behaviors through experience.
- Automatically responding to *stimuli* we do not control is called *respondent behavior.*
- In *associative learning,* we learn that certain events occur together. These associations produce *operant behaviors.*
- Through *cognitive learning,* we acquire mental information, such as by observation, that guides our behavior.

CLASSICAL CONDITIONING

6-2 What is *classical conditioning,* and how does it demonstrate associative learning?

- *Classical conditioning* is a type of learning in which we learn to link two or more stimuli and anticipate events. The process involves stimuli and responses:
  - A *UR (unconditioned response)* is an event that occurs naturally (such as salivation), in response to some stimulus.
  - A *US (unconditioned stimulus)* is something that naturally and automatically

(without learning) triggers the unlearned response (as food in the mouth triggers salivation).

- A CS *(conditioned stimulus)* is originally an NS *(neutral stimulus,* such as a tone) that, after association with a US (such as food), comes to trigger a CR (salivating).
- A CR *(conditioned response)* is the learned response (salivating) to the originally neutral (but now conditioned) stimulus.

6-3 What parts do acquisition, extinction, spontaneous recovery, generalization, and discrimination play in classical conditioning?

- In classical conditioning, the first stage is *acquisition*, or the association of the NS with the US so that the NS begins triggering the CR. Acquisition occurs most readily when the NS is presented just before (ideally, about a half-second before) a US, preparing the organism for the upcoming event. This finding supports the view that classical conditioning is biologically adaptive.
- *Extinction* is diminished responding, which occurs if the CS appears repeatedly by itself (without the US).
- *Spontaneous recovery* is the reappearance of a weakened conditioned response, following a rest period.
- Responses may be triggered by stimuli similar to the CS *(generalization)* but not by dissimilar stimuli *(discrimination)*.

6-4 Why is Pavlov's work important, and how is it being applied?

- Ivan Pavlov taught us how to study a psychological process objectively, and that classical conditioning is a basic form of learning that applies to all species.
- Classical conditioning is applied to further human health and well-being in many areas, including behavioral therapy for some types of psychological disorders.

OPERANT CONDITIONING

6-5 What is *operant conditioning,* and how is operant behavior reinforced and shaped?

- *Operant conditioning* is a type of learning in which behavior becomes more probable if followed by a *reinforcer* or less probable if followed by a punisher.
- Expanding on Edward Thorndike's *law of effect*, B. F. Skinner and others *shaped* the behavior of rats and pigeons placed in *operant chambers* by rewarding successive approximations of a desired behavior.

6-6 How do positive and negative reinforcement differ, and what are the basic types of reinforcers?

- *Positive reinforcers* add a desirable stimulus to increase the frequency of a behavior. *Negative reinforcers* remove or reduce a negative stimulus to increase the frequency of a behavior.
- *Primary reinforcers* (such as receiving food when hungry) are naturally satisfying—no learning is required. *Conditioned* (or secondary) *reinforcers* (such as cash) are satisfying because we have learned to associate them with primary reinforcers.
- Reinforcers may be immediate or delayed.

6-7 How do continuous and partial reinforcement schedules affect behavior?

- A *reinforcement schedule* is a pattern that defines how often a desired response will be reinforced.
- In *continuous reinforcement* (reinforcing desired responses every time they occur), learning is rapid, but so is extinction if reinforcement stops.
- In *partial (intermittent) reinforcement* (reinforcing responses only sometimes), learning is slower, but the behavior is much more resistant to extinction.
  - *Fixed-ratio schedules* reinforce behaviors after a set number of responses.
  - *Variable-ratio schedules* reinforce behaviors after an unpredictable number of responses.
  - *Fixed-interval schedules* reinforce behaviors after set time periods.
  - *Variable-interval schedules* reinforce behaviors after unpredictable time periods.

6-8 How does punishment differ from negative reinforcement, and how does punishment affect behavior?

- *Punishment* aims to decrease the frequency of a behavior (such as a child's disobedience). Punishment administers an undesirable consequence (such as spanking) or withdraws something desirable (such as taking away a favorite toy).
- Negative reinforcement aims to increase the frequency of a behavior (such as putting on your seat belt) by withdrawing something *undesirable* (the annoying beeping).
- Punishment can have unintended drawbacks: it can (1) suppress rather than change unwanted behaviors; (2) fail to provide a direction for appropriate behavior; (3) encourage discrimination (so that the undesirable behavior appears when the punisher is absent); (4) create fear; and (5) increase aggression.

6-9 Why were Skinner's ideas controversial, and how might his operant conditioning principles be applied at school, at work, in sports, in parenting, and for self-improvement?

- Critics say that Skinner's approach dehumanized people by neglecting their personal freedom and seeking to control their actions. Skinner replied that external forces shape us anyway, so we should direct those forces with reinforcement, which is more humane than punishment.
- Teachers can control students' behaviors with *shaping* techniques, and use interactive media to provide immediate feedback. (For example, the LearningCurve and Achieve Read & Practice systems available with this text provide such feedback and allow students to direct the pace of their own learning.)
- Managers can boost productivity and morale by rewarding well-defined and achievable behaviors.
- Coaches can catch and immediately reward players' desirable behaviors.
- Parents can reward desirable behaviors but not undesirable ones.
- We can shape our own behaviors by stating realistic goals, planning how to work toward these goals, monitoring the frequency of our desired behaviors, reinforcing these behaviors, and gradually reducing rewards as our desired behaviors become habitual.

6-10 How does classical conditioning differ from operant conditioning?

- Both types of conditioning are forms of associative learning and involve acquisition, extinction, spontaneous recovery, generalization, and discrimination.
- In classical conditioning, we associate events we do not control and respond automatically (respondent behaviors). In operant conditioning, we link our behaviors (operant behaviors) with their consequences.

BIOLOGY, COGNITION, AND LEARNING

6-11 What limits does biology place on conditioning?

- We come prepared to learn tendencies, such as taste aversions, that aid our survival. Learning is adaptive.
- We most easily learn and retain behaviors that reflect our biological predispositions—associations that are naturally adaptive.

6-12 How do cognitive processes affect classical and operant conditioning?

- More than the *behaviorists* supposed, expectations influence conditioning. In classical conditioning, animals may learn when to expect a US and may be aware of the link between stimuli and responses.
- In operant conditioning, *cognitive mapping* and *latent learning* research illustrate learning that occurs without immediate consequences. This demonstrates the importance of cognitive processes in learning.

LEARNING BY OBSERVATION

6-13 What is *observational learning?*

- *Observational learning* (also called *social learning*) involves learning by watching and imitating, rather than through direct experience.

6-14 How may observational learning be enabled by neural mirroring?

- Our brain's frontal lobes have a demonstrated ability to mirror the activity of another's brain.
- Some psychologists believe *mirror neurons* enable this process. The same areas fire when we perform certain actions (such as responding to pain or moving our mouth to form words) as when we observe someone else performing those actions.

6-15 What is the impact of prosocial modeling and of antisocial modeling?

- Children tend to imitate what a model does and says, whether the behavior *modeled* is *prosocial* (positive, helpful) or antisocial.
- If a model's actions and words are inconsistent, children may imitate the hypocrisy they observe.

6-16 What is the violence-viewing effect?

- Media violence can contribute to aggression. This violence-viewing effect may be prompted by imitation and desensitization.
- Correlation does not equal causation, but study participants have reacted more cruelly to provocations when they have viewed violence (instead of entertaining nonviolence).

CHAPTER 7

Memory

STUDYING MEMORY

7-1 What is *memory,* and how do information-processing models help us study memory?

- *Memory* is the persistence of learning over time through the encoding, storage, and retrieval of information.
- Psychologists use memory models to think about and explain how our brain forms and retrieves memories. Information-processing models involve three processes: *encoding, storage,* and *retrieval.*

7-2 What is the three-stage information-processing model, and how has later research updated this model?

- The three processing stages in the Atkinson and Shiffrin classic three-stage model of memory are *sensory memory, short-term memory,* and *long-term memory.*
- More recent research has updated this model to include two additional concepts: (1) *working memory,* to stress the active processing occurring in the second memory stage; and (2) *automatic processing,* to address the processing of information outside of conscious awareness.

BUILDING MEMORIES: ENCODING

7-3 How do implicit and explicit memories differ?

- *Implicit* (nondeclarative) *memories* are our unconscious memories of learned skills and classically conditioned associations. They happen without our awareness, through *automatic processing.*
- *Explicit* (declarative) *memories* are our conscious memories of general knowledge, facts, and personal experiences. They form through *effortful processing.*

7-4 What information do we process automatically?

- In addition to skills and classically conditioned associations, we automatically process incidental information about space, time, and frequency. Our two-track mind works efficiently with the *parallel processing* of many things at once.

7-5 How does sensory memory work?

- Sensory memory feeds some information into working memory for active processing there.
- An iconic memory is a very brief (a few tenths of a second) picture-image memory of a scene; an echoic memory is a three- or four-second sensory memory of a sound.

7-6 What is our short-term memory capacity?

- Short-term memory capacity is about seven items, give or take two, but this information disappears from memory quickly without rehearsal.
- Our working-memory capacity for active processing varies, depending on age and other factors.

7-7 What are some effortful processing strategies that can help us remember new information?

- Effective effortful processing strategies include *chunking* and *mnemonics.* Such strategies help us remember new information because we then focus our attention and make a conscious effort to remember.

7-8 Why is cramming ineffective, and what is the *testing effect?* Why is it important to make new information meaningful?

- Massed practice, or cramming, results in poorer long-term recall than encoding that is spread over time. Psychologists call this result of distributed practice the *spacing effect.* The *testing effect* is the finding that consciously retrieving, rather than simply rereading information enhances memory.
- If new information is not meaningful, it will be difficult to process. We can avoid some encoding errors by thinking about what we have learned and rephrasing it into personally meaningful terms. The way people better remember personally meaningful information is called the self-reference effect.

MEMORY STORAGE

7-9 What is the capacity of long-term memory? Are our long-term memories processed and stored in specific locations?

- We have an unlimited capacity for storing information permanently in long-term memory.

- Memories are not stored intact in the brain in single specific spots. Many parts of the brain interact as we encode, store, and retrieve memories.

7-10 What roles do the hippocampus and frontal lobes play in memory processing?

- The *hippocampus* and frontal lobes are parts of the brain network dedicated to explicit memory formation.
- Many brain regions send information to the frontal lobes for processing. The hippocampus, with the help of nearby brain networks, registers and temporarily holds elements of explicit memories (which are either *semantic* or *episodic*) before moving them for storage elsewhere *(memory consolidation)*. Sleep supports memory consolidation.

7-11 What roles do the cerebellum and basal ganglia play in memory processing?

- The cerebellum and basal ganglia are parts of the brain network dedicated to implicit memory formation. The cerebellum is important for storing classically conditioned memories. The basal ganglia are involved in motor movement and help form procedural memories for skills.
- As adults, our conscious memory of our first four years is largely blank due to infantile amnesia.

7-12 How do emotions affect our memory processing?

- Emotional arousal causes an outpouring of stress hormones, which leads the amygdala to boost activity in the brain's memory-forming areas. Significantly stressful events can trigger very clear *flashbulb memories*.

7-13 How do changes at the synapse level affect our memory processing?

- *Long-term potentiation (LTP)* is the neural process for learning and memory. It involves an increase in a synapse's firing potential as neurons become more efficient and more connections between neurons develop.

RETRIEVAL: GETTING INFORMATION OUT

7-14 How do psychologists assess memory with recall, recognition, and relearning?

- Evidence of memory may be seen in an ability to *recall* information, *recognize* it, or *relearn* it more easily on a later attempt.
- Psychologists can measure these different forms of memory separately. Some tests, such as the Wechsler Memory Scale (WMS-IV), are global assessments of memory functioning.

7-15 How do external events, internal moods, and order of appearance affect memory retrieval?

- *Retrieval cues*, such as events, feelings, and places, are information bits linked with the original encoded memory. These cues activate associations that help us retrieve memories; this process may occur without our awareness, as it does in *priming*.
- The *encoding specificity principle* is the idea that cues and contexts specific to a particular memory will be most effective in helping us to recall it. Returning to the same physical context or emotional state *(mood congruency)* in which we formed a memory can help us retrieve it.
- The *serial position effect* is our tendency to recall best the last items (which may still be in working memory) and the first items (which we've spent more time rehearsing) in a list.

FORGETTING

7-16 Why do we forget?

- *Anterograde amnesia* is an inability to form new memories. *Retrograde amnesia* is an inability to retrieve old memories. Normal forgetting can happen because we have never encoded information (encoding failure); because the physical *memory trace* has decayed (storage decay); or because we cannot retrieve what we have encoded and stored (retrieval failure).
- Retrieval problems may result from *proactive* (forward-acting) *interference*, when prior learning interferes with recall of new information, or from *retroactive* (backward-acting) *interference*, when new learning disrupts recall of old information.
- Motivated forgetting occurs, but researchers have found little evidence of *repression*.

MEMORY CONSTRUCTION ERRORS

7-17 How do misinformation, imagination, and source amnesia influence our memory construction? How do we decide whether a memory is real or false?

- Memories can be continually revised when retrieved, a process memory researchers call *reconsolidation*.
- *Misinformation* (exposure to misleading information) and imagination effects corrupt our stored memories of what actually happened. *Source amnesia* leads to faulty memories of how, when, or where we learned something, and may help explain *déjà vu*.
- False memories feel like real memories and can be persistent but are usually limited to the gist (the general idea) of the event.

7-18 Why have reports of repressed and recovered memories been so hotly debated?

- The debate focuses on whether memories of early childhood abuse are repressed and can be recovered during therapy. Unless the victim was a child too young to remember, such traumas are usually remembered vividly, not repressed.
- Psychologists agree that childhood sexual abuse happens; injustice happens; forgetting happens; recovered memories are common; memories of events that happened before age 4 are unreliable; memories "recovered" under hypnosis are especially unreliable; and memories, whether real or false, can be emotionally upsetting.

7-19 How reliable are young children's eyewitness descriptions?

- Children's eyewitness descriptions are subject to the same memory influences that distort adult reports. If questioned soon after an event in neutral words they understand, children can accurately recall events and people involved in them.

IMPROVING MEMORY

7-20 How can you use memory research findings to do better in this course and in others?

- Memory research findings suggest the following strategies for improving memory: Rehearse repeatedly, make the material meaningful, activate retrieval cues, use mnemonic devices, minimize proactive and retroactive interference, sleep more, and test yourself to be sure you can retrieve, as well as recognize, material.

CHAPTER 8

Thinking, Language, and Intelligence

THINKING

8-1 What is *cognition*, and what are the functions of concepts?

- *Cognition* refers to all the mental activities associated with thinking, knowing, remembering, and communicating.

• We use *concepts,* mental groupings of similar objects, events, ideas, or people, to simplify and order the world around us. We form most concepts around *prototypes,* or best examples of a category.

8-2 What cognitive strategies help us solve problems, and what tendencies work against us?

• An *algorithm* is a methodical, logical rule or procedure (such as a step-by-step description for evacuating a building during a fire) that guarantees a solution to a problem.

• A *heuristic* is a simpler strategy (such as running for an exit if you smell smoke) that is usually speedier than an algorithm but is also more error-prone.

• *Insight* is not a strategy-based solution, but rather a sudden flash of inspiration (Aha!) that solves a problem.

• Tendencies that work against us in problem solving include *confirmation bias,* which leads us to verify rather than challenge our hypotheses, and *functional fixedness,* which may prevent us from taking the fresh perspective that would lead to a solution.

8-3 What is *intuition,* and how can the representativeness and availability heuristics influence our decisions and judgments?

• *Intuition* involves fast, automatic, unreasoned feelings and thoughts, as contrasted with explicit, conscious reasoning.

• Heuristics enable snap judgments. Using the *representativeness heuristic,* we judge the likelihood of events based on how well they seem to represent particular prototypes. Using the *availability heuristic,* we judge the likelihood of things based on how readily they come to mind.

8-4 What factors exaggerate our fear of unlikely events?

• The availability heuristic often leads us to fear the wrong things. We also fear what our ancestral history has prepared us to fear, what we cannot control, and what is immediate. We fear too little the ongoing threats that claim lives one by one, such as traffic accidents and diseases.

8-5 How are our decisions and judgments affected by overconfidence, belief perseverance, and framing?

• *Overconfidence* can lead us to overestimate the accuracy of our beliefs.

• When a belief we have formed has been discredited, *belief perseverance* may cause us to cling to that belief. A remedy for belief perseverance is to consider how we might have explained an opposite result.

• *Framing* is the way an issue is posed. Subtle differences in presentation can dramatically alter our responses and *nudge* us toward beneficial decisions.

8-6 How do smart thinkers use intuition?

• As people gain expertise, they become skilled at making quick, shrewd judgments. Smart thinkers welcome their intuitions (which are usually adaptive), but when making complex decisions they gather as much information as possible and then take time to let their two-track mind process all available information.

8-7 What is *creativity,* and what fosters it?

• *Creativity,* the ability to produce new and valuable ideas, requires a certain level of aptitude (ability to learn), but it is more than school smarts. Aptitude tests require *convergent thinking,* but creativity requires *divergent thinking.*

• Robert Sternberg has proposed that creativity has five components: expertise; imaginative thinking skills; a venturesome personality; intrinsic motivation; and a creative environment that sparks, supports, and refines creative ideas.

8-8 What do we know about thinking in other species?

• Evidence from studies of various species shows that many other animals use concepts, numbers, and tools, and that they transmit learning from one generation to the next (cultural transmission). And, like humans, some other species also show insight, self-awareness, altruism, cooperation, and grief.

LANGUAGE

8-9 How do we acquire language, and what is *universal grammar?*

• *Language* is our spoken, written, or signed words and the ways we combine them to communicate meaning.

• Noam Chomsky has proposed that humans are born with a predisposition (a built-in readiness) to learn language. He called this predisposition *universal grammar.* The particular language we learn is the result of our experience.

8-10 What are the milestones in language development, and when is the critical period for learning language?

• Receptive language (the ability to understand what is said to or about you) develops before productive language (the ability to produce words).

• Language development's timing varies, but all children follow the same sequence:

  • By about 4 months of age, infants *babble,* making a wide range of sounds found in languages all over the world.

  • By about 10 months, babbling contains only the sounds of the household language.

  • By about 12 months, children begin to speak in *one-word* sentences.

  • *Two-word (telegraphic)* phrases happen around 24 months, followed by full sentences soon after.

• Childhood is a critical period for learning language. A delay in exposure until age 2 or 3 produces a rush of language. But there is no similar rush of learning in children not exposed to either a spoken or a signed language until age 7; such deprived children will never master any language.

8-11 What brain areas are involved in language processing and speech?

• Two important language- and speech-processing areas are *Broca's area,* a region of the frontal lobe that controls language expression, and *Wernicke's area,* a region in the left temporal lobe that controls language reception.

• Language processing is spread across other brain areas as well, with different neural networks handling specific linguistic subtasks.

8-12 How can thinking in images be useful?

• Thinking in images can provide useful mental practice if we focus on the steps needed to reach our goal (rather than fantasize about having achieved the goal).

8-13 What do we know about other species' capacity for language?

• A number of chimpanzees and bonobos have (1) learned to communicate with humans by signing, (2) developed vocabularies of nearly 400 words, (3) communicated by stringing these words together, (4) taught their skills to younger animals, and (5) demonstrated some understanding of syntax. But only humans possess language—verbal or signed expressions of complex grammar.

INTELLIGENCE

8-14 How do psychologists define *intelligence,* and what are the arguments for general intelligence *(g)?*

• *Intelligence* is the ability to learn from experience, solve problems, and use knowledge to adapt to new situations.

• Charles Spearman proposed that we have one *general intelligence (g)* underlying all other specific mental abilities. He helped develop factor analysis, a statistical procedure that searches for clusters of related items.

8-15 How do Gardner's and Sternberg's theories of multiple intelligences differ, and what criticisms have they faced?

• *Savant syndrome* and abilities lost after brain injuries seem to support Howard Gardner's view that we have multiple intelligences. He proposed eight relatively independent intelligences: linguistic, logical-mathematical, musical, spatial, bodily-kinesthetic, intrapersonal, interpersonal, and naturalist. (He later proposed a ninth possible intelligence—existential intelligence.)

• Robert Sternberg's triarchic theory proposes three intelligence areas that predict real-world skills: analytical (academic problem solving), creative (innovative smarts), and practical (everyday tasks).

• Critics note that research has confirmed a general intelligence factor, which widely predicts performance. But highly successful people also tend to be conscientious, well connected, and doggedly energetic; their achievements arise from both ability *and* motivation. The luck of an advantaged home and school also matter.

8-16 What four abilities make up emotional intelligence?

• *Emotional intelligence,* which is an aspect of social intelligence, includes the abilities to perceive, understand, manage, and use emotions. Emotionally intelligent people achieve greater personal and professional success.

8-17 What is an *intelligence test,* and how do achievement and aptitude tests differ?

• *Intelligence tests* assess a person's mental aptitudes and compare them with those of others, using numerical scores.

• *Aptitude tests* measure the ability to learn; *achievement tests* measure what we have already learned.

8-18 When and why were intelligence tests created, and how do today's tests differ from early intelligence tests?

• Alfred Binet started the modern intelligence-testing movement in France in the early 1900s, when he developed questions to help predict children's future progress in the Paris school system. Binet hoped his test, which measured children's *mental age,* would improve children's education; but he feared it might also be used to label children.

• During the early twentieth century, Lewis Terman of Stanford University revised Binet's work for use in the United States (which resulted in the *Stanford-Binet* intelligence test). Terman's belief in an intelligence that was fixed at birth and differed among ethnic groups realized Binet's fears that intelligence tests would be used to limit children's opportunities.

• William Stern contributed the concept of the *IQ (intelligence quotient).*

• The most widely used intelligence tests today are the *Wechsler Adult Intelligence Scale* (WAIS) and Wechsler's tests for children. These tests differ from their predecessors in the way they offer an overall intelligence score as well as scores for verbal comprehension, perceptual reasoning, working memory, and processing speed.

8-19 What is a *normal curve,* and what does it mean to say that a test has been standardized and is reliable and valid?

• The distribution of test scores often forms a *normal* (bell-shaped) *curve* around the central average score, with fewer and fewer scores at the extremes.

• *Standardization* establishes a basis for meaningful score comparisons by giving a test to a representative sample of future test-takers.

• *Reliability* is the extent to which a test yields consistent results (on two halves of the test, on alternative forms of the test, or on retesting).

• *Validity* is the extent to which a test measures or predicts what it is supposed to. A test should have *predictive validity.* (Aptitude tests have predictive validity if they can predict future achievements.)

8-20 What are the traits of people with extremely low and high intelligence scores?

• An intelligence test score of or below 70 is one diagnostic factor in the diagnosis of *intellectual disability;* limited conceptual, social, and practical skills are other factors. Some people with this diagnosis may be able to live independently. One condition included in this category is Down syndrome, a developmental disorder caused by an extra copy of chromosome 21.

• People at the high-intelligence extreme tend to be healthy and well-adjusted, as well as unusually successful academically.

8-21 What is *heritability?* What do twin and adoption studies tell us about the nature and nurture of intelligence?

• *Heritability* is the portion of variation among people in a group that can be attributed to genes. Many genes contribute to intelligence; there is no known "genius" gene.

• Studies of twins, family members, and adoptive parents and siblings indicate a significant hereditary contribution to intelligence scores. But these studies also provide evidence of environmental influences.

8-22 How can environmental influences affect cognitive development?

• Heredity and environment interact: Our genes shape the environments that influence us.

• Studies of children raised in extremely impoverished environments with minimal social interaction indicate that life experiences can significantly influence intelligence test performance. No evidence supports the idea that normal, healthy children can be molded into geniuses by growing up in an exceptionally enriched environment.

• Environments that foster a growth mindset do not alter intelligence, but can positively impact achievement.

8-23 How stable are intelligence test scores over the life span?

• *Cross-sectional studies* and *longitudinal studies* have shown that intelligence endures. The stability of intelligence test scores increases with age, with scores very stable and predictive by age 11.

8-24 What are *crystallized* and *fluid intelligence,* and how does aging affect them?

• *Crystallized intelligence,* our accumulated knowledge and verbal skills, tends to increase with age.

• *Fluid intelligence,* our ability to reason speedily and abstractly, declines in older adults.

8-25 How and why do the genders differ in mental ability scores?

• Males and females tend to have the same average intelligence test scores, but they differ in some specific abilities.

• Girls, on average, are better spellers, more verbally fluent, better at locating objects, better at detecting emotions, and more sensitive to touch, taste, and color.

• Boys outperform girls at spatial ability and complex math, though in math computation and overall math performance, boys and girls hardly differ. Boys also outnumber girls at the low and high extremes of mental abilities.

• Evolutionary and cultural explanations have been proposed for these gender differences.

8-26 How and why do racial and ethnic groups differ in mental ability scores?

• Racial and ethnic groups differ in their average intelligence test scores. Evidence suggests that environmental differences are responsible for these group differences.

8-27 Are intelligence tests biased or unfair? What is *stereotype threat,* and how does it affect test-takers' performance?

• The scientific meaning of bias hinges on a test's ability to predict future behavior for all test-takers, not just for some. In this sense, most experts consider the major aptitude tests unbiased.

• However, if we consider bias to mean that a test may be influenced by the test-taker's cultural experience, then intelligence tests, by that definition, may be considered unfair.

• *Stereotype threat,* a self-confirming concern that we will be judged based on a negative stereotype, affects performance on all kinds of tests.

CHAPTER 9

Motivation and Emotion

MOTIVATIONAL CONCEPTS

9-1 What is *motivation,* and what are three key perspectives that help us understand motivated behaviors?

• *Motivation* is a need or desire that energizes and directs behavior.

• *Drive-reduction theory*: We feel motivated when pushed by a *physiological need* to reduce a drive (such as thirst), or when pulled by an *incentive* in our environment (an ice-cold drink). Drive-reduction's goal is *homeostasis,* maintaining a steady internal state.

• Arousal theory: We also feel motivated to behave in ways that maintain arousal (for example, curiosity-driven behaviors). The *Yerkes-Dodson law* describes the relationship between arousal and performance.

• Maslow's *hierarchy of needs:* Our levels of motivation form a pyramid of human needs, from basic needs up to higher-level needs.

HUNGER

9-2 What physiological factors cause us to feel hungry?

• Hunger's pangs correspond to stomach contractions, but hunger also has other causes. Neural areas in the brain, some within the hypothalamus, monitor blood chemistry (including level of *glucose*) and incoming information about the body's state.

• Appetite hormones include ghrelin (secreted by an empty stomach); orexin (secreted by the hypothalamus); insulin (controls blood glucose); leptin (secreted by fat cells); and PYY (secreted by the digestive tract).

• *Basal metabolic rate* is the body's resting rate of energy output. The body may have a *set point* (a biologically fixed tendency to maintain an optimum weight) or a looser settling point (also influenced by the environment).

9-3 How do cultural and situational factors affect our taste preferences and eating habits?

• Hunger reflects our memory of when we last ate and our expectation of when we should eat again.

• Humans as a species prefer certain tastes (such as sweet and salty). Some taste preferences have survival value.

• Our individual preferences are also influenced by our learning, culture, and situation. Situational influences include the presence of others, serving size, and the variety of foods offered.

9-4 How does obesity affect physical and psychological health? What factors are involved in weight management?

• *Obesity,* defined by a body mass index (BMI) of 30 or above, is associated with increased depression (especially among women) and bullying, and with many physical health risks.

• Genes and environment interact to produce obesity. Storing fat was adaptive to our ancestors, and fat requires less food intake to maintain than it did to gain. Set point and metabolism matter.

• Twin and adoption studies also indicate that body weight is genetically influenced. Environmental influences include sleep loss, social influence, and food and activity levels.

• Those wishing to lose weight are advised to make a lifelong change in habits: Begin only if you feel motivated and self-disciplined; exercise and get enough sleep; minimize exposure to tempting food cues; limit variety and eat healthy foods; reduce portion sizes; space meals throughout the day; beware of the binge; plan ahead to control eating during social events; forgive the occasional lapse; chart your progress online; and connect to a support group.

THE NEED TO BELONG

9-5 What evidence points to our human need to belong?

• Social bonds are adaptive, and having a social identity (feeling part of a group) helps us to be healthier and happier. According to *self-determination theory*, we strive to satisfy our needs for competence, autonomy, and relatedness.

• Feeling loved activates brain regions associated with rewards and satisfaction.

• *Ostracism* is the deliberate exclusion of individuals or groups. Social isolation can put us at risk mentally and physically.

9-6 How does social networking influence us?

• We connect with others through social networking, strengthening our relationships with those we already know and often starting new friendships or romances. When networking, people tend toward increased self-disclosure. People with high *narcissism* are especially active on social networking sites.

• Working out strategies for self-control and disciplined usage can help people maintain a healthy balance between their real-world and online time.

ACHIEVEMENT MOTIVATION

9-7 What is *achievement motivation,* and what are some ways to encourage achievement?

• *Achievement motivation* is a desire for significant accomplishment, for mastery of skills or ideas, for control, and for attaining a high standard. High achievement motivation leads to greater success, especially when combined with determined, persistent *grit*.

• Research shows that excessive rewards (driving *extrinsic motivation*) can undermine *intrinsic motivation*.

- We can encourage achievement by making resolutions; announcing our goals; developing action plans; creating short-term rewards that support long-term goals; monitoring and recording progress; creating a supportive environment; and repeating hard-to-do behaviors to transform them into must-do habits.

EMOTION: AROUSAL, BEHAVIOR, AND COGNITION

9-8 What are the three parts of an emotion, and what theories help us to understand our emotions?

- *Emotions* are responses of the whole organism involving bodily arousal, expressive behaviors, and conscious experience and feelings.
- *James-Lange theory:* Emotional feelings follow our body's response to the emotion-arousing stimuli. (We observe our heart pounding and feel fear.)
- *Cannon-Bard theory:* Our body responds to emotion at the same time that we experience that emotion. (Neither causes the other.)
- Schachter-Singer *two-factor theory:* Emotions have two ingredients, physical arousal and a cognitive label, and the cognitive labels we put on our states of arousal are an essential ingredient of emotion.
- Richard Lazarus agreed that many important emotions arise from our interpretations or inferences. But Robert Zajonc and Joseph LeDoux have contended that some simple emotional responses occur instantly, not only outside our conscious awareness, but before any cognitive processing occurs. This interplay between emotion and cognition illustrates our two-track mind.

EMBODIED EMOTION

9-9 What are some basic emotions?

- Most emotion scientists agree that anger, fear, disgust, sadness, and happiness are basic human emotions. Carroll Izard's 10 basic emotions are joy, interest-excitement, surprise, sadness, anger, disgust, contempt, fear, shame, and guilt.

9-10 What is the link between emotional arousal and the autonomic nervous system?

- The arousal component of emotion is regulated by the autonomic nervous system's sympathetic (arousing) and parasympathetic (calming) divisions.
- In a crisis, the *fight-or-flight response* automatically mobilizes your body for action.

9-11 How do our body states relate to specific emotions?

- The large-scale body changes that accompany fear, anger, and sexual arousal are very similar (increased perspiration, breathing, and heart rate), though they feel different. Emotions may be similarly arousing, but some subtle physiological responses (such as facial muscle movements) distinguish them.
- Emotions use different brain pathways and areas. For example, greater activity in the left frontal lobe signals positive rather than negative moods.

9-12 How effective are polygraphs in using body states to detect lies?

- *Polygraphs* (lie detectors) attempt to measure physical evidence of emotions; they are not accurate enough to justify widespread use in business and law enforcement.
- Using the Concealed Information Test may produce better indications of lying.

EXPRESSED AND EXPERIENCED EMOTION

9-13 How do we communicate nonverbally? How do women and men differ in these abilities?

- We are good at detecting emotions from body movements, facial expressions, and voice tones. Even seconds-long video clips of behavior can reveal feelings.
- Women tend to read emotional cues more easily and to be more empathic. Their faces also express more emotion.

9-14 How are gestures and facial expressions of emotion understood within and across cultures?

- The meaning of gestures varies by culture, but facial expressions, such as those of happiness and sadness, are roughly similar all over the world.
- Cultures differ in the amount of emotion they express.

9-15 How do facial expressions influence our feelings?

- Research on the *facial feedback effect* shows that our facial expressions can trigger emotional feelings and signal our body to respond accordingly. We also mimic others' expressions, which helps us empathize.

CHAPTER 10

Stress, Health, and Human Flourishing

STRESS: SOME BASIC CONCEPTS

10-1 How does our appraisal of an event affect our stress reaction, and what are the three main types of stressors?

- *Stress* is the process by which we appraise and respond to stressors—events that challenge or threaten us. If we appraise an event as challenging, we will be aroused and focused in preparation for success. If we appraise an event as a threat, we will experience a stress reaction, and our health may suffer.
- The three main types of stressors are catastrophes, significant life changes, and daily hassles.

10-2 How does the body respond to stress?

- Walter Cannon viewed our body's response to stress as a *fight-or-flight* system.
- Hans Selye proposed a three-phase (alarm, resistance, exhaustion) *general adaptation syndrome (GAS).*
- People may react to stress by withdrawing. They may also show a *tend-and-befriend response* (more common in women), such as when helping others after natural disasters.

STRESS EFFECTS AND HEALTH

10-3 How does stress influence our immune system?

- Stress takes energy away from the immune system, inhibiting the activities of its B and T lymphocytes, macrophages, and natural killer (NK) cells. This leaves us more vulnerable to illness and disease. *Psychoneuroimmunology* is the study of these mind-body interactions.
- Although stress does not cause diseases such as AIDS and cancer, it may make us more vulnerable to them and influence their progression.

10-4 How does stress increase coronary heart disease risk?

- Stress is directly connected to *coronary heart disease,* the United States' leading cause of death.
- Heart disease has been linked with the competitive, hard-driving, impatient, and (especially) anger-prone *Type A* personality.

Type A people secrete more stress hormones. Chronic stress contributes to persistent inflammation, which is associated with heart and other health problems, including depression.

- *Type B* personalities are more relaxed and easygoing and less likely to experience heart disease.
- The fight-or-flight stress reaction may divert blood from the liver to the muscles, leaving excess cholesterol circulating in the bloodstream.
- Depression and pessimism also increase our risk of heart disease.

10-5 So, does stress *cause* illness?

- Stress may not directly cause illness, but it does make us more vulnerable, by influencing our behaviors and our physiology.

COPING WITH STRESS

10-6 What are two basic ways that people cope with stress?

- We use direct, *problem-focused coping* strategies when we feel a sense of control over a situation.
- When lacking that sense of control, we may need to use *emotion-focused coping* strategies to protect our long-term well-being. These strategies can be harmful if misused.

10-7 How does our sense of control influence stress and health?

- Feelings of loss of *personal control* can trigger physical symptoms, such as increased stress hormones and rising blood pressure. A series of uncontrollable events can lead to *learned helplessness*.
- Those with an *internal locus of control* achieve more in school and work, act more independently, enjoy better health, and feel less depressed than do those with an *external locus of control*.
- Those who develop and maintain *self-control* earn higher income, get better grades, and are healthier.

10-8 How do optimists and pessimists differ, and why does our outlook on life matter?

- *Optimists* (those expecting positive outcomes) tend to be in better health than *pessimists* (those expecting negative outcomes).
- Studies of people with an optimistic outlook show that their immune system is stronger, their blood pressure does not increase as sharply in response to stress, their recovery from heart bypass surgery is faster, and their life expectancy is longer. Yet excessive optimism can blind us to real risks; realistic anxiety over possible future failures can help motivate us to do better.

10-9 How do social support and finding meaning in life influence health?

- Social support promotes health by calming us, by reducing blood pressure and stress hormones, and by fostering stronger immune function. We can significantly reduce our stress and increase our health by building and maintaining relationships with family and friends, and by finding meaning even in difficult times.

MANAGING STRESS EFFECTS

10-10 How well does aerobic exercise help us manage stress and improve well-being?

- *Aerobic exercise* is sustained activity that increases heart and lung fitness, which leads to greater well-being.
- Exercise increases arousal and triggers serotonin activity. It also reduces depression and anxiety.

10-11 In what ways might relaxation and meditation influence stress and health?

- Relaxation and meditation have been shown to lower stress, reduce blood pressure, improve immune functioning, and lessen anxiety and depression. *Mindfulness meditation* is a reflective practice of attending to current experiences in a nonjudgmental and accepting manner. Massage therapy also promotes relaxation and reduces depression.
- Counseling Type A heart attack survivors to slow down and relax has helped lower rates of recurring attacks.

10-12 Does religious involvement relate to health?

- Religious involvement predicts better health and longevity. This may be explained by the healthier lifestyles of religiously active people, the social support that comes along with practicing a faith in community, and the positive emotions often found among people who regularly attend religious services.

HAPPINESS

10-13 What are the causes and consequences of happiness?

- A good mood brightens people's perceptions of the world. Happy people tend to be healthy, energized, and satisfied with life. They also are more willing to help others (the *feel-good, do-good phenomenon*). Tough challenges can foster *resilience*, which helps people cope with stress and adversity.
- Having enough money to assure comfort, security, and a sense of control predicts happiness. Once you satisfy these needs, more money does not mean more happiness. Economic growth in many countries has produced rising inequality, which is a predictor of unhappiness.
- Even significant good or bad events don't usually change our *subjective well-being* for long. Happiness is relative to our own experiences (the *adaptation-level phenomenon*) and to others' success (the *relative deprivation* principle).
- Tips for increasing happiness levels: take charge of your schedule, act happy, seek meaningful work and leisure, buy shared experiences rather than things, exercise, sleep enough, foster friendships, focus beyond the self, challenge negative thinking, and nurture gratitude and spirituality.

CHAPTER 11

Social Psychology

WHAT IS SOCIAL PSYCHOLOGY'S FOCUS?

11-1 What are three main focuses of social psychology?

- *Social psychologists* use scientific methods to study how we think about, influence, and relate to one another. They study the social influences that explain why the same person will act differently in different situations.

SOCIAL THINKING

11-2 How does the fundamental attribution error describe how we tend to explain others' behavior compared with our own?

- We may commit the *fundamental attribution error* (especially if we come from an individualist Western culture) when explaining others' behavior, by underestimating the influence of the situation and overestimating the effects of personality.
- When explaining our own behavior, we more often recognize the influence of the situation.

11-3 What is an *attitude*, and how do attitudes and actions affect each other?

- *Attitudes* are feelings, often based on our beliefs, that predispose us to respond in certain ways. Attitudes that are stable, specific, and easily recalled can affect our actions when other influences are minimal.
- Actions also modify our attitudes, as in the *foot-in-the-door phenomenon* and *role* playing.
- When our attitudes don't fit with our actions, *cognitive dissonance theory* suggests that we will reduce tension by changing our attitudes to match our actions.

11-4 How do *peripheral route persuasion* and *central route persuasion* differ?

- *Peripheral route persuasion* uses incidental cues (such as celebrity endorsement) to try to produce fast but relatively thoughtless changes in attitudes. *Central route persuasion* offers evidence and arguments to influence interested people's thinking, and is more durable.

11-5 How can we share our views more effectively?

- To persuade people with views that differ from your own, avoid yelling at, humiliating, or overloading them with too much complicated information. Instead, identify shared goals and relate your aim to their motives. It also helps to make your message vivid, repeat it, and try to engage others in restating it.

SOCIAL INFLUENCE

11-6 What do experiments on conformity and obedience reveal about the power of social influence?

- Solomon Asch and others found that we are most likely to *conform* to a group standard when we feel incompetent or insecure, our group has at least three people, everyone else agrees, we admire the group, we have not already committed to another response, we know we are being observed, and our culture encourages respect for social standards.
- We may conform to gain approval *(normative social influence)* or because we are willing to accept others' opinions as new information *(informational social influence)*.
- In Stanley Milgram's famous experiments, people usually obeyed the experimenter's orders even when they thought they were harming another person. Obedience was highest when the experimenter was nearby and was a legitimate authority figure supported by an important institution, the victim was not nearby, and there were no role models for defiance.

11-7 What do the social influence studies teach us about ourselves? How much power do we have as individuals?

- These experiments demonstrate that strong social influences affect behavior.
- The power of the individual (personal control) and the power of the situation (social control) interact.
- A small minority consistently expressing its views may sway a group.

11-8 How does the presence of others influence our actions, via social facilitation, social loafing, and deindividuation?

- In *social facilitation,* the presence of others arouses us, improving performance on easy tasks (but decreasing it on difficult ones).
- *Social loafing* is the tendency when participating in a group project to feel less responsible, when we may free ride on others' efforts.
- When the presence of others both arouses us and makes us feel less responsible, we may experience *deindividuation*—loss of self-awareness and self-restraint.

11-9 How can group interaction enable group polarization?

- In *group polarization,* group discussion with like-minded others strengthens shared beliefs and attitudes.

11-10 What role does the internet play in group polarization?

- Internet communication magnifies the effect of connecting like-minded people, for better and for worse. People find support, which strengthens their ideas, but also often isolation from those with different opinions. Separation plus conversation may thus lead to group polarization.

11-11 How can group interaction enable groupthink?

- *Groupthink* is driven by a desire for harmony within a decision-making group, causing its members to overlook important alternatives.

SOCIAL RELATIONS

11-12 What are the three parts of *prejudice?* How do explicit and implicit prejudice differ?

- *Prejudice* is an unfair, usually negative, attitude toward a group and its members. Prejudice's three components are negative feelings, beliefs (often *stereotypes*), and predispositions to action *(discrimination)*.
- Prejudice may be explicit (open), or it may be implicit—an unthinking knee-jerk response operating below conscious awareness. Implicit prejudice can cause discrimination even when people do not consciously intend to discriminate.

11-13 What groups are frequent targets of prejudice?

- Prejudice involves explicit and implicit negative attitudes toward people of a particular racial or ethnic group, gender identity, sexual orientation, or belief system. In the United States, frequently targeted groups include Black Americans, women, religious minorities, and gay, lesbian, and transgender people.

11-14 What are some social, emotional, and cognitive roots of prejudice? What are some ways to combat prejudice?

- The social roots of prejudice include social inequalities and divisions. Favored social groups often justify their higher status with the *just-world phenomenon*.
- We tend to favor our own group *(ingroup bias)* as we divide ourselves into us (the *ingroup*) and them (the *outgroup*).
- We may use prejudice to protect our emotional well-being, such as when focusing anger by blaming events on a *scapegoat*.
- The cognitive roots of prejudice grow from our natural ways of processing information: forming categories, remembering vivid cases, and believing that the world is just (and our group's way of doing things is the right way).

11-15 What biological factors make us more likely to be aggressive?

- *Aggression* is a complex behavior resulting from the interaction of biology and experience.
- Biology influences our threshold for aggressive behaviors at three levels: genetic (inherited traits), biochemical (such as alcohol or excess testosterone in the bloodstream), and neural (activity in key brain areas).

11-16 What psychological and social-cultural factors may trigger aggressive behavior?

- Frustration *(frustration-aggression principle),* getting rewarded for aggression, seeing an aggressive role model, and poor self-control can all contribute to aggression.

- Media violence provides *social scripts* that children learn to follow. Viewing sexual violence contributes to greater aggression toward women. Violent video games can increase aggressive thoughts, emotions, and behaviors.

11-17 Why do we befriend or fall in love with some people but not others?

- Proximity (geographical nearness) increases liking, in part because of the *mere exposure effect*.
- Physical attractiveness increases social opportunities and improves the way we are perceived.
- Similarity of attitudes and interests greatly increases liking, especially as relationships develop. We also like those who like us.

11-18 How does romantic love typically change as time passes?

- Intimate love relationships start with *passionate love*—an intensely aroused state.
- Over time, the strong affection of *companionate love* may develop, especially if enhanced by an *equitable* relationship, intimate *self-disclosure*, and positive support.

11-19 What is *altruism*? When are we most—and least—likely to help?

- *Altruism* is unselfish concern for the well-being of others.
- We are most likely to help when we notice an incident, interpret it as an emergency, and assume responsibility for helping. Other factors, including our mood and our similarity to the victim, also affect our willingness to help.
- We are least likely to help if other bystanders are present (the *bystander effect*).

11-20 How do social norms explain helping behavior?

- Helping results from socialization, in which we are taught guidelines for expected behaviors in social situations, such as the *reciprocity norm* and the *social-responsibility norm*.

11-21 What social processes fuel conflict? How can we transform feelings of prejudice and conflict into behaviors that promote peace?

- *Conflicts*, perceived incompatibilities of actions, goals, or ideas between individuals and cultures, are often fed by distorted *mirror-image perceptions*—each party views itself as ethical and peaceful and the other as untrustworthy and evil-intentioned. Perceptions can be *self-fulfilling prophecies*.
- Peace can result when individuals or groups cooperate to achieve *superordinate* (shared) *goals*.

CHAPTER 12

Personality

WHAT IS PERSONALITY?

12-1 What is *personality,* and what theories inform our understanding of personality?

- *Personality* is an individual's characteristic pattern of thinking, feeling, and acting.
- Psychoanalytic (and later psychodynamic) theory and humanistic theory have become part of our cultural legacy. They also laid the foundation for later theories, such as trait and social-cognitive theories of personality.

PSYCHODYNAMIC THEORIES

12-2 How did Sigmund Freud's treatment of psychological disorders lead to his view of the unconscious mind?

- *Psychodynamic theories* view personality from the perspective that behavior is a lively (dynamic) interaction between the conscious and unconscious mind. The theories trace their origin to Sigmund Freud's theory of *psychoanalysis*.
- In treating patients whose disorders had no clear physical explanation, Freud concluded that these problems reflected unacceptable thoughts and feelings, hidden away in the *unconscious* mind. To explore this hidden part of a patient's mind, Freud used *free association* and dream analysis.

12-3 What was Freud's view of personality?

- Freud believed that personality is a result of conflict among the mind's three systems: the *id* (pleasure-seeking impulses), *ego* (reality-oriented executive), and *superego* (internalized set of ideals, or conscience).

12-4 What developmental stages did Freud propose?

- He believed children pass through five *psychosexual stages* (oral, anal, phallic, latency, and genital). Unresolved conflicts at any stage can leave a person's pleasure-seeking impulses *fixated* (stalled) at that stage.

12-5 How did Freud think people defended themselves against anxiety?

- For Freud, anxiety was the product of tensions between the demands of id and superego.
- The ego copes by using unconscious *defense mechanisms,* such as *repression,* which he viewed as the basic mechanism underlying and enabling all the others.

12-6 Which of Freud's ideas did his followers accept or reject?

- Freud's early followers, the neo-Freudians, accepted many of his ideas. They differed in placing more emphasis on the conscious mind and in stressing social motives more than sex or aggression. Neo-Freudian Carl Jung proposed the *collective unconscious*.
- Contemporary psychodynamic theorists and therapists reject Freud's emphasis on sexual motivation. They stress, with support from modern research findings, that much of our mental life is unconscious, and they believe that our childhood experiences influence our adult personality and attachment patterns.

12-7 What are *projective tests,* how are they used, and what criticisms have they faced?

- *Projective tests* attempt to assess personality by showing people an ambiguous image designed to trigger projection of the test-taker's unconscious thoughts and feelings.
- The *Thematic Apperception Test (TAT)* and the *Rorschach inkblot test* are two such tests. The Rorschach has low reliability and validity, but some clinicians value it as a source of suggestive leads, an icebreaker, or a revealing interview technique.

12-8 How do today's psychologists view Freud's psychoanalysis?

- Freud rightly drew our attention to the vast unconscious, the importance of human sexuality, and the conflict between biological impulses and social restraints.
- But his concept of repression, and his view of the unconscious as a collection of repressed and unacceptable thoughts, wishes, feelings, and memories, cannot survive scientific scrutiny.
- Research does not support many of Freud's specific ideas, such as development

being fixed in childhood. (We now know it is lifelong.)

- Freud offered after-the-fact explanations, which are hard to test scientifically.

12-9 How has modern research developed our understanding of the unconscious?

- Research confirms that we do not have full access to all that goes on in our mind, but the current view of the unconscious is that it is a separate and parallel track of information processing that occurs outside our awareness. Research also supports reaction formation and projection (the false consensus effect).
- This processing includes schemas that control our perceptions, implicit memories of learned skills, instantly activated emotions, and the implicit prejudice and stereotypes that automatically influence how we process information about others.

HUMANISTIC THEORIES

12-10 How did humanistic psychologists view personality, and what was their goal in studying personality?

- Humanistic theories sought to turn psychology's attention toward human growth potential.
- Abraham Maslow thought that human motivations form a *hierarchy of needs.* If basic needs are fulfilled, people will strive toward *self-actualization* and *self-transcendence.*
- Carl Rogers believed that people are basically good, and that showing *unconditional positive regard* and being accepting, genuine, and empathic can help others develop a more realistic and positive *self-concept.*

12-11 How did humanistic psychologists assess a person's sense of self?

- Some rejected any standardized assessments and relied on interviews and conversations.
- Others, like Rogers, sometimes used questionnaires in which people described their ideal and actual selves. These were later used to judge progress during therapy.

12-12 How have humanistic theories influenced psychology? What criticisms have they faced?

- Humanistic psychology helped renew interest in the concept of self, and also laid the groundwork for today's scientific subfield of positive psychology.
- Critics have said that humanistic psychology's concepts are vague and subjective, its values self-centered, and its assumptions naively optimistic.

TRAIT THEORIES

12-13 How do psychologists use traits to describe personality?

- *Trait* theorists see personality as a stable and enduring pattern of behavior. They have been more interested in describing our differences than in explaining them.
- They identify *factors*—clusters of behavior tendencies that occur together.

12-14 What are some common misunderstandings about introversion?

- Western cultures prize extraversion, but introverts have different, equally important skills. Introversion does not equal shyness.
- Introverts handle conflict well, and introverted leaders outperform extraverted leaders in some contexts.

12-15 What are *personality inventories?*

- *Personality inventories* (such as the *MMPI*) are questionnaires on which people respond to items designed to gauge a wide range of feelings and behaviors.
- Unlike projective tests, these tests are objectively scored. But people can fake their answers to create a good impression; objectivity does not guarantee validity.

12-16 Which traits seem to provide the most useful information about personality variation?

- The Big Five personality factors—openness, conscientiousness, extraversion, agreeableness, and neuroticism (OCEAN)—currently offer the clearest picture of personality.
- These factors are generally stable and appear to be found in all cultures.

12-17 Does research support the consistency of personality traits over time and across situations?

- A person's average traits persist over time and are predictable over many different situations. But traits cannot predict behavior in any one particular situation.

SOCIAL-COGNITIVE THEORIES

12-18 How do social-cognitive theorists view personality development, and how do they explore behavior?

- *Reciprocal determinism* describes the interaction and mutual influence of behavior, internal personal factors, and environmental factors.
- Albert Bandura first proposed the *social-cognitive perspective,* which views behavior as the product of the interaction between a person's traits (and their thinking) and the situation—the social world around us.
- Social-cognitive researchers apply principles of learning, cognition, and social behavior to personality.

12-19 What criticisms have social-cognitive theorists faced?

- Critics note that social-cognitive theorists focus so much on the situation that they fail to appreciate a person's inner traits, underemphasizing the importance of unconscious motives, emotions, and personality characteristics.

EXPLORING THE SELF

12-20 Why has psychology generated so much research on the self? How important is self-esteem to our well-being?

- The *self* is the center of personality, organizing our thoughts, feelings, and actions.
- Considering possible selves helps motivate us toward positive development, but focusing too intensely on ourselves can lead to the *spotlight effect.*
- High *self-esteem* is beneficial, but unrealistically high self-esteem, which can be *narcissistic,* is dangerous (linked to aggressive behavior) and fragile. Rather than unrealistically promoting children's feelings of self-worth, it is better to reward their achievements, which leads to feelings of competence.

12-21 What evidence reveals self-serving bias, and how do defensive and secure self-esteem differ?

- *Self-serving bias* is our tendency to perceive ourselves favorably, as when viewing ourselves as better than average or when accepting credit for our successes but not blame for our failures.
- Defensive self-esteem is fragile, focuses on sustaining itself, and views failure or criticism as a threat.
- Secure self-esteem is sturdy, enabling us to feel accepted for who we are.

12-22 How do individualist and collectivist cultures differ in their values and goals?

- Although individuals vary, different cultures tend to emphasize either individualism or collectivism.

- Cultures based on self-reliant *individualism* tend to value personal independence and achievement.
- Cultures based on socially connected *collectivism* tend to value group goals, social identity, and commitments.

CHAPTER 13

Psychological Disorders

WHAT IS A PSYCHOLOGICAL DISORDER?

13-1 How should we draw the line between normality and disorder?

- According to psychologists and psychiatrists, *psychological disorders* are marked by a clinically significant disturbance in an individual's cognition, emotion regulation, or behavior. Such dysfunctional or maladaptive thoughts, emotions, or behaviors interfere with daily life, and thus are disordered.

13-2 Why is there controversy over attention-deficit/hyperactivity disorder?

- A child (or, less commonly, an adult) who displays extreme inattention and/or hyperactivity and impulsivity may be diagnosed with *attention-deficit/hyperactivity disorder (ADHD)*.
- Controversies center on whether the growing number of ADHD cases reflects overdiagnosis or increased awareness of the disorder, and on the long-term effects of stimulant-drug treatment.

13-3 How do the medical model and the biopsychosocial approach influence our understanding of psychological disorders?

- The *medical model* assumes that psychological disorders have physical causes that can be diagnosed, treated, and often cured through therapy, sometimes in a hospital.
- The biopsychosocial approach assumes that disordered behavior comes from the interaction of biological characteristics, psychological dynamics, and social-cultural circumstances.
- This perspective has led to the vulnerability-stress model. Individual characteristics and environmental stressors combine to increase or decrease the likelihood of developing a psychological disorder. This model is supported by *epigenetics* research.

13-4 How and why do clinicians classify psychological disorders, and why do some psychologists criticize the use of diagnostic labels?

- The American Psychiatric Association's *DSM-5 (Diagnostic and Statistical Manual of Mental Disorders,* Fifth Edition) lists and describes psychological disorders. Diagnostic labels provide a common language and shared concepts for communication and research.
- Some critics believe the DSM editions have become too detailed and extensive. The Research Domain Criteria (RDoC) project is a new, related framework that organizes disorders according to behaviors and brain activity along several dimensions. Any classification attempt produces diagnostic labels that may create preconceptions that cause us to view a person differently, and then look for evidence to confirm that view.

ANXIETY DISORDERS, OCD, AND PTSD

13-5 How do generalized anxiety disorder, panic disorder, and phobias differ? How do anxiety disorders differ from the ordinary worries and fears we all experience?

- *Anxiety disorders* are psychological disorders characterized by distressing, persistent anxiety or maladaptive behaviors that reduce anxiety.
    - People with *generalized anxiety disorder* feel, for no apparent reason, persistently and uncontrollably tense and apprehensive.
    - In the more extreme *panic disorder,* anxiety escalates into episodes of intense dread.
    - Those with a *phobia* show an intense and irrational fear and avoidance of a specific object, activity, or situation.

13-6 What is *OCD?*

- Persistent and repetitive thoughts (obsessions), actions (compulsions), or both mark *obsessive-compulsive disorder (OCD)*.

13-7 What is *PTSD?*

- Symptoms of *posttraumatic stress disorder (PTSD)* include four or more weeks of haunting memories, nightmares, hypervigilance, avoidance of trauma-related stimuli, social withdrawal, jumpy anxiety, numbness of feeling, and/or sleep problems following a traumatic event.

13-8 How do conditioning, cognition, and biology contribute to the feelings and thoughts that mark anxiety disorders, OCD, and PTSD?

- The learning perspective views anxiety disorders, OCD, and PTSD as products of fear conditioning, stimulus generalization, fearful-behavior reinforcement, and observational learning of others' fears and cognitions.
- The biological perspective considers genetic predispositions and the role that fears of life-threatening animals, objects, or situations played in natural selection and evolution.

SUBSTANCE USE DISORDERS

13-9 What are *substance use disorders?*

- Those with a *substance use disorder* experience continued substance craving and use despite significant life disruption and/or physical risk. *Psychoactive drugs* are any chemical substances that alter perceptions and moods.

13-10 What roles do tolerance and addiction play in substance use disorders, and how has the concept of *addiction* changed?

- Psychoactive drugs may produce *tolerance*—requiring larger doses to achieve the desired effect—and *withdrawal*—significant discomfort, due to strong addictive cravings, accompanying attempts to quit.
- Addiction prompts users to crave the drug and to continue use, despite adverse consequences. Although psychologists try to avoid overuse of the term "addiction" to label driven, excessive behaviors, there are some behavior addictions (such as gambling disorder) in which behaviors become compulsive and dysfunctional.

13-11 What are *depressants,* and what are their effects?

- *Depressants* (alcohol, *barbiturates, opiates*) reduce neural activity and slow body functions.
- Alcohol disinhibits, increasing the likelihood that we will act on our impulses, whether helpful or harmful. User expectations strongly influence alcohol's behavioral effects.
- Alcohol slows neural processing, disrupts memory, and shrinks the brain in those with *alcohol use disorder* (marked by

tolerance, withdrawal if use is suspended, and a drive to continue problematic use).

13-12 What are *stimulants,* and what are their effects?

- *Stimulants* (caffeine, nicotine, cocaine, the amphetamines, methamphetamine, Ecstasy) excite neural activity and speed up body functions, leading to heightened energy and mood. All are highly addictive.
  - *Nicotine's* effects make tobacco product use difficult to quit, yet repeated attempts seem to pay off.
  - *Cocaine* gives users a fast high, followed shortly by a crash. Its risks include cardiac arrest, respiratory failure, and emotional disturbances.
  - *Amphetamines* stimulate neural activity, leading to heightened energy and mood. *Methamphetamine* use may permanently reduce dopamine levels.
  - *Ecstasy (MDMA),* which is also a mild hallucinogen, may damage serotonin-producing neurons and impair physical and cognitive functions.

13-13 What are *hallucinogens,* and what are their effects?

- *Hallucinogens* (*LSD,* marijuana) distort perceptions and evoke hallucinations, some of which resemble the altered consciousness of *near-death experiences.*
- Marijuana's main ingredient, *THC,* may trigger feelings of disinhibition, euphoria, relaxation, relief from pain, and intense sensitivity to colors, sounds, tastes, and smells. It may also increase the risk of psychological disorders and lead to impaired learning and memory.

13-14 What biological, psychological, and social-cultural factors help explain why some people abuse mind-altering drugs?

- Some people may be biologically more vulnerable to drugs.
- Psychological factors (such as stress, depression, and anxiety) and social-cultural influences (peer pressure, cultural values) combine to lead many people to experiment with—and sometimes become addicted to—drugs.

MAJOR DEPRESSIVE DISORDER AND BIPOLAR DISORDER

13-15 How do major depressive disorder and bipolar disorder differ?

- A person with *major depressive disorder* experiences two or more weeks with five or more symptoms, at least one of which must be either (1) depressed mood or (2) loss of interest or pleasure.
- A person with the less common condition of *bipolar disorder* experiences not only depression but also *mania*—episodes of hyperactive and wildly optimistic, impulsive behavior.

13-16 How can the biological and social-cognitive perspectives help us understand major depressive disorder and bipolar disorder?

- The biological perspective on major depressive disorder and bipolar disorder focuses on genetic predispositions and on abnormalities in brain function, including those found in neurotransmitter systems.
- The social-cognitive perspective views depression as an ongoing cycle of stressful experiences (interpreted through negative beliefs, attributions, and memories) leading to negative moods and actions and fueling new stressful experiences.

SCHIZOPHRENIA

13-17 What patterns of perceiving, thinking, and feeling characterize schizophrenia?

- *Schizophrenia* is a *psychotic disorder* characterized by delusions, hallucinations, disorganized speech, and/or diminished, inappropriate emotional expression.
- *Delusions* are false beliefs; hallucinations are sensory experiences without sensory stimulation.
- Schizophrenia symptoms may be positive (the presence of inappropriate behaviors) or negative (the absence of appropriate behaviors).

13-18 How do *acute schizophrenia* and *chronic schizophrenia* differ?

- Schizophrenia typically strikes during late adolescence, affects slightly more males than females, and occurs in all cultures. In *chronic* (or process) *schizophrenia,* the disorder develops gradually and recovery is doubtful. In *acute* (or reactive) *schizophrenia,* onset is sudden, in reaction to stress, and the prospects for recovery are brighter.

13-19 What brain abnormalities are associated with schizophrenia?

- People with schizophrenia have more receptors for dopamine, which may intensify the positive symptoms such as hallucinations and paranoia.
- Brain scans have revealed abnormal activity in the frontal lobes, thalamus, and amygdala. Brain abnormalities associated with schizophrenia include enlarged, fluid-filled areas and loss of cerebral cortex.

13-20 What prenatal events are associated with increased risk of developing schizophrenia?

- Possible contributing factors include mother's diabetes, father's older age, viral infections or famine conditions during the mother's pregnancy, and low weight or oxygen deprivation at birth.

13-21 How do genes influence schizophrenia?

- Twin and adoption studies indicate that the predisposition to schizophrenia is inherited. Multiple genes probably interact to produce schizophrenia.
- No environmental causes invariably produce schizophrenia, but environmental events (such as prenatal viruses or maternal stress) may "turn on" genes for this disorder in those who are predisposed to it.

OTHER DISORDERS

13-22 What are the three main eating disorders, and how do biological, psychological, and social-cultural influences make people more vulnerable to them?

- In those with eating disorders, psychological factors can overwhelm the body's tendency to maintain a normal weight.
- Despite being significantly underweight, people with *anorexia nervosa* (usually adolescent females) continue to diet and sometimes exercise excessively because they view themselves as fat.
- Those with *bulimia nervosa* secretly binge and then compensate with purging, fasting, or excessively exercising.
- Those with *binge-eating disorder* binge but do not follow with purging, fasting, and exercise.
- Cultural pressures, low self-esteem, and negative emotions interact with stressful life experiences and genetics to produce eating disorders.

13-23 What are *dissociative disorders,* and why are they controversial?

- *Dissociative disorders* are controversial, rare conditions in which conscious awareness seems to become separated (dissociated) from previous memories, thoughts, and feelings.

- Skeptics note that *dissociative identity disorder (DID)* increased dramatically in the late twentieth century, is rarely found outside North America, and may reflect role playing by people vulnerable to therapists' suggestions. Others view DID as a protective response to traumatic experience.

13-24 What are the three clusters of personality disorders? What biological and psychological factors are associated with antisocial personality disorder?

- *Personality disorders* are inflexible and enduring behavior patterns that impair social functioning. The ten DSM-5 disorders tend to form three clusters, characterized by (1) anxiety, (2) eccentric or odd behaviors, and (3) dramatic or impulsive behaviors.
- *Antisocial personality disorder* (in the third cluster) is characterized by a lack of conscience and, sometimes, by aggressive and fearless behavior. Genetic predispositions may interact with the environment to produce the altered brain activity associated with this disorder. Differences in brain structure and function include a smaller amygdala and less active response to emotional stimuli.

RISK OF HARM TO SELF AND OTHERS

13-25 What factors increase the risk of suicide, and what do we know about nonsuicidal self-injury?

- People with disorders such as depression are more at risk for suicide than others are, but health status, social disconnection (including among heavy consumers of social media), feeling trapped by a situation, and economic frustration are also contributing factors.
- Forewarnings of suicide may include verbal hints, giving away possessions, sudden mood changes, or withdrawal and preoccupation with death. People who talk about suicide should be taken seriously: Listen and empathize, connect them to help, and protect those who appear at immediate risk.
- Nonsuicidal self-injury (NSSI) does not usually lead to suicide but may escalate to suicidal thoughts and acts if untreated. People with NSSI generally do not tolerate stress well and tend to be self-critical.

13-26 What is the relationship between psychological disorders and violent acts?

- Mental disorders seldom lead to violence, but when they do, they raise moral and ethical questions about how to protect both disordered individuals and others. Most people with disorders are nonviolent and are more likely to be victims than attackers.

CHAPTER 14

Therapy

TREATING PSYCHOLOGICAL DISORDERS

14-1 How do psychotherapy and the biomedical therapies differ?

- *Psychotherapy* is treatment involving psychological techniques. It consists of interactions between a trained therapist and a person seeking to overcome psychological difficulties or achieve personal growth. The major psychotherapies derive from psychology's psychodynamic, humanistic, behavioral, and cognitive perspectives.
- *Biomedical therapy* treats psychological disorders with medications and other biological treatments.
- Therapists who take an *eclectic approach* combine different techniques tailored to the client's problems.

THE PSYCHOLOGICAL THERAPIES

14-2 What are the goals and techniques of psychoanalysis, and how have they been adapted in psychodynamic therapy?

- Sigmund Freud's *psychoanalysis* aimed to give people self-insight and relief from their disorders by bringing anxiety-laden feelings and thoughts into conscious awareness.
- Techniques included free association, dream analysis, and *interpretation* of instances of *resistance* and *transference*.
- Like psychoanalysis, *psychodynamic therapy* focuses on childhood experiences, therapist interactions, unconscious feelings, and unresolved conflicts. Yet it is briefer, less expensive, and focuses primarily on current symptom relief. Exploring past relationship troubles may help clients understand the origin of their current difficulties.

14-3 What are the basic themes of humanistic therapy, and what are the goals and techniques of Rogers' person-centered approach?

- Both psychodynamic and humanistic therapies are *insight therapies*—they attempt to improve functioning by increasing clients' awareness of motives and defenses.
- Humanistic therapy's goals have included helping clients grow in self-awareness and self-acceptance; promoting personal growth rather than curing illness; helping clients take responsibility for their own growth; focusing on conscious thoughts rather than unconscious motivations; and seeing the present and future as more important than the past.
- Carl Rogers' *person-centered therapy* proposed that therapists' most important contribution is to function as a psychological mirror through *active listening* and to provide a growth-fostering environment of *unconditional positive regard* characterized by acceptance, genuineness, and empathy.

14-4 How does the basic assumption of behavior therapy differ from the assumptions of psychodynamic and humanistic therapies? What techniques are used in exposure therapies and aversive conditioning?

- The psychodynamic and humanistic therapies seek to provide insight to help clients address problems. The *behavior therapies* instead assume that problem behaviors *are* the problem. The goal of behavior therapists is to apply learning principles to modify problem behaviors.
- Classical conditioning techniques, including *exposure therapies* (such as *systematic desensitization* or *virtual reality exposure therapy*) and *aversive conditioning*, attempt to change behaviors through *counterconditioning*—evoking new responses to old stimuli that trigger unwanted behaviors.

14-5 What is the basic idea of operant conditioning therapies?

- A basic operant conditioning concept is that consequences drive our voluntary behaviors. Therapy based on operant conditioning principles therefore uses behavior modification techniques to change unwanted behaviors by positively reinforcing desired behaviors and ignoring or punishing undesirable behaviors.
- Therapists may use a *token economy*, in which desired behavior earns privileges.

14-6 What are the goals and techniques of the cognitive therapies and of cognitive-behavioral therapy?

• *Cognitive therapies,* such as Aaron Beck's therapy for depression, assume that our thinking influences our feelings, and that the therapist's role is to change clients' self-defeating thinking by training them to think in healthier ways.

• The widely researched and practiced *cognitive-behavioral therapy (CBT)* combines cognitive therapy and behavior therapy by helping clients regularly act out their new ways of thinking and behaving in their everyday life. A newer CBT variation, dialectical behavior therapy (DBT), combines cognitive tactics for tolerating distress and regulating emotions with social skills training and mindfulness meditation.

14-7 What are the aims and benefits of group and family therapies?

• *Group therapy* can help more people with less cost than individual therapy. Clients may benefit from learning that others have similar problems and from getting feedback on new ways of behaving.

• *Family therapy* treats a family as an interactive system and attempts to help family members understand their ways of relating to one another and improve communication.

EVALUATING PSYCHOTHERAPIES

14-8 Does psychotherapy work? How can we know?

• Clients' and therapists' positive testimonials cannot prove that psychotherapy is actually effective. Clients believe treatment will be effective, want to justify their investment, tend to speak kindly of their therapists, and often enter therapy in crisis. Sometimes they are healed by time alone. Therapists tend to track only their "success" stories and are, like everyone, vulnerable to cognitive errors.

• Outcome research has found that people who remain untreated often improve, but those who receive psychotherapy are more likely to improve, to improve more quickly, and to improve with less chance of a relapse.

14-9 Are some psychotherapies more effective than others for specific disorders?

• No one psychotherapy is superior to all others. Therapy is most effective for those with clear-cut, specific problems.

• Cognitive and cognitive-behavioral therapies work best for anxiety, PTSD, insomnia, and depression.

• Behavioral conditioning therapies work best with specific behavior problems, such as bed-wetting, phobias, compulsions, marital problems, and sexual dysfunctions.

• Psychodynamic therapy has been effective for depression and anxiety.

• Nondirective (person-centered) counseling often helps with mild to moderate depression.

• *Evidence-based practice* integrates the best available research with clinicians' expertise and patients' characteristics, preferences, and circumstances.

14-10 What three elements are shared by all forms of psychotherapy?

• All effective psychotherapies offer (1) new hope; (2) a fresh perspective; and (3) an empathic, trusting, caring relationship.

• An emotional bond of trust and understanding between therapist and client (the *therapeutic alliance*) is an important element in effective therapy.

14-11 What personal factors influence the client-therapist relationship?

• Therapists differ from one another and from their clients. These differences may create problems if therapists and clients differ in their cultural, religious, or personal values and beliefs.

14-12 What should a person look for when selecting a therapist?

• College health centers are generally good starting points for counseling options, and they offer some free services. Some providers now offer therapy online as well as in person.

• A person seeking therapy may want to ask about the therapist's treatment approach, values, credentials, and fees. An important consideration is whether the therapy seeker feels comfortable and able to establish a bond with the therapist.

THE BIOMEDICAL THERAPIES

14-13 Why is therapeutic lifestyle change considered an effective biomedical therapy, and how does it work?

• Our lifestyle influences our brain and body, which affects our mental health.

• Depressed people who undergo a program of aerobic exercise, adequate sleep, light exposure, social engagement, negative-thought reduction, and better nutrition have gained some relief. The biomedical therapies assume that mind and body are a unit: Affect one and you will affect the other.

14-14 What are the drug therapies? How do double-blind studies help researchers evaluate a drug's effectiveness?

• Drug therapy is the most widely used biomedical therapy by far.

• *Antipsychotic drugs* are used in treating schizophrenia and other forms of severe thought disorders; some block dopamine activity. Side effects may include tardive dyskinesia (with involuntary movements of facial muscles, tongue, and limbs) or increased risk of obesity and diabetes.

• *Antianxiety drugs,* which depress central nervous system activity, are used to treat anxiety disorders, OCD, and PTSD, often in combination with psychotherapy. These drugs can reinforce a person's tendency to take drugs and can also cause physical problems.

• *Antidepressant drugs,* which often increase the availability of various neurotransmitters, are used to treat depression, but also anxiety disorders, OCD, and PTSD, with modest effectiveness. Some professionals prefer the term SSRIs (selective serotonin reuptake inhibitors) for drugs such as Prozac.

• Mood-stabilizing drugs, such as lithium and Depakote, are often prescribed for those with bipolar disorder.

• Studies may use a double-blind procedure to avoid the placebo effect and researchers' and patients' potential bias.

14-15 How are brain stimulation and psychosurgery used in treating specific disorders?

• In *electroconvulsive therapy (ECT),* a brief electric current is sent through the brain of an anesthetized patient. ECT is an effective treatment for severely depressed people who have not responded to other therapy.

• Newer alternative treatments for depression include transcranial direct current stimulation (tDCS), *transcranial magnetic stimulation (TMS),* and deep brain stimulation (DBS).

• *Psychosurgery* (including very precise micropsychosurgery) removes or destroys brain tissue in hopes of modifying behavior. These irreversible psychosurgical procedures are used only as a last resort. *Lobotomies* are no longer performed.

PREVENTING PSYCHOLOGICAL DISORDERS AND BUILDING RESILIENCE

14-16 What may help prevent psychological disorders, and why is it important to develop resilience?

- Preventive mental health programs are based on the idea that many psychological disorders could be prevented by changing stressful social contexts and teaching people to cope better with stress. This may help them become more *resilient,* enabling recovery from adversity.
- Community psychologists work to prevent psychological disorders by turning destructive environments into more nurturing places that foster competence, health, and well-being.

APPENDIX A

Statistical Reasoning in Everyday Life

DESCRIBING DATA

A-1 How do we describe data using three measures of central tendency, and what is the relative usefulness of the two measures of variation?

- Researchers may use descriptive statistics to meaningfully organize the data they've gathered.
- A measure of central tendency is a single score that represents a whole set of scores. Three such measures are the *mode* (the most frequently occurring score), the *mean* (the arithmetic average), and the *median* (the middle score in a group of data).
- Measures of variation tell us how diverse the data are. Two measures of variation are the *range* (which describes the gap between the highest and lowest scores) and the *standard deviation* (which states how much scores vary around the mean, or average, score). The standard deviation uses information from each score, so it is especially useful for showing whether scores are packed together or dispersed.
- Scores often form a *normal* (or bell-shaped) *curve.*

A-2 How do correlations measure relationships between variables?

- When we say two things are correlated, we are saying that they accompany each other in their movements. The strength of their relationship is expressed as a *correlation coefficient,* which ranges from +1.00 (a perfect positive correlation) through 0 (no correlation) to −1.00 (a perfect negative correlation).
- Their relationship may be displayed in a *scatterplot,* in which each dot represents a value for the two *variables.*
- Correlations predict but cannot explain.

A-3 What are *illusory correlations,* and what is *regression toward the mean?*

- An *illusory correlation* is our perceiving a relationship where none exists, or perceiving a stronger-than-actual relationship.
- *Regression toward the mean* is the tendency for extreme or unusual scores to fall back toward their average.

SIGNIFICANT DIFFERENCES

A-4 How do we know whether an observed difference can be generalized to other populations?

- Researchers use inferential statistics to help determine the reliability and significance of a study finding.
- To feel confident about generalizing an observed difference to other populations, we would want to know that the sample studied was representative of the larger population being studied; that the observations, on average, had low variability; that the sample consisted of more than a few cases; and that the observed difference was *statistically significant.*

A-5 What are *cross-sectional studies* and *longitudinal studies,* and why is it important to know which method was used?

- In a *cross-sectional study,* people of different ages are compared. In a *longitudinal study,* a group of people is studied periodically over a long period of time.
- To draw meaningful conclusions about a study's results, we need to know which method was used. Studies of intelligence and aging, for example, have drawn different conclusions depending on whether a cross-sectional or longitudinal study was used.

APPENDIX B

Psychology at Work

WORK AND LIFE SATISFACTION

B-1 What is *flow?*

- *Flow* is a completely involved, focused state of consciousness with lowered awareness of self and time. It results from fully engaging one's skills.
- Interests predict both performance and persistence, so people should seek careers with a strong person-environment fit.

INDUSTRIAL-ORGANIZATIONAL PSYCHOLOGY

B-2 What are industrial-organizational psychology's three key areas of study?

- Three key areas of study related to *industrial-organizational (I/O) psychology* are *human factors, personnel,* and *organizational psychology.* Each uses psychological principles to study and benefit the wide range of today's workers, workplaces, and work activities.

ORGANIZATIONAL PSYCHOLOGY

B-3 Why are organizational psychologists interested in employee satisfaction and engagement?

- Employee satisfaction and engagement tend to correlate with organizational success; in fact, employee attitudes predict future business success.
- Engaged workers know what is expected, have what they need, feel fulfilled, have regular opportunities to do what they do best, feel a part of something significant, and have opportunities to learn and develop.

B-4 How can leaders be most effective?

- Effective leaders set specific, challenging goals and choose an appropriate *leadership* style, which may be goal-oriented *(task leadership),* group-oriented *(social leadership),* or some combination of the two.
- Positive reinforcement, fulfilling the need to belong, and participative management can also make for effective leadership.
- Cultures vary in their leadership expectations; leaders who fulfill expectations tend to be successful. But thriving companies worldwide tend to focus on identifying and enhancing employee strengths; strengths-based leadership pays dividends everywhere.

APPENDIX E

Answers to the *Retrieve & Remember* and *Chapter Test* Questions

CHAPTER 1

Psychology's Roots, Critical Thinking, and Self-Improvement Tools

RETRIEVE & REMEMBER ANSWERS

1. Evaluating evidence, judging the source, assessing conclusions, and examining our own assumptions are essential parts of critical thinking. **2.** The scientific attitude combines (1) curiosity about the world around us, (2) skepticism about unproven claims and ideas, and (3) humility about our own understanding. These three basic attitudes guide psychologists as they consider ideas and test them with scientific methods. Ideas that don't hold up will then be discarded. **3.** Scientific psychology began in Germany in 1879, when Wilhelm Wundt opened the first psychology laboratory. **4.** behaviorism; psychoanalytic psychology. **5.** It led the field back to its early interest in mental processes and made them acceptable topics for scientific study. **6.** social-cultural; behavioral. **7.** i. b, ii. c, iii. a. **8.** We often suffer from hindsight bias: after we've learned a situation's outcome, that outcome seems familiar and therefore obvious. **9.** 1. A good theory *organizes* observed facts and implies hypotheses that offer testable *predictions* and, sometimes, practical applications. It also often stimulates further research. **10.** When others are able to repeat (replicate) an experiment with the same (or stronger) results, scientists can confirm the result and become more confident of its reliability. **11.** Case studies involve only one individual or group, so we can't know for sure whether the principles observed would apply to a larger population. **12.** Researchers are able to carefully observe and record naturally occurring behaviors outside the artificiality of a laboratory. However, outside the lab they are not able to control for all the factors that may influence the everyday interactions they record. **13.** An unrepresentative sample is a group that does not represent the population being studied. *Random sampling* helps researchers form a representative sample, because each member of the population has an equal chance of being included. **14.** a. Negative, b. Positive, c. Positive, d. Negative. **15.** In this case, as in many others, a third factor can explain the correlation: Golden anniversaries and baldness both accompany aging. **16.** Research designed to prevent the placebo effect randomly assigns participants to an *experimental group* (which receives the real treatment) or to a *control group* (which receives a placebo). A double-blind procedure prevents people's beliefs and hopes from affecting the results, because neither the participants nor those collecting the data know who receives the placebo. A comparison of the results will demonstrate whether the real treatment produces better results than *belief* in that treatment. **17.** confounding variables. **18.** i. c, ii. a, iii. b. **19.** We learn more about the drug's effectiveness when we can compare the results of those who took the drug (the experimental group) with the results of those who did not (the control group). If we gave the drug to all 1000 participants, we would have no way of knowing whether the drug is serving as a placebo or is actually medically effective. **20.** Animal protection laws, laboratory regulation and inspection, and local and university ethics committees (which screen research proposals) attempt to safeguard animal welfare. International psychological organizations urge researchers involving human participants to obtain *informed consent*, protect them from greater-than-usual harm and discomfort, treat their personal information confidentially, and *debrief* them fully at the end of the experiment. **21.** testing effect. **22.** Survey, Question, Read, Retrieve, Review.

CHAPTER TEST ANSWERS

1. Critical thinking is smart thinking. When evaluating media claims (even about topics you might not know much about), look for scientific evidence. Ask the following questions in your analysis: Are the claims based on scientific findings? Have several studies replicated the findings and confirmed them? Are any experts cited? If so, are they from a credible institution? Have they conducted or written about scientific research? What agenda might they have? What alternative explanations are possible? **2.** d. **3.** Wilhelm Wundt. **4.** a. **5.** a. **6.** b. **7.** The environment (nurture) has an influence on us, but that influence is limited by our biology (nature). Nature and nurture interact. People predisposed to be very tall (nature), for example, are unlikely to become Olympic gymnasts, no matter how hard they work (nurture). **8.** b. **9.** dual processing. **10.** d. **11.** psychiatrist. **12.** positive psychology. **13.** Hindsight bias. **14.** hypothesis. **15.** c. **16.** random (representative). **17.** negative. **18.** a. **19.** (a) *Alcohol use is associated with violence. (One interpretation: Drinking triggers, or unleashes, aggressive behavior.)* Perhaps anger triggers drinking, or perhaps the same genes or child-raising practices are making both drinking and aggression more likely. (Here researchers have learned that drinking does indeed trigger aggressive behavior.) (b) *Educated people live longer, on average, than less-educated people. (One interpretation: Education lengthens life and improves health.)* Perhaps richer people can afford more education and better health care. (Research supports this conclusion.) (c) *Teens engaged in team sports are less likely to use drugs, smoke, have sex, carry weapons, and eat junk food than are teens who do not engage in team sports. (One interpretation: Team sports encourage healthy living.)* Perhaps some third factor explains this correlation—teens who use drugs, smoke, have sex, carry weapons, and eat junk food may be adolescents who do not enjoy playing on any team. (d) *Adolescents who frequently see smoking in movies are more likely to smoke. (One interpretation: Movie stars' behavior influences impressionable teens.)* Perhaps adolescents who smoke and attend movies frequently have less parental supervision and more access to spending money than do other adolescents. **20.** experiments. **21.** placebo. **22.** c. **23.** independent variable. **24.** b. **25.** d.

CHAPTER 2

The Biology of Behavior and Consciousness

RETRIEVE & REMEMBER ANSWERS

1. Thanks to its *plasticity*, our brain changes in response to the experiences we have. Learning and practicing a new skill, like playing an instrument, can promote the development of new neural pathways and cause lasting changes in brain organization. **2.** dendrites, cell body, axon. **3.** Stronger stimuli (the slap) cause more neurons to fire and to fire more frequently than happens with weaker stimuli (the tap). **4.** Neurons send neurotransmitters (chemical messengers) across this tiny space between one neuron's terminal branch and the next neuron's dendrite or cell body. **5.** neurotransmitters. **6.** i. c, ii. a, iii. b. **7.** The sympathetic division of the autonomic nervous system would have directed arousal (accelerated heartbeat, inhibited digestion, and so forth), and the parasympathetic division would have directed calming. **8.** Responding to signals from the hypothalamus, the pituitary releases hormones that trigger other endocrine glands to secrete hormones, which in turn influence brain and behavior. **9.** Both of these communication systems produce chemical molecules that act on the body's receptors to influence our behavior and emotions. The endocrine system, which secretes hormones into the bloodstream, delivers its messages much more slowly than the speedy nervous system, and the effects of the endocrine system's messages tend to linger much longer than those of the nervous system. **10.** i. b, ii. a, iii. c. **11.** brainstem. **12.** (a) cerebellum, (b) thalamus, (c) reticular formation, (d) medulla. **13.** the sympathetic nervous system. **14.** (1) The *amygdala* is involved in aggression and fear responses. (2) The *hypothalamus* is involved in bodily maintenance, pleasurable rewards, and control of the hormonal systems. (3) The *hippocampus* processes memory of facts and events. **15.** (1) The right limbs' opposed activities interfere with each other because both are controlled by the same (left) side of your brain. (2) Opposite sides of your brain control your left and right limbs, so the reversed motion causes less interference. **16.** somatosensory; motor. **17.** Association areas are involved in higher mental functions—interpreting, integrating, and acting on information processed in other areas. **18.** (a) yes, (b) no, (c) green. **19.** Our *selective attention* allows us to focus on only a limited portion of our surroundings. *Inattentional blindness* explains why we don't perceive some things when we are distracted. *Change blindness,* for example, happens when we fail to notice a relatively unimportant change in our environment. These principles help magicians fool us, as they direct our attention elsewhere to perform their tricks. **20.** With each refugee cycling through the sleep stages independently, at any given time at least one likely will be in an easily awakened stage. **21.** REM (R), NREM-1 (N1), NREM-2 (N2), NREM-3 (N3); normally we move through N1, then N2, then N3, then back up through N2 before we experience REM sleep. **22.** i. b, ii. c, iii. a. **23.** (1) Sleep has survival value. (2) Sleep helps restore the immune system and repair brain tissue. (3) During sleep we strengthen memories. (4) Sleep fuels creativity. (5) Sleep plays a role in the growth process. **24.** quick reaction times; gain weight. **25.** (1) Freud's wish fulfillment (dreams as a psychic safety valve), (2) information processing (dreams sort the day's events and form memories), (3) physiological function (dreams pave neural pathways), (4) making sense of neural static (REM sleep triggers random neural activity that the mind weaves into stories), and (5) cognitive development (dreams reflect the dreamer's developmental stage).

CHAPTER TEST ANSWERS

1. The human brain is uniquely designed to be flexible. It can reorganize after damage and it can build new pathways based on experience. This plasticity enables us to adapt to our changing world. **2.** axon. **3.** c. **4.** a. **5.** neurotransmitters. **6.** b. **7.** b. **8.** autonomic. **9.** central. **10.** a. **11.** adrenal glands. **12.** b. **13.** d. **14.** c. **15.** cerebellum. **16.** b. **17.** amygdala. **18.** b. **19.** hypothalamus. **20.** d. **21.** The visual cortex is a neural network of sensory neurons connected via interneurons to other neural networks, including auditory networks. If you can see and hear, this allows you to integrate visual and auditory information to respond when a friend you recognize greets you at a party. **22.** c. **23.** association areas. **24.** frontal. **25.** c. **26.** ON; HER. **27.** a. **28.** b. **29.** inattentional blindness. **30.** selective. **31.** circadian rhythm. **32.** b. **33.** N3. **34.** It increases in duration. **35.** c. **36.** With narcolepsy, the person periodically falls directly into REM sleep with no warning; with sleep apnea, the person repeatedly awakens during the night. **37.** d. **38.** The information-processing explanation of dreaming proposes that brain activity during REM sleep enables us to sift through the daily events and activities we have been thinking about. **39.** REM rebound.

CHAPTER 3

Developing Through the Life Span

RETRIEVE & REMEMBER ANSWERS

1. nature; nurture. **2.** continuity; stages. **3.** (1) Stage theory is supported by the work of Piaget (cognitive development), Kohlberg (moral development), and Erikson (psychosocial development). (2) Some traits, such as temperament, exhibit remarkable stability across many years. **4.** gene, chromosome, nucleus. **5.** zygote; fetus; embryo. **6.** Researchers use twin and adoption studies to understand how much variation among individuals is due to heredity and how much is due to environmental factors. Some studies compare the traits and behaviors of identical twins (same genes) and fraternal twins (different genes, as in any two siblings). They also compare adopted children with their adoptive and biological parents. Some studies compare traits and behaviors of twins raised together or separately. **7.** maturation. **8.** Object permanence for the sensorimotor stage, pretend play for the preoperational stage, conservation for the concrete operational stage, and abstract logic for the formal operational stage. **9.** i. d, ii. b, iii. c, iv. c, v. a, vi. b. **10.** Theory of mind focuses on our ability to understand our own and others' mental states. Those with autism spectrum disorder struggle with this ability. **11.** The authoritarian style would be described as too hard, the permissive style too soft, the negligent style too uncaring, and the authoritative style just right. Parents using the authoritative style tend to have children with high self-esteem, self-reliance, self-regulation, and social competence. **12.** preconventional; postconventional; conventional. **13.** Kohlberg's work reflected an individualist worldview, so his theory is less culturally universal than he supposed. Kohlberg's theory can also be viewed as male-focused, since women more often emphasize care for others in need over what is "fair." **14.** Adolescents tend to *select* similar others and to sort themselves into like-minded groups. For an athletic teen, this could lead to finding other athletic teens and joining school teams together. **15.** i. g, ii. h, iii. c, iv. f, v. e, vi. d, vii. a, viii. b. **16.** love; work. **17.** Challenges: decline of muscular strength, reaction times, stamina, sensory keenness, cardiac output, and immune system functioning. Risk of cognitive decline increases. Rewards: positive feelings tend to grow; negative emotions subside; and anger, stress, worry, and social-relationship problems decrease.

CHAPTER TEST ANSWERS

1. Cross-sectional studies compare people of different ages at one point in time. Longitudinal studies restudy and retest the same people over a long period of time. **2.** continuity/stages. **3.** b. **4.** chromosomes. **5.** gene. **6.** environments. **7.** c. **8.** teratogens. **9.** a. **10.** c. **11.** Identical (monozygotic). **12.** b. **13.** frontal. **14.** b. **15.** We have little conscious recall of events occurring before age 4, in part because major brain areas have not yet matured. **16.** Infants in Piaget's *sensorimotor stage* tend to be focused only on their own perceptions of the world and may, for example, be unaware that objects continue to exist when unseen. A child in the *preoperational stage* is still egocentric and incapable of appreciating simple logic, such as the reversibility of operations. A preteen in the *concrete operational stage* is beginning to think logically about concrete events but not about abstract concepts. **17.** a. **18.** stranger anxiety. **19.** Before these studies, many psychologists believed that infants simply became attached to those who nourished them. **20.** temperament. **21.** b. **22.** formal operational. **23.** b. **24.** emerging adulthood. **25.** a. **26.** generativity. **27.** c.

CHAPTER 4

Sex, Gender, and Sexuality

RETRIEVE & REMEMBER ANSWERS

1. Women; men. **2.** seven; puberty. **3.** *Gender roles* are social rules or norms for accepted and expected men's and women's behaviors, attitudes, and traits. The norms associated with various roles, including gender roles, vary widely in different cultural contexts, which is proof that we are able to learn and adapt to the social demands of different environments. **4.** estrogens; testosterone. **5.** sexual dysfunction; paraphilia. **6.** Influences include biological factors such as sexual maturity and sex hormones, psychological factors such as environmental stimuli and fantasies, and social-cultural factors such as the values and expectations absorbed from family and the surrounding culture. **7.** a, c, d. **8.** b, c, e. **9.** Evolutionary psychologists theorize that females have inherited their ancestors' tendencies to be more cautious sexually because of the challenges associated with incubating and nurturing offspring. Males have inherited a tendency to be more casual about sex, because their act of fathering requires a smaller investment. **10.** (1) It starts with an effect and works backward to propose an explanation. (2) This explanation may overlook the effects of cultural expectations and socialization. (3) Men could use such explanations to rationalize irresponsible behavior toward women.

CHAPTER TEST ANSWERS

1. sex; gender. **2.** c. **3.** Y. **4.** d. **5.** 11; 12. **6.** intersex. **7.** b. **8.** gender identity. **9.** b. **10.** b. **11.** does; doesn't. **12.** c. **13.** Although nature and nurture work together, researchers have found no evidence of specific environmental factors (parental relationships, childhood sexual experiences, peer relationships, or dating experiences) in the development of our sexual orientation. **14.** *Natural selection* favors traits and behaviors that enable survival and reproduction. Evolutionary psychologists argue that women are choosier about their mates because of the investment required to conceive, birth, protect, and nurse children. Straight women tend to prefer men who seem capable of supporting and protecting their joint offspring. Men, who have less at stake, tend to be more casual about sex, and straight men tend to prefer women whose traits convey health and fertility.

CHAPTER 5

Sensation and Perception

RETRIEVE & REMEMBER ANSWERS

1. *Sensation* is the bottom-up process by which your sensory receptors and your nervous system receive and represent stimuli. *Perception* is the top-down process by which your brain creates meaning by organizing and interpreting what your senses detect. **2.** *Absolute threshold* is the minimum stimulation needed to detect a particular sound (such as an approaching bike on the sidewalk behind you) 50 percent of the time. *Subliminal stimulation* happens when, without your awareness, your sensory system processes a sound that is below your absolute threshold. A *difference threshold* is the minimum difference needed to distinguish between two stimuli (such as between the sound of a bike and the sound of a runner coming up behind you) 50 percent of the time. **3.** The shoes provide constant stimulation. Thanks to *sensory adaptation*, we tend to focus primarily on changing stimuli. **4.** It involves top-down processing, because it draws on your experiences, assumptions, and expectations when interpreting stimuli. **5.** Your blind spot is on the nose side of each retina, which means that objects to your right may fall onto the right eye's blind spot. Objects to your left may fall on the left eye's blind spot. The blind spot does not normally impair your vision, because your eyes are moving and because one eye catches what the other misses. Moreover, even with only one eye open, your brain gives you a perception without a hole in **it.** **6.** rods; cones; color. **7.** pupils. **8.** The *Young-Helmholtz trichromatic theory* shows that the retina contains color receptors for red, green, and blue. The *opponent-process theory* shows that we have opponent-process cells in the retina and thalamus for red-green, blue-yellow, and white-black. These theories make sense together. They outline the two stages of color vision: (1) The retina's receptors for red, green, and blue respond to different color stimuli. (2) The receptors' signals are then processed by the opponent-process cells on their way to the visual cortex in the brain. **9.** Light waves reflect off your friend and travel into your eyes. Receptor cells in your retina convert the light waves' energy into neural impulses sent to your brain. Your brain detector cells and work teams process the different parts of this visual input—including movement, form, depth, and color—on separate but parallel paths. Your brain interprets this information, based on previously stored information and your expectations, and forms a conscious perception of your friend. **10.** figure; ground. **11.** Gestalt psychologists used this saying to describe our perceptual tendency to organize clusters of stimuli into meaningful forms or coherent groups. **12.** We are normally able to perceive depth thanks to (1) binocular cues (such as retinal disparity), and (2) monocular cues (which include relative height, relative size, interposition, linear perspective, light and shadow, and relative motion). **13.** loudness. **14.** lower; lower. **15.** c. **16.** We have four basic touch senses and five basic taste sensations. But we have no specific smell receptors. Instead, different combinations of odor receptors send messages to the brain, enabling us to recognize some 1 trillion different smells. **17.** Kinesthetic receptors are located in our joints, tendons, and muscles. Vestibular sense receptors are located in our inner ear. **18.** The ESP event would need to be reproduced in other scientific studies.

CHAPTER TEST ANSWERS

1. b. **2.** perception. **3.** d. **4.** just noticeable difference. **5.** b. **6.** d. **7.** a. **8.** wavelength. **9.** a. **10.** c. **11.** c. **12.** d. **13.** Your brain constructs this perception of color in two stages. In the first stage, the lemon reflects light energy into your eyes, where it is transformed into neural messages. Three sets of cones, each sensitive to a different light frequency (red, blue, and green) process color. In this case, the light energy stimulates both red-sensitive and green-sensitive cones. In the second stage, opponent-process cells sensitive to paired opposites of color (red-green, blue-yellow, and black-white) evaluate the incoming neural messages as they pass through your optic nerve to the thalamus and visual cortex. When the yellow-sensitive opponent-process cells are stimulated, you identify the lemon as yellow. **14.** feature detectors. **15.** parallel processing. **16.** a. **17.** d. **18.** b. **19.** c. **20.** monocular. **21.** b. **22.** b. **23.** perceptual adaptation. **24.** cochlea. **25.** The outer ear collects sound waves, which are translated into mechanical waves by the *middle ear* and turned into fluid waves in the *inner ear*. The auditory nerve then translates the energy into electrical waves and sends them to the brain, which perceives and interprets the sound. **26.** nociceptors. **27.** c. **28.** Our experience of pain is influenced by biological factors (such as genetic differences in endorphin production), psychological factors (such as our attention), and social-cultural factors (such as the presence of others). **29.** We have specialized receptors for detecting sweet, salty, sour, bitter, and umami tastes. Being able to detect pleasurable tastes enabled our ancestors to seek out energy- or protein-rich foods. Detecting aversive tastes deterred them from eating toxic substances, increasing their chances of survival. **30.** Kinesthesia; vestibular sense. **31.** Your vestibular sense regulates balance and body positioning through kinesthetic receptors triggered by fluid in your inner ear. Wobbly legs and a spinning world are signs that these receptors are still responding to the ride's turbulence. As your vestibular sense adjusts to solid ground, your balance will be restored. **32.** d. **33.** d.

CHAPTER 6

Learning

RETRIEVE & REMEMBER ANSWERS

1. Habits form when we repeat behaviors in a given context and, as a result, learn associations—often without our awareness. For example, we may have eaten a sweet pastry with a cup of coffee often enough to associate the flavor of the coffee with the treat, so that the cup of coffee alone just doesn't seem right anymore! **2.** NS = tone before conditioning; US = air puff; UR = blink to air puff; CS = tone after conditioning; CR = blink to tone. **3.** If viewing an admired actor (a US) elicits a positive response (a UR), then pairing the US with a new NS (the beverage) could turn the beverage into a conditioned stimulus (CS) that also becomes positive, a conditioned response (CR). **4.** acquisition; extinction. **5.** generalization. **6.** The cake (including its taste) is the US. The associated aroma is the CS. Salivation to the aroma is the CR. **7.** The US was the loud noise; the UR was the fear response to the noise; the NS was the rat before it was paired with the noise; the CS was the rat after pairing; the CR was fear of the rat. **8.** do not; resulting. **9.** The baby negatively reinforces her parents' behavior when she stops crying once they grant her wish. Her parents positively reinforce her cries by letting her sleep with them. **10.** Spammers are reinforced on a variable-ratio schedule (after sending a varying number of emails). Cookie checkers are reinforced on a fixed-interval schedule. Coffee rewards programs use a fixed-ratio schedule. **11.** (1) PR (positive reinforcement); (2) NP (negative punishment); (3) PP (positive punishment); (4) NR (negative reinforcement). **12.** If Joslyn is seeking attention, the teacher's scolding may be reinforcing rather than punishing. To change Joslyn's behavior, her teacher could offer reinforcement (such as praise) each time she behaves well. The teacher might encourage Joslyn toward increasingly appropriate behavior through shaping, or by rephrasing rules as rewards instead of punishments ("You can use the blocks if you play nicely with the other children" [reward] rather than "You may not use the blocks if you misbehave!" [punishment]). **13.** respondent; operant. **14.** Garcia and Koelling demonstrated that rats may learn an aversion to tastes, on which their survival depends, but not to sights or sounds. **15.** The success of operant conditioning is affected not just by environmental cues, but also by cognitive factors. **16.** Emily may be more likely to speed. Observational learning studies suggest that children tend to do as others do and say what they say. **17.** i. c (You've probably learned your way by latent learning), ii. d (Observational learning may have contributed to your brother's imitating the actions seen in the movie), iii. a (Through classical conditioning you have associated the smell with the anticipated tasty result), iv. e (You are biologically predisposed to develop a conditioned taste aversion to foods associated with illness), v. b (Through operant conditioning your dog may have come to associate approaching excitedly with attention, petting, and a treat).

CHAPTER TEST ANSWERS

1. information; behaviors. **2.** c. **3.** conditioned. **4.** discrimination. **5.** b. **6.** A sexual image is a US that triggers a UR of interest or arousal. Before the ad pairs a product with a sexual image, the product is an NS. Over time the product can become a CS that triggers the CR of interest or arousal. **7.** Skinner. **8.** shaping. **9.** b. **10.** Your instructor could reinforce your attentive behavior by taking away something you dislike. For example, your instructor could offer to shorten the length of an assigned paper or replace standard lecture time with an interesting in-class activity. In both cases, the instructor would remove something aversive in order to negatively reinforce your focused attention. **11.** partial. **12.** a. **13.** variable-interval. **14.** c. **15.** d. **16.** b. **17.** cognitive map. **18.** latent learning. **19.** observational learning. **20.** vicarious; vicarious. **21.** a. **22.** mirror. **23.** c.

CHAPTER 7

Memory

RETRIEVE & REMEMBER ANSWERS

1. The newer idea of *a working memory* emphasizes the active processing that we now know takes place in Atkinson-Shiffrin's short-term memory stage. While the Atkinson-Shiffrin model viewed short-term memory as a temporary holding space, working memory plays a key role in processing new information and connecting it to previously stored information. **2.** (1) Active processing of incoming sensory information, and (2) focusing our spotlight of attention. **3.** *Automatic* processing occurs unconsciously (automatically) for such things as the sequence and frequency of a day's events, and reading and comprehending words in our own language(s). *Effortful* processing requires attentive awareness and happens, for example, when we work hard to learn new material in a course, or new lines for a play. **4.** sensory memory. **5.** Although cramming and rereading may lead to short-term gains in knowledge, distributed practice and repeated self-testing will result in the greatest long-term retention. **6.** The cerebellum and basal ganglia are important for *implicit* memory processing. The hippocampus and frontal lobes are key to *explicit* memory formation. **7.** Our *explicit* conscious memories of facts and episodes differ from our *implicit* memories of skills (such as tying shoelaces) and classically conditioned responses. The parts of the brain involved in explicit memory processing (the frontal lobes and hippocampus) may have sustained damage in the accident, while the parts involved in implicit memory processing (the cerebellum and basal ganglia) appear to have escaped harm. **8.** the amygdala. **9.** long-term potentiation. **10.** recognition; recall. **11.** It would be better to test your memory with *recall* (such as with short-answer or fill-in-the-blank self-test questions) rather than *recognition* (such as with multiple-choice questions). Recalling information is harder than recognizing it. So if you can recall it, that means your retention of the material is better than if you could only recognize it. Your chances of test success are therefore greater. **12.** *Priming* is the activation (often without our awareness) of associations. Seeing a gun, for example, might temporarily predispose someone to interpret an ambiguous face as threatening, or to recall a boss as nasty. **13.** serial position. **14.** (1) *Encoding failure*: Unattended information never entered our memory system. (2) *Storage decay*: Information fades from our memory. (3) *Retrieval failure*: We cannot access stored information accurately, sometimes due to interference or motivated forgetting. **15.** repress. **16.** Real experiences would be confused with those we dreamed. When seeing someone we know, we might therefore be unsure whether we were reacting to something they previously did or to something we dreamed they did. **17.** It will be important to remember the key points agreed upon by most researchers and professional associations: Sexual abuse, injustice, forgetting, and memory construction all happen; recovered memories are common; memories from before age 4 are unreliable; memories claimed to be recovered through hypnosis are especially unreliable; and memories, whether real or false, can be emotionally upsetting. **18.** Spend more time rehearsing or actively thinking about the material to boost long-term recall. Schedule spaced (not crammed) study times. Make the material personally meaningful, with well-organized and vivid associations. Refresh your memory by returning to contexts and moods to activate retrieval cues. Use mnemonic devices. Minimize proactive and retroactive interference. Plan ahead to ensure a complete night's sleep. Test yourself repeatedly—retrieval practice is a proven retention strategy.

CHAPTER TEST ANSWERS

1. encoding; storage; retrieval. **2.** a. **3.** iconic; echoic. **4.** seven. **5.** mnemonics. **6.** a. **7.** implicit. **8.** c. **9.** recall. **10.** retrieval cues. **11.** Memories are stored within a web of many associations, one of which is mood. When you recall happy moments from your past, you activate these positive links. You may then experience mood-congruent memory and recall other happy moments, which could improve your mood and brighten your interpretation of current events. **12.** a. **13.** d. **14.** d. **15.** retroactive. **16.** repression. **17.** b. **18.** Eliza's immature hippocampus and minimal verbal skills made it impossible for her to encode an explicit memory of the wedding reception at the age of two. It's more likely that Eliza learned information (from hearing the story repeatedly) that she eventually constructed into a memory that feels very real. **19.** source amnesia. **20.** déjà vu. **21.** b. **22.** b.

CHAPTER 8

Thinking, Language, and Intelligence

RETRIEVE & REMEMBER ANSWERS

1. If a tragic event such as a plane crash makes the news, it is noteworthy and unusual, unlike much more common bad events, such as traffic accidents. Knowing this, we can worry less about unlikely events and think more about improving the safety of our everyday activities. (For example, we can wear a seat belt when in a vehicle and use the crosswalk when walking.) **2.** i. b, ii. c, iii. e, iv. d, v. a, vi. f, vii. h, viii. j, ix. i, x. g, xi. k. **3.** Chomsky maintained that humans are biologically predisposed to acquire the grammar rules of language. **4.** Infants normally start developing receptive language skills (ability to understand what is said to and about them) around 4 months of age. Then, starting with babbling at 4 months and beyond, infants normally start building productive language skills (ability to produce sounds and eventually words). **5.** Our brain's *critical period* for language learning is in childhood, when we can absorb language structure almost effortlessly. As we move past that stage in our brain's development, our ability to learn a new language diminishes dramatically. **6.** Broca's area; Wernicke's area. **7.** Mental practice uses visual imagery to mentally rehearse future behaviors, activating some of the same brain areas used during the actual behaviors. Visualizing the details of the process is more effective than visualizing only your end goal. **8.** These are definitely communications. But if language consists of words and the grammatical rules we use to combine them to communicate meaning, few scientists would label a dog's barking and yipping as language. **9.** People with savant syndrome have limited mental ability overall but possess one or more exceptional skills. According to Howard Gardner, this suggests that our abilities come in separate packages rather than being fully expressed by one general intelligence that covers all of our talents. **10.** aptitude; achievement. **11.** Binet hoped that determining the child's mental age (the age that typically corresponds to a certain level of performance) would help identify appropriate school placements. **12.** 125 ($5 \div 4 \times 100 = 125$). **13.** A psychological test must be *standardized* (pretested on a representative sample of people), *reliable* (yielding consistent results), and *valid* (measuring and predicting what it is supposed to). **14.** a. (Heritability—variation explained by genetic influences—will increase as environmental variation decreases.) **15.** Researcher A should develop a *longitudinal study* to examine how intelligence changes in the same people over the life span. Researcher B should develop a *cross-sectional study* to examine the intelligence of people now at various life stages. **16.** Perfectly equal opportunity would create 100 percent heritability, because genes alone would account for any human differences. **17.** A test may be *culturally* biased (unfair) if higher scores are achieved by those with certain cultural experiences. That same test is not scientifically biased as long as it has *predictive validity*—if it predicts what it is supposed to predict. For example, the SAT may favor those with experience in the U.S. school system, but it does still accurately predict U.S. college success. **18.** stereotype threat.

CHAPTER TEST ANSWERS

1. concept. **2.** algorithm. **3.** Oscar will need to guard against *confirmation bias* (searching for support for his own views and ignoring contradictory evidence) as he seeks out opposing viewpoints. Even if Oscar encounters new information that disproves his beliefs, *belief perseverance* may lead him to cling to these views anyway. It will take more compelling evidence to change his beliefs than it took to create them. **4.** c. **5.** availability. **6.** framing. **7.** b. **8.** universal grammar. **9.** c. **10.** telegraphic speech. **11.** a. **12.** general intelligence. **13.** c. **14.** analytical; creative; practical. **15.** d. **16.** d ($9 \div 6 \times 100 = 150$). **17.** c. **18.** reliability. **19.** c. **20.** a. **21.** c. **22.** c. **23.** Writers' work relies more on crystallized intelligence, or accumulated knowledge, which increases with age. For top performance, scientists doing research may need more fluid intelligence (speedy and abstract reasoning), which tends to decrease with age. **24.** Stereotype threat.

CHAPTER 9

Motivation and Emotion

RETRIEVE & REMEMBER ANSWERS

1. (a) Well-practiced runners tend to excel when aroused by competition. (b) High anxiety about a difficult exam may disrupt test-takers' performance. **2.** According to Maslow, our drive to meet the physiological needs of hunger and thirst takes priority over our safety needs, prompting us to take risks at times. **3.** low; high. **4.** You have learned to respond to the sight and aroma that signal the food about to enter your mouth. Both *physiological* cues (low blood sugar) and *psychological* cues (anticipation of the tasty meal) heighten your experienced hunger. **5.** Genetically influenced set/settling points, metabolism, and other factors (such as adequate sleep) influence the way our bodies burn calories. **6.** They engaged in more self-defeating behaviors and displayed more disparaging and aggressive behavior. These students' basic *need to belong* seems to have been disrupted. **7.** strengthen; increase. **8.** self-discipline *(grit)*. **9.** simultaneously; sequentially (first the physiological response, and then the experienced emotion). **10.** cognitive. **11.** Zajonc and LeDoux suggested that we experience some emotions without any conscious, cognitive appraisal. Lazarus, Schachter, and Singer emphasized the importance of appraisal and cognitive labeling in our experience of emotion. **12.** The *sympathetic division* of the ANS arouses us for more intense experiences of emotion, pumping out stress hormones to prepare our body for fight or flight. The *parasympathetic division* of the ANS takes over when a crisis passes, restoring our body to a calm physiological and emotional state. **13.** Women. **14.** gestures. **15.** (a) Most students report feeling more happy than sad when their cheeks are raised upward. (b) Most students report feeling more sad than happy when their cheeks are pulled downward.

CHAPTER TEST ANSWERS

1. a. **2.** incentive. **3.** Arousal. **4.** b. **5.** a. **6.** Maslow's hierarchy of needs best supports this statement because it addresses the primacy of some motives over others. Once our basic physiological needs are met, safety concerns are addressed next, followed by belongingness and love needs (such as the desire to kiss). **7.** set. **8.** c. **9.** low. **10.** basal metabolic. **11.** d. **12.** Sanjay's plan is problematic. After he gains weight, the extra fat will require less energy to maintain than it did to gain in the first place. Sanjay may have a hard time getting rid of it later, when his metabolism slows down in an effort to retain his body weight. **13.** c. **14.** Monitor your time spent online, as well as your feelings about that time. Hide distracting online friends when necessary. Check your devices less often. Get outside and away from technology regularly. **15.** should; should. **16.** James-Lange. **17.** b. **18.** c. **19.** A polygraph measures emotion-linked physiological changes, such as in perspiration, heart rate, and breathing. But the measure cannot distinguish between emotions with similar physiology (such as anxiety and guilt). **20.** facial feedback. **21.** Aiden's droopy posture could negatively affect his mood thanks to the behavior feedback effect, which tends to make us feel the way we act.

CHAPTER 10

Stress, Health, and Human Flourishing

RETRIEVE & REMEMBER ANSWERS

1. sympathetic; increase; muscles; fight-or-flight. **2.** psychoneuroimmunology. **3.** Stress tends to reduce our immune system's ability to function properly, so that higher stress generally leads to greater risk of physical illness. **4.** Feeling angry and negative much of the time. **5.** problem; emotion. **6.** Aerobic exercise, relaxation procedures, mindfulness meditation, and religious engagement. **7.** a. (Age does NOT effectively predict happiness levels. Better predictors are personality traits, sleep and exercise, and religious faith.)

CHAPTER TEST ANSWERS

1. b. **2.** d. **3.** resistance; exhaustion. **4.** tend; befriend. **5.** immune system. **6.** c. **7.** Type A individuals frequently experience negative emotions (such as anger and impatience), during which the sympathetic nervous system diverts blood away from the liver. This leaves fat and cholesterol circulating in the bloodstream for deposit near the heart and other organs, increasing the risk of heart disease and other health problems. Thus, Type A individuals actually harm themselves by directing anger at others. **8.** emotion. **9.** b. **10.** internal. **11.** d. **12.** aerobic. **13.** c. **14.** d. **15.** b. **16.** relative deprivation.

CHAPTER 11

Social Psychology

RETRIEVE & REMEMBER ANSWERS

1. By attributing the other person's behavior to the person ("What a terrible driver") and his own to the situation ("These roads are awful"), Marco has exhibited the fundamental attribution error. **2.** Our attitudes often influence our actions as we behave in ways consistent with our beliefs. However, our actions also influence our attitudes; we come to believe in what we have done. **3.** cognitive dissonance. **4.** Avoid yelling at, humiliating, or boring your audience. It's more effective to identify shared values, appeal to others' admirable motives, make your message vivid and repeat it, and get your audience to actively engage with your message as well. **5.** a. **6.** normative social influence. **7.** Stanley Milgram. **8.** The Milgram studies showed that people were most likely to follow orders when (1) the experimenter was nearby and was perceived to be a legitimate authority figure, (2) the authority figure was supported by a respected institution, (3) the victim was depersonalized or at a distance, and (4) there were no models for defiance. **9.** This improved performance in the presence of others is most likely to occur with a well-learned task, because the added arousal caused by an audience tends to strengthen the most likely response. This also predicts poorer performance on a difficult task in others' presence. **10.** social loafing. **11.** The anonymity provided by the masks, combined with the arousal of the competitive setting, might create deindividuation (lessened self-awareness and self-restraint). **12.** group polarization. **13.** groupthink. **14.** scapegoat. **15.** Our biology (our genes, biochemistry—including testosterone and alcohol levels—and neural systems) influences our aggressive tendencies. Psychological factors (such as frustration, previous rewards for aggressive acts, and observation of others' aggression) can trigger any aggressive tendencies we may have. Social influences, such as exposure to violent media or being personally insulted, and cultural influences, such as whether we've grown up in a "culture of honor" or a father-absent home, can also affect our aggressive responses. **16.** mere exposure effect. **17.** Being physically attractive tends to elicit positive first impressions. People tend to assume that attractive people are healthier, happier, more sensitive, more successful, and more socially skilled than others are. **18.** Emotions consist of (1) physical arousal and (2) our interpretation of that arousal. Researchers have found that any source of arousal may be interpreted as passion in the presence of a desirable person. **19.** equity; self-disclosure. **20.** In the presence of others, an individual is less likely to notice a situation, correctly interpret it as an emergency, and take responsibility for offering help. The Kitty Genovese case demonstrated this bystander effect, as each witness assumed many others were also aware of the event. **21.** Sports fans may feel they are a part of an ingroup that sets itself apart from an outgroup (fans of the archrival team). Ingroup bias tends to develop, leading to prejudice and the view that the outgroup "deserves" misfortune. So, the archrival team's loss may seem justified. In conflicts, this kind of thinking is problematic, especially when each side in the conflict develops mirror-image perceptions of the other (distorted, negative images that are ironically similar). **22.** Peacemakers should encourage equal-status contact and cooperation to achieve superordinate goals (shared goals that override differences).

CHAPTER TEST ANSWERS

1. fundamental attribution. **2.** foot-in-the-door. **3.** Cognitive dissonance theory best supports this suggestion. If Jamala acts confident, her behavior will contradict her negative self-thoughts, creating cognitive dissonance. To relieve the tension, Jamala may realign her attitudes with her actions by viewing herself as more outgoing and confident. **4.** peripheral. **5.** c. **6.** a. **7.** The presence of a large audience generates arousal and strengthens Dr. Huang's most likely response: enhanced performance on a task he has mastered (teaching music history) and impaired performance on a task he finds difficult (statistics). **8.** deindividuation. **9.** group polarization. **10.** stereotypes. **11.** b. **12.** more. **13.** d. **14.** frustration-aggression principle. **15.** c. **16.** c. **17.** c. **18.** mere exposure. **19.** companionate; passionate. **20.** d. **21.** c. **22.** mirror-image. **23.** superordinate.

CHAPTER 12

Personality

RETRIEVE & REMEMBER ANSWERS

1. ego; id; superego. **2.** fixation. **3.** unconsciously; anxiety. **4.** Freud is credited with first drawing attention to the importance of childhood experiences, the existence of the unconscious mind, and our self-protective defense mechanisms. Freud's theory has been criticized as not scientifically testable and offering after-the-fact explanations, focusing too much on sexual conflicts in childhood, and being based on the idea of repression, which has not been supported by modern research. **5.** Today's psychodynamic theorists and therapists still use Freud's interviewing techniques, and they still tend to focus on childhood experiences and attachments, unresolved conflicts, and unconscious influences. However, they are not likely to dwell on fixation at any psychosexual stage, or the idea that sexual issues are the basis of our personality. **6.** The humanistic theories sought to turn psychology's attention away from drives and conflicts and toward our growth potential. This movement's focus on the way people strive for self-determination and self-realization was in contrast to Freudian theory and strict behaviorism. **7.** To be *empathic* is to share and mirror another person's feelings. Carl Rogers believed that people nurture growth in others by being empathic. Abraham Maslow proposed that *self-actualization* is the motivation to fulfill one's potential, and one of the ultimate psychological needs (another is self-transcendence). **8.** extraversion–introversion and emotional stability–instability. **9.** The Big Five personality factors are openness, conscientiousness, extraversion, agreeableness, and neuroticism (emotional stability vs. instability): OCEAN. These factors may be objectively measured, they are relatively stable over the life span, and they apply to all cultures in which they have been studied. **10.** Our scores on personality tests predict our *average* behavior across many situations much better than they predict our specific behavior in any given situation. **11.** social-cognitive; reciprocal determinism. **12.** Examine the person's past behavior patterns in similar situations. **13.** People who feel confident in their abilities are often happier, have greater motivation, and are less susceptible to depression. Inflated self-esteem can lead to self-serving bias, greater aggression, and narcissism. **14.** self-serving bias. **15.** Defensive; Secure. **16.** Individualists give priority to personal goals over group goals and tend to define their identity in terms of their own personal attributes. Collectivists give priority to group goals over individual goals and tend to define their identity in terms of group identifications.

CHAPTER TEST ANSWERS

1. c. **2.** superego. **3.** b. **4.** anxiety. **5.** repression. **6.** d. **7.** a. **8.** Projective. **9.** a. **10.** d. **11.** Freud might argue that the criminal may have lacked the proper guidance as a child for developing a strong superego, allowing the id free rein. Rogers might assert that the criminal was raised in an environment lacking genuineness, acceptance (unconditional positive regard), and empathy, which inhibited psychological growth and led to a negative self-concept. **12.** unconditional positive regard. **13.** Trait. **14.** c. **15.** b. **16.** b. **17.** a. **18.** social-cognitive. **19.** spotlight effect. **20.** b. **21.** Yes, if that self-love is of the *secure* type. Secure self-esteem promotes a focus beyond the self and a higher quality of life. Excessive self-love may promote artificially high or defensive self-esteem, which is fragile. Perceived threats may be met with anger or aggression. **22.** b.

CHAPTER 13

Psychological Disorders

RETRIEVE & REMEMBER ANSWERS

1. dysfunctional or maladaptive. **2.** Some psychological disorders are culture-specific. For example, anorexia nervosa occurs mostly in Western cultures, and *taijin kyofusho* appears largely in Japan. Other disorders, such as major depressive disorder and schizophrenia, are universal—they occur in all cultures. **3.** Biological, psychological, and social-cultural influences combine to produce psychological disorders. This approach helps us understand that our well-being is affected by our genes, brain functioning, inner thoughts and feelings, and the influences of our social and cultural environment. **4.** Therapists and others apply disorder labels to communicate with one another using a common language, and to share concepts during research. Clients may benefit from knowing that they are not the only ones with these symptoms. The dangers of labeling people are that (a) overly broad classifications may pathologize normal behavior, and (b) the labels can trigger assumptions that will change people's behavior toward those labeled. **5.** generalized anxiety. **6.** panic. **7.** phobia. **8.** obsessive-compulsive. **9.** posttraumatic stress. **10.** Biological factors include inherited temperament differences and other gene variations; experience-altered brain pathways; and outdated, inherited responses that had survival value for our distant ancestors. **11.** With repeated exposure to a psychoactive drug, the user's brain chemistry adapts and the drug's effect lessens. Thus, it takes bigger doses to get the desired effect. **12.** Unless it becomes compulsive or dysfunctional, simply having a strong interest in shopping is not the same as having a physical addiction to a drug. It typically does not involve obsessive craving in spite of known negative consequences. **13.** depressants. **14.** Nicotine-withdrawal symptoms include strong cravings, insomnia, anxiety, irritability, distractibility, and difficulty concentrating. However, if your friend sticks with her vow to stop vaping, the craving and withdrawal symptoms will gradually disappear over about 6 months. **15.** Psychoactive drugs create pleasure by altering brain chemistry. With repeated use of the drug, the user develops tolerance and needs more of the drug to achieve the desired effect. (Marijuana is an exception.) Discontinuing use of the substance then produces painful or psychologically unpleasant withdrawal symptoms. **16.** Possible explanations include (a) biological factors (a person could have a biological predisposition to both early use and later abuse, or alcohol use could modify a person's neural pathways); (b) psychological factors (early use could establish taste preferences for alcohol); and (c) social-cultural factors (early use could influence enduring habits, attitudes, activities, or peer relationships that could foster alcohol use disorder). **17.** women's; men's. **18.** Many factors contribute to depression, including the biological influences of genetics and brain function. Social-cognitive factors also matter, including the interaction of explanatory style, mood, our responses to stressful experiences, changes in our patterns of thinking and behaving, and cultural influences. Depression involves the whole body and may disrupt sleep, energy levels, and concentration. **19.** negative. **20.** Biological factors include abnormalities in brain structure and function and a genetic predisposition to the disorder. Environmental factors such as nutritional deprivation, exposure to virus, and maternal stress contribute to activating the genes that increase risk. **21.** anorexia nervosa; bulimia nervosa. **22.** The psychodynamic explanation of DID symptoms is that they are defenses against anxiety generated by unacceptable urges. The learning perspective attempts to explain these symptoms as behaviors that have been reinforced by relieving anxiety. **23.** Twin and adoption studies show that biological relatives of people with this disorder are at increased risk for antisocial behavior. Researchers have also observed differences in the brain activity and structure of antisocial criminals. Negative environmental factors, such as poverty or childhood abuse, may channel genetic traits such as fearlessness in more dangerous directions—toward aggression and away from social responsibility.

CHAPTER TEST ANSWERS

1. major depressive disorder. **2.** No. Anna's behavior is unusual, causes her distress, and may make her a few minutes late on occasion, but it does not appear to significantly disrupt her ability to function. Like most of us, Anna demonstrates some unusual behaviors. Since they are not disabling or dysfunctional, they do not suggest a psychological disorder. **3.** medical. **4.** c. **5.** a. **6.** c. **7.** phobia. **8.** obsessive-compulsive. **9.** c. **10.** tolerance. **11.** a. **12.** Alcohol is a disinhibitor—it makes us more likely to do what we would have done when sober, whether that is being helpful or being aggressive. **13.** d. **14.** hallucinogenic. **15.** a. **16.** b. **17.** d. **18.** norepinephrine; serotonin. **19.** social-cognitive. **20.** b. **21.** hallucination. **22.** Schizophrenia involves the altered perceptions, emotions, and behaviors of a mind split from reality. It does not involve the rapid changes in mood or identity suggested by this comparison. **23.** a. **24.** b. **25.** c. **26.** c. **27.** b. **28.** Men; women.

CHAPTER 14

Therapy

RETRIEVE & REMEMBER ANSWERS

1. transference; resistance; interpretation. **2.** The *insight therapies*—psychodynamic and humanistic therapies—seek to relieve problems by providing an understanding of their origins. *Behavior therapies* assume the problem behavior *is* the problem and treat it directly, paying less attention to its origins. **3.** If a behavior can be learned, it can be *un*learned and replaced by other more adaptive responses. **4.** classical; operant. **5.** By reflecting people's feelings in a nondirective setting, the *humanistic therapies* attempt to foster personal growth by helping people become more self-aware and self-accepting. By making people aware of self-defeating patterns of thinking, *cognitive therapies* guide them toward more adaptive ways of thinking about themselves and their world. **6.** This integrative therapy helps people change self-defeating thinking and behavior. It has been shown to be effective for those with anxiety disorders, OCD, depressive disorders, bipolar disorder, eating disorders, and ADHD. **7.** are. **8.** When using an evidence-based approach, therapists make decisions about treatment based on research evidence, clinical expertise, and knowledge of the client. **9.** more. **10.** Exercise regularly, get enough sleep, get more exposure to light (get outside or use a light box), nurture important relationships, redirect negative thinking, and eat a diet rich in omega-3 fatty acids. **11.** Researchers assign people to treatment and no-treatment conditions to see if those who receive the drug therapy improve more than those who don't. Double-blind controlled studies are most effective. If neither the therapist nor the client knows which participants have received the drug treatment, then any difference between the treated and untreated groups will reflect the drug treatment's actual effect. **12.** antidepressants; antipsychotic. **13.** electroconvulsive therapy; transcranial; transcranial; deep brain. **14.** Psychological and biomedical therapies attempt to relieve people's suffering from psychological disorders. Preventive mental health attempts to prevent suffering by identifying and eliminating the conditions that cause disorders, as well as by building resilience.

CHAPTER TEST ANSWERS

1. a. **2.** Insight. **3.** d. **4.** active listening. **5.** c. **6.** counterconditioning. **7.** systematic desensitization. **8.** Behavior therapies are often the best choice for treating phobias. Viewing Rico's fear of the freeway as a learned response, a behavior therapist might help Rico learn to replace his anxious response to freeway driving with a relaxation response. **9.** token economy. **10.** d. **11.** Cognitive-behavioral. **12.** b. **13.** c. **14.** d. **15.** research evidence, clinical expertise, and knowledge of the patient. **16.** The placebo effect is the healing power of belief in a treatment. When patients expect a treatment to be effective, they may believe it was. **17.** c. **18.** antianxiety. **19.** lithium. **20.** b. **21.** d.

APPENDIX A

Statistical Reasoning in Everyday Life

RETRIEVE & REMEMBER ANSWERS

1. Note how the y-axis of each graph is labeled. The range for the y-axis label in graph (a) is only from 95 to 100. The range for graph (b) is from 0 to 100. All the trucks rank as 95 percent and up, so almost all are still functioning after 10 years, which graph (b) makes clear. **2.** mean; mode; median; range; standard deviation. **3.** The team's poor performance was not their typical behavior. Their return to their normal—their winning streak—may just have been a case of regression toward the mean. **4.** Averages based on fewer courses are more variable, which guarantees a greater number of extremely low and high marks at the end of the first term. **5.** Descriptive; inferential.

APPENDIX TEST ANSWERS

1. b. **2.** d. **3.** normal curve. **4.** a. **5.** negative. **6.** scatterplot. **7.** Without knowing that extreme scores or outcomes tend to return to normal after an unusual event, we may inaccurately decide the return to normal was a result of our own behavior. **8.** cross-sectional. **9.** a.

APPENDIX B

Psychology at Work

RETRIEVE & REMEMBER ANSWERS

1. We become more likely to view our work as fulfilling and socially useful, and we experience higher self-esteem, feelings of competence, and overall well-being. **2.** *Transformational leaders* are able to inspire others to share a vision and commit themselves to a group's mission. They tend to be naturally extraverted and to set high standards.

APPENDIX TEST ANSWERS

1. flow. **2.** human factors, personnel, and organizational. **3.** Personnel; human factors. **4.** Focusing on specific, short-term goals, such as maintaining a regular study schedule, will be more helpful than focusing on more distant general goals, such as earning a good grade in this class. **5.** transformational. **6.** c.

APPENDIX F

The Story of Psychology: A Timeline

Charles L. Brewer, *Furman University*[1]

B.C.E.

387 — Plato, who believed in innate ideas, suggests that the brain is the seat of mental processes.

335 — Aristotle, who denied the existence of innate ideas, suggests that the heart is the seat of mental processes.

C.E.

1604 — Johannes Kepler describes inverted image on the retina.

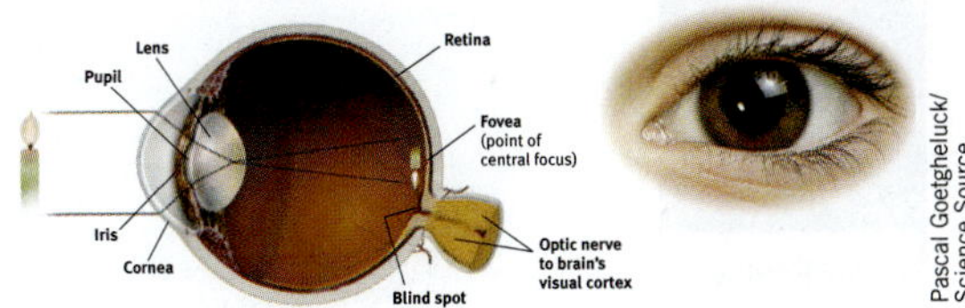

Pascal Goetgheluck/Science Source

Inverted image on the retina

1605 — Francis Bacon publishes *The Proficiency and Advancement of Learning*.

1636 — Harvard College is founded.

1637 — René Descartes, the French philosopher and mathematician who proposed mind–body interaction and the doctrine of innate ideas, publishes *A Discourse on Method*.

1690 — John Locke, the British philosopher who rejected Descartes' notion of innate ideas and insisted that the mind at birth is a "blank slate" *(tabula rasa)*, publishes *An Essay Concerning Human Understanding*, which stresses empiricism over speculation.

1774 — Franz Mesmer, an Austrian physician, performs his first supposed cure using "animal magnetism" (later called mesmerism and hypnosis). In 1777 he was expelled from the practice of medicine in Vienna.

1793 — Philippe Pinel releases the first mental patients from their chains at the Bicêtre Asylum in France and advocates for more humane treatment of mental patients.

1802 — Thomas Young publishes *A Theory of Color Vision* in England. (His theory was later called the trichromatic theory.)

1808 — Franz Joseph Gall, a German physician, describes phrenology, the belief that the shape of a person's skull reveals mental faculties and character traits.

1813 — The first private psychiatric hospital in the United States opens in Philadelphia.

1834 — Ernst Heinrich Weber publishes *The Sense of Touch*, in which he discusses the "just noticeable difference *(jnd)*" and what we now call Weber's law.

1844 — In Philadelphia, 13 superintendents form *The Association of Medical Superintendents of American Institutions for the Insane* (now known as the American Psychiatric Association).

1848 — Phineas Gage suffers massive brain damage when a large iron rod accidentally pierces his brain, leaving his intellect and memory intact but altering his personality.

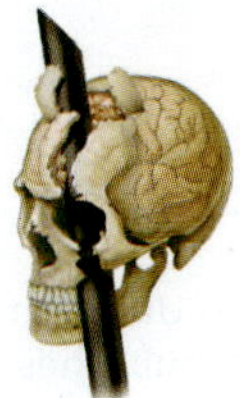

Warren Anatomical Museum in the Francis A. Countway Library of Medicine. Gift of Jack and Beverly Wilgus.

Phineas Gage

1850 — Hermann von Helmholtz measures the speed of the nerve impulse.

1859 — Charles Darwin publishes *On the Origin of Species by Means of Natural Selection*, synthesizing much previous work on the theory of evolution, including that of Herbert Spencer, who coined the phrase "survival of the fittest."

1861 — Paul Broca, a French physician, discovers an area in the left frontal lobe of the brain (now called Broca's area) that is critical for the production of spoken language.

1869 — Francis Galton, Charles Darwin's cousin, publishes *Hereditary Genius*, in which he claims that intelligence is inherited. In 1876 he coins the expression "nature and nurture" to correspond with "heredity and environment."

1874 — Carl Wernicke, a German neurologist and psychiatrist, shows that damage to a specific area in the left temporal lobe (now called Wernicke's area) disrupts ability to comprehend or produce spoken or written language.

1878 — G. Stanley Hall receives from Harvard University's Department of Philosophy the first U.S. Ph.D. degree based on psychological research.

[1] Our friend Charles Brewer died in 2018 after a lifetime devoted to the teaching of psychology. We offer special thanks to Salena Brody (University of Texas at Dallas), who has built on his work and helped us to make this timeline more inclusive of diverse contributions to psychology's development. (Dr. Brody also contributed new activities related to psychology's diversity for our Instructor's Resources in LaunchPad.)

1879 
Wilhelm Wundt
(1832–1920)

Wilhelm Wundt establishes at the University of Leipzig, Germany, the first psychology laboratory, which becomes a mecca for psychology students from all over the world.

1883 G. Stanley Hall, student of Wilhelm Wundt, establishes the first formal U.S. psychology laboratory at Johns Hopkins University.

1885 Hermann Ebbinghaus publishes *On Memory*, summarizing his extensive research on learning and memory, including the "forgetting curve."

1886 Joseph Jastrow receives from Johns Hopkins University the first Ph.D. degree in psychology awarded by a Department of Psychology in the United States.

1889 
Alfred Binet
(1857–1911)

Alfred Binet and Henri Beaunis establish the first psychology laboratory in France at the Sorbonne, and the first International Congress of Psychology meets in Paris.

1890 
William James
(1842–1910)

William James, Harvard University philosopher and psychologist, publishes *The Principles of Psychology*, describing psychology as "the science of mental life."

1891 James Mark Baldwin establishes the first psychology laboratory in the British Commonwealth at the University of Toronto.

1892 G. Stanley Hall spearheads the founding of the American Psychological Association (APA) and becomes its first president.

1893 
Mary Whiton Calkins
(1863–1930)

Mary Whiton Calkins and Christine Ladd-Franklin are the first women elected to membership in the APA.

1894 Margaret Floy Washburn is the first woman to receive a Ph.D. degree in psychology (Cornell University).

Harvard University denies Mary Whiton Calkins admission to doctoral candidacy because of her gender, despite Hugo Münsterberg's claim that she was the best student he had ever had there.

1896 John Dewey publishes "The Reflex Arc Concept in Psychology," helping to formalize the school of psychology called functionalism.

1898 In *Animal Intelligence*, Edward L. Thorndike, Columbia University, describes his learning experiments with cats in "puzzle boxes." In 1905, he proposes the "law of effect."

Doctoral student Alice Lee uses published data from the *Journal of Anatomy* to debunk the popular eugenics argument that skull size is related to intelligence.

1900 Sigmund Freud publishes *The Interpretation of Dreams*, his major theoretical work on psychoanalysis.

1901 Ten founders establish the British Psychological Society.

1904 Ivan Pavlov is awarded the Nobel Prize for Physiology or Medicine for his studies on the physiology of digestion.

1905 Mary Whiton Calkins becomes the first woman president of the APA.

Ivan Pavlov
(1849–1936)

Ivan Petrovich Pavlov begins publishing studies of conditioning in animals.

Alfred Binet and Théodore Simon produce the first intelligence test for assessing the abilities and academic progress of Parisian schoolchildren.

1909 
Sigmund Freud
(1856–1939)

Sigmund Freud makes his only trip to America to deliver a series of lectures at Clark University.

1913 
John Watson
(1878–1958)

John B. Watson outlines the tenets of behaviorism in a *Psychological Review* article, "Psychology as the Behaviorist Views It."

1914 During World War I, Robert Yerkes and his staff develop a group intelligence test for evaluating U.S. military personnel, which increases the U.S. public's acceptance of psychological testing.

Lilian Gilbreth publishes *Principles of Management*, a foundational text for the field of industrial-organizational psychology.

All Portraits: Macmillan Learning

1920 

Leta Stetter Hollingworth publishes *The Psychology of Subnormal Children*, an early classic. In 1921 she is cited in *American Men of Science* for her research on the psychology of women.

Leta Stetter Hollingworth (1886–1939)

Francis Cecil Sumner receives a Ph.D. degree in psychology from Clark University, becoming the first African-American to earn a psychology doctorate.

Francis Cecil Sumner (1895–1954)

John B. Watson and Rosalie Rayner report conditioning a fear reaction in a child called "Little Albert."

1921 Hermann Rorschach, a Swiss psychiatrist, introduces the Rorschach Inkblot Test.

1923 Developmental psychologist Jean Piaget publishes *The Language and Thought of the Child*.

1924 Mary Cover Jones reports reconditioning a fear reaction in a child (Peter), a forerunner of systematic desensitization developed by Joseph Wolpe.

1927 In *Introduction to the Technique of Child Analysis*, Anna Freud discusses psychoanalysis in the treatment of children.

1929 Wolfgang Köhler publishes *Gestalt Psychology*, which criticizes behaviorism and outlines essential elements of the gestalt position and approach.

1931 

Margaret Floy Washburn becomes the first female psychologist (and the second female scientist in any discipline) elected to the U.S. National Academy of Sciences.

Margaret Floy Washburn (1871–1939)

1932 In *The Wisdom of the Body*, Walter B. Cannon coins the term *homeostasis*, discusses the fight-or-flight response, and identifies hormonal changes associated with stress.

1933 

Inez Beverly Prosser becomes the first African-American woman to receive a doctoral degree in psychology from a U.S. institution (Ph.D., University of Cincinnati).

Inez Beverly Prosser (1895–1934)

1934 

Ruth Winifred Howard becomes the second African-American woman to receive a doctoral degree in psychology (Ph.D., University of Minnesota).

Ruth Winifred Howard (1900–1997)

1935 Christiana Morgan and Henry Murray introduce the Thematic Apperception Test to elicit fantasies from people undergoing psychoanalysis.

1936 Egas Moniz, a Portuguese physician, publishes work on the first frontal lobotomies performed on humans.

1938 B. F. Skinner publishes *The Behavior of Organisms*, which describes operant conditioning of animals.

In *Primary Mental Abilities*, Louis L. Thurstone proposes seven such abilities.

Ugo Cerletti and Lucio Bini use electroshock treatment with a human patient.

1939 David Wechsler publishes the Wechsler–Bellevue intelligence test, forerunner of the Wechsler Intelligence Scale for Children (WISC) and the Wechsler Adult Intelligence Scale (WAIS).

Mamie Phipps Clark receives a master's degree from Howard University. In collaboration with Kenneth B. Clark, she later extends her thesis, "The Development of Consciousness of Self in Negro Preschool Children," providing joint research cited in the U.S. Supreme Court's 1954 decision to end racial segregation in public schools.

Mamie Phipps Clark (1917–1983)

Edward Alexander Bott helps found the Canadian Psychological Association. He becomes its first president in 1940.

World War II provides many opportunities for psychologists to enhance the popularity and influence of psychology, especially in applied areas.

1943 Psychologist Starke Hathaway and physician J. Charnley McKinley publish the Minnesota Multiphasic Personality Inventory (MMPI).

1945 

Karen Horney, who criticized Freud's theory of female sexual development, publishes *Our Inner Conflicts*.

Karen Horney (1885–1952)

1946 Benjamin Spock's first edition of *The Commonsense Book of Baby and Child Care* appears; the book will influence child raising in North America for several decades.

1948 Alfred Kinsey and his colleagues publish *Sexual Behavior in the Human Male*, and they publish *Sexual Behavior in the Human Female* in 1953.

B. F. Skinner (1904–1990)

B. F. Skinner's novel, *Walden Two*, describes a Utopian community based on positive reinforcement, which becomes a clarion call for applying psychological principles in everyday living, especially communal living.

Ernest R. Hilgard publishes *Theories of Learning*, which was required reading for several generations of psychology students in North America.

1949 Raymond B. Cattell publishes the Sixteen Personality Factor Questionnaire (16PF).

The scientist-practitioner model of training is approved at The Boulder Conference on Graduate Education in Clinical Psychology.

In *The Organization of Behavior: A Neuropsychological Theory*, Canadian psychologist Donald O. Hebb outlines a new and influential conceptualization of how the nervous system functions.

1950 Solomon Asch publishes studies of effects of conformity on judgments of line length.

In *Childhood and Society*, Erik Erikson outlines his stages of psychosocial development.

1951 Carl Rogers publishes *Client-Centered Therapy*.

1952 The American Psychiatric Association publishes the *Diagnostic and Statistical Manual of Mental Disorders*, an influential book that will be updated periodically.

1953 Eugene Aserinski and Nathaniel Kleitman describe rapid eye movements (REM) that occur during sleep.

Janet Taylor's Manifest Anxiety Scale appears in the *Journal of Abnormal Psychology*.

1954 In *Motivation and Personality*, Abraham Maslow proposes a hierarchy of motives ranging from physiological needs to self-actualization. (Maslow later updates the hierarchy to include self-transcendence needs.)

James Olds and Peter Milner, McGill University neuropsychologists, describe the rewarding effects of electrical stimulation of the hypothalamus in rats.

Gordon Allport publishes *The Nature of Prejudice*.

1956 In his *Psychological Review* article titled "The Magical Number Seven, Plus or Minus Two: Some Limits on Our Capacity for Processing Information," George Miller coins the term *chunk* for memory researchers.

1957 Robert Sears, Eleanor Maccoby, and Harry Levin publish *Patterns of Child Rearing*.

Charles Ferster and B. F. Skinner publish *Schedules of Reinforcement*.

1958 Harry Harlow outlines "The Nature of Love," his work on attachment in monkeys.

1959 Noam Chomsky's critical review of B. F. Skinner's *Verbal Behavior* appears in the journal *Language*.

Keturah Whitehurst (1912–2000)

Keturah Whitehurst becomes the first African-American to be licensed as a psychologist in Virginia.

Eleanor Gibson and Richard Walk report their research on infants' depth perception in "The Visual Cliff."

Lloyd Peterson and Margaret Peterson, in the *Journal of Experimental Psychology* article, "Short-Term Retention of Individual Verbal Items," highlight the importance of rehearsal in memory.

John Thibaut and Harold Kelley publish *The Social Psychology of Groups*.

1960 George Sperling publishes "The Information Available in Brief Visual Presentations."

1961 Georg von Békésy receives a Nobel Prize for research on the physiology of hearing.

David McClelland publishes *The Achieving Society*.

1962 Jerome Kagan and Howard Moss publish *Birth to Maturity*.

Martha E. Bernal (1931–2001)

Martha E. Bernal becomes the first Latina to earn a U.S. doctoral degree (Ph.D., Indiana University).

Stanley Schachter and Jerome Singer publish findings that support the two-factor theory of emotion.

Albert Ellis' *Reason and Emotion in Psychotherapy* is published; it is a milestone in the development of rational-emotive therapy (RET).

1963 Raymond B. Cattell distinguishes between *fluid* and *crystallized* intelligence.

Stanley Milgram's "Behavioral Study of Obedience" appears in the *Journal of Abnormal and Social Psychology*.

1964 Marigold Linton becomes the first Native American to receive a doctoral degree in psychology. She is a founding member of both the Society for Advancement of Chicanos and Native Americans in Science, and the National Indian Education Association.

Marigold Linton (born 1936)

1965 Canadian researcher Ronald Melzack and British researcher Patrick Wall propose the gate-control theory of pain.

Robert Zajonc's "Social Facilitation" is published in *Science*.

The Archives of the History of American Psychology is founded at the University of Akron.

1966 Nancy Bayley becomes the first woman to receive the APA's Distinguished Scientific Contribution Award.

Jerome Bruner and colleagues at Harvard University's Center for Cognitive Studies publish *Studies in Cognitive Growth*.

William Masters and Virginia Johnson publish results of their research in *Human Sexual Responses*.

Allen Gardner and Beatrix Gardner begin training a chimpanzee (Washoe) in American Sign Language at the University of Nevada, Reno. Washoe dies in 2007.

John Garcia and Robert Koelling publish a study on taste aversion in rats.

John Garcia (1917–1983)

David M. Green and John A. Swets publish *Signal Detection Theory and Psychophysics*.

Julian Rotter publishes research on locus of control.

1967 Ulric Neisser's *Cognitive Psychology* helps to steer psychology away from behaviorism and toward cognitive processes.

Martin Seligman and Steven Maier publish the results of their research with "learned helplessness" in dogs.

1968 Richard Atkinson and Richard Shiffrin's influential three-stage memory model appears in *The Psychology of Learning and Motivation*.

Neal E. Miller's article in *Science*, describing instrumental conditioning of autonomic responses, stimulates research on biofeedback.

1969 Albert Bandura publishes *Principles of Behavior Modification*.

The Association for Women in Psychology is founded. E. Kitch Childs was instrumental in this effort, and pioneered therapy techniques that were grounded in intersectionality.

In his APA presidential address, "Psychology as a Means of Promoting Human Welfare," George Miller emphasizes the importance of "giving psychology away."

1970 Psychologist Reiko Homma True lobbies successfully to open the Asian American Community Mental Health program—the first to focus on a minority population.

Reiko Homma True (born 1933)

1971 Kenneth B. Clark becomes the first African-American president of the American Psychological Association.

Kenneth B. Clark (1914–2005)

Albert Bandura publishes *Social Learning Theory*.

Allan Paivio publishes *Imagery and Verbal Processes*.

B. F. Skinner publishes *Beyond Freedom and Dignity*.

1972 Elliot Aronson publishes *The Social Animal*.

Fergus Craik and Robert Lockhart's "Levels of Processing: A Framework for Memory Research" appears in the *Journal of Verbal Learning and Verbal Behavior*.

Robert Rescorla and Allan Wagner publish their associative model of Pavlovian conditioning.

Under the leadership of Derald Wing Sue and Stanley Sue, the Asian American Psychological Association is founded.

Derald Wing Sue (born 1942) Stanley Sue (born 1944)

1973 Ethologists Karl von Frisch, Konrad Lorenz, and Nikolaas Tinbergen receive the Nobel Prize for their research on animal behavior.

1974 APA's Division 2 first publishes its journal, *Teaching of Psychology*, with Robert S. Daniel as editor.

Eleanor Maccoby and Carol Jacklin publish *The Psychology of Sex Differences*.

1975 Biologist Edward O. Wilson's *Sociobiology* is published; it will be a controversial precursor to evolutionary psychology.

1976 Sandra Wood Scarr and Richard A. Weinberg publish "IQ Test Performance of Black Children Adopted by White Families" in *American Psychologist*.

Psychologist Robert V. Guthrie publishes *Even the Rat Was White*, the first history of African-American psychologists in America.

imageBROKER/Alamy

Saundra Murray Nettles chairs the Task Force on Black Women's Priorities, which leads to the creation of APA's Division 35, Section 1: The Psychology of Black Women.

Psychologist Carolyn Payton becomes the first African-American and first woman Director of the U.S. Peace Corps.

All Portraits: Macmillan Learning

1978 Psychologist Herbert A. Simon, Carnegie-Mellon University, wins a Nobel Prize for pioneering research on computer simulations of human thinking and problem solving.

1979 James J. Gibson publishes *The Ecological Approach to Visual Perception.*

Elizabeth Loftus publishes *Eyewitness Testimony.*

1981 David Hubel and Torsten Wiesel receive a Nobel Prize for research on single-cell recordings that identified feature detector cells in the visual cortex.

Roger Sperry receives a Nobel Prize for research on split-brain patients.

Sociologist Harriette Pipe McAdoo publishes *Black Families*, an anthology of work done with John Lewis McAdoo on middle class African-American families. Previous studies had focused on dysfunctional families, such as those in contact with prison and drug treatment programs.

Paleontologist Stephen Jay Gould publishes *The Mismeasure of Man*, highlighting the debate concerning biological determination of intelligence.

1983 In his *Frames of Mind*, Howard Gardner outlines his theory of multiple intelligences.

1984 44 Society for the Psychology of Sexual Orientation and Gender Diversity

The American Psychological Association creates Division 44 (Society for the Psychology of Sexual Orientation and Gender Diversity).

Robert Sternberg proposes the triarchic theory of human intelligence in *Behavioral and Brain Sciences.*

1987 Elizabeth Scarborough and Laurel Furumoto publish *Untold Lives: The First Generation of American Women Psychologists.*

Fluoxetine (Prozac) is introduced as a treatment for depression.

Wilbert J. McKeachie, University of Michigan, receives the first APA Award for Distinguished Career Contributions to Education and Training in Psychology.

1988 The American Psychological Society is founded. It changes its name to Association for Psychological Science in 2006.

1990 Psychiatrist Aaron Beck receives the Distinguished Scientific Award for the Applications of Psychology for advancing understanding and treatment of psychopathology, including pivotal contributions to the development of cognitive therapy.

B. F. Skinner receives APA's first Citation for Outstanding Lifetime Contributions to Psychology and presents his last public address, "Can Psychology Be a Science of Mind?" (He died a few days later at age 86.)

1991 Martin Seligman publishes *Learned Optimism*, which foreshadows the "positive psychology" movement.

1992 Teachers of Psychology in Secondary Schools (TOPSS) is established as part of the APA.

About 3,000 U.S. secondary school students take the first Advanced Placement (AP) Examination in Psychology, hoping to earn exemption from an introductory psychology course at the postsecondary level.

1993 Psychologist Judith Rodin is elected president of the University of Pennsylvania, becoming the first female president of an Ivy League school.

1996 Dorothy Cantor becomes the first president of the APA with a Psy.D. degree.

1998 *The Handbook of Asian American Psychology* is published.

2002 New Mexico becomes the first U.S. state to allow qualified clinical psychologists to prescribe certain drugs.

Psychologist Daniel Kahneman, Princeton University, receives a Nobel Prize for research on decision making.

2009 Psychologist Judy Chu becomes the first Chinese-American woman elected to the U.S. Congress.

2011 Proposed by participants at the 2008 national conference at the University of Puget Sound, the document, "Principles for Quality Undergraduate Education in Psychology," is approved as official APA policy.

Melba J. T. Vasquez is the first Latina president of the American Psychological Association.

Melba J. T. Vasquez (born 1951)

2013 U.S. President Barack Obama announces $100 million in funding for an interdisciplinary project to advance understanding of the human brain.

2014 Social psychologist Jennifer L. Eberhardt is awarded the MacArthur Fellowship ("Genius Grant") to support her implicit bias research.

2015 The *Independent Review Relating to APA Ethics Guidelines, National Security Interrogations, and Torture* is presented to the American Psychological Association.

2018 Kristina Olson becomes the first psychologist to receive the National Science Foundation's Waterman Award. She also receives a 2018 MacArthur Fellowship for her work studying the social and cognitive development of transgender and gender-nonconforming youth.

GLOSSARY

absolute threshold the minimum stimulus energy needed to detect a particular stimulus 50 percent of the time. (p. 133)

accommodation adapting our current understandings (schemas) to incorporate new information. (p. 80)

achievement motivation a desire for significant accomplishment, for mastery of skills or ideas, for control, and for attaining a high standard. (p. 259)

achievement test a test designed to assess what a person has learned. (p. 232)

acquisition in classical conditioning, the initial stage—when we link a neutral stimulus and an unconditioned stimulus so that the neutral stimulus begins triggering the conditioned response. (In operant conditioning, the strengthening of a reinforced response.) (p. 169)

action potential a nerve impulse; a brief electrical charge that travels down an axon. (p. 32)

active listening empathic listening in which the listener echoes, restates, and clarifies. A feature of Rogers' person-centered therapy. (p. 404)

acute schizophrenia (also called *reactive schizophrenia*) a form of schizophrenia that can begin at any age, frequently occurs in response to a traumatic event, and from which recovery is much more likely. (p. 388)

adaptation-level phenomenon our tendency to form judgments (of sounds, of lights, of income) relative to a neutral level defined by our past experiences. (p. 296)

adolescence the transition period from childhood to adulthood, extending from puberty to independence. (p. 90)

adrenal [ah-DREEN-el] **glands** a pair of endocrine glands that sit just above the kidneys and secrete hormones (epinephrine and norepinephrine) that help arouse the body in times of stress. (p. 39)

aerobic exercise sustained exercise that increases heart and lung fitness; also helps reduce depression and anxiety. (p. 288)

aggression any act intended to harm someone physically or emotionally. (pp. 108, 320)

AIDS (acquired immune deficiency syndrome) a life-threatening, sexually transmitted infection caused by the *human immunodeficiency virus (HIV)*. AIDS depletes the immune system, leaving the person vulnerable to infections. (p. 119)

alcohol use disorder (popularly known as *alcoholism*) alcohol use marked by tolerance, withdrawal, and a drive to continue problematic use. (p. 374)

algorithm a methodical, logical rule or procedure that guarantees you will solve a particular problem. Contrasts with the usually speedier—but also more error-prone—use of *heuristics*. (p. 214)

all-or-none response a neuron's reaction of either firing (with a full-strength response) or not firing. (p. 34)

alpha waves relatively slow brain waves of a relaxed, awake state. (p. 57)

altruism unselfish concern for the welfare of others. (p. 328)

amphetamines drugs (such as *methamphetamine*) that stimulate neural activity, causing speeded-up body functions and associated energy and mood changes. (p. 377)

amygdala [uh-MIG-duh-la] two lima bean-sized neural clusters in the limbic system; linked to emotion. (p. 44)

androgyny displaying both traditionally masculine and traditionally feminine psychological characteristics. (p. 114)

anorexia nervosa an eating disorder in which a person (usually an adolescent female) maintains a starvation diet despite being significantly underweight; sometimes accompanied by excessive exercise. (p. 390)

anterograde amnesia an inability to form new memories. (p. 202)

antianxiety drugs drugs used to control anxiety and agitation. (p. 419)

antidepressant drugs drugs used to treat depression, anxiety disorders, obsessive-compulsive disorder, and posttraumatic stress disorder. (Several widely used antidepressant drugs are *selective serotonin reuptake inhibitors—SSRIs*.) (p. 419)

antipsychotic drugs drugs used to treat schizophrenia and other forms of severe thought disorders. (p. 417)

antisocial personality disorder a personality disorder in which a person (usually a man) exhibits a lack of conscience for wrongdoing, even toward friends and family members; may be aggressive and ruthless or a clever con artist. (p. 393)

anxiety disorders psychological disorders characterized by distressing, persistent anxiety or maladaptive behaviors that reduce anxiety. (p. 367)

aptitude test a test designed to predict a person's future performance; *aptitude* is the capacity to learn. (p. 232)

asexual having no sexual attraction toward others. (p. 117)

assimilation interpreting our new experiences in terms of our existing schemas. (p. 80)

association areas cerebral cortex areas involved primarily in higher mental functions, such as learning, remembering, thinking, and speaking. (p. 48)

associative learning learning that certain events occur together. The events may be two stimuli (as in classical conditioning) or a response and its consequence (as in operant conditioning). (p. 166)

attachment an emotional tie with others; shown in young children by their seeking closeness to caregivers and showing distress on separation. (p. 85)

attention-deficit/hyperactivity disorder (ADHD) a psychological disorder marked by extreme inattention and/or hyperactivity and impulsivity. (p. 362)

attitude feelings, often based on our beliefs, that predispose us to respond in a particular way to objects, people, and events. (p. 303)

audition the sense or act of hearing. (p. 150)

autism spectrum disorder (ASD) a disorder that appears in childhood and is marked by significant limitations in communication and social interaction, and by rigidly fixated interests and repetitive behaviors. (p. 84)

automatic processing unconscious encoding of everyday information, such as space, time, and frequency, and of well-learned information, such as word meanings. (p. 191)

autonomic [aw-tuh-NAHM-ik] **nervous system (ANS)** peripheral nervous system division that controls the glands and the muscles of the internal organs (such as the heart). Its *sympathetic* subdivision arouses; its *parasympathetic* subdivision calms. (p. 37)

availability heuristic judging the likelihood of events based on their availability in memory; if an event comes readily to mind (perhaps because it was vivid), we assume it must be common. (p. 216)

aversive conditioning associates an unpleasant state (such as nausea) with an unwanted behavior (such as drinking alcohol). (p. 407)

axon the neuron extension that sends messages to other neurons or to muscles and glands. (p. 32)

babbling stage the stage in speech development, beginning around 4 months, during which an infant spontaneously utters various sounds that are not all related to the household language. (p. 224)

barbiturates drugs that depress central nervous system activity, reducing anxiety but impairing memory and judgment. (p. 374)

basal metabolic rate the body's resting rate of energy output. (p. 252)

basic trust according to Erik Erikson, a sense that the world is predictable and trustworthy; said to be formed during infancy by appropriate experiences with responsive caregivers. (p. 86)

behaviorism the view that psychology (1) should be an objective science that (2) studies behavior without reference to mental processes. Most research psychologists today agree with (1) but not with (2). (pp. 5, 181)

behavior therapy therapy that applies learning principles to the elimination of unwanted behaviors. (p. 405)

belief perseverance clinging to beliefs even after evidence has proven them wrong. (p. 218)

binge-eating disorder significant binge-eating episodes, followed by distress, disgust, or guilt, but without the behavior to compensate that marks bulimia nervosa. (p. 391)

binocular cue a depth cue, such as retinal disparity, that depends on the use of two eyes. (p. 146)

biological psychology the scientific study of the links between biological and psychological processes. (p. 53)

biomedical therapy prescribed medications or procedures that act directly on the person's physiology. (p. 403)

biopsychosocial approach an approach that integrates different but complementary views from biological, psychological, and social-cultural viewpoints. (p. 8)

bipolar disorder a disorder in which a person alternates between the hopelessness and weariness of depression and the overexcited state of mania. (Formerly called *manic-depressive disorder.*) (p. 382)

blind spot the point at which the optic nerve leaves the eye; this part of the retina is "blind" because it has no receptor cells. (p. 140)

bottom-up processing analysis that begins with the sensory receptors and works up to the brain's integration of sensory information. (p. 132)

brainstem the oldest part and central core of the brain, beginning where the spinal cord swells as it enters the skull; responsible for automatic survival functions. (p. 42)

Broca's area a frontal lobe brain area, usually in the left hemisphere, that helps control language expression by directing the muscle movements involved in speech. (p. 226)

bulimia nervosa an eating disorder in which a person's binge eating (usually of high-calorie foods) is followed by inappropriate weight-loss-promoting behavior, such as vomiting, laxative use, fasting, or excessive exercise. (p. 391)

bystander effect the tendency for any given bystander to be less likely to give aid if other bystanders are present. (p. 329)

Cannon-Bard theory the theory that an emotion-arousing stimulus simultaneously triggers (1) physiological responses and (2) the subjective experience of emotion. (p. 262)

case study a descriptive technique in which one individual or group is studied in depth in the hope of revealing universal principles. (p. 16)

cell body the part of a neuron that contains the nucleus; the cell's life-support center. (p. 32)

central nervous system (CNS) the brain and spinal cord. (p. 36)

central route persuasion occurs when interested people's thinking is influenced by considering evidence and arguments. (p. 305)

cerebellum [sehr-uh-BELL-um] the "little brain" at the rear of the brainstem; functions include processing sensory input, coordinating movement output and balance, and enabling nonverbal learning and memory. (p. 43)

cerebral [seh-REE-bruhl] **cortex** a thin layer of interconnected neurons covering the cerebral hemispheres; the body's ultimate control and information-processing center. (p. 46)

change blindness failing to notice changes in the environment; a form of *inattentional blindness.* (p. 56)

chromosomes threadlike structures made of DNA molecules that contain the genes. (p. 72)

chronic schizophrenia (also called *process schizophrenia*) a form of schizophrenia in which symptoms usually appear by late adolescence or early adulthood. As people age, psychotic episodes last longer and recovery periods shorten. (p. 388)

chunking organizing items into familiar, manageable units; often occurs automatically. (p. 193)

circadian [ser-KAY-dee-an] **rhythm** our internal biological clock; regular bodily rhythms (for example, of temperature and wakefulness) that occur on a 24-hour cycle. (p. 56)

classical conditioning a type of learning in which we link two or more stimuli and anticipate events. (p. 167)

clinical psychology a branch of psychology that studies, assesses, and treats people with psychological disorders. (p. 10)

cocaine a powerful and addictive stimulant derived from the coca plant; temporarily increases alertness and produces feelings of euphoria. (p. 376)

cochlea [KOHK-lee-uh] a coiled, bony, fluid-filled tube in the inner ear; sound waves traveling through the cochlear fluid trigger nerve impulses. (p. 151)

cochlear implant a device for converting sounds into electrical signals and stimulating the auditory nerve through electrodes threaded into the cochlea. (p. 152)

cognition all the mental activities associated with thinking, knowing, remembering, and communicating. (pp. 79, 214)

cognitive-behavioral therapy (CBT) a popular integrative therapy that combines cognitive therapy (changing self-defeating thinking) with behavior therapy (changing behavior). (p. 410)

cognitive dissonance theory the theory that we act to reduce the discomfort (dissonance) we feel when two of our thoughts (cognitions) clash. For example, when we become aware that our attitudes and our actions don't match, we may change our attitudes so that we feel more comfortable. (p. 305)

cognitive learning the acquisition of mental information, whether by observing events, by watching others, or through language. (p. 167)

cognitive map a mental image of the layout of one's environment. (p. 182)

cognitive neuroscience the interdisciplinary study of the brain activity linked with cognition (including perception, thinking, memory, and language). (pp. 6, 53)

cognitive psychology the study of mental processes, such as occur when we perceive, learn, remember, think, communicate, and solve problems. (p. 5)

cognitive therapy therapy that teaches people new, more adaptive ways of thinking; based on the assumption that thoughts intervene between events and our emotional reactions. (p. 408)

collective unconscious Carl Jung's concept of a shared, inherited group of memories from our species' history. (p. 340)

collectivism giving priority to the goals of our group (often our extended family or work group) and defining our identity accordingly. (p. 356)

community psychology a branch of psychology that studies how people interact with their social environments and how social institutions (such as schools and neighborhoods) affect individuals and groups. (p. 11)

companionate love the deep affectionate attachment we feel for those with whom our lives are intertwined. (p. 327)

concept a mental grouping of similar objects, events, ideas, or people. (p. 214)

concrete operational stage in Piaget's theory, the stage of cognitive development (from about 7 to 11 years of age) at which children gain the mental operations that enable them to think logically about concrete events. (p. 82)

conditioned reinforcer an event that gains its reinforcing power through its link with a primary reinforcer. (Also known as *secondary reinforcer.*) (p. 174)

conditioned response (CR) in classical conditioning, a learned response to a previously neutral (but now conditioned) stimulus (CS). (p. 168)

conditioned stimulus (CS) in classical conditioning, an originally neutral stimulus that, after association with an unconditioned stimulus (US), comes to trigger a conditioned response (CR). (p. 168)

conduction hearing loss a less common form of hearing loss, caused by damage to the mechanical system that conducts sound waves to the cochlea. (p. 152)

cones retinal receptors that are concentrated near the center of the retina, and that function in daylight or well-lit conditions. Cones detect fine detail and give rise to color sensations. (p. 140)

confirmation bias a tendency to search for information that supports your preconceptions and to ignore or distort evidence that contradicts them. (p. 215)

conflict a perceived incompatibility of actions, goals, or ideas. (p. 330)

conformity adjusting our behavior or thinking to coincide with a group standard. (p. 307)

confounding variable in an experiment, a factor other than the factor being studied that might influence a study's results. (p. 21)

consciousness our subjective awareness of ourselves and our environment. (p. 53)

conservation the principle (which Piaget believed to be a part of concrete operational reasoning) that properties such as mass, volume, and number remain the same despite changes in shapes. (p. 81)

continuous reinforcement reinforcing a desired response every time it occurs. (p. 175)

control group in an experiment, the group *not* exposed to the treatment; the control group serves as a comparison with the experimental group for judging the effect of the treatment. (p. 20)

convergent thinking narrowing the available solutions to determine the single best solution to a problem. (p. 220)

coping reducing stress using emotional, cognitive, or behavioral methods. (p. 282)

coronary heart disease the clogging of the vessels that nourish the heart muscle; the leading cause of death in the United States and many other countries. (p. 281)

corpus callosum [KOR-pus kah-LOW-sum] a large band of neural fibers connecting the two brain hemispheres and carrying messages between them. (p. 51)

correlation a measure of the extent to which two factors vary together, and thus of how well either one predicts the other. The *correlation coefficient* is the mathematical expression of the relationship, ranging from –1.00 to +1.00, with 0 indicating no relationship. (p. 18)

correlation coefficient a statistical index of the relationship between two things (from –1.00 to +1.00). (p. A-4)

counseling psychology a branch of psychology that assists people with problems in living (often related to school, work, or relationships) and in achieving greater well-being. (p. 10)

counterconditioning behavior therapy procedures that use classical conditioning to evoke new responses to stimuli that are triggering unwanted behaviors; includes *exposure therapies* and *aversive conditioning*. (p. 406)

creativity the ability to produce new and valuable ideas. (p. 220)

critical period a period early in life when exposure to certain stimuli or experiences is needed for proper development. (p. 78)

critical thinking thinking that does not blindly accept arguments and conclusions. Rather, it examines assumptions, assesses the source, uncovers hidden values, weighs evidence, and assesses conclusions. (p. 2)

cross-sectional study research that compares people of different ages at the same point in time. (pp. 70, 238, A-6)

crystallized intelligence your accumulated knowledge and verbal skills; tends to increase with age. (p. 239)

culture the enduring behaviors, ideas, attitudes, values, and traditions shared by a group of people and handed down from one generation to the next. (p. 8)

debriefing after an experiment ends, explaining to participants the study's purpose and any deceptions researchers used. (p. 25)

defense mechanisms in psychoanalytic theory, the ego's protective methods of reducing anxiety by unconsciously distorting reality. (p. 339)

deindividuation the loss of self-awareness and self-restraint occurring in group situations that foster arousal and anonymity. (p. 312)

déjà vu that eerie sense that "I've experienced this before." Cues from the current situation may unconsciously trigger retrieval of an earlier experience. (p. 207)

delta waves large, slow brain waves associated with deep sleep. (p. 58)

delusion a false belief, often of persecution or grandeur, that may accompany psychotic disorders. (p. 387)

dendrites neuron extensions that receive and integrate messages and conduct them toward the cell body. (p. 32)

dependent variable in an experiment, the factor that is measured; the variable that may change when the independent variable is manipulated. (p. 21)

depressants drugs (such as alcohol, barbiturates, and opiates) that reduce (depress) neural activity and slow body functions. (p. 372)

depth perception the ability to see objects in three dimensions, although the images that strike the retina are two-dimensional; allows us to judge distance. (p. 145)

developmental psychology a branch of psychology that studies physical, cognitive, and social development throughout the life span. (p. 70)

difference threshold the minimum difference between two stimuli required for detection 50 percent of the time. We experience the difference threshold as a *just noticeable difference* (or *jnd*). (p. 135)

discrimination (1) in classical conditioning, the learned ability to distinguish between a conditioned stimulus and similar stimuli that do not signal an unconditioned stimulus. (In operant conditioning, the ability to distinguish responses that are reinforced from similar responses that are not reinforced.) (2) in social psychology, unfair negative behavior toward a group or its members. (pp. 170, 315)

dissociative disorders controversial, rare disorders in which conscious awareness becomes separated (dissociated) from previous memories, thoughts, and feelings. (p. 392)

dissociative identity disorder (DID) a rare dissociative disorder in which a person exhibits two or more distinct and alternating identities. (Formerly called *multiple personality disorder*.) (p. 392)

divergent thinking expanding the number of possible solutions to a problem; creative thinking that branches out in different directions. (p. 220)

DNA (deoxyribonucleic acid) a molecule containing the genetic information that makes up the chromosomes. (p. 72)

double-blind procedure in an experiment, a procedure in which both the participants and the research staff are ignorant (blind) about who has received the treatment or a placebo. (p. 21)

dream a sequence of images, emotions, and thoughts passing through a sleeping person's mind. (p. 63)

drive-reduction theory the idea that a physiological need creates an aroused state (a drive) that motivates us to satisfy the need. (p. 248)

DSM-5 the American Psychiatric Association's *Diagnostic and Statistical Manual of Mental Disorders*, Fifth Edition; a widely used system for classifying psychological disorders. (p. 365)

dual processing the principle that our mind processes information at the same time on separate conscious and unconscious tracks. (p. 10)

eclectic approach an approach to psychotherapy that uses techniques from various forms of therapy. (p. 402)

Ecstasy (MDMA) a synthetic stimulant and mild hallucinogen. Produces euphoria and social intimacy, but with short-term health risks and longer-term harm to serotonin-producing neurons and to mood and cognition. (p. 377)

EEG (electroencephalograph) a device that uses electrodes placed on the scalp to record waves of electrical activity sweeping across the brain's surface. (The record of those brain waves is an *electroencephalogram*.) (p. 40)

effortful processing encoding that requires attention and conscious effort. (p. 191)

ego the largely conscious, "executive" part of personality that, according to Freud, balances the demands of the id, the superego, and reality. The ego operates on the *reality principle*, satisfying the id's desires in ways that will realistically bring pleasure rather than pain. (p. 337)

egocentrism in Piaget's theory, the preoperational child's difficulty taking another's point of view. (p. 82)

electroconvulsive therapy (ECT) a biomedical therapy for severely depressed patients in which a brief electric current is sent through the brain of an anesthetized patient. (p. 420)

embodied cognition the influence of bodily sensations, gestures, and other states on cognitive preferences and judgments. (p. 160)

embryo the developing human organism from about 2 weeks after fertilization through the second month. (p. 74)

emerging adulthood a period from about age 18 to the mid-twenties, when many in Western cultures are no longer adolescents but have not yet achieved full independence as adults. (p. 96)

emotion a response of the whole organism, involving (1) bodily arousal, (2) expressive behaviors, and (3) conscious experience. (p. 262)

emotion-focused coping attempting to reduce stress by avoiding or ignoring a stressor and attending to emotional needs related to our stress reaction. (p. 282)

emotional intelligence the ability to perceive, understand, manage, and use emotions. (p. 231)

encoding the process of getting information into the memory system. (p. 190)

encoding specificity principle the idea that cues and contexts specific to a particular memory will be most effective in helping us recall it. (p. 200)

endocrine [EN-duh-krin] **system** the body's "slow" chemical communication system; a set of glands that secrete hormones into the bloodstream. (p. 39)

endorphins [en-DOR-fins] "morphine within"—natural, opiate-like neurotransmitters linked to pain control and to pleasure. (p. 36)

environment every external influence, from prenatal nutrition to social support in later life. (p. 73)

epigenetics the study of the molecular ways by which environments can influence gene expression (without a DNA change). (pp. 74, 364)

episodic memory explicit memory of personally experienced events; one of our two conscious memory systems (the other is *semantic memory*). (p. 195)

equity a condition in which people receive from a relationship in proportion to what they give to it. (p. 327)

erectile disorder inability to develop or maintain an erection due to insufficient blood flow to the penis. (p. 118)

estrogens sex hormones, such as estradiol, that contribute to female sex characteristics and are secreted in greater amounts by females than by males. Estrogen levels peak during ovulation. In nonhuman mammals, this promotes sexual receptivity. (p. 117)

evidence-based practice clinical decision making that integrates the best available research with clinical expertise and patient characteristics and preferences. (p. 414)

evolutionary psychology the study of how our behavior and mind have changed in adaptive ways over time due to natural selection. (p. 126)

experiment a method in which researchers vary one or more factors (independent variables) to observe the effect on some behavior or mental process (the dependent variable). By *random assignment* of participants, researchers aim to control other factors. (p. 20)

experimental group in an experiment, the group exposed to the treatment, that is, to one version of the independent variable. (p. 20)

explicit memory retention of facts and personal events you can consciously retrieve. (Also called *declarative memory*.) (p. 191)

exposure therapies behavioral techniques, such as *systematic desensitization* and *virtual reality exposure therapy*, that treat anxieties by exposing people (in imaginary or actual situations) to the things they fear and avoid. (p. 406)

external locus of control the perception that outside forces beyond our personal control determine our fate. (p. 284)

extinction in classical conditioning, the weakening of a conditioned response when an unconditioned stimulus does not follow a conditioned stimulus. (In operant conditioning, the weakening of a response when it is no longer reinforced.) (p. 169)

extrasensory perception (ESP) the controversial claim that perception can occur apart from sensory input; includes telepathy, clairvoyance, and precognition. (p. 160)

extrinsic motivation the desire to perform a behavior to receive promised rewards or avoid threatened punishment. (p. 260)

facial feedback effect the tendency of facial muscle states to trigger corresponding feelings such as fear, anger, or happiness. (p. 271)

factor a cluster of behavior tendencies that occur together. (p. 346)

family therapy therapy that treats people in the context of their family system. Views an individual's unwanted behaviors as influenced by, or directed at, other family members. (p. 411)

feature detectors nerve cells in the brain's visual cortex that respond to specific features of a stimulus, such as shape, angles, or movement. (p. 143)

feel-good, do-good phenomenon our tendency to be helpful when in a good mood. (p. 293)

female orgasmic disorder distress due to infrequently or never experiencing orgasm. (p. 118)

fetal alcohol syndrome (FAS) physical and mental abnormalities in children caused by a pregnant woman's heavy drinking. In severe cases, signs include a small, out-of-proportion head and abnormal facial features. (p. 74)

fetus the developing human organism from 9 weeks after conception to birth. (p. 74)

fight-or-flight response an emergency response, including activity of the sympathetic nervous system, that mobilizes energy and activity for attacking or escaping a threat. (p. 278)

figure-ground the organization of the visual field into objects (the *figures*) that stand out from their surroundings (the *ground*). (p. 145)

fixation in personality theory, according to Freud, a lingering focus of pleasure-seeking energies at an earlier psychosexual stage, in which conflicts were unresolved. (p. 338)

fixed-interval schedule in operant conditioning, a reinforcement schedule that reinforces a response only after a specified time has elapsed. (p. 176)

fixed-ratio schedule in operant conditioning, a reinforcement schedule that reinforces a response only after a specified number of responses. (p. 175)

flashbulb memory a clear memory of an emotionally significant moment or event. (p. 197)

flow a completely involved, focused state, with lowered awareness of self and time; results from full engagement of our skills. (p. B-1)

fluid intelligence your ability to reason speedily and abstractly; tends to decrease with age, especially during late adulthood. (p. 239)

fMRI (functional MRI) a technique for revealing blood flow and, therefore, brain activity by comparing successive MRI scans. fMRI scans show brain function. (p. 41)

foot-in-the-door phenomenon the tendency for people who have first agreed to a small request to comply later with a larger request. (p. 304)

formal operational stage in Piaget's theory, the stage of cognitive development (normally beginning about age 12) at which people begin to think logically about abstract concepts. (p. 82)

framing the way an issue is posed; framing can significantly affect decisions and judgments. (p. 219)

fraternal (dizygotic) twins individuals who developed from separate fertilized eggs. They are genetically no closer than ordinary siblings, but shared a prenatal environment. (p. 76)

free association in psychoanalysis, a method of exploring the unconscious in which the person relaxes and says whatever comes to mind, no matter how unimportant or embarrassing. (p. 337)

frequency the number of complete wavelengths that pass a point in a given time (for example, per second). (p. 151)

frontal lobes the portion of the cerebral cortex lying just behind the forehead; involved in speaking and muscle movements and in making plans and judgments. (p. 46)

frustration-aggression principle the principle that frustration—the blocking of an attempt to achieve some goal—creates anger, which can generate aggression. (p. 321)

functional fixedness in cognition, the inability to see a problem from a new perspective; an obstacle to problem solving. (p. 215)

functionalism an early school of thought promoted by James and influenced by Darwin that focused on how the mind functions. (p. 5)

fundamental attribution error the tendency, when analyzing others' behavior, to overestimate the influence of personal traits and underestimate the influence of the situation. (p. 302)

gender in psychology, the behavioral characteristics that people associate with *boy*, *girl*, *man*, and *woman*. (See also *gender identity*.) (p. 108)

gender identity our sense of being male, female, neither, or some combination of male and female. (p. 114)

gender role a set of expected behaviors, attitudes, and traits for men and for women. (p. 113)

gender typing the acquisition of a traditional masculine or feminine role. (p. 114)

general adaptation syndrome (GAS) Selye's concept of the body's adaptive response to stress in three stages—alarm, resistance, exhaustion. (p. 278)

general intelligence (*g*) according to Spearman and others, underlies all mental abilities and is therefore measured by every task on an intelligence test. (p. 229)

generalization in classical conditioning, the tendency, after conditioning, to respond similarly to stimuli that resemble the conditioned stimulus. (In operant conditioning, *generalization* occurs when responses learned in one situation occur in other, similar situations.) (p. 170)

generalized anxiety disorder an anxiety disorder in which a person is continually tense, fearful, and in a state of autonomic nervous system arousal. (p. 367)

genes the biochemical units of heredity that make up the chromosomes; segments of DNA. (p. 72)

genome the complete instructions for making an organism, consisting of all the genetic material in that organism's chromosomes. (p. 73)

gestalt an organized whole. Gestalt psychologists emphasized our tendency to integrate pieces of information into meaningful wholes. (p. 144)

glial cells (glia) cells in the nervous system that support, nourish, and protect neurons; they also play a role in learning, thinking, and memory. (p. 32)

glucose the form of sugar that circulates in the blood and provides the major source of energy for body tissues. When its level is low, we feel hunger. (p. 251)

grammar in a language, a system of rules that enables us to communicate with and understand others. (p. 225)

grit in psychology, passion and perseverance in the pursuit of long-term goals. (p. 260)

group polarization strengthening of a group's preexisting attitudes through discussions within the group. (p. 313)

group therapy therapy conducted with groups rather than individuals, providing benefits from group interaction. (p. 411)

grouping the perceptual tendency to organize stimuli into meaningful groups. (p. 145)

groupthink the mode of thinking that occurs when the desire for harmony in a decision-making group overrides a realistic appraisal of alternatives. (p. 315)

hallucination a false sensory experience, such as hearing something in the absence of an external auditory stimulus. (p. 48)

hallucinogens psychedelic ("mind-manifesting") drugs, such as LSD, that distort perceptions and trigger sensory images in the absence of sensory input. (p. 377)

heredity the genetic transfer of characteristics from parents to offspring. (p. 72)

heritability the proportion of variation among people in a group that we can attribute to genes. The heritability of a trait may vary, depending on the population and the environment. (p. 235)

heuristic a simple thinking strategy that often allows you to make judgments and solve problems efficiently; usually speedier but also more error-prone than an *algorithm*. (p. 214)

hierarchy of needs Maslow's pyramid of human needs; at the base are physiological needs. These basic needs must be satisfied before higher-level safety needs, and then psychological needs, become active. (pp. 249, 343)

hindsight bias the tendency to believe, after learning an outcome, that we could have predicted it. (Also known as the *I-knew-it-all-along phenomenon.*) (p. 12)

hippocampus a neural center located in the limbic system; helps process for storage explicit (conscious) memories of facts and events. (pp. 44, 195)

homeostasis a tendency to maintain a balanced or constant internal state; the regulation of any aspect of body chemistry, such as blood glucose, around a particular level. (p. 248)

hormones chemical messengers that are manufactured by the endocrine glands, travel through the bloodstream, and affect other tissues. (p. 39)

hue the dimension of color that is determined by the wavelength of light; what we know as the color names *blue, green,* and so forth. (p. 139)

human factors psychology a field of psychology allied with I/O psychology that explores how people and machines interact and how machines and physical environments can be made safe and easy to use. (p. B-3)

humanistic psychology a historically important perspective that emphasized human growth potential. (p. 5)

hypnosis a social interaction in which one person (the hypnotist) suggests to another person (the subject) that certain perceptions, feelings, thoughts, or behaviors will spontaneously occur. (p. 155)

hypothalamus [hi-po-THAL-uh-muss] a neural structure lying below *(hypo)* the thalamus; directs several maintenance activities (eating, drinking, body temperature), helps govern the endocrine system via the pituitary gland, and is linked to emotion and reward. (p. 44)

hypothesis a testable prediction, often implied by a theory. (p. 14)

id a reservoir of unconscious psychic energy that, according to Freud, strives to satisfy basic sexual and aggressive drives. The id operates on the *pleasure principle*, demanding immediate gratification. (p. 337)

identical (monozygotic) twins individuals who developed from a single fertilized egg that split in two, creating two genetically identical siblings. (p. 76)

identification the process by which, according to Freud, children incorporate their parents' values into their developing superegos. (p. 338)

identity our sense of self; according to Erikson, the adolescent's task is to solidify a sense of self by testing and blending various roles. (p. 93)

illusory correlation perceiving a relationship where none exists, or perceiving a stronger-than-actual relationship. (p. A-5)

implicit memory retention of learned skills, or classically conditioned associations, without conscious awareness. (Also called *nondeclarative memory*.) (p. 191)

inattentional blindness failing to see visible objects when our attention is directed elsewhere. (p. 55)

incentive a positive or negative environmental stimulus that motivates behavior. (p. 248)

independent variable in an experiment, the factor that is manipulated; the variable whose effect is being studied. (p. 21)

individualism giving priority to our own goals over group goals and defining our identity in terms of personal traits rather than group membership. (p. 356)

industrial-organizational (I/O) psychology the application of psychological concepts and methods to human behavior in workplaces. (p. B-3)

informational social influence influence resulting from a person's willingness to accept others' opinions about reality. (p. 308)

informed consent giving people enough information about a study to enable them to decide whether they wish to participate. (p. 25)

ingroup "us"—people with whom we share a common identity. (p. 318)

ingroup bias the tendency to favor our own group. (p. 318)

inner ear the innermost part of the ear, containing the cochlea, semicircular canals, and vestibular sacs. (p. 151)

insight a sudden realization of the solution to a problem; contrasts with strategy-based solutions. (p. 214)

insight therapies therapies that aim to improve psychological functioning by increasing a person's awareness of underlying motives and defenses. (p. 404)

insomnia recurring problems in falling or staying asleep. (p. 63)

intellectual disability a condition of limited mental ability, indicated by an intelligence test score of 70 or below and difficulty adapting to the demands of life. (Formerly referred to as *mental retardation*.) (p. 234)

intelligence the ability to learn from experience, solve problems, and use knowledge to adapt to new situations. (p. 229)

intelligence quotient (IQ) defined originally as the ratio of mental age *(ma)* to chronological age *(ca)* multiplied by 100 (thus, IQ = *ma/ca* × 100). On contemporary intelligence tests, the average performance for a given age is assigned a score of 100. (p. 232)

intelligence test a method for assessing an individual's mental aptitudes and comparing them with those of others, using numerical scores. (p. 232)

intensity the amount of energy in a light wave or sound wave, which influences what we perceive as brightness or loudness. Intensity is determined by the wave's amplitude (height). (p. 139)

interaction the interplay that occurs when the effect of one factor (such as environment) depends on another factor (such as heredity). (p. 73)

internal locus of control the perception that we control our own fate. (p. 284)

interneurons neurons within the brain and spinal cord; they communicate internally and process information between sensory inputs and motor outputs. (p. 36)

interpretation in psychoanalysis, the analyst's noting of supposed dream meanings, resistances, and other significant behaviors and events in order to promote insight. (p. 403)

intersex possessing both male and female biological sexual characteristics at birth. (p. 108)

intimacy in Erikson's theory, the ability to form close, loving relationships; a primary developmental task in early adulthood. (p. 94)

intrinsic motivation the desire to perform a behavior well for its own sake. (p. 260)

intuition an effortless, immediate, automatic feeling or thought, as contrasted with explicit, conscious reasoning. (p. 215)

James-Lange theory the theory that our experience of emotion occurs when we become aware of our physiological responses to an emotion-arousing stimulus. (p. 262)

just-world phenomenon the tendency to believe that the world is just and people therefore get what they deserve and deserve what they get. (p. 318)

kinesthesia [kin-ehs-THEE-zhuh] our movement sense—our system for sensing the position and movement of individual body parts. (p. 158)

language our spoken, written, or signed words, and the ways we combine them to communicate meaning. (p. 223)

latent content according to Freud, the underlying meaning of a dream. (p. 64)

latent learning learning that is not apparent until there is an incentive to demonstrate it. (p. 182)

law of effect Thorndike's principle that behaviors followed by favorable consequences become more likely, and that behaviors followed by unfavorable consequences become less likely. (p. 172)

leadership an individual's ability to motivate and influence others to contribute to their group's success. (p. B-5)

learned helplessness the hopelessness and passive resignation an animal or person learns when unable to avoid repeated aversive events. (p. 283)

learning the process of acquiring, through experience, new and relatively enduring information or behaviors. (p. 166)

limbic system neural system (including the *amygdala, hypothalamus,* and *hippocampus*) located below the cerebral hemispheres; associated with emotions and drives. (p. 44)

lobotomy a psychosurgical procedure once used to calm uncontrollably emotional or violent patients. The procedure cut the nerves connecting the frontal lobes to the emotion-controlling centers of the inner brain. (p. 422)

longitudinal study research that follows and retests the same people over time. (pp. 70, 238, A-6)

long-term memory the relatively permanent and limitless storehouse of the memory system. Includes knowledge, skills, and experiences. (p. 190)

long-term potentiation (LTP) an increase in a nerve cell's firing potential after brief, rapid stimulation. LTP is a neural basis for learning and memory. (p. 198)

LSD (lysergic acid diethylamide) a powerful hallucinogenic drug; also known as acid. (p. 378)

major depressive disorder a disorder in which a person experiences, in the absence of drugs or another medical condition, two or more weeks with five or more symptoms, at least one of which must be either (1) depressed mood or (2) loss of interest or pleasure. (p. 381)

mania a hyperactive, wildly optimistic state in which dangerously poor judgment is common. (p. 382)

manifest content according to Freud, the remembered story line of a dream. (p. 64)

maturation biological growth processes leading to orderly changes in behavior, mostly independent of experience. (p. 77)

mean the arithmetic average of a distribution, obtained by adding the scores and then dividing by the number of scores. (p. A-2)

median the middle score in a distribution; half the scores are above it and half are below it. (p. A-2)

medical model the concept that diseases, in this case psychological disorders, have physical causes that can be *diagnosed, treated,* and, in most cases, *cured,* often through treatment in a *hospital.* (p. 364)

medulla [muh-DUL-uh] the base of the brainstem; controls heartbeat and breathing. (p. 42)

MEG (magnetoencephalography) a brain-imaging technique that measures magnetic fields from the brain's natural electrical activity. (p. 40)

memory the persistence of learning over time through the encoding, storage, and retrieval of information. (p. 190)

memory consolidation the neural storage of a long-term memory. (p. 196)

memory trace lasting physical change in the brain as a memory forms. (p. 203)

menarche [meh-NAR-key] the first menstrual period. (p. 112)

menopause the end of menstruation. In everyday use, it can also mean the biological transition a woman experiences from before until after the end of menstruation. (p. 97)

mental age a measure of intelligence test performance devised by Binet; the level of performance typically associated with children of a certain chronological age. Thus, a child who does as well as an average 8-year-old is said to have a mental age of 8. (p. 232)

mere exposure effect the tendency for repeated exposure to novel stimuli to increase our liking of them. (p. 324)

methamphetamine a powerfully addictive drug that stimulates the central nervous system with speeded-up body functions and associated energy and mood changes; over time, reduces baseline dopamine levels. (p. 377)

middle ear the chamber between the eardrum and cochlea containing three tiny bones—hammer (malleus), anvil (incus), and stirrup (stapes)—that concentrate the vibrations of the eardrum on the cochlea's oval window. (p. 151)

mindfulness meditation a reflective practice in which people attend to current experiences in a nonjudgmental and accepting manner. (p. 290)

Minnesota Multiphasic Personality Inventory (MMPI) the most widely researched and clinically used of all personality tests. Originally developed to identify emotional disorders (still considered its most appropriate use), this test is now used for many other screening purposes. (p. 347)

mirror-image perceptions mutual views often held by conflicting groups, as when each side sees itself as ethical and peaceful and views the other side as evil and aggressive. (p. 330)

mirror neuron a neuron that fires when we perform certain actions and when we observe others performing those actions; a neural basis for imitation and observational learning. (p. 183)

misinformation effect occurs when a memory has been corrupted by misleading information. (p. 206)

mnemonics [nih-MON-iks] memory aids, especially techniques that use vivid imagery and organizational devices. (p. 193)

mode the most frequently occurring score(s) in a distribution. (p. A-2)

modeling the process of observing and imitating a specific behavior. (p. 182)

monocular cue a depth cue, such as interposition or linear perspective, available to either eye alone. (p. 146)

mood-congruent memory the tendency to recall experiences that are consistent with your current good or bad mood. (p. 201)

motivation a need or desire that energizes and directs behavior. (p. 248)

motor cortex the cerebral cortex area at the rear of the frontal lobes; controls voluntary movements. (p. 46)

motor neurons neurons that carry outgoing information from the brain and spinal cord to the muscles and glands. (p. 36)

MRI (magnetic resonance imaging) a technique that uses magnetic fields and radio waves to produce computer-generated images of soft tissue. MRI scans show brain anatomy. (p. 40)

narcissism excessive self-love and self-absorption. (pp. 258, 354)

narcolepsy a sleep disorder in which a person has uncontrollable sleep attacks, sometimes lapsing directly into REM sleep. (p. 63)

natural selection the principle that inherited traits that better enable an organism to survive and reproduce in a particular environment will (in competition with other trait variations) most likely be passed on to subsequent generations. (p. 126)

naturalistic observation a descriptive technique of observing and recording behavior in naturally occurring situations without trying to change or control the situation. (p. 16)

nature–nurture issue the age-old controversy over the relative influence of genes and experience in the development of psychological traits and behaviors. Today's psychological science sees traits and behaviors arising from the interaction of nature and nurture. (p. 9)

near-death experience an altered state of consciousness reported after a close brush with death (such as cardiac arrest); often similar to drug-induced hallucinations. (p. 377)

need to belong the need to build and maintain relationships and to feel part of a group. (p. 255)

negative reinforcement increasing behaviors by stopping or reducing aversive stimuli, such as an electric shock. A negative reinforcer is anything that, when *removed* after a response, strengthens the response. (*Note:* Negative reinforcement is *not* punishment.) (p. 174)

nerves bundled axons that form neural cables connecting the central nervous system with muscles, glands, and sense organs. (p. 36)

nervous system the body's speedy, electrochemical communication network, consisting of all the nerve cells of the central and peripheral nervous systems. (p. 36)

neurogenesis the formation of new neurons. (p. 50)

neuron a nerve cell; the basic building block of the nervous system. (p. 32)

neurotransmitters neuron-produced chemicals that cross the synaptic gap to carry messages to other neurons or to muscles and glands. (p. 34)

neutral stimulus (NS) in classical conditioning, a stimulus that evokes no response before conditioning. (p. 168)

nicotine a stimulating and highly addictive psychoactive drug in tobacco products. (p. 375)

night terrors a sleep disorder characterized by high arousal and an appearance of being terrified; unlike nightmares, night terrors occur during N3 sleep and are infrequently remembered. (p. 63)

normal curve a symmetrical, bell-shaped curve that describes the distribution of many types of data. Most scores fall near the average, or *mean* (about 68 percent fall within one *standard deviation* of it) and fewer and fewer scores lie near the extremes. (Also called a *normal distribution*.) (pp. 234, A-3)

normative social influence influence resulting from a person's desire to gain approval or avoid disapproval. (p. 308)

nudge framing choices in a way that encourages people to make decisions that support their personal well-being. (p. 219)

obesity defined as a body mass index (BMI) measurement of 30 or higher, which is calculated from our weight-to-height ratio. (Individuals who are *overweight* have a BMI of 25 or higher.) (p. 253)

object permanence the awareness that things continue to exist even when not perceived. (p. 80)

observational learning learning by observing others. (p. 182)

obsessive-compulsive disorder (OCD) a disorder characterized by unwanted repetitive thoughts (obsessions), actions (compulsions), or both. (p. 368)

occipital [ahk-SIP-uh-tuhl] **lobes** the portion of the cerebral cortex lying at the back of the head; includes areas that receive information from the visual fields. (p. 46)

Oedipus [ED-uh-puss] **complex** according to Freud, a boy's sexual desires toward his mother and feelings of jealousy and hatred for the rival father. (p. 338)

one-word stage the stage in speech development, from about age 1 to 2, during which a child speaks mostly in single words. (p. 224)

operant behavior behavior that operates on the environment, producing a consequence. (p. 167)

operant chamber in operant conditioning research, a chamber (also known as a *Skinner box*) containing a bar or key that an animal can manipulate to obtain a food or water reinforcer; attached devices record the animal's rate of bar pressing or key pecking. (p. 172)

operant conditioning a type of learning in which a behavior becomes more probable if followed by a reinforcer or less probable if followed by a punisher. (p. 172)

operational definition a carefully worded statement of the exact procedures (operations) used in a research study. For example, *human intelligence* may be operationally defined as what an intelligence test measures. (p. 15)

opiates opium and its derivatives, such as morphine and heroin; depress neural activity, temporarily lessening pain and anxiety. (pp. 35, 374)

opponent-process theory the theory that opposing retinal processes (red-green, blue-yellow, white-black) enable color vision. For example, some cells are turned "on" by green and turned "off" by red; others are turned on by red and off by green. (p. 142)

optic nerve the nerve that carries neural impulses from the eye to the brain. (p. 140)

optimism the anticipation of positive outcomes. Optimists are people who expect the best and expect their efforts to lead to good things. (p. 285)

organizational psychology an I/O psychology subfield that examines organizational influences on worker satisfaction and productivity and facilitates organizational change. (p. B-3)

ostracism deliberate social exclusion of individuals or groups. (p. 256)

other-race effect the tendency to recall faces of one's own race more accurately than faces of other races. (p. 318)

outgroup "them"—those perceived as different or apart from our ingroup. (p. 318)

overconfidence the tendency to be more confident than correct—to overestimate the accuracy of our beliefs and judgments. (p. 218)

panic disorder an anxiety disorder marked by unpredictable minutes-long episodes of intense dread in which a person may experience terror and accompanying chest pain, choking, or other frightening sensations; often followed by worry over a possible next attack. (p. 367)

parallel processing processing many aspects of a stimulus or problem at the same time. (pp. 54, 143, 192)

paraphilias sexual arousal from fantasies, behaviors, or urges involving nonhuman objects, the suffering of self or others, and/or nonconsenting persons. (p. 119)

parasympathetic nervous system autonomic nervous system subdivision that calms the body, conserving its energy. (p. 37)

parietal [puh-RYE-uh-tuhl] **lobes** the portion of the cerebral cortex lying at the top of the head and toward the rear; receives sensory input for touch and body position. (p. 46)

partial (intermittent) reinforcement reinforcing a response only part of the time; results in slower acquisition but much greater resistance to extinction than does continuous reinforcement. (p. 175)

passionate love an aroused state of intense positive absorption in another, usually present at the beginning of romantic love. (p. 327)

perception the process by which our brain organizes and interprets sensory information, transforming it into meaningful objects and events. (p. 132)

perceptual adaptation the ability to adjust to changed sensory input, including an artificially displaced or even inverted visual field. (p. 149)

perceptual constancy perceiving objects as unchanging (having consistent color, shape, and size) even as illumination and retinal images change. (p. 148)

perceptual set mental tendencies and assumptions that set us up to perceive one thing and not another. (p. 136)

peripheral nervous system (PNS) the sensory and motor neurons connecting the central nervous system to the rest of the body. (p. 36)

peripheral route persuasion occurs when people are influenced by unimportant cues, such as a speaker's attractiveness. (p. 305)

personal control our sense of controlling our environment rather than feeling helpless. (p. 283)

personality an individual's characteristic pattern of thinking, feeling, and acting. (p. 336)

personality disorders inflexible and enduring behavior patterns that impair social functioning. (p. 393)

personality inventory a questionnaire (often with *true-false* or *agree-disagree* items) on which people respond to items designed to gauge a wide range of feelings and behaviors; used to assess selected personality traits. (p. 347)

person-centered therapy a humanistic therapy, developed by Carl Rogers, in which the therapist uses techniques such as *active listening* within an accepting, genuine, empathic environment to facilitate clients' growth. (Also called *client-centered therapy*.) (p. 404)

personnel psychology an I/O psychology subfield that helps with job seeking, and with employee recruitment, selection, placement, training, appraisal, and development. (p. B-3)

pessimism the anticipation of negative outcomes. Pessimists are people who expect the worst and doubt that their goals will be achieved. (p. 286)

PET (positron emission tomography) scan a view of brain activity showing where a radioactive form of glucose goes while the brain performs a given task. (p. 40)

phobia an anxiety disorder marked by a persistent, irrational fear and avoidance of a specific object, activity, or situation. (p. 368)

physiological need a basic bodily requirement. (p. 248)

pitch a tone's experienced highness or lowness; depends on frequency. (p. 151)

pituitary gland the most influential endocrine gland. Under the influence of the hypothalamus, the pituitary regulates growth and controls other endocrine glands. (p. 40)

placebo [pluh-SEE-bo; Latin for "I shall please"] an inactive substance or condition that is sometimes given to those in a control group in place of the treatment given to the experimental group. (p. 21)

placebo effect results caused by expectations alone. (p. 21)

plasticity the brain's ability to change, especially during childhood, by reorganizing after damage or by building new pathways based on experience. (p. 32)

polygraph a machine often used in attempts to detect lies that measures emotion-linked changes in perspiration, heart rate, and breathing. (p. 267)

population all those in a group being studied, from which random samples may be drawn. (*Note:* Except for national studies, this does *not* refer to a country's whole population.) (p. 17)

positive psychology the scientific study of human flourishing, with the goals of discovering and promoting strengths and virtues that help individuals and communities to thrive. (p. 11)

positive reinforcement increasing behaviors by presenting a pleasurable stimulus, such as food. A positive reinforcer is anything that, when presented after a response, strengthens the response. (p. 174)

posthypnotic suggestion a suggestion, made during a hypnosis session, to be carried out after the subject is no longer hypnotized; used by some clinicians to help control undesired symptoms and behaviors. (p. 156)

posttraumatic growth positive psychological changes as a result of struggling with extremely challenging circumstances and life crises. (p. 424)

posttraumatic stress disorder (PTSD) a disorder characterized by haunting memories, nightmares, hypervigilance, avoidance of trauma-related stimuli, social withdrawal, jumpy anxiety, numbness of feeling, and/or insomnia lingering for four weeks or more after a traumatic experience. (p. 368)

predictive validity the success with which a test predicts the behavior it is designed to predict. (p. 234)

prejudice an unfair and usually negative attitude toward a group and its members. Prejudice generally involves negative feelings, stereotyped beliefs, and a predisposition to discriminatory action. (p. 315)

preoperational stage in Piaget's theory, the stage (from about 2 to 6 or 7 years of age) in which a child learns to use language but cannot yet perform the mental operations of concrete logic. (p. 81)

preregistration publicly communicating planned study design, hypotheses, data collection, and analyses. (p. 15)

primary reinforcer an event that is innately reinforcing, often by satisfying a biological need. (p. 174)

primary sex characteristics the body structures (ovaries, testes, and external genitalia) that make sexual reproduction possible. (p. 111)

priming the activation, often unconsciously, of associations in our mind, thus setting us up to perceive, remember, or respond to objects or events in certain ways. (pp. 134, 200)

proactive interference the forward-acting disruptive effect of older learning on the recall of *new* information. (p. 204)

problem-focused coping attempting to reduce stress directly—by changing the stressor or the way we interact with that stressor. (p. 282)

projective test a personality test, such as the Rorschach or TAT, that provides ambiguous images designed to trigger projection of the test-taker's unconscious thoughts or feelings. (p. 340)

prosocial behavior positive, constructive, helpful behavior. The opposite of antisocial behavior. (p. 184)

prototype a mental image or best example of a category. Matching new items to a prototype provides a quick and easy method for sorting items into categories (as when you compare a feathered creature to a prototypical bird, such as a crow). (p. 214)

psychiatry a branch of medicine dealing with psychological disorders; practiced by physicians who sometimes provide medical (for example, drug) treatments as well as psychological therapy. (p. 10)

psychoactive drug a chemical substance that alters perceptions and mood. (p. 371)

psychoanalysis (1) Freud's theory of personality that attributes thoughts and actions to unconscious motives and conflicts. (2) Freud's therapeutic technique used in treating psychological disorders. Freud believed the patient's free associations, resistances, dreams, and transferences—and the analyst's interpretations of them—released previously repressed feelings, allowing the patient to gain self-insight. (pp. 336, 402)

psychodynamic theories theories that view personality with a focus on the unconscious and the importance of childhood experiences. (p. 336)

psychodynamic therapy therapy deriving from the psychoanalytic tradition; views individuals as responding to unconscious forces and childhood experiences, and seeks to enhance self-insight. (p. 403)

psychological disorder a syndrome marked by a clinically significant disturbance in a person's cognition, emotion regulation, or behavior. (p. 362)

psychology the science of behavior and mental processes. (p. 6)

psychoneuroimmunology the study of how psychological, neural, and endocrine processes combine to affect our immune system and health. (p. 279)

psychosexual stages the childhood stages of development (oral, anal, phallic, latency, genital) during which, according to Freud, the id's pleasure-seeking energies focus on distinct erogenous zones. (p. 338)

psychosurgery surgery that removes or destroys brain tissue in an effort to change behavior. (p. 422)

psychotherapy treatment involving psychological techniques; consists of interactions between a trained therapist and someone seeking to overcome psychological difficulties or achieve personal growth. (p. 402)

psychotic disorders a group of disorders marked by irrational ideas, distorted perceptions, and a loss of contact with reality. (p. 386)

puberty the period of sexual maturation, during which a person becomes capable of reproducing. (pp. 90, 111)

punishment an event that decreases the behavior it follows. (p. 176)

random assignment assigning participants to experimental and control groups by chance, thus minimizing any preexisting differences between the groups. (p. 20)

random sample a sample that fairly represents a population because each member has an equal chance of inclusion. (p. 17)

range the difference between the highest and lowest scores in a distribution. (p. A-2)

recall memory demonstrated by retrieving information learned earlier, as on a fill-in-the-blank test. (p. 198)

reciprocal determinism the interacting influences of behavior, internal personal factors, and environment. (p. 351)

reciprocity norm an expectation that people will help, not hurt, those who have helped them. (p. 330)

recognition memory demonstrated by identifying items previously learned, as on a multiple-choice test. (p. 198)

reconsolidation a process in which previously stored memories, when retrieved, are potentially altered before being stored again. (p. 206)

reflex a simple, automatic response to a sensory stimulus, such as the knee-jerk response. (pp. 38, 75)

refractory period (1) in neural processing, a brief resting pause that occurs after a neuron has fired;

subsequent action potentials cannot occur until the axon returns to its resting state. (2) in human sexuality, a resting pause that occurs after orgasm, during which a person cannot achieve another orgasm. (pp. 34, 118)

regression toward the mean the tendency for extreme or unusual scores or events to fall back (regress) toward the average. (p. A-5)

reinforcement in operant conditioning, any event that *strengthens* the behavior it follows. (p. 173)

reinforcement schedule a pattern that defines how often a desired response will be reinforced. (p. 175)

relational aggression an act of aggression (physical or verbal) intended to harm a person's relationship or social standing. (p. 108)

relative deprivation the perception that we are worse off relative to those with whom we compare ourselves. (p. 296)

relearning memory demonstrated by time saved when learning material again. (p. 198)

reliability the extent to which a test yields consistent results, as assessed by the consistency of scores on two halves of the test, on alternative forms of the test, or on retesting. (p. 234)

REM rebound the tendency for REM sleep to increase following REM sleep deprivation. (p. 65)

REM (R) sleep rapid eye movement sleep; a recurring sleep stage during which vivid dreams commonly occur. Also known as *paradoxical sleep,* because the muscles are relaxed (except for minor twitches) but other body systems are active. (p. 57)

replication repeating the essence of a research study, usually with different participants in different situations, to see whether the basic finding can be reproduced. (p. 15)

representativeness heuristic judging the likelihood of events in terms of how well they seem to represent, or match, particular prototypes; may lead us to ignore other relevant information. (p. 216)

repression in psychoanalytic theory, the basic defense mechanism that banishes from consciousness the thoughts, feelings, and memories that arouse anxiety. (pp. 205, 339)

resilience the personal strength that helps most people cope with stress and recover from adversity and even trauma. (pp. 293, 424)

resistance in psychoanalysis, the blocking from consciousness of anxiety-laden material. (p. 403)

respondent behavior behavior that occurs as an automatic response to some stimulus. (p. 167)

reticular formation nerve network running through the brainstem and into the thalamus; plays an important role in controlling arousal. (p. 43)

retina the light-sensitive inner surface of the eye. Contains the receptor rods and cones plus layers of neurons that begin the processing of visual information. (p. 139)

retinal disparity a binocular cue for perceiving depth. By comparing images from the two eyes, the brain computes distance—the greater the disparity (difference) between the two images, the closer the object. (p. 146)

retrieval the process of getting information out of memory storage. (p. 190)

retrieval cue any stimulus (event, feeling, place, and so on) linked to a specific memory. (p. 200)

retroactive interference the backward-acting disruptive effect of newer learning on the recall of **old** information. (p. 204)

retrograde amnesia an inability to remember information from our past. (p. 202)

reuptake a neurotransmitter's reabsorption by the sending neuron. (p. 34)

rods retinal receptors that detect black, white, and gray, and are sensitive to movement. Rods are necessary for peripheral and twilight vision, when cones don't respond. (p. 140)

role a set of expectations (*norms*) about a social position, defining how those in the position ought to behave. (pp. 113, 304)

Rorschach inkblot test the most widely used projective test; a set of 10 inkblots, designed by Hermann Rorschach; seeks to identify people's inner feelings by analyzing their interpretations of the blots. (p. 341)

savant syndrome a condition in which a person otherwise limited in mental ability has an exceptional specific skill, such as in computation or drawing. (p. 229)

scaffold in Vygotsky's theory, a framework that offers children temporary support as they develop higher levels of thinking. (p. 83)

scapegoat theory the theory that prejudice offers an outlet for anger by providing someone to blame. (p. 318)

scatterplot a graphed cluster of dots, each of which represents the values of two variables. The slope of the points suggests the direction of the relationship between the two variables. The amount of scatter suggests the strength of the correlation (little scatter indicates high correlation). (p. A-4)

schema a concept or framework that organizes and interprets information. (p. 80)

schizophrenia a disorder characterized by delusions, hallucinations, disorganized speech, and/or diminished, inappropriate emotional expression. (p. 386)

secondary sex characteristics nonreproductive sexual traits, such as female breasts and hips, male voice quality, and body hair. (p. 112)

selective attention focusing conscious awareness on a particular stimulus. (p. 54)

self your image and understanding of who you are; in modern psychology, the idea that this is the center of personality, organizing your thoughts, feelings, and actions. (p. 353)

self-actualization according to Maslow, the psychological need that arises after basic physical and psychological needs are met and self-esteem is achieved; the motivation to fulfill our potential. (p. 343)

self-concept all our thoughts and feelings about ourselves, in answer to the question, "Who am I?" (p. 344)

self-control the ability to control impulses and delay short-term gratification for greater long-term rewards. (p. 285)

self-determination theory the theory that we feel motivated to satisfy our needs for competence, autonomy, and relatedness. (p. 256)

self-disclosure revealing intimate aspects of ourselves to others. (p. 328)

self-efficacy our sense of competence and effectiveness. (p. 351)

self-esteem our feelings of high or low self-worth. (p. 354)

self-fulfilling prophecy a belief that leads to its own fulfillment. (p. 330)

self-serving bias our readiness to perceive ourselves favorably. (p. 355)

self-transcendence according to Maslow, the striving for identity, meaning, and purpose beyond the self. (p. 343)

semantic memory explicit memory of facts and general knowledge; one of our two conscious memory systems (the other is *episodic memory*). (p. 195)

sensation the process by which our sensory receptors and nervous system receive and represent stimulus energies from our environment. (p. 132)

sensorimotor stage in Piaget's theory, the stage (from birth to nearly 2 years of age) at which infants know the world mostly in terms of their sensory impressions and motor activities. (p. 80)

sensorineural hearing loss hearing loss caused by damage to the cochlea's receptor cells or to the auditory nerve. The most common form of hearing loss (also called *nerve deafness*). (p. 151)

sensory adaptation reduced sensitivity in response to constant stimulation. (p. 135)

sensory interaction the principle that one sense may influence another, as when the smell of food influences its taste. (p. 159)

sensory memory the immediate, very brief recording of sensory information in the memory system. (p. 190)

sensory neurons neurons that carry incoming information from the body's tissues and sensory receptors to the brain and spinal cord. (p. 36)

sensory receptors sensory nerve endings that respond to stimuli. (p. 132)

sequential processing processing one aspect of a stimulus or problem at a time; generally used to process new information or to solve difficult problems. (p. 54)

serial position effect our tendency to recall best the last and first items in a list. (p. 201)

set point the point at which your "weight thermostat" may be set. When your body falls below this weight, increased hunger and a lowered metabolic rate may combine to restore lost weight. (p. 252)

sex in psychology, the biologically influenced characteristics by which people define *male, female,* and *intersex.* (p. 108)

sexual aggression any physical or verbal behavior of a sexual nature that is intended to harm someone physically or emotionally. Can be expressed as either sexual harassment or *sexual assault*. (p. 114)

sexual dysfunction a problem that consistently impairs sexual arousal or functioning. (p. 118)

sexual orientation the direction of our sexual attractions, as reflected in our longings and fantasies. (p.121)

sexual response cycle the four stages of sexual responding described by Masters and Johnson—excitement, plateau, orgasm, and resolution. (p. 118)

shaping an operant conditioning procedure in which reinforcers guide actions closer and closer toward a desired behavior. (p. 173)

short-term memory activated memory that holds a few items briefly (such as digits of a phone number while calling) before the information is stored or forgotten. (p. 190)

sleep a periodic, natural loss of consciousness—as distinct from unconsciousness resulting from a coma, general anesthesia, or hibernation. (p. 57)

sleep apnea a sleep disorder in which a sleeping person repeatedly stops breathing until blood oxygen is so low the person awakens just long enough to draw a breath. (p. 63)

social clock the culturally preferred timing of social events such as marriage, parenthood, and retirement. (p. 101)

social-cognitive perspective a view of behavior as influenced by the interaction between persons (and their thinking) and their social context. (p. 351)

social facilitation improved performance on simple or well-learned tasks in the presence of others. (p. 311)

social identity the "we" aspect of our self-concept; the part of our answer to "Who am I?" that comes from our group memberships. (p. 93)

social leadership group-oriented leadership that builds teamwork, resolves conflict, and offers support. (p. B-6)

social learning theory the theory that we learn social behavior by observing and imitating and by being rewarded or punished. (p. 114)

social loafing the tendency for people in a group to exert less effort when pooling their efforts toward attaining a common goal than when individually accountable. (p. 312)

social psychology the scientific study of how we think about, influence, and relate to one another. (p. 302)

social-responsibility norm an expectation that people will help those needing their help. (p. 330)

social script a culturally modeled guide for how to act in various situations. (pp. 121, 322)

somatic nervous system peripheral nervous system division that controls the body's skeletal muscles. Also called the *skeletal nervous system*. (p. 36)

somatosensory cortex the cerebral cortex area at the front of the parietal lobes; registers and processes body touch and movement sensations. (p. 48)

source amnesia faulty memory for how, when, or where information was learned or imagined. (p. 207)

spacing effect the tendency for distributed study or practice to yield better long-term retention than is achieved through massed study or practice. (p. 194)

spermarche [sper-MAR-key] the first ejaculation. (p. 112)

split brain a condition resulting from surgery that separates the brain's two hemispheres by cutting the fibers (mainly those of the corpus callosum) connecting them. (p. 51)

spontaneous recovery the reappearance, after a pause, of an extinguished conditioned response. (p. 170)

spotlight effect overestimating others' noticing and evaluating our appearance, performance, and blunders (as if we presume a spotlight shines on us). (p. 353)

SQ3R a study method incorporating five steps: Survey, Question, Read, Retrieve, Review. (p. 26)

standard deviation a computed measure of how much scores vary around the mean score. (p. A-2)

standardization defining uniform testing procedures and meaningful scores by comparison with the performance of a pretested group. (p. 233)

Stanford-Binet the widely used American revision (by Terman at Stanford University) of Binet's original intelligence test. (p. 232)

statistical significance a statistical statement of how likely it is that an obtained result occurred by chance. (p. A-7)

stereotype a generalized (sometimes accurate but often overgeneralized) belief about a group of people. (p. 315)

stereotype threat a self-confirming concern that you will be judged based on a negative stereotype. (p. 243)

stimulants drugs (such as caffeine, nicotine, and the more powerful cocaine, amphetamines, methamphetamine, and Ecstasy) that excite neural activity and speed up body functions. (p. 374)

stimulus any event or situation that evokes a response. (p. 167)

storage the process of retaining encoded information over time. (p. 190)

stranger anxiety the fear of strangers that infants commonly display, beginning by about 8 months of age. (p. 85)

stress the process by which we perceive and respond to certain events, called *stressors*, that we appraise as threatening or challenging. (p. 276)

structuralism an early school of thought promoted by Wundt that focused on the structure of the human mind. (p. 5)

subjective well-being self-perceived happiness or satisfaction with life. Used along with measures of objective well-being (for example, physical and economic indicators) to judge our quality of life. (p. 294)

subliminal below a person's absolute threshold for conscious awareness. (p. 133)

substance use disorder disorder characterized by continued substance craving and use despite significant life disruption and/or physical risk. (p. 371)

superego the part of personality that, according to Freud, represents internalized ideals and provides standards for judgment (the conscience) and for future goals. (p. 338)

superordinate goals shared goals that override differences among people and require their cooperation. (p. 331)

suprachiasmatic nucleus (SCN) a pair of cell clusters in the hypothalamus that controls circadian rhythm. In response to light, the SCN adjusts melatonin production, thus modifying our feelings of sleepiness. (p. 60)

survey a descriptive technique for obtaining the self-reported attitudes or behaviors of a group, usually by questioning a representative, *random sample* of that group. (p. 17)

sympathetic nervous system autonomic nervous system subdivision that arouses the body, mobilizing its energy. (p. 37)

synapse [SIN-aps] the junction between the axon tip of a sending neuron and the dendrite or cell body of a receiving neuron. The tiny gap at this junction is called the *synaptic gap* or *synaptic cleft*. (p. 33)

systematic desensitization a type of exposure therapy that associates a pleasant, relaxed state with gradually increasing, anxiety-triggering stimuli. Commonly used to treat phobias. (p. 406)

task leadership goal-oriented leadership that sets standards, organizes work, and focuses attention on goals. (p. B-6)

telegraphic speech the early speech stage in which a child speaks in compressed sentences, like a telegram—"want milk" or "Daddy go store"—using mostly nouns and verbs. (p. 224)

temperament a person's characteristic emotional reactivity and intensity. (p. 76)

temporal lobes the portion of the cerebral cortex lying roughly above the ears; includes areas that receive information from the ears. (p. 46)

tend-and-befriend response under stress, people (especially women) often provide support to others *(tend)* and bond with and seek support from others *(befriend)*. (p. 278)

teratogens [tuh-RAT-uh-jenz] agents, such as chemicals or viruses, that can reach the embryo or fetus during prenatal development and cause harm. (p, 74)

testing effect enhanced memory after retrieving, rather than simply rereading, information. Also sometimes referred to as a *retrieval practice effect* or *test-enhanced learning*. (pp. 26, 194)

testosterone the most important male sex hormone. Both males and females have it, but the additional testosterone in males stimulates the growth of the male sex organs during the fetal period, and the development of the male sex characteristics during puberty. (p. 111)

thalamus [THAL-uh-muss] the brain's sensory control center, located on top of the brainstem; directs sensory messages to the cortex and transmits replies to the cerebellum and medulla. (p. 42)

THC the major active ingredient in marijuana; triggers a variety of effects, including mild hallucinations. (p. 378)

Thematic Apperception Test (TAT) a projective test in which people express their inner feelings and interests through the stories they make up about ambiguous scenes. (p. 340)

theory an explanation using principles that organize observations and predict behaviors or events. (p. 14)

theory of mind people's ideas about their own and others' mental states—about their feelings, perceptions, and thoughts, and the behaviors these might predict. (p. 84)

therapeutic alliance a bond of trust and mutual understanding between a therapist and client, who work together constructively to overcome the client's problem. (p. 415)

threshold the level of stimulation required to trigger a neural impulse. (p. 34)

token economy an operant conditioning procedure in which people earn a token for exhibiting a desired behavior and can later exchange the tokens for privileges or treats. (p. 408)

tolerance a dwindling effect with regular use of the same dose of a drug, requiring the user to take larger and larger doses before experiencing the drug's effect. (p. 372)

top-down processing information processing guided by higher-level mental processes, as when we construct perceptions drawing on our experience and expectations. (p. 132)

trait a characteristic pattern of behavior or a tendency to feel and act in certain ways, as assessed by self-report inventories and peer reports. (p. 346)

transcranial magnetic stimulation (TMS) the application of repeated pulses of magnetic energy to the brain; used to stimulate or suppress brain activity. (p. 421)

transduction changing one form of energy into another. In sensation, the transforming of stimulus energies (such as sights, sounds, and smells) into neural impulses our brain can interpret. (p. 132)

transference in psychoanalysis, the patient's transfer to the analyst of emotions linked with other relationships (such as love or hatred for a parent). (p. 403)

transgender an umbrella term describing people whose gender identity or expression differs from that associated with their birth-designated sex. (p. 116)

two-factor theory Schachter and Singer's theory that to experience emotion we must (1) be physically aroused and (2) cognitively label the arousal. (p. 263)

two-word stage the stage in speech development, beginning about age 2, during which a child speaks mostly in two-word statements. (p. 224)

Type A Friedman and Rosenman's term for competitive, hard-driving, impatient, verbally aggressive, and anger-prone people. (p. 281)

Type B Friedman and Rosenman's term for easygoing, relaxed people. (p. 281)

unconditional positive regard a caring, accepting, nonjudgmental attitude, which Carl Rogers believed would help people develop self-awareness and self-acceptance. (pp. 344, 405)

unconditioned response (UR) in classical conditioning, an unlearned, naturally occurring response (such as salivation) to an unconditioned stimulus (US) (such as food in the mouth). (p. 168)

unconditioned stimulus (US) in classical conditioning, a stimulus that unconditionally—naturally and automatically—triggers a response (UR). (p. 168)

unconscious according to Freud, a reservoir of mostly unacceptable thoughts, wishes, feelings, and memories. According to contemporary psychologists, information processing of which we are unaware. (p. 336)

validity the extent to which a test measures or predicts what it is supposed to. (See also *predictive validity*.) (p. 234)

variable anything that can vary and is feasible and ethical to measure. (p. A-4)

variable-interval schedule in operant conditioning, a reinforcement schedule that reinforces a response at unpredictable time intervals. (p. 176)

variable-ratio schedule in operant conditioning, a reinforcement schedule that reinforces a response after an unpredictable number of responses. (p. 176)

vestibular sense our sense of balance—our sense of body movement and position that enables our sense of balance. (p. 158)

virtual reality exposure therapy a counterconditioning technique that treats anxiety through creative electronic simulations in which people can safely face their greatest fears, such as airplane flying, spiders, or public speaking. (p. 407)

visual cliff a laboratory device for testing depth perception in infants and young animals. (p. 146)

wavelength the distance from the peak of one light wave or sound wave to the peak of the next. (p. 139)

Weber's law the principle that, to be perceived as different, two stimuli must differ by a constant minimum percentage (rather than a constant amount). (p. 135)

Wechsler Adult Intelligence Scale (WAIS) the WAIS and its companion versions for children are the most widely used intelligence tests; they contain verbal and performance (nonverbal) subtests. (p. 233)

Wernicke's area a brain area, usually in the left temporal lobe, involved in language comprehension and expression. (p. 226)

withdrawal the discomfort and distress that follow ending the use of an addictive drug or behavior. (p. 372)

working memory a newer understanding of short-term memory that adds conscious, active processing of incoming sensory information, and of information retrieved from long-term memory. (p. 190)

X chromosome the sex chromosome found in both males and females. Females typically have two X chromosomes; males typically have one. An X chromosome from each parent produces a female child. (p. 111)

Y chromosome the sex chromosome found only in males. When paired with an X chromosome from the mother, it produces a male child. (p. 111)

Yerkes-Dodson law the principle that performance increases with arousal only up to a point, beyond which performance decreases. (p. 249)

Young-Helmholtz trichromatic (three-color) theory the theory that the retina contains three different types of color receptors—one most sensitive to red, one to green, one to blue. When stimulated in combination, these receptors can produce the perception of any color. (p. 142)

zygote the fertilized egg; it enters a 2-week period of rapid cell division and develops into an embryo. (p. 74)

GLOSARIO

absolute threshold/umbral absoluto Energía de estimulación mínima necesaria para detectar una estimulación dada el 50 por ciento del tiempo. (pág. 133)

accommodation/acomodo Adaptación de nuestros entendimientos (esquemas) actuales de manera que incorporen información nueva. (pág. 80)

achievement motivation/motivación de logro Deseo de lograr algo importante, para el dominio maestral de destrezas o ideas; para el control; deseo de alcanzar una norma alta. (pág. 259)

achievement test/prueba de rendimiento Prueba diseñada para evaluar lo que una persona ha aprendido. (pág. 232)

acquisition/adquisición Según el condicionamiento clásico, etapa inicial en la que relacionamos un estímulo neutral con uno incondicionado, de tal modo que el estímulo neutral comience a desencadenar la respuesta condicionada. (Según el condicionamiento operante, intensificación de una respuesta reforzada). (pág. 169)

action potential/potencial de acción Impulso nervioso. Carga eléctrica de corta duración que viaja a través del axón. (pág. 32)

active listening/escucha activa Escucha empática en la que el oyente hace eco, reitera y aclara. Característica de la terapia de Rogers centrada en la persona. (pág. 404)

acute schizophrenia/esquizofrenia aguda (también se le dice *esquizofrenia reactiva*). Tipo de esquizofrenia que puede comenzar a cualquier edad; se produce con frecuencia en respuesta a un evento emocionalmente traumático y de este tipo de esquizofrenia la recuperación es mucho más probable. (pág. 388)

adaptation-level phenomenon/fenómeno del nivel de adaptación Nuestra tendencia de formar juicios (de sonidos, de luces, de ingresos) con relación a un nivel neutro definido por nuestras vivencias anteriores. (pág. 296)

adolescence/adolescencia Período de transición de la niñez a la madurez, extendiéndose de la pubertad a la independencia. (pág. 90)

adrenal glands/glándulas suprarrenales Par de glándulas endocrinas ubicadas sobre los riñones que segregan hormonas (epinefrina y norepinefrina) que contribuyen a la estimulación del cuerpo en presencia de situaciones de tensión. (pág. 39)

aerobic exercise/ejercicios aeróbicos Actividad sostenida que mejora la salud cardíaca y pulmonar; ayuda a reducir también la depresión y la ansiedad. (pág. 288)

aggression/agresión Toda conducta que tiene por fin hacerle daño a alguien, sea física o emocionalmente. (pág. 108, 320)

AIDS (acquired immune deficiency syndrome)/SIDA (síndrome de inmunodeficiencia adquirida) Infección que se transmite sexualmente y que atenta contra la vida misma, causada por el *virus de inmunodeficiencia humana* (VIH). El SIDA debilita el sistema inmunitario, lo que aumenta la vulnerabilidad de la persona a infecciones. (pág. 119)

alcohol use disorder/trastorno de uso del alcohol (conocido comúnmente como *alcoholismo*) Consumo de alcohol caracterizado por tolerancia, síntomas de abstinencia cuando se interrumpe el consumo y deseo de seguir consumiéndolo de manera problemática. (pág. 374)

algorithm/algoritmo Regla o procedimiento metódico y lógico que garantiza la resolución de un problema dado. Contrasta con el empleo de la *heurística*, un método generalmente más rápido pero también más propenso a registrar errores. (pág. 214)

all-or-none response/respuesta de todo o nada Reacción que produce una neurona al activarse (con una respuesta de máxima intensidad) o al no activarse. (pág. 34)

alpha waves/ritmo alfa Ritmo con ondas cerebrales relativamente lentas que corresponden a un estado relajado y de vigilia. (pág. 57)

altruism/altruismo Consideración desinteresada por el bienestar de los demás. (pág. 328)

amphetamines/anfetaminas Medicamentos que estimulan la actividad neuronal, acelerando las funciones corporales y cambiando el humor y los niveles de energía. (pág. 377)

amygdala/amígdala Dos conjuntos de fibras nerviosas del tamaño de un haba que se hallan en el sistema límbico e intervienen en las emociones. (pág. 44)

androgyny/androginia Que presenta características psicológicas tradicionales tanto masculinas como femeninas. (pág. 114)

anorexia nervosa/anorexia nerviosa Trastorno alimentario en el cual una persona (generalmente una mujer adolescente) se somete a una dieta de hambre a pesar de padecer de delgadez extrema; a veces acompañada de ejercicios excesivos. (pág. 390)

anterograde amnesia/amnesia anterógrada Incapacidad para formar nuevos recuerdos. (pág. 202)

antianxiety drugs/medicamentos ansiolíticos Medicamentos recetados para aliviar los síntomas de la ansiedad y la agitación. (pág. 419)

antidepressant drugs/medicamentos antidepresivos Medicamentos que se usan para tratar la depresión y los trastornos de ansiedad, obsesivo-compulsivo o de estrés postraumático. (Varios de los medicamentos más usados son *inhibidores selectivos de la recaptación de serotonina:* los ISRS). (pág. 419)

antipsychotic drugs/medicamentos antipsicóticos Medicamentos recetados para tratar la esquizofrenia y otros tipos de trastornos graves del pensamiento. (pág. 417)

antisocial personality disorder/trastorno de personalidad antisocial Trastorno de la personalidad que se manifiesta cuando la persona (generalmente un hombre) no exhibe sentimiento de culpa por actuar con maldad, incluso hacia los amigos y miembros de la familia; puede ser agresivo y cruel o puede ser un timador listo. (pág. 393)

anxiety disorders/trastornos de ansiedad Trastornos psicológicos que se caracterizan por la preocupación y tensión crónicas o por comportamientos inadaptados que reducen la ansiedad. (pág. 367)

aptitude test/prueba de aptitud Prueba diseñada para predecir el desempeño de una persona en el futuro; *aptitud* es la capacidad de aprender. (pág. 232)

asexual/asexual Ausencia de atracción sexual hacia otros. (pág. 117)

assimilation/asimilación Interpretación de nuestras experiencias nuevas en términos de nuestros esquemas existentes. (pág. 80)

association areas/áreas de asociación Áreas de la corteza cerebral principalmente relacionadas con las funciones mentales superiores como aprender, recordar, pensar y hablar. (pág. 48)

associative learning/aprendizaje asociativo Aprender que ciertos eventos ocurren juntos. Los eventos pueden ser dos estímulos (como en el condicionamiento clásico) o una respuesta y sus consecuencias (como en el condicionamiento operante). (pág. 166)

attachment/apego Vínculo emocional con otra persona; se observa en niños pequeños que buscan cercanía física con la persona que los cuida. Se observan señales de angustia cuando ocurre una separación. (pág. 85)

attention-deficit/hyperactivity disorder (ADHD)/trastorno por déficit de atención con hiperactividad (TDAH) Trastorno psicológico caracterizado por una falta de atención extrema y/o hiperactividad e impulsividad. (pág. 362)

attitude/actitud Sentimientos, a menudo basados en nuestras creencias, que nos predisponen para responder de una manera particular a los objetos, las personas y los eventos. (pág. 303)

audition/audición Sentido o acto de oír. (pág. 150)

autism spectrum disorder (ASD)/autismo Trastorno que se manifiesta en la niñez y que está marcado por deficiencias en las comunicaciones y en la interacción social, y por conductas repetitivas e intereses rigurosamente fijados. (pág. 84)

automatic processing/procesamiento automático Codificación inconsciente de información cotidiana, por ejemplo, de espacio, de tiempo y de frecuencia, y de información bien asimilada, tal como el significado de las palabras. (pág. 191)

autonomic nervous system (ANS)/sistema nervioso autónomo (SNA) División del sistema nervioso periférico que controla las glándulas y los músculos de los órganos internos (tales como el corazón). La subdivisión *simpática* estimula y la subdivisión *parasimpática* relaja. (pág. 37)

availability heuristic/heurística de disponibilidad Acto de estimar la probabilidad de un evento basándose en su disponibilidad en la memoria. Si un evento viene prontamente a la mente (quizás debido a su intensidad), presumimos que es un evento común. (pág. 216)

aversive conditioning/condicionamiento aversivo Tipo de contracondicionamiento que asocia un estado desagradable (por ejemplo, náuseas) con una conducta no deseada (tal como beber alcohol). (pág. 407)

axon/axón Prolongación de las neuronas que transmite mensajes a otras neuronas o a músculos y glándulas. (pág. 32)

babbling stage/fase balbuciente Fase del desarrollo del lenguaje que se da aproximadamente a los 4 meses de edad, y en la que el bebé espontáneamente emite diversos sonidos que al principio no se relacionan con el lenguaje que se usa en casa. (pág. 224)

barbiturates/barbitúricos Medicamentos que deprimen la actividad del sistema nervioso central, reduciendo la ansiedad pero afectando la memoria y el discernimiento. (pág. 374)

basal metabolic rate/tasa de metabolismo basal Cantidad de energía producida por el organismo en reposo absoluto. (pág. 252)

basic trust/confianza básica Según Erik Erikson, una percepción de que el mundo es predecible y fiable; se dice que se forma durante la primera infancia a través de experiencias apropiadas con cuidadores que responden con sensibilidad. (pág. 86)

behaviorism/conductismo Posición de que la psicología (1) debe ser una ciencia objetiva que (2) estudia el comportamiento sin referencia a los procesos mentales. Hoy, la mayoría de los psicólogos de investigación concuerdan con (1) pero no con (2). (págs. 5, 181)

behavior therapy/terapia del comportamiento Enfoque terapéutico que aplica los principios de aprendizaje para lograr la eliminación de comportamientos no deseados. (pág. 405)

belief perseverance/perseverancia en las creencias Empeño en insistir en las creencias incluso después de presentarse pruebas que las desacreditan. (pág. 218)

binge-eating disorder/trastorno por atracón Ingestión excesiva de alimentos, seguida de angustia, disgusto o culpa, pero sin las purgas, el ayuno o los ejercicios físicos excesivos que caracterizan a la bulimia nerviosa. (pág. 391)

binocular cue/clave binocular Señal de profundidad, por ejemplo la disparidad retiniana, para la que se requiere el uso de ambos ojos. (pág. 146)

biological psychology/psicología biológica Estudio científico de la relación entre los procesos biológicos y los psicológicos. (pág. 53)

biomedical therapy/terapia biomédica Procedimientos o medicamentos recetados que actúan directamente sobre la fisiología de la persona. (pág. 403)

biopsychosocial approach/enfoque biopsicosocial Enfoque que integra diversos conceptos complementarios en los que se combinan perspectivas biológicas, psicológicas y socioculturales. (pág. 8)

bipolar disorder/trastorno bipolar Trastorno en el que la persona alterna entre la desesperanza y el abatimiento de la depresión y el estado eufórico de la manía. (Anteriormente llamado *psicosis maníaco-depresiva*.) (pág. 382)

blind spot/punto ciego Punto en el cual el nervio óptico sale del ojo; esta parte de la retina es "ciega" porque carece de células receptoras. (pág. 140)

bottom-up processing/proceso ascendente Análisis que comienza con los receptores sensoriales y marcha hacia el cerebro y su integración de la información sensorial. (pág. 132)

brainstem/tronco encefálico Parte más antigua y núcleo central del cerebro, empezando donde la médula espinal se amplía al entrar en el cráneo; el tronco encefálico es responsable de las funciones automáticas de supervivencia. (pág. 42)

Broca's area/área de Broca Parte del lóbulo frontal del cerebro, generalmente en el hemisferio izquierdo, que dirige los movimientos musculares relacionados con el habla y que controla la expresión del lenguaje. (pág. 226)

bulimia nervosa/bulimia nerviosa Trastorno alimentario que se caracteriza por episodios de ingestión excesiva de alimentos (generalmente de alto contenido calórico) seguidos de purgas (vómito o uso de laxantes), ayuno o ejercicios físicos excesivos. (pág. 391)

bystander effect/efecto espectador Tendencia que tienen las personas a no brindar ayuda si hay otras personas presentes. (pág. 329)

Cannon-Bard theory/teoría de Cannon-Bard Teoría de que un estímulo que despierta emociones puede provocar simultáneamente (1) respuestas fisiológicas y (2) la experiencia subjetiva de la emoción. (pág. 262)

case study/caso de estudio Técnica de observación en la cual se estudia a un solo individuo o grupo a profundidad con la esperanza de revelar principios universales. (pág. 16)

cell body/cuerpo celular La parte de una neurona que contiene el núcleo; el centro de apoyo a la vida de la célula. (pág. 32)

central nervous system (CNS)/sistema nervioso central (SNC) La cerebro y la médula espinal. (pág. 36)

central route persuasion/ruta de persuasión central Se produce cuando los pensamientos de las personas interesadas se ve influenciada por contemplar los argumentos y la evidencia. (pág. 305)

cerebellum/cerebelo Es el "cerebro pequeño" y está unido a la parte posterior del tronco encefálico. Sus funciones incluyen el procesamiento de la información sensorial, la coordinación de los movimientos y el equilibrio y la habilitación del lenguaje no verbal y la memoria. (pág. 43)

cerebral cortex/corteza cerebral Capa delgada de neuronas conectadas entre sí, que cubre la superficie de los hemisferios cerebrales; es el principal centro de control y procesamiento de información del organismo. (pág. 46)

change blindness/ceguera al cambio No darse cuenta de cambios en el entorno. Una forma de ceguera por falta de atención. (pág. 56)

chromosomes/cromosomas Estructuras semejantes a hilos conformadas de moléculas de ADN que contienen los genes. (pág. 72)

chronic schizophrenia/esquizofrenia crónica (también se le dice *esquizofrenia procesal*) Tipo de esquizofrenia en la que los síntomas aparecen generalmente en la adolescencia tardía o adultez temprana. A medida que las personas envejecen, los episodios psicóticos duran más y se acortan los períodos de recuperación. (pág. 388)

chunking/agrupamiento Organizar artículos en unidades conocidas y manejables; a menudo ocurre automáticamente. (pág. 193)

circadian rhythm/ritmo circadiano Reloj biológico; ritmos periódicos del organismo (por ejemplo, los de temperatura y de estado de vigilia) que ocurren en ciclos de 24 horas. (pág. 56)

classical conditioning/condicionamiento clásico Tipo de aprendizaje en el cual aprendemos a relacionar dos o más estímulos y a anticipar sucesos. (pág. 167)

clinical psychology/psicología clínica Especialización de la psicología que estudia, evalua y trata personas con trastornos psicológicos. (pág. 10)

cocaine/cocaína Estimulante potente y adictivo derivado de la planta de coca; aumenta temporalmente el estado de alerta y produce sensaciones de euforia. (pág. 376)

cochlea/cóclea Estructura tubular en forma de espiral, ósea y rellena de líquido que se halla en el oído interno; las ondas sonoras que pasan por el líquido coclear desencadenan impulsos nerviosos. (pág. 151)

cochlear implant/implante coclear Dispositivo que convierte sonidos en señales eléctricas que estimulan el nervio auditivo mediante electrodos enhebrados en la cóclea. (pág. 152)

cognition/cognición Todas las actividades mentales asociadas con pensar, saber, recordar y comunicar. (págs. 79, 214)

cognitive-behavioral therapy (CBT)/terapia cognitivo-conductual (TCC) Terapia integrada muy difundida que combina la terapia cognitiva (que cambia los pensamientos contraproducentes) con la terapia conductual (que cambia la conducta). (pág. 410)

cognitive dissonance theory/teoría de disonancia cognitiva Teoría según la cual llevamos a cabo una acción con el propósito de reducir la incomodidad (disonancia) que sentimos cuando tenemos dos pensamientos (cogniciones) contradictorios. Por ejemplo, cuando tenemos consciencia de que nuestras actitudes y nuestras acciones entran en conflicto, podríamos cambiar nuestra actitud para sentirnos más cómodos. (pág. 305)

cognitive learning/aprendizaje cognitivo Adquisición de información mental, ya sea a partir de la observación de acontecimientos, a partir de la observación de otras personas o a través del lenguaje. (pág. 167)

cognitive map/mapa cognitivo Imagen mental del trazado de nuestro entorno. (pág. 182)

cognitive neuroscience/neurociencia cognitiva Estudio interdisciplinario de la actividad cerebral relacionada con la cognición (que incluye la percepción, el pensamiento, la memoria y el lenguaje). (págs. 6, 53)

cognitive psychology/psicología cognitiva Estudio de los procesos mentales, tales como los que ocurren cuando percibimos, aprendemos, recordamos, pensamos, nos comunicamos y resolvemos problemas. (pág. 5)

cognitive therapy/terapia cognitiva Enfoque terapéutico en que se les enseña a los pacientes nuevas formas de pensar de un modo más adaptativo. Se basa en el supuesto de que los pensamientos intervienen entre los eventos y nuestras reacciones emocionales. (pág. 408)

collective unconscious/inconsciente colectivo Concepto propuesto por Carl Jung en relación a un grupo común de recuerdos heredados de la historia de nuestra especie. (pág. 340)

collectivism/colectivismo Modo de dar prioridad a las metas del grupo (a menudo de la familia extendida o el grupo de trabajo) y de definir la identidad personal según lo que dicta el grupo. (pág. 356)

community psychology/psicología comunitaria Especialización de la psicología que estudia como las personas se relacionan con sus entornos sociales y como las instituciones sociales (tales como las escuelas y los barrios) afectan a la gente. (pág. 11)

companionate love/amor sociable Apego afectuoso profundo que sentimos por aquellos con quienes nuestras vidas se entrelazan. (pág. 327)

concept/concepto Agrupamiento mental de objetos, eventos, ideas o personas que tienen un parecido. (pág. 214)

concrete operational stage/etapa del pensamiento lógico-concreto En la teoría de Piaget, la fase del desarrollo cognitivo (desde aproximadamente los 7 años hasta los 11 años de edad) durante la cual los niños adquieren las operaciones mentales que les permiten pensar lógicamente sobre eventos concretos. (pág. 82)

conditioned reinforcer/reforzador condicionado (También denominado *reforzador secundario*) Evento que adquiere su poder de reforzamiento mediante su vínculo con el reforzador primario. (pág. 174)

conditioned response (CR)/respuesta condicionada (RC) En el condicionamiento clásico, la respuesta aprendida a un estímulo previamente neutral (pero ahora condicionado). (pág. 168)

conditioned stimulus (CS)/estímulo condicionado (EC) En el condicionamiento clásico, un estímulo originalmente neutral que, después de verse asociado con un estímulo incondicionado (EI) produce una respuesta condicionada. (pág. 168)

cones/conos Receptores que se concentran cerca del centro de la retina; con la luz del día o en lugares bien iluminados, los conos detectan detalles finos y producen las sensaciones del color. (pág. 140)

confirmation bias/sesgo confirmatorio Tendencia a buscar información que confirme nuestras ideas preconcebidas y de hacer caso omiso o de distorsionar las pruebas que las contradigan. (pág. 215)

conflict/conflicto Incompatibilidad percibida de acciones, metas o ideas. (pág. 330)

conformity/conformidad Tendencia a ajustar el comportamiento o la forma de pensar hasta hacerlos coincidir con las normas que tiene un grupo. (pág. 307)

confounding variable/variable de confusión Factor distinto del factor que se está estudiando que podría producir un efecto sobre los resultados de un estudio. (pág. 21)

consciousness/consciencia Percepción subjetiva de nosotros mismos y de nuestro entorno. (pág. 53)

conservation/conservación Principio (que para Piaget forma parte del razonamiento operacional concreto) de que ciertas propiedades (ej., masa, volumen y número) no varían pese a modificaciones en la forma de los objetos. (pág. 81)

continuous reinforcement/reforzamiento continuo Reforzar la respuesta deseada cada vez que ocurre. (pág. 175)

control group/grupo de control En un experimento, el grupo de participantes que *no* se expone al tratamiento; el grupo de control sirve de comparación con el grupo sometido al tratamiento para evaluar el efecto del tratamiento. (pág. 20)

convergent thinking/razonamiento convergente Reducción de las soluciones disponibles con el fin de determinar cuál es la mejor solución a un problema. (pág. 220)

coping/estrategias de afrontamiento Reducción de las tensiones con métodos emocionales, cognitivos o conductuales. (pág. 282)

coronary heart disease/enfermedad coronaria Obstrucción de los vasos que alimentan el músculo cardíaco; causa principal de muerte en Estados Unidos y muchos otros países. (pág. 281)

corpus callosum/cuerpo calloso Banda grande de fibras neuronales que conecta los dos hemisferios del cerebro y transmite mensajes entre ellos. (pág. 51)

correlation/correlación Medida del grado en que dos factores varían juntos y por ende, si es que uno de ellos puede predecir el otro. El *coeficiente de correlación* es la expresión matemática de la relación, la cual abarca desde −1.00 hasta +1.00, con el 0 señalando que no hay relación. (pág. 18)

correlation coefficient/coeficiente de correlación Índice estadístico de la relación entre dos cosas (del −1.00 al +1.00). (pág. A-4)

counseling psychology/psicología de consejería Especialización de la psicología que ayuda a personas con problemas en vivir (a menudo relacionadas con la escuela, el trabajo o las relaciones) y en lograr mayor bienestar. (pág. 10)

counterconditioning/contracondicionamiento Técnicas de terapia conductual que se valen del condicionamiento clásico para provocar respuestas alternativas a estímulos que producen comportamientos no deseados; incluye las *terapias de exposición* y el *condicionamiento aversivo*. (pág. 406)

creativity/creatividad Capacidad para generar ideas novedosas y valiosas. (pág. 220)

critical period/período crítico Etapa al inicio de la vida, en la cual son necesarios ciertos estímulos o experiencias para que se produzca el desarrollo apropiado del organismo. (pág. 78)

critical thinking/pensamiento crítico Forma de pensar en la que no se aceptan razones ni conclusiones ciegamente; por el contrario, se examinan las suposiciones, se evalúa la fuente, se distinguen los valores ocultos, se sopesa la evidencia y se evalúan las conclusiones. (pág. 2)

cross-sectional study/estudio transversal Estudio en el que personas de diferentes edades se comparan unas con otras en un solo momento temporal. (págs. 70, 238, A-6)

crystallized intelligence/inteligencia cristalizada Todos los conocimientos y capacidades verbales que una persona ha acumulado; tiende a aumentar con la edad. (pág. 239)

culture/cultura Comportamientos, ideas, actitudes, valores y tradiciones duraderos que comparte un grupo de personas y que se transmiten de generación en generación. (pág. 8)

debriefing/rendición de informes Después de concluir un experimento, explicación que se les da a los participantes del objetivo del estudio y de toda decepción que los investigadores pudieron haber utilizado. (pág. 25)

defense mechanisms/mecanismos de defensa En la teoría psicoanalítica, los métodos de protección del ego para reducir la ansiedad distorsionando la realidad de manera inconsciente. (pág. 339)

deindividuation/desindividuación Pérdida de la identidad personal y del autocontrol en situaciones de grupo que fomentan la excitación y el anonimato. (pág. 312)

déjà vu/déjà vu Sensación extraña de haber vivido antes una experiencia específica. Señales de la presente situación pueden de manera subconsciente activar la evocación de una vivencia previa. (pág. 207)

delta waves/ondas delta Ondas cerebrales grandes y lentas que se asocian con el sueño profundo. (pág. 58)

delusion/delirios Creencias falsas, a menudo de persecución o de grandeza que pueden acompañar a trastornos psicóticos. (pág. 387)

dendrites/dendritas Prolongaciones de las neuronas que reciben mensajes y envían impulsos hacia el cuerpo neuronal. (pág. 32)

dependent variable/variable dependiente En un experimento, el factor que se mide. Es la variable que puede cambiar cuando se manipula la variable independiente. (pág. 21)

depressants/depresores Agentes químicos (tales como el alcohol, los barbitúricos y los opiáceos) que reducen (deprimen) la actividad neuronal y enlentecen las funciones del organismo. (pág. 372)

depth perception/percepción de la profundidad Capacidad de ver objetos en tres dimensiones aunque las imágenes percibidas por la retina sean bidimensionales. Nos permite evaluar la distancia. (pág. 145)

developmental psychology/psicología evolutiva Especialización de la psicología que estudia los cambios físicos, cognitivos y sociales que se ocasionan a lo largo de la vida. (pág. 70)

difference threshold/umbral de diferencia La diferencia mínima entre dos estímulos que una persona puede detectar el 50 por ciento de las veces. El umbral de diferencia se experimenta como una *diferencia apenas perceptible*. (pág. 135)

discrimination/discriminación (1) Según el condicionamiento clásico, capacidad aprendida de distinguir entre un estímulo condicionado y otros estímulos sin trascendencia. (En el condicionamiento operante, la capacidad de distinguir las respuestas que son reforzadas de las que no lo son.) (2) En la psicología social, el comportamiento negativo injustificado contra un grupo o sus miembros. (págs. 170, 315)

dissociative disorders/trastornos disociativos Trastornos poco comunes y polémicos en los que el conocimiento consciente se separa (se disocia) de los recuerdos, pensamientos y sentimientos anteriores. (pág. 392)

dissociative identity disorder (DID)/trastorno disociativo de identidad (TDI) Trastorno disociativo poco común, en el cual una persona exhibe dos o más personalidades claramente definidas que se alternan entre sí. (También se denomina *trastorno de personalidad múltiple*). (pág. 392)

divergent thinking/pensamiento divergente Expansión del número de soluciones a un problema. Pensamiento creativo que se ramifica en múltiples direcciones. (pág. 220)

DNA (deoxyribonucleic acid)/ADN (ácido desoxirribonucleico) Molécula que contiene la información genética de la que se constituyen los cromosomas. (pág. 72)

double-blind procedure/procedimiento doble ciego En un experimento, procedimiento en el cual tanto los participantes como el personal de investigación desconocen (van a ciegas) quién ha recibido el tratamiento y quién el placebo. (pág. 21)

dream/sueño Secuencia de imágenes, emociones y pensamientos que fluyen en la mente de una persona dormida. (pág. 63)

drive-reduction theory/teoría de la reducción del impulso Concepto de que una necesidad fisiológica crea un estado de excitación (un impulso) que motiva al organismo a satisfacer tal necesidad. (pág. 248)

DSM-5/DSM-5 *Manual diagnóstico y estadístico de los trastornos mentales*, quinta edición, de la Asociación Estadounidense de Psiquiatría. Sistema ampliamente utilizado para clasificar los trastornos psicológicos. (pág. 365)

dual processing/procesamiento dual Principio que sostiene que la información se procesa simultáneamente en vías separadas conscientes e inconscientes en la mente. (pág. 10)

eclectic approach/enfoque ecléctico Enfoque de la psicoterapia que emplea técnicas tomadas de diversas formas de terapia. (pág. 402)

Ecstasy (MDMA)/éxtasis (MDMA) Estimulante sintético y alucinógeno ligero. Produce euforia e intimidad social, pero conlleva riesgos de salud a corto plazo. Además, a largo plazo, perjudica las neuronas que producen la serotonina, y afecta el ánimo y el proceso de cognición. (pág. 377)

EEG (electroencephalograph)/(EEG) electroencefalógrafo Aparato que emplea electrodos colocados sobre el cuero cabelludo, que produce un registro de las ondas de actividad eléctrica que circulan por la superficie del cerebro. (El trazado de dichas ondas cerebrales es un *electroencefalograma*). (pág. 40)

effortful processing/procesamiento con esfuerzo Codificación que precisa atención y esfuerzo conscientes. (pág. 191)

ego/ego Parte consciente y ejecutiva de la personalidad que, según Freud, media entre las exigencias del id, el superego y la realidad. El ego opera según el *principio de realidad*, satisfaciendo los deseos del id en formas que de manera realista le brindarán placer en lugar de dolor. (pág. 337)

egocentrism/egocentrismo Según la teoría de Piaget, la dificultad de los niños en la etapa preoperacional de aceptar el punto de vista ajeno. (pág. 82)

electroconvulsive therapy (ECT)/terapia electroconvulsiva (TEC) Terapia biomédica para pacientes gravemente deprimidos en la que se envía una corriente eléctrica de corta duración a través del cerebro de un paciente anestesiado. (pág. 420)

embodied cognition/cognición encarnada La influencia de las sensaciones del organismo, los movimientos y otros estados en las preferencias y los juicios cognitivos. (pág. 160)

embryo/embrión El organismo humano en desarrollo a partir de las dos semanas después de fertilización hasta el segundo mes. (pág. 74)

emerging adulthood/madurez emergente Etapa que se extiende desde los 18 hasta alrededor de los 25 años, durante la cual muchas personas en los países occidentales ya no son adolescentes pero aún no han alcanzado la independencia plena de un adulto. (pág. 96)

emotion/emoción Reacción que involucra a todo el organismo e incluye (1) excitación fisiológica, (2) comportamientos expresivos y (3) experiencia consciente. (pág. 262)

emotion-focused coping/estrategias de afrontamiento centradas en la emoción Medidas para sobrellevar las tensiones enfocándose en evitar o hacer caso omiso de una situación estresante y atender las necesidades emocionales relacionadas con nuestra reacción al estrés. (pág. 282)

emotional intelligence/inteligencia emocional Capacidad de percibir, entender, manejar y hacer uso de las emociones. (pág. 231)

encoding/codificación El proceso de ingresar información al sistema de memoria. (pág. 190)

encoding specificity principle/principio de especifidad de codificación La idea que las señales y los contextos que pertenecen a una memoria concreta serán los mas eficaces para ayudar a recordarla. (pág. 200)

endocrine system/sistema endocrino Sistema "lento" de comunicación química del cuerpo; conjunto de glándulas que secretan hormonas al torrente sanguíneo. (pág. 39)

endorphins/endorfinas "Morfina adentro"; neurotransmisores naturales similares a los opiáceos que están asociados con el control del dolor y con el placer. (pág. 36)

environment/entorno Toda influencia externa, desde la alimentación prenatal hasta el apoyo social que se recibe más adelante en la vida. (pág. 73)

epigenetics/epigenética Estudio de la influencia ambiental sobre la expresión de los genes que ocurre sin un cambio de ADN. (págs. 74, 364)

episodic memory/memoria episódica Memoria explícita de eventos experimentados personalmente. Uno de los dos sistemas de memoria conscientes (el otro es la *memoria semántica*). (pág. 195)

equity/equidad Condición en la cual la persona recibe de manera proporcional a lo que aporte a una relación. (pág. 327)

erectile disorder/trastorno eréctil Incapacidad de desarrollar o mantener una erección debido a un flujo insuficiente de sangre al pene. (pág. 118)

estrogens/estrógenos Hormonas sexuales, como el estradiol, que contribuyan a las características sexuales femeninas, secretadas en mayor cantidad en la mujer que en el hombre. Los niveles de estrógeno alcanzan su nivel máximo durante la ovulación. En los animales mamíferos no humanos esto facilita la receptividad sexual. (pág. 117)

evidence-based practice/práctica basada en la evidencia Toma de decisiones clínicas que integra lo mejor de las investigaciones disponibles con la pericia clínica y las características y preferencias del paciente. (pág. 414)

evolutionary psychology/psicología evolucionista Estudio de como el comportamiento y la mente humanos han cambiado (con adaptaciones efectivas) a lo largo del tiempo debido a la selección natural. (pág. 126)

experiment/experimento Método de investigación en el cual el investigador manipula uno o más factores (variables independientes) para observar su efecto en un comportamiento o proceso mental (variable dependiente). Al ser los participantes asignados de manera aleatoria, los investigadores procuran controlar otros factores. (pág. 20)

experimental group/grupo experimental Sujetos de un experimento que están expuestos al tratamiento, o sea, a una versión de la variable independiente. (pág. 20)

explicit memory/memoria explícita Retención de hechos y vivencias personales que tenemos la capacidad de recuperar conscientemente. También se le dice *memoria declarativa*. (pág. 191)

exposure therapies/terapias de exposición Técnicas conductuales, como la *desensibilización sistemática* y *la terapia de exposición de realidad virtual* para tratar la ansiedad exponiendo a la persona (en situaciones imaginarias o reales) a las cosas que teme y evita. (pág. 406)

external locus of control/lugar de control externo Impresión de que nuestro destino está determinado por el azar o por fuerzas que están más allá de nuestro control. (pág. 284)

extinction/extinción Según el condicionamiento clásico, disminución de una respuesta condicionada cuando un estímulo incondicionado no sigue a un estímulo condicionado. (En el condicionamiento operante, disminución de una respuesta cuando deja de ser reforzada). (pág. 169)

extrasensory perception (ESP)/percepción extrasensorial (PES) La afirmación polémica de que la percepción puede ocurrir aislada de la recepción sensorial; incluye la telepatía, la clarividencia y la precognición. (pág. 160)

extrinsic motivation/motivación extrínseca Deseo de realizar un comportamiento para obtener una recompensa o evitar el castigo. (pág. 260)

facial feedback effect/efecto de la retroalimentación facial Tendencia de los músculos faciales a provocar sentimientos correspondientes como el miedo, el enojo o la felicidad. (pág. 271)

factor/factor Conjunto de tendencias del comportamiento que ocurren juntos. (pág. 346)

family therapy/terapia familiar Tipo de terapia que trata a la familia como un sistema. Esta terapia considera que los comportamientos no deseados de una persona son influenciados por otros miembros de la familia o están dirigidos hacia ellos. (pág. 411)

feature detectors/detectores de características Células nerviosas del cerebro que responden a características específicas de un estímulo, como las formas, los ángulos y el movimiento. (pág. 143)

feel-good, do-good phenomenon/fenómeno de sentirse bien y hacer el bien Tendencia a ayudar a los demás cuando estamos de buen humor. (pág. 293)

female orgasmic disorder/trastorno orgásmico Sentimiento de angustia debido a nunca haber experimentado un orgasmo o haberlo hecho de manera infrecuente. (pág. 118)

fetal alcohol syndrome (FAS)/síndrome de alcoholismo fetal (SAF) Anomalías físicas y cognitivas en los niños causadas por la intensa ingestión de alcohol de la madre durante el embarazo. En casos agudos, los síntomas incluyen la cabeza demasiado pequeña y desproporciones faciales observables. (pág. 74)

fetus/feto Organismo humano en vías de desarrollo a partir de las 9 semanas de concepción hasta el nacimiento. (pág. 74)

fight-or-flight response/respuesta de luchar o huir Reacción en una emergencia que incluye actividad del sistema nervioso simpático y genera energía y actividad dirigidas a atacar o escapar ante una amenaza. (pág. 278)

figure-ground/figura-fondo Organización del campo visual en objetos (las *figuras*) que se distinguen de sus entornos (los *fondos*). (pág. 145)

fixation/fijación En la teoría de la personalidad, según Freud, un foco persistente de energías en busca del placer en una etapa psicosexual anterior en la que los conflictos todavía no estaban resueltos. (pág. 338)

fixed-interval schedule/calendario de intervalo fijo Según el condicionamiento operante, calendario de reforzamiento que refuerza la respuesta solo después de haber transcurrido un tiempo específico. (pág. 176)

fixed-ratio schedule/calendario de proporción fija Según el condicionamiento operante, calendario de reforzamiento que refuerza la respuesta solo después de darse un número específico de respuestas. (pág. 175)

flashbulb memory/memoria de flash Memoria clara de un momento o evento emocionalmente significativo. (pág. 197)

flow/fluidez Estado de participación y concentración totales, con disminución de la conciencia de uno mismo y del tiempo, que ocurre cuando aprovechamos nuestras destrezas al máximo. (pág. B-1)

fluid intelligence/inteligencia fluida Capacidad que tenemos de razonar de manera rápida y abstracta; tiende a disminuir con la edad, especialmente en la vejez. (pág. 239)

fMRI (functional MRI)/(IRMf) imagen por resonancia magnética funcional Técnica para observar la circulación de la sangre y, por lo tanto, la actividad cerebral. Consiste en comparar imágenes de resonancia magnética sucesivas. Las imágenes de resonancia magnética funcional muestran el funcionamiento del cerebro. (pág. 41)

foot-in-the-door phenomenon/fenómeno de pie en la puerta Tendencia de la gente que ha accedido a algo pequeño en primer lugar, a después satisfacer una exigencia de mayor envergadura. (pág. 304)

formal operational stage/etapa de las operaciones formales En la teoría de Piaget, el período en el desarrollo cognitivo (normalmente empieza a los 12 años) durante el cual la persona empieza a pensar lógicamente sobre conceptos abstractos. (pág. 82)

framing/encuadre Forma en que se presenta un asunto; el encuadre puede influenciar considerablemente las decisiones y las opiniones. (pág. 219)

fraternal (dizygotic) twins/gemelos fraternos (dicigóticos) Se desarrollan de dos óvulos fecundados. Genéticamente no están más cercanos que los hermanos y hermanas, pero comparten un entorno prenatal. (pág. 76)

free association/asociación libre En psicoanálisis, método para explorar el inconsciente en el que la persona se relaja y dice lo primero que le viene a la mente, no importa cuán poco importante o incómodo. (pág. 337)

frequency/frecuencia Número de ondas completas que pasan un punto en un tiempo dado (por ejemplo, por segundo). (pág. 151)

frontal lobes/lóbulos frontales Porción de la corteza cerebral que se halla inmediatamente detrás de la frente; se relaciona con el habla y los movimientos musculares y con la planificación y la formación de opiniones. (pág. 46)

frustration-aggression principle/principio de frustración-agresión Principio de que la frustración —el bloqueo de un intento para lograr alguna meta— crea ira, la cual puede generar agresión. (pág. 321)

functional fixedness/fijación funcional Un sesgo cognitivo que resulta en la incapacidad de ver un problema desde perpectivas nuevas; un obstáculo para resolver problemas. (pág. 215)

functionalism/funcionalismo Una escuela de pensamiento de los primeros años promovido por James e influenciado por Darwin que se centró en como funciona la mente. (pág. 5)

fundamental attribution error/error fundamental de la atribución Tendencia de los observadores, cuando analizan el comportamiento ajeno, a sobrestimar el impacto de las características personales y subestimar el impacto de la situación. (pág. 302)

gender/género En psicología, las características de comportamiento por las cuales la sociedad define *varón* y *mujer*. (pág. 108)

gender identity/identidad de género Nuestra sensación personal de ser varón o mujer, ninguno de estos o combinación de ambos. (pág. 114)

gender role/papel del género Conjunto de comportamientos, actitudes y rasgos esperados para las mujeres y los hombres. (pág. 113)

gender typing/tipificación por género La adquisición de un papel masculino o femenino tradicional. (pág. 114)

general adaptation syndrome (GAS)/síndrome general de adaptación Término usado por Selye para referirse a la respuesta adaptiva del cuerpo al estrés que se da en tres etapas: alarma, resistencia y agotamiento. (pág. 278)

general intelligence (*g*)/factor g de inteligencia general Factor de inteligencia general que, según Spearman y otros, subyace todas las habilidades mentales específicas y es, por tanto, cuantificado por cada función en una prueba de inteligencia. (pág. 229)

generalization/generalización Según el condicionamiento clásico, tendencia posterior al condicionamiento de responder de manera similar a los estímulos que se parecen al estímulo condicionado. (En el condicionamiento operante, se produce una *generalización* cuando las respuestas aprendidas en una situación ocurren en otras situaciones similares.) (pág. 170)

generalized anxiety disorder/trastorno de ansiedad generalizada Trastorno de ansiedad en el cual la persona está constantemente tensa, temerosa y con el *sistema nervioso autónomo* activado. (pág. 367)

genes/genes Unidades bioquímicas de la herencia que forman los cromosomas: segmentos de ADN. (pág. 72)

genome/genoma Instrucciones completas para crear un organismo; consiste en todo el material genético en los cromosomas de ese organismo. (pág. 73)

gestalt/Gestalt Un todo organizado. Los psicólogos de la Gestalt enfatizan nuestra tendencia a integrar segmentos de información en todos significativos. (pág. 144)

glial cells (glia)/células gliales Células del sistema nervioso que apoyan, alimentan y protegen a las neuronas; también desempeñan un papel en el aprendizaje, el razonamiento y la memoria. (pág. 32)

glucose/glucosa Forma de azúcar que circula en la sangre y es la mayor fuente de energía para los tejidos del cuerpo. Cuando su nivel está bajo, sentimos hambre. (pág. 251)

grammar/gramática En un lenguaje específico, sistema de reglas que nos permite comunicarnos y entendernos unos con otros. (pág. 225)

grit/tenacidad En psicología, se refiere a la pasión y la perseverancia en la búsqueda de objetivos a largo plazo. (pág. 260)

group polarization/efecto de polarización de grupo Solidificación y fortalecimiento de las posiciones imperantes en un grupo mediante diálogos en el grupo. (pág. 313)

group therapy/terapia de grupo Tratamiento que se realiza con grupos en lugar de con personas individuales, que genera beneficios de la interacción del grupo. (pág. 411)

grouping/agrupamiento Tendencia de percepción que clasifica los estímulos en grupos que tienen sentido. (pág. 145)

groupthink/pensamiento de grupo Modo de pensar que ocurre cuando el deseo de armonía en un grupo que toma decisiones colectivas anula la evaluación objetiva de las alternativas. (pág. 315)

hallucination/alucinación Experiencia sensorial falsa, por ejemplo, cuando una persona oye algo sin haber ningún estímulo auditivo externo. (pág. 48)

hallucinogens/alucinógenos Drogas psicodélicas (que producen "manifestación de la mente"), como el LSD, que distorsionan las percepciones y desencadenan imágenes sensoriales sin que intervengan estímulos sensoriales. (pág. 377)

heredity/herencia Transferencia genética de características de los padres a los hijos. (pág. 72)

heritability/heredabilidad La proporción de variación entre individuos que le podemos atribuir a los genes. La heredabilidad de un rasgo varía de acuerdo con la población y el entorno. (pág. 235)

heuristic/heurística Estrategia de pensamiento sencilla que a menudo nos permite formar juicios y resolver problemas de manera eficiente. Por lo general es más expedita que utilizar un *algoritmo*, pero también puede conducir a más errores. (pág. 214)

hierarchy of needs/jerarquía de necesidades Pirámide de Maslow de las necesidades humanas. En la base de la pirámide están las necesidades fisiológicas, que deben satisfacerse antes que las necesidades de seguridad personal que son de más alto nivel. Las necesidades psicológicas se activan por último, después de satisfacer las anteriores. (págs. 249, 343)

hindsight bias/sesgo retrospectivo Tendencia a creer después de saber un resultado que uno lo habría previsto. (También conocido como el *fenómeno de ya yo lo sabía*.) (pág. 12)

hippocampus/hipocampo Centro neuronal ubicado en el sistema límbico; ayuda a procesar recuerdos explícitos (conscientes) de hechos y eventos para almacenarlos de manera accesible. (págs. 44, 195)

homeostasis/homeostasis Tendencia a mantener un estado interno constante o equilibrado; la regulación de cualquier aspecto de la química del organismo, tal como los niveles de glucosa, alrededor de un nivel dado. (pág. 248)

hormones/hormonas Mensajeros químicos producidos por las glándulas endocrinas, que circulan por la sangre y tienen efecto en los tejidos del cuerpo. (pág. 39)

hue/tono Dimensión del color determinada por la longitud de onda de la luz; lo que conocemos como los nombres de los colores: *azul*, *verde*, etc. (pág. 139)

human factors psychology/psicología de factores humanos División de la psicología relacionada con la psicología del trabajo y de las organizaciones que explora la interacción entre las personas y las máquinas, y las maneras de hacer que las máquinas y los entornos físicos sean más seguros y fáciles de utilizar. (pág. B-3)

humanistic psychology/psicología humanista Perspectiva de importancia histórica que enfatiza el potencial de crecimiento humano. (pág. 5)

hypnosis/hipnosis Interacción social en la cual una persona (el hipnotizador) le sugiere a otra persona (el sujeto) que ciertas percepciones, sentimientos, pensamientos o comportamientos se producirán espontáneamente. (pág. 155)

hypothalamus/hipotálamo Estructura neuronal localizada debajo *(hipo)* del tálamo; dirige varias actividades de mantenimiento (comer, beber, temperatura corporal); ayuda a dirigir el sistema endocrino a través de la glándula pituitaria y está conectado a las emociones y las recompensas. (pág. 44)

hypothesis/hipótesis Predicción comprobable, a menudo implicada por una teoría. (pág. 14)

id/id Reserva de energía psíquica inconsciente que, según Freud, aspira a satisfacer los impulsos sexuales y agresivos esenciales. El id funciona según el *principio de placer*, exigiendo satisfacción inmediata. (pág. 337)

identical (monozygotic) twins/gemelos idénticos (monocigóticos) Se desarrollan de un solo óvulo fertilizado que se subdivide en dos para así crear dos organismos genéticamente idénticos. (pág. 76)

identification/identificación Proceso en el que, según Freud, los niños incorporan los valores de sus padres en sus superegos en vías de desarrollo. (pág. 338)

identity/identidad Sentido de autorreconocimiento; según Erikson, la tarea del adolescente consiste en solidificar el sentido de sí mismo probando e integrando una variedad de papeles. (pág. 93)

illusory correlation/correlación ilusoria La percepción de una relación donde no la hay o de una relación más fuerte de la que hay. (pág. A-5)

implicit memory/memoria implícita Retención de destrezas aprendidas o asociaciones condicionadas clásicas, sin tener consciencia del aprendizaje. (También se le dice *memoria no declarativa*). (pág. 191)

inattentional blindness/ceguera por falta de atención No ver los objetos visibles cuando nuestra atención se dirige a otra parte. (pág. 55)

incentive/incentivo Estímulo positivo o negativo del entorno que motiva el comportamiento. (pág. 248)

independent variable/variable independiente Factor que se manipula en un experimento; la variable cuyo efecto es el objeto de estudio. (pág. 21)

individualism/individualismo Darle atención prioritaria a las metas personales antes que a las metas del grupo y definir la identidad mediante las cualidades personales y no con la pertenencia al grupo. (pág. 356)

industrial-organizational (I/O) psychology/psicología del trabajo y de las organizaciones Aplicación de conceptos y métodos psicológicos al comportamiento humano en el entorno laboral. (pág. B-3)

informational social influence/influencia social informativa Influencia resultante de la disposición de una persona a aceptar las opiniones de otros acerca de la realidad. (pág. 308)

informed consent/consentimiento informado Darles a las personas información suficiente sobre un estudio para permitirles decidir si desean o no participar. (pág. 25)

ingroup/endogrupo "Nosotros". Personas con quienes uno comparte una identidad común. (pág. 318)

ingroup bias/sesgo endogrupal Tendencia a favorecer al grupo al que se pertenece. (pág. 318)

inner ear/oído interno Parte más interna del oído; contiene la cóclea, los canales semicirculares y los sacos vestibulares. (pág. 151)

insight/percepción Entendimiento repentino de cómo se resuelve un problema; contrasta con las soluciones basadas en estrategias. (pág. 214)

insight therapies/tratamientos por percepción Terapias que aspiran a mejorar el funcionamiento psicológico mediante el aumento en la conciencia de la persona, de los motivos y las defensas subyacentes. (pág. 404)

insomnia/insomnio Dificultades recurrentes para dormirse y permanecer dormido. (pág. 63)

intellectual disability/discapacidad intelectual Estado de capacidad mental limitada, que se expresa a través de una puntuación de prueba de inteligencia de 70 o menos y de la dificultad para adaptarse a las exigencias de la vida. (Anteriormente conocida como *retraso mental*). (pág. 234)

intelligence/inteligencia Capacidad de aprender de las experiencias, de resolver problemas y de utilizar el conocimiento para adaptarse a situaciones nuevas. (pág. 229)

intelligence quotient (IQ)/coeficiente intelectual (CI) Cifra definida originalmente como la edad mental *(em)* dividida entre la edad cronológica *(ec)* y el resultado multiplicado por 100 (por lo tanto, CI = *em* ÷ *ec* × 100). En las pruebas actuales de inteligencia, al desempeño promedio para una edad dada se le asigna una puntuación de 100. (pág. 232)

intelligence test/prueba de inteligencia Método para evaluar las aptitudes mentales de la persona y compararlas con las de otras personas utilizando puntuaciones numéricas. (pág. 232)

intensity/intensidad Cantidad de energía en una onda de luz o en una onda sonora que percibimos como brillo o volumen. La intensidad la determina la amplitud (altura) de la onda. (pág. 139)

interaction/interacción Situación que se produce cuando el efecto de un factor (por ejemplo, el entorno) depende de otro factor (por ejemplo, la herencia). (pág. 73)

internal locus of control/lugar de control interno Impresión de que controlamos nuestro propio destino. (pág. 284)

interneurons/interneuronas Neuronas ubicadas dentro del cerebro y la médula espinal. Se comunican internamente y procesan la información entre los estímulos sensoriales y las respuestas motoras. (pág. 36)

interpretation/interpretación En psicoanálisis, las observaciones del analista con relación al significado de los sueños, las resistencias, y otras conductas y eventos significativos, a fin de promover la percepción. (pág. 403)

intersex/intersexualidad Condición al momento del nacimiento en la que el recién nacido presenta características sexuales biológicas de ambos sexos. (pág. 108)

intimacy/intimidad Según la teoría de Erikson, capacidad de formar relaciones cercanas y cariñosas; función primordial del desarrollo en la adolescencia y al comienzo de la vida adulta. (pág. 94)

intrinsic motivation/motivación intrínseca Deseo de realizar una conducta de manera adecuada simplemente por la mera satisfacción de hacerlo bien. (pág. 260)

intuition/intuición Sentimiento o pensamiento automático e inmediato, que no precisa esfuerzo alguno, que se contrasta con el razonamiento explícito y consciente. (pág. 215)

James-Lange theory/teoría de James-Lange Teoría que expone que nuestra experiencia emocional es la conciencia que tenemos de nuestras respuestas fisiológicas a los estímulos que despiertan emociones. (pág. 262)

just-world phenomenon/hipótesis del mundo justo Tendencia a creer que el mundo es justo y que por tanto, las personas obtienen lo que se merecen y se merecen lo que obtienen. (pág. 318)

kinesthesia/cinestesia Sentido de movimiento. Sistema que siente la posición y el movimiento de las partes individuales del cuerpo. (pág. 158)

language/lenguaje Palabras habladas, escritas o en señas y las maneras en que se combinan para comunicar significado. (pág. 223)

latent content/contenido latente Según Freud, significado subyacente de un sueño. (pág. 64)

latent learning/aprendizaje latente Aprendizaje que no es aparente sino hasta que hay un incentivo para demostrarlo. (pág. 182)

law of effect/ley de efecto Principio propuesto por Thorndike en el que se propone que las conductas seguidas por consecuencias favorables se tornan más comunes, mientras que las conductas seguidas por consecuencias desfavorables se repiten con menos frecuencia. (pág. 172)

leadership/liderazgo La capacidad de un individuo de motivar e influir a los demás para contribuir al éxito del grupo. (pág. B-5)

learned helplessness/indefensión aprendida Desesperación y resignación pasiva que un animal o persona desarrolla cuando es incapaz de evitar repetidos eventos de aversión. (pág. 283)

learning/aprendizaje Proceso de adquirir mediante la experiencia información o conductas nuevas y relativamente permanentes. (pág. 166)

limbic system/sistema límbico Sistema neural (incluye la *amígdala*, *el hipotálamo* y *el hipocampo*) ubicado debajo de los hemisferios cerebrales; se lo asocia con las emociones y los impulsos. (pág. 44)

lobotomy/lobotomía Procedimiento psicoquirúrgico que antes era usado para calmar a pacientes emocionalmente incontrolables o violentos. En el procedimiento se cortaban los nervios entre los lóbulos frontales y los centros en el interior del cerebro que controlan las emociones. (pág. 422)

longitudinal study/estudio longitudinal Investigación en la que las mismas personas se estudian una y otra vez durante un lapso de tiempo prolongado. (págs. 70, 238, A-6)

long-term memory/memoria a largo plazo El almacenaje relativamente permanente e ilimitado del sistema de la memoria. Incluye los conocimientos, las habilidades y las experiencias. (pág. 190)

long-term potentiation (LTP)/potenciación a largo plazo (PLP) Aumento en la eficacia de una célula nerviosa para transmitir impulsos sinápticos después de la estimulación breve y rápida. Se considera la base neuronal del aprendizaje y la memoria. (pág. 198)

LSD (lysergic acid diethylamide)/LSD (dietilamida de ácido lisérgico) Poderosa droga alucinógena; también se conoce como ácido. (pág. 378)

major depressive disorder/trastorno depresivo mayor Trastorno en el cual una persona—sin padecer alguna condición médica y sin usar drogas—pasa dos o más semanas con cinco o más síntomas, de los cuales al menos uno debe ser o (1) un estado de ánimo deprimido o (2) la pérdida de interés o placer. (pág. 381)

mania/manía Estado de ánimo marcado por un estado de hiperactividad y optimismo desenfrenado, caracterizado por la falta de juicio. (pág. 382)

manifest content/contenido manifiesto Según Freud, trama del sueño que se recuerda al despertarse. (pág. 64)

maturation/maduración Procesos de crecimiento biológico que casi siempre conducen a cambios ordenados en el comportamiento y son en gran parte independientes de la experiencia. (pág. 77)

mean/promedio Media aritmética de una distribución que se obtiene sumando los valores y luego dividiendo el total entre el número de valores. (pág. A-2)

median/mediana Valor central de una distribución; la mitad de los valores se encuentran por encima y la mitad se encuentran por debajo de la mediana. (pág. A-2)

medical model/modelo médico Concepto que afirma que las enfermedades, en este caso los trastornos psicológicos, tienen causas físicas que se pueden *diagnosticar*, *tratar* y, en la mayoría de los casos, *curar*, generalmente por medio de tratamientos que se llevan a cabo en un *hospital*. (pág. 364)

medulla/bulbo raquídeo Base del tronco encefálico; controla la frecuencia cardíaca y la respiración. (pág. 42)

MEG (magnetoencephalography)/MEG (magnetoencefalografía) Técnica de obtener imágenes del cerebro a través de la medición de los campos magnéticos de la actividad eléctrica natural del cerebro. (pág. 40)

memory/memoria La persistencia del aprendizaje con el pasar del tiempo a través de la codificación, el almacenaje y la recuperación de la información. (pág. 190)

memory consolidation/consolidación de la memoria Almacenaje neural de una memoria a largo plazo. (pág. 196)

memory trace/rastro de memoria Cambios físicos duraderos que ocurren en el cerebro al formarse un recuerdo. (pág. 203)

menarche/menarquia Primera menstruación. (pág. 112)

menopause/menopausia Cesación de la menstruación. En el uso cotidiano, el término se refiere a la transición biológica que experimenta la mujer desde antes hasta después de acabar de menstruar. (pág. 97)

mental age/edad mental Medida de desempeño en la prueba de inteligencia diseñada por Binet. El nivel de desempeño que corresponde característicamente a un niño de la edad cronológica dada. Por ende, se dice que un niño que se desempeña como una persona normal de 8 años tiene una edad mental de 8 años. (pág. 232)

mere exposure effect/efecto de mera exposición Fenómeno que sostiene que la exposición repetida a estímulos novedosos aumenta la atracción a tales estímulos. (pág. 324)

methamphetamine/metanfetamina Droga poderosamente adictiva que estimula el sistema nervioso central con funciones corporales aceleradas y los cambios correspondientes de la energía y el estado de ánimo. Con el tiempo, parece reducir los niveles básicos de dopamina. (pág. 377)

middle ear/oído medio Cámara ubicada entre el tímpano y la cóclea; contiene tres huesos pequeños (el martillo, el yunque y el estribo) que concentran las vibraciones del tímpano y de la ventana oval de la cóclea. (pág. 151)

mindfulness meditation/meditación de conciencia plena Práctica reflexiva en la que las personas atienden a las vivencias actuales de una manera tolerante y sin juicios. (pág. 290)

Minnesota Multiphasic Personality Inventory (MMPI)/Inventario Multifásico de Personalidad de Minnesota La prueba de personalidad más utilizada e investigada con más profundidad. Se creó originalmente para identificar trastornos emocionales (y aún esto se considera el uso mas apropiado de la prueba). Esta prueba se utiliza en la actualidad para muchas actividades de preselección. (pág. 347)

mirror-image perceptions/percepciones de imagen reflejada Opiniones mutuas que generalmente sostienen los grupos que discrepan o experimentan conflictos entre sí, tal como cuando cada parte se ve a sí misma como ética y pacifica, y a la otra parte la ve como malvada y agresiva. (pág. 330)

mirror neuron/neurona espejo Neurona que se activa cuando llevamos a cabo ciertas acciones y cuando observamos a otros realizando tales acciones; la base neuronal para el aprendizaje por imitación y por observación. (pág. 183)

misinformation effect/efecto de información errónea La corrupción de una memoria que se deforma al recibir información engañosa. (pág. 206)

mnemonics/reglas mnemotécnicas Ayudas para la memoria, sobre todo técnicas que utilizan imágenes vivas y dispositivos organizacionales. (pág. 193)

mode/moda Valor o valores que ocurren con mayor frecuencia en una distribución. (pág. A-2)

modeling/modelar Proceso de observar e imitar un comportamiento en particular. (pág. 182)

monocular cue/clave monocular Señal de profundidad, como la interposición y la perspectiva lineal, que puede ser extraída de las imágenes de cada uno de los ojos. (pág. 146)

mood-congruent memory/memoria congruente con el estado de ánimo Tendencia a recordar experiencias que concuerdan con el buen o mal estado de ánimo que estamos viviendo. (pág. 201)

motivation/motivación Necesidad o deseo que promueve y dirige el comportamiento. (pág. 248)

motor cortex/corteza motora Parte de la corteza cerebral en la parte posterior de los lóbulos frontales. Controla los movimientos voluntarios. (pág. 46)

motor neurons/motoneuronas Neuronas que llevan la información desde el cerebro y la médula espinal hacia los músculos y las glándulas. (pág. 36)

MRI (magnetic resonance imaging)/imagen por resonancia magnética (IRM) Técnica que emplea campos magnéticos y ondas de radio para producir imágenes computarizadas de tejidos blandos. Las imágenes de IRM nos permiten visualizar la anatomía del cerebro. (pág. 40)

narcissism/narcisismo Amor propio y ensimismamiento excesivos. (págs. 258, 354)

narcolepsy/narcolepsia Trastorno del sueño caracterizado por ataques incontrolables de sueño, en el que a veces el individuo entra directamente en el sueño MOR. (pág. 63)

natural selection/selección natural Principio según el cual de entre la variedad de rasgos heredados aquellos que contribuyen al aumento de la reproducción y la supervivencia en un entorno determinado tienen mayor probabilidad de pasar a las generaciones futuras. (pág. 126)

naturalistic observation/observación naturalista Técnica de observar y registrar la conducta en situaciones reales sin tratar de manipular ni controlar la situación. (pág. 16)

nature–nurture issue/cuestión de innato o adquirido Controversia de antaño acerca de la influencia respectiva que ejercen los genes y las vivencias en el desarrollo de los rasgos psicológicos y comportamientos. En la ciencia psicológica actual se opina que los rasgos y comportamientos tienen origen en la interrelación entre lo innato y lo adquirido. (pág. 9)

near-death experience/experiencia cercana a la muerte Estado alterado de consciencia experimentado por personas que tienen un encuentro cercano con la muerte (por ejemplo, cuando se sufre un paro cardíaco). A menudo es similar a las alucinaciones inducidas por las drogas. (pág. 377)

need to belong/necesidad de pertenencia La necesidad de crear y mantener relaciones y sentirse parte de un grupo. (pág. 255)

negative reinforcement/reforzamiento negativo Aumento en la expresión de comportamientos mediante la interrupción o reducción de los estímulos negativos tales como un corrientazo. Un reforzamiento negativo es cualquier cosa que, *cuando se elimina* después de una reacción, refuerza la reacción. (*Nota:* el reforzamiento negativo *no* significa castigo). (pág. 174)

nerves/nervios Haces de axones neuronales que forman "cables" de nervios y conectan el sistema nervioso central con los músculos, las glándulas y los órganos sensoriales. (pág. 36)

nervous system/sistema nervioso Red rápida electroquímica de comunicación del cuerpo que consta de todas las células nerviosas de los sistemas nerviosos central y periférico. (pág. 36)

neurogenesis/neurogénesis Formación de neuronas nuevas. (pág. 50)

neuron/neurona Célula nerviosa; el componente básico del sistema nervioso. (pág. 32)

neurotransmitters/neurotransmisores Agentes químicos producidos por las neuronas que atraviesan la brecha sináptica y transmiten mensajes a otras neuronas o a los músculos y las glándulas. (pág. 34)

neutral stimulus (NS)/estímulo neutro (EN) Según el condicionamiento clásico, un estímulo que no produce respuesta antes del condicionamiento. (pág. 168)

nicotine/nicotina Droga estimulante, altamente adictiva y psicoactiva, que se halla en el tabaco. (pág. 375)

night terrors/terrores nocturnos Trastorno de sueño que se caracteriza por un nivel alto de excitación y la apariencia de un terror extremo. A diferencia de las pesadillas, los terrores nocturnos ocurren durante la fase 3 del sueño NMOR y raramente se recuerdan. (pág. 63)

normal curve/curva normal Curva simétrica en forma de campana que describe la distribución de muchos atributos físicos y psicológicos. La mayoría de las puntuaciones yacen cerca de la media (cerca de 68 por ciento caen entre una desviación estándar) y otras, cada vez menos, yacen cerca de los extremos. (También llamada *distribución normal.*) (págs. 234, A-3)

normative social influence/influencia social normativa Influencia resultante del deseo de una persona de obtener la aprobación o evitar la desaprobación de los demás. (pág. 308)

nudge/empujón El encuadre de las decisiciones de una manera que alienta a las personas a tomar decisiones que apoyan a su bienestar personal. (pág. 219)

obesity/obesidad Índice de masa corporal (IMC) de 30 o más, que se calcula de la proporción peso-estatura. (Personas con *sobrepeso* tienen el IMC de 25 o más.) (pág. 253)

object permanence/permanencia de los objetos Reconocimiento de que las cosas siguen existiendo aunque no las veamos. (pág. 80)

observational learning/aprendizaje observacional Aprender observando a los demás. (pág. 182)

obsessive-compulsive disorder (OCD)/trastorno obsesivo-compulsivo (TOC) Trastorno que se caracteriza por pensamientos (obsesiones) y/o acciones (compulsiones) repetitivos y no deseados. (pág. 368)

occipital lobes/lóbulos occipitales Porción de la corteza cerebral ubicada en la parte posterior de la cabeza; incluye las áreas que reciben información de los campos visuales. (pág. 46)

Oedipus complex/complejo de Edipo Según Freud, los deseos sexuales de un niño hacia su madre y sentimientos de celos y odio hacia el padre rival. (pág. 338)

one-word stage/etapa holofrástica Etapa en el desarrollo del habla, entre el primero y segundo años, en la que el niño se expresa principalmente con palabras aisladas. (pág. 224)

operant behavior/comportamiento operante Comportamiento que opera en el entorno, produciendo consecuencias. (pág. 167)

operant chamber/cámara operante Caja que contiene una barra o tecla que un animal puede manipular para obtener un reforzamiento de comida o agua. Está dotada de un aparato de grabación que registra la frecuencia con la que el animal dentro de la caja presiona la barra u oprime la tecla. Se emplea en investigaciones de condicionamiento operante. (También se conoce como *caja de Skinner*). (pág. 172)

operant conditioning/condicionamiento operante Aprendizaje en el que el comportamiento se torna más probable si está seguido por un reforzamiento o se atenúa si está seguido por un castigo. (pág. 172)

operational definition/definición operacional Declaración redactada con gran cuidado en la que se detallan los procedimientos (operaciones) exactos que se usan en un estudio de investigación. Por ejemplo, *la inteligencia humana* puede ser operacionalmente definida como lo que se mide en una prueba de inteligencia. (pág. 15)

opiates/opiáceos El opio y sus derivados, tales como la morfina y la heroína. Deprimen la actividad neuronal y alivian temporalmente el dolor y la ansiedad. (págs. 35, 374)

opponent-process theory/teoría de procesos oponentes Teoría que manifiesta que los procesos opuestos de la retina (rojo-verde, amarillo-azul, blanco-negro) posibilitan la visualización de los colores. Por ejemplo, el verde "enciende" algunas células y "apaga" otras; y el rojo "enciende" otras células que el verde "apaga". (pág. 142)

optic nerve/nervio óptico Nervio que transporta los impulsos neuronales del ojo al cerebro. (pág. 140)

optimism/optimismo Anticipación de resultados positivos. Son optimistas las personas que esperan lo mejor y creen que sus esfuerzos llevan a obtener buenos resultados. (pág. 285)

organizational psychology/psicología organizacional Subdivisión de la psicología del trabajo y de las organizaciones que examina las influencias organizacionales en la satisfacción y productividad de los trabajadores y facilita cambios organizacionales. (pág. B-3)

ostracism/ostracismo Exclusión social deliberada de individuos o grupos. (pág. 256)

other-race effect/efecto de otra raza Tendencia a recordar caras de la raza de uno mismo con mayor precisión que las caras de otras razas. (pág. 318)

outgroup/exogrupo "Ellos", o sea, las personas a las que percibimos como distintas o separadas, que no forman parte de nuestro grupo. (pág. 318)

overconfidence/exceso de confianza Tendencia a ser más confiado que acertado, o sea, a sobreestimar las creencias y las opiniones propias. (pág. 218)

panic disorder/trastorno de pánico Trastorno de ansiedad marcado por el inicio repentino y recurrente de episodios de aprehensión intensa o terror que pueden durar varios minutos. Pueden incluir dolor de pecho, sofocamiento, y otras sensaciones atemorizantes, a menudo seguidas por preocupaciones de un posible ataque posterior. (pág. 367)

parallel processing/procesamiento en paralelo Procesamiento simultáneo de muchos aspectos de un problema o escena. (págs. 54, 143, 192)

paraphilias/parafilias La excitación sexual en la que las fuentes de placer son fantasías, comportamientos, o impulsos que pertenecen a objetos no humanos, el sufrimiento de uno mismo o de otros y/o personas que no dan su consentimiento. (pág. 119)

parasympathetic nervous system/sistema nervioso parasimpático Subdivisión del sistema nervioso autonómico que calma el cuerpo y conserva su energía. (pág. 37)

parietal lobes/lóbulos parietales Área de la corteza cerebral en la parte superior y hacia la parte posterior de la cabeza; recibe aportes sensoriales del tacto y la posición del cuerpo. (pág. 46)

partial (intermittent) reinforcement/reforzamiento parcial (intermitente) Reforzamiento de una respuesta tan solo una parte del tiempo; tiene como resultado la adquisición más lenta de una respuesta pero mucho más resistente a la extinción que el reforzamiento continuo. (pág. 175)

passionate love/amor apasionado Estado excitado de intensa y positiva absorción en otro ser. Por lo general se observa al comienzo de una relación de amor romántica. (pág. 327)

perception/percepción Proceso mediante el cual el cerebro organiza e interpreta la información sensorial transformándola en objetos y sucesos que tienen sentido. (pág. 132)

perceptual adaptation/adaptación perceptual Capacidad de acomodarnos a un estímulo sensorial cambiado, como por ejemplo un campo visual artificialmente desplazado o incluso invertido. (pág. 149)

perceptual constancy/constancia perceptual Tendencia a percibir objetos como si fueran constantes e inalterables (como si mantuvieran el color, la forma y el tamaño), a pesar de los cambios que se produzcan en la iluminación y en las imágenes que llegan a la retina. (pág. 148)

perceptual set/predisposición perceptiva Predisposición mental para percibir una cosa y no otra. (pág. 136)

peripheral nervous system (PNS)/sistema nervioso periférico (SNP) Neuronas sensoriales y motoras que conectan el sistema nervioso central con el resto del organismo. (pág. 36)

peripheral route persuasion/persuasión de ruta periférica Se produce cuando las personas se ven influenciadas por señales triviales, como el atractivo del orador. (pág. 305)

personal control/control personal Nuestro sentido de controlar el entorno en lugar de sentirnos impotentes. (pág. 283)

personality/personalidad Forma característica de una persona de pensar, sentir y actuar. (pág. 336)

personality disorders/trastornos de la personalidad Patrones de comportamiento inflexibles y duraderos que se interponen ante el desempeño social. (pág. 393)

personality inventory/inventario de personalidad Cuestionario (a menudo de preguntas de *verdadero/falso* o de *desacuerdo/acuerdo*) en el que las personas responden a preguntas diseñadas para medir una amplia gama de sentimientos y conductas. Se usa para evaluar ciertas características seleccionadas de la personalidad. (pág. 347)

person-centered therapy/terapia centrada en la persona Tipo de terapia humanista creada por Rogers, en la cual el terapeuta se vale de técnicas tales como escuchar activamente dentro de un entorno genuino, con aceptación y empatía, para facilitar el crecimiento personal del cliente. (También se denomina terapia centrada en el cliente). (pág. 404)

personnel psychology/psicología de personal Subdivisión de la psicología del trabajo y de las organizaciones que ayuda con la búsqueda de empleo y con el reclutamiento, selección, colocación, capacitación, evaluación y desarrollo de los empleados. (pág. B-3)

pessimism/pesimismo Anticipación de resultados negativos. Son pesimistas las personas que esperan lo peor y dudan de que puedan alcanzar sus metas. (pág. 286)

PET (positron emission tomography) scan/examen TEP (tomografía por emisión de positrones) Muestra visual de la actividad cerebral que detecta hacia dónde se dirige un tipo de glucosa radiactiva en el momento en que el cerebro realiza una función dada. (pág. 40)

phobia/fobia Trastorno de ansiedad marcado por un temor persistente e irracional y la evasión de un objeto, actividad o situación específico. (pág. 368)

physiological need/necesidad fisiológica Exigencia básica del cuerpo. (pág. 248)

pitch/tono Propiedad de los sonidos que los caracteriza como agudos o graves, en función de su frecuencia. (pág. 151)

pituitary gland/glándula pituitaria La glándula más influyente del sistema endocrino. Bajo la influencia del hipotálamo, la glándula pituitaria regula el crecimiento y controla las demás glándulas endocrinas. (pág. 40)

placebo/placebo Substancia o condición inactiva que a veces se suministra a los miembros de un grupo de control en lugar del tratamiento que se le da al grupo experimental. (pág. 21)

placebo effect/efecto placebo Resultados producidos por las expectativas únicamente. (pág. 21)

plasticity/plasticidad Capacidad del cerebro de modificarse, sobre todo durante la niñez, reordenándose después de un daño cerebral o formando nuevas trayectorias basadas en la experiencia. (pág. 32)

polygraph/polígrafo Máquina, utilizada comúnmente con la intención de detectar mentiras, que mide ciertas reacciones corporales (como los cambios en la transpiración, el ritmo cardíaco y la respiración) que acompañan a las emociones. (pág. 267)

population/población Todos aquellos que constituyen el grupo que se está estudiando, a partir del cual se pueden tomar muestras. (*Nota:* Salvo en estudios de alcance nacional, *no* se refiere a la totalidad de la población de un país). (pág. 17)

positive psychology/psicología positiva Estudio científico de la prosperidad humana, que tiene las metas de descubrir y promover las fortalezas y las virtudes que ayudan a los individuos y a las comunidades a fructificar. (pág. 11)

positive reinforcement/reforzamiento positivo Aumento en la expresión de comportamientos mediante la presentación de estímulos positivos, por ejemplo, un alimento. Un reforzamiento positivo es cualquier cosa que, *presentada* después de una respuesta, refuerza la respuesta. (pág. 174)

posthypnotic suggestion/sugestión poshipnótica Sugerencia que se hace durante una sesión de hipnotismo, que el sujeto debe realizar cuando ya no está hipnotizado; la utiliza algunos practicantes para ayudar a controlar síntomas y conductas no deseadas. (pág. 156)

posttraumatic growth/crecimiento postraumático Cambios psicológicos positivos como resultado de la lucha contra circunstancias extremadamente difíciles y crisis de la vida. (pág. 424)

posttraumatic stress disorder (PTSD)/trastorno por estrés postraumático (TEPT) Trastorno de ansiedad caracterizado por recuerdos obsesionantes, pesadillas, hipervigilancia, evitación de estímulos asociados a los sucesos traumáticos, aislamiento social, ansiedad asustadiza, emociones entumecidas y/o insomnio que perdura por cuatro semanas o más después de una experiencia traumática. (pág. 368)

predictive validity/validez predictiva Nivel de éxito con el que una prueba predice el comportamiento para el que ha sido diseñada predecir. (pág. 234)

prejudice/prejuicio Actitud injusta y normalmente negativa hacia un grupo y sus integrantes. El prejuicio generalmente implica creencias estereotipadas, sentimientos negativos y una predisposición a acción discriminatoria. (pág. 315)

preoperational stage/etapa preoperacional En la teoría de Piaget, la etapa (desde alrededor de los 2 hasta los 6 o 7 años de edad) durante la que el niño aprende a utilizar el lenguaje pero todavía no comprende las operaciones mentales de la lógica concreta. (pág. 81)

preregistration/registro previo Comunicación pública del diseño, hipótesis, recopilación de datos y análisis de los ensayos clínicos planificados. (pág. 15)

primary reinforcer/reforzador primario Suceso que es inherentemente reforzador y a menudo satisface una necesidad biológica. (pág. 174)

primary sex characteristics/características sexuales primarias Estructuras del organismo (ovarios, testículos y aparatos genitales externos) que posibilitan la reproducción sexual. (pág. 111)

priming/primado Activación de asociaciones en nuestra mente, a menudo de manera inconsciente, que nos dispone a percibir o recordar objetos o sucesos de una manera determinada. (págs. 134, 200)

proactive interference/interferencia proactiva Efecto interruptor del aprendizaje anterior sobre la manera de recordar información *nueva*. (pág. 204)

problem-focused coping/estrategias de afrontamiento centradas en los problemas Intento de sobrellevar el estrés de manera directa cambiando ya sea lo que produce la tensión o la forma en que nos relacionamos con dicho factor estresante. (pág. 282)

projective test/prueba proyectiva Tipo de prueba de la personalidad, como la prueba de Rorschach, en la cual se le da a una persona una imagen ambigua diseñada para provocar una proyección de pensamientos o sentimientos inconscientes. (pág. 340)

prosocial behavior/comportamiento prosocial Comportamiento positivo, constructivo y útil. Lo contrario del comportamiento antisocial. (pág. 184)

prototype/prototipo Imagen mental o mejor ejemplo de una categoría. Al cotejar artículos nuevos con un prototipo se trabaja con un método rápido y sencillo para clasificar artículos en categorías (tal como cuando se comparan animales de plumas con un ave prototípico, como un cuervo). (pág. 214)

psychiatry/psiquiatría La rama de la medicina que se ocupa de trastornos psicológicos; los médicos que practican psiquiatría suelen proveer tratamientos médicos (por ejemplo, medicamentos) así como terapia psicológica. (pág. 10)

psychoactive drug/psicoactivo Sustancia química que altera las percepciones y el estado de ánimo. (pág. 371)

psychoanalysis/psicoanálisis (1) Teoría de Freud sobre la personalidad que atribuye los pensamientos y las acciones a motivos y conflictos inconscientes; las técnicas utilizadas en el tratamiento de trastornos psicológicos intentando descubrir e interpretar las tensiones inconscientes. (2) El método terapéutico de Freud usado para el tratamiento de trastornos psicológicos. Freud creía que las asociaciones libres, las resistencias, los sueños y las transferencias del paciente (así como la interpretación de ellas por parte del analista) liberaban sentimientos antes reprimidos, permitiendo que el paciente adquiriera autoconocimiento. (págs. 336, 402)

psychodynamic theories/teorías psicodinámicas Visión de la personalidad con una concentración en el subconsciente y en la importancia de las vivencias en la niñez. (pág. 336)

psychodynamic therapy/terapia psicodinámica Enfoque terapéutico que se deriva de la tradición psicoanalítica; se observa a los individuos como si respondieran a fuerzas inconscientes y experiencias de la niñez, y se busca agudizar la introspección. (pág. 403)

psychological disorder/trastorno psicológico Síndrome caracterizado por la alteración clínicamente significativa de los pensamientos, los sentimientos o los comportamientos de una persona. (pág. 362)

psychology/psicología La ciencia del comportamiento y los procesos mentales. (pág. 6)

psychoneuroimmunology/psiconeuroinmunología Estudio de cómo los procesos psicológicos, neuronales y endocrinos se combinan en nuestro organismo para influenciar el sistema inmunitario y la salud en general. (pág. 279)

psychosexual stages/etapas psicosexuales Etapas del desarrollo infantil (oral, anal, fálica, latente, genital), durante las cuales, según Freud, las energías del id que buscan el placer se enfocan en zonas erógenas específicas. (pág. 338)

psychosurgery/psicocirugía Cirugía que extrae o destruye tejido cerebral para cambiar el comportamiento. (pág. 422)

psychotherapy/psicoterapia Tratamiento que incluye técnicas psicológicas; consiste en interacciones entre un terapeuta cualificado y una persona que desea superar dificultades psicológicas o lograr un crecimiento personal. (pág. 402)

psychotic disorders/trastornos psicóticos Grupo de trastornos caracterizados por ideas irracionales, percepciones distorsionadas y pérdida de contacto con la realidad. (pág. 386)

puberty/pubertad Período de maduración sexual durante el cual la persona adquiere la capacidad de reproducirse. (págs. 90, 111)

punishment/castigo Evento que disminuye el comportamiento que le precede. (pág. 176)

random assignment/asignación aleatoria Asignación de participantes a los grupos experimental y de control. Se realiza al azar para minimizar las diferencias preexistentes que pudiese haber entre los asignados. (pág. 20)

random sample/muestra aleatoria Muestra que representa justamente la población, gracias a que cada elemento de la población tiene igual oportunidad de ser seleccionado. (pág. 17)

range/rango Diferencia entre los valores más alta y más baja en una distribución. (pág. A-2)

recall/recuperación Memoria que se demuestra extrayendo información aprendida anteriormente, tal como en las pruebas que consisten en rellenar espacios en blanco. (pág. 198)

reciprocal determinism/determinismo recíproco Influencias de la interacción entre la conducta, los factores personales internos y el entorno. (pág. 351)

reciprocity norm/norma de reciprocidad Expectativa de que las personas ayudarán, y no harán daño, a aquellos que las han ayudado. (pág. 330)

recognition/reconocimiento Memoria que se demuestra identificando cosas que se aprendieron anteriormente, tal como en las pruebas de opciones múltiples. (pág. 198)

reconsolidation/reconsolidación Proceso en el que los recuerdos almacenados, al ser recuperados, son potencialmente alterados antes de ser almacenados nuevamente. (pág. 206)

reflex/reflejo Respuesta simple y automática a un estímulo sensorial. (págs. 38, 75)

refractory period/período refractario (1) En el procesamiento neuronal, una breve fase de descanso que se produce después de que una neurona ha disparado. No se pueden producir potenciales de acción subsiguientes hasta que el axón vuelva a su estado de reposo. (2) En la sexualidad humana, fase de descanso que se produce después del orgasmo, en la que la persona es incapaz de tener otro orgasmo. (págs. 34, 118)

regression toward the mean/regresión hacia la media Tendencia de las puntuaciones o eventos extremos o poco comunes a retornar (regresar) hacia el promedio. (pág. A-5)

reinforcement/reforzamiento Según el condicionamiento operante, todo suceso que *fortalezca* el comportamiento al que sigue. (pág. 173)

reinforcement schedule/calendario de reforzamiento Patrón que define la frecuencia con que se reforzará una respuesta deseada. (pág. 175)

relational aggression/agresión relacional Acto de agresión (sea física o verbal) que tiene por intención hacerle daño a las relaciones de la persona o a su estatus social. (pág. 108)

relative deprivation/privación relativa Impresión de que estamos en peor situación que aquellos con quienes nos comparamos. (pág. 296)

relearning/reaprendizaje Memoria que se demuestra por el tiempo que se ahorra cuando se aprende algo por segunda vez. (pág. 198)

reliability/fiabilidad Grado hasta el que una prueba produce resultados coherentes, comprobados por la uniformidad de las puntuaciones en las dos mitades de la prueba, en formas distintas de la prueba, o al retomar la prueba. (pág. 234)

REM rebound/rebote de MOR Tendencia al aumento del sueño MOR como consecuencia de la privación del sueño MOR. (pág. 65)

REM sleep/sueño MOR (sueño de movimientos oculares rápidos) Etapa recurrente del sueño durante la cual generalmente ocurren sueños gráficos. También se conoce como *sueño paradójico*, porque los músculos están relajados (salvo unos espasmos mínimos) pero los demás sistemas del cuerpo están activos. (pág. 57)

replication/replicación Repetir la esencia de un estudio de investigación, por lo general con participantes diferentes y en situaciones diferentes, para ver si las conclusiones básicas se pueden reproducir. (pág. 15)

representativeness heuristic/heurística de la representatividad Estimar las probabilidades de eventos según cuán bien representen o corresponden con prototipos determinados. Podría llevarnos a ignorar otra información pertinente. (pág. 216)

repression/represión En la teoría del psicoanálisis, el mecanismo básico de defensa por medio del cual el sujeto elimina de su consciente aquellos pensamientos, emociones y recuerdos que le producen ansiedad. (págs. 205, 339)

resilience/resiliencia Fuerza personal que ayuda a la mayoría de las personas a asumir con flexibilidad situaciones de estrés y recuperarse de la adversidad e incluso de un trauma. (págs. 293, 424)

resistance/resistencia En el psicoanálisis, bloquear del consciente aquello que está cargado de ansiedad. (pág. 403)

respondent behavior/comportamiento respondiente Comportamiento que ocurre como respuesta automática a un estímulo. (pág. 167)

reticular formation/formación reticular Red de nervios que atraviesa el tronco encefálico e ingresa en el tálamo y que desempeña un papel importante en el control de la excitación. (pág. 43)

retina/retina Superficie en la parte interior del ojo que es sensible a la luz y que contiene los receptores de luz llamados bastoncillos y conos, además de capas de neuronas que inician el procesamiento de la información visual. (pág. 139)

retinal disparity/disparidad retiniana Clave binocular para la percepción de la profundidad. Mediante la comparación de las imágenes que provienen de ambos ojos, el cerebro calcula la distancia. Cuanto mayor sea la disparidad (diferencia) entre dos imágenes, más cerca estará el objeto. (pág. 146)

retrieval/recuperación Proceso de extraer la información que está almacenada en la memoria. (pág. 190)

retrieval cue/clave de recuperación Todo estímulo (suceso, sentimiento, lugar, etcétera) relacionado con un recuerdo específico. (pág. 200)

retroactive interference/interferencia retroactiva Efecto interruptor de algo nuevo que se ha aprendido en la capacidad de recordar información *vieja*. (pág. 204)

retrograde amnesia/amnesia retrógrada La incapacidad de recordar información antes de un momento en el pasado. (pág. 202)

reuptake/recaptación Reabsorción de un neurotransmisor por la neurona emisora. (pág. 34)

rods/bastoncillos Receptores de la retina que detectan el negro, el blanco y el gris, y que son sensibles al movimiento; necesarios para la visión periférica y crepuscular cuando los conos no responden. (pág. 140)

role/rol social Conjunto de expectativas (normas) acerca de una posición social, que definen la forma en que deben comportarse las personas que ocupan esa posición. (págs. 113, 304)

Rorschach inkblot test/prueba de Rorschach Prueba proyectiva de amplio uso. Conjunto de 10 manchas de tinta, diseñado por Hermann Rorschach; busca identificar los sentimientos internos de las personas mediante el análisis de sus interpretaciones de las manchas. (pág. 341)

savant syndrome/síndrome de savant Condición según la cual una persona de capacidad mental limitada cuenta con una destreza excepcional en un campo como la computación o el dibujo. (pág. 229)

scaffold/andamiaje En la teoría de Vygotsky, un marco que ofrece apoyo temporal a los niños mientras que desarrollan niveles más elevados de pensamiento. (pág. 83)

scapegoat theory/teoría del chivo expiatorio Teoría que expone que el prejuicio ofrece un escape para la cólera porque nos brinda a alguien a quien culpar. (pág. 318)

scatterplot/gráfico de dispersión Conjunto de datos graficados, cada uno de los cuales representa los valores de dos variables. La pendiente de los puntos sugiere el sentido de la relación entre las dos variables. El nivel de dispersión sugiere la fuerza de la correlación (un bajo nivel de dispersión indica alta correlación). (pág. A-4)

schema/esquema Concepto o marco referencial que organiza e interpreta la información. (pág. 80)

schizophrenia/esquizofrenia Trastorno caracterizado por delirios, alucinaciones, habla desorganizada y/o expresión emocional disminuida o inapropiada. (pág. 386)

secondary sex characteristics/características sexuales secundarias Rasgos sexuales no relacionados con la reproducción, tales como los senos y las caderas de las mujeres, la calidad de la voz del varón y el pelo corporal. (pág. 112)

selective attention/atención selectiva Capacidad de enfocar la consciencia en un estímulo en particular. (pág. 54)

self/yo Imagen que tenemos de nosotros mismos y entendimiento de quiénes somos. Según la psicología moderna, el concepto de que este es el centro de la personalidad, que organiza los pensamientos, los sentimientos y las acciones. (pág. 353)

self-actualization/autorrealización Según Maslow, necesidad psicológica que surge después de satisfacer las necesidades físicas y psicológicas y de lograr la autoestima; motivación para realizar nuestro potencial pleno. (pág. 343)

self-concept/autoconcepto Todo lo que pensamos y sentimos acerca de nosotros mismos cuando respondemos a la pregunta "¿Quién soy?" (pág. 344)

self-control/autocontrol Capacidad de controlar los impulsos y demorar la gratificación a corto plazo con el fin de obtener mayores recompensas a largo plazo. (pág. 285)

self-determination theory/teoría de la autodeterminación La teoría que los seres humanos estamos motivados para satisfacer nuestras necesidades de competencia, autonomía y relación. (pág. 256)

self-disclosure/autorevelación Revelación a los demás de cosas íntimas de nuestro ser. (pág. 328)

self-efficacy/autoeficacia Nuestros sentimientos de competencia y eficacia. (pág. 351)

self-esteem/autoestima Sentimientos altos o bajos con que nos valoramos a nosotros mismos. (pág. 354)

self-fulfilling prophecy/profecía autorrealizada Creencia que conduce a su propia realización. (pág. 330)

self-serving bias/sesgo de autoservicio Disposición para percibirnos a nosotros mismos de manera favorable. (pág. 355)

self-transcendence/autotrascendencia Según Maslow, esfuerzo por alcanzar una identidad, un sentido y un propósito que vaya más allá de uno mismo. (pág. 343)

semantic memory/memoria semántica Memoria explícita de hechos y conocimientos generales. Uno de los dos sistemas de memoria conscientes (el otro es la *memoria episódica*). (pág. 195)

sensation/sensación Proceso mediante el cual los receptores sensoriales y el sistema nervioso reciben y representan las energías de los estímulos provenientes de nuestro entorno. (pág. 132)

sensorimotor stage/etapa sensoriomotora En la teoría de Piaget, la etapa (de los 0 a los 2 años de edad) durante la cual los bebés conocen el mundo principalmente en términos de sus impresiones sensoriales y actividades motoras. (pág. 80)

sensorineural hearing loss/pérdida de la audición sensorineuronal Sordera causada por daños a las células receptoras de la cóclea o a los nervios de la audición; la forma más común de sordera. También se le dice *sordera nerviosa*. (pág. 151)

sensory adaptation/adaptación sensorial Disminución en la sensibilidad como respuesta a la estimulación constante. (pág. 135)

sensory interaction/interacción sensorial Principio que un sentido puede influir en otro, como cuando el olor de la comida influye en su sabor. (pág. 159)

sensory memory/memoria sensorial Registro breve e inmediato de la información sensorial en el sistema de la memoria. (pág. 190)

sensory neurons/neuronas sensoriales Neuronas que conducen la información que le llega desde los tejidos del cuerpo y los receptores sensoriales al cerebro y la médula espinal. (pág. 36)

sensory receptors/receptores sensoriales Terminaciones nerviosas sensoriales que responden a estímulos. (pág. 132)

sequential processing/procesamiento secuencial Procesamiento de un aspecto de un problema o estímulo a la vez; se utiliza cuando centramos la atención en tareas nuevas o complejas. (pág. 54)

serial position effect/efecto de posición serial Tendencia a recordar con mayor facilidad los elementos del comienzo y del final de una lista. (pág. 201)

set point/punto fijo Punto de supuesto equilibrio en el "termostato del peso" de una persona. Cuando el cuerpo alcanza un peso por debajo de este punto, se produce un aumento en el hambre y una disminución en el índice metabólico, los cuales pueden actuar para restablecer el peso perdido. (pág. 252)

sex/sexo En psicología, las características biológicas por las cuales la sociedad define al *hombre* y a la *mujer*. (pág. 108)

sexual aggression/agresión sexual Comportamiento físico o verbal de carácter sexual que tiene por objetivo hacerle daño física o emocionalmente a alguien. Puede expresearse como *acoso sexual* o *asalto sexual*. (pág. 114)

sexual dysfunction/disfunción sexual Problema que complica de manera constante la excitación o el funcionamiento sexual. (pág. 118)

sexual orientation/orientación sexual La dirección que toma el deseo sexual de una persona, como se refleja en sus anhelos y fantasías. (pág. 121)

sexual response cycle/ciclo de respuesta sexual Las cuatro etapas de respuesta sexual descritas por Masters y Johnson: excitación, meseta, orgasmo y resolución. (pág. 118)

shaping/moldeamiento Procedimiento del condicionamiento operante en el cual los reforzadores conducen una acción con aproximaciones sucesivas hasta lograr el comportamiento deseado. (pág. 173)

short-term memory/memoria a corto plazo Memoria activada que retiene algunos elementos por un corto tiempo, tales como los siete dígitos de un número telefónico mientras se marca, antes de que la información se almacene o se olvide. (pág. 190)

sleep/sueño Pérdida del conocimiento que es periódica y natural. Es distinta de la inconsciencia que puede resultar del estado de coma, de la anestesia general o de la hibernación. (pág. 57)

sleep apnea/apnea del sueño Trastorno del sueño en el que se interrumpe repetidamente la respiración hasta tal punto de que el nivel de oxígeno en sangre llega a ser tan bajo que la persona tiene que despertarse para respirar. (pág. 63)

social clock/reloj social Manera que la sociedad prefiere para marcar el tiempo adecuado de los eventos sociales, tales como el matrimonio, la paternidad y la jubilación. (pág. 101)

social-cognitive perspective/perspectiva sociocognoscitiva La idea que la conducta es influida por la interacción entre las personas (y sus pensamientos) y su contexto social. (pág. 351)

social facilitation/facilitación social Mejoramiento del desempeño en funciones sencillas o bien aprendidas en la presencia de otros. (pág. 311)

social identity/identidad social Aspecto "nosotros" del concepto de nosotros mismos; parte de nuestra respuesta a "¿Quién soy?" que proviene de nuestra pertenencia a grupos. (pág. 93)

social leadership/liderazgo social Liderazgo orientado hacia el grupo que fortalece el trabajo en equipo, que media en conflictos y que ofrece apoyo. (pág. B-6)

social learning theory/teoría del aprendizaje social Teoría que señala que aprendemos la conducta social observando e imitando, y al ser recompensados o castigados. (pág. 114)

social loafing/pereza social Tendencia de las personas en un grupo de realizar menos esfuerzo cuando juntan sus esfuerzos para lograr una meta común que cuando son responsables individualmente. (pág. 312)

social psychology/psicología social Estudio científico de cómo pensamos, influimos y nos relacionamos con los demás. (pág. 302)

social-responsibility norm/norma de responsabilidad social Expectativa de que las personas ayudarán a aquellos que dependen de ellas. (pág. 330)

social script/guión social Guía modelada culturalmente acerca de cómo actuar en diversas situaciones. (págs. 121, 322)

somatic nervous system/sistema nervioso somático División del sistema nervioso periférico que controla los músculos esqueléticos del cuerpo. También llamado *sistema nervioso esquelético*. (pág. 36)

somatosensory cortex/corteza somatosensorial Área de la corteza cerebral en la parte delantera de los lóbulos parietales. Registra y procesa el tacto y las sensaciones de movimiento. (pág. 48)

source amnesia/amnesia de la fuente La incapacidad de recordar cómo, cuándo o dónde se aprendió o se imaginó la información. (pág. 207)

spacing effect/efecto de memoria espaciada Tendencia a que el estudio o la práctica distribuidos logren mejor retención a largo plazo que la que se logra a través del estudio o la práctica en volumen masivo. (pág. 194)

spermarche/espermarquia Primera eyaculación. (pág. 112)

split brain/cerebro dividido Condición en la que los dos hemisferios cerebrales se privan de la comunicación mediante el corte quirúrgico de las fibras que los conectan (principalmente las del cuerpo calloso). (pág. 51)

spontaneous recovery/recuperación espontánea Reaparición, después de una pausa, de una respuesta condicionada extinguida. (pág. 170)

spotlight effect/efecto foco Sobreestimación de lo que los demás notan y evalúan de nuestro aspecto, desempeño y desatinos (como si nos estuviera iluminando un foco). (pág. 353)

SQ3R/inspeccionar, preguntar, leer, recitar, repasar Método de estudio en el que se siguen cinco pasos: inspeccionar, preguntar, leer, recitar y repasar. (pág. 26)

standard deviation/desviación estándar Medición computada de cuánto varían los valores con respecto al valor medio. (pág. A-2)

standardization/estandarización Definir procedimientos de medición uniformes y puntuaciones significativos mediante la comparación del desempeño de un grupo examinado con anterioridad. (pág. 233)

Stanford-Binet/escala de inteligencia Stanford-Binet Revisión norteamericana (por Terman en la Universidad de Stanford) de la prueba original de inteligencia de Binet. Esta prueba se usa extensamente. (pág. 232)

statistical significance/significación estadística Declaración estadística de la probabilidad de que un resultado obtenido haya sido producto del azar. (pág. A-7)

stereotype/estereotipo Creencia (a veces acertada, pero frecuentemente demasiado generalizada) sobre las características de un grupo. (pág. 315)

stereotype threat/amenaza del estereotipo Preocupación autoconfirmadora de que nos evaluarán con base en un estereotipo negativo. (pág. 243)

stimulants/estimulantes Drogas (tales como la cafeína, la nicotina y las más poderosas, cocaína, anfetaminas, metanfetamina y éxtasis) que excitan la actividad neuronal y aceleran las funciones corporales. (pág. 374)

stimulus/estímulo Todo suceso o situación que provoca una respuesta. (pág. 167)

storage/almacenamiento Retención a través del tiempo de información codificada. (pág. 190)

stranger anxiety/ansiedad ante extraños Miedo a los extraños que manifiestan los bebés normalmente a partir de alrededor de los 8 meses de edad. (pág. 85)

stress/estrés Proceso mediante el cual percibimos y respondemos a ciertos eventos llamados *estresores*, los cuales evaluamos como amenazantes o desafiantes. (pág. 276)

structuralism/estructuralismo Una escuela de pensamiento de los primeros años promovido por Wundt que se centró en la estructura de la mente humana. (pág. 5)

subjective well-being/bienestar subjetivo Felicidad o satisfacción autopercibida con la vida de uno mismo. Se emplea junto con medidas de bienestar objetivas (por ejemplo, con indicadores físicos y económicos) para evaluar nuestra calidad de vida. (pág. 294)

subliminal/subliminal Aquello que ocurre por debajo de nuestro umbral absoluto de la consciencia. (pág. 133)

substance use disorder/trastornos por uso de sustancias Trastorno caracterizado por la continuación de las ansias y el uso de sustancias pese a que han interrumpido el estilo de vida de manera significativa y/o representan un riesgo físico. (pág. 371)

superego/superego En el psicoanálisis freudiano, componente de la personalidad que representa ideales internalizados y proporciona parámetros de juicio (la consciencia) y para fijarse metas futuras. (pág. 338)

superordinate goals/metas superordinadas Metas compartidas que hacen caso omiso de las diferencias entre las personas y que requieren su cooperación. (pág. 331)

suprachiasmatic nucleus (SCN)/núcleo supraquiasmático (NSQ) Par de grupos de células en el hipotálamo que controlan el ritmo circadiano. En respuesta a la luz, el núcleo supraquiasmático ajusta la producción de melatonina, modificando de esta manera los niveles de somnolencia. (pág. 60)

survey/encuesta Técnica descriptiva para obtener actitudes o conductas del grupo autodeclaradas por las personas; generalmente mediante preguntas que se le plantean a una *muestra aleatoria* y representativa de dicho grupo. (pág. 17)

sympathetic nervous system/sistema nervioso simpático Subdivisión del sistema nervioso autonómico que despierta al cuerpo y moviliza su energía. (pág. 37)

synapse/sinapsis Intersección entre el extremo del axón de una neurona que envía un mensaje y la dendrita o cuerpo celular de la neurona receptora. El pequeño espacio entre estos puntos de contacto se denomina *brecha sináptica* o *hendidura sináptica*. (pág. 33)

systematic desensitization/desensibilización sistemática Tipo de terapia de exposición en la cual se asocia un estado tranquilo y agradable con estímulos que van aumentando paulatinamente y que provocan ansiedad. De uso común para tratar fobias. (pág. 406)

task leadership/liderazgo específico Liderazgo orientado a metas específicas que establece las normas, organiza el trabajo y centra la atención en metas. (pág. B-6)

telegraphic speech/habla telegráfica Etapa inicial del habla de un niño, que tiene forma de telegrama y está formada mayormente por sustantivos y verbos; por ejemplo, "quiero leche" o "papá va tienda". (pág. 224)

temperament/temperamento Reactividad e intensidad emocionales características de una persona. (pág. 76)

temporal lobes/lóbulos temporales Porción de la corteza cerebral que yace más o menos encima de las orejas; incluye las áreas que reciben información de los oídos. (pág. 46)

tend-and-befriend response/respuesta de cuidar y hacer amistad En situaciones de estrés, las personas (sobre todo las mujeres) a menudo se dan apoyo *(cuidar)* y a la vez forman vínculos y buscan apoyo de otros *(hacer amistad)*. (pág. 278)

teratogens/teratógenos Agentes, podrían ser químico o viral, que pueden afectar al embrión o al feto durante el desarrollo prenatal produciéndole daño. (pág. 74)

testing effect/efecto de prueba Recuerdo aumentado después de recuperar la información, en lugar de simplemente volver a leerla. También conocido como *efecto de práctica de recuperación* o *aprendizaje intensificado por pruebas*. (págs. 26, 194)

testosterone/testosterona La hormona sexual masculina más importante. La tienen tanto los varones como las mujeres pero la cantidad adicional en los varones estimula el crecimiento de los órganos sexuales masculinos durante el período fetal y el desarrollo de las características sexuales masculinas secundarias en la pubertad. (pág. 111)

thalamus/tálamo Centro sensorial de control del cerebro ubicado encima del tronco encefálico; dirige mensajes sensoriales a la corteza cerebral y transmite respuestas al cerebelo y el bulbo raquídeo. (pág. 42)

THC/THC Principal sustancia activa que se encuentra en la marihuana; produce distintos efectos, inclusive alucinaciones leves. (pág. 378)

Thematic Apperception Test (TAT)/Test de apercepción temática (T.A.T.) Prueba proyectiva en la que el individuo expresa sus sentimientos e intereses internos mediante historias que inventa en torno a escenas ambiguas. (pág. 340)

theory/teoría Explicación que emplea principios que organizan observaciones y predicen comportamientos o sucesos. (pág. 14)

theory of mind/teoría de la mente Conceptos que tienen las personas acerca de sus propios procesos mentales y de los de los demás; es decir, de sus sentimientos, percepciones y pensamientos y de los comportamientos que estos podrían predecir. (pág. 84)

therapeutic alliance/alianza terapéutica Vínculo de confianza y comprensión mutua que se establece entre el terapeuta y el cliente, que trabajan juntos de manera constructiva para superar el problema del cliente. (pág. 415)

threshold/umbral Nivel de estimulación requerido para activar un impulso neuronal. (pág. 34)

token economy/economía de fichas Procedimiento del condicionamiento operante en el que las personas ganan una ficha cuando exhiben un comportamiento deseado y luego pueden intercambiar las fichas ganadas por privilegios o para darse algún gusto. (pág. 408)

tolerance/tolerancia Disminución del efecto con el uso regular de la misma dosis de una sustancia, lo que requiere que el usuario tome dosis cada vez mayores para poder experimentar el efecto de la sustancia. (pág. 372)

top-down processing/proceso descendente Procesamiento de la información orientado por procesos mentales de alto nivel, como cuando construimos percepciones basándonos en nuestras vivencias y expectativas. (pág. 132)

trait/rasgo Patrón de comportamiento característico o disposición a sentirse y actuar de cierta forma, según se evalúa en los inventarios de autoinformes e informes de pares. (pág. 346)

transcranial magnetic stimulation (TMS)/estimulación magnética transcraneana (EMT) Aplicación repetitiva de pulsos de energía magnética al cerebro. Se utiliza para estimular o suprimir la actividad cerebral. (pág. 421)

transduction/transducción Transformación de un tipo de energía en otro. En términos de la sensación, transformación de las energías de los estímulos, tales como las imágenes, los sonidos y los olores, en impulsos neuronales que el cerebro tiene la capacidad de interpretar. (pág. 132)

transference/transferencia En el psicoanálisis, la transferencia (que realiza el paciente) de emociones ligadas a otras relaciones al analista (tales como el amor o el odio hacia el padre o la madre). (pág. 403)

transgender/transgénero Término genérico que describe a personas cuya identidad o expresión de género difiere de la que se asocia con su asignación de sexo al nacer. (pág. 116)

two-factor theory/teoría de los dos factores Teoría de Schachter y Singer que propone que para experimentar emociones debemos (1) recibir estimulación física y (2) identificar el estímulo a nivel cognitivo. (pág. 263)

two-word stage/etapa de dos palabras A partir de los 2 años de edad, etapa del desarrollo del lenguaje durante la cual el niño emite mayormente frases de dos palabras. (pág. 224)

Type A/Tipo A Término de Friedman y Rosenman para referirse a las personas competitivas, compulsivas, impacientes, verbalmente agresivas y con tendencia a enojarse. (pág. 281)

Type B/Tipo B Término de Friedman y Rosenman para referirse a las personas tolerantes, relajadas y tranquilas. (pág. 281)

unconditional positive regard/consideración positiva incondicional Actitud de cuidado, aceptación y sin prejuicios. Según Rogers, así los clientes desarrollarían consciencia y aceptación de sí mismos. (págs. 344, 405)

unconditioned response (UR)/respuesta incondicionada (RI) En el condicionamiento clásico, la respuesta no aprendida e innata que es producida por un estímulo incondicionado (EI) (como la salivación cuando la comida está en la boca). (pág. 168)

unconditioned stimulus (US)/estímulo incondicionado (EI) En el condicionamiento clásico, estímulo que provoca una respuesta incondicionalmente (RI) y de manera natural y automática. (pág. 168)

unconscious/inconsciente Según Freud, un depósito de pensamientos, deseos, sentimientos y recuerdos, en su mayoría inaceptables. Según los psicólogos contemporáneos, el procesamiento de información del cual no tenemos consciencia. (pág. 336)

validity/validez Grado en que una prueba mide o predice lo que se supone debe medir o predecir. (Ver también *validez predictiva.*) (pág. 234)

variable/variable cualquier cosa que puede variar y que es factible y ético medir. (pág. A-4)

variable-interval schedule/calendario de intervalo variable Según el condicionamiento operante, calendario de reforzamientos que refuerza una respuesta en intervalos de tiempo impredecibles. (pág. 176)

variable-ratio schedule/calendario de proporción variable En el condicionamiento operante, calendario de reforzamientos que refuerza una respuesta después de un número impredecible de respuestas. (pág. 176)

vestibular sense/sentido vestibular Sentido de movimiento y posición del cuerpo, inclusive el sentido de equilibrio. (pág. 158)

virtual reality exposure therapy/terapia de exposición de realidad virtual Técnica del contracondicionamiento que trata la ansiedad mediante estimulaciones electrónicas creativas en la que las personas pueden hacerles frente a sus mayores temores, tales como volar en avión, ver una araña o hablar en público. (pág. 407)

visual cliff/vacío visual Dispositivo del laboratorio con el que se examina la percepción de profundidad en los bebés y en animales de corta edad. (pág. 146)

wavelength/longitud de onda Distancia entre la cresta de una onda de luz o de sonido y la cresta de la siguiente onda. (pág. 139)

Weber's law/ley de Weber Principio que sostiene que para que dos estímulos se perciban como distintos, estos deben diferir por un porcentaje mínimo constante (en vez de por una cantidad constante). (pág. 135)

Wechsler Adult Intelligence Scale (WAIS)/escala de la Inteligencia de Wechsler para adultos (EIWA) La prueba EIWA y sus versiones adaptadas para niños son las pruebas de inteligencia más ampliamente utilizadas. Incluyen subpruebas verbales y de desempeño (no verbales). (pág. 233)

Wernicke's area/área de Wernicke Parte del cerebro generalmente ubicada en el lóbulo temporal izquierdo, que participa en la comprensión y la expresión del lenguaje. (pág. 226)

withdrawal/síndrome de abstinencia La incomodidad y angustia que sigue cuando se deja de utilizar una droga adictiva o se suspende una conducta adictiva. (pág. 372)

working memory/memoria de trabajo Entendimiento más reciente de la memoria a corto plazo que añade el procesamiento consciente y activo de información auditiva y visual-espacial, y de información recuperada de la memoria a largo plazo. (pág. 190)

X chromosome/cromosoma X Cromosoma del sexo que se encuentra en el varón y la mujer. Las mujeres por lo general tienen dos cromosomas X; los hombres por lo general tienen un cromosoma X y un cromosoma Y. Con un cromosoma X del padre y otro de la madre, se produce una mujer. (pág. 111)

Y chromosome/cromosoma Y Cromosoma del sexo que solamente se halla en los hombres. Cuando se aparea con un cromosoma X de la madre, se produce un varón. (pág. 111)

Yerkes-Dodson law/Ley de Yerkes-Dodson Principio que establece que el rendimiento aumenta con la excitación solamente hasta un punto; más allá de este punto el rendimiento disminuye. (pág. 249)

Young-Helmholtz trichromatic (three-color) theory/teoría tricromática de Young-Helmholtz Teoría de que la retina contiene tres tipos distintos de receptores de color: uno más sensible al rojo, otro al verde y otro al azul. Al estimularse en combinación, estos receptores son capaces de producir la percepción de cualquier color. (pág. 142)

zygote/cigoto Huevo fertilizado. Atraviesa por un período de dos semanas de división celular rápida y se convierte en un embrión. (pág. 74)

REFERENCES

AAA. (2010). *Asleep at the wheel: the prevalence and impact of drowsy driving* [PDF file]. Retrieved from aaafoundation.org/pdf/2010DrowsyDrivingReport.pdf

AAA. (2015). *Teen driver safety: Environmental factors and driver behaviors in teen driver crashes* [PDF file]. Retrieved from newsroom.aaa.com/wp-content/uploads/2015/03/TeenCrashCausation_2015_FACTSHEET3.pdf

AAMC. (2014). *Medical students, selected years, 1965–2013.* Association of American Medical Colleges (aamc.org).

AAMC. (2016). *Total enrollment by U.S. medical school and sex, 2011–2012 through 2015–2016.* Association of American Medical Colleges (aamc.org).

AAS. (2009, April 25). *USA suicide: 2006 final data.* Prepared for the American Association of Suicidology by J. L. McIntosh (suicidology.org).

Abrams, D. B., & Wilson, G. T. (1983). Alcohol, sexual arousal, and self-control. *Journal of Personality and Social Psychology, 45,* 188–198.

Abrams, L. (2008). Tip-of-the-tongue states yield language insights. *American Scientist, 96,* 234–239.

Abrams, M. (2002, June). Sight unseen—Restoring a blind man's vision is now a real possibility through stem-cell surgery. But even perfect eyes cannot see unless the brain has been taught to use them. *Discover, 23,* 54–60.

Abramson, L. Y., Metalsky, G. I., & Alloy, L. B. (1989). Hopelessness depression: A theory-based subtype. *Psychological Review, 96,* 358–372.

Abramson, L. Y., Seligman, M. E. P., & Teasdale, J. D. (1978). Learned helplessness in humans: Critique and reformulation. *Journal of Abnormal Psychology, 87,* 49–74.

Academy of Science of South Africa. (2015). *Diversity in human sexuality: Implications for policy in Africa.* Retrieved from dx.doi.org/10.17159/assaf/0022

Acevedo, B. P., & Aron, A. (2009). Does a long-term relationship kill romantic love? *Review of General Psychology, 13,* 59–65.

Acevedo, B. P., Aron, A., Fisher, H. E., & Brown, L. L. (2012). Neural correlates of long-term intense romantic love. *Social Cognitive and Affective Neuroscience, 7,* 145–159.

ACHA. (2009). *American College Health Association-National College Health Assessment II: Reference group executive summary Fall 2008.* Baltimore: American College Health Association.

Ackerman, D. (2004). *An alchemy of mind: The marvel and mystery of the brain.* New York: Scribner.

Adachi, T., Fujino, H., Nakae, A., Mashimo, T., & Sasaki, J. (2014). A meta-analysis of hypnosis for chronic pain problems: A comparison between hypnosis, standard care, and other psychological interventions. *International Journal of Clinical and Experimental Hypnosis, 62,* 1–28.

Adams, H. E., Wright, L. W., Jr., & Lohr, B. A. (1996). Is homophobia associated with homosexual arousal? *Journal of Abnormal Psychology, 105,* 440–446.

Adelmann, P. K., Antonucci, T. C., Crohan, S. F., & Coleman, L. M. (1989). Empty nest, cohort, and employment in the well-being of midlife women. *Sex Roles, 20,* 173–189.

Aderka, I. M., Nickerson, A., Bøe, H. J., & Hofmann, S. G. (2012). Sudden gains during psychological treatments of anxiety and depression: A meta-analysis. *Journal of Consulting and Clinical Psychology, 80,* 93–101.

Adler, J. M., Lodi-Smith, J., Philippe, F. L., & Houle, I. (2016). The incremental validity of narrative identity in predicting well-being: A review of the field and recommendations for the future. *Personality and Social Psychology Review, 20,* 142–175.

Adolph, K. E., Kretch, K. S., & LoBue, V. (2014). Fear of heights in infants? *Current Directions in Psychological Science, 23,* 60–66.

Affleck, G., Tennen, H., Urrows, S., & Higgins, P. (1994). Person and contextual features of daily stress reactivity: Individual differences in relations of undesirable daily events with mood disturbance and chronic pain intensity. *Journal of Personality and Social Psychology, 66,* 329–340.

Agerström, J., Björklund, F., Carlsson, R., & Rooth, D.-O. (2012). Warm and competent Hassan = cold and incompetent Eric: A harsh equation of real-life hiring discrimination. *Basic and Applied Social Psychology, 34,* 359–366.

Agrillo, C. (2011). Near-death experience: Out-of-body and out-of-brain? *Review of General Psychology, 15,* 1–10.

Agudelo, L. Z., Femenía, T., Orhan, F., Porsmyr-Palmertz, M., Goiny, M., Martinez-Redondo, V., . . . Ruas, J. L. (2014). Skeletal muscle PGC-1 1 modulates kynurenine metabolism and mediates resilience to stress-induced depression. *Cell, 159,* 33–45.

Ahrén, J. C., Chiesa, F., Koupil, I., Magnusson, C., Dalman, C., & Goodman, A. (2013). We are family—parents, siblings, and eating disorders in a prospective total-population study of 250,000 Swedish males and females. *International Journal of Eating Disorders, 46,* 693–700.

Aiello, J. R., Thompson, D. D., & Brodzinsky, D. M. (1983). How funny is crowding anyway? Effects of room size, group size, and the introduction of humor. *Basic and Applied Social Psychology, 4,* 193–207.

Aimone, J. B., Jessberger, S., & Gage, F. H. (2010). Adult neurogenesis. *Scholarpedia, 2*(2), 2100. Retrieved from scholarpedia.org/article/adult_neurogenesis

Ainsworth, M. D. S. (1973). The development of infant-mother attachment. In B. Caldwell & H. Ricciuti (Eds.), *Review of child development research* (Vol. 3). Chicago: University of Chicago Press.

Ainsworth, M. D. S. (1979). Infant-mother attachment. *American Psychologist, 34,* 932–937.

Ainsworth, M. D. S. (1989). Attachments beyond infancy. *American Psychologist, 44,* 709–716.

Airan, R. D., Meltzer, L. A., Roy, M., Gong, Y., Chen, H., & Deisseroth, K. (2007). High-speed imaging reveals neurophysiological links to behavior in an animal model of depression. *Science, 317,* 819–823.

Akhtar, S., Justice, L. V., Morrison, C. M., & Conway, M. A. (2018). Fictional first memories. *Psychological Science, 29,* 1612–1619.

Akiyama, M., Okada, Y., Kanai, M., Takahashi, A., Momozawa, Y., Ikeda, M., . . . Iwasaki, M. (2017). Genome-wide association study identifies 112 new loci for body mass index in the Japanese population. *Nature Genetics, 49,* 1458–1467.

Aknin, L. B., Barrington-Leigh, C. P., Dunn, E. W., Helliwell, J. F., Burns, J., Biswas-Diener, R., & Norton, M. I. (2013). Prosocial spending and well-being: Cross-cultural evidence for a psychological universal. *Journal of Personality and Social Psychology, 104,* 635–652.

Aknin, L. B., Broesch, T., Kiley Hamlin, J., & Van de Vondervoort, J. W. (2015). Pro-social behavior leads to happiness in a small-scale rural society. *Journal of Experimental Psychology: General, 144,* 788–795.

Akpinar, E., & Berger, J. (2015). Drivers of cultural success: The case of sensory metaphors. *Journal of Personality and Social Psychology, 109,* 20–34.

Al Ibraheem, B., Kira, I. A., Aljakoub, J., & Al Ibraheem, A. (2017). The health effect of the Syrian conflict on IDPs and refugees. *Peace and Conflict: Journal of Peace Psychology, 23,* 140–152.

al-Asaadi, M. (2016). 'We sleep afraid, we wake up afraid': A child's life in Yemen. *The New York Times* (nytimes.com).

Al-Sayegh, H., Lowry, J., Polur, R. N., Hines, R. B., Liu, F., & Zhang, J. (2015). Suicide history and mortality: A follow-up of a national cohort in the United States. *Archives of Suicide Research, 19,* 35–47.

Alanko, K., Santtila, P., Harlaar, N., Witting, K., Varjonen, M., Jern, P., . . . Sandnabba, N. K. (2010). Common genetic effects of gender atypical behavior in childhood and sexual orientation in adulthood: A study of Finnish twins. *Archives of Sexual Behavior, 39,* 81–92.

Albee, G. W. (1986). Toward a just society: Lessons from observations on the primary prevention of psychopathology. *American Psychologist, 41,* 891–898.

Albee, G. W. (2006). Historical overview of primary prevention of psychopathology: Address to the 3rd world conference on the promotion of mental health and prevention of mental and behavioral disorders. September 15–17, 2004, Auckland, New Zealand. *The Journal of Primary Prevention, 27,* 449–456.

Albert, D., Chein, J., & Steinberg, L. (2013). Peer influences on adolescent decision making. *Current Directions in Psychological Science, 22,* 80–86.

Alcock, J. E. (2011, March/April). Back from the future: Parapsychology and the Bem affair. *Skeptical Inquirer,* pp. 31–39.

Aldao, A., & Nolen-Hoeksema, S. (2010). Emotion-regulation strategies across psychopathology: A meta-analytic review. *Clinical Psychology Review, 30,* 217–237.

Aleman, A., Kahn, R. S., & Selten, J.-P. (2003). Sex differences in the risk of schizophrenia: Evidence from meta-analysis. *Archives of General Psychiatry, 60,* 565–571.

Alexander, L., & Tredoux, C. (2010). The spaces between us: A spatial analysis of informal segregation. *Journal of Social Issues, 66,* 367–386.

Allan, B. A. (2017). Task significance and meaningful work: A longitudinal study. *Journal of Vocational Behavior, 102,* 174–182.

Allen, J. P., Uchino, B. N., & Hafen, C. A. (2015). Running with the pack: Teen peer-relationship qualities as predictors of adult physical health. *Psychological Science, 26,* 1574–1583.

Allen, K. (2003). Are pets a healthy pleasure? The influence of pets on blood pressure. *Current Directions in Psychological Science, 12,* 236–239.

Allen, M., D'Alessio, D., & Emmers-Sommer, T. M. (2000). Reactions of criminal sexual offenders to pornography: A meta-analytic summary. In M. Roloff (Ed.), *Communication Yearbook 22* (pp. 139–169). Thousand Oaks, CA: Sage.

Allen, M., Emmers, T. M., Gebhardt, L., & Giery, M. (1995). Pornography and rape myth acceptance. *Journal of Communication, 45*, 5–26.

Allen, M. S., & Jones, M. V. (2014). The "home advantage" in athletic competitions. *Current Directions in Psychological Science, 23*, 48–53.

Allen, M. W., Gupta, R., & Monnier, A. (2008). The interactive effect of cultural symbols and human values on taste evaluation. *Journal of Consumer Research, 35*, 294–308.

Allen, N. B., & Badcock, P. B. T. (2003). The social risk hypothesis of depressed mood: Evolutionary, psychosocial, and neurobiological perspectives. *Psychological Bulletin, 129*, 887–913.

Allen, T. D., Golden, T. D., & Shockley, K. M. (2015). How effective is telecommuting? Assessing the status of our scientific findings. *Psychological Science in the Public Interest, 16*, 40–68.

Allen, T., & Sherman, J. (2011). Ego threat and intergroup bias: A test of motivated-activation versus self-regulatory accounts. *Psychological Science, 22*, 331–333.

Alloy, L. B., Hamilton, J. L., Hamlat, E. J., & Abramson, L. Y. (2016). Pubertal development, emotion regulatory styles, and the emergence of sex differences in internalizing disorders and symptoms in adolescence. *Clinical Psychological Science, 4*, 867–881.

Allport, G. W. (1954). *The nature of prejudice*. New York: Addison-Wesley.

Ally, B. A., Hussey, E. P., & Donahue, M. J. (2013). A case of hyperthymesia: Rethinking the role of the amygdala in autobiographical memory. *Neurocase, 19*, 166–181.

Almas, A. N., Degnan, K. A., Nelson, C. A., Zeanah, C. H., & Fox, N. A. (2017). IQ at age 12 following a history of institutional care: Findings from the Bucharest Early Intervention Project. *Developmental Psychology, 52*, 1858–1866.

Alonso, J., Mortier, P., Auerbach, R. P., Bruffaerts, R., Vilagut, G., Cuijpers, P., . . . & Green, J. G. (2018). Severe role impairment associated with mental disorders: Results of the WHO World Mental Health Surveys International College Student Project. *Depression and Anxiety, 35*, 802–814.

AlShebli, B. K., Rahwan, T., & Woon, W. L. (2018). The preeminence of ethnic diversity in scientific collaboration. *Nature Communications, 9*, 5163.

Altamirano, L. J., Miyake, A., & Whitmer, A. J. (2010). When mental inflexibility facilitates executive control: Beneficial side effects of ruminative tendencies on goal maintenance. *Psychological Science, 21*, 1377–1382.

Alter, A. (2017). *Irresistible: The rise of addictive technology and the business of keeping us hooked*. New York: Penguin.

Alter, A. L., & Hershfield, H. E. (2014). People search for meaning when they approach a new decade in chronological age. *PNAS, 111*, 17066–17070.

Alter, A. L., Stern, C., Granot, Y., & Balcetis, E. (2016). The "bad is black" effect: Why people believe evildoers have darker skin than do-gooders. *Personality & Social Psychology Bulletin, 42*, 1653–1665.

Alves, H. (2018). Sharing rare attitudes attracts. *Personality and Social Psychology Bulletin, 44*, 1270–1283.

Alwin, D. F. (1990). Historical changes in parental orientations to children. In N. Mandell (Ed.), *Sociological studies of child development (Vol. 3)*. Greenwich, CT: JAI Press.

Amabile, T. M. (1983). *The social psychology of creativity*. New York: Springer-Verlag.

Amabile, T. M., & Hennessey, B. A. (1992). The motivation for creativity in children. In A. K. Boggiano & T. S. Pittman (Eds.), *Achievement and motivation: A social-developmental perspective*. New York: Cambridge University Press.

Amabile, T. M., & Kramer, S. J. (2011). *The progress principle: Using small wins to ignite joy, engagement, and creativity at work*. Cambridge, MA: Harvard Business Review Press.

Ambady, N. (2010). The perils of pondering: Intuition and thin slice judgments. *Psychological Inquiry, 21*, 271–278.

Ambrose, C. T. (2010). The widening gyrus. *American Scientist, 98*, 270–274.

Amedi, A., Merabet, L. B., Bermpohl, F., & Pascual-Leone, A. (2005). The occipital cortex in the blind: Lessons about plasticity and vision. *Current Directions in Psychological Science, 14*, 306–311.

Amen, D. G., Stubblefield, M., Carmichael, B., & Thisted, R. (1996). BrainSPECT findings and aggressiveness. *Annals of Clinical Psychiatry, 8*, 129–137.

American Enterprise. (1992, January/February). Women, men, marriages & ministers. p. 106.

American Psychiatric Association. (2013). *Diagnostic and statistical manual of mental disorders* (Fifth ed.). Arlington, VA: American Psychiatric Publishing.

Amick, H. R., Gartlehner, G., Gaynes, B. N., Forneris, C., Asher, G. N., Morgan, L. C., . . . Lohr, K. N. (2015). Comparative benefits and harms of second generation antidepressants and cognitive behavioral therapies in initial treatment of major depressive disorder: Systematic review and meta-analysis. *BMJ, 351*, h6019.

Ammori, B. (2013, January 4). Viewpoint: Benefits of bariatric surgery. *GP* (gponline.com).

Andersen, R. A., Hwang, E. J., & Mulliken, G. H. (2010). Cognitive neural prosthetics. *Annual Review of Psychology, 61*, 169–190.

Andersen, S. M. (1998, September). *Service learning: A national strategy for youth development*. Washington, DC: Institute for Communitarian Policy Studies, George Washington University.

Anderson, B. L. (2002). Biobehavioral outcomes following psychological interventions for cancer patients. *Journal of Consulting and Clinical Psychology, 70*, 590–610.

Anderson, C. A. (2004). An update on the effects of playing violent video games. *Journal of Adolescence, 27*, 113–122.

Anderson, C. A. (2013, June). Guns, games, and mass shootings in the U.S. *Bulletin of the International Society for Research on Aggression*, pp. 14–19.

Anderson, C. A., Brion, S., Moore, D. A., & Kennedy, J. A. (2012). A status enhancement account of overconfidence. *Journal of Personality and Social Psychology, 103*, 718–735.

Anderson, C. A., Bushman, B. J., & Groom, R. W. (1997). Hot years and serious and deadly assault: Empirical tests of the heat hypothesis. *Journal of Personality and Social Psychology, 73*, 1213–1223.

Anderson, C. A., & Delisi, M. (2011). Implications of global climate change for violence in developed and developing countries. In J. Forgas, A. Kruglanski., & K. Williams (Eds.), *The psychology of social conflict and aggression* (pp. 249–265). New York: Psychology Press.

Anderson, C. A., & Dill, K. E. (2000). Video games and aggressive thoughts, feelings, and behavior in the laboratory and in life. *Journal of Personality and Social Psychology, 78*, 772–790.

Anderson, C. A., Shibuya, A., Ihori, N., Swing, E. L., Bushman, B. J., Sakamoto, A., . . . Saleem, M. (2010a). Violent video game effects on aggression, empathy, and prosocial behavior in Eastern and Western countries: A meta-analytic review. *Psychological Bulletin, 136*, 151–173.

Anderson, C. A., Suzuki, K., Swing, E. L., Groves, C. L., Gentile, D. A., Prot, S., . . . Jelic, M. (2017). Media violence and other aggression risk factors in seven nations. *Personality and Social Psychology Bulletin, 43*, 986–998.

Anderson, C. A., & Warburton, W. A. (2012). The impact of violent video games: An overview. In W. Warburton & D. Braunstein (Eds.), *Growing up fast and furious: Reviewing the impacts of violent and sexualized media on children* (pp. 56–84). Annandale, New South Wales, Australia: Federation Press.

Anderson, J. R., Gillies, A., & Lock, L. C. (2010). Pan thanatology. *Current Biology, 20*, R349–R351.

Anderson, M. & Jiang, J. (2018). *Teens, social media and technology 2018*. Pew Research Center, Internet & Technology (pewinternet.org).

Anderson, P. L., Edwards, S. M., & Goodnight, J. R. (2017). Virtual reality and exposure group therapy for social anxiety disorder: Results from a 4-6 year follow-up. *Cognitive Therapy and Research, 41*, 230–236.

Anderson, R. C., Pichert, J. W., Goetz, E. T., Schallert, D. L., Stevens, K. V., & Trollip, S. R. (1976). Instantiation of general terms. *Journal of Verbal Learning and Verbal Behavior, 15*, 667–679.

Anderson, S. E., Dallal, G. E., & Must, A. (2003). Relative weight and race influence average age at menarche: Results from two nationally representative surveys of U.S. girls studied 25 years apart. *Pediatrics, 111*, 844–850.

Andreasen, N. C. (1997). Linking mind and brain in the study of mental illnesses: A project for a scientific psychopathology. *Science, 275*, 1586–1593.

Andreasen, N. C. (2001). *Brave new brain: Conquering mental illness in the era of the genome*. New York: Oxford University Press.

Andrews, G., Basu, A., Cuijpers, P., Craske, M. G., McEvoy, P., English, C. L., & Newby, J. M. (2018). Computer therapy for the anxiety and depression disorders is effective, acceptable and practical health care: An updated meta-analysis. *Journal of Anxiety Disorders, 55*, 70–78.

Andrews, P. W., & Thomson, J. A., Jr. (2009a). The bright side of being blue: Depression as an adaptation for analyzing complex problems. *Psychological Review, 116*, 620–654.

Andrews, P. W., & Thomson, J. A., Jr. (2009b). Depression's evolutionary roots. *Scientific American Mind, 20*, 56–61.

Andrillon, T., Nir, Y., Cirelli, C., Tononi, G., & Fried, I. (2015). Single-neuron activity and eye movements during human REM sleep and awake vision. *Nature Communications, 6*, Article 7884. doi:10.1038/ncomms8884

Anestis, M. D., & Anestis, J. C. (2015). Suicide rates and state laws regulating access and exposure to handguns. *American Journal of Public Health, 105*, 2049–2058.

Anestis, M. D., Khazem, L. R., Law, K. C., Houtsma, C., LeTard, R., Moberg, F., & Martin, R. (2015). The association between state laws regulating handgun ownership and statewide suicide rates. *American Journal of Public Health, 105*, 2059–2067.

Angermeyer, M. C., & Dietrich, S. (2006). Public beliefs about and attitudes towards people with mental illness: a review of population studies. *Acta Psychiatrica Scandinavica*, 113, 163–179.

Anglemyer, A., Horvath, T., & Rutherford, G. (2014). The accessibility of firearms and risk for suicide and homicide victimization among household members. *Annals of Internal Medicine*, 160, 101–112.

Ansari, A., Purtell, K., & Gershoff, E. (2015). Classroom age composition and the school readiness of 3- and 4-year-olds in the Head Start program. *Psychological Science*, 27, 53–63.

Anton, B. S. (2015, June). Quoted in, "APA applauds President Obama's call to end use of therapies intended to change sexual orientation." *Monitor*, 46, p. 10.

Antonaccio, O., Botchkovar, E. V., & Tittle, C. R. (2011). Attracted to crime: Exploration of criminal motivation among respondents in three European cities. *Criminal Justice and Behavior*, 38, 1200–1221.

Antony, M. M., Brown, T. A., & Barlow, D. H. (1992). Current perspectives on panic and panic disorder. *Current Directions in Psychological Science*, 1, 79–82.

Antrobus, J. (1991). Dreaming: Cognitive processes during cortical activation and high afferent thresholds. *Psychological Review*, 98, 96–121.

Anzures, G., Quinn, P. C., Pascalis, O., Slater, A. M., Tanaka, J. W., & Lee, K. (2013). Developmental origins of the other-race effect. *Current Directions in Psychological Science*, 22, 173–178.

AP. (2009, May 9). AP-mtvU AP 2009 Economy, College Stress and Mental Health Poll. Associated Press (ap.org).

AP. (2017, July 11). Strangers on beach form 80-link human chain, rescue family from rip current. CBC. Retrieved from cbc.ca/news/world/human-chain-saves-family-in-water-1.4199181

AP. (2018, April 19). Two black men arrested at Philadelphia Starbucks push for lasting change. Associated Press. Retrieved from cbc.ca/news/business/starbucks-arrest-1.4626158

APA. (2006). Evidence-based practice in psychology (from APA Presidential Task Force on Evidence-Based Practice). *American Psychologist*, 61, 271–285.

APA. (2007). *Report of the task force on the sexualization of girls*. Washington, DC: American Psychological Association (apa.org).

APA. (2009). *Stress in America 2009*. American Psychological Association (apa.org).

APA. (2010). *Answers to your questions about transgender individuals and gender identity*. American Psychological Association (apa.org).

APA. (2012). *Guidelines for ethical conduct in the care and use of nonhuman animals in research*. Washington, DC: American Psychological Association.

Archer, J. (2000). Sex differences in aggression between heterosexual partners: A meta-analytic review. *Psychological Bulletin*, 126, 651–680.

Archer, J. (2004). Sex differences in aggression in real-world settings: A meta-analytic review. *Review of General Psychology*, 8, 291–322.

Archer, J. (2007). A cross-cultural perspective on physical aggression between partners. *Issues in Forensic Psychology*, 6, 125–131.

Archer, J. (2009). Does sexual selection explain human sex differences in aggression? *Behavioral and Brain Sciences*, 32, 249–311.

Arent, S. M., Landers, D. M., & Etnier, J. L. (2000). The effects of exercise on mood in older adults: A meta-analytic review. *Journal of Aging and Physical Activity*, 8, 407–430.

Ariel, R., & Karpicke, J. D. (2018). Improving self-regulated learning with a retrieval practice intervention. *Journal of Experimental Psychology: Applied*, 24, 43–56.

Ariely, D. (2010). *Predictably irrational, revised and expanded edition: The hidden forces that shape our decisions*. New York: Harper Perennial.

Ariely, D., & Loewenstein, G. (2006). The heat of the moment: The effect of sexual arousal on sexual decision making. *Journal of Behavioral Decision Making*, 19, 87–98.

Aries, E. (1987). Gender and communication. In P. Shaver & C. Henrick (Eds.), *Review of Personality and Social Psychology*, 7, 149–176.

Arkowitz, H., & Lilienfeld, S. O. (2006, April/May). Psychotherapy on trial. *Scientific American: Mind*, pp. 42–49.

Armony, J. L., Quirk, G. J., & LeDoux, J. E. (1998). Differential effects of amygdala lesions on early and late plastic components of auditory cortex spike trains during fear conditioning. *Journal of Neuroscience*, 18, 2592–2601.

Armstrong, E. A., England, P., & Fogarty, A. C. K. (2012). Accounting for women's orgasm and sexual enjoyment in college hookups and relationships. *American Sociological Review*, 77, 435–462.

Arnedo, J., Mamah, D., Baranger, D. A., Harms, M. P., Barch, D. M., Svrakic, D. M., . . . Zwir, I. (2015). Decomposition of brain diffusion imaging data uncovers latent schizophrenias with distinct patterns of white matter anisotropy. *NeuroImage*, 120, 43–54.

Arneson, J. J., Sackett, P. R., & Beatty, A. S. (2011). Ability-performance relationships in education and employment settings: Critical tests of the more-is-better and the good-enough hypotheses. *Psychological Science*, 22, 1336–1342.

Arnett, J. J. (2006). Emerging adulthood: Understanding the new way of coming of age. In J. J. Arnett & J. L. Tanner (Eds.), *Emerging adults in America: Coming of age in the 21st century* (pp. 3–19). Washington, DC: American Psychological Association.

Arnett, J. J. (2007). Socialization in emerging adulthood: From the family to the wider world, from socialization to self-socialization. In J. E. Grusec & P. D. Hastings (Eds.), *Handbook of socialization: Theory and research* (pp. 208–230). New York: Guilford Press.

Arnold, K. M., Umanath, S., Thio, K., Reilly, W. B., McDaniel, M. A., & Marsh, E. J. (2017). Understanding the cognitive processes involved in writing to learn. *Journal of Experimental Psychology: Applied*, 23, 115–127

Aron, A., Melinat, E., Aron, E. N., Vallone, R. D., & Bator, R. J. (1997). The experimental generation of interpersonal closeness: A procedure and some preliminary findings. *Personality and Social Psychology Bulletin*, 23, 363–377.

Aron, A., Norman, C. C., Aron, E. N., McKenna, C., & Heyman, R. E. (2000). Couples' shared participation in novel and arousing activities and experienced relationship quality. *Journal of Personality and Social Psychology*, 78, 273–284.

Aronson, E. (2001, April 13). *Newsworthy violence* [Email to Society for Personality and Social Psychology discussion list, drawing from *Nobody left to hate: Teaching compassion after Columbine*. (2000). New York: Freeman].

Arriaga, P., Adrião, J., Madeira, F., Cavaleiro, I., Maia e Silva, A., Barahona, I., & Esteves, F. (2015). A "dry eye" for victims of violence: Effects of playing a violent video game on pupillary dilation to victims and on aggressive behavior. *Psychology of Violence*, 5, 199–208.

Arsenio, W. F. (2018). The wealth of nations: International judgments regarding actual and ideal resource distributions. *Current Directions in Psychological Science*, 27, 357–362.

Ascády, L., & Harris, K. D. (2017). Synaptic scaling in sleep. *Science*, 355, 457.

Asch, S. E. (1955). Opinions and social pressure. *Scientific American*, 193, 31–35.

Aserinsky, E. (1988, January 17). Personal communication.

Askay, S. W., & Patterson, D. R. (2007). Hypnotic analgesia. *Expert Review of Neurotherapeutics*, 7, 1675–1683.

Aspinwall, L. G., & Tedeschi, R. G. (2010). The value of positive psychology for health psychology: Progress and pitfalls in examining the relation of positive phenomena to health. *Annals of Behavioral Medicine*, 39, 4–15.

Aspy, C. B., Vesely, S. K., Oman, R. F., Rodine, S., Marshall, L., & McLeroy, K. (2007). Parental communication and youth sexual behaviour. *Journal of Adolescence*, 30, 449–466.

Assanand, S., Pinel, J. P. J., & Lehman, D. R. (1998). Personal theories of hunger and eating. *Journal of Applied Social Psychology*, 28, 998–1015.

Atir, S., & Ferguson, M. J. (2018). How gender determines the way we speak about professionals. *PNAS*, 115, 7278–7283.

Atkinson, R. C., & Shiffrin, R. M. (1968). Human memory: A control system and its control processes. In K. Spence (Ed.), *The psychology of learning and motivation* (Vol. 2). New York: Academic Press.

Atkinson, R. C., & Shiffrin, R. M. (2016). Human memory: A proposed system and its control processes. In R. J. Sternberg, S. T. Fiske, & D. J. Foss (Eds.), *Scientists making a difference: One hundred eminent behavioral and brain scientists talk about their most important contributions*. New York: Cambridge University Press.

Atlas, D. (2016, January 29). Autism's first-ever patient, now 82, "has continued to grow his whole life." *People* (people.com/article/donald-triplett-first-ever-autism-case).

Austin, E. J., Deary, I. J., Whiteman, M. C., Fowkes, F. G. R., Pedersen, N. L., Rabbitt, P., . . . McInnes, L. (2002). Relationships between ability and personality: Does intelligence contribute positively to personal and social adjustment? *Personality and Individual Differences*, 32, 1391–1411.

Averill, J. R. (1993). William James's other theory of emotion. In M. E. Donnelly (Ed.), *Reinterpreting the legacy of William James*. Washington, DC: American Psychological Association.

Aviezer, H., Hassin, R. R., Ryan, J., Grady, C., Susskind, J., Anderson, A., . . . Bentin, S. (2008). Angry, disgusted, or afraid? Studies on the malleability of emotion perception. *Psychological Science*, 19, 724–732.

Aviv, R. (2017, June 19). Remembering the murder you didn't commit. *New Yorker* (newyorker.com).

Ax, A. F. (1953). The physiological differentiation of fear and anger in humans. *Psychosomatic Medicine*, 15, 433–442.

Ayan, S. (2009). Laughing matters. *Scientific American Mind*, 20, 24–31.

Azar, B. (1998, June). Why can't this man feel whether or not he's standing up? *APA Monitor* (apa.org/monitor/jun98/touch.html).

Azevedo, F. A., Carvalho, L. R., Grinberg, L. T., Farfel, J. M., Ferretti, R. E., Leite, R. E., . . . Herculano-Houzel, S. (2009). Equal numbers of neuronal and nonneuronal cells make the human brain an isometrically scaled-up primate brain. *Journal of Comparative Neurology*, 513, 532–541.

Baas, M., De Dreu, C. K. W., & Nijstad, B. A. (2008). A meta-analysis of 25 years of mood-creativity research: Hedonic tone, activation, or regulatory focus? *Psychological Bulletin, 134*, 779–806.

Babyak, M., Blumenthal, J. A., Herman, S., Khatri, P., Doraiswamy, M., Moore, K., . . . Krishnan, K. R. (2000). Exercise treatment for major depression: Maintenance of therapeutic benefit at ten months. *Psychosomatic Medicine, 62*, 633–638.

Bachman, J., O'Malley, P. M., Schulenberg, J. E., Johnston, L. D., Freedman-Doan, P., & Messersmith, E. E. (2007). *The education-drug use connection: How successes and failures in school relate to adolescent smoking, drinking, drug use, and delinquency.* Mahwah, NJ: Earlbaum.

Back, M. D., Stopfer, J. M., Vazire, S., Gaddis, S., Schmukle, S. C., Egloff, B., & Gosling, S. D. (2010). Facebook profiles reflect actual personality, not self-idealization. *Psychological Science, 21*, 372–374.

Backman, L., & MacDonald, S. W. S. (2006). Death and cognition: Synthesis and outlook. *European Psychologist, 11*, 224 –235.

Baddeley, A. D. (1982). *Your memory: A user's guide.* New York: Macmillan.

Baddeley, A. D., Thomson, N., & Buchanan, M. (1975). Word length and the structure of short-term memory. *Journal of Verbal Learning and Verbal Behavior, 14*, 575–589.

Baddeley, J. L., & Singer, J. A. (2009). A social interactional model of bereavement narrative disclosure. *Review of General Psychology, 13*, 202–218.

Bagemihl, B. (1999). *Biological exuberance: Animal homosexuality and natural diversity.* New York: St. Martins.

Bagge, C. L., Littlefield, A. K., & Glenn, C. R. (2017). Trajectories of affective response as warning signs for suicide attempts: An examination of the 48 hours prior to a recent suicide attempt. *Clinical Psychological Science, 5*, 259–271.

Baglioni, C., Nanovska, S., Regen, W., Spiegelhalder, K., Feige, B., Nissen, C., . . . Riemann, D. (2016). Sleep and mental disorders: A meta-analysis of polysomnographic research. *Psychological Bulletin, 142*, 969–990.

Bahrick, H. P. (1984). Semantic memory content in permastore: 50 years of memory for Spanish learned in school. *Journal of Experimental Psychology: General, 111*, 1–29.

Bahrick, H. P., Bahrick, P. O., & Wittlinger, R. P. (1975). Fifty years of memory for names and faces: A cross-sectional approach. *Journal of Experimental Psychology: General, 104*, 54–75.

Bailey, J. M., Dunne, M. P., & Martin, N. G. (2000). Genetic and environmental influences on sexual orientation and its correlates in an Australian twin sample. *Journal of Personality and Social Psychology, 78*, 524–536.

Bailey, J. M., Vasey, P. L., Diamond, L. M., Breedlove, S. M., Vilain, E., & Epprecht, M. (2016). Sexual orientation, controversy, and science. *Psychological Science in the Public Interest, 17*, 45–101.

Bailey, R. E., & Gillaspy, J. A., Jr. (2005). Operant psychology goes to the fair: Marian and Keller Breland in the popular press, 1947–1966. *The Behavior Analyst, 28*, 143–159.

Baillargeon, R. (2008). Innate ideas revisited: For a principle of persistence in infants' physical reasoning. *Perspectives in Psychological Science, 3*, 2–13.

Baillargeon, R., Scott, R. M., & Bian, L. (2016). Psychological reasoning in infancy. *Annual Review of Psychology, 67*, 159–186.

Baio, J., Wiggins, L., Christensen, D. L., Maenner, M. J., Daniels, J., Warren, Z., . . . & Durkin, M. S. (2018). Prevalence of autism spectrum disorder among children aged 8 years—Autism and Developmental Disabilities Monitoring Network, 11 Sites, United States, 2014. *MMWR Surveillance Summaries, 67*, 1.

Baker, T. B., McFall, R. M., & Shoham, V. (2008). Current status and future prospects of clinical psychology: Toward a scientifically principled approach to mental and behavioral health care. *Psychological Science in the Public Interest, 9*, 67–103.

Baker, T. B., Piper, M. E., McCarthy, D. E., Majeskie, M. R., & Fiore, M. C. (2004). Addiction motivation reformulated: An affective processing model of negative reinforcement. *Psychological Review, 111*, 33–51.

Bakermans-Kranenburg, M. J., van IJzendoorn, M. H., & Juffer, F. (2003). Less is more: Meta-analyses of sensitivity and attachment interventions in early childhood. *Psychological Bulletin, 129*, 195–215.

Bakshy, E., Messing, S., & Adamic, L. A. (2015). Exposure to ideologically diverse news and opinion on Facebook. *Science, 348*, 1130–1132.

Balcetis, E., & Dunnin, D. (2010). Wishful seeing: More desired objects are seen as closer. *Psychological Science, 21*, 147–152.

Ball, G., Adamson, C., Beare, R., & Seal, M. L. (2017). Modelling neuroanatomical variation due to age and sex during childhood and adolescence. Unpublished manuscript:biorxiv.org/content/early/2017/07/16/126441

Balsam, K. F., Beauchaine, T. P., Rothblum, E. S., & Solomon, S. E. (2008). Three-year follow-up of same-sex couples who had civil unions in Vermont, same-sex couples not in civil unions, and heterosexual married couples. *Developmental Psychology, 44*, 102–116.

Balter, M. (2010). Animal communication helps reveal roots of language. *Science, 328*, 969–970.

Balter, M. (2014). Science misused to justify Ugandan antigay law. *Science, 343*, 956.

Balter, M. (2015). Can epigenetics explain homosexuality puzzle? *Science, 350*, 148.

Banaji, M. R., & Greenwald, A. G. (2013). *Blindspot: Hidden biases of good people.* New York: Delacorte Press.

Bancroft, J., Loftus, J., & Long, J. S. (2003). Distress about sex: A national survey of women in heterosexual relationships. *Archives of Sexual Behavior, 32*, 193–208.

Bandura, A. (1977). Self-efficacy: Toward a unifying theory of behavior. *Psychological Review, 84*, 191–215.

Bandura, A. (1982). The psychology of chance encounters and life paths. *American Psychologist, 37*, 747–755.

Bandura, A. (1986). *Social foundations of thought and action: A social-cognitive theory.* Englewood Cliffs, NJ: Prentice-Hall.

Bandura, A. (2005). The evolution of social cognitive theory. In K. G. Smith & M. A. Hitt (Eds.), *Great minds in management: The process of theory development* (pp. 9–35). Oxford: Oxford University Press.

Bandura, A. (2006). Toward a psychology of human agency. *Perspectives on Psychological Science, 1*, 164–180.

Bandura, A. (2008). An agentic perspective on positive psychology. In S. J. Lopez (Ed.), *The science of human flourishing.* Westport, CT: Praeger.

Bandura, A. (2018). Toward a psychology of human agency: Pathways and reflections. *Perspectives on Psychological Science, 13*, 130–136.

Bandura, A., Ross, D., & Ross, S. A. (1961). Transmission of aggression through imitation of aggressive models. *Journal of Abnormal and Social Psychology, 63*, 575–582.

Bang, J. W., Shibata, K., Frank, S. M., Walsh, E. G., Greenlee, M. W., Watanabe, T., & Sasaki, Y. (2018). Consolidation and reconsolidation share behavioural and neurochemical mechanisms. *Nature Human Behaviour, 2*, 507–513.

Bansak, K., Hainmueller, J., & Hangartner, D. (2016). How economic, humanitarian, and religious concerns shape European attitudes toward asylum seekers. *Science, 354*, 217–222.

Barash, D. P. (2012). *Homo mysterius: Evolutionary puzzles of human nature.* New York: Oxford University Press.

Barbaresi, W. J., Katusic, S. K., Colligan, R. C., Weaver, A. L., & Jacobsen, S. J. (2007). Modifiers of long-term school outcomes for children with attention deficit/hyperactivity disorder: Does treatment with stimulant medication make a difference? Results from a population-based study. *Journal of Developmental and Behavioral Pediatrics, 28*, 274–287.

Barberá, P., Jost, J. T., Nagler, J., Tucker, J. A., & Bonneau, R. (2015). Tweeting from left to right: Is online political communication more than an echo chamber? *Psychological Science, 26*, 1531–1542.

Bargh, J. A., & Chartrand, T. L. (1999). The unbearable automaticity of being. *American Psychologist, 54*, 462–479.

Bargh, J. A., & McKenna, K. Y. A. (2004). The internet and social life. *Annual Review of Psychology, 55*, 573–590.

Bargh, J. A., McKenna, K. Y. A., & Fitzsimons, G. M. (2002). Can you see the real me? Activation and expression of the "true self" on the internet. *Journal of Social Issues, 58*, 33–48.

Bar-Haim, Y., Lamy, D., Pergamin, L., Bakermans-Kranenburg, M. J., & van IJzendoorn, M. H. (2007). Threat-related attentional bias in anxious and nonanxious individuals: A meta-analytic study. *Psychological Bulletin, 133*, 1–24.

Barinaga, M. B. (1997). How exercise works its magic. *Science, 276*, 1325.

Barkley, R. A., Cook, E. H., Diamond, A., Zametkin, A., Thapar, A., & Teeter, A. (2002). International consensus statement on ADHD. (January 2002). *Clinical Child and Family Psychology Review, 5*, 89–111.

Barnett, P. A., & Gotlib, I. H. (1988). Psychosocial functioning and depression: Distinguishing among antecedents, concomitants, and consequences. *Psychological Bulletin, 104*, 97–126.

Barnier, A. J., & McConkey, K. M. (2004). Defining and identifying the highly hypnotizable person. In M. Heap, R. J. Brown, & D. A. Oakley (Eds.), *The highly hypnotizable person: Theoretical, experimental and clinical issues* (pp. 30–60). London: Brunner-Routledge.

Baron, C. E., Smith, T. W., Uchino, B. N., Baucom, B. R., & Birmingham, W. C. (2016). Getting along and getting ahead: Affiliation and dominance predict ambulatory blood pressure. *Health Psychology, 35*, 253–261.

Baron-Cohen, S. (2017). The eyes as window to the mind. *American Journal of Psychiatry, 174*, 1–2.

Baron-Cohen, S., Bowen, D. C., Rosemary, J. H., Allison, C., Auyeung, B., Lombardo, M. V., & Lai, M.-C. (2015). The "reading the mind in the eyes" test: Complete absence of typical difference in ~400 men and women with autism. *PLOS ONE, 10*, e0136521.

Barr, S. M., Budge, S. L., & Adelson, J. L. (2016). Transgender community belongingness as a mediator between strength of transgender identity and well-being. *Journal of Counseling Psychology, 63*, 87.

Barrera, T. L., Mott, J. M., Hofstein, R. F., & Teng, E. J. (2013). A meta-analytic review of exposure in group cognitive behavioral therapy for posttraumatic stress disorder. *Clinical Psychology Review, 33*, 24–32.

Barrett, D. (2011, November/December). Answers in your dreams. *Scientific American Mind*, 26–33.

Barrett, H. C., Bolyanatz, A., Crittenden, A. N., Fessler, D. M., Fitzpatrick, S., Gurven, M., . . . Scelza, B. A. (2016). Small-scale societies exhibit fundamental variation in the role of intentions in moral judgment. *PNAS, 113*, 4688–4693.

Barrett, L. F. (2006). Are emotions natural kinds? *Perspectives on Psychological Science, 1*, 28–58.

Barrett, L. F. (2017). *How emotions are made: The secret life of the brain.* New York: Houghton Mifflin Harcourt.

Barretto, R. P., Gillis-Smith, S., Chandrashekar, J., Yarmolinsky, D. A., Schnitzer, M. J., Ryba, N. J., & Zuker, C. S. (2015). The neural representation of taste quality at the periphery. *Nature, 517*, 373–376.

Barrington-Trimis, J. L., Berhane, K., Unger, J. B., Cruz, T. B., Urman, R., Chou, C. P., . . . Huh, J. (2016). The e-cigarette social environment, e-cigarette use, and susceptibility to cigarette smoking. *Journal of Adolescent Health, 59*, 75–80.

Barry, C. L., McGinty, E. E., Vernick, J. S., & Webster, D. W. (2013). After Newtown—Public opinion on gun policy and mental illness. *New England Journal of Medicine, 368*, 1077–1081.

Bartels, J. M., Milovich, M. M., & Moussier, S. (2016). Coverage of the Stanford prison experiment in introductory psychology courses: A survey of introductory psychology instructors. *Teaching of Psychology, 43*, 136–141.

Bartels, M. (2015). Genetics of wellbeing and its components with life, happiness, and quality of life: A review of meta-analysis of heritability studies. *Behavior Genetics, 45*, 137–156.

Bashore, T. R., Ridderinkhof, K. R., & van der Molen, M. W. (1997). The decline of cognitive processing speed in old age. *Current Directions in Psychological Science, 6*, 163–169.

Baskind, D. E. (1997, December 14). Personal communication, from Delta College.

Basu, S., & Basu, D. (2015). The relationship between psychoactive drugs, the brain and psychosis. *International Archives of Addiction Research and Medicine*, 1(003).

Bates, T. C. (2015). The glass is half full and half empty: A population-representative twin study testing if optimism and pessimism are distinct systems. *Journal of Positive Psychology, 10*, 533–542.

Bathje, G. J., & Pryor, J. B. (2011). The relationships of public and self-stigma to seeking mental health services. *Journal of Mental Health Counseling, 33*, 161–177.

Batsell, W. R., Perry, J. L., Hanley, E., & Hostetter, A. B. (2017). Ecological validity of the testing effect: The use of daily quizzes in introductory psychology. *Teaching of Psychology, 44*, 18–23.

Batz-Barbarich, C., Tay, L., Kuykendall, L., & Cheung, H. K. (2018). A meta-analysis of gender differences in subjective well-being: Estimating effect sizes and associations with gender inequality. *Psychological Science, 29*, 1491–1503.

Bauer, C. M., Hirsch, G. V., Zajac, L., Koo, B-B., Collignon, O., & Merabet, L. B. (2017). Multimodal MR-imaging reveals large-scale structural and functional connectivity changes in profound early blindness. *PLOS ONE, 12*, e0173064.

Bauer, M., Cassar, A., Chytilová, J., & Henrich, J. (2014). War's enduring effects on the development of egalitarian motivations and in-group biases. *Psychological Science, 25*, 47–57.

Baumann, J., & DeSteno, D. (2010). Emotion guided threat detection: Expecting guns where there are none. *Journal of Personality and Social Psychology, 99*, 595–610.

Baumeister, H., & Härter, M. (2007). Prevalence of mental disorders based on general population surveys. *Social Psychiatry and Psychiatric Epidemiology, 42*, 537–546.

Baumeister, R. F. (2001). Violent pride: Do people turn violent because of self-hate, or self-love? *Scientific American, 17*, 96–101.

Baumeister, R. F. (2010). *Is there anything good about men? How cultures flourish by exploiting men.* New York: Oxford.

Baumeister, R. F. (2015). Toward a general theory of motivation: Problems, challenges, opportunities, and the big picture. *Motivation and Emotion, 40*, 1–10.

Baumeister, R. F., & Bratslavsky, E. (1999). Passion, intimacy, and time: Passionate love as a function of change in intimacy. *Personality and Social Psychology Review, 3*, 49–67.

Baumeister, R. F., Bratslavsky, E., Muraven, M., & Tice, D. M. (1998). Ego depletion: Is the active self a limited resource? *Journal of Personality and Social Psychology, 74*, 1252–1265.

Baumeister, R. F., Campbell, J. D., Krueger, J. I., & Vohs, K. D. (2003). Does high self-esteem cause better performance, interpersonal success, happiness, or healthier lifestyles? *Psychological Science in the Public Interest, 4*, 1–44.

Baumeister, R. F., Catanese, K. R., & Vohs, K. D. (2001). Is there a gender difference in strength of sex drive? Theoretical views, conceptual distinctions, and a review of relevant evidence. *Personality and Social Psychology Review, 5*, 242–273.

Baumeister, R. F., Dale, K., & Sommer, K. L. (1998b). Freudian defense mechanisms and empirical findings in modern personality and social psychology: Reaction formation, projection, displacement, undoing, isolation, sublimation, and denial. *Journal of Personality, 66*, 1081–1125.

Baumeister, R. F., & Leary, M. R. (1995). The need to belong: Desire for interpersonal attachments as a fundamental human motivation. *Psychological Bulletin, 117*, 497–529.

Baumeister, R. F., & Tice, D. M. (1986). How adolescence became the struggle for self: A historical transformation of psychological development. In J. Suls & A. G. Greenwald (Eds.), *Psychological perspectives on the self* (Vol. 3, pp. 183–201). Hillsdale, NJ: Erlbaum.

Baumeister, R. F., Tice, D. M., & Vohs, K. D. (2018). The strength model of self-regulation: Conclusions from the second decade of willpower research. *Perspectives on Psychological Science, 13*, 141–145.

Baumeister, R. F., & Vohs, K. D. (2016). Strength model of self-regulation as limited resource: Assessment, controversies, update. *Advances in Experimental Social Psychology, 54*, 67–127.

Baumeister, R. F., & Vohs, K. D. (2018). Revisiting our reappraisal of the (surprisingly few) benefits of high self-esteem. *Perspectives on Psychological Science, 13*, 137–140.

Baumgardner, A. H., Kaufman, C. M., & Levy, P. E. (1989). Regulating affect interpersonally: When low esteem leads to greater enhancement. *Journal of Personality and Social Psychology, 56*, 907–921.

Baumrind, D. (1966). Effects of authoritative parental control on child behavior. *Child Development*, 37(4), 887–907.

Baumrind, D. (1967). Child care practices anteceding three patterns of preschool behavior. *Genetic Psychology Monographs, 75*, 43–88.

Baumrind, D. (1996). The discipline controversy revisited. *Family Relations, 45*, 405–414.

Baumrind, D. (2013). Is a pejorative view of power assertion in the socialization process justified? *Review of General Psychology, 17*, 420–427.

Baumrind, D., Larzelere, R. E., & Cowan, P. A. (2002). Ordinary physical punishment: Is it harmful? Comment on Gershoff (2002). *Psychological Bulletin, 128*, 602–611.

Baur, E., Forsman, M., Santtila, P., Johansson, A., Sandnabba, K., & Långström, N. (2016). Paraphilic sexual interests and sexually coercive behavior: A population-based twin study. *Archives of Sexual Behavior, 45*, 1163–1172.

Bavelier, D., Newport, E. L., & Supalla, T. (2003). Children need natural languages, signed or spoken. *Cerebrum, 5*, 19–32.

Bavelier, D., Tomann, A., Hutton, C., Mitchell, T., Corina, D., Liu, G., & Neville, H. (2000). Visual attention to the periphery is enhanced in congenitally deaf individuals. *Journal of Neuroscience, 20*, 1–6.

Baxter, M. G., & Burwell, R. D. (2017). Promoting transparency and reproducibility in *Behavioral Neuroscience*: Publishing replications, registered reports, and null results. *Behavioral Neuroscience, 131*, 275–276.

BBC. (2018). Santa Fe school shooting: Suspect 'was rejected' by victim Shana Fisher. Retrieved from bbc.com

Beam, C. R., Emery, R. E., Reynolds, C. A., Gatz, M., Turkheimer, R., & Pedersen, N. L. (2016). Widowhood and the stability of late life depressive symptomatology in the Swedish Adoption Twin Study of Aging. *Behavior Genetics, 46*, 100–113.

Beaman, A. L., & Klentz, B. (1983). The supposed physical attractiveness bias against supporters of the women's movement: A meta-analysis. *Personality and Social Psychology Bulletin, 9*, 544–550.

Beames, J. R., Schofield, T. P., & Denson, T. F. (2017). A meta-analysis of improving self-control with practice. In D. T. D. de Ridder, M. A. Adriaanse, & K. Fujita (Eds.), *Handbook of self-control in health and well-being.* New York: Routledge.

Beauchamp, G. K. (1987). The human preference for excess salt. *American Scientist, 75*, 27–33.

Beauchamp, M. R., Puterman, E., & Lubans, D. R. (2018). Physical inactivity and mental health in late adolescence. *JAMA Psychiatry, 75*, 543–544.

Beauvois, J.-L., Courbet, D., & Oberlé, D. (2012). The prescriptive power of the television host: A transposition of Milgram's obedience paradigm to the context of TV game show. *European Review of Applied Psychology/Revue Européenne de Psychologie Appliquée, 62*, 111–119.

Becerra-Culqui, T. A., Liu, Y., Nash, R., Cromwell, L., Flanders, W. D., Getahun, D., . . . & Quinn, V. P. (2018). Mental health of transgender and gender nonconforming youth compared with their peers. *Pediatrics*, 141, e20173845.

Beck, A. T., & Bredemeier, K. (2016). A unified model of depression: Integrating clinical, cognitive, biological, and evolutionary perspectives. *Clinical Psychological Science, 4*, 596–619.

Beck, A. T., Rush, A. J., Shaw, B. F., & Emery, G. (1979). *Cognitive therapy of depression.* New York: Guilford Press.

Becker, D. V., Kenrick, D. T., Neuberg, S. L., Blackwell, K. C., & Smith, D. M. (2007). The confounded nature of angry men and happy women. *Journal of Personality and Social Psychology, 92*, 179–190.

Becker, J. E., Maley, C., Shultz, E., & Taylor, W. D. (2016). Update on transcranial magnetic stimulation for depression and other neuropsychiatric illnesses. *Psychiatric Annals, 46*, 637–641.

Becker, M., Cortina, K. S., Tsai, Y., & Eccles, J. S. (2014). Sexual orientation, psychological well-being, and mental health: A longitudinal analysis from adolescence to young adulthood. *Psychology of Sexual Orientation and Gender Diversity, 1*, 132–145.

Becker, S., & Wojtowicz, J. M. (2007). A model of hippocampal neurogenesis in memory and mood disorders. *Trends in Cognitive Sciences, 11*, 70–76.

Becklen, R., & Cervone, D. (1983). Selective looking and the noticing of unexpected events. *Memory and Cognition, 11,* 601–608.

Beckman, M. (2004). Crime, culpability, and the adolescent brain. *Science, 305,* 596–599.

Bediou, B., Adams, D. M., Mayer, R. E., Tipton, E., Green, C. S., & Bavelier, D. (2018). Meta-analysis of action video game impact on perceptual, attentional, and cognitive skills. *Psychological Bulletin, 144,* 77–110.

Beeman, M. J., & Chiarello, C. (1998). Complementary right- and left-hemisphere language comprehension. *Current Directions in Psychological Science, 7,* 2–8.

Beer, J. S., & Hughes, B. L. (2010). Neural systems of social comparison and the "above-average" effect. *NeuroImage, 49,* 2671–2679.

Bègue, L., Subra, B., Arvers, P., Muller, D., Bricout, V., & Zorman, M. (2009). A message in a bottle: Extra-pharmacological effects of alcohol on aggression. *Journal of Experimental Social Psychology, 45,* 137–142.

Beilock, S. (2010). *Choke: What the secrets of the brain reveal about getting it right when you have to.* New York: Free Press.

Beintner, I., Jacobi, C., & Taylor, C. B. (2012). Effects of an Internet-based prevention programme for eating disorders in the USA and Germany: A meta-analytic review. *European Eating Disorders Review, 20,* 1–8.

Bell, A. P., Weinberg, M. S., & Hammersmith, S. K. (1981). *Sexual preference: Its development in men and women.* Bloomington: Indiana University Press.

Bell, S. B., & DeWall, N. (2018). Does transcranial direct current stimulation to the prefrontal cortex affect social behavior? A meta-analysis. *Social Cognitive and Affective Neuroscience, 13,* 899–906.

Belluck, P. (2013, February 5). People with mental illness more likely to be smokers, study finds. *The New York Times* (nytimes.com).

Belot, M., & Francesconi, M. (2006, November). *Can anyone be "the one"? Evidence on mate selection from speed dating.* London: Centre for Economic Policy Research (cepr.org).

Belson, K. (2015, September 6). No foul mouths on this field: Football with a New Age twist. *The New York Times* (nytimes.com).

Belson, K. (2017, September 21). Aaron Hernandez had severe C.T.E. when he died at age 27. *The New York Times* (nytimes.com).

Bem, D. J. (1984). Quoted in *The Skeptical Inquirer, 8,* 194.

Bem, D. J. (2011). Feeling the future: Experimental evidence for anomalous retroactive influences on cognition and affect. *Journal of Personality and Social Psychology, 100,* 407–425.

Bem, D., Tressoldi, P. E., Rabeyron, T., & Duggan, M. (2014, April 11). *Feeling the future: A meta-analysis of 90 experiments on the anomalous anticipation of random future events.* Retrieved from ncbi.nlm.nih.gov/pmc/articles/PMC4706048.1/

Bem, S. L. (1987). Masculinity and femininity exist only in the mind of the perceiver. In J. M. Reinisch, L. A. Rosenblum, & S. A. Sanders (Eds.), *Masculinity/femininity: Basic perspectives* (pp. 304–311). New York: Oxford University Press.

Bem, S. L. (1993). *The lenses of gender: Transforming the debate on sexual inequality.* New Haven, CT: Yale University Press.

Ben-Shakhar, G., & Elaad, E. (2003). The validity of psychophysiological detection of information with the guilty knowledge test: A meta-analytic review. *Journal of Applied Psychology, 88,* 131–151.

Benartzi, S., Beshears, J., Milkman, K. L., Sunstein, C. R., Thaler, R. H., Shankar, M., . . . Galing, S. (2017). Should governments invest more in nudging? *Psychological Science, 28,* 1041–1055.

Bendixen, M., Asao, K., Wyckoff, J. P., Buss, D. M., & Kennair, L. E. O. (2017). Sexual regret in US and Norway: Effects of culture and individual differences in religiosity and mating strategy. *Personality and Individual Differences, 116,* 246–251.

Benedict, C., Brooks, S. J., O'Daly, O. G., Almen, M. S., Morell, A., Åberg, K., . . . Schiöth, H. B. (2012). Acute sleep deprivation enhances the brain's response to hedonic food stimuli: An fMRI study. *Journal of Clinical Endocrinology and Metabolism, 97,* 2011–2759.

Benner, A. D., Wang, Y., Shen, Y., Boyle, A. E., Polk, R., & Cheng, Y. P. (2018). Racial/ethnic discrimination and well-being during adolescence: A meta-analytic review. *American Psychologist, 73,* 855–883.

Bennett, W. I. (1995). Beyond overeating. *New England Journal of Medicine, 332,* 673–674.

Bensley, D. A., Lilienfeld, S. O., & Powell, L. A. (2014). A new measure of psychological misconceptions: Relations with academic background, critical thinking, and acceptance of paranormal and pseudoscientific claims. *Learning and Individual Differences, 36,* 9–18.

Benson, P. L., Sharma, A. R., & Roehlkepartain, E. C. (1994). *Growing up adopted: A portrait of adolescents and their families.* Minneapolis: Search Institute.

Berg, J. M., Wall, M., Larson, N., Eisenberg, M. E., Loth, K. A., & Neumark-Sztainer, D. (2014). The unique and additive associations of family functioning and parenting practices with disordered eating behaviors in diverse adolescents. *Journal of Behavioral Medicine, 37,* 205–217.

Bergen, B. K. (2014). Universal grammar. Response to 2014 Edge question: What scientific idea is ready for retirement? *Edge* (edge.org).

Berger, B. G., & Motl, R. W. (2000). Exercise and mood: A selective review and synthesis of research employing the profile of mood states. *Journal of Applied Sports Psychology, 12,* 69–92.

Berk, L. E. (1994). Why children talk to themselves. *Scientific American, 271,* 78–83.

Berk, L. S., Felten, D. L., Tan, S. A., Bittman, B. B., & Westengard, J. (2001). Modulation of neuroimmune parameters during the eustress of humor-associated mirthful laughter. *Alternative Therapies, 7,* 62–76.

Berken, J. A., Gracco, V. L., Chen, J., Soles, J., Watkins, K. E., Baum, S., . . . Klein, D. (2015). Neural activation in speech production and reading aloud in native and non-native languages. *NeuroImage, 112,* 208–217.

Berkovich-Ohana, A., Glickson, J., & Goldstein, A. (2014). Studying the default mode and its mindfulness-induced changes using EEF functional connectivity. *Social Cognitive and Affective Neuroscience, 9,* 1616–1624.

Berkowitz, L. (1983). Aversively stimulated aggression: Some parallels and differences in research with animals and humans. *American Psychologist, 38,* 1135–1144.

Berkowitz, L. (1989). Frustration-aggression hypothesis: Examination and reformulation. *Psychological Bulletin, 106,* 59–73.

Berman, M. G., Jonides, J., & Kaplan, S. (2008). The cognitive benefits of interacting with nature. *Psychological Science, 19,* 1207–1212.

Bernieri, F., Davis, J., Rosenthal, R., & Knee, C. (1994). Interactional synchrony and rapport: Measuring synchrony in displays devoid of sound and facial affect. *Personality and Social Psychology Bulletin, 20,* 303–311.

Bernstein, D. M., & Loftus, E. F. (2009). The consequences of false memories for food preferences and choices. *Perspectives on Psychological Science, 4,* 135–139.

Bernstein, M. J., & Claypool, H. M. (2012). Social exclusion and pain sensitivity: Why exclusion sometimes hurts and sometimes numbs. *Personality and Social Psychology Bulletin, 38,* 185–196.

Berridge, K. C., Robinson, T. E., & Aldridge, J. W. (2009). Dissecting components of reward: "liking", "wanting", and learning. *Current Opinion in Pharmacology, 9,* 65–73.

Berry, C. M., & Zhao, P. (2015). Addressing criticisms of existing predictive bias research: Cognitive ability test scores still overpredict African Americans' job performance. *Journal of Applied Psychology, 100,* 162–179.

Berscheid, E. (1981). An overview of the psychological effects of physical attractiveness and some comments upon the psychological effects of knowledge of the effects of physical attractiveness. In G. W. Lucker, K. Ribbens, & J. A. McNamara (Eds.), *Psychological aspects of facial form* (Craniofacial Growth Series). Ann Arbor: Center for Human Growth and Development, University of Michigan.

Berscheid, E., Gangestad, S. W., & Kulakowski, D. (1984). Emotion in close relationships: Implications for relationship counseling. In S. D. Brown & R. W. Lent (Eds.), *Handbook of counseling psychology* (pp. 435–476). New York: Wiley.

Berti, A., Cottini, G., Gandola, M., Pia, L., Smania, N., Stracciari, A., . . . Paulesu, E. (2005). Shared cortical anatomy for motor awareness and motor control. *Science, 309,* 488–491.

Bertrand, M., & Mullainathan, S. (2004). Are Emily and Greg more employable than Lakisha and Jamal? A field experiment on labor market discrimination. *American Economic Review, 94,* 991–1013.

Bettergarcia, J. N., & Israel, T. (2018). Therapist reactions to transgender identity exploration: Effects on the therapeutic relationship in an analogue study. *Psychology of Sexual Orientation and Gender Diversity, 5,* 423–431.

Bhatt, R. S., Wasserman, E. A., Reynolds, W. F., Jr., & Knauss, K. S. (1988). Conceptual behavior in pigeons: Categorization of both familiar and novel examples from four classes of natural and artificial stimuli. *Journal of Experimental Psychology: Animal Behavior Processes, 14,* 219–234.

Bianchi, E. C., Hall, E. V., & Lee, S. (2018). Reexamining the link between economic downturns and racial antipathy: Evidence that prejudice against blacks rises during recessions. *Psychological Science, 29,* 1584–1597.

Bick, J., Zhu, T., Stamoulis, C., Fox, N. A., Zeanah, C., & Nelson, C. A. (2015). Effect of early institutionalization and foster care on long-term white matter development: A randomized clinical trial. *JAMA Pediatrics, 169,* 211–219.

Biederman, I., & Vessel, E. A. (2006). Perceptual pleasure and the brain. *American Scientist, 94,* 247–253.

Bienvenu, O. J., Davydow, D. S., & Kendler, K. S. (2011). Psychiatric "diseases" versus behavioral disorders and degree of genetic influence. *Psychological Medicine, 41,* 33–40.

Bilefsky, D. (2009, March 11). Europeans debate castration of sex offenders. *The New York Times* (nytimes.com).

Billock, V. A., & Tsou, B. H. (2012). Elementary visual hallucinations and their relationships to neural pattern-forming mechanisms. *Psychological Bulletin, 138,* 744–774.

Bird, C. D., & Emery, N. J. (2009). Rooks use stones to raise the water level to reach a floating worm. *Current Biology, 19,* 1410–1414.

Birkeland, M. S., Blix, I., Solberg, Ø., & Heir, T. (2016). Does optimism act as a buffer against posttraumatic stress over time? A longitudinal study of the protective role of optimism after the 2011 Oslo bombing. *Psychological Trauma: Theory, Research, Practice, and Policy, 9,* 207–213.

Birnbaum, G. E. (2018). The fragile spell of desire: A functional perspective on changes in sexual desire across relationship development. *Personality and Social Psychology Review, 22*, 101–127.

Birnbaum, G. E., & Reis, H. T. (2012). When does responsiveness pique sexual interest? Attachment and sexual desire in initial acquaintanceships. *Personality and Social Psychology Bulletin, 38*, 946–958.

Birnbaum, G. E., Reis, H. T., Mikulincer, M., Gillath, O., & Orpaz, A. (2006). When sex is more than just sex: Attachment orientations, sexual experience, and relationship quality. *Journal of Personality and Social Psychology, 91*, 929–943.

Birnbaum, S. G., Yuan, P. X., Wang, M., Vijayraghavan, S., Bloom, A. K., Davis, D. J., . . . Arnsten, A. F. T. (2004). Protein kinase C overactivity impairs prefrontal cortical regulation of working memory. *Science, 306*, 882–884.

Biro, D., Humle, T., Koops, K., Sousa, C., Hayashi, M., & Matsuzawa, T. (2010a). Chimpanzee mothers at Bossou, Guinea carry the mummified remains of their dead infants. *Current Biology, 20*, R351–R352.

Biro, F. M., Galvez, M. P., Greenspan, L. C., Succop, P. A., Vangeepuram, N., Pinney, S. M., . . . Wolff, M. S. (2010b). Pubertal assessment method and baseline characteristics in a mixed longitudinal study of girls. *Pediatrics, 126*, e583–e590.

Biro, F. M., Greenspan, L. C., & Galvez, M. P. (2012). Puberty in girls of the 21st century. *Journal of Pediatric and Adolescent Gynecology, 25*, 289–294.

Bishop, G. D. (1991). Understanding the understanding of illness: Lay disease representations. In J. A. Skelton & R. T. Croyle (Eds.), *Mental representation in health and illness* (pp. 32–59). New York: Springer-Verlag.

Bjork, E. L., & Bjork, R. (2011). Making things hard on yourself, but in a good way: Creating desirable difficulties to enhance learning. In M. A. Gernsbacher, M. A. Pew, L. M. Hough, & J. R. Pomerantz (Eds.), *Psychology and the real world* (pp. 55–64). New York: Worth.

Bjorklund, D. F., & Green, B. L. (1992). The adaptive nature of cognitive immaturity. *American Psychologist, 47*, 46–54.

BJS. (2017). *Data collection: National Crime Victimization Survey (NCVS)*. Retrieved from bjs.gov/index.cfm?ty-dcdetail&iid-245

Black, M. C., Basile, K. C., Breiding, M. J., Smith, S. G., Walters, M. L., Merrick, M. T., . . . Stevens, M. R. (2011). *The National Intimate Partner and Sexual Violence Survey (NISVS): 2010 summary report*. Atlanta, GA: National Center for Injury Prevention and Control, Centers for Disease Control and Prevention.

Blake, A., Nazarian, M., & Castel, A. (2015). The Apple of the mind's eye: Everyday attention, metamemory, and reconstructive memory for the Apple logo. *Quarterly Journal of Experimental Psychology, 68*, 858–865.

Blake, W. (2013, March). Voices from solitary: A sentence worse than death. Retrieved from solitarywatch.com

Blakemore, S. (2018). Avoiding social risk in adolescence. *Current Directions in Psychological Science, 27*, 116–122.

Blakemore, S. J. (2008). Development of the social brain during adolescence. *Quarterly Journal of Experimental Psychology, 61*, 40–49.

Blakeslee, S. (2006, January 10). Cells that read minds. *The New York Times* (nytimes.com).

Blanchard, R. (2004). Quantitative and theoretical analyses of the relation between older brothers and homosexuality in men. *Journal of Theoretical Biology, 230*, 173–187.

Blanchard, R. (2008). Review and theory of handedness, birth order, and homosexuality in men. *Laterality, 13*, 51–70.

Blanchard, R. (2018). Fraternal birth order, family size, and male homosexuality: Meta-analysis of studies spanning 25 years. *Archives of Sexual Behavior, 47*, 1–15.

Blanchard-Fields, F. (2007). Everyday problem solving and emotion: An adult developmental perspective. *Current Directions in Psychological Science, 16*, 26–31.

Blanke, O. (2012). Multisensory brain mechanisms of bodily self-consciousness. *Nature Reviews Neuroscience, 13*, 556–571.

Blascovich, J., & Mendes, W. B. (2010). Social psychophysiology and embodiment. In S. T. Fiske, D. T. Gilbert, & G. Lindzey (Eds.), *The handbook of social psychology*, 5th ed. (pp. 194–227). New York: Wiley.

Blasi, D. E., Wichmann, S., Hammarström, H., Stadler, P. F., & Christiansen, M. H. (2016). Sound-meaning association biases evidenced across thousands of languages. *PNAS, 113*, 10818–10823.

Blass, T. (1999). The Milgram paradigm after 35 years: Some things we now know about obedience to authority. *Journal of Applied Social Psychology, 29*, 955–978.

Blechert, J., Testa, G., Georgii, C., Klimesch, W., & Wilhelm, F. H. (2016). The Pavlovian craver: Neural and experiential correlates of single trial naturalistic food conditioning in humans. *Physiology & Behavior, 158*, 18–25.

Bleidorn, W., Arslan, R. C., Denissen, J. J. A., Rentfrow, P. J., Gebauer, J. E., Potter, J., & Gosling, S. D. (2016). Age and gender differences in self-esteem—A cross-cultural window. *Journal of Personality and Social Psychology, 111*, 396–410.

Bleidorn, W., Hopwood, C. J., & Lucas, R. E. (2018). Life events and personality trait change. *Journal of Personality, 86*, 83–96.

Blinkhorn, V., Lyons, M., & Almond, L. (2015). The ultimate femme fatale: Narcissism predicts serious and aggressive sexually coercive behavior in females. *Personality and Individual Differences, 87*, 219–223.

Blix, I., & Brennen, T. (2011). Mental time travel after trauma: The specificity and temporal distribution of autobiographical memories and future-directed thoughts. *Memory, 19*, 956–967.

Bloom, B. C. (Ed.). (1985). *Developing talent in young people*. New York: Ballantine.

Bloom, F. E. (1993, January/February). What's new in neurotransmitters. *Brain-Work*, pp. 7–9.

Bloom, P. (2000). *How children learn the meanings of words*. Cambridge, MA: MIT Press.

Blow, C. M. (2015, March 26). Officers' race matters less than you think. *The New York Times* (nytimes.com).

Boag, S. (2006). Freudian repression, the common view, and pathological science. *Review of General Psychology, 10*, 74–86.

Bockting, W. O. (2014). Transgender identity development. In D. L. Tolman & L. M. Diamond (Eds.), *APA handbook of sexuality and psychology: Vol. 1. Person-based approaches* (pp. 739–758). Washington, DC: American Psychological Association.

Boecker, H., Sprenger, T., Spilker, M. E., Henriksen, G., Koppenhoefer, M., Wagner, K. J., . . . Tolle, T. R. (2008). The runner's high: Opioidergic mechanisms in the human brain. *Cerebral Cortex, 18*, 2523–2531.

Boehm, J. K., & Kubzansky, L. D. (2012). The heart's content: The association between positive psychological well-being and cardiovascular health. *Psychological Bulletin, 138*, 655–691.

Boehm, J. K., Trudel-Fitzgerald, C., Kivimaki, M., & Kubzansky, L. D. (2015). The prospective association between positive psychological well-being and diabetes. *Health Psychology, 34*, 1013–1021.

Boenigk, S., & Mayr, M. L. (2016). The happiness of giving: Evidence from the German socioeconomic panel that happier people are more generous. *Journal of Happiness Studies, 17*, 1825–1846.

Boesch-Achermann, H., & Boesch, C. (1993). Tool use in wild chimpanzees: New light from dark forests. *Current Directions in Psychological Science, 2*, 18–21.

Bogaert, A. F. (2003). Number of older brothers and sexual orientation: New texts and the attraction/behavior distinction in two national probability samples. *Journal of Personality and Social Psychology, 84*, 644–652.

Bogaert, A. F. (2004). Asexuality: Prevalence and associated factors in a national probability sample. *Journal of Sex Research, 41*, 279–287.

Bogaert, A. F. (2006). Biological versus nonbiological older brothers and men's sexual orientation. *PNAS, 103*, 10771–10774.

Bogaert, A. F. (2015). Asexuality: What it is and why it matters. *Journal of Sex Research, 52*, 362–379.

Bogaert, A. F., Skorska, M. N., Wang, C., Gabrie, J., MacNeil, A. J., Hoffarth, M. R., . . . Blanchard, R. (2018). Male homosexuality and maternal immune responsivity to the Y-linked protein NLGN4Y. *PNAS, 115*, 302–306.

Boggiano, A. K., Harackiewicz, J. M., Bessette, M. M., & Main, D. S. (1985). Increasing children's interest through performance-contingent reward. *Social Cognition, 3*, 400–411.

Boggiano, M. M., Chandler, P. C., Viana, J. B., Oswald, K. D., Maldonado, C. R. and Wauford, P. K. (2005). Combined dieting and stress evoke exaggerated responses to opioids in binge-eating rats. *Behavioral Neuroscience, 119*, 1207–1214.

Bohannon, J. (2016). Government "nudges" prove their worth. *Science, 352*, 1042.

Bohlken, M. M., Brouwer, R. M., Mandl, R. C. W., Van, d. H., Hedman, A. M., De Hert, M., . . . Hulshoff Pol, H. E. (2016). Structural brain connectivity as a genetic marker for schizophrenia. *JAMA Psychiatry, 73*, 11–19.

Boldrini, M., Fulmore, C. A., Tartt, A. N., Simeon, L. R., Pavlova, I, Poposka, V., . . . Mann, J. J. (2018). Human hippocampal neurogenesis persists throughout aging. *Cell Stem Cell, 22*, 589–599.

Bolger, N., DeLongis, A., Kessler, R. C., & Schilling, E. A. (1989). Effects of daily stress on negative mood. *Journal of Personality and Social Psychology, 57*, 808–818.

Bolmont, M., Cacioppo, J. T., & Cacioppo, S. (2014). Love is in the gaze: An eye-tracking study of love and sexual desire. *Psychological Science, 25*, 1748–1756.

Boly, M., Garrido, M. I., Gosseries, O., Bruno, M.-A., Boveroux, P., Schnakers, C., . . . Friston, K. (2011). Preserved feed-forward but impaired top-down processes in the vegetative state. *Science, 332*, 858–862.

Bonanno, G. A. (2004). Loss, trauma, and human resilience: Have we underestimated the human capacity to thrive after extremely aversive events? *American Psychologist, 59*, 20–28.

Bonanno, G. A. (2005). Adult resilience to potential trauma. *Current Directions in Psychological Science, 14*, 135–137.

Bonanno, G. A. (2009). *The other side of sadness: What the new science of bereavement tells us about life after loss*. New York: Basic Books.

Bonanno, G. A., Brewin, C. R., Kaniasty, K., & La Greca, A. M. (2010). Weighing the costs of disaster: Consequences, risks, and resilience in individuals, families, and communities. *Psychological Science in the Public Interest, 11*, 1–49.

Bonanno, G. A., Galea, S., Bucciarelli, A., & Vlahov, D. (2006). Psychological resilience after disaster. *Psychological Science, 17*, 181–186.

Bonanno, G. A., Galea, S., Bucciarelli, A., & Vlahov, D. (2007). What predicts psychological resilience after disaster? The role of demographics, resources, and life stress. *Journal of Consulting and Clinical Psychology, 75*, 671–682.

Bonanno, G. A., & Kaltman, S. (1999). Toward an integrative perspective on bereavement. *Psychological Bulletin, 125*, 760–777.

Bonanno, G. A., Kennedy, P., Galatzer-Levy, I. R., Lude, P., & Elfström, M. L. (2012). Trajectories of resilience, depression, and anxiety following spinal cord injury. *Rehabilitation Psychology, 57*, 236–247.

Bonanno, G. A., Westphal, M., & Mancini, A. D. (2011). Resilience to loss and potential trauma. *Annual Review of Clinical Psychology, 11*, 511–535.

Bond, C. F., Jr., & DePaulo, B. M. (2006). Accuracy of deception judgments. *Personality and Social Psychology Review, 10*, 214–234.

Bond, M. H., Lun, V. M.-C., Chan, J., Chan, W. W.-Y., & Wong, D. (2012). Enacting modesty in Chinese culture: The joint contribution of personal characteristics and contextual features. *Asian Journal of Social Psychology, 15*, 14–25.

Bond, R., & Smith, P. B. (1996). Culture and conformity: A meta-analysis of studies using Asch's (1952, 1956) line judgment task. *Psychological Bulletin, 119*, 111–137.

Bonezzi, A., Brendl, C. M., & DeAngelis, M. (2011). Stuck in the middle: The psychophysics of goal pursuit. *Psychological Science, 22*, 607–612.

Bonfils, K. A., Lysaker, P. H., Minor, K. S., & Salyers, M. P. (2016). Affective empathy in schizophrenia: A meta-analysis. *Schizophrenia Research, 175*, 109–117.

Bono, J. E., & Judge, T. A. (2004). Personality and transformational and transactional leadership: A meta-analysis. *Journal of Applied Psychology, 89*, 901–910.

Bonos, L. (2018, March 8). A legislator has a bill to ban *The Bachelor's* Arie Luyendyk Jr. from Minnesota. *The Washington Post* (washingtonpost.com).

Boone, A. P., & Hegarty, M. (2017). Sex differences in mental rotation tasks: Not just in the mental rotation process! *Journal of Experimental Psychology: Learning, Memory, and Cognition, 43*, 1005–1019.

Bora, E., & Pantelis, C. (2013). Theory of mind impairments in first-episode psychosis, individuals at ultra-high risk for psychosis and in first-degree relatives of schizophrenia: Systematic review and meta-analysis. *Schizophrenia Research, 144*, 31–36.

Bornstein, M. H., Cote, L. R., Maital, S., Painter, K., Park, S.-Y., Pascual, L., . . . Vyt, A. (2004). Cross-linguistic analysis of vocabulary in young children: Spanish, Dutch, French, Hebrew, Italian, Korean, and American English. *Child Development, 75*, 1115–1139.

Bornstein, M. H., Tal, J., Rahn, C., Galperin, C. Z., Pêcheux, M.-G., Lamour, M., . . . Tamis-LeMonda, C. S. (1992a). Functional analysis of the contents of maternal speech to infants of 5 and 13 months in four cultures: Argentina, France, Japan, and the United States. *Developmental Psychology, 28*, 593–603.

Bornstein, M. H., Tamis-LeMonda, C. S., Tal, J., Ludemann, P., Toda, S., Rahn, C. W., . . . Vardi, D. (1992b). Maternal responsiveness to infants in three societies: The United States, France, and Japan. *Child Development, 63*, 808–821.

Bornstein, R. F. (1989). Exposure and affect: Overview and meta-analysis of research, 1968–1987. *Psychological Bulletin, 106*, 265–289.

Bornstein, R. F. (1999). Source amnesia, misattribution, and the power of unconscious perceptions and memories. *Psychoanalytic Psychology, 16*, 155–178.

Bornstein, R. F., Galley, D. J., Leone, D. R., & Kale, A. R. (1991). The temporal stability of ratings of parents: Test-retest reliability and influence of parental contact. *Journal of Social Behavior and Personality, 6*, 641–649.

Bos, H. M. W., Knox, J. R., van Rijn-van Gelderen, L., & Gartrell, N. K. (2016). Same-sex and different-sex parent households and child health outcomes: Findings from the national survey of children's health. *Journal of Developmental and Behavioral Pediatrics, 37*, 179–187.

Bostwick, J. M., & Pankratz, V. S. (2000). Affective disorders and suicide risk: A re-examination. *American Journal of Psychiatry, 157*, 1925–1932.

Bosworth, R. G., & Dobkins, K. R. (1999). Left-hemisphere dominance for motion processing in deaf signers. *Psychological Science, 10*, 256–262.

Bothwell, R. K., Brigham, J. C., & Malpass, R. S. (1989). Cross-racial identification. *Personality and Social Psychology Bulletin, 15*, 19–25.

Bouchard, T. J., Jr. (2004). Genetic influence on human psychological traits. *Current Directions in Psychological Science, 13*, 148–151.

Boucher, J., Mayes, A., & Bigham, S. (2012). Memory in autistic spectrum disorder. *Psychological Bulletin, 138*, 458–496.

Bowden, E. M., & Beeman, M. J. (1998). Getting the right idea: Semantic activation in the right hemisphere may help solve insight problems. *Psychological Science, 9*, 435–440.

Bower, B. (2009, February 14). The dating go round. *Science News*, pp. 22–25.

Bower, G. H. (1986). Prime time in cognitive psychology. In P. Eelen (Ed.), *Cognitive research and behavior therapy: Beyond the conditioning paradigm*. Amsterdam: North Holland Publishers.

Bower, G. H., & Morrow, D. G. (1990). Mental models in narrative comprehension. *Science, 247*, 44–48.

Bower, J. M., & Parsons, L. M. (2003, August). Rethinking the "lesser brain." *Scientific American*, pp. 50–57.

Bowers, J. S., Mattys, S. L., & Gage, S. H. (2009). Preserved implicit knowledge of a forgotten childhood language. *Psychological Science, 20*, 1064–1069.

Bowker, E., & Dorstyn, D. (2016). Hypnotherapy for disability-related pain: A meta-analysis. *Journal of Health Psychology, 21*, 526–539.

Bowling, N. A., Eschleman, K. J., & Wang, Q. (2010). A meta-analytic examination of the relationship between job satisfaction and subjective well-being. *Journal of Occupational and Organizational Psychology, 83*, 915–934.

Boxer, P., Huesmann, L. R., Bushman, B. J., O'Brien, M., & Moceri, D. (2009). The role of violent media preference in cumulative developmental risk for violence and general aggression. *Journal of Youth and Adolescence, 38*, 417–428.

Boyatzis, C. J. (2012). Spiritual development during childhood and adolescence. In L. J. Miller (Ed.), *The Oxford handbook of psychology and spirituality* (pp. 151–164). New York: Oxford University Press.

Boyatzis, C. J., Matillo, G. M., & Nesbitt, K. M. (1995). Effects of the "Mighty Morphin Power Rangers" on children's aggression with peers. *Child Study Journal, 25*, 45–55.

Boyce, C. J., & Wood, A. M. (2011). Personality prior to disability determines adaptation: Agreeable individuals recover lost life satisfaction faster and more completely. *Psychological Science, 22*, 1397–1402.

Braden, J. P. (1994). *Deafness, deprivation, and IQ*. New York: Plenum.

Bradley, D. R., Dumais, S. T., & Petry, H. M. (1976). Reply to Cavonius. *Nature, 261*, 78.

Bradley, R. B., Binder, E. B., Epstein, M. P., Tang, Y., Nair, H. P., Liu, W., . . . Ressler, K. J. (2008). Influence of child abuse on adult depression: Moderation by the corticotropin-releasing hormone receptor gene. *Archives of General Psychiatry, 65*, 190–200.

Bradshaw, C., Sawyer, A., & O'Brennan, L. (2009). A social disorganization perspective on bullying-related attitudes and behaviors: The influence of school context. *American Journal of Community Psychology, 43*, 204–220.

Brainerd, C. J. (1996). Piaget: A centennial celebration. *Psychological Science, 7*, 191–195.

Brand, B. L., Sar, V., Stavropoulos, P., Krüger, C., Korzekwa, M., Martínez-Taboas, A., & Middleton, W. (2016). Separating fact from fiction: An empirical examination of six myths about dissociative identity disorder. *Harvard Review of Psychiatry, 24*, 257–270.

Brandon, S., Boakes, J., Glaser, D., & Green, R. (1998). Recovered memories of childhood sexual abuse: Implications for clinical practice. *British Journal of Psychiatry, 172*, 294–307.

Brang, D., Edwards, L., Ramachandran, V. S., & Coulson, S. (2008). Is the sky 2? Contextual priming in grapheme-color synaesthesia. *Psychological Science, 19*, 421–428.

Brannan, D., Biswas-Diener, R., Mohr, C., Mortazavi, S., & Stein, N. (2013). Friends and family: A cross-cultural investigation of social support and subjective well-being among college students. *Journal of Positive Psychology, 8*, 65–75.

Bransford, J. D., & Johnson, M. K. (1972). Contextual prerequisites for understanding: Some investigations of comprehension and recall. *Journal of Verbal Learning and Verbal Behavior, 11*, 717–726.

Brasel, S. A., & Gips, J. (2011). Media multitasking behavior: Concurrent television and computer usage. *Cyberpsychology, Behavior, and Social Networking, 14*, 527–534.

Braun, S. (1996). New experiments underscore warnings on maternal drinking. *Science, 273*, 738–739.

Braun, S. (2001, Spring). Seeking insight by prescription. *Cerebrum*, pp. 10–21.

Braunstein, G. D., Sundwall, D. A., Katz, M., Shifren, J. L., Buster, J. E., Simon, J. A., . . . Watts, N. B. (2005). Safety and efficacy of a testosterone patch for the treatment of hypoactive sexual desire disorder in surgically menopausal women: A randomized, placebo-controlled trial. *Archives of Internal Medicine, 165*, 1582–1589.

Bray, D. W., & Byham, W. C. (1991, Winter). Assessment centers and their derivatives. *Journal of Continuing Higher Education*, pp. 8–11.

Bray, D. W., & Byham, W. C., interviewed by Mayes, B. T. (1997). Insights into the history and future of assessment centers: An interview with Dr. Douglas W. Bray and Dr. William Byham. *Journal of Social Behavior and Personality, 12*, 3–12.

Brayne, C., Spiegelhalter, D. J., Dufouil, C., Chi, L.-Y., Dening, T. R., Paykel, E. S., . . . Huppert, F. A. (1999). Estimating the true extent of cognitive decline in the old old. *Journal of the American Geriatrics Society, 47*, 1283–1288.

Breedlove, S. M. (1997). Sex on the brain. *Nature, 389*, 801.

Breedvelt, J. J. F., Kandola, A., Kousoulis, A. A., Brouwer, M. E., Karyotaki, E., Bockting, C. L. H., & Cuijpers, P. M. W. (2018). What are the effects of preventative interventions on major depressive disorder (MDD) in young adults? A systematic review and meta-analysis of randomized controlled trials. *Journal of Affective Disorders, 239*, 18–29.

Brehm, S., & Brehm, J. W. (1981). *Psychological reactance: A theory of freedom and control.* New York: Academic Press.

Breslau, J., Gilman, S. E., Stein, B. D., Ruder, T., Gmelin, T., & Miller, E. (2017). Sex differences in recent first-onset depression in an epidemiological sample of adolescents. *Translational Psychiatry, 7*, e1139.

Breslin, C. W., & Safer, M. A. (2011). Effects of event valence on long-term memory for two baseball championship games. *Psychological Science, 22*, 1408–1412.

Brewer, W. F. (1977). Memory for the pragmatic implications of sentences. *Memory & Cognition, 5*, 673–678.

Brewin, C. R., & Andrews, B. (2017). Creating memories for false autobiographical events in childhood: A systematic review. *Applied Cognitive Psychology, 31*, 2–23.

Brewin, C. R., Andrews, B., Rose, S., & Kirk, M. (1999). Acute stress disorder and posttraumatic stress disorder in victims of violent crime. *American Journal of Psychiatry, 156*, 360–366.

Briley, D. A., & Tucker-Drob, E. (2014). Genetic and environmental continuity in personality development: A meta-analysis. *Psychological Bulletin, 140*, 1303–1331.

Briscoe, D. (1997, February 16). Women lawmakers still not in charge. *Grand Rapids Press*, p. A23.

Brislin, R. W. (1988). Increasing awareness of class, ethnicity, culture, and race by expanding on students' own experiences. In I. Cohen (Ed.), *The G. Stanley Hall Lecture Series*. Washington, DC: American Psychological Association.

Broadbent, E., Kahokehr, A., Booth, R. J., Thomas, J., Windsor, J. A., Buchanan, C. M., . . . Hill, A. G. (2012). A brief relaxation intervention reduces stress and improves surgical wound healing response: A randomized trial. *Brain, Behavior, and Immunity, 26*, 212–217.

Brodbeck, F. C., Chhokar, J. S., & House, R. J. (2008). Culture and leadership in 25 societies: Integration, conclusions, and future directions. In J. S. Chhokar, F. C. Brodbeck & R. J. House (Eds.), *Culture and leadership across the world: The GLOBE book of in-depth studies of 25 societies* (pp. 1023–1099). Mahwah, NJ: Erlbaum.

Brody, S., & Tillmann, H. C. (2006). The post-orgasmic prolactin increase following intercourse is greater than following masturbation and suggests greater satiety. *Biological Psychology, 71*, 312–315.

Broman, C. L. (1996). Coping with personal problems. In H. W. Neighbors & J. S. Jackson (Eds.), *Mental health in Black America* (pp. 117–129). Thousand Oaks, CA: Sage.

Brooks, R. (2012). "Asia's missing women" as a problem in applied evolutionary psychology? *Evolutionary Psychology, 12*, 910–925.

Brooks, S. (2015). Does personal social media usage affect efficiency and well-being? *Computers in Human Behavior, 46*, 26–37.

Brose, A., de Roover, K., Ceulemans, E., & Kuppens, P. (2015). Older adults' affective experiences across 100 days are less variable and less complex than younger adults'. *Psychology and Aging, 30*, 194–208.

Brown, A. (2017, November 8). Republicans, Democrats have starkly different views on transgender issues. Pew Research Center (pewresearch.org).

Brown, A. S., Begg, M. D., Gravenstein, S., Schaefer, C. A., Wyatt, R. J., Bresnahan, M., . . . Susser, E. S. (2004). Serologic evidence of prenatal influenza in the etiology of schizophrenia. *Archives of General Psychiatry, 61*, 774–780.

Brown, A. S., & Marsh, E. (2009). Creating illusions of past encounter through brief exposure. *Psychological Science, 20*, 534–538.

Brown, A. S., & Patterson, P. H. (2011). Maternal infection and schizophrenia: Implications for prevention. *Schizophrenia Bulletin, 37*, 284–290.

Brown, A. S., Schaefer, C. A., Wyatt, R. J., Goetz, R., Begg, M. D., Gorman, J. M., & Susser, E. S. (2000). Maternal exposure to respiratory infections and adult schizophrenia spectrum disorders: A prospective birth cohort study. *Schizophrenia Bulletin, 26*, 287–295.

Brown, E. L., & Deffenbacher, K. (1979). *Perception and the senses.* New York: Oxford University Press.

Brown, J. A. (1958). Some tests of the decay theory of immediate memory. *Quarterly Journal of Experimental Psychology, 10*, 12–21.

Brown, K. W., Creswell, J. D., & Ryan, R. M. (Eds.). (2016). *Handbook of mindfulness: Theory, research, and practice.* New York: Guilford.

Brown, K. W., Goodman, R. J., & Inzlicht, M. (2013). Dispositional mindfulness and the attenuation of neural responses to emotional stimuli. *Social Cognitive and Affective Neuroscience, 8*, 93–99.

Brown, L. A., Gallagher, T., Petersen, J., Benhamou, K., Foa, E. B., & Asnaani, A. (2018). Does CBT for anxiety-related disorders alter suicidal ideation? Findings from a naturalistic sample. *Journal of Anxiety Disorders, 59*, 10–16.

Brown, R. P., Imura, M., & Mayeux, L. (2014). Honor and the stigma of mental healthcare. *Personality and Social Psychology Bulletin, 40*, 1119–1131.

Brown, R. P., Osterman, L. L., & Barnes, C. D. (2009). School violence and the culture of honor. *Psychological Science, 20*, 1400–1405.

Brown, S. L., Brown, R. M., House, J. S., & Smith, D. M. (2008). Coping with spousal loss: Potential buffering effects of self-reported helping behavior. *Personality and Social Psychology Bulletin, 34*, 849–861.

Browning, C. (1992). *Ordinary men: Reserve police battalion 101 and the final solution in Poland.* New York: HarperCollins.

Browning, R. (1868). "The ring and the book. IV—Tertium quid." New York: Thomas Y. Crowell.

Bruck, M., & Ceci, S. J. (1999). The suggestibility of children's memory. *Annual Review of Psychology, 50*, 419–439.

Bruck, M., & Ceci, S. J. (2004). Forensic developmental psychology: Unveiling four common misconceptions. *Current Directions in Psychological Science, 15*, 229–232.

Bruer, J. T. (1999). *The myth of the first three years: A new understanding of early brain development and lifelong learning.* New York: Free Press.

Brummelman, E., Thomaes, S., Nelemans, S. A., Orobio de Castro, B., Overbeek, G., & Bushman, B. J. (2015). Origins of narcissism in children. *PNAS, 112*, 3659–3662.

Bruni, F. (2018, October 30). The internet will be the death of us. *The New York Times* (nytimes.com).

Brunner, M., Gogol, K. M., Sonnleitner, P., Keller, U., Krauss, S., & Preckel, F. (2013). Gender differences in the mean level, variability, and profile shape of student achievement: Results from 41 countries. *Intelligence, 41*, 378–395.

Bruno, M.-A., Bernheim, J. L., Ledoux, D., Pellas, F., Demertzi, A., & Laureys, S. (2011). A survey on self-assessed well-being in a cohort of chronic locked-in syndrome patients: Happy majority, miserable minority. *BMJ Open, 1*, e000039.

Bruno, M.-A., Pellas, F., & Laureys, S. (2008). Quality of life in locked-in syndrome survivors. In J. L. Vincent (Ed.), *2008 yearbook of intensive care and emergency medicine.* New York: Springer.

Brunoni, A. R., Chaimani, A., Moffa, A. H., Razza, L. B., Gattaz, W. F., Daskalakis, Z. J., & Carvalho, A. F. (2017). Repetitive transcranial magnetic stimulation for the acute treatment of major depressive episodes: A systematic review with network meta-analysis. *JAMA Psychiatry, 74*, 143–152.

Bryan, A. E. B., & Arkowitz, H. (2015). Meta-analysis of the effects of peer-administered psychosocial interventions on symptoms of depression. *American Journal of Community Psychology, 55*, 455–471.

Bryant, G. A., Fessler, D. M. T., Fusaroli, R., Clint, E., Amir, D., Chávez, B., . . . Zhou, Y. (2018). The perception of spontaneous and volitional laughter across 21 societies. *Psychological Science, 29*, 1515–1525.

Bub, K. L., Robinson, L. E., & Curtis, D. S. (2016). Longitudinal associations between self-regulation and health across childhood and adolescence. *Health Psychology, 35*, 1235–1245.

Buchanan, R. W., Kreyenbuhl, J., Kelly, D. L., Noel, J. M., Boggs, D. L., Fischer, B. A., . . . Keller, W. (2010). The 2009 schizophrenia PORT psychopharmacological treatment recommendations and summary statements. *Schizophrenia Bulletin, 36*, 71–93.

Buchanan, T. W. (2007). Retrieval of emotional memories. *Psychological Bulletin, 133*, 761–779.

Buck, L. B., & Axel, R. (1991). A novel multigene family may encode odorant receptors: A molecular basis for odor recognition. *Cell, 65*, 175–187.

Buckels, E. E., Trapnell, P. D., & Paulhus, D. L. (2014). Trolls just want to have fun. *Personality and Individual Differences, 67*, 97–102.

Buckholtz, J. W., Treadway, M. T., Cowan, R. L., Woodward, N. D., Benning, S. D., Li, R., . . . Zald, D. H. (2010). Mesolimbic dopamine reward system hypersensitivity in individuals with psychopathic traits. *Nature Neuroscience, 13*, 419–421.

Buckingham, M. (2007). *Go put your strengths to work: 6 powerful steps to achieve outstanding performance.* New York: Free Press.

Buckingham, M., & Clifton, D. O. (2001). *Now, discover your strengths.* New York: Free Press.

Buckley, C. (2007, January 3). Man is rescued by stranger on subway tracks. *The New York Times* (nytimes.com).

Buehler, R., Griffin, D., & Ross, M. (1994). Exploring the "planning fallacy": Why people underestimate their task completion times. *Journal of Personality and Social Psychology, 67*, 366–381.

Buehler, R., Griffin, D., & Ross, M. (2002). Inside the planning fallacy: The causes and consequences of optimistic time predictions. In T. Gilovich, D. Griffin, & D. Kahneman (Eds.), *Heuristics and biases: The psychology of intuitive judgment* (pp. 250–270). Cambridge: Cambridge University Press.

Buffardi, L. E., & Campbell, W. K. (2008). Narcissism and social networking web sites. *Personality and Social Psychology Bulletin, 34*, 1303–1314.

Buhle, J. T., Silvers, J. A., Wager, T. D., Lopez, R., Onyemekwu, C., Kober, H., . . . Ochsner, K. N. (2014). Cognitive reappraisal of emotion: A meta-analysis of human neuroimaging studies. *Cerebral Cortex, 24*, 2981–2990.

Buhle, J. T., Stevens, B. L., Friedman, J. J., & Wager, T. D. (2012). Distraction and placebo: Two separate routes to pain control. *Psychological Science, 23,* 246–253.

Buka, S. L., Tsuang, M. T., Torrey, E. F., Klebanoff, M. A., Wagner, R. L., & Yolken, R. H. (2001). Maternal infections and subsequent psychosis among offspring. *Archives of General Psychiatry, 58,* 1032–1037.

Bullock, B., & Murray, G. (2014). Reduced amplitude of the 24-hour activity rhythm: A biomarker of vulnerability to bipolar disorder? *Clinical Psychological Science, 2,* 86–96.

Burger, J. M. (2009). Replicating Milgram: Would people still obey today? *American Psychologist, 64,* 1–11.

Burger, J. M., Bender, T. J., Day, L., DeBolt, J. A., Guthridge, L., How, H. W., . . . Taylor, S. (2015). The power of one: The relative influence of helpful and selfish models. *Social Influence, 10,* 77–84.

Buri, J. R., Louiselle, P. A., Misukanis, T. M., & Mueller, R. A. (1988). Effects of parental authoritarianism and authoritativeness on self-esteem. *Personality and Social Psychology Bulletin, 14,* 271–282.

Burish, T. G., & Carey, M. P. (1986). Conditioned aversive responses in cancer chemotherapy patients: Theoretical and developmental analysis. *Journal of Counseling and Clinical Psychology, 54,* 593–600.

Burke, D. M., & Shafto, M. A. (2004). Aging and language production. *Current Directions in Psychological Science, 13,* 21–24.

Burke, K. (2018). How many texts do people send every day (2018)? Retrieved from textrequest.com/blog /how-many-texts-people-send-per-day/

Burkhauser, R. V., De Neve, J.-E., & Powdthavee, N. (2016, January). *Top incomes and human well-being around the world.* London School of Economic and Political Science: Centre for Economic Performance, CEP Discussion Paper No. 1400.

Burlingame, G. M., Seebeck, J. D., Janis, R. A., Whitcomb, K. E., Barkowski, S., Rosendahl, J., & Strauss, B. (2016). Outcome differences between individual and group formats when identical and nonidentical treatments, patients, and doses are compared: A 25-year meta-analytic perspective. *Psychotherapy, 53,* 446–461.

Burns, B. C. (2004). The effects of speed on skilled chess performance. *Psychological Science, 15,* 442–447.

Burt, M. R. (1980). Cultural myths and supports for rape. *Journal of Personality and Social Psychology, 38,* 217–230.

Busby, D. M., Carroll, J. S., & Willoughby, B. J. (2010). Compatibility or restraint? The effects of sexual timing on marriage relationships. *Journal of Family Psychology, 24,* 766–774.

Bushdid, C., Magnasco, M. O., Vosshall, L. B., & Keller, A. (2014). Humans can discriminate more than 1 trillion olfactory stimuli. *Science, 343,* 1370–1372.

Bushman, B. J. (2016). Violent media and hostile appraisals: A meta-analytic review. *Aggressive Behavior, 42,* 605–613.

Bushman, B. J. (2018). Teaching students about violent media effects. *Teaching of Psychological Science, 45,* 200–206.

Bushman, B. J., & Anderson, C. A. (2009). Comfortably numb: Desensitizing effects of violent media on helping others. *Psychological Science, 20,* 273–277.

Bushman, B. J., Bonacci, A. M., van Dijk, M., & Baumeister, R. F. (2003). Narcissism, sexual refusal, and aggression: Testing a narcissistic reactance model of sexual coercion. *Journal of Personality and Social Psychology, 84,* 1027–1040.

Bushman, B. J., DeWall, C. N., Pond, R. S., Jr., & Hanus, M. D. (2014). Low glucose relates to greater aggression in married couples. *PNAS, 111,* 6254–6257.

Bushman, B. J., & Huesmann, L. R. (2010). Aggression. In S. T. Fiske, D. T. Gilbert, & G. Lindzey (Eds.), *Handbook of social psychology* (5th ed., Ch. 23, pp. 833–863). New York: John Wiley & Sons.

Bushman, B. J., Moeller, S. J., & Crocker, J. (2011). Sweets, sex, or self-esteem? Comparing the value of self-esteem boosts with other pleasant rewards. *Journal of Personality, 79,* 993–1012.

Bushman, B. J., Ridge, R. D., Das, E., Key, C. W., & Busath, G. L. (2007). When God sanctions killing: Effects of scriptural violence on aggression. *Psychological Science, 18,* 204–207.

Buss, A. H. (1989). Personality as traits. *American Psychologist, 44,* 1378–1388.

Buss, D. M. (1994). The strategies of human mating: People worldwide are attracted to the same qualities in the opposite sex. *American Scientist, 82,* 238–249.

Buss, D. M. (1995). Evolutionary psychology: A new paradigm for psychological science. *Psychological Inquiry, 6,* 1–30.

Buss, D. M. (2008). *Female sexual psychology.* Retrieved from edge.org/q2008/q08_12.html#buss

Buster, J. E., Kingsberg, S. A., Aguirre, O., Brown, C., Breaux, J. G., Buch, A., . . . Casson, P. (2005). Testosterone patch for low sexual desire in surgically menopausal women: A randomized trial. *Obstetrics and Gynecology, 105,* 944–952.

Butler, A., Oruc, I., Fox, C. J., & Barton, J. J. S. (2008). Factors contributing to the adaptation aftereffects of facial expression. *Brain Research, 1191,* 116–126.

Butler, R. A. (1954, February). Curiosity in monkeys. *Scientific American,* pp. 70–75.

Butts, M. M., Casper, W. J., & Yang, T. S. (2013). How important are work-family support policies? A meta-analytic investigation of their effects on employee outcomes. *Journal of Applied Psychology, 98,* 1–25.

Buxton, O. M., Cain, S. W., O'Connor, S. P., Porter, J. H., Duffy, J. F., Wang, W., . . . Shea, S. A. (2012). Adverse metabolic consequences in humans of prolonged sleep restriction combined with circadian disruption. *Science Translational Medicine, 4,* 129–143.

Byrc, K., Durand, E. Y., Macpherson, J. M., Reich, D., & Mountain, J. L. (2015). The genetic ancestry of African Americans, Latinos, and European Americans across the United States. *American Journal of Human Genetics 96,* 37–53.

Byrd, A. L., & Manuck, S. B. (2014). MAOA, childhood maltreatment, and antisocial behavior: Meta-analysis of a gene-environment interaction. *Biological Psychiatry, 75,* 9–17.

Byrne, D. (1982). Predicting human sexual behavior. In A. G. Kraut (Ed.), *The G. Stanley Hall Lecture Series* (Vol. 2, pp. 211–254). Washington, DC: American Psychological Association.

Byrne, R. W. (1991, May/June). Brute intellect. *The Sciences,* pp. 42–47.

Byrne, R. W., Bates, L. A., & Moss, C. J. (2009). Elephant cognition in primate perspective. *Comparative Cognition & Behavior Reviews, 4,* 1–15.

Byron, K., & Khazanchi, S. (2011). A meta-analytic investigation of the relationship of state and trait anxiety to performance on figural and verbal creative tasks. *Personality and Social Psychology Bulletin, 37,* 269–283.

Cacioppo, J. T., Cacioppo, S., Capitanio, J. P., & Cole, S. W. (2015). The neuroendocrinology of social isolation. *Annual Review of Psychology, 66,* 733–767.

Cacioppo, J. T., Cacioppo, S., Gonzaga, G. C., Ogburn, E. L., & VanderWeele, T. J. (2013). Marital satisfaction and break-ups differ across on-line and off-line meeting venues. *PNAS, 110,* 10135–10140.

Cacioppo, J. T., & Patrick, C. (2008). *Loneliness.* New York: W. W. Norton.

Caddick, A., & Porter, L. E. (2012). Exploring a model of professionalism in multiple perpetrator violent crime in the UK. *Criminological & Criminal Justice: An International Journal, 12,* 61–82.

Cain, S. (2012). *Quiet: The power of introverts in a world that can't stop talking.* New York: Crown.

Calati, R., De Ronchi, D., Bellini, M., Serretti, A. (2011). The 5-HTTLPR polymorphism and eating disorders: A meta-analysis. *International Journal of Eating Disorders, 44,* 191–199.

Calcutt, S. E., Proctor, D., Berman, S. M., & de Waal, F. B. (2019). Chimpanzees (Pan troglodytes) are more averse to social than nonsocial risk. *Psychological Science, 30,* 105–115.

Caldwell, J. A. (2012). Crew schedules, sleep deprivation, and aviation performance. *Current Directions in Psychological Science, 21,* 85–89.

Cale, E. M., & Lilienfeld, S. O. (2002). Sex differences in psychopathy and antisocial personality disorder: A review and integration. *Clinical Psychology Review, 22,* 1179–1207.

Caliskan, A., Bryson, J. J., & Narayanan, A. (2017). Semantics derived automatically from language corpora contain human-like biases. *Science, 356,* 183–186.

Callaghan, T., Rochat, P., Lillard, A., Claux, M. L., Odden, H., Itakura, S., . . . Singh, S. (2005). Synchrony in the onset of mental-state reasoning. *Psychological Science, 16,* 378–384.

Calvert, S. L., Appelbaum, M., Dodge, K. A., Graham, S., Nagayama Hall, G. C., Hamby, S., . . . Hedges, L. V. (2017). The American Psychological Association Task Force assessment of violent video games: Science in the service of public interest. *American Psychologist, 72,* 126–143.

Calvin, C. M., Batty, G. D., Der, G., Brett, C. E., Taylor, A., Pattie, A., . . . Deary, I. J. (2017). Childhood intelligence in relation to major causes of death in 68-year follow-up: Prospective population study. *BMJ: British Medical Journal, 357,* j2708.

Calvo-Merino, B., Glaser, D. E., Grèzes, J., Passingham, R. E., & Haggard, P. (2004). Action observation and acquired motor skills: An fMRI study with expert dancers. *Cerebral Cortex, 15,* 1243–1249.

Camerer, C. F., Dreber, A., Holzmeister, F., Ho, T. H., Huber, J., Johannesson, M., . . . & Altmejd, A. (2018). Evaluating the replicability of social science experiments in *Nature* and *Science* between 2010 and 2015. *Nature Human Behaviour, 2,* 637–644.

Campbell, A. (2010). Oxytocin and human social behavior. *Personality and Social Psychology Review, 14,* 281–205.

Campbell, D. T. (1975). On the conflicts between biological and social evolution and between psychology and moral tradition. *American Psychologist, 30,* 1103–1126.

Campbell, D. T., & Specht, J. C. (1985). Altruism: Biology, culture, and religion. *Journal of Social and Clinical Psychology, 3,* 33–42.

Campbell, L., & Marshall, T. (2011). Anxious attachment and relationship processes: An interactionist perspective. *Journal of Personality, 79,* 1219–1249.

Campbell, S. (1986). *The Loch Ness Monster: The evidence.* Willingborough, Northamptonshire, U.K.: Acquarian Press.

Camperio-Ciani, A., Corna, F., & Capiluppi, C. (2004). Evidence for maternally inherited factors favouring male homosexuality and promoting female fecundity. *Proceedings of the Royal Society of London B, 271,* 2217–2221.

Camperio-Ciani, A., Lemmola, F., & Blecher, S. R. (2009). Genetic factors increase fecundity in female maternal relatives of bisexual men as in homosexuals. *Journal of Sexual Medicine, 6,* 449–455.

Camperio-Ciani, A., & Pellizzari, E. (2012). Fecundity of paternal and maternal non-parental female relatives of homosexual and heterosexual men. *PLOS ONE, 7,* e51088.

Campitelli, G., & Gobet, F. (2011). Deliberate practice: Necessary but not sufficient. *Current Directions in Psychological Science, 20,* 280–285.

Campos, J. J., Bertenthal, B. I., & Kermoian, R. (1992). Early experience and emotional development: The emergence of wariness of heights. *Psychological Science, 3,* 61–64.

Canetta, S., Sourander, A., Surcel, H., Hinkka-Yli-Salomäki, S., Leiviskä, J., Kellendonk, C., . . . Brown, A. S. (2014). Elevated maternal C-reactive protein and increased risk of schizophrenia in a national birth cohort. *American Journal of Psychiatry, 171,* 960–968.

Canli, T., Desmond, J. E., Zhao, Z., & Gabrieli, J. D. E. (2002). Sex differences in the neural basis of emotional memories. *PNAS, 99,* 10789–10794.

Cannon, W. B. (1929). *Bodily changes in pain, hunger, fear, and rage.* New York: Branford.

Cannon, W. B., & Washburn, A. L. (1912). An explanation of hunger. *American Journal of Physiology, 29,* 441–454.

Cantor, N., & Kihlstrom, J. F. (1987). *Personality and social intelligence.* Englewood Cliffs, NJ: Prentice-Hall.

Canuso, C. M., Singh, J. B., Fedgchin, M., Alphs, L., Lane, R., Lim, P., . . . Drevets, W. C. (2018). Efficacy and safety of intranasal esketamine for the rapid reduction of symptoms of depression and suicidality in patients at imminent risk for suicide: Results of a double-blind, randomized, placebo-controlled study. *American Journal of Psychiatry, 175,* 620–630.

Caplan, N., Choy, M. H., & Whitmore, J. K. (1992, February). Indochinese refugee families and academic achievement. *Scientific American,* pp. 36–42.

Caprariello, P. A., & Reis, H. T. (2013). To do, to have, or to share? Valuing experiences over material possessions depends on the involvement of others. *Journal of Personality and Social Psychology, 104,* 199–215.

Carey, B. (2007, September 4). Bipolar illness soars as a diagnosis for the young. *The New York Times* (nytimes .com).

Carey, B. (2009, November 27). Surgery for mental ills offers both hope and risk. *The New York Times* (nytimes .com).

Carey, B. (2011, February 14). Wariness on surgery of the mind. *The New York Times* (nytimes.com).

Carey, B. (2016, December 29). Did Debbie Reynolds die of a broken heart? *The New York Times* (nytimes.com).

Carey, G. (1990). Genes, fears, phobias, and phobic disorders. *Journal of Counseling and Development, 68,* 628–632.

Carhart-Harris, R. L., Muthukumaraswamy, S., Roseman, L., Kaelen, M., Droog, W., Murphy, K., . . . Leech, R. (2016). Neural correlates of the LSD experience revealed by multimodal neuroimaging. *PNAS, 113,* 4853–4858.

Carlbring, P., Andersson, G., Cuijpers, P., Riper, H., & Hedman-Lagerlöf, E. (2018). Internet-based vs. face-to-face cognitive behavior therapy for psychiatric and somatic disorders: An updated systematic review and meta-analysis. *Cognitive Behaviour Therapy, 47,* 1–18.

Carli, L. L., & Leonard, J. B. (1989). The effect of hindsight on victim derogation. *Journal of Social and Clinical Psychology, 8,* 331–343.

Carlson, M. (1995, August 29). Quoted by S. Blakeslee, In brain's early growth, timetable may be crucial. *The New York Times,* pp. C1, C3.

Carlson, M., Charlin, V., & Miller, N. (1988). Positive mood and helping behavior: A test of six hypotheses. *Journal of Personality and Social Psychology, 55,* 211–229.

Carmeli, A., Ben-Hador, B., Waldman, D. A., & Rupp, D. E. (2009). How leaders cultivate social capital and nurture employee vigor: Implications for job performance. *Journal of Applied Psychology, 94,* 1553–1561.

Carney, D. R., Cuddy, A. J. C., & Yap, A. J. (2015). Review and summary of research on the embodied effects of expansive (vs. contractive) nonverbal displays. *Psychological Science, 26,* 657–663.

Caroll, H. (2013, October). Teen fashion model Georgina got so thin her organs were failing. But fashion designers still queued up to book her. Now she's telling her story to shame the whole industry. *The Daily Mail* (dailymail.co.uk).

Carpusor, A., & Loges, W. E. (2006). Rental discrimination and ethnicity in names. *Journal of Applied Social Psychology, 36,* 934–952.

Carr, E. W., Brady, T. F., & Winkielman, P. (2017). Are you smiling, or have I seen you before? Familiarity makes faces look happier. *Psychological Science, 28,* 1087–1102.

Carroll, J. M., & Russell, J. A. (1996). Do facial expressions signal specific emotions? Judging emotion from the face in context. *Journal of Personality and Social Psychology, 70,* 205–218.

Carstensen, L. L. (2011). *A long bright future: Happiness, health and financial security in an age of increased longevity.* New York: PublicAffairs.

Carstensen, L. L., & Mikels, J. A. (2005). At the intersection of emotion and cognition: Aging and the positivity effect. *Current Directions in Psychological Science, 14,* 117–121.

Carstensen, L. L., Turan, B., Scheibe, S., Ram, N., Ersner-Hershfield, H., Samanez-Larkin, G. R., . . . Nesselroade, J. R. (2011). Emotional experience improves with age: Evidence based on over 10 years of experience sampling. *Psychology and Aging, 26,* 21–33.

Carter, C. S., Bearden, C. E., Bullmore, E. T., Geschwind, D. H., Glahn, D. C., Gur, R. E., . . . Weinberger, D. R. (2017). Enhancing the informativeness and replicability of imaging genomics studies. *Biological Psychiatry, 82,* 157–164.

Carver, C. S., Johnson, S. L., & Joormann, J. (2008). Serotonergic function, two-mode models of self-regulation, and vulnerability to depression: What depression has in common with impulsive aggression. *Psychological Bulletin, 134,* 912–943.

Carver, C. S., Scheier, M. F., & Segerstrom, S. C. (2010). Optimism. *Clinical Psychology Review, 30,* 879–889.

CASA. (2003). *The formative years: Pathways to substance abuse among girls and young women ages 8–22.* New York: National Center on Addiction and Substance Use, Columbia University.

Casey, B. J., & Caudle, K. (2013). The teenage brain: Self-control. *Current Directions in Psychological Science, 22,* 82–87.

Caspi, A., McClay, J., Moffitt, T., Mill, J., Martin, J., Craig, I. W., . . . Poulton, R. (2002). Role of genotype in the cycle of violence in maltreated children. *Science, 297,* 851–854.

Cassidy, J., & Shaver, P. R. (1999). *Handbook of attachment.* New York: Guilford.

Castillo-Gualda, R., Cabello, R., Herrero, M., Rodríguez-Carvajal, R., & Fernández-Berrocal, P. (2017). A three-year emotional intelligence intervention to reduce adolescent aggression: The mediating role of unpleasant affectivity. *Journal of Research on Adolescence, 28,* 286–198.

CATO Institute. (2017). *Criminal immigrants: Their numbers, demographics, and countries of origin* [PDF file]. Retrieved from object.cato.org/sites/cato.org/files/pubs /pdf/immigration_brief-1.pdf

Cattell, R. B. (1963). Theory of fluid and crystallized intelligence: A critical experiment. *Journal of Educational Psychology, 54,* 1–22.

Cavalli-Sforza, L., Menozzi, P., & Piazza, A. (1994). *The history and geography of human genes.* Princeton, NJ: Princeton University Press.

Cawley, B. D., Keeping, L. M., & Levy, P. E. (1998). Participation in the performance appraisal process and employee reactions: A meta-analytic review of field investigations. *Journal of Applied Psychology, 83,* 615–633.

CDC. (2014). *Pregnant women need a flu shot* [PDF file]. Retrieved from cdc.gov/flu/pdf/freeresources/pregnant /flushot_pregnant_factsheet.pdf

CDC. (2016a, accessed August 23, 2018). *HIV Surveillance Report: Diagnoses of HIV Infection in the United States and Dependent Areas,* Vol. 28 [PDF file]. Retrieved from cdc.gov/hiv/pdf/library/reports/surveillance/cdc-hiv-surveillance-report-2016-vol-28.pdf

CDC. (2016b, accessed January 21). *Reproductive health: Teen pregnancy.* Retrieved from cdc.gov/teenpregnancy

CDC. (2017). Heart disease fact sheet. Retrieved from cdc.gov/dhdsp/data_statistics/fact_sheets/fs_heart_ disease.htm

CDC. (2018, March 18). What you need to know about marijuana use and pregnancy. Retrieved from cdc.gov /marijuana/factsheets/pregnancy.htm

CDC. (2018). *Distracted driving.* Retrieved from cdc.gov /motorvehiclesafety/distracted_driving/index.html

CDC. (2018a). Estimated HIV incidence and prevalence in the United States, 2010-2015. *HIV Surveillance Supplemental Report, 23.*

CDC. (2018b). *Notes from the field: Use of electronic cigarettes and any tobacco product among middle and high school students — United States, 2011–2018.* (cdc.gov).

CDC. (2018c). *Smoking in the movies.* (cdc.gov).

CDC. (2018d). *Tobacco-related mortality.* (cdc.gov).

CDC. (2018e). *Underlying cause of death, 1999–2017.* (wonder.cdc.gov).

CDC. (2018f). *Youth risk behavior survey: Data summary and trends report 2007-2017.* [PDF file]. Retrieved from cdc.gov/healthyyouth/data/yrbs/pdf/trendsreport.pdf

CEA. (2014). *Nine facts about American families and work.* Office of the President of the United States: Council of Economic Advisers.

Ceci, S. J. (1993). *Cognitive and social factors in children's testimony.* Master lecture presented at the Annual Convention of the American Psychological Association.

Ceci, S. J., & Bruck, M. (1993). Child witnesses: Translating research into policy. *Social Policy Report (Society for Research in Child Development), 7,* 1–30.

Ceci, S. J., & Bruck, M. (1995). *Jeopardy in the courtroom: A scientific analysis of children's testimony.* Washington, DC: American Psychological Association.

Ceci, S. J., Ginther, D. K., Kahn, S., & Williams, W. M. (2014). Women in academic science: A changing landscape. *Psychological Science in the Public Interest, 15,* 75–141.

Ceci, S. J., Huffman, M. L. C., Smith, E., & Loftus, E. F. (1994). Repeatedly thinking about a non-event: Source misattributions among preschoolers. *Consciousness and Cognition, 3,* 388–407.

Ceci, S. J., & Williams, W. M. (1997). Schooling, intelligence, and income. *American Psychologist, 52,* 1051–1058.

Ceci, S. J., & Williams, W. M. (2009). *The mathematics of sex: How biology and society conspire to limit talented women and girls.* New York: Oxford University Press.

Census Bureau. (2014). Industry and occupation. Table 1: Full-time, year-round workers and median earnings in the past 12 months by sex and detailed occupation. Washington, DC: Bureau of the Census.

Centerwall, B. S. (1989). Exposure to television as a risk factor for violence. *American Journal of Epidemiology, 129,* 643–652.

Cepeda, N. J., Pashler, H., Vul, E., Wixted, J. T., & Rohrer, D. (2006). Distributed practice in verbal recall tasks: A review and quantitative synthesis. *Psychological Bulletin, 132,* 354–380.

Cepeda, N. J., Vul, E., Rohrer, D., Wixed, J. T., & Pashler, H. (2008). Spacing effects in learning: A temporal ridgeline of optimal retention. *Psychological Science, 19,* 1095–1102.

Cerasoli, C. P., Nicklin, J. M., & Ford, M. T. (2014). Intrinsic motivation and extrinsic incentives jointly predict performance: A 40-year meta-analysis. *Psychological Bulletin, 140,* 980–1008.

Cerrillo-Urbina, A. J., García-Hermoso, A., Sánchez-López, M., Pardo-Guijarro, M. J., Santos Gómez, J. L., & Martínez-Vizcaíno, V. (2015). The effects of physical exercise in children with attention deficit hyperactivity disorder: A systematic review and meta-analysis of randomized control trials. *Child: Care, Health and Development, 41,* 779–788.

CFI. (2003, July). *International developments.* Report. Amherst, NY: Center for Inquiry International.

Cha, C. B., Augenstein, T. M., Frost, K. H., Gallagher, K., D'Angelo, E. J., & Nock, M. K. (2016). Using implicit and explicit measures to predict nonsuicidal self-injury among adolescent inpatients. *Journal of the American Academy of Child & Adolescent Psychiatry, 55,* 62–68.

Chabris, C. (2015, February 9). Quoted by T. Parker-Pope, Was Brian Williams a victim of false memory? *The New York Times* (nytimes.com).

Chabris, C. F., & Simons, D. (2010). *The invisible gorilla: And other ways our intuitions deceive us.* New York: Crown.

Chamove, A. S. (1980). Nongenetic induction of acquired levels of aggression. *Journal of Abnormal Psychology, 89,* 469–488.

Champagne, F. A. (2010). Early adversity and developmental outcomes: Interaction between genetics, epigenetics, and social experiences across the life span. *Perspectives on Psychological Science, 5,* 564–574.

Chance News. (1997, 25 November). More on the frequency of letters in texts. Dartmouth College (Chance@Dartmouth.edu).

Chandler, J. J., & Pronin, E. (2012). Fast thought speed induces risk taking. *Psychological Science, 23,* 370–374.

Chandra, A., Mosher, W. D., & Copen, C. (2011, March 3). *Sexual behavior, sexual attraction, and sexual identity in the United States: Data from the 2006–2008 National Survey of Family Growth* (National Health Statistics Report No. 36). Retrieved from cdc.gov/nchs/data/nhsr/nhsr036.pdf

Chang, A.-M., Aeschbach, D., Duggy, J. F., & Czeisler, C. A. (2015). Evening use of light-emitting eReaders negatively affects sleep, circadian timing, and next-morning alertness. *PNAS, 112,* 1232–1237.

Chang, E. C. (2001). Cultural influences on optimism and pessimism: Differences in Western and Eastern construals of the self. In E. C. Chang (Ed.), *Optimism and pessimism* (pp. 257–280). Washington, DC: APA Books.

Chaplin, T. M. (2015). Gender and emotion expression: A developmental contextual perspective. *Emotion Review, 7,* 14–21.

Chaplin, T. M., & Aldao, A. (2013). Gender differences in emotion expression in children: A meta-analytic review. *Psychological Bulletin, 139,* 735–765.

Chaplin, W. F., Phillips, J. B., Brown, J. D., Clanton, N. R., & Stein, J. L. (2000). Handshaking, gender, personality, and first impressions. *Journal of Personality and Social Psychology, 79,* 110–117.

Charness, N., & Boot, W. R. (2009). Aging and information technology use. *Current Directions in Psychological Science, 18,* 253–258.

Charpak, G., & Broch, H. (2004). *Debunked! ESP, telekinesis, and other pseudoscience.* Baltimore, MD: Johns Hopkins University Press.

Chartrand, T. L., & Bargh, J. A. (1999). The chameleon effect: The perception-behavior link and social interaction. *Journal of Personality and Social Psychology, 76,* 893–910.

Chartrand, T. L., & van Baaren, R. (2009). Human mimicry. In M. P. Zanna (Ed.), *Advances in experimental social psychology* (pp. 219–274). San Diego, CA: Elsevier Academic Press.

Chassy, P., & Gobet, F. (2011). A hypothesis about the biological basis of expert intuition. *Review of General Psychology, 15,* 198–212.

Chatard, A., & Selimbegović, L. (2011). When self-destructive thoughts flash through the mind: Failure to meet standards affects the accessibility of suicide-related thoughts. *Journal of Personality and Social Psychology, 100,* 587–605.

Chatterjee, R. (2015, October 3). Out of the darkness. *Science, 350,* 372–375.

Chaudhary, U., Xia, B., Silvoni, S., Cohen, L. G., & Birbaumer, N. (2017). Brain–computer interface–based communication in the completely locked-in state. *PLOS Biology, 15,* 25.

Cheek, J. M., & Melchior, L. A. (1990). Shyness, self-esteem, and self-consciousness. In H. Leitenberg (Ed.), *Handbook of social and evaluation anxiety.* New York: Plenum.

Chein, J. M., & Schneider, W. (2012). The brain's learning and control architecture. *Current Directions in Psychological Science, 21,* 78–84.

Chein, J., Albert, D., O'Brien, L., Uckert, K., & Steinberg, L. (2011). Peers increase adolescent risk taking by enhancing activity in the brain's reward circuitry. *Developmental Science, 14,* F1–F10.

Cheit, R. E. (1998). Consider this, skeptics of recovered memory. *Ethics & Behavior, 8,* 141–160.

Chen, A. W., Kazanjian, A., & Wong, H. (2009). Why do Chinese Canadians not consult mental health services: Health status, language or culture? *Transcultural Psychiatry, 46,* 623–640.

Chen, E., Turiano, N. A., Mroczek, D. K., & Miller, G. E. (2016). Association of reports of childhood abuse and all-cause mortality rates in women. *JAMA Psychiatry, 73,* 920–927.

Chen, J. (2017, June 28). Katy Perry defends her livestream therapy session: 'People think it's weird'. *Rolling Stone* (rollingstone.com).

Chen, M.-H., Lan, W.-H., Bai, Y.-M., Huang, K.-L., Su, T.-P., Tsai, S.-J., . . . Hsu, J.-W. (2016). Influence of relative age on diagnosis and treatment of attention-deficit hyperactivity disorder in Taiwanese children. *Journal of Pediatrics, 172,* 162–167.

Cheng, C., & Li, A. Y. L. (2014). Internet addiction prevalence and quality of (real) life: A meta-analysis of 31 nations across seven world regions. *Cyberpsychology, Behavior, and Social Networking, 17,* 755–760.

Chennu, S., Pinoia, P., Kamau, E., Allanson, J., Williams, G. B., Monti, M. M., . . . Bekinschtein, T. A. (2014). Spectral signatures of reorganised brain network in disorders of consciousness. *PLOS Computational Biology, 10,* e1003887.

Cherniss, C. (2010a). Emotional intelligence: New insights and further clarifications. *Industrial and Organizational Psychology, 3,* 183–191.

Cherniss, C. (2010b). Emotional intelligence: Toward clarification of a concept. *Industrial and Organizational Psychology, 3,* 110–126.

Chess, S., & Thomas, A. (1987). *Know your child: An authoritative guide for today's parents.* New York: Basic Books.

Chetty, N., & Alathur, S. (2018). Hate speech review in the context of online social networks. *Aggression and Violent Behavior, 40,* 108–118.

Cheung, B. Y., Chudek, M., & Heine, S. J. (2011). Evidence for a sensitive period for acculturation: Younger immigrants report acculturating at a faster rate. *Psychological Science, 22,* 147–152.

Cheung, F. (2018). Income redistribution predicts greater life satisfaction across individual, national, and cultural characteristics. *Journal of Personality and Social Psychology, 115,* 867–882.

Cheung, F., & Lucas, R. E. (2015). When does money matter most? Examining the association between income and life satisfaction over the life course. *Psychology and Aging, 30,* 120–135.

Cheung, F., & Lucas, R. E. (2016). Income inequality is associated with stronger social comparison effects: The effect of relative income on life satisfaction. *Journal of Personality and Social Psychology, 110,* 332–341.

Chick, C. F. (2015). Reward processing in the adolescent brain: Individual differences and relation to risk taking. *Journal of Neuroscience, 35,* 13539–13541.

Chida, Y., & Hamer, M. (2008). Chronic psychosocial factors and acute physiological responses to laboratory-induced stress in healthy populations: A quantitative review of 30 years of investigations. *Psychological Bulletin, 134,* 829–885.

Chida, Y., & Steptoe, A. (2009). The association of anger and hostility with future coronary heart disease: A meta-analytic review of prospective evidence. *Journal of the American College of Cardiology, 17,* 936–946.

Chida, Y., Steptoe, A., & Powell, L. H. (2009). Religiosity/spirituality and mortality. *Psychotherapy and Psychosomatics, 78,* 81–90.

Chida, Y., & Vedhara, K. (2009). Adverse psychosocial factors predict poorer prognosis in HIV disease: A meta-analytic review of prospective investigations. *Brain, Behavior, and Immunity, 23,* 434–445.

Chiles, J. A., Lambert, M. J., & Hatch, A. L. (1999). The impact of psychological interventions on medical cost offset: A meta-analytic review. *Clinical Psychology: Science and Practice, 6,* 204–220.

Chisholm, D., Sweeny, K., Sheehan, P., Rasmussen, B., Smit, F., Cuijpers, P., & Saxena, S. (2016). Scaling-up treatment of depression and anxiety:

A global return on investment analysis. *The Lancet Psychiatry, 3*, 415–424.

Chivers, M. L., Seto, M. C., Lalumière, M. L., Laan, E., & Grimbos, T. (2010). Agreement of self-reported and genital measures of sexual arousal in men and women: A meta-analysis. *Archives of Sexual Behavior, 39*, 5–56.

Chmielewski, M., Zhu, J., Burchett, D., Bury, A. S., & Bagby, R. M. (2017). The comparative capacity of the Minnesota Multiphasic Personality Inventory–2 (MMPI–2) and MMPI–2 Restructured Form (MMPI-2-RF) validity scales to detect suspected malingering in a disability claimant sample. *Psychological Assessment, 29*, 199–208.

Cho, K. W., Neely, J. H., Crocco, S., & Vitrano, D. (2017). Testing enhances both encoding and retrieval for both tested and untested items. *The Quarterly Journal of Experimental Psychology, 70*, 1211–1235.

Choi, C. Q. (2008, March). Do you need only half your brain? *Scientific American*, p. 104.

Chomsky, N. (1972). *Language and mind*. New York: Harcourt Brace.

Chopik, W. J., Edelstein, R. S., & Fraley, R. C. (2013). From the cradle to the grave: Age differences in attachment from early adulthood to old age. *Journal of Personality, 81*, 171–183.

Chopik, W. J., & Kitayama, S. (2018). Personality change across the life span: Insights from a cross-cultural, longitudinal study. *Journal of Personality, 86*, 508–521.

Choudhary, E., Smith, M., & Bossarte, R. M. (2012). Depression, anxiety, and symptom profiles among female and male victims of sexual violence. *American Journal of Men's Health, 6*, 28–36.

Christakis, D. A., Garrison, M. M., Herrenkohl, T., Haggerty, K., Rivara, K. P., Zhou, C., & Liekweg, K. (2013). Modifying media content for preschool children: A randomized control trial. *Pediatrics, 131*, 431–438.

Christakis, N. A., & Fowler, J. H. (2007). The spread of obesity in a large social network over 32 years. *New England Journal of Medicine, 357*, 370–379.

Christensen, A., & Jacobson, N. S. (1994). Who (or what) can do psychotherapy: The status and challenge of nonprofessional therapies. *Psychological Science, 5*, 8–14.

Christophersen, E. R., & Edwards, K. J. (1992). Treatment of elimination disorders: State of the art 1991. *Applied & Preventive Psychology, 1*, 15–22.

Chu, C., Podlogar, M. C., Hagan, C. R., Buchman-Schmitt, J. M., Silva, C., Chiurliza, B., . . . Joiner, T. E. (2016). The interactive effects of the capability for suicide and major depressive episodes on suicidal behavior in a military sample. *Cognitive Therapy and Research, 40*, 22–30.

Chu, C., Walker, K. L., Stanley, I. H., Hirsch, J. K., Greenberg, J. H., Rudd, M. D., & Joiner, T. E. (2018). Perceived problem-solving deficits and suicidal ideation: Evidence for the explanatory roles of thwarted belongingness and perceived burdensomeness in five samples. *Journal of Personality and Social Psychology, 115*, 137–160.

Chu, P. S., Saucier, D. A., & Hafner, E. (2010). Meta-analysis of the relationships between social support and well-being in children and adolescents. *Journal of Social and Clinical Psychology, 29*, 624–645.

Chua, H. F., Boland, J. E., & Nisbett, R. E. (2005). Cultural variation in eye movements during scene perception. *PNAS, 102*, 12629–12633.

Chugani, H. T., & Phelps, M. E. (1986). Maturational changes in cerebral function in infants determined by 18FDG positron emission tomography. *Science, 231*, 840–843.

Chulov, M. (2014, December 11). ISIS: The inside story. *The Guardian* (theguardian.com).

Church, A. T., Katigbak, M. S., Mazuera Arias, R., Rincon, B. C., Vargas-Flores, J., Ibáñez-Reyes, J., . . . Ortiz, F. A. (2014). A four-culture study of self-enhancement and adjustment using the social relations model: Do alternative conceptualizations and indices make a difference? *Journal of Personality and Social Psychology, 106*, 997–1014.

Churchland, P. S. (2013). *Touching a nerve: The self as brain*. New York: Norton.

Cialdini, R. B. (1993). *Influence: Science and practice* (3rd ed.). New York: HarperCollins.

Cialdini, R. B., & Richardson, K. D. (1980). Two indirect tactics of image management: Basking and blasting. *Journal of Personality and Social Psychology, 39*, 406–415.

Ciardelli, L. E., Weiss, A., Powell, D. M., & Reiss, D. (2017). Personality dimensions of the captive California sea lion (*Zalophus californianus*). *Journal of Comparative Psychology, 131*, 50–58.

Cin, S. D., Gibson, B., Zanna, M. P., Shumate, R., & Fong, G. T. (2007). Smoking in movies, implicit associations of smoking with the self, and intentions to smoke. *Psychological Science, 18*, 559–563.

Cipriani, A., Furukawa, T. A., Salanti, G., Chaimani, A., Atkinson, L. Z., Ogawa, Y., . . . Geddes, J. R. (2018). Comparative efficacy and acceptability of 21 antidepressant drugs for the acute treatment of adults with major depressive disorder: A systematic review and network meta-analysis. *The Lancet, 391*, 1357–1366.

Clack, B., Dixon, J., & Tredoux, C. (2005). Eating together apart: Patterns of segregation in a multi-ethnic cafeteria. *Journal of Community and Applied Social Psychology, 15*, 1–16.

Clancy, S. A. (2005). *Abducted: How people come to believe they were kidnapped by aliens*. Cambridge, MA: Harvard University Press.

Clark, A., Seidler, A., & Miller, M. (2001). Inverse association between sense of humor and coronary heart disease. *International Journal of Cardiology, 80*, 87–88.

Clark, C. J., Luguri, J. B., Ditto, P. H., Knobe, J., Shariff, A. F., & Baumeister, R. F. (2014). Free to punish: A motivated account of free will belief. *Journal of Personality and Social Psychology, 106*, 501–513.

Clark, I. A., & Maguire, E. A. (2016). Remembering preservation in hippocampal amnesia. *Annual Review of Psychology, 67*, 51–82.

Clark, K. B., & Clark, M. P. (1947). Racial identification and preference in Negro children. In T. M. Newcomb & E. L. Hartley (Eds.), *Readings in social psychology*. New York: Holt.

Clark, R. D., III, & Hatfield, E. (1989). Gender differences in receptivity to sexual offers. *Journal of Psychology & Human Sexuality, 2*, 39–55.

Clarke, E., Reichard, U. H., & Zuberbuehler, K. (2015). Context-specific close-range "hoo" calls in wild gibbons (Hylobates lar). *BMC Evolutionary Biology, 15*, 56.

Clausen, J., Fetz, E., Donoghue, J., Ushiba, J., Spöhase, J., Birbaummer, N., & Soekadar, S. R. (2017). Help, hope, and hype: Ethical dimensions of neuroprosthetics. *Science, 356*, 1338–1339.

Claxton, S. E., DeLuca, H. K., & van Dulmen, M. H. (2015). The association between alcohol use and engagement in casual sexual relationships and experiences: A meta-analytic review of non-experimental studies. *Archives of Sexual Behavior, 44*, 837–856.

Cleary, A. M., & Claxton, A. B. (2018). Déjà vu: An illusion of prediction. *Psychological Science, 29*, 635–644.

Clements, C. C., Zoltowski, A. R., Yankowitz, L. D., Yerys, B. E., Schultz, R. T., & Herrington, J. D. (2018). Evaluation of the social motivation hypothesis of autism: A systematic review and meta-analysis. *JAMA Psychiatry, 75*, 797–808.

Clynes, T. (2016). How to raise a genius. *Nature, 537*, 152–155.

Coan, J. A., Schaefer, H. S., & Davidson, R. J. (2006). Lending a hand: Social regulation of the neural response to threat. *Psychological Science, 17*, 1032–1039.

Cohen, A. O., Breiner, K., Steinberg, L., Bonnie, R. J., Scott, E. S., Taylor-Thompson, K. A., . . . Silverman, M. R. (2016). When is an adolescent an adult? Assessing cognitive control in emotional and nonemotional contexts. *Psychological Science, 27*, 549–562.

Cohen, G. L., & Sherman, D. K. (2014). The psychology of change: Self-affirmation and social psychological intervention. *Annual Review of Psychology, 65*, 333–371.

Cohen, P. (2010, June 11). Long road to adulthood is growing even longer. *The New York Times* (nytimes.com).

Cohen, S. (2004). Social relationships and health. *American Psychologist, 59*, 676–684.

Cohen, S., Alper, C. M., Doyle, W. J., Treanor, J. J., & Turner, R. B. (2006). Positive emotional style predicts resistance to illness after experimental exposure to rhinovirus or influenza A virus. *Psychosomatic Medicine, 68*, 809–815.

Cohen, S., Doyle, W. J., Skoner, D. P., Rabin, B. S., & Gwaltney, J. M., Jr. (1997). Social ties and susceptibility to the common cold. *Journal of the American Medical Association, 277*, 1940–1944.

Cohen, S., Doyle, W. J., Turner, R., Alper, C. M., & Skoner, D. P. (2003). Sociability and susceptibility to the common cold. *Psychological Science, 14*, 389–395.

Cohen, S., Janicki-Deverts, D., Turner, R. B., & Doyle, W. J. (2015). Does hugging provide stress-buffering social support? A study of susceptibility to upper respiratory infection and illness. *Psychological Science, 26*, 135–147.

Cohen, S., Kamarck, T., Mermelstein, R. (1983). A global measure of perceived stress. *Journal of Health and Social Behavior, 24*, 385–396.

Cohen, S., Kaplan, J. R., Cunnick, J. E., Manuck, S. B., & Rabin, B. S. (1992). Chronic social stress, affiliation, and cellular immune response in nonhuman primates. *Psychological Science, 3*, 301–304.

Cohen, S., & Pressman, S. D. (2006). Positive affect and health. *Current Directions in Psychological Science, 15*, 122–125.

Cohen, S., Tyrrell, D. A. J., & Smith, A. P. (1991). Psychological stress and susceptibility to the common cold. *New England Journal of Medicine, 325*, 606–612.

Coker, A. L., Bush, H. M., Cook-Craig, P. G., DeGue, S. A., Clear, E. R., Brancato, C. J., . . . Recktenwald, E. A. (2017). RCT testing bystander effectiveness to reduce violence. *American Journal of Preventative Medicine, 52*, 566–578.

Colapinto, J. (2000). *As nature made him: The boy who was raised as a girl*. New York: HarperCollins.

Colarelli, S. M., Spranger, J. L., & Hechanova, M. R. (2006). Women, power, and sex composition in small groups: An evolutionary perspective. *Journal of Organizational Behavior, 27*, 163–184.

Cole, M. W., Ito, T., & Braver, T. S. (2015). Lateral prefrontal cortex contributes to fluid intelligence through multinetwork connectivity. *Brain Connectivity, 5*, 497–504.

Collier, K. L., Bos, H. M. W., & Sandfort, T. G. M. (2012). Intergroup contact, attitudes toward homosexuality, and the role of acceptance of gender non-conformity in young adolescents. *Journal of Adolescence, 35,* 899–907.

Collins, G. (2009, March 9). The rant list. *The New York Times* (nytimes.com).

Collins, R. L., Elliott, M. N., Berry, S. H., Danouse, D. E., Kunkel, D., Hunter, S. B., & Miu, A. (2004). Watching sex on television predicts adolescent initiation of sexual behavior. *Pediatrics, 114,* 280–289.

Collinson, S. L., MacKay, C. E., James, A. C., Quested, D. J., Phillips, T., Roberts, N., & Crow, T. J. (2003). Brain volume, asymmetry and intellectual impairment in relation to sex in early-onset schizophrenia. *British Journal of Psychiatry, 183,* 114–120.

Colvert, E., Beata, T., McEwen, F., Stewart, C., Curran, S. R., Woodhouse, E., . . . Bolton, P. (2015). Heritability of autism spectrum disorder in a UK population-based twin sample. *JAMA Psychiatry, 72,* 415–423.

Compton, W. C. (2018). Self-actualization myths: What did Maslow really say? *Journal of Humanistic Psychology.* Advance online publication. doi.org/10.1177/0022167818761929

Confer, J. C., Easton, J. A., Fleischman, D. S., Goetz, C. D., Lewis, D. M. G., Perilloux, C., & Buss, D. M. (2010). Evolutionary psychology: Controversies, questions, prospects, and limitations. *American Psychologist, 65,* 110–126.

Conley, T. D. (2011). Perceived proposer personality characteristics and gender differences in acceptance of casual sex offers. *Journal of Personality and Social Psychology, 100,* 300–329.

Connor, C. E. (2010). A new viewpoint on faces. *Science, 330,* 764–765.

Conroy-Beam, D., Buss, D. M., Pham, M. N., & Shackelford, T. K. (2015). How sexually dimorphic are human mate preferences? *Personality and Social Psychology Bulletin, 41,* 1082–1093.

Consumer Reports. (1995, November). Does therapy help? pp. 734–739.

Conway, A. R. A., Skitka, L. J., Hemmerich, J. A., & Kershaw, T. C. (2009). Flashbulb memory for 11 September 2001. *Applied Cognitive Psychology, 23,* 605–623.

Conway, M. A., Wang, Q., Hanyu, K., & Haque, S. (2005). A cross-cultural investigation of autobiographical memory: On the universality and cultural variation of the reminiscence bump. *Journal of Cross-Cultural Psychology, 36,* 739–749.

Cook, S., Kokmotou, K., Soto, V., Fallon, N., Tyson-Carr, J., Thomas, A., . . . Stancak, A. (2017). Pleasant and unpleasant odour-face combinations influence face and odour perception: An event-related potential study. *Behavioural Brain Research, 333,* 304–313.

Cooke, L. J., Wardle, J., & Gibson, E. L. (2003). Relationship between parental report of food neophobia and everyday food consumption in 2–6-year-old children. *Appetite, 41,* 205–206.

Cooper, W. H., & Withey, M. J. (2009). The strong situation hypothesis. *Personality and Social Psychology Review, 13,* 62–72.

Coopersmith, S. (1967). *The antecedents of self-esteem.* San Francisco: Freeman.

Copen, C. E., Chandra, A., & Febo-Vazquez, I. (2016, January 7). Sexual behavior, sexual attraction, and sexual orientation among adults aged 18–44 in the United States: Data from the 2011–2013 National Survey of Family Growth. Centers for Disease Control and Prevention, *National Health Statistics Reports,* Number 88.

Corcoran, D. W. J. (1964). The relation between introversion and salivation. *The American Journal of Psychology, 77,* 298–300.

Coren, S. (1996). *Sleep thieves: An eye-opening exploration into the science and mysteries of sleep.* New York: Free Press.

Corey, D. P., Garcia-Añoveros, J., Holt, J. R., Kwan, K. Y., Lin, S. Y., Vollrath, M. A., & Zhang, D. S. (2004). TRPA1 is a candidate for the mechanosensitive transduction channel of vertebrate hair cells. *Nature, 432,* 723–730.

Corina, D. P. (1998). The processing of sign language: Evidence from aphasia. In B. Stemmer & H. A. Whittaker (Eds.), *Handbook of neurolinguistics* (pp. 313–329). San Diego, CA: Academic Press.

Corina, D. P., Vaid, J., & Bellugi, U. (1992). The linguistic basis of left hemisphere specialization. *Science, 255,* 1258–1260.

Corkin, S. (2013). *Permanent present tense: The unforgettable life of the amnesic patient.* New York: Basic Books.

Corkin, S., quoted by R. Adelson. (2005, September). Lessons from H. M. *Monitor on Psychology,* p. 59.

Cormier, Z. (2016). Brain scans reveal how LSD affects consciousness. *Nature* (nature.com).

Cornier, M.-A. (2011). Is your brain to blame for weight regain? *Physiology & Behavior, 104,* 608–612.

Correa, C., & Louttit, M. (2018, January 24). More than 160 women say Larry Nassar sexually abused them. Here are his accusers in their own words. *The New York Times* (nytimes.com).

Correll, J., Park, B., Judd, C. M., Wittenbrink, B., Sadler, M. S., & Keesee, T. (2007). Across the thin blue line: Police officers and racial bias in the decision to shoot. *Journal of Personality and Social Psychology, 92,* 1006–1023.

Correll, J., Wittenbrink, B., Crawford, M. T., & Sadler, M. S. (2015). Stereotypic vision: How stereotypes disambiguate visual stimuli. *Journal of Personality and Social Psychology, 108,* 219–233.

Corrigan, P. (2004). How stigma interferes with mental health care. *American Psychologist, 59,* 614–625.

Corrigan, P. W. (2014). Can there be false hope in recovery? *British Journal of Psychiatry, 205,* 423–424.

Corrigan, P. W., & Watson, A. C. (2002). Understanding the impact of stigma on people with mental illness. *World Psychiatry, 1,* 16–20.

Costa, P. T., Jr., & McCrae, R. R. (2011). The five-factor model, five factor theory, and interpersonal psychology. In L. M. Horowitz & S. Strack (Eds.), *Handbook of interpersonal psychology: Theory, research, assessment, and therapeutic interventions* (pp. 91–104). Hoboken, NJ: John Wiley & Sons.

Costa, P. T., Jr., Terracciano, A., & McCrae, R. R. (2001). Gender differences in personality traits across cultures: Robust and surprising findings. *Journal of Personality and Social Psychology, 81,* 322–331.

Costello, E. J., Compton, S. N., Keeler, G., & Angold, A. (2003). Relationships between poverty and psychopathology: A natural experiment. *Journal of the American Medical Association, 290,* 2023–2029.

Costello, T. H., Unterberger, A., Watts, A. L., & Lilienfeld, S. O. (2018). Psychopathy and pride: Testing Lykken's hypothesis regarding the implications of fearlessness for prosocial and antisocial behavior. *Frontiers in Psychology, 9,* 185.

Coulter, K. C., & Malouff, J. M. (2013). Effects of an intervention designed to enhance romantic relationship excitement: A randomized-control trial. *Couple and Family Psychology: Research and Practice, 2,* 34–44.

Courtney, J. G., Longnecker, M. P., Theorell, T., & de Verdier, M. G. (1993). Stressful life events and the risk of colorectal cancer. *Epidemiology, 4,* 407–414.

Cowan, N. (2010). The magical mystery four: How is working memory capacity limited, and why? *Current Directions in Psychological Science, 19,* 51–57.

Cowan, N. (2015). George Miller's magical number of immediate memory in retrospect: Observations on the faltering progression of science. *Psychological Review, 122,* 536–541.

Cowan, N. (2016). Working memory maturation: Can we get at the essence of cognitive growth? *Perspectives on Psychological Science, 11,* 239–264.

Cowart, B. J. (1981). Development of taste perception in humans: Sensitivity and preference throughout the life span. *Psychological Bulletin, 90,* 43–73.

Cox, J. J., Reimann, F. Nicholas, A. K., Thornton, G., Roberts, E., Springell, K., & Woods, C. G. (2006). An SCN9A channelopathy causes congenital inability to experience pain. *Nature, 444,* 894–898.

Coye, C., Ouattara, K., Zuberbühler, K., & Lemasson, A. (2015). Suffixation influences receivers' behaviour in non-human primates. *Proceedings of the Royal Society B, 282,* 1807.

Coyne, S. M., Padilla-Walker, L., Holmgren, H. G., Davis, E. J., Collier, K. M., Memmott-Elison, M., & Hawkins, A. J. (2018). A meta-analysis of prosocial media on prosocial behavior, aggression, and empathic concern: A multidimensional approach. *Developmental Psychology, 54,* 331–347.

Crabbe, J. C. (2002). Genetic contributions to addiction. *Annual Review of Psychology, 53,* 435–462.

Crabtree, S. (2005, January 13). Engagement keeps the doctor away. *Gallup Management Journal* (gmj.gallup.com).

Crabtree, S. (2011, December 12). *U.S. seniors maintain happiness highs with less social time.* Gallup Poll (gallup.com).

Crandall, C. S., Miller, J. M., & White, M. H. (2018). Changing norms following the 2016 U.S. presidential election: The Trump effect on prejudice. *Social Psychological and Personality Science, 9,* 186–192.

Crawford, M., Chaffin, R., & Fitton, L. (1995). Cognition in social context. *Learning and Individual Differences, 7,* 341–362.

Credé, M., & Kuncel, N. R. (2008). Study habits, skills, and attitudes: The third pillar supporting collegiate academic performance. *Perspectives on Psychological Science, 3,* 425–453.

Credé, M., Tynan, M. C., & Harms, P. D. (2017). Much ado about grit: A meta-analytic synthesis of the grit literature. *Journal of Personality and Social Psychology, 113,* 492–511.

Creswell, J. D., Bursley, J. K., & Satpute, A. B. (2013). Neural reactivation links unconscious thought to decision making performance. *Social Cognitive and Affective Neuroscience, 8,* 863–869.

Creswell, J. D., Way, B. M., Eisenberger, N. I., & Lieberman, M. D. (2007). Neural correlates of dispositional mindfulness during affect labeling. *Psychosomatic Medicine, 69,* 560–565.

Crews, F. T., He, J., & Hodge, C. (2007). Adolescent cortical development: A critical period of vulnerability for addiction. *Pharmacology, Biochemistry and Behavior, 86,* 189–199.

Crews, F. T., Mdzinarishvilli, A., Kim, D., He, J., & Nixon, K. (2006). Neurogenesis in adolescent brain is potently inhibited by ethanol. *Neuroscience, 137,* 437–445.

Crivelli, C., Jarillo, S., Russell, J. A., & Fernández-Dols, J. M. (2016a). Reading emotions from faces in two indigenous societies. *Journal of Experimental Psychology: General, 145,* 830–843.

Crivelli, C., Russell, J. A., Jarillo, S., & Fernández-Dols, J. M. (2016b). The fear gasping face as a threat display in a Melanesian society. *PNAS, 113,* 12403–12407.

Crocker, J., & Park, L. E. (2004). The costly pursuit of self-esteem. *Psychological Bulletin, 130,* 392–414.

Crocker, J., Thompson, L. L., McGraw, K. M., & Ingerman, C. (1987). Downward comparison, prejudice, and evaluation of others: Effects of self-esteem and threat. *Journal of Personality and Social Psychology, 52,* 907–916.

Crockett, M. J., Kurth-Nelson, Z., Siegel, J. Z., Dayan, P., & Dolan, R. J. (2014). Harm to others outweighs harm to self in moral decision making. *PNAS, 111,* 17320–17325.

Crockford, C., Wittig, R. M., & Zuberbühler, K. (2017). Vocalizing in chimpanzees is influenced by social-cognitive processes. *Science Advances, 3,* e1701742.

Croft, A., Schmader, T., Block, K., & Baron, A. S. (2014). The second shift reflected in the second generation: Do parents' gender roles at home predict children's aspirations? *Psychological Science, 25,* 1418–1428.

Croft, R. J., Klugman, A., Baldeweg, T., & Gruzelier, J. H. (2001). Electrophysiological evidence of serotonergic impairment in long-term MDMA ("Ecstasy") users. *American Journal of Psychiatry, 158,* 1687–1692.

Crook, T. H., & West, R. L. (1990). Name recall performance across the adult lifespan. *British Journal of Psychology, 81,* 335–340.

Crosier, B. S., Webster, G. D., & Dillon, H. M. (2012). Wired to connect: Evolutionary psychology and social networks. *Review of General Psychology, 16,* 230–239.

Cross-National Collaborative Group. (1992). The changing rate of major depression. *Journal of the American Medical Association, 268,* 3098–3105.

Crouse, K. (2017, September 21). Michael Phelps: A golden shoulder to lean on. *The New York Times* (nytimes.com).

Crowell, J. A., & Waters, E. (1994). Bowlby's theory grown up: The role of attachment in adult love relationships. *Psychological Inquiry, 5,* 1–22.

Csikszentmihalyi, M. (1990). *Flow: The psychology of optimal experience.* New York: Harper & Row.

Csikszentmihalyi, M. (1999). If we are so rich, why aren't we happy? *American Psychologist, 54,* 821–827.

Csikszentmihalyi, M., & Hunter, J. (2003). Happiness in everyday life: The uses of experience sampling. *Journal of Happiness Studies, 4,* 185–199.

Cucchi, A., Ryan, D., Konstantakopoulos, G., Stroumpa, S., Kaçar, A. Ş., Renshaw, S., . . . Kravariti, E. (2016). Lifetime prevalence of non-suicidal self-injury in patients with eating disorders: A systematic review and meta-analysis. *Psychological Medicine, 46,* 1345–1358.

Cuijpers, P. (2017). Four decades of outcome research on psychotherapies for adult depression: An overview of a series of meta-analyses. *Canadian Psychology/Psychologie Canadienne, 58,* 7–19.

Cuijpers, P., Driessen, E., Hollon, S. D., van Oppen, P., Barth, J., & Andersson, G. (2012). The efficacy of non-directive supportive therapy for adult depression: A meta-analysis. *Clinical Psychology Review, 32,* 280–291.

Cuijpers, P., van Straten, A., Schuurmans, J., van Oppen, P., Hollon, S. D., & Andersson, G. (2010). Psychotherapy for chronic major depression and dysthymia: A meta-analysis. *Clinical Psychology Review, 30,* 51–62.

Culbert, K. M., Burt, S. A., McGue, M., Iacono, W. G., & Klump, K. L. (2009). Puberty and the genetic diathesis of disordered eating attitudes and behaviors. *Journal of Abnormal Psychology, 118,* 788–796.

Culbert, K. M., Racine, S. E., & Klump, K. L. (2015). Research review: What we have learned about the causes of eating disorders—a synthesis of sociocultural, psychological, and biological research. *Journal of Child Psychology and Psychiatry, 56,* 1141–1164.

Cunningham, W. A., Johnson, M. K., Raye, C. L., Gatenby, J. C., Gore, J. C., & Banaji, M. R. (2004). Separable neural components in the processing of Black and White faces. *Psychological Science, 15,* 806–813.

Curci, A., Lanciano, T., Mastandrea, S., & Sartori, G. (2015). Flashbulb memories of the Pope's resignation: Explicit and implicit measure across different religious groups. *Memory, 23,* 529–544.

Currie, T. E., & Little, A. C. (2009). The relative importance of the face and body in judgments of human physical attractiveness. *Evolution and Human Behavior, 30,* 409–416.

Curry, J., Silva, S., Rohde, P., Ginsburg, G., Kratochvil, C., Simons, A., . . . March, J. (2011). Recovery and recurrence following treatment for adolescent major depression. *Archives of General Psychiatry, 68,* 263–269.

Curtis, R. C., & Miller, K. (1986). Believing another likes or dislikes you: Behaviors making the beliefs come true. *Journal of Personality and Social Psychology, 51,* 284–290.

Custers, R., & Aarts, H. (2010). The unconscious will: How the pursuit of goals operates outside of conscious awareness. *Science, 329,* 47–50.

Cyders, M. A., & Smith, G. T. (2008). Emotion-based dispositions to rash action: Positive and negative urgency. *Psychological Bulletin, 134,* 807–828.

Czarna, A. Z., Leifeld, P., Śmieja, M., Dufner, M., & Salovey, P. (2016). Do narcissism and emotional intelligence win us friends? Modeling dynamics of peer popularity using inferential network analysis. *Personality and Social Psychology Bulletin, 42,* 1588–1599.

Dai, H., Milkman, K. L., & Riis, J. (2014). The fresh start effect: Temporal landmarks motivate aspirational behavior. *Management Science, 60,* 2563–2582.

Dake, L. (2016, June 16). Jamie Shupe becomes first legally non-binary person in the U.S. *The Guardian* (theguardian.com).

Daley, J. (2011, July/August). What you don't know can kill you. *Discover* (discovermagazine.com).

Daly, M., Delaney, L., Egan, R. F., & Baumeister, R. F. (2015). Childhood self-control and unemployment throughout the life span: Evidence from two British cohort studies. *Psychological Science, 26,* 709–723.

Damasio, A. R. (2003). *Looking for Spinoza: Joy, sorrow, and the feeling brain.* New York: Harcourt.

Dambacher, F., Sack, A. T., Lobbestael, J., Arntz, A., Brugman, S., & Schuhmann, T. (2015). Out of control: Evidence for anterior insula involvement in motor impulsivity and reactive aggression. *Social Cognitive and Affective Neuroscience, 10,* 508–516.

Damian, R. I., & Roberts, B. W. (2015). The associations of birth order with personality and intelligence in a representative sample of U.S. high school students. *Journal of Research in Personality, 58,* 96–105.

Damian, R. I., Spengler, M., Sutu, A., & Roberts, B. W. (2018). Sixteen going on sixty-six: A longitudinal study of personality stability and change across 50 years. *Journal of Personality and Social Psychology.* Advance online publication. doi.org/10.1037/pspp0000210

Danek, A. H., & Salvi, C. (2018). Moment of truth: Why aha! experiences are correct. *The Journal of Creative Behavior.* Advance online publication. doi.org/10.1002/jocb.380

Danelli, L., Cossu, G., Berlingeri, M., Bottini, G., Sberna, M., & Paulesu, E. (2013). Is a lone right hemisphere enough? Neurolinguistic architecture in a case with a very early left hemispherectomy. *Neurocase, 19,* 209–231.

Daniel, T. A., & Katz, J. S. (2018). Primacy and recency effects for taste. *Journal of Experimental Psychology: Learning, Memory, and Cognition, 44,* 399–405.

Danner, D. D., Snowdon, D. A., & Friesen, W. V. (2001). Positive emotions in early life and longevity: Findings from the Nun Study. *Journal of Personality and Social Psychology, 80,* 804–813.

Danso, H., & Esses, V. (2001). Black experimenters and the intellectual test performance of white participants: The tables are turned. *Journal of Experimental Social Psychology, 37,* 158–165.

Darley, J. M., & Alter, A. (2013). Behavioral issues of punishment, retribution, and deterrence. In E. Shafir (Ed.), *The behavioral foundations of public policy* (pp. 181–194). Princeton, NJ: Princeton University Press.

Darley, J. M., & Latané, B. (1968a). Bystander intervention in emergencies: Diffusion of responsibility. *Journal of Personality and Social Psychology, 8,* 377–383.

Darley, J. M., & Latané, B. (1968b, December). When will people help in a crisis? *Psychology Today,* pp. 54–57, 70–71.

Darwin, C. (1872). *The expression of the emotions in man and animals.* London, England: John Murray.

Daum, I., & Schugens, M. M. (1996). On the cerebellum and classical conditioning. *Psychological Science, 5,* 58–61.

Davey, G. C. L. (1995). Preparedness and phobias: Specific evolved associations or a generalized expectancy bias? *Behavioral and Brain Sciences, 18,* 289–297.

Davey, G., & Rato, R. (2012). Subjective well-being in China: A review. *Journal of Happiness Studies, 13,* 333–346.

Davidson, J. R. T., Connor, K. M., & Swartz, M. (2006). Mental illness in U.S. presidents between 1776 and 1974: A review of biographical sources. *Journal of Nervous and Mental Disease, 194,* 47–51.

Davidson, R. J., & Begley, S. (2012). *The emotional life of your brain: How its unique patterns affect the way you think, feel, and live—and how you can change them.* New York: Hudson Street Press.

Davidson, R. J., Kabat-Zinn, J., Schumacher, J., Rosenkranz, M., Muller, D., Santorelli, S. F., . . . Sheridan, J. F. (2003). Alterations in brain and immune function produced by mindfulness meditation. *Psychosomatic Medicine, 65,* 564–570.

Davidson, R. J., Pizzagalli, D., Nitschke, J. B., & Putnam, K. (2002). Depression: Perspectives from affective neuroscience. *Annual Review of Psychology, 53,* 545–574.

Davidson, R. J., Putnam, K. M., & Larson, C. L. (2000). Dysfunction in the neural circuitry of emotion regulation—a possible prelude to violence. *Science, 289,* 591–594.

Davidson, T. L., & Riley, A. L. (2015). Taste, sickness, and learning. *American Scientist, 103,* 204–211.

Davies, P. (2007). *Cosmic jackpot: Why our universe is just right for life.* Boston: Houghton Mifflin.

Davis, B. E., Moon, R. Y., Sachs, H. C., & Ottolini, M. C. (1998). Effects of sleep position on infant motor development. *Pediatrics, 102,* 1135–1140.

Davis, D. E., Choe, E., Meyers, J., Wade, N., Varias, K., Gifford, A., . . . Worthington, E. L. (2016). Thankful for the little things: A meta-analysis of gratitude interventions. *Journal of Counseling Psychology, 63*, 20–31.

Davis, E. P., Stout, S. A., Molet, J., Vegetabile, B., Glynn, L. M., Sandman, C. A., . . . Baram, T. Z. (2017). Exposure to unpredictable maternal sensory signals influences cognitive development across species. *PNAS, 114*, 10390–10395.

Davis, J. O., & Phelps, J. A. (1995). Twins with schizophrenia: Genes or germs? *Schizophrenia Bulletin, 21*, 13–18.

Davis, J. O., Phelps, J. A., & Bracha, H. S. (1995). Prenatal development of monozygotic twins and concordance for schizophrenia. *Schizophrenia Bulletin, 21*, 357–366.

Davis, J. P., Lander, K., & Jansari, A. (2013). I never forget a face. *The Psychologist, 26*, 726–729.

Davis, K., Christodoulou, J., Seider, S., & Gardner, H. (2011). The theory of multiple intelligences. In R. J. Sternberg & S. B. Kaufman (Eds.), *Cambridge handbook of intelligence* (pp. 485–503). Cambridge, UK; New York: Cambridge University Press.

Davison, S. L., & Davis, S. R. (2011). Androgenic hormones and aging—The link with female function. *Hormones and Behavior, 59*, 745–753.

Dawes, R. M. (1994). *House of cards: Psychology and psychotherapy built on myth.* New York: Free Press.

Dawkins, L., Shahzad, F.-Z., Ahmed, S. S., & Edmonds, C. J. (2011). Expectation of having consumed caffeine can improve performance and moods. *Appetite, 57*, 597–600.

Day, F. R., Thompson, D. J., Helgason, H., Chasman, D. I., Finucane, H., Sulem, P., . . . Altmaier, E. (2017). Genomic analyses identify hundreds of variants associated with age at menarche and support a role for puberty timing in cancer risk. *Nature Genetics, 49*, 834–841.

de Boysson-Bardies, B., Halle, P., Sagart, L., & Durand, C. (1989). A cross-linguistic investigation of vowel formants in babbling. *Journal of Child Language, 16*, 1–17.

de Courten-Myers, G. M. (2005, February 4). Personal communication.

De Dreu, C. K. W., Greer, L. L., Handgraaf, M. J. J., Shalvi, S., Van Kleef, G. A., Baas, M., . . . Feith, S. W. W. (2010). The neuropeptide oxytocin regulated parochial altruism in intergroup conflict among humans. *Science, 328*, 1409–1411.

De Dreu, C. K. W., Nijstad, B. A., Baas, M., Wolsink, I., & Roskes, M. (2012). Working memory benefits creative insight, musical improvisation, and original ideation through maintained task-focused attention. *Personality and Social Psychology Bulletin, 38*, 656–669.

de Gee, J., Knapen, T., & Donner, T. H. (2014). Decision-related pupil dilation reflects upcoming choice and individual bias. *PNAS, 111*, E618–E625.

de Hoogh, A. H. B., den Hartog, D. N., Koopman, P. L., Thierry, H., van den Berg, P. T., van der Weide, J. G., & Wilderom, C. P. M. (2004). Charismatic leadership, environmental dynamism, and performance. *European Journal of Work and Organisational Psychology, 13*, 447–471.

de la Vega, A., Chang, L. J., Banich, M. T., Wager, T. D., & Yarkoni, T. (2016). Large-scale meta-analysis of human medial frontal cortex reveals tripartite functional organization. *The Journal of Neuroscience, 36*, 6553–6562.

de Lange, M., Debets, L., Ruitenberg, K., & Holland, R. (2012). Making less of a mess: Scent exposure as a tool for behavioral change. *Social Influence, 7*, 90–97.

De Neve, J.-E., Diener, E., Tay, L., & Xuereb, C. (2013). The objective benefits of subjective well-being. In J. F. Helliwell, R. Layard, & J. Sachs (Eds.), *World happiness report 2013. Volume 2.* (pp. 54–79). New York: UN Sustainable Network Development Solutions Network.

De Neve, K. M., & Cooper, H. (1998). The happy personality: A meta-analysis of 137 personality traits and subjective well-being. *Psychological Bulletin, 124*, 197–229.

de Waal, F. (2011). Back cover quote for D. Blum, *Love at Goon Park: Harry Harlow and the science of affection.* New York: Basic Books.

de Waal, F. (2016). *Are we smart enough to know how smart animals are?* New York: Norton.

de Wit, L., Luppino, F., van Straten, A., Penninx, B., Zitman, F., & Cuijpers, P. (2010). Depression and obesity: A meta-analysis of community-based studies. *Psychiatry Research, 178*, 230–235.

De Wolff, M. S., & van IJzendoorn, M. H. (1997). Sensitivity and attachment: A meta-analysis on parental antecedents of infant attachment. *Child Development, 68*, 571–591.

Dean, M., Harwood, R., & Kasari, C. (2017). The art of camouflage: Gender differences in the social behaviors of girls and boys with autism spectrum disorder. *Autism, 21*, 678–689.

Deary, I. J., Batty, G. D., & Gale, C. R. (2008). Bright children become enlightened adults. *Psychological Science, 19*, 1–6.

Deary, I. J., Pattie, A., & Starr, J. M. (2013). The stability of intelligence from age 11 to age 90 years: The Lothian birth cohort of 1921. *Psychological Science, 24*, 2361–2368.

Deary, I. J., & Ritchie, S. J. (2016). Processing speed differences between 70- and 83-year-olds matched on childhood IQ. *Intelligence, 55*, 28–33.

Deary, I. J., Thorpe, G., Wilson, V., Starr, J. M., & Whalley, L. J. (2003). Population sex differences in IQ at age 11: The Scottish mental survey 1932. *Intelligence, 31*, 533–541.

Deary, I. J., Whalley, L. J., & Starr, J. M. (2009). *A lifetime of intelligence: Follow-up studies of the Scottish Mental Surveys of 1932 and 1947.* Washington, DC: American Psychological Association.

Deary, I. J., Whiteman, M. C., Starr, J. M., Whalley, L. J., & Fox, H. C. (2004). The impact of childhood intelligence on later life: Following up the Scottish mental surveys of 1932 and 1947. *Journal of Personality and Social Psychology, 86*, 130–147.

Deary, I. J., Yang, J., Davies, G., Harris, S. E., Tenesa, A., Liewald, D., . . . Visscher, P. M. (2012). Genetic contributions to stability and change in intelligence from childhood to old age. *Nature, 481*, 212–215.

Dechêne, A., Stahl, C., Hansen, J., & Wänke, M. (2010). The truth about the truth: A meta-analytic review of the truth effect. *Personality and Social Psychology Review, 14*, 238–257.

Dechesne, M., Pyszczynski, T., Arndt, J., Ransom, S., Sheldon, K. M., van Knippenberg, A., & Janssen, J. (2003). Literal and symbolic immortality: The effect of evidence of literal immortality on self-esteem striving in response to mortality salience. *Journal of Personality and Social Psychology, 84*, 722–737.

Deci, E. L., & Ryan, R. M. (2012). Motivation, personality, and development within embedded social contexts: An overview of self-determination theory. In R. M. Ryan (Ed.), *Oxford handbook of human motivation* (pp. 85–107). Oxford: Oxford University Press.

Deckman, T., DeWall, C. N., Way, B., Gilman, R., & Richman, S. (2014). Can marijuana reduce social pain? *Social Psychological and Personality Science, 5*, 131–139.

DeFina, R., & Hannon, L. (2015). The changing relationship between unemployment and suicide. *Suicide and Life-Threatening Behavior, 45*, 217–229.

Dehne, K. L., & Riedner, G. (2005). *Sexually transmitted infections among adolescents: The need for adequate health services.* Geneva: World Health Organization.

DeLamater, J. D. (2012). Sexual expression in later life: A review and synthesis. *Journal of Sex Research, 49*, 125–141.

DeLamater, J. D., & Sill, M. (2005). Sexual desire in later life. *Journal of Sex Research, 42*, 138–149.

Delaney, H. D., Miller, W. R., & Bisonó, A. M. (2007). Religiosity and spirituality among psychologists: A survey of clinician members of the American Psychological Association. *Professional Psychology: Research and Practice, 38*, 538–546.

Delaunay-El Allam, M., Soussignan, R., Patris, B., Marlier, L., & Schaal, B. (2010). Long-lasting memory for an odor acquired at the mother's breast. *Developmental Science, 13*, 849–863.

DeLoache, J. S., & Brown, A. L. (1987, October-December). Differences in the memory-based searching of delayed and normally developing young children. *Intelligence, 11*, 277–289.

DeLoache, J. S., Chiong, C., Sherman, K., Islam, N., Vanderborght, M., Troseth, G. L., . . . O'Doherty, K. (2010). Do babies learn from baby media? *Psychological Science, 21*, 1570–1574.

Dement, W. C. (1978). *Some must watch while some must sleep.* New York: Norton.

Dement, W. C. (1999). *The promise of sleep.* New York: Delacorte Press.

Dement, W. C., & Wolpert, E. A. (1958). The relation of eye movements, body mobility, and external stimuli to dream content. *Journal of Experimental Psychology, 55*, 543–553.

Dempster, E., Viana, J., Pidsley, R., & Mill, J. (2013). Epigenetic studies of schizophrenia: Progress, predicaments, and promises for the future. *Schizophrenia Bulletin, 39*, 11–16.

Denissen, J. J. A., Bleidorn, W., Hennecke, M., Luhmann, M., Orth, U., Specht, J., & Zimmermann, J. (2018). Uncovering the power of personality to shape income. *Psychological Science, 29*, 3–13.

Dennehy, T. C., & Dasgupta, N. (2017). Female peer mentors early in college increase women's positive academic experiences and retention in engineering. *PNAS, 114*, 5964–5969.

Denny, B. T., Inhoff, M. C., Zerubavel, N., Davachi, L., & Ochsner, K. N. (2015). Getting over it: Long-lasting effects of emotion regulation on amygdala response. *Psychological Science, 26*, 1377–1388.

Denton, K., & Krebs, D. (1990). From the scene to the crime: The effect of alcohol and social context on moral judgment. *Journal of Personality and Social Psychology, 59*, 242–248.

Denyer, S., & Gowen, A. (2018, April 18). Too many men. *The Washington Post* (www.washingtonpost.com).

Depla, M. F. I. A., ten Have, M. L., van Balkom, A. J. L. M., & de Graaf, R. (2008). Specific fears and phobias in the general population: Results from the Netherlands Mental Health Survey and Incidence Study (NEMESIS). *Social Psychiatry and Psychiatric Epidemiology, 43*, 200–208.

Derebery, M. J., Vermiglio, A., Berliner, K. I., Potthoff, M., & Holguin, K. (2012). Facing the music: Pre- and postconcert assessment of hearing in teenagers. *Otology & Neurotology, 33*, 1136–1141.

Deri, S., Davidai, S., & Gilovich, T. (2017). Home alone: Why people believe others' social lives are richer than their own. *Journal of Personality and Social Psychology, 113*, 858–877.

Dermer, M., Cohen, S. J., Jacobsen, E., & Anderson, E. A. (1979). Evaluative judgments of aspects of life as a function of vicarious exposure to hedonic extremes. *Journal of Personality and Social Psychology, 37*, 247–260.

Desikan, R. S., Cabral, H. J., Hess, C. P., Dillon, W. P., Glastonbury, C. M., Weiner, M. W., . . . Alzheimer's Disease Neuroimaging Initiative. (2009). Automated MRI measures identify individuals with mild cognitive impairment and Alzheimer's disease. *Brain, 132*, 2048–2057.

DeSteno, D., Petty, R. E., Wegener, D. T., & Rucker, D. D. (2000). Beyond valence in the perception of likelihood: The role of emotion specificity. *Journal of Personality and Social Psychology, 78*, 397–416.

Dettman, S. J., Pinder, D., Briggs, R. J. S., Dowell, R. C., & Leigh, J. R. (2007). Communication development in children who receive the cochlear implant younger than 12 months: Risk versus benefits. *Ear and Hearing, 28*(2), Supplement 11S–18S.

Deutsch, J. A. (1972, July). Brain reward: ESP and ecstasy. *Psychology Today*, 46–48.

DeValois, R. L., & DeValois, K. K. (1975). Neural coding of color. In E. C. Carterette & M. P. Friedman (Eds.), *Handbook of perception: Vol. V. Seeing*. New York: Academic Press.

Dew, M. A., Hoch, C. C., Buysse, D. J., Monk, T. H., Begley, A. E., Houck, P. R., . . . Reynolds, C. F., III. (2003). Healthy older adults' sleep predicts all-cause mortality at 4 to 19 years of follow-up. *Psychosomatic Medicine, 65*, 63–73.

DeWall, C. N., Lambert, N. M., Slotter, E. B., Pond, R. S., Jr., Deckman, T., Finkel, E. J., . . . Fincham, F. D. (2011). So far away from one's partner, yet so close to romantic alternatives: Avoidant attachment, interest in alternatives, and infidelity. *Journal of Personality and Social Psychology, 101*, 1302–1316.

DeWall, C. N., MacDonald, G., Webster, G. D., Masten, C. L., Baumeister, R. F., Powell, C., . . . Eisenberger, N. I. (2010). Acetaminophen reduces social pain: Behavioral and neural evidence. *Psychological Science, 21*, 931–937.

DeWall, C. N., & Pond, R. S., Jr. (2011). Loneliness and smoking: The costs of the desire to reconnect. *Self and Identity, 10*, 375–385.

DeWall, C. N., Pond, R. S., Jr., Carter, E. C., McCullough, M. E., Lambert, N. M., Fincham, F. D., & Nezlek, J. B. (2014). Explaining the relationship between religiousness and substance use: Self-control matters. *Journal of Personality and Social Psychology, 107*, 339–351.

Dewar, M., Alber, J., Butler, C., Cowan, N., & Sala, S. D. (2012). Brief wakeful resting boosts new memories over the long term. *Psychological Science, 23*, 955–960.

DeYoung, C. G., & Allen, T. A. (2019). Personality neuroscience: A developmental perspective. In D. P. McAdams, Rebecca L. Shiner & Jennifer L. Tackett (Eds.), *Handbook of personality development*. New York: Guilford Press.

Di Tella, R., Haisken-De New, J., & MacCulloch, R. (2010). Happiness adaptation to income and to status in an individual panel. *Journal of Economic Behavior & Organization, 76*, 834–852.

Diaconis, P., & Mosteller, F. (1989). Methods for studying coincidences. *Journal of the American Statistical Association, 84*, 853–861.

Diamond, L. M., Dickenson, J. A., & Blair, K. L. (2017). Stability of sexual attractions across different timescales: The roles of bisexuality and gender. *Archives of Sexual Behavior, 46*, 193–204.

Dickens, L. R. (2017). Using gratitude to promote positive change: A series of meta-analyses investigating the effectiveness of gratitude interventions. *Basic and Applied Social Psychology, 39*, 193–208.

Dickens, W. T., & Flynn, J. R. (2006). Black Americans reduce the racial IQ gap: Evidence from standardization samples. *Psychological Science, 17*, 913–920.

Dickson, B. J. (2005, June 3). Quoted in E. Rosenthal, For fruit flies, gene shift tilts sex orientation. *The New York Times* (nytimes.com).

Dickson, N., van Roode, T., Cameron, C., & Paul, C. (2013). Stability and change in same-sex attraction, experience, and identity by sex and age in a New Zealand birth cohort. *Archives of Sexual Behavior, 42*, 753–763.

Diener, E., Nickerson, C., Lucas, R. E., & Sandvik, E. (2002). Dispositional affect and job outcomes. *Social Indicators Research, 59*, 229–259.

Diener, E., & Oishi, S. (2000). Money and happiness: Income and subjective well-being across nations. In E. Diener & E. M. Suh (Eds.), *Subjective well-being across cultures*. Cambridge, MA: MIT Press.

Diener, E., Oishi, S., & Lucas, R. E. (2003). Personality, culture, and subjective well-being: Emotional and cognitive evaluations of life. *Annual Review of Psychology, 54*, 403–425.

Diener, E., Oishi, S., & Lucas, R. E. (2015). National accounts of subjective well-being. *American Psychologist, 70*, 234–242.

Diener, E., Oishi, S., & Park, J. Y. (2014). An incomplete list of eminent psychologists of the modern era. *Archives of Scientific Psychology, 21*, 20–31.

Diener, E., & Tay, L. (2015). Subjective well-being and human welfare around the world as reflected in the Gallup world poll. *International Journal of Psychology, 50*, 135–149.

Diener, E., Tay, L., & Myers, D. G. (2011). The religion paradox: If religion makes people happy, why are so many dropping out? *Journal of Personality and Social Psychology, 101*, 1278–1290.

Diener, E., Wolsic, B., & Fujita, F. (1995). Physical attractiveness and subjective well-being. *Journal of Personality and Social Psychology, 69*, 120–129.

DiFranza, J. R. (2008). Hooked from the first cigarette. *Scientific American, 298*, 82–87.

Dijksterhuis, A., & Strick, M. (2016). A case for thinking without consciousness. *Perspectives on Psychological Science, 11*, 117–132.

Dik, B. J., & Duffy, R. D. (2012). *Make your job a calling: How the psychology of vocation can change your life at work*. Conshohocken, PA: Templeton Press.

Dik, B. J., & Rottinghaus, P. J. (2013). Assessments of interests. In K. F. Geisinger & six others (Eds.), *APA handbook of testing and assessment in psychology*, Vol. 2. Washington, DC: APA.

DiLalla, D. L., Carey, G., Gottesman, I. I., & Bouchard, T. J., Jr. (1996). Heritability of MMPI personality indicators of psychopathology in twins reared apart. *Journal of Abnormal Psychology, 105*, 491–499.

Dimberg, U., Thunberg, M., & Elmehed, K. (2000). Unconscious facial reactions to emotional facial expressions. *Psychological Science, 11*, 86–89.

Ding, F., O'Donnell, J., Xu, Q., Kang, N., Goldman, N., & Nedergaard, M. (2016). Changes in the composition of brain interstitial ions control the sleep-wake cycle. *Science, 352*, 550–555.

Dinges, C. W., Varnon, C. A., Cota, L. D., Slykerman, S., & Abramson, C. I. (2017). Studies of learned helplessness in honey bees (*Apis mellifera ligustica*). *Journal of Experimental Psychology: Animal Learning and Cognition, 43*, 147–158.

Dingfelder, S. F. (2010, November). A second chance for the Mexican wolf. *Monitor on Psychology*, pp. 20–21.

Ditre, J. W., Brandon, T. H., Zale, E. L., & Meagher, M. M. (2011). Pain, nicotine, and smoking: Research findings and mechanistic considerations. *Psychological Bulletin, 137*, 1065–1093.

Ditto, P., Wojcik, S., Chen, E., Grady, R., & Ringel, M. (2015). Political bias is tenacious. *Behavioral and Brain Sciences, 38*. doi:10.1017/S0140525X14001186

Dixon, M. L., Thiruchselvam, R., Todd, R., & Christoff, K. (2017). Emotion and the prefrontal cortex: An integrative review. *Psychological Bulletin, 143*, 1033–1081.

Dobbs, D. (2009). The post-traumatic stress trap. *Scientific American, 300*, 64–69.

Dodge, K. A. (2009). Mechanisms of gene-environment interaction effects in the development of conduct disorder. *Perspectives on Psychological Science, 4*, 408–414.

Doherty, C., & Kiley, J. (2016, June 22). Key facts about partisanship and political animosity in America. Pew Research (pewresearch.org).

Dohrenwend, B. P., Pearlin, L., Clayton, P., Hamburg, B., Dohrenwend, B. S., Riley, M., & Rose, R. (1982). Report on stress and life events. In G. R. Elliott & C. Eisdorfer (Eds.), *Stress and human health: Analysis and implications of research* (A study by the Institute of Medicine/National Academy of Sciences). New York: Springer.

DOL. (2015, accessed March 4). *Women in the labor force*. Retrieved from dol.gov/wb/stats/facts_over_time.htm

Dolezal, H. (1982). *Living in a world transformed*. New York: Academic Press.

Doliński, D., Grzyb, T., Folwarczny, M., Grzybała, P., Krzyszycha, K., Martynowska, K., & Trojanowski, J. (2017). Would you deliver an electric shock in 2015? Obedience in the experimental paradigm developed by Stanley Milgram in the 50 years following the original studies. *Social Psychological and Personality Science, 8*, 927–933.

Dollfus, S., Lecardeur, L., Morello, R., & Etard, O. (2016). Placebo response in repetitive transcranial magnetic stimulation trials of auditory hallucinations in schizophrenia: A meta-analysis. *Schizophrenia Bulletin, 42*, 301–308.

Domany, Y., Bleich-Cohen, M., Tarrasch, R., Meidan, R. Litvak-Lazar, O., Stoppleman, N., . . . Sharon, H. (2019). Repeated oral ketamine for out-patient treatment of resistant depression: Randomised, double-blind, place-controlled, proof-of-concept study. *British Journal of Psychiatry, 214*, 20–26.

Domhoff, G. W. (1996). *Finding meaning in dreams: A quantitative approach*. New York: Plenum.

Domhoff, G. W. (2003). *The scientific study of dreams: Neural networks, cognitive development, and content analysis*. Washington, DC: American Psychological Association.

Domhoff, G. W. (2007). Realistic simulations and bizarreness in dream content: Past findings and suggestions for future research. In D. Barrett & P. McNamara (Eds.), *The new science of dreaming: Content, recall, and personality characteristics* (Vol. 2, pp. 1–27). Westport, CT: Praeger.

Domhoff, G. W. (2010). *The case for a cognitive theory of dreams*. Retrieved from www2.ucsc.edu/dreams/Library/domhoff_2010a.html

Domhoff, G. W. (2011). The neural substrate for dreaming: Is it a subsystem of the default network? *Consciousness and Cognition, 20,* 1163–1174.

Domjan, M. (1992). Adult learning and mate choice: Possibilities and experimental evidence. *American Zoologist, 32,* 48–61.

Domjan, M. (1994). Formulation of a behavior system for sexual conditioning. *Psychonomic Bulletin & Review, 1,* 421–428.

Domjan, M. (2005). Pavlovian conditioning: A functional perspective. *Annual Review of Psychology, 56,* 179–206.

Domo. (2018). Data never sleeps 5.0 infographic. Domo. Retrieved from domo.com/learn/data-never-sleeps-5?aid=DPR072517

Donald, J. N., Sahdra, B. K., Van Zanden, B., Duineveld, J. J., Atkins, P. W., Marshall, S. L., & Ciarrochi, J. (2018). Does your mindfulness benefit others? A systematic review and meta-analysis of the link between mindfulness and prosocial behaviour. *British Journal of Psychology, 110,* 101–125.

Dong, X., Talhelm, T., & Ren, X. (2018). Teens in Rice County are more interdependent and think more holistically than nearby Wheat County. *Social Psychological and Personality Science.* Advance online publication. doi.org/10.1177/1948550618808868

Donnellan, M. B., Trzesniewski, K. H., Robins, R. W., Moffitt, T. E., & Caspi, A. (2005). Low self-esteem is related to aggression, antisocial behavior, and delinquency. *Psychological Science, 16,* 328–335.

Donnerstein, E. (1998). *Why do we have those new ratings on television?* Invited address to the National Institute on the Teaching of Psychology.

Dorfman, P., Javidan, M., Hanges, P., Dastmalchian, A., & House, R. (2012). GLOBE: A twenty-year journey into the intriguing world of culture and leadership. *Journal of World Business, 47,* 504–518.

Douglas, K. S., Guy, L. S., & Hart, S. D. (2009). Psychosis as a risk factor for violence to others: A meta-analysis. *Psychological Bulletin, 135,* 679–706.

Dovidio, J. F., & Gaertner, S. L. (1999). Reducing prejudice: Combating intergroup biases. *Current Directions in Psychological Science, 8,* 101–105.

Downs, E., & Smith, S. L. (2010). Keeping abreast of hypersexuality: A video game character content analysis. *Sex Roles, 62,* 721–733.

Doyle, R. (2005, March). Gay and lesbian census. *Scientific American,* p. 28.

Doyle, R. A., & Voyer, R. A. (2016). Stereotype manipulation effects on math and spatial test performance: A meta-analysis. *Learning and Individual Differences, 47,* 103–116.

Draganski, B., Gaser, C., Busch, V., Schuierer, G., Bogdahn, U., & May, A. (2004). Neuroplasticity: Changes in grey matter induced by training. *Nature, 427,* 311–312.

Drake, B., & Poushter, J. (2016, July 12). In views of diversity, many Europeans are less positive than Americans. Pew Research Center (pewresearch.org).

Drew, T., Võ, M. L. H., & Wolfe, J. M. (2013). The invisible gorilla strikes again: Sustained inattentional blindness in expert observers. *Psychological Science, 24,* 1848–1853.

Driessen, E., Cuijpers, P., de Maat, S. C. M., Abbas, A. A., de Jonghe, F., & Dekker, J. J. M. (2010). The efficacy of short-term psychodynamic psychotherapy for depression: A meta-analysis. *Clinical Psychology Review, 30,* 25–36.

Driessen, E., Van, H. L., Peen, J., Don, F. J., Twisk, J. W. R., Cuijpers, P., & Dekker, J. J. M. (2017). Cognitive-behavioral versus psychodynamic therapy for major depression: Secondary outcomes of a randomized clinical trial. *Journal of Consulting and Clinical Psychology, 85,* 653–663.

Drydakis, N. (2009). Sexual orientation discrimination in the labour market. *Labour Economics, 16,* 364–372.

Drydakis, N. (2015). Sexual orientation discrimination in the United Kingdom's labour market: A field experiment. *Human Relations, 68,* 1769–1796.

Dubé, S., Lavoie, F., Blais, M., & Hébert, M. (2017). Consequences of casual sex relationships and experiences on adolescents' psychological well-being: A prospective study. *Journal of Sex Research, 54,* 1006–1017.

Ducasse, D., Loas, G., Dassa, D., Gramaglia, C., Zeppegno, P., Guillaume, S., . . . & Courtet, P. (2018). Anhedonia is associated with suicidal ideation independently of depression: A meta-analysis. *Depression and Anxiety, 35,* 382–392.

Duckworth, A. (2016). *Grit: The power of passion and perseverance.* New York: Scribner.

Duckworth, A. L., & Seligman, M. E. P. (2005). Discipline outdoes talent: Self-discipline predicts academic performance in adolescents. *Psychological Science, 12,* 939–944.

Duckworth, A. L., & Seligman, M. E. P. (2006). Self-discipline gives girls the edge: Gender in self-discipline, grades, and achievement tests. *Journal of Educational Psychology, 98,* 198–208.

Duckworth, A. L., Gendler, T. S., & Gross, J. J. (2016). Situational strategies for self-control. *Perspectives on Psychological Science, 11,* 35–55.

Duckworth, A. L., Quinn, P. D., Lynam, D. R., Loeber, R., & Stouthamer-Loeber, M. (2011). Role of test motivation in intelligence testing. *PNAS, 108,* 7716–7720.

Duckworth, A. L., Tsukayama, E., & Kirby, T. A. (2013). Is it really self-control? Examining the predictive power of the delay of gratification task. *Personality and Social Psychology Bulletin, 39,* 843–855.

Duclos, S. E., Laird, J. D., Sexter, M., Stern, L., & Van Lighten, O. (1989). Emotion-specific effects of facial expressions and postures on emotional experience. *Journal of Personality and Social Psychology, 57,* 100–108.

Dufner, M., Gebauer, J. E., Sedikides, C., & Denissen, J. J. (2018). Self-enhancement and psychological adjustment: A meta-analytic review. *Personality and Social Psychology Review, 23,* 48–72.

Duggan, J. P., & Booth, D. A. (1986). Obesity, overeating, and rapid gastric emptying in rats with ventromedial hypothalamic lesions. *Science, 231,* 609–611.

Duits, P., Cath, D. C., Lissek, S., Hox, J. J., Hamm, A. O., Engelhard, I. M., . . . Baas, J. M. P. (2015). Updated meta-analysis of classical fear conditioning in the anxiety disorders. *Depression and Anxiety, 32,* 239–253.

DuMont, K. A., Widom, C. S., & Czaja, S. J. (2007). Predictors of resilience in abused and neglected children grown-up: The role of individual and neighborhood characteristics. *Child Abuse & Neglect, 31,* 255–274.

Dunbar, R. I. M., Baron, R., Frangou, A., Pearce, E., van Leeuwin, E. J. C., Stow, J., . . . van Vugt, M. (2011). Social laughter is correlated with an elevated pain threshold. *Proceedings of the Royal Society B, 279,* 1161–1167.

Duncan, L. E., Ratanatharathorn, A., Aiello, A. E., Almli, L. M., Amstadter, A. B., Ashley-koch, A., . . . Koenen, K. C. (2018). Largest GWAS of PTSD (N=20 070) yields genetic overlap with schizophrenia and sex differences in heritability. *Molecular Psychiatry, 23,* 666–673.

Dunn, A. (2018, October 4). Partisans are divided over the fairness of the U.S. economy—and why people are rich or poor. Pew Research Center (pewresearch.org).

Dunn, A. L., Trivedi, M. H., Kampert, J. B., Clark, C. G., & Chambliss, H. O. (2005). Exercise treatment for depression: Efficacy and dose response. *American Journal of Preventive Medicine, 28,* 1–8.

Dunn, E. W., Aknin, L. B., & Norton, M. I. (2008). Spending money on others promotes happiness. *Science, 319,* 1687–1688.

Dunn, E. W., Aknin, L. B., & Norton, M. I. (2014). Pro-social spending and happiness: Using money to benefit others pays off. *Current Directions in Psychological Science, 13,* 347–355.

Dunn, E., & Norton, M. (2013). *Happy money: The science of smarter spending.* New York: Simon & Schuster.

Dunn, M., & Searle, R. (2010). Effect of manipulated prestige-car ownership on both sex attractiveness ratings. *British Journal of Psychology, 101,* 69–80.

Dunson, D. B., Colombo, B., & Baird, D. D. (2002). Changes with age in the level and duration of fertility in the menstrual cycle. *Human Reproduction, 17,* 1399–1403.

Dunster, G. P., de la Iglesia, L., Ben-Hamo, M., Nave, C., Fleischer, J. G., Panda, S., & Horacio, O. (2018). Sleepmore in Seattle: Later school start times are associated with more sleep and better performance in high school students. *Science Advances, 4,* eaau6200.

Dutton, D. G., & Aron, A. P. (1974). Some evidence for heightened sexual attraction under conditions of high anxiety. *Journal of Personality and Social Psychology, 30,* 510–517.

Dutton, D. G., & Aron, A. P. (1989). Romantic attraction and generalized liking for others who are sources of conflict-based arousal. *Canadian Journal of Behavioural Sciences, 21,* 246–257.

Dweck, C. (2018, August 20). Growth mindset interventions yield impressive results. *Character & Context* (spsp.org).

Dweck, C. S. (2012a). Implicit theories. In P.A.M. Van Lange, A. Kruglanski, & E. T. Higgins (Eds.), *Handbook of theories of social psychology* (Vol. 2, pp. 43–61). Thousand Oaks, CA: Sage.

Dweck, C. S. (2012b). Mindsets and human nature: Promoting change in the Middle East, the schoolyard, the racial divide, and willpower. *American Psychologist, 67,* 614–622.

Dweck, C. S. (2015, January 1). The secret to raising smart kids. *Scientific American.* Retrieved from scientificamerican.com/article/the-secret-to-raising-smart-kids1/

Eagan, K., Stolzenberg, E. B., Bates, A. K., Aragon, M. C. Suchard, M. R., & Rios-Aguilar, C. R. (2016). *The American freshman: National norms 2015.* Los Angeles, Higher Education Research Institute, UCLA.

Eagan, K., Stolzenberg, E. B., Zimmerman, H. B., Aragon, M. C., Sayson, H. W., and Rios-Aguilar, C. (2017). *The American freshman: National norms fall 2016.* Higher Education Research Institute, UCLA.

Eagly, A. H. (2007). Female leadership advantage and disadvantage: Resolving the contradictions. *Psychology of Women Quarterly, 31,* 1–12.

Eagly, A. H. (2009). The his and hers of prosocial behavior: An examination of the social psychology of gender. *American Psychologist, 64,* 644–658.

Eagly, A. H. (2013, March 20). Hybrid style works, and women are best at it. *The New York Times* (nytimes.com).

Eagly, A. H., Ashmore, R. D., Makhijani, M. G., & Kennedy, L. C. (1991). What is beautiful is good, but . . .: A meta-analytic review of research on the physical attractiveness stereotype. *Psychological Bulletin, 110,* 109–128.

Eagly, A. H., & Carli, L. (2007). *Through the labyrinth: The truth about how women become leaders.* Cambridge, MA: Harvard University Press.

Eagly, A. H., & Wood, W. (1999). The origins of sex differences in human behavior: Evolved dispositions versus social roles. *American Psychologist, 54,* 408–423.

Eagly, A. H., & Wood, W. (2013). The nature-nurture debates: 25 years of challenges in understanding the psychology of gender. *Perspectives on Psychological Science, 8,* 340–357.

Eastwick, P. W., Luchies, L. B., Finkel, E. J., & Hunt, L. L. (2014a). The many voices of Darwin's descendants: Reply to Schmitt (2014). *Psychological Bulletin, 140,* 673–681.

Eastwick, P. W., Luchies, L. B., Finkel, E. J., & Hunt, L. L. (2014b). The predictive validity of ideal partner preferences: A review and meta-analysis. *Psychological Bulletin, 140,* 623–665.

Ebbinghaus, H. (1885/1964). *Memory: A contribution to experimental psychology* (H. A. Ruger & C. E. Bussenius, Trans.). New York: Dover.

Eberhardt, J. L. (2005). Imaging race. *American Psychologist, 60,* 181–190.

Ebert, D. D., Van Daele, T., Nordgreen, T., Karekla, M., Compare, A., Zarbo, C., . . . Taylor, J. (2018). Internet- and mobile-based psychological interventions: Applications, efficacy, and potential for improving mental health: A report of the EFPA E-health taskforce. *European Psychologist, 23,* 167–187.

Eccles, J. S., Jacobs, J. E., & Harold, R. D. (1990). Gender role stereotypes, expectancy effects, and parents' socialization of gender differences. *Journal of Social Issues, 46,* 183–201.

Eckensberger, L. H. (1994). Moral development and its measurement across cultures. In W. J. Lonner & R. Malpass (Eds.), *Psychology and culture.* Boston: Allyn & Bacon.

Eckert, E. D., Heston, L. L., & Bouchard, T. J., Jr. (1981). MZ twins reared apart: Preliminary findings of psychiatric disturbances and traits. In L. Gedda, P. Paris, & W. D. Nance (Eds.), *Twin research: Vol. 3. Pt. B. Intelligence, personality, and development.* New York: Alan Liss.

Economist. (2001, December 20). An anthropology of happiness. *The Economist* (economist.com/world/asia).

Eddy, K. T., Tabri, N., Thomas, J. J., Murray, H. B., Keshaviah, A., Hastings, E., . . . Franko, D. L. (2017). Recovery from anorexia nervosa and bulimia nervosa at 22-year follow-up. *Journal of Clinical Psychiatry, 78,* 184–189.

Edelman, B., Luca, M., & Svirsky, D. (2017). Racial discrimination in the sharing economy: Evidence from a field experiment. *American Economic Journal: Applied Economics, 9,* 1–22.

Edelman, S., & Kidman, A. D. (1997). Mind and cancer: Is there a relationship? A review of the evidence. *Australian Psychologist, 32,* 1–7.

Editorial Board of The New York Times. (2015, December 15). Don't blame mental illness for gun violence. *The New York Times* (nytimes.com).

Edwards, R. R., Campbell, C., Jamison, R. N., & Wiech, K. (2009). The neurobiological underpinnings of coping with pain. *Current Directions in Psychological Science, 18,* 237–241.

Egeland, M., Zunszain, P. A., & Pariante, C. M. (2015). Molecular mechanisms in the regulation of adult neurogenesis during stress. *Nature Reviews Neuroscience, 16,* 189–200.

Eichstaedt, J. C., Schwartz, H. A., Kern, M. L., Park, G., Labarthe, D. R., Merchant, R. M., . . . Seligman, M. E. P. (2015). Psychological language on Twitter predicts county-level heart disease mortality. *Psychological Science, 26,* 159–169.

Eippert, F., Finsterbush, J., Bingel, U., & Bùchel, C. (2009). Direct evidence for spinal cord involvement in placebo analgesia. *Science, 326,* 404.

Eisenberg, N., & Lennon, R. (1983). Sex differences in empathy and related capacities. *Psychological Bulletin, 94,* 100–131.

Eisenberger, N. I., Master, S. L., Inagaki, T. K., Taylor, S. E., Shirinyan, D., Lieberman, M. D., & Nalifoff, B. D. (2011). Attachment figures activate a safety signal-related neural region and reduce pain experience. *PNAS, 108,* 11721–11726.

Eisenberger, R., & Aselage, J. (2009). Incremental effects of reward on experienced performance pressure: Positive outcomes for intrinsic interest and creativity. *Journal of Organizational Behavior, 30,* 95–117.

Eklund, A., Nichols, T. E., & Knutsson, H. (2016). Cluster failure: Why fMRI inferences for spatial extent have inflated false-positive rates. *PNAS, 113,* 7900–7905.

Ekman, P. (1994). Strong evidence for universals in facial expressions: A reply to Russell's mistaken critique. *Psychological Bulletin, 115,* 268–287.

Ekman, P. (2016). What scientists who study emotion agree about. *Perspectives on Psychological Science, 11,* 31–34.

Ekman, P., & Friesen, W. V. (1971). Constants across cultures in the face and emotion. *Journal of Personality and Social Psychology, 17,* 124–129.

Ekman, P., & Friesen, W. V. (1975). *Unmasking the face.* Englewood Cliffs, NJ: Prentice-Hall.

Ekman, P., Friesen, W. V., O'Sullivan, M., Chan, A., Diacoyanni-Tarlatzis, I., Heider, K., . . . Tzavaras, A. (1987). Universals and cultural differences in the judgments of facial expressions of emotion. *Journal of Personality and Social Psychology, 53,* 712–717.

Elbogen, E. B., Dennis, P. A., & Johnson, S. C. (2016). Beyond mental illness: Targeting stronger and more direct pathways to violence. *Clinical Psychological Science, 4,* 747–759.

Elfenbein, H. A., & Ambady, N. (2002). On the universality and cultural specificity of emotion recognition: A meta-analysis. *Psychological Bulletin, 128,* 203–235.

Elkind, D. (1970). The origins of religion in the child. *Review of Religious Research, 12,* 35–42.

Ellenbogen, J. M., Hu, P. T., Payne, J. D., Titone, D., & Walker, M. P. (2007). Human relational memory requires time and sleep. *PNAS, 104,* 7723–7728.

Ellis, B. J., Bates, J. E., Dodge, K. A., Fergusson, D. M., John, H. L., Pettit, G. S., & Woodward, L. (2003). Does father absence place daughters at special risk for early sexual activity and teenage pregnancy? *Child Development, 74,* 801–821.

Ellis, B. J., Bianchi, J., Griskevicius, V., & Frankenhuis, W. E. (2017). Beyond risk and protective factors: An adaptation-based approach to resilience. *Perspectives on Psychological Science, 12,* 561–587.

Ellis, B. J., & Boyce, W. T. (2008). Biological sensitivity to context. *Current Directions in Psychological Science, 17,* 183–187.

Ellis, B. J., Schlomer, G. L., Tilley, E. H., & Butler, E. A. (2012). Impact of fathers on risky sexual behavior in daughters: A genetically and environmentally controlled sibling study. *Development and Psychopathology, 24,* 317–332.

Ellis, L., & Ames, M. A. (1987). Neurohormonal functioning and sexual orientation: A theory of homosexuality-heterosexuality. *Psychological Bulletin, 101,* 233–258.

Ellison, K. (2015, November 9). A.D.H.D. rates rise around globe, but sympathy often lags. *The New York Times* (nytimes.com).

Else-Quest, N. M., Hyde, J. S., & Linn, M. C. (2010). Cross-national patterns of gender differences in mathematics: A meta-analysis. *Psychological Bulletin, 136,* 103–127.

Elsey, J. W. B., Van Ast, V. A., & Kindt, M. (2018). Human memory reconsolidation: A guiding framework and critical review of the evidence. *Psychological Bulletin, 144,* 797–848.

Elzinga, B. M., Ardon, A. M., Heijnis, M. K., De Ruiter, M. B., Van Dyck, R., & Veltman, D. J. (2007). Neural correlates of enhanced working-memory performance in dissociative disorder: A functional MRI study. *Psychological Medicine, 37,* 235–245.

Emmons, S., Geisler, C., Kaplan, K. J., & Harrow, M. (1997). *Living with schizophrenia.* Muncie, IN: Taylor and Francis (Accelerated Development).

Endler, N. S. (1982). *Holiday of darkness: A psychologist's personal journey out of his depression.* New York: Wiley.

Engen, T. (1987). Remembering odors and their names. *American Scientist, 75,* 497–503.

Epley, N., Keysar, B., Van Boven, L., & Gilovich, T. (2004). Perspective taking as egocentric anchoring and adjustment. *Journal of Personality and Social Psychology, 87,* 327–339.

Epley, N., Savitsky, K., & Gilovich, T. (2002). Empathy neglect: Reconciling the spotlight effect and the correspondence bias. *Journal of Personality and Social Psychology, 83,* 300–312.

Epstein, J., Stern, E., & Silbersweig, D. (1998). Mesolimbic activity associated with psychosis in schizophrenia: Symptom-specific PET studies. In J. F. McGinty (Ed.), *Advancing from the ventral striatum to the extended amygdala: Implications for neuropsychiatry and drug use: In honor of Lennart Heimer. Annals of the New York Academy of Sciences, 877,* 562–574.

Epstein, S. (1983a). Aggregation and beyond: Some basic issues on the prediction of behavior. *Journal of Personality, 51,* 360–392.

Epstein, S. (1983b). The stability of behavior across time and situations. In R. Zucker, J. Aronoff, & A. I. Rabin (Eds.), *Personality and the prediction of behavior.* San Diego: Academic Press.

Equal Employment Opportunity Commission. (2018, accessed February 20). *Sexual harassment.* Equal Employment Opportunity Commission (eeoc.gov).

Eranti, S. V., MacCabe, J. H., Bundy, H., & Murray, R. M. (2013). Gender difference in age at onset of schizophrenia: A meta-analysis. *Psychological Medicine, 43,* 155–167.

Erdelyi, M. H. (1985). *Psychoanalysis: Freud's cognitive psychology.* New York: Freeman.

Erdelyi, M. H. (1988). Repression, reconstruction, and defense: History and integration of the psychoanalytic and experimental frameworks. In J. Singer (Ed.), *Repression: Defense mechanism and cognitive style.* Chicago: University of Chicago Press.

Erdelyi, M. H. (2006). The unified theory of repression. *Behavioral and Brain Sciences, 29,* 499–551.

Erickson, K. I., Raji, C. A., Lopez, O. L., Becker, J. T., Rosano, C., Newman, A. B., . . . Kuller, L. H. (2010). Physical activity predicts gray matter volume in late adulthood: The Cardiovascular Health Study. *Neurology, 75,* 1415–1422.

Erickson, M. F., & Aird, E. G. (2005). *The motherhood study: Fresh insights on mothers' attitudes and concerns.* New York: The Motherhood Project, Institute for American Values.

Ericsson, K. A. (2001). Attaining excellence through deliberate practice: Insights from the study of expert performance. In M. Ferrari (Ed.), *The pursuit of excellence in education.* Hillsdale, NJ: Erlbaum.

Ericsson, K. A. (2006). The influence of experience and deliberate practice on the development of superior expert performance. In K. A. Ericsson, N. Charness, P. J. Feltovich, & R. R. Hoffman (Eds.), *The Cambridge handbook of expertise and expert performance.* Cambridge: Cambridge University Press.

Ericsson, K. A. (2007). Deliberate practice and the modifiability of body and mind: Toward a science of the structure and acquisition of expert and elite performance. *International Journal of Sport Psychology, 38,* 4–34.

Ericsson, K. A., Cheng, X., Pan, Y., Ku, Y., Ge, Y., & Hu, Y. (2017). Memory skills mediating superior memory in a world-class memorist. *Memory, 25,* 1294–1302.

Ericsson, K. A., & Pool, R. (2016). *PEAK: Secrets from the new science of expertise.* Boston: Houghton Mifflin.

Erikson, E. H. (1963). *Childhood and society.* New York: Norton.

Erlich, N., Lipp, O. V., & Slaughter, V. (2013). Of hissing snakes and angry voices: Human infants are differentially responsive to evolutionary fear-relevant sounds. *Developmental Science, 16,* 894–904.

Ermer, E., Kahn, R. E., Salovey, P., & Kiehl, K. A. (2012). Emotional intelligence in incarcerated men with psychopathic traits. *Journal of Personality and Social Psychology, 103,* 194–204.

Ertmer, D. J., Young, N. M., & Nathani, S. (2007). Profiles of focal development in young cochlear implant recipients. *Journal of Speech, Language, and Hearing Research, 50,* 393–407.

Escasa, M. J., Casey, J. F., & Gray, P. B. (2011). Salivary testosterone levels in men at a U.S. sex club. *Archives of Sexual Behavior, 40,* 921–926.

Escobar-Chaves, S. L., Tortolero, S. R., Markham, C. M., Low, B. J., Eitel, P., & Thickstun, P. (2005). Impact of the media on adolescent sexual attitudes and behaviors. *Pediatrics, 116,* 303–326.

Esposito, G., Yoshida, S., Ohnishi, R., Tsuneoka, Y., Rostagno, M., Yokota, S., . . . Kuroda, K. O. (2013). Infant calming responses during maternal carrying in humans and mice. *Current Biology, 23,* 739–745.

Esser, J. K., & Lindoerfer, J. S. (1989). Groupthink and the space shuttle *Challenger* accident: Toward a quantitative case analysis. *Journal of Behavioral Decision Making, 2,* 167–177.

Esterling, B. A., L'Abate, L., Murray, E. J., & Pennebaker, J. W. (1999). Empirical foundations for writing in prevention and psychotherapy: Mental and physical health outcomes. *Clinical Psychology Review, 19,* 79–96.

Esterson, A. (2001). The mythologizing of psychoanalytic history: Deception and self-deception in Freud's accounts of the seduction theory episode. *History of Psychiatry, 12,* 329–352.

Eurich, T. L., Krause, D. E., Cigularov, K., & Thornton, G. C., III. (2009). Assessment centers: Current practices in the United States. *Journal of Business Psychology, 24,* 387–407.

Euston, D. R., Tatsuno, M., & McNaughton, B. L. (2007). Fast-forward playback of recent memory sequences in prefrontal cortex during sleep. *Science, 318,* 1147–1150.

Evans, C. R., & Dion, K. L. (1991). Group cohesion and performance: A meta-analysis. *Small Group Research, 22,* 175–186.

Evenson, K. R., Wen, F., & Herring, A. H. (2016). Associations of accelerometry-assessed and self-reported physical activity and sedentary behavior with all-cause and cardiovascular mortality among U.S. adults. *American Journal of Epidemiology, 184,* 621–632.

Everaert, J., Bronstein, M. V., Cannon, T. D., & Joormann, J. (2018). Looking through tinted glasses: Depression and social anxiety are related to both interpretation biases and inflexible negative interpretations. *Clinical Psychological Science, 6,* 517–528.

Everett, J. A. C., Caviola, L., Kahane, G., Savulescu, J., & Faber, N. S. (2015). Doing good by doing nothing? The role of social norms in explaining default effects in altruistic contexts. *European Journal of Social Psychology, 45,* 230–241.

Evers, A., Muñiz, J., Bartram, D., Boben, D., Egeland, J., Fernández-Hermida, J. R., . . . Urbánek, T. (2012). Testing practices in the 21st century: Developments and European psychologists' opinions. *European Psychologist, 17,* 300–319.

Everson, S. A., Goldberg, D. E., Kaplan, G. A., Cohen, R. D., Pukkala, E., Tuomilehto, J., & Salonen, J. T. (1996). Hopelessness and risk of mortality and incidence of myocardial infarction and cancer. *Psychosomatic Medicine, 58,* 113–121.

Exelmans, L., Custers, K., & Van den Bulck, J. (2015). Violent video games and delinquent behavior in adolescents: A risk factor perspective. *Aggressive Behavior, 41,* 267–279.

Eysenck, H. J. (1952). The effects of psychotherapy: An evaluation. *Journal of Consulting Psychology, 16,* 319–324.

Eysenck, H. J. (1990, April 30). An improvement on personality inventory. *Current Contents: Social and Behavioral Sciences, 22,* 20.

Eysenck, H. J. (1992). Four ways five factors are *not* basic. *Personality and Individual Differences, 13,* 667–673.

Eysenck, H. J., & Grossarth-Maticek, R. (1991). Creative novation behavior therapy as a prophylactic treatment for cancer and coronary heart disease: Part II—Effects of treatment. *Behaviour Research and Therapy, 29,* 17–31.

Eysenck, H. J., Wakefield, J. A., Jr., & Friedman, A. F. (1983). Diagnosis and clinical assessment: The DSM-III. *Annual Review of Psychology, 34,* 167–193.

Eysenck, S. B. G., & Eysenck, H. J. (1963). The validity of questionnaire and rating assessments of extraversion and neuroticism, and their factorial stability. *British Journal of Psychology, 54,* 51–62.

Fabiano, G. A., Pelham, W. E., Jr., Coles, E. K., Gnagy, E. M., Chronis-Tuscano, A., & O'Connor, B. C. (2008). A meta-analysis of behavioral treatments for attention-deficit/hyperactivity disorder. *Clinical Psychology Review, 29,* 129–140.

Fagan, J. F., & Holland, C. R. (2007). Racial equality in intelligence: Predictions from a theory of intelligence as processing. *Intelligence, 35,* 319–334.

Fagan, J. F., & Holland, C. R. (2009). Culture-fair prediction of academic achievement. *Intelligence, 37,* 62–67.

Faheem, S., Petti, V., & Mellos, G. (2017). Disruptive mood dysregulation disorder and its effect on bipolar disorder. *Annals of Clinical Psychiatry, 29,* e1–e8.

Fairbairn, C. E., & Sayette, M. A. (2014). A social-attributional analysis of alcohol response. *Psychological Bulletin, 140,* 1361–1382.

Fairfield, H. (2012, February 4). Girls lead in science exam, but NOT in the United States. *The New York Times* (nytimes.com).

Fales, M. R., Frederick, D. A., Garcia, J. R., Gildersleeve, K. A., Haselton, M. G., & Fisher, H. E. (2016). Mating markets and bargaining hands: Mate preferences for attractiveness and resources in two national U.S. studies. *Personality and Individual Differences, 88,* 78–87.

Falk, C. F., Heine, S. J., Yuki, M., & Takemura, K. (2009a). Why do Westerners self-enhance more than East Asians? *European Journal of Personality, 23,* 183–203.

Falk, R., Falk, R., & Ayton, P. (2009b). Subjective patterns of randomness and choice: Some consequences of collective responses. *Journal of Experimental Psychology: Human Perception and Performance, 35,* 203–224.

Falkner, A. L., Grosenick, L., Davidson, T. J., Deisseroth, K., & Lin, D. (2016). Hypothalamic control of male aggression-seeking behavior. *Nature Neuroscience, 19,* 596–604.

Fan, W., & Williams, C. (2018). The mediating role of student motivation in the linking of perceived school climate and academic achievement in reading and mathematics. *Frontiers in Education, 3,* 50.

Fanti, K. A., Vanman, E., Henrich, C. C., & Avraamides, M. N. (2009). Desensitization to media violence over a short period of time. *Aggressive Behavior, 35,* 179–187.

Farah, M. J. (2017). The neuroscience of socioeconomic status: Correlates, causes, and consequences. *Neuron, 96,* 56–71.

Farah, M. J., Rabinowitz, C., Quinn, G. E., & Liu, G. T. (2000). Early commitment of neural substrates for face recognition. *Cognitive Neuropsychology, 17,* 117–124.

Farb, N. A. S., Anderson, A. K., Mayberg, H., Bean, J., McKeon, D., & Segal, Z. V. (2010). Minding one's emotions: Mindfulness training alters the neural expression of sadness. *Emotion, 10,* 25–33.

Farina, A. (1982). The stigma of mental disorders. In A. G. Miller (Ed.), *In the eye of the beholder.* New York: Praeger.

Farnia, V., Shakeri, J., Tatari, F., Juibari, T. A., Yazdchi, K., Bajoghli, H., . . . Aghaei, A. (2014). Randomized controlled trial of aripiprazole versus risperidone for the treatment of amphetamine-induced psychosis. *The American Journal of Drug and Alcohol Abuse, 40,* 10–15.

Farr, R. H. (2017). Does parental sexual orientation matter? A longitudinal follow-up of adoptive families with school-age children. *Developmental Psychology, 53,* 252–264.

Farr, R. H., Bruun, S. T., Doss, K. M., & Patterson, C. J. (2018). Children's gender-typed behavior from early to middle childhood in adoptive families with lesbian, gay, and heterosexual parents. *Sex Roles, 78,* 528–541.

Farrington, D. P. (1991). Antisocial personality from childhood to adulthood. *The Psychologist: Bulletin of the British Psychological Society, 4,* 389–394.

Farsalinos, K. E., Kistler, K. A., Gillman, G., & Voudris, V. (2014). Evaluation of electronic cigarette liquids and aerosol for the presence of selected inhalation toxins. *Nicotine and Tobacco Research, 17,* 168–174.

Farstad, S. M., McGeown, L. M., & von Ranson, K. M. (2016). Eating disorders and personality, 2004–2016: A systematic review and meta-analysis. *Clinical Psychology Review, 46,* 91–105.

Fatemi, S. H., & Folsom, T. D. (2009). The neurodevelopmental hypothesis of schizophrenia, revisted. *Schizophrenia Bulletin, 35,* 528–548.

Fattore, L. (2016). Synthetic cannabinoids—further evidence supporting the relationship between cannabinoids and psychosis. *Biological Psychiatry, 79,* 539–548.

Fazel, S., Langstrom, N., Hjern, A., Grann, M., & Lichtenstein, P. (2009). Schizophrenia, substance abuse, and violent crime. *JAMA, 301,* 2016–2023.

Fazel, S., Lichtenstein, P., Grann, M., Goodwin, G. M., & Långström, N. (2010). Bipolar disorder and violent crime: New evidence from population-based longitudinal studies and systematic review. *Archives of General Psychiatry, 67,* 931–938.

Fazio, L. K., Brashier, N. M., Payne, B. K., & Marsh, E. J. (2015). Knowledge does not protect against illusory truth. *Journal of Experimental Psychology: General, 144,* 993–1002.

FBI. (2018). Hate crime statistics. Federal Bureau of Investigation (www.ucr.fbi.gov/hate-crime).

Fedorenko, E., Scott, T. L., Brunner, P., Coon, W. G., Pritchett, B., Schalk, G., & Kanwisher, N. (2016). Neural correlate of the construction of sentence meaning. *PNAS, 113,* E6256–E6262.

Feinberg, T. E., & Mallatt, J. (2016). The nature of primary consciousness: A new synthesis. *Consciousness and Cognition, 43,* 113–127.

Feingold, A. (1992). Good-looking people are not what we think. *Psychological Bulletin, 111,* 304–341.

Feingold, A., & Mazzella, R. (1998). Gender differences in body image are increasing. *Psychological Science, 9,* 190–195.

Feinstein, J. S., Buzza, C., Hurlemann, R., Follmer, R. L., Dahdaleh, N. S., Coryell, W. H., . . . Wemmie, J. A. (2013). Fear and panic in humans with bilateral amygdala damage. *Nature Neuroscience, 16,* 270–272.

Feinstein, J. S., Duff, M. C., & Tranel, D. (2010, April 27). Sustained experiences of emotion after loss of memory in patients with amnesia. *PNAS, 107,* 7674–7679.

Feldman, M. B., & Meyer, I. H. (2010). Comorbidity and age of onset of eating disorders in gay men, lesbians, and bisexuals. *Psychiatry Research, 180,* 126–131.

Feldman, R., Rosenthal, Z., & Eidelman, A. I. (2014). Maternal-preterm skin-to-skin contact enhances child physiologic organization and cognitive control across the first 10 years of life. *Biological Psychiatry, 75,* 56–64.

Fenigstein, A. (2015). Milgram's shock experiments and the Nazi perpetrators: A contrarian perspective on the role of obedience pressures during the Holocaust. *Theory and Psychology, 25,* 581–598.

Fenn, K. M., & Hambrick, D. Z. (2012). Individual differences in working memory capacity predict sleep-dependent memory consolidation. *Journal of Experimental Psychology: General, 141,* 404–410.

Fenton, W. S., & McGlashan, T. H. (1991). Natural history of schizophrenia subtypes: II. Positive and negative symptoms and long-term course. *Archives of General Psychiatry, 48,* 978–986.

Fenton, W. S., & McGlashan, T. H. (1994). Antecedents, symptom progression, and long-term outcome of the deficit syndrome in schizophrenia. *American Journal of Psychiatry, 151,* 351–356.

Ferguson, C. J. (2009, June 14). Not every child is secretly a genius. *The Chronicle Review* (chronicle.com).

Ferguson, C. J. (2013a). Spanking, corporal punishment and negative long-term outcomes: A meta-analytic review of longitudinal studies. *Clinical Psychology Review, 33,* 196–208.

Ferguson, C. J. (2013b). Violent video games and the Supreme Court: Lessons for the scientific community in the wake of *Brown v. Entertainment Merchants Association. American Psychologist, 68,* 57–74.

Ferguson, C. J. (2014). Is video game violence bad? *The Psychologist, 27,* 324–327.

Ferguson, C. J. (2015). Do angry birds make for angry children? A meta-analysis of video game influences on children's and adolescents' aggression, mental health, prosocial behavior, and academic performance. *Perspectives on Psychological Science, 10,* 646–666.

Ferguson, C. J., Winegard, B., & Winegard, B. M. (2011). Who is the fairest one of all? How evolution guides peer and media influences on female body dissatisfaction. *Review of General Psychology, 15,* 11–28.

Ferguson, M. J., & Zayas, V. (2009). Automatic evaluation. *Current Directions in Psychological Science, 18,* 362–366.

Fernández-Dols, J.-M., & Ruiz-Belda, M.-A. (1995). Are smiles a sign of happiness? Gold medal winners at the Olympic Games. *Journal of Personality and Social Psychology, 69,* 1113–1119.

Fernie, G., Peeters, M., Gullo, M. J., Christianson, P., Cole, J. C., Sumnall, H., & Field, M. (2013). Multiple behavioral impulsivity tasks predict prospective alcohol involvement in adolescents. *Addiction, 108,* 1916–1923.

Fernyhough, C. (2008). Getting Vygotskian about theory of mind: Mediation, dialogue, and the development of social understanding. *Developmental Review, 28,* 225–262.

Ferriman, K., Lubinski, D., & Benbow, C. P. (2009). Work preferences, life values, and personal views of top math/science graduate students and the profoundly gifted: Developmental changes and gender differences during emerging adulthood and parenthood. *Journal of Personality and Social Psychology, 97,* 517–522.

Ferris, C. F. (1996, March). The rage of innocents. *The Sciences,* pp. 22–26.

Fetterman, A. K., Wilkowski, B. M., & Robinson, M. D. (2018). On feeling warm and being warm: Daily perceptions of physical warmth fluctuate with interpersonal warmth. *Social Psychological and Personality Science, 9,* 560–567.

Fetvadjiev, V. H., Meiring, D., van de Vijver, F. J., Nel, J. A., Sekaja, L., & Laher, S. (2017). Personality and behavior prediction and consistency across cultures: A multimethod study of blacks and whites in South Africa. *Journal of Personality and Social Psychology, 114,* 465–481.

Fichter, M. M., & Quadflieg, N. (2016). Mortality in eating disorders—results of a large prospective clinical longitudinal study. *International Journal of Eating Disorders, 49,* 391–401.

Ficks, C. A., & Waldman, I. D. (2014). Candidate genes for aggression and antisocial behavior: A meta-analysis of association studies of the 5HTTLPR and MAOA-uVNTR. *Behavior Genetics, 44,* 427–444.

Fiedler, F. E. (1981). Leadership effectiveness. *American Behavioral Scientist, 24,* 619–632.

Fiedler, F. E. (1987, September). When to lead, when to stand back. *Psychology Today,* pp. 26–27.

Field, A. P. (2006). Is conditioning a useful framework for understanding the development and treatment of phobias? *Clinical Psychology Review, 26,* 857–875.

Field, T. (2010). Touch for socioemotional and physical well-being: A review. *Developmental Review, 30,* 367–383.

Fielder, R. L., Walsh, J. L., Carey, K. B., & Carey, M. P. (2013). Predictors of sexual hookups: A theory-based, prospective study of first-year college women. *Archives of Sexual Behavior, 42,* 1425–1441.

Fields, R. D. (2011, May/June). The hidden brain. *Scientific American,* pp. 53–59.

Fikke, L. T., Melinder, A., & Landrø, N. I. (2011). Executive functions are impaired in adolescents engaging in non-suicidal self-injury. *Psychological Medicine, 41,* 601–610.

Fincham, F. D., & Bradbury, T. N. (1993). Marital satisfaction, depression, and attributions: A longitudinal analysis. *Journal of Personality and Social Psychology, 64,* 442–452.

Finer, L. B., & Philbin, J. M. (2014). Trends in ages at key reproductive transitions in the United States, 1951–2010. *Women's Health Issues, 24,* e271–279.

Fingelkurts, A. A., & Fingelkurts, A. A. (2009). Is our brain hardwired to produce God, or is our brain hardwired to perceive God? A systematic review on the role of the brain in mediating religious experience. *Cognitive Processes, 10,* 293–326.

Fingerman, K. L., & Charles, S. T. (2010). It takes two to tango: Why older people have the best relationships. *Current Directions in Psychological Science, 19,* 172–176.

Fink, M. (2009). *Electroconvulsive therapy: A guide for professionals and their patients.* New York: Oxford University Press.

Finkel, E. J. (2017). *The all-or-nothing marriage.* New York: Dutton.

Finkel, E. J., & Eastwick, P. W. (2008). Speed-dating. *Current Directions in Psychological Science, 17,* 193–197.

Finkel, E. J., & Eastwick, P. W. (2009). Arbitrary social norms influence sex differences in romantic selectivity. *Psychological Science, 20,* 1290–1295.

Finkel, E. J., DeWall, C. N., Slotter, E. B., McNulty, J. K., Pond, R. S., Jr., & Atkins, D. C. (2012a). Using I3 theory to clarify when dispositional aggressiveness predicts intimate partner violence perpetration. *Journal of Personality and Social Psychology, 102,* 533–549.

Finkel, E. J., Eastwick, P. W., Karney, B. R., Reis, H. T., & Sprecher, S. (2012b, September/October). Dating in a digital world. *Scientific American Mind,* pp. 26–33.

Finkenauer, C., Buyukcan-Tetik, A., Baumeister, R. F., Schoemaker, K., Bartels, M., & Vohs, K. D. (2015). Out of control: Identifying the role of self-control strength in family violence. *Current Directions in Psychological Science, 24,* 261–266.

Finnigan, K. M., & Vazire, S. (2018). The incremental validity of average state self-reports over global self-reports of personality. *Journal of Personality and Social Psychology, 115,* 321–337.

Fiore, M. C., Jaén, C. R., Baker, T. B., Bailey, W. C., Benowitz, N. L., Curry, S. J., . . . Wewers, M. E. (2008). *Treating tobacco use and dependence: 2008 update. Clinical practice guideline.* Rockville, MD: U.S. Department of Health and Human Services, Public Health Service.

Fischer, A., & LaFrance, M. (2015). What drives the smile and the tear: Why women are more emotionally expressive than men. *Emotion Review, 7,* 22–29.

Fischer, P., & Greitemeyer, T. (2006). Music and aggression: The impact of sexual-aggressive song lyrics on aggression-related thoughts, emotions, and behavior toward the same and the opposite sex. *Personality and Social Psychology Bulletin, 32,* 1165–1176.

Fischer, P., Greitemeyer, T., Kastenmüller, A., Vogrincic, C., & Sauer, A. (2011). The effects of risk-glorifying media exposure on risk-positive cognitions, emotions, and behaviors: A meta-analytic review. *Psychological Bulletin, 137,* 367–390.

Fischer, R., & Boer, D. (2011). What is more important for national well-being: money or autonomy? A meta-analysis of well-being, burnout, and anxiety across 63 societies. *Journal of Personality and Social Psychology, 101,* 164–184.

Fischhoff, B., Slovic, P., & Lichtenstein, S. (1977). Knowing with certainty: The appropriateness of extreme confidence. *Journal of Experimental Psychology: Human Perception and Performance, 3*, 552–564.

Fishbach, A., Dhar, R., & Zhang, Y. (2006). Subgoals as substitutes or complements: The role of goal accessibility. *Journal of Personality and Social Psychology, 91*, 232–242.

Fisher, G., & Rangel, A. (2014). Symmetry in cold-to-hot and hot-to-cold valuation gaps. *Psychological Science, 25*, 120–127.

Fisher, H. E. (1993, March/April). After all, maybe it's biology. *Psychology Today*, pp. 40–45.

Fisher, H. T. (1984). Little Albert and Little Peter. *Bulletin of the British Psychological Society, 37*, 269.

Flack, W. F. (2006). Peripheral feedback effects of facial expressions, bodily postures, and vocal expressions on emotional feelings. *Cognition and Emotion, 20*, 177–195.

Flaherty, D. K. (2011). The vaccine-autism connection: A public health crisis caused by unethical medical practices and fraudulent science. *Annals of Pharmacotherapy, 45*, 1302–1304.

Flegal, K. M., Carroll, M. D., Kit, B. K., & Ogden, C. L. (2012). Prevalence of obesity and trends in the distribution of body mass index among US adults, 1999–2010. *JAMA, 307*, 491–497.

Flegal, K. M., Carroll, M. D., Ogden, C. L., & Curtin, L. R. (2010). Prevalence and trends in obesity among US adults, 1999–2008. *JAMA, 303*, 235–241.

Flegal, K. M., Kruszon-Moran, D., Carroll, M. D., Fryar, C. D., & Ogden, C. L. (2016). Trends in obesity among adults in the United States, 2005 to 2014. *JAMA, 315*, 2284–2291.

Fleming, I., Baum, A., & Weiss, L. (1987). Social density and perceived control as mediator of crowding stress in high-density residential neighborhoods. *Journal of Personality and Social Psychology, 52*, 899–906.

Fleming, J. H. (2001, Winter/Spring). Introduction to the special issue on linkage analysis. *Gallup Research Journal*, pp. i–vi.

Fleming, J. H., & Scott, B. A. (1991). The costs of confession: The Persian Gulf War POW tapes in historical and theoretical perspective. *Contemporary Social Psychology, 15*, 127–138.

Fletcher, G. J. O., Fitness, J., & Blampied, N. M. (1990). The link between attributions and happiness in close relationships: The roles of depression and explanatory style. *Journal of Social and Clinical Psychology, 9*, 243–255.

Flora, S. R. (2004). *The power of reinforcement*. Albany, NY: SUNY Press.

Flora, S. R., & Bobby, S. E. (2008, September/October). The bipolar bamboozle. *Skeptical Inquirer*, pp. 41–45.

Flores, A. R., Herman, J. L., Gates, G. J., & Brown, T. N. T. (2016, June). *How many adults identify as transgender in the United States?* Los Angeles, CA: Williams Institute.

Flueckiger, L., Lieb, R., Meyer, A., Witthauer, C., & Mata, J. (2016). The importance of physical activity and sleep for affect on stressful days: Two intensive longitudinal studies. *Emotion, 16*(4), 488–497.

Flynn, J. R. (2012). *Are we getting smarter? Rising IQ in the twenty-first century*. Cambridge: Cambridge University Press.

Flynn, J. R. (2018). Reflections about intelligence over 40 years. *Intelligence, 70*, 73–83.

Flynn, M. (2018, November 5). 'I wanted him to feel compassion': The Jewish nurse who treated the synagogue shooting suspect tells his story. *The Washington Post* (washingtonpost.com).

Foa, E. B., & Kozak, M. J. (1986). Emotional processing of fear: Exposure to corrective information. *Psychological Bulletin, 99*, 20–35.

Foa, E. B., & McLean, C. P. (2016). The efficacy of exposure therapy for anxiety-related disorders and its underlying mechanisms: The case of OCD and PTSD. *Annual Review of Clinical Psychology, 12*, 1–28.

Foer, J. (2011). *Moonwalking with Einstein: The art and science of remembering everything*. New York: Penguin.

Foley, M. A. (2015). Setting the records straight: Impossible memories and the persistence of their phenomenological qualities. *Review of General Psychology, 19*, 230–248.

Foley, R. T., Whitwell, R. L., & Goodale, M. A. (2015). The two-visual-systems hypothesis and the perspectival features of visual experience. *Consciousness and Cognition, 35*, 225–233.

Fong, C. J., Zaleski, D. J., & Leach, J. K. (2015). The challenge–skill balance and antecedents of flow: A meta-analytic investigation. *Journal of Positive Psychology, 10*, 425–446.

Fong, K., & Mar, R. A. (2015). What does my avatar say about me? Inferring personality from avatars. *Personality and Social Psychology Bulletin, 41*, 237–249.

Forbes, L., Graham, J., Berglund, C., & Bell, R. (2018). Dietary change during pregnancy and women's reasons for change. *Nutrients, 10*, 1032.

Forbes, M. K., Eaton, N. R., & Krueger, R. F. (2017). Sexual quality of life and aging: A prospective study of a nationally representative sample. *Journal of Sex Research, 54*, 137–148.

Ford, E. S. (2002). Does exercise reduce inflammation? Physical activity and B-reactive protein among U.S. adults. *Epidemiology, 13*, 561–569.

Ford, M. T., Cerasoli, C. P., Higgins, J. A., & Deccesare, A. L. (2011). Relationships between psychological, physical, and behavioural health and work performance: A review and meta-analysis. *Work & Stress, 25*, 185–204.

Foree, D. D., & LoLordo, V. M. (1973). Attention in the pigeon: Differential effects of food-getting versus shock-avoidance procedures. *Journal of Comparative and Physiological Psychology, 85*, 551–558.

Forest, A. L., Kille, D. R, Wood, J. V., & Stehouwer, L. R. (2015). Turbulent times, rocky relationships: Relational consequences of experiencing physical instability. *Psychological Science, 26*, 1261–1271.

Forgas, J. (2017, May 14). Why bad moods are good for you: The surprising benefits of sadness. *The Conversation* (theconversation.com).

Forgas, J. P. (2008). Affect and cognition. *Perspectives on Psychological Science, 3*, 94–101.

Forgas, J. P. (2009, November/December). Think negative! *Australian Science*, pp. 14–17.

Forgas, J. P., Bower, G. H., & Krantz, S. E. (1984). The influence of mood on perceptions of social interactions. *Journal of Experimental Social Psychology, 20*, 497–513.

Forrin, N. D., & MacLeod, C. M. (2018). This time it's personal: The memory benefit of hearing oneself. *Memory, 26*, 574–579.

Forsyth, D. R., Lawrence, N. K., Burnette, J. L., & Baumeister, R. F. (2007). Attempting to improve academic performance of struggling college students by bolstering their self-esteem: An intervention that backfired. *Journal of Social and Clinical Psychology, 26*, 447–459.

Foss, D. J., & Hakes, D. T. (1978). *Psycholinguistics: An introduction to the psychology of language*. Englewood Cliffs, NJ: Prentice-Hall.

Foss, D. J., & Pirozzolo, J. W. (2017). Four semesters investigating frequency of testing, the testing effect, and transfer of training. *Journal of Educational Psychology, 109*, 1067.

Foster, J. (2011). Our deadly anorexic pact. *The Daily Mail* (dailymail.co.uk).

Fothergill, E., Guo, J., Howard, L., Kerns, J. C., Knuth, J. D., Brychta, R., . . . Hall, K. D. K. (2016). Persistent metabolic adaptation 6 years after "The Biggest Loser" competition. *Obesity, 24*, 1612–1619.

Foubert, J. D., Brosi, M. W., & Bannon, R. S. (2011). Pornography viewing among fraternity men: Effects on bystander intervention, rape myth acceptance, and behavioral intent to commit sexual assault. *Sexual Addiction & Compulsivity, 18*, 212–231.

Foulkes, D. (1999). *Children's dreaming and the development of consciousness*. Cambridge, MA: Harvard University Press.

Fournier, J. C., DeRubeis, R. J., Hollon, S. D., Dimidjian, S., Amsterdam, J. D., Shelton, R. C., & Fawcett, J. (2010). Antidepressant drug effects and depression severity: A patient-level meta-analysis. *Journal of the American Medical Association, 303*, 47–53.

Fouts, R. S. (1992). Transmission of a human gestural language in a chimpanzee mother-infant relationship. *Friends of Washoe, 12/13*, pp. 2–8.

Fouts, R. S. (1997). *Next of kin: What chimpanzees have taught me about who we are*. New York: Morrow.

Fowles, D. C. (1992). Schizophrenia: Diathesis-stress revisited. *Annual Review of Psychology, 43*, 303–336.

Fowles, D. C., & Dindo, L. (2009). Temperament and psychopathy: A dual-pathway model. *Current Directions in Psychological Science, 18*, 179–183.

Fox, A. S., Oler, J. A., Shackman, A. J., Shelton, S. E., Raveendran, M., McKay, D. R., . . . Rogers, J. (2015). Intergenerational neural mediators of early-life anxious temperament. *PNAS, 112*, 9118–9122.

Fox, B. H. (1998). Psychosocial factors in cancer incidence and prognosis. In J. C. Holland (Ed.), *Psycho-oncology* (pp. 110–124). New York: Oxford University Press.

Fox, D. (2010, June). The insanity virus. *Discover*, pp. 58–64.

Fox, E., Lester, V., Russo, R., Bowles, R. J., Pichler, A., & Dutton, K. (2000). Facial expression of emotion: Are angry faces detected more efficiently? *Cognition and Emotion, 14*, 61–92.

Fox, M. L., Dwyer, D. J., & Ganster, D. C. (1993). Effects of stressful job demands and control on physiological and attitudinal outcomes in a hospital setting. *Academy of Management Journal, 36*, 289–318.

Fox, N. A., Bakermans-Kranenburg, M., Yoo, K. H., Bowman, L. C., Cannon, E. N., Vanderwert, R. E., . . . van IJzendoorn, M. H. (2016). Assessing human mirror activity with EEG mu rhythm: A meta-analysis. *Psychological Bulletin, 142*, 291–313.

Fraley, R. C., & Tancredy, C. M. (2012). Twin and sibling attachment in a nationally representative sample. *Personality and Social Psychology Bulletin, 38*, 308–316.

Fraley, R. C., Roisman, G. I., Booth-LaForce, C., Owen, M. T., & Holland, A. S. (2013). Interpersonal and genetic origins of adult attachment styles: A longitudinal study from infancy to early adulthood. *Journal of Personality and Social Psychology, 104*, 817–838.

Fraley, R. C., Vicary, A. M., Brumbaugh, C. C., & Roisman, G. I. (2011). Patterns of stability in adult attachment: An empirical test of two models of continuity and change. *Journal of Personality and Social Psychology, 101*, 974–992.

Frances, A. J. (2013). *Saving normal: An insider's revolt against out-of-control psychiatric diagnosis, DSM-5, Big Pharma, and the medicalization of ordinary life.* New York: HarperCollins.

Frances, A. J. (2014, September/October). No child left undiagnosed. *Psychology Today,* pp. 49–50.

Frank, J. D. (1982). Therapeutic components shared by all psychotherapies. In J. H. Harvey & M. M. Parks (Eds.), *The Master Lecture Series: Vol. 1. Psychotherapy research and behavior change.* Washington, DC: American Psychological Association.

Frankenburg, W., Dodds, J., Archer, P., Shapiro, H., & Bresnick, B. (1992). The Denver II: A major revision and restandardization of the Denver Developmental Screening Test. *Pediatrics, 89,* 91–97.

Frankl, V. E. (1962). *Man's search for meaning: An introduction to logotherapy.* Boston: Beacon Press.

Franklin, M., & Foa, E. B. (2011). Treatment of obsessive-compulsive disorder. *Annual Review of Clinical Psychology, 7,* 229–243.

Frasure-Smith, N., & Lesperance, F. (2005). Depression and coronary heart disease: Complex synergism of mind, body, and environment. *Current Directions in Psychological Science, 14,* 39–43.

Frattaroli, J. (2006). Experimental disclosure and its moderators: A meta-analysis. *Psychological Bulletin, 132,* 823–865.

Fredrickson, B. L. (2013). Updated thinking on positivity ratios. *American Psychologist, 68,* 814–822.

Freedman, D. H. (2011, February). How to fix the obesity crisis. *Scientific American,* pp. 40–47.

Freedman, D. J., Riesenhuber, M., Poggio, T., & Miller, E. K. (2001). Categorical representation of visual stimuli in the primate prefrontal cortex. *Science, 291,* 312–316.

Freedman, J. L., & Perlick, D. (1979). Crowding, contagion, and laughter. *Journal of Experimental Social Psychology, 15,* 295–303.

Freedman, R., Lewis, D. A., Michels, R., Pine, D. S., Schultz, S. K., Tamminga, C. A., . . . Yager, J. (2013). The initial field trials of DSM-5: New blooms and old thorns. *American Journal of Psychiatry, 170,* 1–5.

Freeman, D., & Freeman, J. (2013). *The stressed sex: Uncovering the truth about men, women, and mental health.* Oxford, England: Oxford University Press.

Freeman, D., Haselton, P., Freeman, J., Spanlang, B., Kishore, S., Albery, E., . . . Nickless, A. (2018). Automated psychological therapy using immersive virtual reality for treatment of fear of heights: A single-blind, parallel-group, randomised controlled trial. *The Lancet Psychiatry, 5,* 625–632.

Freeman, E. C., & Twenge, J. M. (2010, January). *Using MySpace increases the endorsement of narcissistic personality traits.* Poster presented at the annual conference of the Society for Personality and Social Psychology, Las Vegas, NV.

Freeman, S., Eddy, S. L., McDonough, M., Smith, M. K., Okoroafor, N., Jordt, H., & Wenderoth, M. P. (2014). Active learning increases student performance in science, engineering, and mathematics. *PNAS, 111,* 8410–8415.

Freeman, W. J. (1991, February). The physiology of perception. *Scientific American,* pp. 78–85.

Frenda, S. J., Patihis, L., Loftus, E. F., Lewis, H. C., & Fenn, K. M. (2014). Sleep deprivation and false memories. *Clinical Psychological Science, 25,* 1674–1681.

Freyd, J. J., DePrince, A. P., & Gleaves, D. H. (2007). The state of betrayal trauma theory: Reply to McNally—Conceptual issues and future directions. *Memory, 15,* 295–311.

Friedel, J. E., DeHart, W. B., Madden, G. J., & Odum, A. L. (2014). Impulsivity and cigarette smoking: Discounting of monetary and consumable outcomes in current and non-smokers. *Psychopharmacology, 231,* 4517–4526.

Friedman, H. S., & Martin, L. R. (2012). *The longevity project.* New York: Penguin (Plume).

Friedman, M., & Ulmer, D. (1984). *Treating Type A behavior—and your heart.* New York: Knopf.

Friedman, R. A. (2012, December 17). In gun debate, a misguided focus on mental illness. *The New York Times* (nytimes.com).

Friedman, R. A. (2017, October 11). Psychiatrists can't stop mass killers. *The New York Times* (nytimes.com).

Friedman, R., & James, J. W. (2008). The myth of the stages of dying, death and grief. *Skeptic, 14,* 37–41.

Friedrich, M., Wilhelm, I., Born, J., & Friederici, A. D. (2015). Generalization of word meanings during infant sleep. *Nature Communications, 6,* Article 6004.

Friend, T. (2004). *Animal talk: Breaking the codes of animal language.* New York: Free Press.

Friesen, J. P., Campbell, T. H., & Kay, A. C. (2015). The psychological advantage of unfalsifiability: The appeal of untestable religious and political ideologies. *Journal of Personality and Social Psychology, 108,* 515–529.

Frisell, T., Pawitan, Y., Långström, N., & Lichtenstein, P. (2012). Heritability, assortative mating and gender differences in violent crime: Results from a total population sample using twin, adoption, and sibling models. *Behavior Genetics, 42,* 3–18.

Frith, U., & Frith, C. (2001). The biological basis of social interaction. *Current Directions in Psychological Science, 10,* 151–155.

Fritz, N., & Paul, B. (2018). From orgasms to spanking: A content analysis of the agentic and objectifying sexual scripts in feminist, for women, and mainstream pornography, *Sex Roles, 77,* 639–652.

Fromkin, V., & Rodman, R. (1983). *An introduction to language* (3rd ed.). New York: Holt, Rinehart & Winston.

Frühauf, S., Gerger, H., Schmidt, H. M., Munder, T., & Barth, J. (2013). Efficacy of psychological interventions for sexual dysfunction: A systematic review and meta-analysis. *Archives of Sexual Behavior, 42,* 915–933.

Fry, A. F., & Hale, S. (1996). Processing speed, working memory, and fluid intelligence: Evidence for a developmental cascade. *Psychological Science, 7,* 237–241.

Fry, D. P. (2012). Life without war. *Science, 336,* 879–884.

Fry, R. (2017, May 5). It's becoming more common for young adults to live at home—and for longer stretches. Pew Research Center (pewresearch.org).

Fuhrmann, D., Knoll, L. J., & Blakemore, S. J. (2015). Adolescence as a sensitive period of brain development. *Trends in Cognitive Sciences,* 19(10), 558–566.

Fuller, T. D., Edwards, J. N., Sermsri, S., & Vorakitphokatorn, S. (1993). Housing, stress, and physical well-being: Evidence from Thailand. *Social Science & Medicine, 36,* 1417–1428.

Fuller-Thomson, E., Agbeyaka, S., LaFond, D. M., & Bern-Klug, M. (2016). Flourishing after depression: Factors associated with achieving complete mental health among those with a history of depression. *Psychiatry Research, 242,* 111–120.

Fulmer, C. A., Gelfand, M. J., Kruglanski, A. W., Kim-Prieto, C., Diener, E., Pierro, A., & Higgins, E. T. (2010). On "feeling right" in cultural contexts: How person–culture match affects self-esteem and subjective well-being. *Psychological Science, 21,* 1563–1569.

Funder, D. C., & Block, J. (1989). The role of ego-control, ego-resiliency, and IQ in delay of gratification in adolescence. *Journal of Personality and Social Psychology, 57,* 1041–1050.

Furnham, A. (1982). Explanations for unemployment in Britain. *European Journal of Social Psychology, 12,* 335–352.

Furnham, A. (2016). Whether you think you can, or you think you can't—you're right. In R. J. Sternberg, S. T. Fiske, & D. J. Foss (Eds.), *Scientists making a difference: One hundred eminent behavioral and brain scientists talk about their most important contributions.* New York: Cambridge University Press.

Furnham, A., & Baguma, P. (1994). Cross-cultural differences in the evaluation of male and female body shapes. *International Journal of Eating Disorders, 15,* 81–89.

Furr, R. M., & Funder, D. C. (1998). A multimodal analysis of personal negativity. *Journal of Personality and Social Psychology, 74,* 1580–1591.

Furukawa, T. A., Levine, S. Z., Tanaka, S., Goldberg, Y., Samara, M., Davis, J. M., . . . Leucht, S. (2015). Initial severity of schizophrenia and efficacy of antipsychotics: Participant-level meta-analysis of 6 placebo-controlled studies. *JAMA Psychiatry, 72,* 14–21.

Fuss, J., Steinle, J., Bindila, L., Auer, M. K., Kirchherr, H., Lutz, B., & Gass, P. (2015). A runner's high depends on cannabinoid receptors in mice. *PNAS, 112,* 13105–13108.

Futrell, R., Mahowald, K., & Gibson, E. (2015). Large-scale evidence of dependency length minimization in 37 languages. *PNAS, 112,* 10336–10341.

Gaddy, M. A., & Ingram, R. E. (2014). A meta-analytic review of mood-congruent implicit memory in depressed mood. *Clinical Psychology Review, 34,* 402–416.

Gaertner, L., Iuzzini, J., & O'Mara, E. M. (2008). When rejection by one fosters aggression against many: Multiple-victim aggression as a consequence of social rejection and perceived groupness. *Journal of Experimental Social Psychology, 44,* 958–970.

Gaissmaier, W., & Gigerenzer, G. (2012). 9/11, Act II: A fine-grained analysis of regional variations in traffic fatalities in the aftermath of the terrorist attacks. *Psychological Science, 23,* 1449–1454.

Gaither, S. E., & Sommers, S. R. (2013). Living with another-race roommate shapes whites' behavior in subsequent diverse settings. *Journal of Experimental Social Psychology, 49,* 272–276.

Galak, J., Leboeuf, R. A., Nelson, L. D., & Simmons, J. P. (2012). Correcting the past: Failures to replicate psi. *Journal of Personality and Social Psychology, 103,* 933–948.

Galambos, N. L. (1992). Parent-adolescent relations. *Current Directions in Psychological Science, 1,* 146–149.

Galanter, E. (1962). Contemporary psychophysics. In R. Brown, E. Galanter, E. H. Hess, & G. Mandler (Eds.), *New directions in psychology.* New York: Holt Rinehart & Winston.

Gale, C. R., Batty, G. D., & Deary, I. J. (2008). Locus of control at age 10 years and health outcomes and behaviors at age 30 years: The 1970 British Cohort Study. *Psychosomatic Medicine, 70,* 397–403.

Galinsky, A. M., & Sonenstein, F. L. (2013). Relationship commitment, perceived equity, and sexual enjoyment among young adults in the United States. *Archives of Sexual Behavior, 42,* 93–104.

Galla, B. M., & Duckworth, A. L. (2015). More than resisting temptation: Beneficial habits mediate the relationship between self-control and positive life outcomes. *Journal of Personality and Social Psychology, 109,* 508–525.

Gallace, A. (2012). Living with touch. *The Psychologist, 25,* 896–899.

Gallace, A., & Spence, C. (2011). To what extent do Gestalt grouping principles influence tactile perception? *Psychological Bulletin, 137,* 538–561.

Gallese, V., Gernsbacher, M. A., Heyes, C., Hickok, G., & Iacoboni, M. (2011). Mirror neuron forum. *Perspectives on Psychological Science, 6,* 369–407.

Gallup. (2004, August 16). 65% of Americans receive NO praise or recognition in the workplace. E-mail from Tom Rath: bucketbook@gallup.com.

Gallup. (2016). *Islamophobia: Understanding anti-Muslim sentiment in the West.* Gallup News (news.gallup.com).

Gallup. (2017). *State of the global workplace.* Gallup (gallup.com).

Gallup, G. G., Jr., & Frederick, D. A. (2010). The science of sex appeal: An evolutionary perspective. *Review of General Psychology, 14,* 240–250.

Gallup, G. H. (1972). *The Gallup poll: Public opinion 1935–1971* (Vol. 3). New York: Random House.

Gandhi, A. V., Mosser, E. A., Oikonomou, G., & Prober, D. A. (2015). Melatonin is required for the circadian regulation of sleep. *Neuron, 85,* 1193–1199.

Gandhi, T. K., Ganesh, S., & Sinha, P. (2014). Improvement in spatial imagery following sight onset late in childhood. *Psychological Science, 25,* 693–701.

Gandhi, T. K., Singh, A. K., Swami, P., Ganesh, S., & Sinha, P. (2017). Emergence of categorical face perception after extended early-onset blindness. *PNAS, 114,* 6139–6143.

Gangestad, S. W., Thornhill, R., & Garver-Apgar, C. E. (2010). Men's facial masculinity predicts changes in their female partners' sexual interests across the ovulatory cycle, whereas men's intelligence does not. *Evolution and Human Behavior, 31,* 412–424.

Gangwisch, J. E., Babiss, L. A., Malaspina, D., Turner, J. B., Zammit, G. K., & Posner, K. (2010). Earlier parental set bedtimes as a protective factor against depression and suicidal ideation. *Sleep, 33,* 97–106.

Gao, Y., Raine, A., Venables, P. H., Dawson, M. E., & Mednick, S. A. (2010). Association of poor child fear conditioning and adult crime. *American Journal of Psychiatry, 167,* 56–60.

Garcia-Falgueras, A., & Swaab, D. F. (2010). Sexual hormones and the brain: An essential alliance for sexual identity and sexual orientation. *Endocrine Development, 17,* 22–35.

Garcia, J. R., Reiber, C., Massey, S. G., & Merriwether, A. M. (2013, February). Sexual hook-up culture. *Monitor on Psychology,* pp. 60–66.

Garcia, J., & Gustavson, A. R. (1997, January). Carl R. Gustavson (1946–1996): Pioneering wildlife psychologist. *APS Observer,* pp. 34–35.

Garcia, J., & Koelling, R. A. (1966). Relation of cue to consequence in avoidance learning. *Psychonomic Science, 4,* 123–124.

Gardner, H. (1983). *Frames of mind: The theory of multiple intelligences.* New York: Basic Books.

Gardner, H. (1998, March 19). An intelligent way to progress. *The Independent* (London), p. E4.

Gardner, H. (1999). *Multiple views of multiple intelligence.* New York: Basic Books.

Gardner, H. (2006). *The development and education of the mind: The selected works of Howard Gardner.* New York: Routledge/Taylor & Francis.

Gardner, H. (2011). *The theory of multiple intelligences: As psychology, as education, as social science.* Address on the receipt of an honorary degree from José Cela University in Madrid and the Prince of Asturias Prize for Social Science.

Gardner, J., & Oswald, A. J. (2007). Money and mental well-being: A longitudinal study of medium-sized lottery wins. *Journal of Health Economics, 6,* 49–60.

Gardner, R. A., & Gardner, B. I. (1969). Teaching sign language to a chimpanzee. *Science, 165,* 664–672.

Garfield, C. (1986). *Peak performers: The new heroes of American business.* New York: Morrow.

Garon, N., Bryson, S. E., & Smith, I. M. (2008). Executive function in preschoolers: A review using an integrative framework. *Psychological Bulletin,134,* 31–60.

Garry, M., Loftus, E. F., & Brown, S. W. (1994). Memory: A river runs through it. *Consciousness and Cognition, 3,* 438–451.

Gartrell, N., & Bos, H. (2010). U.S. national longitudinal lesbian family study: Psychological adjustment of 17-year-old adolescents. *Pediatrics, 126,* 28–36.

Gaskins, A. J., Rich-Edwards, J. W., Williams, P. L., Toth, T. L., Missmer, S. A., & Chavarro, J. E. (2018). Pre-pregnancy caffeine and caffeinated beverage intake and risk of spontaneous abortion. *European Journal of Nutrition, 57,* 107–117.

Gatchel, R. J., Peng, Y. B., Peters, M. L., Fuchs, P. N., & Turk, D. C. (2007). The biopsychosocial approach to chronic pain: Scientific advances and future directions. *Psychological Bulletin, 133,* 581–624.

Gavin, K. (2004, November 9). *U-M team reports evidence that smoking affects human brain's natural "feel good" chemical system* [Press release]. Retrieved from med .umich.edu/

Gazzaniga, M. S. (1967, August). The split brain in man. *Scientific American,* pp. 24–29.

Gazzaniga, M. S. (1983). Right hemisphere language following brain bisection: A 20-year perspective. *American Psychologist, 38,* 525–537.

Gazzaniga, M. S. (1988). Organization of the human brain. *Science, 245,* 947–952.

Gazzaniga, M. S. (2016). *Tales from both sides of the brain: A life in neuroscience.* New York: Ecco.

Gazzola, V., Spezio, M. L., Etzel, J. A., Catelli, F., Adolphs, R., & Keysers, C. (2012). Primary somatosensory cortex discriminates affective significance in social touch. *PNAS, 109,* E1657–E1666.

GBD. (2017). Smoking prevalence and attributable disease burden in 195 countries and territories, 1990–2015: A systematic analysis from the Global Burden of Disease Study 2015. *The Lancet, 389,* 1885–1906.

GBD 2015 Obesity Collaborators. (2017). Health effects of overweight and obesity in 195 countries over 25 years. *New England Journal of Medicine, 377,* 13–27.

Ge, X., & Natsuaki, M. N. (2009). In search of explanations for early pubertal timing effects on developmental psychopathology. *Current Directions in Psychological Science, 18,* 327–441.

Ge, Y., Knittel, C. R., MacKenzie, D., & Zoepf, S. (2016, October). *Racial and gender discrimination in transportation network companies.* NBER Working Paper No. 22776. Retrieved from nber.org/papers/w2276

Geary, D. C. (1996). Sexual selection and sex differences in mathematical abilities. *Behavioral and Brain Sciences, 19,* 229–247.

Gecewicz, C. (2018, October 1). 'New Age' beliefs common among both religious and nonreligious Americans. Pew Research Center (www.pewresearch.org).

Gehring, W. J., Wimke, J., & Nisenson, L. G. (2000). Action monitoring dysfunction in obsessive-compulsive disorder. *Psychological Science, 11,* 1–6.

Geier, A. B., Rozin, P., & Doros, G. (2006). Unit bias: A new heuristic that helps explain the effects of portion size on food intake. *Psychological Science, 17,* 521–525.

Gellis, L. A., Arigo, D., & Elliott, J. C. (2013). Cognitive refocusing treatment for insomnia: A randomized controlled trial in university students. *Behavior Therapy, 44,* 100–110.

Gentile, D. A. (2009). Pathological video-game use among youth ages 8 to 18: A national study. *Psychological Science, 20,* 594–602.

Gentile, D. A., & Bushman, B. J. (2012). Reassessing media violence effects using a risk and resilience approach to understanding aggression. *Psychology of Popular Media Culture, 1,* 138–151.

Gentile, D. A., Coyne, S., & Walsh, D. A. (2011). Media violence, physical aggression and relational aggression in school age children: A short-term longitudinal study. *Aggressive Behavior, 37,* 193–206.

Gentzkow, M., Shapiro, J. M., & Taddy, M. (2016, July). *Measuring polarization in high-dimensional data: Method and application to congressional speech.* NBER Working Paper 22423. Retrieved from nber.org/papers /w22423

Geraerts, E., Bernstein, D. M., Merckelbach, H., Linders, C., Raymaekers, L., & Loftus, E. F. (2008). Lasting false beliefs and their behavioral consequences. *Psychological Science, 19,* 749–753.

Geraerts, E., Schooler, J. W., Merckelbach, H., Jelicic, M., Hauer, B. J. A., & Ambadar, Z. (2007). The reality of recovered memories: Corroborating continuous and discontinuous memories of childhood sexual abuse. *Psychological Science, 18,* 564–568.

Gerber, J., & Wheeler, L. (2009). On being rejected: A meta-analysis of experimental research on rejection. *Perspectives on Psychological Science, 4,* 468–488.

Germain, A. (2013). Sleep disturbances as the hallmark of PTSD: Where are we now? *Archives of Journal of Psychiatry, 170,* 372–382.

Gershoff, E. T., & Grogan-Kaylor, A. (2016). Spanking and child outcomes: Old controversies and new meta-analyses. *Journal of Family Psychology, 30,* 453–469.

Gershoff, E. T., Grogan-Kaylor, A., Lansford, J. E., Chang, L., Zelli, A., Deater-Deckard, K., & Dodge, K. A. (2010). Parent discipline practices in an international sample: Associations with child behaviors and moderation by perceived normativeness. *Child Development, 81,* 487–502.

Gershoff, E. T., Sattler, K. M. P., & Ansari, A. (2018). Strengthening causal estimates for links between spanking and children's externalizing behavior problems. *Psychological Science, 29,* 110–120.

Gershon, A., Ram, N., Johnson, S. L., Harvey, A. G., & Zeitzer, J. M. (2016). Daily actigraphy profiles distinguish depressive and interepisode states in bipolar disorder. *Clinical Psychological Science, 4,* 641–650.

Geukes, K., Nestler, S., Hutteman, R., Dufner, M., Küfner, A. C., Egloff, B., . . . Back, M. D. (2016). Puffed-up but shaky selves: State self-esteem level and variability in narcissists. *Journal of Personality and Social Psychology, 11,* 769–786.

Giancola, P. R., & Corman, M. D. (2007). Alcohol and aggression: A test of the attention-allocation model. *Psychological Science, 18,* 649–655.

Giancola, P. R., Josephs, R. A., Parrott, D. J., & Duke, A. A. (2010). Alcohol myopia revisited: Clarifying aggression and other acts of disinhibition through a distorted lens. *Perspectives on Psychological Science, 5,* 265–278.

Gibbons, F. X. (1986). Social comparison and depression: Company's effect on misery. *Journal of Personality and Social Psychology, 51,* 140–148.

Gibson, E. J., & Walk, R. D. (1960, April). The "visual cliff." *Scientific American*, pp. 64–71.

Giesbrecht, T., Lynn, S. J., Lilienfeld, S. O., & Merckelbach, H. (2008). Cognitive processes in dissociation: An analysis of core theoretical assumptions. *Psychological Bulletin, 134*, 617–647.

Giesbrecht, T., Lynn, S. J., Lilienfeld, S. O., & Merckelbach, H. (2010). Cognitive processes, trauma, and dissociation—Misconceptions and misrepresentations: Reply to Bremmer (2010). *Psychological Bulletin, 136*, 7–11.

Gigerenzer, G. (2004). Dread risk, September 11, and fatal traffic accidents. *Psychological Science, 15*, 286–287.

Gigerenzer, G. (2006). Out of the frying pan into the fire: Behavioral reactions to terrorist attacks. *Risk Analysis, 26*, 347–351.

Gigerenzer, G. (2010). *Rationality for mortals: How people cope with uncertainty*. New York: Oxford University Press.

Gigerenzer, G. (2015). *Simply rational: Decision making in the real world*. New York: Oxford University Press.

Gilbert, D. T. (2006). *Stumbling on happiness*. New York: Knopf.

Gilbert, D. T., King, G., Pettigrew, S., & Wilson, T. D. (2016). Comment on "Estimating the reproducibility of psychological science." *Science, 351*, 1037.

Gillen-O'Neel, C., Huynh, V. W., & Fuligni, A. J. (2013). To study or to sleep? The academic costs of extra studying at the expense of sleep. *Child Development, 84*, 133–142.

Gilligan, C. (1982). *In a different voice: Psychological theory and women's development*. Cambridge, MA: Harvard University Press

Gilligan, C. (2015). In a different voice: Women's conceptions of self and morality. In V. Burr (Ed.), *Gender and psychology* (Vol. II, pp. 33–74). New York: Routledge/Taylor & Francis Group.

Gilmore, R. O., & Adolph, K. E. (2017). Video can make behavioural science more reproducible. *Nature Human Behaviour, 1*, s41562–017.

Gilovich, T. (1991). *How we know what isn't so: The fallibility of human reason in everyday life*. New York: Free Press.

Gilovich, T. D. (1996). *The spotlight effect: Exaggerated impressions of the self as a social stimulus*. Unpublished manuscript, Cornell University.

Gilovich, T. D., & Medvec, V. H. (1995). The experience of regret: What, when, and why. *Psychological Review, 102*, 379–395.

Gilovich, T. D., & Savitsky, K. (1999). The spotlight effect and the illusion of transparency: Egocentric assessments of how we are seen by others. *Current Directions in Psychological Science, 8*, 165–168.

Gingerich, O. (1999, February 6). *Is there a role for natural theology today?* Retrieved from http://www.origins.org/real/n9501/natural.html

Gino, G., Wilmuth, C. A., & Brooks, A. W. (2015). Compared to men, women view professional advancement as equally attainable, but less desirable. *PNAS, 112*, 12354–12359.

Giuliano, T. A., Barnes, L. C., Fiala, S. E., & Davis, D. M. (1998). *An empirical investigation of male answer syndrome*. Paper presented at the Southwestern Psychological Association convention.

Glasman, L. R., & Albarracin, D. (2006). Forming attitudes that predict future behavior: A meta-analysis of the attitude-behavior relation. *Psychological Bulletin, 132*, 778–822.

Glass, R. M. (2001). Electroconvulsive therapy: Time to bring it out of the shadows. *Journal of the American Medical Association, 285*, 1346–1348.

Glasser, M. F., Coalson, T. S., Robinson, E. C., Hacker, C. D., Harwell, J., Yacoub, E., . . . Van Essen, D. C. (2016). A multi-modal parcellation of human cerebral cortex. *Nature, 536*, 171–178.

Gleaves, D. H. (1996). The sociocognitive model of dissociative identity disorder: A reexamination of the evidence. *Psychological Bulletin, 120*, 42–59.

Glenn, A. L., Raine, A. (2014). Neurocriminology: Implications for the punishment, prediction and prevention of criminal behavior. *Nature Reviews Neuroscience, 15*, 54–63.

Gliklich, E., Guo, R., & Bergmark, R. W. (2016). Texting while driving: A study of 1211 U.S. adults with the Distracted Driving Survey. *Preventive Medicine Reports, 4*, 486–489.

Global Burden of Disease Study 2013 Collaborators. (2015). Global, regional, and national incidence, prevalence, and years lived with disability for 301 acute and chronic diseases and injuries in 188 countries, 1990–2013: A systematic analysis for the Global Burden of Disease Study 2013. *The Lancet, 386*, 743–800.

Glocalities. (2018). Majority of humanity say we are not alone in the universe. Retrieved from glocalities.com/reports/majority-of-humanity-say-we-are-not-alone-in-the-universe

GLSEN. (2012). *The 2011 national school climate survey*. New York: Gay, Lesbian & Straight Education Network (glsen.org).

Glynn, T. R., Gamarel, K. E., Kahler, C. W., Iwamoto, M., Operario, D., & Nemoto, T. (2017). The role of gender affirmation in psychological well-being among transgender women. *Psychology of Sexual Orientation and Gender Diversity, 3*, 336–344.

Gnambs, T., & Appel, M. (2018). Narcissism and social networking behavior: A meta-analysis. *Journal of Personality, 86*, 200–212.

Godart, F. C., Maddux, W. W., Shipilov, A. V., & Galinsky, A. D. (2015). Fashion with a foreign flair: Professional experiences abroad facilitate the creative innovations of organizations. *Academy of Management Journal, 58*, 195–220.

Godden, D. R., & Baddeley, A. D. (1975). Context-dependent memory in two natural environments: On land and underwater. *British Journal of Psychology, 66*, 325–331.

Goethals, G. R., & Allison, S. T. (2014). Kings and charisma, Lincoln and leadership: An evolutionary perspective. In G. R. Goethals, S. T. Allison, R. M. Kramer, & D. M. Messick (Eds.), *Conceptions of leadership: Enduring ideas and emerging insights* (pp. 111–124). New York: Palgrave Macmillan.

Goff, D. C., Falkai, P., Fleischhacker, W. W., Girgis, R. R., Kahn, R. M., Uchida, H., . . . Lieberman, J. A. (2017). The long-term effects of antipsychotic medication on clinical course in schizophrenia. *The American Journal of Psychiatry, 174*, 840–849.

Goff, D. C., & Simms, C. A. (1993). Has multiple personality disorder remained consistent over time? *Journal of Nervous and Mental Disease, 181*, 595–600.

Gold, M. (2019, January 21). New York passes a ban on 'conversion therapy' after years-long efforts. *The New York Times* (nytimes.com).

Gold, M., & Yanof, D. S. (1985). Mothers, daughters, and girlfriends. *Journal of Personality and Social Psychology, 49*, 654–659.

Goldberg, J. (2007, accessed May 31). *Quivering bundles that let us hear*. Howard Hughes Medical Institute (hhmi.org/senses/c120.html).

Goldberg, L. R. (1992). The development of markers for the Big-Five factor structure. *Psychological Assessment, 4*, 26–42.

Golder, S. A., & Macy, M. W. (2011). Diurnal and seasonal mood vary with work, sleep, and day length across diverse cultures. *Science, 333*, 1878–1881.

Goldfried, M. R. (2001). Integrating gay, lesbian, and bisexual issues into mainstream psychology. *American Psychologist, 56*, 977–988.

Goldfried, M. R., Raue, P. J., & Castonguay, L. G. (1998). The therapeutic focus in significant sessions of master therapists: A comparison of cognitive-behavioral and psychodynamic–interpersonal interventions. *Journal of Consulting and Clinical Psychology, 66*, 803–810.

Goldinger, S. D., & Papesh, M. H. (2012). Pupil dilation reflects the creation and retrieval of memories. *Current Directions in Psychological Science, 21*, 90–95.

Goldman, A. L., Pezawas, L., Mattay, V. S., Fischl, B., Verchinski, B. A., Chen, Q., . . . Meyer-Lindenberg, A. (2009). Widespread reductions of cortical thickness in schizophrenia and spectrum disorders and evidence of heritability. *Archives of General Psychiatry, 66*, 467–477.

Goldstein, I., Lue, T. F., Padma-Nathan, H., Rosen, R. C., Steers, W. D., & Wicker, P. A. (1998). Oral sildenafil in the treatment of erectile dysfunction. *New England Journal of Medicine, 338*, 1397–1404.

Goleman, D. (1980, February). 1,528 little geniuses and how they grew. *Psychology Today*, pp. 28–53.

Goleman, D. (1995). *Emotional intelligence*. New York: Bantam.

Goleman, D. (2006). *Social intelligence*. New York: Bantam Books.

Golkar, A., Selbing, I., Flygare, O., Öhman, A., & Olsson, A. (2013). Other people as means to a safe end: Vicarious extinction blocks the return of learned fear. *Psychological Science, 24*, 2182–2190.

Gollwitzer, P. M., & Oettingen, G. (2012). Goal pursuit. In P. M. Gollwitzer & G. Oettingen (Eds.), *The Oxford handbook of human motivation* (pp. 208–231). New York: Oxford University Press.

Gollwitzer, P. M., & Sheeran, P. (2006). Implementation intentions and goal achievement: A meta-analysis of effects and processes. *Advances in Experimental Social Psychology, 38*, 69–119.

Gómez-Robles, A., Hopkins, W. D., Schapiro, S. J., & Sherwood, C. C. (2015). Relaxed genetic control of cortical organization in human brains compared with chimpanzees. *PNAS, 112*, 14799–14804.

Gong, H., Liu, Y.-Z., Zhang, Y., Su, W.-J., Lian, Y.-J., Peng, W., & Jiang, C.-L. (2016). Mindfulness meditation for insomnia: A meta-analysis of randomized controlled trials. *Journal of Psychosomatic Research, 89*, 1–6.

Gongola, J., Scurich, N., & Quas, J. A. (2017). Detecting deception in children: A meta-analysis. *Law and Human Behavior, 41*, 44–54.

Goodale, M. A., & Milner, D. A. (2004). *Sight unseen: An exploration of conscious and unconscious vision*. Oxford: Oxford University Press.

Goodale, M. A., & Milner, D. A. (2006). One brain—two visual systems. *The Psychologist, 19*, 660–663.

Goodall, J. (1986). *The chimpanzees of Gombe: Patterns of behavior*. Cambridge, MA: Harvard University Press.

Goode, E. (1999, April 13). If things taste bad, 'phantoms' may be at work. *The New York Times* (nytimes.com).

Goode, E. (2012, June 19). Senators start a review of solitary confinement. *The New York Times* (nytimes.com).

Goodhart, D. E. (1986). The effects of positive and negative thinking on performance in an achievement situation. *Journal of Personality and Social Psychology, 51*, 117–124.

Goodman, G. S., Ghetti, S., Quas, J. A., Edelstein, R. S., Alexander, K. W., Redlich, A. D., . . . Jones, D. P. H. (2003). A prospective study of memory for child sexual abuse: New findings relevant to the repressed-memory controversy. *Psychological Science, 14*, 113–118.

Goodman, G. S., & Quas, J. A. (2008). Repeated interviews and children's memory. *Current Directions in Psychological Science, 17*, 386–389.

Goodwin, P. Y., Mosher, W. D., & Chandra, A. (2010, February). *Marriage and cohabitation in the United States: A statistical portrait based on Cycle 6 (2002) of the National Survey of Family Growth* (Vital Health Statistics Series 23, No. 28). Washington, DC: U.S. Department of Health and Human Service, Centers for Disease Control and Prevention, National Center for Health Statistics.

Gopnik, A. (2016). *The carpenter and the gardener.* New York: Farrar, Straus, and Giroux.

Gopnik, A., Griffiths, T. L., & Lucas, C. G. (2015). When younger learners can be better (or at least more open-minded) than older ones. *Current Directions in Psychological Science, 24*, 87–92.

Goranson, A., Ritter, R. S., Waytz, A., Norton, M. I., & Gray, K. (2017). Dying is unexpectedly positive. *Psychological Science, 28*, 988–999.

Goranson, R. E. (1978). *The hindsight effect in problem solving.* Unpublished manuscript cited in G. Wood (1984), Research methodology: A decision-making perspective. In A. M. Rogers & C. J. Scheirer (Eds.), *The G. Stanley Hall Lecture Series* (Vol. 4, pp. 193–217). Washington, DC: American Psychological Association.

Gorchoff, S. M., John, O. P., & Helson, R. (2008). Contextualizing change in marital satisfaction during middle age. *Psychological Science, 19*, 1194–1200.

Gordon, A. M., & Chen, S. (2010). When you accept me for me: The relational benefits of intrinsic affirmations from one's relationship partner. *Personality and Social Psychology Bulletin, 36*, 1439–1453.

Gordon, A. M., & Chen, S. (2014). The role of sleep in interpersonal conflict: Do sleepless nights mean worse fights? *Social Psychological and Personality Science, 5*, 168–175.

Gore-Felton, C., Koopman, C., Thoresen, C., Arnow, B., Bridges, E., & Spiegel, D. (2000). Psychologists' beliefs and clinical characteristics: Judging the veracity of childhood sexual abuse memories. *Professional Psychology: Research and Practice, 31*, 372–377.

Gore, J., & Sadler-Smith, E. (2011). Unpacking intuition: A process and outcome framework. *Review of General Psychology, 15*, 304–316.

Gorka, S. M., Lieberman, L., Shankman, S. A., & Phan, K. L. (2017). Startle potentiation to uncertain threat as a psychophysiological indicator of fear-based psychopathology: An examination across multiple internalizing disorders. *Journal of Abnormal Psychology, 126*, 8.

Gorlick, A. (2010, January 13). Stanford scientists link brain development to chances of recovering vision after blindness. *Stanford Report* (news.stanford.edu).

Gorman, J. (2014, January 6). The brain, in exquisite detail. *The New York Times* (nytimes.com).

Gorrese, A., & Ruggieri, R. (2012). Peer attachment: A meta-analytic review of gender and age differences and associations with parent attachment. *Journal of Youth and Adolescence, 41*, 650–672.

Gosling, S. D. (2008). *Snoop: What your stuff says about you.* New York: Basic Books.

Gosling, S. D., Kwan, V. S. Y., & John, O. P. (2003). A dog's got personality: A cross-species comparative approach to personality judgments in dogs and humans. *Journal of Personality and Social Psychology, 85*, 1161–1169.

Gotink, R. A., Meijboom, R., Vernooij, M. W., Smits, M., & Hunink, M. G. M. (2016). 8-week mindfulness based stress reduction induces brain changes similar to traditional long-term meditation practice—A systematic review. *Brain and Cognition, 108*, 32–41.

Gotlib, I. H., & Hammen, C. L. (1992). *Psychological aspects of depression: Toward a cognitive-interpersonal integration.* New York: Wiley.

Gottesman, I. I. (1991). *Schizophrenia genesis: The origins of madness.* New York: Freeman.

Gottesman, I. I. (2001). Psychopathology through a life span—genetic prism. *American Psychologist, 56*, 867–881.

Gottfredson, L. S. (2002a). Where and why *g* matters: Not a mystery. *Human Performance, 15*, 25–46.

Gottfredson, L. S. (2002b). *g*: Highly general and highly practical. In R. J. Sternberg & E. L. Grigorenko (Eds.), *The general factor of intelligence: How general is it?* (pp. 331–380). Mahwah, NJ: Erlbaum.

Gottfredson, L. S. (2003a). Dissecting practical intelligence theory: Its claims and evidence. *Intelligence, 31*, 343–397.

Gottfredson, L. S. (2003b). On Sternberg's "Reply to Gottfredson." *Intelligence, 31*, 415–424.

Gottfried, A. W., Gottfried, A. E., & Guerin, D. W. (2006). The Fullerton Longitudinal Study: A long-term investigation of intellectual and motivational giftedness. *Journal for the Education of the Gifted, 29*, 430–450.

Gould, E. (2007). How widespread is adult neurogenesis in mammals? *Nature Neuroscience, 8*, 481–488.

Gould, S. J. (1981). *The mismeasure of man.* New York: Norton.

Gow, A. J., Bastin, M. E., Maniega, S. M., Hernández, M. C. V., Morris, Z., Murray, C., . . . Wardlaw, J. M. (2012). Neuroprotective lifestyles and the aging brain: Activity, atrophy, and white matter integrity. *Neurology, 79*, 1802–1808.

Goyal, M., Singh, S., Sibinga, E. S., Gould, N. F., Rowland-Seymour, A., Sharma, R., . . . Haythornthwaite, J. A. (2014). Meditation programs for psychological stress and well-being: A systematic review and meta-analysis. *JAMA Internal Medicine, 174*, 357–368.

Goyer, J. P., Garcia, J., Purdie-Vaughns, V., Binning, K. R., Cook, J. E., Reeves, S. L., . . . Cohen, G. L. (2017). Self-affirmation facilitates minority middle schoolers' progress along college trajectories. *PNAS, 114*(29), 7594–7599.

Graafland, J., & Lous, B. (2018). Income inequality, life satisfaction inequality and trust: A cross country panel analysis. *Journal of Happiness Studies.* Retrieved from https://doi.org/10.1007/s10902-018-0021-0

Grabo, A., & van Vugt, M. (2016). Charismatic leadership and the evolution of cooperation. *Evolution and Human Behavior, 37*, 399–406.

Grady, C. L., McIntosh, A. R., Horwitz, B., Maisog, J. M., Ungeleider, L. G., Mentis, M. J., . . . Haxby, J. V. (1995). Age-related reductions in human recognition memory due to impaired encoding. *Science, 269*, 218–221.

Graf, S., Paolini, S., & Rubin, M. (2014). Negative intergroup contact is more influential, but positive intergroup contact is more common: Assessing contact prominence and contact prevalence in five central European countries. *European Journal of Social Psychology, 44*, 536–547.

Graham, C., Laffan, K., & Pinto, S. (2018). Well-being in metrics and policy. *Science, 362*, 287–288.

Graham, J., Nosek, B. A., & Haidt, J. (2012, December 12). The moral stereotypes of liberals and conservatives: Exaggeration of differences across the political spectrum. *PLOS ONE 7*, e50092.

Grand, J. A. (2016). Brain drain? An examination of stereotype threat effects during training on knowledge acquisition and organizational effectiveness. *Journal of Applied Psychology, 102*, 115–150.

Granic, I., Lobel, A., & Engels, R. C. M. E. (2014). The benefits of playing video games. *American Psychologist, 69*, 66–78.

Grant, A. M., Gino, F., & Hofmann, D. A. (2011a). Reversing the extraverted leadership advantage: The role of employee proactivity. *Academy of Management Journal, 54*, 528–550.

Grant, J. M., Mottet, L. A., Tanis, J., Herman, J. L., Harrison, J., & Keisling, M. (2011b). *National transgender discrimination survey: Full report.* Retrieved from https://transequality.org/issues/resources/national-transgender-discrimination-survey-full-report

Grassegger, H., & Krogerus, M. (2017, January 28). How Cambridge Analytica used your Facebook data to help the Donald Trump campaign in the 2016 election. Retrieved from motherboard.vice.com

Gray-Little, B., & Burks, N. (1983). Power and satisfaction in marriage: A review and critique. *Psychological Bulletin, 93*, 513–538.

Graybiel, A. M., & Smith, K. S. (2014, June). Good habits, bad habits. *Scientific American*, pp. 39–43.

Green, J. D., Sedikides, C., & Gregg, A. P. (2008). Forgotten but not gone: The recall and recognition of self-threatening memories. *Journal of Experimental Social Psychology, 44*, 547–561.

Green, J. T., & Woodruff-Pak, D. S. (2000). Eyeblink classical conditioning: Hippocampal formation is for neutral stimulus associations as cerebellum is for association-response. *Psychological Bulletin, 126*, 138–158.

Green, M. F., & Horan, W. P. (2010). Social cognition in schizophrenia. *Current Directions in Psychological Science, 19*, 243–248.

Greenaway, K. H., Cruwys, T., Haslam, S. A., & Jetten, J. (2016). Social identities promote well-being because they satisfy global psychological needs. *European Journal of Social Psychology, 46*, 294–307.

Greenaway, K. H., Haslam, S. A., Cruwys, T., Branscombe, N. R., Ysseldyk, R., & Heldreth, C. (2015). From "we" to "me": Group identification enhances perceived personal control with consequences for health and well-being. *Journal of Personality and Social Psychology, 109*, 53–74.

Greenberg, J. (2008). Understanding the vital human quest for self-esteem. *Perspectives on Psychological Science, 3*, 48–55.

Greene, J., Sommerville, R. B., Nystrom, L. E., Darley, J. M., & Cohen, J. D. (2001). An fMRI investigation of emotional engagement in moral judgment. *Science, 293*, 2105.

Greenwald, A. G. (1992). *Subliminal semantic activation and subliminal snake oil.* Paper presented to the American Psychological Association Convention, Washington, DC.

Greenwald, A. G., Banaji, M. R., & Nosek, B. A. (2015). Statistically small effects of the implicit association test can have societally large effects. *Journal of Personality and Social Psychology, 108*, 553–561.

Greenwald, A. G., & Pettigrew, T. F. (2014). With malice toward none and charity for some: Ingroup favoritism enables discrimination. *American Psychologist, 69*, 645–655.

Greenwald, A. G., Spangenberg, E. R., Pratkanis, A. R., & Eskenazi, J. (1991). Double-blind tests of subliminal self-help audiotapes. *Psychological Science, 2*, 119–122.

Greer, S. G., Goldstein, A. N., & Walker, M. P. (2013). The impact of sleep deprivation on food desire in the human brain. *Nature Communications, 4*, Article 3259.

Gregory, A. M., Rijksdijk, F. V., Lau, J. Y., Dahl, R. E., & Eley, T. C. (2009). The direction of longitudinal associations between sleep problems and depression symptoms: A study of twins aged 8 and 10 years. *Sleep, 32*, 189–199.

Gregory, R. L. (1978). *Eye and brain: The psychology of seeing* (3rd ed.). New York: McGraw-Hill.

Gregory, R. L., & Gombrich, E. H. (Eds.). (1973). *Illusion in nature and art*. New York: Charles Scribner's Sons.

Greist, J. H., Jefferson, J. W., & Marks, I. M. (1986). *Anxiety and its treatment: Help is available*. Washington, DC: American Psychiatric Press.

Greitemeyer, T., & Mügge, D. O. (2014). Video games do affect social outcomes: A meta-analytic review of the effects of violent and prosocial video game play. *Personality and Social Psychology Bulletin, 40*, 578–589.

Greyson, B. (2010). Implications of near-death experiences for a postmaterialist psychology. *Review of Religion and Spirituality, 2*, 37–45.

Grèzes, J., & Decety, J. (2001). Functional anatomy of execution, mental simulation, observation, and verb generation of actions: A meta-analysis. *Human Brain Mapping, 12*, 1–19.

Griffiths, M. (2001). Sex on the internet: Observations and implications for internet sex addiction. *Journal of Sex Research, 38*, 333–342.

Griggs, R. (2014). Coverage of the Stanford Prison Experiment in introductory psychology textbooks. *Teaching of Psychology, 41*, 195–203.

Grijalva, E., Newman, D. A., Tay, L., Donnellan, M. B., Harms, P. D., Robins, R. W., & Yan, T. (2015). Gender differences in narcissism: A meta-analytic review. *Psychological Bulletin, 141*, 261–310.

Grillon, C., Quispe-Escudero, D., Mathur, A., & Ernst, M. (2015). Mental fatigue impairs emotion regulation. *Emotion, 15*, 383–389.

Grilo, C. M., & Pogue-Geile, M. F. (1991). The nature of environmental influences on weight and obesity: A behavior genetic analysis. *Psychological Bulletin, 110*, 520–537.

Grobstein, C. (1979, June). External human fertilization. *Scientific American*, pp. 57–67.

Grønnerød, C., Grønnerød, J. S., & Grøndahl, P. (2015). Psychological treatment of sexual offenders against children: A meta-analytic review of treatment outcome studies. *Trauma, Violence, & Abuse, 16*, 280–290.

Gross, A. E., & Crofton, C. (1977). What is good is beautiful. *Sociometry, 40*, 85–90.

Gross, J. J. (2013). Emotion regulation: Taking stock and moving forward. *Emotion, 13*, 359–365.

Grossberg, S. (1995). The attentive brain. *American Scientist, 83*, 438–449.

Grossmann, I., Na, J., Varnum, M. E. W., Park, D. C., Kitayama, S., & Nisbett, R. E. (2010). Reasoning about social conflicts improves into old age. *PNAS, 107*, 7246–7250.

Grossmann, I., & Varnum, M. E. W. (2015). Social structure, infectious diseases, disasters, secularism, and cultural change in America. *Psychological Science, 26*, 311–324.

Groß, J., Blank, H., & Bayen U. J. (2017). Hindsight bias in depression. *Clinical Psychological Science, 5*, 771–788.

Gruder, C. L. (1977). Choice of comparison persons in evaluating oneself. In J. M. Suls & R. L. Miller (Eds.), *Social comparison processes*. New York: Hemisphere.

Gu, J., Strauss, C., Bond, R., & Cavanagh, K. (2015). How do mindfulness-based cognitive therapy and mindfulness-based stress reduction improve mental health and wellbeing? A systematic review and meta-analysis of mediation studies. *Clinical Psychology Review, 37*, 1–12.

Guardino, C. M., Schetter, C. D., Saxbe, D. E., Adam, E. K., Ramey, S. L., & Shalowitz, M. U. (2016). Diurnal salivary cortisol patterns prior to pregnancy predict infant birth weight. *Health Psychology, 35*, 625–633.

Guéguen, N. (2011). Effects of solicitor sex and attractiveness on receptivity to sexual offers: A field study. *Archives of Sexual Behavior, 40*, 915–919.

Guiso, L., Monte, F., Sapienza, P., & Zingales, L. (2008). Culture, gender, and math. *Science, 320*, 1164–1165.

Gunaydin, G., Selcuk, E., & Zayas, V. (2017). Impressions based on a portrait predict, 1-month later, impressions following a live interaction. *Social Psychological and Personality Science, 8*, 36–44.

Gunderson, E. A., Gripshover, S. J., Romero, C., Dweck, C. S., Goldin-Meadow, S., & Levine, S. C. (2013). Parent praise to 1- to 3-year-olds predicts children's motivational frameworks 5 years later. *Child Development, 84*, 1526–1541.

Guo, J., He, H., Qu, Z., Wang, X., & Liu, C. (2017). Post-traumatic stress disorder and depression among adult survivors 8 years after the 2008 Wenchuan earthquake in China. *Journal of Affective Disorders, 210*, 27–34.

Guo, M., Gan, Y., & Tong, J. (2013). The role of meaning-focused coping in significant loss. *Anxiety, Stress, & Coping, 26*, 87–102.

Guo, X., Zhai, J., Liu, Z., Fang, M., Wang, B., Wang, C., . . . Zhao, J. (2010). Effect of antipsychotic medication alone vs combined with psychosocial intervention on outcomes of early-stage schizophrenia. *Archives of General Psychiatry, 67*, 895–904.

Gupta, M. D. (2017, September). Return of the missing daughters. *Scientific American*, pp. 78–85.

Gustavson, C. R., Garcia, J., Hankins, W. G., & Rusiniak, K. W. (1974). Coyote predation control by aversive conditioning. *Science, 184*, 581–583.

Gustavson, C. R., Kelly, D. J., & Sweeney, M. (1976). Prey lithium aversions I: Coyotes and wolves. *Behavioral Biology, 17*, 61–72.

Gutchess, A. (2014). Plasticity in the aging brain: New directions in cognitive neuroscience. *Science, 346*, 579–582.

Guttmacher Institute. (1994). *Sex and America's teenagers*. New York: Alan Guttmacher Institute.

H., Sally. (1979, August). Videotape recording number T-3, Fortunoff Video Archive of Holocaust Testimonies. New Haven, CT: Yale University Library.

Haapakoski, R., Mathieu, J., Ebmeier, K. P., Alenius, H., & Kivimäki, M. (2015). Cumulative meta-analysis of interleukins 6 and 1b, tumour necrosis factor a and C-reactive protein in patients with major depressive disorder. *Brain, Behavior, and Immunity, 49*, 206–215.

Haas, A. P., Eliason, M., Mays, V. M., Mathy, R. M., Cochran, S. D., D'Augelli, A. R., . . . Clayton, P. J. (2011). Suicide and suicide risk in lesbian, gay, bisexual, and transgender populations: Review and recommendations. *Journal of Homosexuality, 58*, 10–51.

Habashi, M. M., Graziano, W. G., & Hoover, A. E. (2016). Searching for the prosocial personality: A big five approach to linking personality and prosocial behavior. *Personality and Social Psychology Bulletin, 42*, 1177–1192.

Habel, U., Koch, K., Kellerman, T., Reske, M., Frommann, N., Wolwer, W., . . . Schneider, F. (2010). Training of affect recognition in schizophrenia: Neurobiological correlates. *Social Neuroscience, 5*, 92–104.

Hadjistavropoulos, T., Craig, K. D., Duck, S., Cano, A., Goubert, L., Jackson, P. L., . . . Fitzgerald, T. D. (2011). A biopsychosocial formulation of pain communication. *Psychological Bulletin, 137*, 910–939.

Hafenbrack, A. C., & Vohs, K. D. (2018). Mindfulness meditation impairs task motivation but not performance. *Organizational Behavior and Human Decision Processes, 147*, 1–15.

Hagger, M. S., Chatzisarantis, N. L. D., Alberts, H., Anggono, C. O., Birt, A., Brand, R., . . . Cannon, T. (2016). A multi-lab pre-registered replication of the ego-depletion effect. *Perspectives on Psychological Science, 11*, 546–573.

Haidt, J. (2002). The moral emotions. In R. J. Davidson, K. Scherer, & H. H. Goldsmith (Eds.), *Handbook of affective sciences* (pp. 852–870). New York: Oxford University Press.

Haidt, J. (2006). *The happiness hypothesis: Finding modern truth in ancient wisdom*. New York: Basic Books.

Haidt, J. (2010). Moral psychology must not be based on faith and hope: Commentary on Narvaez. *Perspectives on Psychological Science, 5*, 182–184.

Hainey, M. (2016). Lin-Manuel Miranda thinking the key to parenting is a little less parenting. *GQ Magazine* (gq.com).

Hajhosseini, B., Stewart, B., Tan, J. C., Busque, S., & Melcher, M. L. (2013). Evaluating deceased donor registries: Identifying predictive factors of donor designation. *American Surgeon, 79*, 235–241.

Hakuta, K., Bialystok, E., & Wiley, E. (2003). Critical evidence: A test of the critical-period hypothesis for second-language acquisition. *Psychological Science, 14*, 31–38.

Halberstadt, J. B., Niedenthal, P. M., & Kushner, J. (1995). Resolution of lexical ambiguity by emotional state. *Psychological Science, 6*, 278–281.

Halberstadt, J., Sherman, S. J., & Sherman, J. W. (2011). Why Barack Obama is Black. *Psychological Science, 22*, 29–33.

Haldeman, D. C. (1994). The practice and ethics of sexual orientation conversion therapy. *Journal of Consulting and Clinical Psychology, 62*, 221–227.

Haldeman, D. C. (2002). Gay rights, patient rights: The implications of sexual orientation conversion therapy. *Professional Psychology: Research and Practice, 33*, 260–264.

Hales, A. H., Kassner, M. P., Williams, K. D., & Graziano, W. G. (2016). Disagreeableness as a cause and consequence of ostracism. *Personality and Social Psychology Review, 42*, 782–797.

Hall, C. S., Dornhoff, W., Blick, K. A., & Weesner, K. E. (1982). The dreams of college men and women in 1950 and 1980: A comparison of dream contents and sex differences. *Sleep, 5*, 188–194.

Hall, C. S., & Lindzey, G. (1978). *Theories of personality* (2nd ed.). New York: Wiley.

Hall, D. T., & Chandler, D. E. (2005). Psychological success: When the career is a calling. *Journal of Organizational Behavior, 26*, 155–176.

Hall, G. (1997). Context aversion, Pavlovian conditioning, and the psychological side effects of chemotherapy. *European Psychologist, 2*, 118–124.

Hall, J. A., Gunnery, S. D., & Horgan, T. G. (2016). Gender differences in interpersonal accuracy. In J. A. Hall, M. S. Mast & T. V. West (Eds.), *The social psychology of perceiving others accurately* (pp. 309–327), New York: Cambridge University Press.

Hall, K. M., Knudson, S. T., Wright, J., Charlifue, S. W., Graves, D. E., & Warner, P. (1999). Follow-up study of individuals with high tetraplegia (C1-C4) 14 to 24 years postinjury. *Archives of Physical Medicine and Rehabilitation, 80*, 1507–1513.

Hall, S. S. (2004, May). The good egg. *Discover*, pp. 30–39.

Hall, S. S., Knox, D., & Shapiro, K. (2017). "I have," "I would," "I won't": hooking up among sexually diverse groups of college students. *Psychology of Sexual Orientation and Gender Diversity, 4*, 233–240.

Hallal, P. C., Andersen, L. B., Bull, F. C., Guthold, R., Haskell, W., & Ekelund, U. (2012). Global physical activity levels: Surveillance progress, pitfalls, and prospects. *The Lancet, 380*, 247–257.

Haller, R., Rummel, C., Henneberg, S., Pollmer, U., & Köster, E. P. (1999). The influence of early experience with vanillin on food preference later in life. *Chemical Senses, 24*, 465–467.

Halpern, D. (2015). The rise of psychology in policy: The UK's de facto council of psychological science advisers. *Perspectives on Psychological Science, 10*, 768–771.

Halpern, D. F., Benbow, C. P., Geary, D. C., Gur, R. C., Hyde, J. S., & Gernsbacher, M. A. (2007). The science of sex differences in science and mathematics. *Psychological Science in the Public Interest, 8*, 1–51.

Halpern, D., Valenzuela, S., & Katz, J. E. (2016). "Selfie-ists" or "Narci-selfiers"?: A cross-lagged panel analysis of selfie taking and narcissism. *Personality and Individual Differences, 97*, 98–101.

Hambrick, D. Z. (2014, December 2). Brain training doesn't make you smarter. Retrieved from scientificamerican .com

Hamid, A. A., Pettibone, J. R., Mabrouk, O. S., Hetrick, V. L., Schmidt, R., Vander Weele, C. M., . . . Berke, J. D. (2016). Mesolimbic dopamine signals the value of work. *Nature Neuroscience, 19*, 117–126.

Hammack, P. L., (2005). The life course development of human sexual orientation: An integrative paradigm. *Human Development, 48*, 267–290.

Hammersmith, S. K. (1982, August). *Sexual preference: An empirical study from the Alfred C. Kinsey Institute for Sex Research*. Paper presented at the 90th Annual Convention of the American Psychological Association, Washington, DC.

Hammond, D. C. (2008). Hypnosis as sole anesthesia for major surgeries: Historical and contemporary perspectives. *American Journal of Clinical Hypnosis, 51*, 101–121.

Hampshire, A., Highfield, R. R., Parkin, B. L., & Owen, A. M. (2012). Fractionating human intelligence. *Neuron, 76*, 1225–1237.

Hamza, C. A., Willoughby, T., & Heffer, T. (2015). Impulsivity and nonsuicidal self-injury: A review and meta-analysis. *Clinical Psychology Review, 38*, 13–24.

Haney, C., Haslam, A., Reicher, S., & Zimbardo, P. (2018, September 27). Consensus statement on the Stanford Prison Experiment and BBC Prison Study (bbcprisonstudy.org).

Hänggi, J., Koeneke, S., Bezzola, L., Jäncke, L. (2010). Structural neuroplasticity in the sensorimotor network of professional female ballet dancers. *Human Brain Mapping, 31*, 1196–1206.

Hankin, B. L., & Abramson, L. Y. (2001). Development of gender differences in depression: An elaborated cognitive vulnerability-transactional stress theory. *Psychological Bulletin, 127*, 773–796.

Hannikainen, I., Cabral, G., Machery, E., & Struchiner, N. (2016). A deterministic worldview promotes approval of state paternalism. *Journal of Experimental Social Psychology, 70*, 251–259.

Harackiewicz, J. M., Canning, E. A., Tibbetts, Y., Giffen, C. J., Blair, S. S., Rouse, D. I., & Hyde, J. S. (2014). Closing the social class achievement gap for first-generation students in undergraduate biology. *Journal of Educational Psychology, 106*, 375–389.

Harackiewicz, J. M., Canning, E. A., Tibbetts, Y., Priniski, S. J., & Hyde, J. S. (2016). Closing achievement gaps with a utility-value intervention: Disentangling race and social class. *Journal of Personality and Social Psychology, 111*, 745–765.

Harari, G. M., Lane, N. D., Wang, R., Crosier, B. S., Campbell, A. T., & Gosling, S. D. (2016). Using smartphones to collect behavioral data in psychological science: Opportunities, practical considerations, and challenges. *Perspectives on Psychological Science, 11*, 838–854.

Harbaugh, W. T., Mayr, U., & Burghart, D. R. (2007). Neural responses to taxation and voluntary giving reveal motives for charitable donations. *Science, 316*, 1622–1625.

Harden, K. P. (2012). True love waits? A sibling-comparison study of age at first sexual intercourse and romantic relationships in young adulthood. *Psychological Science, 23*, 1324–1336.

Harden, K. P., & Mendle, J. (2011). Why don't smart teens have sex? A behavioral genetic approach. *Child Development, 82*, 1327–1344.

Hardt, O., Einarsson, E. O., & Nader, K. (2010). A bridge over troubled water: Reconsolidation as a link between cognitive and neuroscientific memory research traditions. *Annual Review of Psychology, 61*, 141–167.

Hare, R. D. (1975). Psychophysiological studies of psychopathy. In D. C. Fowles (Ed.), *Clinical applications of psychophysiology*. New York: Columbia University Press.

Harenski, C. L., Harenski, K. A., Shane, M. W., & Kiehl, K. A. (2010). Aberrant neural processing of moral violations in criminal psychopaths. *Journal of Abnormal Psychology, 119*, 863–874.

Harkin, B., Webb, T. L., Chang, B. P. I., Prestwich, A., Conner, M., Kellar, I., . . . Sheeran, P. (2016). Does monitoring goal progress promote goal attainment? A meta-analysis of the experimental evidence. *Psychological Bulletin, 142*, 198–229.

Harkins, S. G., & Szymanski, K. (1989). Social loafing and group evaluation. *Journal of Personality and Social Psychology, 56*, 934–941.

Harlow, H. F., Harlow, M. K., & Suomi, S. J. (1971). From thought to therapy: Lessons from a primate laboratory. *American Scientist, 59*, 538–549.

Harmon-Jones, E., Abramson, L. Y., Sigelman, J., Bohlig, A., Hogan, M. E., & Harmon-Jones, C. (2002). Proneness to hypomania/mania symptoms or depression symptoms and asymmetrical frontal cortical responses to an anger-evoking event. *Journal of Personality and Social Psychology, 82*, 610–618.

Harms, P. D., Roberts, B. W., & Winter, D. (2006). Becoming the Harvard man: Person-environment fit, personality development, and academic success. *Personality and Social Psychology Bulletin, 32*, 851–865.

Harnett, N. G., Shumen, J. R., Wagle, P. A., Wood, K. H., Wheelock, M. D., Baños, J. H., & Knight, D. C. (2016). Neural mechanisms of human temporal fear conditioning. *Neurobiology of Learning and Memory, 136*, 97–104.

Harold, C. M., Oh, I.-S., Holtz, B. C., Han, S., & Giacalone, R. A. (2016). Fit and frustration as drivers of targeted counterproductive work behaviors: A multifoci perspective. *Journal of Applied Psychology, 101*, 1513–1535.

Harper, C., & McLanahan, S. (2004). Father absence and youth incarceration. *Journal of Research on Adolescence, 14*, 369–397.

Harris, B. (1979). Whatever happened to Little Albert? *American Psychologist, 34*, 151–160.

Harris, J. R. (1998). *The nurture assumption*. New York: Free Press.

Harris, J. R. (2002). Beyond the nurture assumption: Testing hypotheses about the child's environment. In J. G. Borkowski, S. L. Ramey, & M. Bristol-Power (Eds.), *Parenting and the child's world: Influences on academic, intellectual, and social-emotional development* (pp. 3–20). Mahwah, NJ: Erlbaum.

Harris, J. R. (2009). *The nurture assumption: Why children turn out the way they do, revised and updated*. New York: Free Press.

Harris, M. A., Brett, C. E., Johnson, W., & Deary, I. J. (2016). Personality stability from age 14 to age 77 years. *Psychology and Aging, 31*, 862–874.

Harris, R. J. (1994). The impact of sexually explicit media. In J. Brant & D. Zillmann (Eds.), *Media effects: Advances in theory and research* (pp. 247–272). Hillsdale, NJ: Erlbaum.

Harrison, G., Hopper, K. I. M., Craig, T., Laska, E., Siegel, C., Wanderling, J., . . . Holmberg, S. K. (2001). Recovery from psychotic illness: A 15-and 25-year international follow-up study. *The British Journal of Psychiatry, 178*, 506–517.

Harrison, L. A., Hurlemann, R., & Adolphs, R. (2015). An enhanced default approach bias following amygdala lesions in humans. *Psychological Science, 26*, 1543–1555.

Harriston, K. A. (1993, December 24). 1 shakes, 1 snoozes: Both win $45 million. *Washington Post* release (in *Tacoma News Tribune*, pp. A1, A2).

Harter, J. K., Schmidt, F. L., & Hayes, T. L. (2002). Business-unit-level relationship between employee satisfaction, employee engagement, and business outcomes: A meta-analysis. *Journal of Applied Psychology, 87*, 268–279.

Harter, J. K., Schmidt, F. L., Asplund, J. W., Killham, E. A., & Agrawal, S. (2010). Causal impact of employee work perceptions on the bottom line of organizations. *Perspectives on Psychological Science, 5*, 378–389.

Hartshorne, J. K., Tenenbaum, J. B., & Pinker, S. (2018). A critical period for second language acquisition: Evidence from 2/3 million English speakers. *Cognition, 177*, 263–277.

Hartwig, M., & Bond, C. F., Jr. (2011). Why do lie-catchers fail? A lens model meta-analysis of human lie judgments. *Psychological Bulletin, 137*, 643–659.

Harvey, S. B., Øverland, S., Hatch, S. L., Wessely, S., Mykletun, A., & Hotopf, M. (2018). Exercise and the prevention of depression: Results of the HUNT Cohort Study. *American Journal of Psychiatry, 175*, 28–36.

Harward, S. C., Hedrick, N. G., Hall, C. E., Parra-Bueno, P., Milner, T. A., Pan, E., . . . McNamara, J. O. (2016). Autocrine BDNF–TrkB signalling within a single dendritic spine. *Nature, 538*, 99–103.

Haselton, M. (2018). *Hormonal: The hidden intelligence of hormones—how they drive desire, shape relationships, influence our choices, and make us wiser*. New York: Little, Brown and Company.

Haselton, M. G., & Gildersleeve, K. (2011). Can men detect ovulation? *Current Directions in Psychological Science, 20*, 87–92.

Haselton, M. G., & Gildersleeve, K. (2016). Human ovulation cues. *Current Opinion in Psychology, 7*, 120–125.

Hasin, D. S., Sarvet, A. L., Meyers, J. L. (2018). Epidemiology of adult DSM-5 major depressive disorder and its specifiers in the United States. *JAMA Psychiatry, 75*, 334–336.

Haslam, S. A., & Reicher, S. (2007). Beyond the banality of evil: Three dynamics of an interactionist social psychology of tyranny. *Personality and Social Psychology Bulletin, 33*, 615–622.

Haslam, S. A., & Reicher, S. D. (2012). Contesting the "nature" of conformity: What Milgram and Zimbardo's studies really show. *PLOS Biology, 10*, e1001426.

Haslam, S. A., Reicher, S. D., & Van Bavel, J. J. (2018). Rethinking the 'nature' of brutality: Uncovering the role of identity leadership in the Stanford Prison Experiment. *American Psychologist* (preprint at psyarxiv .com/b7crx/).

Hassin, R. R. (2013). Yes it can: On the functional abilities of the human unconscious. *Perspectives on Psychological Science, 8*, 195–207.

Hatfield, E. (1988). Passionate and companionate love. In R. J. Sternberg & M. L. Barnes (Eds.), *The psychology of love* (pp. 191–217). New Haven, CT: Yale University Press.

Hatfield, E. (2016). Love and sex in the marketplace. In R. J. Sternberg, S. T. Fiske, & D. J. Foss (Eds.), *Scientists making a difference: One hundred eminent behavioral and brain scientists talk about their most important contributions*. New York: Cambridge University Press.

Hatfield, E., Mo, Y., & Rapson, R. L. (2015). Love, sex, and marriage across cultures. *Oxford Handbooks Online* (oxfordhandbooks.com).

Hatfield, E., & Sprecher, S. (1986). *Mirror, mirror . . . The importance of looks in everyday life*. Albany: State University of New York Press.

Hatzenbuehler, M. L. (2011). The social environment and suicide attempts in lesbian, gay, and bisexual youth. *Pediatrics, 127*, 896–903.

Hatzenbuehler, M. L. (2014). Structural stigma and the health of lesbian, gay, and bisexual populations. *Current Directions in Psychological Science, 23*, 127–132.

Havas, D. A., Glenberg, A. M., Gutowski, K. A., Lucarelli, M. J., & Davidson, R. J. (2010). Cosmetic use of botulinum toxin-A affects processing of emotional language. *Psychological Science, 21*, 895–900.

Haworth, C. M. A., Wright, M. J., Martin, N. W., Martin, N. G., Boomsma, D. I., Bartels, M., . . . Plomin, R. (2009). A twin study of the genetics of high cognitive ability selected from 11,000 twin pairs in six studies from four countries. *Behavior Genetics, 39*, 359–370.

Haxby, J. V. (2001, July 7). Quoted by B. Bower, Faces of perception. *Science News*, pp. 10–12. See also J. V. Haxby, M. I. Gobbini, M. L. Furey, A. Ishai, J. L. Schouten & P. Pietrini (2001), Distributed and overlapping representations of faces and objects in ventral temporal cortex. *Science, 293*, 2425–2430.

Hayashi, Y., Kashiwagi, M., Yasuda, K., Ando, R., Kanuka, M., Sakai, K., & Itohara, S. (2015). Cells of a common developmental origin regulate REM/non-REM sleep and wakefulness in mice. *Science, 350*, 957–961.

Hays, C., & Carver, L. J. (2014). Follow the liar: The effects of adult lies on children's honesty. *Developmental Science, 17*, 977–983.

HBS. (2018). Admissions: Class of 2020 profile. Retrieved from https://www.hbs.edu/mba/admissions/class-profile/Pages/default.aspx

HBVA. (2018, accessed February 20). *Honour killings by region, South and Central Asia*. Honour Based Violence Awareness Network. Retrieved from hbv-awareness.com

He, Q., Turel, O., & Bechara, A. (2017). Brain anatomy alterations associated with Social Networking Site (SNS) addiction. *Scientific Reports, 7*, 45064.

He, Z., & Jin, Y. (2016). Intrinsic control of axon regeneration. *Neuron, 90*, 437–451.

Headey, B., Muffels, R., & Wagner, G. G. (2010). Long-running German panel survey shows that personal and economic choices, not just genes, matter for happiness. *PNAS, 107*, 17922–17926.

Healy, A. F., Jones, M., Lalchandani, L. A., & Tack, L. A. (2017). Timing of quizzes during learning: Effects on motivation and retention. *Journal of Experimental Psychology: Applied, 23*, 128–137.

Heathcote, R. J., Darden, S. K., Troscianko, J., Lawson, M. R., Brown, A. M., Laker, P. R., . . . & Croft, D. P. (2018). Dynamic eye colour as an honest signal of aggression. *Current Biology, 28*, R652–R653.

Heberle, A. E., & Carter, A. S. (2015). Cognitive aspects of young children's experience of economic disadvantage. *Psychological Bulletin, 141*, 723–746.

Heck, P. R., Simons, D. J., & Chabris, C. F. (2018). 65% of Americans believe they are above average in intelligence: Results of two nationally representative surveys. *PLOS ONE, 13*, e0200103.

Heckert, J. (2012, November 15). The hazards of growing up painlessly. *The New York Times* (nytimes.com).

Heider, F. (1958). *The psychology of interpersonal relations*. New York: Wiley.

Heiman, J. R. (1975, April). The physiology of erotica: Women's sexual arousal. *Psychology Today*, pp. 90–94.

Hein, G., Morishima, Y., Leiberg, S., Sul, S., & Fehr, E. (2016). The brain's functional network architecture reveals human motives. *Science, 351*, 1074–1078.

Heine, S. J., Proulx, T., & Vohs, K. D. (2006). Meaning maintenance model: On the coherence of human motivations. *Personality and Social Psychology Review, 10*, 88–110.

Heinz, A. J., Meffert, B. N., Halvorson, M. A., Blonigen, D., Timko, C., & Cronkite, R. (2018). Employment characteristics, work environment, and the course of depression over 23 years: Does employment help foster resilience? *Depression and Anxiety, 35*, 861–867.

Hejmadi, A., Davidson, R. J., & Rozin, P. (2000). Exploring Hindu Indian emotion expressions: Evidence for accurate recognition by Americans and Indians. *Psychological Science, 11*, 183–187.

Helfand, D. (2011, January 7). An assault on rationality. *The New York Times* (nytimes.com).

Heller, A. S., Johnstone, T., Schackman, A. J., Light, S. N., Peterson, M. J., Kolden, G. G., . . . Davidson, R. J. (2009). Reduced capacity to sustain positive emotion in major depression reflects diminished maintenance of fronto-striatal brain activation. *PNAS, 106*, 22445–22450.

Heller, S. B. (2014). Summer jobs reduce violence among disadvantaged youth. *Science, 346*, 1219–1222.

Heller, W. (1990, May/June). Of one mind: Second thoughts about the brain's dual nature. *The Sciences*, pp. 38–44.

Helliwell, J., Layard, R., & Sachs, J. (Eds.) (2013). *World happiness report*. New York: The Earth Institute, Columbia University.

Helliwell, J. F., & Wang, S. (2015). How was the weekend? How the social context underlies weekend effects in happiness and other emotions for US workers. *PLOS ONE, 10*, e0145123.

Helmreich, W. B. (1992). *Against all odds: Holocaust survivors and the successful lives they made in America*. New York: Simon & Schuster.

Helmreich, W. B. (1994). Personal correspondence. Department of Sociology, City University of New York.

Helms, J. E., Jernigan, M., & Mascher, J. (2005). The meaning of race in psychology and how to change it: A methodological perspective. *American Psychologist, 60*, 27–36.

Helmuth, L. (2001). Boosting brain activity from the outside in. *Science, 292*, 1284–1286.

Helsen, K., Goubert, L., Peters, M. L., & Vlaeyen, J. W. S. (2011). Observational learning and pain-related fear: An experimental study with colored cold pressor tasks. *The Journal of Pain, 12*, 1230–1239.

Hembree, R. (1988). Correlates, causes, effects, and treatment of test anxiety. *Review of Educational Research, 58*, 47–77.

Hemmings, S. M. J., Malan-Müller, S., van den Heuvel, L. L., Demmitt, B. A., Stanislawski, M. A., Smith, D. G., . . . Lowry, C. A. (2017). The microbiome in posttraumatic stress disorder and trauma-exposed controls: An exploratory study. *Psychosomatic Medicine, 79*, 936–946.

Henderlong, J., & Lepper, M. R. (2002). The effects of praise on children's intrinsic motivation: A review and synthesis. *Psychological Bulletin, 128*, 774–795.

Henig, R. M. (2010, August 18). What is it about 20-somethings? *The New York Times* (nytimes.com).

Hennenlotter, A., Dresel, C., Castrop, F., Ceballos Baumann, A., Wohschlager, A., & Haslinger, B. (2008). The link between facial feedback and neural activity within central circuitries of emotion: New insights from botulinum toxin-induced denervation of frown muscles. *Cerebral Cortex, 19*, 537–542.

Hennessey, B. A., & Amabile, T. M. (2010). Creativity. *Annual Review of Psychology, 61*, 569–598.

Henrich, J., Heine, S. J., & Norenzayan, A. (2010). The weirdest people in the world? *Behavioral and Brain Sciences, 33*, 61–135.

Hensley, C., Browne, J. A., & Trentham, C. E. (2018). Exploring the social and emotional context of childhood animal cruelty and its potential link to adult human violence. *Psychology, Crime & Law, 24*, 489–499.

Herbenick, D., Reece, M., Schick, V., & Sanders, S. A. (2014). Erect penile length and circumference dimensions of 1,661 sexually active men in the United States. *Journal of Sexual Medicine, 11*, 93–101.

Herculano-Houzel, S. (2012). The remarkable, yet not extraordinary, human brain as a scaled-up primate brain and its associated cost. *PNAS, 109*(suppl 1), 10661–10668.

Herholz, S. C., & Zatorre, R. J. (2012). Musical training as a framework for brain plasticity: Behavior, function, and structure. *Neuron, 76*, 486–502.

Herman, C. P., & Polivy, J. (1980). Restrained eating. In A. J. Stunkard (Ed.), *Obesity*. Philadelphia: Saunders.

Herman, C. P., Polivy, J., Pliner, P., & Vartanian, L. R. (2015). Mechanisms underlying the portion-size effect. *Physiology & Behavior, 144*, 129–136.

Herman, C. P., Roth, D. A., & Polivy, J. (2003). Effects of the presence of others on food intake: A normative interpretation. *Psychological Bulletin, 129*, 873–886.

Herman-Giddens, M. E. (2013). The enigmatic pursuit of puberty in girls. *Pediatrics, 132*, 1125–1126.

Herman-Giddens, M. E., Steffes, J., Harris, D., Slora, E., Hussey, M., Dowshen, S. A., . . . Reiter, E. O. (2012). Secondary sexual characteristics in boys: Data from the pediatric research in office settings network. *Pediatrics, 130*, 1058–1068.

Hernandez, A. E., & Li, P. (2007). Age of acquisition: Its neural and computational mechanisms. *Psychological Bulletin, 133*, 638–650.

Hernandez, R., Kershaw, K. N., Siddique, J., Boehm, J. K., Kubzansky, L. D., Diez-Roux, A., . . . Lloyd-Jones, D. M. (2015). Optimism and cardiovascular health: Multi-Ethnic Study of Atherosclerosis (MESA). *Health Behavior and Policy Review, 2*, 62–73.

Heron, M. (2018). Deaths: Leading causes for 2016. *National Vital Statistics Reports, 67*(6[PDF file]). Retrieved from cdc.gov/nchs/data/nvsr/nvsr65/nvsr65_05.pdf

Herrnstein, R. J., & Loveland, D. H. (1964). Complex visual concept in the pigeon. *Science, 146,* 549–551.

Hertenstein, M. J., Hansel, C., Butts, S., Hile, S. (2009). Smile intensity in photographs predicts divorce later in life. *Motivation and Emotion, 33,* 99–105.

Hertenstein, M. J., Keltner, D., App, B., Bulleit, B., & Jaskolka, A. (2006). Touch communicates distinct emotions. *Emotion, 6,* 528–533.

Herz, R. (2012, January 28). You eat that? *The Wall Street Journal* (online.wsj.com).

Herz, R. S. (2001, October). Ah, sweet skunk! Why we like or dislike what we smell. *Cerebrum,* pp. 31–47.

Hess, E. H. (1956, July). Space perception in the chick. *Scientific American,* pp. 71–80.

Hess, U., & Thibault, P. (2009). Darwin and emotion expression. *American Psychologist, 64,* 120–128.

Hetherington, M. M., Anderson, A. S., Norton, G. N. M., & Newson, L. (2006). Situational effects on meal intake: A comparison of eating alone and eating with others. *Physiology and Behavior, 88,* 498–505.

Hewett, R., & Conway, N. (2015). The undermining effect revisited: The salience of everyday verbal rewards and self-determined motivation. *Journal of Organizational Behavior, 37,* 436–455.

Hickok, G. (2014). *The myth of mirror neurons: The real neuroscience of communication and cognition.* New York: Norton.

Hickok, G., Bellugi, U., & Klima, E. S. (2001, June). Sign language in the brain. *Scientific American,* pp. 58–65.

Hidden Brain. (2018, Nov. 19). Nature, nurture, and our evolving debates about gender. National Public Radio (npr.org).

Hilgard, E. R. (1986). *Divided consciousness: Multiple controls in human thought and action.* New York: Wiley.

Hilgard, E. R. (1992). Dissociation and theories of hypnosis. In E. Fromm & M. R. Nash (Eds.), *Contemporary hypnosis research.* New York: Guilford.

Hilker, R., Helenius, D., Fagerlund, B., Skytthe, A., Christensen, K., Werge, T. M., . . . & Glenthøj, B. (2018). Heritability of schizophrenia and schizophrenia spectrum based on the nationwide Danish twin register. *Biological Psychiatry, 83,* 492–498.

Hill, C. E., & Nakayama, E. Y. (2000). Client-centered therapy: Where has it been and where is it going? A comment on Hathaway. *Journal of Clinical Psychology, 56,* 961–875.

Hills, P. J., Werno, M. A., & Lewis, M. B. (2011). Sad people are more accurate at face recognition than happy people. *Consciousness and Cognition, 20,* 1502–1517.

Hines, M. (2004). *Brain gender.* New York: Oxford University Press.

Hingson, R. W., Heeren, T., & Winter, M. R. (2006). Age at drinking onset and alcohol dependence. *Archives of Pediatrics & Adolescent Medicine, 160,* 739–746.

Hintzman, D. L. (1978). *The psychology of learning and memory.* San Francisco: Freeman.

Hinz, L. D., & Williamson, D. A. (1987). Bulimia and depression: A review of the affective variant hypothesis. *Psychological Bulletin, 102,* 150–158.

Hirsh-Pasek, K., Adamson, L. B., Bakeman, R., Owen, M. T., Golinkoff, R. M., Pace, A., . . . Suma, K. (2015). The contribution of early communication quality to low-income children's language success. *Psychological Science, 26,* 1071–1083.

Hirst, W., & Phelps, E. A. (2016). Flashbulb memories. *Current Directions in Psychological Science, 25,* 36–41.

Hirst, W., Phelps, E. A., Buckner, R. L., Budson, A. E., Cuc, A., Gabrieli, J. D., . . . Vaidya, C. J. (2009). Long-term memory for the terrorist attack of September 11: Flashbulb memories, event memories, and the factors that influence their retention. *Journal of Experimental Psychology: General, 138,* 161–176.

Hjelmborg, J. V. B., Fagnani, C., Silventoinen, K., McGue, M., Korkeila, M., Christensen, K., . . . Kaprio, J. (2008). Genetic influences on growth traits of BMI: A longitudinal study of adult twins. *Obesity, 16,* 847–852.

HMHL. (2007, February). Electroconvulsive therapy. *Harvard Mental Health Letter,* Harvard Medical School, pp. 1–4.

Ho, T., Chong, J. K., & Xia, X. (2017). Yellow taxis have fewer accidents than blue taxis because yellow is more visible than blue. *PNAS, 114,* 3074–3078.

Hoang, T. D., Reis, J., Zhu, N., Jacobs, D. R., Jr., Launer, L. J., Whitmer, R. A., . . . Yaffe, K. (2016). Effect of early adult patterns of physical activity and television viewing on midlife cognitive function. *JAMA Psychiatry, 73,* 73–79.

Hobaiter, C., Poisot, T., Zuberbühler, K., Hoppitt, W., & Gruber, T. (2014). Social network analysis shows direct evidence for social transmission of tool use in wild chimpanzees. *PLOS Biology, 12,* e1001960.

Hobbs, W. R., Burke, M., Christakis, N. A., & Fowler, J. H. (2016). Online social integration is associated with reduced mortality risk. *PNAS, 113,* 12980–12984.

Hobson, J. A. (2003). *Dreaming: An introduction to the science of sleep.* New York: Oxford.

Hobson, J. A. (2004). *13 dreams Freud never had: The new mind science.* New York: Pi Press.

Hobson, J. A. (2009). REM sleep and dreaming: Towards a theory of protoconsciousness. *Nature Reviews, 10,* 803–814.

Hoby, H. (2012, September 1). Angel Haze: 'Right now, no one can beat me'. *The Guardian* (theguardian .com).

Hochmair, I. (2013, September). Cochlear implants: The size of the task concerning children born deaf. MED-EL (medel.com).

Hoebel, B. G., & Teitelbaum, P. (1966). Effects of forcefeeding and starvation on food intake and body weight in a rat with ventromedial hypothalamic lesions. *Journal of Comparative and Physiological Psychology, 61,* 189–193.

Hoeft, F., Watson, C. L., Kesler, S. R., Bettinger, K. E., & Reiss, A. L. (2008). Gender differences in the mesocorticolimbic system during computer game-play. *Journal of Psychiatric Research, 42,* 253–258.

Hofer, M. K., Whillans, A. V., & Chen, F. S. (2018). Olfactory cues from romantic partners and strangers influence women's responses to stress. *Journal of Personality and Social Psychology, 114,* 1–9.

Hoffman, B. M., Babyak, M. A., Craighead, W. E., Sherwood, A., Doraiswamy, P. M., Coons, M. J., & Blumenthal, J. A. (2011). Exercise and pharmacotherapy in patients with major depression: One-year follow-up of the SMILE study. *Psychosomatic Medicine, 73,* 127–133.

Hoffman, D. D. (1998). *Visual intelligence: How we create what we see.* New York: Norton.

Hoffman, H. (2012). Considering the role of conditioning in sexual orientation. *Archives of Sexual Behavior, 41,* 63–71.

Hoffman, H. G. (2004, August). Virtual-reality therapy. *Scientific American,* pp. 58–65.

Hoffman, Y. S. G., Shrira, A., Cohen-Fridel, S., Grossman, E. S., & Bodner, E. (2016). The effect of exposure to missile attacks on posttraumatic stress disorder symptoms as a function of perceived media control and locus of control. *Psychiatry Research, 244,* 51–56.

Hofmann, S. G., Sawyer, A. T., Witt, A. A., & Oh, D. (2010). The effect of mindfulness-based therapy on anxiety and depression: A meta-analytic review. *Journal of Consulting and Clinical Psychology, 78,* 169–183.

Hogan, C. L., Catalino, L. I., Mata, J., & Fredrickson, B. L. (2015). Beyond emotional benefits: Physical activity and sedentary behavior affect psychosocial resources through emotions. *Psychology & Health, 30,* 354–369.

Hoge, C. W., Terhakopian, A., Castro, C. A., Messer, S. C., & Engel, C. C. (2007). Association of posttraumatic stress disorder with somatic symptoms, health care visits, and absenteeism among Iraq War veterans. *American Journal of Psychiatry, 164,* 150–153.

Hogg, M. A. (1996). Intragroup processes, group structure and social identity. In W. P. Robinson (Ed.), *Social groups and identities: Developing the legacy of Henri Tajfel.* Oxford: Butterworth Heinemann.

Hogg, M. A. (2006). Social identity theory. In P. J. Burke (Ed.), *Contemporary social psychological theories* (pp. 111–136). Stanford, CA: Stanford University Press.

Hohmann, G. W. (1966). Some effects of spinal cord lesions on experienced emotional feelings. *Psychophysiology, 3,* 143–156.

Holahan, C. K., & Sears, R. R. (1995). *The gifted group in later maturity.* Stanford, CA: Stanford University Press.

Holden, C. (2008). Poles apart. *Science, 321,* 193–195.

Holden, G. W., & Miller, P. C. (1999). Enduring and different: A meta-analysis of the similarity in parents' child rearing. *Psychological Bulletin, 125,* 223–254.

Holland, D., Chang, L., Ernst, T. M., Curran, M., Buchthal, S. D., Alicata, D., . . . Dale, A. M. (2014). Structural growth trajectories and rates of change in the first 3 months of infant brain development. *JAMA Neurology, 71,* 1266–1274.

Holland, J. L. (1996). Exploring careers with a typology: What we have learned and some new directions. *American Psychologist, 51,* 397–406.

Holland, K. J., Cortina, L. M., & Freyd, J. J. (2018). Compelled disclosure of college sexual assault. *American Psychologist, 73,* 256–268.

Holle, H., Warne, K., Seth, A. K., Critchley, H. D., & Ward, J. (2012). Neural basis of contagious itch and why some people are more prone to it. *PNAS, 109,* 19816–19821.

Hollis, K. L. (1997). Contemporary research on Pavlovian conditioning: A "new" functional analysis. *American Psychologist, 52,* 956–965.

Hollon, S. D., DeRubeis, R. J., Fawcett, J., Amsterdam, J. D., Shelton, R. C., Zajecka, J., . . . Gallop, R. (2014). Effect of cognitive therapy with antidepressant medications vs. antidepressants alone on the rate of recovery in major depressive disorder. *JAMA Psychiatry, 71,* 1157–1164.

Holman, E. A., Garfin, D. R., & Silver, R. C. (2014). Media's role in broadcasting acute stress following the Boston marathon bombings. *PNAS, 111,* 93–98.

Holmes, L. (2015, February 18). Kate Middleton has an empowering message for those facing mental health stigma. *The New York Times* (nytimes.com).

Holstege, G., Georgiadis, J. R., Paans, A. M. J., Meiners, L. C., van der Graaf, F. H. C. E., & Reinders, A. A. T. S. (2003a). Brain activation during male ejaculation. *Journal of Neuroscience, 23,* 9185–9193.

Holstege, G., Reinders, A. A. T., Paans, A. M. J., Meiners, L. C., Pruim, J., & Georgiadis, J. R. (2003b).

Brain activation during female sexual orgasm (Annual Conference Abstract Viewer/Itinerary Planner Program No. 727.7). Washington, DC: Society for Neuroscience.

Holtgraves, T. (2011). Text messaging, personality, and the social context. *Journal of Research in Personality, 45*, 92–99.

Homer, B. D., Solomon, T. M., Moeller, R. W., Mascia, A., DeRaleau, L., & Halkitis, P. N. (2008). Methamphetamine abuse and impairment of social functioning: A review of the underlying neurophysiological causes and behavioral implications. *Psychological Bulletin, 134*, 301–310.

Hoogman, M., Bralten, J., Hibar, D. P., Mennes, M., Zwiers, M. P., Schweren, L. S., . . . de Zeeuw, P. (2017). Subcortical brain volume differences in participants with attention deficit hyperactivity disorder in children and adults: A cross-sectional mega-analysis. *The Lancet Psychiatry, 4*, 310–319.

Hooks, K. B., Konsman, J. P., & O'Malley, M. A. (2019). Microbiota-gut-brain research: A critical analysis. *Behavioral and Brain Sciences*, 1–40.

Hooper, J., & Teresi, D. (1986). *The three-pound universe.* New York: Macmillan.

Hopkins, E. D., & Cantalupo, C. (2008). Theoretical speculations on the evolutionary origins of hemispheric specialization. *Current Directions in Psychological Science, 17*, 233–237.

Hopman, E. W. M., & MacDonald, M. C. (2018). Production practice during language learning improves comprehension. *Psychological Science, 29*, 961–971.

Hoppenbrouwers, S. S., Bulten, B. H., & Brazil, I. A. (2016). Parsing fear: A reassessment of the evidence for fear deficits in psychopathy. *Psychological Bulletin, 142*, 573–600.

Horne, J. (2011). The end of sleep: "Sleep debt" versus biological adaptation of human sleep to waking needs. *Biological Psychology, 87*, 1–14.

Horne, Z., Powell, D., Hummel, J. E., & Holyoak, K. J. (2015). Countering antivaccination attitudes. *PNAS, 112*, 10321–10324.

Horowitz, S. S. (2012). The science and art of listening. *The New York Times* (nytimes.com).

Horta, L., de Mola, C. L., & Victora, C. G. (2015). Breastfeeding and intelligence: Systematic review and meta-analysis. *Acta Paediatrica, 104*, 14–19.

Horváth, K., Hannon, B., Ujma, P. P., Gombos, F., & Plunkett, K. (2017). Memory in 3-month-old infants benefits from a short nap. *Developmental Science, 21*, e12587.

Horwood, L. J., & Fergusson, D. M. (1998). Breastfeeding and later cognitive and academic outcomes. *Pediatrics, 101*(1), e9.

Hostinar, C. E., Sullivan, R., & Gunnar, M. R. (2014). Psychobiological mechanisms underlying the social buffering of the hypothalamic-pituitary-adrenocortical axis: A review of animal models and human studies across development. *Psychological Bulletin, 140*, 256–282.

Hou, W.-H., Chiang, P.-T., Hsu, T.-Y., Chiu, S.-Y., & Yen, Y.-C. (2010). Treatment effects of massage therapy in depressed people: A meta-analysis. *Journal of Clinical Psychiatry, 71*, 894–901.

House, R., Javidan, M., & Dorfman, P. (2001). Project GLOBE: An introduction. *Applied Psychology: An International Review, 50*, 489–505.

Houser-Marko, L., & Sheldon, K. M. (2008). Eyes on the prize or nose to the grindstone? The effects of level of goal evaluation on mood and motivation. *Personality and Social Psychology Bulletin, 34*, 1556–1569.

Houts, A. C., Berman, J. S., & Abramson, H. (1994). Effectiveness of psychological and pharmacological treatments for nocturnal enuresis. *Journal of Consulting and Clinical Psychology, 62*, 737–745.

Hovatta, I., Tennant, R. S., Helton, R., Marr, R. A., Singer, O., Redwine, J. M., . . . Barlow, C. (2005). Glyoxalase 1 and glutathione reductase 1 regulate anxiety in mice. *Nature, 438*, 662–666.

Howard, J. L., Gagné, M., & Bureau, J. S. (2017). Testing a continuum structure of self-determined motivation: A meta-analysis. *Psychological Bulletin, 143*, 1346–1377.

Hsee, C. K., & Ruan, B. (2016). The Pandora effect: The power and peril of curiosity. *Psychological Science, 27*, 659–666.

Hsee, C. K., Yang, A. X., & Wang, L. (2010). Idleness aversion and the need for justifiable busyness. *Psychological Science, 21*, 926–930.

Hsiang, S. M., Burke, M., & Miguel, E. (2013). Quantifying the influence of climate on human conflict. *Science, 341*, 1212.

Huang, C. (2010). Mean-level change in self-esteem from childhood through adulthood: Meta-analysis of longitudinal studies. *Review of General Psychology, 14*, 251–260.

Huang, C. (2015). Relation between attributional style and subsequent depressive symptoms: A systematic review and meta-analysis of longitudinal studies. *Cognitive Therapy and Research, 39*, 721–735.

Huang, J., Chaloupka, F. J., & Fong, G. T. (2013). Cigarette graphic warning labels and smoking prevalence in Canada: A critical examination and reformulation of the FDA regulatory impact analysis. *Tobacco Control, 23*, i7–i12.

Huang, M.-E., Wu, Z.-Q., & Tang, G.-Q. (2010). How does personality relate to mental health in service industry setting? The mediating effects of emotional labor strategies. *Acta Psychologica Sinica, 42*, 1175–1189.

Hubbard, E. M., Arman, A. C., Ramachandran, V. S., & Boynton, G. M. (2005). Individual differences among grapheme-color synesthetes: Brain-behavior correlations. *Neuron, 45*, 975–985.

Hubel, D. H. (1979, September). The brain. *Scientific American*, pp. 45–53.

Hubel, D. H., & Wiesel, T. N. (1979, September). Brain mechanisms of vision. *Scientific American*, pp. 150–162.

Hucker, S. J., & Bain, J. (1990). Androgenic hormones and sexual assault. In W. L. Marshall, D. R. Laws, & H. E. Barbaree (Eds.), *Handbook of sexual assault: Issues, theories, and treatment of the offender* (pp. 209–229). New York: Plenum Press.

Huckins, L. M. (2017). Linking cannabis use to depression and suicidal thoughts and behaviours. *The Lancet Psychiatry, 4*, P654–656.

Hudson, N. W., & Roberts, B. W. (2014). Goals to change personality traits: Concurrent links between personality traits, daily behavior, and goals to change oneself. *Journal of Research in Personality, 53*, 68–83.

Huey, E. D., Krueger, F., & Grafman, J. (2006). Representations in the human prefrontal cortex. *Current Directions in Psychological Science, 15*, 167–171.

Hugenberg, K., & Bodenhausen, G. V. (2003). Facing prejudice: Implicit prejudice and the perception of facial threat. *Psychological Science, 14*, 640–643.

Hugenberg, K., Young, S. G., Bernstein, M. J., & Sacco, D. F. (2010). The categorization–individuation model: An integrative account of the other-race recognition deficit. *Psychological Review, 117*, 1168–1187.

Hughes, J. R., Peters, E. N., & Naud, S. (2008). Relapse to smoking after 1 year of abstinence: A meta-analysis. *Addictive Behaviors, 33*, 1516–1520.

Hughes, M. L., Geraci, L., & De Forrest, R. L. (2013). Aging 5 years in 5 minutes: The effect of taking a memory test on older adults' subjective age. *Psychological Science, 24*, 2481–2488.

Hull, J. G., & Bond, C. F., Jr. (1986). Social and behavioral consequences of alcohol consumption and expectancy: A meta-analysis. *Psychological Bulletin, 99*, 347–360.

Hull, J. M. (1990). *Touching the rock: An experience of blindness.* New York: Vintage Books.

Hull, S. J., Hennessy, M., Bleakley, A., Fishbein, M., & Jordan, A. (2011). Identifying the causal pathways from religiosity to delayed adolescent sexual behavior. *Journal of Sex Research, 48*, 543–553.

Human Connectome Project. (2013). The Human Connectome Project (humanconnectome.org).

Hummer, R. A., Rogers, R. G., Nam, C. B., & Ellison, C. G. (1999). Religious involvement and U.S. adult mortality. *Demography, 36*, 273–285.

Humphrey, S. E., Nahrgang, J. D., & Morgeson, F. P. (2007). Integrating motivational, social, and contextual work design features: A meta-analytic summary and theoretical extension of the work design literature. *Journal of Applied Psychology, 92*, 1332–1356.

Hunsley, J., & Bailey, J.M. (1999). The clinical utility of the Rorschach: Unfulfilled promises and an uncertain future. *Psychological Assessment, 11*, 266–277.

Hunsley, J., & Di Giulio, G. (2002). Dodo bird, phoenix, or urban legend? The question of psychotherapy equivalence. *Scientific Review of Mental Health Practice, 1*, 11–22.

Hunt, C., Slade, T., & Andrews, G. (2004). Generalized anxiety disorder and major depressive disorder comorbidity in the National Survey of Mental Health and Well-Being. *Depression and Anxiety, 20*, 23–31.

Hunt, J. M. (1982). Toward equalizing the developmental opportunities of infants and preschool children. *Journal of Social Issues, 38*, 163–191.

Hunt, L. L., Eastwick, P. W., & Finkel, E. J. (2015). Leveling the playing field: Longer acquaintance predicts reduced assortative mating on attractiveness. *Psychological Science, 26*, 1046–1053.

Hunt, M. (1990). *The compassionate beast: What science is discovering about the humane side of humankind.* New York: William Morrow.

Hunt, M. (1993). *The story of psychology.* New York: Doubleday.

Hunter, S., & Sundel, M. (Eds.). (1989). *Midlife myths: Issues, findings, and practice implications.* Newbury Park, CA: Sage.

Hutchinson, R. (2006). *Calum's road.* Edinburgh, Scotland: Burlinn Limited.

Hutchison, K. A., Smith, J. L., & Ferris, A. (2013). Goals can be threatened to extinction using the Stroop task to clarify working memory depletion under stereotype threat. *Social and Personality Psychological Science, 4*, 74–81.

Hutteman, R., Nestler, S., Wagner, J., Egloff, B., & Back, M. D. (2015). Wherever I may roam: Processes of self-esteem development from adolescence to emerging adulthood in the context of international student exchange. *Journal of Personality and Social Psychology, 108*, 767–783.

Hvistendahl, M. (2011). China's population growing slowly, changing fast. *Science, 332*, 650–651.

Hyde, J. S. (2014). Gender similarities and differences. *Annual Review of Psychology, 65*, 373–398.

Hyde, J. S., & Mertz, J. E. (2009). Gender, culture, and mathematics performance. *PNAS, 106,* 8801–8807.

Iacoboni, M. (2009). Imitation, empathy, and mirror neurons. *Annual Review of Psychology, 60,* 653–670.

Ibbotson, P., & Tomasello, M. (2016, November). Language in a new key. *Scientific American,* pp. 71–75.

Ibos, G., & Freedman, D. J. (2014). Dynamic integration of task-relevant visual features in posterior parietal cortex. *Neuron, 83,* 1468–1480.

Idson, L. C., & Mischel, W. (2001). The personality of familiar and significant people: The lay perceiver as a social-cognitive theorist. *Journal of Personality and Social Psychology, 80,* 585–596.

IJzerman, H., & Semin, G. R. (2009). The thermometer of social relations: Mapping social proximity on temperature. *Psychological Science, 20,* 1214–1220.

Ikizer, E. G., & Blanton, H. (2016). Media coverage of "wise" interventions can reduce concern for the disadvantaged. *Journal of Experimental Psychology: Applied, 22,* 135–147.

Ilardi, S. (2016, accessed May 2). *Therapeutic lifestyle change (TLC).* University of Kansas (tlc.ku.edu).

Ilardi, S. S. (2009). *The depression cure: The six-step program to beat depression without drugs.* Cambridge, MA: De Capo Lifelong Books.

Ilieva, I. P., Hook, C. J., & Farah, M. J. (2015). Prescription stimulants' effects on healthy inhibitory control, working memory, and episodic memory: A meta-analysis. *Journal of Cognitive Neuroscience, 27,* 1069–1089.

Imuta, K., Henry, J. D., Slaughter, V., Selcuk, B., & Ruffman, T. (2016). Theory of mind and prosocial behavior in childhood: A meta-analytic review. *Developmental Psychology,* 52, 1192–1205.

Inbar, Y., Cone, J., & Gilovich, T. (2010). People's intuitions about intuitive insight and intuitive choice. *Journal of Personality and Social Psychology, 99,* 232–247.

Infurna, F. J., & Luthar, S. S. (2016a). The multidimensional nature of resilience to spousal loss. *Journal of Personality and Social Psychology, 112,* 926–947.

Infurna, F. J., & Luthar, S. S. (2016b). Resilience to major life stressors is not as common as thought. *Perspectives on Psychological Science, 11,* 175–194.

Ingalhalikar, M., Smith, A., Parker, D., Satterthwaite, T. D., Elliott, M. A., Ruparel, K., . . . Verma, R. (2013). Sex differences in the structural connectome of the human brain. *PNAS, 111,* 823–828.

Ingham, A. G., Levinger, G., Graves, J., & Peckham, V. (1974). The Ringelmann effect: Studies of group size and group performance. *Journal of Experimental Social Psychology, 10,* 371–384.

Inglehart, R. (1990). *Culture shift in advanced industrial society.* Princeton, NJ: Princeton University Press.

Inglehart, R., Foa, R., Peterson, C., & Welzel, C. (2008). Development, freedom, and rising happiness: A global perspective (1981–2007). *Perspectives on Psychological Science, 3,* 264–285.

Ingraham, C. (2016, May 1). Toddlers have shot at least 23 people this year. *The Washington Post* (washingtonpost.com).

Innocence Project. (2018, accessed September 19). DNA exonerations in the United States. Retrieved from innocenceproject.org/dna-exonerations-in-the-united-states

Insel, T., Cuthbert, B., Garvey, M., Heinssen, R., Pine, D. S., Quinn, K., . . . Wang, P. (2010). Research Domain Criteria (RDoC): Toward a new classification framework for research on mental disorders. *American Journal of Psychiatry, 167,* 748–751.

Insel, T. R. (2010). Faulty circuits. *Scientific American, 302,* 44–51.

Insel, T. R., & Cuthbert, B. N. (2015). Brain disorders? Precisely. *Science, 348,* 499–500.

Insel, T. R., & Lieberman, J. A. (2013, May 13). *DSM-5 and RDoC: Shared interests. National Institute of Mental Health.* [Press release.] Retrieved from nimh.nih.gov/news/science-news/2013/dsm-5-and-rdoc-shared-interests.shtml

Inzlicht, M., & Kang, S. K. (2010). Stereotype threat spillover: How coping with threats to social identity affects aggression, eating, decision making, and attention. *Journal of Personality and Social Psychology, 99,* 467–481.

Ion, A., Mindu, A., & Gorbănescu, A. (2017). Grit in the workplace: Hype or ripe? *Personality and Individual Differences, 111,* 163–168.

IPU. (2018). *Women in parliament in 2017: The year in review.* Retrieved from https://www.ipu.org/resources/publications/reports/2018-03/women-in-parliament-in-2017-year-in-review

Ireland, M. E., & Pennebaker, J. W. (2010). Language style matching in writing: Synchrony in essays, correspondence, and poetry. *Journal of Personality and Social Psychology, 99,* 549–571.

Ironson, G., Solomon, G. F., Balbin, E. G., O'Cleirigh, C., George, A., Kumar, M., . . . Woods, T. E. (2002). The Ironson-Woods spiritual/religiousness index is associated with long survival, health behaviors, less distress, and low cortisol in people with HIV/AIDS. *Annals of Behavioral Medicine, 24,* 34–48.

Isaacowitz, D. M. (2012). Mood regulation in real time: Age differences in the role of looking. *Current Directions in Psychological Science, 21,* 237–242.

Ishiyama, S., & Brecht, M. (2017). Neural correlates of ticklishness in the rat somatosensory cortex. *Science, 354,* 757–760.

Ising, H. K., Smit, F., Veling, W., Rietdijk, J., Dragt, S., Klaassen, R. M. C., . . . van der Gaag, M. (2015). Cost-effectiveness of preventing first-episode psychosis in ultra-high-risk subjects: Multi-centre randomized controlled trial. *Psychological Medicine, 45,* 1435–1446.

Islam, S. S., & Johnson, C. (2003). Correlates of smoking behavior among Muslim Arab-American adolescents. *Ethnicity & Health, 8,* 319–337.

Iso-Markku, P., Waller, K., Vuoksimaa, E., Heikkilä, K., Rinne, J., Kaprio, J., & Kujala, U. M. (2016). Midlife physical activity and cognition later in life: A prospective twin study. *Journal of Alzheimer's Disease, 54,* 1303–1317.

Iso, H., Simoda, S., & Matsuyama, T. (2007). Environmental change during postnatal development alters behaviour. *Behavioural Brain Research, 179,* 90–98.

ITU. (2016, accessed April 20). *ICT facts and figures* [PDF file]. Retrieved from itu.int/en/ITU-D/Statistics/Documents/facts/ICTFactsFigures2015.pdf

Ives-Deliperi, V. L., Solms, M., & Meintjes, E. M. (2011). The neural substrates of mindfulness: An fMRI investigation. *Social Neuroscience, 6,* 231–242.

Iyengar, S. S., & Lepper, M. R. (2000). When choice is demotivating: Can one desire too much of a good thing? *Journal of Personality and Social Psychology, 79,* 995–1006.

Iyengar, S., & Westwood, S. J. (2015). Fear and loathing across party lines: New evidence on group polarization. *American Journal of Political Science, 59,* 690–707.

Izard, C. E. (1977). *Human emotions.* New York: Plenum Press.

Izard, C. E. (1994). Innate and universal facial expressions: Evidence from developmental and cross-cultural research. *Psychological Bulletin, 114,* 288–299.

Jääskeläinen, E., Juola, P., Hirvonen, N., McGrath, J. J., Saha, S., Isohanni, M., . . . Miettunen, J. (2013). A systematic review and meta-analysis of recovery in schizophrenia. *Schizophrenia Bulletin, 39,* 1296–1306.

Jablensky, A. (1999). Schizophrenia: Epidemiology. *Current Opinion in Psychiatry, 12,* 19–28.

Jablensky, A., Sartorius, N., Ernberg, G., Anker, M., Korten, A., Cooper, J. E., . . . & Bertelsen, A. (1992). Schizophrenia: manifestations, incidence and course in different cultures. A World Health Organization ten-country study. *Psychological Medicine Monograph Supplement, 20,* 1–97.

Jachimowicz, J., Wihler, A., Bailey, E., & Galinsky, A. (2018). Why grit requires perseverance and passion to positively predict performance. *PNAS, 115,* 9980–9985.

Jack, R. E., Garrod, O. G. B., Yu, H., Caldara, R., & Schyns, P. G. (2012). Facial expressions of emotion are not culturally universal. *PNAS, 109,* 7241–7244.

Jackson, G. (2009). Sexual response in cardiovascular disease. *Journal of Sex Research, 46,* 233–236.

Jackson, J. M., & Williams, K. D. (1988). *Social loafing: A review and theoretical analysis.* Unpublished manuscript, Fordham University.

Jackson, S. W. (1992). The listening healer in the history of psychological healing. *American Journal Psychiatry, 149,* 1623–1632.

Jacobs, B. L. (2004). Depression: The brain finally gets into the act. *Current Directions in Psychological Science, 13,* 103–106.

Jacobson, L. (2015, August 27). More Americans killed by guns since 1968 than in all U.S. wars, columnist Nicholas Kristof writes. *Politifact* (politifact.com).

Jacques, C., & Rossion, B. (2006). The speed of individual face categorization. *Psychological Science, 17,* 485–492.

Jaffe, E. (2004, October). Peace in the Middle East may be impossible: Lee D. Ross on naive realism and conflict resolution. *APS Observer,* pp. 9–11.

Jakubiak, B. K., & Feeney, B. C. (2017). Affectionate touch to promote relational, psychological, and physical well-being in adulthood: A theoretical model and review of the research. *Personality and Social Psychology Review, 21,* 228–252.

Jakubowski, K. P., Cundiff, J. M., & Matthews, K. A. (2018). Cumulative childhood adversity and adult cardiometabolic disease: A meta-analysis. *Health Psychology, 37,* 701–715.

James, S. E., Herman, J. L., Rankin, S., Keisling, M., Mottet, L., & Anafi, M. (2016). *The report of the 2015 U.S. Transgender Survey* [PDF file]. Retrieved from https://transequality.org/sites/default/files/docs/usts/USTS-Full-Report-Dec17.pdf

James, S. L., Abate, D., Abate, K. H., Abay, S. M., Abbafati, C., Abbasi, N., . . . & Abdollahpour, I. (2018). Global, regional, and national incidence, prevalence, and years lived with disability for 354 diseases and injuries for 195 countries and territories, 1990–2017: A systematic analysis for the Global Burden of Disease Study 2017. *The Lancet, 392,* 1789–1858.

James, W. (1890). *The principles of psychology* (Vol. 2). New York: Holt.

Jamieson, J. P. (2010). The home field advantage in athletics: A meta-analysis. *Journal of Applied Social Psychology, 40,* 1819–1848.

Jamieson, J. P., Peters, B. J., Greenwood, E. J., & Altose, A. J. (2016). Reappraising stress arousal improves performance and reduces evaluation anxiety in classroom exam situations. *Social Psychological and Personality Science, 7,* 579–587.

Jamison, K. R. (1993). *Touched with fire: Manic-depressive illness and the artistic temperament.* New York: Free Press.

Jamison, K. R. (1995). *An unquiet mind.* New York: Knopf.

Janis, I. L. (1982). *Groupthink: Psychological studies of policy decisions and fiascoes.* Boston: Houghton Mifflin.

Janis, I. L. (1986). Problems of international crisis management in the nuclear age. *Journal of Social Issues, 42,* 201–220.

Janoff-Bulman, R., Timko, C., & Carli, L. L. (1985). Cognitive biases in blaming the victim. *Journal of Experimental Social Psychology, 21,* 161–177.

Jayakar, R., King, T. Z., Morris, R., & Na, S. (2015). Hippocampal volume and auditory attention on a verbal memory task with adult survivors of pediatric brain tumor. *Neuropsychology, 29,* 303–319.

Jebb, A. T., Tay, L., Diener, E., & Oishi, S. (2018). Happiness, income satiation and turning points around the world. *Nature: Human Behaviour, 2,* 33–38.

Jedrychowski, W., Perera, F., Jankowski, J., Butscher, M., Mroz, E., Flak, E., . . . Sowa, A. (2012). Effect of exclusive breastfeeding on the development of children's cognitive function in the Krakow prospective birth cohort study. *European Journal of Pediatrics, 171,* 151–158.

Jeffrey, K., Mahoney, S., Michaelson, J., & Abdallah, S. (2014). Well-being at work: A review of the literature. Retrieved from neweconomics.org /2014/03/wellbeing-at-work

Jena, A. B., Jain, A., & Hicks, T. R. (2018). Do 'Fast and 'Furious' movies cause a rise in speeding? *The New York Times* (nytimes.com).

Jenkins, J. G., & Dallenbach, K. M. (1924). Obliviscence during sleep and waking. *American Journal of Psychology, 35,* 605–612.

Jenkins, J. M., & Astington, J. W. (1996). Cognitive factors and family structure associated with theory of mind development in young children. *Developmental Psychology, 32,* 70–78.

Jensen, J. P., & Bergin, A. E. (1988). Mental health values of professional therapists: A national interdisciplinary survey. *Professional Psychology: Research and Practice, 19,* 290–297.

Jeon, D. W., Jung, D. U., Kim, S. J., Shim, J. C., Moon, J. J., Seo, Y. S., . . . & Kim, Y. N. (2018). Adjunct transcranial direct current stimulation improves cognitive function in patients with schizophrenia: A double-blind 12-week study. *Schizophrenia Research, 197,* 378–385.

Jepson, C., Krantz, D. H., & Nisbett, R. E. (1983). Inductive reasoning: Competence or skill. *The Behavioral and Brain Sciences, 3,* 494–501.

Jessberger, S., Aimone, J. B., & Gage, F. H. (2008). Neurogenesis. In J. H. Byrne (Ed.), *Learning and memory: A comprehensive reference: Vol. 4. Molecular mechanisms of memory* (pp. 839–858). Oxford: Elsevier.

Jiang, H., White, M. P., Greicius, M. D., Waelde, L. C., & Spiegel, D. (2016). Brain activity and functional connectivity associated with hypnosis. *Cerebral Cortex, 27,* 4083–4093.

Jiang, J. (2018, August 22). How teens and parents navigate screen time and device distractions. Pew Research Center (pewinternet.org).

Jimenez, J. C., Su, K., Goldberg, A. R., Luna, V. M., Biane, J. S., Ordek, G., . . . & Paninski, L. (2018). Anxiety cells in a hippocampal-hypothalamic circuit. *Neuron, 97,* 670–683.

Job, V., Dweck, C. S., & Walton, G. M. (2010). Ego depletion—Is it all in your head?: Implicit theories about willpower affect self-regulation. *Psychological Science, 21,* 1686–1693.

Jobe, T. H., & Harrow, M. (2010). Schizophrenia course, long-term outcome, recovery, and prognosis. *Current Directions in Psychological Science, 19,* 220–225.

Joel, D., Berman, Z, Tavor, I., Wexler, N., Gaber, O., Stein, Y., . . . Assaf, Y. (2015, December) Sex beyond the genitalia: The human brain mosaic. *PNAS, 112*(50), 15468–15473.

Joel, S., Eastwick, P. W., & Finkel, E. J. (2017). Is romantic desire predictable? Machine learning applied to initial romantic attraction. *Psychological Science, 28,* 1478–1489.

Johnson, D. L., Wiebe, J. S., Gold, S. M., Andreasen, N. C., Hichwa, R. D., Watkins, G. L., & Ponto, L. L. B. (1999). Cerebral blood flow and personality: A positron emission tomography study. *American Journal of Psychiatry, 156,* 252–257.

Johnson, D. P., Rhee, S. H., Friedman, N. P., Corley, R. P., Munn-Chernoff, M., Hewitt, J. K., & Whisman, M. A. (2016). A twin study examining rumination as a transdiagnostic correlate of psychopathology. *Clinical Psychological Science, 4,* 971–987.

Johnson, E. J., & Goldstein, D. (2003). Do defaults save lives? *Science, 302,* 1338–1339.

Johnson, J. A. (2007, June 26). Not so situational. Commentary on the SPSP listserv (spsp-discuss@stolaf.edu).

Johnson, J. G., Cohen, P., Kotler, L., Kasen, S., & Brook, J. S. (2002). Psychiatric disorders associated with risk for the development of eating disorders during adolescence and early adulthood. *Journal of Consulting and Clinical Psychology, 70,* 1119–1128.

Johnson, J. S., & Newport, E. L. (1991). Critical period affects on universal properties of language: The status of subjacency in the acquisition of a second language. *Cognition, 39,* 215–258.

Johnson, M. D., & Chen, J. (2015). Blame it on the alcohol: The influence of alcohol consumption during adolescence, the transition to adulthood, and young adulthood on one-time sexual hookups. *Journal of Sex Research, 52,* 570–579.

Johnson, M. H., & Morton, J. (1991). *Biology and cognitive development: The case of face recognition.* Oxford, England: Blackwell.

Johnson, M. P. (2008). *A typology of domestic violence: Intimate terrorism, violent resistance, and situational couple violence.* Boston: Northeastern University Press.

Johnson, R. (2017, August 12). The mystery of S., the man with an impossible memory. *The New Yorker* (newyorker.com).

Johnson, W. (2010). Understanding the genetics of intelligence: Can height help? Can corn oil? *Current Directions in Psychological Science, 19,* 177–182.

Johnson, W., Carothers, A., & Deary, I. J. (2008). Sex differences in variability in general intelligence: A new look at the old question. *Perspectives on Psychological Science, 3,* 518–531.

Johnston, L. D., Miech, R. A., O'Malley, P. M., Bachman, J. G., Schulenberg, J. E., & Patrick, M. E. (2018). *Monitoring the Future national survey results on drug use: 1975–2017: Overview, key findings on adolescent drug use.* Ann Arbor: Institute for Social Research, The University of Michigan.

Johnston, L. D., O'Malley, P. M., Bachman, J. G., & Schulenberg, J. E. (2007, May). *Monitoring the Future national results on adolescent drug use: Overview of key findings, 2006.* Bethesda, MD: National Institute on Drug Abuse.

Joiner, T. E., Jr. (2006). *Why people die by suicide.* Cambridge, MA: Harvard University Press.

Jonason, P. K., Garcia, J. R., Webster, G. D., Li, N. P., & Fisher, H. E. (2015). Relationship dealbreakers: Traits people avoid in potential mates. *Personality and Social Psychology Bulletin, 41,* 1697–1711.

Jones, A. C., & Gosling, S. D. (2005). Temperament and personality in dogs *(Canis familiaris)*: A review and evaluation of past research. *Applied Animal Behaviour Science, 95,* 1–53.

Jones, B., Reedy, E. J., & Weinberg, B. A. (2014, January). *Age and scientific genius.* Retrieved from nber .org/papers/w19866

Jones, E. (1957). *Sigmund Freud: Life and Work,* Vol. 3, Pt. 1., Ch. 4. New York: Basic Books.

Jones, J. M. (2016, November 21). *Record-high 77% of Americans perceive nation as divided.* Gallup Poll (gallup .com).

Jones, M. (2018, February 7). What teenagers are learning from online porn. *The New York Times Magazine* (nytimes.com).

Jones, M. C. (1924). A laboratory study of fear: The case of Peter. *Journal of Genetic Psychology, 31,* 308–315.

Jones, S. (2017). Can newborn infants imitate? *WIREs Cognitive Science, 8*(1-2), 1–13.

Jones, S. S. (2007). Imitation in infancy: The development of mimicry. *Psychological Science, 18,* 593–599.

Jorm, A. F., Reavley, N. J., & Ross, A. M. (2012). Belief in the dangerousness of people with mental disorders: A review. *Australian and New Zealand Journal of Psychiatry, 46,* 1029–1045.

Jose, A., O'Leary, D., & Moyer, A. (2010). Does premarital cohabitation predict subsequent marital stability and marital quality? A meta-analysis. *Journal of Marriage and Family, 72,* 105–116.

Joshi, S. H., Espinoza, R. T., Pirnia, T., Shi, J., Wang, Y., Ayers, B., . . . Narr, K. L. (2016). Structural plasticity of the hippocampus and amygdala induced by electroconvulsive therapy in major depression. *Biological Psychiatry, 79,* 282–292.

Jost, J. T. (2019). The IAT is dead, long live the IAT: Context-sensitive measures of implicit attitudes are indispensable to social and political psychology. *Current Directions in Psychological Science, 28,* 10–19.

Jost, J. T., Kay, A. C., & Thorisdottir, H. (Eds.) (2009). *Social and psychological bases of ideology and system justification.* New York: Oxford University Press.

Judge, T. A., Thoresen, C. J., Bono, J. E., & Patton, G. K. (2001). The job satisfaction/job performance relationship: A qualitative and quantitative review. *Psychological Bulletin, 127,* 376–407.

Jung-Beeman, M., Bowden, E. M., Haberman, J., Frymiare, J. L., Arambel-Liu, S., Greenblatt, R., . . . Kounios, J. (2004). Neural activity when people solve verbal problems with insight. *PLOS Biology, 2,* e111.

Just, M. A., Keller, T. A., & Cynkar, J. (2008). A decrease in brain activation associated with driving when listening to someone speak. *Brain Research, 1205,* 70–80.

Kable, J. W., Caulfield, M. K., Falcone, M., McConnell, M., Bernardo, L., Parthasarathi, T., . . . & Diefenbach, P. (2017). No effect of commercial cognitive training on brain activity, choice behavior, or cognitive performance. *Journal of Neuroscience, 37,* 7390–7402.

Kadohisa, M. (2013). Effects of odor on emotion, with implications. *Frontiers in Systems Neuroscience, 7,* 6.

Kagan, J. (1976). Emergent themes in human development. *American Scientist, 64,* 186–196.

Kagan, J. (1984). *The nature of the child.* New York: Basic Books.

Kagan, J. (1995). On attachment. *Harvard Review of Psychiatry, 3,* 104–106.

Kagan, J. (1998). *Three seductive ideas.* Cambridge, MA: Harvard University Press.

Kagan, J. (2010). *The temperamental thread: How genes, culture, time, and luck make us who we are.* Washington, DC: Dana Press.

Kagan, J., & Snidman, N. (2004). *The long shadow of temperament.* Cambridge, MA: Belknap Press.

Kagan, J., Lapidus, D. R., & Moore, M. (1978, December). Infant antecedents of cognitive functioning: A longitudinal study. *Child Development, 49*(4), 1005–1023.

Kahan, D. M. (2015). What is the "science of science communication"? *Journal of Science Communication,* 14, 1–10.

Kahneman, D. (1985, June). Quoted by K. McKean, Decisions, decisions. *Discover,* pp. 22–31.

Kahneman, D. (1999). Assessments of objective happiness: A bottom-up approach. In D. Kahneman, E. Diener, & N. Schwartz (Eds.), *Understanding well-being: Scientific perspectives on enjoyment and suffering.* New York: Russell Sage Foundation.

Kahneman, D. (2005a, January 13). What were they thinking? Q&A with Daniel Kahneman. *Gallup Management Journal* (gmj.gallup.com).

Kahneman, D. (2005b, January 13). What were they thinking? Q&A with Daniel Kahneman. *Gallup Management Journal* (gmj.gallup.com).

Kahneman, D. (2011). *Thinking, fast and slow.* New York: Farrar, Straus, and Giroux.

Kahneman, D., & Tversky, A. (1972). Subjective probability: A judgment of representativeness. *Cognitive Psychology* 3, 430–454.

Kahneman, D., Fredrickson, B. L., Schreiber, C. A., & Redelmeier, D. A. (1993). When more pain is preferred to less: Adding a better end. *Psychological Science,* 4, 401–405.

Kahneman, D., Krueger, A. B., Schkade, D. A., Schwarz, N., & Stone, A. A. (2004). A survey method for characterizing daily life experience: The day reconstruction method. *Science, 306,* 1776–1780.

Kail, R. (1991). Developmental change in speed of processing during childhood and adolescence. *Psychological Bulletin, 109,* 490–501.

Kail, R., & Hall, L. K. (2001). Distinguishing short-term memory from working memory. *Memory & Cognition, 29,* 1–9.

Kaiser Family Foundation. (2010, January). *Generation M2: Media in the lives of 8- to 18-year-olds* (by V. J. Rideout, U. G. Foeher, & D. F. Roberts). Menlo Park, CA: Henry J. Kaiser Family Foundation.

Kakinami, L., Barnett, T. A., Séguin, L., & Paradis, G. (2015). Parenting style and obesity risk in children. *Preventive Medicine, 75,* 18–22.

Kalokerinos, E. K., Kjelsaas, K., Bennetts, S., & von Hippel, C. (2018). Men in pink-collars: Stereotype threat and disengagement among male teachers and child protection workers. *European Journal of Social Psychology, 47,* 553–565.

Kambeitz, J., Kambelitz-Hankovic, L., Cabral, C., Dwyer, D. B., Calhoun, V. C., van den Heuvel, M. P., . . . Malchow, B. (2016). Aberrant functional whole-brain network architecture in patients with schizophrenia: A meta-analysis. *Schizophrenia Bulletin, 42,* Suppl. no. 1, S13–S21.

Kamel, N. S., & Gammack, J. K. (2006). Insomnia in the elderly: Cause, approach, and treatment. *American Journal of Medicine, 119,* 463–469.

Kamenica, E., Naclerio, R., & Malani, A. (2013). Advertisements impact the physiological efficacy of a branded drug. *PNAS, 110,* 12931–12935.

Kamil, A. C., & Cheng, K. (2001). Way-finding and landmarks: The multiple-bearings hypothesis. *Journal of Experimental Biology, 204,* 103–113.

Kaminski, J., Cali, J., & Fischer, J. (2004). Word learning in a domestic dog: Evidence for "fast mapping." *Science, 304,* 1682–1683.

Kamp, K. S., & Due, H. (2018). How many bereaved people hallucinate about their loved one? A systematic review and meta-analysis of bereavement hallucinations. *Journal of Affective Disorders, 243,* 463–476.

Kämpf, M. S., Liebermann, H., Kerschreiter, R., Krause, S., Nestler, S., & Schmukle, S. C. (2018). Disentangling the sources of mimicry: Social relations analyses of the link between mimicry and liking. *Psychological Science, 29,* 131–138.

Kandel, E. (2008, October/November). Quoted in S. Avan, Speaking of memory. *Scientific American Mind,* pp. 16–17.

Kandel, E. (2013, September 6). The new science of mind. *The New York Times* (nytimes.com).

Kandel, E. R. (2012, March 5). Interview by Claudia Dreifus: A quest to understand how memory works. *The New York Times* (nytimes.com).

Kandel, E. R., & Schwartz, J. H. (1982). Molecular biology of learning: Modulation of transmitter release. *Science, 218,* 433–443.

Kandler, C., & Riemann, R. (2013). Genetic and environmental sources of individual religiousness: The roles of individual personality traits and perceived environmental religiousness. *Behavior Genetics, 43,* 297–313.

Kandler, C., Riemann, R., & Angleitner, A. (2013). Patterns and sources of continuity and change of energetic and temporal aspects of temperament in adulthood: A longitudinal twin study of self and peer reports. *Developmental Psychology, 49,* 1739–1753.

Kane, G. D. (2010). Revisiting gay men's body image issues: Exposing the fault lines. *Review of General Psychology, 14,* 311–317.

Kane, J. M., & Mertz, J. E. (2012). Debunking myths about gender and mathematics performance. *Notices of the American Mathematical Society, 59,* 10–21.

Kaplan, H. I., & Saddock, B. J. (Eds.). (1989). *Comprehensive textbook of psychiatry,* V. Baltimore, MD: Williams and Wilkins.

Kaprio, J., Koskenvuo, M., & Rita, H. (1987). Mortality after bereavement: A prospective study of 95,647 widowed persons. *American Journal of Public Health, 77,* 283–287.

Karacan, I., Goodenough, D. R., Shapiro, A., & Starker, S. (1966). Erection cycle during sleep in relation to dream anxiety. *Archives of General Psychiatry, 15,* 183–189.

Karasik, L. B., Adolph, K. E., Tamis-LeMonda, C. S., & Bornstein, M. H. (2010). WEIRD walking: Cross-cultural research on motor development. *Behavioral and Brain Sciences, 33,* 95–96.

Karau, S. J., & Williams, K. D. (1993). Social loafing: A meta-analytic review and theoretical integration. *Journal of Personality and Social Psychology, 65,* 681–706.

Karazsia, B. T., Murnen, S. K., & Tylka, T. L. (2017). Is body dissatisfaction changing across time? A cross-temporal meta-analysis. *Psychological Bulletin, 143,* 293–320.

Kark, J. D., Shemi, G., Friedlander, Y., Martin, O., Manor, O., & Blondheim, S. H. (1996). Does religious observance promote health? Mortality in secular vs. religious kibbutzim in Israel. *American Journal of Public Health, 86,* 341–346.

Karlén, J., Ludvigsson, J., Hedmark, M., Faresjö, Å., Theodorsson, E., & Faresjö, T. (2015). Early psychosocial exposures, hair cortisol levels, and disease risk. *Pediatrics, 135,* e1450–e1457.

Karlsgodt, K. H., Sun, D., & Cannon, T. D. (2010). Structural and functional brain abnormalities in schizophrenia. *Current Directions in Psychological Science, 19,* 226–231.

Karpicke, J. D. (2012). Retrieval-based learning: Active retrieval promotes meaningful learning. *Current Directions in Psychological Science, 21,* 157–163.

Karremans, J. C., Frankenhis, W. E., & Arons, S. (2010). Blind men prefer a low waist-to-hip ratio. *Evolution and Human Behavior, 31,* 182–186.

Kasen, S., Chen, H., Sneed, J., Crawford, T., & Cohen, P. (2006). Social role and birth cohort influences on gender-linked personality traits in women: A 20-year longitudinal analysis. *Journal of Personality and Social Psychology, 91,* 944–958.

Kashdan, T. B. (2009). *Curious? Discover the missing ingredient to a fulfilling life.* New York: William Morrow.

Katz-Wise, S. L., & Hyde, J. S. (2012). Victimization experiences of lesbian, gay, and bisexual individuals: A meta-analysis. *Journal of Sex Research, 49,* 142–167.

Katz-Wise, S. L., Priess, H. A., & Hyde, J. S. (2010). Gender-role attitudes and behavior across the transition to parenthood. *Developmental Psychology, 46,* 18–28.

Kaufman, J. C., & Baer, J. (2002). I bask in dreams of suicide: Mental illness, poetry, and women. *Review of General Psychology, 6,* 271–286.

Kaufman, L., & Kaufman, J. H. (2000). Explaining the moon illusion. *PNAS, 97,* 500–505.

Kawakami, K., Dunn, E., Karmali, F., & Dovidio, J. F. (2009). Mispredicting affective and behavioral responses to racism. *Science, 323,* 276–278.

Kawamichi, H., Yoshihara, K., Sugawara, S. K., Matsunaga, M., Makita, K., Hamano, Y. H., . . . Sadato, N. (2015). Helping behavior induced by empathic concern attenuates anterior cingulate activation in response to others' distress. *Social Neuroscience, 11,* 109–122.

Kay, A. C., Baucher, D., Peach, J. M., Laurin, K., Friesen, J., Zanna, M. P., & Spencer, S. J. (2009). Inequality, discrimination, and the power of the status quo: Direct evidence for a motivation to see the way things are as the way they should be. *Journal of Personality and Social Psychology, 97,* 421–434.

Kayser, C. (2007, April/May). Listening with your eyes. *Scientific American Mind,* pp. 24–29.

Kazantzis, N., & Dattilio, F. M. (2010). Definitions of homework, types of homework and ratings of the importance of homework among psychologists with cognitive behavior therapy and psychoanalytic theoretical orientations. *Journal of Clinical Psychology, 66,* 758–773.

Kazantzis, N., Whittington, C., & Dattilio, F. M. (2010). Meta-analysis of homework effects in cognitive and behavioral therapy: A replication and extension. *Clinical Psychology: Science and Practice, 17,* 144–156.

Kazdin, A. E. (2015). Editor's introduction to the special series: Targeted training of cognitive processes for behavioral and emotional disorders. *Clinical Psychological Science, 3,* 38.

Kean, S. (2016, September). The audacious plan to save this man's life by transplanting his head. *The Atlantic* (theatlantic.com).

Keesey, R. E., & Corbett, S. W. (1983). Metabolic defense of the body weight set-point. In A. J. Stunkard & E. Stellar (Eds.), *Eating and its disorders* (pp. 87–96). New York: Raven Press.

Keiser, H. N., Sackett, P. R., Kuncel, N. R., & Brothen, T. (2016). Why women perform better in college than admission scores would predict: Exploring the roles of conscientiousness and course-taking patterns. *Journal of Applied Psychology, 101*, 569–581.

Keith, S. W., Redden, D. T., Katzmarzyk, P. T., Boggiano, M. M., Hanlon, E. C., Benca, R. M., . . . Allison, D. B. (2006). Putative contributors to the secular increase in obesity: Exploring the roads less traveled. *International Journal of Obesity, 30*, 1585–1594.

Kell, H. J., Lubinski, D., & Benbow, C. P. (2013). Who rises to the top? Early indicators. *Psychological Science, 24*, 648–659.

Keller, C., Hartmann, C., & Siegrist, M. (2016). The association between dispositional self-control and longitudinal changes in eating behaviors, diet quality, and BMI. *Psychology & Health, 31*, 1311–1327.

Kellerman, J., Lewis, J., & Laird, J. D. (1989). Looking and loving: The effects of mutual gaze on feelings of romantic love. *Journal of Research in Personality, 23*, 145–161.

Kelling, S. T., & Halpern, B. P. (1983). Taste flashes: Reaction times, intensity, and quality. *Science, 219*, 412–414.

Kellner, C. H., Knapp, R. G., Petrides, G., Rummans, T. A., Husain, M. M., Rasmussen, K., . . . Fink, M. (2006). Continuation electroconvulsive therapy vs. pharmacotherapy for relapse prevention in major depression: A multisite study from the Consortium for Research in Electroconvulsive Therapy (CORE). *Archives of General Psychiatry, 63*, 1337–1344.

Kelly, A. E. (2000). Helping construct desirable identities: A self-presentational view of psychotherapy. *Psychological Bulletin, 126*, 475–494.

Kelly, D. J., Quinn, P. C., Slater, A. M., Lee, K., Ge, L., & Pascalis, O. (2007). The other-race effect develops during infancy: Evidence of perceptual narrowing. *Psychological Science, 18*, 1084–1089.

Kelly, T. A. (1990). The role of values in psychotherapy: A critical review of process and outcome effects. *Clinical Psychology Review, 10*, 171–186.

Kendall-Tackett, K. A., Williams, L. M., & Finkelhor, D. (1993). Impact of sexual abuse on children: A review and synthesis of recent empirical studies. *Psychological Bulletin, 113*, 164–180.

Kendler, K. S. (1996). Parenting: A genetic-epidemiologic perspective. *The American Journal of Psychiatry, 153*, 11–20.

Kendler, K. S. (1998, January). Major depression and the environment: A psychiatric genetic perspective. *Pharmacopsychiatry, 31*, 5–9.

Kendler, K. S. (2011). A statement from Kenneth S. Kendler, M.D., on the proposal to eliminate the grief exclusion criterion from major depression. American Psychiatric Association DSM-5 Development (www.dsm5.org).

Kendler, K. S., Maes, H. H., Lönn, S. L., Morris, N. A., Lichtenstein, P., Sundquist, J., & Sundquist, K. (2015a). A Swedish national twin study of criminal behavior and its violent, white-collar and property subtypes. *Psychological Medicine, 45*, 2253–2262.

Kendler, K. S., Myers, J., & Zisook, S. (2008). Does bereavement-related major depression differ from major depression associated with other stressful life events? *American Journal of Psychiatry, 165*, 1449–1455.

Kendler, K. S., Neale, M. C., Thornton, L. M., Aggen, S. H., Gilman, S. E., & Kessler, R. C. (2002). Cannabis use in the last year in a U.S. national sample of twin and sibling pairs. *Psychological Medicine, 32*, 551–554.

Kendler, K. S., Ohlsson, H., Lichtenstein, P., Sundquist, J., & Sundquist, K. (2018). The genetic epidemiology of treated major depression in Sweden. *The American Journal of Psychiatry, 175*, 1137–1144.

Kendler, K. S., Ohlsson, H., Sundquist, J., & Sundquist, K. (2016). Alcohol use disorder and mortality across the lifespan: A longitudinal cohort and co-relative analysis. *JAMA Psychiatry, 73*, 575–581.

Kendler, K. S., Sundquist, K., Ohlsson, H., Palmer, K., Maes, H., Winkleby, M. A., & Sundquist, J. (2012). Genetic and familiar environmental influences on the risk for drug abuse: A Swedish adoption study. *Archives of General Psychiatry, 69*, 690–697.

Kendler, K. S., Turkheimer, E., Ohlsson, H., Sundquist, J., & Sundquist, K. (2015b). Family environment and the malleability of cognitive ability: A Swedish national home-reared and adopted-away cosibling control study. *PNAS, 112*, 4612–4617.

Kendrick, K. M., & Feng, J. (2011). Neural encoding principles in face perception revealed using non-primate models. In G. Rhodes, A. Calder, M. Johnson, & J. V. Haxby (Eds.), *The Oxford handbook of face perception.* Oxford: Oxford University Press.

Kennard, B. D., Emslie, G. J., Mayes, T. L., Nakonezny, P. A., Jones, J. M., Foxwell, A. A., & King, J. (2014). Sequential treatment of fluoxetine and relapse-prevention CBT to improve outcomes in pediatric depression. *American Journal of Psychiatry, 171*, 1083–1090.

Kennedy, M., Kreppner, J., Knights, N., Kumsta, R., Maughan, B., Golm, D., . . . Sonuga-Barke, E. J. (2016). Early severe institutional deprivation is associated with a persistent variant of adult attention-deficit/hyperactivity disorder: Clinical presentation, developmental continuities and life circumstances in the English and Romanian Adoptees study. *Journal of Child Psychology and Psychiatry, 57*, 1113–1125.

Kenrick, D. T., & Gutierres, S. E. (1980). Contrast effects and judgments of physical attractiveness: When beauty becomes a social problem. *Journal of Personality and Social Psychology, 38*, 131–140.

Kenrick, D. T., Nieuweboer, S., & Bunnk, A. P. (2009). Universal mechanisms and cultural diversity: Replacing the blank slate with a coloring book. In M. Schaller, S. Heine, A. Norenzayan, T. Yamagishi, & T. Kameda (Eds.), *Evolution, culture, and the human mind* (pp. 257–271). Mahwah, NJ: Erlbaum.

Kensinger, E. A. (2007). Negative emotion enhances memory accuracy: Behavioral and neuroimaging evidence. *Current Directions in Psychological Science, 16*, 213–218.

Keough, K. A., Zimbardo, P. G., & Boyd, J. N. (1999). Who's smoking, drinking, and using drugs? Time perspective as a predictor of substance use. *Basic and Applied Social Psychology, 2*, 149–164.

Keramati, M., Durand, A., Girardeau, P., Gutkin, B., & Ahmed, S. H. (2017). Cocaine addiction as a homeostatic reinforcement learning disorder. *Psychological Review, 124*, 130–153.

Keresztes, A., Bender, A. R., Bodammer, N. C., Lindenberger, U., Shing, Y. L., & Werkle-Bergner, M. (2017). Hippocampal maturity promotes memory distinctiveness in childhood and adolescence. *PNAS, 114*, 9212–9217.

Kern, M. L., Eichstaedt, J. C., Schwartz, H. A., Dziurzynski, L., Ungar, L. H., Stillwell, D. J., . . . Seligman, M. E. P. (2014). The online social self: An open vocabulary approach to personality. *Assessment, 21*, 158–169.

Kernis, M. H. (2003). Toward a conceptualization of optimal self-esteem. *Psychological Inquiry, 14*, 1–26.

Kerns, J. C., Guo, J., Fothergill, E., Howard, L., Knuth, N. D., Brychta, R., . . . Hall, K. D. (2017). Increased physical activity associated with less weight regain six years after "The Biggest Loser" competition. *Obesity, 25*, 1838–1843.

Kerr, N. L., & Bruun, S. E. (1983). Dispensability of member effort and group motivation losses: Free-rider effects. *Journal of Personality and Social Psychology, 44*, 78–94.

Kessler, M., & Albee, G. (1975). Primary prevention. *Annual Review of Psychology, 26*, 557–591.

Kessler, R. C., Brinbaum, H. G., Shahly, V., Bromet, E., Hwang, I., McLaughlin, K. A., . . . Stein, D. J. (2010). Age differences in the prevalence and co-morbidity of DSM-IV major depressive episodes: Results from the WHO World Mental Health Survey Initiative. *Depression and Anxiety, 27*, 351–364.

Keyes, K. M., Maslowsky, J., Hamilton, A., & Schulenberg, J. (2015). The great sleep recession: Changes in sleep duration among U.S. adolescents, 1991–2012. *Pediatrics, 135*, 460–468.

Keynes, M. (1980, December 20/27). Handel's illnesses. *The Lancet*, pp. 1354–1355.

Keys, A., Brozek, J., Henschel, A., Mickelsen, O., & Taylor, H. L. (1950). *The biology of human starvation.* Minneapolis: University of Minnesota Press.

Khazanoy, G. K., & Ruscio, A. M. (2016). Is low positive emotionality a specific risk factor for depression? A meta-analysis of longitudinal studies. *Psychological Bulletin, 142*, 991–1015.

Khera, M., Bhattacharya, R. K., Blick, G., Kushner, H., Nguyen, D., & Miner, M. M. (2011). Improved sexual function with testosterone replacement therapy in hypogonadal men: Real-world data from the Testim Registry in the United States (TriUS). *Journal of Sexual Medicine, 8*, 3204–3213.

Khodagholy, D., Gelinas, J. N., & Buzsáki, G. (2018). Learning-enhanced coupling between ripple oscillations in association cortices and hippocampus. *Science, 358*, 369–372.

Kiatpongsan, S., & Norton, M. (2014). How much (more) should CEOs make? A universal desire for more equal pay. *Perspectives on Psychological Science, 9*, 587–593.

Kiecolt-Glaser, J. K. (2009). Psychoneuroimmunology: Psychology's gateway to the biomedical future. *Perspectives on Psychological Science, 4*, 367–369.

Kiecolt-Glaser, J. K., Page, G. G., Marucha, P. T., MacCallum, R. C., & Glaser, R. (1998). Psychological influences on surgical recovery: Perspectives from psychoneuroimmunology. *American Psychologist, 53*, 1209–1218.

Kiehl, K. A., & Buckholtz, J. W. (2010). Inside the mind of a psychopath. *Scientific American Mind, 21*, 22–29.

Kihlstrom, J. F. (1990). *Awareness, the psychological unconscious, and the self.* Address to the American Psychological Association convention.

Kihlstrom, J. F. (2005). Dissociative disorders. *Annual Review of Clinical Psychology, 1*, 227–253.

Kihlstrom, J. F. (2006). Repression: A unified theory of a will-o'-the-wisp. *Behavioral and Brain Sciences, 29*, 523.

Kilgore, A. (2017, November 9). Aaron Hernandez suffered from most severe CTE ever found in a person his age. *The Washington Post* (washingtonpost.com).

Kille, D. R., Forest, A. L., & Wood, J. V. (2013). Tall, dark, and stable: Embodiment motivates mate selection preferences. *Psychological Science, 24*, 112–114.

Killingsworth, M. A., & Gilbert, D. T. (2010). A wandering mind is an unhappy mind. *Science, 330*, 932.

Kilpatrick, L. A., Suyenobu, B. Y., Smith, S. R., Bueller, J. A., Goodman, T., Creswell, J. D., . . . Naliboff, B. D. (2011). Impact of mindfulness-based stress reduction training on intrinsic brain activity. *Neuroimage, 56*, 290–298.

Kilpeläinen, T. O., Qi, L. Brage, S., Sharp, S. J., Sonestedt, E., Demerath, E., . . . Loos, R. J. F. (2012). Physical activity attenuates the influence of FTO variants on obesity risk: A meta-analysis of 218,166 adults and 19,268 children. *PLOS Medicine, 8,* e1001116.

Kim, B. S. K., Ng, G. F., & Ahn, A. J. (2005). Effects of client expectation for counseling success, client-counselor worldview match, and client adherence to Asian and European American cultural values on counseling process with Asian Americans. *Journal of Counseling Psychology, 52,* 67–76.

Kim, E. S., Hagan, K. A., Grodstein, F., DeMeo, D. L., De Vivo, I., & Kubzansky, L. D. (2017). Optimism and cause-specific mortality: A prospective cohort study. *American Journal of Epidemiology, 185,* 21–29.

Kim, H., & Markus, H. R. (1999). Deviance or uniqueness, harmony or conformity? A cultural analysis. *Journal of Personality and Social Psychology, 77,* 785–800.

Kim, H., Schimmack, U., Oishi, S., & Tsutsui, Y. (2018). Extraversion and life satisfaction: A cross-cultural examination of student and nationally representative samples. *Journal of Personality, 86,* 604–618.

Kim, J., Wang, C., Nunez, N., Kim, S., Smith, T., & Sahgal, N. (2015). Paranormal Beliefs: Using Survey Trends from the USA to Suggest a New Area of Research in Asia. *Asian Journal for Public Opinion Research, 2,* 279–306.

Kim, J. L., & Ward, L. M. (2012). Striving for pleasure without fear: Short-term effects of reading a women's magazine on women's sexual attitudes. *Psychology of Women Quarterly, 36,* 326–336.

Kim, M., Kim, C.-H., Jung, H. H., Kim, S. J., & Chang, J. W. (2018). Treatment of major depressive disorder via magnetic resonance-guided focused ultrasound surgery. *Biological Psychiatry, 83,* e17–e18.

Kim, S. H., Vincent, L. C., & Goncalo, J. A. (2013). Outside advantage: Can social rejection fuel creative thought? *Journal of Experimental Psychology: General, 142,* 605–611.

Kimata, H. (2001). Effect of humor on allergen-induced wheal reactions. *Journal of the American Medical Association, 285,* 737.

King, D. W., King, L. A., Park, C. L., Lee, L. O., Pless Kaiser, A., Spiro, A., . . . Keane, T. M. (2015). Positive adjustment among American repatriated prisoners of the Vietnam War: Modeling the long-term effects of captivity. *Clinical Psychological Science, 3,* 861–876.

King, L. A., Heintzelman, S. J., & Ward, S. J. (2016). Beyond the search for meaning: A contemporary science of the experience of meaning in life. *Current Directions in Psychological Science, 25,* 211–216.

King, S., St.-Hilaire, A., & Heidkamp, D. (2010). Prenatal factors in schizophrenia. *Current Directions in Psychological Science, 19,* 209–213.

Kinnier, R. T., & Metha, A. T. (1989). Regrets and priorities at three stages of life. *Counseling and Values, 33,* 182–193.

Kinsella, E. L., Ritchie, T. D., & Igou, E. R. (2015). Zeroing in on heroes: A prototype analysis of hero features. *Journal of Personality and Social Psychology, 108,* 114–127.

Kinsey, A. C., Pomeroy, W. B., & Martin, C. E. (1948). *Sexual behavior in the human male.* Bloomington: Indiana University Press.

Kinsey, A. C., Pomeroy, W. B., Martin, C. E., & Gebhard, P. H. (1953). *Sexual behavior in the human female.* Philadelphia: W. B. Saunders.

Kipnis, J. (2018, August). The seventh sense. *Scientific American,* pp. 28–35.

Kirby, D. (2002). Effective approaches to reducing adolescent unprotected sex, pregnancy, and childbearing. *Journal of Sex Research, 39,* 51–57.

Kirkpatrick, B., Fenton, W. S., Carpenter, W. T., Jr., & Marder, S. R. (2006). The NIMH-MATRICS consensus statement on negative symptoms. *Schizophrenia Bulletin, 32,* 214–219.

Kirsch, I. (2010). *The emperor's new drugs: Exploding the antidepressant myth.* New York: Basic Books.

Kirsch, I. (2016). *The emperor's new drugs: Medication and placebo in the treatment of depression.* Presentation given at the Behind and Beyond the Brain symposium conducted by the Bial Foundation, March 30–April 2 (www.bial.com/imagem/Programa_e%20_Resumos-Program_and_Abstracts.pdf).

Kirsch, I., Deacon, B. J., Huedo-Medina, T. B., Scoboria, A., Moore, T. J., & Johnson, B. T. (2008). Initial severity and antidepressant benefits: A meta-analysis of data submitted to the Food and Drug Administration. *Public Library of Science Medicine, 5,* e45.

Kirsch, I., Kong, J., Sadler, P., Spaeth, R., Cook, A., Kaptchuk, T. J., & Gollub, R. (2014). Expectancy and conditioning in placebo analgesia: Separate or connected processes? *Psychology of Consciousness; Theory, Research, and Practice, 1,* 51–59.

Kirsch, I., & Sapirstein, G. (1998). Listening to Prozac but hearing placebo: A meta-analysis of antidepressant medication. *Prevention & Treatment, 1,* 2a.

Kirsch, I., Wampold, B., & Kelley, J. M. (2016). Controlling for the placebo effect in psychotherapy: Noble quest or tilting at windmills? *Psychology of Consciousness: Theory, Research, and Practice, 3,* 121–131.

Kisely, S., Li, A., Warren, N., & Siskind, D. (2018). A systematic review and meta-analysis of deep brain stimulation for depression. *Depression and Anxiety, 35,* 468–480.

Kitahara, C. M., Flint, A. J., de Gonzalez, A. B., Bernstein, L., Brotzman, M., MacInnis, R. J., . . . Hartge, P. (2014, July 8). Association between class III obesity (BMI of 40–59 kg/m2) and mortality: A pooled analysis of 20 prospective studies. *PLOS Medicine, 11,* e1001673.

Kitaoka, A. (2016, September 11). Facebook post. Retrieved from facebook.com/photo.php?fbid=10207806660899237&set=a.2215289656523.1183661076035621&type=3&theater

Kitayama, S., Park, J., Boylan, J. M., Miyamoto, Y., Levine, C. S., Markus, H. R., . . . Ryff, C. D. (2015). Expression of anger and ill health in two cultures: An examination of inflammation and cardiovascular risk. *Psychological Science, 26,* 211–220.

Kivipelto, M., & Håkansson, K. (2017, April). A rare success against Alzheimer's. *Scientific American,* pp. 33–37.

Kivlighan, D. M., Goldberg, S. B., Abbas, M., Pace, B. T., Yulish, N. E., Thomas, J. G., . . . Wampold, B. E. (2015). The enduring effects of psychodynamic treatments vis-à-vis alternative treatments: A multilevel longitudinal meta-analysis. *Clinical Psychology Review, 40,* 1–14.

Klahr, A. M., & Burt, S. A. (2014). Elucidating the etiology of individual differences in parenting: A meta-analysis of behavioral genetic research. *Psychological Bulletin, 140,* 544–586.

Klayman, J., & Ha, Y.-W. (1987). Confirmation, disconfirmation, and information in hypothesis testing. *Psychological Review, 94,* 211–228.

Klein, D. N. (2010). Chronic depression: Diagnosis and classification. *Current Directions in Psychological Science, 19,* 96–100.

Klein, D. N., & Kotov, R. (2016). Course of depression in a 10-year prospective study: Evidence for qualitatively distinct subgroups. *Journal of Abnormal Psychology, 125,* 337–348.

Klein, D. N., Schwartz, J. E., Santiago, N. J., Vivian, D., Vocisano, C., Castonguay, L. G., . . . Keller, M. B. (2003). Therapeutic alliance in depression treatment: Controlling for prior change and patient characteristics. *Journal of Consulting and Clinical Psychology, 71,* 997–1006.

Klein, R. A., Ratliff, K. A., Vianello, M., Adams, R. B., Jr., Bahník, Š., Bernstein, M. J., . . . Nosek, B. A. (2014). Investigating variation in replicability: A "many labs" replication project. *Social Psychology, 45,* 142–152.

Kleinke, C. L. (1986). Gaze and eye contact: A research review. *Psychological Bulletin, 1000,* 78–100.

Kleinmuntz, B., & Szucko, J. J. (1984). A field study of the fallibility of polygraph lie detection. *Nature, 308,* 449–450.

Kleitman, N. (1960, November). Patterns of dreaming. *Scientific American,* pp. 82–88.

Klemm, W. R. (1990). Historical and introductory perspectives on brainstem-mediated behaviors. In W. R. Klemm & R. P. Vertes (Eds.), *Brainstem mechanisms of behavior* (pp. 3–32). New York: Wiley.

Klimstra, T. A., Hale, W. W., III, Raaijmakers, Q. A. W., Branje, S. J. T., & Meeus, W. H. J. (2009). Maturation of personality in adolescence. *Journal of Personality and Social Psychology, 96,* 898–912.

Klimstra, T. A., Noftle, E. E., Luyckx, K., Goossens, L., & Robins, R. W. (2018). Personality development and adjustment in college: A multifaceted, cross-national view. *Journal of Personality and Social Psychology, 115,* 338–361.

Kline, D., & Schieber, F. (1985). Vision and aging. In J. E. Birren & K. W. Schaie (Eds.), *Handbook of the psychology of aging* (2nd ed., pp. 296–331). New York: Van Nostrand Reinhold.

Kline, N. S. (1974). *From sad to glad.* New York: Ballantine Books.

Klinke, R., Kral, A., Heid, S., Tillein, J., & Hartmann, R. (1999). Recruitment of the auditory cortex in congenitally deaf cats by long-term cochlear electrostimulation. *Science, 285,* 1729–1733.

Kluemper, D. H., McLarty, B. D., Bishop, T. R., & Sen, A. (2015). Interviewee selection test and evaluator assessments of general mental ability, emotional intelligence and extraversion: Relationships with structured behavioral and situational interview performance. *Journal of Business and Psychology, 30,* 543–563.

Klump, K. L., Suisman, J. L., Burt, S. A., McGue, M., & Iacono, W. G. (2009). Genetic and environmental influences on disordered eating: An adoption study. *Journal of Abnormal Psychology, 118,* 797–805.

Klüver, H., & Bucy, P. C. (1939). Preliminary analysis of functions of the temporal lobes in monkeys. *Archives of Neurology and Psychiatry, 42,* 979–1000.

Knapp, S., & VandeCreek, L. (2000). Recovered memories of childhood abuse: Is there an underlying professional consensus? *Professional Psychology: Research and Practice, 31,* 365–371.

Knickmeyer, E. (2001, August 7). In Africa, big is definitely better. *Seattle Times,* p. A7.

Knight, R. T. (2007). Neural networks debunk phrenology. *Science, 316,* 1578–1579.

Knight, W. (2004, August 2). Animated face helps deaf with phone chat. *NewScientist.com.*

Knouse, L. E., Teller, J., & Brooks, M. A. (2017). Meta-analysis of cognitive–behavioral treatments for adult ADHD. *Journal of Consulting and Clinical Psychology, 85,* 737–750.

Knuts, I. J. E., Cosci, F., Esquivel, G., Goossens, L., van Duinen, M., Bareman, M., . . . Schruers, K. R. J. (2010). Cigarette smoking and 35% CO_2 induced panic in panic disorder patients. *Journal of Affective Disorders, 124,* 215–218.

Koch, C. (2015, January/February). The face as entryway to the self. *Scientific American Mind,* pp. 26–29.

Koch, C. (2017, November). How to make a consciousness meter. *Scientific American,* pp. 28–33.

Koch, C. (2018, June). What is consciousness? *Scientific American,* pp. 61–64.

Kocsis, J. H. (2018). Internet-based psychotherapy: How far can we go? *American Journal of Psychiatry, 175,* 202–203.

Kodal, A., Fjermestad, K., Bjelland, I., Gjestad, R., Öst, L. G., Bjaastad, J. F., . . . & Wergeland, G. J. (2018). Long-term effectiveness of cognitive behavioral therapy for youth with anxiety disorders. *Journal of Anxiety Disorders, 53,* 58–67.

Koenen, K. C., Moffitt, T. E., Roberts, A. L., Martin, L. T., Kubzansky, L., Harrington, H., . . . Caspi, A. (2009). Childhood IQ and adult mental disorders: A test of the cognitive reserve hypothesis. *American Journal of Psychiatry, 166,* 50–57.

Koenig, H. G., King, D. E., & Carson, V. B. (2012). *Handbook of religion and health* (2nd ed.). New York: Oxford University Press.

Koenig, H. G., & Larson, D. B. (1998). Use of hospital services, religious attendance, and religious affiliation. *Southern Medical Journal, 91,* 925–932.

Koenig, L. B., & Vaillant, G. E. (2009). A prospective study of church attendance and health over the lifespan. *Health Psychology, 28,* 117–124.

Koenigs, M., Young, L., Adolphs, R., Tranel, D., Cushman, F., Hauser, M., & Damasio, A. (2007). Damage to the prefrontal cortex increases utilitarian moral judgements. *Nature, 446,* 908–911.

Kofler, M. J., Raiker, J. S., Sarver, D. E., Wells, E. L., & Soto, E. F. (2016). Is hyperactivity ubiquitous in ADHD or dependent on environmental demands? Evidence from meta-analysis. *Clinical Psychology Review, 46,* 12–24.

Koh, A. W. L., Lee, S. C., & Lim, S. W. H. (2018). The learning benefits of teaching: A retrieval practice hypothesis. *Applied Cognitive Psychology, 32,* 401–410.

Kohlberg, L. (1981). *The philosophy of moral development: Essays on moral development* (Vol. I). San Francisco: Harper & Row.

Kohlberg, L. (1984). *The psychology of moral development: Essays on moral development* (Vol. II). San Francisco: Harper & Row.

Kohler, C. G., Walker, J. B., Martin, E. A., Healey, K. M., & Moberg, P. J. (2010). Facial emotion perception in schizophrenia: A meta-analytic review. *Schizophrenia Bulletin, 36,* 1009–1019.

Kohler, I. (1962, May). Experiments with goggles. *Scientific American,* pp. 62–72.

Köhler, W. (1925; reprinted 1957). *The mentality of apes.* London: Pelican.

Kolb, B. (1989). Brain development, plasticity, and behavior. *American Psychologist, 44,* 1203–1212.

Kolb, B., & Whishaw, I. Q. (1998). Brain plasticity and behavior. *Annual Review of Psychology, 49,* 43–64.

Kolovos, S., van Tulder, M. W., Cuijpers, P., Prigent, A., Chevreul, K., Riper, H., & Bosmans, J. E. (2017). The effect of treatment as usual on major depressive disorder: A meta-analysis. *Journal of Affective Disorders, 210,* 72–81.

Koltko-Rivera, M. E. (2006). Rediscovering the later version of Maslow's hierarchy of needs: Self-transcendence and opportunities for theory, research, and unification. *Review of General Psychology, 10,* 302–317.

Komisaruk, B. R., & Whipple, B. (2011). Non-genital orgasms. *Sexual and Relationship Therapy, 26,* 356–372.

Kondoh, K., Lu, Z., Olson, D. P., Lowell, B. B., & Buck, L. B. (2016). A specific area of olfactory cortex involved in stress hormone responses to predator odours. *Nature, 532,* 103–106.

Konkle, T., Brady, T. F., Alvarez, G. A., & Oliva, A. (2010). Conceptual distinctiveness supports detailed visual long-term memory for real-world objects. *Journal of Experimental Psychology: General, 139,* 558–578.

Koops, S., Blom, J. D., Bouachmir, O., Slot, M. I., Neggers, B., & Sommer, I. E. (2018). Treating auditory hallucinations with transcranial direct current stimulation in a double-blind, randomized trial. *Schizophrenia Research, 201,* 329–336.

Kosslyn, S. M. (2005). Reflective thinking and mental imagery: A perspective on the development of post-traumatic stress disorder. *Development and Psychopathology, 17,* 851–863.

Kosslyn, S. M., & Koenig, O. (1992). *Wet mind: The new cognitive neuroscience.* New York: Free Press.

Kotchick, B. A., Shaffer, A., & Forehand, R. (2001). Adolescent sexual risk behavior: A multi-system perspective. *Clinical Psychology Review, 21,* 493–519.

Kotkin, M., Daviet, C., & Gurin, J. (1996). The *Consumer Reports* mental health survey. *American Psychologist, 51,* 1080–1082.

Kounios, J., & Beeman, M. (2014). The cognitive neuroscience of insight. *Annual Review of Psychology, 65,* 71–93.

Kovelman, I., Shalinsky, M. H., Berens, M. S., & Petitto, L. (2014). Words in the bilingual brain: An fNIRS brain imaging investigation of lexical processing in sign-speech bimodal bilinguals. *Frontiers in Human Neuroscience, 8,* article 606.

Kowalski, R. M., Limber, S. P., & McCord, A. (2018). A developmental approach to cyberbullying: Prevalence and protective factors. *Aggression and Violent Behavior, 45,* 20–32.

Kraft, T., & Pressman, S. (2012). Grin and bear it: The influence of the manipulated facial expression on the stress response. *Psychological Science, 23,* 1372–1378.

Krahé, B., & Berger, A. (2017). Longitudinal pathways of sexual victimization, sexual self-esteem, and depression in women and men. *Psychological Trauma: Theory, Research, Practice, and Policy, 9,* 147–155.

Krahé, B., Lutz, J., & Sylla, I. (2018). Lean back and relax: Reclined seating position buffers the effect of frustration on anger and aggression. *European Journal of Social Psychology, 48,* 718–723.

Krakow, B., Germain, A., Warner, T. D., Schrader, R., Koss, M. P., Hollifeld, M., . . . Johnston, L. (2001). The relationship of sleep quality and posttraumatic stress to potential sleep disorders in sexual assault survivors with nightmares, insomnia, and PTSD. *Journal of Traumatic Stress, 14,* 647–665.

Krakow, B., Schrader, R., Tandberg, D., Hollifeld, M., Koss, M. P., Yau, C. L., & Cheng, D. T. (2002). Nightmare frequency in sexual assault survivors with PTSD. *Journal of Anxiety Disorders, 16,* 175–190.

Kramer, A. (2010). Personal communication.

Kramer, A. D. I. (2012). The spread of emotion via Facebook. *Proceedings of the SIGCHI Conference on Human Factors in Computing Systems.* ACM (Association for Computing Machinery), New York, 767–770.

Kramer, A. F., & Colcombe, S. (2018). Fitness effects on the cognitive function of older adults: A meta-analytic study—revisited. *Perspectives on Psychological Science, 13,* 213–217.

Kranz, F., & Ishai, A. (2006). Face perception is modulated by sexual preference. *Current Biology, 16,* 63–68.

Kranz, G. S., Hahn, A., Kaufmann, U., Küblböck, M., Hummer, A., Ganger, S., . . . Lanzenberger, R. (2014). White matter microstructure in transsexuals and controls investigated by diffusion tensor imaging. *The Journal of Neuroscience, 34,* 15466–15475.

Kraul, C. (2010, October 12). Chief engineer knew it would take a miracle. *The Los Angeles Times* (latimes.com).

Kring, A. M., & Caponigro, J. M. (2010). Emotion in schizophrenia: Where feeling meets thinking. *Current Directions in Psychological Science, 19,* 255–259.

Kring, A. M., & Gordon, A. H. (1998). Sex differences in emotion: Expression, experience, and physiology. *Journal of Personality and Social Psychology, 74,* 686–703.

Kringelbach, M. L., & Berridge, K. C. (2012, August). The joyful mind. *Scientific American,* pp. 40–45.

Kristof, N. (2017, February 11). Husbands are deadlier than terrorists. *The New York Times* (nytimes.com).

Krizan, Z., & Herlache, A. D. (2018). The narcissism spectrum model: A synthetic view of narcissistic personality. *Personality and Social Psychology Review, 22,* 3–31.

Kroes, M. C. W., Tendolkar, I., van Wingen, G. A., van Waarde, J. A., Strange, B. A., & Fernández, G. (2014). An electroconvulsive therapy procedure impairs reconsolidation of episodic memories in humans. *Nature Neuroscience, 17,* 204–206.

Krosnick, J. A., & Alwin, D. F. (1989). Aging and susceptibility to attitude change. *Journal of Personality and Social Psychology, 57,* 416–425.

Krosnick, J. A., Betz, A. L., Jussim, L. J., & Lynn, A. R. (1992). Subliminal conditioning of attitudes. *Personality and Social Psychology Bulletin, 18,* 152–162.

Kross, E., Bruehlman-Senecal, E., Park, J., Burson, A., Dougherty, A., Shablack, H., . . . Ayduk, O. (2014). Self-talk as a regulatory mechanism: How you do it matters. *Journal of Personality and Social Psychology, 106,* 304–324.

Krueger, J., & Killham, E. (2006, March 9). Why Dilbert is right: Uncomfortable work environments make for disgruntled employees—just like the cartoon says. *Gallup Management Journal* (gmj.gallup.com).

Krueze, L. J., Pijnenborg, G. H. M., de Jonge, Y. B., & Nauta, M. H. (2018). Cognitive-behavior therapy for children and adolescents with anxiety disorders: A meta-analysis of secondary outcomes. *Journal of Anxiety Disorders, 60,* 43–57.

Kruger, J., Epley, N., Parker, J., & Ng, Z.-W. (2005). Egocentrism over e-mail: Can we communicate as well as we think? *Journal of Personality and Social Psychology, 89,* 925–936.

Krumhansl, C. L. (2010). Plink: "Thin slices" of music. *Music Perception, 27,* 337–354.

Kteily, N. S., & Bruneau, E. (2017). Darker demons of our nature: The need to (re)focus attention on blatant forms of dehumanization. *Current Directions in Psychological Science, 26,* 487–494.

Kubzansky, L. D., Sparrow, D., Vokanas, P., & Kawachi, I. (2001). Is the glass half empty or half full? A prospective study of optimism and coronary heart disease in the normative aging study. *Psychosomatic Medicine, 63,* 910–916.

Kuchynka, S. L., Salomon, K., Bosson, J. K., El-Hout, M., Kiebel, E., Cooperman, C., & Toomey, R. (2018). Hostile and benevolent sexism and college women's STEM outcomes. *Psychology of Women Quarterly, 42,* 72–87.

Kuehner, C. (2017). Why is depression more common among women than among men? *The Lancet Psychiatry, 4,* 146–158.

Kuhl, P. K., & Meltzoff, A. N. (1982). The bimodal perception of speech in infancy. *Science, 218*, 1138–1141.

Kuhl, P. K., Ramírez, R. R., Bosseler, A., Lin, J. L., & Imada, T. (2014). Infants' brain responses to speech suggest analysis by synthesis. *PNAS, 111*, 11238–11245.

Kumar, A., & Gilovich, T. (2015). Some "thing" to talk about? Differential story utility from experiential and material purchases. *Personality and Social Psychology Bulletin, 41*, 1320–1331.

Kupfer, D. J. (2012, June 1). *Dr. Kupfer defends DSM-5.* medscape.com/viewarticle/764735

Kupper, N., & Denollet, J. (2007). Type D personality as a prognostic factor in heart disease: Assessment and mediating mechanisms. *Journal of Personality Assessment, 89*, 265–276.

Kurtycz, L. M. (2015). Choice and control for animals in captivity. *The Psychologist, 28*, 892–893.

Kutas, M. (1990). Event-related brain potential (ERP) studies of cognition during sleep: Is it more than a dream? In R. R. Bootzin, J. F. Kihlstrom, & D. Schacter (Eds.), *Sleep and cognition* (pp. 43–57). Washington, DC: American Psychological Association.

Kuttler, A. F., La Greca, A. M., & Prinstein, M. J. (1999). Friendship qualities and social–emotional functioning of adolescents with close, cross-sex friendships. *Journal of Research on Adolescence, 9*, 339–366.

Kuyken, W., Warren, F. C., Taylor, R. S., Whalley, B., Crane, C., Bondolfi, G., . . . Dalgleish, T. (2016). Efficacy of mindfulness-based cognitive therapy in prevention of depressive relapse: An individual patient data meta-analysis from randomized trials. *JAMA Psychiatry, 73*, 565–574.

Kvam, S., Kleppe, C. L., Nordhus, I. H., & Hovland, A. (2016). Exercise as a treatment for depression: A meta-analysis. *Journal of Affective Disorders, 202*, 67–86.

La Londe, K. B., Mahoney, A., Edwards, T. L., Cox, C., Weetjens, B., Durgin, A., & Poling, A. (2015). Training pouched rats to find people. *Journal of Applied Behavior Analysis, 48*, 1–10.

Labella, M. H., Johnson, W. F., Martin, J., Ruiz, S. K., Shankman, J. L., Englund, M. M., . . . Simpson, J. A. (2018). Multiple dimensions of childhood abuse and neglect prospectively predict poorer adult romantic functioning. *Personality and Social Psychology Bulletin, 44*, 238–251.

LaCapria, K. (2015, December 17). Kindergarten, stop. Snopes.com.

Lacayo, R. (1995, June 12). Violent reaction. *Time*, pp. 25–39.

Lacey, M. (2010, December 11). He found bag of cash, but did the unexpected. *The New York Times* (nytimes.com).

Laeng, B., & Sulutvedt, U. (2014). The eye pupil adjusts to imaginary light. *Psychological Science, 25*, 188–197.

Laird, J. D. (1974). Self-attribution of emotion: The effects of expressive behavior on the quality of emotional experience. *Journal of Personality and Social Psychology, 29*, 475–486.

Laird, J. D. (1984). The real role of facial response in the experience of emotion: A reply to Tourangeau and Ellsworth, and others. *Journal of Personality and Social Psychology, 47*, 909–917.

Laird, J. D., & Lacasse, K. (2014). Bodily influences on emotional feelings: Accumulating evidence and extensions of William James's theory of emotion. *Emotion Review, 6*, 27–34.

Lakin, J. L., Chartrand, T. L., & Arkin, R. M. (2008). I am too just like you: Nonconscious mimicry as an automatic behavioral response to social exclusion. *Psychological Science, 19*, 816–822.

Lally, P., Van Jaarsveld, C. H. M., Potts, H. W. W., & Wardle, J. (2010). How are habits formed: Modelling habit formation in the real world. *European Journal of Social Psychology, 40*, 998–1009.

Lam, C. B., & McBride-Chang, C. A. (2007). Resilience in young adulthood: The moderating influences of gender-related personality traits and coping flexibility. *Sex Roles, 56*, 159–172.

Lambert, N. M., DeWall, C. N., Bushman, B. J., Tillman, T. F., Fincham, F. D., Pond, R. S., Jr., & Gwinn, A. M. (2011). *Lashing out in lust: Effect of pornography on nonsexual, physical aggression against relationship partners.* Paper presentation at the Society for Personality and Social Psychology convention.

Lambert, N. M., Negash, S., Stillman, T. F., Olmstead, S. B., & Fincham, F. D. (2012). A love that doesn't last: Pornography consumption and weakened commitment to a romantic partner. *Journal of Social and Clinical Psychology, 31*, 410–438.

Lambird, K. H., & Mann, T. (2006). When do ego threats lead to self-regulation failure? Negative consequences of defensive high self-esteem. *Personality and Social Psychology Bulletin, 32*, 1177–1187.

Lammers, J., & Baldwin, M. (2018). Past-focused temporal communication overcomes conservatives' resistance to liberal political ideas. *Journal of Personality and Social Psychology, 114*, 599–619.

Landau, E., Verjee, Z., & Mortensen, A. (2014, February 24). Uganda president: Homosexuals are "disgusting." CNN (cnn.com).

Landauer, T. (2001, September). Quoted in R. Herbert, You must remember this. *APS Observer*, p. 11.

Landberg, J., & Norström, T. (2011). Alcohol and homicide in Russia and the United States: A comparative analysis. *Journal of Studies on Alcohol and Drugs, 72*, 723–730.

Landry, M. J. (2002). MDMA: A review of epidemiologic data. *Journal of Psychoactive Drugs, 34*, 163–169.

Lange, S., Probst, C., Gmel, G., Rehm, J., Burd, L., & Popova, S. (2017). Global prevalence of fetal alcohol spectrum disorder among children and youth: A systematic review and meta-analysis. *JAMA Pediatrics, 171*, 948–956.

Langer, E. J. (1983). *The psychology of control.* Beverly Hills, CA: Sage.

Langer, E. J., & Abelson, R. P. (1974). A patient by any other name . . .: Clinician group differences in labeling bias. *Journal of Consulting and Clinical Psychology, 42*, 4–9.

Langer, E. J., & Imber, L. (1980). The role of mindlessness in the perception of deviance. *Journal of Personality and Social Psychology, 39*, 360–367.

Langkaas, T. F., Hoffart, A., Øktedalen, T., Ulvenes, P., Hembree, E. A., & Smucker, M. (2017). Exposure to non-fear emotions: A randomized controlled study of exposure-based and rescripting-based imagery in PTSD treatment. *Behavior Research Therapy, 97*, 33–42.

Langmeyer, A., Guglhör-Rudan, A., & Tarnai, C. (2012). What do music preferences reveal about personality? A cross-cultural replication using self-ratings and ratings of music samples. *Journal of Individual Differences, 33*, 119–130.

Långström, N. H., Rahman, Q., Carlström, E., & Lichtenstein, P. (2010). Genetic and environmental effects on same-sex sexual behavior: A population study of twins in Sweden. *Archives of Sexual Behavior, 39*, 75–80.

Lankford, A. (2009). Promoting aggression and violence at Abu Ghraib: The U.S. military's transformation of ordinary people into torturers. *Aggression and Violent Behavior, 14*, 388–395.

Lapidos, R. (2016, August 2). Five things we learned from Kristen Stewart's struggle with anxiety. Retrieved from https://www.wellandgood.com/good-advice/kristen-stewart-anxiety/

Larkin, J. E., Brasel, A. M., & Pines, H. A. (2013). Cross-disciplinary applications of I/O psychology concepts: Predicting student retention and employee turnover. *Review of General Psychology, 17*, 82–92.

Larkin, K., Resko, J. A., Stormshak, F., Stellflug, J. N., & Roselli, C. E. (2002, November). *Neuroanatomical correlates of sex and sexual partner preference in sheep.* Paper presented at the annual meeting of the Society for Neuroscience, Orlando, FL.

Larrick, R. P., Timmerman, T. A., & Carton, A. M., & Abrevaya, J. (2011). Temper, temperature, and temptation: Heat-related retaliation in baseball. *Psychological Science, 22*, 423–428.

Larson, R. W., & Verma, S. (1999). How children and adolescents spend time across the world: Work, play, and developmental opportunities. *Psychological Bulletin, 125*, 701–736.

Larzelere, R. E. (2000). Child outcomes of non-abusive and customary physical punishment by parents: An updated literature review. *Clinical Child and Family Psychology Review, 3*, 199–221.

Larzelere, R. E., & Kuhn, B. R. (2005). Comparing child outcomes of physical punishment and alternative disciplinary tactics: A meta-analysis. *Clinical Child and Family Psychology Review, 8*, 1–37.

Larzelere, R. E., Kuhn, B. R., & Johnson, B. (2004). The intervention selection bias: An underrecognized confound in intervention research. *Psychological Bulletin, 130*, 289–303.

Lassiter, G. D., & Irvine, A. A. (1986). Video-taped confessions: The impact of camera point of view on judgments of coercion. *Journal of Personality and Social Psychology, 16*, 268–276.

Latané, B. (1981). The psychology of social impact. *American Psychologist, 36*, 343–356.

Latané, B., & Dabbs, J. M., Jr. (1975). Sex, group size and helping in three cities. *Sociometry, 38*, 180–194.

Latzman, R. D., Freeman, H. D., Schapiro, S. J., & Hopkins, W. D. (2015). The contribution of genetics and early rearing experiences to hierarchical personality dimensions in chimpanzees (*Pan troglodytes*). *Journal of Personality and Social Psychology, 109*, 889–900.

Latzman, R. D., Patrick, C. J., Freeman, H. D., Schapiro, S. J., & Hopkins, W. D. (2017). Etiology of triarchic psychopathy dimensions in chimpanzees (*Pan troglodytes*). *Clinical Psychological Science, 5*, 341–354.

Laukka, P., Elfenbein, H. A., Thingujam, N. S., Rockstuhl, T., Iraki, F. K., Chui, W., & Althoff, J. (2016). The expression and recognition of emotions in the voice across five nations: A lens model analysis based on acoustic features. *Journal of Personality and Social Psychology, 111*, 686–705.

Laws, K. R., & Kokkalis, J. (2007). Ecstasy (MDMA) and memory function: A meta-analytic update. *Human Psychopharmacology: Clinical and Experimental, 22*, 381–388.

Layous, K., Davis, E. M., Garcia, J., Purdie-Vaughns, V., Cook, J. E., & Cohen, G. L. (2017). Feeling left out, but affirmed: Protecting against the negative effects of low belonging in college. *Journal of Experimental Social Psychology, 69*, 227–231.

Layous, K., & Lyubomirsky, S. (2014). The how, who, what, when, and why of happiness: Mechanisms underlying the success of positive activity interventions. In J. Gruber & J. T. Moskowitz (Eds.), *Positive emotions: Integrating the light and dark sides* (pp. 473–495). New York: Oxford University Press.

Lazarus, R. S. (1990). Theory-based stress measurement. *Psychological Inquiry, 1*, 3–13.

Lazarus, R. S. (1991). Progress on a cognitive-motivational-relational theory of emotion. *American Psychologist, 46*, 352–367.

Lazarus, R. S. (1998). *Fifty years of the research and theory of R. S. Lazarus: An analysis of historical and perennial issues*. Mahwah, NJ: Erlbaum.

Lea, S. E. G. (2000). Towards an ethical use of animals. *The Psychologist, 13*, 556–557.

Leaper, C., & Ayres, M. M. (2007). A meta-analytic review of gender variations in adults' language use: Talkativeness, affiliative speech, and assertive speech. *Personality and Social Psychology Review, 11*, 328–363.

Leary, M. R. (1999). The social and psychological importance of self-esteem. In R. M. Kowalski & M. R. Leary (Eds.), *The social psychology of emotional and behavioral problems*. Washington, DC: APA Books.

Leary, M. R. (2012). Sociometer theory. In L. Van Lange, A. W. Kruglanski, & E. T. Higgins (Eds.), *Handbook of theories of social psychology* (Vol. 2, pp. 141–159). Los Angeles: Sage.

Leary, M. R. (2018). Self-awareness, hypo-egoicism, and psychological well-being. In J. E. Maddux (Ed.), *Subjective well-being and life satisfaction* (pp. 392–408). New York: Routledge.

Leary, M. R., Kowalski, R. M., Smith, L., & Phillips, S. (2003). Teasing, rejection, and violence: Case studies of the school shootings. *Aggressive Behavior, 29*, 202–214.

Lebedev, A. V., Lövdén, M., Rosenthal, G., Feilding, A., Nutt, D. J., & Carhart-Harris, R. L. (2015). Finding the self by losing the self: Neural correlates of ego-dissolution under psilocybin. *Human Brain Mapping, 36*, 3137–3153.

Leckelt, M., Küfner, A. C. P., Nestler, S., & Back, M. D. (2015). Behavioral processes underlying the decline of narcissists' popularity over time. *Journal of Personality and Social Psychology, 109*, 856–871.

LeDoux, J. (2015). *Anxious: Using the brain to understand and treat fear and anxiety*. New York: Viking.

LeDoux, J. E. (1996). *The emotional brain: The mysterious underpinnings of emotional life*. New York: Simon & Schuster.

LeDoux, J. E. (2002). *The synaptic self*. London: Macmillan.

LeDoux, J. E. (2009, July/August). Quoted by K. McGowan, Out of the past. *Discover*, pp. 28–37.

LeDoux, J. E., & Armony, J. (1999). Can neurobiology tell us anything about human feelings? In D. Kahneman, E. Diener, & N. Schwartz (Eds.), *Well-being: The foundations of hedonic psychology* (pp. 489–499). New York: Sage.

LeDoux, J. E., & Brown, R. (2017). A higher-order theory of emotional consciousness. *PNAS, 114*, E2016–E2025.

Lee, B. S., McIntyre, R. S., Gentle, J. E., Park, N. S., Chiriboga, D. A., Lee, Y., . . . & McPherson, M. A. (2018). A computational algorithm for personalized medicine in schizophrenia. *Schizophrenia Research, 192*, 131–136.

Lee, C. A., Derefinko, K. J., Milich, R., Lynam, D. R., & DeWall, C. N. (2017). Longitudinal and reciprocal relations between delay discounting and crime. *Personality and Individual Differences, 111*, 193–198.

Lee, D. S., Kim, E., & Schwarz, N. (2015). Something smells fishy: Olfactory suspicion cues improve performance on the Moses illusion and Wason rule discovery task. *Journal of Experimental Social Psychology, 59*, 47–50.

Lee, J. C., Hall, D. L., & Wood, W. (2018). Experiential or material purchases? Social class determines purchase happiness. *Psychological Science, 29*, 1031–1039.

Lee, J. J., Wedow, R., Okbay, A., Kong, E., Maghzian, O., Zacher, M., . . . & Fontana, M. A. (2018). Gene discovery and polygenic prediction from a genome-wide association study of educational attainment in 1.1 million individuals. *Nature Genetics, 50*, 1112–1121.

Lee, L., Frederick, S., & Ariely, D. (2006). Try it, you'll like it: The influence of expectation, consumption, and revelation on preferences for beer. *Psychological Science, 17*, 1054–1058.

Lee, S. W. S., & Schwarz, N. (2012). Bidirectionality, mediation, and moderation of metaphorical effects: The embodiment of social suspicions and fishy smells. *Journal of Personality and Social Psychology, 103*, 737–749.

Lefcourt, H. M. (1982). *Locus of control: Current trends in theory and research*. Hillsdale, NJ: Erlbaum.

Leger, K. A., Charles, S. T., & Almeida, D. M. (2018). Let it go: Lingering negative affect in response to daily stressors is associated with physical health years later. *Psychological Science, 29*, 1283–1290.

Lehman, D. R., Wortman, C. B., & Williams, A. F. (1987). Long-term effects of losing a spouse or child in a motor vehicle crash. *Journal of Personality and Social Psychology, 52*, 218–231.

Leichsenring, F., & Leweke, F. (2017). Social anxiety disorder. *The New England Journal of Medicine, 376*, 2255–2264.

Leichsenring, F., & Rabung, S. (2008). Effectiveness of long-term psychodynamic psychotherapy: A meta-analysis. *JAMA, 300*, 1551–1565.

Leitenberg, H., & Henning, K. (1995). Sexual fantasy. *Psychological Bulletin, 117*, 469–496.

Lemonick, M. D. (2002, June 3). Lean and hungrier. *Time*, p. 54.

LeMoult, J., & Gotlib, I. H. (2019). Depression: A cognitive perspective. *Clinical Psychology Review, 69*, 51–66.

Lench, H. C., Flores, S. A., & Bench, S. W. (2011). Discrete emotions predict changes in cognition, judgment, experience, behavior, and physiology: A meta-analysis of experimental emotion elicitations. *Psychological Bulletin, 137*, 834–855.

Lenhart, A. (2015a, April 9). *Mobile access shifts social media use and other online activities*. Pew Research Center (pewresearch.org).

Lenneberg, E. H. (1967). *Biological foundations of language*. New York: Wiley.

Lennox, B. R., Bert, S., Park, G., Jones, P. B., & Morris, P. G. (1999). Spatial and temporal mapping of neural activity associated with auditory hallucinations. *The Lancet, 353*, 644.

Lenton, A. P., & Francesconi, M. (2010). How humans cognitively manage an abundance of mate options. *Psychological Science, 21*, 528–533.

Lenton, A. P., & Francesconi, M. (2012). Too much of a good thing? Variety is confusing in mate choice. *Biology Letters, 7*, 528–531.

LePort, A. K. R., Mattfeld, A. T., Dickinson-Anson, H., Fallon, J. H., Stark, C. E. L., Kruggel, F., . . . McGaugh, J. L. (2012). Behavioral and neuroanatomical investigation of highly superior autobiographical memory (HSAM). *Neurobiology of Learning and Memory, 98*, 78–92.

Lepp, A., Barkley, J. E., & Karpinski, A. C. (2014). The relationship between cell phone use, academic performance, anxiety, and satisfaction with life in college students. *Computers in Human Behavior, 31*, 343–350.

Lereya, S. T., Copeland, W. E., Costello, E. J., & Wolke, D. (2015). Adult mental health consequences of peer bullying and maltreatment in childhood: Two cohorts in two countries. *The Lancet Psychiatry, 2*, 524–531.

Leucht, S., Barnes, T. R. E., Kissling, W., Engel, R. R., Correll, C., & Kane, J. M. (2003). Relapse prevention in schizophrenia with new-generation antipsychotics: A systematic review and exploratory meta-analysis of randomized, controlled trials. *American Journal of Psychiatry, 160*, 1209–1222.

Leucht, S., Leucht, C., Huhn, M., Chaimani, A., Mavridis, D., Helfer, B., . . . Geddes, J. R. (2017). Sixty years of placebo-controlled antipsychotic drug trials in acute schizophrenia: Systematic review, Bayesian meta-analysis, and meta-regression of efficacy predictors. *American Journal of Psychiatry, 174*, 927–942.

LeVay, S. (1991). A difference in hypothalamic structure between heterosexual and homosexual men. *Science, 253*, 1034–1037.

LeVay, S. (2011). *Gay, straight, and the reason why: The science of sexual orientation*. New York: Oxford University Press.

Levenson, R. M., Krupinski, E. A., Navarro, V. M., & Wasserman, E. A. (2015, November 18). Pigeons (*Columba livia*) as trainable observers of pathology and radiology breast cancer images. *PLOS ONE*, 10:e0141357.

Levenson, R. W. (1992). Autonomic nervous system differences among emotions. *Psychological Science, 3*, 23–27.

Levin, B., Nolan, J. J., & Reitzel, J. D. (2018, June 16). New data shows US hate crimes continued to rise in 2017. Retrieved from theconversation.com/new-data-shows-us-hate-crimes-continued-to-rise-in-2017-97989

Levin, K. H., Shanafelt, T. D., Keran, C. M., Busis, N. A., Foster, L. A., Molano, J. R. V., . . . Cascino, T. L. (2017). Burnout, career satisfaction, and well-being among US neurology residents and fellows in 2016. *Neurology, 89*, 492–501.

Levin, M. E., Stocke, K., Pierce, B., & Levin, C. (2018). Do college students use online self-help? A survey of intentions and use of mental health resources. *Journal of College Student Psychotherapy, 32*, 181–198.

Levine, J. A., Lanningham-Foster, L. M., McCrady, S. K., Krizan, A. C., Olson, L. R., Kane, P. H., . . . Clark, M. M. (2005). Interindividual variation in posture allocation: Possible role in human obesity. *Science, 307*, 584–586.

Levine, R. (2016). *Stranger in the mirror: The scientific search for self*. Princeton, NJ: Princeton University Press.

Levine, R., Sato, S., Hashimoto, T., & Verma, J. (1995). Love and marriage in eleven cultures. *Journal of Cross-Cultural Psychology, 26*, 554–571.

Levy, D. J., Heissel, J. A., Richeson, J. A., & Adam, E. K. (2016). Psychological and biological responses to race-based social stress as pathways to disparities in educational outcomes. *American Psychologist, 71*, 455–473.

Lewandowski, G. W., Jr., Aron, A., & Gee, J. (2007). Personality goes a long way: The malleability of opposite-sex physical attractiveness. *Personality Relationships, 14*, 571–585.

Lewinsohn, P. M., Hoberman, H., Teri, L., & Hautziner, M. (1985). An integrative theory of depression. In S. Reiss & R. Bootzin (Eds.), *Theoretical issues in behavior therapy* (pp. 331–359). Orlando, FL: Academic Press.

Lewinsohn, P. M., Petit, J., Joiner, T. E., Jr., & Seeley, J. R. (2003). The symptomatic expression of major depressive disorder in adolescents and young adults. *Journal of Abnormal Psychology, 112*, 244–252.

Lewinsohn, P. M., Rohde, P., & Seeley, J. R. (1998). Major depressive disorder in older adolescents: Prevalence, risk factors, and clinical implications. *Clinical Psychology Review, 18*, 765–794.

Lewis, D. M. G., Al-Shawaf, L., Conroy-Beam, D., Asao, K., & Buss, D. M. (2017). Evolutionary psychology: A how-to guide. *American Psychologist, 72,* 353–373.

Lewis, D. M. G., Russell, E. M., Al-Shawaf, L., & Buss, D. M. (2015). Lumbar curvature: A previously undiscovered standard of attractiveness. *Evolution and Human Behavior, 36,* 345–350.

Lewis, D. O., Yeager, C. A., Swica, Y., Pincus, J. H., & Lewis, M. (1997). Objective documentation of child abuse and dissociation in 12 murderers with dissociative identity disorder. *American Journal of Psychiatry, 154,* 1703–1710.

Lewis, M. B. (2018). The interactions between botulinum-toxin-based facial treatments and embodied emotions. *Scientific Reports, 8,* 14720.

Li, C.-M., Zhang, X., Hoffman, H. J., Cotch, M. F., Themann, C. L., & Wilson, M. R. (2014). Hearing impairment associated with depression in US adults, National Health and Nutrition Examination Survey 2005–2010. *Otolaryngology—Head & Neck Surgery, 140,* 293–302.

Li, J., Laursen, T. M., Precht, D. H., Olsen, J., & Mortensen, P. B. (2005). Hospitalization for mental illness among parents after the death of a child. *New England Journal of Medicine, 352,* 1190–1196.

Li, J., Zhao, Y., Lin, L., Chen, J., & Wang, S. (2018). The freedom to persist: Belief in free will predicts perseverance for long-term goals among Chinese adolescents. *Personality and Individual Differences, 121,* 7–10.

Li, N. P., & Kanazawa, S. (2016). Country roads, take me home . . . to my friends: How intelligence, population density, and friendship affect modern happiness. *British Journal of Psychology, 107,* 675–697.

Li, S., Stampfer, M. J., Williams, D. R., & VanderWeele, T. J. (2016). Association of religious service attendance with mortality among women. *JAMA Internal Medicine, 176,* 777–785.

Li, T., Yan, X., Li, Y., Wang, J., Li, Q., Li, H., & Li, J. (2017). Neuronal correlates of individual differences in the Big Five personality traits: evidences from cortical morphology and functional homogeneity. *Frontiers in Neuroscience, 11,* 414.

Li, W., Ma, L., Yang, G., & Gan, W. B. (2017). REM sleep selectively prunes and maintains new synapses in development and learning. *Nature Neuroscience, 20,* 427–437.

Liberman, M. C. (2015, August). Hidden hearing loss. *Scientific American,* pp. 49–53.

Licata, A., Taylor, S., Berman, M., & Cranston, J. (1993). Effects of cocaine on human aggression. *Pharmacology Biochemistry and Behavior, 45,* 549–552.

Lichtenstein, E., Zhu, S.-H., & Tedeschi, G. J. (2010). Smoking cessation quitlines: An underrecognized intervention success story. *American Psychologist, 65,* 252–261.

Liddle, J. R., Shackelford, T. K., & Weekes-Shackelford, V. W. (2012). Why can't we all just get along? Evolutionary perspectives on violence, homicide, and war. *Review of General Psychology, 16,* 24–36.

Lieberman, M. D., & Eisenberger, N. I. (2015). The dorsal anterior cingulate is selective for pain: Results from large-scale fMRI reverse inference. *PNAS, 12,* 15250–15255.

Lieberman, M. D., Eisenberger, N. L., Crockett, M. J., Tom, S. M., Pfeifer, J. H., & Way, B. M. (2007). Putting feelings into words: Affect labeling disrupts amygdala activity in response to affective stimuli. *Psychological Science, 18,* 421–428.

Lifton, R. J. (1961). *Thought reform and the psychology of totalism: A study of "brainwashing" in China.* New York: Norton.

Lilienfeld, S. O. (2009, Winter). Tips for spotting psychological pseudoscience: A student-friendly guide. *Eye on Psi Chi,* pp. 23–26.

Lilienfeld, S. O., Lynn, S. J., Kirsch, I., Chaves, J. F., Sarbin, T. R., Ganaway, G. K., & Powell, R. A. (1999). Dissociative identity disorder and the sociocognitive model: Recalling the lessons of the past. *Psychological Bulletin, 125,* 507–523.

Lilienfeld, S. O., Marshall, J., Todd, J. T., & Shane, H. C. (2015). The persistence of fad interventions in the face of negative scientific evidence: Facilitated communication for autism as a case example. *Evidence-Based Communication Assessment and Intervention, 8,* 62–101.

Lilienfeld, S. O., Ritschel, L. A., Lynn, S. J., Cautin, R. L., & Latzman, R. D. (2015). Science–practice gap. *Encyclopedia of Clinical Psychology.* New York: Wiley, 1–7.

Lilienfeld, S. O., Ritschel, L. A., Lynn, S. J., Cautin, R. L., & Latzman, R. D. (2013). Why many clinical psychologists are resistant to evidence-based practice: Root causes and constructive remedies. *Clinical Psychology Review, 33,* 883–900.

Lilienfeld, S. O., Sauvigné, K. C., Reber, J., Watts, A. L., Hamann, S., Smith, S. F., . . . Tranel, D. (2017). Potential effects of severe bilateral amygdala damage on psychopathic features: A case report. *Personality Disorders: Theory, Research, and Treatment, 9,* 112–121.

Lim, D., & DeSteno, D. (2016). Suffering and compassion: The links among adverse life experiences, empathy, compassion, and prosocial behavior. *Emotion, 16*(2), 175–182.

Lim, J., & Dinges, D. F. (2010). A meta-analysis of the impact of short-term sleep deprivation on cognitive variables. *Psychological Bulletin, 136,* 375–389.

Lin, P. (2016). Risky behaviors: Integrating adolescent egocentrism with the theory of planned behavior. *Review of General Psychology, 20,* 392–398.

Lin, Z., & Murray, S. O. (2015). More power to the unconscious: Conscious, but not unconscious, exogenous attention requires location variation. *Psychological Science, 26,* 221–230.

Linardon, J., Wade, T. D., de la Piedad Garcia, X., & Brennan, L. (2017). The efficacy of cognitive-behavioral therapy for eating disorders: A systematic review and meta-analysis. *Journal of Consulting and Clinical Psychology, 85,* 1080–1094.

Lindau, S. T., Schumm, L. P., Laumann, E. O., Levinson, W., O'Muircheartaigh, C. A., & Waite, L. J. (2007). A study of sexuality and health among older adults in the United States. *New England Journal of Medicine, 357,* 762–774.

Lindberg, S. M., Hyde, J. S., Linn, M. C., & Petersen, J. L. (2010). New trends in gender and mathematics performance: A meta-analysis. *Psychological Bulletin, 136,* 1125–1135.

Lindner, I., Echterhoff, G., Davidson, P. S. R., & Brand, M. (2010). Observation inflation: Your actions become mine. *Psychological Science, 21,* 1291–1299.

Lindson-Hawley, N., Banting, M., West, R., Michie, S., Shinkins, B., & Aveyard, P. (2016). Gradual versus abrupt smoking cessation: A randomized, controlled noninferiority trial. *Annals of Internal Medicine, 164,* 585–592.

Linehan, M. M., Korslund, K. E., Harned, M. S., Gallop, R. J., Lungu, A., Neacsiu, A. D., . . . Murray-Gregory, A. M. (2015). Dialectical behavior therapy for high suicide risk in individuals with borderline personality disorder: A randomized clinical trial and component analysis. *JAMA Psychiatry, 72,* 475–482.

Lippa, R. A. (2007). The relation between sex drive and sexual attraction to men and women: A cross-national study of heterosexual, bisexual, and homosexual men and women. *Archives of Sexual Behavior, 36,* 209–222.

Lippa, R. A. (2009). Sex differences in sex drive, sociosexuality, and height across 53 nations: Testing evolutionary and social structural theories. *Archives of Sexual Behavior, 38,* 631–651.

Lipsitt, L. P. (2003). Crib death: A biobehavioral phenomenon? *Current Directions in Psychological Science, 12,* 164–170.

Littman, R. (2018). Perpetrating violence increases identification with violent groups: Survey evidence from former combatants. *Personality and Social Psychology Bulletin, 44,* 1077–1089.

Liu, D., & Baumeister, R. F. (2016). Social networking online and personality of self-worth: A meta-analysis. *Journal of Research in Personality, 64,* 79–89.

Liu, J., Zhao, S., Chen, X., Falk, E., & Albarracín, D. (2017). The influence of peer behavior as a function of social and cultural closeness: A meta-analysis of normative influence on adolescent smoking initiation and continuation. *Psychological Bulletin, 143,* 1082–1115.

Liu, X., Hodgson, J. J., & Buchon, N. (2017). Drosophila as a model for homeostatic, antibacterial, and antiviral mechanisms in the gut. *PLOS Pathogens, 13,* e1006.

Liu, Y., Balaraman, Y., Wang, G., Nephew, K. P., & Zhou, F. C. (2009). Alcohol exposure alters DNA methylation profiles in mouse embryos at early neurulation. *Epigenetics, 4,* 500–511.

Livingstone, M., & Hubel, D. (1988). Segregation of form, color, movement, and depth: Anatomy, physiology, and perception. *Science, 240,* 740–749.

Lo, J. C., Chong, P. L., Ganesan, S., Leong, R. L., & Chee, M. W. (2016). Sleep deprivation increases formation of false memory. *Journal of Sleep Research, 25,* 673–682.

LoBello, S. G. (2017). The validity of major depression with seasonal pattern: Reply to young. *Clinical Psychological Science, 5,* 755–757.

Locke, K. D., Church, A. T., Mastor, K. A., Curtis, G. J., Sadler, P., McDonald, K., . . . Cabrera, H. F. (2017). Cross-situational self-consistency in nine cultures: The importance of separating influences of social norms and distinctive dispositions. *Personality and Social Psychology Bulletin, 43,* 1033–1049.

Loehlin, J. C. (2016). What can an adoption study tell us about the effect of prenatal environment on a trait? *Behavior Genetics, 46,* 329–333.

Loewenstein, G., & Furstenberg, F. (1991). Is teenage sexual behavior rational? *Journal of Applied Social Psychology, 21,* 957–986.

Loftus, E. F. (2012, July). *Manufacturing memories.* Invited address to the International Congress of Psychology, Cape Town.

Loftus, E. F., & Ketcham, K. (1994). *The myth of repressed memory: False memories and allegations of sexual abuse.* New York: St. Martin's Press.

Loftus, E. F., & Loftus, G. R. (1980). On the permanence of stored information in the human brain. *American Psychologist, 35,* 409–420.

Loftus, E. F., & Palmer, J. C. (October, 1974). Reconstruction of automobile destruction: An example of the interaction between language and memory. *Journal of Verbal Learning & Verbal Behavior, 13,* 585–589.

Loftus, E. F., Levidow, B., & Duensing, S. (1992). Who remembers best? Individual differences in memory for events that occurred in a science museum. *Applied Cognitive Psychology, 6,* 93–107.

Logan, T. K., Walker, R., Cole, J., & Leukefeld, C. (2002). Victimization and substance abuse among women: Contributing factors, interventions, and implications. *Review of General Psychology, 6*, 325–397.

Logue, A. W. (1998a). Laboratory research on self-control: Applications to administration. *Review of General Psychology, 2*, 221–238.

Logue, A. W. (1998b). Self-control. In W. T. O'Donohue (Ed.), *Learning and behavior therapy* (pp. 252–273). Boston: Allyn & Bacon.

London, P. (1970). The rescuers: Motivational hypotheses about Christians who saved Jews from the Nazis. In J. Macaulay & L. Berkowitz (Eds.), *Altruism and helping behavior*. New York: Academic Press.

Lonergan, M. H., Olivera-Figueroa, L., Pitman, R. K., & Brunet, A. (2013). Propranolol's effects on the consolidation and reconsolidation of long-term emotional memory in healthy participants: A meta-analysis. *Journal of Psychiatry & Neuroscience, 38*, 222–231.

Loomes, R., Hull, L., & Mandy, W. P. L. (2017). What is the male-to-female ratio in autism spectrum disorder? A systematic review and meta-analysis. *Journal of the American Academy of Child & Adolescent Psychiatry, 56*, 466–474.

Lopez-Quintero, C., de los Cobos, P., Hasin, D. S., Okuda, M., Wang, S., Grant, B. F., & Blanco, C. (2011). Probability and predictors of transition from first use to dependence on nicotine, alcohol, cannabis, and cocaine: Results of the national epidemiologic survey on alcohol and related conditions (NESARC). *Drug and Alcohol Dependence, 115*, 120–130.

Loprinzi, P. D., Loenneke, J. P., & Blackburn, E. H. (2015). Movement-based behaviors and leukocyte telomere length among US adults. *Medical Science and Sports Exercise, 47*, 2347–2352.

Lord, C. G., Lepper, M. R., & Preston, E. (1984). Considering the opposite: A corrective strategy for social judgment. *Journal of Personality and Social Psychology, 47*, 1231–1247.

Lord, C. G., Ross, L., & Lepper, M. (1979). Biased assimilation and attitude polarization: The effects of prior theories on subsequently considered evidence. *Journal of Personality and Social Psychology, 37*, 2098–2109.

Louie, K., & Wilson, M. A. (2001). Temporally-structured replay of awake hippocampal ensemble activity during rapid eye movement sleep. *Neuron, 29*, 145–156.

Lourenco, O., & Machado, A. (1996). In defense of Piaget's theory: A reply to 10 common criticisms. *Psychological Review, 103*, 143–164.

Lovaas, O. I. (1987). Behavioral treatment and normal educational and intellectual functioning in young autistic children. *Journal of Consulting and Clinical Psychology, 55*, 3–9.

Low, P. (2012). *The Cambridge Declaration on Consciousness.* Publicly proclaimed in Cambridge, UK, on July 7, 2012, at the Francis Crick Memorial Conference on Consciousness in Human and non-Human Animals (fcmconference.org /img/CambridgeDeclarationOnConsciousness.pdf).

Lowry, P. E. (1997). The assessment center process: New directions. *Journal of Social Behavior and Personality, 12*, 53–62.

Lozano, A., Mayberg, H., Giacobbe, P., Hami, C., Craddock, R., & Kennedy, S. (2008). Subcallosal cingulate gyrus deep brain stimulation for treatment-resistant depression. *Biological Psychiatry, 64*, 461–467.

Lu, J.G., Martin, A., Usova, A., & Galinsky, A.D. (2018). Creativity and humor across cultures: Where Aha meets Haha. In S.R. Luria, J. Baer, & J.C. Kaufman (Eds.) *Creativity and humor* (pp. 183–203). San Diego, CA: Academic Press.

Luan, Z., Poorthuis, A. M., Hutteman, R., Denissen, J. J., Asendorpf, J. B., & van Aken, M. A. (2019). Unique predictive power of other-rated personality: An 18-year longitudinal study. *Journal of Personality, 87*, 532–545.

Lubinski, D. (2009a). Cognitive epidemiology: With emphasis on untangling cognitive ability and socioeconomic status. *Intelligence, 37*, 625–633.

Lubinski, D. (2009b). Exceptional cognitive ability: The phenotype. *Behavioral Genetics, 39*, 350–358.

Lubinski, D. (2016). From Terman to today: A century of findings on intellectual precocity. *Review of Educational Research, 86*, 900–944.

Lubinski, D., Benbow, C. P., & Kell, H. J. (2014). Life paths and accomplishments of mathematically precocious males and females four decades later. *Psychological Science, 25*, 2217–2232.

Lucas, A., Morley, R., Cole, T. J., Lister, G., & Leeson-Payne, C. (1992). Breast milk and subsequent intelligence quotient in children born preterm. *The Lancet, 339*, 261–264.

Lucas, R. E., Clark, A. E., Georgellis, Y., & Diener, E. (2004). Unemployment alters the set point for life satisfaction. *Psychological Science, 15*, 8–13.

Lucas, R. E., & Donnellan, M. B. (2007). How stable is happiness? Using the STARTS model to estimate the stability of life satisfaction. *Journal of Research in Personality, 41*, 1091–1098.

Lucas, R. E., & Donnellan, M. B. (2011). Personality development across the life span: Longitudinal analyses with a national sample from Germany. *Journal of Personality and Social Psychology, 101*, 847–861.

Ludwig, A. M. (1995). *The price of greatness: Resolving the creativity and madness controversy.* New York: Guilford Press.

Ludwig, D. S., & Friedman, M. I. (2014). Increasing adiposity: Consequence or cause of overeating? *JAMA, 311*, 2167–2168.

Luethi, M. S., Friese, M., Binder, J., Boesiger, P., Luechinger, R., & Rasch, B. (2016). Motivational incentives lead to a strong increase in lateral prefrontal activity after self-control exertion. *Social Cognitive and Affective Neuroscience, 10*, 1618–1626.

Lukaszewski, A. W., Simmons, Z. L., Anderson, C., & Roney, J. R. (2016). The role of physical formidability in human social status allocation. *Journal of Personality and Social Psychology, 110*, 385–406.

Lund, T. J., & Dearing, E. (2012). Is growing up affluent risky for adolescents or is the problem growing up in an affluent neighborhood? *Journal of Research on Adolescence, 23*, 274–282.

Luppino, F. S., de Wit, L. M., Bouvy, P. F., Stijnen, T., Cuijpers, P., Penninx, W. J. H., & Zitman, F. G. (2010). Overweight, obesity, and depression. *Archives of General Psychiatry, 67*, 220–229.

Luria, A. M. (1968). In L. Solotaroff (Trans.), *The mind of a mnemonist*. New York: Basic Books.

Lutgendorf, S. K., & Andersen, B. L. (2015). Biobehavioral approaches to cancer progression and survival. *American Psychologist, 70*, 186–197.

Lutgendorf, S. K., Lamkin, D. M., Jennings, N. B., Arevalo, J. M. G., Penedo, F., DeGeest, K., . . . Sood, A. K. (2008). Biobehavioral influences on matrix metalloproteinase expression in ovarian carcinoma. *Clinical Cancer Research, 14*, 6839–6846.

Lutgendorf, S. K., Russell, D., Ullrich, P., Harris, T. B., & Wallace, R. (2004). Religious participation, interleukin-6, and mortality in older adults. *Health Psychology, 23*, 465–475.

Luthar, S. S., Barkin, S. H., & Crossman, E. J. (2013). "I can, therefore I must": Fragility in the upper-middle classes. *Development and Psychopathology, 25*, 1529–1549.

Lutz, P. E., Gross, J. A., Dhir, S. K., Maussion, G., Yang, J., Bramoullé, A., . . . Turecki, G. (2017). Epigenetic regulation of the kappa opioid receptor by child abuse. *Biological Psychiatry, 84*, 751–761.

Luyckx, K., Tildesley, E. A., Soenens, B., Andrews, J. A., Hampson, S. E., Peterson, M., & Duriez, B. (2011). Parenting and trajectories of children's maladaptive behaviors: A 12-year prospective community study. *Journal of Clinical Child and Adolescent Psychology, 40*, 468–478.

Lykken, D. T. (1991). *Science, lies, and controversy: An epitaph for the polygraph.* Invited address upon receipt of the Senior Career Award for Distinguished Contribution to Psychology in the Public Interest, American Psychological Association convention.

Lykken, D. T. (1995). *The antisocial personalities.* New York: Erlbaum.

Lykken, D. T. (2006). The mechanism of emergenesis. *Genes, Brain & Behavior, 5*, 306–310.

Lynch, G. (2002). Memory enhancement: The search for mechanism-based drugs. *Nature Neuroscience, 5* (suppl.), 1035–1038.

Lynch, G., & Staubli, U. (1991). Possible contributions of long-term potentiation to the encoding and organization of memory. *Brain Research Reviews, 16*, 204–206.

Lynn, M. (1988). The effects of alcohol consumption on restaurant tipping. *Personality and Social Psychology Bulletin, 14*, 87–91.

Lynn, R., & Vanhanen, T. (2012). *Intelligence: A unifying construct for the social sciences.* London, England: Ulster Institute for Social Research.

Lynn, S. J., Laurence, J., & Kirsch, I. (2015). Hypnosis, suggestion, and suggestibility: An integrative model. *American Journal of Clinical Hypnosis, 57*, 314–329.

Lynn, S. J., Lilienfeld, S. O., Merckelbach, H., Giesbrecht, T., McNally, R. J., Loftus, E. F., . . . Malaktaris, A. (2014). The trauma model of dissociation: Inconvenient truths and stubborn fictions. Comment on Dalenberg et al. (2012). *Psychological Bulletin, 140*, 896–910.

Lynn, S. J., Rhue, J. W., & Weekes, J. R. (1990). Hypnotic involuntariness: A social cognitive analysis. *Psychological Review, 97*, 169–184.

Lyons, A. (2015). Resilience in lesbians and gay men: A review and key findings from a nationwide Australian survey. *International Review of Psychiatry, 27*, 435–443.

Lyons, B. D., Hoffman, B. J., Michel, J. W., & Williams, K. J. (2011). On the predictive efficiency of past performance and physical ability: The case of the National Football League. *Human Performance, 24*, 158–172.

Lyons, H. A., Manning, W. D., Longmore, M. A., & Giordano, P. C. (2015). Gender and casual sexual activity from adolescence to emerging adulthood: Social and life course correlates. *Journal of Sex Research, 52*, 543–557.

Lyons, M. J., Panizzon, M. S., Liu, W., McKenzie, R., Bluestone, N. J., Grant, M. D., . . . Xian, H. (2017). A longitudinal twin study of general cognitive ability over four decades. *Developmental Psychology, 53*, 1170–1177.

Lyubomirsky, S. (2001). Why are some people happier than others? The role of cognitive and motivational processes in well-being. *American Psychologist, 56*, 239–249.

Lyubomirsky, S. (2008). *The how of happiness.* New York: Penguin.

Ma, A., Landau, M. J., Narayanan, J., & Kay, A. C. (2017). Thought-control difficulty motivates structure seeking. *Journal of Experimental Psychology: General, 146*, 1067–1072.

Maas, J. B., & Robbins, R. S. (2010). *Sleep for success: Everything you must know about sleep but are too tired to ask.* Bloomington, IN: Author House.

MacCabe, J. H., Lambe, M. P., Cnattingius, S., Torrång, A., Björk, C., Sham, P. C., . . . Hultman, C. M. (2008). Scholastic achievement at age 16 and risk of schizophrenia and other psychoses: A national cohort study. *Psychological Medicine, 38,* 1133–1140.

Maccoby, E. E. (1990). Gender and relationships: A developmental account. *American Psychologist, 45,* 513–520.

Maccoby, E. E. (1998). *The paradox of gender.* Cambridge, MA: Harvard University Press.

Maccoby, E. E. (2002). Gender and group process: A developmental perspective. *Current Directions in Psychological Science, 11,* 54–58.

MacCormack, J. K., & Lindquist, K. A. (2016). Bodily contribution to emotion: Schachter's legacy for a psychological constructionist view on emotion. *Emotion Review, 9,* 36–45.

MacDonald, G., & Leary, M. R. (2005). Why does social exclusion hurt? The relationship between social and physical pain. *Psychological Bulletin, 131,* 202–223.

MacDonald, T. K., & Hynie, M. (2008). Ambivalence and unprotected sex: Failure to predict sexual activity and decreased condom use. *Journal of Applied Social Psychology, 38,* 1092–1107.

MacDonald, T. K., Zanna, M. P., & Fong, G. T. (1995). Decision making in altered states: Effects of alcohol on attitudes toward drinking and driving. *Journal of Personality and Social Psychology, 68,* 973–985.

MacFarlane, A. (1978, February). What a baby knows. *Human Nature,* pp. 74–81.

Mackenzie, A. K., & Harris, J. M. (2017). A link between attentional function, effective eye movements, and driving ability. *Journal of Experimental Psychology: Human Perception and Performance, 43,* 381–394.

Mackenzie, J. L., Aggen, S. H., Kirkpatrick, R. M., Kendler, K. S., & Amstadter, A. B. (2015). A longitudinal twin study of insomnia symptoms in adults. *Sleep, 38,* 1423–1430.

MacKenzie, M. J., Nicklas, E., Waldfogel, J., & Brooks-Gunn, J. (2013). Spanking and child development across the first decade of life. *Pediatrics, 132,* e1118–e1125.

MacKerron, G., & Mourato, S. (2013). Happiness is greater in natural environments. *Global Environmental Change, 23,* 992–1000.

MacLeod, C., & Clarke, P. J. F. (2015). The attentional bias modification approach to anxiety intervention. *Clinical Psychological Science, 3,* 58–78.

MacLeod, C. M., & Bodner, G. E. (2017). The production effect in memory. *Current Directions in Psychological Science, 26,* 390–395.

Macmillan, M., & Lena, M. L. (2010). Rehabilitating Phineas Gage. *Neuropsychological Rehabilitation, 17,* 1–18.

Macnamara, B. N., Hambrick, D. Z., & Oswald, F. L. (2014). Deliberate practice and performance in music, games, sports, education, and professions: A meta-analysis. *Psychological Science, 25,* 1608–1618.

Macnamara, B. N., Moreau, D., & Hambrick, D. Z. (2016). The relationship between deliberate practice and performance in sports: A meta-analysis. *Perspectives on Psychological Science, 11,* 333–350.

MacNeilage, P. F., Rogers, L. J., & Vallortigara, G. (2009, July). Origins of the left and right brain. *Scientific American,* pp. 60–67.

MacPherson, S. E., Turner, M. S., Bozzali, M., Cipolotti, L., & Shallice, T. (2016). The Doors and People Test: The effect of frontal lobe lesions on recall and recognition memory performance. *Neuropsychology, 30,* 332–337.

Macur, J. (2018, January 24). In Larry Nassar's case, a single voice eventually raised an army. *The New York Times* (nytimes.com).

Madison, G., Mosling, M. A., Verweij, K. J. H., Pedersen, N. L., & Ullen, F. (2016). Common genetic influences on intelligence and auditory simple reaction time in a large Swedish sample. *Intelligence, 59,* 157–162.

Maeda, Y., & Yoon, S. Y. (2013). A meta-analysis on gender differences in mental rotation ability measured by the Purdue spatial visualization tests: Visualization of rotations (PSVT:R). *Educational Psychology Review, 25,* 69–94.

Maes, H. H. M., Neale, M. C., & Eaves, L. J. (1997). Genetic and environmental factors in relative body weight and human adiposity. *Behavior Genetics, 27,* 325–351.

Maes, H. H., Neale, M. C., Ohlsson, H., Zahery, M., Lichtenstein, P., Sundquist, K., . . . Kendler, K. S. (2016). A bivariate genetic analysis of drug abuse ascertained through medical and criminal registries in Swedish twins, siblings and half-siblings. *Behavior Genetics, 46,* 735–741.

Magnusson, D. (1990). Personality research—challenges for the future. *European Journal of Personality, 4,* 1–17.

Maguire, E. A., Gadian, D. G., Johnsrude, I. S., Good, C. D., Ashburner, J., Frackowiak, R. S. J., & Frith, C. D. (2000). Navigation-related structural change in the hippocampi of taxi drivers. *PNAS, 97,* 4398–4403.

Maguire, E. A., Valentine, E. R., Wilding, J. M., & Kapur, N. (2003). Routes to remembering: The brains behind superior memory. *Nature Neuroscience, 6,* 90–95.

Maguire, E. A., Woollett, & Spiers, H. J. (2006). London taxi drivers and bus drivers: A structural MRI and neuropsychological analysis. *Hippocampus, 16,* 1091–1101.

Maher, S., Ekstrom, T., & Chen, Y. (2014). Greater perceptual sensitivity to happy facial expression. *Perception, 43,* 1353–1364.

Maia, T. V., & Frank, M. J. (2017). An integrative perspective on the role of dopamine in schizophrenia. *Biological Psychiatry, 81,* 52–66.

Maier, S. F., & Seligman, M. E. P. (2016). Learned helplessness at fifty: Insights from neuroscience. *Psychological Review, 123,* 349–367.

Maier, S. F., Watkins, L. R., & Fleshner, M. (1994). Psychoneuroimmunology: The interface between behavior, brain, and immunity. *American Psychologist, 49,* 1004–1017.

Major, B., Carrington, P. I., & Carnevale, P. J. D. (1984). Physical attractiveness and self-esteem: Attribution for praise from an other-sex evaluator. *Personality and Social Psychology Bulletin, 10,* 43–50.

Major, B., Schmidlin, A. M., & Williams, L. (1990). Gender patterns in social touch: The impact of setting and age. *Journal of Personality and Social Psychology, 58,* 634–643.

Makel, M. C., Kell, H. J., Lubinski, D., Putallaz, M., & Benbow, C. P. (2016). When lightning strikes twice: Profoundly gifted, profoundly accomplished. *Psychological Science, 27,* 1004–1018.

Makin, S. (2015a, November/December). What really causes autism. *Scientific American,* pp. 57–63.

Malamuth, N. (2018). "Adding fuel to the fire"? Does exposure to non-consenting adult or to child pornography increase risk of sexual aggression? *Aggression and Violent Behavior, 41,* 74–89.

Malani, P., Singer, D., Clark, S., Kirch, M., & Solway, E. (2018, May). *Let's talk about sex.* National poll on healthy aging. Retrieved from https://www.healthyagingpoll.org/report/lets-talk-about-sex

Malle, B. F. (2006). The actor–observer asymmetry in attribution: A (surprising) meta-analysis. *Psychological Bulletin, 132,* 895–919.

Malle, B. F., Knobe, J. M., & Nelson, S. E. (2007). Actor–observe asymmetries in explanations of behavior: New answers to an old question. *Journal of Personality and Social Psychology, 93,* 491–514.

Malmquist, C. P. (1986). Children who witness parental murder: Post-traumatic aspects. *Journal of the American Academy of Child Psychiatry, 25,* 320–325.

Mandelli, L., Arminio, A., Atti, A. R., & De Ronchi, D. (2018). Suicide attempts in eating disorder subtypes: A meta-analysis of the literature employing DSM-IV, DSM-5, or ICD-10 diagnostic criteria. *Psychological Medicine, 49,* 1237–1249.

Mandsager, K., Harb, S., Cremer, P., Phelan, D., Nissen, S. E., & Jaber, W. (2018). Association of cardiorespiratory fitness with long-term mortality among adults undergoing exercise treadmill testing. *JAMA Network Open, 1,* e183605–e183605.

Maner, J. K., Kenrick, D. T., Neuberg, S. L., Becker, D. V., Robertson, T., Hofer, B., . . . Schaller, M. (2005). Functional projection: How fundamental social motives can bias interpersonal perception. *Journal of Personality and Social Psychology, 88,* 63–78.

Mann, T., Tomiyama, A. J., & Ward, A. (2015). Promoting public health in the context of the "obesity epidemic": False starts and promising new directions. *Perspectives on Psychological Science, 10,* 706–710.

Manning, W., & Cohen, J. A. (2012). Premarital cohabitation and marital dissolution: An examination of recent marriages. *Journal of Marriage and Family, 74,* 377–387.

Manson, J. E. (2002). Walking compared with vigorous exercise for the prevention of cardiovascular events in women. *New England Journal of Medicine, 347,* 716–725.

Maquet, P. (2001). The role of sleep in learning and memory. *Science, 294,* 1048–1052.

Mar, R. A., & Oatley, K. (2008). The function of fiction is the abstraction and simulation of social experience. *Perspectives on Psychological Science, 3,* 173–192.

Marangolo, P., Fiori, V., Sabatini, U., De Pasquale, G., Razzano, C., Caltagirone, C., & Gili, T. (2016). Bilateral transcranial direct current stimulation language treatment enhances functional connectivity in the left hemisphere: Preliminary data from aphasia. *Journal of Cognitive Neuroscience, 28,* 724–738.

Marcinkowska, U. M., Kaminski, G., Little, A. C., & Jasienska, G. (2018). Average ovarian hormone levels, rather than daily values and their fluctuations, are related to facial preferences among women. *Hormones and Behavior, 102,* 114–119.

Marinak, B. A., & Gambrell, L. B. (2008). Intrinsic motivation and rewards: What sustains young children's engagement with text? *Literacy Research and Instruction, 47,* 9–26.

Marjonen, H., Sierra, A., Nyman, A., Rogojin, V., Gröhn, O., Linden, A. M., . . . Kaminen-Ahola, N. (2015). Early maternal alcohol consumption alters hippocampal DNA methylation, gene expression and volume in a mouse model. *PLOS ONE, 10*(5), e0124931.

Marks, A. K., Patton, F., & Coll, C. G. (2011). Being bicultural: A mixed-methods study of adolescents' implicitly and explicitly measured multiethnic identities. *Developmental Psychology, 47,* 270–288.

Marks, E. H., Franklin, A. R., & Zoellner, L. A. (2018). Can't get it out of my mind: A systematic review of predictors of intrusive memories of distressing events. *Psychological Bulletin, 144*, 584–640.

Markus, H. R., & Kitayama, S. (1991). Culture and the self: Implications for cognition, emotion, and motivation. *Psychological Review, 98*, 224–253.

Markus, H. R., & Nurius, P. (1986). Possible selves. *American Psychologist, 41*, 954–969.

Marley, J., & Bulia, S. (2001). Crimes against people with mental illness: Types, perpetrators and influencing factors. *Social Work, 46*, 115–124.

Marsh, A. A., Rhoads, S. A., & Ryan, R. M. (2019). A multi-semester classroom demonstration yields evidence in support of the facial feedback effect. *Emotion*. doi:10.1037/emo0000532

Marsh, N., Scheele, D., Gerhardt, H., Strang, S., Enax, L., Weber, B., . . . Hurlemann, R. (2017). The neuropeptide oxytocin induces a social altruism bias. *Journal of Neuroscience, 35*, 15696–15701.

Marshall, M. J. (2002). *Why spanking doesn't work*. Springville, UT: Bonneville Books.

Marshall, P. J., & Meltzoff, A. N. (2014). Neural mirroring mechanisms and imitation in human infants. *Philosophical Transactions of the Royal Society: Series B, 369*(1644).

Marteau, T. M. (1989). Framing of information: Its influences upon decisions of doctors and patients. *British Journal of Social Psychology, 28*, 89–94.

Marteau, T. M., Hollands, G. J., & Fletcher, P. C. (2012). Changing human behavior to prevent disease: The importance of targeting automatic processes. *Science, 337*, 1492–1495.

Martel, M. M., Levinson, C. A., Langer, J. K., & Nigg, J. T. (2016). A network analysis of developmental change in ADHD symptom structure from preschool to adulthood. *Clinical Psychological Science, 4*, 988–1001.

Martela, F., & Steger, M. F. (2016). The three meanings of meaning in life: Distinguishing coherence, purpose, and significance. *The Journal of Positive Psychology, 11*, 531–545.

Martin, C. K., Anton, S. D., Walden, H., Arnett, C., Greenway, F. L., & Williamson, D. A. (2007). Slower eating rate reduces the food intake of men, but not women: Implications for behavioural weight control. *Behaviour Research and Therapy, 45*, 2349–2359.

Martin, C. L., & Ruble, D. (2004). Children's search for gender cues. *Current Directions in Psychological Science, 13*, 67–70.

Martin, C. L., Ruble, D. N., & Szkrybalo, J. (2002). Cognitive theories of early gender development. *Psychological Bulletin, 128*, 903–933.

Martín, R., Bajo-Grañeras, R., Moratalla, R., Perea, G., & Araque, A. (2015). Circuit-specific signaling in astrocyte-neuron networks in basal ganglia pathways. *Science, 349*, 730–734.

Martins, Y., Preti, G., Crabtree, C. R., & Wysocki, C. J. (2005). Preference for human body odors is influenced by gender and sexual orientation. *Psychological Science, 16*, 694–701.

Mashour, G. A. (2018). The controversial correlates of consciousness. *Science, 360*, 493–494.

Maslow, A. H. (1970). *Motivation and personality* (2nd ed.). New York: Harper & Row.

Maslow, A. H. (1971). *The farther reaches of human nature*. New York: Viking Press.

Mason, C., & Kandel, E. R. (1991). Central visual pathways. In E. R. Kandel, J. H. Schwartz, & T. M. Jessell (Eds.), *Principles of neural science* (3rd ed.). New York: Elsevier.

Mason, R. A., & Just, M. A. (2004). How the brain processes causal inferences in text. *Psychological Science, 15*, 1–7.

Massimini, M., Ferrarelli, F., Huber, R., Esser, S. K., Singh, H., & Tononi, G. (2005). Breakdown of cortical effective connectivity during sleep. *Science, 309*, 2228–2232.

Masters, K. S. (2010). The role of religion in therapy: Time for psychologists to have a little faith? *Cognitive and Behavioral Practice, 17*, 393–400.

Masters, K. S., & Hooker, S. A. (2013). Religiousness/spirituality, cardiovascular disease, and cancer: Cultural integration for health research and intervention. *Journal of Consulting and Clinical Psychology, 81*, 206–216.

Masters, W. H., & Johnson, V. E. (1966). *Human sexual response*. Boston: Little, Brown.

Mastroianni, G. R. (2015). Obedience in perspective: Psychology and the Holocaust. *Theory and Psychology, 25*, 657–669.

Mastroianni, G. R., & Reed, G. (2006). Apples, barrels, and Abu Ghraib. *Sociological Focus, 39*, 239–250.

Mata, R., Josef, A. K., & Hertwig, R. (2016). Propensity for risk taking across the life span and around the globe. *Psychological Science, 27*, 231–243.

Mataix-Cols, D., Rosario-Campos, M. C., & Leckman, J. F. (2005). A multidimensional model of obsessive-compulsive disorder. *American Journal of Psychiatry, 162*, 228–238.

Mataix-Cols, D., Wooderson, S., Lawrence, N., Brammer, M. J., Speckens, A., & Phillips, M. L. (2004). Distinct neural correlates of washing, checking, and hoarding symptom dimensions in obsessive-compulsive disorder. *Archives of General Psychiatry, 61*, 564–576.

Mather, M. (2016). The affective neuroscience of aging. *Annual Review of Psychology, 67*, 213–238.

Mather, M., & Sutherland, M. (2012, February). The selective effects of emotional arousal on memory. APA Science Brief (apa.org).

Matson, J. L., & Boisjoli, J. A. (2009). The token economy for children with intellectual disability and/or autism: A review. *Research on Developmental Disabilities, 30*, 240–248.

Matsumoto, D., & Ekman, P. (1989). American-Japanese cultural differences in intensity ratings of facial expressions of emotion. *Motivation and Emotion, 13*, 143–157.

Matsumoto, D., Frank, M. G., & Hwang, H. C. (2015). The role of intergroup emotions on political violence. *Current Directions in Psychological Science, 24*, 369–373.

Matsumoto, D., & Willingham, B. (2006). The thrill of victory and the agony of defeat: Spontaneous expressions of medal winners of the 2004 Athens Olympic Games. *Journal of Personality and Social Psychology, 91*, 568–581.

Matsumoto, D., & Willingham, B. (2009). Spontaneous facial expressions of emotion of congenitally and noncongenitally blind individuals. *Journal of Personality and Social Psychology, 96*, 1–10.

Mattheisen, M., Samuels, J. F., Wang, Y., Greenberg, B. D., Fyer, A. J., McCracken, J. T., . . . Riddle, M. A. (2015). Genome-wide association study in obsessive-compulsive disorder: Results from OCGAS. *Molecular Psychiatry, 20*, 337–344.

Matthews, R. N., Domjan, M., Ramsey, M., & Crews, D. (2007). Learning effects on sperm competition and reproductive fitness. *Psychological Science, 18*, 758–762.

Matz, S. C., Kosinski, M., Nave, G., & Stillwell, D. J. (2017). Psychological targeting as an effective approach to digital mass persuasion. *PNAS, 114*, 12714–12719.

Maurer, D., & Maurer, C. (1988). *The world of the newborn*. New York: Basic Books

Mauss, I. B., Shallcross, A. J., Troy, A. S., John, O. P., Ferrer, E., Wilhelm, F. H., & Gross, J. J. (2011). Don't hide your happiness! Positive emotion dissociation, social connectedness, and psychological functioning. *Journal of Personality and Social Psychology, 100*, 738–748.

Mautz, B., Wong, B., Peters, R., & Jennions, M. (2013). Penis size interacts with body shape and height to influence male attractiveness. *PNAS, 110*, 6925–6693.

Maxwell, S. E., Lau, M. Y., & Howard, G. S. (2015). Is psychology suffering from a replication crisis? What does "failure to replicate" really mean? *American Psychologist, 70*, 487–498.

May, C., & Hasher, L. (1998). Synchrony effects in inhibitory control over thought and action. *Journal of Experimental Psychology: Human Perception and Performance, 24*, 363–380.

May, P. A., Chambers, C. D., Kalberg, W. O., Zellner, J., Feldman, H., Buckley, D., . . . Hoyme, E. (2018). Prevalence of fetal alcohol spectrum disorders in 4 US communities. *JAMA, 319*, 474–482.

May, R. (1982). The problem of evil: An open letter to Carl Rogers. *Journal of Humanistic Psychology, 22*, 10–21.

Mayberg, H. S., Lozano, A. M., Voon, V., McNeely, H. E., Seminowicz, D., Hamani, C., . . . Kennedy, S. H. (2005). Deep brain stimulation for treatment-resistant depression. *Neuron, 45*, 651–660.

Mayer, J. D., Caruso, D. R., & Salovey, P. (2016). The ability model of emotional intelligence: Principles and updates. *Emotion Review, 8*, 290–300.

Mayer, J. D., Salovey, P., & Caruso, D. R. (2002). *The Mayer-Salovey-Caruso emotional intelligence test (MSCEIT)*. Toronto, Canada: Multi-Health Systems, Inc.

Mayer, J. D., Salovey, P., & Caruso, D. R. (2012). The validity of the MSCEIT: Additional analyses and evidence. *Emotion Review, 4*, 403–408.

Mazure, C., Keita, G., & Blehar, M. (2002). *Summit on women and depression: Proceedings and recommendations* [PDF file]. Retrieved from apa.org/pi/women/programs/depression/summit-2002.pdf

Mazza, S., Gerbier, E., Gustin, M. P., Kasikci, Z., Koenig, O., Toppino, T. C., & Magnin, M. (2016). Relearn faster and retain longer: Along with practice, sleep makes perfect. *Psychological Science, 27*, 1321–1330.

Mazzei, P. (2019, March 24). After 2 apparent student suicides, Parkland grieves again. *The New York Times* (nytimes.com).

Mazzoni, G., Scoboria, A., & Harvey, L. (2010). Nonbelieved memories. *Psychological Science, 21*, 1334–1340.

McAdams, D. P., & Guo, J. (2015). Narrating the generative life. *Psychological Science, 26*, 475–483.

McBurney, D. H. (1996). *How to think like a psychologist: Critical thinking in psychology*. Upper Saddle River, NJ: Prentice-Hall.

McBurney, D. H., & Collings, V. B. (1984). *Introduction to sensation and perception* (2nd ed.). Englewood Cliffs, NJ: Prentice-Hall.

McBurney, D. H., & Gent, J. F. (1979). On the nature of taste qualities. *Psychological Bulletin, 86*, 151–167.

McCabe, K. O., & Fleeson, W. (2016). Are traits useful? Explaining trait manifestations as tools in the pursuit of goals. *Journal of Personality and Social Psychology, 110*, 287–301.

McCain, J. (2017, February 18). McCain attacks Trump administration and inability to "separate truth from lies." Retrieved from https://www.theguardian.com/us-news/2017/feb/18/john-mccain-savages-donald-trump-administration-inability-separate-truth-from-lies

McCann, I. L., & Holmes, D. S. (1984). Influence of aerobic exercise on depression. *Journal of Personality and Social Psychology, 46,* 1142–1147.

McCann, U. D., Eligulashvili, V., & Ricaurte, G. A. (2001). (+–)3,4–Methylenedioxymethamphetamine ('Ecstasy')-induced serotonin neurotoxicity: Clinical studies. *Neuropsychobiology, 42,* 11–16.

McCarthy, J. (2016, August 8). *One in eight U.S. adults say they smoke marijuana.* Gallup Poll (gallup.com).

McCarthy, P. (1986, July). Scent: The tie that binds? *Psychology Today,* pp. 6, 10.

McCauley, C. R. (2002). Psychological issues in understanding terrorism and the response to terrorism. In C. E. Stout (Ed.), *The psychology of terrorism* (Vol. 3, pp. 3–29). Westport, CT: Praeger/Greenwood.

McCauley, C. R., & Segal, M. E. (1987). Social psychology of terrorist groups. In C. Hendrick (Ed.), *Group processes and intergroup relations: Review of personality and social psychology* (Vol. 9, pp. 231–256). Beverly Hills, CA: Sage.

McCauley, E., Berk, M. S., Asarnow, J. R., Adrian, M., Cohen, J., Korslund, K., . . . & Linehan, M. M. (2018). Efficacy of dialectical behavior therapy for adolescents at high risk for suicide: A randomized clinical trial. *JAMA Psychiatry, 75,* 777–785.

McClendon, B. T., & Prentice-Dunn, S. (2001). Reducing skin cancer risk: An intervention based on protection motivation theory. *Journal of Health Psychology, 6,* 321–328.

McClintock, M. K., & Herdt, G. (1996, December). Rethinking puberty: The development of sexual attraction. *Current Directions in Psychological Science, 5,* 178–183.

McClung, M., & Collins, D. (2007). "Because I know it will!": Placebo effects of an ergogenic aid on athletic performance. *Journal of Sport & Exercise Psychology, 29,* 382–394.

McClure, E. B. (2000). A meta-analytic review of sex differences in facial expression processing and their development in infants, children, and adolescents. *Psychological Bulletin, 126,* 424–453.

McClure, M. J., & Lydon, J. E. (2014). Anxiety doesn't become you: How attachment compromises relational opportunities. *Journal of Personality and Social Psychology, 106,* 89–111.

McConnell, A. R., Brown, C. M., Shoda, T. M., Stayton, L. E., & Martin, C. E. (2011). Friends with benefits: On the positive consequences of pet ownership. *Journal of Personality and Social Psychology, 101,* 1239–1252.

McCrae, R. R., & Costa, P. T., Jr. (1986). Clinical assessment can benefit from recent advances in personality psychology. *American Psychologist, 41,* 1001–1003.

McCrae, R. R., & Costa, P. T., Jr. (2008). The Five-Factor Theory of personality. In O. P. John, R. W., Robins, & L. A. Pervin (Eds.), *Handbook of personality: Theory and research* (3rd ed.). New York: Guilford.

McCrae, R. R., Costa, P. T., Jr., Ostendorf, F., Angleitner, A., Hrebicková, M., Avia, M. D., . . . Smith, P. B. (2000). Nature over nurture: Temperament, personality, and life span development. *Journal of Personality and Social Psychology, 78,* 173–186.

McCrae, R. R., Terracciano, A., & 78 members of the Personality Profiles and Cultures Project. (2005). Universal features of personality traits from the observer's perspective: Data from 50 cultures. *Journal of Personality and Social Psychology, 88,* 547–561.

McCrae, R. R., Terracciano, A., & Khoury, B. (2007). Dolce far niente: The positive psychology of personality stability and invariance. In A. D. Ong & M. H. Van Dulmen (Eds.), *Oxford handbook of methods in positive psychology* (pp. 176–188). New York: Oxford University Press.

McCullough, M. E., Hoyt, W. T., Larson, D. B., Koenig, H. G., & Thoresen, C. (2000). Religious involvement and mortality: A meta-analytic review. *Health Psychology, 19,* 211–222.

McCullough, M. E., & Laurenceau, J.-P. (2005). Religiousness and the trajectory of self-rated health across adulthood. *Personality and Social Psychology Bulletin, 31,* 560–573.

McCullough, M. E., & Willoughby, B. L. B. (2009). Religion, self-regulation, and self-control: Associations, explanations, and implications. *Psychological Bulletin, 135,* 69–93.

McDaniel, M. A., Bugg, J. M., Liu, Y., & Brick, J. (2015). When does the test-study-test sequence optimize learning and retention? *Journal of Experimental Psychology: Applied, 21,* 370–382.

McDaniel, M. A., Howard, D. C., & Einstein, G. O. (2009). The read-recite-review study strategy: Effective and portable. *Psychological Science, 20,* 516–522.

McDonald, P. (2012). Workplace sexual harassment 30 years on: A review of the literature. *International Journal of Management Reviews, 14,* 1–17.

McDuff, D., Kodra, E., el Kallouby, R., & LaFrance, M. (2017). A large-scale analysis of sex differences in facial expressions. *PLOS ONE, 12,* e0173942.

McEvoy, S. P., Stevenson, M. R., McCartt, A. T., Woodward, M., Haworth, C., Palamara, P., & Ceracelli, R. (2005). Role of mobile phones in motor vehicle crashes resulting in hospital attendance: A case-crossover study. *British Medical Journal, 331,* 428.

McEvoy, S. P., Stevenson, M. R., & Woodward, M. (2007). The contribution of passengers versus mobile phone use to motor vehicle crashes resulting in hospital attendance by the driver. *Accident Analysis and Prevention, 39,* 1170–1176.

McGaugh, J. L. (1994). Quoted by B. Bower, Stress hormones hike emotional memories. *Science News, 146,* 262.

McGaugh, J. L. (2003). *Memory and emotion: The making of lasting memories.* New York: Columbia University Press.

McGaugh, J. L. (2015). Consolidating memories. *Annual Review of Psychology, 66,* 1–24.

McGaugh, J. L., & LePort, A. (2014, February). Remembrance of all things past. *Scientific American,* pp. 41–45.

McGeehan, P. (February 6, 2018). Failure to screen for sleep apnea led to two recent train crashes. *The New York Times* (nytimes.com).

McGhee, P. E. (1976, June). Children's appreciation of humor: A test of the cognitive congruency principle. *Child Development, 47,* 420–426.

McGrath, J. J., & Welham, J. L. (1999). Season of birth and schizophrenia: A systematic review and meta-analysis of data from the Southern hemisphere. *Schizophrenia Research, 35,* 237–242.

McGrath, J. J., Welham, J., & Pemberton, M. (1995). Month of birth, hemisphere of birth and schizophrenia. *British Journal of Psychiatry, 167,* 783–785.

McGue, M., & Bouchard, T. J., Jr. (1998). Genetic and environmental influences on human behavioral differences. *Annual Review of Neuroscience, 21,* 1–24.

McGue, M., Bouchard, T. J., Jr., Iacono, W. G., & Lykken, D. T. (1993). Behavioral genetics of cognitive ability: A life-span perspective. In R. Plomin & G. E. McClearn (Eds.), *Nature, nurture and psychology.* Washington, DC: American Psychological Association.

McGurk, H., & MacDonald, J. (1976). Hearing lips and seeing voices. *Nature, 264,* 746–748.

McHugh, P. R. (1995b). Witches, multiple personalities, and other psychiatric artifacts. *Nature Medicine, 1,* 110–114.

McIntosh, A. M., & Relton, C. (2018). Do depression and stressful events cause premature aging? *American Journal of Psychiatry, 175,* 714–715.

McKinnon, M. C., Palombo, D. J., Nazarov, A., Kumar, N., Khuu, W., & Levine, B. (2015). Threat of death and autobiographical memory a study of passengers from flight AT236. *Clinical Psychological Science, 3,* 487–502.

McLaughlin, M. (2010, October 2). J. K. Rowling: Depression, the "terrible place that allowed me to come back stronger." *The Scotsman* (scotsman.com).

McLean, C. P., & Anderson, E. R. (2009). Brave men and timid women? A review of the gender differences in fear and anxiety. *Clinical Psychology Review, 29,* 496–505.

McMurray, B. (2007). Defusing the childhood vocabulary explosion. *Science, 317,* 631.

McNally, R. J. (2003). *Remembering trauma.* Cambridge, MA: Harvard University Press.

McNally, R. J. (2007). Betrayal trauma theory: A critical appraisal. *Memory, 15,* 280–294.

McNally, R. J. (2012). Are we winning the war against posttraumatic stress disorder? *Science, 336,* 872–874.

McNally, R. J., & Geraerts, E. (2009). A new solution to the recovered memory debate. *Perspectives on Psychological Science, 4,* 126–134.

McNeil, B. J., Pauker, S. G., & Tversky, A. (1988). On the framing of medical decisions. In D. E. Bell, H. Raiffa, & A. Tversky (Eds.), *Decision making: Descriptive, normative, and prescriptive interactions* (pp. 562–568). New York: Cambridge University Press.

McNeil, J., Ellis, S. J., & Eccles, F. J. R. (2017). Suicide in trans populations: A systematic review of prevalence and correlates. *Psychology of Sexual Orientation and Gender Diversity, 4,* 341–353.

McNulty, J. K., Olson, M. A., Meltzer, A. L., & Shaffer, M. J. (2013). Though they may be unaware, newlyweds implicitly know whether their marriage will be satisfying. *Science, 342,* 1119–1120.

Meador, B. D., & Rogers, C. R. (1984). Person-centered therapy. In R. J. Corsini (Ed.), *Current psychotherapies* (3rd ed.). Itasca, IL: Peacock.

Medda, P., Toni, C., Mariani, M. G., De Simone, L., Mauri, M., & Perugi, G. (2015). Electroconvulsive therapy in 197 patients with a severe, drug-resistant bipolar mixed state: Treatment outcome and predictors of response. *The Journal of Clinical Psychiatry, 76,* 1168–1173.

Mednick, S. A., Huttunen, M. O., & Machon, R. A. (1994). Prenatal influenza infections and adult schizophrenia. *Schizophrenia Bulletin, 20,* 263–267.

Medvec, V. H., Madey, S. F., & Gilovich, T. (1995). When less is more: Counterfactual thinking and satisfaction among Olympic medalists. *Journal of Personality and Social Psychology, 69,* 603–610.

Meerwijk, E. L., & Sevelius, J. M. (2017). Transgender population size in the United States: a meta-regression of population-based probability samples. *American Journal of Public Health, 107,* e1–e8.

Mehlum, L., Ramberg, M., Tørmoen, A. J., Haga, E., Diep, L. M., Stanley, B. H., . . . Grøholt, B. (2016). Dialectical behavior therapy compared with enhanced usual care for adolescents with repeated suicidal and self-harming behavior: Outcomes over a one-year follow-up. *Journal of the American Academy of Child & Adolescent Psychiatry, 55,* 295–300.

Mehta, D., Klengel, T., Conneely, K. N., Smith, A. K., Altmann, A., Pace, T. W., . . . Binder, E. B. (2013). Childhood maltreatment is associated with distinct genomic and epigenetic profiles in posttraumatic stress disorder. *PNAS, 110*, 8302–8307.

Meichenbaum, D. (1977). *Cognitive-behavior modification: An integrative approach*. New York: Plenum Press.

Meichenbaum, D. (1985). *Stress inoculation training*. New York: Pergamon.

Melby-Lervåg, M., Redick, T. S., & Hulme, C. (2016). Working memory training does not improve performance on measures of intelligence or other measures of "far transfer": Evidence from a meta-analytic review. *Perspectives on Psychological Science, 11*, 512–534.

Melioli, T., Bauer, S., Franko, D. L., Moessner, M., Ozer, F., Chabrol, H., & Rodgers, R. F. (2016). Reducing eating disorder symptoms and risk factors using the internet: A meta-analytic review. *International Journal of Eating Disorders, 49*, 19–31.

Meltzer, A. L., Makhanova, A., Hicks, L. L., French, J. E., McNulty, J. K., & Bradbury, T. N. (2017). Quantifying the sexual afterglow: The lingering benefits of sex and their implications for pair-bonded relationships. *Psychological Science, 28*, 587–598.

Meltzoff, A. N., Kuhl, P. K., Movellan, J., & Sejnowski, T. J. (2009). Foundations for a new science of learning. *Science, 325*, 284–288.

Meltzoff, A. N., & Moore, M. K. (1997). Explaining facial imitation: A theoretical model. *Early Development and Parenting, 6*, 179–192.

Melvill, H. (1855). Partaking in other men's sins. Sermon at St. Margaret's Church, Lothbury, England. No. 2,365 in the "Penny Pulpit" series. Reprinted in *The golden lecture: Forty-five sermons delivered at St. Margaret's Church, Lothbury*. London, England: James Paul.

Melzack, R. (1992, April). Phantom limbs. *Scientific American*, pp. 120–126.

Melzack, R. (2005). Evolution of the neuromatrix theory of pain. *Pain Practice, 5*, 85–94.

Melzack, R., & Katz, J. (2013). Pain. *Wiley Interdisciplinary Reviews: Cognitive Science, 4*, 1–15.

Melzack, R., & Wall, P. D. (1965). Pain mechanisms: A new theory. *Science, 150*, 971–979.

Melzack, R., & Wall, P. D. (1983). *The challenge of pain*. New York: Basic Books.

Mendelson, J. L., Gates, J. A., & Lerner, M. D. (2016). Friendship in school-age boys with autism spectrum disorders: A meta-analytic summary and developmental, process-based model. *Psychological Bulletin, 142*, 601–622.

Mendolia, M., & Kleck, R. E. (1993). Effects of talking about a stressful event on arousal: Does what we talk about make a difference? *Journal of Personality and Social Psychology, 64*, 283–292.

Merari, A. (2002). *Explaining suicidal terrorism: Theories versus empirical evidence*. Invited address to the American Psychological Association.

Mercado, M. C., Holland, K., Leemis, R. W., Stone, D. M., & Wang, J. (2017). Trends in emergency department visits for nonfatal self-inflicted injuries among youth aged 10 to 24 years in the United States, 2001–2015. *JAMA, 318*, 1931–1933.

Mercer, T. (2015). Wakeful rest alleviates interference-based forgetting. *Memory, 23*, 127–137.

Merskey, H. (1992). The manufacture of personalities: The production of multiple personality disorder. *British Journal of Psychiatry, 160*, 327–340.

Merzenich, M. (2007). Quoted at Posit Science Brain Fitness Program (positscience.com).

Mesman, J., van Ijzendoorn, M., Behrens, K., Carbonell, O. A., Cárcamo, R., Cohen-Paraira, I., . . . Kondo-Ikemura, K. (2015). Is the ideal mother a sensitive mother? Beliefs about early childhood parenting in mothers across the globe. *International Journal of Behavioral Development, 40*, 385–397.

Messerli, F. H. (2012). Chocolate consumption, cognitive function, and Nobel laureates. *The New England Journal of Medicine, 367*, 1562–1564.

Messias, E., Eaton, W. W., & Grooms, A. N. (2011). Economic grand rounds: Income inequality and depression prevalence across the United States: An ecological study. *Psychiatric Services, 62*, 710–712.

Meston, C. M., & Buss, D. M. (2007). Why humans have sex. *Archives of Sexual Behavior, 36*, 477–507.

Metzler, D. (2011, Spring). Vocabulary growth in adult cross-fostered chimpanzees. *Friends of Washoe, 32*(3), 11–13.

Meyer, A., Proudfit, G. H., Bufferd, S. J., Kujawa, A. J., Laptook, R. S., Torpey, D. C., & Klein, D. N. (2015). Self-reported and observed punitive parenting prospectively predicts increased error-related brain activity in six-year-old children. *Journal of Abnormal Child Psychology, 43*, 821–829.

Meyer-Bahlburg, H. F. L. (1995). Psychoneuroendocrinology and sexual pleasure: The aspect of sexual orientation. In P. R. Abramson & S. D. Pinkerton (Eds.), *Sexual nature/sexual culture* (pp. 135–153). Chicago: University of Chicago Press.

Meyerhoff, J., & Rohan, K. J. (2016). Treatment expectations for cognitive-behavioral therapy and light therapy for seasonal affective disorder: Change across treatment and relation to outcome. *Journal of Consulting and Clinical Psychology, 84*, 898–906.

Mez, J., Daneshvar, D. H., Kiernan, P. T., Abdolmohammadi, B., Alvarez, V. E., Huber, B. R., . . . & Cormier, K. A. (2017). Clinicopathological evaluation of chronic traumatic encephalopathy in players of American football. *Journal of the American Medical Association, 318*, 360–370.

Miao, C., Humphrey, R. H., & Qian, S. (2016). Leader emotional intelligence and subordinate job satisfaction: A meta-analysis of main, mediator, and moderator effects. *Personality and Individual Differences, 102*, 13–24.

Michael, R. B., Garry, M., & Kirsch, I. (2012). Suggestion, cognition, and behavior. *Current Directions in Psychological Science, 21*, 151–156.

Middlebrooks, J. C., & Green, D. M. (1991). Sound localization by human listeners. *Annual Review of Psychology, 42*, 135–159.

Miech, R. A., Johnston, L. D., O'Malley, P. M., Bachman, J. G., & Schulenberg, J. E. (2016). *Monitoring the Future national survey results on drug use, 1975–2015: Volume I, Secondary school students*. Ann Arbor: Institute for Social Research, The University of Michigan.

Miers, R. (2009, Spring). Calum's road. *Scottish Life*, pp. 36–39, 75.

Mikalson, P., Pardo, S., & Green, J. (2012). *First, do no harm: Reducing disparities for lesbian, gay, bisexual, transgender, queer and questioning populations in California*. National Council on Crime & Delinquency. Retrieved from https://www.nccdglobal.org/newsroom/news-of-interest/first-do-no-harm-reducing-disparities-lesbian-gay-bisexual-transgender

Mikulincer, M., & Shaver, P. R. (2001). Attachment theory and intergroup bias: Evidence that priming the secure base schema attenuates negative reactions to out-groups. *Journal of Personality and Social Psychology, 81*, 97–115.

Milan, R. J., Jr., & Kilmann, P. R. (1987). Interpersonal factors in premarital contraception. *Journal of Sex Research, 23*, 289–321.

Milek, A., Butler, E. A., Tackman, A. M., Kaplan, D. M., Raison, C. L., Sbarra, D. A., . . . Mehl, M. R. (2018). "Eavesdropping on happiness" revisited: A pooled, multisample replication of the association between life satisfaction and observed daily conversation quantity and quality. *Psychological Science, 29*, 1451–1462.

Miles, D. R., & Carey, G. (1997). Genetic and environmental architecture of human aggression. *Journal of Personality and Social Psychology, 72*, 207–217.

Miles-Novelo, A., & Anderson, C. A. (2019). Climate change and psychology: Effects of rapid global warming on violence and aggression. *Current Climate Change Reports, 5*, 36–46.

Milgram, S. (1963). Behavioral study of obedience. *Journal of Abnormal & Social Psychology, 67*, 371–378.

Milgram, S. (1974). *Obedience to authority*. New York: Harper & Row.

Miller, B. G., Kors, S., & Macfie, J. (2017). No differences? Meta-analytic comparisons of psychological adjustment in children of gay fathers and heterosexual parents. *Psychology of Sexual Orientation and Gender Diversity, 4*, 14–22.

Miller, C. H., Hamilton, J. P., Sacchet, M. D., & Gotlib, I. H. (2015). Meta-analysis of functional neuroimaging of major depressive disorder in youth. *JAMA Psychiatry, 72*(10), 1045–1053.

Miller, D. I., Nolla, K. M., Eagly, A. H., & Uttal, D. H. (2018). The development of children's gender-science stereotypes: A meta-analysis of 5 decades of U.S. Draw-A-Scientist studies. *Child Development, 89*, 1943–1955.

Miller, G. (2004). Axel, Buck share award for deciphering how the nose knows. *Science, 306*, 207.

Miller, G. (2012). Drone wars: Are remotely piloted aircraft changing the nature of war? *Science, 336*, 842–843.

Miller, G. A. (1956). The magical number seven, plus or minus two: Some limits on our capacity for processing information. *Psychological Review, 63*, 81–97.

Miller, J. G., Goyal, N., & Wice, M. (2017). A cultural psychology of agency: Morality, motivation, and reciprocity. *Perspectives on Psychological Science, 12*, 867–875.

Miller, L. K. (1999). The savant syndrome: Intellectual impairment and exceptional skill. *Psychological Bulletin, 125*, 31–46.

Miller, M., Azrael, D., & Hemenway, D. (2002). Household firearm ownership levels and suicide across U.S. regions and states, 1988–1997. *Epidemiology, 13*, 517–524.

Miller, M., Swanson, S. A., & Azrael, D. (2016). Are we missing something pertinent? A bias analysis of unmeasured confounding in the firearm-suicide literature. *Epidemiologic Reviews, 38*, 62–69.

Miller, P. (2012, January). A thing or two about twins. *National Geographic*, pp. 38–65.

Milojev, P., & Sibley, C. G. (2017). Normative personality trait development in adulthood: A 6-year cohort-sequential growth model. *Journal of Personality and Social Psychology, 112*, 510–526.

Mineka, S. (1985). The frightful complexity of the origins of fears. In F. R. Brush & J. B. Overmier (Eds.), *Affect, conditioning and cognition: Essays on the determinants of behavior*. Hillsdale, NJ: Erlbaum.

Mineka, S. (2002). Animal models of clinical psychology. In N. Smelser & P. Baltes (Eds.), *International encyclopedia of the social and behavioral sciences*. Oxford, England: Elsevier Science.

Mineka, S., & Oehlberg, K. (2008). The relevance of recent developments in classical conditioning to understanding the etiology and maintenance of anxiety disorders. *Acta Psychologica, 127*, 567–580.

Mineka, S., & Zinbarg, R. (1996). Conditioning and ethological models of anxiety disorders: Stress-in-dynamic-context anxiety models. In D. Hope (Ed.), *Perspectives on anxiety, panic, and fear* (Nebraska Symposium on Motivation). Lincoln: University of Nebraska Press.

Minns, S., Levihn-Coon, A., Carl, E., Smits, J. A., Miller, W., Howard, D., . . . & Carlbring, P. (2019). Immersive 3D exposure-based treatment for spider fear: A randomized controlled trial. *Journal of Anxiety Disorders, 61*, 37–44.

Mischel, W. (1968). *Personality and assessment.* New York: Wiley.

Mischel, W. (1981). Current issues and challenges in personality. In L. T. Benjamin, Jr. (Ed.), *The G. Stanley Hall Lecture Series* (Vol. 1). Washington, DC: American Psychological Association.

Mischel, W. (2014). *The marshmallow test: Mastering self-control.* Boston: Little, Brown.

Mishkin, M. (1982). A memory system in the monkey. *Philosophical Transactions of the Royal Society of London: Biological Sciences, 298*, 83–95.

Mishkin, M., Suzuki, W. A., Gadian, D. G., & Vargha-Khadem, F. (1997). Hierarchical organization of cognitive memory. *Philosophical Transactions of the Royal Society of London: Biological Sciences, 352*, 1461–1467.

Mita, T. H., Dermer, M., & Knight, J. (1977). Reversed facial images and the mere-exposure hypothesis. *Journal of Personality and Social Psychology, 35*, 597–601.

Mitani, J. C., Watts, D. P., & Amsler, S. J. (2010). Lethal intergroup aggression leads to territorial expansion in wild chimpanzees. *Current Biology, 20*, R507–R509.

Mitchell, G. (2012). Revisiting truth or triviality: The external validity of research in the psychological laboratory. *Perspectives on Psychological Science, 7*, 109–117.

Mitte, K. (2008). Memory bias for threatening information in anxiety and anxiety disorders: A meta-analytic review. *Psychological Bulletin, 134*, 886–911.

Miu, A. S., & Yeager, D. S. (2015). Preventing symptoms of depression by teaching adolescents that people can change: Effects of a brief incremental theory of personality intervention at 9-month follow-up. *Clinical Psychological Science, 3*, 726–743.

Miyamoto, Y., & Kitayama, S. (2018). Cultural differences in correspondence bias are systematic and multifaceted. *Advances in Methods and Practices in Psychological Science, 1*, 497–498.

Miyatsu, T., Nguyen, K., & McDaniel, M. A. (2018). Five popular study strategies: Their pitfalls and optimal implementations. *Perspectives on Psychological Science, 13*, 390–407.

Mobbs, D., Yu, R., Meyer, M., Passamonti, L., Seymour, B., Calder, A. J., . . . Dalgeish, T. (2009). A key role for similarity in vicarious reward. *Science, 324*, 900.

Moffitt, T. E., Arsenault, L., Belsky, D., Dickson, N., Hancox, R. J., Harrington, H., . . . Caspi, A. (2011). A gradient of childhood self-control predicts health, wealth, and public safety. *PNAS, 108*, 2693–2698.

Moffitt, T. E., Caspi, A., Harrington, H., & Milne, B. J. (2002). Males on the life-course-persistent and adolescence-limited antisocial pathways: Follow-up at age 26 years. *Development and Psychopathology, 14*, 179–207.

Moffitt, T. E., Harrington, H., Caspi, A., Kim-Cohen, J., Goldberg, D., Gregory, A. M., & Poulton, R. (2007). Depression and generalized anxiety disorder: Cumulative and sequential comorbidity in a birth cohort followed prospectively to age 32 years. *Archives of General Psychiatry, 64*, 651–660.

Moghaddam, F. M. (2005). The staircase to terrorism: A psychological exploration. *American Psychologist, 60*, 161–169.

Molenberghs, P., Ogilivie, C., Louis, W. R., Decety, J., Bagnall, J., & Bain, P. G. (2015). The neural correlates of justified and unjustified killing: An fMRI study. *Social Cognitive and Affective Neuroscience, 10*, 1397–1404.

Möller-Levet, C. S., Archer, S. N., Bucca, G., Laing, E. E., Slak, A., Kabijo, R., . . . Dijk, D.-J. (2013). Effects of insufficient sleep on circadian rhythmicity and expression amplitude of the human blood transcriptome. *PNAS, 110*, E1132–E1141.

Mondloch, C. J., Lewis, T. L., Budreau, D. R., Maurer, D., Dannemiller, J. L., Stephens, B. R., & Kleiner-Gathercoal, K. A. (1999). Face perception during early infancy. *Psychological Science, 10*, 419–422.

Money, J. (1987). Sin, sickness, or status? Homosexual gender identity and psychoneuroendocrinology. *American Psychologist, 42*, 384–399.

Money, J., Berlin, F. S., Falck, A., & Stein, M. (1983). *Antiandrogenic and counseling treatment of sex offenders.* Baltimore: Johns Hopkins University School of Medicine, Department of Psychiatry and Behavioral Sciences.

Monroe, S. M., & Reid, M. W. (2009). Life stress and major depression. *Currents Directions in Psychological Science, 18*, 68–72.

Monroe, S. M., & Simons, A. D. (1991). Diathesis-stress theories in the context of life stress research: Implications for the depressive disorders. *Psychological Bulletin, 110*, 406–425.

Montoya, R. M., & Horton, R. S. (2013). A meta-analytic investigation of the processes underlying the similarity-attraction effect. *Journal of Social and Personal Relationships, 30*, 64–94.

Montoya, R. M., & Horton, R. S. (2014). A two-dimensional model for the study of interpersonal attraction. *Personality and Social Psychology Review, 18*, 59–86.

Montoya, R. M., Horton, R. S., Vevea, J. L., Citkowicz, M., & Lauber, E. A. (2017). A re-examination of the mere exposure effect: The influence of repeated exposure on recognition, familiarity, and liking. *Psychological Bulletin, 143*, 459–498.

Mook, D. G. (1983). In defense of external invalidity. *American Psychologist, 38*, 379–387.

Moore, D. M., D'Mello, A. M., McGrath, L. M., & Stoodley, C. J. (2017). The developmental relationship between specific cognitive domains and grey matter in the cerebellum. *Developmental Cognitive Neuroscience, 24*, 1–11.

Moore, D. W. (2004, December 17). *Sweet dreams go with a good night's sleep.* Gallup News Service (gallup.com).

Moore, S. C., Lee, I., Weiderpass, E., Campbell, P. T., Sampson, J. N., Kitahara, C. M., . . . Patel, A. V. (2016). Association of leisure-time physical activity with risk of 26 types of cancer in 1.44 million adults. *JAMA Internal Medicine, 176*, 816–825.

Mor, N., & Winquist, J. (2002). Self-focused attention and negative affect: A meta-analysis. *Psychological Bulletin, 128*, 638–662.

Moreira, M. T., Smith, L. A., & Foxcroft, D. (2009). Social norms interventions to reduce alcohol misuse in university or college students. *Cochrane Database of Systematic Reviews.* 2009, Issue 3., Art. No. CD006748.

Moreland, R. L., & Zajonc, R. B. (1982). Exposure effects in person perception: Familiarity, similarity, and attraction. *Journal of Experimental Social Psychology, 18*, 395–415.

Morelli, G. A., Rogoff, B., Oppenheim, D., & Goldsmith, D. (1992). Cultural variation in infants' sleeping arrangements: Questions of independence. *Developmental Psychology, 26*, 604–613.

Moreno, C., Laje, G., Blanco, C., Jiang, H., Schmidt, A. B., & Olfson, M. (2007). National trends in the outpatient diagnosis and treatment of bipolar disorder in youth. *Archives of General Psychiatry, 64*, 1032–1039.

Morey, R. A., Inan, S., Mitchell, T. V., Perkins, D. O., Lieberman, J. A., & Belger, A. (2005). Imaging frontostriatal function in ultra-high-risk, early, and chronic schizophrenia during executive processing. *Archives of General Psychiatry, 62*, 254–262.

Morgan, A. B., & Lilienfeld, S. O. (2000). A meta-analytic review of the relation between antisocial behavior and neuropsychological measures of executive function. *Clinical Psychology Review, 20*, 113–136.

Morgenthaler, T. I., Hashmi, S., Croft, J. B., Dort, L., Heald, J. L., & Mullington, J. (2016). High school start times and the impact on high school students: What we know and what we hope to learn. *Journal of Clinical Sleep Medicine, 12*, 1681–1689.

Mori, K., & Mori, H. (2009). Another test of the passive facial feedback hypothesis: When you face smiles, you feel happy. *Perceptual and Motor Skills, 109*, 1–3.

Morris, M. (2015, September 18). Damaging labels do transgender people a disservice. Retrieved from https://edmontonjournal.com/news/politics/opinion-damaging-labels-do-transgender-people-a-disservice

Morrison, A. R. (2003). The brain on night shift. *Cerebrum, 5*, 23–36.

Morrison, M., Tay, L., & Diener, E. (2014). *Subjective well-being across the lifespan worldwide.* Paper presented at the Society for Personality and Social Psychology convention, Austin, Texas.

Mortensen, P. B. (1999). Effects of family history and place and season of birth on the risk of schizophrenia. *New England Journal of Medicine, 340*, 603–608.

Moruzzi, G., & Magoun, H. W. (1949). Brain stem reticular formation and activation of the EEG. *Electroencephalography and Clinical Neurophysiology, 1*, 455–473.

Moscovici, S. (1985). Social influence and conformity. In G. Lindzey & E. Aronson (Eds.), *The handbook of social psychology* (3rd ed., pp. 347–412). Hillsdale, NJ: Erlbaum.

Moses, E. B., & Barlow, D. H. (2006). A new unified treatment approach for emotional disorders based on emotion science. *Current Directions in Psychological Science, 15*, 146–150.

Mosher, C. E., & Danoff-Burg, S. (2008). Agentic and communal personality traits: Relations to disordered eating behavior, body shape concern, and depressive symptoms. *Eating Behaviors, 9*, 497–500.

Mosing, M. A., Zietsch, B. P., Shekar, S. N., Wright, M. J., & Martin, N. G. (2009). Genetic and environmental influences on optimism and its relationship to mental and self-rated health: A study of aging twins. *Behavior Genetics, 39*, 597–604.

Moskowitz, T. J., & Wertheim, L. J. (2011). *Scorecasting: The hidden influences behind how sports are played and games are won.* New York: Crown Archetype.

Moss-Racusin, C. A., Pietri, E. S., Hennes, E. P., Dovidio, J. F., Brescoll, V. L., Roussos, G., & Handelsman, J. (2018). Reducing STEM gender bias with VIDS (video interventions for diversity in STEM). *Journal of Experimental Psychology: Applied, 24*, 236–260.

Motivala, S. J., & Irwin, M. R. (2007). Sleep and immunity: Cytokine pathways linking sleep and health outcomes. *Current Directions in Psychological Science, 16*, 21–25.

Moulin, S., Waldfogel, J., & Washbrook, E. (2014). Baby bonds: Parenting, attachment, and a secure base for children. *Sutton Trust*, 1–42.

Moyer, K. E. (1983). The physiology of motivation: Aggression as a model. In C. J. Scheier & A. M. Rogers (Eds.), *The G. Stanley Hall Lecture Series* (Vol. 3, pp. 123–139). Washington, DC: American Psychological Association.

Mroczek, D. K., & Kolarz, D. M. (1998). The effect of age on positive and negative affect: A developmental perspective on happiness. *Journal of Personality and Social Psychology, 75*, 1333–1349.

Mueller, P. A., & Oppenheimer, D. M. (2014). The pen is mightier than the keyboard: Advantages of longhand over laptop note-taking. *Psychological Science, 25*, 1159–1168.

Mueller, S. C., De Cuypere, G., & T'Sjoen, G. (2017). Transgender research in the 21st century: A selective critical review from a neurocognitive perspective. *The American Journal of Psychiatry, 174*, 1155–1162.

Muldoon, S., Taylor, S. C., & Norma, C. (2016). The survivor master narrative in sexual assault. *Violence Against Women, 22*, 565–587.

Mulick, A., Walker, J., Puntis, S., Burke, K., Symeonides, S., Gourley, C., . . . Sharpe, M. (2018). Does depression treatment improve the survival of depressed patients with cancer? A long-term follow-up of participants in the SMaRT oncology-2 and 3 trials. *The Lancet Psychiatry, 5*, 321–326.

Muller, J. E., & Verrier, R. L. (1996). Triggering of sudden death—Lessons from an earthquake. *New England Journal of Medicine, 334*, 461.

Muller, J. E., Mittleman, M. A., Maclure, M., Sherwood, J. B., & Tofler, G. H. (1996). Triggering myocardial infarction by sexual activity. *Journal of the American Medical Association, 275*, 1405–1409.

Müller, M. J., Bosy-Westphal, A., & Heymsfield, S. B. (2010). Is there evidence for a set point that regulates human body weight? *F1000 Medicine Reports, 2*.

Mullin, C. R., & Linz, D. (1995). Desensitization and resensitization to violence against women: Effects of exposure to sexually violent films on judgments of domestic violence victims. *Journal of Personality and Social Psychology, 69*, 449–459.

Murayama, K., Pekrun, R., Lichtenfeld, S., & vom Hofe, R. (2013). Predicting long-term growth in students' mathematics achievement: The unique contributions of motivation and cognitive strategies. *Child Development, 84*, 1475–1490.

Murray, H. (1938). *Explorations in personality*. New York: Oxford University Press.

Murray, H. A., & Wheeler, D. R. (1937). A note on the possible clairvoyance of dreams. *Journal of Psychology, 3*, 309–313.

Murray, R., Jones, P., O'Callaghan, E., Takei, N., & Sham, P. (1992). Genes, viruses, and neurodevelopmental schizophrenia. *Journal of Psychiatric Research, 26*, 225–235.

Musick, M. A., Herzog, A. R., & House, J. S. (1999). Volunteering and mortality among older adults: Findings from a national sample. *Journals of Gerontology, 54B*, 173–180.

Mustanski, B. S., & Bailey, J. M. (2003). A therapist's guide to the genetics of human sexual orientation. *Sexual and Relationship Therapy, 18*, 1468–1479.

Muusses, L. D., Kerkhof, P., & Finkenauer, C. (2015). Internet pornography and relationship quality: A longitudinal study of within and between partner effects of adjustment, sexual satisfaction and sexually explicit internet material among newlyweds. *Computers in Human Behavior, 45*, 77–84.

Myers, D. G. (1993). *The pursuit of happiness*. New York: Harper.

Myers, D. G. (2000). *The American paradox: Spiritual hunger in an age of plenty*. New Haven, CT: Yale University Press.

Myers, D. G. (2010). *Social psychology*, 10th edition. New York: McGraw-Hill.

Myers, D. G. (2018, August 23). Do more immigrants equal greater acceptance or greater fear of immigrants? TalkPsych (TalkPsych.com).

Myers, D. G. (2019, May). The likely aftermath of adversity: harm, resilience, or growth? *APS Observer*, in press.

Myers, D. G., & Bishop, G. D. (1970). Discussion effects on racial attitudes. *Science, 169*, 778–779.

Myers, D. G., & Diener, E. (1995). Who is happy? *Psychological Science, 6*, 10–19.

Myers, D. G., & Diener, E. (1996, May). The pursuit of happiness. *Scientific American* (scientificamerican.com/article/the-pursuit-of-happiness/).

Myers, D. G., & Scanzoni, L. D. (2005). *What God has joined together?* San Francisco: Harper.

Myers, T. A., & Crowther, J. H. (2009). Social comparison as a predictor of body dissatisfaction: A meta-analytic review. *Journal of Abnormal Psychology, 118*, 683–698.

Myre, G. (2000, April 27). McCain still can't forgive guards at "Hanoi Hilton." The *Washington Post*. Retrieved from washingtonpost.com/wp-dyn/content/article/2008/08/13/AR2008081302644.html

Nagourney, A. (2002, September 25). For remarks on Iraq, Gore gets praise and scorn. *The New York Times* (nytimes.com).

Nagourney, A., Sanger, D. E., & Barr, J. (2018, January 13). Hawaii panics after alert about incoming missile is sent in error. *The New York Times* (nytimes.com).

Nam, B., Wilcox, H. C., Hilimire, M., & DeVylder, J. E. (2018). Perceived need for care and mental health service utilization among college students with suicidal ideation. *Journal of American College Health, 66*, 713–719.

Nanni, V., Uher, R., & Danese, A. (2012). Childhood maltreatment predicts unfavorable course of illness and treatment outcome in depression: A meta-analysis. *American Journal of Psychiatry, 169*, 141–151.

Napolitan, D. A., & Goethals, G. R. (1979). The attribution of friendliness. *Journal of Experimental Social Psychology, 15*, 105–113.

Nathan, D. (2011). *Sybil exposed: The extraordinary story behind the famous multiple personality case*. New York: Free Press.

Nathanson, L., Rivers, S. E., Flynn, L. M., & Brackett, M. A. (2016). Creating emotionally intelligent schools with RULER. *Emotion Review, 8*, 1–6.

National Academy of Sciences. (2001). *Exploring the biological contributions to human health: Does sex matter?* Washington, DC: Institute of Medicine, National Academy Press.

National Academies of Sciences, Engineering, and Medicine. (2017). *The health effects of cannabis and cannabinoids: The current state of evidence and recommendations for research*. Washington, DC: National Academies Press.

National Center for Health Statistics. (1990). *Health, United States, 1989*. Washington, DC: U.S. Department of Health and Human Services.

National Safety Council. (2017). *Injury Facts®, 2017 Edition*, pp. 156–157. Itasca, IL: National Safety Council.

Naumann, L. P., Vazire, S., Rentfrow, P. J., & Gosling, S. D. (2009). Personality judgments based on physical appearance. *Personality and Social Psychology Bulletin, 35*, 1661–1671.

Nausheen, B., Carr, N. J., Peveler, R. C., Moss-Morris, R., Verrill, C., Robbins, E., . . . Gidron, Y. (2010). Relationship between loneliness and proangiogenic cytokines in newly diagnosed tumors of colon and rectum. *Psychosomatic Medicine, 72*, 912–916.

Nave, G., Minxha, J., Greenberg, D. M., Kosinski, M., Stillwell, D., & Rentfrow, J. (2018). Musical preferences predict personality: Evidence from active listening and Facebook likes. *Psychological Science, 29*, 1145–1158.

NCD Risk Factor Collaboration. (2016). Trends in adult body-mass index in 200 countries from 1975 to 2014: A pooled analysis of 1698 population-based measurement studies with 19.2 million participants. *The Lancet, 387*, 1377–1396.

Neal, D. T., Wood, W., & Drolet, A. (2013). How do people adhere to goals when willpower is low? The profits (and pitfalls) of strong habits. *Journal of Personality and Social Psychology, 104*, 959–975.

Nedeltcheva, A. V., Kilkus, J. M., Imperial, J., Schoeller, D. A., & Penev, P. D. (2010). Insufficient sleep undermines dietary efforts to reduce adiposity. *Annals of Internal Medicine, 153*, 435–441.

NEEF. (2015). Fact sheet: Children's health and nature. National Environmental Education Foundation. Retrieved from neefusa.org/resource/children%E2%80%99s-health-and-nature-fact-sheet

Neel, R., Kenrick, D. T., White, A. E., & Neuberg, S. L. (2016). Individual differences in fundamental social motives. *Journal of Personality and Social Psychology, 110*, 887–907.

Neese, R. M. (1991, November/December). What good is feeling bad? The evolutionary benefits of psychic pain. *The Sciences*, pp. 30–37.

Neimeyer, R. A., & Currier, J. M. (2009). Grief therapy: Evidence of efficacy and emerging directions. *Current Directions in Psychological Science, 18*, 352–356.

Neisser, U. (1979). The control of information pickup in selective looking. In A. D. Pick (Ed.), *Perception and its development: A tribute to Eleanor J. Gibson* (pp. 209–219). Hillsdale, NJ: Erlbaum.

Neisser, U., Boodoo, G., Bouchard, T. J., Jr., Boykin, A. W., Brody, N., Ceci, S. J., . . . Urbina, S. (1996). Intelligence: Knowns and unknowns. *American Psychologist, 51*, 77–101.

Neitz, J., Carroll, J., & Neitz, M. (2001). Color vision: Almost reason enough for having eyes. *Optics & Photonics News, 12*, 26–33.

Nelson, C. A., III, Fox, N. A., & Zeanah, C. H., Jr. (2013, April). Anguish of the abandoned child. *Scientific American*, pp. 62–67.

Nelson, C. A., III, Fox, N. A., & Zeanah, C. H., Jr. (2014). *Romania's abandoned children*. Cambridge, MA: Harvard University Press.

Nelson, C. A., III, Furtado, E. Z., Fox, N. A., & Zeanah, C. H., Jr. (2009). The deprived human brain. *American Scientist, 97*, 222–229.

Nelson, J., Klumparendt, A., Doebler, P., & Ehring, T. (2017). Childhood maltreatment and characteristics of adult depression: A meta-analysis. *The British Journal of Psychiatry, 210*, 96–104.

Nelson, L. D., Simmons, J., & Simonsohn, U. (2018). Psychology's renaissance. *Annual Review of Psychology, 69*, 511–534.

Nelson, M. D., Saykin, A. J., Flashman, L. A., & Riordan, H. J. (1998). Hippocampal volume reduction in schizophrenia as assessed by magnetic resonance imaging. *Archives of General Psychiatry, 55*, 433–440.

Nelson, S. K., Kushlev, K., English, T., Dunn, E. W., & Lyubomirsky, S. (2013). In defense of parenthood: Children are associated with more joy than misery. *Psychological Science, 24*, 3–10.

Nes, R. B. (2010). Happiness in behaviour genetics: Findings and implications. *Journal of Happiness Studies, 11*, 369–381.

Nes, R. B., Czajkowski, N., & Tambs, K. (2010). Family matters: Happiness in nuclear families and twins. *Behavior Genetics, 40*, 577–590.

Ness, E. (2016, January/February). FDA OKs sex drug for women. *Discover*, p. 45.

Nestler, E. J. (2011). Hidden switches in the mind. *Scientific American, 305*, 76–83.

Nestoriuc, Y., Rief, W., & Martin, A. (2008). Meta-analysis of biofeedback for tension-type headache: Efficacy, specificity, and treatment moderators. *Journal of Consulting and Clinical Psychology, 76*, 379–396.

Nettle, D., Andrews, C., & Bateson, M. (2017). Food insecurity as a driver of obesity in humans: The insurance hypothesis. *Behavioral and Brain Sciences, 40*, e105.

Neubauer, D. N. (1999). Sleep problems in the elderly. *American Family Physician, 59*, 2551–2558.

Neumann, R., & Strack, F. (2000). "Mood contagion": The automatic transfer of mood between persons. *Journal of Personality and Social Psychology, 79*, 211–223.

Newcomb, M. D., & Harlow, L. L. (1986). Life events and substance use among adolescents: Mediating effects of perceived loss of control and meaninglessness in life. *Journal of Personality and Social Psychology, 51*, 564–577.

Newell, B. R. (2015). "Wait! Just let me not think about that for a minute": What role do implicit processes play in higher-level cognition? *Current Directions in Psychological Science, 24*, 65–70.

Newport, C., Wallis, G., Reshitnyk, Y., & Siebeck, U. E. (2016). Discrimination of human faces by archerfish *(Toxotes chatareus)*. *Scientific Reports, 6*, 27523.

Newport, E. L. (1990). Maturational constraints on language learning. *Cognitive Science, 14*, 11–28.

Newport, F. (2001, February). Americans see women as emotional and affectionate, men as more aggressive. *The Gallup Poll Monthly*, pp. 34–38.

Newport, F. (2012, December 19). *To stop shootings, Americans focus on police, mental health.* Gallup Poll (gallup.com).

Newport, F. (2013a, July 25). *In U.S. 87% approve of Black-White marriage, vs. 4% in 1958.* Gallup Poll (gallup .com).

Newport, F. (2013b, July 31). *Former smokers say best way to quit is just to stop "cold turkey."* Gallup Poll (Gallup Poll.com).

Newport, F. (2015, July 9). *Most U.S. smartphone owners check phone at least hourly.* Gallup Poll (gallup.com).

Newport, F. (2018, May 22). *In U.S. estimate of LGBT population rises to 4.5%.* Gallup Poll (gallup.com).

Newport, F., Argrawal, S., & Witters, D. (2010, December 23). *Very religious Americans lead healthier lives.* Gallup Poll (gallup.com).

Newport, F., & Pelham, B. (2009, December 14). *Don't worry, be 80: Worry and stress decline with age.* Gallup Poll (gallup.com).

Newport, F., & Wilke, J. (2013, August 2). *Most in U.S. want marriage, but its importance has dropped.* Gallup Poll (gallup.com).

Newton, I. (1704). *Opticks: Or, a treatise of the reflexions, refractions, inflexions and colours of light.* London, England: Royal Society.

Ng, J. Y. Y., Ntoumanis, N., Thøgersen-Ntoumani, C., Deci, E. L., Ryan, R. M., Duda, J. L., & Williams, G. C. (2012). Self-determination theory applied to health contexts: A meta-analysis. *Perspectives on Psychological Science, 7*, 325–340.

Ng, T. W. H., Sorensen, K. L., & Eby, L. T. (2006). Locus of control at work: A meta-analysis. *Journal of Organizational Behavior, 27*, 1057–1087.

Ng, T. W. H., Sorensen, K. L., & Yim, F. H. K. (2009). Does the job satisfaction—job performance relationship vary across cultures? *Journal of Cross-Cultural Psychology, 40*, 761–796.

Nguyen, H.-H. D., & Ryan, A. M. (2008). Does stereotype threat affect test performance of minorities and women? A meta-analysis of experimental evidence. *Journal of Applied Psychology, 93*, 1314–1334.

Nguyen, T. T., Ryan, R. M., & Deci, E. L. (2018). Solitude as an approach to affective self-regulation. *Personality and Social Psychology Bulletin, 44*, 92–106.

Nickell, J. (2005, July/August). The case of the psychic detectives. *Skeptical Inquirer* (skeptically.org/skepticism /id10.html).

Nickell, J. (Ed.). (1994). *Psychic sleuths: ESP and sensational cases.* Buffalo, NY: Prometheus Books.

Nickerson, R. S. (2002). The production and perception of randomness. *Psychological Review, 109*, 330–357.

Nickerson, R. S. (2005). Bertrand's chord, Buffon's needles, and the concept of randomness. *Thinking & Reasoning, 11*, 67–96.

Nicolas, S., & Levine, Z. (2012). Beyond intelligence testing: Remembering Alfred Binet after a century. *European Psychologist, 17*, 320–325.

NIDA. (2002). Methamphetamine abuse and addiction. *Research Report Series.* National Institute on Drug Abuse, NIH Publication Number 02-4210.

NIDA. (2005, May). Methamphetamine. *NIDA Info Facts.* National Institute on Drug Abuse.

NIDA. (2018). Overdose death rates. National Institute on Drug Abuse. Retrieved from drugabuse.gov /related-topics/trends-statistics/overdose-death-rates

Nietzsche, F. (1889/1990). *Twilight of the idols* and the Anti-Christ: Or how to philosophize with a hammer (R. J. Hollindale, translator). New York: Penguin Classics.

Nieuwenstein, M. R., Wierenga, T., Morey, R. D., Wicherts, J. M., Blom, T. N., Wagenmakers, E., & van Rijn, H. (2015). On making the right choice: A meta-analysis and large-scale replication attempt of the unconscious thought advantage. *Judgment and Decision Making, 10*, 1–17.

NIH. (2001, July 20). *Workshop summary: Scientific evidence on condom effectiveness for sexually transmitted disease (STD) prevention.* Bethesda, MD: National Institute of Allergy and Infectious Diseases, National Institutes of Health.

NIH. (2010). *Teacher's guide: Information about sleep.* National Institutes of Health (nih.gov/).

Nikles, M., Stiefel, F., & Bourquin, C. (2017). What medical students dream of: A standardized and data-driven approach. *Dreaming, 27*, 177–192.

Nikolas, M. A., & Burt, A. (2010). Genetic and environmental influences on ADHD symptom dimensions of inattention and hyperactivity: A meta-analysis. *Journal of Abnormal Psychology, 119*, 1–17.

Nikolova, H., & Lamberton, C. (2016). Men and the middle: Gender differences in dyadic compromise effects. *Journal of Consumer Research, 43*, 355–371.

Niles, A. N., Craske, M. G., Lieberman, M. D., & Hur, C. (2015). Affect labeling enhances exposure effectiveness for public speaking anxiety. *Behavior Research and Therapy, 68*, 27–36.

NIMH. (2015). *Any mental illness (AMI) among U.S. adults.* National Institute of Mental Health (nimh.nih.gov /health/statistics/prevalence/any-mental-illness-ami -among-us-adults.shtml).

NIMH. (2017, accessed February 27). *Research Domain Criteria (RDoC).* National Institute of Mental Health (nimh.nih.gov/research-priorities/rdoc).

NIMH. (2018). *Suicide.* National Institute of Mental Health. Retrieved from nimh.nih.gov/health/statistics /suicide.shtml

Ninio, J., & Stevens, K. A. (2000). Variations on the Hermann grid: an extinction illusion. *Perception, 29*, 1209–1217.

Nisbett, R. E. (2003). *The geography of thought: How Asians and Westerners think differently . . . and why.* New York: Free Press.

Nisbett, R. E., Aronson, J., Blair, C., Dickens, W., Flynn, J., Halpern, D. F., & Turkheimer, E. (2012). Intelligence: New findings and theoretical developments. *American Psychologist, 67*, 130–159.

Nisbett, R. E., & Ross, L. (1980). *Human inference: Strategies and shortcomings of social judgment.* Englewood Cliffs, NJ: Prentice-Hall.

Nizzi, M. C., Demertzi, A., Gosseries, O., Bruno, M. A., Jouen, F., & Laureys, S. (2012). From armchair to wheelchair: How patients with a locked-in syndrome integrate bodily changes in experienced identity. *Consciousness and Cognition, 21*, 431–437.

Noah, T., Schul, Y., & Mayo, R. (2018). When both the original study and its failed replication are correct: Feeling observed eliminates the facial-feedback effect. *Journal of Personality and Social Psychology, 114*, 657–664.

Nock, M. K., & Kessler, R. C. (2006). Prevalence of and risk factors for suicide attempts versus suicide gestures: Analysis of the National Comorbidity Survey. *Journal of Abnormal Psychology, 115*, 616–623.

Nolen-Hoeksema, S. (2001). Gender differences in depression. *Current Directions in Psychological Science, 10*, 173–176.

Nolen-Hoeksema, S. (2003). *Women who think too much: How to break free of overthinking and reclaim your life.* New York: Holt.

Nolen-Hoeksema, S., & Larson, J. (1999). *Coping with loss.* Mahwah, NJ: Erlbaum.

Nook, E. C., Ong, D. C., Morelli, S. A., Mitchell, J. P., & Zaki, J. (2016). Prosocial conformity: Prosocial norms generalize across behavior and empathy. *Personality and Social Psychology Bulletin, 42*, 1045–1062.

Nørby, S. (2015). Why forget? On the adaptive value of memory loss. *Perspectives on Psychological Science, 10*, 551–578.

NORC. (2016a). *General Social Survey data, 1972 through 2014.* Retrieved from sda.berkeley.edu

NORC. (2016b). *New insights into Americans' perceptions and misperceptions of obesity treatments, and the struggles many face.* Chicago: National Opinion Research Center and the American Society for Metabolic and Bariatric Surgery (norc.org).

Nordgren, L. F., van Harreveld, F., & van der Pligt, J. (2009). The restraint bias: How the illusion of self-restraint promoted impulsive behavior. *Psychological Science, 20*, 1523–1528.

Norem, J. K. (2001). *The positive power of negative thinking: Using defensive pessimism to harness anxiety and perform at your peak.* New York: Basic Books.

Norris, A. L., Marcus, D. K., & Green, B. A. (2015). Homosexuality as a discrete class. *Psychological Science, 26*, 1843–1853.

Northey, J. M., Cherbuin, N., Pumpa, K. L., Smee, D. J., & Rattray, B. (2018). Exercise interventions for cognitive function in adults older than 50: A systematic review with meta-analysis. *British Journal of Sports Medicine, 52*, 154.

Nosek, B. A., Alter, G., Banks, G. C., Borsboom, D., Bowman, S. D., Breckler, S. J., . . . Yarkoni, T. (2015). Promoting an open research culture: Author guidelines for journals could help to promote transparency, openness, and reproducibility. *Science, 348,* 1422–1425.

Nosek, B. A., Ebersole, C. R., DeHaven, A. C., & Mellor, D. T. (2018). The preregistration revolution. *PNAS, 115,* 2600–2606.

Nowak, A., Gelfand, M. J., Borkowski, W., Cohen, D., & Hernandez, I. (2016). The evolutionary basis of honor cultures. *Psychological Science, 27,* 12–24.

NPR. (2009, July 11). Afraid to fly? Try living on a plane. National Public Radio (npr.org).

NSC. (2019). Odds of dying. Chicago: National Safety Council (injuryfacts.nsc.org/all-injuries/preventable-death-overview/odds-of-dying/data-details).

NSF. (2013). *2013 International Bedroom Poll: Summary of findings.* National Sleep Foundation (sleepfoundation.org).

NSF. (2016, accessed November 29). *Sleepwalking.* National Sleep Foundation (sleepfoundation.org).

Nurmikko, A. V., Donoghue, J. P., Hochberg, L. R., Patterson, W. R., Song, Y.-K., Bull, C. W., . . . Aceros, J. (2010). Listening to brain microcircuits for interfacing with external world—Progress in wireless implantable microelectronic neuroengineering devices. *Proceedings of the IEEE, 98,* 375–388.

Nussinovitch, U., & Shoenfeld, Y. (2012). The role of gender and organ specific autoimmunity. *Autoimmunity Reviews, 11,* A377–A385.

Nuttin, J. M., Jr. (1987). Affective consequences of mere ownership: The name letter effect in twelve European languages. *European Journal of Social Psychology, 17,* 381–402.

Nye, C. D., Su, R., Rounds, J., & Drasgow, F. (2012). Vocational interests and performance: A quantitative summary of over 60 years of research. *Perspectives on Psychological Science, 7,* 384–403.

O'Brien, F., Bible, J., Liu, D., & Simons-Morton, B. (2017). Do young drivers become safer after being involved in a collision? *Psychological Science, 28,* 407–413.

O'Brien, L., Albert, D., Chein, J., & Steinberg, L. (2011). Adolescents prefer more immediate rewards when in the presence of their peers. *Journal of Research on Adolescence, 21,* 747–753.

O'Connor, P., & Brown, G. W. (1984). Supportive relationships: Fact or fancy? *Journal of Social and Personal Relationships, 1,* 159–175.

O'Donnell, L., Stueve, A., O'Donnell, C., Duran, R., San Doval, A., Wilson, R. F., . . . Pleck, J. H. (2002). Long-term reduction in sexual initiation and sexual activity among urban middle schoolers in the reach for health service learning program. *Journal of Adolescent Health, 31,* 93–100.

O'Donovan, A., Neylan, T. C., Metzler, T., & Cohen, B. E. (2012). Lifetime exposure to traumatic psychological stress is associated with elevated inflammation in the Heart and Soul Study. *Brain, Behavior, and Immunity, 26,* 642–649.

O'Hara, R. E., Gibbons, F. X., Gerrard, M., Li, Z., & Sargent, J. D. (2012). Greater exposure to sexual content in popular movies predicts earlier sexual debut and increased sexual risk taking. *Psychological Science, 23,* 984–993

O'Leary, T., Williams, A. H., Franci, A., & Marder, E. (2014). Cell types, network homeostasis, and pathological compensation from a biologically plausible ion channel expression model. *Neuron, 82,* 809–821.

O'Sullivan, M., Frank, M. G., Hurley, C. M., & Tiwana, J. (2009). Police lie detection accuracy: The effect of lie scenario. *Law and Human Behavior, 33,* 530–538.

Oakley, D. A., & Halligan, P. W. (2013). Hypnotic suggestion: Opportunities for cognitive neuroscience. *Nature Reviews Neuroscience, 14,* 565–576.

Obama, B. (2017, January 10). President Obama's farewell address. *The New York Times* (nytimes.com).

Obschonka, M., Zhou, M., Zhou, Y., Zhang, J., & Silbereisen, R. K. (2018). "Confucian" traits, entrepreneurial personality, and entrepreneurship in China: a regional analysis. *Small Business Economics.* doi: 10.1007/s11187-018-0103-8

Oelschläger, M., Pfannmöller, J., Langer, I., & Lotze, M. (2014). Usage of the middle finger shapes reorganization of the primary somatosensory cortex in patients with index finger amputation. *Restorative Neurology and Neuroscience, 32,* 507–515.

Offer, D., Ostrov, E., Howard, K. I., & Atkinson, R. (1988). *The teenage world: Adolescents' self-image in ten countries.* New York: Plenum.

Offner, M., Coles, A., Decou, M. L., Minh, T. D. Bienek, A., Snider, J., & Ugnat, A-M. (2018). *Autism Spectrum Disorder among children and youth in Canada 2018:* A report of the National Autism Spectrum Disorder Surveillance System. Public Health Agency of Canada (www.canada.ca).

Ogden, J. (2012, January 16). HM, the man with no memory. *Psychology Today* (psychologytoday.com).

Ohi, K., Shimada, T., Nitta, Y., Kihara, H., Okubo, H., Uehara, T., & Kawasaki, Y. (2016). The five-factor model personality traits in schizophrenia: A meta-analysis. *Psychiatry Research, 240,* 34–41.

Öhman, A. (1986). Face the beast and fear the face: Animal and social fears as prototypes for evolutionary analyses of emotion. *Psychophysiology, 23,* 123–145.

Öhman, A., Lundqvist, D., & Esteves, F. (2001). The face in the crowd revisited: A threat advantage with schematic stimuli. *Journal of Personality and Social Psychology, 80,* 381–396.

Oishi, S., & Diener, E. (2014). Can and should happiness be a policy goal? *Policy Insights from Behavioral and Brain Sciences, 1,* 195–203.

Oishi, S., Diener, E. F., Lucas, R. E., & Suh, E. M. (1999). Cross-cultural variations in predictors of life satisfaction: Perspectives from needs and values. *Personality and Social Psychology Bulletin, 25,* 980–990.

Oishi, S., Kesebir, S., & Diener, E. (2011). Income inequality and happiness. *Psychological Science, 22,* 1095–1100.

Oishi, S., Schiller, J., & Blair, E. G. (2013). Felt understanding and misunderstanding affect the perception of pain, slant, and distance. *Social Psychological and Personality Science, 4,* 259–266.

Oishi, S., & Schimmack, U. (2010). Culture and well-being: A new inquiry into the psychological wealth of nations. *Perspectives in Psychological Science, 5,* 463–471.

Okbay, A., Beauchamp, J. P., Fontana, M. A., Lee, J. J., Pers, T. H., Rietveld, C. A., . . . Oskarsson, S. (2016). Genome-wide association study identifies 74 loci associated with educational attainment. *Nature, 533,* 539–542.

Okimoto, T. G., & Brescoll, V. L. (2010). The price of power: Power seeking and backlash against female politicians. *Personality and Social Psychology Bulletin, 36,* 923–936.

Olds, J. (1975). Mapping the mind onto the brain. In F. G. Worden, J. P. Swazey, & G. Adelman (Eds.), *The neurosciences: Paths of discovery* (pp. 375–400). Cambridge, MA: MIT Press.

Olds, J., & Milner, P. (1954). Positive reinforcement produced by electrical stimulation of the septal area and other regions of rat brain. *Journal of Comparative and Physiological Psychology, 47,* 419–427.

Olff, M., Langeland, W., Draijer, N., & Gersons, B. P. R. (2007). Gender differences in posttraumatic stress disorder. *Psychological Bulletin, 135,* 183–204.

Olfson, M., Gerhard, T., Huang, C., Crystal, S., & Stroup, T. S. (2015). Premature mortality among adults with schizophrenia in the United States. *JAMA Psychiatry, 72,* 1172–1181.

Olfson, M., & Marcus, S. C. (2009). National patterns in antidepressant medication treatment. *Archives of General Psychiatry, 66,* 848–856.

Olfson, M., Wall, M. M., Liu, S-M., & Blanco, C. (2017). Cannabis use and risk of prescription opioid use disorder in the United States. *American Journal of Psychiatry, 175,* 47–53.

Olfson, M., Wang, S., Wall, M., Marcus, S. C., & Blanco, C. (2019). Trends in serious psychological distress and outpatient mental health care of U.S. adults. *JAMA Psychiatry, 76,* 152–161.

Oliner, S. P., & Oliner, P. M. (1988). *The altruistic personality: Rescuers of Jews in Nazi Europe.* New York: Free Press.

Olivé, I., Templemann, C., Berthoz, A., & Heinze, H.-J. (2015). Increased functional connectivity between superior colliculus and brain regions implicated in bodily self-consciousness during the rubber band illusion. *Human Brain Mapping, 36,* 717–730.

Olson, K. R., Key, A. C., & Eaton, N. R. (2015). Gender cognition in transgender children. *Psychological Science, 26,* 467–474.

Olson, R. L., Hanowski, R. J., Hickman, J. S., & Bocanegra, J. (2009, September). *Driver distraction in commercial vehicle operations.* Washington, DC: U.S. Department of Transportation, Federal Motor Carrier Safety Administration.

Olsson, A., Nearing, K. I., & Phelps, E. A. (2007). Learning fears by observing others: The neural systems of social fear transmission. *Social Cognitive and Affective Neuroscience, 2,* 3–11.

Oman, D., Kurata, J. H., Strawbridge, W. J., & Cohen, R. D. (2002). Religious attendance and cause of death over 31 years. *International Journal of Psychiatry in Medicine, 32,* 69–89.

Ooi, J., Dodd, H. F., Stuijfzand, B. G., Walsh, J., & Broeren, S. (2016). Do you think I should be scared? The effect of peer discussion on children's fears. *Behaviour Research and Therapy, 87,* 23–33.

Open Science Collaboration. (2015). Estimating the reproducibility of psychological science. *Science, 349,* 943.

Open Science Collaboration. (2017). Maximizing the reproducibility of your research. In S. O. Lilienfeld & I. D. Waldman (Eds.), *Psychological science under scrutiny: Recent challenges and proposed solutions* (pp. 1–21). New York: Wiley.

Opp, M. R., & Krueger, J. M. (2015). Sleep and immunity: A growing field with clinical impact. *Brain, Behavior, and Immunity, 47,* 1–3.

Oquendo, M. A., Galfalvy, H. C., Currier, D., Grunebaum, M. F., Sher, L., Sullivan, G. M., . . . Mann, J. J. (2011). Treatment of suicide attempters with bipolar disorder: A randomized clinical trial comparing lithium and valproate in the prevention of suicidal behavior. *The American Journal of Psychiatry, 168,* 1050–1056.

Orben, A., & Baukney-Przybylski, A. K. (2019). The association between adolescent well-being and digital technology use. *Nature Human Behaviour.* Retrieved from nature.com/articles/s41562-018-0506-1

Orehek, E., & Human, L. J. (2017). Self-expression on social media: Do tweets present accurate and positive portraits of impulsivity, self-esteem, and attachment style? *Personality and Social Psychology Bulletin, 43*, 60–70.

Orth, U., Erol, R. Y., & Luciano, E. C. (2018). Development of self-esteem from age 4 to 94 years: A meta-analysis of longitudinal studies. *Psychological Bulletin, 144*, 1045–1080.

Orth, U., & Robins, R. W. (2014). The development of self-esteem. *Current Directions in Psychological Science, 23*, 381–387.

Orth, U., Robins, R. W., Meier, L. L., & Conger, R. D. (2016). Refining the vulnerability model of low self-esteem and depression: Disentangling the effects of genuine self-esteem and narcissism. *Journal of Personality and Social Psychology, 110*, 133–149.

Orth, U., Robins, R. W., Trzesniewski, K. H., Maes, J., & Schmitt, M. (2009). Low self-esteem is a risk factor for depressive symptoms from young adulthood to old age. *Journal of Abnormal Psychology, 118*, 472–478.

Osborne, L. (1999, October 27). A linguistic big bang. *The New York Times Magazine* (nytimes.com).

Oskarsson, A. T., Van Voven, L., McClelland, G. H., & Hastie, R. (2009). What's next? Judging sequences of binary events. *Psychological Bulletin, 135*, 262–285.

Osoegawa, C., Gomes, J. S., Grigolon, R. B., Brietzke, E., Gadelha, A., Lacerda, A. L., . . . & Daskalakis, Z. J. (2018). Non-invasive brain stimulation for negative symptoms in schizophrenia: An updated systematic review and meta-analysis. *Schizophrenia Research, 197*, 34–44.

Ossher, L., Flegal, K. E., & Lustig, C. (2012). Everyday memory errors in older adults. *Aging, Neuropsychology, and Cognition, 20*, 220–242.

Öst, L. G., Havnen, A., Hansen, B., & Kvale, G. (2015). Cognitive behavioral treatments of obsessive–compulsive disorder. A systematic review and meta-analysis of studies published 1993–2014. *Clinical Psychology Review, 40*, 156–169.

Öst, L. G., & Hugdahl, K. (1981). Acquisition of phobias and anxiety response patterns in clinical patients. *Behaviour Research and Therapy, 16*, 439–447.

Österman, K., Björkqvist, K., & Wahlbeck, K. (2014). Twenty-eight years after the complete ban on the physical punishment of children in Finland: Trends and psychosocial concomitants. *Aggressive Behavior, 40*, 568–581.

Ostfeld, A. M., Kasl, S. V., D'Atri, D. A., & Fitzgerald, E. F. (1987). *Stress, crowding, and blood pressure in prison*. Hillsdale, NJ: Erlbaum.

Osvath, M., & Karvonen, E. (2012). Spontaneous innovation for future deception in a male chimpanzee. *PLOS ONE, 7*, e36782.

Oswald, F. L., Mitchell, G., Blanton, H., Jaccard, J., & Tetlock, P. E. (2013). Predicting ethnic and racial discrimination: A meta-analysis of IAT criterion studies. *Journal of Personality and Social Psychology, 105*, 171–192.

Oswald, F. L., Mitchell, G., Blanton, H., Jaccard, J., & Tetlock, P. E. (2015). Using the IAT to predict ethnic and racial discrimination: Small effect sizes of unknown societal significance. *Journal of Personality and Social Psychology, 108*, 562–571.

Otgaar, H., & Baker, A. (2018). When lying changes memory for the truth. *Memory, 1*, 2–14.

Ott, B. (2007, June 14). Investors, take note: Engagement boosts earnings. *Gallup Management Journal* (gallup.com).

Overall, N. C., Fletcher, G. J. O., Simpson, J. A., & Fillo, J. (2015). Attachment insecurity, biased perceptions of romantic partners' negative emotions, and hostile relationship behavior. *Journal of Personality and Social Psychology, 108*, 730–749.

Owen, A. (2017). *Into the gray zone: A neuroscientist explores the border between life and death*. New York: Scribner.

Owen, A. M., Coleman, M. R., Boly, M., Davis, M. H., Laureys, S., & Pickard, J. D. (2006). Detecting awareness in the vegetative state. *Science, 313*, 1402.

Owen, R. (1814). First essay in *New view of society or the formation of character*. Quoted in *The story of New Lamark*. New Lamark Mills, Lamark, Scotland: New Lamark Conservation Trust, 1993.

OWN. (2018, April 20). *Oprah and Amy Schumer on being secret introverts* [Video file]. Retrieved from http://www.oprah.com/own-supersoulsessions/oprah-and-amy-schumer-on-being-secret-introverts-video_2

Oxfam. (2005, March 26). *Three months on: New figures show tsunami may have killed up to four times as many women as men*. Oxfam Press Release (oxfam.org.uk).

Ozer, E. J., Best, S. R., Lipsey, T. L., & Weiss, D. S. (2003). Predictors of posttraumatic stress disorder and symptoms in adults: A meta-analysis. *Psychological Bulletin, 1*, 52–73.

Ozer, E. J., & Weiss, D. S. (2004). Who develops posttraumatic stress disorder? *Current Directions in Psychological Science, 13*, 169–172.

Pace-Schott, E. F., Germain, A., & Milad, M. R. (2015). Effects of sleep on memory for conditioned fear and fear extinction. *Psychological Bulletin, 141*, 835–857.

Pachankis, J. E., & Bränström, R. (2018). Hidden from happiness: Structural stigma, sexual orientation concealment, and life satisfaction across 28 countries. *Journal of Consulting and Clinical Psychology, 86*, 403–415.

Pachankis, J. E., Hatzenbuehler, M. L., Wang, K., Burton, C. L., Crawford, F. W., Phelan, J. C., & Link, B. G. (2018). The burden of stigma on health and well-being: A taxonomy of concealment, course, disruptiveness, aesthetics, origin, and peril across 93 stigmas. *Personality and Social Psychology Bulletin, 44*, 451–474.

Pacifici, R., Zuccaro, P., Farre, M., Pichini, S., Di Carlo, S., Roset, P. N., . . . de la Torre, R. (2001). Effects of repeated doses of MDMA ("Ecstasy") on cell-mediated immune response in humans. *Life Sciences, 69*, 2931–2941.

Palejwala, M. H., & Fine, J. G. (2015). Gender differences in latent cognitive abilities in children aged 2 to 7. *Intelligence, 48*, 96–108.

Pallier, C., Colomé, A., & Sebastián-Gallés, N. (2001). The influence of native-language phonology on lexical access: Exemplar-based versus abstract lexical entries. *Psychological Science, 12*, 445–448.

Palmer, D. C. (1989). A behavioral interpretation of memory. In L. J. Hayes (Ed.), *Dialogues on verbal behavior: The first international institute on verbal relations* (pp. 261–279). Reno, NV: Context Press.

Palombo, D. J., McKinnon, M. C., McIntosh, A. R., Anderson, A. K., Todd, R. M., & Levine, B. (2015). The neural correlates of memory for a life-threatening event: An fMRI study of passengers from Flight AT236. *Clinical Psychological Science, 4*, 312–319.

Paluck, E. L., Green, S. A., & Green, D. P. (2018). The contact hypothesis re-evaluated. *Behavioural Public Policy*, 1–30.

Pan, S. C., & Rickard, T. C. (2018). Transfer of test-enhanced learning: Meta-analytic review and synthesis. *Psychological Bulletin, 144*, 710–756.

Pandey, J., Sinha, Y., Prakash, A., & Tripathi, R. C. (1982). Right-left political ideologies and attribution of the causes of poverty. *European Journal of Social Psychology, 12*, 327–331.

Pänkäläinen, M., Kerola, T., Kampman, O., Kauppi, M., & Hintikka, J. (2016). Pessimism and risk of death from coronary heart disease among middle-aged and older Finns: An eleven-year follow-up study. *BMC Public Health, 16*, 1124.

Panksepp, J. (2007). Neurologizing the psychology of affects: How appraisal-based constructivism and basic emotion theory can coexist. *Perspectives on Psychological Science, 2*, 281–295.

Pantev, C., Oostenveld, R., Engelien, A., Ross, B., Roberts, L. R., & Hoke, M. (1998). Increased auditory cortical representation in musicians. *Nature, 392*, 811–814.

Paolini, S., Harwood, J., Rubin, M., Husnu, S., Joyce, N., & Hewstone, M. (2014). Positive and extensive intergroup contact in the past buffers against the disproportionate impact of negative contact in the present. *European Journal of Social Psychology, 44*, 548–562.

Pardiñas, A. F., Holmans, P., Pocklington, A. J., Escott-Price, V., Ripke, S., Carrera, N., . . . & Han, J. (2018). Common schizophrenia alleles are enriched in mutation-intolerant genes and in regions under strong background selection. *Nature Genetics, 50*, 381–389.

Pardini, D. A., Raine, A., Erickson, K., & Loeber, R. (2014). Lower amygdala volume in men is associated with childhood aggression, early psychopathic traits, and future violence. *Biological Psychiatry, 75*, 73–80.

Park, C. L. (2007). Religiousness/spirituality and health: A meaning systems perspective. *Journal of Behavioral Medicine, 30*, 319–328.

Park, D. C., & McDonough, I. M. (2013). The dynamic aging mind: Revelations from functional neuroimaging research. *Perspectives on Psychological Science, 8*, 62–67.

Park, G., Schwartz, H. A., Eichstaedt, J. C., Kern, M. L., Kosinski, M., Stillwell, D. J., . . . Seligman, M. E. P. (2015). Automatic personality assessment through social media language. *Journal of Personality and Social Psychology, 108*, 934–952.

Park, G., Yaden, D. R., Schwartz, H. A., Kern, M. L., Eichstaedt, J. C., Kosinski, M., . . . Seligman, M. E. P. (2016). Women are warmer but no less assertive than men: Gender and language on Facebook. *PLOS ONE, 11*, e0155885.

Parker, C. P., Baltes, B. B., Young, S. A., Huff, J. W., Altmann, R. A., LaCost, H. A., & Roberts, J. E. (2003). Relationships between psychological climate perceptions and work outcomes: A meta-analytic review. *Journal of Organizational Behavior, 24*, 389–416.

Parker, E. S., Cahill, L., & McGaugh, J. L. (2006). A case of unusual autobiographical remembering. *Neurocase, 12*, 35–49.

Parker, K., & Wang, W. (2013, March 14). Modern parenthood: Roles of moms and dads converge as they balance work and family. *Pew Research Center's Social & Demographic Trends Project, 14*.

Parkes, A., Wight, D., Hunt, K., Henderson, M., & Sargent, J. (2013). Are sexual media exposure, parental restrictions on media use and co-viewing TV and DVDs with parents and friends associated with teenagers' early sexual behavior? *Journal of Adolescence, 36*, 1121–1133.

Parnia, S., Spearpoint, K., de Vos, G., Fenwick, P., Goldberg, D., Yang, J., . . . Wood, M. (2014). AWARE—AWAreness during REsuscitation—A prospective study. *Resuscitation, 85*, 1799–1805.

Parsaik, A. K., Mascarenhas, S. S., Hashmi, A., Prokop, L. J., John, V., Okusaga, O., & Singh, B. (2016). Role of botulinum toxin in depression. *Journal of Psychiatric Practice, 22*, 99–110.

Parthasarathy, S., Vasquez, M. M., Halonen, M., Bootzin, R., Quan, S. F., Martinez, F. D., & Guerra, S. (2015). Persistent insomnia is associated with mortality risk. *American Journal of Medicine, 128,* 268–275.

Pascoe, E. A., & Richman, L. S. (2009). Perceived discrimination and health: A meta-analytic review. *Psychological Bulletin, 135,* 531–554.

Patihis, L. (2016). Individual differences and correlates of highly superior autobiographical memory. *Memory, 24,* 961–978.

Patihis, L. (2018). Why there is no false memory trait and why everyone is susceptible to memory distortions: The dual encoding interference hypothesis (Commentary on Bernstein, Scoboria, Desjarlais, & Soucie, 2018). *Psychology of Consciousness: Theory, Research, and Practice, 5,* 180–184.

Patihis, L., Ho, L. Y., Tingen, I. W., Lilienfeld, S. O., & Loftus, E. F. (2014a). Are the "memory wars" over? A scientist-practitioner gap in beliefs about repressed memory. *Psychological Science, 25,* 519–530.

Patihis, L., Lilienfeld, S. O., Ho, L. Y., & Loftus, E. F. (2014b). Unconscious repressed memory is scientifically questionable. *Psychological Science, 25,* 1967–1968.

Patterson, F. (1978, October). Conversations with a gorilla. *National Geographic,* pp. 438–465.

Patterson, G. R., Chamberlain, P., & Reid, J. B. (1982). A comparative evaluation of parent training procedures. *Behavior Therapy, 13,* 638–650.

Patterson, M., Warr, P., & West, M. (2004). Organizational climate and company productivity: The role of employee affect and employee level. *Journal of Occupational and Organizational Psychology, 77,* 193–216.

Pauker, K., Weisbuch, M., Ambady, N., Sommers, S. R., Adams, R. B., Jr., & Ivcevic, Z. (2009). Not so Black and White: Memory for ambiguous group members. *Journal of Personality and Social Psychology, 96,* 795–810.

Pauletti, R. E., Menon, M., Cooper, P. J., Aults, C. D., & Perry, D. G. (2017). Psychological androgyny and children's mental health: A new look with new measures. *Sex Roles, 76,* 705–718.

Paunesku, D., Walton, G. M., Romero, C., Smith, E. N., Yeager, D. S., & Dweck, C. S. (2015). Mindset interventions are a scalable treatment for academic underachievement. *Psychological Science, 26,* 784–793.

Paus, T., Zijdenbos, A., Worsley, K., Collins, D. L., Blumenthal, J., Giedd, J. N., Rapaport, J. L., & Evans, A. C. (1999). Structural maturation of neural pathways in children and adolescents: In vivo study. *Science, 283,* 1908–1911.

Pavlov, I. (1927). *Conditioned reflexes: An investigation of the physiological activity of the cerebral cortex.* Oxford, England: Oxford University Press.

Payne, B. K. (2006). Weapon bias: Split-second decisions and unintended stereotyping. *Current Directions in Psychological Science, 15,* 287–291.

Payne, K. (2017). *The broken ladder: How inequality affects the way we think, live, and die.* New York: Viking.

Pearce, M. J., Koenig, H. G., Robins, C. J., Nelson, B., Shaw, S. F., Cohen, H. J., & King, M. B. (2015). Religiously integrated cognitive behavioral therapy: A new method of treatment for major depression in patients with chronic medical illness. *Psychotherapy, 52,* 56–66.

Peck, E. (2015, April 29). Harvard Business School launches new effort to attract women. *Huffington Post* (huffingtonpost.com).

Pelham, B., & Crabtree, S. (2008, October 8). *Worldwide, highly religious more likely to help others.* Gallup Poll (gallup.com).

Pelham, B. W. (1993). On the highly positive thoughts of the highly depressed. In R. F. Baumeister (Ed.), *Self-esteem: The puzzle of low self-regard.* New York: Plenum.

Pelham, W. E., Jr., Fabiano, G. A., Waxmonsky, J. G., Greiner, A. R., Gnagy, E. M., Pelham, W. E., . . . Murphy, S. A. (2016). Treatment sequencing for childhood ADHD: A multiple-randomization study of adaptive medication and behavioral interventions. *Journal of Clinical Child and Adolescent Psychology, 45,* 396–415.

Pennebaker, J. (1990). *Opening up: The healing power of confiding in others.* New York: William Morrow.

Pennebaker, J. W. (2011). *The secret life of pronouns: What our words say about us.* New York: Bloomsbury Press.

Pennebaker, J. W., Barger, S. D., & Tiebout, J. (1989). Disclosure of traumas and health among Holocaust survivors. *Psychosomatic Medicine, 51,* 577–589.

Pennebaker, J. W., Gosling, S. D., & Ferrell, J. D. (2013). Daily online testing in large classes: Boosting college performance while reducing achievement gaps. *PLOS ONE, 8,* e79774.

Pennebaker, J. W., & O'Heeron, R. C. (1984). Confiding in others and illness rate among spouses of suicide and accidental death victims. *Journal of Abnormal Psychology, 93,* 473–476.

Pennisi, E. (2016). The power of personality. *Science, 352,* 644–647.

Peplau, L. A., & Fingerhut, A. W. (2007). The close relationships of lesbians and gay men. *Annual Review of Psychology, 58,* 405–424.

Pepperberg, I. M. (2009). *Alex & me: How a scientist and a parrot discovered a hidden world of animal intelligence—and formed a deep bond in the process.* New York: Harper.

Pepperberg, I. M. (2012). Further evidence for addition and numerical competence by a grey parrot *(Psittacus erithacus). Animal Cognition, 15,* 711–717.

Pepperberg, I. M. (2013). Abstract concepts: Data from a grey parrot. *Behavioural Processes, 93,* 82–90.

Pereg, D., Gow, R., Mosseri, M., Lishner, M., Rieder, M., Van Uum, S., & Koren, G. (2011). Hair cortisol and the risk for acute myocardial infarction in adult men. *Stress, 14,* 73–81.

Pereira, A. C., Huddleston, D. E., Brickman, A. M., Sosunov, A. A., Hen, R., McKhann, G. M., . . . Small, S. A. (2007). An *in vivo* correlate of exercise-induced neurogenesis in the adult dentate gyrus. *PNAS, 104,* 5638–5643.

Pereira, G. M., & Osburn, H. G. (2007). Effects of participation in decision making on performance and employee attitudes: A quality circles meta-analysis. *Journal of Business Psychology, 22,* 145–153.

Pergamin-Hight, L., Naim, R., Bakermans-Kranenburg, M. J., van IJzendoorn, M. H., & Bar-Haim, Y. (2015). Content specificity of attention bias to threat in anxiety disorders: A meta-analysis. *Clinical Psychology Review, 35,* 10–18.

Perilloux, H. K., Webster, G. D., & Gaulin, S. J. (2010). Signals of genetic quality and maternal investment capacity: The dynamic effects of fluctuating asymmetry and waist-to-hip ratio on men's ratings of women's attractiveness. *Social Psychological and Personality Science, 1,* 34–42.

Perkins, A., & Fitzgerald, J. A. (1997). Sexual orientation in domestic rams: Some biological and social correlates. In L. Ellis & L. Ebertz (Eds.), *Sexual orientation: Toward biological understanding* (pp. 107–128). Westport, CT: Praeger.

Perkins, A. M., Inchley-Mort, S. L., Pickering, A. D., Corr, P. J., & Burgess, A. P. (2012). A facial expression for anxiety. *Journal of Personality and Social Psychology, 102,* 910–924.

Perrachione, T. K., Del Tufo, S. N., & Gabrieli, J. D. E. (2011). Human voice recognition depends on language ability. *Science, 333,* 595.

Perry, G. (2018). *The lost boys: Inside Muzafer Sherif's Robbers Cave experiment.* Melbourne/London: Scribe.

Person, C., Tracy, M., & Galea, S. (2006). Risk factors for depression after a disaster. *Journal of Nervous and Mental Disease, 194,* 659–666.

Pert, C. B., & Snyder, S. H. (1973). Opiate receptor: Demonstration in nervous tissue. *Science, 179,* 1011–1014.

Perugini, E. M., Kirsch, I., Allen, S. T., Coldwell, E., Meredith, J., Montgomery, G. H., & Sheehan, J. (1998). Surreptitious observation of responses to hypnotically suggested hallucinations: A test of the compliance hypothesis. *International Journal of Clinical and Experimental Hypnosis, 46,* 191–203.

Peschel, E. R., & Peschel, R. E. (1987). Medical insights into the castrati in opera. *American Scientist, 75,* 578–583.

Pesko, M. F. (2014). Stress and smoking: Associations with terrorism and causal impact. *Contemporary Economic Policy, 32,* 351–371.

Peter, J., & Valkenburg, P. M. (2016). Adolescents and pornography: A review of 20 years of research. *Journal of Sex Research, 53,* 509–531.

Peters, K., & Kashima, Y. (2015). A multimodal theory of affect diffusion. *Psychological Bulletin, 141,* 966–992.

Peters, M., Rhodes, G., & Simmons, L. W. (2007). Contributions of the face and body to overall attractiveness. *Animal Behaviour, 73,* 937–942.

Petersen, J. L., & Hyde, J. S. (2010). A meta-analytic review of research on gender differences in sexuality, 1993–2007. *Psychological Bulletin, 136,* 21–38.

Petersen, J. L., & Hyde, J. S. (2011). Gender differences in sexual attitudes and behaviors: A review of meta-analytic results and large datasets. *Journal of Sex Research, 48,* 149–165.

Peterson, C., Peterson, J., & Skevington, S. (1986). Heated argument and adolescent development. *Journal of Social and Personal Relationships, 3,* 229–240.

Peterson, L. R., & Peterson, M. J. (1959). Short-term retention of individual verbal items. *Journal of Experimental Psychology, 58,* 193–198.

Petitto, L. A., & Marentette, P. F. (1991). Babbling in the manual mode: Evidence for the ontogeny of language. *Science, 251,* 1493–1496.

Pettegrew, J. W., Keshavan, M. S., & Minshew, N. J. (1993). 31P nuclear magnetic resonance spectroscopy: Neurodevelopment and schizophrenia. *Schizophrenia Bulletin, 19,* 35–53.

Petticrew, C., Bell, R., & Hunter, D. (2002). Influence of psychological coping on survival and recurrence in people with cancer: Systematic review. *British Medical Journal, 325,* 1066.

Petticrew, M., Fraser, J. M., & Regan, M. F. (1999). Adverse life events and risk of breast cancer: A meta-analysis. *British Journal of Health Psychology, 4,* 1–17.

Pettigrew, T. F., & Tropp, L. R. (2011). *When groups meet: The dynamics of intergroup contact.* New York: Psychology Press.

Pew. (2007, July 18). *Modern marriage: "I like hugs. I like kisses. But what I really love is help with the dishes."* Pew Research Center (pewresearch.org).

Pew. (2009, November 4). *Social isolation and new technology: How the internet and mobile phones impact Americans' social networks.* Pew Research Center (pewresearch.org).

Pew. (2010, July 1). *Gender equality universally embraced, but inequalities acknowledged.* Pew Research Center Publications (pewresearch.org).

Pew. (2013, June 4). *The global divide on homosexuality.* Pew Research Center, Global Attitudes Project (pewglobal.org).

Pew. (2013a, June 4). *The global divide on homosexuality.* Pew Research Center, Global Attitudes Project (pewglobal.org).

Pew. (2013b, June 13). *A survey of LGBT Americans.* Pew Research Center. Retrieved from https://www.pewsocialtrends.org/2013/06/13/a-survey-of-lgbt-americans/

Pew. (2014). *Global views of morality.* Pew Research Center, Global Attitudes Project (pewglobal.org).

Pew. (2015, November 4). *Raising kids and running a household: How working parents share the load.* Pew Research Center (pewsocialtrends.org).

Pew. (2016, September 28). *Where the public stands on religious liberty vs. nondiscrimination.* Pew Forum (pewforum.org).

Pew. (2017). Internet/broadband technology fact sheet. Pew Research Center. Retrieved from pewinternet.org /fact-sheet/internet-broadband/

Pfaff, L. A., Boatwright, K. J., Potthoff, A. L., Finan, C., Ulrey, L. A., & Huber, D. M. (2013). Perceptions of women and men leaders following 360-degree feedback evaluations. *Performance Improvement Quarterly, 26,* 35–56.

Pfundmair, M., Zwarg, C., Paulus, M., & Rimpel, A. (2017). Oxytocin promotes attention to social cues regardless of group membership. *Hormones and Behavior, 90,* 136–140.

Phelps, J. A., Davis J. O., & Schartz, K. M. (1997). Nature, nurture, and twin research strategies. *Current Directions in Psychological Science, 6,* 117–120.

Phillips, A. C., Batty, G. D., Gale, C. R., Deary, I. J., Osborn, D., MacIntyre, K., & Carroll, D. (2009). Generalized anxiety disorder, major depressive disorder, and their comorbidity as predictors of all-cause and cardiovascular mortality: The Vietnam Experience Study. *Psychosomatic Medicine, 71,* 395–403.

Phillips, A. L. (2011). A walk in the woods. *American Scientist, 69,* 301–302.

Phillips, D. (2018). Ban was lifted, but transgender recruits still can't join up. *The New York Times* (nytimes .com).

Phillips, W. J., Fletcher, J. M., Marks, A. D. G., & Hine, D. W. (2016). Thinking styles and decision making: A meta-analysis. *Psychological Bulletin, 142,* 260–290.

Piaget, J. (1930). *The child's conception of physical causality* (M. Gabain, Trans.). London: Routledge & Kegan Paul.

Piaget, J. (1932). *The moral judgment of the child.* New York: Harcourt, Brace & World.

Piazza, J. R., Charles, S. T., Silwinski, M. J., Mogle, J., & Almeida, D. M. (2013). Affective reactivity to daily stressors and long-term risk of reporting a chronic health condition. *Annals of Behavioral Medicine, 45,* 110–120.

Picchioni, M. M., & Murray, R. M. (2007). Schizophrenia. *British Medical Journal, 335,* 91–95.

Picci, G., & Scherf, K. S. (2016). From caregivers to peers: Puberty shapes human face perception. *Psychological Science, 27,* 1461–1473.

Piekarski, D. J., Routman, D. M., Schoomer, E. E., Driscoll, J. R., Park, J. H., Butler, M. P., & Zucker, I. (2009). Infrequent low dose testosterone treatment maintains male sexual behavior in Syrian hamsters. *Hormones and Behavior, 55,* 182–189.

Pierce, L. J., Klein, D., Chen, J., Delcenserie, A., & Genesee, F. (2014). Mapping the unconscious maintenance of a lost first language. *PNAS, 111,* 17314–17319.

Pietschnig, J., & Voracek, M. (2015). One century of global IQ gains: A formal meta-analysis of the Flynn effect (1909–2013). *Perspectives on Psychological Science, 10,* 282–306.

Piliavin, J. A. (2003). Doing well by doing good: Benefits for the benefactor. In C. L. M. Keyes & J. Haidt (Eds.), *Flourishing: Positive psychology and the life well-lived.* Washington, DC: American Psychological Association.

Pillemer, D. B. (1998). *Momentous events, vivid memories.* Cambridge, MA: Harvard University Press.

Pilley, J. W. (2013). Chaser: Unlocking the genius of the dog who knows a thousand words. Boston: Houghton Mifflin.

Pinker, S. (1995). The language instinct. *The General Psychologist, 31,* 63–65.

Pinker, S. (1998). Words and rules. *Lingua, 106,* 219–242.

Pinker, S. (2005, April 22). The science of gender and science: A conversation with Elizabeth Spelke. Harvard University. *Edge* (edge.org).

Pinker, S. (2008). *The sexual paradox: Men, women, and the real gender gap.* New York: Scribner.

Pinker, S. (2010, June 10). Mind over mass media. *The New York Times,* A31.

Pinker, S. (2010). 2010: How is the Internet changing the way you think? Not at all. *Edge* (edge.org).

Pinker, S. (2011, September 27). A history of violence. *Edge* (edge.org).

Pinker, S. (2014). *The village effect: Why face-to-face contact matters.* Toronto: Random House Canada.

Pinker, S. (2015, June 8). The trauma of residential schools is passed down through the generations. *The Globe and Mail* (globeandmail.com).

Pinquart, M. (2015). Associations of parenting styles and dimensions with academic achievement in children and adolescents: A meta-analysis. *Educational Psychology Review,* 1–19.

Pinto, Y., de Haan, E. H. F., Lamme, V. A. F. (2017). The split-brain phenomenon revisited: A single conscious agent with split perception. *Trends in Cognitive Sciences, 21,* 835–851.

Pipe, M.-E., Lamb, M. E., Orbach, Y., & Esplin, P. W. (2004). Recent research on children's testimony about experienced and witnessed events. *Developmental Review, 24,* 440–468.

Pittinsky, T. L., & Diamante, N. (2015). Global bystander nonintervention. *Peace and Conflict: Journal of Peace Psychology, 21,* 226–247.

Place, S. S., Todd, P. M., Penke, L., & Asendorph, J. B. (2009). The ability to judge the romantic interest of others. *Psychological Science, 20,* 22–26.

Plant, E. A., & Peruche, B. M. (2005). The consequences of race for police officers' responses to criminal suspects. *Psychological Science, 16,* 180–183.

Plassmann, H., O'Doherty, J., Shiv, B., & Rangel, A. (2008). Marketing actions can modulate neural representations of experienced pleasantness. *PNAS, 105,* 1050–1054.

Platek, S. M., & Singh, D. (2010) Optimal waist-to-hip ratios in women activate neural reward centers in men. *PLOS ONE 5*(2): e9042.

Plomin, R. (2011). Why are children in the same family so different? Nonshared environment three decades later. *International Journal of Epidemiology, 40,* 582–592.

Plomin, R., & Daniels, D. (1987). Why are children in the same family so different from one another? *Behavioral and Brain Sciences, 10,* 1–60.

Plomin, R., & DeFries, J. C. (1998). The genetics of cognitive abilities and disabilities. *Scientific American, 278,* 62–69.

Plomin, R., & McGuffin, P. (2003). Psychopathology in the postgenomic era. *Annual Review of Psychology, 54,* 205–228.

Plomin, R., DeFries, J. C., Knopik, V. S., & Neiderhiser, J. M. (2016). Top 10 replicated findings from behavioral genetics. *Perspectives on Psychological Science, 11,* 3–23.

Plomin, R., DeFries, J. C., McClearn, G. E., & Rutter, M. (1997). *Behavioral genetics.* New York: Freeman.

Plomin, R., McClearn, G. E., Pedersen, N. L., Nesselroade, J. R., & Bergeman, C. S. (1988). Genetic influence on childhood family environment perceived retrospectively from the last half of the life span. *Developmental Psychology, 24,* 37–45.

Plomin, R., & von Stumm, S. (2018). The new genetics of intelligence. *Nature Reviews Neuroscience, 19,* 148–159.

Plous, S., & Herzog, H. A. (2000). Poll shows researchers favor lab animal protection. *Science, 290,* 711.

Pluess, M., & Belsky, J. (2013). Vantage sensitivity: Individual differences in response to positive experiences. *Psychological Bulletin, 139,* 901–916.

Poelmans, G., Pauls, D. L., Buitelaar, J. K., & Franke, B. (2011). Integrated genomewide association study findings: Identification of a neurodevelopmental network for attention deficit hyperactivity disorder. *American Journal of Psychiatry, 168,* 365–377.

Polanin, J. R., Espelage, D. L., & Pigott, T. D. (2012). A meta-analysis of school-based bully prevention programs' effects on bystander intervention behavior. *School Psychology Review, 41,* 47–65.

Polderman, T. J. C., Benyamin, B., de Leeuw, C. A., Sullivan, P. F., van Bochoven, A., Visscher, P. M., & Posthuma, D. (2015). Meta-analysis of the heritability of human traits based on fifty years of twin studies. *Nature Genetics, 47,* 702–709.

Poldrack, R. A., Halchenko, Y. O., & Hanson, S. J. (2009). Decoding the large-scale structure of brain function by classifying mental states across individuals. *Psychological Science, 20,* 1364–1372.

Polivy, J., Herman, C. P., & Coelho, J. S. (2008). Caloric restriction in the presence of attractive food cues: External cues, eating, and weight. *Physiology and Behavior, 94,* 729–733.

Pollak, S., Cicchetti, D., & Klorman, R. (1998). Stress, memory, and emotion: Developmental considerations from the study of child maltreatment. *Developmental Psychopathology, 10,* 811–828.

Poole, D. A., & Lindsay, D. S. (1995). Interviewing preschoolers: Effects of nonsuggestive techniques, parental coaching and leading questions on reports of nonexperienced events. *Journal of Experimental Child Psychology, 60,* 129–154.

Poole, D. A., & Lindsay, D. S. (2001). Children's eyewitness reports after exposure to misinformation from parents. *Journal of Experimental Psychology: Applied, 7,* 27–50.

Pope, D., & Simonsohn, U. (2011). Round numbers as goals: Evidence from baseball, SAT takers, and the lab. *Psychological Science, 22,* 71–79.

Pope Francis. (2015). *Encyclical Letter Laudato Si' of the Holy Father Francis on care for our common home (official English-language text of encyclical).* Retrieved from w2.vatican.va

Poropat, A. E. (2014). Other-rated personality and academic performance: Evidence and implications. *Learning and Individual Differences, 34,* 24–32.

Porter, S., & Peace, K. A. (2007). The scars of memory: A prospective, longitudinal investigation of the consistency of traumatic and positive emotional memories in adulthood. *Psychological Science, 18,* 435–441.

Poulton, R., Moffitt, T. E., & Silva, P. A. (2015). The Dunedin multidisciplinary health and development study: Overview of the first 40 years, with an eye to the future. *Social Psychiatry and Psychiatric Epidemiology, 50,* 679–693.

Poundstone, W. (2014). *How to predict the unpredictable. The art of outsmarting almost everyone.* London, England: OneWorld.

Poushter, J. (2016, February 22). *Smartphone ownership and internet usage continues to climb in emerging economies.* Pew Research Center (pewglobal.org).

Powell, R., Digdon, N. A., Harris, B., & Smithson, C. (2014). Correcting the record on Watson, Rayner and Little Albert: Albert Barger as "Psychology's Lost Boy." *American Psychologist, 69,* 600–611.

Powell, R. A., & Boer, D. P. (1994). Did Freud mislead patients to confabulate memories of abuse? *Psychological Reports, 74,* 1283–1298.

Powell, R. A., & Schmaltz, R. M. (2017, July). *Did Little Albert actually acquire a conditioned fear of animals? What the film evidence tells us.* Paper presented at the Vancouver International Conference on the Teaching of Psychology.

Prather, A. A., Janicki-Deverts, D., Hall, M. H., & Cohen, S. (2015). Behaviorally assessed sleep and susceptibility to the common cold. *Sleep, 38,* 1353–1359.

Pratt, L. A., Brody, D. J., & Gu, Q. (2017, August). Antidepressant use among persons aged 12 and over: United States, 2011–2014. *NCHS Data Brief, 283,* 1–8.

Prentice, D. A., & Miller, D. T. (1993). Pluralistic ignorance and alcohol use on campus: Some consequences of misperceiving the social norm. *Journal of Personality and Social Psychology, 64,* 243–256.

Prescott, A. T., Sargent, J. D., & Hull, J. G. (2018). Metaanalysis of the relationship between violent video game play and physical aggression over time. *PNAS, 115,* 9882–9888.

Pronin, E. (2007). Perception and misperception of bias in human judgment. *Trends in Cognitive Sciences, 11,* 37–43.

Pronin, E. (2013). When the mind races: Effects of thought speed on feeling and action. *Current Directions in Psychological Science, 22,* 283–288.

Pronin, E., & Ross, L. (2006). Temporal differences in trait self-ascription: When the self is seen as another. *Journal of Personality and Social Psychology, 90,* 197–209.

Prot, S., Gentile, D., Anderson, C. A., Suzuli, K., Swing, E., Lim, K. M., . . . Lam, B. C. P. (2014). Long-term relations among prosocial-media use, empathy, and prosocial behavior. *Psychological Science, 25,* 358–368.

Protzko, J., Aronson, J., & Blair, C. (2013). How to make a young child smarter: Evidence from the database of raising intelligence. *Perspectives on Psychological Science, 8,* 25–40.

Provine, R. R. (2012). *Curious behavior: Yawning, laughing, hiccupping, and beyond.* Cambridge, MA: Harvard University Press.

Provine, R. R., Krosnowski, K. A., & Brocato, N. W. (2009). Tearing: Breakthrough in human emotional signaling. *Evolutionary Psychology, 7,* 52–56.

Pryor, J. H., Hurtado, S., DeAngelo, L., Blake, L. P., & Tran, S. (2011). *The American freshman: National norms fall 2010.* Los Angeles: Higher Education Research Institute, UCLA.

Pryor, J. H., Hurtado, S., Saenz, V. B., Korn, J. S., Santos, J. L., & Korn, W. S. (2006). *The American freshman: National norms for fall 2006.* Los Angeles: UCLA Higher Education Research Institute.

Pryor, J. H., Hurtado, S., Sharkness, J., & Korn, W. S. (2007). *The American freshman: National norms for fall 2007.* Los Angeles: UCLA Higher Education Research Institute.

Przybylski, A. K., Weinstein, N., & Murayama, K. (2017). Internet gaming disorder: Investigating the clinical relevance of a new phenomenon. *American Journal of Psychiatry, 174,* 230–236.

Psychologist. (2003). Who's the greatest? *The Psychologist, 16,* 170–175.

Puhl, R. M., Latner, J. D., O'Brien, K., Luedicke, J., Forhan, M., & Danielsdottir, S. (2015). Cross-national perspectives about weight-based bullying in youth: Nature, extent and remedies. *Pediatric Obesity, 11,* 241–250.

Putnam, A. L., Ross, M. Q., Soter, L. K., & Roediger, H. L. (2018). Collective narcissism: Americans exaggerate the role of their home state in appraising U.S. history. *Psychological Science, 29,* 1414–1422.

Putnam, F. W. (1991). Recent research on multiple personality disorder. *Psychiatric Clinics of North America, 14,* 489–502.

Pyszczynski, T. A., Motyl, M., Vail, K. E., III, Hirschberger, G., Arndt, J., & Kesebir, P. (2012). Drawing attention to global climate change decreases support for war. *Peace and Conflict: Journal of Peace Psychology, 18,* 354–368.

Pyszczynski, T. A., Rothschild, Z., & Abdollahi, A. (2008). Terrorism, violence, and hope for peace: A terror management perspective. *Current Directions in Psychological Science 17,* 318–322.

Pyszczynski, T. A., Solomon, S., & Greenberg, J. (2002). *In the wake of 9/11: The psychology of terror.* Washington, DC: American Psychological Association.

Qaseem, A., Kansagara, D., Forciea, M. A., Cooke, M., & Denberg, T. D., for the Clinical Guidelines Committee of the American College of Physicians. (2016). Management of chronic insomnia disorder in adults: A clinical practice guideline from the American College of Physicians. *Annals of Internal Medicine, 165,* 125–133.

Qin, H.-F., & Piao, T.-J. (2011). Dispositional optimism and life satisfaction of Chinese and Japanese college students: Examining the mediating effects of affects and coping efficacy. *Chinese Journal of Clinical Psychology, 19,* 259–261.

Qirko, H. N. (2004). "Fictive kin" and suicide terrorism. *Science, 304,* 49–50.

Qiu, L., Lin, H., Ramsay, J., & Yang, F. (2012). You are what you tweet: Personality expression and perception on Twitter. *Journal of Research in Personality, 46,* 710–718.

Quaedflieg, C. W. E. M., & Schwabe, L. (2017). Memory dynamics under stress. *Memory, 26,* 364–376.

Quinn, P. C., Bhatt, R. S., Brush, D., Grimes, A., & Sharpnack, H. (2002). Development of form similarity as a Gestalt grouping principle in infancy. *Psychological Science, 13,* 320–328.

Quoidbach, J., Gilbert, D. T., & Wilson, T. D. (2013). The end of history illusion. *Science, 339,* 96–98.

Raby, K. L., Roisman, G. I., Fraley, R. C., & Simpson, J. A. (2014). The enduring predictive significance of early maternal sensitivity: Social and academic competence through age 32 years. *Child Development, 86,* 695–708.

Racsmány, M., Conway, M. A., & Demeter, G. (2010). Consolidation of episodic memories during sleep: Long-term effects of retrieval practice. *Psychological Science, 21,* 80–85.

Radford, B. (2010, March 5). Missing persons and abductions reveal psychics' failures. *DiscoveryNews* (news.discovery.com).

Radua, J., Schmidt, A., Borgwardt, S., Heinz, A., Schlagenhauf, F., McGuire, P., & Fusar-Poli, P. (2015). Ventral striatal activation during reward processing in psychosis: A neurofunctional meta-analysis. *JAMA Psychiatry, 72,* 1243–1251.

Rahman, Q. (2015, July 24). "Gay genes": Science is on the right track, we're born this way. Let's deal with it. *The Guardian* (theguardian.com).

Rahman, Q., & Koerting, J. (2008). Sexual orientation-related differences in allocentric spatial memory tasks. *Hippocampus, 18,* 55–63.

Rahman, Q., & Wilson, G. D. (2003). Born gay? The psychobiology of human sexual orientation. *Personality and Individual Differences, 34,* 1337–1382.

Rahman, Q., Wilson, G. D., & Abrahams, S. (2004). Biosocial factors, sexual orientation and neurocognitive functioning. *Psychoneuroendocrinology, 29,* 867–881.

Raila, H., Scholl, B. J., & Gruber, J. (2015). Seeing the world through rose-colored glasses: People who are happy and satisfied with life preferentially attend to positive stimuli. *Emotion, 15,* 449–462.

Raine, A. (1999). Murderous minds: Can we see the mark of Cain? *Cerebrum: The Dana Forum on Brain Science 1,* 15–29.

Raine, A. (2005). The interaction of biological and social measures in the explanation of antisocial and violent behavior. In D. M. Stoff & E. J. Susman (Eds.), *Developmental psychobiology of aggression.* New York: Cambridge University Press.

Raine, A. (2013). *The anatomy of violence: The biological roots of crime.* New York: Pantheon.

Raine, A., Lencz, T., Bihrle, S., LaCasse, L., & Colletti, P. (2000). Reduced prefrontal gray matter volume and reduced autonomic activity in antisocial personality disorder. *Archives of General Psychiatry, 57,* 119–127.

Rainie, L., Purcell, K., Goulet, L. S., & Hampton, K. H. (2011, June 16). *Social networking sites and our lives.* Pew Research Center (pewresearch.org).

Rainville, P., Duncan, G. H., Price, D. D., Carrier, B., & Bushnell, M. C. (1997). Pain affect encoded in human anterior cingulate but not somatosensory cortex. *Science, 277,* 968–971.

Rajendran, G., & Mitchell, P. (2007). Cognitive theories of autism. *Developmental Review, 27,* 224–260.

Raji, C. A., Merrill, D. A., Eyre, H., Mallam, S., Torosyan, N., Erickson, K.I. . . . Kuller, L. H. (2016). Longitudinal relationships between caloric expenditure and gray matter in the cardiovascular health study. *Journal of Alzheimer's Disease, 52,* 719–729.

Ramachandran, V. S., & Blakeslee, S. (1998). *Phantoms in the brain: Probing the mysteries of the human mind.* New York: Morrow.

Ramos, M. R., Cassidy, C., Reicher, S., & Haslam, S. A. (2012). A longitudinal investigation of the rejection-identification hypothesis. *British Journal of Social Psychology, 51,* 642–660.

Randall, D. K. (2012, September 22). Rethinking sleep. *The New York Times* (nytimes.com).

Randi, J. (1999, February 4). 2000 club mailing list e-mail letter.

Rapoport, J. L. (1989). The biology of obsessions and compulsions. *Scientific American, 260,* 83–89.

Räsänen, S., Pakaslahti, A., Syvalahti, E., Jones, P. B., & Isohanni, M. (2000). Sex differences in schizophrenia: A review. *Nordic Journal of Psychiatry, 54,* 37–45.

Rasmussen, H. N., Scheier, M. F., & Greenhouse, J. B. (2009). Optimism and physical health: A meta-analytic review. *Annals of Behavioral Medicine, 37,* 239–256.

Rasmussen, K. (2016). Entitled vengeance: A meta-analysis relating narcissism to provoked aggression. *Aggressive Behavior, 42,* 362–379.

Rath, T., & Harter, J. K. (2010, August 19). Your friends and your social well-being: Close friendships are vital to health, happiness, and even workplace productivity. *Gallup Management Journal* (gmj.gallup.com).

Rathbone, C. J., Salgado, S., Akan, M., Havelka, J., & Berntsen, D. (2016). Imagining the future: A cross-cultural perspective on possible selves. *Consciousness and Cognition, 42,* 113–124.

Rattan, A., Savani, K., Naidu, N. V. R., & Dweck, C. S. (2012). Can everyone become highly intelligent? Cultural differences in and societal consequences of beliefs about the universal potential for intelligence. *Journal of Personality and Social Psychology, 103,* 787–803.

Ravizza, S. M., Uitvlught, M. G., & Fenn, K. M. (2017). Logged in and zoned out. *Psychological Science, 28,* 171–180.

Ray, J., & Kafka, S. (2014, May 6). *Life in college matters for life after college.* Gallup Poll (gallup.com).

Ray, O., & Ksir, C. (1990). *Drugs, society, and human behavior* (5th ed.). St. Louis: Times Mirror/Mosby.

Raynor, H. A., & Epstein, L. H. (2001). Dietary variety, energy regulation, and obesity. *Psychological Bulletin, 127,* 325–341.

Reason, J., & Mycielska, K. (1982). *Absent-minded? The psychology of mental lapses and everyday errors.* Englewood Cliffs, NJ: Prentice-Hall.

Rebar, A. L., Stanton, R., Geard, D., Short, C., Duncan, M. J., & Vandelanotte, C. (2015). A meta-meta-analysis of the effect of physical activity on depression and anxiety in non-clinical adult populations. *Health Psychology Review, 9,* 366–378.

Redden, J. P., Mann, T., Vickers, Z., Mykerezi, E., Reicks, M., & Elsbernd, E. (2015). Serving first in isolation increases vegetable intake among elementary schoolchildren. *PLOS ONE, 10,* e0121283.

Redick, T. S., Unsworth, N., Kane, M. J., & Hambrick, D. Z. (2017). Don't shoot the messenger: Still no evidence that video-game experience is related to cognitive abilities—A reply to Green et al. (2017). *Psychological Science, 28,* 683–686.

Reebs, A., Yuval, K., & Bernstein, A. (2017). Remembering and responding to distressing autobiographical memories: Exploring risk and intervention targets for posttraumatic stress in traumatized refugees. *Clinical Psychological Science, 5,* 789–797.

Reed, P. (2000). Serial position effects in recognition memory for odors. *Journal of Experimental Psychology: Learning, Memory, and Cognition, 26,* 411–422.

Reeves, A., McKee, M., & Stuckler, D. (2014). Economic suicides in the Great Recession in Europe and North America. *British Journal of Psychiatry, 205,* 246–247.

Reichenberg, A., Cederlöf, M., McMillan, A., Trzaskowski, M., Kapara, O., Fruchter, E., . . . Plomin, R. (2016). Discontinuity in the genetic and environmental causes of the intellectual disability spectrum. *PNAS, 113,* 1098–1103.

Reichenberg, A., & Harvey, P. D. (2007). Neuropsychological impairments in schizophrenia: Integration of performance-based and brain imaging findings. *Psychological Bulletin, 133,* 833–858.

Reicher, S., Haslam, S. A., & Van Bavel, J. J. (2018, August). Breaking free from Stanford. *The Psychologist,* pp. 2–3.

Reichert, R. A., Robb, M. B., Fender, J. G., & Wartella, E. (2010). Word learning from baby videos. *Archives of Pediatrics & Adolescent Medicine, 164,* 432–437.

Reichow, B. (2012). Overview of meta-analyses on early intensive behavioral intervention for young children with autism spectrum disorders. *Journal of Autism and Developmental Disorders, 42,* 512–520.

Reid, V. M., Dunn, K., Young, R. J., Amu, J., Donovan, T., & Reissland, N. (2017). The human fetus preferentially engages with face-like visual stimuli. *Current Biology, 27,* 1825–1828.

Reifman, A. S., Larrick, R. P., & Fein, S. (1991). Temper and temperature on the diamond: The heat-aggression relationship in Major League Baseball. *Personality and Social Psychology Bulletin, 17,* 580–585.

Reimann, F., Cox, J. J., Belfer, I., Diatchenko, L., Zaykin, D. V., McHale, D. P., . . . Woods, C. G. (2010). Pain perception is altered by a nucleotide polymorphism in SCN9A. *PNAS, 107,* 5148–5153.

Reimão, R. N., & Lefévre, A. B. (1980). Prevalence of sleep-talking in childhood. *Brain and Development, 2,* 353–357.

Reiner, W. G., & Gearhart, J. P. (2004). Discordant sexual identity in some genetic males with cloacal exstrophy assigned to female sex at birth. *New England Journal of Medicine, 350,* 333–341.

Reis, H. T., & Aron, A. (2008). Love: What is it, why does it matter, and how does it operate? *Perspectives on Psychological Science, 3,* 80–86.

Reis, M., Ramiro, L., Camacho, I., Tomé, G., Brito, C., & Gaspar de Matos, G. (2017). Does having a pet make a difference? Highlights from the HBSC Portuguese study. *European Journal of Developmental Psychology, 15,* 548–564.

Reis, S. M. (2001). Toward a theory of creativity in diverse creative women. In M. Bloom & T. Gullotta (Eds.), *Promoting creativity across the life span* (pp. 231–275). Washington, DC: CWLA Press.

Reisenzein, R. (1983). The Schachter theory of emotion: Two decades later. *Psychological Bulletin, 94,* 239–264.

Reiser, M. (1982). *Police psychology.* Los Angeles: LEHI.

Reitz, A. K., Motti-Stefanidi, F., & Asendorpf, J. B. (2016). Me, us, and them: Testing sociometer theory in a socially diverse real-life context. *Journal of Personality and Social Psychology, 110,* 908–920.

Reivich, K., Gillham, J. E., Chaplin, T. M., & Seligman, M. E. P. (2013). From helplessness to optimism: The role of resilience in treating and preventing depression in youth. In S. Goldstein & R. B. Brooks (Eds.), *Handbook of resilience in children* (2nd ed., pp. 201–214). New York: Springer.

Rekker, R., Keijsers, L., Branje, S., & Meeus, W. (2015). Political attitudes in adolescence and emerging adulthood: Developmental changes in mean level, polarization, rank-order stability, and correlates. *Journal of Adolescence, 41,* 136–147.

Remick, A. K., Polivy, J., & Pliner, P. (2009). Internal and external moderators of the effect of variety on food intake. *Psychological Bulletin, 135,* 434–451.

Remington, A., Swettenham, J., Campbell, R., & Coleman, M. (2009). Selective attention and perceptual load in autism spectrum disorder. *Psychological Science, 20,* 1388–1393.

Remley, A. (1988, October). From obedience to independence. *Psychology Today,* pp. 56–59.

Ren, D., Wesselmann, E., & Williams, K. D. (2016). Evidence for another response to ostracism: Solitude seeking. *Social Psychological and Personality Science, 7*(3), 204–212.

Renner, M. J., & Renner, C. H. (1993). Expert and novice intuitive judgments about animal behavior. *Bulletin of the Psychonomic Society, 31,* 551–552.

Renner, M. J., & Rosenzweig, M. R. (1987). *Enriched and impoverished environments: Effects on brain and behavior.* New York: Springer-Verlag.

Renninger, K. A., & Granott, N. (2005). The process of scaffolding in learning and development. *New Ideas in Psychology, 23,* 111–114.

Rentfrow, P. J., & Gosling, S. D. (2003). The do re mi's of everyday life: The structure and personality correlates of music preferences. *Journal of Personality and Social Psychology, 84,* 1236–1256.

Rentfrow, P. J., & Gosling, S. D. (2006). Message in a ballad: The role of music preferences in interpersonal perception. *Psychological Science, 17,* 236–242.

Rescorla, R. A., & Wagner, A. R. (1972). A theory of Pavlovian conditioning: Variations in the effectiveness of reinforcement and nonreinforcement. In A. H. Black & W. F. Perokasy (Eds.), *Classical conditioning II: Current theory.* New York: Appleton-Century-Crofts.

Resnick, M. D., Bearman, P. S., Blum, R. W., Bauman, K. E., Harris, K. M., Jones, J., . . . Udry, J. R. (1997). Protecting adolescents from harm: Findings from the National Longitudinal Study on Adolescent Health. *Journal of the American Medical Association, 278,* 823–832.

Resnick, S. M. (1992). Positron emission tomography in psychiatric illness. *Current Directions in Psychological Science, 1,* 92–98.

Reuters. (2000, July 5). *Many teens regret decision to have sex* (National Campaign to Prevent Teen Pregnancy survey). Retrieved from washingtonpost.com.

Reyna, V. F., & Farley, F. (2006). Risk and rationality in adolescent decision making: Implications for theory, practice, and public policy. *Psychological Science in the Public Interest, 7,* 1–44.

Reyna, V. F., Chick, C. F., Corbin, J. C., & Hsia, A. N. (2014). Developmental reversals in risky decision making: Intelligence agents show larger decision biases than college students. *Psychological Science, 25,* 76–84.

Rhodes, M. G., & Anastasi, J. S. (2012). The own-age bias in face recognition: A meta-analytic and theoretical review. *Psychological Bulletin, 138,* 146–174.

Rhodes, S. R. (1983). Age-related differences in work attitudes and behavior: A review and conceptual analysis. *Psychological Bulletin, 93,* 328–367.

Riccelli, R., Toschi, N., Nigro, S., Terracciano, A., & Passamonti, L. (2017). Surface-based morphometry reveals the neuroanatomical basis of the five-factor model of personality. *Social Cognitive and Affective Neuroscience, 12,* 671–684.

Ricciardelli, L. A., & McCabe, M. P. (2004). A biopsychosocial model of disordered eating and the pursuit of muscularity in adolescent boys. *Psychological Bulletin, 130,* 179–205.

Rice, M. E., & Grusec, J. E. (1975). Saying and doing: Effects on observer performance. *Journal of Personality and Social Psychology, 32,* 584–593.

Richardson, G. B., La Guardia, A. C., & Klay, P. M. (2018). Determining the roles of father absence and age at menarche in female psychosocial acceleration. *Evolution and Human Behavior, 39,* 437–446.

Richardson, M., Abraham, C., & Bond, R. (2012). Psychological correlates of university students' academic performance: A systematic review and meta-analysis. *Psychological Bulletin, 138,* 353–387.

Richeson, J. A., & Shelton, J. N. (2007). Negotiating interracial interactions. *Current Directions in Psychological Science, 16,* 316–320.

Richtel, M., & Kaplan, S. (2018, August 27). Did Juul lure teenagers and get 'customers for life'? *The New York Times* (nytimes.com).

Rieff, P. (1979). *Freud: The mind of a moralist* (3rd ed.). Chicago: University of Chicago Press.

Rigoni, J. B., & Asplund, J. (2016a, July 7). *Strengths-based development: The business results.* The Gallup Organization (gallup.com).

Rigoni, J. B., & Asplund, J. (2016b, July 12). *Global study: ROI for strengths-based development.* The Gallup Organization (gallup.com).

Rindermann, H., & Ceci, S. J. (2009). Educational policy and country outcomes in international cognitive competence studies. *Perspectives on Psychological Science, 4,* 551–577.

Riordan, M. (2013, March 19). *Tobacco warning labels: Evidence of effectiveness.* Washington, DC: The Campaign for Tobacco-Free Kids (tobaccofreekids.org).

Ritchey, A. J., & Ruback, R. B. (2018). Predicting lynching atrocity: The situational norms of lynchings in Georgia. *Personality and Social Psychology Bulletin, 44,* 619–637.

Ritchie, S. J., Dickie, D. A., Cox, S. R., Hernandez, M. del C. V., Corley, J., Royle, N. A., . . . Deary, I. J. (2015). Brain volumetric changes and cognitive ageing during the eighth decade of life. *Human Brain Mapping, 36,* 4910–4925.

Ritchie, S. J., & Tucker-Drob, E. M. (2018). How much does education improve intelligence? A meta-analysis. *Psychological Science, 29,* 1358–1369.

Ritchie, S. J., Wiseman, R., & French, C. C. (2012). Failing the future: Three unsuccessful attempts to replicate Bem's "retroactive facilitation of recall" effect. *PLOS ONE, 7*(3), e33r23.

Rith-Najarian, L. R., Mesri, B., Park, A. L., Sun, M., Chavira, D. A., & Chorpita, B. F. (2018). Durability of cognitive behavioral therapy effects for youth and adolescents with anxiety, depression, or traumatic stress: A meta-analysis on long-term follow-ups. *Behavior Therapy, 50,* 225–240.

Ritter, S. M., Damian, R. I., Simonton, D. K., van Baaren, R. B., Strick, M., Derks, J., & Dijksterhuis, A. (2012). Diversifying experiences enhance cognitive flexibility. *Journal of Experimental Social Psychology, 48,* 961–964.

Rizzolatti, G., Fadiga, L., Fogassi, L., & Gallese, V. (2002). From mirror neurons to imitation: Facts and speculations. In A. N. Meltzoff & W. Prinz (Eds.), *The imitative mind: Development, evolution, and brain bases.* Cambridge, UK: Cambridge University Press.

Rizzolatti, G., Fogassi, L., & Gallese, V. (2006, November). Mirrors in the mind. *Scientific American,* pp. 54–61.

Roberti, J. W., Storch, E. A., & Bravata, E. A. (2004). Sensation seeking, exposure to psychosocial stressors, and body modifications in a college population. *Personality and Individual Differences, 37,* 1167–1177.

Roberts, B. W., Caspi, A., & Moffitt, T. E. (2001). The kids are alright: Growth and stability in personality development from adolescence to adulthood. *Journal of Personality and Social Psychology, 81,* 670–683.

Roberts, L. (1988). Beyond Noah's ark: What do we need to know? *Science, 242,* 1247.

Roberts, T.-A. (1991). Determinants of gender differences in responsiveness to others' evaluations. *Dissertation Abstracts International, 51*(8–B).

Robinson, F. P. (1970). *Effective study.* New York: Harper & Row.

Robinson, J. P., & Martin, S. (2008). What do happy people do? *Social Indicators Research, 89,* 565–571.

Robinson, J. P., & Martin, S. (2009). Changes in American daily life: 1965–2005. *Social Indicators Research, 93,* 47–56.

Robinson, O. J., Cools, R., Carlisi, C. O., & Drevets, W. C. (2012). Ventral striatum response during reward and punishment reversal learning in unmedicated major depressive disorder. *American Journal of Psychiatry, 169,* 152–159.

Robinson, T. E., & Berridge, K. C. (2003). Addiction. *Annual Review of Psychology, 54,* 25–53.

Robinson, T. N., Borzekowski, D. L. G., Matheson, D. M., & Kraemer, H. C. (2007). Effects of fast food branding on young children's taste preferences. *Archives of Pediatric and Adolescent Medicine, 161,* 792–797.

Robinson, V. M. (1983). Humor and health. In P. E. McGhee & J. H. Goldstein (Eds.), *Handbook of humor research: Vol. II. Applied studies.* New York: Springer-Verlag.

Robles, T. F. (2015). Marital quality and health: Implications for marriage in the 21st century. *Current Directions in Psychological Science, 23,* 427–432.

Rochat, F. (1993). *How did they resist authority? Protecting refugees in Le Chambon during World War II.* Paper presented at the American Psychological Association convention.

Rock, I., & Palmer, S. (1990, December). The legacy of Gestalt psychology. *Scientific American,* pp. 84–90.

Rodin, J. (1986). Aging and health: Effects of the sense of control. *Science, 233,* 1271–1276.

Roediger, H. L., III. (2013). Applying cognitive psychology to education: Translational educational science. *Psychological Science in the Public Interest, 14,* 1–3.

Roediger, H. L., III., & DeSoto, K. A. (2016). Was Alexander Hamilton president? *Psychological Science, 27,* 644–650.

Roediger, H. L., III, & Finn, B. (2010, March/April). The pluses of getting it wrong. *Scientific American Mind,* pp. 39–41.

Roediger, H. L., III, & Karpicke, J. D. (2006). Test-enhanced learning: Taking memory tests improves long-term retention. *Psychological Science, 17,* 249–255.

Roediger, H. L., III, & Karpicke, J. D. (2018). Reflections on the resurgence of interest in the testing effect. *Perspectives on Psychological Science, 13,* 236–241.

Roediger, H. L., III, & McDermott, K. B. (1995). Creating false memories: Remembering words not presented in lists. *Journal of Experimental Psychology: Learning, Memory, and Cognition, 21,* 803–814.

Roediger, H. L., III, Meade, M. L., & Bergman, E. T. (2001). Social contagion of memory. *Psychonomic Bulletin & Review, 8,* 365–371.

Roediger, H. L., III, Wheeler, M. A., & Rajaram, S. (1993). Remembering, knowing, and reconstructing the past. In D. L. Medin (Ed.), *The psychology of learning and motivation: Advances in research and theory* (Vol. 30). Orlando, FL: Academic Press.

Roehling, P. V., Roehling, M. V., & Moen, P. (2001). The relationship between work-life policies and practices and employee loyalty: A life course perspective. *Journal of Family and Economic Issues, 22,* 141–170.

Roelofs, T. (2010, September 22). Somali refugee takes oath of U.S. citizenship year after his brother. *The Grand Rapids Press* (mlive.com).

Roenneberg, T., Kuehnle, T., Pramstaller, P. P., Ricken, J., Havel, M., Guth, A., & Merrow, M. (2004). A marker for the end of adolescence. *Current Biology, 14,* R1038–R1039.

Roepke, A. M. (2015). Psychosocial interventions and posttraumatic growth: A meta-analysis. *Journal of Consulting and Clinical Psychology, 83,* 129.

Roepke, A. M., & Seligman, M. E. P. (2015). Doors opening: A mechanism for growth after adversity. *Journal of Positive Psychology, 10,* 107–115.

Roese, N. J., & Summerville, A. (2005). What we regret most . . . and why. *Personality and Social Psychology Bulletin, 31,* 1273–1285.

Roese, N. J., & Vohs, K. D. (2012). Hindsight bias. *Perspectives on Psychological Science, 7,* 411–426.

Roesser, R. (1998). What you should know about hearing conservation. *Better Hearing Institute* (betterhearing.org).

Rogers, C. R. (1961). *On becoming a person: A therapist's view of psychotherapy.* Boston: Houghton Mifflin.

Rogers, C. R. (1980). *A way of being.* Boston: Houghton Mifflin.

Rogers, C. R. (1985, February). Quoted by M. L. Wallach & L. Wallach, How psychology sanctions the cult of the self. *Washington Monthly,* pp. 46–56.

Rogers, T., & Milkman, K. L. (2016). Reminders through association. *Psychological Science, 27,* 973–986.

Rohner, R. P., & Veneziano, R. A. (2001). The importance of father love: History and contemporary evidence. *Review of General Psychology, 5,* 382–405.

Rohrer, J. M., Egloff, B., Kosinski, M., Stillwell, D., & Schmukle, S. C. (2018). In your eyes only? Discrepancies and agreement between self- and other-reports of personality from age 14 to 29. *Journal of Personality and Social Psychology, 115,* 304–320.

Rohrer, J. M., Egloff, B., & Schmukle, S. C. (2015). Examining the effects of birth order on personality. *PNAS, 112,* 14224–14229.

Rohrer, J. M., Richter, D., Brümmer, M., Wagner, G. G., & Schmukle, S. C. (2018). Successfully striving for happiness: Socially engaged pursuits predict increases in life satisfaction. *Psychological Science, 29,* 1291–1298.

Roiser, J. P., Cook, L. J., Cooper, J. D., Rubinsztein, D. C., & Sahakian, B. J. (2005). Association of a functional polymorphism in the serotonin transporter gene with abnormal emotional processing in Ecstasy users. *American Journal of Psychiatry, 162,* 609–612.

Romano, A., Balliet, D., Yamagishi, T., & Liu, J. H. (2017). Parochial trust and cooperation across 17 societies. *PNAS, 114,* 12702–12707.

Romens, S. E., McDonald, J., Svaren, J., & Pollak, S. D. (2015). Associations between early life stress and gene methylation in children. *Child Development, 86,* 303–309.

Ronay, R., & von Hippel, W. (2010). The presence of an attractive woman elevates testosterone and physical risk taking in young men. *Social Psychology and Personality Science, 1,* 57–64.

Root, T. L., Thornton, L. M., Lindroos, A. K., Stunkard, A. J., Lichtenstein, P., Pedersen, N. L., . . . Bulik, C. M. (2010). Shared and unique genetic and environmental influences on binge eating and night eating: A Swedish twin study. *Eating Behaviors, 11,* 92–98.

Roper, K. R. (2016, July 19). Public Facebook post. Retrieved from facebook.com/kate.riffleroper/posts/1746348308987959

Roper, S. D., & Chaudhari, N. (2017). Taste buds: Cells, signals, and synapses. *Nature Reviews Neuroscience, 18,* 485–497.

Roque, L., Verissimo, M., Oliveira, T. F., & Oliveira, R. F. (2012). Attachment security and HPA axis reactivity to positive and challenging emotional situations in child–mother dyads in naturalistic settings. *Developmental Psychobiology, 54,* 401–411.

Rosch, E. (1978). Principles of categorization. In E. Rosch & B. L. Lloyd (Eds.), *Cognition and categorization* (pp. 27–48). Hillsdale, NJ: Erlbaum.

Rose, A. J., & Rudolph, K. D. (2006). A review of sex differences in peer relationship processes: Potential trade-offs for the emotional and behavioral development of girls and boys. *Psychological Bulletin, 132,* 98–131.

Roselli, C. E., Larkin, K., Schrunk, J. M., & Stormshak, F. (2004). Sexual partner preference, hypothalamic morphology and aromatase in rams. *Physiology and Behavior, 83,* 233–245.

Roselli, C. E., Resko, J. A., & Stormshak, F. (2002). Hormonal influences on sexual partner preference in rams. *Archives of Sexual Behavior, 31,* 43–49.

Rosenbaum, M. (1986). The repulsion hypothesis: On the nondevelopment of relationships. *Journal of Personality and Social Psychology, 51,* 1156–1166.

Rosenberg, N. A., Pritchard, J. K., Weber, J. L., Cann, H. M., Kidd, K. K., Zhivotosky, L. A., & Feldman, M. W. (2002). Genetic structure of human populations. *Science, 298,* 2381–2385.

Rosenberg, T. (2010, November 1). The opt-out solution. *The New York Times.* Retrieved from http://opinionator.blogs.nytimes.com/2010/11/01/the-opt-out-solution/

Rosenblum, L. D. (2013, January). A confederacy of senses. *Scientific American,* pp. 73–78.

Rosenfeld, M. J. (2013, August 26). Personal communication.

Rosenfeld, M. J. (2014). Couple longevity in the era of same-sex marriage in the United States. *Journal of Marriage and Family, 76,* 905–911.

Rosenfeld, M. J., & Thomas, R. J. (2012). Searching for a mate: The rise of the internet as a social intermediary. *American Sociological Review, 77,* 523–547.

Rosenhan, D. L. (1973). On being sane in insane places. *Science, 179,* 250–258.

Rosenkranz, M. A., Davidson, R. J., Maccoon, D. G., Sheridan, J. F., Kalin, N. H., & Lutz, A. (2013). A comparison of mindfulness-based stress reduction and an active control in modulation of neurogenic inflammation. *Brain, Behavior, and Immunity, 27,* 174–184.

Rosenquist, P. B., McCall, W. V., & Youssef, N. (2016). Charting the course of electroconvulsive therapy: Where have we been and where are we headed? *Psychiatric Annals, 46,* 647–651.

Rosenthal, R., Hall, J. A., Archer, D., DiMatteo, M. R., & Rogers, P. L. (1979). The PONS test: Measuring sensitivity to nonverbal cues. In S. Weitz (Ed.), *Nonverbal communication* (2nd ed.). New York: Oxford University Press.

Rosenzweig, M. R. (1984). Experience, memory, and the brain. *American Psychologist, 39,* 365–376.

Rosenzweig, M. R., Krech, D., Bennett, E. L., & Diamond, M. C. (1962). Effects of environmental complexity and training on brain chemistry and anatomy: A replication and extension. *Journal of Comparative and Physiological Psychology, 55,* 429–437.

Roseth, C. J., Johnson, D. W., & Johnson, R. T. (2008). Promoting early adolescents' achievement and peer relationships: The effects of cooperative, competitive, and individualistic goal structures. *Psychological Bulletin, 134,* 223–246.

Ross, E. L., Zivin, K., & Maixner, D. F. (2018a). Cost-effectiveness of electroconvulsive therapy vs pharmacotherapy/psychotherapy for treatment-resistant depression in the United States. *JAMA Psychiatry, 75,* 713–722.

Ross, L. E., Salway, T., Tarasoff, L. A., MacKay, J. M., Hawkins, B. W., & Fehr, C. P. (2018b). Prevalence of depression and anxiety among bisexual people compared to gay, lesbian, and heterosexual individuals: A systematic review and meta-analysis. *Journal of Sex Research, 55,* 435–456.

Rossi, P. J. (1968). Adaptation and negative aftereffect to lateral optical displacement in newly hatched chicks. *Science, 160,* 430–432.

Rotge, J.-Y., Lemogne, C., Hinfray, S., Huguet, P., Grynszpan, O., Tartour, E., . . . Fossati, P. (2015). A meta-analysis of the anterior cingulate contribution to social pain. *Social Cognitive and Affective Neuroscience, 10,* 19–27.

Roth, B., Becker, N., Romeyke, S., Schäfer, S., Domnick, F., & Spinath, F. M. (2015). Intelligence and school grades: A meta-analysis. *Intelligence, 53,* 118–137.

Rothbart, M., Fulero, S., Jensen, C., Howard, J., & Birrell, P. (1978). From individual to group impressions: Availability heuristics in stereotype formation. *Journal of Experimental Social Psychology, 14,* 237–255.

Rothbart, M. K. (2007). Temperament, development, and personality. *Current Directions in Psychological Science, 16,* 207–212.

Rotheneichner, P., Lange, S., O'Sullivan, A., Marschallinger, J., Zaunmair, P., Geretsegger, C., . . . Couillard-Despres, S. (2014). Hippocampal neurogenesis and antidepressive therapy: Shocking relations. *Neural Plasticity, 2014,* 723915.

Rothman, A. J., & Salovey, P. (1997). Shaping perceptions to motivate healthy behavior: The role of message framing. *Psychological Bulletin, 121,* 3–19.

Rottensteiner, M., Leskinen, T., Niskanen, E., Aaltonen, S., Mutikainen, S., Wikgren, J., . . . Kujala, U. M. (2015). Physical activity, fitness, glucose homeostasis, and brain morphology in twins. *Medicine and Science in Sports and Exercise, 47,* 509–518.

Rounds, J., & Su, R. (2014). The nature and power of interests. *Current Directions in Psychological Science, 23,* 98–103.

Rovee-Collier, C. (1989). The joy of kicking: Memories, motives, and mobiles. In P. R. Solomon, G. R. Goethals, C. M. Kelley, & B. R. Stephens (Eds.), *Memory: Interdisciplinary approaches* (pp. 151–179). New York: Springer-Verlag.

Rovee-Collier, C. (1999). The development of infant memory. *Current Directions in Psychological Science, 8,* 80–85.

Rowe, D. C. (1990). As the twig is bent? The myth of child-rearing influences on personality development. *Journal of Counseling and Development, 68,* 606–611.

Rowe, D. C., Vazsonyi, A. T., & Flannery, D. J. (1994). No more than skin deep: Ethnic and racial similarity in developmental process. *Psychological Review, 101,* 396.

Rozin, P., Dow, S., Mosovitch, M., & Rajaram, S. (1998). What causes humans to begin and end a meal? A role for memory for what has been eaten, as evidenced by a study of multiple meal eating in amnesic patients. *Psychological Science, 9,* 392–396.

Ruau, D., Liu, L. Y., Clark, J. D., Angst, M. S., & Butte, A. J. (2012). Sex differences in reported pain across 11,000 patients captured in electronic medical records. *Journal of Pain, 13,* 228–234.

Ruback, R. B., Carr, T. S., & Hopper, C. H. (1986). Perceived control in prison: Its relation to reported crowding, stress, and symptoms. *Journal of Applied Social Psychology, 16,* 375–386.

Rubenstein, J. S., Meyer, D. E., & Evans, J. E. (2001). Executive control of cognitive processes in task switching. *Journal of Experimental Psychology: Human Perception and Performance, 27,* 763–797.

Ruberton, P. M., Gladstone, J., & Lyubomirsky, S. (2016). How your bank balance buys happiness. *Emotion, 16,* 575–580.

Rubin, D. C., Rahhal, T. A., & Poon, L. W. (1998). Things learned in early adulthood are remembered best. *Memory and Cognition, 26,* 3–19.

Rubin, L. B. (1985). *Just friends: The role of friendship in our lives.* New York: Harper & Row.

Rubin, Z. (1970). Measurement of romantic love. *Journal of Personality and Social Psychology, 16,* 265–273.

Rubio-Fernández, P., & Geurts, B. (2013). How to pass the false-belief task before your fourth birthday. *Psychological Science, 24,* 27–33.

Ruchlis, H. (1990). *Clear thinking: A practical introduction.* Buffalo, NY: Prometheus Books.

Rueckert, L., Doan, T., & Branch, B. (2010). *Emotion and relationship effects on gender differences in empathy.* Presented at the annual meeting of the Association for Psychological Science, Boston, MA, May, 2010.

Rueger, S. Y., Malecki, C. K., Pyun, Y., Aycock, C., & Coyle, S. (2016). A meta-analytic review of the association between perceived social support and depression in childhood and adolescence. *Psychological Bulletin, 142,* 1017–1067.

Ruffin, C. L. (1993). Stress and health—little hassles vs. major life events. *Australian Psychologist, 28,* 201–208.

Rule, B. G., & Ferguson, T. J. (1986). The effects of media violence on attitudes, emotions, and cognitions. *Journal of Social Issues, 42,* 29–50.

Rumbaugh, D. M. (1977). *Language learning by a chimpanzee: The Lana project.* New York: Academic Press.

Rumbaugh, D. M., & Washburn, D. A. (2003). *Intelligence of apes and other rational beings.* New Haven, CT: Yale University Press.

Runeson, B., Haglund, A., Lichtenstein, P., & Tidemalm, C. (2016). Suicide risk after nonfatal self-harm: A national cohort study, 2000–2008. *Journal of Clinical Psychiatry, 77,* 240–256.

Ruotsalainen, H., Kyngäs, H., Tammelin, T., & Kääriäinen, M. (2015). Systematic review of physical activity and exercise interventions on body mass indices, subsequent physical activity and psychological symptoms in overweight and obese adolescents. *Journal of Advanced Nursing, 71,* 2461–2477.

Rushton, J. P. (1975). Generosity in children: Immediate and long-term effects of modeling, preaching, and moral judgment. *Journal of Personality and Social Psychology, 31,* 459–466.

Rutledge, R. B., Skandali, N., Dayan, P., & Dolan, R. J. (2014). A computational and neural model of momentary subjective well-being. *PNAS, 111,* 12252–12257.

Rutz, C., Klump, B. C., Komarczyk, L., Leighton, R., Kramer, R., Wischnewski, S., . . . Masuda, B. M. (2016). Discovery of species-wide tool use in the Hawaiian crow. *Nature, 537,* 403–407.

Ryan, B. (2016, March 8). *Women's life ratings get better with full-time jobs.* Gallup World Poll (gallup.com).

Ryan, R. M., & Deci, E. L. (2000). Self-determination theory and the facilitation of intrinsic motivation, social development, and well-being. *American Psychologist, 55,* 68–78.

Ryan, R. M., & Deci, E. L. (2004). Avoiding death or engaging life as accounts of meaning and culture: Comment on Pyszczynski et al. (2004). *Psychological Bulletin, 130,* 473–477.

Rydell, M., Lundström, S., Gillberg, C., Lichtenstein, P., & Larsson, H. (2018). Has the attention deficit hyperactivity disorder phenotype become more common in children between 2004 and 2014? Trends over 10 years from a Swedish general population sample. *Journal of Child Psychology and Psychiatry, 59,* 863–871.

Rydell, R. J., Rydell, M. T., & Boucher, K. L. (2010). The effect of negative performance stereotypes on learning. *Journal of Personality and Social Psychology, 99,* 883–896.

Saad, L. (2002, November 21). *Most smokers wish they could quit.* Gallup News Service (gallup.com).

Saad, L. (2015, July 13). *Nearly half of smartphone users can't imagine life without it.* Gallup Poll (gallup.com).

Saad, L. (2017, December 20). *Eight in 10 Americans afflicted by stress.* Gallup Poll (gallup.com).

Sabbagh, M. A., Xu, F., Carlson, S. M., Moses, L. J., & Lee, K. (2006). The development of executive functioning and theory of mind: A comparison of Chinese and U.S. preschoolers. *Psychological Science, 17,* 74–81.

Sabesan, R., Schmidt, B. P., Tuten, W. S., & Roorda, A. (2016). The elementary representation of spatial and color vision in the human retina. *Science Advances, 2,* e1600797.

Sachdev, P., & Sachdev, J. (1997). Sixty years of psychosurgery: Its present status and its future. *Australian and New Zealand Journal of Psychiatry, 31,* 457–464.

Sachs, A. (2007, August 27). A memoir of schizophrenia. *Time* (time.com).

Sackett, P. R., & Walmsley, P. T. (2014). Which personality attributes are most important in the workplace? *Perspectives on Psychological Science, 9,* 538–551.

Sacks, O. (1985). *The man who mistook his wife for a hat.* New York: Summit Books.

Sadler, M. S., Correll, J., Park, B., & Judd, C. M. (2012a). The world is not Black and White: Racial bias in the decision to shoot in a multiethnic context. *Journal of Social Issues, 68,* 286–313.

Sadler, M. S., Meagor, E. L., & Kaye, M. E. (2012b). Stereotypes of mental disorders differ in competence and warmth. *Social Science and Medicine, 74,* 915–922.

Sagan, C. (1977). *The dragons of Eden: Speculations on the evolution of human intelligence.* New York: Ballantine.

Saint Louis, C. (2017, February 2). Pregnant women turn to marijuana, perhaps harming infants. *The New York Times.* Retrieved from https://www.nytimes.com/2017/02/02/health/marijuana-and-pregnancy.html

Sala, G., Tatlidil, K. S., & Gobet, F. (2018). Video game training does not enhance cognitive ability: A comprehensive meta-analytic investigation. *Psychological Bulletin, 144,* 111–139.

Salas-Wright, C. P., Vaughn, M. G., Hodge, D. R., & Perron, B. E. (2012). Religiosity profiles of American youth in relation to substance use, violence, and delinquency. *Journal of Youth and Adolescence, 41,* 1560–1575.

Salehi, I., Hosseini, S. M., Haghighi, M., Jahangard, L., Bajoghli, H., Gerber, M., . . . Brand, S. (2016). Electroconvulsive therapy (ECT) and aerobic exercise training (AET) increased plasma BDNF and ameliorated depressive symptoms in patients suffering from major depressive disorder. *Journal of Psychiatric Research, 76,* 1–8.

Salgado, J. F., & Moscoso, S. (2002). Comprehensive meta-analysis of the construct validity of the employment interview. *European Journal of Work and Organizational Psychology, 11,* 299–326.

Salk, R. H., Hyde, J. S., & Abramson, L. Y. (2017). Gender differences in depression in representative national samples: Meta-analyses of diagnoses and symptoms. *Psychological Bulletin, 143,* 783–822.

Salmon, P. (2001). Effects of physical exercise on anxiety, depression, and sensitivity to stress: A unifying theory. *Clinical Psychology Review, 21,* 33–61.

Salovey, P. (1990, January/February). Interview. *American Scientist,* pp. 25–29.

Salthouse, T. A. (2009). When does age-related cognitive decline begin? *Neurobiology of Aging, 30,* 507–514.

Salthouse, T. A. (2010). Selective review of cognitive aging. *Journal of the International Neuropsychological Society, 16,* 754–760.

Salthouse, T. A. (2013). Within-cohort age-related differences in cognitive functioning. *Psychological Science, 24,* 123–130.

Salthouse, T. A. (2014). Why are there different age relations in cross-sectional and longitudinal comparisons of cognitive functioning? *Current Directions in Psychological Science, 23,* 252–256.

Salthouse, T. A., & Mandell, A. R. (2013). Do age-related increases in tip-of-the tongue experiences signify episodic memory impairments? *Psychological Science, 24,* 2489–2497.

Samson, D. R., Crittenden, A. N., Mabulla, I. A., Mabulla, A. Z. P., & Nunn, C. L. (2017). Chronotype variation drives night-time sentinel-like behaviour in hunter-gatherers. *Processing of the Royal Society B, 284*(1858), 20170967.

Sánchez-Álvarez, N., Extremera, N., & Fernández-Berrocal, P. (2016). The relation between emotional intelligence and subjective well-being: A meta-analytic investigation. *Journal of Positive Psychology, 11,* 276–285.

Sánchez-Villegas, A., Henríquez-Sánchez, P., Ruiz-Canela, M., Lahortiga, F., Molero, P., Toledo, E., & Martínez-González, M. A. (2015). A longitudinal analysis of diet quality scores and the risk of incident depression in the SUN Project. *BMC Medicine, 13,* 1.

Sanders, A. R., Beecham, G. W., Guo, S., Dawood, K., Rieger, G., Badner, J. A., ... Martin, E. R. (2017). Genome-wide association study of male sexual orientation. *Nature: Scientific Reports, 7*(1), 16950.

Sanders, A. R., Martin, E. R., Beecham, G. W., Guo, S., Dawood, K. Rieger, G. . . Bailey, J. M. (2015). Genome-wide scan demonstrates significant linkage for male sexual orientation. *Psychological Medicine, 45,* 1379–1388.

Sandler, W., Meir, I., Padden, C., & Aronoff, M. (2005). The emergence of grammar: Systematic structure in a new language. *PNAS, 102,* 2261–2265.

Sandoval, M., Leclerc, J. A., & Gómez, R. L. (2017). Words to sleep on: Naps facilitate verb generalization in habitually and nonhabitually napping preschoolers. *Child Development, 88*(5), 1615–1626.

Sandstrom, A. (2015, December 2). *Religious groups' policies on transgender members vary widely.* Pew Research Center (pewresearch.org).

Santangelo, V., Cavallina, C., Colucci, P., Santori, A., Macri, S., McGaugh, J. L., & Campolongo, P. (2018). Enhanced brain activity associated with memory access in highly superior autobiographical memory. *PNAS, 115,* 7795–7800.

Santavirta, T., Santavirta, N., & Gilman, S. E. (2018). Association of the World War II Finnish evacuation of children with psychiatric hospitalization in the next generation. *JAMA Psychiatry, 75,* 21–27.

Santos, H. C., Varnum, M. E. W., & Grossmann, I. (2017). Global increases in individualism. *Psychological Science, 28,* 1228–1239.

Sanz, C., Blicher, A., Dalke, K., Gratton-Fabri, L., McClure-Richards, T., & Fouts, R. (1998, Winter-Spring). Enrichment object use: Five chimpanzees' use of temporary and semi-permanent enrichment objects. *Friends of Washoe, 19*(1,2), 9–14.

Sanz, C., Morgan, D., & Gulick, S. (2004). New insights into chimpanzees, tools, and termites from the Congo Basin. *American Naturalist, 164,* 567–581.

Sapadin, L. A. (1988). Friendship and gender: Perspectives of professional men and women. *Journal of Social and Personal Relationships, 5,* 387–403.

Saphire-Bernstein, S., Way, B. M., Kim, H. S, Sherman, D. K., & Taylor, S. E. (2011). Oxytocin receptor gene (OXTR) is related to psychological resources. *PNAS, 108,* 15118–15122.

Sapolsky, R. (2005). The influence of social hierarchy on primate health. *Science, 308,* 648–652.

Sapolsky, R. (2015, September 3). Caitlyn Jenner and our cognitive dissonance. *Nautilus.* Retrieved from nautil.us/issue/28/2050/caitlyn-jenner-and-our-cognitive-dissonance

Sapolsky, R. M. (2018, November). The science of inequality. *Scientific American,* pp. 54–67.

Saposnik, G., Redelmeier, D., Ruff, C. C., & Tobler, P. N. (2016). Cognitive biases associated with medical decisions: A systematic review. *BMC Medical Informatics and Decision Making, 16,* 138.

Sarrasin, J. B., Nenciovici, L., Foisy, L.-M. B., Allaire-Duquette, G., Riopel, M., Masson, S. (2018). Effects of teaching the concept of neuroplasticity to induce a growth mindset on motivation, achievement, and brain activity: A meta-analysis. *Trends in Neuroscience and Education, 12,* 22–31.

Sarro, E. C., Wilson, D. A., & Sullivan, R. M. (2014). Maternal regulation of infant brain state. *Current Biology, 24,* 1664–1669.

Sauce, B., & Matzel, L. D. (2018). The paradox of intelligence: Heritability and malleability coexist in hidden gene-environment interplay. *Psychological Bulletin, 144,* 26–47.

Saunders, G. R. B., Elkins, I. J., Christensen, K., & McGue, M. (2018). The relationship between subjective well-being and mortality within discordant twin pairs from two independent samples. *Psychology and Aging, 33,* 439–447.

Savage, J. E., Jansen, P. R., Stringer, S., Watanabe, K., Bryois, J., de Leeuw, C. A., . . . & Grasby, K. L. (2018). Genome-wide association meta-analysis in 269,867 individuals identifies new genetic and functional links to intelligence. *Nature Genetics, 50,* 912–919.

Savage-Rumbaugh, E. S., Murphy, J., Sevcik, R. A., Brakke, K. E., Williams, S. L., & Rumbaugh, D. M., with commentary by Bates, E. (1993). Language comprehension in ape and child. *Monographs of the Society for Research in Child Development,* 58(233), 1–254.

Savage-Rumbaugh, E. S., Rumbaugh, D., & Fields, W. M. (2009). Empirical Kanzi: The ape language controversy revisited. *Skeptic, 15,* 25–33.

Savani, K., & Job, V. (2017). Reverse ego-depletion: Acts of self-control can improve subsequent performance in Indian cultural contexts. *Journal of Personality and Social Psychology, 113,* 589–607.

Savani, K., & Rattan, A. (2012). A choice mind-set increases the acceptance and maintenance of wealth inequality. *Psychological Science, 23,* 796–804.

Savic, I., Berglund, H., & Lindstrom, P. (2005). Brain response to putative pheromones in homosexual men. *PNAS, 102,* 7356–7361.

Savin-Williams, R., Joyner, K., & Rieger, G. (2012). Prevalence and stability of self-reported sexual orientation identity during young adulthood. *Archives of Sexual Behavior, 41,* 103–110.

Savitsky, K., Epley, N., & Gilovich, T. D. (2001). Do others judge us as harshly as we think? Overestimating the impact of our failures, shortcomings, and mishaps. *Journal of Personality and Social Psychology, 81,* 44–56.

Savitsky, K., & Gilovich, T. D. (2003). The illusion of transparency and the alleviation of speech anxiety. *Journal of Experimental Social Psychology, 39,* 618–625.

Savoy, C., & Beitel, P. (1996). Mental imagery for basketball. *International Journal of Sport Psychology, 27,* 454–462.

Sawyer, A. C. P., Miller-Lewis, L. R., Searle, A. K., & Sawyer, M. G. (2015). Is greater improvement in early self-regulation associated with fewer behavioral problems later in childhood? *Developmental Psychology,* 51, 1740–1755.

Sawyer, J., & Gampa, A. (2018). Implicit and explicit racial attitudes changed during Black Lives Matter. *Personality and Social Psychology Bulletin, 44,* 1039–1059.

Sayer, L. C. (2016). Trends in women's and men's time use, 1965–2012: Back to the future? In S. M. McHale, V. King, J. Van Hook, and A. Booth (Eds.), *Gender and couple relationships.* Cham, Switzerland: Springer International Publishing.

Sayette, M. A., Schooler, J. W., & Reichle, E. D. (2010). Out for a smoke: The impact of cigarette craving on zoning out during reading. *Psychological Science, 21*, 26–30.

Sbarra, D. A., Hasselmo, K., & Bourassa, K. J. (2015). Divorce and health: Beyond individual differences. *Current Directions in Psychological Science, 24*, 109–113.

Scaini, S., Belotti, R., Ogliari, A., & Battaglia, M. (2016). A comprehensive meta-analysis of cognitive-behavioral interventions for social anxiety disorder in children and adolescents. *Journal of Anxiety Disorders, 42*, 105–112.

Scarf, D., Boy, K., Reinert, A. U., Devine, J., Güntürkün, O., & Colombo, M. (2016). Orthographic processing in pigeons (*Columba livia*). *PNAS, 113*, 11272–11276.

Scarr, S. (1984, May). What's a parent to do? A conversation with E. Hall. *Psychology Today*, pp. 58–63.

Scarr, S. (1989). Protecting general intelligence: Constructs and consequences for interventions. In R. J. Linn (Ed.), *Intelligence: Measurement, theory, and public policy*. Champaign: University of Illinois Press.

Scarr, S. (1993, May/June). Quoted in Nature's thumbprint: So long, superparents. *Psychology Today*, p. 16.

Schab, F. R. (1991). Odor memory: Taking stock. *Psychological Bulletin, 109*, 242–251.

Schachter, S., & Singer, J. E. (1962). Cognitive, social and physiological determinants of emotional state. *Psychological Review, 69*, 379–399.

Schacter, D. L. (1992). Understanding implicit memory: A cognitive neuroscience approach. *American Psychologist, 47*, 559–569.

Schacter, D. L. (1996). *Searching for memory: The brain, the mind, and the past*. New York: Basic Books.

Schaffer, A., Isometsä, E. T., Tondo, L., Moreno, D., Turecki, G., Reis, C., . . . Ha, K. (2015). International society for bipolar disorders task force on suicide: Meta-analyses and meta-regression of correlates of suicide attempts and suicide deaths in bipolar disorder. *Bipolar Disorders, 17*, 1–16.

Schaie, K. W., & Geiwitz, J. (1982). *Adult development and aging*. Boston: Little, Brown.

Schalock, R. L., Borthwick-Duffy, S., Bradley, V. J., Buntinx, W. H. E., Coulter, D. L., Craig, E. M. (2010). *Intellectual disability: Definition, classification, and systems of supports* (11th edition). Washington, DC: American Association on Intellectual and Developmental Disabilities.

Scheier, M. F., & Carver, C. S. (1992). Effects of optimism on psychological and physical well-being: Theoretical overview and empirical update. *Cognitive Therapy and Research, 16*, 201–228.

Schein, E. H. (1956). The Chinese indoctrination program for prisoners of war: A study of attempted brainwashing. *Psychiatry, 19*, 149–172.

Schick, V., Herbenick, D., Reece, M., Sanders, S. A., Dodge, B., Middlestadt, S. E., & Fortenberry, J. D. (2010). Sexual behaviors, condom use, and sexual health of Americans over 50: Implications for sexual health promotion for older adults. *Journal of Sexual Medicine, 7*(suppl 5), 315–329.

Schiffenbauer, A., & Schiavo, R. S. (1976). Physical distance and attraction: An intensification effect. *Journal of Experimental Social Psychology, 12*, 274–282.

Schilt, T., de Win, M. M. L, Koeter, M., Jager, G., Korf, D. J., van den Brink, W., & Schmand, B. (2007). Cognition in novice Ecstasy users with minimal exposure to other drugs. *Archives of General Psychiatry, 64*, 728–736.

Schizophrenia Working Group of the Psychiatric Genomics Consortium. (2014). Biological insights from 108 schizophrenia-associated genetic loci. *Nature, 511*, 421–427.

Schlomer, G. L., Del Giudice, M., & Ellis, B. J. (2011). Parent-offspring conflict theory: An evolutionary framework for understanding conflict within human families. *Psychological Review, 118*, 496–521.

Schmidt, F. L., & Hunter, J. E. (1998). The validity and utility of selection methods in personnel psychology: Practical and theoretical implications of 85 years of research findings. *Psychological Bulletin, 124*, 262–274.

Schmidt, F. T. C., Nagy, G., Fleckenstein, J., Möller, J., & Retelsdorf, J. (2018). Same same, but different? Relations between facets of conscientiousness and grit. *European Journal of Personality, 32*, 705–720.

Schmitt, D. P. (2003). Universal sex differences in the desire for sexual variety; tests from 52 nations, 6 continents, and 13 islands. *Journal of Personality and Social Psychology, 85*, 85–104.

Schmitt, D. P. (2007). Sexual strategies across sexual orientations: How personality traits and culture relate to sociosexuality among gays, lesbians, bisexuals, and heterosexuals. *Journal of Psychology and Human Sexuality, 18*, 183–214.

Schmitt, D. P., & Allik, J. (2005). Simultaneous administration of the Rosenberg Self-esteem Scale in 53 nations: Exploring the universal and culture-specific features of global self-esteem. *Journal of Personality and Social Psychology, 89*, 623–642.

Schmitt, D. P., Allik, J., McCrae, R. R., & Benet-Martínez, V., Reips, U.-D. (2007). The geographic distribution of Big Five personality traits: Patterns and profiles of human self-description across 56 nations. *Journal of Cross-Cultural Psychology, 38*, 173–212.

Schmitt, D. P., & Fuller, R. C. (2015). On the varieties of sexual experience: Cross-cultural links between religiosity and human mating strategies. *Psychology of Religion and Spirituality, 7*, 314–326.

Schmitt, D. P., Jonason, P. K., Byerley, G. J., Flores, S. D., Illbeck, B. E., O'Leary, K. N., & Qudrat, A. (2012). A reexamination of sex differences in sexuality: New studies reveal old truths. *Current Directions in Psychological Science, 21*, 135–139.

Schnall, E., Wassertheil-Smnoller, S., Swencionis, C., Zemon, V., Tinker, L., O'Sullivan, M. J., . . . Goodwin, M. (2010). The relationship between religion and cardiovascular outcomes and all-cause mortality in the Women's Health Initiative Observational Study. *Psychology and Health, 25*, 249–263.

Schneider, S. L. (2001). In search of realistic optimism: Meaning, knowledge, and warm fuzziness. *American Psychologist, 56*, 250–263.

Schneier, B. (2007, May 17). Virginia Tech lesson: Rare risks breed irrational responses. *Wired* (wired.com).

Schoeneman, T. J. (1994). Individualism. In V. S. Ramachandran (Ed.), *Encyclopedia of human behavior* (Vol. 2, pp. 631–643). San Diego: Academic Press.

Schofield, J. W. (1986). Black-White contact in desegregated schools. In M. Hewstone & R. Brown (Eds.), *Contact and conflict in intergroup encounters* (pp. 79–92). Oxford, England: Basil Blackwell.

Scholtz, S., Miras, A. D., Chhina, N., Prechtl, C. G., Sleeth, M. L., Daud, N. M., . . . Vincent, R. P. (2013). Obese patients after gastric bypass surgery have lower brain-hedonic responses to food than after gastric banding. *Gut, 63*, 891–902.

Schonfield, D., & Robertson, B. A. (1966). Memory storage and aging. *Canadian Journal of Psychology, 20*, 228–236.

Schooler, J. W., Gerhard, D., & Loftus, E. F. (1986). Qualities of the unreal. *Journal of Experimental Psychology: Learning, Memory, and Cognition, 12*, 171–181.

Schorr, E. A., Fox, N.A., van Wassenhove, V., & Knudsen, E. I. (2005). Auditory-visual fusion in speech perception in children with cochlear implants. *PNAS, 102*, 18748–18750.

Schreiber, F. R. (1973). *Sybil*. Chicago: Regnery.

Schroeder, J., Caruso, E. M., & Epley, N. (2016). Many hands make overlooked work: Over-claiming of responsibility increases with group size. *Journal of Experimental Psychology: Applied, 22*, 238–246.

Schroeder, J., & Epley, N. (2015). The sound of intellect: Speech reveals a thoughtful mind, increasing a job candidate's appeal. *Psychological Science, 26*, 877–891.

Schroeder, J., & Epley, N. (2016). Mistaking minds and machines: How speech affects dehumanization and anthropomorphism. *Journal of Experimental Psychology: General, 145*, 1427–1437.

Schuch, F. B., Vancampfort, D., Rosenbaum, S., Richards, J., Ward, P. B., & Stubbs, B. (2016). Exercise improves physical and psychological quality of life in people with depression: A meta-analysis including the evaluation of control group response. *Psychiatry Research, 241*, 47–54.

Schuch, F., Vancampfort, D., Firth, J., Rosenbaum, S., Ward, P., Silva, E. S., . . . Stubbs, B. (2018). Physical activity and incident depression: A meta-analysis of prospective cohort studies. *American Journal of Psychiatry, 175*, 631–648.

Schultheiss, O., Wiemers, U. & Wolf, O. (2014). Implicit need for achievement predicts attenuated cortisol responses to difficult tasks. *Journal of Research in Personality, 48*, 84–92.

Schuman, H., & Scott, J. (June, 1989). Generations and collective memories. *American Sociological Review, 54*, 359–381.

Schumann, K., & Ross, M. (2010). Why women apologize more than men: Gender differences in thresholds for perceiving offensive behavior. *Psychological Science, 21*, 1649–1655.

Schutte, N. S., Malouff, J. M., Thorsteinsson, E. B., Bhullar, N., & Rooke, S. E. (2007). A meta-analytic investigation of the relationship between emotional intelligence and health. *Personality and Individual Differences, 42*, 921–933.

Schutte, N. S., Palanisamy, S. K. A., & McFarlane, J. R. (2016). The relationship between positive characteristics and longer telomeres. *Psychology & Health, 31*, 1466–1480.

Schuyler, A. C., Kintzle, S., Lucas, C. L., Moore, H., & Castro, C. A. (2017). Military sexual assault (MSA) among veterans in Southern California: Associations with physical health, psychological health, and risk behaviors. *Traumatology, 23*, 223–234.

Schwartz, B. (1984). *Psychology of learning and behavior* (2nd ed.). New York: Norton.

Schwartz, B. (2000). Self-determination: The tyranny of freedom. *American Psychologist, 55*, 79–88.

Schwartz, B. (2004). *The paradox of choice: Why more is less*. New York: Ecco/HarperCollins.

Schwartz, H. W., Eichstaedt, J., Kern, M. L., Dziurzynski, L., Ramones, S., Agrawal, M., . . . Ungar, L. (2013). Personality, gender, and age in the language of social media: The open-vocabulary approach. *PLOS ONE, 8*, e73791.

Schwartz, J. M., Stoessel, P. W., Baxter, L. R., Jr., Martin, K. M., & Phelps, M. E. (1996). Systematic changes in cerebral glucose metabolic rate after successful behavior modification treatment of obsessive-compulsive disorder. *Archives of General Psychiatry, 53*, 109–113.

Schwartz, P. J. (2011). Season of birth in schizophrenia: A maternal-fetal chronobiological hypothesis. *Medical Hypotheses, 76*, 785–793.

Schwartz, S. H., & Rubel-Lifschitz, T. (2009). Cross-national variation in the size of sex differences in values: Effects of gender equality. *Journal of Personality and Social Psychology, 97*, 171–185.

Schwartzman-Morris, J., & Putterman, C. (2012). Gender differences in the pathogenesis and outcome of lupus and of lupus nephritis. *Clinical and Developmental Immunology, 2012*, 604892.

Schwarz, A. (2012, June 9). Risky rise of the good-grade pill. *The New York Times* (nytimes.com).

Schwarz, A., & Cohen, S. (2013, March 31). A.D.H.D. seen in 11% of U.S. children as diagnoses rise. *The New York Times* (nytimes.com).

Schwarz, N., Strack, F., Kommer, D., & Wagner, D. (1987). Soccer, rooms, and the quality of your life: Mood effects on judgments of satisfaction with life in general and with specific domains. *European Journal of Social Psychology, 17*, 69–79.

Sclafani, A. (1995). How food preferences are learned: Laboratory animal models. *PNAS, 54*, 419–427.

Scoboria, A., Wade, K. A., Lindsay, D. S., Azad, T., Strange, D., Ost, J., & Hyman, I. E. (2017). A mega-analysis of memory reports from eight peer-reviewed false memory implantation studies. *Memory, 25*, 146–163.

Scopelliti, I., Loewenstein, G., & Vosgerau, J. (2015). You call it "self-exuberance"; I call it "bragging": Miscalibrated predictions of emotional responses to self-promotion. *Psychological Science, 26*, 903–914.

Scott-Sheldon, L., Carey, K. B., Elliott, J. C., Garey, L., & Carey, M. P. (2014). Efficacy of alcohol interventions for first-year college students: A meta-analytic review of randomized controlled trials. *Journal of Consulting and Clinical Psychology, 82*, 177–188.

Scott-Sheldon, L. A. J., Terry, D. L., Carey, K. B., Garey, L., & Carey, M. P. (2012). Efficacy of expectancy challenge interventions to reduce college student drinking: A meta-analytic review. *Psychology of Addictive Behaviors, 26*, 393–405.

Scott, D. J., Stohler, C. S., Egnatuk, C. M., Wang, H., Koeppe, R. A., & Zubieta, J.-K. (2007). Individual differences in reward responding explain placebo-induced expectations and effects. *Neuron, 55*, 325–336.

Scott, K. M., Wells, J. E. Angermeyer, M., Brugha, T. S., Bromet, E., Demyttenaere, K., . . . Kessler, R. C. (2010). Gender and the relationship between marital status and first onset of mood, anxiety and substance use disorders. *Psychological Medicine, 40*, 1495–1505.

Scullin, M. K., & Bliwise, D. L. (2015). Sleep, cognition, and normal aging: Integrating a half century of multidisciplinary research. *Perspectives on Psychological Science, 10*, 97–137.

Scullin, M. K., & McDaniel, M. A. (2010). Remembering to execute a goal: Sleep on it! *Psychological Science, 21*, 1028–1035.

Sdorow, L. M. (2005). The people behind psychology. In B. Perlman, L. McCann, & W. Buskist (Eds.), *Voices of experience: Memorable talks from the National Institute on the Teaching of Psychology*. Washington, DC: American Psychological Society.

Seal, K. H., Bertenthal, D., Miner, C. R., Sen, S., & Marmar, C. (2007). Bringing the war back home: Mental health disorders among 103,788 U.S. veterans returning from Iraq and Afghanistan seen at Department of Veterans Affairs facilities. *Archives of Internal Medicine, 167*, 467–482.

Sechrest, L., Stickle, T. R., & Stewart, M. (1998). The role of assessment in clinical psychology. In A. Bellack, M. Hersen (series eds.), & C. R. Reynolds (vol. ed.), *Comprehensive clinical psychology: Vol. 4. Assessment* (pp. 1–32). New York: Pergamon.

Sedley, W., Gander, P. E., Kumar, S., Oya, H., Kovach, C. K., Nourski, K. V., . . . Griffiths, T. D. (2015). Intracranial mapping of a cortical tinnitus system using residual inhibition. *Current Biology, 25*, 1208–1214.

Sedlmeier, P., Eberth, J., Schwarz, M., Zimmermann, D., Haarig, F., Jaeger, S., & Kunze, S. (2012). The psychological effects of meditation: A meta-analysis. *Psychological Bulletin, 138*, 1139–1171.

Seehagen, S., Konrad, C., Herbert, J. S., & Schneider, S. (2015). Timely sleep facilitates declarative memory consolidation in infants. *PNAS, 112*, 1625–1629.

Seeman, P., Guan, H.-C., & Van Tol, H. H. M. (1993). Dopamine D4 receptors elevated in schizophrenia. *Nature, 365*, 441–445.

Seery, M. D. (2011). Resilience: A silver lining to experiencing adverse life events. *Current Directions in Psychological Science, 20*, 390–394.

Segal, N. L. (2005). *Indivisible by two: Lives of extraordinary twins*. Cambridge: Harvard University Press.

Segal, N. L., McGuire, S. A., & Stohs, J. H. (2012). What virtual twins reveal about general intelligence and other behaviors. *Personality and Individual Differences, 53*, 405–410.

Segall, M. H., Dasen, P. R., Berry, J. W., & Poortinga, Y. H. (1990). *Human behavior in global perspective: An introduction to cross-cultural psychology*. New York: Pergamon.

Sege, R., Nykiel-Bub, L., & Selk, S. (2015). Sex differences in institutional support for junior biomedical researchers. *Journal of American Medical Association, 314*, 1175–1177.

Segerstrom, S. C., Taylor, S. E., Kemeny, M. E., & Fahey, J. L. (1998). Optimism is associated with mood, coping, and immune change in response to stress. *Journal of Personality and Social Psychology, 74*, 1646–1655.

Seibert, S. E., Wang, G., & Courtright, S. H. (2011). Antecedents and consequences of psychological and team empowerment in organizations: A meta-analytic review. *Journal of Applied Psychology, 96*, 981–1003.

Sejnowski, T. (2016, January 20). Quoted in "Memory capacity of brain is 10 times more than previously thought." *KurzweilAI Accelerating Intelligence News* (kurzweilai.net).

Self, C. E. (1994). *Moral culture and victimization in residence halls*. Unpublished master's thesis. Bowling Green University.

Seligman, M. E. P. (1975). *Helplessness: On depression, development and death*. San Francisco: Freeman.

Seligman, M. E. P. (1991). *Learned optimism: How to change your mind and your life*. New York: Knopf.

Seligman, M. E. P. (1994). *What you can change and what you can't*. New York: Knopf.

Seligman, M. E. P. (1995). The efffectiveness of psychotherapy: The *Consumer Reports* study. *American Psychologist, 50*, 965–974.

Seligman, M. E. P. (2002). *Authentic happiness: Using the new positive psychology to realize your potential for lasting fulfillment*. New York: Free Press.

Seligman, M. E. P. (2011). *Flourish: A visionary new understanding of happiness and well-being*. New York: Free Press.

Seligman, M. E. P. (2012, May 8). Quoted in A. C. Brooks, America and the value of "earned success." *The Wall Street Journal* (wsj.com).

Seligman, M. E. P., Ernst, R. M., Gillham, J., Reivich, K., & Linkins, M. (2009). Positive education: Positive psychology and classroom interventions. *Oxford Review of Education, 35*, 293–311.

Seligman, M. E. P., & Maier, S. F. (1967). Failure to escape traumatic shock. *Journal of Experimental Psychology, 74*, 1–9.

Seligman, M. E. P., Steen, T. A., Park, N., & Peterson, C. (2005). Positive psychology progress: Empirical validation of interventions. *American Psychologist, 60*, 410–421.

Seligman, M. E. P., & Yellen, A. (1987). What is a dream? *Behavior Research and Therapy, 25*, 1–24.

Sellers, H. (2010). *You don't look like anyone I know*. New York: Riverhead Books.

Selye, H. (1936). A syndrome produced by diverse nocuous agents. *Nature, 138*, 32.

Selye, H. (1976). *The stress of life*. New York: McGraw-Hill.

Senghas, A., & Coppola, M. (2001). Children creating language: How Nicaraguan Sign Language acquired a spatial grammar. *Psychological Science, 12*, 323–328.

Senju, A., Southgate, V., White, S., & Frith, U. (2009). Mindblind eyes: An absence of spontaneous theory of mind in Asperger syndrome. *Science, 325*, 883–885.

Serpeloni, F., Radtke, K, de Assis, S. G., Henning, F., Nätt, D., & Elbert, T. (2017). Grandmaternal stress during pregnancy and DNA methylation of the third generation: an epigenome-wide association study. *Translational Psychiatry, 7*(8), e1202.

Service, R. F. (1994). Will a new type of drug make memory-making easier? *Science, 266*, 218–219.

Sest, N., & March, E. (2017). Constructing the cyber-troll: Psychopathy, sadism, and empathy. *Personality and Individual Differences, 119*, 69–72.

Sexton, C. E., Betts, J. F., Demnitz, N., Dawes, H., Ebmeier, K. P., & Johansen-Berg, H. (2016). A systematic review of MRI studies examining the relationship between physical fitness and activity and the white matter of the ageing brain. *NeuroImage, 131*, 81–90.

Shackman, A. J., Tromp, D. P., Stockbridge, M. D., Kaplan, C. M., Tillman, R. M., & Fox, A. S. (2016). Dispositional negativity: An integrative psychological and neurobiological perspective. *Psychological Bulletin, 142*, 1275–1314.

Shadish, W. R., & Baldwin, S. A. (2005). Effects of behavioral marital therapy: A meta-analysis of randomized controlled trials. *Journal of Consulting and Clinical Psychology, 73*, 6–14.

Shafir, E., & LeBoeuf, R. A. (2002). Rationality. *Annual Review of Psychology, 53*, 491–517.

Shaki, S. (2013). What's in a kiss? Spatial experience shapes directional bias during kissing. *Journal of Nonverbal Behavior, 37*, 43–50.

Shallcross, A. J., Ford, B. Q., Floerke, V. A., & Mauss, I. B. (2013). Getting better with age: The relationship between age, acceptance, and negative affect. *Journal of Personality and Social Psychology, 104*, 734–749.

Shanahan, L., McHale, S. M., Osgood, D. W., & Crouter, A. C. (2007). Conflict frequency with mothers and fathers from middle childhood to late adolescence: Within- and between-families comparisons. *Developmental Psychology, 43*, 539–550.

Shane, S. (2015, June 24). Homegrown extremists tied to deadlier toll than jihadis in U.S. since 9/11. *The New York Times* (nytimes.com).

Shannon, B. J., Raichle, M. E., Snyder, A. Z., Fair, D. A., Mills, K. L., Zhang, D., . . . Kiehl, K. A. (2011). Premotor functional connectivity predicts impulsivity in juvenile offenders. *PNAS, 108*, 11241–11245.

Shapiro, F. (1999). Eye movement desensitization and reprocessing (EMDR) and the anxiety disorders: Clinical and research implications of an integrated psychotherapy treatment. *Journal of Anxiety Disorders, 13*, 35–67.

Shapiro, K. A., Moo, L. R., & Caramazza, A. (2006). Cortical signatures of noun and verb production. *PNAS, 103*, 1644–1649.

Shargorodsky, J., Curhan, S. G., Curhan, G. C., & Eavey, R. (2010). Changes of prevalence of hearing loss in US adolescents. *Journal of the American Medical Association, 304*, 772–778.

Shariff, A. F., Greene, J. D., Karremans, J. C., Luguri, J. B., Clark, C. J., Schooler, J. W., . . . Vohs, K. D. (2014). Free will and punishment: A mechanistic view of human nature reduces retribution. *Psychological Science, 25*, 1563–1570.

Shaver, P. R., Morgan, H. J., & Wu, S. (1996). Is love a basic emotion? *Personal Relationships, 3*, 81–96.

Shaw, B. A., Liang, J., & Krause, N. (2010). Age and race differences in the trajectories of self-esteem. *Psychology and Aging, 25*, 84–94.

Shaw, J., & Porter, S. (2015). Constructing rich false memories of committing crime. *Psychological Science, 26*, 291–301.

Shedler, J. (2009, March 23). *That was then, this is now: Psychoanalytic psychotherapy for the rest of us.* Unpublished manuscript, Department of Psychiatry, University of Colorado Health Sciences Center, Aurora, CO.

Shedler, J. (2010). The efficacy of psychodynamic psychotherapy. *American Psychologist, 65*, 98–109.

Sheeber, L. B., Feil, E. G., Seeley, J. R., Leve, C., Gau, J. M., Davis, B., . . . Allan, S. (2017). Mom-net: Evaluation of an internet-facilitated cognitive behavioral intervention for low-income depressed mothers. *Journal of Consulting and Clinical Psychology, 85*, 355–366.

Sheehan, S. (1982). *Is there no place on earth for me?* Boston: Houghton Mifflin.

Sheldon, K. M., & Lyubomirsky, S. (2012). The challenge of staying happier: Testing the hedonic adaptation prevention model. *Personality and Social Psychology Bulletin, 38*, 670–680.

Sheltzer, J. M., & Smith, J. C. (2014). Elite male faculty in the life sciences employ fewer females. *PNAS, 111*, 10107–10112.

Shenton, M. E. (1992). Abnormalities of the left temporal lobe and thought disorder in schizophrenia: A quantitative magnetic resonance imaging study. *New England Journal of Medicine, 327*, 604–612.

Shepard, R. N. (1990). *Mind sights.* New York: Freeman.

Shepperd, J. A., Waters, E., Weinstein, N. D., & Klein, W. M. P. (2015). A primer on unrealistic optimism. *Current Directions in Psychological Science, 24*, 232–237.

Shergill, S. S., Bays, P. M., Frith, C. D., & Wolpert, D. M. (2003). Two eyes for an eye: The neuroscience of force escalation. *Science, 301*, 187.

Sherif, M. (1966). *In common predicament: Social psychology of intergroup conflict and cooperation.* Boston: Houghton Mifflin.

Sherif, M., Radhakrishnan, R., D'Souza, D. C., & Ranganathan, M. (2016). Human laboratory studies on cannabinoids and psychosis. *Biological Psychiatry, 79*, 526–538.

Sherman, L. E., Payton, A. A., Hernandez, L. M., Greenfield, P. M., & Dapretto, M. (2016). The power of the like in adolescence: Effects of peer influence on neural and behavioral responses to social media. *Psychological Science, 27*, 1027–1035.

Sherman, R. A., Rauthmann, J. F., Brown, N. A., Serfass, D. S., & Jones, A. B. (2015). The independent effects of personality and situations on real-time expressions of behavior and emotion. *Journal of Personality and Social Psychology, 109*, 872–888.

Sherry, D., & Vaccarino, A. L. (1989). Hippocampus and memory for food caches in black-capped chickadees. *Behavioral Neuroscience, 103*, 308–318.

Shettleworth, S. J. (1973). Food reinforcement and the organization of behavior in golden hamsters. In R. A. Hinde & J. Stevenson-Hinde (Eds.), *Constraints on learning.* London, England: Academic Press.

Shettleworth, S. J. (1993). Where is the comparison in comparative cognition? Alternative research programs. *Psychological Science, 4*, 179–184.

Shiell, M. M., Champoux, F., & Zatorre, R. (2014). Enhancement of visual motion detection thresholds in early deaf people. *PLOS ONE, 9*, e90498.

Shilsky, J. D., Hartman, T. J., Kris-Etherton, P. M., Rogers, C. J., Sharkey, N. A., & Nickols-Richardson, S. M. (2012). Partial sleep deprivation and energy balance in adults: An emerging issue for consideration by dietetics practitioners. *Journal of the Academy of Nutrition and Dietetics, 112*, 1785–1797.

Shiromani, P. J., Horvath, T., Redline, S., & Van Cauter E. (Eds.) (2012). *Sleep loss and obesity: Intersecting epidemics.* New York: Springer Science.

Shockley, K. M., Ispas, D., Rossi, M. E., & Levine, E. L. (2012). A meta-analytic investigation of the relationship between state affect, discrete emotions, and job performance. *Human Performance, 25*, 377–411.

Shor, E., Roelfs, D. J., & Yogev, T. (2013). The strength of family ties: A meta-analysis and meta-regression of self-reported social support and mortality. *Social Networks, 35*, 626–638.

Shor, E., Roelfs, D. J., Bugyi, P., & Schwartz, J. E. (2012). Meta-analysis of marital dissolution and mortality: Reevaluating the intersection of gender and age. *Social Science & Medicine, 75*, 46–59.

Shors, T. J. (2014). The adult brain makes new neurons, and effortful learning keeps them alive. *Current Directions in Psychological Science, 23*, 311–318.

Short, M., Gradisar, M., Wright, H., Dewald, J., Wolfson, A., & Carskadon, M. (2013). A cross-cultural comparison of sleep duration between U.S. and Australian adolescents: The effect of school start time, parent-set bedtimes, and extra-curricular load. *Health Education Behavior, 40*, 323–330.

Showers, C. (1992). The motivational and emotional consequences of considering positive or negative possibilities for an upcoming event. *Journal of Personality and Social Psychology, 63*, 474–484.

Shrestha, A., Nohr, E. A., Bech, B. H., Ramlau-Hansen, C. H., & Olsen, J. (2011). Smoking and alcohol during pregnancy and age of menarche in daughters. *Human Reproduction, 26*, 259–265.

Shuffler, M. L., Burke, C. S., Kramer, W. S., & Salas, E. (2013). Leading teams: Past, present, and future perspectives. In M. G. Rumsey (Ed.), *The Oxford handbook of leadership.* New York: Oxford University Press.

Shuffler, M. L., DiazGranados, D., & Salas, E. (2011). There's a science for that: Team development interventions in organizations. *Current Directions in Psychological Science, 20*, 365–372.

Shuwairi, S. M., & Johnson, S. P. (2013). Oculomotor exploration of impossible figures in early infancy. *Infancy, 18*, 221–232.

Siegel, E. H., Sands, M. K., Van den Noortgate, W., Condon, P., Chang, Y., Dy, J., . . . & Barrett, L. F. (2018). Emotion fingerprints or emotion populations? A meta-analytic investigation of autonomic features of emotion categories. *Psychological Bulletin, 144*, 343–393.

Siegel, J. M. (2012). Suppression of sleep for mating. *Science, 337*, 1610–1611.

Siegel, R. K. (1977, October). Hallucinations. *Scientific American*, pp. 132–140.

Siegel, R. K. (1980). The psychology of life after death. *American Psychologist, 35*, 911–931.

Siegel, R. K. (1982, October). Quoted by J. Hooper, Mind tripping. *Omni*, pp. 72–82, 159–160.

Siegel, R. K. (1984, March 15). Personal communication.

Siegel, R. K. (1990). *Intoxication: Life in pursuit of artificial paradise.* New York: Pocket Books.

Siegel, S. (2005). Drug tolerance, drug addiction, and drug anticipation. *Current Directions in Psychological Science, 14*, 296–300.

Siegler, R. S., & Ellis, S. (1996). Piaget on childhood. *Psychological Science, 7*, 211–215.

Silber, M. H., Ancoli-Israel, S., Bonnet, M. H., Chokroverty, S., Grigg-Damberger, M. M., Hirshkowitz, M., . . . Iber, C. (2007). The visual scoring of sleep in adults. *Journal of Clinical Sleep Medicine, 3*, 121–131.

Silbersweig, D. A., Stern, E., Frith, C., Cahill, C., Holmes, A., Grootoonk, S., Seaward, J., . . . Frackowiak, R. S. J. (1995). A functional neuroanatomy of hallucinations in schizophrenia. *Nature, 378*, 176–179.

Silva, C. E., & Kirsch, I. (1992). Interpretive sets, expectancy, fantasy proneness, and dissociation as predictors of hypnotic response. *Journal of Personality and Social Psychology, 63*, 847–856.

Silver, M., & Geller, D. (1978). On the irrelevance of evil: The organization and individual action. *Journal of Social Issues, 34*, 125–136.

Silver, N. (2012). *The signal and the noise: Why so many predictions fail—but some don't.* New York: Penguin.

Silver, R. C., Holman, E. A., Anderson, J. P., Poulin, M., McIntosh, D. N., & Gil-Rivas, V. (2013). Mental- and physical-health effects of acute exposure to media images of the September 11, 2001 attacks and Iraq War. *Psychological Science, 24*, 1623–1634.

Silver, R. C., Holman, E. A., McIntosh, D. N., Poulin, M., & Gil-Rivas, V. (2002). Nationwide longitudinal study of psychological responses to September 11. *Journal of the American Medical Association, 288*, 1235–1244.

Silverman, K., Evans, S. M., Strain, E. C., & Griffiths, R. R. (1992). Withdrawal syndrome after the double-blind cessation of caffeine consumption. *New England Journal of Medicine, 327*, 1109–1114.

Silverstein, B. H., Snodgrass, M., Shevrin, H., & Kushwaha, R. (2015). P3b, consciousness, and complex unconscious processing. *Cortex, 73*, 216–227.

Silwa, J., & Frehwald, W. A. (2017). A dedicated network for social interaction processing in the primate brain. *Science, 356*, 745–749.

Simon, H. A., & Chase, W. G. (1973). Skill in chess. *American Scientist, 61*, 394–403.

Simon, V., Czobor, P., Bálint, S., Mésáros, A., & Bitter, I. (2009). Prevalence and correlates of adult attention-deficit hyperactivity disorder: Meta-analysis. *British Journal of Psychiatry, 194*, 204–211.

Simons, D. J., & Chabris, C. F. (1999). Gorillas in our midst: Sustained inattentional blindness for dynamic events. *Perception, 28*, 1059–1074.

Simons, D. J., & Levin, D. T. (1998). Failure to detect changes to people during a real-world interaction. *Psychonomic Bulletin & Review, 5*, 644–649.

Simons, D. J., Boot, W. R., Charness, N., Gathercole, S. E., Chabris, C. F., Hambrick, D. Z., & Stine-Morrow, E. A. L. (2016). Do "brain-training" programs work? *Psychological Science in the Public Interest, 17*, 103–186.

Simonton, D. K. (1988). Age and outstanding achievement: What do we know after a century of research? *Psychological Bulletin, 104*, 251–267.

Simonton, D. K. (1990). Creativity in the later years: Optimistic prospects for achievement. *The Gerontologist, 30,* 626–631.

Simonton, D. K. (1992). The social context of career success and course for 2,026 scientists and inventors. *Personality and Social Psychology Bulletin, 18,* 452–463.

Simonton, D. K. (2012a). Teaching creativity: Current findings, trends, and controversies in the psychology of creativity. *Teaching of Psychology, 39,* 217–222.

Simonton, D. K. (2012b, November–December). The science of genius. *Scientific American Mind,* pp. 35–41.

Simpson, A., & Rios, K. (2016). How do U.S. Christians and atheists stereotype one another's moral values? *International Journal for the Psychology of Religion, 26,* 320–336.

Sin, N. L., Graham-Engeland, J. E., Ong, A. D., & Almeida, D. M. (2015). Affective reactivity to daily stressors is associated with elevated inflammation. *Health Psychology, 34,* 154–1165.

Sin, N. L., & Lyubomirsky, S. (2009). Enhancing well-being and alleviating depressive symptoms with positive psychology interventions: A practice-friendly meta-analysis. *Journal of Clinical Psychology: In session, 65,* 467–487.

Sinclair, R. C., Hoffman, C., Mark, M. M., Martin, L. L., & Pickering, T. L. (1994). Construct accessibility and the misattribution of arousal: Schachter and Singer revisited. *Psychological Science, 5,* 15–18.

Singer, J. L. (1981). Clinical intervention: New developments in methods and evaluation. In L. T. Benjamin, Jr. (Ed.), *The G. Stanley Hall Lecture Series* (Vol. 1). Washington, DC: American Psychological Association.

Singer, T., Seymour, B., O'Doherty, J., Kaube, H., Dolan, R. J., & Frith, C. (2004). Empathy for pain involves the affective but not sensory components of pain. *Science, 303,* 1157–1162.

Singh, S. (1997). *Fermat's enigma: The epic quest to solve the world's greatest mathematical problem.* New York: Bantam Books.

Singh, S., & Riber, K. A. (1997, November). Fermat's last stand. *Scientific American,* pp. 68–73.

Sio, U. N., Monahan, P., & Ormerod, T. (2013). Sleep on it, but only if it is difficult: Effects of sleep on problem solving. *Memory and Cognition, 41,* 159–166.

Sireteanu, R. (1999). Switching on the infant brain. *Science, 286,* 59, 61.

Skeem, J., Kennealy, P., Monahan, J., Peterson, J., & Appelbaum, P. (2016). Psychosis uncommonly and inconsistently precedes violence among high-risk individuals. *Clinical Psychological Science, 4,* 40–49.

Skeem, J. L., & Cooke, D. J. (2010). Is criminal behavior a central component of psychopathy? Conceptual directions for resolving the debate. *Psychological Assessment, 22,* 433–445.

Skinner, B. F. (1953). *Science and human behavior.* New York: Macmillan.

Skinner, B. F. (1956). A case history in scientific method. *American Psychologist, 11,* 221–233.

Skinner, B. F. (1961, November). Teaching machines. *Scientific American,* pp. 91–102.

Skinner, B. F. (1966). *The behavior of organisms: An experimental analysis.* New York: Appleton-Century-Crofs. (Original work published 1938.)

Skinner, B. F. (1983, September). Origins of a behaviorist. *Psychology Today,* pp. 22–33.

Skinner, B. F. (1989). Teaching machines. *Science, 243,* 1535.

Sklar, L. S., & Anisman, H. (1981). Stress and cancer. *Psychological Bulletin, 89,* 369–406.

Skov, R. B., & Sherman, S. J. (1986). Information-gathering processes: Diagnosticity, hypothesis-confirmatory strategies, and perceived hypothesis confirmation. *Journal of Experimental Social Psychology, 22,* 93–121.

Slatcher, R. B., Selcuk, E., & Ong, A. (2015). Perceived partner responsiveness predicts diurnal cortisol profiles 10 years later. *Psychological Science, 26,* 972–982.

Slaughter, V., Imuta, K., Peterson, C. C., & Henry, J. D. (2015). Meta-analysis of theory of mind and peer popularity in the preschool and early school years. *Child Development, 86,* 1159–1174.

Slovic, P., Västfjälla, D., Erlandsson, A., & Gregory, R. (2017). Iconic photographs and the ebb and flow of empathic response to humanitarian disasters. PNAS, 114, 640–644.

Slutske, W. S., Moffitt, T. E., Poulton, R., & Caspi A. (2012). Undercontrolled temperament at age 3 predicts disordered gambling at age 32: A longitudinal study of a complete birth cohort. *Psychological Science, 23,* 510–516.

Smalarz, L., & Wells, G. L. (2015). Contamination of eyewitness self-reports and the mistaken identification problem. *Current Directions in Psychological Science, 24,* 120–124.

Small, M. F. (1997). Making connections. *American Scientist, 85,* 502–504.

Smedley, A., & Smedley, B. D. (2005). Race as biology is fiction, racism as a social problem is real: Anthropological and historical perspectives on the social construction of race. *American Psychologist, 60,* 16–26.

Smith, A. (1983). Personal correspondence.

Smith, A. (2016, February 11). 15% of American adults have used online dating sites or mobile dating apps. Pew Research Center (pewresearch.org).

Smith, B. C. (2011, January 16). The senses and the multi-sensory. World Question Center, *Edge* (edge.org).

Smith, G. E. (2016). Healthy cognitive aging and dementia prevention. *American Psychologist, 71,* 268–275.

Smith, H. J., Pettigrew, T. F. & Huo, Y. J. (2019). Advances in relative deprivation theory and applications. In Suls, J., Collins, B. & Wheeler, L. (Eds.), *Social comparison, judgment and behavior.* New York: Oxford University Press.

Smith, J. A., & Rhodes, J. E. (2014). Being depleted and being shaken: An interpretative phenomenological analysis of the experiential features of a first episode of depression. *Psychology and Psychotherapy: Theory, Research and Practice, 88,* 197–209.

Smith, J. C., Nielson, K. A., Woodard, J. L., Seidenberg, M., Durgerian, S., Hazlett, K. E., . . . Rao, S. M. (2014, April 23). Physical activity reduces hippocampal atrophy in elders at genetic risk for Alzheimer's disease. *Frontiers in Aging Neuroscience, 6,* 61.

Smith, K. (2018). Sex and drugs and self-control: How the teen brain navigates risk. *Nature,* 554, 426-428.

Smith, M. B. (1978). Psychology and values. *Journal of Social Issues, 34,* 181–199.

Smith, M. L., & Glass, G. V. (1977). Meta-analysis of psychotherapy outcome studies. *American Psychologist, 32,* 752–760.

Smith, M. L., Glass, G. V., & Miller, R. L. (1980). *The benefits of psychotherapy.* Baltimore: Johns Hopkins Press.

Smith, M. M., Sherry, S. B., Chen, S., Saklofske, D. H., Mushquash, C., Flett, G. L., & Hewitt, P. L. (2018). The perniciousness of perfectionism: A meta-analytic review of the perfectionism–suicide relationship. *Journal of Personality, 86,* 522–542.

Smith, P. B., & Tayeb, M. (1989). Organizational structure and processes. In M. Bond (Ed.), *The cross-cultural challenge to social psychology.* Newbury Park, CA: Sage.

Smith, S. F., Lilienfeld, S. O., Coffey, K., & Dabbs, J. M. (2013). Are psychopaths and heroes twigs off the same branch? Evidence from college, community, and presidential samples. *Journal of Research in Personality, 47,* 634–646.

Smith, S. L., Pieper, K., & Choueiti, M. (2017, February). *Inclusion in the director's chair? Gender, race, & age of film directors across 1,000 films from 2007–2016.* Media, Diversity, & Social Change Initiative, University of Southern California Annenberg School for Communications and Journalism.

Smith, S. M., Nichols, T. E., Vidaurre, D., Winkler, A. M., Behrens, T. E., Glasser, M. F., . . . Miller, K. L. (2015). A positive-negative mode of population covariation links brain connectivity, demographics, and behavior. *Nature Neuroscience, 18,* 1565–1567.

Smith, T. W., & Baucom, B. R. W. (2017). Intimate relationships, individual adjustment, and coronary heart disease: Implications of overlapping associations in psychosocial risk. *American Psychologist, 72,* 578–589.

Smith, T. W., Marsden, P. V., & Hout, M. (2017). *General social surveys, 1972–2016 cumulative file* (ICPSR31521-v1). Chicago: National Opinion Research Center. Ann Arbor, MI: Inter-university Consortium for Political and Social Research. doi:10.3886/ICPSR31521.v1

Smithers, L. G., Sawyer, A. C., Chittleborough, C. R., Davies, N. M., Smith, G. D., & Lynch, J. W. (2018). A systematic review and meta-analysis of effects of early life non-cognitive skills on academic, psychosocial, cognitive and health outcomes. *Nature Human Behaviour, 2,* 867–880.

Smits, I. A. M., Dolan, C. V., Vorst, H. C. M., Wicherts, J. M., & Timmerman, M. E. (2011). Cohort differences in big five personality traits over a period of 25 years. *Journal of Personality and Social Psychology, 100,* 1124–1138.

Snedeker, J., Geren, J., & Shafto, C. L. (2007). Starting over: International adoption as a natural experiment in language development. *Psychological Science, 18,* 79–86.

Sniekers, S., Stringer, S., Watanabe, K., Jansen, P. R., Coleman, J. R. I., Krapohl, E., . . . Posthuma, D. (2017). Genome-wide association meta-analysis of 78,308 individuals identifies new loci and genes influencing human intelligence. *Nature Genetics, 49,* 1107–1112.

Snipes, D. J., Calton, J. M., Green, B. A., Perrin, P. B., & Benotsch, E. G. (2017). Rape and posttraumatic stress disorder (PTSD): Examining the mediating role of explicit sex-power beliefs for men versus women. *Journal of Interpersonal Violence, 32,* 2453–2470.

Snippe, E., Simons, C. J., Hartmann, J. A., Menne-Lothmann, C., Kramer, I., Booij, S. H., . . . Wichers, M. (2016). Change in daily life behaviors and depression: Within-person and between-person associations. *Health Psychology, 35,* 433–441.

Snyder, S. H. (1984). Neurosciences: An integrative discipline. *Science, 225,* 1255–1257.

Snyder, S. H. (1986). *Drugs and the brain.* New York: Scientific American Library.

Social Trends Institute (2017). *World family map 2017: Mapping family change and child well-being outcomes.* Social Trends Institute (www.socialtrendsinstitute.org).

Soderstrom, N. C., Kerr, T. K., & Bjork, R. A. (2016). The critical importance of retrieval—and spacing—for learning. *Psychological Science, 27,* 223–230.

Solomon, D. A., Keitner, G. I., Miller, I. W., Shea, M. T., & Keller, M. B. (1995). Course of illness and maintenance treatments for patients with bipolar disorder. *Journal of Clinical Psychiatry, 56,* 5–13.

Solomon, Z., Greene, T., Ein-Dor, T., Zerach, G., Benyamini, Y., & Ohry, A. (2014). The long-term implications of war captivity for mortality and health. *Journal of Behavioral Medicine, 37,* 849–859.

Solomon, Z., Tsur, N., Levin, Y., Uziel, O., Lahav, M., & Ohry, A. (2017). The implications of war captivity and long-term psychopathology trajectories for telomere length. *Psychoneuroendocrinology, 81,* 122–128.

Song, S. (2006, March 27). Mind over medicine. *Time,* p. 47.

Sood, A. K., Armaiz-Pena, G. N., Halder, J., Nick, A. M., Stone, R. L., Hu, W., . . . Lutgendorf, S. K. (2010). Adrenergic modulation of focal adhesion kinase protects human ovarian cancer cells from anoikis. *Journal of Clinical Investigation, 120,* 1515–1523.

Sorrells, S., Alvarez-Buylla, A. A., & Paredes, M. (2018). No evidence for new adult neurons. *American Scientist, 106,* 152–155.

Soto, C. J., & John, O. P. (2017). The next big five inventory (BFI-2): Developing and assessing a hierarchical model with 15 facets to enhance bandwidth, fidelity, and predictive power. *Journal of Personality and Social Psychology, 113,* 117–143.

South, S. C., Krueger, R. F., Johnson, W., & Iacono, W. G. (2008). Adolescent personality moderates genetic and environmental influences on relationships with parents. *Journal of Personality and Social Psychology, 94,* 899–912.

Spanos, N. P., & Coe, W. C. (1992). A social-psychological approach to hypnosis. In E. Fromm & M. R. Nash (Eds.), *Contemporary hypnosis research.* New York: Guilford.

Sparks, S., Cunningham, S. J., & Kritikos, A. (2016). Culture modulates implicit ownership-induced self-bias in memory. *Cognition, 153,* 89–98.

Sparrow, B., Liu, J., & Wegner, D. M. (2011). Google effects on memory: Cognitive consequences of having information at our fingertips. *Science, 333,* 776–778.

Spearman, C. (1904). "General intelligence," objectively determined and measured. *American Journal of Psychology, 15,* 201–292.

Speer, N. K., Reynolds, J. R., Swallow, K. M., & Zacks, J. M. (2009). Reading stories activates neural representations of visual and motor experiences. *Psychological Science, 20,* 989–999.

Spencer, S. J., Logel, C., & Davies, P. G. (2016). Stereotype threat. *Annual Review of Psychology, 67,* 415–437.

Spencer, S. J., Steele, C. M., & Quinn, D. M. (1997). *Stereotype threat and women's math performance.* Unpublished manuscript, Hope College.

Sperling, G. (1960). The information available in brief visual presentations. *Psychological Monographs, 74* (Whole No. 498).

Sperry, R. W. (1964). *Problems outstanding in the evolution of brain function.* The James Arthur Lecture, delivered at the American Museum of Natural History, New York, NY. Cited by R. Ornstein (1977), *The psychology of consciousness* (2nd ed.). New York: Harcourt Brace Jovanovich.

Spiegel, A. (2015, January 8). Dark thoughts. From "Invisibilia," National Public Radio (npr.org).

Spiegel, D. (2007). The mind prepared: Hypnosis in surgery. *Journal of the National Cancer Institute, 99,* 1280–1281.

Spielberger, C., & London, P. (1982). Rage boomerangs. *American Health, 1,* 52–56.

Spinhoven, P., van Hemert, A. M., & Penninx, B. W. (2018). Repetitive negative thinking as a predictor of depression and anxiety: A longitudinal cohort study. *Journal of Affective Disorders, 241,* 216–225.

Spring, B., Pingitore, R., Bourgeois, M., Kessler, K. H., & Bruckner, E. (1992). *The effects and non-effects of skipping breakfast: Results of three studies.* Paper presented at the American Psychological Association convention.

Sproesser, G., Schupp, H. T., & Renner, B. (2014). The bright side of stress-induced eating: Eating more when stressed but less when pleased. *Psychological Science, 25,* 58–65.

Squire, L. R., & Zola-Morgan, S. (1991, September 20). The medial temporal lobe memory system. *Science, 253,* 1380–1386.

Srivastava, S., McGonigal, K. M., Richards, J. M., Butler, E. A., & Gross, J. J. (2006). Optimism in close relationships: How seeing things in a positive light makes them so. *Journal of Personality and Social Psychology, 91,* 143–153.

St. Clair, D., Xu, M., Wang, P., Yu, Y., Fang, Y., Zhang, F., Zheng, X., . . . He, L. (2005). Rates of adult schizophrenia following prenatal exposure to the Chinese famine of 1959–1961. *Journal of the American Medical Association, 294,* 557–562.

St-Onge, M. P., McReynolds, A., Trivedi, Z. B., Roberts, A. L., Sy, M., & Hirsch, J. (2012). Sleep restriction leads to increased activation of brain regions sensitive to food stimuli. *American Journal of Clinical Nutrition, 95,* 818–824.

Stacey, D., Bilbao, A., Maroteaux, M., Jia, T., Easton, A. E., Longueville, S., . . . the IMAGEN Consortium. (2012). *RASGRF2* regulates alcohol-induced reinforcement by influencing mesolimbic dopamine neuron activity and dopamine release. *PNAS, 109,* 21128–21133.

Stafford, T., & Dewar, M. (2014). Tracing the trajectory of skill learning with a very large sample of online game players. *Psychological Science, 25,* 511–518.

Stager, C. L., & Werker, J. F. (1997). Infants listen for more phonetic detail in speech perception than in word-learning tasks. *Nature, 388,* 381–382.

Stahl, A. E., & Feigenson, L. (2015). Observing the unexpected enhances infants' learning and exploration. *Science, 348,* 91–94.

Stanley, D., Phelps, E., & Banaji, M. (2008). The neural basis of implicit attitudes. *Current Directions in Psychological Science, 17,* 164–170.

Stanley, S. M., Rhoades, G. K., Amato, P. R., Markman, H. J., & Johnson, C. A. (2010). The timing of cohabitation and engagement: Impact on first and second marriages. *Journal of Marriage and Family, 72,* 906–918.

Stanley, T. D., Carter, E. C., & Doucouliagos, H. (2018). What meta-analyses reveal about the replicability of psychological research. *Psychological Bulletin, 144,* 1325–1346.

Stanovich, K. (1996). *How to think straight about psychology.* New York: HarperCollins.

Stanovich, K. E., & West, R. F. (2014a). The assessment of rational thinking: IQ ≠ RQ. *Teaching of Psychology, 41,* 265–271.

Stanovich, K. E., & West, R. F. (2014b). What intelligence tests miss. *Psychologist, 27,* 80–83.

Stanovich, K. E., West, R. F., & Toplak, M. E. (2013). My side bias, rational thinking, and intelligence. *Current Directions in Psychological Science, 22,* 259–264.

Starcke, K., & Brand, M. (2016). Effects of stress on decisions under uncertainty: A meta-analysis. *Psychological Bulletin, 142,* 909–933.

Stark, R. (2003a). *For the glory of God: How monotheism led to reformations, science, witch-hunts, and the end of slavery.* Princeton, NJ: Princeton University Press.

Stark, R. (2003b, October-November). False conflict: Christianity is not only compatible with science—it created it. *American Enterprise,* pp. 27–33.

Starzynski, L. L., Ullman, S. E., & Vasquez, A. L. (2017). Sexual assault survivors' experiences with mental health professionals: A qualitative study. *Women & Therapy, 40,* 228–246.

State, M. W., & Šestan, N. (2012). The emerging biology of autism spectrum disorders. *Science, 337,* 1301–1304.

Statista. (2018). Matchmaking – United States. Statista. Retrieved from statista.com/outlook/371/109/matchmaking/united-states#market-users

Statista. (2017). *Reported violent crime in the United States from 1990 to 2015.* Retrieved from statista.com/statistics/191219/reported-violent-crime-rate-in-the-usa-since-1990

Statistics Canada. (2011). *Marital status: Overview, 2011.* Table 2: Divorces and crude divorce rates, Canada, provinces and territories, 1981 to 2008. Retrieved from statcan.gc.ca/pub/91-209-x/2013001/article/11788/tbl/tbl2-eng.htm

Stavrinos, D., Pope, C. N., Shen, J., & Schwebel, D. C. (2017). Distracted walking, bicycling, and driving: Systematic review and meta-analysis of mobile technology and youth crash risk. *Child Development, 89*(1), 118–128.

Steel, P., Schmidt, J., & Schultz, J. (2008). Refining the relationship between personality and subject well-being. *Psychological Bulletin, 134,* 138–161.

Steele, C. M. (1990, May). A conversation with Claude Steele. *APS Observer,* pp. 11–17.

Steele, C. M. (1995, August 31). Black students live down to expectations. *The New York Times* (nytimes.com).

Steele, C. M. (2010). *Whistling Vivaldi: And other clues to how stereotypes affect us.* New York: Norton.

Steele, C. M., & Josephs, R. A. (1990). Alcohol myopia: Its prized and dangerous effects. *American Psychologist, 45,* 921–933.

Steele, C. M., Spencer, S. J., & Aronson, J. (2002). Contending with group image: The psychology of stereotype and social identity threat. *Advances in Experimental Social Psychology, 34,* 379–440.

Steinberg, L. (1987, September). Bound to bicker. *Psychology Today,* pp. 36–39.

Steinberg, L. (2001). We know some things: Parent–adolescent relationships in retrospect and prospect. *Journal of Research on Adolescence, 11,* 1–19.

Steinberg, L. (2010, March). Analyzing adolescence. Interview with Sara Martin. *Monitor on Psychology,* pp. 26–29.

Steinberg, L. (2013). The influence of neuroscience on U.S. Supreme Court decisions involving adolescents' criminal culpability. *Nature Reviews Neuroscience, 14,* 513–518.

Steinberg, L., Cauffman, E., Woolard, J., Graham, S., & Banich, M. (2009). Are adolescents less mature than adults? Minors' access to abortion, the juvenile death penalty, and the alleged APA "flip-flop." *American Psychologist, 64,* 583–594.

Steinberg, L., Lamborn, S. D., Darling, N., Mounts, N. S., & Dornbusch, S. M. (1994). Overtime changes in adjustment and competence among adolescents from authoritative, authoritarian, indulgent, and neglectful families. *Child Development, 65,* 754–770.

Steinberg, L., & Morris, A. S. (2001). Adolescent development. *Annual Review of Psychology, 52,* 83–110.

Steinberg, L., & Scott, E. S. (2003). Less guilty by reason of adolescence: Developmental immaturity, diminished responsibility, and the juvenile death penalty. *American Psychologist, 58,* 1009–1018.

Steinberg, N. (1993, February). Astonishing love stories (from an earlier United Press International report). *Games,* p. 47.

Steinert, C., Munder, T., Rabung, S., Hoyer, J., & Leichsenring, F. (2017). Psychodynamic therapy: As efficacious as other empirically supported treatments? A meta-analysis testing equivalence of outcomes. *American Journal of Psychiatry, 174,* 943–953.

Steinglass, J. E, Glasofer, D. R., Walsh, E., Guzman, G., Peterson, C. B., Walsh, B. T., Attia, E., & Wonderlich, S. A. (2018). Targeting habits in anorexia nervosa: A proof-of-concept randomized trial. *Psychological Medicine, 48,* 2584–2591.

Stellar, J. E., John-Henderson, N., Anderson, C. L., Gordon, A. M., McNeil, G. D., & Keltner, D. (2015). Positive affect and markers of inflammation: Discrete positive emotions predict lower levels of inflammatory cytokines. *Emotion, 15,* 129–133.

Stephan, Y., Sutin, A. R., Kornadt, A., Caudroit, J., & Terracciano, A. (2018). Higher IQ in adolescence is related to a younger subjective age in later life: Findings from the Wisconsin Longitudinal Study. *Intelligence, 69,* 195199.

Stephens-Davidowitz, S. (2017). *Everybody lies: Big data, new data, and what the internet can tell us about who we really are.* New York: HarperCollins.

Steptoe, A., & Wardle, J. (2011). Positive affect measured using ecological momentary assessment and survival in older men and woman. *PNAS, 108,* 18244–18248.

Steptoe, A., & Wardle, J. (2017). Life skills, wealth, health, and wellbeing later in life. *PNAS, 114,* 4354–4359.

Sterling, R. (2003). *The traveling curmudgeon: Irreverent notes, quotes, and anecdotes on dismal destinations, excess baggage, the full upright position, and other reasons not to go there* (p. 102). Seattle: Sasquatch Book.

Sternberg, R. J. (1985). *Beyond IQ: A triarchic theory of human intelligence.* New York: Cambridge University Press.

Sternberg, R. J. (1988). Applying cognitive theory to the testing and teaching of intelligence. *Applied Cognitive Psychology, 2,* 231–255.

Sternberg, R. J. (2003). Our research program validating the triarchic theory of successful intelligence: Reply to Gottfredson. *Intelligence, 31,* 399–413.

Sternberg, R. J. (2006). The Rainbow Project: Enhance the SAT through assessments of analytical, practical, and creative skills. *Intelligence, 34,* 321–350.

Sternberg, R. J. (2011). The theory of successful intelligence. In R. J. Sternberg & S. B. Kaufman (Eds.), *The Cambridge handbook of intelligence.* New York: Cambridge University Press.

Sternberg, R. J., & Grajek, S. (1984). The nature of love. *Journal of Personality and Social Psychology, 47,* 312–329.

Sternberg, R. J., & Kaufman, J. C. (1998). Human abilities. *Annual Review of Psychology, 49,* 479–502.

Sternberg, R. J., & Lubart, T. I. (1991). An investment theory of creativity and its development. *Human Development, 34,* 1–31.

Sternberg, R. J., & Lubart, T. I. (1992). Buy low and sell high: An investment approach to creativity. *Psychological Science, 1,* 1–5.

Stetter, F., & Kupper, S. (2002). Autogenic training: A meta-analysis of clinical outcome studies. *Applied Psychophysiology and Biofeedback, 27,* 45–98.

Stevenson, H. W. (1992, December). Learning from Asian schools. *Scientific American,* pp. 70–76.

Stevenson, R. J. (2014). Flavor binding: Its nature and cause. *Psychological Bulletin, 140,* 487–510.

Stice, E., Ng, J., & Shaw, H. (2010). Risk factors and prodromal eating pathology. *Journal of Child Psychology and Psychiatry, 51,* 518–525.

Stice, E., Spangler, D., & Agras, W. S. (2001). Exposure to media-portrayed thin-ideal images adversely affects vulnerable girls: A longitudinal experiment. *Journal of Social and Clinical Psychology, 20,* 270–288.

Stickgold, R. (2000, March 7). Quoted by S. Blakeslee, For better learning, researchers endorse, "sleep on it" adage. *The New York Times,* p. F2.

Stickgold, R. (2012). Sleep, memory and dreams: Putting it all together. In *Aquém e além do cérebro* [Behind and beyond the brain]. Bial: Fundação Bial Institution of Public Utility.

Stillman, T. F., Baumeister, R. F., Vohs, K. D., Lambert, N. M., Fincham, F. D., & Brewer, L. E. (2010). Personal philosophy and personnel achievement: Belief in free will predicts better job performance. *Social Psychological and Personality Science, 1,* 43–50.

Stillman, T. F., Lambet, N. M., Fincham, F. D., & Baumeister, R. F. (2011). Meaning as magnetic force: Evidence that meaning in life promotes interpersonal appeal. *Social Psychological and Personality Science, 2,* 13–20.

Stith, S. M., Rosen, K. H., Middleton, K. A., Busch, A. L., Lunderberg, K., & Carlton, R. P. (2000). The intergenerational transmission of spouse abuse: A meta-analysis. *Journal of Marriage and the Family, 62,* 640–654.

Stjepanovic, D. & LaBar, K. S. (2018). Fear learning. In J. T. Wixted (Ed.), *Stevens' Handbook of Experimental Psychology, 4th Ed., Vol. 1.* New York: Wiley.

Stockton, M. C., & Murnen, S. K. (1992, June). *Gender and sexual arousal in response to sexual stimuli: A meta-analytic review.* Paper presented at the Fourth Annual Convention of the American Psychological Society, San Diego, CA.

Stoet, G., & Geary, D. C. (2018). The gender-equality paradox in science, technology, engineering, and mathematics education. *Psychological Science, 29,* 581–593.

Stoll, G., Rieger, S., Lüdtke, O., Nagengast, B., Trautwein, U., & Roberts, B. W. (2017). Vocational interests assessed at the end of high school predict life outcomes assessed 10 years later over and above IQ and big five personality traits. *Journal of Personality and Social Psychology, 113,* 167–184.

Stone, A. A., & Neale, J. M. (1984). Effects of severe daily events on mood. *Journal of Personality and Social Psychology, 46,* 137–144.

Stone, A. A., Schwartz, J. E., Broderick, J. E., & Deaton, A. (2010). A snapshot of the age distribution of psychological well-being in the United States. *PNAS, 107,* 9985–9990.

Stop Street Harassment. (2018). *The facts behind the #metoo movement: A national study on sexual harassment and assault* [PDF file]. Retrieved from http://www.stopstreetharassment.org/wp-content/uploads/2018/01/Full-Report-2018-National-Study-on-Sexual-Harassment-and-Assault.pdf

Storbeck, J., Robinson, M. D., & McCourt, M. E. (2006). Semantic processing precedes affect retrieval: The neurological case for cognitive primary in visual processing. *Review of General Psychology, 10,* 41–55.

Storm, B. C., & Jobe, T. A. (2012). Retrieval-induced forgetting predicts failure to recall negative autobiographical memories. *Psychological Science, 23,* 1356–1363.

Storms, M. D. (1973). Videotape and the attribution process: Reversing actors' and observers' points of view. *Journal of Personality and Social Psychology, 27,* 165–175.

Storms, M. D., & Thomas, G. C. (1977). Reactions to physical closeness. *Journal of Personality and Social Psychology, 35,* 412–418.

Stowell, J. R., Oldham, T., & Bennett, D. (2010). Using student response systems ("clickers") to combat conformity and shyness. *Teaching of Psychology, 37,* 135–140.

Strack, F. (2016). Reflection on the Smiling Registered Replication Report. *Perspectives on Psychological Science, 11,* 929–930.

Strain, J. F., Womack, K. B., Didenbani, N., Spence, J. S., Conover, H., Hart, J., Jr., . . . Cullum, C. M. (2015). Imaging correlates of memory and concussion history in retired National Football League athletes. *JAMA Neurology, 72,* 773–780.

Strand, L. B., Mukamal, K. J., Halasz, J., Vatten, L. J., & Janszky, I. (2016). Short-term public health impact of the July 22, 2011, terrorist attacks in Norway: A nationwide register-based study. *Psychosomatic Medicine, 78,* 525–531.

Strange, B. A., & Dolan, R. J. (2004). b-Adrenergic modulation of emotional memory-evoked human amygdala and hippocampal responses. *PNAS, 101,* 11454–11458.

Strange, D., Hayne, H., & Garry, M. (2008). A photo, a suggestion, a false memory. *Applied Cognitive Psychology, 22,* 587–603.

Strasburger, V. C., Jordan, A. B., & Donnerstein, E. (2010). Health effects of media on children and adolescents. *Pediatrics, 125,* 756–767.

Stratton, G. M. (1896). Some preliminary experiments on vision without inversion of the retinal image. *Psychological Review, 3,* 611–617.

Straub, R. O., Seidenberg, M. S., Bever, T. G., & Terrace, H. S. (1979). Serial learning in the pigeon. *Journal of the Experimental Analysis of Behavior, 32,* 137–148.

Straus, M. A., Sugarman, D. B., & Giles-Sims, J. (1997). Spanking by parents and subsequent antisocial behavior of children. *Archives of Pediatric Adolescent Medicine, 151,* 761–767.

Strawbridge, W. J. (1999). *Mortality and religious involvement: A review and critique of the results, the methods, and the measures.* Paper presented at a Harvard University conference on religion and health, sponsored by the National Institute for Health Research and the John Templeton Foundation.

Strawbridge, W. J., Cohen, R. D., & Shema, S. J. (1997). Frequent attendance at religious services and mortality over 28 years. *American Journal of Public Health, 87,* 957–961.

Strick, M., Dijksterhuis, A., & van Baaren, R. B. (2010). Unconscious thought effects take place off-line, not on-line. *Psychological Science, 21,* 484–488.

Stringaris, A., Vidal-Ribas Belil, P., Artiges, E., Lemaitre, H., Gollier-Briant, F., Wolke, S., . . . Fadai, T. (2015). The brain's response to reward anticipation and depression in adolescence: Dimensionality, specificity, and longitudinal predictions in a community-based sample. *American Journal of Psychiatry, 172,* 1215–1223.

Stroebe, M., Finenauer, C., Wijngaards-de Meij, L., Schut, H., van den Bout, J., & Stroebe, W. (2013). Partner-oriented self-regulation among bereaved parents: The costs of holding in grief for the partner's sake. *Psychological Science, 24,* 395–402.

Stroebe, W., Schut, H., & Stroebe, M. S. (2005). Grief work, disclosure and counseling: Do they help the bereaved? *Clinical Psychology Review, 25,* 395–414.

Stroud, L. R., Panadonatos, G. D., Rodriguez, D., McCallum, M., Salisbury, A. L., Phipps, M. G., . . . Marsit, C. J. (2014). Maternal smoking during pregnancy and infant stress response: Test of a prenatal programming hypothesis. *Psychoneuroendocrinology, 48,* 29–40.

Strully, K. W. (2009). Job loss and health in the U.S. labor market. *Demography, 46*, 221–246.

Stuart, G. J., & Spruston, N. (2015). Dendritic integration: 60 years of progress. *Nature Neuroscience, 18*, 1713–1721.

Štulhofer, A., Šoh, D., Jelaska, N., Baćak, V., & Landripet, I. (2011). Religiosity and sexual risk behavior among Croatian college students, 1998–2008. *Journal of Sex Research, 48*, 360–371.

Stutzer, A., & Frey, B. S. (2006). Does marriage make people happy, or do happy people get married? *Journal of Socio-Economics, 35*, 326–347.

Suddath, R. L., Christison, G. W., Torrey, E. F., Casanova, M. F., & Weinberger, D. R. (1990). Anatomical abnormalities in the brains of monozygotic twins discordant for schizophrenia. *New England Journal of Medicine, 322*, 789–794.

Sue, S., Zane, N., Hall, G. C. N., & Berger, L. K. (2009). The case for cultural competency in psychotherapeutic interventions. *Annual Review of Psychology, 60*, 525–548.

Suedfeld, P., & Mocellin, J. S. P. (1987). The "sensed presence" in unusual environments. *Environment and Behavior, 19*, 33–52.

Suglia, S. F., Kara, S., & Robinson, W. R. (2014). Sleep duration and obesity among adolescents transitioning to adulthood: Do results differ by sex? *The Journal of Pediatrics, 165*, 750–754.

Sulik, M. J., Blair, C., Mills-Koonce, R., Berry, D., Greenberg, M., & Family Life Project Investigators. (2015). Early parenting and the development of externalizing behavior problems: Longitudinal mediation through children's executive function. *Child Development, 86*, 1588–1603.

Sullivan, P. F., Børglum, A. D., Faraone, S. V., & Smoller, J. W. (2018). Psychiatric genomics: An update and an agenda. *American Journal of Psychiatry, 175*, 15–27.

Sullivan, P. F., Neale, M. C., & Kendler, K. S. (2000). Genetic epidemiology of major depression: Review and meta-analysis. *American Journal of Psychiatry, 157*, 1552–1562.

Suls, J. M., & Tesch, F. (1978). Students' preferences for information about their test performance: A social comparison study. *Journal of Experimental Social Psychology, 8*, 189–197.

Summers, M. (1996, December 9). Mister Clean. *People Weekly*, pp. 139–142.

Sundstrom, E., De Meuse, K. P., & Futrell, D. (1990). Work teams: Applications and effectiveness. *American Psychologist, 45*, 120–133.

Sung, S., Simpson, J. A., Griskevicius, V., Sally, I., Kuo, C., Schlomer, G. L., & Belsky, J. (2016). Secure infant-mother attachment buffers the effect of early-life stress on age of menarche. *Psychological Science, 27*, 667–674.

Sunstein, C. R., Bobadilla-Suarez, S., Lazzaro, S. C., & Sharot, T. (2016). How people update beliefs about climate change: Good news and bad news. Social Science Research Network (ssrn.com).

Suomi, S. J. (1986). Anxiety-like disorders in young nonhuman primates. In R. Gettleman (Ed.), *Anxiety disorders of childhood*. New York: Guilford Press.

Suomi, S. J., Collins, M. L., Harlow, H. F., & Ruppenthal, G. C. (1976). Effects of maternal and peer separations on young monkeys. *Journal of Child Psychology and Psychiatry, 17*, 101–112.

Surgeon General. (1986). *The Surgeon General's workshop on pornography and public health*, June 22–24. Report prepared by E. P. Mulvey & J. L. Haugaard and released by Office of the Surgeon General on August 4, 1986.

Surgeon General. (1999). *Mental health: A report of the Surgeon General*. Rockville, MD: U.S. Department of Health and Human Services.

Susser, E., & Martínez-Alés, G. (2018). Putting psychosis into sociocultural context: An international study in 17 locations. *JAMA Psychiatry, 75*, 9–10.

Susser, E. S., Neugenbauer, R., Hoek, H. W., Brown, A. S., Lin, S., Labovitz, D., & Gorman, J. M. (1996). Schizophrenia after prenatal famine. *Archives of General Psychiatry, 53*, 25–31.

Swami, V. (2015). Cultural influences on body size ideals: Unpacking the impact of Westernization and modernization. *European Psychologist, 20*, 44–51.

Swami, V., Frederick, D. A., Aavik, T., Alcalay, L., Allik, J., Anderson, D., . . . Zivcic-Becirevic, I. (2010). The attractive female body weight and female body dissatisfaction in 26 countries across 10 world regions: Results of the International Body Project I. *Personality and Social Psychology Bulletin, 36*, 309–325.

Swann, W. B., Jr., Chang-Schneider, C., & McClarty, K. L. (2007). Do people's self-views matter: Self-concept and self-esteem in everyday life. *American Psychologist, 62*, 84–94.

Swift, A. (2013, October 28). *Personal safety top reason Americans own guns today*. Gallup (gallup.com).

Swift, A. (2016, November 9). *Americans' perceptions of U.S. crime problem are steady*. Gallup Poll (gallup.com).

Symbaluk, D. G., Heth, C. D., Cameron, J., & Pierce, W. D. (1997). Social modeling, monetary incentives, and pain endurance: The role of self-efficacy and pain perception. *Personality and Social Psychology Bulletin, 23*, 258–269.

Symonds, A. (2014, February 4). The emancipation of Angel Haze. *Out Magazine* (www.out.com).

Symons, C. S., & Johnson, B. T. (1997). The self-reference effect in memory: A meta-analysis. *Psychological Bulletin, 121*, 371–394.

Szkodny, L. E., Newman, M. G., & Goldfried, M. R. (2014). Clinical experiences in conducting empirically supported treatments for generalized anxiety disorder. *Behavior Therapy, 45*, 7–20.

Szutorisz, H., & Hurd, J. L. (2016). Epigenetic effects of cannabis exposure. *Biological Psychiatry, 79*, 586–594.

Tackett, J. L., Herzhoff, K., Kushner, S. C., & Rule, N. (2016). Thin slices of child personality: Perceptual, situational, and behavioral contributions. *Journal of Personality and Social Psychology, 110*, 150–166.

Taheri, S. (2004, December 20). Does the lack of sleep make you fat? *University of Bristol Research News* (bristol.ac.uk).

Taheri, S., Lin, L., Austin, D., Young, T., & Mignot, E. (2004). Short sleep duration is associated with reduced leptin, elevated ghrelin, and increased body mass index. *PLOS Medicine, 1*, e62.

Tajfel, H. (Ed.). (1982). *Social identity and intergroup relations*. New York: Cambridge University Press.

Takizawa, R., Maughan, B., & Arseneault, L. (2014). Adult health outcomes of childhood bullying victimization: Evidence from a five-decade longitudinal British birth cohort. *American Journal of Psychiatry, 171*, 777–784.

Talarico, J. M., & Moore, K. M. (2012). Memories of "The Rivalry": Differences in how fans of the winning and losing teams remember the same game. *Applied Cognitive Psychology, 26*, 746–756.

Talhelm, T., Zhang, X., & Oishi, S. (2018). Moving chairs in Starbucks: Observational studies find rice-wheat cultural differences in daily life in China. *Science Advances, 4*, eaap8469.

Talhelm, T., Zhang, X., Oishi, S., Shimin, C., Duan, D., Lan, X., & Kitayama, S. (2014). Large-scale psychological differences within China explained by rice versus wheat agriculture. *Science, 344*, 603–608.

Tam, T. (2018). *The Chief Public Health Officer's report on the state of public health in Canada: Preventing problematic substance use in youth*. Public Health Agency of Canada (canada.ca/en/public-health.html).

Tamres, L. K., Janicki, D., & Helgeson, V. S. (2002). Sex differences in coping behavior: A meta-analytic review and an examination of relative coping. *Personality and Social Psychology Review, 6*, 2–30.

Tannen, D. (1990). *You just don't understand: Women and men in conversation*. New York: Morrow.

Tanner, J. M. (1978). *Fetus into man: Physical growth from conception to maturity*. Cambridge, MA: Harvard University Press.

Tardif, T., Fletcher, P., Liang, W., Zhang, Z., Kaciroti, N., & Marchman, V. A. (2008). Baby's first 10 words. *Developmental Psychology, 44*, 929–938.

Tatlow, D. K. (2016, June 11). Doctor's plan for full-body transplants raises doubts even in daring China. *The New York Times* (nytimes.com).

Taubes, G. (2001). The soft science of dietary fat. *Science, 291*, 2536–2545.

Taubes, G. (2002, July 7). What if it's all been a big fat lie? *The New York Times* (nytimes.com).

Tausch, N., Hewstone, M., Kenworthy, J. B., Psaltis, C., Schmid, K., Popan, J. R., . . . Hughes, J. (2010). Secondary transfer effects of intergroup contact: Alternative accounts and underlying processes. *Journal of Personality and Social Psychology, 99*, 282–302.

Tavernier, R., & Willoughby, T. (2014). Bidirectional associations between sleep (quality and duration) and psychosocial functioning across the university years. *Developmental Psychology, 50*, 674–682.

Tavernise, S. (2013, February 13). To reduce suicide rates, new focus turns to guns. *The New York Times* (nytimes.com).

Tavernise, S. (2016, February 29). "Female Viagra" only modestly increases sexual satisfaction, study finds. *The New York Times* (nytimes.com).

Taylor, C. (2017). Creativity and mood disorder: A systematic review and meta-analysis. *Perspectives on Psychological Science, 12*, 1040–1076.

Taylor, C. A., Manganello, J. A., Lee, S. J., & Rice, J. C. (2010). Mothers' spanking of 3-year-old children and subsequent risk of children's aggressive behavior. *Pediatrics, 125*, 1057–1065.

Taylor, L. E., Swerdfeger, A. L., & Eslick, G. D. (2014). Vaccines are not associated with autism: An evidence-based meta-analysis of case-control and cohort studies. *Vaccine, 32*, 3623–3629.

Taylor, P. J., Gooding, P., Wood, A. M., & Tarrier, N. (2011). The role of defeat and entrapment in depression, anxiety, and suicide. *Psychological Bulletin, 137*, 391–420.

Taylor, S. (2013). Molecular genetics of obsessive-compulsive disorder: A comprehensive meta-analysis of genetic association studies. *Molecular Psychiatry, 18*, 799–805.

Taylor, S. E. (1983). Adjustment to threatening events: A theory of cognitive adaptation. *American Psychologist, 38*, 1161–1173.

Taylor, S. E. (2002). *The tending instinct: How nurturing is essential to who we are and how we live*. New York: Times Books.

Taylor, S. E. (2006). Tend and befriend: Biobehavioral bases of affiliation under stress. *Current Directions in Psychological Science, 15*, 273–277.

Taylor, S. E., Pham, L. B., Rivkin, I. D., & Armor, D. A. (1998). Harnessing the imagination: Mental simulation, self-regulation, and coping. *American Psychologist, 53,* 429–439.

Taylor, S. F., Bhati, M. T., Dubin, M. J., Hawkins, J. M., Lisanby, S. H., Morales, O., . . . Watcharotone, K. (2017). A naturalistic, multi-site study of repetitive transcranial magnetic stimulation therapy for depression. *Journal of Affective Disorders, 208,* 284–290.

Tedeschi, R. G., & Calhoun, L. G. (2004). Posttraumatic growth: Conceptual foundations and empirical evidence. *Psychological Inquiry, 15,* 1–18.

Teghtsoonian, R. (1971). On the exponents in Stevens' law and the constant in Ekman's law. *Psychological Review, 78,* 71–80.

Teicher, M. H., & Samson, J. A. (2016). Annual research review: Enduring neurobiological effects of childhood abuse and neglect. *Journal of Child Psychology and Psychiatry, 57,* 241–266.

Teller. (2009, April 20). Quoted by J. Lehrer, Magic and the brain: Teller reveals the neuroscience of illusion. *Wired Magazine* (wired.com).

Telzer, E. H., Flannery, J., Shapiro, M., Humphreys, K. L., Goff, B., Gabard-Durman, L., . . . Tottenham, N. (2013). Early experience shapes amygdala sensitivity to race: An international adoption design. *Journal of Neuroscience, 33,* 13484–13488.

ten Brinke, L., Vohs, K. D., & Carney. D. (2016). Can ordinary people detect deception after all? *Trends in Cognitive Sciences, 20,* 579–588.

Tenenbaum, H. R., & Leaper, C. (2002). Are parents' gender schemas related to their children's gender-related cognitions? A meta-analysis. *Developmental Psychology, 38,* 615–630.

Tenney, E. R., Logg, J. M., & Moore, D. A. (2015). (Too) optimistic about optimism: The belief that optimism improves performance. *Journal of Personality and Social Psychology, 108,* 377–399.

Terada, S., Sakurai, Y., Nakahara, H., & Fujisawa, S. (2017). Temporal and rate coding for discrete event sequences in the hippocampus. *Neuron, 94,* 1248–1262.

Terrace, H. S. (1979, November). How Nim Chimpsky changed my mind. *Psychology Today,* pp. 65–76.

Terrell, J., Kofink, A., Middleton, J., Rainear, C., Murphy-Hill, E., Parnin, C., & Stallings, J. (2017). Gender differences and bias in open source: Pull request acceptance of women versus men. *PeerJ Computer Science, 3,* e111.

Tesser, A., Forehand, R., Brody, G., & Long, N. (1989). Conflict: The role of calm and angry parent-child discussion in adolescent development. *Journal of Social and Clinical Psychology, 8,* 317–330.

Testa, R. J., Michaels, M. S., Bliss, W., Rogers, M. L., Balsam, K. F., & Joiner, T. (2017). Suicidal ideation in transgender people: Gender minority stress and interpersonal factors. *Journal of Abnormal Psychology, 126,* 125–136.

Teter, C. J., DiRaimo, C. G., West, B. T., Schepis, T. S., & McCabe, S. E. (2018). Nonmedical use of prescription stimulants among U.S. high school students to help study: Results from a national survey. *Journal of Pharmacy Practice.* doi.org/10.1177/0897190018783887

Tetlock, P. E. (1998). Close-call counterfactuals and belief-system defenses: I was not almost wrong but I was almost right. *Journal of Personality and Social Psychology, 75,* 639–652.

Tetlock, P. E. (2005). *Expert political judgement: How good is it? How can we know?* Princeton, NJ: Princeton University Press.

Tetlock, P. E., & Gardner, D. (2016). *Superforecasting: The art and science of prediction.* New York: Broadway Books.

Thaler, L., Arnott, S. R., & Goodale, M. A. (2011). Neural correlates of natural human echolocation in early and late blind echolocation experts. *PLOS ONE, 6,* e20162.

Thaler, L., Milne, J. L., Arnott, S. R., Kish, D., & Goodale, M. A. (2014). Neural correlates of motion processing through echolocation, source hearing, and vision in blind echolocation experts and sighted echolocation novices. *Journal of Neurophysiology, 111,* 112–127.

Thaler, R. H. (2015, May 8). Unless you are Spock, irrelevant things matter in economic behavior. *The New York Times* (nytimes.com).

Thaler, R. H., & Sunstein, C. R. (2008). *Nudge: Improving decisions about health, wealth, and happiness.* New Haven, CT: Yale University Press.

Thalmann, M., Souza, A. S., & Oberauer, K. (2018). How does chunking help working memory? *Journal of Experimental Psychology: Learning, Memory, and Cognition, 45,* 37–55.

Thatcher, R. W., Walker, R. A., & Giudice, S. (1987). Human cerebral hemispheres develop at different rates and ages. *Science, 236,* 1110–1113.

The Guardian. (2014, August 12). Maryam Mirzakhani: "The more I spent time on maths, the more excited I got." *The Guardian* (theguardian.com).

Thibodeau, R., Jorgensen, R. S., & Kim, S. (2006). Depression, anxiety, and resting frontal EEG asymmetry: A meta-analytic review. *Journal of Abnormal Psychology, 115,* 715–729.

Thiel, A., Hadedank, B., Herholz, K., Kessler, J., Winhuisen, L., Haupt, W. F., & Heiss, W. D. (2006). From the left to the right: How the brain compensates progressive loss of language function. *Brain and Language, 98,* 57–65.

Thomas, A., & Chess, S. (1986). The New York Longitudinal Study: From infancy to early adult life. In R. Plomin & J. Dunn (Eds.), *The study of temperament: Changes, continuities, and challenges.* Hillsdale, NJ: Erlbaum.

Thomas, L. (1992). *The fragile species.* New York: Scribner's.

Thompson, G. (2010). The $1 million dollar challenge. *Skeptic Magazine, 15,* 8–9.

Thompson-Hollands, J., Marx, B. P., Lee, D. J., Resick, P. A., & Sloan, D. M. (2018). Long-term treatment gains of a brief exposure-based treatment for PTSD. *Depression and Anxiety, 35,* 985–991.

Thompson, J. K., Jarvie, G. J., Lahey, B. B., & Cureton, K. J. (1982). Exercise and obesity: Etiology, physiology, and intervention. *Psychological Bulletin, 91,* 55–79

Thompson, P. M., Giedd, J. N., Woods, R. P., MacDonald, D., Evans, A. C., & Toga, A. W. (2000). Growth patterns in the developing brain detected by using continuum mechanical tensor maps. *Nature, 404,* 190–193.

Thompson, R., Emmorey, K., & Gollan, T. H. (2005). "Tip of the fingers" experiences by Deaf signers. *Psychological Science, 16,* 856–860.

Thompson-Schill, S. L., Ramscar, M., & Chrysikou, E. G. (2009). Cognition without control: When a little frontal lobe goes a long way. *Current Directions in Psychological Science, 18,* 259–263.

Thorndike, E. L. (1898). Animal intelligence: An experimental study of the associative processes in animals. *Psychological Review Monograph Supplement, 2,* 4–160.

Thorne, J., with Larry Rothstein. (1993). *You are not alone: Words of experience and hope for the journey through depression.* New York: HarperPerennial.

Thornicroft, G., Chatterji, S., Evans-Lacko, S., Gruber, M., Sampson, N., Aguilar-Gaxiola, S., . . . Bruffaerts, R. (2017). Undertreatment of people with major depressive disorder in 21 countries. *British Journal of Psychiatry, 210,* 119–124.

Thornton, B., & Moore, S. (1993). Physical attractiveness contrast effect: Implications for self-esteem and evaluations of the social self. *Personality and Social Psychology Bulletin, 19,* 474–480.

Thorpe, W. H. (1974). *Animal nature and human nature.* London, England: Metheun.

Tick, B., Bolton, P., Happé, F., Rutter, M., & Rijsdijk, F. (2015). Heritability of autism spectrum disorders: a meta-analysis of twin studies. *Journal of Child Psychology and Psychiatry, 57,* 585–595.

Tickle, J. J., Hull, J. G., Sargent, J. D., Dalton, M. A., & Heatherton, T. F. (2006). A structural equation model of social influences and exposure to media smoking on adolescent smoking. *Basic and Applied Social Psychology, 28,* 117–129.

Tiggemann, M., & Miller, J. (2010). The Internet and adolescent girls' weight satisfaction and drive for thinness. *Sex Roles, 63,* 79–90.

Tiihonen, J., Lönnqvist, J., Wahlbeck, K., Klaukka, T., Niskanen, L., Tanskanen, A., & Haukka, J. (2009). 11-year follow-up of mortality in patients with schizophrenia: A population-based cohort study (FIN11 study). *The Lancet, 374,* 260–267.

Time/CNN Survey. (1994, December 19). Vox pop: Happy holidays, *Time.*

Timerman, J. (1980). *Prisoner without a name, cell without a number.* Madison: University of Wisconsin Press.

Timmerman, T. A. (2007) "It was a thought pitch": Personal, situational, and target influences on hit-by-pitch events across time. *Journal of Applied Psychology, 92,* 876–884.

Tirrell, M. E. (1990). Personal communication.

Tobin, D. D., Menon, M., Menon, M., Spatta, B. C., Hodges, E. V. E., & Perry, D. G. (2010). The intrapsychics of gender: A model of self-socialization. *Psychological Review, 117,* 601–622.

Todd, R. M., MacDonald, M. J., Sedge, P., Robertson, A., Jetly, R., Taylor, M. J., & Pang, E. W. (2015). Soldiers with posttraumatic stress disorder see a world full of threat: Magnetoencephalography reveals enhanced tuning to combat-related cues. *Biological Psychiatry, 78,* 821–829.

Todes, D. P. (2014). *Ivan Pavlov: A Russian life in science.* New York: Oxford University Press.

Toews, P. (2004, December 30). *Dirk Willems: A heart undivided.* Mennonite Brethren Historical Commission (nbhistory.org/profiles/dirk.en.html).

Tolin, D. F. (2010). Is cognitive-behavioral therapy more effective than other therapies? A meta-analytic review. *Clinical Psychology Review, 30,* 710–720.

Tolman, E. C., & Honzik, C. H. (1930). Introduction and removal of reward, and maze performance in rats. *University of California Publications in Psychology, 4,* 257–275.

Tomaka, J., Blascovich, J., & Kelsey, R. M. (1992). Effects of self-deception, social desirability, and repressive coping on psychophysiological reactivity to stress. *Personality and Social Psychology Bulletin, 18,* 616–624.

Topolinski, S., & Reber, R. (2010). Gaining insight into the "aha" experience. *Current Directions in Psychological Science, 19,* 401–405.

Torrey, E. F. (1986). *Witchdoctors and psychiatrists.* New York: Harper & Row.

Torrey, E. F., & Miller, J. (2002). *The invisible plague: The rise of mental illness from 1750 to the present.* New Brunswick, NJ: Rutgers University Press.

Torrey, E. F., Miller, J., Rawlings, R., & Yolken, R. H. (1997). Seasonality of births in schizophrenia and bipolar disorder: A review of the literature. *Schizophrenia Research, 28*, 1–38.

Toschi, N., Riccelli, R., Indovina, I., Terracciano, A., & Passamonti, L. (2018). Functional connectome of the five-factor model of personality. *Personality Neuroscience, 1*, e2.

Tovee, M. J., Mason, S. M., Emery, J. L., McCluskey, S. E., & Cohen-Tovee, E. M. (1997). Supermodels: Stick insects or hourglasses? *The Lancet, 350*, 1474–1475.

Townsend, S. S. M., Stephens, N. M., Smallets, S., & Hamedani, M. G. (2019). Empowerment through difference: An online difference-education intervention closes the social class achievement gap. *Personality and Social Psychology Bulletin*. Advance online publication. doi.org/10.1177/0146167218804548

Tracey, J. L., & Robins, R. W. (2004). Show your pride: Evidence for a discrete emotion expression. *Psychological Science, 15*, 194–197.

Traffanstedt, M. K., Mehta, S., & LoBello, S. G. (2016). Major depression with seasonal variation: Is it a valid construct? *Clinical Psychological Science, 4*, 825–834.

Trahan, L. H., Stuebing, K. K., Fletcher, J. M., & Hiscock, M. (2014). The Flynn effect: A meta-analysis. *Psychological Bulletin, 140*, 1332–1360.

Treanor, M., Brown, L. A., Rissman, J., & Craske, M. G. (2017). Can memories of traumatic experiences or addiction be erased or modified? A critical review of research on the disruption of memory reconsolidation and its applications. *Perspectives on Psychological Science, 12*, 290–305.

Treffert, D. A. (2010). *Islands of genius: The beautiful mind of the autistic, acquired, and sudden savant*. Philadelphia, PA: Jessica Kinsley.

Treffert, D. A., & Christensen, D. D. (2005, December). Inside the mind of a savant. *Scientific American*, pp. 108–113.

Treisman, A. (1987). Properties, parts, and objects. In K. R. Boff, L. Kaufman, & J. P. Thomas (Eds.), *Handbook of perception and human performance* (pp. 35-1–35-70). New York: Wiley.

Triandis, H. C. (1994). *Culture and social behavior*. New York: McGraw-Hill.

Trickett, E. (2009). Community psychology: Individuals and interventions in community context. *Annual Review of Psychology, 60*, 395–419.

Trillin, C. (2006, March 27). Alice off the page. *The New Yorker*, p. 44.

Triplett, N. (1898). The dynamogenic factors in pacemaking and competition. *American Journal of Psychology, 9*, 507–533.

Tropp, L. R., & Barlow, F. K. (2018). Making advantaged racial groups care about inequality: Intergroup contact as a route to psychological investment. *Current Directions in Psychological Science, 27*, 194–199.

Trotter, J. (2014). The power of positive coaching. *Sports Illustrated* (mmqb.si.com).

Trumbo, M. C., Leiting, K. A., McDaniel, M. A., & Hodge, G. K. (2016). Effects of reinforcement on test-enhanced learning in a large, diverse introductory college psychology course. *Journal of Experimental Psychology: Applied, 22*, 148–160.

Tsai, J. L., Ang, J. Y. Z., Blevins, E., Goernandt, J., Fung, H. H., Jiang, D., . . . Haddouk, L. (2016). Leaders' smiles reflect cultural differences in ideal affect. *Emotion, 16*, 183–195.

Tsai, J. L., Knutson, B., & Fung, H. H. (2006). Cultural variation in affect valuation. *Journal of Personality and Social Psychology, 90*, 288–307.

Tsang, Y. C. (1938). Hunger motivation in gastrectomized rats. *Journal of Comparative Psychology, 26*, 1–17.

Tskhay, K. O., Zhu, R., Zou, C., & Rule, N. O. (2018). Charisma in everyday life: Conceptualization and validation of the General Charisma Inventory. *Journal of Personality and Social Psychology, 114*, 131–152.

Tsvetkova, M., & Macy, M. W. (2014). The social contagion of generosity. *PLOS ONE, 9*(2), e87275.

Tuber, D. S., Miller, D. D., Caris, K. A., Halter, R., Linden, F., & Hennessy, M. B. (1999). Dogs in animal shelters: Problems, suggestions, and needed expertise. *Psychological Science, 10*, 379–386.

Tucker-Drob, E. M., & Bates, T. C. (2016). Large cross-national differences in gene x socioeconomic status interaction on intelligence. *Psychological Science, 27*, 138–149.

Tuerk, P. W. (2005). Research in the high-stakes era: Achievement, resources, and No Child Left Behind. *Psychological Science, 16*, 419–425.

Tuk, M. A., Zhang, K., & Sweldens, S. (2015). The propagation of self-control: Self-control in one domain simultaneously improves self-control in other domains. *Journal of Experimental Psychology: General, 144*, 639–654.

Tullett, A. M., Kay, A. C., & Inzlicht, M. (2015). Randomness increases self-reported anxiety and neurophysiological correlates of performance monitoring. *Social Cognitive and Affective Neuroscience, 10*, 628-635.

Turner, J. C. (1987). Rediscovering the social group: A self-categorization theory. New York: Basil Blackwell.

Turner, J. C. (2007) Self-categorization theory. In R. Baumeister & K. Vohs (Eds.), *Encyclopedia of social psychology* (pp. 793–795). Thousand Oaks, CA: Sage.

Turner, N., Barling, J., & Zacharatos, A. (2002). Positive psychology at work. In C. R. Snyder & S. J. Lopez (Eds.), *The handbook of positive psychology*. New York: Oxford University Press.

Tversky, A. (1985, June). Quoted in K. McKean, Decisions, decisions. *Discover*, pp. 22–31.

Tversky, A., & Kahneman, D. (1974). Judgment under uncertainty: Heuristics and biases. *Science, 185*, 1124–1131.

Twenge, J. M. (2017). *iGen: Why today's super-connected kids are growing up less rebellious, more tolerant, less happy—and completely unprepared for adulthood—and what that means for the rest of us*. New York: Artria.

Twenge, J. M., Baumeister, R. F., Tice, D. M., & Stucke, T. S. (2001). If you can't join them, beat them: Effects of social exclusion on aggressive behavior. *Journal of Personality and Social Psychology, 81*, 1058–1069.

Twenge, J. M., & Campbell, W. K. (2008). Increases in positive self-views among high school students: Birth-cohort changes in anticipated performance, self-satisfaction, self-liking, and self-competence. *Psychological Science, 19*, 1082–1086.

Twenge, J. M., Campbell, W. K., & Freeman, E. C. (2012). Generational differences in young adults' life goals, concern for others, and civic orientation, 1966–2009. *Journal of Personality and Social Psychology, 102*, 1045–1062.

Twenge, J. M., Gentile, B., DeWall, C. N., Ma, D., Lacefield, K., & Schurtz, D. R. (2010b). Birth cohort increases in psychopathology among young Americans, 1938–2007: A cross-temporal meta-analysis of the MMPI. *Clinical Psychology Review, 30*, 145–154.

Twenge, J. M., Joiner, T. E., Rogers, M. L., & Martin, G. N. (2018a). Increases in depressive symptoms, suicide-related outcomes, and suicide rates among U.S. adolescents after 2010 and links to increased new media screen time. *Clinical Psychological Science,6*, 3–17.

Twenge, J. M., Martin, G. N., & Campbell, W. K. (2018b). Decreases in psychological well-being among American adolescents after 2012 and links to screen time during the rise of smartphone technology. *Emotion, 18*, 765–780.

Twenge, J. M., & Park, H. (2019). The decline in adult activities among U.S. adolescents, 1976–2016. *Child Development, 90*, 638–654.

Twenge, J. M., Sherman, R. A., & Wells, B. E. (2016). Sexual inactivity during young adulthood is more common among U.S. millennials and iGen: Age, period, and cohort effects on having no sexual partners after age 18. *Archives of Sexual Behavior, 6*, 1–8.

Twenge, J. M., Sherman, R. A., & Wells, B. E. (2017). Declines in sexual frequency among American adults, 1989–2014. *Archives of Sexual Behavior, 46*, 2389–2401.

Twenge, J. M., Zhang, L., & Im, C. (2004). It's beyond my control: A cross-temporal meta-analysis of increasing externality in locus of control, 1960–2002. *Personality and Social Psychology Review, 8*, 308–319.

Twiss, C., Tabb, S., & Crosby, F. (1989). Affirmative action and aggregate data: The importance of patterns in the perception of discrimination. In F. Blanchard & F. Crosby (Eds.), *Affirmative action: Social psychological perspectives*. New York: Springer-Verlag.

U.S. Senate Select Committee on Intelligence. (2004, July 9). *Report of the Select Committee on Intelligence on the U.S. intelligence community's prewar intelligence assessments on Iraq*. Washington, DC: U.S. Senate Select Committee on Intelligence.

Uchida, Y., & Kitayama, S. (2009). Happiness and unhappiness in East and West: Themes and variations. *Emotion, 9*, 441–456.

Uchino, B. N., Cacioppo, J. T., & Kiecolt-Glaser, J. K. (1996). The relationship between social support and physiological processes: A review with emphasis on underlying mechanisms and implications for health. *Psychological Bulletin, 119*, 488–531.

Uchino, B. N., & Way, B. M. (2017). Integrative pathways linking close family ties to health: A neurochemical perspective. *American Psychologist, 72*, 590–600.

Udo, T., & Grilo, C. M. (2018). Prevalence and correlates of DSM-5–defined eating disorders in a nationally representative sample of U.S. adults. *Biological Psychiatry, 84*, 345–354.

Udry, J. R. (2000). Biological limits of gender construction. *American Sociological Review, 65*, 443–457.

Uhlhaas, P. J., Grent-Jong, T., & Gross, J. (2018). Magnetoencephalography and translational neuroscience in psychiatry. *JAMA Psychiatry, 75*, 969–971.

Ullsperger, J. M., & Nikolas, M. A. (2017). A meta-analytic review of the association between pubertal timing and psychopathology in adolescence: Are there sex differences in risk? *Psychological Bulletin, 143*, 903–938.

UN. (2015a). *Human development report 2015*. New York: United Nations Development Programme.

UN. (2015b). *The world's women: Trends and statistics*. United Nations Statistics Division.

UNAIDS. (2013, accessed May 17). *Data and analysis*. Joint United Nations Programme on HIV/AIDS. Retrieved from unaids.org/en/data-analysis

Underwood, E. (2016). Cadaver study challenges brain stimulation methods. *Science, 352*, 397.

Underwood, E. (2017). Brain implant trials spur ethical discussions. *Science, 358*, 710.

Ungar, L. (2014). Quiz: How long will you live? *Time Magazine*. Retrieved from http://time.com/3485579/when-will-i-die-life-expectancy-calculator/?xid=time_socialflow_twitter&utm_campaign=time&utm_source=twitter.com&utm_medium=social

United Nations. (2011, November 17). *Discriminatory laws and practices and acts of violence against individuals based on their sexual orientation and gender identity.* Report of the United Nations High Commissioner for Human Rights.

United States Department of Justice. (Retrieved 2018, Dec. 1). Sexual assault. Office on Violence Against Women (justice.gov/ovw/sexual-assault).

Urbain, C., De Tiège, X., De Beeck, M. O., Bourguignon, M., Wens, V., Verheulpen, D., . . . Peigneux, P. (2016). Sleep in children triggers rapid reorganization of memory-related brain processes. *NeuroImage, 134,* 213–222.

Urry, H. L., & Gross, J. J. (2010). Emotion regulation in older age. *Current Directions in Psychological Science, 19,* 352–357.

Urry, H. L., Nitschke, J. B., Dolski, I., Jackson, D. C., Dalton, K. M., Mueller, C. J., . . . Davidson, R. J. (2004). Making a life worth living: Neural correlates of well-being. *Psychological Science, 15,* 367–372.

Vaillant, G. (2013, May). What makes us happy, revisited? *The Atlantic* (theatlantic.com/magazine/archive/2013/05/thanks-mom/309287/).

Vaillant, G. E. (2002). *Aging well: Surprising guideposts to a happier life from the landmark Harvard study of adult development.* Boston: Little, Brown.

Valenstein, E. S. (1986). *Great and desperate cures: The rise and decline of psychosurgery.* New York: Basic Books.

Valentine, S. E., & Shipherd, J. C. (2018). A systematic review of social stress and mental health among transgender and gender non-conforming people in the United States. *Clinical Psychology Review, 66,* 24–38.

Valkenburg, P. M., & Peter, J. (2009). Social consequences of the Internet for adolescents: A decade of research. *Current Directions in Psychological Science, 18,* 1–5.

Vallone, R. P., Griffin, D. W., Lin, S., & Ross, L. (1990). Overconfident prediction of future actions and outcomes by self and others. *Journal of Personality and Social Psychology, 58,* 582–592.

van Anders, S. M. (2012). Testosterone and sexual desire in healthy women and men. *Archives of Sexual Behavior, 41,* 1471–1484.

Van Blerkom, D. L. (2012). *Orientation to learning* (7th ed.). Boston: Wadsworth.

Van Bockstaele, B., Verschuere, B., Tibboel, H., De Houwer, J., Crombez, G., & Koster, E. H. W. (2014). A review of current evidence for the causal impact of attentional bias on fear and anxiety. *Psychological Bulletin, 140,* 682–721.

Van Dam, N. T., van Vugt, M. K., Vago, D. R., Schmalzl, L., Saron, C. D., Olendzki, A., . . . Meyer, D. E. (2018). Mind the hype: A critical evaluation and prescriptive agenda for research on mindfulness and meditation. *Perspectives on Psychological Science, 13,* 36–61.

van de Bongardt, D., Reitz, E., Sandfort, T., & Deković, M. (2015). A meta-analysis of the relations between three types of peer norms and adolescent sexual behavior. *Personality and Social Psychology Review, 19,* 203–234.

Van den Akker, A. L., Asscher, J., & Prinzie, P. (2014). Mean-level personality development across childhood and adolescence: A temporary defiance of the maturity principle and bidirectional associations with parenting. *Journal of Personality and Social Psychology, 107,* 736–750.

van den Boom, D. C. (1990). Preventive intervention and the quality of mother-infant interaction and infant exploration in irritable infants. In W. Koops, H. J. G. Soppe, J. L. van der Linden, P. C. M. Molenaar, & J. J. F. Schroots (Eds.), *Developmental psychology research in The Netherlands.* The Netherlands: Uitgeverij Eburon. Cited by C. Hazan & P. R. Shaver (1994). Deeper into attachment theory. *Psychological Inquiry, 5,* 68–79.

van den Boom, D. C. (1995). Do first-year intervention effects endure? Follow-up during toddlerhood of a sample of Dutch irritable infants. *Child Development, 66,* 1798–1816.

van den Bos, K., & Spruijt, N. (2002). Appropriateness of decisions as a moderator of the psychology of voice. *European Journal of Social Psychology, 32,* 57–72.

Van den Bulck, J., Çetin, Y., Terzi, Ö., & Bushman, B. J. (2016). Violence, sex, and dreams: Violent and sexual media content infiltrate our dreams at night. *Dreaming, 26,* 271–279.

van der Lee, R., & Ellemers, N. (2015). Gender contributes to personal research funding success in The Netherlands. *PNAS, 112,* 12349–12353.

van der Linden, S. L., Leiserowitz, A. A., Feinberg, G. D, & Maibach, E. W. (2015). The scientific consensus on climate change as a gateway belief: Experimental evidence. *PLOS ONE, 10,* e0118489.

Van Dessel, P., Mertens, G., Smith, C. T., & De Houwer, J. (2019). Mere exposure effects on implicit stimulus evaluation: The moderating role of evaluation task, number of stimulus presentations, and memory for presentation frequency. *Personality and Social Psychology Bulletin, 45,* 447–460.

van Dijk, W. W., Van Koningsbruggen, G. M., Ouwerkerk, J. W., & Wesseling, Y. M. (2011). Self-esteem, self-affirmation, and schadenfreude. *Emotion, 11,* 1445–1449.

Van Dyke, C., & Byck, R. (1982, March). Cocaine. *Scientific American,* pp. 128–141.

van Engen, M. L., & Willemsen, T. M. (2004). Sex and leadership styles: A meta-analysis of research published in the 1990s. *Psychological Reports, 94,* 3–18.

van Geel, M., Goemans, A., & Vedder, P. (2015). A meta-analysis on the relation between peer victimization and adolescent non-suicidal self-injury. *Psychiatry Research, 230,* 364–368.

van Haren, N. E., Rijsdijk, F., Schnack, H. G., Picchioni, M. M., Toulopoulou, T., Weisbrod, M., . . . Kahn, R. S. (2012). The genetic and environmental determinants of the association between brain abnormalities and schizophrenia: The schizophrenia twins and relatives consortium. *Biological Psychiatry, 71,* 915–921.

van Haren, N. E., Schnack, H. G., Koevoets, M. G., Cahn, W., Pol, H. E. H., & Kahn, R. S. (2016). Trajectories of subcortical volume change in schizophrenia: A 5-year follow-up. *Schizophrenia Research, 173,* 140–145.

van Honk, J., Schutter, D. J., Bos, P. A., Kruijt, A.-W., Lentje, E. G., & Baron-Cohen, S. (2011). Testosterone administration impairs cognitive empathy in women depending on second-to-fourth digit ratio. *PNAS, 108,* 3448–3452.

Van Horn, J., Irimia, A., Torgerson, C., Chambers, M., Kikinis, R., & Toga, A. (2012). Mapping connectivity damage in the case of Phineas Gage. *PLOS ONE, 7*(5), e37454.

van IJzendoorn, M., Fearon, P., & Bakermans-Kranenburg, M. (2017). Attachment—public and scientific. *The Psychologist, 30,* 6–9.

van IJzendoorn, M. H., & Kroonenberg, P. M. (1988). Cross-cultural patterns of attachment: A meta-analysis of the strange situation. *Child Development, 59,* 147–156.

van IJzendoorn, M. H., Luijk, M. P. C. M., & Juffer, F. (2008). IQ of children growing up in children's homes: A meta-analysis on IQ delays in orphanages. *Merrill-Palmer Quarterly, 54,* 341–366.

Van Kesteren, P. J. M., Asscheman, H., Megens, J. A. J., & Gooren, J. G. (1997). Mortality and morbidity in transsexual subjects treated with cross-sex hormones. *Clinical Endocrinology, 47,* 337–342.

Van Tongeren, D. R., DeWall, C. N., Green, J. D., Cairo, A. H., Davis, D. E., & Hook, J. N. (2018). Self-regulation facilitates meaning in life. *Review of General Psychology, 22,* 95–106.

Van Yperen, N. W., & Buunk, B. P. (1990). A longitudinal study of equity and satisfaction in intimate relationships. *European Journal of Social Psychology, 20,* 287–309.

Van Zeijl, J., Mesman, J., van IJzendoorn, M. H., Bakermans-Kranenburg, M. J., Juffer, F., Stolk, M. N., . . . Alink, L. R. A. (2006). Attachment-based intervention for enhancing sensitive discipline in mothers of 1- to 3-year-old children at risk for externalizing behavior problems: A randomized controlled trial. *Journal of Consulting and Clinical Psychology, 74,* 994–1005.

vanDellen, M. R., Campbell, W. K., Hoyle, R. H., & Bradfield, E. K. (2011). Compensating, resisting, and breaking: A meta-analytic examination of reactions to self-esteem threat. *Personality and Social Psychological Review, 15,* 51–74.

VanderLaan, D. P., Forrester, D. L., Petterson, L. J., & Vasey, P. L. (2012). Offspring production among the extended relatives of Samoan men and fa'afafine. *PLOS ONE, 7,* e36088.

VanderLaan, D. P., & Vasey, P. L. (2011). Male sexual orientation in Independent Samoa: Evidence for fraternal birth order and maternal fecundity effects. *Archives of Sexual Behavior, 40,* 495–503.

VanderWeele, T. J. (2017, May 30). What the *New York Times* gets wrong about marriage, health, and well-being. Institute for Family Studies (www.ifstudies.org).

VanderWeele, T. J. (2018, September 18). Religious upbringing and adolescence. Institute for Family Studies (www.ifstudies.org).

VanderWeele, T. J., Li, S., Tsai, A. C., & Kawachi, I. (2016). Association between religious service attendance and lower suicide rates among US women. *JAMA Psychiatry, 73,* 845–851.

Vanhalst, J., Soenens, B., Luyckx, K., Van Petegem, S., Weeks, M. S., & Asher, S. R. (2015). Why do the lonely stay lonely? Chronically lonely adolescents' attributions and emotions in situations of social inclusion and exclusion. *Journal of Personality and Social Psychology, 109,* 932–948.

Vaughn, K. B., & Lanzetta, J. T. (1981). The effect of modification of expressive displays on vicarious emotional arousal. *Journal of Experimental Social Psychology, 17,* 16–30.

Vecera, S. P., Vogel, E. K., & Woodman, G. F. (2002). Lower region: A new cue for figure-ground assignment. *Journal of Experimental Psychology: General, 13,* 194–205.

Veenhoven, R. (2014, accessed March 17). *World database of happiness.* Retrieved from worlddatabaseofhappiness.eur.nl

Veenhoven, R. (2015). Informed pursuit of happiness: What we should know, do know and can get to know. *Journal of Happiness Studies, 16,* 1035–1071.

Verdolini, N., Pacchiarotti, I., Köhler, C. A., Reinares, M., Samalin, L., Colom, F., . . . & Murru, A. (2018). Violent criminal behavior in the context of bipolar disorder: Systematic review and meta-analysis. *Journal of Affective Disorders, 239,* 161–170.

Verduyn, P., Ybarra, O., Résibois, M., Jonides, J., & Kross, E. (2017). Do social network sites enhance or undermine subjective well-being? A critical review. *Social Issues and Policy Review, 11,* 274–302.

Vergauwe, J., Wille, B., Hofmans, J., Kaiser, R. B., & De Fruyt, F. (2018). The double-edged sword of leader charisma: Understanding the curvilinear relationship between charismatic personality and leader effectiveness. *Journal of Personality and Social Psychology, 114,* 110–130.

Verhaeghen, P., & Salthouse, T. A. (1997). Meta-analyses of age-cognition relations in adulthood: Estimates of linear and nonlinear age effects and structural models. *Psychological Bulletin, 122,* 231–249.

Vermetten, E., Schmahl, C., Lindner, S., Loewenstein, R. J., & Bremner, J. D. (2006). Hippocampal and amygdalar volumes in dissociative identity disorder. *American Journal of Psychiatry, 163,* 630–636.

Verschuere, B., & Meijer, E. H. (2014). What's on your mind? Recent advances in memory detection using the concealed information test. *European Psychologist, 19,* 162–171.

Vezzali, L., Stathi, S., Giovannini, D., Capozza, D., & Trifiletti, E. (2015). The greatest magic of Harry Potter: Reducing prejudice. *Journal of Applied Social Psychology, 45,* 105–121.

Victora, C. G., Horta, B. L., de Mola, C. L., Quevedo, L., Pinheiro, R. T., Gigante, D. P., . . . Barros, F. C. (2015). Association between breastfeeding and intelligence, educational attainment, and income at 30 years of age: A prospective birth cohort study from Brazil. *The Lancet Global Health, 3,* e199–205.

Vieselmeyer, J., Holguin, J., & Mezulis, A. (2017). The role of resilience and gratitude in posttraumatic stress and growth following a campus shooting. *Psychological Trauma: Theory, Research, Practice, and Policy, 9,* 62–69.

Vigil, J. M. (2009). A socio-relational framework of sex differences in the expression of emotion. *Behavioral and Brain Sciences, 32,* 375–428.

Vigliocco, G., & Hartsuiker, R. J. (2002). The interplay of meaning, sound, and syntax in sentence production. *Psychological Bulletin, 128,* 442–472.

Vining, E. P. G., Freeman, J. M., Pillas, D. J., Uematsu, S., Carson, B. S., Brandt, J., . . . Zukerberg, A. (1997). Why would you remove half a brain? The outcome of 58 children after hemispherectomy—The Johns Hopkins Experience: 1968 to 1996. *Pediatrics, 100,* 163–171.

Visich, P. S., & Fletcher, E. (2009). Myocardial infarction. In J. K. Ehrman, P. M. Gordon, P. S. Visich, & S. J. Keleyian (Eds.), *Clinical exercise physiology* (2nd ed.). Champaign, IL: Human Kinetics.

Vitello, P. (2012, August 1). George A. Miller, a pioneer in cognitive psychology, is dead at 92. *The New York Times* (nytimes.com).

Vlasic, B. (2015, Feb. 4). Despite recalls, G.M. pays workers a big bonus. *The New York Times* (nytimes.com).

Vliegenthart, J., Noppe, G., van Rossum, E. F. C., Koper, J. W., Raat, H., & van den Akker, E. L. T. (2016). Socioeconomic status in children is associated with hair cortisol levels as a biological measure of chronic stress. *Psychoneuroendocrinology, 65,* 9–14.

Vocks, S., Tuschen-Caffier, B., Pietrowsky, R., Rustenbach, S. J., Kersting, A., & Herpertz, S. (2010). Meta-analysis of the effectiveness of psychological and pharmacological treatments for binge eating disorder. *International Journal of Eating Disorders, 43,* 205–217.

Vogel, G. (2010). Long-fought compromise reached on European animal rules. *Science, 329,* 1588–1589.

Vogel, N., Schilling, Wahl, H.-W., Beekman, A. T. F., & Penninx, B. W. J. H. (2013). Time-to-death-related change in positive and negative affect among older adults approaching the end of life. *Psychology and Aging, 28,* 128–141.

Vohs, K. D., Baumeister, R. F., & Schmeichel, B. J. (2012). Motivation, personal beliefs, and limited resources all contribute to self-control. *Journal of Experimental Social Psychology, 48,* 943–947.

Volkow, N. D., Swanson, J. M., Evins, A. E., DeLisi, L. E., Meier, M. H., Gonzalez, R., . . . Baler, R. (2016). Effects of cannabis use on human behavior, including cognition, motivation, and psychosis: a review. *JAMA Psychiatry, 73,* 292–297.

Volkow, N. D., Wang, G. J., Kollins, S. H., Wigal, T. L., Newcorn, J. H., Telang, F., . . . Swanson, J. M. (2009). Evaluating dopamine reward pathway in ADHD: Clinical implications. *Journal of the American Medical Association, 302,* 1084–1091.

von Dawans, B., Ditzen, B., Trueg, A., Fischbacher, U., & Heinrichs, M. (2019). Effects of acute stress on social behavior in women. *Psychoneuroendocrinology, 99,* 137–144.

von Hippel, W. (2007). Aging, executive functioning, and social control. *Current Directions in Psychological Science, 16,* 240–244.

von Hippel, W. (2015, July 17). Do people become more prejudiced as they grow older? Retrieved from bbc.com/news/magazine-33523313

von Hippel, W. & Trivers, R. (2011). The evolution and psychology of self-deception. *Behavioral and Brain Sciences, 34,* 1–56.

von Senden, M. (1932). *The perception of space and shape in the congenitally blind before and after operation.* Glencoe, IL: Free Press.

von Soest, T., Wagner, J., Hansen, T., & Gerstorf, D. (2017). Self-esteem across the second half of life: The role of socioeconomic status, physical health, social relationships, and personality factors. *Journal of Personality and Social Psychology, 114,* 945–958.

von Stumm, S., Hell, B., & Chamorro-Premuzic, T. (2011). The hungry mind: Intellectual curiosity is the third pillar of academic performance. *Perspectives on Psychological Science, 6,* 574–588.

von Stumm, S., & Plomin, R. (2015). Breastfeeding and IQ growth from toddlerhood through adolescence. *PLOS ONE, 10*(9), e0138676.

Vonk, J., Jett, S. E., & Mosteller, K. W. (2012). Concept formation in American black bears, *Ursus americanus. Animal Behaviour, 84,* 953–964.

Vorona, R. D., Szklo-Coxe, M., Wu, A., Dubik, M., Zhao, Y., & Ware, J. C. (2011). Dissimilar teen crash rates in two neighboring Southeastern Virginia cities with different high school start times. *Journal of Clinical Sleep Medicine, 7,* 145–151.

Vosoughi, S., Roy, D., & Aral, S. (2018). The spread of true and false news online. *Science, 359,* 1146–1151.

Voyer, D., & Voyer, S. D. (2014). Gender differences in scholastic achievement: A meta-analysis. *Psychological Bulletin, 140,* 1174–1204.

VPC. (2016, January 4). States with weak gun laws and higher gun ownership lead nation in gun deaths, new data for 2014 confirms. Violence Policy Center (vpc.org).

Vrij, A., & Fisher, R. P. (2016). Which lie detection tools are ready for use in the criminal justice system? *Journal of Applied Research in Memory and Cognition, 5,* 302–307.

Vukasovi, T., & Bratko, D. (2015). Heritability of personality: A meta-analysis of behavior genetic studies. *Psychological Bulletin, 141,* 769–785.

Vyse, S. (2016, March/April). Guns: feeling safe ≠ being safe. *Skeptical Inquirer,* pp. 27–30.

Waber, R. L., Shiv, B., Carmon, Z., & Ariely, D. (2008). Commercial features of placebo and therapeutic efficacy. *Journal of the American Medical Association, 299,* 1016–1017.

Wade, K. A., Garry, M., & Pezdek, K. (2018). Deconstructing rich false memories of committing crime: Commentary on Shaw and Porter (2015). *Psychological Science, 29,* 471–476.

Wade, K. A., Garry, M., Read, J. D., & Lindsay, D. S. (2002). A picture is worth a thousand lies: Using false photographs to create false childhood memories. *Psychonomic Bulletin & Review, 9,* 597–603.

Wagar, B. M., & Cohen, D. (2003). Culture, memory, and the self: An analysis of the personal and collective self in long-term memory. *Journal of Experimental Social Psychology, 39,* 458–475.

Wagenmakers, E.-J. (2014, June 25). Bem is back: A skeptic's review of a meta-analysis on psi. Open Science Collaboration (centerforopenscience.github.io/osc/2014/06/25/a-skeptics-review).

Wagenmakers, E.-J., Wetzels, R., Borsboom, D., & van der Maas, H. (2011). Why psychologists must change the way they analyze their data: The case of psi. *Journal of Personality and Social Psychology, 100,* 1–12.

Wager, R. D., & Atlas, L. Y. (2013). How is pain influenced by cognition? Neuroimaging weighs in. *Perspectives on Psychological Science, 8,* 91–97.

Wagner, D. D., Altman, M., Boswell, R. G., Kelley, W. M., & Heatherton, T. F. (2013). Self-regulatory depletion enhances neural responses to rewards and impairs top-down control. *Psychological Science, 24,* 2262–2271.

Wagner, D., Becker, B., Koester, P., Gouzoulis-Mayfrank, E., & Daumann, J. (2012). A prospective study of learning, memory, and executive function in new MDMA users. *Addiction, 108,* 136–145.

Wagner, K., & Dobkins, K. R. (2011). Synaesthetic associations decrease during infancy. *Psychological Science, 22,* 1067–1072.

Wagstaff, G. (1982). Attitudes to rape: The "just world" strikes again? *Bulletin of the British Psychological Society, 13,* 275–283.

Wakefield, J. C., & Spitzer, R. L. (2002). Lowered estimates—but of what? *Archives of General Psychiatry, 59,* 129–130.

Walfisch, A., Sermer, C., Cressman, A., & Koren, G. (2014). Breast milk and cognitive development—the role of confounders: A systematic review. *BMJ Open, 3*(8), e003259.

Walker, E., Shapiro, D., Esterberg, M., & Trotman, H. (2010). Neurodevelopment and schizophrenia: Broadening the focus. *Current Directions in Psychological Science, 19,* 204–208.

Walker, M. P., & van der Helm, E. (2009). Overnight therapy? The role of sleep in emotional brain processing. *Psychological Bulletin, 135,* 731–748.

Walker, W. R., Skowronski, J. J., & Thompson, C. P. (2003). Life is pleasant—and memory helps to keep it that way! *Review of General Psychology, 7,* 203–210.

Wallace, L. E., Anthony, R., End, C. M., & Way, B. M. (2018). Does religion stave off the grave? Religious affiliation in one's obituary and longevity. *Social Psychological and Personality Science.* Advance online publication. doi.org/10.1177/1948550618779820

Wallach, M. A., & Wallach, L. (1983). *Psychology's sanction for selfishness: The error of egoism in theory and therapy.* New York: Freeman.

Walsh, J. L., Fielder, R. L., Carey, K. B., & Carey, M. P. (2013). Female college students' media use and academic outcomes: Results from a longitudinal cohort study. *Emerging Adulthood, 1,* 219–232.

Walsh, L. C., Boehm, J. K., & Lyubomirsky, S. (2018). Does happiness promote career success? Revisiting the evidence. *Journal of Career Assessment, 26,* 199–219.

Walsh, R. (2011). Lifestyle and mental health. *American Psychologist, 66,* 579–592.

Walster (Hatfield), E., Aronson, V., Abrahams, D., & Rottman, L. (1966). Importance of physical attractiveness in dating behavior. *Journal of Personality and Social Psychology, 4*, 508–516.

Walters, G. D. (2018). Predicting short- and long-term desistance from crime with the NEO personality inventory-short form: Domain scores and interactions in high risk delinquent youth. *Journal of Research in Personality, 75*, 37–45.

Walton, G. M., & Spencer, S. J. (2009). Latent ability: Grades and test scores systematically underestimate the intellectual ability of negatively stereotyped students. *Psychological Science, 20*, 1132–1139.

Walton, G. M., & Wilson, T. D. (2018). Wise interventions: Psychological remedies for social and personal problems. *Psychological Review, 125*, 617–655.

Wampold, B. E. (2001). *The great psychotherapy debate: Models, methods, and findings*. Mahwah, NJ: Erlbaum.

Wampold, B. E. (2007). Psychotherapy: The humanistic (and effective) treatment. *American Psychologist, 62*, 857–873.

Wampold, B. E., Flückiger, C., Del Re, A. C., Yulish, N. E., Frost, N. D., Pace, B. T., . . . Hilsenroth, M. J. (2017). In pursuit of truth: A critical examination of meta-analyses of cognitive behavior therapy. *Psychotherapy Research, 27*, 14–32.

Wang, F., DesMeules, M., Luo, W., Dai, S., Lagace, C., & Morrison, H. (2011). Leisure-time physical activity and marital status in relation to depression between men and women: A prospective study. *Health Psychology, 30*, 204–211.

Wang, J., Häusermann, M., Wydler, H., Mohler-Kuo, M., & Weiss, M. G. (2012). Suicidality and sexual orientation among men in Switzerland: Findings from 3 probability surveys. *Journal of Psychiatric Research, 46*, 980–986.

Wang, J., He, L., Liping, J., Tian, J., & Benson, V. (2015a). The "positive effect" is present in older Chinese adults: Evidence from an eye tracking study. *PLOS ONE, 10*, e0121372.

Wang, J., Leu, J., & Shoda, Y. (2011b). When the seemingly innocuous "stings": Racial microaggressions and their emotional consequences. *Personality and Social Psychology Bulletin, 37*, 1666–1678.

Wang, J., Plöderl, M., Häusermann, M., & Weiss, M. G. (2015b). Understanding suicide attempts among gay men from their self-perceived causes. *Journal of Nervous and Mental Disease, 203*, 499–506.

Wang, J., Rao, Y., & Houser, D. E. (2017a). An experimental analysis of acquired impulse control among adult humans intolerant to alcohol. *PNAS, 114*, 1299–1304.

Wang, J., Wei, Q., Bai, T., Zhou, X., Sun, H., Becker, B., . . . Kendrick, K. (2017b). Electroconvulsive therapy selectively enhanced feedforward connectivity from fusiform face area to amygdala in major depressive disorder. *Social Cognitive and Affective Neuroscience 2*, 1983–1992.

Wang, J. X., Rogers, L. M., Gross, E. Z., Ryals, A. J., Dokucu, M. E., Brandstatt, K. L., . . . Voss, J. L. (2014). Targeted enhancement of cortical-hippocampal brain networks and associative memory. *Science, 345*, 1054–1057.

Wang, Y., Highhouse, S., Lake, C. J., Petersen, N. L., & Rada, T. B. (2017). Meta-analytic investigations of the relation between intuition and analysis. *Journal of Behavioral Decision Making, 30*, 15–25.

Wang, Z., Lukowski, S. L., Hart, S. A., Lyons, I. M., Thompson, L. A., Kovas, Y., . . . Petrill, S. A. (2015). Is math anxiety always bad for math learning? The role of math motivation. *Psychological Science, 26*, 1863–1876.

Wann, J. P. Poulter, D. R., & Purcell, C. (2011). Reduced sensitivity to visual looming inflates the risk posed by speeding vehicles when children try to cross the road. *Psychological Science, 22*, 429–434.

Ward, A., & Mann, T. (2000). Don't mind if I do: Disinhibited eating under cognitive load. *Journal of Personality and Social Psychology, 78*, 753–763.

Ward, C. (1994). Culture and altered states of consciousness. In W. J. Lonner & R. Malpass (Eds.), *Psychology and culture*. Boston: Allyn & Bacon.

Ward, J. (2003). State of the art synaesthesia. *The Psychologist, 16*, 196–199.

Ward, K. D., Klesges, R. C., & Halpern, M. T. (1997). Predictors of smoking cessation and state-of-the-art smoking interventions. *Journal of Social Issues, 53*, 129–145.

Wardle, J., Cooke, L. J., Gibson, L., Sapochnik, M., Sheiham, A., & Lawson, M. (2003). Increasing children's acceptance of vegetables: A randomized trial of parent-led exposure. *Appetite, 40*, 155–162.

Warne, R. T., & Burningham, C. (2019). Spearman's *g* found in 31 non-Western nations: Strong evidence that *g* is universal. *Psychological Bulletin, 145*, 237–272.

Washington Post. (2017). Fatal force. Retrieved from washingtonpost.com/graphics/national/police-shootings/

Wason, P. C. (1960). On the failure to eliminate hypotheses in a conceptual task. *Quarterly Journal of Experimental Psychology, 12*, 129–140.

Wasserman, E. A. (1993). Comparative cognition: Toward a general understanding of cognition in behavior. *Psychological Science, 4*, 156–161.

Wasserman, E. A. (1995). The conceptual abilities of pigeons. *American Scientist, 83*, 246–255.

Waters, E. A., Klein, W. M. P., Moser, R. P., Yu, M., Waldron, W. R., McNeel, T. S., & Freedman, A. N. (2011). Correlates of unrealistic risk beliefs in a nationally representative sample. *Journal of Behavioral Medicine, 34*, 225–235.

Watson, D. (2000). *Mood and temperament*. New York: Guilford Press.

Watson, J. B. (1913). Psychology as the behaviorist views it. *Psychological Review, 20*, 158–177.

Watson, J. B. (1924). The unverbalized in human behavior. *Psychological Review, 31*, 339–347.

Watson, J. B., & Rayner, R. (1920). Conditioned emotional reactions. *Journal of Experimental Psychology, 3*, 1–14.

Watson, R. I., Jr. (1973). Investigation into deindividuation using a cross-cultural survey technique. *Journal of Personality and Social Psychology, 25*, 342–345.

Watts, T. W., Duncan, G. J., & Quan, H. (2018). Revisiting the marshmallow task: A conceptual replication investigating links between early delay of gratification and later outcomes. *Psychological Science, 29*, 1159–1177.

Way, B. M., Creswell, J. D., Eisenberger, N. I., & Lieberman, M. D. (2010). Dispositional mindfulness and depressive symptomatology: Correlations with limbic and self-referential neural activity during rest. *Emotion, 10*, 12–24.

Wayment, H. A., & Peplau, L. A. (1995). Social support and well-being among lesbian and heterosexual women: A structural modeling approach. *Personality and Social Psychology Bulletin, 21*, 1189–1199.

Waytz, A., Young, L. L., & Ginges, J. (2014). Motive attribution asymmetry for love vs. hate drives intractable conflict. *PNAS, 111*, 15687–15692.

Webb, C. E., Rossignac-Milon, M., & Higgins, E. T. (2017). Stepping forward together: Could walking facilitate interpersonal conflict resolution? *American Psychologist, 72*, 374–385.

Weber, A., Fernald, A., & Diop, Y. (2017). When cultural norms discourage talking to babies: Effectiveness of a parenting program in rural Senegal. *Child Development, 88*, 1513–1526.

Webster, G. D., DeWall, C. N., Pond, R. S., Jr., Deckman, T., Jonason, P. K., Le, B. M., . . . Bator, R. J. (2014). The Brief Aggression Questionnaire: Psychometric and behavioral evidence for an efficient measure of trait aggression. *Aggressive Behavior, 40*, 120–139.

Wechsler, D. (1972). "Hold" and "Don't Hold" tests. In S. M. Chown (Ed.), *Human aging*. New York: Penguin.

Wegner, D. M., & Ward, A. F. (2013). How Google is changing your brain. *Scientific American, 309*, 58–61.

Weichbold, V., Holzer, A., Newesely, G., & Stephan, K. (2012). Results from high-frequency hearing screening in 14- to 15-year old adolescents and their relation to self-reported exposure to loud music. *International Journal of Audiology, 51*, 650–654.

Weinberger, D. R. (2019). Thinking about schizophrenia in an era of genomic medicine. *American Journal of Psychiatry, 176*, 12–20.

Weiner, B., Perry, R. P., & Magnusson, J. (1988). An attributional analysis of reactions to stigmas. *Journal of Personality and Social Psychology, 55*, 738–748.

Weingarden, H., & Renshaw, K. D. (2012). Early and late perceived pubertal timing as risk factors for anxiety disorders in adult women. *Journal of Psychiatric Research, 46*, 1524–1529.

Weingarten, G. (2002, March 10). Below the beltway. *The Washington Post*, p. WO3.

Weinstein, N. D. (1980). Unrealistic optimism about future life events. *Journal of Personality and Social Psychology, 39*, 806–820.

Weinstein, N. D., Ryan, W. S., DeHaan, C. R., Przbylski, A. K., Legate, N., & Ryan, R. M. (2012). Parental autonomy support and discrepancies between implicit and explicit sexual identities: Dynamics of self-acceptance and defense. *Journal of Personality and Social Psychology, 102*, 815–832.

Weinstein, Y., Levav, I., Gelkopf, M., Roe, D., Yoffe, R., Pugachova, I., & Levine, S. Z. (2018). Association of maternal exposure to terror attacks during pregnancy and the risk of schizophrenia in the offspring: A population-based study. *Schizophrenia Research, 199*, 163–167.

Weir, K. (2013, May). Captive audience. *Monitor on Psychology*, pp. 44–49.

Weisbuch, M., Ivcevic, Z., & Ambady, N. (2009). On being liked on the web and in the "real world": Consistency in first impressions across personal webpages and spontaneous behavior. *Journal of Experimental Social Psychology, 45*, 573–576.

Weiser, E. B. (2015). #Me: Narcissism and its facets as predictors of selfie-posting frequency. *Personality and Individual Differences, 86*, 477–481.

Weiss, A., Wilson, M. L., Collins, D. A., Mhungu, D., Kamenya, S., Foerster, S., & Pusey, A. E. (2017). Personality in the chimpanzees of Gombe National Park. *Nature: Scientific Data, 4*, #170146.

Weissman, M. M., Wickramaratne, P., Gameroff, M. J., Warner, V., Pilowsky, D., Kohad, R. G., . . . Talati, A. (2016). Offspring of depressed parents: 30 years later. *American Journal of Psychiatry, 173*, 1024–1032.

Weisz, J. R., Kuppens, S., Ng, M. Y., Eckshtain, D., Ugueto, A. M., Vaughn-Coaxum, R., . . . Weersing, V. R. (2017). What five decades of research tells us about the effects of youth psychological therapy:

A multilevel meta-analysis and implications for science and practice. *American Psychologist, 72*, 79–117.

Welborn, B. L., Gunter, B. C., Vesich, I. S., & Lieberman, M. D. (2017). Neural correlates of the false consensus effect: Evidence for motivated projection and regulatory restraint. *Journal of Cognitive Neuroscience, 29*, 708–717.

Welch, W. W. (2005, February 28). Trauma of Iraq war haunting thousands returning home. *USA Today* (usatoday.com).

Welker, K. M., Baker, L., Padilla, A., Holmes, H., Aron, A., & Slatcher, R. B. (2014). Effects of self-disclosure and responsiveness between couples on passionate love within couples. *Personal Relationships, 21*, 692–708.

Weller, S., & Davis-Beaty, K. (2002). The effectiveness of male condoms in prevention of sexually transmitted diseases (protocol). *Cochrane Database of Systematic Reviews*, Issue 4, Art. No. CD004090.

Wells, D. L. (2009). The effects of animals on human health and well-being. *Journal of Social Issues, 65*, 523–543.

Wells, G. L. (1981). Lay analyses of causal forces on behavior. In J. Harvey (Ed.), *Cognition, social behavior and the environment*. Hillsdale, NJ: Erlbaum.

Wenze, S. J., Gunthert, K. C., & German, R. E. (2012). Biases in affective forecasting and recall in individuals with depression and anxiety symptoms. *Personality and Social Psychology Bulletin, 38*, 895–906.

Westen, D. (1996). *Is Freud really dead? Teaching psychodynamic theory to introductory psychology*. Presentation to the Annual Institute on the Teaching of Psychology, St. Petersburg Beach, FL.

Westen, D. (1998). The scientific legacy of Sigmund Freud: Toward a psychodynamically informed psychological science. *Psychological Bulletin, 124*, 333–371.

Westen, D. (2007). *The political brain: The role of emotion in deciding the fate of the nation*. New York: PublicAffairs.

Westen, D., & Morrison, K. (2001). A multidimensional meta-analysis of treatments for depression, panic, and generalized anxiety disorder: An empirical examination of the status of empirically supported therapies. *Journal of Consulting and Clinical Psychology, 69*, 875–899.

Wetherell, J. L., Petkus, A. J., White, K. S., Nguyen, H., Kornblith, S., Andreescu, C., . . . Lenze, E. J. (2013). Antidepressant medication augmented with cognitive-behavioral therapy for generalized anxiety disorder in older adults. *American Journal of Psychiatry, 170*, 782–789.

Whelan, R., Conrod, P. J., Poline, J.-B., Lourdusamy, A., Banaschewski, T., Barker, G. J., . . . the IMAGEN Consortium. (2012). Adolescent impulsivity phenotypes characterized by distinct brain networks. *Nature Neuroscience, 15*, 920–925.

Whillans, A. V., Christie, C. D., Cheung, S., Jordan, A. H., & Chen, F. S. (2017). From misperception to social connection: Correlates and consequences of overestimating others' social connectedness. *Personality and Social Psychology Bulletin, 43*, 1696–1711.

Whisman, M. A., Johnson, D. P., & Rhee, S. H. (2014). A behavior genetic analysis of pleasant events, depressive symptoms, and their covariation. *Clinical Psychological Science, 2*, 535–544.

White, H. R., Brick, J., & Hansell, S. (1993). A longitudinal investigation of alcohol use and aggression in adolescence. *Journal of Studies on Alcohol, Supplement 11*, 62–77.

White, L., & Edwards, J. (1990). Emptying the nest and parental well-being: An analysis of national panel data. *American Sociological Review, 55*, 235–242.

White, P. H., Kjelgaard, M. M., & Harkins, S. G. (1995). Testing the contribution of self-evaluation to goal-setting effects. *Journal of Personality and Social Psychology, 69*, 69–79.

Whitehead, B. D., & Popenoe, D. (2001). *The state of our unions 2001: The social health of marriage in America*. Rutgers University: The National Marriage Project.

Whitehurst, L. N., Cellini, N., McDevitt, E. A., Duggan, K. A., & Mednick, S. C. (2016). Autonomic activity during sleep predicts memory consolidation in humans. *PNAS, 113*, 7272–7277.

Whiten, A., & Boesch, C. (2001, January). Cultures of chimpanzees. *Scientific American*, pp. 60–67.

Whiting, B. B., & Edwards, C. P. (1988). *Children of different worlds: The formation of social behavior*. Cambridge, MA: Harvard University Press.

Whitley, B. E., Jr. (1999). Right-wing authoritarianism, social dominance orientation, and prejudice. *Journal of Personality and Social Psychology, 77*, 126–134.

Whitlock, J. R., Heynen, A. L., Shuler, M. G., & Bear, M. F. (2006). Learning induces long-term potentiation in the hippocampus. *Science, 313*, 1093–1097.

WHO (World Health Organization). (2000). *Effectiveness of male latex condoms in protecting against pregnancy and sexually transmitted infections*. World Health Organization (who.int).

WHO. (2003). *The male latex condom: Specification and guidelines for condom procurement*. Department of Reproductive Health and Research, Family and Community Health, World Health Organization. Retrieved from who.int

WHO. (2012, May). *Tobacco: Fact sheet N339*. (who.int).

WHO. (2013, November). *Sexually transmitted infections (STIs)* (Fact Sheet No. 110). Retrieved from who.int /mediacentre/factsheets/fs110/en/

WHO. (2014a, accessed September 20). *Chain-free initiative*. Retrieved from emro.who.int/mental-health /chain-free-initiative

WHO. (2014b). *Global status report on alcohol and health 2014*. (who.int).

WHO. (2016, November). *Violence against women. Intimate partner and sexual violence against* women. Fact Sheet. Retrieved from who.int/mediacentre/factsheets/fs239/en/

WHO. (2017a). *Depression*. Retrieved from who.int /mediacentre/factsheets/fs369/en

WHO. (2017b). *The determinants of health*. Retrieved from who.int/hia/evidence/doh/en/

WHO. (2017c). *Mental disorders*. Retrieved from who.int /mediacentre/factsheets/fs396/en

WHO. (2018a). *Depression*. (who.int).

WHO. (2018b). *Gaming disorder*. (who.int).

WHO. (2018c). *Monitoring health for sustainable development goals*. (who.int).

Wicherts, J. M., Dolan, C. V., Carlson, J. S., & van der Maas, H. L. J. (2010). Raven's test performance of sub-Saharan Africans: Mean level, psychometric properties, and the Flynn effect. *Learning and Individual Differences, 20*, 135–151.

Wickelgren, I. (2009, September/October). I do not feel your pain. *Scientific American Mind*, pp. 51–57.

Wickelgren, W. A. (1977). *Learning and memory*. Englewood Cliffs, NJ: Prentice-Hall.

Widiger, T. A., Gore, W. L., Crego, C., Rojas, S. L., & Oltmanns, J. R. (2016). Five factor model and personality disorder. In T. A. Widiger (Ed.), *The Oxford handbook of the five factor model of personality*. New York: Oxford University Press.

Widom, C. S. (1989a). Does violence beget violence? A critical examination of the literature. *Psychological Bulletin, 106*, 3–28.

Widom, C. S. (1989b). The cycle of violence. *Science, 244*, 160–166.

Wiens, A. N., & Menustik, C. E. (1983). Treatment outcome and patient characteristics in an aversion therapy program for alcoholism. *American Psychologist, 38*, 1089–1096.

Wierson, M., & Forehand, R. (1994). Parent behavioral training for child noncompliance: Rationale, concepts, and effectiveness. *Current Directions in Psychological Science, 3*, 146–149.

Wierzbicki, M. (1993). Psychological adjustment of adoptees: A meta-analysis. *Journal of Clinical Child Psychology, 22*, 447–454.

Wiese, C. W., Kuykendall, L., & Tay, L. (2018). Get active? A meta-analysis of leisure-time physical activity and subjective well-being. *The Journal of Positive Psychology, 13*, 57–66.

Wiesel, T. N. (1982). Postnatal development of the visual cortex and the influence of environment. *Nature, 299*, 583–591.

Wigdor, A. K., & Garner, W. R. (1982). *Ability testing: Uses, consequences, and controversies*. Washington, DC: National Academy Press.

Wilcox, W. B., & Wolfinger, N. H. (2017, February). *Men & marriage: Debunking the ball and chain myth* [PDF file]. Retrieved from ifstudies.org/wp-content /uploads/2017/02/IFSMenandMarriageResearchBrief2.pdf

Wilder, D. A. (1981). Perceiving persons as a group: Categorization and intergroup relations. In D. L. Hamilton (Ed.), *Cognitive processes in stereotyping and intergroup behavior* (pp. 213–257). Hillsdale, NJ: Erlbaum.

Wiley, J., & Jarosz, A. F. (2012). Working memory capacity, attentional focus, and problem solving. *Current Directions in Psychological Science, 21*, 258–262.

Wilkey, E. D., Cutting, L. E., & Price, G. R. (2018). Neuroanatomical correlates of performance in a statewide test of math achievement. *Developmental Science, 21*, e12545.

Wilkinson, R., & Pickett, K. (2009). *The spirit level: Why greater equality makes societies stronger*. London: Bloomsbury Press.

Wilkinson, R. G., & Pickett, K. E. (2017a). The enemy between us: The psychological and social costs of inequality. *European Journal of Social Psychology, 47*, 11–24.

Wilkinson, R. G., & Pickett, K. (2017b). Inequality and mental illness. *The Lancet Psychiatry, 4*, 512–513.

Willett, L. L., Halvorsen, A. J., McDonald, F. S., Chaudhry, S. I., & Arora, V. M. (2015). Gender differences in salary of internal medicine residency directors: A national survey. *The American Journal of Medicine, 128*, 659–665.

Williams, J. E., & Best, D. L. (1990). *Measuring sex stereotypes: A multination study*. Newbury Park, CA: Sage.

Williams, K. D. (2007). Ostracism. *Annual Review of Psychology, 58*, 425–452.

Williams, K. D. (2009). Ostracism: A temporal need-threat model. *Advances in Experimental Social Psychology, 41*, 275–313.

Williams, K. D., & Sommer, K. L. (1997). Social ostracism by coworkers: Does rejection lead to loafing or compensation? *Personality and Social Psychology Bulletin, 23*, 693–706.

Williams, L. E., & Bargh, J. A. (2008). Experiencing physical warmth promotes interpersonal warmth. *Science, 322*, 606–607.

Williams, N. M., Zaharieva, I., Martin, A., Langley, K., Mantripragada, K., Fossdal, R., . . . Thapar, A. (2010). Rare chromosomal deletions and duplications in attention-deficit hyperactivity disorder: A genome-wide analysis. *The Lancet, 376*, 1401–1408.

Williams, N. R., Heifets, B. D., Blasey, C., Sudheimer, K., Pannu, J., Pankow, H., . . . & Schatzberg, A. F. (2018). Attenuation of antidepressant effects of ketamine by opioid receptor antagonism. *American Journal of Psychiatry, 175*, 1205–1215.

Williams, S. L. (1987). *Self-efficacy and mastery-oriented treatment for severe phobias.* Paper presented to the American Psychological Association convention.

Williams, T. (2015, March 17). Missouri executes killer who had brain injury. *The New York Times* (nytimes.com).

Williams, W. W., & Ceci, S. (2015). National hiring experiments reveal 2:1 faculty preference for women on tenure track. *PNAS, 112*, 5360–5365.

Willingham, D. T. (2010, Summer). Have technology and multitasking rewired how students learn? *American Educator, 42*, 23–28.

Willis, J., & Todorov, A. (2006). First impressions: Making up your mind after a 100-ms. exposure to a face. *Psychological Science, 17*, 592–598.

Willmuth, M. E. (1987). Sexuality after spinal cord injury: A critical review. *Clinical Psychology Review, 7*, 389–412.

Willoughby, B. J., Carroll, J. S., & Busby, D. M. (2014). Differing relationship outcomes when sex happens before, on, or after first dates. *Journal of Sex Research, 51*, 52–61.

Willoughby, T., Heffer, T., & Hamza, C. A. (2015). The link between nonsuicidal self-injury and acquired capability for suicide: A longitudinal study. *Journal of Abnormal Psychology, 124*, 1110–1115.

Wilson, A. E., & Ross, M. (2001). From chump to champ: People's appraisals of their earlier and present selves. *Journal of Personality and Social Psychology, 80*, 572–584.

Wilson, R. S. (1979). Analysis of longitudinal twin data: Basic model and applications to physical growth measures. *Acta Geneticae Medicae et Gemellologiae, 28*, 93–105.

Wilson, R. S., Beck, T. L., Bienias, J. L., & Bennett, D. A. (2007). Terminal cognitive decline: Accelerated loss of cognition in the last years of life. *Psychosomatic Medicine, 69*, 131–137.

Wilson, T. D., Reinhard, D. A., Westgate, E. C., Gilbert, D. T., Ellerbeck, N., Hahn, C., . . . Shaked, A. (2014). Just think: The challenges of the disengaged mind. *Science, 345*, 75–77.

Wimber, M., Alink, A., Charest, I., Kriegeskorte, N., & Anderson, M. C. (2015). Retrieval induces adaptive forgetting of competing memories via cortical pattern suppression. *Nature Neuroscience, 18*, 582–589.

Wimmer, R. D., Schmitt, L. I., Davidson, T. J., Nakajima, M., Deisseroth, K., & Halassa, M. M. (2015). Thalamic control of sensory selection in divided attention. *Nature, 526*, 705–709.

Windholz, G. (1989, April-June). The discovery of the principles of reinforcement, extinction, generalization, and differentiation of conditional reflexes in Pavlov's laboratories. *Pavlovian Journal of Biological Science, 26*, 64–74.

Windholz, G. (1997). Ivan P. Pavlov: An overview of his life and psychological work. *American Psychologist, 52*, 941–946.

Winkler, A., Dòrsing, B., Rief, W., Shen, Y., & Glombiewski, J. A. (2013). Treatment of internet addiction: A meta-analysis. *Clinical Psychology Review, 33*, 317–329.

Wirth, J. H., Sacco, D. F., Hugenberg, K., & Williams, K. D. (2010). Eye gaze as relational evaluation: Averted eye gaze leads to feelings of ostracism and relational devaluation. *Personality and Social Psychology Bulletin, 36*, 869–882.

Wiseman, R., & Greening, E. (2002). The Mind Machine: A mass participation experiment into the possible existence of extra-sensory perception. *British Journal of Psychology, 93*, 487–499.

Witt, J. K., & Brockmole, J. R. (2012). Action alters object identification: Wielding a gun increases the bias to see guns. *Journal of Experimental Psychology: Human Perception and Performance, 38*, 1159–1167.

Witt, J. K., & Proffitt, D. R. (2005). See the ball, hit the ball: Apparent ball size is correlated with batting average. *Psychological Science, 16*, 937–938.

Witters, D. (2014, October 20). *U.S. adults with children at home have greater joy, stress.* Gallup Poll (gallup.com).

Witters, D., & Wood, J. (2015, January 14). *Heart attacks and depression closely linked.* Gallup Poll (gallup.com).

Wittgenstein, L. (1922). *Tractatus logico-philosophicus* (C. K. Ogden, Trans.). New York: Harcourt, Brace.

Witvliet, C. V. O., & Vrana, S. R. (1995). Psychophysiological responses as indices of affective dimensions. *Psychophysiology, 32*, 436–443.

Wixted, J. T., & Ebbesen, E. B. (1991). On the form of forgetting. *Psychological Science, 2*, 409–415.

WKYT. (2017). Kentucky fans set crowd roar world record. Retrieved from wkyt.com/content/news/Kentucky-fans-set-crowd-roar-world-record-412059133.html

Wölfer, R., & Hewstone, M. (2015, August). Intra- versus intersex aggression. Testing theories of sex differences using aggression networks. *Psychological Science, 26*, 1285–1294.

Wolfinger, N. H. (2015). *Want to avoid divorce? Wait to get married, but not too long.* Retrieved from family-studies.org/want-to-avoid-divorce-wait-to-get-married-but-not-too-long/

Wolfson, A. R., & Carskadon, M. A. (1998). Sleep schedules and daytime functioning in adolescents. *Child Development, 69*, 875–887.

Wolpe, J. (1958). *Psychotherapy by reciprocal inhibition.* Stanford, CA: Stanford University Press.

Wolpe, J., & Plaud, J. J. (1997). Pavlov's contributions to behavior therapy: The obvious and the not so obvious. *American Psychologist, 52*, 966–972.

Wondra, J. D., & Ellsworth, P. C. (2015). An appraisal theory of empathy and other vicarious emotional experiences. *Psychological Review, 122*, 411–428.

Wong, D. F., Wagner, H. N., Tune, L. E., Dannals, R. F., Pearlson, G. D., Links, J. M., . . . Gjedde, A. (1986). Positron emission tomography reveals elevated D_2 dopamine receptors in drug-naive schizophrenics. *Science, 234*, 1588–1593.

Wong, M. M., & Csikszentmihalyi, M. (1991). Affiliation motivation and daily experience: Some issues on gender differences. *Journal of Personality and Social Psychology, 60*, 154–164.

Wood, D., Bruner, J., & Ross, G. (1976). The role of tutoring in problem solving. *Journal of Child Psychology and Child Psychiatry, 17*, 89–100.

Wood, J. M. (2003, May 19). Quoted in R. Mestel, Rorschach tested: Blot out the famous method? Some experts say it has no place in psychiatry. *The Los Angeles Times.* Retrieved from articles.latimes.com/2003/may/19/health/he-rorschach19

Wood, J. M., Bootzin, R. R., Kihlstrom, J. F., & Schacter, D. L. (1992). Implicit and explicit memory for verbal information presented during sleep. *Psychological Science, 3*, 236–239.

Wood, J. M., Nezworski, M. T., Garb, H. N., & Lilienfeld, S. O. (2006). The controversy over the Exner Comprehensive System and the Society for Personality Assessment's white paper on the Rorschach. *Independent Practitioner, 26.*

Wood, W. (1987). Meta-analytic review of sex differences in group performance. *Psychological Bulletin, 102*, 53–71.

Wood, W. (2017). Habit in personality and social psychology. *Personality and Social Psychology Review, 21*, 389–403.

Wood, W., & Eagly, A. H. (2002). A cross-cultural analysis of the behavior of women and men: Implications for the origins of sex differences. *Psychological Bulletin, 128*, 699–727.

Wood, W., & Eagly, A. H. (2007). Social structural origins of sex differences in human mating. In S. W. Gagestad & J. A. Simpson (Eds.), *The evolution of mind: Fundamental questions and controversies* (pp. 383–390). New York: Guilford Press.

Wood, W., Kressel, L., Joshi, P. D., & Louie, B. (2014). Meta-analysis of menstrual cycle effects on women's mate preferences. *Emotion Review, 6*, 229–249.

Wood, W., Lundgren, S., Ouellette, J. A., Busceme, S., & Blackstone, T. (1994). Minority influence: A meta-analytic review of social influence processes. *Psychological Bulletin, 115*, 323–345.

Woolett, K., & Maguire, E. A. (2011). Acquiring "the knowledge" of London's layout drives structural brain changes. *Current Biology, 21*, 2109–2114.

Woolley, A. W., Chabris, C. F., Pentland, A., Hasmi, N., & Malone, T. W. (2010). Evidence for a collective intelligence factor in the performance of human groups. *Science, 330*, 686–688.

Woolley, K., & Fishbach, A. (2017). Immediate rewards predict adherence to long-term goals. *Personality and Social Psychology Bulletin, 43*, 151–162.

World Federation for Mental Health. (2005). ADHD: The hope behind the hype. World Federation for Mental Health (wfmh.org).

World Inequality Lab. (2018). *World inequality report 2018: Executive summary.* World Inequality Database (WIR2018.WID.World).

Worldwatch Institute. (2017). Meat production continues to rise. Retrieved July 24, 2017, from worldwatch.org/node/5443

Worthman, C. M., & Trang, K. (2018). Dynamics of body time, social time and life history at adolescence. *Nature, 554*, 451–457.

Wortman, C. B., & Silver, R. C. (1989). The myths of coping with loss. *Journal of Consulting and Clinical Psychology, 57*, 349–357.

Wren, C. S. (1999, April 8). Drug survey of children finds middle school a pivotal time. *The New York Times* (nytimes.com).

Wright, P., Takei, N., Rifkin, L., & Murray, R. M. (1995). Maternal influenza, obstetric complications, and schizophrenia. *American Journal of Psychiatry, 152*, 1714–1720.

Wright, P. H. (1989). Gender differences in adults' same- and cross-gender friendships. In R. G. Adams & R. Blieszner (Eds.), *Older adult friendships: Structure and process.* Newbury Park, CA: Sage.

Wright, P. J., Bridges, A. J., Sun, C., Ezzell, M. B., Johnson, J. A. (2018). Personal pornography viewing and sexual satisfaction: A quadratic analysis. *Journal of Sex and Marital Therapy, 44*, 308–315.

Wrzesniewski, A., & Dutton, J. E. (2001). Crafting a job: Revisioning employees as active crafters of their work. *Academy of Management Review, 26*, 179–201.

Wrzesniewski, A., Schwartz, B., Cong, X., Kane, M., Omar, A., & Kolditz, T. (2014). Multiple types of motives don't multiply the motivation of West Point cadets. *PNAS, 111*, 10990–10995.

Wu, X., Kaminga, A. C., Dai, W., Deng, J., Wang, Z., Pan, X., & Liu, A. (2018). The prevalence of moderate-to-high posttraumatic growth: A systematic review and meta-analysis. *Journal of Affective Disorders, 243*, 408–415.

Wu, X., Zhang, Z., Zhao, F., Wang, W., Li, Y., Bi, L., . . . Sun, Y. (2016). Prevalence of internet addiction and its association with social support and other related factors among adolescents in China. *Journal of Adolescence, 52*, 103–111.

Wucherpfennig, F., Rubel, J. A., Hofmann, S. G., & Lutz, W. (2017). Processes of change after a sudden gain and relation to treatment outcome—Evidence for an upward spiral. *Journal of Consulting and Clinical Psychology, 85*, 1199–1210.

Wuethrich, B. (2001, March). Features—GETTING STUPID—Surprising new neurological behavioral research reveals that teenagers who drink too much may permanently damage their brains and seriously compromise their ability to learn. *Discover, 56*, 56–64.

Wulsin, L. R., Vaillant, G. E., & Wells, V. E. (1999). A systematic review of the mortality of depression. *Psychosomatic Medicine, 61*, 6–17.

Wyatt, J. K., & Bootzin, R. R. (1994). Cognitive processing and sleep: Implications for enhancing job performance. *Human Performance, 7*, 119–139.

Wynn, K., Bloom, P., Jordan, A., Marshall, J., & Sheskin, M. (2018). Not noble savages after all: Limits to early altruism. *Current Directions in Psychological Science, 27*, 3–8.

Wynne, C. D. L. (2004). *Do animals think?* Princeton, NJ: Princeton University Press.

Wynne, C. D. L. (2008). Aping language: A skeptical analysis of the evidence for nonhuman primate language. *Skeptic, 13*, 10–13.

Xie, L., Kang, H., Xu, Q., Chen, M. J., Liao, Y., Thiyagarajan, M., . . . Nedergaard, M. (2013). Sleep drives metabolite clearance from the adult brain. *Science, 342*, 373–377.

Xu, J., & Potenza, M. N. (2012). White matter integrity and five-factor personality measures in healthy adults. *NeuroImage, 59*, 800–807.

Xu, J., Murphy, S. L., Kochanek, K. D., & Bastian B. A. (2016, February 16). Deaths: Final data for 2013. *National Vital Statistics Report, 64*(2). (cdc.gov).

Xu, Y., & Corkin, S. (2001). H. M. revisits the Tower of Hanoi puzzle. *Neuropsychology, 15*, 69–79.

Yamaguchi, M., Masuchi, A., Nakanishi, D., Suga, S., Konishi, N., Yu, Y. Y., & Ohtsubo, Y. (2015). Experiential purchases and prosocial spending promote happiness by enhancing social relationships. *The Journal of Positive Psychology, 11*, 1–9.

Yang, G., Lai, G. S. W., Cichon, J., Ma, L., Li, W., & Gan, W. B. (2014). Sleep promotes branch-specific formation of dendritic spines after learning. *Science, 344*, 173–1178.

Yang, S., Martin, R.M., Oken, E., Hameza, M., Doniger, G., Amit S, . . . Kramer, M. S. (2018). Breastfeeding during infancy and neurocognitive function in adolescence: 16-year follow-up of the PROBIT cluster-randomized trial. *PLOS Med, 15*, e1002554.

Yang, Y. C., Boen, C., Gerken, K., Li, T., Schorpp, K., & Harris, K. M. (2016). Social relationships and physiological determinants of longevity across the human life span. *PNAS, 113*, 578–583.

Yang, Y., Cao, S., Shields, G. S., Teng, Z., & Liu, Y. (2017). The relationships between rumination and core executive functions: A meta-analysis. *Depression and Anxiety, 34*, 37–50.

Yang, Y., & Raine, A. (2009). Prefrontal structural and functional brain imaging findings in antisocial, violent, and psychopathic individuals: A meta-analysis. *Psychiatry Research: Neuroimaging, 174*, 81–88.

Yarnell, P. R., & Lynch, S. (1970, April 25). Retrograde memory immediately after concussion. *The Lancet, 1*, 863–865.

Yates, A. (1989). Current perspectives on the eating disorders: I. History, psychological and biological aspects. *Journal of the American Academy of Child and Adolescent Psychiatry, 28*, 813–828.

Yates, A. (1990). Current perspectives on the eating disorders: II. Treatment, outcome, and research directions. *Journal of the American Academy of Child and Adolescent Psychiatry, 29*, 1–9.

Ybarra, O. (1999). Misanthropic person memory when the need to self-enhance is absent. *Personality and Social Psychology Bulletin, 25*, 261–269.

Yeager, D. S., Johnson, R., Spitzer, B. J., Trzesniewski, K. H., Powers, J., & Dweck, C. S. (2014). The far-reaching effects of believing people can change: Implicit theories of personality shape stress, health, and achievement during adolescence. *Journal of Personality and Social Psychology, 106*, 867–884.

Yeager, D. S., Lee, H. Y., & Jamieson, J. P. (2016). How to improve adolescent stress responses: Insights from integrating implicit theories of personality and biopsychosocial models. *Psychological Science, 27*, 1078–1091.

Yeager, D. S., Miu, A. S., Powers, J., & Dweck, C. S. (2013). Implicit theories of personality and attributions of hostile intent: A meta-analysis, an experiment, and a longitudinal intervention. *Child Development, 84*, 1651–1667.

Yeager, D. S., Walton, G. M., Brady, S. T., Akcinar, E. N., Paunesku, D., Keane, L., . . . Gomez, E. M. (2016b). Teaching a lay theory before college narrows achievement gaps at scale. *PNAS, 113*, E3341–E3348.

Yengo, L., Robinson, M. R., Keller, M. C., Kemper, K. E., Yang, Y., Trzaskowski, M., . . . & Wray, N. R. (2018). Imprint of assortative mating on the human genome. *Nature Human Behaviour, 2*, 948–954.

Yerkes, R. M., & Dodson, J. D. (1908). The relation of strength of stimulus to rapidity of habit-formation. *Journal of Comparative Neurology and Psychology, 18*, 459–482.

Yesavage, J. A., Fairchild, J. K., Mi, Z., Biswas, K., Davis-Karim, A., Phibbs, C. S., . . . George, M. S. (2018). Effect of repetitive transcranial magnetic stimulation on treatment-resistant major depression in US veterans: A randomized clinical trial. *JAMA Psychiatry, 75*, 884–893.

Yiend, J., Parnes, C., Shepherd, K., Roche, M.-K., & Cooper, M. J. (2014). Negative self-beliefs in eating disorders: A cognitive-bias-modification study. *Clinical Psychological Science, 2*, 756–766.

Yoshimoto, C., & Frauenheim, E. (2018, February 27). The best companies to work for are beating the marketplace. Retrieved from fortune.com/2018/02/27/the-best-companies-to-work-for-are-beating-the-market

YOU. (2009, September 10). Wow, look at Caster now! *YOU* (you.co.za/). (p. 168)

Young, C., & Lim, C. (2014). Time as a network good: Evidence from unemployment and the standard workweek. *Sociological Science, 1*, 10–27.

Young, S. G., Hugenberg, K., Bernstein, M. J., & Sacco, D. F. (2012). Perception and motivation in face recognition: A critical review of theories of the cross-race effect. *Personality and Social Psychology Review, 16*, 116–142.

Younger, J., Aron, A., Parke, S., Chatterjee, N., & Mackey, S. (2010) Viewing pictures of a romantic partner reduces experimental pain: Involvement of neural reward systems. *PLOS ONE, 5*, e13309.

Yount, K. M., James-Hawkins, L., Cheong, Y. F., & Naved, R. T. (2017). Men's perpetration of partner violence in Bangladesh: Community gender norms and violence in childhood. *Psychology of Men & Masculinity, 19*, 117–130.

Youyou, W., Kosinski, M., & Stillwell, D. (2015). Computer-based personality judgments are more accurate than those made by humans. *PNAS, 112*, 1036–1040.

Yuval, K., Zvielli, A., & Bernstein, A. (2017). Attentional bias dynamics and posttraumatic stress in survivors of violent conflict and atrocities: New directions in clinical psychological science of refugee mental health. *Clinical Psychological Science, 5*, 64–73.

Zagorsky, J. L. (2007). Do you have to be smart to be rich? The impact of IQ on wealth, income and financial distress. *Intelligence, 35*, 489–501.

Zahrt, O. H., & Crum, A. J. (2017). Perceived physical activity and mortality: Evidence from three nationally representative U.S. samples. *Health Psychology, 36*, 1017–1025.

Zainulbhai, H. (2016, March 8). Strong global support for gender equality, especially among women. Pew Research Center (pewresearch.org).

Zajonc, R. B. (1980). Feeling and thinking: Preferences need no inferences. *American Psychologist, 35*, 151–175.

Zajonc, R. B. (1984). On the primacy of affect. *American Psychologist, 39*, 117–123.

Zajonc, R. B. (2001). Mere exposure: A gateway to the subliminal. *Current Directions in Psychological Science, 10*, 224–228.

Zajonc, R. B., & Markus, G. B. (1975). Birth order and intellectual development. *Psychological Review, 82*, 74–88.

Zanarini, M. C., Williams, A. A., Lewis, R. E., Reich, R. B., Vera, S. C., Marino, M. F., . . . Frankenburg, R. F. (1997). Reported pathological childhood experiences associated with the development of borderline personality disorder. *American Journal of Psychiatry, 154*, 1101–1106.

Zannas, A. S., Provençal, N., & Binder, E. B. (2015). Epigenetics of posttraumatic stress disorder: current evidence, challenges, and future directions. *Biological Psychiatry, 78*, 327–335.

Zauberman, G., & Lynch, J. G., Jr. (2005). Resource slack and propensity to discount delayed investments of time versus money. *Journal of Experimental Psychology: General, 134*, 23–37.

Zeidner, M. (1990). Perceptions of ethnic group modal intelligence: Reflections of cultural stereotypes or intelligence test scores? *Journal of Cross-Cultural Psychology, 21*, 214–231.

Zell, E., & Alicke, M. D. (2010). The local dominance effect in self-evaluation: Evidence and explanations. *Personality and Social Psychology Review, 14*, 368–384.

Zell, E., Krizan, Z., & Teeter, S. R. (2015). Evaluating gender similarities and differences using metasynthesis. *American Psychologist, 70*, 10–20.

Zentner, M., & Eagly, A. H. (2015). A sociocultural framework for understanding partner preferences of women and men: Integration of concepts and evidence. *European Journal of Social Psychology, 26*, 328–373.

Zerr, C. L., Berg, J. J., Nelson, S. M., Fishell, A. K., Savalia, N. K., & McDermott, K. B. (2018). Learning efficiency: Identifying individual differences in learning rate and retention in healthy adults. *Psychological Science, 29*, 1436–1450.

Zerubavel, N., Hoffman, M. A., Reich, A., Ochsner, K. N., & Bearman, P. (2018). Neural precursors of future liking and affective reciprocity. *PNAS, 115*, 4375–4380.

Zhang, J., Fang, L., Yow-Wu, B. W., & Wieczorek, W. F. (2013). Depression, anxiety, and suicidal ideation among

Chinese Americans: A study of immigration-related factors. *The Journal of Nervous and Mental Disease, 201,* 17–22.

Zhong, C.-B., Dijksterhuis, A., & Galinsky, A. D. (2008). The merits of unconscious thought in creativity. *Psychological Science, 19,* 912–918.

Zilbergeld, B. (1983). *The shrinking of America: Myths of psychological change.* Boston: Little, Brown.

Zillmann, D. (1989). Effects of prolonged consumption of pornography. In D. Zillmann & J. Bryant (Eds.), *Pornography: Research advances and policy considerations* (pp. 127–157). Hillsdale, NJ: Erlbaum.

Zillmann, D., & Bryant, J. (1984). Effects of massive exposure to pornography. In N. Malamuth & E. Donnerstein (Eds.), *Pornography and sexual aggression* (pp. 115–138). Orlando, FL: Academic Press.

Zimbardo, P. G. (1970). The human choice: Individuation, reason, and order versus deindividuation, impulse, and chaos. In W. J. Arnold & D. Levine (Eds.), *Nebraska Symposium on Motivation, 1969.* Lincoln, NE: University of Nebraska Press.

Zimbardo, P. G. (1972, April). Pathology of imprisonment. *Society, 9,* pp. 4–8.

Zimbardo, P. G. (2001, September 16). *Fighting terrorism by understanding man's capacity for evil.* Op-ed essay distributed by spsp-discuss@stolaf.edu.

Zimbardo, P. G. (2007, September). Person x situation x system dynamics. *The Observer* (Association for Psychological Science), p. 43.

Zimbardo, P., Wilson, G., & Coulombe, N. (2016). How porn is messing with your manhood. Retrieved from skeptic.com/reading_room/how-porn-is-messing-with-your-manhood

Zimmerman, J. (2018). One group that definitely faces prejudice in college admissions. *The Washington Post* (washingtonpost.com).

Zinzow, H. M., Amstadter, A. B., McCauley, J. L., Ruggiero, K. J., Resnick, H. S., & Kilpatrick, D. G. (2011). Self-rated health in relation to rape and mental health disorders in a national sample of college women. *Journal of American College Health, 59,* 588–594.

Zogby, J. (2006, March). *Survey of teens and adults about the use of personal electronic devices and headphones.* Utica, NY: Zogby International.

Zoma, M., & Gielen, U. P. (2015). How many psychologists are there in the world? *International Psychology Bulletin, 19,* 47–50.

Zou, L. Q., van Hartevelt, T. J., Kringelbach, M. L., Cheung, E. F., & Chan, R. C. (2016). The neural mechanism of hedonic processing and judgment of pleasant odors: An activation likelihood estimation meta-analysis. *Neuropsychology, 30,* 970–979.

Zubieta, J.-K., Bueller, J. A., Jackson, L. R., Scott, D. J., Xu, Y., Koeppe, R. A., . . . Stohler, C. S. (2005). Placebo effects mediated by endogenous opioid activity on μ-opioid receptors. *Journal of Neuroscience, 25,* 7754–7762.

Zubieta, J.-K., Heitzeg, M. M., Smith, Y. R., Bueller, J. A., Xu, K., Xu, Y., . . . Goldman, D. (2003). COMT val158met genotype affects μ-opioid neurotransmitter responses to a pain stressor. *Science, 299,* 1240–1243.

Zucker, G. S., & Weiner, B. (1993). Conservatism and perceptions of poverty: An attributional analysis. *Journal of Applied Social Psychology, 23,* 925–943.

Zuckerberg, M. (2012, February 1). Letter to potential investors. Quoted by S. Sengupta & C. C. Miller, "Social mission" vision meets Wall Street. *The New York Times* (nytimes.com).

Zuckerman, M. (1979). *Sensation seeking: Beyond the optimal level of arousal.* Hillsdale, NJ: Erlbaum.

Zuckerman, M. (1999). *Vulnerability to psychopathology: A biosocial model.* Washington, DC: American Psychological Association.

Zuckerman, M. (2009). Sensation seeking. In M. R. Leary & R. H. Hoye (Eds.), *Handbook of individual differences in social behavior* (pp. 455–465). New York: Guilford Press.

Zuckerman, M., Li, C., & Hall, J. A. (2016). When men and women differ in self-esteem and when they don't: A meta-analysis. *Journal of Research in Personality, 64,* 34–51.

Zvolensky, M. J., & Bernstein, A. (2005). Cigarette smoking and panic psychopathology. *Current Directions in Psychological Science, 14,* 301–305.

Zvolensky, M. J., Bakhshaie, J., Sheffer, C., Perez, A., & Goodwin, R. D. (2015). Major depressive disorder and smoking relapse among adults in the United States: A 10-year, prospective investigation. *Psychiatry Research, 226,* 73–77.

Zych, I., Farrington, D. P., & Ttofi, M. M. (2018). Protective factors against bullying and cyberbullying: A systematic review of meta-analyses. *Aggression and Violent Behavior, 45,* 4–19.

NAME INDEX

Note: Page numbers preceded by A, B, or C indicate Appendices.

SUBJECT INDEX

Note: Page numbers preceded by A, B, or C indicate Appendices.

How Does Psychology Apply to YOUR Everyday Life?

(CONTINUED FROM INSIDE FRONT COVER.)